U.S. FOREIGN RELATIONS LAW

CASES, MATERIALS, AND SIMULATIONS

Fourth Edition

■ ■ ■

By

Thomas M. Franck (1931–2009)
Murry and Ida Becker Professor of Law Emeritus
New York University
School of Law

Michael J. Glennon
Professor of International Law
Fletcher School of Law & Diplomacy
Tufts University

Sean D. Murphy
Patricia Roberts Harris Research Professor of Law
George Washington University
School of Law

Edward T. Swaine
Professor of Law
George Washington University
School of Law

AMERICAN CASEBOOK SERIES®

WEST®

A Thomson Reuters business

Mat #41074063

610 Opperman Drive
St. Paul, MN 55123
1–800–313–9378

Printed in the United States of America

ISBN: 978–0–314–26833–4

Dedication

This edition is dedicated to
Thomas M. Franck
1931–2009
Scholar, colleague, mentor and friend

PREFACE

Every decade seems to present a cataclysm in the field of U.S. foreign relations and national security, whether it be the dramatic withdrawal of U.S. forces from Vietnam, the collapse of communism in the Soviet Union and Eastern Europe, the horrific terrorist attacks of September 11, the ensuing U.S. interventions in Afghanistan and Iraq, or the revolutionary wave of uprisings in the Arab world during 2011, triggering in part military intervention in Libya.

Between those cataclysms, less dramatic transnational events also occur that can deeply affect the U.S. polity, such as adherence to trade agreements that both help and hurt U.S. industry; pursuit of litigation in U.S. courts that seeks to promote respect for human rights abroad; enactment of state-level sanctions directed at foreign governments, which might also impede federal policy; leaking of national security information to the media; or the pursuit, extradition, and prosecution of alleged criminals located abroad.

The hard-cover version of this course book introduces law students, and upper-level undergraduate students, to the constitutional rules, principal statutes, and landmark judicial decisions applicable to such cataclysms and events in both the fields of "foreign relations law" and "national security law." The nine chapters cover the core areas of substantive law and procedure, addressing the manner in which international law (the law of nations and treaties) becomes a part of U.S. law, and the manner in which power is allocated within the federal government and between the federal government and the several states. Each chapter is further sub-divided into topics appropriate for coverage during one or two classes. The cases and materials are designed to inform the reader and to provoke discussion about *de lege lata* (the law as it is) and *de lege ferenda* (the law as it should be). Detailed notes guide the reader through the major thematic elements, pose questions for further analysis, and provide suggestions for additional reading. An appendix sets forth various simulations related to the readings that may be used to enhance the classroom experience, by having students play particular roles for addressing fictional (but realistic) problems.

Why use this particular course book? Course books in constitutional, criminal, and international law touch upon various aspects of the field of foreign relations and national security law, but largely in a hit-or-miss fashion. Course books on particular subjects of transnational affairs, such as on trade law, terrorism, or human rights, provide a detailed look at a slice of the field, but at the expense of the broader range of substance and structure. By contrast, this course book provides a comprehensive overview of the field of foreign relations and national security law, thereby laying the groundwork for more detailed study. There are some course books that do focus on foreign relations law, but do not address issues that more squarely fall in the field of national security law, such as the handling of national security information. Other course books focus on national security law, but neglect broader aspects of foreign relations law, such as the division of authority between the federal government and the several states on matters of international relations. This course book provides a survey of the law relating to both fields, allowing professors and students to select all or some of the topics spanning these fields, and to see their inter-relationship.

At the same time, some instructors may wish to teach only the foreign relations or national security materials, while leaving out the other materials. To support such courses, two soft-cover versions of this course book are available that focus exclusively on one or the other field. Thus, soft-cover versions exist for:

> *U.S. Foreign Relations Law*: reproducing Chapters 1, 2 (Sections 1–6 only), 3, 4 (Sections 1–4 only), 6, and 7, as well as Appendix I and II
>
> *U.S. National Security Law*: reproducing Chapters 1, 2 (Sections 1–2 and 7–8 only), 3 (Sections 1–4 only), 4, 5, 7 (Sections 1–2 only), 8, and 9, as well as Appendix I and II

These soft-cover versions retain the pagination of the hard-cover version, thus the soft-cover versions contain "gaps" where material from the hard-cover version was not reproduced. Our belief was that this will permit more convenient use of all three versions should instructors find a need to do so from year-to-year.

The issues addressed in this course book are of enormous importance—perhaps the most monumental that any lawyer ever confronts. In times of national emergency, such as a large-scale terrorist attack, how should one think about the relative allocation of the powers of Congress and the President? What are the effects on U.S. law and policy when the United States adheres to a treaty that, for example, prohibits torture? Should rules developed through the practice of nations worldwide be used as a part of internal U.S. law, including for interpretation of the U.S. Constitution? When can the President introduce U.S. armed forces into hostilities without congressional authorization? To what extent can individual rights—such as freedom of the press and freedom from otherwise illegal searches or seizures—constitutionally be constricted for reasons of "national security"? What role can the courts play in adjudicating such disputes?

Such questions have been hotly debated, of course, since the earliest days of the Republic, and many contemporary arguments are but replays of previous disputes. Consequently materials once written on parchment retain an enduring relevance. Yet, as the nation moves forward in the twenty-first century, with parchment replaced by hard drives, old controversies do take on new forms. Unprecedented threats are posed, not only to the nation but also to the values at the heart of our legal structure. These cases and materials provide students an opportunity to confront these difficult choices of law, policy, and social values in both an historical and contemporary context.

We welcome the comments of instructors and students who use this book. Subsequent editions will benefit greatly from your advice and counsel.

MICHAEL J. GLENNON
SEAN D. MURPHY
EDWARD T. SWAINE

November 2011

ACKNOWLEDGMENTS

The authors wish to acknowledge the invaluable help of the following research assistants: Ashley Belyea, Jeff Brundage, Bonnie Chen, Kelly J. Dunn, Rachel A. Goldbrenner, Matthew Hoisington, Kevin Futch, Nitya Kumar, Susannah Norvell, Emily Pierce, Mat Trachok, Christian Westra, and Jocelyn Wiesner. The authors' students at George Washington University, New York University, and Tufts University made helpful comments on ways of improving the prior editions, as did instructors at other colleges and universities who taught from those editions. Finally, the authors acknowledge, with appreciation, the permission granted to reprint copyrighted material contained herein.

Summary of Contents

TABLE OF CONTENTS

TABLE OF CASES

The principal cases are in bold type. Cases cited or discussed in the text are in roman type. References are to pages. Cases cited in principal cases and within other quoted materials are not included.

Page numbers 232–272, 558–748, and 1054–1363, set out below, are found in Franck's Foreign Relations and National Security Law.

U.S. Foreign Relations Law

CASES, MATERIALS, AND SIMULATIONS

CHAPTER 1

FOREIGN RELATIONS LAW: NATURE AND CONSTITUTIONAL STRUCTURE

■ ■ ■

SECTION 1. ORIGINS AND NATURE OF U.S. FOREIGN RELATIONS LAW

INTRODUCTORY NOTE

Studying the constitutional origins of U.S. foreign relations law is important for at least two reasons. First, in the *Curtiss-Wright* case (*infra* Section 2), Supreme Court Justice Sutherland articulated a theory of the foreign affairs power that was predicated on a particular historical interpretation. According to Justice Sutherland, at the time of the American Revolution, the foreign affairs power relating to the thirteen colonies was transferred from the British government to the government of the Articles of Confederation. Upon ratification of the U.S. Constitution, the foreign affairs power then transferred from the government of the Articles of Confederation to the government of the U.S. Constitution. As such, the several states never exercised the foreign affairs power, and therefore that power should be viewed differently from Article I powers of Congress, which were generally exercised by the several states until the U.S. Constitution enumerated them as part of the powers of the federal government. Is this view of history accurate?

Second, to understand the types of powers accorded to the federal government under the U.S. Constitution, it is useful to know what governmental powers existed under the Articles of Confederation and why those powers were regarded as deficient. After all, the U.S. Constitution was written against the backdrop of the Articles of Confederation. The framers were trying to fix certain problems of the previous government. By understanding these problems, we can understand better what the framers were trying to do in creating certain federal foreign affairs powers and what they were trying to avoid.

Consequently, as you read the materials below, consider the following. The ability to represent the American colonies in matters of foreign relations resided with the British government up until 1776. Where did that foreign relations power reside after the U.S. Declaration of Independence? Where did it reside after the formation of the new government under the U.S. Constitution in 1789? To the extent that concern about the foreign affairs power was one impetus to shift from the Articles of Confederation to the U.S. Constitution, what exactly was the problem under the Articles of Confederation? Was it a concern with the division of powers within the central government or the division of powers between the central government and the states?

AKHIL REED AMAR, AMERICA'S CONSTITUTION: A BIOGRAPHY*

27–29 (2005) (footnotes omitted).

[C]onfusion about the pre–1787 location of sovereignty has arisen because later readers have often misunderstood what sovereignty did and did not mean to late-eighteenth-century American lawyers. Sovereign states under traditional legal principles were free to enter multilateral treaties, leagues, federations, and confederations without surrendering their ultimate sovereignty. In the words of Swiss jurist Emmerich de Vattel, whose *Law of Nations* was widely read and cited in Revolutionary America, "Several sovereign and independent states may unite themselves together by a *perpetual confederacy*, without each in particular ceasing to be a perfect state. They will form together a federal republic: the deliberations in common will offer no violence to the sovereignty of each member." In his influential *Second Treatise*, Locke had offered a similar account of the ongoing sovereignty of governments merely "in league" with one another, who had not combined "to make one body politic." William Blackstone's *Commentaries* also affirmed the continuing sovereignty of nation-states that merely joined together in "foederate alliance." Hence, the mere fact that each of the thirteen states agreed to what the Articles [of Confederation] called a "perpetual" "union" in no way negated each state's continuing sovereign status.

Nor was each state's ultimate legal sovereignty undermined by the fact that Congress—basing its authority initially on the Declaration [of Independence] and de facto alliance and later on the formal Articles—acted and spoke on behalf of the individual states in diplomatic dealings with foreign powers. Classic leagues of sovereign states, such as the eighteenth-century Dutch and Swiss confederacies, often coordinated the military and diplomatic affairs of the individual member states. Vis-à-vis the rest of the world, the thirteen American states could act as a unit, so long as their league held together and each state consented to be represented by Congress. Yet this apparent external unity while the Confederation continued intact said little about whether and how a formally "sovereign" state might one day lawfully exit the league.

What, then, *did* each state's ultimate "sovereignty" mean, and how was a "confederation" or "league" any different than a single sovereign nation-state? Within the interior of daily arrangements, a very strong confederacy might well approximate a decentralized nation-state. A con-

* Reprinted by permission of Random House Inc.

federacy might give important powers, including all powers over foreign affairs, to its common council, while a nation might leave many issues to be decided by local subunits. But at crucial junctures of system creation, amendment, and abolition, the differences would be dramatic. A *confederacy* essentially rested on the ongoing voluntary participation of its sovereign member states. Each sovereign member of a classic confederacy was free not to join at the moment of creation, typically free to refuse to accede to any later proposed amendment, and ultimately free to leave if, in its good-faith judgment, the core purposes of the confederation were going unfulfilled. Based on the Latin *foedus* (meaning treaty or covenant) and its cognate *fides* (faith), a traditional "confederated" union ultimately depended on the good faith and voluntary compliance of member states. Thus the precise language of the Articles' closing clause—in which the delegates of sovereign states agreed to "solemnly plight and engage the faith of our respective constituents"—confirmed the basic structure announced in the document's opening words.

Alas, plighted faith did not always translate into actual performance. Although on paper the Congress under the Articles enjoyed some important powers, it had no effective means of carrying them out. It could not directly tax individuals or legislate upon them; it had no explicit "legislative" or "governmental" power to make binding "law" enforceable in state courts; it lacked broad authority to set up its own general courts; and it could raise troops and money only by "requisitioning" contributions from each state. On paper, such requisitions were "binding." In practice, they were mere requests. As one wag put it, Congress "may declare every thing, but do nothing." By 1787, the Confederation was in shambles. Various states failed to honor requisitions, enacted laws violating duly ratified treaties, waged unauthorized local wars against Indian tribes, and maintained standing armies without congressional permission—all in plain contravention of the Articles.

America needed a new system. But how to launch it?

ANDREW C. McLAUGHLIN, A CONSTITUTIONAL HISTORY OF THE UNITED STATES

125–146 (1935) (footnote omitted).

. . . The powers granted to Congress [under the Articles of Confederation, which were ratified in 1781,] bear a general resemblance to those exercised by the Crown and Parliament in the old colonial system in which the colonies had grown to maturity; and if one compares the Articles with the Constitution adopted at Philadelphia in 1787, he will find a considerable similarity in the scheme of distribution. Time was to show the defects of the system; but the actual merits of the system agreed upon are noteworthy. No power to lay taxes was bestowed on Congress, and no power to regulate commerce, the two things about which there had been so much dispute in the preceding decade. These omissions were largely instrumental in bringing into existence the Constitutional Convention of 1787.

Without the consent of Congress, the states were expressly forbidden to send an embassy to a foreign state, receive an embassy, enter into any agreement with a foreign power, form any treaty of combination among themselves, maintain ships of war or troops in time of peace—though a militia must be provided and sufficiently armed—, or engage in war unless actually invaded or in immediate danger of Indian attack. All charges of war and other expenses incurred for the common defense and general welfare were to be defrayed out of a common treasury supplied by the several states. To Congress was given, among other powers, the general powers of determining on war and peace, carrying on foreign affairs, though with some restrictions, regulating the alloy and value of coin, fixing the standard of weights and measures, regulating the trade and managing all the affairs with the Indians "not members of any of the States", establishing and regulating post offices from one state to another, appointing important army officers and all naval officers, borrowing money, building and equipping a navy, and making requisitions upon the states for troops. . . .

While the Articles granted to Congress considerable authority, its powers were qualified, in some respects carefully, for the protection of the states' rights. Although Congress was given power to enter into treaties, the states were not totally forbidden to lay imposts, but they were forbidden to levy such duties as might interfere with "stipulations in treaties entered into by the United States . . . in pursuance of any treaties already proposed by Congress to the courts of France and Spain." Congress could make no treaty of commerce whereby the states should be restrained from imposing such imposts on foreigners as their own people were subjected to; and apparently the states could freely prohibit the exportation or importation of any kind of goods. The failure to grant Congress complete power to regulate commerce rendered it difficult or impossible to make a commercial treaty with a foreign nation and to have assurance that the states would comply with its provisions. The years that followed disclosed the fact that the want of authority to make treaties which would bind the states was one of the cardinal defects of the system.

. . . .

The industrial and commercial conditions after the [revolutionary] war were in considerable confusion. Readjustments were necessary, especially for the resuscitation of the New England shipping industry. Some improvement came fairly quickly, and there is evidence that by 1786 the clouds of depression were beginning to lift. But it was hard to make much headway, especially as Britain was not ready to treat her former colonies as if they deserved particular favors or consideration; they had made their own beds, now let them lie there—a condition of retirement not suited to the restless spirit of the New England skippers whose ships were soon plowing the seas, even on to the Orient as well as to the ports of continental Europe. Commercial treaties were desirable, and some steps were taken in that direction; but it was hard to do anything effectively as long as the individual states could not be relied on to fulfill their obligations. Foreign nations naturally queried whether America was one or many, or, perhaps, one to-day and thirteen to-morrow.

The [1783 U.S.–Great Britain] treaty of peace was not carried out. Britain still held the western posts from Lake Champlain to Mackinaw and thus retained control of the northern fur trade and influence over the Indians. Spain holding the mouth of the Mississippi was unwilling to allow free navigation through her territory. Trouble was brewing because of American treatment of loyalists and because the stipulation in the treaty, that there should be no unlawful impediment to the collection of debts due British creditors, received no particular attention. John Jay declared in 1786 that the treaty had been constantly violated by one state or another from the time of its signing and ratification. The Barbary powers, eager to take advantage of a helpless country, to seize American seamen, and to hold them for ransom, entered upon the game with lusty vigor. A nation which was not yet a nation in terms of law and political authority could do nothing to resist scorn and humiliation.

. . . .

But what was the very center of the difficulty? What was the chief problem of the time? The trouble and confusion were manifestly caused by the failure of the states to abide by their obligations. The problem was to find a method, if union was to subsist at all, for overcoming the difficulty, to find therefore some arrangement, some scheme or plan of organization wherein there would be reasonable assurance that the states would fulfill their obligations and play their part under established articles of union and not make mockery of union by willful disregard or negligent delay. That was the *chief problem* of the day. . . .

THE FEDERALIST PAPERS NO. 41 (MADISON)

255–59 (Clinton Rossiter ed., 1961).

The Constitution proposed by the convention may be considered under two general points of view. The first relates to the sum or quantity of power which it vests in the government, including the restraints imposed on the States. The second, to the particular structure of the government and the distribution of this power among its several branches.

Under the first view of the subject, two important questions arise: 1. Whether any part of the powers transferred to the general government be unnecessary or improper? 2. Whether the entire mass of them be dangerous to the portion of jurisdiction left in the several States?

. . . .

It cannot have escaped those who have attended with candor to the arguments employed against the extensive powers of the government that the authors of them have very little considered how far these powers were necessary means of attaining a necessary end. They have chosen rather to dwell on the inconveniences which must be unavoidably blended with all political advantages; and on the possible abuses which must be incident to every power or trust of which a beneficial use can be made. . . .

That we may form a correct judgment on this subject, it will be proper to review the several powers conferred on the government of the Union; and that this may be the more conveniently done they may be reduced into different classes as they relate to the following different objects: 1. Security against foreign danger; 2. Regulation of the intercourse with foreign nations; 3. Maintenance of harmony and proper intercourse among the States; 4. Certain miscellaneous objects of general utility; 5. Restraint of the States from certain injurious acts; 6. Provisions for giving due efficacy to all these powers.

. . . .

Security against foreign danger is one of the primitive objects of civil society. It is an avowed and essential object of the American Union. The powers requisite for attaining it must be effectually confided to the federal councils.

. . . .

. . . The Union itself, which it cements and secures, destroys every pretext for a military establishment which could be dangerous. America united, with a handful of troops, or without a single soldier, exhibits a more forbidding posture to foreign ambition than America disunited, with a hundred thousand veterans ready for combat. . . . Instead of deriving from our situation the precious advantage which Great Britain has derived from hers, the face of America [in the absence of union] will be but a copy of that of the continent of Europe. It will present liberty everywhere crushed between standing armies and perpetual taxes. The fortunes of disunited America will be even more disastrous than those of Europe. The sources of evil in the latter are confined to her own limits. No superior powers of another quarter of the globe intrigue among her rival nations, inflame their mutual animosities, and render them the instruments of foreign ambition, jealousy, and revenge. In America the miseries springing from her internal jealousies, contentions, and wars would form a part only of her lot. A plentiful addition of evils would have their source in that relation in which Europe stands to this quarter of the earth, and which no other quarter of the earth bears to Europe.

THE FEDERALIST PAPERS NO. 42 (MADISON)

264–65 (Clinton Rossiter ed., 1961).

The *second* class of powers lodged in the general government consist of those which regulate the intercourse with foreign nations, to wit: to make treaties; to send and receive ambassadors, other public ministers, and consuls;[1] to define and punish piracies and felonies committed on the high seas, and offenses against the law of nations; to regulate foreign

1. [Authors' Note: *See* U.S. CONST. art. II, § 2, cl. 2.]

commerce. . . .[2]

This class of powers forms an obvious and essential branch of federal administration. If we are to be one nation in any respect, it clearly ought to be in respect to other nations.

The powers to make treaties and to send and receive ambassadors speak their own propriety. Both of them are comprised in the Articles of Confederation, with this difference only, that the former is disembarrassed by the plan of the convention, of an exception under which treaties might be substantially frustrated by regulations of the States; and that a power of appointing and receiving "other public ministers and consuls" is expressly and very properly added to the former provision concerning ambassadors. . . .

. . . .

The power to define and punish piracies and felonies committed on the high seas and offenses against the law of nations belongs with equal propriety to the general government, and is a still greater improvement on the Articles of Confederation. These articles contain no provision for the case of offenses against the law of nations; and consequently leave it in the power of any indiscreet member to embroil the Confederacy with foreign nations. . . .

THE FEDERALIST PAPERS NO. 44 (MADISON)

280–86 (Clinton Rossiter ed., 1961).

A *fifth* class of provisions in favor of the federal authority consists of the following restrictions on the authority of the several States.

1. "No State shall enter into any treaty, alliance, or confederation; [or] grant letters of marque and reprisal. . . ."[1]

The prohibition against treaties, alliances, and confederations makes a part of the existing [Articles of Confederation]; and for reasons which need no explanation, is copied into the new Constitution. The prohibition of letters of marque is another part of the old system, but is somewhat extended in the new. According to the former, letters of marque could be granted by the States after a declaration of war; according to the latter, these licenses must be obtained, as well during war as previous to its declaration, from the government of the United States. This alteration is fully justified by the advantage of uniformity in all points which relate to foreign powers; and of immediate responsibility to the nation in all those for whose conduct the nation itself is to be responsible.

. . . .

2. "No state shall, without the consent of Congress, lay any imposts or duties on imports or exports, except what may be absolutely necessary for executing its inspection laws, and the net produce of all duties and

2. [Authors' Note: *See* U.S. CONST. art. I, § 8.]

1. [Authors' Note: U.S. CONST. art. I, § 10, cl. 1.]

imposts laid by any State on imports or exports shall be for the use of the treasury of the United States; and all such laws shall be subject to the revision and control of the Congress. No State shall, without the consent of Congress, lay any duty on tonnage, keep troops or ships of war in time of peace, enter into any agreement or compact with another State, or with a foreign power, or engage in war unless actually invaded, or in such imminent danger as will not admit of delay."[2]

The restraint on the power of the States over imports and exports is enforced by all the arguments which prove the necessity of submitting the regulation of trade to the federal councils. It is needless, therefore, to remark further on this head, than that the manner in which the restraint is qualified seems well calculated at once to secure to the States a reasonable discretion in providing for the conveniency of their imports and exports, and to the United States a reasonable check against the abuse of this discretion. The remaining particulars of this clause fall within reasonings which are either so obvious, or have been so fully developed, that they may be passed over without remark.

The *sixth* and last class consists of the several powers and provisions by which efficacy is given to all the rest.

1. Of these the first is the "power to make all laws which shall be necessary and proper for carrying into execution the foregoing powers, and all other powers vested by this Constitution in the government of the United States, or in any department or officer thereof."[3]

Few parts of the Constitution have been assailed with more intemperance than this; yet on a fair investigation of it, as has been elsewhere shown, no part can appear more completely invulnerable. Without the *substance* of this power, the whole Constitution would be a dead letter. . . .

. . . .

2. "This Constitution and the laws of the United States which shall be made in pursuance thereof, and all treaties made, or which shall be made, under the authority of the United States, shall be the supreme law of the land, and the judges in every State shall be bound thereby, anything in the constitution or laws of any State to the contrary notwithstanding."[4]

The indiscreet zeal of the adversaries to the Constitution has betrayed them into an attack on this part of it also, without which it would have been evidently and radically defective. To be fully sensible of this, we need only to suppose for a moment that the supremacy of the State constitutions had been left complete by a saving clause in their favor.

CHAE CHAN PING v. UNITED STATES [THE CHINESE EXCLUSION CASE]

130 U.S. 581, 603–06, 9 S.Ct. 623, 32 L.Ed. 1068 (1889).

[Following the anti-Chinese riots of 1885–86 in San Francisco, the United States and China took measures to limit emigration from China to

2. [Authors' Note: U.S. CONST. art. I, § 10, cl. 2 & 3.]
3. [Authors' Note: U.S. CONST. art. I, § 8, cl. 18.]
4. [Authors' Note: *See* U.S. CONST. art. VI, cl. 2.]

America. Under the Bayard–Zhang Treaty (1888), China agreed to suspend immigration for twenty years. In return, the American government pledged to protect Chinese assets in the United States. Massive protests erupted in China following the signing of the Bayard–Zhang Treaty, and the agreement was never formally ratified by the Chinese government. Congress proceeded legislatively, enacting the Scott Act in 1888, which permanently banned the immigration or return of Chinese to the United States. In 1889, the Supreme Court considered the legality of the Scott Act.]

MR. JUSTICE FIELD delivered the opinion of the Court.

. . . .

There being nothing in the treaties between China and the United States to impair the validity of the act of Congress of October 1, 1888, was it on any other ground beyond the competency of Congress to pass it? If so, it must be because it was not within the power of Congress to prohibit Chinese laborers who had at the time departed from the United States, or should subsequently depart, from returning to the United States. Those laborers are not citizens of the United States; they are aliens. That the government of the United States, through the action of the legislative department, can exclude aliens from its territory is a proposition which we do not think open to controversy. Jurisdiction over its own territory to that extent is an incident of every independent nation. It is a part of its independence. If it could not exclude aliens it would be to that extent subject to the control of another power. . . .

While under our Constitution and form of government the great mass of local matters is controlled by local authorities, the United States, in their relation to foreign countries and their subjects or citizens are one nation, invested with powers which belong to independent nations, the exercise of which can be invoked for the maintenance of its absolute independence and security throughout its entire territory. The powers to declare war, make treaties, suppress insurrection, repel invasion, regulate foreign commerce, secure republican governments to the States, and admit subjects of other nations to citizenship, are all sovereign powers, restricted in their exercise only by the Constitution itself and considerations of public policy and justice which control, more or less, the conduct of all civilized nations. . . .

. . . .

To preserve its independence, and give security against foreign aggression and encroachment, is the highest duty of every nation, and to attain these ends nearly all other considerations are to be subordinated. It matters not in what form such aggression and encroachment come, whether from the foreign nation acting in its national character, or from vast hordes of its people crowding in upon us. The government, possessing the powers which are to be exercised for protection and security, is clothed with authority to determine the occasion on which the powers shall be called forth; and its determinations, so far as the subjects affected are concerned, are necessarily conclusive upon all its departments and officers. If, therefore, the government of the United States, through its legislative department, considers the presence of foreigners of a different race in this country, who will not assimilate with us, to be dangerous to its peace and security, their exclusion is not to be stayed because at the time there are no actual hostilities with the nation of which the foreigners are subjects. The existence of war would render the necessity of the proceeding only more obvious and pressing. The same necessity, in a less pressing degree, may arise when war does not exist, and the same authority which adjudges the necessity in one case must also determine it in the other. In both cases its determination is conclusive upon the judiciary. If the government of the country of which the foreigners excluded are subjects is dissatisfied with this action, it can make complaint to the executive head of our government, or resort to any other measure which, in its judgment, its interests or dignity may demand; and there lies its only remedy.

NOTE ON THE CONTENT OF U.S. FOREIGN RELATIONS POWERS

1. *Content of U.S. Foreign Relations Powers*. At the end of this casebook, the U.S. Constitution is appended (*see* Appendix I). Look through the Constitution and identify what powers relating to foreign affairs have been expressly allocated to the federal government. In doing so, you may wish to divide them up based on whether they were allocated to the legislative, executive, or judicial branches. To which branch are the most powers accorded? To which the least? Note that in some instances specific foreign affairs powers (such as the power to make treaties) were expressly denied to the several states. Are any significant foreign affairs powers left unaddressed? Do any appear to have been allocated to the several states? The division of power between the federal government and the states in the area of foreign affairs remains an important issue today. For cases and commentary, see Chapter 6.

2. *Nature of U.S. Foreign Relations Powers*. Do you think the foreign relations powers of the United States emanate solely from the U.S. Constitution or from other sources? Do you see in the *Chinese Exclusion Case* a reliance upon sovereignty as a source of extra-constitutional congressional authority? Is the foreign relations power of a nature that it trumps protections that might otherwise exist for individuals or must the foreign relations power be read consonant with individual rights and liberties, as they existed at the founding and as they have evolved over time? Consider the view of Professor Louis Henkin in *Essays Commemorating the One Hundredth Anniversary of the Harvard Law Review: The Constitution and United States Sovereignty: A Century of* Chinese Exclusion *and Its Progeny*, 100 HARV. L. REV. 853, 862–63 (1987) (footnotes omitted):

> As a blanket exemption of immigration laws from constitutional limitations, *Chinese Exclusion* is a "relic from a different era." That era was one in which constitutional restraints were deemed inapplicable to

actions by the United States outside its territory; when orotund generalities about sovereignty and national security were a substitute for significant scrutiny of governmental action impinging on individual rights; when the Bill of Rights had not yet become our national hallmark and the principal justification and preoccupation of judicial review. It was an era before United States commitment to international human rights; before enlightenment in and out of the United States brought an end both to official racial discrimination at home and to national-origins immigration laws; before important freedoms were recognized as preferred, inviting strict scrutiny if they were invaded and requiring a compelling public interest to uphold their invasion. Since that era, the Supreme Court has held that the Bill of Rights applies to foreign as well as to domestic affairs, in war as well as in peace, to aliens as well as to citizens, abroad as well as at home. The Court has left only immigration and deportation outside the reach of fundamental constitutional protections.

The power of Congress to control immigration and to regulate alienage and naturalization is plenary. But even plenary power is subject to constitutional restraints. I cannot believe that the Court would hold today that the Constitution permits either exclusion on racial or religious grounds or deportation of persons lawfully admitted who have resided peacefully here. I do not believe that the Constitution permits indefinite detention of persons for no reason other than that our government wishes not to admit them and cannot deport them because no other country will take them or that it wishes to mistreat them in order to discourage others from coming here.

Chinese Exclusion—its very name is an embarrassment—must go.

3. *Further Reading*. An important commentary on the foreign relations law of the United States, with useful references to constitutional origins and early case law, is the *Restatement (Third) of the Foreign Relations Law of the United States* (1987) (2 vols.). Although now two decades old, the *Restatement* remains an important starting place for courts, practitioners, and scholars working in this field.

For other works that discuss foreign affairs and the founding of the American Republic, see Michael Ramsey, *The Constitution's Text in Foreign Affairs* (2007); Frederick W. Marks III, *Independence on Trial: Foreign Affairs and the Making of the Constitution* (1986); Jack N. Rakove, *Original Meanings: Politics and Ideas in the Making of the Constitution* (1996); Abraham D. Sofaer, *War, Foreign Affairs, and Constitutional Power: The Origins* (1984); *The Constitution and the Conduct of American Foreign Policy* (David Gray Adler & Larry N. George eds., 1996); Cecil V. Crabb Jr. & Pat M. Holt, *Invitation to Struggle: Congress, the President, and Foreign Policy* (1989); Michael J. Glennon, *Constitutional Diplomacy* (1990); Louis Henkin, *Foreign Affairs and the United States Constitution* (2d ed. 1996); Louis Henkin, *Constitutionalism, Democracy and Foreign Affairs* (1990); Harold Hongju Koh, *The National Security Constitution: Sharing Power After the Iran–Contra Affair* (1990); James M. Lindsay, *Congress and the Politics of U.S. Foreign Policy* (1994).

SECTION 2. INTERPRETIVE THEORY

INTRODUCTORY NOTE

Constitutional questions that arise in the realm of foreign relations frequently relate to matters not addressed directly by the constitutional text. The issues fall within the gaps between textual provisions; they are "interstitial." No provision in the text of the document, for example, indicates expressly which branch is possessed of the power to recognize and de-recognize foreign states. To what interpretive theory does a decision-maker turn in resolving such an issue? This is a seminal question in the on-going debate over constitutional interpretation generally. The focus can be somewhat different, however, when the issue is discussed in connection with constitutional subjects other than foreign relations law, such as the Bill of Rights. There, attention centers on such topics as personal autonomy and minority rights, issues that have been debated for centuries by moral philosophers; as a consequence, the discussion over interpretive theory tends to tie into a particular philosophical tradition. The allocation of governmental power to carry out a specific international act, on the other hand, while surely no less contentious a topic, raises issues of a different character. These tend to be questions of institutional right rather than of individual right. As the following materials indicate, there clearly is a good deal of overlap. Because textual ambiguities concerning each can be treated differently, however, it is important to be clear about what methodologies are available to resolve those ambiguities, and their strengths and weaknesses. The following materials address these issues. How much weight should be accorded constitutional text and structure? The intent of the framers? The intent of the ratifying conventions? Subsequent custom and practice? On what other sources would reliance be permissible?

GLENNON, CONSTITUTIONAL DIPLOMACY

35–49 (1990) (some footnotes omitted).

THE SEPARATION-OF-POWERS DOCTRINE IN FOREIGN-AFFAIRS DISPUTES

. . . .

Despite the frequency and import of separation cases, the Court has failed to articulate a consistent theoretical framework for determining the significance of these sources. In some cases, such as *Dames & Moore v. Regan* and *Haig v. Agee*, the Court has relied heavily upon custom, apparently viewing it as determinative. In other cases, such as *Nixon v. Administrator of General Services* and *INS v. Chadha*, custom has been virtually ignored. The Court's references in these cases to the separation-of-powers doctrine—a nebulous concept finding no express articulation in the constitutional text—seem to reduce it to a concept consisting of aggregated historical precedent more than articulated constitutional principle.

A separation-of-powers doctrine of independent vitality must apply a prescriptive norm different from the rule or rules that might be drawn from other jurisprudential approaches necessarily subsumed within it; it must direct an outcome that would not otherwise obtain. In this sense, separation of powers is not a distinct analytical doctrine. The cases that the Supreme Court has purportedly resolved by relying on the doctrine have in fact been decided by referring to other traditional sources of decisional authority directly relevant to the specific matter in dispute: the constitutional text, constitutional custom, the intent of the Framers, and functional considerations. The essential task for the Court in separation-of-powers disputes has thus been to discover which of these sources will be determinative.

THE SEPARATION-OF-POWERS DOCTRINE

. . . .

The Court has often referred to the doctrine as the juridical principle on which a decision is based. And it has attempted to spell out a more precise test for determining whether a statute violates the doctrine.... [An] examination of its decisions indicates that the Court has relied ultimately not upon the application of any such test but upon the same jurisprudential sources ordinarily used to resolve other constitutional controversies. These are the constitutional text, custom, the intent of the Framers, and on rare occasions, functional considerations. Most often, the Court applies a combination of the four approaches.

A survey of separation cases reveals no discernible system for deciding which of these sources of authority should be regarded as controlling. Most of these cases do not involve claims of plenary power by the Executive, and few involve foreign relations; they do, however, shed light on the allocation of power generally between the political branches and thus inform any effort to devise a methodology for allocating power in foreign affairs.

Reliance Upon the Constitutional Text

The Court on occasion disposes of a case simply by categorizing the challenged activity as legislative, executive, or judicial, and assigning the activity accordingly. Few cases lend themselves to this treatment, probably because a controversy will reach the Court only if there is room for reasonable dispute and because there can be no dispute if the Constitution has explicitly allocated the activity. *Springer v. Philippine Islands* is illustrative, involving a challenge to the validity of several acts of the Philippine legislature when the Philippines was a United States territory. The legislature had divested the Governor–General of his authority to appoint the directors and officers of several government-owned corporations and placed that function instead in the hands of the legislature. The acts were challenged as conflicting with the Organic Act, the fundamental law governing the Philippine Islands. The Court found that the Organic Act was the functional equivalent of a state constitution, containing the same if not stricter separation principles as those set forth in the United States Constitution. The Court declared that the appointment of business managers or of any other agents charged with carrying out the law was an inherently executive function; it thus held that the assignment of that function to the legislative branch was invalid. Similarly, ... the Court held in the *Steel Seizure Case* that President Truman could not order the Secretary of Commerce to seize the nation's steel mills because the order had a predominantly legislative character. The Court based its conclusion squarely on the text of the Constitution, which specifies that legislative powers shall vest in Congress; except for a limited authority to recommend and veto legislation, the Court found that the Constitution restricts the President's power to the faithful execution of the law.

Reliance Upon the Framers' Intent

When the constitutional text is not dispositive, the Court frequently turns to other sources of authority, including the Framers' intent. In *Myers v. United States*, for example, the issue was whether a president could remove a postmaster without the consent of the Senate when Senate concurrence was required by law. The Court found that no express provision in the constitutional text addressed the issue but nonetheless held that the statute requiring Senate consent was invalid based on the Framers' intent as inferred from the First Congress.

Nine years later, when the Court limited the scope of the *Myers* opinion in *Humphrey's Executor v. United States*, it again looked to the Framers' intent in restricting the President's power to remove commission members. Referring to the First Congress's grant of exclusive removal power to the President, the Court drew support from statements of the Framers that had construed the grant as limited to officers whose functions are wholly executive. In addition to legislation enacted when many Framers were members of Congress, the Court has relied upon the debates of the Philadelphia Convention to divine the Framers' intent. In *Powell v. McCormack*, the Court held that the article I, section 5, grant of power to both houses of Congress to pass on the "qualifications" of their members was limited to applying the textual requirements for membership set forth in that clause. And in *Morrison v. Olson*, the Court canvassed debate at the Convention in concluding that the Framers did not intend to deny Congress the power to provide for interbranch appointments.

Reliance Upon Custom

The Court has frequently relied upon custom as a source of decisional authority. As early as 1803, the Court so relied in upholding the power of the Supreme Court justices to sit as circuit judges in *Stuart v. Laird.* Noting that the practice was several years old—dating, in fact, from the inception of the federal judiciary—and that it enjoyed general acceptance, the Court held that the challenged practice itself provided "a contemporary interpretation ... too strong and obstinate to be shaken or controlled."

Stuart was cited with approval in what is perhaps the seminal custom case, *United States v. Midwest Oil Co.* At issue was the President's power to withdraw specified public lands from private acquisition in the face of a congressional declaration that such lands be "free and open to occupation, exploration and purchase by a citizen of the United States." The President's action was upheld on the basis of a long-standing executive practice. The Court was aware of the apparent circularity involved in relying on the challenged practice to justify its holding but defended its conclusion by reasoning that unchallenged executive actions create a presumption of authority and that such a presumption serves the need for continuity and stability in the proper administration of laws.

The Court again emphasized the probity of custom when in 1925 it found in *Ex parte Grossman* that the practice of several United States attorneys general in pardoning contempts had established that criminal contempt of court was an "offense against the United States" within the meaning of article II, section 2, clause 1, and that that provision thus conferred power upon the President. Specifically, the Court held that such a practice, when combined with legislative acquiescence, "strongly sustains the construction it is based on." Four years later, custom again played a role in the *Pocket Veto Cases*. At issue was the President's power to veto legislation presented to him within ten days of an adjournment of Congress without returning the bill to Congress for an "override" vote. Although the Court's holding was based on its interpretation of the Constitution, it also noted that its construction of the provision was "confirmed by the practical construction that has been given to it by the Presidents through a long course of years, in which Congress has acquiesced." Most recently, in *Mistretta v. United States*, the Court reviewed practices from Chief Justice (and treaty negotiator) John Jay to Chief Justice (and assassination investigator) Earl Warren in concluding that the assumption of extrajudicial duties was not unconstitutional.

Reliance Upon Functionalism

The functional approach, as we saw in Justice Sutherland's opinion in *Curtiss-Wright*, relies upon the institutional attributes of the branches as a standard for the allocation of power; powers are assigned based upon the functional advantages and disadvantages of one branch compared with the other. There appears to be no case in which the approach was solely relied upon by the Court, and indeed even passing references to functional considerations are fairly rare. One such case was *United States v. Nixon*, where the Court noted that "[t]he President's need for complete candor and objectivity from advisers calls for great deference from the courts." Similarly, in *Myers v. United States*, the Court observed that a power to dismiss was necessarily lodged in the President to maintain discipline in the ranks of governmental employees.

ANALYSIS OF THE COURT'S METHODOLOGY

Weaknesses of Each Approach

The Supreme Court's vacillation among these approaches reflects a recognition that none of the four, taken alone, is equal to the task of resolving the full range of separation-of-powers conflicts. An examination of the weaknesses of each approach helps explain the absence of a more principled decisional framework. The Court has seldom employed only one such juridical device for resolving separation-of-powers issues; in *Bowsher v. Synar*, for example, it employed three. For analytical purposes, however, each is considered below as an exclusive approach.

Textualism

The strict textualist approach to constitutional construction insists upon express textual authority for any assertion of constitutional power. Constitutional provisions are thus viewed as essentially "self-contained units, [to be] interpreted on the basis of their language ... without significant injection of content from outside the provision."[58] The fundamental justification for textualism is usually the perception that the discretion to disregard textual limitations is inconsistent with a government of laws.

Although the differences between textualist and nontextualist approaches are most salient with respect to issues that touch fundamental rights, the two approaches also yield significantly different results with regard to separation-of-powers disputes. In the *Steel Seizure Case*, for example, Justice Black relied upon the commander-in-chief clause and article I to dispose of the Executive's claim of authority to seize the nation's steel mills. Justice Black could not conceive of any concept of "theater of war" or executive power that would support President Truman's assumption of what was essentially a legislative function. Hence, the seizure order could only have been issued by Congress, in which all "authority to make laws" was vested by the Constitution. Justices Frankfurter and Jackson, concurring, doubted the power of the words' plain meaning. For Justice Frankfurter, "the considerations relevant to the legal enforcement of the principle of separations of powers seem ... more complicated and flexible than may appear from what Mr. Justice Black has written." Justice Jackson's concurring opinion seems implicitly to assume that the constitutional text alone cannot resolve all separation-of-powers disputes.

The appeal of textualism is understandable. The job of judges is to interpret, not to rewrite, and they are most clearly doing that job when their decisions are grounded firmly in the Constitution's text. But as *INS v. Chadha* serves to point out, the illusory simplicity of the textualist approach obscures the real elements of the judges' work. In *Chadha*, Chief Justice Burger relied largely upon the text of article I to find the legislative veto unconstitutional. The Court found that because the rules of the electoral branches in the legislative process were prescribed by "[e]xplicit and unambiguous provisions of the Constitution," no deviation from that method was allowable. In his dissent, however, Justice White persuasively argued that "[t]he constitutionality of the legislative-veto

58. J. Ely, Democracy and Distrust 12–13 (1980).

provision is anything but clearcut." He observed that the controversy was a direct result of the Constitution's silence "on the precise question" at issue.

In the realm of separation-of-powers, therefore, no less than that of fundamental rights, the strict textualist approach masks the tangle of values and methodologies that compose the process of judicial decision making. Moreover, rigid textual adherence fails to account for the Constitution's silence with respect to some subjects, nor does it address the need to afford other "enumerated powers the scope and elasticity" necessitated by the practical implications of their exercise. Applied to the few truly explicit constitutional provisions, textualism may be an appropriate means of judicial decision making. In the vast majority of separation disputes, however, the textualist approach represents result-oriented jurisprudence masquerading as commonsense reliance upon the constitutional text.

Intentionalism

Unlike textualism, the intentionalist approach eschews complete reliance on the constitutional text and allows resort to other expressions of the Framers' intent in determining the meaning of the original document. This intent is inferred from such sources as Madison's notes on the Constitutional Convention, the *Federalist* papers, records of the states' ratifying conventions, and the writings of participants. Subsequent custom and practice are of no constitutional relevance. The approach assumes that the states that ratified the work of the Constitutional Convention approved only the text before them, not a malleable instrument.

Although the pure intentionalist approach is not as limited in applicability as textualism, its weaknesses are no less evident. First, it is doubtful that the Framers themselves were strict intentionalists. They may have intended that their purposes, or at least some of their purposes, be viewed as tentative. Madison, describing the organization of the new Executive to the Virginia ratifying convention, emphasized the difficulty in delineating its responsibilities and acknowledged that the "mode which was judged most expedient was adopted, till experience should point out one more eligible."[75] In addition, as Professor Sandalow has pointed out, the intentions of the Framers can be described on a number of different levels of generality: "[A]ll the decisions shaping constitutional law to contemporary values can be understood as coming within the general intentions of the framers. All that is necessary is to state those intentions at a sufficiently high level of abstraction."[76]

Second, fifty-five men took part in the Philadelphia Convention, and it is always dubious to infer the intent of an assembly from the statement of an individual. Moreover, the records of the Philadelphia Convention, as well as those of the ratifying conventions, are incomplete. No verbatim

75. 3 [Debates in the Several State Conventions on the Adoption of the Federal Constitution (J. Elliot 2d ed. 1836)] at 531.

76. Sandalow, *Constitutional Interpretation*, 79 Mich. L. Rev. 1033, 1045 (1984).

notes were kept, and all meetings in Philadelphia were secret. Madison's notes were not published until 1840, and after the earlier publication of his *Journal,* he attempted to revise his account. The intentions of the Framers must, as Mr. Justice Jackson said, "be divined from materials almost as enigmatic as the dreams Joseph was called upon to interpret for Pharaoh."

Third, it is doubtful that the Framers themselves intended that their intent be sought to resolve conflicts concerning the document's meaning. The words of Thomas Jefferson bear note:

> Some men look at Constitutions with sanctimonious reverence, and deem them like the ark of the covenant, too sacred to be touched. They ascribe to the men of the preceding age a wisdom more than human, and suppose what they did to be beyond amendment. I knew that age well; I belonged to it, and labored with it. It deserved well of its country. It was very like the present, but without the experience of the present; and forty years of experience in government is worth a century of book-reading; and this [the Framers] would say themselves, were they to rise from the dead.... Let us ... avail ourselves of our reason and experience, to correct the crude essays of our first and unexperienced, although wise, virtuous, and well-meaning councils.[80]

Finally, the Framers' consent to the Constitution—whether divined from the text or other sources—does not establish the legitimacy of the system of government that exists two hundred years later. Few would argue that in a democratic society, decisions about the allocation of power made by a majority of the populace can be wholly displaced by the actions and beliefs of generations long dead.

Adaptivism

The adaptivist approach relies upon custom to determine the Constitution's meaning. It addresses the deficiencies of the first two methodologies by down-playing the primacy of the Constitution as originally conceived; the approach relies instead upon subsequent practice. Adherents to the adaptivist model emphasize the inability of the Framers to divine the exigencies likely to be confronted by the federal government in a dimly foreseen future. Karl Llewellyn, an eloquent advocate of the adaptivist perspective, found it "utterly fantastic that a document framed 150 years ago to initiate the operation of a government for three million agricultural, sea-board people could be presumed to control the present-day governing of an industrial nation of 130 million."[82] Dean Sandalow has written that constitutional law is not an exegesis, but "a process by which each generation gives formal expression to the values it holds fundamental in the operations of government."[83]

80. Letter to Samuel Kercheval, July 12, 1816, *in* 15 Writings of Thomas Jefferson 40–42 (1903).

82. Llewellyn, *The Constitution as an Institution*, 34 Colum. L. Rev. 1, 3 (1934).

83. Sandalow, *supra* note 76, at 1068....

The flexibility and pragmatism that are the chief virtues of the adaptivist model suggest its deficiencies as well. In place of a "filiopietistic" regard for the wisdom of the ancients, it substitutes a crypto-iconoclastic reverence for the "street smarts" of contemporaries. It equates what *is* with what ought to be and regards patterns of practice as principles of law. Acts inconsistent with the intent of the Framers represent not a usurpation of power but in effect an alternative means of amending the Constitution. Washington recognized the occasional value of such an approach to the resolution of constitutional conflicts, but cautioned that it was also "the customary weapon by which free governments are destroyed."[85]

Functionalism

It is easy to see why cases employing a functional approach are too few to indicate any doctrinal pattern. Indeed, in the most recent separation cases, the Court has seemed to take pains to *reject* the use of functional criteria. In an important passage in *INS v. Chadha*, the Court said that "the fact that a given law is efficient, convenient, and useful in facilitating functions of government, standing alone, will not save it if it is contrary to the Constitution. Convenience and efficiency are not the primary objectives—or the hallmarks—of democratic government." This repudiation of functionalism was reiterated in *Bowsher v. Synar*.

Thus one cannot normally argue for a given allocation of power on the basis of functional considerations, for a simple reason: The Constitution has already taken those considerations into account. Functional considerations animated the Framers' debate in Philadelphia; functional considerations impelled them to draft the constitutional text as they did; functional considerations engendered the customs that have grown from the way government actually works. Functional considerations, in short, are for a Constitution's *makers*, not its interpreters. It is therefore impermissible to contend that the Senate is better suited to determine whether a given foreign government should be recognized and that the Senate, not the President, possesses the recognition power. This is a judgment that the Constitution makes for us. Similarly, it would not be satisfactory to think of the Constitution as now permitting the President, without statutory authority, to invade Mexico to collect delinquent American bank loans because the President is functionally better able to act quickly. Functional considerations inform constitutional interpretation, providing explanatory reasons *why* the Constitution allocates power as it does. But they are *not* criteria to be applied to resolve allocation disputes controlled by other sources of constitutional power. "[T]he Framers," the Court said in *Chadha*, "ranked other values higher than efficiency."

Summary

None of the four approaches is capable of meeting reasonable objections leveled against its use as an exclusive methodology of constitutional

85. 35 The Writings of George Washington 228–29 (J. Fitzpatrick ed. 1940). . . .

interpretation. The pure textualist approach proceeds from the fiction that the language of the Constitution alone is dispositive; in contentious circumstances, it is not. On the other hand, the adaptivist approach prefers a Constitution that is all sail, threatening the very purpose of a written Constitution, and the intentionalist approach opts for a charter that is all anchor, presupposing a rigid constitutional order not subject to modification. The functionalist approach, finally, stands upon the appealing premise "You too can be a Framer," permitting ephemeral administrative variables to supplant enduring constitutional norms.

The Court has apparently recognized the shortcomings of sole reliance on any one of the four approaches, and has therefore generally employed a combination of approaches. First, it seeks to resolve the controversy by reference to the constitutional text, as it has been interpreted in the case law. If the text is not found dispositive, the Court next looks to other sources of authority: custom, the Framers' intent, and (on rare occasions) functional considerations.

Recognition of the methodology's general contours, however, only begins the inquiry. Both litigants and courts must be able to discern a principled process or framework for applying text, custom, and intent consistently in separation disputes. An examination of the Court's decisions in this area, however, reveals no such apparent framework for identifying the source of authority that should be regarded as controlling in a case. The Court has shifted from one approach to another, or emphasized one while deemphasizing another, without articulating any principled basis for favoring the approach selected. And as Leonard Levy has pointed out in discussing the "jurisprudence of original intent," the Court is not alone in lacking a principled approach.

In many cases, an approach other than the one employed would have seemed equally justified. In a dissenting opinion in *Myers*, for example, Justice Brandeis detailed the instances in which Congress had conditioned executive removal of an official upon legislative concurrence. Yet such precedents were accorded no weight by the Court's majority, who elected to view the Framers' intent as controlling. In *Chadha*, the Court declined even to consider what weight should be given the practice of "legislative-veto" review of executive activities—even though the practice comprised hundreds of precedents over a history of nearly fifty years. The long-standing use of executive agreements to settle international claims disputes was nonetheless found by the Court, in light of the provisions of the International Emergency Economic Powers Act, to be dispositive of the question of the validity of the United States–Iran Claims Settlement Agreement, although significant authority exists for the position that such circumvention of the advice and consent of the Senate by using an executive agreement is at odds with the intent of the Framers. The one analytic constant in such cases seems to be a recognition by the Court that its starting point must be the constitutional text—a sound theoretical instinct, but one that often produces little practical guidance.

JOHN HART ELY, DEMOCRACY AND DISTRUST*

12–13 (1981) (footnotes omitted).

Interpretivism does seem to retain the substantial virtue of fitting better our ordinary notion of how law works: if your job is to enforce the Constitution then the Constitution is what you should be enforcing, not whatever may happen to strike you as a good idea at the time. Thus stated, the conclusion possesses the unassailability of a truism, and if acceptance of *that* were all it took to make someone an interpretivist, no sane person could be anything else. But the debate over interpretivism is not an argument about the truth of a tautology, for interpretivism involves a further claim, that "enforcing the Constitution" necessarily means proceeding from premises that are explicit or clearly implicit in the document itself.

. . . .

. . . The suggestion . . . is usually that the various provisions of the Constitution be approached essentially as self-contained units and interpreted on the basis of their language, with whatever interpretive help the legislative history can provide, without significant injection of content from outside the provision. We shall see, however, that this standard form of interpretivism runs into trouble—trouble precisely on its own terms, and so serious as to be dispositive. For the constitutional document itself, the interpretivist's Bible, contains several provisions whose invitation to look beyond their four corners—whose invitation, if you will, to become at least to that extent a noninterpretivist—cannot be construed away.

Constitutional provisions exist on a spectrum ranging from the relatively specific to the extremely open-textured. At one extreme—for example the requirement that the President "have attained to the Age of thirty five years"—the language is so clear that a conscious reference to purpose seems unnecessary. Other provisions, such as the one requiring that the President be a "natural born Citizen," may need a reference to historical usage so as to exclude certain alternative constructions—conceivably if improbably here, a requirement of legitimacy (or illegitimacy!) or non-Caesarian birth—but once that "dictionary function" is served, the provision becomes relatively easy to apply. Others, such as the First Amendment's prohibition of congressional laws "abridging the freedom of speech," seem to need more. For one thing, a phrase as terse as the others I have mentioned is here expected to govern a broader and more important range of problems. For another, and this may have something to do with the first, we somehow sense that a line of growth was intended, that the language was not intended to be restricted to its 1791 meaning. This realization would not faze Justice Black or most other interpretivists: the job of the person interpreting the provision, they would respond, is to identify the *sorts of evils* against which the provision was directed and to move against their contemporary counterparts. Obviously this will be difficult, but it will remain interpretivism—a determination of "the present scope and meaning of a decision that the nation, at an earlier time, articulated and enacted into the constitutional text."

WILLIAM J. BRENNAN, JR., THE CONSTITUTION OF THE UNITED STATES: CONTEMPORARY RATIFICATION

19 U.C. Davis L. Rev. 2, 3–7 (1985).

The Constitution is fundamentally a public text—the monumental charter of a government and a people—and a Justice of the Supreme Court must apply it to resolve public controversies. For, from our beginnings, a most important consequence of the constitutionally created separation of powers has been the American habit, extraordinary to other democracies, of casting social, economic, philosophical and political questions in the form of lawsuits, in an attempt to secure ultimate resolution by the Supreme Court. In this way, important aspects of the most fundamental issues confronting our democracy may finally arrive in the Supreme Court for judicial determination. Not infrequently, these are the issues upon which contemporary society is most deeply divided. They arouse our deepest emotions. The main burden of my twenty-nine Terms on the Supreme Court has thus been to wrestle with the Constitution in this heightened public context, to draw meaning from the text in order to resolve public controversies.

Two other aspects of my relation to this text warrant mention. First, constitutional interpretation for a federal judge is, for the most part, obligatory. When litigants approach the bar of court to adjudicate a constitutional dispute, they may justifiably demand an answer. Judges cannot avoid a definitive interpretation because they feel unable to, or would prefer not to, penetrate to the full meaning of the Constitution's provisions. Unlike literary critics, judges cannot merely savor the tensions or revel in the ambiguities inhering in the text—judges must resolve them.

Second, consequences flow from a Justice's interpretation in a direct and immediate way. A judicial decision respecting the incompatibility of Jim Crow with a constitutional guarantee of equality is not simply a contemplative exercise in defining the shape of a just society. It is an order—supported by the full coercive power of the State—that the present society change in a fundamental aspect. Under such circumstances the process of deciding can be a lonely, troubling experience for fallible human beings conscious that their best may not be adequate to the challenge. We Justices are certainly aware that we are not final because we are infallible; we know that we are infallible only because we are final. One does not forget how much may depend on the decision. More than the litigants may be affected. The course of vital social, economic and political currents may be directed.

These three defining characteristics of my relation to the constitutional text—its public nature, obligatory character, and consequentialist aspect—cannot help but influence the way I read that text. When Justices interpret the Constitution they speak for their community, not for themselves alone. The act of interpretation must be undertaken with full consciousness that it is, in a very real sense, the community's interpretation that is sought. Justices are not platonic guardians appointed to wield authority according to their personal moral predilections. Precisely because coercive force must attend any judicial decision to countermand the will of a contemporary majority, the Justices must render constitutional interpretations that are received as legitimate....

There are those who find legitimacy in fidelity to what they call "the intentions of the Framers." In its most doctrinaire incarnation, this view demands that Justices discern exactly what the Framers thought about the question under consideration and simply follow that intention in resolving the case before them. It is a view that feigns self-effacing deference to the specific judgments of those who forged our original social compact. But in truth it is little more than arrogance cloaked as humility. It is arrogant to pretend that from our vantage we can gauge accurately the intent of the Framers on application of principle to specific, contemporary questions. All too often, sources of potential enlightenment such as records of the ratification debates provide sparse or ambiguous evidence of the original intention. Typically, all that can be gleaned is that the Framers themselves did not agree about the application or meaning of particular constitutional provisions, and hid their differences in cloaks of generality. Indeed, it is far from clear whose intention is relevant—that of the drafters, the congressional disputants, or the ratifiers in the states?—or even whether the idea of an original intention is a coherent way of thinking about a jointly drafted document drawing its authority from a general assent of the states. And apart from the problematic nature of the sources, our distance of two centuries cannot but work as a prism refracting all we perceive. One cannot help but speculate that the chorus of lamentations calling for interpretation faithful to "original intention"—and proposing nullification of interpretations that fail this quick litmus test—must inevitably come from persons who have no familiarity with the historical record.

....

We current Justices read the Constitution in the only way that we can: as Twentieth Century Americans. We look to the history of the time of framing and to the intervening history of interpretation. But the ultimate question must be, what do the words of the text mean in our time? For the genius of the Constitution rests not in any static meaning it might have had in a world that is dead and gone, but in the adaptability of its great principles to cope with current problems and current needs. What the constitutional fundamentals meant to the wisdom of other times cannot be their measure to the vision of our time. . . .

ANTONIN SCALIA, CONSTITUTIONAL INTERPRETATION

Remarks to the Woodrow Wilson International Center for Scholars (March 14, 2005).

I am one of a small number of judges, small number of anybody—judges, professors, lawyers—who are known as originalists. Our manner of interpreting the Constitution is to begin with the text, and to give that text the meaning that it bore when it was adopted by the people. I'm not a "strict constructionist" . . . I don't like the term "strict construction." I do not think the Constitution, or any text should be interpreted either strictly or sloppily; it should be interpreted reasonably. Many of my interpretations do not deserve the description "strict." I do believe, however, that you give the text the meaning it had when it was adopted.

This is such a minority position in modern academia and in modern legal circles that on occasion I'm asked when I've given a talk like this a question from the back of the room—"Justice Scalia, when did you first become an originalist?"—as though it is some kind of weird affliction that seizes some people—"When did you first start eating human flesh?"

Although it is a minority view now, the reality is that, not very long ago, originalism was orthodoxy. Everybody, at least purported to be an originalist. If you go back and read the commentaries on the Constitution by Joseph Story, he didn't think the Constitution evolved or changed. He said it means and will always mean what it meant when it was adopted.

. . . .

Now, in asserting that originalism used to be orthodoxy, I do not mean to imply that judges did not distort the Constitution now and then, of course they did. We had willful judges then, and we will have willful judges until the end of time. But the difference is that prior to the last 50 years or so, prior to the advent of the "Living Constitution," judges did their distortions the good old fashioned way, the honest way—they lied about it. They said the Constitution means such and such, when it never meant such and such.

It's a big difference that you now no longer have to lie about it, because we are in the era of the evolving Constitution. And the judge can simply say, "Oh yes, the Constitution didn't used to mean that, but it does now." We are in the age in which not only judges, not only lawyers, but even school children have come to learn the Constitution changes. I have grammar school students come into the Court now and then, and they recite very proudly what they have been taught: "The Constitution is a living document." You know, it morphs.

. . . .

What are the arguments usually made in favor of the Living Constitution? As the name of it suggests, it is a very attractive philosophy, and it's hard to talk people out of it—the notion that the Constitution grows. The major argument is the Constitution is a living organism, it has to grow with the society that it governs or it will become brittle and snap.

This is the equivalent of, an anthropomorphism equivalent to what you hear from your stockbroker, when he tells you that the stock market is resting for an assault on the 11,000 level. The stock market panting at some base camp. The stock market is not a mountain climber and the Constitution is not a living organism for Pete's sake; it's a legal document, and like all legal documents, it says some things, and it doesn't say other things. And if you think that the aficionados of the Living Constitution want to bring you flexibility, think again.

My Constitution is a very flexible Constitution. You think the death penalty is a good idea—persuade your fellow citizens and adopt it. You think it's a bad idea—persuade them the other way and eliminate it. You want a right to abortion—create it the way most rights are created in a democratic society, persuade your fellow citizens it's a good idea and enact it. You want the opposite—persuade them the other way. . . .

. . . Some people also seem to like [the Living Constitution] because they think it's a good liberal thing—that somehow this is a conservative / liberal battle, and conservatives like the old-fashioned originalist Constitution and liberals ought to like the Living Constitution. That's not true either. The dividing line between those who believe in the Living Constitution and those who don't is not the dividing line between conservatives and liberals.

Conservatives are willing to grow the Constitution to cover their favorite causes just as liberals are. . . .

. . . .

Some people are in favor of the Living Constitution because they think it always leads to greater freedom—there's just nothing to lose, the evolving Constitution will always provide greater and greater freedom, more and more rights. Why would you think that? It's a two-way street. And indeed, under the aegis of the Living Constitution, some freedoms have been taken away.

. . . .

Well, I've talked about some of the false virtues of the Living Constitution, let me tell you what I consider its principle vices are. Surely the greatest—you should always begin with principle—its greatest vice is its illegitimacy. The only reason federal courts sit in judgment of the constitutionality of federal legislation is not because they are explicitly authorized to do so in the Constitution. Some modern constitutions give the constitutional court explicit authority to review German legislation or French legislation for its constitutionality; our Constitution doesn't say anything like that. But John Marshall says in *Marbury v. Madison*: Look, this is lawyers' work. What you have here is an apparent conflict between the Constitution and the statute. And, all the time, lawyers and judges have to reconcile these conflicts—they try to read the two to comport with each other. If they can't, it's judges' work to decide which ones prevail. When there are two statutes, the more recent one prevails. It implicitly repeals the older one. But when the Constitution is at issue, the Constitution prevails because it is a "superstatute." I mean, that's what Marshall says: It's judges' work.

If you believe, however, that the Constitution is not a legal text, like the texts involved when judges reconcile or decide which of two statutes prevail; if you think the Constitution is some exhortation to give effect to the most fundamental values of the society as those values change from year to year; if you think that it is meant to reflect, as some of the Supreme Court cases say, particularly those involving the Eighth Amendment, if you think it is simply meant to reflect the evolving standards of decency that mark the progress of a maturing society—if that is what you think it is, then why in the world would you have it interpreted by nine lawyers? What do I know about the evolving standards of decency of American society? I'm afraid to ask.

If that is what you think the Constitution is, then *Marbury v. Madison* is wrong. It shouldn't be up to the judges, it should be up to the legislature. We should have a system like the English—whatever the legislature thinks is constitutional is constitutional. They know the evolving standards of American society, I don't. So in principle, it's incompatible with the legal regime that America has established.

. . . You see, I have my rules that confine me. I know what I'm looking for. When I find it—the original meaning of the Constitution—I am handcuffed. If I believe that the First Amendment meant when it was adopted that you are entitled to burn the American flag, I have to come out that way even though I don't like to come out that way. When I find that the original meaning of the jury trial guarantee is that any additional time you spend in prison which depends upon a fact must depend upon a fact found by a jury—once I find that's what the jury trial guarantee means, I am handcuffed. Though I'm a law-and-order type, I cannot do all the mean conservative things I would like to do to this society. You got me.

Now, if you're not going to control your judges that way, what other criterion are you going to place before them? What is the criterion that governs the Living Constitutional judge? What can you possibly use, besides original meaning? Think about that. Natural law? We all agree on that, don't we? The philosophy of John Rawls? That's easy. There really is nothing else. You either tell your judges, "Look, this is a law, like all laws, give it the meaning it had when it was adopted." Or, you tell your judges, "Govern us. You tell us whether people under 18, who committed their crimes when they were under 18, should be executed. You tell us whether there ought to be an unlimited right to abortion or a partial right to abortion. You make these decisions for us." I have put this question—you know I speak at law schools with some frequency just to make trouble—and I put this question to the faculty all the time, or incite the students to ask their Living Constitutional professors: "Okay professor, you are not an originalist, what is your criterion?" There is none other.

PHILLIP R. TRIMBLE, INTERNATIONAL LAW: UNITED STATES FOREIGN RELATIONS LAW

27–31 (2002).

Original Intent includes statements of participants in the Philadelphia convention or the ratifying conventions held in individual states, and contemporaneous statements by these "Framers," such as the Federalist papers. Original Intent also can be found in speeches, judicial decisions and other writings by the Framers in the early years of the Republic, and actions of the early Presidents and Congresses who were well aware of the Framers' intent. Thus, at the Philadelphia convention, Madison explained that a proposed amendment—later adopted—would make it clear that the "President could repel sudden attacks." From this it has generally been agreed that the President may use military force to defend the country in the event of invasion (and perhaps in other situations as well), even though nothing in the text states or implies such an authority.

There are, nevertheless, several problems with finding and using Original Intent as a definitive source of constitutional interpretation. First, it is difficult to impute a unified intent to any deliberative body, where different participants may have had different intentions and understandings (not to mention motives). Second, the product of deliberation inevitably includes compromises that may mask inconsistent intentions of the different participants or may simply defer arguments over matters that could not be resolved. Third, it is inevitably hazardous to impute a collective purpose based on an isolated statement by one individual. Fourth, there were 14 deliberative bodies involved in the drafting and ratification of the Constitution and some of these deliberations were secret. Fifth, the surviving evidence of what happened is quite fragmentary. As Justice Jackson remarked:

> Just what our forefathers did envision, or would have envisioned had they foreseen modern conditions, must be divined from materials almost as enigmatic as the dreams Joseph was called upon to interpret for Pharaoh. A century and a half of partisan debate and scholarly speculation yields no net result but only supplies more or less apt quotations from respected sources on each side of any question.[11]

Sixth, the surviving evidence may not be wholly reliable. One of the best sources consists of Madison's notes on the deliberations in Philadel-

11. [Youngstown Sheet & Tube Co. v. Sawyer, 343 U.S.] at 634–35 [(concurring op.)].

phia which were revised 30 years after the fact. Seventh, the materials are often contradictory.

Justice Jackson was wrong to brush aside the Vesting Clause as an important source of presidential authority, but he was correct to note that the quotations of the Framers employed by advocates of particular political outcomes "largely cancel each other.... A Hamilton may be matched against a Madison."[12] Indeed a Hamilton may be matched against a Hamilton, and a Madison against a Madison. Hamilton defended the Vesting Clause in his Publius article ... but he later argued that Senate consent was required for removal of a (Federalist) official. Madison, who as Helvidius argued for restriction of presidential authority and who disparaged the Vesting Clause, took the opposite position on the removal issue. The point is that individual statements are unreliable guides to understanding the original meaning of the Constitution.

Another kind of problem with using Original Intent is that any statement or point made can be expressed at different levels of generality to support different conclusions. For example, Madison's statement about presidential authority to "repel sudden attack" could be taken to justify responding to an invasion of the United States, or more generally, to any unanticipated emergency situation thrust upon the nation. Finally, perhaps the Framers themselves did not intend that their intent be conclusive in resolving issues in the future. Original Intent thus may tell us that Original Intent should not govern!

The many problems with persuasively demonstrating an Original Intent reinforce the need to refer to language, structure and context as preferable guides in constitutional interpretation. Indeed it seems more realistic to attempt to fathom an *original understanding* of constitutional text, based on general contextual analysis as opposed to specific statements of particular Framers. Original Intent in this sense provides a more secure foundation for interpreting the ambiguous constitutional text, but it would be unrealistic to ignore the fact that isolated statements of Framers and the other contextual components of Original Intent identified above form an important component of legal rhetoric in this field, whether in a legal brief, an academic article, or a political forum. Original Intent is also frequently supplemented with other approaches to constitutional interpretation.

NOTES ON INTERPRETIVE THEORY

1. *Interpreting the Interpreters*. Professor Glennon asserts that, in the field of foreign relations law, "the Court has failed to articulate a consistent theoretical framework for determining the significance of" text, constitutional framework, original intent, subsequent practice, and other potential sources. Over the course of this chapter, you will read a number of cases in the field—*Little v. Barreme*, *Curtiss-Wright*, *Youngstown*, *Korematsu*, and *Hamdi*. As

12. Id. at 635....

you do so, consider whether you agree with Professor Glennon's assertion. Does the Supreme Court generally apply an informal hierarchy of sources to its jurisprudence? If so, how are the elements of this informal hierarchy ordered?

2. *Charting a Course for Foreign Affairs Law.* The nineteenth-century British poet and historian Thomas Babington Macaulay is said to have told an American acquaintance, "Your constitution is all sail and no anchor." Given the dramatic developments in foreign relations since the founding of the American Republic, including the emergence of air power, the development of weapons of mass destruction, and the rise of transnational terrorism, is this an area of the law where "sailing" is especially called for? Or are there dangers of relying on a "Living Constitution," which tacks with the changing values of society?

3. *Laying Anchor.* Justice Scalia suggests that once he has determined the original intent of the framers he is "handcuffed." Is such an approach especially necessary in the field of foreign relations and national security law, where core values of American society are severely tested? Or is the approach especially infeasible in this field of law? In the *Youngstown* case (next section), Justice Jackson suggests that the intent of the framers ". . . must be divined from materials almost as enigmatic as the dreams Joseph was called upon to interpret for Pharaoh"? Even if it is possible to divine the intent of the framers in certain areas of the law, what should the Court do (or not do) when considering matters on which the framers were arguably silent?

4. *Using Foreign and International Law.* A further interpretive issue that arises is the extent to which foreign or international law should be consulted when interpreting the U.S. Constitution. For cases and commentary, see Chapter 2, Section 4.

SECTION 3. BALANCING CONCURRENT CONGRESSIONAL–PRESIDENTIAL POWER

LITTLE v. BARREME

6 U.S. (2 Cranch) 170, 2 L.Ed. 243 (1804).

[Relations between the United States and France, two allies during the American Revolutionary War, deteriorated rapidly following ratification of the Jay Treaty between America and Britain in 1795. Within just a few years, French privateers were raiding U.S. vessels, including in the Chesapeake Bay. Consequently, during 1798–1800, the United States fought an undeclared naval war with France.

Little v. Barreme was one of three Supreme Court cases to address this so-called "quasi-war" with France. In this case, U.S. frigates in 1799 captured a Danish vessel (the *Flying Fish*) near the island of Hispaniola (a large island that is now home to the countries of Haiti and the Dominican Republic). The *Flying Fish* was en route from Jeremie (a port on the French-controlled part of Hispaniola, now in Haiti) to the island of St.

Thomas (part of the Virgin Islands then under Danish control). The U.S. captain (Little) brought the vessel to Boston, thinking that he was acting in accordance with the 1799 Non–Intercourse Law, which allowed for seizure on the high seas of vessels bound for France if thought to be carrying cargo for France.]

February 27. MARSHALL, CHIEF JUSTICE, now delivered the opinion of the Court.

The *Flying-Fish*, a Danish vessel, having on board Danish and neutral property, was captured on the 2d of December 1799, on a voyage from Jeremie to St. Thomas's, by the United States frigate *Boston*, commanded by Captain Little, and brought into the port of Boston, where she was libelled as an American vessel that had violated the non-intercourse law.

The judge before whom the cause was tried, directed a restoration of the vessel and cargo as neutral property, but refused to award damages for the capture and detention, because in his opinion, there was probable cause to suspect the vessel to be American.

On an appeal to the circuit court this sentence was reversed, because the *Flying-Fish* was on a voyage *from*, not *to*, a French port, and was therefore, had she even been an American vessel, not liable to capture on the high seas.

During the hostilities between the United States and France, an act for the suspension of all intercourse between the two nations was annually passed. That under which the *Flying-Fish* was condemned, declared every vessel, owned, hired or employed wholly or in part by an American, which should be employed in any traffic or commerce with or for any person resident within the jurisdiction or under the authority of the French republic, to be forfeited together with her cargo; the one half to accrue to the United States, and the other to any person or persons, citizens of the United States, who will inform and prosecute for the same.

The 5th section of this act authorizes the president of the United States, to instruct the commanders of armed vessels, "to stop and examine any ship or vessel of the United States on the high seas, which there may be reason to suspect to be engaged in any traffic or commerce contrary to the true tenor of the act, and if upon examination it should appear that such ship or vessel is bound, or sailing *to* any port or place within the territory of the French republic or her dependencies, it is rendered lawful to seize such vessel, and send her into the United States for adjudication."

It is by no means clear that the president of the United States whose high duty it is to "take care that the laws be faithfully executed," and who is commander in chief of the armies and navies of the United States, might not, without any special authority for that purpose, in the then existing state of things, have empowered the officers commanding the armed vessels of the United States, to seize and send into port for adjudication, American vessels which were forfeited by being engaged in this illicit commerce. But when it is observed that the general clause of the first section of the "act, which declares that such vessels may be seized, and may be prosecuted in any district or circuit court, which shall be holden within or for the district where the seizure shall be made," obviously contemplates a seizure within the United States; and that the 5th section gives a special authority to seize on the high seas, and limits that authority to the seizure of vessels bound or sailing *to* a French port, the legislature seems to have prescribed that the manner in which this law shall be carried into execution, was to exclude a seizure of any vessel not bound *to* a French port. Of consequence, however strong the circumstances might be, which induced Captain Little to suspect the *Flying-Fish* to be an American vessel, they could not excuse the detention of her, since he would not have been authorised to detain her had she been really American.

It was so obvious, that if only vessels sailing to a French port could be seized on the high seas, that the law would be very often evaded, that this act of congress appears to have received a different construction from the executive of the United States; a construction much better calculated to give it effect.

A copy of this act was transmitted by the secretary of the navy, to the captains of the armed vessels, who were ordered to consider the 5th section as a part of their instructions. The same letter contained the following clause. "A proper discharge of the important duties enjoined on you, arising out of this act, will require the exercise of a sound and an impartial judgment. You are not only to do all that in you lies, to prevent all intercourse, whether direct or circuitous, between the ports of the United States and those of France or her dependencies, where the vessels *are apparently as well as really* American, and protected by American papers only, but you are to be vigilant that vessels or cargoes really American, but covered by Danish or other foreign papers, and bound *to* or *from* French ports, do not escape you."

These orders given by the executive under the construction of the act of congress made by the department to which its execution was assigned, enjoin the seizure of American vessels sailing from a French port. Is the officer who obeys them liable for damages sustained by this misconstruction of the act, or will his orders excuse him? If his instructions afford him no protection, then the law must take its course, and he must pay such damages as are legally awarded against him; if they excuse an act not otherwise excusable, it would then be necessary to inquire whether this is a case in which the probable cause which existed to induce a suspicion that the vessel was American, would excuse the captor from damages when the vessel appeared in fact to be neutral.

I confess the first bias of my mind was very strong in favor of the opinion that though the instructions of the executive could not give a right, they might yet excuse from damages. I was much inclined to think that a distinction ought to be taken between acts of civil and those of military officers; and between proceedings within the body of the country and those on the high seas. That implicit obedience which military men usually pay to the orders of their superiors, which indeed is indispensably necessary to every military system, appeared to me strongly to imply the principle that those orders, if not to perform a prohibited act, ought to justify the person whose general duty it is to obey them, and who is placed by the laws of his country in a situation which in general requires that he should obey them. I was strongly inclined to think that where, in consequence of orders from the legitimate authority, a vessel is seized with pure intention, the claim of the injured party for damages would be against that government from which the orders proceeded, and would be a proper subject for negotiation. But I have been convinced that I was mistaken, and I have receded from this first opinion. I acquiesce in that of my brethren, which is, that the instructions cannot change the nature of the transaction, or legalize an act which without those instructions would have been a plain trespass.

It becomes therefore unnecessary to inquire whether the probable cause afforded by the conduct of the *Flying-Fish* to suspect her of being an American, would excuse Captain Little from damages for having seized and sent her into port, since had she actually been an American, the seizure would have been unlawful?

Captain Little then must be answerable in damages to the owner of this neutral vessel, and as the account taken by order of the circuit court is not objectionable on its face, and has not been excepted to by council before the proper tribunal, this court can receive no objection to it.

There appears then to be no error in the judgment of the circuit court, and it must be affirmed with costs.

NOTES ON LITTLE V. BARREME

1. *Congressional Power.* What constitutional power of Congress was at play in *Little v. Barreme*? The power to declare war? To make rules concerning captures on water? To make rules for the governing and regulation of naval forces? To regulate foreign commerce?

2. *Presidential Power.* Is there any constitutional power of the President that should have been relevant in *Little v. Barreme*? Of what significance is it that the Court does not discuss whether the President has "inherent" or "independent" power to conduct U.S. foreign policy, especially in the context of an informal war? Why does the Court not discuss the constitutionality of the statute in question, *i.e.*, the ability of Congress to inhibit the President's conduct in waging an informal war?

3. *Relating Congressional Power to Executive Power.* What specific act of the Executive was challenged in *Little v. Barreme*? With respect to that challenged act, what was the posture of Congress? Did Congress approve of the act? Oppose it? Neither? Does the constitutionality of the President's act turn on how you answer that question? Would the President's act have been constitutional if Congress had been silent?

4. *Implying Congressional Approval.* Assuming that the non-intercourse statute is the relevant source of law, might the Secretary of the Navy have *implied* a broader congressional restriction on trade with France from the statute? Is Justice Marshall's interpretation the only viable one? What if Congress had appropriated funding for naval patrols off the coast of Port-au-Prince? The question of implied congressional authorization is one that has arisen repeatedly and will be revisited in the materials to come.

5. *Precedential Value. Little v. Barreme* is frequently cited as a case dealing with the distribution of war powers between Congress and the President, one that helps define the scope of presidential power in the face of congressional disapproval. How significant is it that the congressional statute at issue authorized the seizure of American vessels engaged in *commerce* with France, given Congress' express constitutional power to regulate foreign commerce? Further, should the case be read narrowly as concerning merely the liability of a military official for damages during a period of hostilities? One scholar has suggested that "the Court instead viewed the provisions of the act as primarily pertaining to Congress's power to regulate commerce with other nations," Gregory J. Sidak, *The Quasi–War Cases*, 28 HARV. J.L. & PUB. POL'Y 465, 493 (2005), while another has argued that *Barreme* does not reach the issue of presidential war powers because the Court was asked only to consider Captain Little's liability. *See* John C. Yoo, *The Continuation of Politics by Other Means: The Original Understanding of War Powers*, 84 CAL. L. REV. 167, 294–95 n.584 (1996). Do you agree?

UNITED STATES v. CURTISS–WRIGHT EXPORT CORP.

299 U.S. 304, 57 S.Ct. 216, 81 L.Ed. 255 (1936) (footnotes and some citations omitted).

[From 1932 to 1935, Bolivia and Paraguay fought a war for control of a large part of the Chaco region of South America, which was thought to contain vast oil resources. In 1934, Congress enacted and the President signed into law a joint resolution providing that, if the President made certain findings and issued a proclamation to the effect that a ban on arms sales to Bolivia and Paraguay would serve the cause of regional peace, then such arms sales would be illegal. Thereafter, the President made the findings and issued the proclamation. Upon being charged in 1936 with violating the law by selling arms to Bolivia, defendant Curtiss–Wright Corporation challenged the law's constitutionality inter alia on a theory that it invalidly delegated legislative power to the executive.]

MR. JUSTICE SUTHERLAND delivered the opinion of the Court.

. . . .

Whether, if the Joint Resolution had related solely to internal affairs it would be open to the challenge that it constituted an unlawful delegation of legislative power to the Executive, we find it unnecessary to determine. The whole aim of the resolution is to affect a situation entirely external to the United States, and falling within the category of foreign affairs. The determination which we are called to make, therefore, is whether the Joint Resolution, as applied to that situation, is vulnerable to attack under the rule that forbids a delegation of the law-making power. In other words, assuming (but not deciding) that the challenged delegation, if it were confined to internal affairs, would be invalid, may it nevertheless be sustained on the ground that its exclusive aim is to afford a remedy for a hurtful condition within foreign territory?

It will contribute to the elucidation of the question if we first consider the differences between the powers of the federal government in respect of foreign or external affairs and those in respect of domestic or internal affairs. That there are differences between them, and that these differences are fundamental, may not be doubted.

The two classes of powers are different, both in respect of their origin and their nature. The broad statement that the federal government can exercise no powers except those specifically enumerated in the Constitution, and such implied powers as are necessary and proper to carry into effect the enumerated powers, is categorically true only in respect of our internal affairs. In that field, the primary purpose of the Constitution was to carve from the general mass of legislative powers *then possessed by the states* such portions as it was thought desirable to vest in the federal government, leaving those not included in the enumeration still in the states. *Carter v. Carter Coal Co.*, 298 U.S. 238, 294. That this doctrine applies only to powers which the states had, is self evident. And since the states severally never possessed international powers, such powers could not have been carved from the mass of state powers but obviously were transmitted to the United States from some other source. During the colonial period, those powers were possessed exclusively by and were entirely under the control of the Crown. By the Declaration of Independence, "the Representatives of the United States of America" declared the United [not the several] Colonies to be free and independent states, and as such to have "full Power to levy War, conclude Peace, contract Alliances, establish Commerce and to do all other Acts and Things which Independent States may of right do."

As a result of the separation from Great Britain by the colonies acting as a unit, the powers of external sovereignty passed from the Crown not to the colonies severally, but to the colonies in their collective and corporate capacity as the United States of America. Even before the Declaration, the colonies were a unit in foreign affairs, acting through a common agency—namely, the Continental Congress, composed of delegates from the thirteen colonies. That agency exercised the powers of war and peace, raised an army, created a navy, and finally adopted the Declaration of Independence. Rulers come and go; governments end and forms of government change; but sovereignty survives. A political society cannot endure without a supreme will somewhere. Sovereignty is never held in suspense. When, therefore, the external sovereignty of Great Britain in respect of the colonies ceased, it immediately passed to the Union. *See Penhallow v. Doane*, 3 Dall. 54, 80–81. That fact was given practical application almost at once. The treaty of peace, made on September 23, 1783, was concluded between his Brittanic Majesty and the "United States of America."

The Union existed before the Constitution, which was ordained and established among other things to form "a more perfect Union." Prior to that event, it is clear that the Union, declared by the Articles of Confederation to be "perpetual," was the sole possessor of external sovereignty and in the Union it remained without change save in so far as the Constitution in express terms qualified its exercise. The Framers' Convention was called and exerted its powers upon the irrefutable postulate that though the states were several their people in respect of foreign affairs were one. Compare *The Chinese Exclusion Case*, 130 U.S. 581, 604, 606. In that convention, the entire absence of state power to deal with those affairs was thus forcefully stated by Rufus King:

> "The states were not 'sovereigns' in the sense contended for by some. They did not possess the peculiar features of sovereignty,—they could not make war, nor peace, nor alliances, nor treaties. Considering them as political beings, they were dumb, for they could not speak to any foreign sovereign whatever. They were deaf, for they could not hear any propositions from such sovereign. They had not even the organs or faculties of defence or offence, for they could not of themselves raise troops, or equip vessels, for war." 5 Elliot's Debates 212.

It results that the investment of the federal government with the powers of external sovereignty did not depend upon the affirmative grants of the Constitution. The powers to declare and wage war, to conclude peace, to make treaties, to maintain diplomatic relations with other sovereignties, if they had never been mentioned in the Constitution, would have vested in the federal government as necessary concomitants of nationality. Neither the Constitution nor the laws passed in pursuance of it have any force in foreign territory unless in respect of our own citizens; and operations of the nation in such territory must be governed by treaties, international understandings and compacts, and the principles of international law. As a member of the family of nations, the right and power of the United States in that field are equal to the right and power of the other members of the international family. Otherwise, the United States is not completely sovereign. The power to acquire territory by discovery and occupation, the power to expel undesirable aliens, the power to make such international agreements as do not constitute treaties in the constitutional sense, none of which is expressly affirmed by the Constitution, nevertheless exist as inherently inseparable from the conception of nationality. This the court recognized, and in each of the cases cited found the warrant for its conclusions not in the provisions of the Constitution, but in the law of nations.

In *Burnet v. Brooks*, 288 U.S. 378, 396, we said, "As a nation with all the attributes of sovereignty, the United States is vested with all the powers of government necessary to maintain an effective control of international relations." *Cf. Carter v. Carter Coal Co.*

Not only, as we have shown, is the federal power over external affairs in origin and essential character different from that over internal affairs, but participation in the exercise of the power is significantly limited. In this vast external realm, with its important, complicated, delicate and manifold problems, the President alone has the power to speak or listen as a representative of the nation. He *makes* treaties with the advice and consent of the Senate; but he alone negotiates. Into the field of negotiation the Senate cannot intrude; and Congress itself is powerless to invade it. As Marshall said in his great argument of March 7, 1800, in the House of Representatives, "The President is the sole organ of the nation in its external relations, and its sole representative with foreign nations." Annals, 6th Cong., col. 613. The Senate Committee on Foreign Relations at a very early day in our history (February 15, 1816), reported to the Senate, among other things, as follows:

> "The President is the constitutional representative of the United States with regard to foreign nations. He manages our concerns with foreign nations and must necessarily be most competent to determine when, how, and upon what subjects negotiation may be urged with the greatest prospect of success. For his conduct he is responsible to the Constitution. The committee considers this responsibility the surest pledge for the faithful discharge of his duty. They think the interference of the Senate in the direction of foreign negotiations calculated to diminish that responsibility and thereby to impair the best security for the national safety. The nature of transactions with foreign nations, moreover, requires caution and unity of design, and their success frequently depends on secrecy and dispatch." U.S. Senate, Reports, Committee on Foreign Relations, vol. 8, p. 24.

It is important to bear in mind that we are here dealing not alone with an authority vested in the President by an exertion of legislative power, but with such an authority plus the very delicate, plenary and exclusive power of the President as the sole organ of the federal government in the field of international relations—a power which does not require as a basis for its exercise an act of Congress, but which, of course, like every other governmental power, must be exercised in subordination to the applicable provisions of the Constitution. It is quite apparent that if, in the maintenance of our international relations, embarrassment—perhaps serious embarrassment—is to be avoided and success for our aims achieved, congressional legislation which is to be made effective through negotiation and inquiry within the international field must often accord to the President a degree of discretion and freedom from statutory restriction which would not be admissible were domestic affairs alone involved. Moreover, he, not Congress, has the better opportunity of knowing the conditions which prevail in foreign countries, and especially is this true in time of war. He has his confidential sources of information. He has his agents in the form of diplomatic, consular and other officials. Secrecy in respect of information gathered by them may be highly necessary, and the premature disclosure of it productive of harmful results. Indeed, so clearly is this true that the first President refused to accede to a request to lay before the House of Representatives the instructions, correspondence and documents relating to the negotiation of the Jay Treaty—a refusal the wisdom of which was recognized by the House itself and has never since been doubted. In his reply to the request, President Washington said:

> "The nature of foreign negotiations requires caution, and their success must often depend on secrecy; and even when brought to a conclusion a full disclosure of all the measures, demands, or eventual concessions which may have been proposed or contemplated would be extremely impolitic; for this might have a pernicious influence on future negotiations, or produce immediate inconveniences, perhaps danger and mischief, in relation to other powers. The necessity of such caution and secrecy was one cogent reason for vesting the power of making treaties in the President, with the advice and consent of the Senate, the principle on which that body was formed confining it to a small number of members. To admit, then, a right in the House of Representatives to demand and to have as a matter of course all the papers respecting a negotiation with a foreign power would be to establish a dangerous precedent." 1 Messages and Papers of the Presidents, p. 144.

The marked difference between foreign affairs and domestic affairs in this respect is recognized by both houses of Congress in the very form of their requisitions for information from the executive departments. In the case of every department except the Department of State, the resolution *directs* the official to furnish the information. In the case of the State Department, dealing with foreign affairs, the President is *requested* to furnish the information "if not incompatible with the public interest." A statement that to furnish the information is not compatible with the public interest rarely, if ever, is questioned.

When the President is to be authorized by legislation to act in respect of a matter intended to affect a situation in foreign territory, the legislator properly bears in mind the important consideration that the form of the President's action—or, indeed, whether he shall act at all—may well depend, among other things, upon the nature of the confidential information which he has or may thereafter receive, or upon the effect which his action may have upon our foreign relations. This consideration, in connection with what we have already said on the subject, discloses the unwisdom of requiring Congress in this field of governmental power to lay down narrowly definite standards by which the President is to be governed. As this court said in *Mackenzie v. Hare*, 239 U.S. 299, 311, "As a government, the United States is invested with all the attributes of sovereignty. As it has the character of nationality it has the powers of nationality, especially those which concern its relations and intercourse with other countries. *We should hesitate long before limiting or embarrassing such powers.*" (Italics supplied.)

In the light of the foregoing observations, it is evident that this court should not be in haste to apply a general rule which will have the effect of condemning legislation like that under review as constituting an unlawful delegation of legislative power. The principles which justify such legislation find overwhelming support in the unbroken legislative practice which has prevailed almost from the inception of the national government to the present day.

. . . .

The uniform, long-continued and undisputed legislative practice just disclosed rests upon an admissible view of the Constitution which, even if the practice found far less support in principle than we think it does, we should not feel at liberty at this late day to disturb.

We deem it unnecessary to consider, *seriatim*, the several clauses which are said to evidence the unconstitutionality of the Joint Resolution as involving an unlawful delegation of legislative power. It is enough to summarize by saying that, both upon principle and in accordance with precedent, we conclude there is sufficient warrant for the broad discretion vested in the President to determine whether the enforcement of the statute will have a beneficial effect upon the reestablishment of peace in the affected countries; whether he shall make proclamation to bring the resolution into operation; whether and when the resolution shall cease to operate and to make proclamation accordingly; and to prescribe limitations and exceptions to which the enforcement of the resolution shall be subject.

. . . .

The judgment of the court below must be reversed and the cause remanded for further proceedings in accordance with the foregoing opinion.

Reversed.

MR. JUSTICE MCREYNOLDS does not agree. He is of opinion that the court below reached the right conclusion and its judgment ought to be affirmed.

MR. JUSTICE STONE took no part in the consideration or decision of this case.

NOTES ON CURTISS-WRIGHT

1. *Extra-Constitutional Source for Foreign Affairs Power?* Is the notion of a source of power outside of the Constitution compatible with the concept of a government of limited powers? If such a source of power does exist, why should constitutional limitations be deemed to apply to the exercise of that power? Moreover, if sovereignty provides a source of presidential power, should limitations implicit in the concept of sovereignty also apply? For example, if sovereign states are precluded by international law from waging aggressive war, should that prohibition be seen as applicable, constitutionally, to exercises of presidential power?

Is there any support in practice for Justice Sutherland's notion of extra-constitutional power? In analyzing *Curtiss-Wright*, Professor Sarah Cleveland notes, "the Court has also relied on inherent sovereign powers derived from international law to establish national quasi-constitutional or extra-constitutional authority in a variety of areas, including immigration and the governance of Native American tribes and territorial inhabitants, as well as the power of eminent domain.... In each of these contexts, the Court has looked to international law, not to inform constitutional text, but to supplant it." Sarah H. Cleveland, *Our International Constitution*, 31 YALE J. INT'L L. 1, 39 (2006); *see* Sarah H. Cleveland, *Powers Inherent in Sovereignty: Indians, Aliens, Territories, and the Nineteenth Century Origins of Plenary Power over Foreign Affairs*, 81 TEX. L. REV. 1, 7 (2002).

2. *Hindsight*. Is Justice Sutherland's view of history correct? For the view that sovereignty resided in the states for at least some period of time between 1776 and 1789, see the excerpt by Akhil Amar (*supra* this chapter, Section 1); Merrill Jensen, *The Articles of Confederation* 176 (1970) ("according to the constitution which united the thirteen states from 1781 to 1789, the several states were *de facto* and *de jure* sovereign"); Claude H. Van Tyne, *Sovereignty in the American Revolution: An Historical Study*, 12 AM. HIST. REV. 529 (1907) (arguing that both psychologically and legally the states were regarded as sovereign throughout the period). According to Professor David Levitan, Justice Sutherland had proffered his theory in a 1910 article and, upon becoming a member of the Court, waited for the opportunity to make it "law of the land." David M. Levitan, *The Foreign Relations Power: An Analysis of Mr. Justice Sutherland's Theory*, 55 YALE L.J. 467, 478 (1946).

Justice Sutherland's reliance upon Marshall's "sole organ" formulation has also been challenged. Dr. Louis Fisher has argued that Marshall's statement was taken out of context; read in context, Fisher suggests, Marshall's statement offers a very limited view of presidential power. At issue was President Adams' authority to turn over to Britain an individual charged with murder. Marshall took to the floor of the House to argue against efforts to impeach Adams, and was simply stating that the President was that sole organ for carrying out "legislative policy, either in the form of a statute or a treaty." Louis Fisher, *Congressional Abdication on War and Spending* 31 (2000). Neither Marshall nor Adams was arguing that the president was the "sole organ" for *making* foreign policy.

3. *Why the President?* If Justice Sutherland's view concerning the devolution of sovereignty is correct, does it follow that powers incident to sovereignty now reside exclusively within the Executive? Or does it simply mean that the powers reside in the federal government, and leave unaddressed the allocation of that power as among the three branches?

4. *Delegation Theory*. Unlike *Little v. Barreme*, *Curtiss-Wright* presents a case where Congress and the President are marching in lockstep. As such, is any significant constitutional issue presented by the facts of *Curtiss-Wright*? Was it necessary for the Court to discuss the scope of the President's "inherent" powers? Is the discussion of sovereignty and its effect on executive power holding or dictum? What exactly is the holding of the case? Is it surprising that the Supreme Court should take the case?

Part of the explanation may lie in two cases decided during the year before *Curtiss-Wright* was handed down. In these cases, the Supreme Court struck down key pieces of New Deal legislation on the theory that the statutes unconstitutionally delegated legislative power to the Executive. Arguably, some clarification was required concerning the extent to which the "non-delegation doctrine" applied in the realm of foreign affairs. In *Panama Refining Co. v. Ryan*, 293 U.S. 388, 421, 55 S.Ct. 241, 79 L.Ed. 446 (1935), the Court had said that, while the Constitution allows Congress to "lay [] down policies and establish [] standards, while leaving to selected instrumentalities the making of subordinate rules within prescribed limits," the Constitution does not allow Congress "to abdicate, or to transfer to others, the essential legislative functions with which it is [] vested." The Court then held that, "[t]hough the authority delegated [in the case at issue] was clearly defined, Congress had not set up a standard for the President's action; instead, it gave the President an unlimited authority to lay down the prohibition or not, as he might see fit." Bernard Schwartz, *Administrative Law* 39 (2d ed. 1984). Four months later, in *A.L.A. Schechter Poultry Corp. v. United States*, 295 U.S. 495, 55 S.Ct. 837, 79 L.Ed. 1570 (1935), the Court struck down a law that conferred standardless discretion on the President; delegation, in Justice Cardozo's phrase, "running riot." *Id.* at 553. In light of those decisions, it is perhaps not surprising that Curtiss–Wright Corporation mounted the defense that it did.

5. *An Executive Stalwart.* The *Curtiss-Wright* case is often cited by the executive branch to support wide-ranging presidential powers in the field of foreign affairs, even though on the facts of that case Congress fully supported the executive action. For example, Colonel Oliver North invoked *Curtiss-Wright* during congressional hearings on the Iran–Contra affair in 1987. Several years earlier, Congress had enacted a series of provisions known collectively as the Boland Amendments, which effectively barred U.S. assistance to the Contras, a group of Nicaraguan insurrectionists at war with the Marxist Sandinistas (*see* Chapter 5, Section 3). President Reagan signed the first of the Boland Amendments into law as a rider to the Defense Appropriations Act of 1983. Subsequently, it emerged that members of the staff of the National Security Council (NSC) had been channeling money to the Contras from covert arms sales to Iran. There was little question that the actions of the NSC staff violated the Boland Amendments. Those who defended the arms sales tended to base their defense on Justice Sutherland's appraisal of the President's power in foreign affairs:

> [The] Constitution gives the President some power to act on his own in foreign affairs. What kinds of activities are set aside for him? The most obvious—other than the Commander-in-Chief power and others explicitly listed in Article II—is the one named in *Curtiss-Wright*: the President is the "sole organ" of the government in foreign affairs. . . .
>
> . . . .
>
> Congress may not use its control over appropriations, including salaries, to prevent the executive or judiciary from fulfilling Constitutionally mandated obligations. The implications for the Boland amendments is obvious. If any part of the amendments would have used Congress's

control over salaries to prevent executive actions that Congress may not prohibit directly, the amendments would be just as unconstitutional as if they had dealt with the subject directly.

Report of the Congressional Committees Investigating the Iran–Contra Affair, S. Rep. No. 100–216, H. Rep. No. 100–433 (1987), at 473, 478 (minority report). On the facts of the Iran–Contra affair, do you think it makes sense to rely on *Curtiss-Wright*?

6. *Relating Congressional Power to Executive Power*. The means for balancing congressional power and executive power in the field of foreign affairs were more squarely addressed in the next case, *Youngstown Sheet & Tube Co. v. Sawyer*, especially in Justice Jackson's famous concurring opinion. That case arose in the midst of the Korean War and concerned the ability of the President to seize control of U.S. steel mills as a means of ensuring that labor unrest would not imperil the supply of steel for the war effort. As you read the case, consider whether you think it provides a template for analyzing the concurrent foreign affairs power.

YOUNGSTOWN SHEET & TUBE CO. v. SAWYER

343 U.S. 579, 72 S.Ct. 863, 96 L.Ed. 1153 (1952) (some footnotes and citations omitted).

MR. JUSTICE BLACK delivered the opinion of the Court.

We are asked to decide whether the President was acting within his constitutional power when he issued an order directing the Secretary of Commerce to take possession of and operate most of the Nation's steel mills. The mill owners argue that the President's order amounts to lawmaking, a legislative function which the Constitution has expressly confided to the Congress and not to the President. The Government's position is that the order was made on findings of the President that his action was necessary to avert a national catastrophe which would inevitably result from a stoppage of steel production, and that in meeting this grave emergency the President was acting within the aggregate of his constitutional powers as the Nation's Chief Executive and the Commander in Chief of the Armed Forces of the United States. The issue emerges here from the following series of events:

In the latter part of 1951, a dispute arose between the steel companies and their employees over terms and conditions that should be included in new collective bargaining agreements. Long-continued conferences failed to resolve the dispute. On December 18, 1951, the employees' representative, United Steelworkers of America, C.I.O., gave notice of an intention to strike when the existing bargaining agreements expired on December 31. The Federal Mediation and Conciliation Service then intervened in an effort to get labor and management to agree. This failing, the President on December 22, 1951, referred the dispute to the Federal Wage Stabilization Board to investigate and make recommendations for fair and equitable terms of settlement. This Board's report resulted in no settlement. On April 4, 1952, the Union gave notice of a nation-wide strike called to begin at 12:01 a.m. April 9. The indispensability of steel as a component of substantially all weapons and other war materials led the President to believe that the proposed work stoppage would immediately jeopardize our national defense and that governmental seizure of the steel mills was necessary in order to assure the continued availability of steel. Reciting these considerations for his action, the President, a few hours before the strike was to begin, issued Executive Order 10340. The order directed the Secretary of Commerce to take possession of most of the steel mills and keep them running. The Secretary immediately issued his own possessory orders, calling upon the presidents of the various seized companies to serve as operating managers for the United States. They were directed to carry on their activities in accordance with regulations and directions of the Secretary. The next morning the President sent a message to Congress reporting his action. Twelve days later he sent a second message. Congress has taken no action.

Obeying the Secretary's orders under protest, the companies brought proceedings against him in the District Court. Their complaints charged that the seizure was not authorized by an act of Congress or by any constitutional provisions. The District Court was asked to declare the orders of the President and the Secretary invalid and to issue preliminary and permanent injunctions restraining their enforcement. Opposing the motion for preliminary injunction, the United States asserted that a strike disrupting steel production for even a brief period would so endanger the well-being and safety of the Nation that the President had "inherent power" to do what he had done—power "supported by the Constitution, by historical precedent, and by court decisions." The Government also contended that in any event no preliminary injunction should be issued because the companies had made no showing that their available legal remedies were inadequate or that their injuries from seizure would be irreparable. Holding against the Government on all points, the District Court on April 30 issued a preliminary injunction restraining the Secretary from "continuing the seizure and possession of the plants . . . and from acting under the purported authority of Executive Order No. 10340." On the same day the Court of Appeals stayed the District Court's injunction. Deeming it best that the issues raised be promptly decided by this Court, we granted certiorari on May 3 and set the cause for argument on May 12.

. . . .

The President's power, if any, to issue the order must stem either from an act of Congress or from the Constitution itself. There is no statute that expressly authorizes the President to take possession of property as he did here. Nor is there any act of Congress to which our attention has been directed from which such a power can fairly be implied. Indeed, we do not understand the Government to rely on statutory authorization for this seizure. There are two statutes which do authorize the President to take both personal and real property under certain conditions. However, the Government admits that these conditions were not met and that the President's order was not rooted in either of the statutes. The Government refers to the seizure provisions of one of these statutes as "much too cumbersome, involved, and time-consuming for the crisis which was at hand."

Moreover, the use of the seizure technique to solve labor disputes in order to prevent work stoppages was not only unauthorized by any congressional enactment; prior to this controversy, Congress had refused to adopt that method of settling labor disputes. When the Taft–Hartley Act was under consideration in 1947, Congress rejected an amendment which would have authorized such governmental seizures in cases of emergency. Apparently it was thought that the technique of seizure, like that of compulsory arbitration, would interfere with the process of collective bargaining. Consequently, the plan Congress adopted in that Act did not provide for seizure under any circumstances. Instead, the plan sought to bring about settlements by use of the customary devices of mediation, conciliation, investigation by boards of inquiry, and public reports. In some instances temporary injunctions were authorized to provide cooling-off periods. All this failing, unions were left free to strike after a secret vote by employees as to whether they wished to accept their employers' final settlement offer.

It is clear that if the President had authority to issue the order he did, it must be found in some provisions of the Constitution. And it is not claimed that express constitutional language grants this power to the President. The contention is that presidential power should be implied from the aggregate of his powers under the Constitution. Particular reliance is placed on provisions in Article II which say that "The executive Power shall be vested in a President . . ."; that "he shall take Care that the Laws be faithfully executed"; and that he "shall be Commander in Chief of the Army and Navy of the United States."

The order cannot properly be sustained as an exercise of the President's military power as Commander in Chief of the Armed Forces. The Government attempts to do so by citing a number of cases upholding broad powers in military commanders engaged in day-to-day fighting in a theater of war. Such cases need not concern us here. Even though "theater of war" be an expanding concept, we cannot with faithfulness to our constitutional system hold that the Commander in Chief of the Armed Forces has the ultimate power as such to take possession of private property in order to keep labor disputes from stopping production. This is a job for the Nation's lawmakers, not for its military authorities.

Nor can the seizure order be sustained because of the several constitutional provisions that grant executive power to the President. In the framework of our Constitution, the President's power to see that the laws are faithfully executed refutes the idea that he is to be a lawmaker. The Constitution limits his functions in the lawmaking process to the recommending of laws he thinks wise and the vetoing of laws he thinks bad. And the Constitution is neither silent nor equivocal about who shall make laws which the President is to execute. The first section of the first article says that "All legislative Powers herein granted shall be vested in a Congress of the United States...." After granting many powers to the Congress, Article I goes on to provide that Congress may "make all Laws which shall be necessary and proper for carrying into Execution the foregoing Powers, and all other Powers vested by this Constitution in the Government of the United States, or in any Department or Officer thereof."

The President's order does not direct that a congressional policy be executed in a manner prescribed by Congress—it directs that a presidential policy be executed in a manner prescribed by the President. The preamble of the order itself, like that of many statutes, sets out reasons why the President believes certain policies should be adopted, proclaims these policies as rules of conduct to be followed, and again, like a statute, authorizes a government official to promulgate additional rules and regulations consistent with the policy proclaimed and needed to carry that policy into execution. The power of Congress to adopt such public policies as those proclaimed by the order is beyond question. It can authorize the taking of private property for public use. It can make laws regulating the relationships between employers and employees, prescribing rules designed to settle labor disputes, and fixing wages and working conditions in certain fields of our economy. The Constitution does not subject this lawmaking power of Congress to presidential or military supervision or control.

It is said that other Presidents without congressional authority have taken possession of private business enterprises in order to settle labor disputes. But even if this be true, Congress has not thereby lost its exclusive constitutional authority to make laws necessary and proper to carry out the powers vested by the Constitution "in the Government of the United States, or in any Department or Officer thereof."

The Founders of this Nation entrusted the lawmaking power to the Congress alone in both good and bad times. It would do no good to recall the historical events, the fears of power and the hopes for freedom that lay behind their choice. Such a review would but confirm our holding that this seizure order cannot stand.

The judgment of the District Court is

Affirmed.

....

MR. JUSTICE JACKSON, concurring in the judgment and opinion of the Court.

That comprehensive and undefined presidential powers hold both practical advantages and grave dangers for the country will impress anyone who has served as legal adviser to a President in time of transition and public anxiety. While an interval of detached reflection may temper teachings of that experience, they probably are a more realistic influence on my views than the conventional materials of judicial decision which seem unduly to accentuate doctrine and legal fiction. But as we approach the question of presidential power, we half overcome mental hazards by recognizing them. The opinions of judges, no less than executives and publicists, often suffer the infirmity of confusing the issue of a power's validity with the cause it is invoked to promote, of confounding the permanent executive office with its temporary occupant. The tendency is strong to emphasize transient results upon policies—such as wages or stabilization—and lose sight of enduring consequences upon the balanced power structure of our Republic.

A judge, like an executive adviser, may be surprised at the poverty of really useful and unambiguous authority applicable to concrete problems of executive power as they actually present themselves. Just what our forefathers did envision, or would have envisioned had they foreseen modern conditions, must be divined from materials almost as enigmatic as the dreams Joseph was called upon to interpret for Pharaoh. A century and a half of partisan debate and scholarly speculation yields no net result but only supplies more or less apt quotations from respected sources on each side of any question. They largely cancel each other.[1] And court decisions are indecisive because of the judicial practice of dealing with the largest questions in the most narrow way.

The actual art of governing under our Constitution does not and cannot conform to judicial definitions of the power of any of its branches based on isolated clauses or even single Articles torn from context. While the Constitution diffuses power the better to secure liberty, it also contemplates that practice will integrate the dispersed powers into a workable government. It enjoins upon its branches separateness but interdependence, autonomy but reciprocity. Presidential powers are not fixed but fluctuate, depending upon their disjunction or conjunction with those of Congress. We may well begin by a somewhat over-simplified grouping of practical situations in which a President may doubt, or others may challenge, his powers, and by distinguishing roughly the legal consequences of this factor of relativity.

1. When the President acts pursuant to an express or implied authorization of Congress, his authority is at its maximum, for it includes all that he possesses in his own right plus all that Congress can delegate.[2] In these circumstances, and in these only, may he be said (for what it may

---

1. A Hamilton may be matched against a Madison. 7 The Works of Alexander Hamilton, 76–117; 1 Madison, Letters and Other Writings, 611–654. Professor Taft is counterbalanced by Theodore Roosevelt. Taft, Our Chief Magistrate and His Powers, 139–140; Theodore Roosevelt, Autobiography, 388–389. It even seems that President Taft cancels out Professor Taft. Compare his "Temporary Petroleum Withdrawal No. 5" of September 27, 1909, *United States v. Midwest Oil Co.*, 236 U.S. 459, 467, 468, with his appraisal of executive power in "Our Chief Magistrate and His Powers" 139–140.

2. It is in this class of cases that we find the broadest recent statements of presidential power, including those relied on here. *United States v. Curtiss–Wright Export Corp.*, 299 U.S. 304, involved, not the question of the President's power to act without congressional authority, but the question of his right to act under and in accord with an Act of Congress. The constitutionality of the Act under which the President had proceeded was assailed on the ground that it delegated legislative powers to the President. Much of the Court's opinion is *dictum*, but the *ratio decidendi* is contained in the following language:

"When the President is to be authorized by legislation to act in respect of a matter intended to affect a situation in foreign territory, the legislator properly bears in mind the important be worth), to personify the federal sovereignty. If his act is held unconstitutional under these circumstances, it usually means that the Federal Government as an undivided whole lacks power. A seizure executed by the President pursuant to an Act of Congress would be supported by the strongest of presumptions and the widest latitude of judicial interpretation, and the burden of persuasion would rest heavily upon any who might attack it.

2. When the President acts in absence of either a congressional grant or denial of authority, he can only rely upon his own independent powers, but there is a zone of twilight in which he and Congress may have concurrent authority, or in which its distribution is uncertain. Therefore, congressional inertia, indifference or quiescence may sometimes, at least as a practical matter, enable, if not invite, measures on independent presidential responsibility. In this area, any actual test of power is likely to depend on the imperatives of events and contemporary imponderables rather than on abstract theories of law.[3]

3. When the President takes measures incompatible with the expressed or implied will of Congress, his power is at its lowest ebb, for then he can rely only upon his own constitutional powers minus any constitutional powers of Congress over the matter. Courts can sustain exclusive presidential control in such a case only by disabling the Congress from acting upon the subject.[4] Presidential claim to a power at once so conclu-

consideration that the form of the President's action—or, indeed, whether he shall act at all—may well depend, among other things, upon the nature of the confidential information which he has or may thereafter receive, or upon the effect which his action may have upon our foreign relations. This consideration, in connection with what we have already said on the subject, discloses the unwisdom of requiring Congress in this field of governmental power to lay down narrowly definite standards by which the President is to be governed. As this court said in *Mackenzie v. Hare*, 239 U.S. 299, 311, 'As a government, the United States is invested with all the attributes of sovereignty. As it has the character of nationality it has the powers of nationality, especially those which concern its relations and intercourse with other countries. *We should hesitate long before limiting or embarrassing such powers.*' (Italics supplied.)" *Id.*, at 321–322.

That case does not solve the present controversy. It recognized internal and external affairs as being in separate categories, and held that the strict limitation upon congressional delegations of power to the President over internal affairs does not apply with respect to delegations of power in external affairs. It was intimated that the President might act in external affairs without congressional authority, but not that he might act contrary to an Act of Congress.

Other examples of wide definition of presidential powers under statutory authorization are *Chicago & Southern Air Lines v. Waterman Steamship Corp.*, 333 U.S. 103, and *Hirabayashi v. United States*, 320 U.S. 81. But see, *Jecker v. Montgomery*, 13 How. 498, 515; *Western Union Telegraph Co. v. United States*, 272 F. 311, aff'd, 272 F. 893; rev'd on consent of the parties, 260 U.S. 754; *United States Harness Co. v. Graham*, 288 F. 929.

3. Since the Constitution implies that the writ of habeas corpus may be suspended in certain circumstances but does not say by whom, President Lincoln asserted and maintained it as an executive function in the face of judicial challenge and doubt. *Ex parte Merryman*, 17 Fed. Cas. 144; *Ex parte Milligan*, 4 Wall. 2, 125; see *Ex parte Bollman*, 4 Cranch 75, 101. Congress eventually ratified his action. Habeas Corpus Act of March 3, 1863, 12 Stat. 755. See Hall, Free Speech in War Time, 21 Col. L. Rev. 526. Compare *Myers v. United States*, 272 U.S. 52, with *Humphrey's Executor v. United States*, 295 U.S. 602; and *Hirabayashi v. United States*, 320 U.S. 81, with the case at bar. Also compare *Ex parte Vallandigham*, 1 Wall. 243, with *Ex parte Milligan*, *supra*.

4. President Roosevelt's effort to remove a Federal Trade Commissioner was found to be contrary to the policy of Congress and impinging upon an area of congressional control, and so his sive and preclusive must be scrutinized with caution, for what is at stake is the equilibrium established by our constitutional system.

Into which of these classifications does this executive seizure of the steel industry fit? It is eliminated from the first by admission, for it is conceded that no congressional authorization exists for this seizure. That takes away also the support of the many precedents and declarations which were made in relation, and must be confined, to this category.[5]

Can it then be defended under flexible tests available to the second category? It seems clearly eliminated from that class because Congress has not left seizure of private property an open field but has covered it by three statutory policies inconsistent with this seizure. In cases where the purpose is to supply needs of the Government itself, two courses are provided: one, seizure of a plant which fails to comply with obligatory orders placed by the Government; another, condemnation of facilities, including temporary use under the power of eminent domain. The third is applicable where it is the general economy of the country that is to be protected rather than exclusive governmental interests. None of these were invoked. In choosing a different and inconsistent way of his own, the President cannot claim that it is necessitated or invited by failure of Congress to legislate upon the occasions, grounds and methods for seizure of industrial properties.

This leaves the current seizure to be justified only by the severe tests under the third grouping, where it can be supported only by any remainder of executive power after subtraction of such powers as Congress may have over the subject. In short, we can sustain the President only by holding that seizure of such strike-bound industries is within his domain and beyond control by Congress. Thus, this Court's first review of such seizures occurs under circumstances which leave presidential power most vulnerable to attack and in the least favorable of possible constitutional postures.

---

removal power was cut down accordingly. *Humphrey's Executor v. United States*. However, his exclusive power of removal in executive agencies, affirmed in *Myers v. United States*, continued to be asserted and maintained. *Morgan v. Tennessee Valley Authority*, 115 F.2d 990, cert. denied, 312 U.S. 701; *In re Power to Remove Members of the Tennessee Valley Authority*, 39 Op. Atty. Gen. 145; President Roosevelt's Message to Congress of March 23, 1938, The Public Papers and Addresses of Franklin D. Roosevelt, 1938 (Rosenman), 151.

5. The oft-cited Louisiana Purchase had nothing to do with the separation of powers as between the President and Congress, but only with state and federal power. The Louisiana Purchase was subject to rather academic criticism, not upon the ground that Mr. Jefferson acted without authority from Congress, but that neither had express authority to expand the boundaries of the United States by purchase or annexation. Mr. Jefferson himself had strongly opposed the doctrine that the State's delegation of powers to the Federal Government could be enlarged by resort to implied powers. Afterwards in a letter to John Breckenridge, dated August 12, 1803, he declared:

> "The Constitution has made no provision for our holding foreign territory, still less for incorporating foreign nations into our Union. The executive in seizing the fugitive occurrence which so much advances the good of their country, have done an act beyond the Constitution. The Legislature in casting behind them metaphysical subtleties, and risking themselves like faithful servants, must ratify and pay for it, and throw themselves on their country for doing for them unauthorized, what we know they would have done for themselves had they been in a situation to do it." 10 The Writings of Thomas Jefferson 407, 411.

I did not suppose, and I am not persuaded, that history leaves it open to question, at least in the courts, that the executive branch, like the Federal Government as a whole, possesses only delegated powers. The purpose of the Constitution was not only to grant power, but to keep it from getting out of hand. However, because the President does not enjoy unmentioned powers does not mean that the mentioned ones should be narrowed by a niggardly construction. Some clauses could be made almost unworkable, as well as immutable, by refusal to indulge some latitude of interpretation for changing times. I have heretofore, and do now, give to the enumerated powers the scope and elasticity afforded by what seem to be reasonable practical implications instead of the rigidity dictated by a doctrinaire textualism.

The Solicitor General seeks the power of seizure in three clauses of the Executive Article, the first reading, "The executive Power shall be vested in a President of the United States of America." Lest I be thought to exaggerate, I quote the interpretation which his brief puts upon it: "In our view, this clause constitutes a grant of all the executive powers of which the Government is capable." If that be true, it is difficult to see why the forefathers bothered to add several specific items, including some trifling ones.[9]

The example of such unlimited executive power that must have most impressed the forefathers was the prerogative exercised by George III, and the description of its evils in the Declaration of Independence leads me to doubt that they were creating their new Executive in his image. Continental European examples were no more appealing. And if we seek instruction from our own times, we can match it only from the executive powers in those governments we disparagingly describe as totalitarian. I cannot accept the view that this clause is a grant in bulk of all conceivable executive power but regard it as an allocation to the presidential office of the generic powers thereafter stated.

The clause on which the Government next relies is that "The President shall be Commander in Chief of the Army and Navy of the United States. . . ." These cryptic words have given rise to some of the most persistent controversies in our constitutional history. Of course, they imply something more than an empty title. But just what authority goes with the name has plagued presidential advisers who would not waive or narrow it by nonassertion yet cannot say where it begins or ends. It undoubtedly puts the Nation's armed forces under presidential command. Hence, this loose appellation is sometimes advanced as support for any presidential action, internal or external, involving use of force, the idea being that it vests power to do anything, anywhere, that can be done with an army or navy.

---

9. ". . . he may require the Opinion, in writing, of the principal Officer in each of the executive Departments, upon any Subject relating to the Duties of their respective Offices. . . ." U.S. Const., Art. II, § 2. He ". . . shall Commission all the Officers of the United States." U.S. Const., Art. II, § 3. Matters such as those would seem to be inherent in the Executive if anything is.

That seems to be the logic of an argument tendered at our bar—that the President having, on his own responsibility, sent American troops abroad derives from that act "affirmative power" to seize the means of producing a supply of steel for them. To quote, "Perhaps the most forceful illustrations of the scope of Presidential power in this connection is the fact that American troops in Korea, whose safety and effectiveness are so directly involved here, were sent to the field by an exercise of the President's constitutional powers." Thus, it is said, he has invested himself with "war powers."

I cannot foresee all that it might entail if the Court should indorse this argument. Nothing in our Constitution is plainer than that declaration of a war is entrusted only to Congress. Of course, a state of war may in fact exist without a formal declaration. But no doctrine that the Court could promulgate would seem to me more sinister and alarming than that a President whose conduct of foreign affairs is so largely uncontrolled, and often even is unknown, can vastly enlarge his mastery over the internal affairs of the country by his own commitment of the Nation's armed forces to some foreign venture.[10] I do not, however, find it necessary or appropriate to consider the legal status of the Korean enterprise to discountenance argument based on it.

Assuming that we are in a war *de facto,* whether it is or is not a war *de jure,* does that empower the Commander in Chief to seize industries he thinks necessary to supply our army? The Constitution expressly places in Congress power "to raise and *support* Armies" and "to *provide* and *maintain* a Navy." (Emphasis supplied.) This certainly lays upon Congress primary responsibility for supplying the armed forces. Congress alone controls the raising of revenues and their appropriation and may determine in what manner and by what means they shall be spent for military and naval procurement. I suppose no one would doubt that Congress can take over war supply as a Government enterprise. On the other hand, if Congress sees fit to rely on free private enterprise collectively bargaining with free labor for support and maintenance of our armed forces, can the

---

10. How widely this doctrine espoused by the President's counsel departs from the early view of presidential power is shown by a comparison. President Jefferson, without authority from Congress, sent the American fleet into the Mediterranean, where it engaged in a naval battle with the Tripolitan fleet. He sent a message to Congress on December 8, 1801, in which he said:

> "Tripoli, the least considerable of the Barbary States, had come forward with demands unfounded either in right or in compact, and had permitted itself to denounce war on our failure to comply before a given day. The style of the demand admitted but one answer. I sent a small squadron of frigates into the Mediterranean ... with orders to protect our commerce against the threatened attack.... Our commerce in the Mediterranean was blockaded and that of the Atlantic in peril.... One of the Tripolitan cruisers having fallen in with and engaged the small schooner *Enterprise,* ... was captured, after a heavy slaughter of her men.... Unauthorized by the Constitution, without the sanction of Congress, to go beyond the line of defense, the vessel being disabled from committing further hostilities, was liberated with its crew. The Legislature will doubtless consider whether, by authorizing measures of offense also, they will place our force on an equal footing with that of its adversaries. I communicate all material information on this subject, that in the exercise of the important function confided by the Constitution to the Legislature exclusively their judgment may form itself on a knowledge and consideration of every circumstance of weight." I Richardson, Messages and Papers of the Presidents, 314.

Executive, because of lawful disagreements incidental to that process, seize the facility for operation upon Government-imposed terms?

There are indications that the Constitution did not contemplate that the title Commander in Chief *of the Army and Navy* will constitute him also Commander in Chief of the country, its industries and its inhabitants. He has no monopoly of "war powers," whatever they are. While Congress cannot deprive the President of the command of the army and navy, only Congress can provide him an army or navy to command. It is also empowered to make rules for the "Government and Regulation of land and naval Forces," by which it may to some unknown extent impinge upon even command functions.

That military powers of the Commander in Chief were not to supersede representative government of internal affairs seems obvious from the Constitution and from elementary American history. Time out of mind, and even now in many parts of the world, a military commander can seize private housing to shelter his troops. Not so, however, in the United States, for the Third Amendment says, "No Soldier shall, in time of peace be quartered in any house, without the consent of the Owner, nor in time of war, but in a manner to be prescribed by law." Thus, even in war time, his seizure of needed military housing must be authorized by Congress. It also was expressly left to Congress to "provide for calling forth the Militia to execute the Laws of the Union, suppress Insurrections and repel Invasions. . . ."[11] Such a limitation on the command power, written at a time when the militia rather than a standing army was contemplated as the military weapon of the Republic, underscores the Constitution's policy that Congress, not the Executive, should control utilization of the war power as an instrument of domestic policy. Congress, fulfilling that function, has authorized the President to use the army to enforce certain civil rights. On the other hand, Congress has forbidden him to use the army for the purpose of executing general laws except when *expressly* authorized by the Constitution or by Act of Congress.

While broad claims under this rubric often have been made, advice to the President in specific matters usually has carried overtones that powers, even under this head, are measured by the command functions usual to the topmost officer of the army and navy. Even then, heed has been taken of any efforts of Congress to negative his authority.[14]

---

11. U.S. Const., Art. I, § 8, cl. 15.

14. In 1940, President Roosevelt proposed to transfer to Great Britain certain overage destroyers and small patrol boats then under construction. He did not presume to rely upon any claim of constitutional power as Commander in Chief. On the contrary, he was advised that such destroyers—if certified not to be essential to the defense of the United States—could be "transferred, exchanged, sold, or otherwise disposed of," because Congress had so authorized him. Accordingly, the destroyers were exchanged for air bases. In the same opinion, he was advised that Congress had prohibited the release or transfer of the so-called "mosquito boats" then under construction, so those boats were not transferred. *Acquisition of Naval and Air Bases in Exchange for Over-age Destroyers*, 39 Op. Atty. Gen. 484. See also *Training of British Flying Students in the United States*, 40 Op. Atty. Gen. 58.

We should not use this occasion to circumscribe, much less to contract, the lawful role of the President as Commander in Chief. I should indulge the widest latitude of interpretation to sustain his exclusive function to command the instruments of national force, at least when turned against the outside world for the security of our society. But, when it is turned inward, not because of rebellion but because of a lawful economic struggle between industry and labor, it should have no such indulgence. His command power is not such an absolute as might be implied from that office in a militaristic system but is subject to limitations consistent with a constitutional Republic whose law and policy-making branch is a representative Congress. The purpose of lodging dual titles in one man was to insure that the civilian would control the military, not to enable the military to subordinate the presidential office. No penance would ever expiate the sin against free government of holding that a President can escape control of executive powers by law through assuming his military role. What the power of command may include I do not try to envision, but I think it is not a military prerogative, without support of law, to seize persons or property because they are important or even essential for the military and naval establishment.

The third clause in which the Solicitor General finds seizure powers is that "he shall take Care that the Laws be faithfully executed. . . ."[15] That authority must be matched against words of the Fifth Amendment that "No person shall be ... deprived of life, liberty or property, without due process of law. . . ." One gives a governmental authority that reaches so far as there is law, the other gives a private right that authority shall go no farther. These signify about all there is of the principle that ours is a government of laws, not of men, and that we submit ourselves to rulers only if under rules.

The Solicitor General lastly grounds support of the seizure upon nebulous, inherent powers never expressly granted but said to have accrued to the office from the customs and claims of preceding administrations. The plea is for a resulting power to deal with a crisis or an emergency according to the necessities of the case, the unarticulated assumption being that necessity knows no law.

Loose and irresponsible use of adjectives colors all non-legal and much legal discussion of presidential powers. "Inherent" powers, "implied" powers, "incidental" powers, "plenary" powers, "war" powers and "emergency" powers are used, often interchangeably and without fixed or ascertainable meanings.

The vagueness and generality of the clauses that set forth presidential powers afford a plausible basis for pressures within and without an administration for presidential action beyond that supported by those whose responsibility it is to defend his actions in court. The claim of inherent and unrestricted presidential powers has long been a persuasive dialectical weapon in political controversy. While it is not surprising that counsel should grasp support from such unadjudicated claims of power, a

15. U.S. Const., Art. II, § 3.

judge cannot accept self-serving press statements of the attorney for one of the interested parties as authority in answering a constitutional question, even if the advocate was himself. But prudence has counseled that actual reliance on such nebulous claims stop short of provoking a judicial test.[16]

. . . .

Germany, after the First World War, framed the Weimar Constitution, designed to secure her liberties in the Western tradition. However, the President of the Republic, without concurrence of the Reichstag, was empowered temporarily to suspend any or all individual rights if public safety and order were seriously disturbed or endangered. This proved a temptation to every government, whatever its shade of opinion, and in 13 years suspension of rights was invoked on more than 250 occasions. Finally, Hitler persuaded President Von Hindenberg to suspend all such rights, and they were never restored.[20]

The French Republic provided for a very different kind of emergency government known as the "state of siege." It differed from the German

16. President Wilson, just before our entrance into World War I, went before the Congress and asked its approval of his decision to authorize merchant ships to carry defensive weapons. He said:

> "No doubt I already possess that authority without special warrant of law, by the plain implication of my constitutional duties and powers; but I prefer, in the present circumstances, not to act upon general implication. I wish to feel that the authority and the power of the Congress are behind me in whatever it may become necessary for me to do. We are jointly the servants of the people and must act together and in their spirit, so far as we can divine and interpret it." XVII Richardson, *op.cit.*, 8211.

When our Government was itself in need of shipping whilst ships flying the flags of nations overrun by Hitler, as well as belligerent merchantmen, were immobilized in American harbors where they had taken refuge, President Roosevelt did not assume that it was in his power to seize such foreign vessels to make up our own deficit. He informed Congress: "I am satisfied, after consultation with the heads of the interested departments and agencies of the Government, that we should have statutory authority to take over such vessels as our needs require. . . ." 87 Cong. Rec. 3072 (77th Cong., 1st Sess.); The Public Papers and Addresses of Franklin D. Roosevelt, 1941 (Rosenman), 94. The necessary statutory authority was shortly forthcoming. 55 Stat. 242.

In his first inaugural address President Roosevelt pointed out two courses to obtain legislative remedies, one being to enact measures he was prepared to recommend, the other to enact measures "the Congress may build out of its experience and wisdom." He continued, "But in the event that the Congress shall fail to take one of these two courses, and in the event that the national emergency is still critical, I shall not evade the clear course of duty that will then confront me. *I shall ask the Congress for the one remaining instrument to meet the crisis*—broad Executive power to wage a war against the emergency, as great as the power that would be given to me if we were in fact invaded by a foreign foe." (Emphasis supplied.) The Public Papers and Addresses of Franklin D. Roosevelt, 1933 (Rosenman), 15.

On March 6, 1933, President Roosevelt proclaimed the Bank Holiday. The Proclamation did not invoke constitutional powers of the Executive but expressly and solely relied upon the Act of Congress of October 6, 1917, 40 Stat. 411, § 5(b), as amended, 50. He relied steadily on legislation to empower him to deal with economic emergency. The Public Papers and Addresses of Franklin D. Roosevelt, 1933 (Rosenman), 24.

It is interesting to note Holdsworth's comment on the powers of legislation by proclamation when in the hands of the Tudors. "The extent to which they could be legally used was never finally settled in this century, because the Tudors made so tactful a use of their powers that no demand for the settlement of this question was raised." 4 Holdsworth, History of English Law, 104.

20. 1 Nazi Conspiracy and Aggression 126–127; Rossiter, Constitutional Dictatorship, 33–61; Brecht, Prelude to Silence, 138.

emergency dictatorship, particularly in that emergency powers could not be assumed at will by the Executive but could only be granted as a parliamentary measure. And it did not, as in Germany, result in a suspension or abrogation of law but was a legal institution governed by special legal rules and terminable by parliamentary authority.[21]

Great Britain also has fought both World Wars under a sort of temporary dictatorship created by legislation.[22] As Parliament is not bound by written constitutional limitations, it established a crisis government simply by delegation to its Ministers of a larger measure than usual of its own unlimited power, which is exercised under its supervision by Ministers whom it may dismiss. This has been called the "high-water mark in the voluntary surrender of liberty," but, as Churchill put it, "Parliament stands custodian of these surrendered liberties, and its most sacred duty will be to restore them in their fullness when victory has crowned our exertions and our perseverance."[23] Thus, parliamentary control made emergency powers compatible with freedom.

This contemporary foreign experience may be inconclusive as to the wisdom of lodging emergency powers somewhere in a modern government. But it suggests that emergency powers are consistent with free government only when their control is lodged elsewhere than in the Executive who exercises them. That is the safeguard that would be nullified by our adoption of the "inherent powers" formula. Nothing in my experience convinces me that such risks are warranted by any real necessity, although such powers would, of course, be an executive convenience.

In the practical working of our Government we already have evolved a technique within the framework of the Constitution by which normal executive powers may be considerably expanded to meet an emergency. Congress may and has granted extraordinary authorities which lie dormant in normal times but may be called into play by the Executive in war or upon proclamation of a national emergency. In 1939, upon congressional request, the Attorney General listed ninety-nine such separate statutory grants by Congress of emergency or wartime executive powers. They were invoked from time to time as need appeared. Under this procedure we retain Government by law—special, temporary law, perhaps, but law nonetheless. The public may know the extent and limitations of the powers that can be asserted, and persons affected may be informed from the statute of their rights and duties.

In view of the ease, expedition and safety with which Congress can grant and has granted large emergency powers, certainly ample to embrace this crisis, I am quite unimpressed with the argument that we should affirm possession of them without statute. Such power either has no beginning or it has no end. If it exists, it need submit to no legal

---

21. Rossiter, Constitutional Dictatorship, 117–129.

22. Defense of the Realm Act, 1914, 4 & 5, Geo. V. c. 29, as amended, c. 63; Emergency Powers (Defence) Act, 1939, 2 & 3 Geo. VI, c. 62; Rossiter, Constitutional Dictatorship, 135–184.

23. Churchill, The Unrelenting Struggle, 13. See also *id.,* at 279–281.

restraint. I am not alarmed that it would plunge us straightway into dictatorship, but it is at least a step in that wrong direction.

. . . .

But I have no illusion that any decision by this Court can keep power in the hands of Congress if it is not wise and timely in meeting its problems. A crisis that challenges the President equally, or perhaps primarily, challenges Congress. If not good law, there was worldly wisdom in the maxim attributed to Napoleon that "The tools belong to the man who can use them." We may say that power to legislate for emergencies belongs in the hands of Congress, but only Congress itself can prevent power from slipping through its fingers.

The essence of our free Government is "leave to live by no man's leave, underneath the law"—to be governed by those impersonal forces which we call law. Our Government is fashioned to fulfill this concept so far as humanly possible. The Executive, except for recommendation and veto, has no legislative power. The executive action we have here originates in the individual will of the President and represents an exercise of authority without law. No one, perhaps not even the President, knows the limits of the power he may seek to exert in this instance and the parties affected cannot learn the limit of their rights. We do not know today what powers over labor or property would be claimed to flow from Government possession if we should legalize it, what rights to compensation would be claimed or recognized, or on what contingency it would end. With all its defects, delays and inconveniences, men have discovered no technique for long preserving free government except that the Executive be under the law, and that the law be made by parliamentary deliberations.

Such institutions may be destined to pass away. But it is the duty of the Court to be last, not first, to give them up.[27]

MICHAEL J. GLENNON, CONSTITUTIONAL DIPLOMACY

12–16 (1990) (footnotes omitted).

CONGRESSIONAL DISAPPROVAL

When the President acts in the face of congressional *disapproval,* that action falls into Jackson's third category, and the Court, if it is to decide the case, faces a difficult task: It must determine whether the President or Congress has exclusive power over the matter. If the Court finds that the President has such power (variously, *independent, plenary, inherent,* or *implied),* then Congress is by definition disabled from acting. Understandably, few cases have been decided in this category. Virtually all have been

27. We follow the judicial tradition instituted on a memorable Sunday in 1612, when King James took offense at the independence of his judges and, in rage, declared: "Then I am to be *under* the law—which it is treason to affirm." Chief Justice Coke replied to his King: "Thus wrote Bracton, 'The King ought not to be under any man, but he is under God and the Law.' " 12 Coke 65 (as to its verity, 18 Eng. Hist. Rev. 664–675); 1 Campbell, Lives of the Chief Justices (1849), 272.

decided against the Executive. In *Little*, as we have seen, an implied congressional prohibition against certain naval seizures prevailed over the President's constitutional power as commander-in-chief. Similarly, in the *Steel Seizure Case,* the President was found to lack the power to seize the nation's steel mills in the face of an implied statutory prohibition....

....

CONCURRENT POWER

The term *concurrent power* is often used to refer to Jackson's middle tier, the "zone of twilight." But this usage is inaccurate, for properly speaking, the concept of concurrent power refers not to the congressional will or lack thereof but to the posture of the Constitution. The Constitution sometimes appears silent with respect to issues of decision-making authority. In such circumstances, concurrent power is said to exist in both political branches. Congress may act, and if it does, the President must comply with its will, since he *ex hypothesi* lacks plenary power. Congress may fail to act, and if it fails, the President may initiate action, subject to congressional countermand.

Thus, concurrent presidential power in a subject area connotes a presidential initiating power. If Congress has enacted no governing statute, the President can take the lead in implementing a policy, but that policy can later be restricted by Congress. (If Congress cannot restrict it, the President has a plenary power to act.) Acts within this realm of concurrent power can be performed constitutionally by the President, but only so long as Congress fails to act. The President's initiatives here are contingently constitutional; their validity depends upon congressional *inaction*. Dicta in *Little v. Barreme* and the *Steel Seizure Case* imply that presidential action might have been permissible had Congress remained silent. Implied congressional disapproval in those cases, however, placed the question in Justice Jackson's third tier, where the President's powers are weakest....

***NOTES ON* YOUNGSTOWN**

1. *The Majority's Theory on Presidential Power*. Justice Black wrote for the Court that the President had engaged in a law-making function, one that the Constitution assigns to Congress. What standard does Justice Black apply to distinguish a "legislative act" from an "executive act"? What guidance is provided by the Constitution? Is the distinction useful? Do you think that the result would have been different if substantial United States casualties in Korea had been directly traceable to the strike against the steel companies? Should it? In his memoirs, President Truman stated:

> Secretary of Defense Lovett said emphatically that any stoppage of steel production, even for a short time, would increase the risk we had taken in the "stretch-out" of the armament program. He also pointed out that our entire combat technique in all three services depended on the fullest use of our industrial facilities. Stressing the situation in Korea, he

said that "we are holding the line with ammunition, and not with the lives of our troops." Any curtailment of steel production, he warned, would endanger the lives of our fighting men.

. . . .

With [Secretary of State] Dean Acheson I discussed the impact which this threatening paralysis of our defense economy might have on our relations with the rest of the world. Any failure on our part to deliver what we had promised to furnish our allies under the Mutual Defense Assistance Program would seriously undermine their faith in our ability to aid them in critical moments. Russia would be cheered by such evidence of a slowdown in our rearmament. We could not overlook even the possibility that Russia would believe us so weakened by an extended strike as to invite further aggression, and there might be other "Koreas."

Harry S. Truman, II *Memoirs* 465–71 (1955). Viewed in this light, should the President's conduct have been viewed as an exercise of executive power to address a growing national security crisis?

2. *Wither Curtiss–Wright?* Justice Black makes no reference to *Curtiss-Wright*—even though it had been decided only sixteen years earlier. Could not the President's seizure of the steel mills have been justified under the *Curtiss-Wright* wide-ranging "sovereignty" theory? Does Justice Black mean to repudiate the theory when he writes, that "[t]he President's power, if any, ... must stem either from an act of Congress or from the Constitution itself"?

3. *Justice Jackson's Theory*. Although set forth in a concurring opinion, Justice Jackson's tripartite framework generated widespread praise and was employed by the Supreme Court in assessing the validity of the Iranian claims settlement agreement in *Dames & Moore v. Regan* (see note 5 below). Is Justice Jackson correct in placing the executive act in *Youngstown* in category three? Why should it not be placed in the "zone of twilight"? As Justice Rehnquist (a former clerk of Justice Jackson) wrote in *Dames & Moore*, "Justice Jackson himself recognized that his three categories represented 'a somewhat oversimplified grouping,' and it is doubtless the case that executive action in any particular instance falls, not neatly in one of three pigeonholes, but rather at some point along a spectrum running from explicit congressional authorization to explicit congressional prohibition." 453 U.S. 654, 669 (1981). What do you think Justice Rehnquist means?

Is the only inquiry required under Justice Jackson's analysis an assessment of the intent of Congress? Suppose the conclusion is that Congress intended to prohibit the presidential act in question; does Justice Jackson regard that will as necessarily dispositive? Note that, in such circumstances, Jackson suggests that the President's power is merely "at its lowest ebb," not that the President is then without any power to act. If the conclusion is that the congressional intent is negative, does not the Jackson analysis require a second inquiry into whether the act in question falls within the exclusive powers of the President—whether, in Justice Jackson's calculus, the "constitutional powers of Congress over the matter" amount to zero?

Compare *Nixon v. Administrator of General Services*, 433 U.S. 425, 443, 97 S.Ct. 2777, 53 L.Ed.2d 867 (1977):

> [I]n determining whether [the statute under separation-of-powers attack] disrupts the proper balance between the coordinate branches, the proper inquiry focuses on the extent to which it prevents the Executive Branch from accomplishing its constitutionally assigned functions. *United States v. Nixon*, 418 U.S., at 711–712. Only where the potential for disruption is present must we then determine whether that impact is justified by an overriding need to promote objectives within the constitutional authority of Congress.

Does this approach differ from Jackson's? If this second level of inquiry is necessary, by what methodology does Justice Jackson suggest that the existence of an exclusive presidential power is determined?

4. *Political Question Doctrine*. Why didn't *Youngstown* present a non-justiciable "political question"? If Congress had been silent, would such a question have presented itself? What is the relationship between the "zone of twilight" and the political question doctrine? *See* Chapter 7.

5. *Playing with Jackson's Categories*. Into which of Justice Jackson's three categories does the particular executive act in *Little v. Barreme* fall? The executive act in *Curtiss-Wright*? Note the parallel between Justice Jackson's third category and the reasoning of Chief Justice Marshall in *Little v. Barreme*. Does Chief Justice Marshall also suggest that the President's powers fluctuate as a function of action taken by Congress? Yet, conceptually, how can a statute alter the scope of a constitutional power? Do these opinions discuss constitutional power or statutory power—or some amalgam of the two? Compare the approach of *Dames & Moore v. Regan*, 453 U.S. 654, 678–79, 101 S.Ct. 2972, 69 L.Ed.2d 918 (1981):

> Although we have declined to conclude that the [International Emergency Economic Powers Act] or the Hostage Act directly authorizes the President's suspension of claims . . ., we cannot ignore the general tenor of Congress' legislation in this area in trying to determine whether the President is acting alone or at least with the acceptance of Congress. . . . Congress cannot anticipate and legislate with regard to every possible action the President may find it necessary to take or every possible situation in which he might act. Such failure of Congress specifically to delegate authority does not, "especially . . . in the areas of foreign policy and national security," imply "congressional disapproval" of action taken by the Executive. *Haig v. Agee*, 453 U.S. 280, 291. On the contrary, the enactment of legislation closely related to the question of the President's authority in a particular case which evinces legislative intent to accord the President broad discretion may be considered to "invite" "measures on independent presidential responsibility," *Youngstown*, 343 U.S., at 637 (Jackson, J., concurring). At least this is so where there is no contrary indication of legislative intent and when, as here, there is a history of congressional acquiescence in conduct of the sort engaged in by the President. . . .

Does this collapse Jackson's first and second categories, suggesting that congressional silence can constitute consent?

6. *The Non-Delegation Doctrine*. As discussed in the notes following the *Curtiss-Wright* case, the non-delegation doctrine in U.S. constitutional law is

the principle that the Congress, being vested with "all legislative powers" by Article I, section 1 of the Constitution, cannot delegate that power to anyone else. Yet when one looks at the foreign affairs powers accorded to the Congress under the Constitution and the foreign affairs powers exercised by the President in practice, it seems that there is a considerable amount of delegation to the President in the field of foreign affairs. What is the current viability of this doctrine and to what extent does it apply to foreign affairs legislation?

GLENNON, CONSTITUTIONAL DIPLOMACY

197–202 (1990) (some footnotes omitted).

THE DELEGATION DOCTRINE IN FOREIGN RELATIONS

Curtiss–Wright does *not* hold that the delegation doctrine has *no* application to international relations; rather, it does not have *equal* application. The distinction is of obvious importance and has often been overlooked. Thus, the case could be restricted to its facts or at least not extended to "powers to go to war, or to use the armed forces." But it was unnecessary to reach even that question. As Professor Bickel suggested, the Court could have found simply that the standards encompassed in the law met delegation requirements.

More important, the central policy reasons underpinning the delegation doctrine militate in favor of applying it to foreign-affairs matters. Justice Rehnquist has said that the delegation doctrine serves three important functions. "First, and most abstractly, it ensures to the extent consistent with orderly governmental administration that important choices of social policy are made by Congress, the branch of our government most responsive to the popular will."[37] It would be hard to imagine a "choice of social policy" more important than the choice to go to war, or the choice, once the armed forces are involved in hostilities, to use nuclear weapons. The responsiveness of Congress (as opposed to that of the Senate and the President) to the popular will apparently represented the precise reason that the Framers placed the decision to go to war in congressional hands. A power allocated to one branch by the Constitution ought not be subject to reassignment to another branch by a vote of Congress, let alone the Senate. This is why the Constitution provides for amendments. There is no apparent reason why that should be less true of a power relating to foreign affairs.

"Second," Justice Rehnquist wrote, "the doctrine guarantees that, to the extent Congress finds it necessary to delegate authority, it provides the recipient of that authority with an intelligible principle to guide the exercise of the delegated discretion."[39] In this sense, the doctrine is not unlike other provisions of the Constitution directed at curbing the exercise of "naked preferences"—the dormant commerce, privileges-and-immunities, equal-protection, due-process, contract, and eminent-domain clauses.

---

37. Industrial Union Dep't v. American Petroleum Inst., 448 U.S. 607, 685 (1986).

39. *Industrial Union Dep't*, 448 U.S. at 685–86.

The delegation decisions require that Congress "lay down the general policy and standards that animate the law, leaving the agency to refine those standards, [to] fill in the blanks, or [to] apply those standards to particular cases."[41] The exercise of arbitrary power is precluded. This concern seems particularly pertinent in foreign affairs. Given the broad presidential powers in the field, additional uncircumscribed discretion—discretion intended by the Framers to reside in the legislature—would write out of the Constitution any meaningful notion of separation of powers in the realm of foreign relations.

"Third, and derivative of the second," Rehnquist wrote, "the doctrine ensures that courts charged with reviewing the exercise of delegated legislative discretion will be able to test that exercise against ascertainable standards."[42] Because the courts have traditionally played a lesser role in foreign affairs, this consideration may be less relevant, although it clearly is not without some application.

The reasons for exempting foreign-affairs powers from the operation of the delegation doctrine are thus less than compelling. The Court has backed steadily away from the exception suggested by *Curtiss–Wright*. The first major step was taken in 1952 with *Youngstown Sheet & Tube v. Sawyer*, the famous *Steel Seizure Case*. President Truman justified the seizure on the ground that the continued operation of the steel mills was necessary for the successful continuation of the war effort in Korea and was therefore permitted under his powers as commander in chief. The Court rejected the argument and held that President Truman's action in effect represented an exercise of *legislative* authority. No examination was made of congressional enactments (such as defense authorization or appropriation acts) from which delegation might conceivably have been inferred. Nor was any reference made to powers that President Truman might have derived from the nation's "sovereignty" or from the "law of nations." Indeed, no reference was made to *Curtiss–Wright*.

Six years later, the Court moved further from Justice Sutherland's constitutional exegesis. In *Kent v. Dulles*, the Court invalidated a passport revocation as beyond the statutory authority of the Secretary of State. If the "power is [to be] delegated," the Court said, "the standards must be adequate to pass scrutiny by the accepted tests."[46] In that case, as in the *Steel Seizure Case*, the Court indicated its willingness to invalidate acts of the Executive in foreign affairs.

CURRENT VIABILITY OF THE DELEGATION DOCTRINE

The invalidation of executive acts notwithstanding, no federal statute has been struck down through application of the delegation doctrine in fifty years.[1] Although rumors of the doctrine's death have been frequently

41. *Industrial Union Dep't*, 448 U.S. at 675.

42. *Id.* at 686.

46. [357 U.S.] at 129.

1. [Authors' Note: In *Clinton v. City of New York*, 524 U.S. 417 (1998), the Supreme Court found that the Line Item Veto Act of 1996, authorizing the President to selectively void portions of appropriation bills, was an unconstitutional delegation of the legislative power of Congress.]

reported, they are probably exaggerated. In the 1980 *Benzene Case*, the plurality opinion relied upon the delegation doctrine in construing narrowly a federal statute conferring rule-making authority on the Secretary of Labor. Justice Rehnquist, concurring, argued that the statute should have been invalidated through use of the doctrine. He repeated the opinion the following term in the *Cotton Dust Case* and was joined by the Chief Justice. On at least two occasions, Justice Brennan expressed a measure of approval for continued application of the doctrine. It is one thing to use the doctrine as a canon of statutory construction and quite another to employ it as a criterion of validity; some justices willing to do the latter would doubtless agree on the doctrine's applicability in a given case. Nonetheless, it is not farfetched to believe that in the right case, for the right purpose, the doctrine could indeed command a majority of the current Supreme Court.

However, in three recent passport cases—*Zemel v. Rusk*, *Haig v. Agee*, and *Wald v. Regan*—the Court once again relied upon the *Curtiss–Wright* notion of generalized deference to the President. Chief Justice Warren noted in *Zemel* that "Congress—in giving the President authority over matters of foreign affairs—must of necessity paint with a brush broader than customarily it wields in domestic areas."[58] The Chief Justice reiterated, however, that *Curtiss–Wright* did "not mean that simply because a statute deals with foreign relations, it can grant the Executive totally unrestricted freedom of choice."[59]

The great deference shown by the Court to the independent constitutional powers of the President in foreign affairs heightens doubts about the continued viability of the delegation doctrine in foreign affairs. Nevertheless, delegating authority to the Executive to limit the international travel of private citizens is fundamentally different from conferring congressional war-making power on the President. If the magnitude of relevant social choices represents one criterion, then the policy considerations are manifestly incomparable: That an aspect of the foreign commerce power happens to be delegable says little or nothing about the delegability of central elements of the war power.

Whether there is a war-powers exception from the delegation doctrine is unclear. In *Dames & Moore v. Regan*, the Iran claims-settlement agreement was upheld through the application of the analytical framework developed in the *Steel Seizure Case*. The majority opinion made no reference to *Curtiss–Wright* or to any notion of presidential power deriving from sovereignty or the law of nations.

More important, perhaps, is the Court's 1983 opinion in *Immigration and Naturalization Service v. Chadha*. In invalidating use of the "legislative veto," the Court mandated that Congress must adhere strictly to constitutionally required procedures for the enactment of legislation. "Convenience and efficiency"—apparently considerations foremost on Jus-

58. 381 U.S. at 17.

59. *Id.* . . .

tice Sutherland's mind in upholding the broad delegation in *Curtiss-Wright*—were insufficient to save a statute "contrary to the Constitution." "Convenience and efficiency ... are not the primary objectives—or the hallmarks—of democratic government."[63]

On the other hand, *Chadha* may be seen as reflecting the Supreme Court's indifference to the delegation doctrine. In some cases, the legislative veto was the only check on the unbridled exercise of presidential powers; its absence might be viewed in those instances as a standardless delegation of legislative power. Justice White's dissent noted that the majority opinion invalidated a number of "foreign affairs" vetos, including those present in legislation concerning war powers and arms exports. A Court concerned about rejuvenating the delegation doctrine would seemingly go about the task differently.

If the state of the delegation doctrine is confused as it applies to domestic affairs, it is thus thoroughly confused as it applies to foreign affairs. Yet one thing is clear: To whatever extent the doctrine has continued vitality, no persuasive reasons have been advanced to exempt from its application questions of war-making authority. And alive or not, the Framers' clear intent to include the House of Representatives in any decision to go to war would raise serious doubts about the validity of any treaty purporting to impose an "automatic" commitment on the United States to use armed force.

INS v. CHADHA

462 U.S. 919, 103 S.Ct. 2764, 77 L.Ed.2d 317 (1983)
(some footnotes and citations omitted).

CHIEF JUSTICE BURGER delivered the opinion of the Court.

. . . .

I

Chadha is an East Indian who was born in Kenya and holds a British passport. He was lawfully admitted to the United States in 1966 on a nonimmigrant student visa. His visa expired on June 30, 1972. On October 11, 1973, the District Director of the Immigration and Naturalization Service ordered Chadha to show cause why he should not be deported for having "remained in the United States for a longer time than permitted." ... [A] deportation hearing was held before an Immigration Judge on January 11, 1974. Chadha conceded that he was deportable for overstaying his visa and the hearing was adjourned to enable him to file an application for suspension of deportation....

After Chadha submitted his application for suspension of deportation, the deportation hearing was resumed on February 7, 1974. On the basis of evidence adduced at the hearing, affidavits submitted with the application, and the results of a character investigation conducted by the INS, the

63. [462 U.S.] at 944.

Immigration Judge, on June 25, 1974, ordered that Chadha's deportation be suspended....

Pursuant to § 244(c)(1) of the Act, the Immigration Judge suspended Chadha's deportation and a report of the suspension was transmitted to Congress....

Once the Attorney General's recommendation for suspension of Chadha's deportation was conveyed to Congress, Congress had the power under [the Act] to veto the Attorney General's determination that Chadha should not be deported....

....

On December 12, 1975, Representative Eilberg, Chairman of the Judiciary Subcommittee on Immigration, Citizenship, and International Law, introduced a resolution opposing "the granting of permanent residence in the United States to [six] aliens," including Chadha.... The resolution was passed without debate or recorded vote. Since the House action was pursuant to § 244(c)(2), the resolution was not treated as an Art. I legislative act; it was not submitted to the Senate or presented to the President for his action.

....

... We begin, of course, with the presumption that the challenged statute is valid. Its wisdom is not the concern of the courts; if a challenged action does not violate the Constitution, it must be sustained....

By the same token, the fact that a given law or procedure is efficient, convenient, and useful in facilitating functions of government, standing alone, will not save it if it is contrary to the Constitution. Convenience and efficiency are not the primary objectives—or the hallmarks—of democratic government and our inquiry is sharpened rather than blunted by the fact that congressional veto provisions are appearing with increasing frequency in statutes which delegate authority to executive and independent agencies:

> "Since 1932, when the first veto provision was enacted into law, 295 congressional veto-type procedures have been inserted in 196 different statutes as follows: from 1932 to 1939, five statutes were affected; from 1940–49, nineteen statutes; between 1950–59, thirty-four statutes; and from 1960–69, forty-nine. From the year 1970 through 1975, at least one hundred sixty-three such provisions were included in eighty-nine laws." Abourezk, The Congressional Veto: A Contemporary Response to Executive Encroachment on Legislative Prerogatives, 52 Ind. L. Rev. 323, 324 (1977)....

JUSTICE WHITE undertakes to make a case for the proposition that the one-House veto is a useful "political invention," and we need not challenge that assertion. We can even concede this utilitarian argument although the long-range political wisdom of this "invention" is arguable. It has been vigorously debated, and it is instructive to compare the views of the protagonists. But policy arguments supporting even useful "political inventions" are subject to the demands of the Constitution which defines powers and, with respect to this subject, sets out just how those powers are to be exercised.

Explicit and unambiguous provisions of the Constitution prescribe and define the respective functions of the Congress and of the Executive in the legislative process. Since the precise terms of those familiar provisions are critical to the resolution of these cases, we set them out verbatim. Article I provides:

> "All legislative Powers herein granted shall be vested in a Congress of the United States, which shall consist of a Senate *and* House of Representatives." Art. I, § 1. (Emphasis added.)
>
> "Every Bill which shall have passed the House of Representatives *and* the Senate, *shall,* before it becomes a law, be presented to the President of the United States...." Art. I, § 7, cl. 2. (Emphasis added.)
>
> "*Every* Order, Resolution, or Vote to which the Concurrence of the Senate and House of Representatives may be necessary (except on a question of Adjournment) *shall be* presented to the President of the United States; and before the Same shall take Effect, *shall be* approved by him, or being disapproved by him, *shall be* repassed by two thirds of the Senate and House of Representatives, according to the Rules and Limitations prescribed in the Case of a Bill." Art. I, § 7, cl. 3. (Emphasis added.)

These provisions of Art. I are integral parts of the constitutional design for the separation of powers. We have recently noted that "[t]he principle of separation of powers was not simply an abstract generalization in the minds of the Framers: it was woven into the document that they drafted in Philadelphia in the summer of 1787." *Buckley v. Valeo,* 424 U.S. at 124. Just as we relied on the textual provision of Art. II, § 2, cl. 2, to vindicate the principle of separation of powers in *Buckley,* we see that the purposes underlying the Presentment Clauses, Art. I, § 7, cls. 2, 3, and the bicameral requirement of Art. I, § 1, and § 7, cl. 2, guide our resolution of the important question presented in these cases....

....

We see therefore that the Framers were acutely conscious that the bicameral requirement and the Presentment Clauses would serve essential constitutional functions. The President's participation in the legislative process was to protect the Executive Branch from Congress and to protect the whole people from improvident laws. The division of the Congress into two distinctive bodies assures that the legislative power would be exercised only after opportunity for full study and debate in separate settings. The President's unilateral veto power, in turn, was limited by the power of two-thirds of both Houses of Congress to overrule a veto thereby precluding final arbitrary action of one person. See *id.,* at 99–104. It emerges clearly that the prescription for legislative action in Art. I, §§ 1,

7, represents the Framers' decision that the legislative power of the Federal Government be exercised in accord with a single, finely wrought and exhaustively considered, procedure.

. . . .

The Constitution sought to divide the delegated powers of the new Federal Government into three defined categories, Legislative, Executive, and Judicial, to assure, as nearly as possible, that each branch of government would confine itself to its assigned responsibility. The hydraulic pressure inherent within each of the separate Branches to exceed the outer limits of its power, even to accomplish desirable objectives, must be resisted.

Although not "hermetically" sealed from one another, the powers delegated to the three Branches are functionally identifiable. When any Branch acts, it is presumptively exercising the power the Constitution has delegated to it. When the Executive acts, he presumptively acts in an executive or administrative capacity as defined in Art. II. And when, as here, one House of Congress purports to act, it is presumptively acting within its assigned sphere.

Beginning with this presumption, we must nevertheless establish that the challenged action under § 244(c)(2) is of the kind to which the procedural requirements of Art. I, § 7, apply. Not every action taken by either House is subject to the bicameralism and presentment requirements of Art. I. See *infra* ... nn. 20, 21. Whether actions taken by either House are, in law and fact, an exercise of legislative power depends not on their form but upon "whether they contain matter which is properly to be regarded as legislative in its character and effect." S. Rep. No. 1335, 54th Cong., 2d Sess., 8 (1897).

Examination of the action taken here by one House pursuant to § 244(c)(2) reveals that it was essentially legislative in purpose and effect. In purporting to exercise power defined in Art. I, § 8, cl. 4, to "establish an uniform Rule of Naturalization," the House took action that had the purpose and effect of altering the legal rights, duties, and relations of persons, including the Attorney General, Executive Branch officials and Chadha, all outside the Legislative Branch. Section 244(c)(2) purports to authorize one House of Congress to require the Attorney General to deport an individual alien whose deportation otherwise would be canceled under § 244. The one-House veto operated in these cases to overrule the Attorney General and mandate Chadha's deportation; absent the House action, Chadha would remain in the United States. Congress has *acted* and its action has altered Chadha's status.

The legislative character of the one-House veto in these cases is confirmed by the character of the congressional action it supplants. Neither the House of Representatives nor the Senate contends that, absent the veto provision in § 244(c)(2), either of them, or both of them acting together, could effectively require the Attorney General to deport an alien once the Attorney General, in the exercise of legislatively delegated authority,[16] had determined the alien should remain in the United States. Without the challenged provision in § 244(c)(2), this could have been achieved, if at all, only by legislation requiring deportation.[17] Similarly, a veto by one House of Congress under § 244(c)(2) cannot be justified as an attempt at amending the standards set out in § 244(a)(1), or as a repeal of § 244 as applied to Chadha. Amendment and repeal of statutes, no less than enactment, must conform with Art. I.[18]

The nature of the decision implemented by the one-House veto in these cases further manifests its legislative character. After long experience with the clumsy, time-consuming private bill procedure, Congress made a deliberate choice to delegate to the Executive Branch, and specifically to the Attorney General, the authority to allow deportable aliens to remain in this country in certain specified circumstances. It is not disputed that this choice to delegate authority is precisely the kind of decision that can be implemented only in accordance with the procedures set out in Art. I. Disagreement with the Attorney General's decision on Chadha's deportation—that is, Congress' decision to deport Chadha—no less than Congress' original choice to delegate to the Attorney General the authority to make that decision, involves determinations of policy that Congress can

16. Congress protests that affirming the Court of Appeals in these cases will sanction "lawmaking by the Attorney General.... Why is the Attorney General exempt from submitting his proposed changes in the law to the full bicameral process?" To be sure, some administrative agency action—rulemaking, for example—may resemble "lawmaking." See 5 U.S.C. § 551(4), which defines an agency's "rule" as "the whole or part of an agency statement of general or particular applicability and future effect designed to implement, interpret, or prescribe *law* or policy...." This Court has referred to agency activity as being "quasi-legislative" in character. *Humphrey's Executor v. United States*, 295 U.S. 602, 628 (1938). Clearly, however, "[i]n the framework of our Constitution, the President's power to see that the laws are faithfully executed refutes the idea that he is to be a lawmaker." *Youngstown Sheet & Tube Co. v. Sawyer*, 343 U.S. 579, 587 (1952). See *Buckley v. Valeo*, 424 U.S. at 123. When the Attorney General performs his duties pursuant to § 244, he does not exercise "legislative" power. The bicameral process is not necessary as a check on the Executive's administration of the laws because his administrative activity cannot reach beyond the limits of the statute that created it—a statute duly enacted pursuant to Art. I, §§ 1, 7. The constitutionality of the Attorney General's execution of the authority delegated to him by § 244 involves only a question of delegation doctrine. The courts, when a case or controversy arises, can always "ascertain whether the will of Congress has been obeyed," and can enforce adherence to statutory standards. See *Youngstown Sheet & Tube Co. v. Sawyer*. It is clear, therefore, that the Attorney General acts in his presumptively Art. II capacity when he administers the Immigration and Nationality Act. Executive action under legislatively delegated authority that might resemble "legislative" action in some respects is not subject to the approval of both Houses of Congress and the President for the reason that the Constitution does not so require. That kind of Executive action is always subject to check by the terms of the legislation that authorized it; and if that authority is exceeded it is open to judicial review as well as the power of Congress to modify or revoke the authority entirely. A one-House veto is clearly legislative in both character and effect and is not so checked; the need for the check provided by Art. I, §§ 1, 7, is therefore clear. Congress' authority to delegate portions of its power to administrative agencies provides no support for the argument that Congress can constitutionally control administration of the laws by way of a congressional veto....

17. We express no opinion as to whether such legislation would violate any constitutional provision.

18. During the Convention of 1787, the application of the President's veto to repeals of statutes was addressed, and the Framers were apparently content with Madison's comment that "[a]s to the difficulty of repeals, it was probable that in doubtful cases the policy would soon take place of limiting the duration of laws as to require renewal instead of repeal." 2 Farrand 587. There is no provision allowing Congress to repeal or amend laws by other than legislative means pursuant to Art. I.

implement in only one way; bicameral passage followed by presentment to the President. Congress must abide by its delegation of authority until that delegation is legislatively altered or revoked.[19]

Finally, we see that when the Framers intended to authorize either House of Congress to act alone and outside of its prescribed bicameral legislative role, they narrowly and precisely defined the procedure for such action. [The Court then discusses four constitutional provisions by which one House may act alone, such as according to the House of Representatives the sole power to initiate impeachments. *See* U.S. CONST. Art. I, § 2, cl. 5.]

. . . .

Since it is clear that the action by the House under § 244(c)(2) was not within any of the express constitutional exceptions authorizing one House to act alone, and equally clear that it was an exercise of legislative power, that action was subject to the standards prescribed in Art. I. The bicameral requirement, the Presentment Clauses, the President's veto, and Congress' power to override a veto were intended to erect enduring checks on each Branch and to protect the people from the improvident exercise of power by mandating certain prescribed steps. To preserve those checks, and maintain the separation of powers, the carefully defined limits on the power of each Branch must not be eroded. To accomplish what has been attempted by one House of Congress in this case requires action in conformity with the express procedures of the Constitution's prescription for legislative action: passage by a majority of both Houses and presentment to the President.

The veto authorized by § 244(c)(2) doubtless has been in many respects a convenient shortcut; the "sharing" with the Executive by Congress of its authority over aliens in this manner is, on its face, an appealing compromise. In purely practical terms, it is obviously easier for action to be taken by one House without submission to the President; but it is crystal clear from the records of the Convention, contemporaneous writings and debates, that the Framers ranked other values higher than efficiency. The records of the Convention and debates in the states preceding ratification underscore the common desire to define and limit the exercise of the newly created federal powers affecting the states and the people. There is unmistakable expression of a determination that legislation by the national Congress be a step-by-step, deliberate and deliberative process.

The choices we discern as having been made in the Constitutional Convention impose burdens on governmental processes that often seem

19. This does not mean that Congress is required to capitulate to "the accretion of policy control by forces outside its chambers." Javits Klein, Congressional Oversight and the Legislative Veto: A Constitutional Analysis, 52 N.Y.U.L. Rev. 455, 462 (1997). The Constitution provides Congress with abundant means to oversee and control its administrative creatures. Beyond the obvious fact that Congress ultimately controls administrative agencies in the legislation that creates them, other means of control, such as durational limits on authorizations and formal reporting requirements, lie well within Congress' constitutional power. See *id.*, at 460–61.

clumsy, inefficient, even unworkable, but those hard choices were consciously made by men who had lived under a form of government that permitted arbitrary governmental acts to go unchecked. There is no support in the Constitution or decisions of this Court for the proposition that the cumbersomeness and delays often encountered in complying with explicit constitutional standards may be avoided, either by the Congress or by the President. See *Youngstown Sheet & Tube Co. v. Sawyer,* 343 U.S. 579 (1952). With all the obvious flaws of delay, untidiness, and potential for abuse, we have not yet found a better way to preserve freedom than by making the exercise of power subject to the carefully crafted restraints spelled out in the Constitution.

Affirmed.

. . . .

JUSTICE WHITE, dissenting.

Today the Court not only invalidates § 244(c)(2) of the Immigration and Nationality Act, but also sounds the death knell for nearly 200 other statutory provisions in which Congress has reserved a "legislative veto." For this reason, the Court's decision is of surpassing importance. And it is for this reason that the Court would have been well advised to decide the cases, if possible, on the narrower grounds of separation of powers, leaving for full consideration the constitutionality of other congressional review statutes operating on such varied matters as war powers and agency rulemaking, some of which concern the independent regulatory agencies.

The prominence of the legislative veto mechanism in our contemporary political system and its importance to Congress can hardly be overstated. It has become a central means by which Congress secures the accountability of executive and independent agencies. Without the legislative veto, Congress is faced with a Hobson's choice: either to refrain from delegating the necessary authority, leaving itself with a hopeless task of writing laws with the requisite specificity to cover endless special circumstances across the entire policy landscape, or in the alternative, to abdicate its law-making function to the Executive Branch and independent agencies. To choose the former leaves major national problems unresolved; to opt for the latter risks unaccountable policymaking by those not elected to fill that role. Accordingly, over the past five decades, the legislative veto has been placed in nearly 200 statutes.[2] The device is known in every field of governmental concern: reorganization, budgets, foreign affairs, war powers, and regulation of trade, safety, energy, the environment, and the economy.

. . . .

The legislative veto developed initially in response to the problems of reorganizing the sprawling Government structure created in response to the Depression. The Reorganization Acts established the chief model for the legislative veto. . . .

2. A selected list and brief description of these provisions is appended to this opinion.

Shortly after adoption of the Reorganization Act of 1939, Congress and the President applied the legislative veto procedure to resolve the delegation problem for national security and foreign affairs. World War II occasioned the need to transfer greater authority to the President in these areas. The legislative veto offered the means by which Congress could confer additional authority while preserving its own constitutional role. During World War II, Congress enacted over 30 statutes conferring powers on the Executive with legislative veto provisions. President Roosevelt accepted the veto as the necessary price for obtaining exceptional authority.

. . . .

During the 1970's the legislative veto was important in resolving a series of major constitutional disputes between the President and Congress over claims of the President to broad impoundment, war, and national emergency powers. The key provision of the War Powers Resolution authorizes the termination by concurrent resolution of the use of armed forces in hostilities. . . .

. . . .

Even this brief review suffices to demonstrate that the legislative veto is more than "efficient, convenient, and useful." It is an important if not indispensable political invention that allows the President and Congress to resolve major constitutional and policy differences, assures the accountability of independent regulatory agencies, and preserves Congress' control over lawmaking. Perhaps there are other means of accommodation and accountability, but the increasing reliance of Congress upon the legislative veto suggests that the alternatives to which Congress must now turn are not entirely satisfactory.

. . . .

APPENDIX TO OPINION OF WHITE, J., DISSENTING, STATUTES WITH PROVISIONS AUTHORIZING CONGRESSIONAL REVIEW

This compilation, reprinted from the Brief for the United States Senate, identifies and describes briefly current statutory provisions for a legislative veto by one or both Houses of Congress. . . .

A.

FOREIGN AFFAIRS AND NATIONAL SECURITY

1. Act for International Development of 1961 (Funds made available for foreign assistance under the Act may be terminated by concurrent resolution).

2. War Powers Resolution (Absent declaration of war, President may be directed by concurrent resolution to remove United States armed forces engaged in foreign hostilities.)

3. Department of Defense Appropriation Authorization Act, 1974 (National defense contracts obligating the United States for any amount

in excess of $25,000,000 may be disapproved by resolution of either House).

4. Department of Defense Appropriation Authorization Act, 1975 (Applications for export of defense goods, technology or techniques may be disapproved by concurrent resolution).

5. H.R.J. Res. 683 (1975) (Assignment of civilian personnel to Sinai may be disapproved by concurrent resolution).

6. International Development and Food Assistance Act of 1975 (Foreign assistance to countries not meeting human rights standards may be terminated by concurrent resolution).

7. International Security Assistance and Arms [Export] Control Act of 1976 (President's letter of offer to sell major defense equipment may be disapproved by concurrent resolution).

8. National Emergencies Act (Presidentially declared national emergency may be terminated by concurrent resolution).

9. International Navigational Rules Act of 1977 (Presidential proclamation of International Regulations for Preventing Collisions at Sea may be disapproved by concurrent resolution).

10. International Security Assistance Act of 1977 (President's proposed transfer of arms to a third country may be disapproved by concurrent resolution).

11. Act of December [28], 1977 (Presidentially declared national emergency and exercise of conditional powers may be terminated by concurrent resolution).

12. Nuclear Non–Proliferation Act of 1978 (Cooperative agreements concerning storage and disposition of spent nuclear fuel, proposed export of nuclear facilities, materials or technology and proposed agreements for international cooperation in nuclear reactor development may be disapproved by concurrent resolution).

[the remaining statutes on Justice White's list are omitted]

NOTES ON CHADHA

1. *Thwarting a Congressional Claw-back*. As indicated in *Chadha*, the increased effort to use legislative vetoes was probably the result of an increased delegation of power from Congress to the President over the past 70 years. As a matter of constitutional theory, why is the Court willing to tolerate extensive delegation of power to the President that is legislative in nature, but is unwilling to allow Congress to try to maintain some kind of check on that power through a legislative veto? Do you think *Chadha* is constitutionally sound or does it rely upon an overly rigid conception of separation of powers?

2. *Types of Congressional Measures*. Four kinds of measures are used by Congress: bills, joint resolutions, concurrent resolutions, and simple resolu-

tions. A *bill* is passed by both houses and presented to the president for his signature or veto. If enacted, it has the force of law. A *joint resolution* is different in name only: it too is passed by both houses and presented to the president for his signature or veto. The two can be used interchangeably, although proposals to amend the Constitution typically are set forth in joint resolutions. A *concurrent resolution* is passed by both houses, but not sent to the president. Consequently, it does not have the force and effect of law. Concurrent resolutions often are used for "sense-of-the-Congress" statements. A *simple resolution* is passed by only one house and thus also lacks the force of law. It is used to amend the standing rules of that house and for "sense-of-the-House" or "sense-of-the-Senate" declarations. *Chadha* involved use of a simple resolution. Does the reasoning of the Court apply equally to a legislative veto consisting of a concurrent resolution? Should it matter that the one-house veto in *Chadha* was not enacted as a "bolt out of the blue" but was incorporated in an otherwise valid statute?

3. *Convenience and Efficiency*. Is the Court correct in assuming that congressional use of the legislative veto is motivated by concerns of "convenience and efficiency"? Could not the alternative—a statute spelling out specific limits on executive discretion—actually be more convenient and efficient, inasmuch as it would involve no subsequent congressional approval or disapproval procedure? Is not the real reason for the legislative veto, or at least some legislative vetoes, a belief that certain executive activities require regulation but cannot be regulated with specific, *prospective* statutory limitation?

4. *Post-Enactment Contingencies*. There are numerous statutes that delegate authority to an executive official so long as certain statutorily-specified contingencies occur after enactment of the statutes. That contingency is often a finding by the President that a certain event has (or has not) occurred. For example, under a 1985 statutory provision known as the Pressler Amendment to the 1961 Foreign Assistance Act, extensive economic and military sanctions were to be imposed on Pakistan unless the President could certify on an annual basis that Pakistan does not possess a nuclear device and that U.S. aid would reduce the risk of Pakistan possessing such a device. *See* 22 U.S.C. § 2375(e) (2006). In 1990, President George H.W. Bush decided that he could no longer issue such a certification and the sanctions were imposed. (A later amendment adopted in 1999 gave the president permanent authority to waive the Pressler amendment sanctions.)

The contingency need not turn solely on an executive branch determination. For example, in January 2004 Congress passed and President George W. Bush signed into law the Millennium Challenge Act of 2003 (MCA). *See* 22 U.S.C. § § 7701–18 (2006). Under the statute, a developing country may qualify for foreign aid if it demonstrates commitment to three broad criteria: good governance; health and education for its people; and sound economic policies. A "Millennium Challenge Corporation" (MCC) was established as a government corporation to administer the MCA. The MCC uses sixteen "indicators" drawn from reputable sources (*e.g.*, Freedom House, the World Bank Institute, the Heritage Foundation) to measure developing country performance on the three criteria. Based on these indicators, the MCC selects those countries eligible for MCA assistance. If the MCC decides that the criteria have not been met for a country seeking aid, then that country cannot receive aid under the MCA.

The Supreme Court has previously upheld the constitutionality of statutes which condition the authority granted therein upon the occurrence or nonoccurrence of a specified contingent event. *See, e.g.,* J. W. Hampton & Co. v. United States, 276 U.S. 394, 48 S.Ct. 348, 72 L.Ed. 624 (1927) (statute authorizing the President to raise tariff rates if he determines it necessary to equalize foreign and domestic production costs); Hirabayashi v. United States, 320 U.S. 81, 63 S.Ct. 1375, 87 L.Ed. 1774 (1943) (statute authorizing a military commander to determine that danger existed warranting imposition of a curfew).

Why is it that the effectiveness of action legislative in character may be conditioned upon decisions by organizations such as Freedom House or the Heritage Foundation, but under *Chadha,* may not be conditioned on the vote of the two legislative bodies of the Congress? Is it sufficient to say that the effect accorded to Freedom House or the Heritage Foundation is not governed by the presentment clause?

5. *Functional Effects of Chadha.* In considering this issue it may be useful to examine the functional effect of the *Chadha* decision. A good vehicle for illustrating that effect is the Arms Export Control Act, Pub. L. No. 94–329, 90 Stat. 729 (1976), as amended. In 1976, following concerns about arms sales abuses, the Senate Foreign Relations Committee proposed sweeping revisions of the Foreign Military Sales Act, including renaming it the "Arms Export Control Act." President Ford vetoed the original version of the Act, objecting, inter alia, to various legislative veto provisions. *See* President's Message to the Senate Returning S. 2662 Without His Approval, 12 WEEKLY COMP. PRES. DOC. 828 (May 7, 1976). A new version was considered and several of the legislative vetoes were dropped, but the Act continued to provide, in section 36(b), that Congress could disapprove certain presidentially-proposed arms sales in excess of $25 million in value through the use of a concurrent resolution. After *Chadha,* such use of the concurrent resolution is no longer permissible, and the Act was amended to preclude such sales when prohibited by joint resolution. *See* 22 U.S.C. § 2753 (2006).

Clearly, however, the Act could have been re-written to permit presidential arms sales in excess of $25 million only if approved by a bill or joint resolution. Under such circumstances, to make the proposed sale, the President would have to persuade a majority in each house of Congress to vote for the proposed sale. In other words, where before it took *two* houses of Congress to block presidential action, after *Chadha* a majority of only *one* house might be required to do so. It thus seems doubtful that the decision in all circumstances benefits the President. Moreover, could it not be argued that, viewed functionally, certain pre-*Chadha* procedures better served principles of bicameralism than those now required by the Court?

6. *Interpretive Theory.* Why should the Court's inquiry be "sharpened rather than blunted by the fact that Congressional veto provisions are appearing with greater frequency . . . ?" Does not practice provide a "gloss" on the constitutional text? The original version of the Arms Export Control Act (discussed in the prior note) included seven legislative veto provisions. *See*

S. 2662, 94th Cong., 1st Sess. (1975). In justifying those provisions constitutionally, the Senate Foreign Relations Committee said that, "[i]f custom has tended to validate otherwise questionable practices engaged in by the executive branch, custom would seem just as surely to have validated the congressional practice embodied in the legislative veto." S. Rep. No. 94–605, 94th Cong., 2d Sess., at 15 (1976).

7. *Relation to War Powers Resolution.* Should it matter whether the presidential act subject to the veto is authorized by the Constitution rather than by a statute? See the materials concerning the legislative veto in section 5(c) of the War Powers Resolution set forth in Chapter 4, Section 5.

SECTION 4. BALANCING CONCURRENT POWER IN EMERGENCIES

JOHN LOCKE, SECOND TREATISE OF GOVERNMENT

84 (C.B. Macpherson ed., 1980).

. . . This power to act according to discretion, for the public good, without the prescription of the law, and sometimes even against it, *is* that which is called *prerogative*: for since in some governments the lawmaking power is not always in being, and is usually too numerous, and so too slow, for the dispatch requisite to execution; and because also it is impossible to foresee, and so by laws to provide for, all accidents and necessities that may concern the public, or make such laws as will do no harm, if they are executed with an inflexible rigour, on all occasions, and upon all persons that may come in their way; therefore there is a latitude left to the executive power, to do many things of choice which the laws do not prescribe.

EX PARTE MERRYMAN

17 F. Cas. 144 (C.C.D. Md. 1861).

[Following the April 1861 bombardment of Fort Sumter by Confederate troops under the command of General P.G.T. Beauregard, President Lincoln called for reinforcements to defend the city of Washington, D.C. As soldiers from the Sixth Massachusetts Regiment passed through Maryland, a slave state, riots erupted across Baltimore. President Lincoln ordered General Winfield Scott, his commanding general, to suspend the writ of habeas corpus along the "military line" between Philadelphia and Washington. During the arrests that followed, Lieutenant John Merryman, an officer of the Maryland cavalry, was imprisoned on suspicion of sabotage. Merryman filed a habeas petition. Over Lincoln's protests, Chief Justice Roger Taney, a native of Maryland, delivered the following opinion as a judge on the Circuit Court for the District of Maryland.]

TANEY, CIRCUIT JUSTICE.

. . . .

As the case comes before me, therefore, I understand that the president not only claims the right to suspend the writ of habeas corpus himself, at his discretion, but to delegate that discretionary power to a military officer, and to leave it to him to determine whether he will or will not obey judicial process that may be served upon him. No official notice has been given to the courts of justice, or to the public, by proclamation or otherwise, that the president claimed this power, and had exercised it in the manner stated in the return. And I certainly listened to it with some surprise, for I had supposed it to be one of those points of constitutional law upon which there was no difference of opinion, and that it was admitted on all hands, that the privilege of the writ could not be suspended, except by act of congress.

. . . .

The clause of the constitution, which authorizes the suspension of the privilege of the writ of habeas corpus, is in the 9th section of the first article. This article is devoted to the legislative department of the United States, and has not the slightest reference to the executive department. . . .

. . . .

It is the second article of the constitution that provides for the organization of the executive department, enumerates the powers conferred on it, and prescribes its duties. And if the high power over the liberty of the citizen now claimed, was intended to be conferred on the president, it would undoubtedly be found in plain words in this article; but there is not a word in it that can furnish the slightest ground to justify the exercise of the power.

. . . .

With such provisions in the constitution, expressed in language too clear to be misunderstood by any one, I can see no ground whatever for supposing that the president, in any emergency, or in any state of things, can authorize the suspension of the privileges of the writ of habeas corpus, or the arrest of a citizen, except in aid of the judicial power. He certainly does not faithfully execute the laws, if he takes upon himself legislative power, by suspending the writ of habeas corpus, and the judicial power also, by arresting and imprisoning a person without due process of law.

. . . .

[Following the circuit court's decision, Merryman was released on bail. He was never tried.]

NOTES ON EMERGENCY POWERS

1. *Locke and Load.* Do you think John Locke is correct that there are times when governmental authorities must be allowed to act "without the prescription of the law, and sometimes even against it," when society is severely threatened? Is the field of foreign relations and national security law

one where this is most likely to happen? What are the dangers of allowing such action? Of prohibiting it?

2. *State of Emergency and the U.S. Constitution*. The U.S. Constitution, unlike the constitutions of some other countries, does not contain a "state of emergency" provision. Nor is there any notion of "derogable" rights in United States constitutional jurisprudence. The only provision of the Constitution that expressly provides for its own suspension is the Habeas Corpus Clause, article I, section 9, clause 2, which provides that the writ "shall not be suspended, unless when in cases of rebellion or invasion the public safety may require it." Does this mean that the scope of the President's constitutional power is constant, or does it expand during a national emergency? If the latter, does this mean that the power of the President and Congress, acting together, also expands so that what would otherwise be unconstitutional (even though within Justice Jackson's first category) is rendered permissible?

3. *The Ticking Time Bomb*. The story is told that Justice Hugo Black, the quintessential "absolutist" in favor of civil rights, was asked whether, if a terrorist who was known to have planted a nuclear device in New York City were captured, and if the only way to locate and disarm the device before detonation were to torture the person, he would allow it. His response allegedly was, "Yes—but we could never say that." Does this mean that the U.S. Constitution permits extra-constitutional conduct in times of *extremis*—but merely does not say so? If so, the ticking time bomb presents an extreme end of the spectrum, and perhaps an unhelpful one since the scenario is relatively unlikely. The real question may be how far along that spectrum for events of lesser significance is extra-constitutional conduct still warranted? Suppose instead of a nuclear bomb, it is a conventional bomb? Suppose you are only fifty percent certain that the person in detention knows where the bomb is? Twenty percent? Is torture still to be tolerated? For commentary on the "ticking time bomb" hypothetical, see Michael J. Glennon, *Terrorism and the Limits of Law*, WILSON Q. 2 (Spring 2002).

4. *Judicial Complicity*. Is the "bending" process greater if the courts consider and legitimate what would otherwise be a transgression? In *The Imperial Presidency*, Arthur Schlesinger writes that, while the Founding Fathers did not rule out the possibility that "crisis might require the executive to act outside the Constitution," neither they did intend to confer constitutional legitimacy on such acts, believing that the "legal order would be better preserved if departures from it were frankly identified as such than if they were anointed with a factitious legality and thereby enabled to serve as constitutional precedents for future action." Arthur Schlesinger, Jr., *The Imperial Presidency* 8 (1973). In this connection, consider in particular the dissent of Justice Jackson in the following case.

KOREMATSU v. UNITED STATES

323 U.S. 214, 65 S.Ct. 193, 89 L.Ed. 194 (1944) (some footnotes omitted).

MR. JUSTICE BLACK delivered the opinion of the Court.

The petitioner, an American citizen of Japanese descent, was convicted in a federal district court for remaining in San Leandro, California, a

"Military Area", contrary to Civilian Exclusion Order No. 34 of the Commanding General of the Western Command, U.S. Army, which directed that after May 9, 1942, all persons of Japanese ancestry should be excluded from that area. No question was raised as to petitioner's loyalty to the United States. The Circuit Court of Appeals affirmed,[1] and the importance of the constitutional question involved caused us to grant certiorari.

It should be noted, to begin with, that all legal restrictions which curtail the civil rights of a single racial group are immediately suspect. That is not to say that all such restrictions are unconstitutional. It is to say that courts must subject them to the most rigid scrutiny. Pressing public necessity may sometimes justify the existence of such restrictions; racial antagonism never can.

In the instant case prosecution of the petitioner was begun by information charging violation of an Act of Congress, of March 21, 1942, 56 Stat. 173, which provides that

> "... whoever shall enter, remain in, leave, or commit any act in any military area or military zone prescribed, under the authority of an Executive order of the President, by the Secretary of War, or by any military commander designated by the Secretary of War, contrary to the restrictions applicable to any such area or zone or contrary to the order of the Secretary of War or any such military commander, shall, if it appears that he knew or should have known of the existence and extent of the restrictions or order and that his act was in violation thereof, be guilty of a misdemeanor and upon conviction shall be liable to a fine of not to exceed $5,000 or to imprisonment for not more than one year, or both, for each offense."

Exclusion Order No. 34, which the petitioner knowingly and admittedly violated, was one of a number of military orders and proclamations, all of which were substantially based upon Executive Order No. 9066, 7 Fed. Reg. 1407. That order, issued after we were at war with Japan, declared that "the successful prosecution of the war requires every possible protection against espionage and against sabotage to national-defense material, national-defense premises, and national-defense utilities...."

One of the series of orders and proclamations, a curfew order, which like the exclusion order here was promulgated pursuant to Executive Order 9066, subjected all persons of Japanese ancestry in prescribed West Coast military areas to remain in their residences from 8 p.m. to 6 a.m. As is the case with the exclusion order here, that prior curfew order was designed as a "protection against espionage and against sabotage." In *Hirabayashi v. United States*, 320 U.S. 81, we sustained a conviction obtained for violation of the curfew order. The Hirabayashi conviction and this one thus rest on the same 1942 Congressional Act and the same basic executive and military orders, all of which orders were aimed at the twin dangers of espionage and sabotage.

---

1. 140 F.2d 289.

The 1942 Act was attacked in the *Hirabayashi* case as an unconstitutional delegation of power; it was contended that the curfew order and other orders on which it rested were beyond the war powers of the Congress, the military authorities and of the President, as Commander in Chief of the Army; and finally that to apply the curfew order against none but citizens of Japanese ancestry amounted to a constitutionally prohibited discrimination solely on account of race. To these questions, we gave the serious consideration which their importance justified. We upheld the curfew order as an exercise of the power of the government to take steps necessary to prevent espionage and sabotage in an area threatened by Japanese attack.

In the light of the principles we announced in the *Hirabayashi* case, we are unable to conclude that it was beyond the war power of Congress and the Executive to exclude those of Japanese ancestry from the West Coast war area at the time they did. True, exclusion from the area in which one's home is located is a far greater deprivation than constant confinement to the home from 8 p.m. to 6 a.m. Nothing short of apprehension by the proper military authorities of the gravest imminent danger to the public safety can constitutionally justify either. But exclusion from a threatened area, no less than curfew, has a definite and close relationship to the prevention of espionage and sabotage. The military authorities, charged with the primary responsibility of defending our shores, concluded that curfew provided inadequate protection and ordered exclusion. They did so, as pointed out in our *Hirabayashi* opinion, in accordance with Congressional authority to the military to say who should, and who should not, remain in the threatened areas.

In this case the petitioner challenges the assumptions upon which we rested our conclusions in the *Hirabayashi* case. He also urges that by May 1942, when Order No. 34 was promulgated, all danger of Japanese invasion of the West Coast had disappeared. After careful consideration of these contentions we are compelled to reject them.

Here, as in the *Hirabayashi* case, *supra*, at p. 99, "... we cannot reject as unfounded the judgment of the military authorities and of Congress that there were disloyal members of that population, whose number and strength could not be precisely and quickly ascertained. We cannot say that the war-making branches of the Government did not have ground for believing that in a critical hour such persons could not readily be isolated and separately dealt with, and constituted a menace to the national defense and safety, which demanded that prompt and adequate measures be taken to guard against it."

Like curfew, exclusion of those of Japanese origin was deemed necessary because of the presence of an unascertained number of disloyal members of the group, most of whom we have no doubt were loyal to this country. It was because we could not reject the finding of the military authorities that it was impossible to bring about an immediate segregation of the disloyal from the loyal that we sustained the validity of the curfew order as applying to the whole group. In the instant case, temporary exclusion of the entire group was rested by the military on the same ground. The judgment that exclusion of the whole group was for the same reason a military imperative answers the contention that the exclusion was in the nature of group punishment based on antagonism to those of Japanese origin. That there were members of the group who retained loyalties to Japan has been confirmed by investigations made subsequent to the exclusion. Approximately five thousand American citizens of Japanese ancestry refused to swear unqualified allegiance to the United States and to renounce allegiance to the Japanese Emperor, and several thousand evacuees requested repatriation to Japan.[2]

We uphold the exclusion order as of the time it was made and when the petitioner violated it.... In doing so, we are not unmindful of the hardships imposed by it upon a large group of American citizens.... But hardships are part of war, and war is an aggregation of hardships. All citizens alike, both in and out of uniform, feel the impact of war in greater or lesser measure. Citizenship has its responsibilities as well as its privileges, and in time of war the burden is always heavier. Compulsory exclusion of large groups of citizens from their homes, except under circumstances of direst emergency and peril, is inconsistent with our basic governmental institutions. But when under conditions of modern warfare our shores are threatened by hostile forces, the power to protect must be commensurate with the threatened danger.

....

It is said that we are dealing here with the case of imprisonment of a citizen in a concentration camp solely because of his ancestry, without evidence or inquiry concerning his loyalty and good disposition towards the United States. Our task would be simple, our duty clear, were this a case involving the imprisonment of a loyal citizen in a concentration camp because of racial prejudice. Regardless of the true nature of the assembly and relocation centers—and we deem it unjustifiable to call them concentration camps with all the ugly connotations that term implies—we are dealing specifically with nothing but an exclusion order. To cast this case into outlines of racial prejudice, without reference to the real military dangers which were presented, merely confuses the issue. Korematsu was not excluded from the Military Area because of hostility to him or his race. He *was* excluded because we are at war with the Japanese Empire, because the properly constituted military authorities feared an invasion of our West Coast and felt constrained to take proper security measures, because they decided that the military urgency of the situation demanded that all citizens of Japanese ancestry be segregated from the West Coast temporarily, and finally, because Congress, reposing its confidence in this

2. Hearings before the Subcommittee on the National War Agencies Appropriation Bill for 1945, Part II, 608–726; Final Report, Japanese Evacuation from the West Coast, 1942, 309–327; Hearings before the Committee on Immigration and Naturalization, House of Representatives, 78th Cong., 2d Sess., on H.R. 2701 and other bills to expatriate certain nationals of the United States, pp. 37–42, 49–58.

time of war in our military leaders—as inevitably it must—determined that they should have the power to do just this. There was evidence of disloyalty on the part of some, the military authorities considered that the need for action was great, and time was short. We cannot—by availing ourselves of the calm perspective of hindsight—now say that at that time these actions were unjustified.

Affirmed.

MR. JUSTICE FRANKFURTER, concurring.

. . . .

The provisions of the Constitution which confer on the Congress and the President powers to enable this country to wage war are as much part of the Constitution as provisions looking to a nation at peace. And we have had recent occasion to quote approvingly the statement of former Chief Justice Hughes that the war power of the Government is "the power to wage war successfully." *Hirabayashi v. United States, supra* at 93. Therefore, the validity of action under the war power must be judged wholly in the context of war. That action is not to be stigmatized as lawless because like action in times of peace would be lawless. To talk about a military order that expresses an allowable judgment of war needs by those entrusted with the duty of conducting war as "an unconstitutional order" is to suffuse a part of the Constitution with an atmosphere of unconstitutionality. The respective spheres of action of military authorities and of judges are of course very different. But within their sphere, military authorities are no more outside the bounds of obedience to the Constitution than are judges within theirs. "The war power of the United States, like its other powers . . . is subject to applicable constitutional limitations". *Hamilton v. Kentucky Distilleries Co.*, 251 U.S. 146, 156. To recognize that military orders are "reasonably expedient military precautions" in time of war and yet to deny them constitutional legitimacy makes of the Constitution an instrument for dialectic subtleties not reasonably to be attributed to the hard-headed Framers, of whom a majority had had actual participation in war. If a military order such as that under review does not transcend the means appropriate for conducting war, such action by the military is as constitutional as would be any authorized action by the Interstate Commerce Commission within the limits of the constitutional power to regulate commerce. And being an exercise of the war power explicitly granted by the Constitution for safeguarding the national life by prosecuting war effectively, I find nothing in the Constitution which denies to Congress the power to enforce such a valid military order by making its violation an offense triable in the civil courts. Compare *Interstate Commerce Commission v. Brimson*, 154 U.S. 447; 155 U.S. 3, and *Monongahela Bridge Co. v. United States,* 216 U.S. 177. To find that the Constitution does not forbid the military measures now complained of does not carry with it approval of that which Congress and the Executive did. That is their business, not ours.

MR. JUSTICE ROBERTS.

I dissent, because I think the indisputable facts exhibit a clear violation of Constitutional rights.

This is not a case of keeping people off the streets at night as was *Hirabayashi v. United States*, 320 U.S. 81, nor a case of temporary exclusion of a citizen from an area for his own safety or that of the community, nor a case of offering him an opportunity to go temporarily out of an area where his presence might cause danger to himself or to his fellows. On the contrary, it is the case of convicting a citizen as a punishment for not submitting to imprisonment in a concentration camp, based on his ancestry, and solely because of his ancestry, without evidence or inquiry concerning his loyalty and good disposition towards the United States. If this be a correct statement of the facts disclosed by this record, and facts of which we take judicial notice, I need hardly labor the conclusion that Constitutional rights have been violated.

. . . .

I would reverse the judgment of conviction.

MR. JUSTICE MURPHY, dissenting.

This exclusion of "all persons of Japanese ancestry, both alien and non-alien," from the Pacific Coast area on a plea of military necessity in the absence of martial law ought not to be approved. Such exclusion goes over "the very brink of constitutional power" and falls into the ugly abyss of racism.

In dealing with matters relating to the prosecution and progress of a war, we must accord great respect and consideration to the judgments of the military authorities who are on the scene and who have full knowledge of the military facts. The scope of their discretion must, as a matter of necessity and common sense, be wide. And their judgments ought not to be overruled lightly by those whose training and duties ill-equip them to deal intelligently with matters so vital to the physical security of the nation.

At the same time, however, it is essential that there be definite limits to military discretion, especially where martial law has not been declared. Individuals must not be left impoverished of their constitutional rights on a plea of military necessity that has neither substance nor support. Thus, like other claims conflicting with the asserted constitutional rights of the individual, the military claim must subject itself to the judicial process of having its reasonableness determined and its conflicts with other interests reconciled. "What are the allowable limits of military discretion, and whether or not they have been overstepped in a particular case, are judicial questions." *Sterling v. Constantin*, 287 U.S. 378, 401.

The judicial test of whether the Government, on a plea of military necessity, can validly deprive an individual of any of his constitutional rights is whether the deprivation is reasonably related to a public danger that is so "immediate, imminent, and impending" as not to admit of delay and not to permit the intervention of ordinary constitutional processes to alleviate the danger. *United States v. Russell*, 13 Wall. 623, 627, 628; *Mitchell v. Harmony*, 13 How. 115, 134, 135; *Raymond v. Thomas*, 91 U.S. 712, 716. Civilian Exclusion Order No. 34, banishing from a prescribed area of the Pacific Coast "all persons of Japanese ancestry, both alien and non-alien," clearly does not meet that test. Being an obvious racial discrimination, the order deprives all those within its scope of the equal protection of the laws as guaranteed by the Fifth Amendment. It further deprives these individuals of their constitutional rights to live and work where they will, to establish a home where they choose and to move about freely. In excommunicating them without benefit of hearings, this order also deprives them of all their constitutional rights to procedural due process. Yet no reasonable relation to an "immediate, imminent, and impending" public danger is evident to support this racial restriction which is one of the most sweeping and complete deprivations of constitutional rights in the history of this nation in the absence of martial law.

It must be conceded that the military and naval situation in the spring of 1942 was such as to generate a very real fear of invasion of the Pacific Coast, accompanied by fears of sabotage and espionage in that area. The military command was therefore justified in adopting all reasonable means necessary to combat these dangers. In adjudging the military action taken in light of the then apparent dangers, we must not erect too high or too meticulous standards; it is necessary only that the action have some reasonable relation to the removal of the dangers of invasion, sabotage and espionage. But the exclusion, either temporarily or permanently, of all persons with Japanese blood in their veins has no such reasonable relation. And that relation is lacking because the exclusion order necessarily must rely for its reasonableness upon the assumption that *all* persons of Japanese ancestry may have a dangerous tendency to commit sabotage and espionage and to aid our Japanese enemy in other ways. It is difficult to believe that reason, logic or experience could be marshalled in support of such an assumption.

That this forced exclusion was the result in good measure of this erroneous assumption of racial guilt rather than bona fide military necessity is evidenced by the Commanding General's Final Report on the evacuation from the Pacific Coast area. In it he refers to all individuals of Japanese descent as "subversive," as belonging to "an enemy race" whose "racial strains are undiluted," and as constituting "over 112,000 potential enemies ... at large today" along the Pacific Coast. In support of this blanket condemnation of all persons of Japanese descent, however, no reliable evidence is cited to show that such individuals were generally disloyal, or had generally so conducted themselves in this area as to constitute a special menace to defense installations or war industries, or had otherwise by their behavior furnished reasonable ground for their exclusion as a group.

Justification for the exclusion is sought, instead, mainly upon questionable racial and sociological grounds not ordinarily within the realm of expert military judgment, supplemented by certain semi-military conclusions drawn from an unwarranted use of circumstantial evidence. Individuals of Japanese ancestry are condemned because they are said to be "a large, unassimilated, tightly knit racial group, bound to an enemy nation by strong ties of race, culture, custom and religion." They are claimed to be given to "emperor worshipping ceremonies" and to "dual citizenship." Japanese language schools and allegedly pro-Japanese organizations are cited as evidence of possible group disloyalty, together with facts as to certain persons being educated and residing at length in Japan. It is intimated that many of these individuals deliberately resided "adjacent to strategic points," thus enabling them "to carry into execution a tremendous program of sabotage on a mass scale should any considerable number of them have been inclined to do so." The need for protective custody is also asserted. The report refers without identity to "numerous incidents of violence" as well as to other admittedly unverified or cumulative incidents. From this, plus certain other events not shown to have been connected with the Japanese Americans, it is concluded that the "situation was fraught with danger to the Japanese population itself" and that the general public "was ready to take matters into its own hands." Finally, it is intimated, though not directly charged or proved, that persons of Japanese ancestry were responsible for three minor isolated shellings and bombings of the Pacific Coast area, as well as for unidentified radio transmissions and night signalling.

The main reasons relied upon by those responsible for the forced evacuation, therefore, do not prove a reasonable relation between the group characteristics of Japanese Americans and the dangers of invasion, sabotage and espionage. The reasons appear, instead, to be largely an accumulation of much of the misinformation, half-truths and insinuations that for years have been directed against Japanese Americans by people with racial and economic prejudices—the same people who have been among the foremost advocates of the evacuation. A military judgment based upon such racial and sociological considerations is not entitled to the great weight ordinarily given the judgments based upon strictly military considerations. Especially is this so when every charge relative to race, religion, culture, geographical location, and legal and economic status has been substantially discredited by independent studies made by experts in these matters.

. . . .

MR. JUSTICE JACKSON, dissenting.

Korematsu was born on our soil, of parents born in Japan. The Constitution makes him a citizen of the United States by nativity and a citizen of California by residence. No claim is made that he is not loyal to this country. There is no suggestion that apart from the matter involved here he is not law-abiding and well disposed. Korematsu, however, has been convicted of an act not commonly a crime. It consists merely of being present in the state whereof he is a citizen, near the place where he was born, and where all his life he has lived.

Even more unusual is the series of military orders which made this conduct a crime. They forbid such a one to remain, and they also forbid him to leave. They were so drawn that the only way Korematsu could avoid violation was to give himself up to the military authority. This meant submission to custody, examination, and transportation out of the territory, to be followed by indeterminate confinement in detention camps.

A citizen's presence in the locality, however, was made a crime only if his parents were of Japanese birth. Had Korematsu been one of four—the others being, say, a German alien enemy, an Italian alien enemy, and a citizen of American-born ancestors, convicted of treason but out on parole—only Korematsu's presence would have violated the order. The difference between their innocence and his crime would result, not from anything he did, said, or thought, different than they, but only in that he was born of different racial stock.

Now, if any fundamental assumption underlies our system, it is that guilt is personal and not inheritable. Even if all of one's antecedents had been convicted of treason, the Constitution forbids its penalties to be visited upon him, for it provides that "no attainder of treason shall work corruption of blood, or forfeiture except during the life of the person attained." But here is an attempt to make an otherwise innocent act a crime merely because this prisoner is the son of parents as to whom he had no choice, and belongs to a race from which there is no way to resign. If Congress in peace-time legislation should enact such a criminal law, I should suppose this Court would refuse to enforce it.

But the "law" which this prisoner is convicted of disregarding is not found in an act of Congress, but in a military order. Neither the Act of Congress nor the Executive Order of the President, nor both together, would afford a basis for this conviction. It rests on the orders of General DeWitt. And it is said that if the military commander had reasonable military grounds for promulgating the orders, they are constitutional and become law, and the Court is required to enforce them. There are several reasons why I cannot subscribe to this doctrine.

It would be impracticable and dangerous idealism to expect or insist that each specific military command in an area of probable operations will conform to conventional tests of constitutionality. When an area is so beset that it must be put under military control at all, the paramount consideration is that its measures be successful, rather than legal. The armed services must protect a society, not merely its Constitution. The very essence of the military job is to marshal physical force, to remove every obstacle to its effectiveness, to give it every strategic advantage. Defense measures will not, and often should not, be held within the limits that bind civil authority in peace. No court can require such a commander in such circumstances to act as a reasonable man; he may be unreasonably cautious and exacting. Perhaps he should be. But a commander in temporarily focusing the life of a community on defense is carrying out a military program; he is not making law in the sense the courts know the term. He issues orders, and they may have a certain authority as military commands, although they may be very bad as constitutional law.

But if we cannot confine military expedients by the Constitution, neither would I distort the Constitution to approve all that the military may deem expedient. That is what the Court appears to be doing, whether consciously or not. I cannot say, from any evidence before me, that the orders of General DeWitt were not reasonably expedient military precautions, nor could I say that they were. But even if they were permissible military procedures, I deny that it follows that they are constitutional. If, as the Court holds, it does follow, then we may as well say that any military order will be constitutional and have done with it.

The limitation under which courts always will labor in examining the necessity for a military order are illustrated by this case. How does the Court know that these orders have a reasonable basis in necessity? No evidence whatever on that subject has been taken by this or any other court. There is sharp controversy as to the credibility of the DeWitt report. So the Court, having no real evidence before it, has no choice but to accept General DeWitt's own unsworn, self-serving statement, untested by any cross-examination, that what he did was reasonable. And thus it will always be when courts try to look into the reasonableness of a military order.

In the very nature of things, military decisions are not susceptible of intelligent judicial appraisal. They do not pretend to rest on evidence, but are made on information that often would not be admissible and on assumptions that could not be proved. Information in support of an order could not be disclosed to courts without danger that it would reach the enemy. Neither can courts act on communications made in confidence. Hence courts can never have any real alternative to accepting the mere declaration of the authority that issued the order that it was reasonably necessary from a military viewpoint.

Much is said of the danger to liberty from the Army program for deporting and detaining these citizens of Japanese extraction. But a judicial construction of the due process clause that will sustain this order is a far more subtle blow to liberty than the promulgation of the order itself. A military order, however unconstitutional, is not apt to last longer than the military emergency. Even during that period a succeeding commander may revoke it all. But once a judicial opinion rationalizes such an order to show that it conforms to the Constitution, or rather rationalizes the Constitution to show that the Constitution sanctions such an order, the Court for all time has validated the principle of racial discrimination in criminal procedure and of transplanting American citizens. The principle then lies about like a loaded weapon ready for the hand of any authority that can bring forward a plausible claim of an urgent need. Every repetition imbeds that principle more deeply in our law and thinking and expands it to new purposes. All who observe the work of courts are familiar with what Judge Cardozo described as "the tendency of a principle to expand itself to the limit of its logic."[1] A military commander may overstep the bounds of constitutionality, and it is an incident. But if we review and approve, that passing incident becomes the doctrine of the Constitution. There it has a generative power of its own, and all that it creates will be in its own image. Nothing better illustrates this danger than does the Court's opinion in this case.

. . . .

I should hold that a civil court cannot be made to enforce an order which violates constitutional limitations even if it is a reasonable exercise of military authority. The courts can exercise only the judicial power, can apply only law, and must abide by the Constitution, or they cease to be civil courts and become instruments of military policy.

Of course the existence of a military power resting on force, so vagrant, so centralized, so necessarily heedless of the individual, is an inherent threat to liberty. But I would not lead people to rely on this Court for a review that seems to me wholly delusive. The military reasonableness of these orders can only be determined by military superiors. If the people ever let command of the war power fall into irresponsible and unscrupulous hands, the courts wield no power equal to its restraint. The chief restraint upon those who command the physical forces of the country, in the future as in the past, must be their responsibility to the political judgments of their contemporaries and to the moral judgments of history.

My duties as a justice as I see them do not require me to make a military judgment as to whether General DeWitt's evacuation and detention program was a reasonable military necessity. I do not suggest that the courts should have attempted to interfere with the Army in carrying out its task. But I do not think they may be asked to execute a military expedient that has no place in law under the Constitution. I would reverse the judgment and discharge the prisoner.

NOTES ON KOREMATSU

1. *Detaining Americans as Threats to National Security.* To what extent might *Korematsu* serve as precedent for the detention without trial of other civilians thought to pose a threat to national security? How might such a group constitutionally be identified? If race can serve as the basis for detention, can expressive activity? Could the government properly take into account, for example, a person's contributions to certain charitable organizations in the Middle East? Could it consider one's membership in a religious congregation deemed to be "radical"?

2. *Applying Justice Jackson's Categories.* Would the challenged executive order have been constitutional if Congress had been silent? If Congress had opposed?

3. *Post-Script.* In 1980, a special commission appointed by President Jimmy Carter determined that the internment of Japanese–Americans during

1. Nature of the Judicial Process, p. 51.

World War II occurred because of race prejudice, war hysteria, and a failure of political leadership. In 1984, Fred Korematsu petitioned the government for a writ of *coram nobis* to vacate his 1944 conviction on the grounds of governmental misconduct. A district court judge for the Northern District of California granted the writ, holding that "the government knowingly withheld information from the courts when they were considering the critical question of military necessity [as to the detention of Japanese–Americans]." 584 F.Supp. 1406 (N.D. Cal. 1984). In particular, the court cited the "erroneous" sabotage statistics included in the *Final Report of General DeWitt* (1943). In 1988, Congress apologized for the detentions and granted personal compensation of $20,000 to each surviving prisoner or their spouse/parent. *See* Civil Liberties Act of 1988, 50 U.S.C. § 1989b (2006). In 1998, President Clinton awarded Korematsu the Presidential Medal of Freedom, seven years before his death in 2005.

Despite these measures, the Supreme Court's decision in *Korematsu v. United States* has never been overruled and remains valid law.

NOTE ON DUE PROCESS FOR AMERICAN "ENEMY COMBATANTS"

After the terrorist attacks of September 11, 2001, Congress enacted a statute referred to as the Authorization to Use Military Force (AUMF). The AUMF states:

> That the President is authorized to use all necessary and appropriate force against those nations, organizations, or persons he determines planned, authorized, committed, or aided the terrorist attacks that occurred on September 11, 2001, or harbored such organizations or persons, in order to prevent any future acts of international terrorism against the United States by such nations, organizations or persons.

Pub. L. No. 107–40, § 2(a), 115 Stat. 224 (2001). The Executive Branch then embarked on an aggressive campaign against the terrorist organization Al Qaeda, by invading its stronghold in Afghanistan, toppling its allied Afghan government (the Taliban), and disrupting its activities in other countries, including Pakistan, the Philippines, and Yemen.

In the process of that campaign, a handful of American citizens were taken into custody in the United States and abroad, and held as "enemy combatants" because of their relationship to Al Qaeda. Yasir Esam Hamdi was a dual U.S.-Saudi national (he was born in Louisiana) who was captured in Afghanistan in late 2001, brought to the United States, and detained as an "enemy combatant" in naval brigs in Norfolk, Virginia and Charleston, South Carolina. He was not charged with any crime. The U.S. government took the position that, while it did not view Hamdi as a prisoner of war, Hamdi could be held for the duration of hostilities against Al Qaeda without any judicial or quasi-judicial proceedings. In June 2002, Hamdi's father filed a habeas petition in U.S. court on behalf of his son. The habeas petition in part relied on the Non–Detention Act of 1948, which states that "[n]o citizen shall be imprisoned or otherwise detained by the United States except pursuant to an Act of Congress." 18 U.S.C. § 4001(a) (2006).

The Supreme Court's decision in *Hamdi v. Rumsfeld*, 542 U.S. 507, 124 S.Ct. 2633, 159 L.Ed.2d 578 (2004), contains various interesting components for U.S. foreign relations law. One component concerns the Court's use of the law of war as a source of law, an issue that is addressed in Chapter 2, Section 7. A different component concerns the Court's consideration of whether Congress and the President, even when working together in the field of foreign relations, are limited by due process concerns. For the plurality, Justice O'Connor determined that "Congress has in fact authorized Hamdi's detention" through the AUMF. 542 U.S. at 517; *see also* Chapter 4, Section 11. Nevertheless, the plurality held that "due process concerns" required that Hamdi be given the opportunity to contest the factual basis for his detention. Do you agree with the plurality's analysis or do you find Justice Thomas' dissent compelling?

HAMDI v. RUMSFELD

542 U.S. 507, 124 S.Ct. 2633, 159 L.Ed.2d 578 (2004) (footnotes and citations omitted).

JUSTICE O'CONNOR announced the judgment of the Court and delivered an opinion, in which THE CHIEF JUSTICE, JUSTICE KENNEDY, and JUSTICE BREYER join.

. . . .

This case arises out of the detention of a man whom the Government alleges took up arms with the Taliban during this conflict. His name is Yaser Esam Hamdi. Born in Louisiana in 1980, Hamdi moved with his family to Saudi Arabia as a child. By 2001, the parties agree, he resided in Afghanistan. At some point that year, he was seized by members of the Northern Alliance, a coalition of military groups opposed to the Taliban government, and eventually was turned over to the United States military. The Government asserts that it initially detained and interrogated Hamdi in Afghanistan before transferring him to the United States Naval Base in Guantanamo Bay in January 2002. In April 2002, upon learning that Hamdi is an American citizen, authorities transferred him to a naval brig in Norfolk, Virginia, where he remained until a recent transfer to a brig in Charleston, South Carolina. The Government contends that Hamdi is an "enemy combatant," and that this status justifies holding him in the United States indefinitely—without formal charges or proceedings—unless and until it makes the determination that access to counsel or further process is warranted.

. . . .

[The district court] ordered the Government to turn over numerous materials for *in camera* review, including copies of all of Hamdi's statements and the notes taken from interviews with him that related to his reasons for going to Afghanistan and his activities therein; a list of all interrogators who had questioned Hamdi and their names and addresses; statements by members of the Northern Alliance regarding Hamdi's surrender and capture; a list of the dates and locations of his capture and subsequent detentions; and the names and titles of the United States

Government officials who made the determinations that Hamdi was an enemy combatant and that he should be moved to a naval brig. The court indicated that all of these materials were necessary for "meaningful judicial review" of whether Hamdi's detention was legally authorized and whether Hamdi had received sufficient process to satisfy the Due Process Clause of the Constitution and relevant treaties or military regulations.

. . . .

It is beyond question that substantial interests lie on both sides of the scale in this case. Hamdi's "private interest ... affected by the official action" is the most elemental of liberty interests—the interest in being free from physical detention by one's own government. *Foucha v. Louisiana*, 504 U.S. 71, 80 (1992) ("Freedom from bodily restraint has always been at the core of the liberty protected by the Due Process Clause from arbitrary governmental action"); *see also Parham v. J. R.*, 442 U.S. 584, 600 (1979) (noting the "substantial liberty interest in not being confined unnecessarily")....

. . . .

On the other side of the scale are the weighty and sensitive governmental interests in ensuring that those who have in fact fought with the enemy during a war do not return to battle against the United States. As discussed above, the law of war and the realities of combat may render such detentions both necessary and appropriate, and our due process analysis need not blink at those realities. Without doubt, our Constitution recognizes that core strategic matters of warmaking belong in the hands of those who are best positioned and most politically accountable for making them. *Department of Navy v. Egan*, 484 U.S. 518, 530 (1988) (noting the reluctance of the courts "to intrude upon the authority of the Executive in military and national security affairs"); *Youngstown Sheet & Tube Co. v. Sawyer*, 343 U.S. 579, 587 (1952) (acknowledging "broad powers in military commanders engaged in day-to-day fighting in a theater of war").

. . . .

Striking the proper constitutional balance here is of great importance to the Nation during this period of ongoing combat. But it is equally vital that our calculus not give short shrift to the values that this country holds dear or to the privilege that is American citizenship. It is during our most challenging and uncertain moments that our Nation's commitment to due process is most severely tested; and it is in those times that we must preserve our commitment at home to the principles for which we fight abroad....

. . . .

With due recognition of these competing concerns, we believe that neither the process proposed by the Government nor the process apparently envisioned by the District Court below strikes the proper constitutional balance when a United States citizen is detained in the United

States as an enemy combatant. That is, "the risk of erroneous deprivation" of a detainee's liberty interest is unacceptably high under the Government's proposed rule, while some of the "additional or substitute procedural safeguards" suggested by the District Court are unwarranted in light of their limited "probable value" and the burdens they may impose on the military in such cases. *Mathews*, 424 U.S., at 335.

We therefore hold that a citizen-detainee seeking to challenge his classification as an enemy combatant must receive notice of the factual basis for his classification, and a fair opportunity to rebut the Government's factual assertions before a neutral decisionmaker.... "For more than a century the central meaning of procedural due process has been clear: 'Parties whose rights are to be affected are entitled to be heard; and in order that they may enjoy that right they must first be notified.' It is equally fundamental that the right to notice and an opportunity to be heard 'must be granted at a meaningful time and in a meaningful manner.'" *Fuentes v. Shevin*, 407 U.S. 67, 80 (1972) (quoting *Baldwin v. Hale*, 1 Wall. 223, 233 (1864)).... These essential constitutional promises may not be eroded.

At the same time, the exigencies of the circumstances may demand that, aside from these core elements, enemy-combatant proceedings may be tailored to alleviate their uncommon potential to burden the Executive at a time of ongoing military conflict. Hearsay, for example, may need to be accepted as the most reliable available evidence from the Government in such a proceeding. Likewise, the Constitution would not be offended by a presumption in favor of the Government's evidence, so long as that presumption remained a rebuttable one and fair opportunity for rebuttal were provided. Thus, once the Government puts forth credible evidence that the habeas petitioner meets the enemy-combatant criteria, the onus could shift to the petitioner to rebut that evidence with more persuasive evidence that he falls outside the criteria. A burden-shifting scheme of this sort would meet the goal of ensuring that the errant tourist, embedded journalist, or local aid worker has a chance to prove military error while giving due regard to the Executive once it has put forth meaningful support for its conclusion that the detainee is in fact an enemy combatant. In the words of *Mathews*, process of this sort would sufficiently address the "risk of erroneous deprivation" of a detainee's liberty interest while eliminating certain procedures that have questionable additional value in light of the burden on the Government. 424 U.S., at 335.

We think it unlikely that this basic process will have the dire impact on the central functions of warmaking that the Government forecasts. The parties agree that initial captures on the battlefield need not receive the process we have discussed here; that process is due only when the determination is made to *continue* to hold those who have been seized. The Government has made clear in its briefing that documentation regarding battlefield detainees already is kept in the ordinary course of military affairs. Any factfinding imposition created by requiring a knowledgeable affiant to summarize these records to an independent tribunal is a minimal one. Likewise, arguments that military officers ought not have to wage war under the threat of litigation lose much of their steam when factual disputes at enemy-combatant hearings are limited to the alleged combatant's acts. This focus meddles little, if at all, in the strategy or conduct of war, inquiring only into the appropriateness of continuing to detain an individual claimed to have taken up arms against the United States. While we accord the greatest respect and consideration to the judgments of military authorities in matters relating to the actual prosecution of a war, and recognize that the scope of that discretion necessarily is wide, it does not infringe on the core role of the military for the courts to exercise their own time-honored and constitutionally mandated roles of reviewing and resolving claims like those presented here. Cf. *Korematsu v. United States*, 323 U.S. 214, 233–234 (1944) (Murphy, J., dissenting) ("[L]ike other claims conflicting with the asserted constitutional rights of the individual, the military claim must subject itself to the judicial process of having its reasonableness determined and its conflicts with other interests reconciled")....

In sum, while the full protections that accompany challenges to detentions in other settings may prove unworkable and inappropriate in the enemy-combatant setting, the threats to military operations posed by a basic system of independent review are not so weighty as to trump a citizen's core rights to challenge meaningfully the Government's case and to be heard by an impartial adjudicator.

....

In so holding, we necessarily reject the Government's assertion that separation of powers principles mandate a heavily circumscribed role for the courts in such circumstances. Indeed, the position that the courts must forgo any examination of the individual case and focus exclusively on the legality of the broader detention scheme cannot be mandated by any reasonable view of separation of powers, as this approach serves only to *condense* power into a single branch of government. We have long since made clear that a state of war is not a blank check for the President when it comes to the rights of the Nation's citizens. *Youngstown Sheet & Tube*, 343 U.S., at 587. Whatever power the United States Constitution envisions for the Executive in its exchanges with other nations or with enemy organizations in times of conflict, it most assuredly envisions a role for all three branches when individual liberties are at stake. *Mistretta v. United States*, 488 U.S. 361, 380 (1989) (it was "the central judgment of the Framers of the Constitution that, within our political scheme, the separation of governmental powers into three coordinate Branches is essential to the preservation of liberty"); *Home Building & Loan Assn. v. Blaisdell*, 290 U.S. 398, 426 (1934) (The war power "is a power to wage war successfully, and thus it permits the harnessing of the entire energies of the people in a supreme cooperative effort to preserve the nation. But even the war power does not remove constitutional limitations safeguarding essential liberties"). Likewise, we have made clear that, unless Congress acts to suspend it, the Great Writ of habeas corpus allows the

Judicial Branch to play a necessary role in maintaining this delicate balance of governance, serving as an important judicial check on the Executive's discretion in the realm of detentions. *See St. Cyr*, 533 U.S., at 301 ("At its historical core, the writ of habeas corpus has served as a means of reviewing the legality of Executive detention, and it is in that context that its protections have been strongest"). Thus, while we do not question that our due process assessment must pay keen attention to the particular burdens faced by the Executive in the context of military action, it would turn our system of checks and balances on its head to suggest that a citizen could not make his way to court with a challenge to the factual basis for his detention by his Government, simply because the Executive opposes making available such a challenge. Absent suspension of the writ by Congress, a citizen detained as an enemy combatant is entitled to this process.

. . . .

The judgment of the United States Court of Appeals for the Fourth Circuit is vacated, and the case is remanded for further proceedings.

It is so ordered.

. . . .

JUSTICE THOMAS, dissenting.

The Executive Branch, acting pursuant to the powers vested in the President by the Constitution and with explicit congressional approval, has determined that Yaser Hamdi is an enemy combatant and should be detained. This detention falls squarely within the Federal Government's war powers, and we lack the expertise and capacity to second-guess that decision. As such, petitioners' habeas challenge should fail, and there is no reason to remand the case. The plurality reaches a contrary conclusion by failing adequately to consider basic principles of the constitutional structure as it relates to national security and foreign affairs and by using the balancing scheme of *Mathews v. Eldridge*, 424 U.S. 319 (1976). I do not think that the Federal Government's war powers can be balanced away by this Court. Arguably, Congress could provide for additional procedural protections, but until it does, we have no right to insist upon them. But even if I were to agree with the general approach the plurality takes, I could not accept the particulars. The plurality utterly fails to account for the Government's compelling interests and for our own institutional inability to weigh competing concerns correctly. I respectfully dissent.

. . . .

"It is 'obvious and unarguable' that no governmental interest is more compelling than the security of the Nation." *Haig v. Agee*, 453 U.S. 280, 307 (1981) (quoting *Aptheker v. Secretary of State*, 378 U.S. 500, 509 (1964)). The national security, after all, is the primary responsibility and purpose of the Federal Government. . . . But because the Founders understood that they could not foresee the myriad potential threats to national security that might later arise, they chose to create a Federal Government that necessarily possesses sufficient power to handle any threat to the security of the Nation. The power to protect the Nation

> "ought to exist without limitation ... *[b]ecause it is impossible to foresee or define the extent and variety of national exigencies, or the correspondent extent & variety of the means which may be necessary to satisfy them.* The circumstances that endanger the safety of nations are infinite; and for this reason no constitutional shackles can wisely be imposed on the power to which the care of it is committed." [The Federalist No. 23, p. 147 (J. Cooke ed. 1961) (A. Hamilton)]....

The Founders intended that the President have primary responsibility—along with the necessary power—to protect the national security and to conduct the Nation's foreign relations. They did so principally because the structural advantages of a unitary Executive are essential in these domains. "Energy in the executive is a leading character in the definition of good government. It is essential to the protection of the community against foreign attacks." *Id.*, No. 70, at 471 (A. Hamilton). The principle "ingredient[t]" for "energy in the executive" is "unity." *Id.*, at 472. This is because "[d]ecision, activity, secrecy, and dispatch will generally characterise the proceedings of one man, in a much more eminent degree, than the proceedings of any greater number." *Ibid.*

These structural advantages are most important in the national-security and foreign-affairs contexts. "Of all the cares or concerns of government, the direction of war most peculiarly demands those qualities which distinguish the exercise of power by a single hand." *Id.*, No. 74, at 500 (A. Hamilton). Also for these reasons, John Marshall explained that "[t]he President is the sole organ of the nation in its external relations, and its sole representative with foreign nations." 10 Annals of Cong. 613 (1800); see *id.*, at 613–614. To this end, the Constitution vests in the President "[t]he executive Power," Art. II, § 1, provides that he "shall be Commander in Chief of the" Armed Forces, § 2, and places in him the power to recognize foreign governments, § 3.

This Court has long recognized these features and has accordingly held that the President has *constitutional* authority to protect the national security and that this authority carries with it broad discretion.

> "If a war be made by invasion of a foreign nation, the President is not only authorized but bound to resist force by force. He does not initiate the war, but is bound to accept the challenge without waiting for any special legislative authority.... Whether the President in fulfilling his duties, as Commander in-chief, in suppressing an insurrection, has met with such armed hostile resistance ... is a question to be decided *by him*." *Prize Cases*, 2 Black 635, 668, 670 (1863).

The Court has acknowledged that the President has the authority to "employ [the Nation's Armed Forces] in the manner he may deem most effectual to harass and conquer and subdue the enemy." *Fleming v. Page*, 9 How. 603, 615 (1850). With respect to foreign affairs as well, the Court has recognized the President's independent authority and need to be free from interference. See, *e.g.*, *United States v. Curtiss–Wright Export Corp.*, 299 U.S. 304, 320 (1936) (explaining that the President "has his confidential sources of information. He has his agents in the form of diplomatic, consular and other officials. Secrecy in respect of information gathered by them may be highly necessary, and the premature disclosure of it productive of harmful results"); *Chicago & Southern Air Lines, Inc. v. Waterman S. S. Corp.*, 333 U.S. 103, 111 (1948).

Congress, to be sure, has a substantial and essential role in both foreign affairs and national security. But it is crucial to recognize that *judicial* interference in these domains destroys the purpose of vesting primary responsibility in a unitary Executive. I cannot improve on Justice Jackson's words, speaking for the Court:

> "The President, both as Commander-in-Chief and as the Nation's organ for foreign affairs, has available intelligence services whose reports are not and ought not to be published to the world. It would be intolerable that courts, without the relevant information, should review and perhaps nullify actions of the Executive taken on information properly held secret. Nor can courts sit *in camera* in order to be taken into executive confidences. But even if courts could require full disclosure, the very nature of executive decisions as to foreign policy is political, not judicial. Such decisions are wholly confided by our Constitution to the political departments of the government, Executive and Legislative. They are delicate, complex, and involve large elements of prophecy. They are and should be undertaken only by those directly responsible to the people whose welfare they advance or imperil. They are decisions of a kind for which the Judiciary has neither aptitude, facilities nor responsibility and which has long been held to belong in the domain of political power not subject to judicial intrusion or inquiry." *Ibid.*

Several points, made forcefully by Justice Jackson, are worth emphasizing. First, with respect to certain decisions relating to national security and foreign affairs, the courts simply lack the relevant information and expertise to second-guess determinations made by the President based on information properly withheld. Second, even if the courts could compel the Executive to produce the necessary information, such decisions are simply not amenable to judicial determination because "[t]hey are delicate, complex, and involve large elements of prophecy." *Ibid.* Third, the Court in *Chicago & Southern Air Lines* and elsewhere has correctly recognized the primacy of the political branches in the foreign-affairs and national-security contexts.

For these institutional reasons and because "Congress cannot anticipate and legislate with regard to every possible action the President may find it necessary to take or every possible situation in which he might act," it should come as no surprise that "[s]uch failure of Congress . . . does not, 'especially . . . in the areas of foreign policy and national security,' imply 'congressional disapproval' of action taken by the Executive." *Dames & Moore v. Regan*, 453 U.S. 654, 678 (1981) (quoting *Agee*, 453 U.S., at 291). Rather, in these domains, the fact that Congress has provided the President with broad authorities does not imply—and the Judicial Branch should not infer—that Congress intended to deprive him of particular powers not specifically enumerated. See *Dames & Moore*, 453 U.S., at 678. As far as the courts are concerned, "the enactment of legislation closely related to the question of the President's authority in a particular case which evinces legislative intent to accord the President broad discretion may be considered to 'invite' 'measures on independent presidential responsibility.'" *Ibid.* (quoting *Youngstown,* 343 U.S., at 637 (Jackson, J., concurring)).

Finally, and again for the same reasons, where "the President acts pursuant to an express or implied authorization from Congress, he exercises not only his powers but also those delegated by Congress[, and i]n such a case the executive action 'would be supported by the strongest of presumptions and the widest latitude of judicial interpretation, and the burden of persuasion would rest heavily upon any who might attack it.'" *Dames & Moore, supra,* at 668 (quoting *Youngstown, supra,* at 637 (Jackson, J., concurring)). That is why the Court has explained, in a case analogous to this one, that "the detention[,] ordered by the President in the declared exercise of his powers as Commander in Chief of the Army in time of war and of grave public danger[, is] not to be set aside by the courts without the clear conviction that [it is] in conflict with the Constitution or laws of Congress constitutionally enacted." *Ex parte Quirin*, 317 U.S. 1, 25 (1942). See also *Ex parte Milligan,* 4 Wall. 2, 133 (1866) (Chase, C. J., concurring in judgment) (stating that a sentence imposed by a military commission "must not be set aside except upon the clearest conviction that it cannot be reconciled with the Constitution and the constitutional legislation of Congress"). This deference extends to the President's determination of all the factual predicates necessary to conclude that a given action is appropriate....

....

Although the President very well may have inherent authority to detain those arrayed against our troops, I agree with the plurality that we need not decide that question because Congress has authorized the President to do so. The Authorization for Use of Military Force (AUMF), 115 Stat. 224, authorizes the President to "use all necessary and appropriate force against those nations, organizations, or persons he determines planned, authorized, committed, or aided the terrorist attacks" of September 11, 2001....

NOTES ON HAMDI

1. *The Least Dangerous Branch.* The *Hamdi* case reminds us that while the foreign affairs power is largely one exercised concurrently by the two political branches, the judicial branch can play a pivotal role as well, even when the two political branches are acting in apparent harmony. In times of

extremis, should courts be more deferential to the political branches, or is that the situation where judicial oversight is most needed?

2. *Deferring to the President*. How much deference should a court give to the Executive Branch's determination that Yaser Hamdi is an enemy combatant? By what standards would a court determine that the executive branch is mistaken? Are courts equipped to make such judgments? Recall the Court's treatment of the *Final Report of General DeWitt* (1943) in *Korematsu;* would that deference be more appropriate? Or are you troubled by what happened in the *Korematsu* case? Given that the Executive Branch makes such determinations based in part on highly classified information, how could that information be properly shared with the court and with the alleged terrorist? For further discussion, see Chapter 8.

3. *Interpreting Congressional Action*. Does the existence of a statute authorizing the use of force by the Executive mean that courts should be more deferential to executive detention of U.S. citizens without charge? Note that Justice Thomas places the President's authority to detain U.S. citizens as enemy combatants in Justice Jackson's first category where "the President acts pursuant to an express or implied authorization of Congress" and "his authority is at its maximum." Do you agree with the plurality, and with Justice Thomas, that Congress authorized the detention of U.S. citizens when it enacted the AUMF?

4. *Targeting an American by Drone Aircraft*. If some kind of due process is owed to U.S. nationals who are taken into custody as suspect Al Qaeda operatives, is there any due process owed to U.S. nationals abroad who are targeted by the U.S. government to be killed? In a case filed in 2010, *Al-Aulaqi v. Obama*, a father maintained that the Obama Administration was targeting his son (a dual U.S.-Yemeni national named Anwar Al-Aulaqi) in Yemen by means of "drone" (unmanned) aircraft due to Al-Aulaqi's association with Al Qaeda. The lawsuit sought an injunction from the court on grounds that the alleged U.S. government conduct violates both the U.S. Constitution and international law. The case was ultimately dismissed on standing and justiciability grounds. *See* Al–Aulaqi v. Obama, 727 F.Supp.2d 1 (2010). On September 30, 2011, Al-Aulaqi was killed in Yemen when a drone attacked his convoy.

Do you think the targeting of a U.S. national abroad suspected of being a terrorist constitutes unlawful extrajudicial killing? The U.S. State Department Legal Adviser, Harold Koh, has said that "a state that is engaged in an armed conflict or in legitimate self-defense is not required to provide targets with legal process before the state may use lethal force." Nor do such killings violate the domestic ban on assassinations, Koh maintained. "[U]nder domestic law, the use of lawful weapons systems—consistent with the applicable laws of war—for precision targeting of specific high-level belligerent leaders when acting in self-defense or during an armed conflict is not unlawful, and hence does not constitute assassination." Harold Hongju Koh, Legal Adviser, U.S. Dep't of State, Address at the Annual Meeting of the American Society of International Law (Mar. 25, 2010), http://www.state.gov/s/1/releases/remarks/139119.htm. Do you agree?

5. *Never Mind*. The Supreme Court's decision in *Hamdi* remanded the case for further proceedings on the issue of what procedures would be implemented in order to ensure Yaser Hamdi's due process rights. However, this issue was never resolved. Rather than granting Hamdi a hearing, in the fall of 2004 the U.S. government brokered a deal in which Hamdi—a U.S. citizen raised in Saudi Arabia—was freed from detention in exchange for agreeing to return to Saudi Arabia, renouncing his American citizenship and adhering to prescribed travel restrictions. *See* Eric Lichtblau, *U.S., Bowing to Court Ruling, Will Free "Enemy Combatant,"* N.Y. TIMES, Sept. 23, 2004.

6. *Preventive Detentions*. Separate from the detention of certain U.S. citizens, in the aftermath of the September 11 attacks the Executive Branch embarked on an aggressive domestic law enforcement campaign that involved the detention of thousands of aliens in the United States as a preventive strategy against future terrorist activity. Consider the following description:

> Such arrests—which were on a scale not seen in the United States since the Second World War—were conducted under great secrecy. Gag orders and other rules (including rules relating to the grand jury and to the detainees' privacy) prevented officials from discussing the detainees, and defense lawyers were sometimes allowed to see documents only at the courthouse. A *Washington Post* analysis of 235 detainees revealed that the largest groups came from Egypt, Pakistan, and Saudi Arabia; virtually all were men in their twenties and thirties; and the greatest concentration were in U.S. states with large Islamic populations that included what law enforcement officials identified as Al Qaeda sympathizers: California, Florida, Michigan, New Jersey, New York, and Texas. Many were arrested because they were in the same places or engaged in the same kinds of activities as the hijackers (for example, taking flying lessons); many others apparently were detained because they came from certain countries or had violated U.S. immigration law. Further, the Justice Department announced a new policy that it would monitor communications between lawyers and persons being held on suspicion of being terrorists.

Sean D. Murphy, *United States Practice in International Law, Vol. 1: 1999–2001* 437 (2002) (footnotes omitted). When combined with the detention of some U.S. citizens as "enemy combatants," does this development suggest that a new approach should be considered for handling foreign relations law in times of crisis? By trying to adhere to the normal rules, do we risk watering down those rules by trying to make them fit extreme circumstances? By shifting to another model, do we risk jettisoning core values just when they are needed most?

BRUCE ACKERMAN, THE EMERGENCY CONSTITUTION

113 Yale L.J. 1029, 1029, 1037, 1047 (2004) (footnotes omitted).

Terrorist attacks will be a recurring part of our future ... The attack of September 11 is the prototype for many events that will litter the twenty-first century. We should be looking at it in a diagnostic spirit:

What can we learn that will permit us to respond more intelligently the next time around?

. . . .

When a terrorist attack places the state's effective sovereignty in doubt, government must act visibly and decisively to demonstrate to its terrorized citizens that the breach was only temporary, and that it is taking aggressive action to contain the crisis and to deal with the prospect of its recurrence. Most importantly, my proposal for an emergency constitution authorizes the government to detain suspects without the criminal law's usual protections of probable cause or even reasonable suspicion.

. . . .

The Executive should be given the power to act unilaterally only for the briefest period—long enough for the legislature to convene and consider the matter, but no longer. If the legislature is already in session, one week seems the longest tolerable period; if not, two weeks at most.

The state of emergency then should expire unless it gains majority approval. But this is only the beginning. Majority support should serve to sustain the emergency for a short time—two or three months. Continuation should require an escalating cascade of supermajorities: sixty percent for the next two months; seventy for the next; eighty thereafter.

DAVID COLE, THE PRIORITY OF MORALITY: THE EMERGENCY CONSTITUTION'S BLIND SPOT

113 Yale L.J. 1753, 1753, 1755–56, 1758 (2004) (footnotes omitted).

In the wake of the terrorist attacks of September 11, Attorney General John Ashcroft announced a campaign of aggressive preventive detention . . . By any measure, the program has been spectacularly unsuccessful.

. . . .

In light of this history . . . Bruce Ackerman's proposal to legitimate the practice of suspicionless preventive detention during emergencies is strikingly ill-advised. History suggests that we ought to do everything we can to *restrict* suspicionless preventive detention, not to *expand* it.

[Ackerman's] basic idea is to give the Executive extraordinary emergency powers—including suspicionless preventive detention—while conditioning the state of emergency on a political process check—the "supermajoritarian escalator"—designed to forestall "permanent" emergencies.

. . . .

At bottom, what is most troubling about Ackerman's proposal is that in his fascination with the idea of the "supermajoritarian escalator" he never addresses the fundamental normative question presented by his proposal. As a normative matter, it is one thing to say, as the Framers did, that in response to a "rebellion" or "invasion," habeas corpus may be suspended when "the public safety may require it"; it is another thing entirely to argue, as Ackerman does, that we should empower the Executive to incarcerate individuals for up to two months without suspicion merely to "reassure" a public in "panic" ... While a political process check may be an important *supplement* to a regime of limited emergency powers, it is no *substitute* for the hard work of striking an appropriate normative balance between liberty and security. Call it the priority of morality.

OREN GROSS, CHAOS AND RULES: SHOULD RESPONSES TO VIOLENT CRISES ALWAYS BE CONSTITUTIONAL?

112 Yale L.J. 1011, 1014–15, 1023–24 (2003) (some footnotes omitted).

The terrorist attacks of September 11, 2001, and the ensuing "war on terrorism" brought to center stage issues that have previously lurked in a dark corner at the edge of the legal universe, such as how a constitutional regime should respond to violent challenges ... The dilemma confronting a constitutional democracy having to respond to emergencies has been famously captured by Abraham Lincoln's rhetorical question: "[A]re all the laws *but* one to go unexecuted, and the Government itself go to pieces, lest that one be violated?"[6] ...

. . . .

I argue that there may be circumstances where the appropriate method of tackling grave dangers and threats entails going outside the constitutional order, at times even violating otherwise accepted constitutional principles, rules, and norms. Such a response, if pursued in appropriate circumstances and properly applied, may strengthen rather than weaken, and result in more rather than less, long-term constitutional fidelity and commitment to the rule of law....

While going outside the legal order may be a "little wrong," it is advocated here in order to facilitate the attainment of a "great right," namely the preservation not only of the constitutional order, but also of its most fundamental principles and tenets. Significantly, I argue that the Extra–Legal Measures model promotes, and is promoted by, ethical concepts of political and popular responsibility, political morality, and candor.

---

6. Abraham Lincoln, Message to Congress in Special Session (July 4, 1861), in 4 THE COLLECTED WORKS OF ABRAHAM LINCOLN 421, 429–30 (Roy P. Basler ed., 1953)....

CHAPTER 2

CUSTOMARY INTERNATIONAL LAW

■ ■ ■

SECTION 1. INTRODUCTION TO CUSTOMARY INTERNATIONAL LAW

NOTE: RELEVANT CONCEPTS IN INTERNATIONAL LAW

This book is not a treatise on international law, a discipline that has produced a vast literature in its own right. Mastering some basic concepts in international law, however, is key for any student of U.S. foreign relations law. This section will briefly illuminate several of those concepts, including that of customary international law, the subject of this chapter as a whole.

International law is traditionally described as those rules that govern relations between states. Its origins, in the West, can be traced back to the Treaty of Westphalia in 1648, which inaugurated the concept of the sovereign nation-state.

Early American jurists, including the founding fathers, used the term "law of nations" to refer to this and related sources of law. One influential commentary was William Blackstone's *Commentaries on the Laws of England.*[1] Blackstone described a "law of nations" that concerned not just the rights and obligations of states to one another, but also the law governing intercourse between individuals of different states. In 1789, Jeremy Bentham invented the term "international law" to describe the rights and obligations of states to one another, but apparently not to address transnational relations of individuals. *See* Mark Janis, *The American Tradition of International Law: Great Expectations, 1789–1914*, at 11–15 (2004). Today, the term "international law" is broadly used to address various types of international rules that govern states, international organizations, and individuals; its main purview, though, remains the state.

International law is generally understood to derive from two main sources: treaties and customary international law.[2] While treaties have proli-

---

1. William Blackstone, *Commentaries on the Laws of England* [1765–1769] (1979 ed., University of Chicago Press, 4 vols.).

2. A third, less-invoked source of international law is that of "general principles of law." *See* Statute of the International Court of Justice, art. 38(1), June 26, 1945, 59 Stat. 1055. Judicial ferated in recent years and thus constitute the dominant form of international law today, customary international law predominated for many centuries and today retains an important role in the international system, sometimes as a "gap-filler" in areas where a recognizable custom has evolved but has not yet been codified by treaty. The role of treaties in U.S. foreign relations law will be treated in Chapter 3; this chapter is concerned with customary international law.

As such, this chapter will consider numerous questions depicted as involving the "law of nations," a term that retains considerable significance. Blackstone used the term to refer broadly to the field of what is now known as international law, thus encompassing both treaties and customary international law. Hence, in cases such as *Ware v. Hylton* (*see* Section 2 below), reference is made broadly to the "law of nations," even though what is actually at issue is the interpretation of a treaty (in that case, the 1783 Treaty of Paris ending the U.S. Revolutionary War). More often the term "law of nations" was used to refer to international law *other than treaties*. Thus, in the First Judiciary Act of 1789, Congress adopted a statute that refers to violations of "the law of nations *or* a treaty of the United States."[3] In this sense, the term "law of nations" is a synonym for customary international law, rather than international law generally. As the *Restatement (Third) of U.S. Foreign Relations Law* puts it: "The term 'law of nations' was used to describe the customary rules and obligations that regulated conduct between states and certain aspects of state conduct towards individuals." *See Restatement (Third)* § 111, Introductory Note (1987).

While treaties, as explored in Chapter 3, are ordinarily expressed as formally-adopted, written documents, customary international law may appear more elusive. How does one determine the existence of a norm of customary international law? The *Restatement (Third)* asserts: "Customary international law results from a general and consistent practice of states followed by them from a sense of legal obligation." *Id.*, § 102(2). As that quote suggests, there are two components to customary international law: (1) a general and consistent practice of states and (2) some sense of legal obligation to engage in that practice, otherwise known as *opinio juris*. A state that does not agree with an emergent trend in customary international law may register its dissent and thereby gain the status of "persistent objector," in which case that state is not bound by the particular rule.

A key threshold question for U.S. foreign relations and national security law is how international law becomes part of the U.S. legal system. Two main schools of thought suggest differing views on the role of international law in relation to domestic legal systems. *Monism* contends that all law is part of the same system and constitutes a spectrum wherein domestic law is hierarchically inferior to and governed by international law. *Dualism*, on the other hand, rejects this ordering and views both systems as entirely separate. At the same time, dualism accepts that a domestic legal system can adopt rules (such as in

decisions and the teachings of highly qualified publicists are also often relied upon, on a subsidiary basis, as a means of understanding the basic sources of international law. *Id.*

3. Alien Tort Statute, 28 U.S.C. § 1350 (2006) (emphasis added).

a constitution) that incorporate any aspects of international law to which the domestic system wishes to adhere.

Most countries in the world today, the United States included, fall somewhere along the spectrum between these extremes, but they tend more toward dualism. *See, e.g., Restatement (Third)*, Part I, Chapter 2, Introductory Note: "International law and the law of the United States are two different and discrete bodies of law, but often they impinge on the same conduct, relations, and interests." The next section addresses U.S. incorporation of "international law" into the domestic U.S. legal system.

SECTION 2. INCORPORATION OF INTERNATIONAL CUSTOM INTO U.S. LAW

RESTATEMENT (THIRD) OF THE FOREIGN RELATIONS LAW OF THE UNITED STATES § 111

(1987).

§ 111. *International Law and Agreements as Law of the United States*

(1) International law and international agreements of the United States are law of the United States and supreme over the law of the several States.

(2) Cases arising under international law or international agreements of the United States are within the Judicial Power of the United States and, subject to Constitutional and statutory limitations and requirements of justiciability, are within the jurisdiction of the federal courts.

. . . .

Comments to § 111:

. . . .

d. International law and agreements as supreme federal law. Treaties made under the authority of the United States, like the Constitution itself and the laws of the United States, are expressly declared to be "supreme Law of the Land" by Article VI of the Constitution. International agreements of the United States other than treaties (see § 303), and customary international law, while not mentioned explicitly in the Supremacy Clause, are also federal law and as such are supreme over State law. Interpretations of international agreements by the United States Supreme Court are binding on the States. Customary international law is considered to be like common law in the United States, but it is federal law. A determination of international law by the Supreme Court is binding on the States and on State courts. . . .

NOTE: HIERARCHICAL STATUS OF INTERNATIONAL CUSTOM IN U.S. LAW

Customary international law's place within the domestic hierarchy of U.S. law is generally as described by Section 111 of the *Restatement (Third)*, though in recent years this ordering has become subject to some dispute. The debate is due in part to the relative silence of the Constitution itself and its disparate treatment of international law's two main sources, treaties and custom.

Treaties, according to the Supremacy Clause of the Constitution, constitute the "supreme law of the land" and are binding on the states. But the Constitution is less clear as to the role of customary international law. That term does not appear as such in the Supremacy Clause, nor anywhere else in the Constitution, which is not surprising, given that it had not yet been coined when the framers met in Philadelphia in 1787. There is a reference to the "law of nations" (potentially encompassing, as noted previously, both treaties and custom) in Article 1, § 8, clause 10 of the Constitution, which authorizes Congress to "define and punish ... Offenses against the Law of Nations." Under that power, Congress may criminally and civilly regulate individuals who violate the law of nations, and punish foreign and domestic states that do so. *See* J. Andrew Kent, *Congress' Under-Appreciated Power to Define and Punish Offenses Against the Law of Nations*, 85 TEX. L. REV. 843 (2007). A striking recent application of customary international law can be seen in the June 2006 Supreme Court decision in *Hamdan v. Rumsfeld*, in which a plurality of the justices held that the minimum protections of Common Article 3 of the 1949 Geneva Conventions (which arise in situations of non-international armed conflict) applied to the conflict between the United States and the terrorist organization Al Qaeda, and that the provisions of Article 75 of Protocol I to those conventions, while not ratified by the United States, also applied as a matter of customary international law. Hamdan v. Rumsfeld, 548 U.S. 557, 631–35, 126 S.Ct. 2749, 165 L.Ed.2d 723 (2006). In that case, a U.S. statute provided that military commissions established by the President must operate in accordance with the "law of war," which the Court read to refer to both treaty law and customary international law. *See also* Chapter 4, Section 11.

If Congress has not legislated with respect to a norm of customary international law, what is the norm's status in U.S. law? It is undisputed that the Constitution is the highest form of law in the United States and that it controls all forms of law within the United States, including customary international law. After the Constitution, statutes and treaties come next in the U.S. hierarchy of law; their interplay and relative status is assessed in Chapter 3, Section 6. Federal common law, a body of law greatly circumscribed since the decision of the Supreme Court in *Erie R.R. Co. v. Tompkins*, 304 U.S. 64, 58 S.Ct. 817, 82 L.Ed. 1188 (1938), rests below these, but is superior to state law.

According to the prevailing contemporary position, customary international law is distinct from but hierarchically equivalent to federal common law. In *Sosa v. Alvarez-Machain* (addressed further in Section 5 below), the U.S. Supreme Court noted that "[f]or two centuries we have affirmed that the domestic law of the United States recognizes the law of nations," and identified such law as one of the "limited enclaves in which federal courts may derive some substantive law in a common law way." 542 U.S. 692, 729, 124 S.Ct. 2739, 159 L.Ed.2d 718 (2004). Understood in this way, customary international law cannot override the Constitution, treaties, or statutes, but it is superior to executive acts and state law. *See Restatement (Third)* § 111, comment *d* above.

Some scholars have advanced views that would accord customary international law either a higher or lower status in U.S. law. For example, Professor Louis Henkin has argued that customary international law might properly be considered equal in status to treaties and statutes, but this position is controversial and has been rejected in some recent cases. *Compare* Louis Henkin, *International Law as Law in the U.S.*, 82 MICH. L. REV. 1555, 1561–69 (1984) ("[I]n principle, the argument for according customary law equal authority [as is accorded to treaties and statutes], and for applying the later-in-time rule to it as well, is not unpersuasive."), *with* United States v. Yousef, 327 F.3d 56, 91 (2d Cir. 2003) (arguing that "United States law is not subordinate to customary international law or necessarily subordinate to treaty-based international law and, in fact, may conflict with both.") (for excerpts, see Section 3 below). Conversely, some scholars inspired by the changed function of federal common law after *Eric R.R. Co. v. Tompkins*, have recently challenged whether customary international law is indeed "supreme federal law." *See* the concluding notes of this section below.

Such debates must come to grips with the fact that customary international law is deeply rooted in the U.S. constitutional and common law heritage. In the words of the oft-quoted *Paquete Habana* case—indeed, quoted in 2004 by the U.S. Supreme Court in the *Sosa* case—"international law is part of our law." 175 U.S. 677, 700, 20 S.Ct. 290, 44 L.Ed. 320 (1900).

The courts' tendency to speak of customary international law as implicitly incorporated into common law can be traced back to pre-revolutionary English and to eighteenth- century American cases. *See* Triquet v. Bath, 3 Burr. 1478 (K.B. 1764) (upholding diplomatic immunity because the law of nations was a part of the law of England); Republica v. De Longchamps, Court of Oyer and Terminer (Pa.), 11 (1784) (holding that the case "must be determined on the principles of the law of nations, which form a part of the municipal law of Pennsylvania.").

That tendency continued in the early American republic, as is indicated by the readings that follow. In the trial of Gideon Henfield, Chief Justice John Jay delivered a much quoted charge to the grand jury empanelled in Richmond, Virginia, in connection with an alleged illegal enlisting of Henfield for service with a French privateer.

TRIAL OF GIDEON HENFIELD

U.S. Circuit Court for the Pennsylvania District, 1793.
Reprinted in Wharton, State Trials 49, 52–53 (1849).

JUSTICE JAY:

That you may perceive more clearly the extent and objects of your inquiries, it may be proper to observe, that the laws of the United States admit of being classed under three heads of descriptions.

1st. All treaties made under the authority of the United States.

2d. The laws of nations.

3dly. The constitution, and statutes of the United States.

Treaties between independent nations, are contracts or bargains which derive all their force and obligation from mutual consent and agreement; and consequently, when once fairly made and properly concluded, cannot be altered or annulled by one of the parties, without the consent and concurrence of the other. Wide is the difference between treaties and statutes—we may negotiate and make contracts with other nations, but we can neither legislate for them, nor they for us; we may repeal or alter our statutes, but no nation can have authority to vacate or modify treaties at discretion. Treaties, therefore, necessarily become the supreme law of the land, and so they are very properly declared to be by the sixth article of the constitution.

Whenever doubts and questions arise relative to the validity, operation or construction of treaties, or of any articles in them, those doubts and questions must be settled according to the maxims and principles of the laws of nations applicable to the case.

The peace, prosperity, and reputation of the United States, will always greatly depend on their fidelity to their engagements; and every virtuous citizen (for every citizen is a party to them) will concur in observing and executing them with honour and good faith; and that, whether they be made with nations respectable and important, or with nations weak and inconsiderable, our obligation to keep our faith results from our having pledged it, and not from the character or description of the state or people, to whom, neither impunity nor the right of retaliation can sanctify perfidy; for although perfidy may deserve chastisement, yet it can never merit imitation.

As to the laws of nations—they are those laws by which nations are bound to regulate their conduct towards each other, both in peace and war. Providence has been pleased to place the United States among the nations of the earth, and therefore, all those duties, as well as rights, which spring from the relation of nation to nation, have devolved upon us. We are with other nations, tenants in common of the sea—it is a highway for all, and all are bound to exercise that common right, and use that common highway in the manner which the laws of nations and treaties require.

On this occasion, it is proper to observe to you, gentlemen, that various circumstances and considerations now unite in urging the people of the United States to be particularly exact and circumspect in observing the obligation of treaties, and the laws of nations, which, as has been already remarked, form a very important part of the laws of our nation. I allude to the facts and injunctions specified in the President's late proclamation; it is in these words:

> "Whereas, it appears that a state of war exists between Austria, Prussia, Sardinia, Great Britain, and the United Netherlands of the one part, and France of the other, and the duty and interest of the United States, require that they should with sincerity and good faith, adopt and pursue a conduct friendly and impartial towards the belligerent powers:
>
> > "I have, therefore, thought fit by these presents, to declare the disposition of the United States to observe the conduct aforesaid towards these powers respectively, and to exhort and warn the citizens of the United States, carefully to avoid all acts and proceedings whatsoever, which may in any manner tend to contravene such disposition.
> >
> > "And I do hereby also make known, that whosoever of the citizens of the United States, shall render himself liable to punishment or forfeiture, under the law of nations, by committing, aiding, or abetting hostilities against any of the said powers, or by carrying to them those articles which are deemed contraband, by the modern usage of nations, will not receive the protection of the United States against such punishment or forfeiture: and further, that I have given instructions to those officers to whom it belongs, to cause prosecutions to be instituted against all persons who shall within the cognizance of the Courts of the United States, violate the law of nations, with respect to the powers at war, or any of them."

WARE v. HYLTON

3 U.S. (3 Dall.) 199, 281, 1 L.Ed. 568 (1796).

[The 1783 Treaty of Paris, which ended the U.S. Revolutionary War, provided that British creditors would meet with no impediment to the recovery of their debts. After the U.S. Constitution took effect in 1788, a case arose concerning the refusal of a Virginian to pay a debt owed to a British subject. While the case is important on the issue of whether, under the new Constitution, the Treaty of Paris could override an otherwise valid state law (*see* Chapter 6, Section 3), Justice Wilson in his separate opinion spoke broadly to the role of the law of nations in U.S. law.]

JUSTICE WILSON:

. . . .

When the United States declared their independence, they were bound to receive the law of nations, in its modern state of purity and refinement. By every nation, whatever is its form of government, the confiscation of debts has long been considered disreputable: and, we know, that not a single confiscation of that kind stained the code of any of the European powers, who were engaged in the war, which our revolution produced. Nor did any authority for the confiscation of debts proceed from Congress (that body, which clearly possessed the right of confiscation, as an incident of the powers of war and peace) and, therefore, in no instance can the act of confiscation be considered as an act of the nation.

THE CHARMING BETSY

6 U.S. (2 Cranch) 64, 115–21, 2 L.Ed. 208 (1804).

[During 1798–1800, the United States and France faced off in an undeclared war (or "quasi-war") involving attacks and seizures of each other's vessels on the high seas. By statute enacted in February 1800, Congress prohibited all commercial intercourse by U.S. nationals with France. In this case, that prohibition was interpreted by the Supreme Court in light of the rule under the law of nations obliging belligerents not to seize the persons and property of neutral countries.]

MR. CHIEF JUSTICE MARSHALL delivered the opinion of the court:

The *Charming Betsy* was an American built vessel, belonging to citizens of the United States, and sailed from Baltimore, under the name of the *Jane*, on the 10th of April, 1800, with a cargo of flour for St. Bartholomew's; she was sent out for the purpose of being sold. The cargo was disposed of at St. Bartholomew's; but finding it impossible to sell the vessel at that place, the captain proceeded with her to the island of St. Thomas, where she was disposed of to Jared Shattuck, who changed her name to that of the *Charming Betsy*, and having put on board her a cargo consisting of American produce, cleared her out, as a Danish vessel, for the island of Guadaloupe.

On her voyage, she was captured by a French privateer, and eight hands were put on board her for the purpose of taking her into Guadaloupe as a prize. She was afterwards re-captured by Captain Murray, commander of the *Constellation* frigate, and carried into Martinique. It appears, that the captain of the *Charming Betsy* was not willing to be taken into that island; but when there, he claimed to have his vessel and cargo restored, as being the property of Jared Shattuck, a Danish burgher.

Jared Shattuck was born in the United States, but had removed to the island of St. Thomas while an infant, and was proved to have resided there ever since the year 1789 or 1790. He had been accustomed to carry on trade as a Danish subject; had married a wife and acquired real property in the island, and also taken the oath of allegiance to the crown of Denmark in 1797.

Considering him as an American citizen, who was violating the law prohibiting all intercourse between the United States and France or its dependencies, or the sale of the vessel as a mere cover to evade that law, Captain Murray sold the cargo of the *Charming Betsy*, which consisted of American produce, in Martinique, and brought the vessel into the port of Philadelphia, where she was libelled under what is termed the non-intercourse law. The vessel and cargo were claimed by the consul of Denmark as being the *bonâ fide* property of a Danish subject.

. . . .

. . . Is the *Charming Betsy* subject to seizure and condemnation for having violated a law of the United States?

The libel claims this forfeiture under the act passed in February, 1800, further to suspend the commercial intercourse between the United States and France and the dependencies thereof.

That act declares "that all commercial intercourse," & c. It has been very properly observed, in argument, that the building of vessels in the United States for sale to neutrals, in the islands, is, during war, a profitable business, which Congress cannot be intended to have prohibited, unless that intent be manifested by express words or a very plain and necessary implication.

It has also been observed that an act of Congress ought never to be construed to violate the law of nations if any other possible construction remains, and consequently can never be construed to violate neutral rights, or to affect neutral commerce, further than is warranted by the law of nations as understood in this country.

These principles are believed to be correct, and they ought to be kept in view, in construing the act now under consideration.

The first sentence of the act which describes the persons whose commercial intercourse with France or her dependencies is to be prohibited, names any person or persons, resident within the United States or under their protection. Commerce carried on by persons within this description is declared to be illicit.

From persons the act proceeds to things, and declares explicitly the cases in which the vessels employed in this illicit commerce shall be forfeited. Any vessel owned, hired or employed wholly or in part by any person residing within the United States, or by any citizen thereof residing elsewhere, which shall perform certain acts recited in the law, becomes liable to forfeiture. It seems to the court to be a correct construction of these words to say, that the vessel must be of this description, not at the time of the passage of the law, but at the time when the act of forfeiture shall be committed. . . .

The *Jane* having been completely transferred in the island of St. Thomas, by a *bonâ fide* sale to Jared Shattuck, and the forfeiture alleged to have accrued on a fact subsequent to that transfer, the liability of the vessel to forfeiture must depend on the inquiry whether the purchaser was within the description of the act.

Jared Shattuck having been born within the United States, and not being proved to have expatriated himself according to any form prescribed by law, is said to remain a citizen, entitled to the benefit and subject to the disabilities imposed upon American citizens; and, therefore, to come expressly within the description of the act which comprehends American citizens residing elsewhere.

Whether a person born within the United States, or becoming a citizen according to the established laws of the country, can divest himself absolutely of that character otherwise than in such manner as may be prescribed by law, is a question which it is not necessary at present to decide. The cases cited at bar and the arguments drawn from the general conduct of the United States on this interesting subject, seem completely to establish the principle that an American citizen may acquire in a foreign country, the commercial privileges attached to his domicil, and be exempted from the operation of an act expressed in such general terms as that now under consideration. Indeed the very expressions of the act would seem to exclude a person under the circumstances of Jared Shattuck. He is not a person under the protection of the United States. The American citizen who goes into a foreign country, although he owes local and temporary allegiance to that country, is yet, if he performs no other act changing his condition, entitled to the protection of our government; and if, without the violation of any municipal law, he should be oppressed unjustly, he would have a right to claim that protection, and the interposition of the American government in his favor, would be considered as a justifiable interposition. But his situation is completely changed, where by his own act he has made himself the subject of a foreign power. Although this act may not be sufficient to rescue him from punishment for any crime committed against the United States, a point not intended to be decided, yet it certainly places him out of the protection of the United States while within the territory of the sovereign to whom he has sworn allegiance, and consequently takes him out of the description of the act.

It is therefore the opinion of the court, that the *Charming Betsy*, with her cargo, being at the time of her re-capture the *bonâ fide* property of a Danish burgher, is not forfeitable, in consequence of her being employed in carrying on trade and commerce with a French island.

THE NEREIDE

13 U.S. (9 Cranch) 388, 418–23, 3 L.Ed. 769 (1815).

[In 1813, during the U.S.-British War of 1812–14, a Spanish subject named Pinto contracted to have goods transported on board a British vessel, *The Nereide*, for a voyage from London to Buenos Aries. On the voyage, *The Nereide* was separated from her convoy, was captured by an American privateer, and was brought into the port of New York, where the vessel and cargo were libeled and condemned as a prize of war, including the cargo owned by Pinto and other Spanish subjects. On appeal, the captors argued that neutral property forfeits its character of neutrality by being put on board an armed ship of an enemy. The Spaniards argued that the property of a neutral country (in this case, Spain) and its nationals (in this case, Spain) was not liable to condemnation under the law of nations.]

MARSHALL, Ch. J. after stating the facts of the case, delivered the opinion of the court as follows:

. . . .

The rule that the goods of an enemy found in the vessel of a friend are prize of war, and that the goods of a friend found in the vessel of an enemy are to be restored, is believed to be a part of the original law of nations, as generally, perhaps universally, acknowledged. Certainly it has been fully and unequivocally recognized by the United States. This rule is founded on the simple and intelligible principle that war gives a full right to capture the goods of an enemy, but gives no right to capture the goods of a friend. In the practical application of this principle, so as to form the rule, the propositions that the neutral flag constitutes no protection to enemy property, and that the belligerent flag communicates no hostile character to neutral property, are necessarily admitted. The character of the property, taken distinctly and separately from all other considerations, depends in no degree upon the character of the vehicle in which it is found.

. . . .

The . . . captors [argue that] the ordinances of [the Spanish] government would subject American property, under similar circumstances, to confiscation, and therefore the property, claimed by Spanish subjects in this case, ought to be condemned as prize of war.

The ordinances themselves have not been produced, nor has the Court received such information respecting them as would enable it to decide certainly either on their permanent existence, or on their application to the United States. But be this as it may, the Court is decidedly of opinion that reciprocating to the subjects of a nation, or retaliating on them, its unjust proceedings towards our citizens, is a political not a legal measure. It is for the consideration of the government not of its Courts. The degree and the kind of retaliation depend entirely on considerations foreign to this tribunal. It may be the policy of the nation to avenge its wrongs in a manner having no affinity to the injury sustained, or it may be its policy to recede from its full rights and not to avenge them at all. It is not for its Courts to interfere with the proceedings of the nation and to thwart its views. It is not for us to depart from the beaten track prescribed for us, and to tread the devious and intricate path of politics. Even in the case of salvage, a case peculiarly within the discretion of Courts, because no fixed rule is prescribed by the law of nations, congress has not left it to this department to say whether the rule of foreign nations shall be applied to them, but has by law applied that rule. If it be the will of the government to apply to Spain any rule respecting captures which Spain is supposed to apply to us, the government will manifest that will by passing an act for the purpose. Till such an act be passed, the Court is bound by the law of nations which is a part of the law of the land.

THE LOTTAWANNA

88 U.S. (21 Wall.) 558, 571–78, 22 L.Ed. 654 (1874).

[In an 1819 case called *The General Smith*, the Supreme Court decided that when repairs or other services are furnished to a ship in the port of a state to which she belongs, no lien is implied unless it is recognized by the local law of the state. By contrast, when such services are furnished to a foreign vessel, maritime and admiralty law recognizes a lien for the party providing the service on the vessel so as to secure payment for the services provided. In this case, a Louisiana vessel called the *Lottawanna* was provided repairs in the port of New Orleans and then became the subject of a lien, even though Louisiana law did not provide for such a lien. Despite the Supreme Court's earlier finding in *The General Smith*, the lower court upheld the lien.]

JUSTICE BRADLEY:

. . . .

The ground on which we are asked to overrule the judgment in the case of *The General Smith* is, that by the general maritime law, those who furnish necessary materials, repairs, and supplies to a vessel, upon her credit, have a lien on such a vessel therefor, as well when furnished in her home port as when furnished in a foreign port, and that the courts of admiralty are bound to give effect to that lien.

The proposition assumes that the general maritime law governs this case, and is binding on the courts of the United States.

But it is hardly necessary to argue that the maritime law is only so far operative as law in any country as it is adopted by the laws and usages of that country. In this respect it is like international law or the laws of war, which have the effect of law in no country any further than they are accepted and received as such; or, like the case of the civil law, which forms the basis of most European laws, but which has the force of law in each state only so far as it is adopted therein, and with such modifications as are deemed expedient. The adoption of the common law by the several States of this Union also presents an analogous case. It is the basis of all the State laws; but is modified as each sees fit. Perhaps the maritime law is more uniformly followed by commercial nations than the civil and common laws are by those who use them. But, like those laws, however fixed, definite, and beneficial the theoretical code of maritime law may be, it can have only so far the effect of law in any country as it is permitted to have. But the actual maritime law can hardly be said to have a fixed and definite form as to all the subjects which may be embraced within its scope. Whilst it is true that the great mass of maritime law is the same in all commercial countries, yet, in each country, peculiarities exist either as to some of the rules, or in the mode of enforcing them. Especially is this the case on the outside boundaries of the law, where it comes in contact with, or shades off into the local or municipal law of the particular country and affects only its own merchants or people in their relations to each other. Whereas, in matters affecting the stranger or foreigner, the commonly received law of the whole commercial world is more assiduously observed—as, in justice, it should be. No one doubts that every nation may adopt its own maritime code. France may adopt one; England another; the United States a third; still, the convenience of the commercial world, bound together, as it is, by mutual relations of trade and intercourse, demands that, in all essential things wherein those relations bring them in contact, there should be a uniform law founded on natural reason and justice. Hence the adoption by all commercial nations (our own included) of the general maritime law as the basis and groundwork of all their maritime regulations. But no nation regards itself as precluded from making occasional modifications suited to its locality and the genius of its own people and institutions, especially in matters that are of merely local and municipal consequence and do not affect other nations. It will be found, therefore, that the maritime codes of France, England, Sweden, and other countries, are not one and the same in every particular; but that whilst there is a general correspondence between them arising from the fact that each adopts the essential principles, and the great mass of the general maritime law, as the basis of its system, there are varying shades of difference corresponding to the respective territories, climate, and genius of the people of each country respectively. Each state adopts the maritime law, not as a code having any independent or inherent force, *proprio vigore,* but as its own law, with such modifications and qualifications as it sees fit. Thus adopted and thus qualified in each case, it becomes the maritime law of the particular nation that adopts it. And without such voluntary adoption it would not be law. And thus it happens, that, from the general practice of commercial nations in making the same general law the basis and groundwork of their respective maritime systems, the great mass of maritime law which is thus received by these nations in common, comes to be the common maritime law of the world.

This account of the maritime law, if correct, plainly shows that in particular matters, especially such as approach a merely municipal character, the received maritime law may differ in different countries without affecting the general integrity of the system as a harmonious whole. The government of one country may be willing to give to its citizens, who supply a ship with provisions at her home port where the owner himself resides, a lien on the ship; whilst that of another country may take a contrary view as to the expediency of such a rule. The difference between them in a matter that concerns only their own citizens, in each case, cannot seriously affect the harmony and consistency of the common maritime law which each adopts and observes.

This view of the subject does not in the slightest degree detract from the proper authority and respect due to that venerable law of the sea, which has been the subject of such high encomiums from the ablest jurists of all countries; it merely places it upon the just and logical grounds upon which it is accepted, and with proper qualifications, received with the binding force of law in all countries.

The proposition, therefore, that by the general maritime law a lien is given in cases of the kind now under consideration, does not advance the argument a single step, unless it be shown to be in accordance with the maritime law as accepted and received in the United States. It certainly has not been the maritime law of England for more than two centuries past; and whether it is the maritime law of this country depends upon questions which are not answered by simply turning to the ordinary European treatises on maritime law, or the codes or ordinances of any particular country.

. . . .

. . . [A]ccording to the maritime law as accepted and received in this country, we feel bound to declare that no such lien exists as is claimed by the appellees in this case. The adjudications in this court before referred to, which it is unnecessary to review, are conclusive on the subject; and we see no sufficient ground for disturbing them.

UNITED STATES v. ARJONA

120 U.S. 479, 484–88, 7 S.Ct. 628, 30 L.Ed. 728 (1887).

[In this case, the Supreme Court considered the constitutionality of a law by which Congress had declared it a punishable offense to counterfeit notes of a foreign bank or corporation. Although the law did not state that this was "an offense against the Law of Nations" the Supreme Court nevertheless found it to be so.]

CHIEF JUSTICE WAITE:

. . . .

The law of nations requires every national government to use "due diligence" to prevent a wrong being done within its own dominion to another nation with which it is at peace, or to the people thereof; and because of this the obligation of one nation to punish those who within its own jurisdiction counterfeit the money of another nation has long been recognized. Vattel, in his Law of Nations, which was first printed at Neuchâtel in 1758, and was translated into English and published in England in 1760, uses this language: "From the principles thus laid down, it is easy to conclude, that if one nation counterfeits the money of another, or if she allows and protects false coiners who presume to do it, she does that nation an injury." When this was written money was the chief thing of this kind that needed protection, but still it was added: "There is another custom more modern, and of no less use to commerce than the establishment of coin, namely, *exchange,* or the traffic of bankers, by means of which a merchant remits immense sums from one end of the world to the other, at very trifling expense, and, if he pleases, without risk. For the same reason that sovereigns are obliged to protect commerce, they are obliged to support this custom, by good laws, in which every merchant, whether citizen or foreigner, may find security. In general, it is equally the interest and duty of every nation to have wise and equitable commercial laws established in the country." Vattel, Law of Nations, Phil. ed. 1876, Book I, chap. 10, pages 46, 47. In a note by Mr. Chitty in his London edition of 1834 it is said: "This is a sound principle, which ought to be extended so as to deny effect to any fraud upon a foreign nation or its subjects." Id. 47, note 50.

This rule was established for the protection of nations in their intercourse with each other. If there were no such intercourse, it would be a matter of no special moment to one nation that its money was counterfeited in another. Its own people could not be defrauded if the false coin did not come among them, and its own sovereignty would not be violated if the counterfeit could not under any circumstances be made to take the place of the true money. But national intercourse includes commercial intercourse between the people of different nations. It is as much the duty of a nation to protect such an intercourse as it is any other, and that is what Vattel meant when he said: "For the same reason that sovereigns are obliged to protect commerce, they are obliged to support this custom;" "namely, *exchange,* or the traffic of bankers, by means of which a merchant remits immense sums from one end of the world to the other," "by good laws, in which every merchant, whether citizen or foreigner, may find security."

. . . .

No nation can be more interested in this question than the United States. Their money is practically composed of treasury notes or certificates issued by themselves, or of bank bills issued by banks created under their authority and subject to their control. Their own securities, and those of the states, the cities, and the public corporations, whose interests abroad they alone have the power to guard against foreign national neglect, are found on sale in the principal money markets of Europe. If these securities, whether national, municipal, or corporate, are forged and counterfeited with impunity at the places where they are sold, it is easy to see that a great wrong will be done to the United States and their people. Any uncertainty about the genuineness of the security necessarily depreciates its value as a merchantable commodity, and against this international comity requires that national protection shall, as far as possible, be afforded. If there is neglect in that, the United States may, with propriety, call on the proper government to provide for the punishment of such an offence, and thus secure the restraining influences of a fear of the consequences of wrong doing. A refusal may not, perhaps, furnish sufficient cause for war, but it would certainly give just ground of complaint, and thus disturb that harmony between the governments which each is bound to cultivate and promote.

But if the United States can require this of another, that other may require it of them, because international obligations are of necessity reciprocal in their nature. The right, if it exists at all, is given by the law of nations, and what is law for one is, under the same circumstances, law for the other. A right secured by the law of nations to a nation, or its people, is one the United States as the representatives of this nation are bound to protect. Consequently, a law which is necessary and proper to afford this protection is one that Congress may enact, because it is one that is needed to carry into execution a power conferred by the Constitution on the Government of the United States exclusively. There is no authority in the United States to require the passage and enforcement of such a law by the states. Therefore the United States must have the power to pass it and enforce it themselves, or be unable to perform a duty which they may owe to another nation, and which the law of nations has imposed on them as part of their international obligations. . . .

It remains only to consider those questions which present the point whether, in enacting a statute to define and punish an offence against the law of nations, it is necessary, in order "to define" the offence, that it be declared in the statute itself to be "an offence against the law of nations." This statute defines the offence, and if the thing made punishable is one which the United States are required by their international obligations to use due diligence to prevent, it is an offence against the law of nations. Such being the case, there is no more need of declaring in the statute that it is such an offence than there would be in any other criminal statute to declare that it was enacted to carry into execution any other particular power vested by the Constitution in the Government of the United States. Whether the offence as defined is an offence against the law of nations depends on the thing done, not on any declaration to that effect by Congress. As has already been seen, it was incumbent on the United States as a nation to use due diligence to prevent any injury to another nation or its people by counterfeiting its money, or its public or *quasi* public securities. This statute was enacted as a means to that end, that is to say, as a means of performing a duty which had been cast on the United States by the law of nations, and it was clearly appropriate legislation for that purpose. Upon its face, therefore, it defines an offence against the law of nations as clearly as if Congress had in express terms so declared. Criminal statutes passed for enforcing and preserving the neutral relations of the United States with other nations were passed by Congress at a very early date; June 5, 1794, c. 50, 1 Stat. 381; June 14, 1797, c. 1, 1 Stat. 520; March 3, 1817, c. 58, 3 Stat. 370; April 20, 1818, c. 88, 3 Stat. 447: and those now in force are found in Title LXVII of the Revised Statutes. These all rest on the same power of Congress that is here invoked, and it has never been supposed they were invalid because they did not expressly declare that the offences there defined were offences against the law of nations.

THE PAQUETE HABANA

175 U.S. 677, 20 S.Ct. 290, 44 L.Ed. 320 (1900).

MR. JUSTICE GRAY delivered the opinion of the court.

These are two appeals from decrees of the District Court of the United States for the Southern District of Florida, condemning two fishing vessels and their cargoes as prize of war.

Each vessel was a fishing smack, running in and out of Havana, and regularly engaged in fishing on the coast of Cuba; sailed under the Spanish flag; was owned by a Spanish subject of Cuban birth, living in the city of Havana; was commanded by a subject of Spain, also residing in Havana; and her master and crew had no interest in the vessel, but were entitled to shares, amounting in all to two thirds, of her catch, the other third belonging to her owner. Her cargo consisted of fresh fish, caught by her crew from the sea, put on board as they were caught, and kept and sold alive. Until stopped by the blockading squadron, she had no knowledge of the existence of the war, or of any blockade. She had no arms or ammunition on board, and made on attempt to run the blockade after she knew of its existence, nor any resistance at the time of the capture.

The *Paquete Habana* was a sloop, 43 feet long on the keel, and of 25 tons burden, and had a crew of three Cubans, including the master, who had a fishing license from the Spanish Government, and no other commission or license. She left Havana March 25, 1898; sailed along the coast of Cuba to Cape San Antonio at the western end of the island, and there fished for twenty-five days, lying between the reefs off the cape, within the territorial waters of Spain; and then started back for Havana, with a cargo of about 40 quintals of live fish. On April 25, 1898, about 2 miles off Mariel, and eleven miles from Havana, she was captured by the United States gunboat *Castine*.

The *Lola* was a schooner, 51 feet long on the keel, and of 35 tons burden, and had a crew of six Cubans, including the master, and no commission or license. She left Havana April 11, 1898, and proceeded to Campeachy Sound off Yucatan, fished there eight days, and started back for Havana with a cargo of about 10,000 pounds of live fish. On April 26, 1898, near Havana, she was stopped by the United States steamship *Cincinnati*, and was warned not to go into Havana, but was told that she would be allowed to land at Bahia Honda. She then changed her course, and put for Bahia Honda, but on the next morning, when near that port, was captured by the United States steamship *Dolphin*.

Both the fishing vessels were brought by their captors into Key West. A libel for the condemnation of each vessel and her cargo as prize of war was there filed on April 27, 1898; a claim was interposed by her master, on behalf of himself and the other members of the crew, and of her owner; evidence was taken, showing the facts above stated; and on May 30, 1898, a final decree of condemnation and sale was entered, "the court not being satisfied that as a matter of law, without any ordinance, treaty or proclamation, fishing vessels of this class are exempt from seizure."

Each vessel was thereupon sold by auction; the *Paquete Habana* for the sum of $490; and the *Lola* for the sum of $800. There was no other evidence in the record of the value of either vessel or of her cargo.

. . . .

We are then brought to the consideration of the question whether, upon the facts appearing in these records, the fishing smacks were subject to capture by the armed vessels of the United States during the recent war with Spain.

By an ancient usage among civilized nations, beginning centuries ago, and gradually ripening into a rule of international law, coast fishing vessels, pursuing their vocation of catching and bringing in fresh fish, have been recognized as exempt, with their cargoes and crews, from capture as prize of war.

This doctrine, however, has been earnestly contested at the bar; and no complete collection of the instances illustrating it is to be found, so far as we are aware, in a single published work although many are referred to and discussed by the writers on international law, notably in 2 Ortolan, Regles Internationales et Diplomatie de la Mer (4th ed.) lib. 3, c. 2, pp. 51–56; in 4 Calvo, Droit International, (5th ed.) §§ 2367–2373; in De Boeck, Propriete Privee Ennemie sous Pavillon Ennemi, §§ 191–196; and in Hall, International Law, (4th ed.) § 148. It is therefore worth the while to trace the history of the rule, from the earliest accessible sources, through the increasing recognition of it, with occasional setbacks, to what we may now justly consider as its final establishment in our own country and generally throughout the civilized world.

. . . .

Since the English orders in council of 1806 and 1810, before quoted, in favor of fishing vessels employed in catching and bringing to market fresh fish, no instance has been found in which the exemption from capture of private coast fishing vessels, honestly pursuing their peaceful industry, has been denied by England, or by any other nation. And the Empire of Japan, (the last state admitted into the rank of civilized nations,) by an ordinance promulgated at the beginning of its war with China in August, 1894, established prize courts, and ordained that "the following enemy's vessels are exempt from detention"—including in the exemption "boats engaged in coast fisheries," as well as "ships engaged exclusively on a voyage of scientific discovery, philanthropy or religious mission." Takahashi, International Law, 11, 178.

International law is part of our law, and must be ascertained and administered by the courts of justice of appropriate jurisdiction, as often as questions of right depending upon it are duly presented for their determination. For this purpose, where there is no treaty, and no controlling executive or legislative act or judicial decision, resort must be had to the customs and usages of civilized nations; and, as evidence of these, to the works of jurists and commentators, who by years of labor, research and experience, have made themselves peculiarly well acquainted with the subjects of which they treat. Such works are resorted to by judicial tribunals, not for the speculations of their authors concerning what the law ought to be, but for trustworthy evidence of what the law really is. *Hilton v. Guyot,* 159 U.S. 113, 163, 164, 214, 215.

. . . .

This review of the precedents and authorities on the subject appears to us abundantly to demonstrate that at the present day, by the general consent of the civilized nations of the world, and independently of any express treaty or other public act, it is an established rule of international law, founded on considerations of humanity to a poor and industrious order of men, and of the mutual convenience of belligerent States, that coast fishing vessels, with their implements and supplies, cargoes and crews, unarmed, and honestly pursuing their peaceful calling of catching and bringing in fresh fish, are exempt from capture as prize of war.

The exemption, of course, does not apply to coast fishermen or their vessels if employed for a warlike purpose, or in such a way as to give aid or information to the enemy; nor when military or naval operations create a necessity to which all private interests must give way.

Nor has the exemption been extended to ships or vessels employed on the high sea in taking whales or seals, or cod or other fish which are not brought fresh to market, but are salted or otherwise cured and made a regular article of commerce.

This rule of international law is one which prize courts, administering the law of nations, are bound to take judicial notice of, and to give effect to, in the absence of any treaty or other public act of their own government in relation to the matter.

. . . .

By the practice of all civilized nations, vessels employed only for the purposes of discovery or science are considered as exempt from the contingencies of war, and therefore not subject to capture. It has been usual for the government sending out such an expedition to give notice to other powers; but it is not essential. 1 Kent Com. 91, note; Halleck, c. 20, § 22; Calvo, § 2376; Hall, § 138.

. . . .

To this subject, in more than one aspect, are singularly applicable the words uttered by Mr. Justice Strong, speaking for this court: "Undoubtedly, no single nation can change the law of the sea. The law is of universal obligation, and no statute of one or two nations can create obligations for the world. Like all the laws of nations, it rests upon the common consent of civilized communities. It is of force, not because it was prescribed by any superior power, but because it has been generally accepted as a rule of conduct. Whatever may have been its origin, whether in the usages of navigation, or in the ordinances of maritime States, or in both, it has become the law of the sea only by the concurrent sanction of those nations who may be said to constitute the commercial world. Many of the usages which prevail, and which have the force of law, doubtless originated in the positive prescriptions of some single State, which were at first of limited effect, but which, when generally accepted, became of universal obligation." "This is not giving to the statutes of any nation extraterritorial effect. It is not treating them as general maritime laws; but it is recognition of the historical fact that by common consent of mankind these rules have been acquiesced in as of general obligation. Of that fact, we think, we may take judicial notice. Foreign municipal laws must indeed be proved as facts, but it is not so with the law of nations." *The Scotia*, 14 Wall. 170, 187, 188.

The position taken by the United States during the recent war with Spain was quite in accord with the rule of international law, now generally recognized by civilized nations, in regard to coast fishing vessels.

On April 21, 1898, the Secretary of the Navy gave instructions to Admiral Sampson, commanding the North Atlantic Squadron, to "immediately institute a blockade of the north coast of Cuba, extending from Cardenas on the east to Bahia Honda on the west." Bureau of Navigation Report of 1898, appx. 175. The blockade was immediately instituted accordingly. On April 22, the President issued a proclamation, declaring that the United States had instituted and would maintain that blockade, "in pursuance of the laws of the United States, and the law of nations applicable to such cases." 30 Stat. 1769. And by the act of Congress of April 25, 1898, c. 189, it was declared that the war between the United States and Spain existed on that day, and had existed since and including April 21. 30 Stat. 364.

On April 26, 1898, the President issued another proclamation, which, after reciting the existence of the war, as declared by Congress, contained this further recital: "It being desirable that such war should be conducted upon principles in harmony with the present views of nations and sanctioned by their recent practice." This recital was followed by specific declarations of certain rules for the conduct of the war by sea, making no mention of fishing vessels. 30 Stat. 1770. But the proclamation clearly manifests the general policy of the Government to conduct the war in accordance with the principles of international law sanctioned by the recent practice of nations.

On April 28, 1898, (after the capture of the two fishing vessels now in question,) Admiral Sampson telegraphed to the Secretary of the Navy as follows: "I find that a large number of fishing schooners are attempting to get into Havana from their fishing grounds near the Florida reefs and coasts. They are generally manned by excellent seamen, belonging to the maritime inscription of Spain, who have already served in the Spanish navy, and who are liable to further service. As these trained men are naval reserves, have a semi-military character, and would be most valuable to the Spaniards as artillerymen, either afloat or ashore, I recommend that they should be detained prisoners of war, and that I should be authorized to deliver them to the commanding officer of the army at Key West." To that communication the Secretary of the Navy, on April 30, 1898, guardedly answered: "Spanish fishing vessels attempting to violate blockade are subject, with crew, to capture, and any such vessel or crew considered likely to aid enemy may be detained." Bureau of Navigation Report of 1898, appx. 178. The Admiral's despatch assumed that he was not authorized, without express order, to arrest coast fishermen peaceably pursuing their calling; and the necessary implication and evident intent of the response of the Navy Department were that Spanish coast fishing vessels and their crews should not be interfered with, so long as they neither attempted to violate the blockade, nor were considered likely to aid the enemy.

. . . .

Upon the facts proved in either case, it is the duty of this court, sitting as the highest prize court of the United States, and administering the law of nations, to declare and adjudge that the capture was unlawful, and without probable cause; and it is therefore, in each case, *Ordered, that the decree of the District Court be reversed*, and the proceeds of the sale of the vessel, together with the proceeds of any sale of her cargo, be restored to the claimant, with damages and costs.

JUSTICE SANDRA DAY O'CONNOR, FEDERALISM OF FREE NATIONS

28 N.Y.U. J. Int'l L. & Pol. 35, 36–42 (1996) (some footnotes omitted).

... In some of the oldest statements from the Court, we have observed that the laws of the United States incorporate fundamental principles of the law of nations. Those who are familiar with our domestic law no doubt know the traditional canon that our courts ordinarily will not construe a statute to conflict with constitutional principles. Instead, we often try to read a law so as not to call into question its constitutional validity. Less well known than the canon is its origins. This cardinal principle has its roots in *Murray v. The Charming Betsy*.[10] In that case, decided in 1804, Chief Justice Marshall wrote not about the violation of constitutional rights, but rather of international obligations. He stated: "[A]n Act of Congress ought never to be construed to violate the law of nations if any other possible construction remains."[11] In this early exposition of interpretive principles that would define our jurisprudence, we thus acknowledged that the law of nations is an integral part of that

10. 6 U.S. (2 Cranch) 64 (1804); *Edward J. DeBartolo Corp. v. Florida Gulf Coast Bldg. and Constr. Trades Council*, 485 U.S. 568 (1988).

11. *Murray v. The Charming Betsy*, 6 U.S. (2 Cranch) at 118; *Edward J. DeBartolo Corp. v. Florida Gulf Coast Bldg. and Constr. Trades Council*, 485 U.S. at 575 (citing *Murray v. The Charming Betsy*).

jurisprudence. We repeated this basic principle in the famous case of *The Paquete Habana*,[12] where the opinion stated unequivocally that,

> [i]nternational law is part of our law, and must be ascertained and administered by the courts of justice of appropriate jurisdiction. . . . . . . For this purpose, where there is no treaty and no controlling executive or legislative act or judicial decision, resort must be had to the customs and usages of civilized nations.[13]

Our membership in the family of civilized nations demands no less than this reciprocal recognition of rights and responsibilities—an obligation that the Supreme Court of the United States has on occasion acknowledged and observed.

Some may wonder how this professed respect for the law of nations comports with the Court's abstention from issues touching on international relations. A skeptical observer perhaps would argue that the Court merely pays lip service to the rule of international law, while at the same time shirks its responsibility to uphold those principles. In fact, our precedents demonstrate an attempt to strike a balance between the requirements of international law with a respect for the judgment of the political branches in matters of foreign policy. It is obviously a delicate balance, and one that continues to be refined in the cases that require us to apply these doctrines.

. . . .

How does the recent trend toward the proliferation of multilateral and international tribunals fit in this doctrinal framework? By enacting legislation creating or consenting to the creation of such tribunals, the political branches in our country have obviously judged that they further America's foreign interests. To the extent that these new tribunals necessitate the involvement of the federal judiciary, Congress and the President are in effect seeking judicial involvement in these matters. . . . By negotiating and approving treaties and agreements which create transnational tribunals and prescribe their relationship with our domestic courts, the political branches of our government are asking the judiciary to not abstain from its usual adjudicatory function. They are ascribing a role for the courts in these specified areas of international relations, a role that is limited by the terms of the authorizing laws and treaties.

. . . .

Having served as a state court judge before taking my seat on the Supreme Court, I have spent considerable time on the Supreme Court explaining the virtues of federalism as applied to the judiciary. The basic feature of this notion of federalism is a judicial comity borne of dialogue and trust. I think the great advantage of our federal system is that it permits state and federal courts to talk with each other—to engage in healthy debate on questions over which there is conflict or to forge

---

12. 175 U.S. 677 (1900).

13. *Id.* at 700.

consensus on issues of mutual interest. In the same light, I think that both federal and state courts are part of one dual system, and we federal judges must trust our state counterparts to do their best in carrying out their duties under the Constitution, which they, like we, have taken an oath to uphold.

As our country moves toward a more international regime of dispute resolution, this federalist ideal of healthy dialogue and mutual trust may possibly be adapted to describe the proper relationship between domestic courts and transnational tribunals. It is a relationship which might be described as "the federalism of free nations," to use a phrase of the philosopher Immanuel Kant.[17] Just as our domestic laws develop through a free exchange of ideas among state and federal courts, so too should international law evolve through a dialogue between national courts and transnational tribunals and through the interdependent effect of their judgments. This dialogue has been rather one-sided with respect to the opinions of the Supreme Court of the United States. The flow of ideas from our Court to other tribunals around the world is well-chronicled, but we have not seen fit to reciprocate in kind. I think this will change, as we are asked to define our role within the international regime. The Supreme Court of the United States observed in *The Paquete Habana* that, in order to discern the rule of law among nations, we resort "to the works of jurists and commentators, who by years of labor, research and experience, have made themselves peculiarly well acquainted with the subjects of which they treat."[18] As our domestic courts are increasingly asked to resolve disputes that involve questions of foreign and international law about which we have no special competence, I think there is great potential for our Court to learn from the experience and logic of foreign courts and international tribunals—just as we have offered these courts some helpful approaches from our own legal traditions.

The other essential element of our federalist tradition is mutual trust and respect. Through the development of abstention doctrines, federal courts have refrained from exercising their authority in certain cases so as not to disrupt proceedings in state courts or to intrude in the processes of state governments. And our precedents, especially in the area of habeas corpus, reflect a healthy respect for the opinions of state courts and recognize the need to protect the finality of their judgments. By the same token, I think it is fair to expect that international tribunals, in discharging their functions, should be mindful of their effect on domestic courts and should heed our prerogatives as a sovereign nation. The trust and respect, of course, is mutual. Just as state courts are expected to follow the dictates of the Constitution and federal statutes, I think domestic courts should faithfully recognize the obligations imposed by international law. The Supremacy Clause of the United States Constitution gives legal

---

17. IMMANUEL KANT, THE ETERNAL PEACE, *reprinted in* THE PHILOSOPHY OF KANT: KANT'S MORAL AND POLITICAL WRITINGS 441 (Carl J. Friedrich ed., 1949).

18. 175 U.S. at 700.

force to foreign treaties, and our status as a free nation demands faithful compliance with the law of free nations.

CONCLUDING NOTES

1. *Powerful or Pious?* In reflecting on the early cases on incorporation of customary international law into U.S. law—such as Judge Jay's charge to the jury in the *Trial of Gideon Henfield* or Justice Wilson's language in *Ware v. Hylton*—as well as the views expressed more recently by Justice O'Connor, does the doctrine of incorporation strike you as a significant U.S. legal phenomenon or more as rhetoric by a few visionary (or pious) judges?

2. *Three Faces of Customary International Law in U.S. Law*. The cases above suggest three important ways that customary international law can affect U.S. law. First, as demonstrated in cases such as *The Nereide* and *The Paquete Habana*, norms contained in customary international law can directly serve as a part of the law of the United States. Thus, even without enactment of a statute, customary international law can be the basis for a governing rule in a particular case. Second, as demonstrated in the *Arjona* case, Congress may adopt a statute that explicitly or implicitly seeks to implement a norm of customary international law. Third, as demonstrated in *The Charming Betsy*, customary international law may give rise to an interpretive presumption, which U.S. courts will apply when construing U.S. statutory or executive exercises of authority.

3. *Direct Incorporation of Customary International Law*. Cases like *The Paquete Habana* are sometimes read to suggest a seamless transition from the international plane to the domestic plane, such that neither incorporation nor translation of customary international law is required, but direct incorporation does not necessarily entail that understanding. To the extent that customary international law is directly applied as a part of U.S. law, should the customary norm in all aspects become a part of U.S. law, or should the norm be adapted to special circumstances of the U.S. legal system? Does *The Lottawanna* help explain when and how U.S. courts should take an international custom and treat it as part of U.S. common law?

As previously noted, the answer to these and other questions regarding direct incorporation may have evolved over time. For 150 years, U.S. courts applied the law of nations as a matter of general common law. Students of U.S. civil procedure will recall that during the reign of *Swift v. Tyson*, 41 U.S. (16 Pet.) 1, 10 L.Ed. 865 (1842), federal judges in diversity cases were free to develop a body of common law distinct from and unbound by the common law of the states in which they sat. Judges were driven by a belief in natural law, by which legal principles could be discerned and applied even absent explicit legislation. Thus, during this time, customary international law was applied as common law by both federal and state courts independently of one another.

When the Supreme Court decided the case of *Erie R.R. Co. v. Tompkins*, nearly 100 years of common law as established by the federal courts was abolished. *Erie* declared that thenceforth, "[e]xcept in matters governed by the Federal Constitution or by acts of Congress, the law to be applied in any case is the law of the state," 304 U.S. 64, 78, 58 S.Ct. 817, 82 L.Ed. 1188

(1938). In such cases, federal courts sitting in diversity would be required to apply the common law of the states in which they sat. The decision marked a shift in jurisprudential philosophy from natural law to positivist thinking. It also left open the question of how the law of nations should be properly applied. Would the law of nations now be applied only under state law? Would it be applied only in limited circumstances where a constitutional or statutory grant of authority was conferred? Or did questions on the law of nations "arise under" the Constitution as per Article III and thus appropriately belong wholly to the federal courts to decide?

In the immediate aftermath of *Erie*, Professor Philip Jessup—later judge of the International Court of Justice—urged that *Erie* not be read as granting states the exclusive power to apply the law of nations. Professor Jessup argued that the United States—and not the fifty states—was the relevant entity under international law, and that therefore federal law was inherently a better repository for law of nations. He wrote:

> [A]ny attempt to extend the doctrine of [*Erie*] to international law should be repudiated by the Supreme Court.... Any question of applying international law in our courts involves the foreign relations of the United States and can thus be brought within a federal power.... The several states of the Union are entities unknown to international law. It would be as unsound as it would be unwise to make our state courts our ultimate authority for pronouncing the rules of international law.

Philip C. Jessup, *The Doctrine of Erie Railroad v. Tompkins Applied to International Law*, 33 AM. J. INT'L L. 740, 743 (1939). Professor Jessup's view proved influential in subsequent jurisprudence. In *Banco Nacional de Cuba v. Sabbatino*, 376 U.S. 398, 84 S.Ct. 923, 11 L.Ed.2d 804 (1964) (excerpted below in Section 5), Justice Harlan, writing for the Court and citing Professor Jessup, upheld the proposition that international law was rightly within the province of federal law.

In 2004, the Supreme Court affirmed that federal courts retain jurisdiction for certain claims under the law of nations and can decide such cases as an element of federal common law. Sosa v. Alvarez–Machain, 542 U.S. 692, 124 S.Ct. 2739, 159 L.Ed.2d 718 (2004) (excerpted below in Section 5); *see* William S. Dodge, *Bridging Erie: Customary International Law in the U.S. Legal System After Sosa v. Alvarez–Machain*, 12 TULSA J. COMP. & INT'L L. 87 (2004); Thomas H. Lee, *The Safe–Conduct Theory of the Alien Tort Statute*, 106 COLUM. L. REV. 830 (2006).

4. *The Academic Debate*. The *Sosa* decision intervened in, without wholly resolving, a sprawling academic debate that revisited how customary international law should be reconciled with *Erie*. For scholarship supportive of the application of customary international law as federal law, see Ralph G. Steinhardt, *Laying One Bankrupt Critique to Rest:* Sosa v. Alvarez–Machain *and the Future of International Human Rights Litigation*, 57 VANDERBILT L. REV. 2241 (2004); Harold Hongju Koh, *Is International Law Really State Law?*, 111 HARV. L. REV. 1824 (1998); Gerald L. Neuman, *Sense and Nonsense About Customary International Law: A Response to Professors Bradley and Goldsmith*, 66 FORDHAM L. REV. 371 (1997); Louis Henkin, *International Law as Law in the United States*, 82 MICH. L. REV. 1555 (1984).

For objections to the "modern position," arguing that customary international law should not provide a federal rule of decision unless incorporated into U.S. law by the political branches, see Curtis A. Bradley, Jack L. Goldsmith & David H. Moore, Sosa, *Customary International Law, and the Continuing Relevance of Erie,* 120 HARV. L. REV. 869 (2007); David H. Moore, *An Emerging Uniformity for International Law,* 75 GEO. WASH. L. REV. 1 (2006); Curtis A. Bradley and & Jack L. Goldsmith, *Customary International Law as Federal Common Law: A Critique of the Modern Position,* 110 HARV. L. REV. 815 (1997).

For a "functionalist" argument that there ought to be a "state-led" system of customary international law development, subject to federal preemption by the Executive, see Julian Ku & John Yoo, *Beyond Formalism in Foreign Affairs: A Functional Approach to the Alien Tort Statute,* 2004 SUP. CT. REV. 153.

5. *The Judicial Debate.* While the debate over the status of customary international law has mostly raged within the academy, it has occasionally been reflected in judicial opinions. *See, e.g.,* Al–Bihani v. Obama, 619 F.3d 1, 16–19 (D.C. Cir. 2010) (Kavanaugh, J., concurring in the denial of rehearing en banc) (siding with objections to the "modern position"). *But cf. Al-Bihani,* 619 F.3d at 53–56 (statement of Williams, J., respecting the denial of rehearing en banc) (distinguishing use of customary international law as a tool for statutory construction); *Al-Bihani,* 619 F.3d at 1 (Sentelle, C.J., and Ginsburg, Henderson, Rogers, Tatel, Garland, and Griffith, JJ., concurring in the denial of rehearing en banc) (indicating that discussions of international law principles in the panel opinion by Judge Kavanaugh and others were dicta).

6. *Statutory Incorporation of Customary International Law.* How important is it that a customary international law norm be incorporated into U.S. law by means of a statute, as opposed to simply being recognized by judges as a part of U.S. law? Critics of direct incorporation frequently distinguish circumstances in which there is political branch authorization for incorporating customary international law, and statutory incorporation is the clearest possible means of providing such authorization. That said, statutory incorporation is not invariably clear. Congress may allude to customary international law without providing clear guidance as to the metes and bounds of that inquiry; as considered in the remainder of this chapter, this has bedeviled domestic application of the international law of war, piracy, and human rights (perhaps particularly in relation to the Alien Tort Statute). In other instances, U.S. statutes may depend on terms or concepts that have resonance in international law, at least arguably inviting courts to rely on those terms or concepts in applying the statutes. *See, e.g.,* Republic of Argentina v. Weltover, Inc., 504 U.S. 607, 612, 112 S.Ct. 2160, 119 L.Ed.2d 394 (1992) (reckoning that the term "commercial" in the Foreign Sovereign Immunities Act should be construed in light of Congress' incorporation of the theory of restrictive immunity as it then prevailed). The *Arjona* case is in some respects at the extreme, insofar as the Supreme Court indicated that the law of nations, while not directly invoked by Congress, might explain the constitutional basis for federal authority.

The significance of the distinction between direct and statutory incorporation may also turn in part on the nature of the norm in question. For example, when customary international law is invoked as a constraint on presidential authority, courts have been particularly leery of assuming direct incorporation. (They may also, alternatively, consider expressions of presidential authority as limits on the force and effect of direct incorporation—a prospect considered in greater detail in the next section.) To a degree this reflects principles that have little to do with customary international law in particular. Do you think that the act of forgery in *Arjona* would have been treated as illegal under federal common law (thereby permitting seizure of the forgers' plates by treasury officials, for example) in the *absence* of a law by Congress specifically making such forgery illegal? More generally, in your view, what kinds of customary international law norms must be incorporated by statute before a U.S. court can give them cognizance?

7. *Interpretive Presumption Based on Customary International Law.* Throughout U.S. history, the idea "that an act of congress ought never to be construed to violate the law of nations, if any other possible construction remains," as enunciated by Chief Justice Marshall in *Charming Betsy*, has remained a guiding principle in U.S jurisprudence. *See, e.g.*, F. Hoffman–La Roche Ltd. v. Empagran, 542 U.S. 155, 164–65, 124 S.Ct. 2359, 159 L.Ed.2d 226 (2004); Vilas v. Manila, 220 U.S. 345, 31 S.Ct. 416, 55 L.Ed. 491 (1911); Chicago, Rock Island and & Pacific R.R. Co. v. McGlinn, 114 U.S. 542, 5 S.Ct. 1005, 29 L.Ed. 270 (1885). If a law can be interpreted either in congruity, or in conflict, with international law, why precisely should courts strive for congruity? Perhaps Congress, as a predictive matter, is unlikely to have intended to conflict with international law; perhaps, regardless of congressional intent, courts are well advised to avoid unnecessary conflicts with other nations as a matter of comity; or perhaps courts should avoid creating unnecessary conflicts between Congress and the President, since it is the latter's responsibility to direct U.S. foreign relations and to respond to claims that the United States has violated customary international law. *See* Curtis A. Bradley, *The* Charming Betsy *Canon and Separation of Powers: Rethinking the Interpretive Role of International Law*, 86 GEO. L.J. 479 (1998). When Congress itself expresses the interpretive presumption, of course, the line between statutory incorporation and the *Charming Betsy* canon is blurred. *See, e.g.*, 33 U.S.C. § 1902(i) (2006) (describing ships subject to preventive measures, subject to savings clause providing that "[n]othing in this section shall be construed to restrict in a manner inconsistent with international law navigational rights and freedoms as defined by United States law, treaty, convention, or customary international law").

8. *Evidence of Customary International Law (Including Treaties to Which the United States Is Not a Party).* Customary international law is widely considered to be more difficult to ascertain than some of other forms of law, and the more controversial the means for establishing that law, the more questions may be raised about its hierarchical status. As made evident in cases contemplating the customary international law of human rights, considered in Section 5 below, courts have reacted differently to claims that customary international law may be divined from treaties to which the United States is not a party. The issue is not, however, merely one of judicial

authority. Suppose the President decides not to submit a global treaty to the Senate for advice and consent, but nevertheless declares that a portion of the treaty reflects customary international law binding upon the United States—and suppose further that, as a matter of international law, the United States may assume some but not all of a treaty's obligations, even in situations where the treaty was a package deal. Does such action by the President subvert the constitutional process for ratification of treaty obligations? As discussed in Chapter 3, Section 8, the President appears to have taken such action in the context of the U.N. Convention on the Law of the Sea, Dec. 10, 1982, 1833 U.N.T.S. 3. The executive branch decided that the United States would not ratify the treaty principally because of a few unacceptable provisions relating to seabed mining, but also asserted that there were many things in the treaty that restate or clarify customary law or that are useful and acceptable developments.

9. *Relevance for Inter–State Conflicts*. Is customary international law that regulates *inter-country* matters relevant when considering regulation of *inter-state* matters in the United States? For use of international legal principles to determine territorial disputes between states of the United States and between states and the federal government, see United States v. Louisiana, 470 U.S. 93, 105 S.Ct. 1074, 84 L.Ed.2d 73 (1985); Iowa v. Illinois, 147 U.S. 1, 13 S.Ct. 239, 37 L.Ed. 55 (1893); Louisiana v. Mississippi, 202 U.S. 1, 26 S.Ct. 408, 50 L.Ed. 913 (1906); Arkansas v. Tennessee, 246 U.S. 158, 38 S.Ct. 301, 62 L.Ed. 638 (1918); Minnesota v. Wisconsin, 252 U.S. 273, 40 S.Ct. 313, 64 L.Ed. 558 (1920); New Jersey v. Delaware, 291 U.S. 361, 54 S.Ct. 407, 78 L.Ed. 847 (1934); Louisiana Boundary Case, 394 U.S. 11, 89 S.Ct. 773, 22 L.Ed.2d 44 (1969).

SECTION 3. LIMITATIONS ON INCORPORATION

INTRODUCTORY NOTE

The Paquete Habana (*supra* Section 2) famously declared that "international law is part of our law." At the same time, Justice Gray suggested that a "controlling executive or legislative act or judicial decision" might override the "customs and usages of civilized nations." Technically that further statement was merely dictum, as no party in the case at bar claimed that such a controlling act existed. Yet the concept of some "controlling" authority in U.S. law defeating the application of customary international law has persisted, and it has given rise to sharp debates as to whether and when Congress and/or the President may disobey customary international law.

Should Congress be able to adopt a statute that places the United States in violation of customary international law? The Second Circuit's decision in *United States v. Yousef* (excerpted below) addresses that issue. For purposes of understanding that case, it is important to know that, over the centuries, states have developed through their practice (and in some instances, through treaties) rules on what kinds of national jurisdiction are acceptable as a matter of international law. Generally, these rules view the permissible scope of a state's exercise of national jurisdiction over persons or conduct as a function of the state's linkages with those persons or conduct. The stronger the link (e.g., regulating only conduct occurring in the state's territory or only conduct abroad undertaken by the state's own nationals), the more likely the exercise of jurisdiction will be regarded as permissible under customary international law. Where the link between the state and the person or conduct is weak or unreasonable, customary international law precludes the exercise of the jurisdiction.

What about the President? Should he or she be able to issue an executive order or decision, or adopt a policy, that places the United States in violation of customary international law? Bear in mind not only that "international law is a part of our law," but also that the President is charged under Article 2, § 3 of the U.S. Constitution with taking care that the laws be "faithfully executed." The Eleventh Circuit's decision in *Garcia-Mir v. Meese* (also below) addresses that issue, as does the commentary that follows it.

What about the courts? Can U.S. courts choose to apply or not to apply customary international law as they wish? Justice Blackmun's remarks, excerpted below, suggest that the Supreme Court at least exercises considerable discretion (not always in the manner he would have preferred). If customary international law is like federal common law, then should federal courts be allowed to construe it in whatever manner they see appropriate? Or is customary international law different because it is not formed by U.S. federal courts, but rather through the practice of countries worldwide, such that federal courts do not have the same discretion as they do for "normal" federal common law? Regardless of whether federal courts have discretion, are state courts absolutely bound to apply customary international law when it arises in cases before them, just as they would any federal common law?

RESTATEMENT (THIRD) OF THE FOREIGN RELATIONS LAW OF THE UNITED STATES §§ 114, 115

(1987).

§ 114. *Interpretation of Federal Statute in Light of International Law or Agreement*

Where fairly possible, a United States statute is to be construed so as not to conflict with international law or with an international agreement of the United States.

. . . .

§ 115. *Inconsistency Between International Law or Agreement and Domestic Law: Law of the United States*

(1)(a) An act of Congress supersedes an earlier rule of international law or a provision of an international agreement as law of the United States if the purpose of the act to supersede the earlier rule or provision is clear or if the act and the earlier rule or provision cannot be fairly reconciled.

(b) That a rule of international law or a provision of an international agreement is superseded as domestic law does not relieve the United States of its international obligation or of the consequences of a violation of that obligation.

(2) A provision of a treaty of the United States that becomes effective as law of the United States supersedes as domestic law any inconsistent preexisting provision of a law or treaty of the United States.

(3) A rule of international law or a provision of an international agreement of the United States will not be given effect as law in the United States if it is inconsistent with the United States Constitution.

UNITED STATES v. YOUSEF

327 F.3d 56 (2d Cir. 2003) (some footnotes omitted).

INTRODUCTION

. . . In the first trial, Yousef, Murad, and Wali Khan Amin Shah were tried on charges relating to a conspiracy to bomb United States commercial airliners in Southeast Asia. In the second trial, Yousef and Ismoil were tried for their involvement in the February 1993 bombing of the World Trade Center in New York City. Yousef, Ismoil, and Murad now appeal from their convictions, asserting a number of claims. Yousef and Ismoil also appeal from the District Court's denial of several of their post-judgment motions. . . .

GENERAL BACKGROUND

. . . .

I. World Trade Center Bombing

The conspiracy to bomb the World Trade Center began in the Spring of 1992, when Yousef met Ahmad Mohammad Ajaj at a terrorist training camp on the border of Afghanistan and Pakistan. After formulating their terrorist plot, Yousef and Ajaj traveled to New York together in September 1992. . . .

Once in New York, Yousef began to put together the manpower and the supplies that he would need to carry out his plan to bomb the World Trade Center. . . .

. . . .

On February 26, 1993, Yousef and Ismoil drove a bomb-laden van onto the B–2 level of the parking garage below the World Trade Center. They then set the bomb's timer to detonate minutes later. At approximately 12:18 p.m. that day, the bomb exploded, killing six people, injuring more than a thousand others, and causing widespread fear and more than $500 million in property damage.

Soon after the bombing, Yousef and Ismoil fled from the United States. Yousef and Ismoil were indicted for their participation in the bombing on March 31, 1993 and August 8, 1994, respectively. Yousef was captured in Pakistan nearly two years after the bombing, and Ismoil was arrested in Jordan a little over two years after the attack. Both were returned to the United States to answer the charges in the indictment.

II. Airline Bombing

A year and a half after the World Trade Center bombing, Yousef entered Manila, the capital of the Philippines, under an assumed name. By September 1994, Yousef had devised a plan to attack United States airliners. According to the plan, five individuals would place bombs aboard twelve United States-flag aircraft that served routes in Southeast Asia. The conspirators would board an airliner in Southeast Asia, assemble a bomb on the plane, and then exit the plane during its first layover. As the planes continued on toward their next destinations, the time-bombs would detonate. Eleven of the twelve flights targeted were ultimately destined for cities in the United States.

Yousef and his co-conspirators performed several tests in preparation for the airline bombings. In December 1994, Yousef and Wali Khan Amin Shah placed one of the bombs they had constructed in a Manila movie theater. The bomb exploded, injuring several patrons of the theater. Ten days later, Yousef planted another test bomb under a passenger's seat during the first leg of a Philippine Airlines flight from Manila to Japan. Yousef disembarked from the plane during the stopover and then made his way back to Manila. During the second leg of the flight, the bomb exploded, killing one passenger, a Japanese national, and injuring others.

The plot to bomb the United States-flag airliners was uncovered in January 1995, only two weeks before the conspirators intended to carry it out. Yousef and Murad were burning chemicals in their Manila apartment and accidentally caused a fire. An apartment security guard saw the smoke coming from the apartment and called the fire department. After the firemen left, the Philippine police arrived at the apartment, where they discovered chemicals and bomb components, a laptop computer on which Yousef had set forth the aircraft bombing plans, and other incriminating evidence. Philippine authorities arrested Murad and Shah, though Shah escaped and was not recaptured until nearly a year later. Yousef fled the country, but was captured in Pakistan the next month.

* * *

On February 21, 1996, a grand jury in the Southern District of New York filed a twenty-count superseding indictment against the defendants and others. Counts One through Eleven charged Yousef and Ismoil with various offenses arising from their participation in the February 26, 1993 bombing of the World Trade Center. Counts Twelve through Nineteen charged Yousef, Murad, and Shah with various crimes relating to their conspiracy to bomb United States airliners in Southeast Asia in 1994 and 1995. [The defendants were convicted on all counts.]

. . . .

AIRLINE BOMBING CASE

. . . .

DISCUSSION

. . . .

Yousef contends that the Government exceeded its authority by trying him in the United States for his conduct in the aircraft bombing case. In particular, he asserts that the charges alleged in Counts Twelve, Thirteen, Fourteen and Nineteen should be dismissed because 18 U.S.C. § 32 cannot be applied to conduct outside the United States.[1] He further claims that he cannot be convicted of the charge set forth in Count Nineteen because he was not "found" within the United States as required by 18 U.S.C. § 32(b).[2] Yousef also contends that his prosecution violates customary international law limiting a nation's jurisdiction to proscribe conduct outside its borders. . . .

A. Jurisdiction to Prosecute Defendants' Extraterritorial Conduct Under Federal Law

1. Applicable Law

It is beyond doubt that, as a general proposition, Congress has the authority to "enforce its laws beyond the territorial boundaries of the United States." *EEOC v. Arabian Am. Oil Co.*, 499 U.S. 244, 248 (1991). Although there is a presumption that Congress does not intend a statute to apply to conduct outside the territorial jurisdiction of the United States, *see Foley Bros. v. Filardo,* 336 U.S. 281, 285 (1949), that presumption can be overcome when Congress clearly expresses its intent to do so, *id.; Sale v. Haitian Ctrs. Council, Inc.,* 509 U.S. 155, 188 (1993); *United States v. Gatlin*, 216 F.3d 207, 211 (2d Cir. 2000). As long as Congress has indicated its intent to reach such conduct, a United States court is "bound to follow the Congressional direction unless this would violate the due process clause of the Fifth Amendment." *United States v. Pinto–Mejia*, 720 F.2d

1. [Authors' Note: 18 U.S.C. § 32(a)(2006) provided that whoever willfully

(1) sets fire to, damages, destroys, disables, or wrecks any aircraft in the special aircraft jurisdiction of the United States or any civil aircraft used, operated, or employed in interstate, overseas, or foreign air commerce; [or]

(2) places or causes to be placed a destructive device or substance in, upon, or in proximity to, or otherwise makes or causes to be made unworkable or unusable or hazardous to work or use, any such aircraft, or any part or other materials used or intended to be used in connection with the operation of such aircraft, if such placing or causing to be placed or such making or causing to be made is likely to endanger the safety of any such aircraft . . .

shall be fined under this title or imprisoned not more than twenty years or both.]

2. [Authors' Note: 18 U.S.C. § 32(b)(3) (2006) provided that whoever willfully

places or causes to be placed on a civil aircraft registered in a country other than the United States while such aircraft is in service, a device or substance which is likely to destroy that aircraft, or to cause damage to that aircraft which renders that aircraft incapable of flight or which is likely to endanger that aircraft's safety in flight . . . shall be fined under this title or imprisoned not more than twenty years, or both. There is jurisdiction over an offense under this subsection if a national of the United States was on board, or would have been on board, the aircraft; an offender is a national of the United States; or an offender is afterwards found in the United States.]

248, 259 (2d Cir. 1983) (internal quotation marks omitted). Moreover, the presumption against extraterritorial application does not apply to those "criminal statutes which are, as a class, not logically dependent on their locality for the Government's jurisdiction." *United States v. Bowman*, 260 U.S. 94, 98 (1922).

In determining whether Congress intended a federal statute to apply to overseas conduct, "an act of Congress ought never to be construed to violate the law of nations if any other possible construction remains." *McCulloch v. Sociedad Nacional de Marineros de Honduras*, 372 U.S. 10, 21 (1963) (internal quotation marks omitted). Nonetheless, in fashioning the reach of our criminal law, "Congress is not bound by international law." *Pinto-Mejia*, 720 F.2d at 259. "If it chooses to do so, it may legislate with respect to conduct outside the United States, in excess of the limits posed by international law." *Id.; see also United States v. Quemener,* 789 F.2d 145, 156 (2d Cir. 1986); *United States v. Allen,* 760 F.2d 447, 454 (2d Cir. 1985).

. . . .

3. Count Twelve

In Count Twelve, the defendants were charged with violating 18 U.S.C. § 371 by conspiring to place bombs on board aircraft and destroy aircraft, in violation of 18 U.S.C. § 32(a)(1) and (2). The District Court concluded that, because it had jurisdiction over the substantive crimes charged—including attempted destruction of aircraft in the special aircraft jurisdiction of the United States—it also had derivative jurisdiction over the conspiracy charges. United States v. Yousef, 927 F.Supp. 673, 682 (S.D.N.Y.1996).

We agree. Indeed, this conclusion is a simple application of the rule enunciated by the Supreme Court as long ago as 1922 in *Bowman*, that Congress is presumed to intend extraterritorial application of criminal statutes where the nature of the crime does not depend on the locality of the defendants' acts and where restricting the statute to United States territory would severely diminish the statute's effectiveness. *See* Bowman, 260 U.S. at 98, 43 S.Ct. 39.... In the instant case, if Congress intended United States courts to have jurisdiction over the substantive crime of placing bombs on board the aircraft at issue, it is reasonable to conclude that Congress also intended to vest in United States courts the requisite jurisdiction over an extraterritorial conspiracy to commit that crime....

4. Count Nineteen

In Count Nineteen, Yousef alone was charged with violating 18 U.S.C. § 32(b)(3) for placing a bomb on a civil aircraft registered in another country. Specifically, Yousef was charged with planting a bomb on board a Philippine Airlines flight traveling from the Philippines to Japan on December 11, 1994. The aircraft was a civil aircraft registered in the Philippines.

There is no dispute that Congress intended § 32(b) to apply to attacks on non-United States-flag aircraft. The statute applies expressly to placing a bomb on aircraft registered in other countries while in flight, no matter where the attack is committed, and provides for jurisdiction over such extraterritorial crimes whenever, inter alia, "an offender is afterwards found in the United States." 18 U.S.C. § 32(b).

. . . .

B. Exercise of United States Extraterritorial Jurisdiction and Customary International Law

On appeal, Yousef challenges the District Court's jurisdiction over Counts Twelve through Nineteen of the indictment by arguing that customary international law does not provide a basis for jurisdiction over these counts and that United States law is subordinate to customary international law and therefore cannot provide a basis for jurisdiction.[24] . . . He particularly contests the District Court's conclusion that customary international law permits the United States to prosecute him under the so-called universality principle for the bombing of Philippine Airline Flight 434 charged in Count Nineteen. Yousef claims that, absent a universally agreed-upon definition of "terrorism" and an international consensus that terrorism is a subject matter over which universal jurisdiction may be exercised, the United States cannot rest jurisdiction over him for this "terrorist" act *either* on the universality principle or on any United States positive law, which, he claims, necessarily is subordinate to customary international law.

Yousef's arguments fail. First, irrespective of whether customary international law provides a basis for jurisdiction over Yousef for Counts Twelve through Nineteen, United States law provides a separate and complete basis for jurisdiction over each of these counts and, contrary to Yousef's assertions, United States law is not subordinate to customary international law or necessarily subordinate to treaty-based international

24. Customary international law is comprised of those practices and customs that States view as obligatory and that are engaged in or otherwise acceded to by a preponderance of States in a uniform and consistent fashion. Ian Brownlie, *Principles of Public International Law* 5–7 (5th ed. 1999). *See also* Restatement (Third) § 102(2) (stating that customary international law "results from . . . [the] consistent practice of states followed by them from a sense of legal obligation"). Customary international law recognizes five bases on which a State may exercise criminal jurisdiction over a citizen or non-citizen for acts committed outside of the prosecuting State. These five well-recognized bases of criminal jurisdiction are: (1) the "objective territorial principle," which provides for jurisdiction over conduct committed outside a State's borders that has, or is intended to have, a substantial effect within its territory; (2) the "nationality principle," which provides for jurisdiction over extraterritorial acts committed by a State's own citizen; (3) the "protective principle," which provides for jurisdiction over acts committed outside the State that harm the State's interests; (4) the "passive personality principle," which provides for jurisdiction over acts that harm a State's citizens abroad; and (5) the "universality principle," which provides for jurisdiction over extraterritorial acts by a citizen or non-citizen that are so heinous as to be universally condemned by all civilized nations. *See generally In re Marc Rich & Co.,* 707 F.2d 663, 666 (2d Cir. 1983) (citing *Introductory Comment to Research on International Law, Part II, Draft Convention on Jurisdiction with Respect to Crime,* 29 Am. J. Int'l L. 435, 445 (Supp. 1935)); *United States v. Pizzarusso,* 388 F.2d 8, 10–11 (2d Cir. 1968); *see also Tel–Oren v. Libyan Arab Republic,* 726 F.2d 774, 781 n. 7 (D.C. Cir. 1984) (Edwards, J., concurring); *United States v. Marino–Garcia,* 679 F.2d 1373, 1380–83 & nn. 13–16 (11th Cir. 1982).

law and, in fact, may conflict with both. Further contrary to Yousef's claims, customary international law *does* provide a substantial basis for jurisdiction by the United States over each of these counts, although not (as the District Court held) under the universality principle.

....

1. Bases of Jurisdiction over the Counts Charged

a. Relationship between Domestic and International Law in Yousef's Prosecution

Jurisdiction over Yousef on Counts Twelve through Nineteen was based on 18 U.S.C. § 32. Yousef argues that this statute cannot give rise to jurisdiction because his prosecution thereunder conflicts with established principles of customary international law. Yousef's argument fails because, while customary international law may inform the judgment of our courts in an appropriate case, it cannot alter or constrain the making of law by the political branches of the government as ordained by the Constitution.

Principles of customary international law reflect the practices and customs of States in the international arena that are applied in a consistent fashion and that are generally recognized by what used to be called "civilized states." That is, principles of customary international law consist of the "*settled* rule[s] of international law" as recognized through "the general assent of civilized nations."[25] *The Paquete Habana,* 175 U.S. 677, 694 (1900) (emphasis added); *id.* at 686; *see generally* Ian Brownlie, *Principles of International Law* 5–7 (5th ed. 1999) (explaining generally the principles of customary international law).

It has long been established that customary international law is part of the law of the United States to the limited extent that "where there is *no treaty,* and *no controlling executive or legislative act or judicial decision,* resort must be had to the customs and usages of civilized nations." *The Paquete Habana,* 175 U.S. at 700 (emphasis added); *see also Garcia–Mir v. Meese,* 788 F.2d 1446, 1453 (11th Cir. 1986) (noting that "public international law is controlling only" in the absence of controlling positive law or judicial precedent).

While it is permissible for United States law to conflict with customary international law, where legislation is susceptible to multiple interpretations, the interpretation that does not conflict with "the law of nations" is preferred. *Murray v. Charming Betsy,* 6 U.S. (2 Cranch) 64, 118 (1804).[26] The *Charming Betsy* canon comes into play only where Con-

25. While it is not possible to claim that the practice or policies of any one country, including the United States, has such authority that the contours of customary international law may be determined by reference only to that country, it is highly unlikely that a purported principle of customary international law in direct conflict with the recognized practices and customs of the United States and/or other prominent players in the community of States could be deemed to qualify as a *bona fide* customary international law principle.

26. As explained further below, the interpretive canon established by *Charming Betsy* does not impinge upon our analysis of jurisdiction over Yousef for Counts Twelve through Nineteen because such exercise of jurisdiction is consistent with principles of customary international law.

gress's intent is ambiguous. *Attorney General of Canada v. R.J. Reynolds Tobacco Holdings, Inc.*, 268 F.3d 103, 128 (2d Cir. 2001) (stating that United States courts " 'are not to read *general words* ... without regard to the limitations customarily observed by nations upon the exercise of their powers.' " (quoting *United States v. Aluminum Co. of Am.*, 148 F.2d 416, 443 (2d Cir. 1945) (emphasis added))).

If a statute makes plain Congress's intent (instead of employing ambiguous or "general" words), then Article III courts, which can overrule Congressional enactments only when such enactments conflict with the Constitution, *see, e.g., Sinclair Refining Co. v. Atkinson*, 370 U.S. 195, 215 (1962) (stating that, "[i]n dealing with problems of interpretation and application of federal statutes, we have no power to change deliberate choices of legislative policy that Congress has made within its constitutional powers"), must enforce the intent of Congress irrespective of whether the statute conforms to customary international law. Thus the Supreme Court stated in *The Nereide*, 13 U.S. (9 Cranch) 388 (1815) (Marshall, C.J.), that while courts are "bound by the law of nations which is a part of the law of the land," Congress may "manifest [its] will" to apply a different rule "by passing an act for the purpose." *Id.* at 423. The Court reaffirmed this principle in *McCulloch v. Sociedad Nacional de Marineros de Honduras*, 372 U.S. 10 (1963), stating that Congress may enact laws superseding "the law of nations" if "the affirmative intention of the Congress [is] clearly expressed." *Id.* at 21–22; *see also, e.g., Comm. of United States Citizens Living in Nicaragua v. Reagan*, 859 F.2d 929, 939 (D.C. Cir. 1988) (holding that "under domestic law, statutes supersede customary international law" and that statutes are not subject to challenge on the basis of a violation of customary international law); *United States v. Howard–Arias*, 679 F.2d 363, 371–72 (4th Cir. 1982) (holding that "the United States may violate international law principles" if Congress enacts federal statutes that conflict with international law). It also is established that Congress "may legislate with respect to conduct outside the United States, in excess of the limits posed by international law." *United States v. Pinto–Mejia*, 720 F.2d 248, 259 (2d Cir. 1983).

In the event that there is no "controlling executive or legislative act or judicial decision" that the court must apply, *The Paquete Habana*, 175 U.S. at 700, a court should identify the norms of customary international law by looking to "the general usage and practice of nations[,] or by [looking to] judicial decisions recognizing and enforcing that law ... [, or by] consulting the works of jurists writing professedly on public law," *United States v. Smith*, 18 U.S. (5 Wheat.) 153 (1820) (Story, J.). However, materials beyond the laws and practices of States, such as the writings of jurists, may serve only as "evidence" of these principles of customary international law, to which courts may look "not for the speculations of their authors concerning what the law *ought to be*, but for trustworthy evidence of *what the law really is*." *The Paquete Habana*, 175 U.S. at 700 (emphasis added); *see also Tel–Oren v. Libyan Arab Republic*, 726 F.2d 774, 789 (D.C. Cir. 1984) (Edwards, J., concurring) (relying on *The*

Paquete Habana *for the proposition that courts should identify the "law of nations" primarily from the official acts and practices of States and, secondarily, as "evidence" of existing state practices, from the writings of scholars). We adopted the teaching of* The Paquete Habana *and* Smith *on the appropriate use of the sources of international law in* Kadic v. Karadzic, *70 F.3d 232, 238–39 (2d Cir. 1995) (quoting* Smith, *18 U.S. at 160–61), and in* Filartiga v. Pena–Irala, *630 F.2d 876 (2d Cir. 1980), in which we emphasized that, to the extent that we rely on secondary writings by publicists as evidence of international law, we do so only for evidence of "what the law* really is," id. *at 881 (emphasis added) (internal quotation marks and citation omitted).*

b. Treaty–Based Jurisdiction: The Hague and Montreal Conventions

Treaty law also may provide a basis for a State's action independent of the principles of customary international law. A treaty creates obligations in States parties to it that may differ from those of customary international law, and it generally is immaterial whether customary international law points in the same or in a different direction than the treaty obligation....

....

2. Jurisdiction over Counts Twelve through Eighteen

Jurisdiction over Counts Twelve through Eighteen is straight-forward, and we affirm both the District Court's finding of jurisdiction and its reasoning. United States domestic law provides a complete basis for jurisdiction over the conduct charged in these counts, independent of customary international law. Nevertheless, contrary to Yousef's claims, jurisdiction is consistent with three of the five principles of customary international law criminal jurisdiction—the objective, protective, and passive personality principles, described at note 24, ante.

First, jurisdiction over Counts Twelve through Eighteen is consistent with the "passive personality principle" of customary international jurisdiction because each of these counts involved a plot to bomb United States-flag aircraft that would have been carrying United States citizens and crews and that were destined for cities in the United States. Moreover, assertion of jurisdiction is appropriate under the "objective territorial principle" because the purpose of the attack was to influence United States foreign policy and the defendants intended their actions to have an effect—in this case, a devastating effect—on and within the United States. Finally, there is no doubt that jurisdiction is proper under the "protective principle" because the planned attacks were intended to affect the United States and to alter its foreign policy.

I. Jurisdiction over Count Nineteen

....

a. The District Court's Holding and Yousef's Challenges on Appeal

Count Nineteen, the bombing of Philippine Airlines Flight 434, appears to present a less straight-forward jurisdictional issue because the airplane that was bombed was not a United States-flag aircraft, it was flying between two destinations outside of the United States, and there is no evidence that any United States citizens were aboard the flight or were targets of the bombing. The District Court nevertheless concluded that jurisdiction over Yousef for the offenses charged in Count Nineteen was proper, inter alia, under the principle of "universal jurisdiction." Yousef, 927 F.Supp. at 681–82.

Yousef makes a two-part argument on appeal challenging the District Court's holding with respect to the Court's jurisdiction over Count Nineteen. First, he claims that the District Court erred in holding that the universality principle provides jurisdiction over Count Nineteen. He bases this claim on the argument that, if his placing the bomb on the Philippine Airlines plane constituted terrorism, then jurisdiction under the universality principle is improper because terrorism is not universally condemned by the community of States and, therefore, is not subject to universal jurisdiction under customary international law. Second, he argues that because customary international law does not provide for the punishment of terrorist acts under the universality principle, such failure precludes or invalidates United States laws that provide for the prosecution of such acts that occur extraterritorially.

... We hold that the District Court erred as a matter of law in relying upon the universality principle as a basis for jurisdiction over the acts charged in Count Nineteen and further hold that customary international law currently does not provide for the prosecution of "terrorist" acts under the universality principle, in part due to the failure of States to achieve anything like consensus on the definition of terrorism. However, ... we hold that Yousef's conduct charged in Count Nineteen—regardless of whether it is termed "terrorist"—constitutes the core conduct proscribed by the Montreal Convention and its implementing legislation. Accordingly, Yousef's prosecution and conviction on this Count is both consistent with and required by the United States' treaty obligations and domestic laws. We therefore reject Yousef's claim that jurisdiction over Count Nineteen was lacking and affirm the substance of the District Court's ruling.

....

To summarize our conclusions, with respect to the airline bombing trial we hold: ... The District Court had jurisdiction over the defendants' extraterritorial conduct pursuant to federal law.

RESTATEMENT (THIRD) OF THE FOREIGN RELATIONS LAW OF THE UNITED STATES § 111, cmt. c

(1987).

International law and agreements as law of the United States. ...

That international law and agreements of the United States are law of the United States means also that the President has the obligation and the necessary authority to take care that they be faithfully executed. United States Constitution, Article II, Section 2. But under the President's constitutional authority, as "sole organ of the nation in its external relations" or as Commander in Chief ..., the President has the power to take various measures including some that might constitute violations of international law by the United States. ...

GARCIA–MIR v. MEESE

788 F.2d 1446 (11th Cir. 1986) (some footnotes and citations omitted).

JOHNSON, CIRCUIT JUDGE:

These cases pose the question whether unadmitted aliens properly may claim the protection of the Due Process Clause of the United States Constitution to secure parole revocation hearings. We earlier determined that, for unadmitted aliens, the right to such hearings is not resident in the core values of the Due Process Clause *per se*. We are today asked to determine whether some actionable liberty interest exists, not based on a core value, which is nonetheless protected by the Fifth Amendment's guarantee of due process of law. For the reasons explained herein, we find it unnecessary to reach that question within the confines of this controversy. It is our opinion that, assuming that undocumented aliens may have actionable nonconstitutionally-based liberty interests, these particular aliens have not stated a viable claim for relief under the Due Process Clause. We also determine that customary international law does not afford these aliens a remedy in American courts.

I.

This is an appeal and cross-appeal from the final decision of the trial court ordering the government to prepare and implement a plan to provide individual parole revocation hearings for unadmitted aliens. The appellees-cross appellants ["appellees" or "aliens" or "Mariels"] are a certified class of Mariel Cuban refugees who were accorded a special immigration parole status by the Refugee Education Assistance Act of 1980, Pub.L. No. 96–422, § 501(e), 94 Stat. 1799 (1980), *reprinted at* 8 U.S.C.A. § 1522 note (1985).[2] The district court has broken the class into

2. The Act defines a "Cuban and Haitian entrant" as:

(1) any individual granted parole status as a Cuban/Haitian Entrant (Status Pending) or granted any other special status subsequently established under the immigration laws for

two sub-classes. The "First Group" includes those who are guilty of crimes committed in Cuba before the boat lift or who are mentally incompetent. They have never been paroled into this country. The "Second Group" consists of all other Mariels—those who, because there was no evidence of criminal or mental defect, were paroled under the provisions of the general alien parole statute, 8 U.S.C.A. § 1182(d)(5) (1985), but whose parole was subsequently revoked. All are currently detained in the Atlanta Penitentiary.

. . . .

II.

We are asked to determine: A) whether the trial court correctly found a nonconstitutionally-based liberty interest; B) whether it correctly held international law inapplicable to this case; and C) whether this matter was properly considered below as a class action. These are questions of law subject to plenary review on appeal.

. . . .

B. *International Law*:

The public law of nations was long ago incorporated into the common law of the United States. *The Paquete Habana*, 175 U.S. 677, 700 (1900); *The Nereide*, 13 U.S. (9 Cranch) 388, 423 (1815); *Restatement of the Law of Foreign Relations Law of the United States (Revised)* § 131 comment d (Tent. Draft No. 6, 1985) [hereinafter cited as "*Restatement 6*"]. To the extent possible, courts must construe American law so as to avoid violating principles of public international law. *Murray v. The Schooner Charming Betsy*, 6 U.S. (2 Cranch) 64, 102 (1804); *Lauritzen v. Larsen*, 345 U.S. 571, 578 (1953). But public international law is controlling only "where there is no treaty and no controlling executive or legislative act or judicial decision. ..." 175 U.S. at 700. Appellees argue that, because general principles of international law forbid prolonged arbitrary detention, we should hold that their current detention is unlawful.

We have previously determined that the general deportation statute, 8 U.S.C.A. § 1227(a) (1985), does not *restrict* the power of the Attorney General to detain aliens indefinitely. *Fernandez–Roque II*, 734 F.2d at 580 n. 6. But this does not resolve the question whether there has been an *affirmative legislative grant* of authority to detain. As to the First Group

nationals of Cuba or Haiti, regardless of the status of the individual at the time assistance or services are provided; and

(2) any other national of Cuba or Haiti

(A) who

(i) was paroled into the United States and has not acquired any other status under the Immigration and Nationality Act;

(ii) is the subject of exclusion or deportation proceedings under the Immigration and Nationality Act; or

(iii) has an application pending with the Immigration and Naturalization Service; and

(B) with respect to whom a final, nonappealable, and legally enforceable order of deportation or exclusion has not been entered.

there is sufficiently express evidence of congressional intent as to interdict the application of international law: Pub. L. No. 96–533, Title VII, § 716, 94 Stat. 3162 (1980), *reprinted at* 8 U.S.C.A. § 1522 note.[9]

The trial court found, correctly, that there has been no affirmative legislative grant to the Justice Department to detain the Second Group without hearings because 8 U.S.C.A. § 1227(c) does not expressly authorize indefinite detention. Thus we must look for a controlling executive act. The trial court found that there was such a controlling act in the Attorney General's termination of the status review plan and in his decision to incarcerate indefinitely pending efforts to deport. The appellees and the *amicus* challenge this by arguing that a controlling executive act can only come from an act by or expressly sanctioned by the President himself, not one of his subordinates. They rely for that proposition upon *The Paquete Habana* and upon the *Restatement of the Law of Foreign Relations Law of the United States (Revised)* § 131 comment c (Tent. Draft No. 1, 1980) [hereinafter cited as "*Restatement 1*"].

As to *The Paquete Habana*, that case involved the capture and sale as war prize of several fishing boats during the Spanish–American War. The Supreme Court found this contrary to the dictates of international law. . . . The Court held that the ships were seized in violation of international law because they were used solely for fishing. It was the *admiral* who acted in excess of the clearly delimited authority granted by the Secretary, who instructed him to act only consistent with international law. Thus *The Paquete Habana* does not support the proposition that the acts of cabinet officers cannot constitute controlling executive acts. At best it suggests that lower level officials cannot by their acts render international law inapplicable. That is not an issue in this case, where the challenge is to the acts of the Attorney General.

[The *Restatement 1*] notes that the President, "acting within his constitutional authority, may have the power under the Constitution to act in ways that constitute violations of international law by the United States." The Constitution provides for the creation of executive departments, *U.S. Const.* art. 2, § 2, and the power of the President to delegate his authority to those departments to act on his behalf is unquestioned. Likewise, in *Restatement 6*, § 135 Reporter's Note 3, the power of the President to disregard international law in service of domestic needs is

9. That enactment provides:

The Congress finds that the United States Government has already incarcerated recently arrived Cubans who are admitted criminals, are security threats, or have incited civil disturbances in Federal processing facilities. The Congress urges the Executive branch, consistent with United States law, to seek the deportation of such individuals.

Admittedly, the legislation encourages the Executive Branch to act in accordance with United States law. That would implicitly incorporate international law prohibiting detention without a hearing, assuming for argument's sake that the international norm appellees invoke actually applies to circumstances of this sort. But the language suggests that Congress clearly anticipated that the First Group was being and would continue to be held until they could be deported. Congress made no attempt to undo what the Justice Department has already done. In fact they encouraged it to deport these persons. We hold that the First Group is subject to a controlling legislative enactment and hence unprotected by international law.

reaffirmed. Thus we hold that the executive acts here evident constitute a sufficient basis for affirming the trial court's finding that international law does not control.

Even if we were to accept, *arguendo*, the appellees' interpretation of "controlling executive act," *The Paquete Habana* also provides that the reach of international law will be interdicted by a controlling judicial decision. In *Jean v. Nelson*, we interpreted the Supreme Court's decision in *Mezei* to hold that even an indefinitely incarcerated alien "could not challenge his continued detention without a hearing." 727 F.2d at 974–75. This reflects the obligation of the courts to avoid any ruling that would "inhibit the flexibility of the political branches of government to respond to changing world conditions. . . ." *Mathews v. Diaz*, 426 U.S. 67, 81 (1976). We find this decision sufficient to meet the test of *The Paquete Habana*.

. . . .

III.

For the reasons we have explained, we hold that the appellees are entitled to no relief on their claim of a nonconstitutionally-based liberty interest. To that extent, the judgment of the trial court is *reversed*. We also hold that the appellees have stated no basis for relief under international law because any rights there extant have been extinguished by controlling acts of the executive and judicial branches. To that extent the judgment of the trial court is *affirmed*. The third claim, regarding the continued maintenance of this action in a class form, is *dismissed as moot*.

AGORA: MAY THE PRESIDENT VIOLATE CUSTOMARY INTERNATIONAL LAW?*

80 Am. J. Int'l L. 913 (1986) (some footnotes omitted).

THE POWER OF THE EXECUTIVE BRANCH OF THE UNITED STATES GOVERNMENT TO VIOLATE CUSTOMARY INTERNATIONAL LAW

In its decision in *The Paquete Habana,* the United States Supreme Court wrote that customary international law is part of the law of the United States to be administered by the courts, "where there is no treaty and no controlling executive or legislative act or judicial decision." The U.S. capture of the foreign fishing vessels in question was determined to have violated customary international law protecting enemy fishing vessels in time of war, and the Supreme Court ordered that compensatory damages were due. The remedy was ordered, notwithstanding the fact that the capture was undertaken to enforce a presidential proclamation establishing a naval blockade of Cuba. The arguments of the Solicitor General and the Assistant Attorney General supporting the capture went unheeded.

Recently, the United States Court of Appeals for the Eleventh Circuit held that an action authorized by the United States Attorney General, even though it violates customary international law, is a "controlling executive ... act" that overrides customary international law to be applied in that court.[3] As a consequence, the customary international law prohibition on prolonged arbitrary detention was not available to the plaintiff Cubans who entered the United States in the 1980 "freedom flotilla" from Mariel harbor. The Supreme Court may now face the difficult question of determining the meaning of "controlling executive ... act" as used in *The Paquete Habana.* The answer to that question will determine the extent to which the United States is bound under domestic law to abide by rules of customary international law.

. . . .

How, then, does one mesh the formal structure of a domestic legal system with the community law structure of customary international law? In the international system, the United States must have the power to engage in the lawmaking process. This participation may involve actions that put the United States in violation of existing customary international law. If the executive branch is restrained by the rule that customary international law is domestic law of the United States and that it may not be violated, U.S. participation in the international system will be handicapped. The alternative solution that the executive branch has no domestic legal obligation to conform to customary international law is equally unpalatable and is contrary to the holding in *The Paquete Habana.*

Some writers maintain that the Executive is obligated under domestic law to conform to customary law, but may be exempted by statute only. Thus, a proposed violation would require the approval of Congress. In the *Garcia–Mir* case, the Eleventh Circuit found such combined action of Congress and the Executive sufficient to establish a controlling action that was determinative for some, but not all, of the issues before it.

... But in the present system, required congressional approval would place unacceptable obstacles in the way of U.S. participation in the international legal system. The evolution of the community law system would not be amenable to case-by-case authorization by Congress. Just as the international system requires that the President be able to enter into executive agreements and, apparently, to terminate treaties unilaterally, so must the President have the unilateral power to enter into the international lawmaking process. The Supreme Court appeared to have assumed that this power resides in the President when, in *The Paquete Habana,* it spoke of a "controlling executive or legislative act." Compared to making and terminating international agreements, this process is more subtle. Thus, it requires greater executive flexibility.

The plaintiffs and amicus in the *Garcia–Mir* case have argued that the Executive is bound under domestic law by customary international law

3. *Garcia–Mir v. Meese*, 788 F.2d 1446 (11th Cir. 1986), *reviewing Fernandez–Roque v. Smith*, 622 F.Supp. 887 (N.D. Ga. 1985).

unless the President officially declares that the United States no longer will be bound by it. This approach would permit the Executive to interact in the international system, but at a price. The President must squarely address the legal obligations of the United States and declare that they will be abrogated. Such direct abrogation would be extremely difficult. In fact, it would never be done. . . .

[T]here are several considerations that ought to be taken into account in a search for the appropriate solution to this debate over the power to take a "controlling . . . act." First, customary international law is law of the United States and is binding as such on all, including members of the executive branch. Second, the United States must have the power to engage effectively in the customary lawmaking process; this process requires that, from time to time, the United States break that law. Third, restrictions on those branches of the Government charged with conducting U.S. foreign relations that inhibit this function are not tolerable; members of the executive branch cannot be subject to enforcement as violators of domestic law if they are participating in the legitimate process of developing customary international law. Fourth, the authority of the executive branch to participate in legitimate customary lawmaking activities should not be so broad that, in fact, it is not bound by customary law in the domestic legal system.

Certainly, if congressional approval were given by statute for an action, that approval would eliminate any domestic law questions so long as there was no violation of the U.S. Constitution. Furthermore, violations of customary law by the President, in the face of a contrary statute, would be unacceptable. Even though an official declaration by the President might be appropriate, more flexibility in the Executive is necessary. That flexibility, however, should not extend either to all members of the executive branch or to all actions by high officials. . . .

. . . .

The President's special role in the United States Government, including the conduct of the nation's foreign relations, suggests that the President, acting alone, may have the authority under domestic law to place the United States in violation of customary international law. The President sits at the intersection of the domestic and international responsibilities of the United States. Other officers, such as the Attorney General, the Secretary of State and the Secretary of the Navy, do not have the same combination of domestic and international responsibilities that would permit them to authorize U.S. violations of international and domestic law in the circumstances under consideration here.

This interpretation of *The Paquete Habana* would best conform with that case and the system of separation of powers established by the Constitution. Requiring actual resort to the President when the United States is contemplating a violation of customary law in the absence of legislation makes likely a serious review of the domestic and international options and consequences. . . .

JONATHAN I. CHARNEY

CAN THE PRESIDENT DO NO WRONG?

. . . .

Customary international law is part of federal common law. Federal common law is binding on every executive branch official, including the President. Congress can by statute create a different rule, however, because federal common law is interstitial; it fills in gaps between statutes and gives way when an inconsistent law is enacted. Consequently, with congressional authorization, the Chief Executive can disregard any norm of customary international law. But in the face of congressional silence, he is required to respect a clearly defined and widely accepted norm of customary international law. . . .

What if the President's action falls within the scope of his plenary constitutional powers? Would not an exercise of such a power as "sole organ"—variously termed exclusive, inherent, independent or implied—prevail as against any contrary assertion of authority? Suppose, for example, that under the facts of *The Paquete Habana,* the President had ordered the seizure of coastal fishing vessels, and suppose that that act lay within his plenary power as commander-in-chief; would his act not be legal?

The answer is that the question is tautological. As the question is posed, it answers itself: the exercise of a plenary power *by definition* is not susceptible of abridgment. . . .

. . . .

We know, however, from the constitutional text that the President has no plenary power to act in violation of international law. Article I, section 8, clause 10 explicitly confers upon Congress the power to define and punish offenses against the law of nations. Congress in clear terms is directly empowered to prohibit violations of international law. It simply cannot be, therefore, that the Constitution gives the President plenary power to carry out an act that violates international law. An act of Congress that prohibits him from doing so will prevail.

. . . .

But it does not follow, one may object, that the *courts* might properly prohibit him from doing such things. After all, the powers enumerated in Article I, section 8 of the Constitution are powers conferred on Congress, not on the judiciary. For the courts to so bind the Executive, it might be argued, would be to usurp the powers of Congress.

. . . Henkin notes that federal courts have "made" law relevant to foreign affairs. In the subsequent section, concerning customary international law, he observes that international law is part of the law of the United States. An earlier draft of the revision of the *Restatement of Foreign Relations Law of the United States* saw no problem in denominating customary international law as federal common law.

. . . .

This reference to "common law" was dropped, however, and subsequent drafts have stated that customary international law is "like" federal common law. Professor Henkin elsewhere has said that he views customary international law as *sui generis* for domestic purposes. ... Whatever the vocabulary—whether customary international law is denominated as federal common law or something else—the policy considerations raised in its domestic incorporation are the same. So is the history of that process: many times since *Erie,* federal courts have applied their own rules—court-made rules, not statutes—to acts of the Executive. In this application those rules have been accorded the same legal weight as acts of Congress. As Professor Henkin has put it, "In principle, any authority exercised by the courts under their own constitutional authority ought to be equal to the authority of Congress or of the treaty-makers, and their 'enactments' entitled to equal weight. ..."

. . . .

Recognition that no plenary power inheres in the Executive to breach customary international law also removes any rationale for giving subordinates immunity. ... [T]he Chief Executive cannot give what he does not have: *no one* in the executive branch has the authority to breach customary international law in the absence of congressional authorization. ...

. . . .

This is, in any event, a question of power, not immunity. The governing law is provided by the separation-of-powers doctrine. ...

. . . .

... Changes in customary international law ordinarily involve many acts by many states, carried out over an extended period of time. The result may be a gradual alteration of existing norms, or it may be a series of acts that fall short of a new custom (or lack *opinio juris*) and thus represent violations. But the point is that the process normally is gradual. Participation in that process thus admits of little need for sole executive action. ...

It is hard to see how the distribution of authority I have outlined could have any appreciable effect on the exercise of legitimate executive "flexibility." An Executive indifferent to international law or unable to make a persuasive case for its violation could face constraints. But that is as it should be. ... If it is imperative that the United States violate customary international law, then the President should have no difficulty in persuading Congress that it is in our national interest to authorize that violation. If he cannot persuade Congress, then the United States should continue to honor international law.

. . . .

This does not mean that the President can *never* act alone. The Executive, for example, may indicate its dissent while a customary rule is being developed. That nascent rule, should it develop into a customary norm, would then have no application to acts of the United States, either internationally or domestically. This measure of discretion is permitted because, at the time the Executive objects, the rule is not yet part of customary international law, and a fortiori not yet part of federal common law, thus lacking wide acceptance and perhaps even clear definition.

... Acting without congressional consent, the President does not have the constitutional power to breach a clearly defined and widely accepted norm of customary international law. It is within the constitutional power of the courts to order any such violation stopped.

MICHAEL J. GLENNON

THE PRESIDENT AND INTERNATIONAL LAW

....

I.

....

... The federal Government is a government of enumerated powers, and each branch of government has only the powers allocated to it. No branch of government is given a power to violate international law, as such. But any act within the authority of a branch of the Government under the Constitution is valid as law of the United States and will be given effect by the courts. The question is whether such an act will be given effect if it would put the United States in violation of international law.

Not by reference to any theory, but principally by construction of the Supremacy Clause of the Constitution, the Supreme Court has established that treaties are subordinate to the Constitution. Therefore, a provision of a treaty cannot be given effect as law in the United States if it is inconsistent with the Constitution. Also, a treaty and an act of Congress have the same status in United States law, and in case of conflict between treaty and statute, the later in time prevails. Therefore, those obligated to enforce the law—the Executive and the courts—are constitutionally obligated to give effect to a treaty provision even in the face of an earlier act of Congress, and to an act of Congress even in the face of an earlier treaty provision. ... A treaty will not be given effect in the face of a "controlling," i.e., a later, act of Congress.

....

The place of customary law in the hierarchy of United States law has never been expounded by the Supreme Court. The Court has accepted that customary law is part of the law of the United States, but it has not considered whether a principle of customary law is subordinate to the Constitution, or where a principle of customary law stands in relation to a treaty or an act of Congress.

....

In the end, I think, the courts will probably conclude that customary law, being equal to treaties in international law, has the same status as treaties in the domestic legal hierarchy as well. And since the Constitution has been read to mean that treaties and statutes are equal, customary law—now read into the Supremacy Clause and treated as law of the United States for other constitutional purposes—should be put on the same level as treaties and statutes. If so, like a treaty, a principle of customary law will not be given effect if supervening national legislation is inconsistent with it. But a supervening principle of customary law will not be denied domestic effect because of some earlier act of Congress.

. . . .

II.

. . . .

. . . The President's duty to take care that the laws be faithfully executed includes not only statutes of Congress and judge-made law, but also treaties and principles of customary law. As with any other law, however, the President need not take care that international law be faithfully executed if (1) it has ceased to be law, or (2) it is superseded by some other law and it is his duty to execute the superseding law.

1. . . .

When a treaty or a principle of law terminates as a result of circumstances, or of an action by another state, it ceases to be an international obligation for the United States, and ceases to be law in the United States. There, no action by the President is involved and no question of presidential power arises. But a treaty or a principle of law can be terminated or modified also by action of the United States, and the authority to take such actions on behalf of the United States lies in the President. I think the President, as "sole organ," has constitutional authority to terminate a treaty, whether in accordance with or in violation of its terms. When the President terminates a treaty, it is no longer law of the United States, and neither the President nor the courts will give it effect.

The same is true when the President, acting within his authority as sole organ, does something that has the effect of terminating or modifying a principle of international law. . . .

In either case, I stress, the constitutional question is not whether the President has authority to violate international law; the question is whether he has constitutional authority to do the act that terminated the treaty or superseded the customary principle. . . .

2. The President need not, may not, execute a principle of international law or a provision in a treaty if it is superseded in United States law by another law that has higher or equal status. Thus, the President will not execute a treaty or customary principle that conflicts with the Constitution. The President will not execute a principle of international law if it is superseded by an intervening treaty provision or a new principle of

international law. Under established doctrine, he may not execute a treaty provision if it is superseded by an intervening act of Congress and, as indicated, the same principle would probably apply to require the President to give effect to an act of Congress that is inconsistent with a preexisting principle of customary law.

A case can be made also that, in some cases, the President can supersede a principle of international law or a treaty by law made under his own authority, in those special circumstances when the President has constitutional authority to make law in the United States. For example, the courts have found that he has such "legislative authority" to determine sovereign immunity. Legislative effect has been given to executive agreements incidental to the President's power to recognize governments, as in the Litvinov Assignment of 1933, and to agreements to settle international claims, as in the Iranian hostage accord of 1980.

... It is argued that, in his conduct of the foreign relations of the United States, the President may decide that it is in the interest of the United States to take some action without regard to international law, e.g., to overfly foreign territory without the state's consent, bring down a foreign airplane, violate a diplomat's immunity. Such acts, contrary to international law, do not ordinarily impinge on international law incorporated as domestic law in the United States. ...

....

A presidential act that terminates the obligation of the United States and therefore its place in the law of the United States, or a presidential act that makes law in the United States and supersedes a principle of customary law as United States law, is a "controlling executive act" within the meaning of *The Paquete Habana*. Perhaps, an act within the President's constitutional authority as sole organ or as commander-in-chief is controlling and will not be enjoined even if it violates a treaty or principle of law. I know of no other kind of acts that would relieve the Executive of the duty to take care that international law be faithfully executed.

III.

If I am correct, *Garcia–Mir* misinterpreted and misapplied *The Paquete Habana*. The court apparently considered any act of the President "controlling" and extended that to include an act by the Attorney General. It took the view that the President—and the Attorney General—had power "to disregard international law in service of domestic needs." There is no such principle. ... There was no suggestion that the President, acting under his constitutional power, had by executive agreement or executive order, made law that superseded the rule of international law forbidding arbitrary detention as domestic law. There was no suggestion that the President ordered the detention in the exercise of his independent constitutional authority as sole organ or as commander-in-chief.

Only such presidential acts would constitute "controlling executive acts" permitting disregard of international law as the law of this land. In the absence of such controlling acts, the court should have required the Attorney General to take care that international law be faithfully executed.

LOUIS HENKIN

In a Letter to the Editor submitted to the *American Journal of International Law*, 81 AM. J. INT'L L. 637 (1987) (footnotes omitted), one commentator rendered the following response to the trilogy of essays by Charney, Glennon, and Henkin:

[T]here are many scholars willing to write at length about *The Paquete Habana,* but few disposed to read the case from beginning to end. ... [T]he lack of attention to the case as a whole helps to perpetuate a totally unfounded, yet slavishly honored misinterpretation of the short, but notorious clause "*where there is no treaty, and no controlling executive or legislative act or judicial decision.*"

To make my point quickly, I suggest we look at the second paragraph of the dissenting opinion by Chief Justice Fuller, in which two of his brethren concurred. It is a succinct, and what we may reasonably presume to be an accurate, summary of the position of the majority. He wrote: "This court holds ... [fishing vessels exempt from seizure] not because such exemption is to be found in *any treaty, legislation, proclamation or instruction, granting it,* but on the ground that the vessels were exempt by reason of an established rule of international law applicable to them. ..."

The Chief Justice disagreed with the majority because he was unwilling to hold fishing vessels exempt from capture *unless the exemption could be found in some treaty, legislation, proclamation or instruction.* Justice Gray, writing for the majority, obviously could have held the vessels exempt from capture had an exemption been provided by a treaty or other public act. But there was no such treaty or other public act and it is to this fact that the notorious clause refers, albeit by implication rather than expressly. Properly understood, it means: where there is no treaty, and no executive or legislative act or judicial opinion, *exempting fishing vessels from capture.* ...

... The clause occurs in a paragraph that opens with an assertion justly famous: "International law is part of our law. ..." The statement, plain and unadorned, is powerful for its very simplicity. It appears to be a declaration of faith in the rule of international law by a man who sounds as if he honestly means what he says. Nevertheless, we are invited to believe [Justice Gray] was a cynic of the first rank who, having said that international law is part of our law, rushed to say in the next sentence that it could be disregarded at will, *by treaty, executive or legislative act or judicial decision.*

. . . .

It is the difference between the two views of international law that explains the meaning of the clause, and its presence in the sentence where it appears. As far as Chief Justice Fuller was concerned, fishing vessels were not exempted from capture by customary international law. Hence, such vessels were subject to capture unless there was a treaty, or controlling executive or legislative act or judicial precedent, exempting them. As far as Justice Gray was concerned, it was just the reverse. Where there was no such treaty, or controlling executive or legislative act or judicial decision, they were exempted from capture nevertheless, by a rule of customary international law.

I submit that this is the proper interpretation of the notorious clause. It remains to be seen how long (*quousque tandem*) judges and scholars will continue to abuse it, and the good name of *The Paquete Habana.*

JOSEPH MODESTE SWEENEY

RESTATEMENT (THIRD) OF THE FOREIGN RELATIONS LAW OF THE UNITED STATES § 111, cmt. c

(1987).

International law and agreements as law of the United States. The proposition that international law and agreements are law in the United States is addressed largely to the courts. In appropriate cases they apply international law or agreements without the need of enactment by Congress or proclamation by the President. . . . Much customary law and many international agreements, however, do not have the quality of law for the courts in that they do not regulate activities, relations, or interests in the United States. . . .

HARRY A. BLACKMUN, THE SUPREME COURT AND THE LAW OF NATIONS

104 Yale L.J. 39, 39–45, 49 (1994).

I. FIRST PRINCIPLES

The Declaration of Independence opens with the following memorable passage:

> When in the Course of human Events, it becomes necessary for one People to dissolve the Political Bands which have connected them with another, and to assume among the Powers of the Earth, the separate and equal Station to which the Laws of Nature and of Nature's God entitle them, *a decent Respect to the Opinions of Mankind* requires that they should declare the causes which impel them to the Separation.[1]

1. THE DECLARATION OF INDEPENDENCE para. 1 (U.S. 1776) (emphasis added).

As Professor Louis Henkin has noted, the early architects of our Nation understood that the customs of nations—the global opinions of mankind—would be binding upon the newly forged union.[2] John Jay, the first Chief Justice of the United States, observed in *Chisolm v. Georgia* that the United States "had, by taking a place among the nations of the earth, become amenable to the laws of nations."[3] Although the Constitution gives Congress the power to "define and punish ... Offenses against the Law of Nations"[4] and identifies treaties as part of "the supreme Law of the Land,"[5] the task of further defining the role of international law in the nation's legal fabric has fallen to the federal courts.

Several first principles have been established. As early as 1804, in *Murray v. Schooner Charming Betsy,* the Supreme Court recognized that "an act of congress ought never to be construed to violate the law of nations if any other possible construction remains."[6] In a trilogy of cases in the 1880's, the Court established that treaties are on equal footing with federal statutes and that, where a treaty and statute cannot be reconciled, the later in time is controlling.[7] Finally, in the case of *The Paquete Habana,*[8] decided in 1900, the Supreme Court addressed the ability of courts to enforce customary international law. In invalidating the wartime seizure of private fishing vessels as contrary to the law of nations, the Court observed: "International law is part of our law, and must be ascertained and administered by the courts. ... [W]here there is no treaty, and no controlling executive or legislative act or judicial decision, resort must be had to the customs and usages of civilized nations. ..."[9] Although commentators continue to debate the extent of executive, legislative, or judicial power to trump customary international law, the import of *The Paquete Habana* is clear: Customary international law informs the construction of domestic law, and, at least in the absence of any superseding positive law, is controlling.

The Paquete Habana left many questions unanswered, and courts since have backed away from some of that decision's more sweeping promises. The principles established during the Supreme Court's first century, however, continue to define the relationship between the law of nations and domestic American law....

---

2. *See* Louis Henkin, *A Decent Respect to the Opinions of Mankind*, 25 J. MARSHALL L. REV. 215 (1992).

3. 2 U.S. (2 Dall.) 419, 474 (1793).

4. U.S. CONST. art. I, § 8, cl. 10.

5. 5 *Id.* art. VI, cl. 2.

6. 6 U.S. (2 Cranch) 64, 118 (1804).

7. *See Head Money Cases*, 112 U.S. 580, 597–99 (1884); *Whitney v. Robertson*, 124 U.S. 190, 194 (1888); *The Chinese Exclusion Case*, 130 U.S. 581, 600, 602–03 (1889).

8. 175 U.S. 677 (1900).

9. *Id.* at 700.

II. CONSTRUING INTERNATIONAL INSTRUMENTS

A. *United States v. Alvarez–Machain*

Two Terms ago, in the case of *United States v. Alvarez–Machain,* the Supreme Court was asked to consider whether the forced abduction of a Mexican national by United States agents violated a U.S.—Mexico extradition treaty.[14] Over the vehement protest of the Mexican government, Dr. Humberto Alvarez–Machain was kidnaped in Mexico and brought to the United States to stand charges for the kidnaping, torture, and murder of a U.S. Drug Enforcement Administration agent. The district court dismissed the charges, concluding that the abduction violated the U.S.—Mexico extradition treaty.[15]

The Supreme Court disagreed, holding, by a 6–3 vote, that the abduction had not violated the extradition treaty. . . . In the absence of an express prohibition, the majority reasoned, the kidnaping must be allowed. Ignoring the hornbook principle that a treaty shall be interpreted according to its ordinary meaning and in light of its object and purpose, the majority rejected the contention that its interpretation would eviscerate the treaty's purpose,[17] even while acknowledging that the abduction "may be in violation of general international law principles."[18]

. . . .

In so doing, the Supreme Court also ignored customary international law. Quoting an article by Professor Henkin, the dissenting opinion observed that with or without an extradition treaty, abducting a person from a foreign country without the foreign government's consent " 'is a gross violation of international law and gross disrespect for a norm high in the opinion of mankind. It is a blatant violation of the territorial integrity of another state; [and] it eviscerates the [global] extradition system.' "[20] Even *with* the consent of the foreign sovereign, kidnaping a foreign national flagrantly violates peremptory human rights norms. . . .

. . . .

In my view, the Supreme Court's *Alvarez-Machain* decision did tremendous damage to the fabric of both conventional and customary international law. . . .

We perhaps can take some comfort in the fact that although the Supreme Court is the highest court in the land, its rulings are not necessarily the final word on questions of international law. The *Alvarez-Machain* decision provoked domestic and international outcry and was deemed by the Inter–American Juridical Committee to be "contrary to the

14. *See* Extradition Treaty, May 4, 1978, U.S.–Mex., 31 U.S.T. 5059.

15. *United States v. Caro–Quintero*, 745 F.Supp.599 (C.D. Cal. 1990).

17. *See Alvarez–Machain*, 112 S. Ct. at 2194.

18. *Id.* at 2196.

20. *Id.* at 2202 (quoting Henkin, *supra* note 2, at 231) (alteration in original).

rules of international law."[23] And the decision and its aftermath inspired a searching reexamination, in both Congress and the Justice Department, of the Government's kidnapping policy.[24] In June 1993, the United States and Mexico formally agreed to negotiate a ban on the practice of trans-border kidnapping.[25] Thus, as is often the case, it appears to have taken a troublesome Supreme Court decision to launch the process of bringing domestic law in line with international practice.

B. *Sale v. Haitian Centers Council, Inc.*

Last Term, the Supreme Court again was called upon to construe an international treaty, with equally disturbing results for the opinions of mankind. *Sale v. Haitian Centers Council, Inc.*[26] concerned a challenge by Haitian refugees to the U.S. policy of interdicting all Haitians who fled Haiti on the high seas and summarily returning them to Haiti, without any inquiry into their asylum claims or even their intended destination. Central to the Haitian plaintiffs' challenge was Article 33.1 of the United Nations Convention Relating to the Status of Refugees. That Article provides: "No Contracting State shall expel or return *('refouler')* a refugee in any manner whatsoever to the frontiers of territories where his life or freedom would be threatened."[27] The principle of *nonrefoulement* expressed in Article 33.1—that no refugee may be returned to a country where he will suffer persecution—guarantees one of the most fundamental international rights of refugees. More than 120 nations, including the United States, have acceded to the binding obligations of Article 33.1.[28] In 1980, Congress adopted § 243(h) of the Immigration and Nationality Act,[29] which mirrors the language of Article 33.1, in order to bring U.S. law expressly into compliance with the Refugee Convention.

In construing § 243(h) and Article 33.1 in *Haitian Centers Council,* the Court once again failed to respect its first principles of international law. Turning first to the statute, the Court remarkably applied a presumption against extraterritoriality to § 243(h) without considering the fact that the statute was enacted pursuant to a multilateral treaty, and without acknowledging the primacy of the principle of *nonrefoulement* in customary international law.[30] The Court thus ignored a maxim recognized since *Schooner Charming Betsy:* An Act of Congress—and particularly a statute enacted pursuant to a treaty—ought never to be construed

23. *Legal Opinion on the Decision of the Supreme Court of the United States of America,* CJI/Res. II–15/92, Inter–Am. Juridical Comm., OEA/ser. G/CP/doc. 2302/92 (Sept. 1, 1992), *reprinted in* 4 CRIM. L.F. 119 (1993).

24. *See Kidnapping Suspects Abroad: Hearings Before the Subcomm. on Civil and Constitutional Rights of the House Comm. on the Judiciary,* 102d Cong., 2d Sess. (1992); Paul Hoffman, *U.S. Must Not Kidnap Suspects Abroad,* NEWSDAY, Dec. 2, 1993, at 114 (noting internal Justice Department review ordered by Attorney General Janet Reno in response to *Alvarez-Machain*).

25. Steven A. Holmes, *U.S. Gives Mexico Abduction Pledge,* N.Y. TIMES, June 22, 1993, at A11.

26. 113 S. Ct. 2549 (1993).

27. Convention Relating to the Status of Refugees, July 28, 1951, art. 33.1, 19 U.S.T. 6259, 6276, 189 U.N.T.S. 150, 176, *as incorporated in* Protocol Relating to the Status of Refugees, Jan. 31, 1967, 19 U.S.T. 6223, 606 U.N.T.S. 267.

28. U.S. DEP'T OF STATE, TREATIES IN FORCE 399–400 (1994).

29. Refugee Act of 1980, Pub. L. No. 96–212, § 203(e), 94 Stat. 107 (codified as amended at 8 U.S.C. § 1253(h) (1988 & Supp. IV 1992)).

30. *See Haitian Ctrs. Council,* 113 S. Ct. at 2563.

to violate a coextensive treaty or otherwise to contradict customary international law.

. . . .

Do not the decisions in the *Alvarez-Machain* and *Haitian Centers Council* cases reflect a disturbing disregard on the part of the Supreme Court of its obligations when construing international law? Treaties are contracts among nations and thus must be interpreted with sensitivity toward the customs of the world community. In each of these cases, however, the Court ignored its first principles and construed the challenged treaty in a manner directly contrary to the opinions of mankind.

. . . .

IV. CONCLUSION

Professor Henkin poignantly has observed that "almost all nations observe almost all principles of international law and almost all of their obligations almost all of the time."[71] Unfortunately, as the cases I have discussed illustrate, the Supreme Court's own recent record in the area is somewhat more qualified. At best, I would say that the present Supreme Court enforces *some* principles of international law and *some* of its obligations *some* of the time.

. . . .

Never before, however, has an understanding of international law been more important. During my thirty-four years of service on the federal bench, the United States has become economically and politically intertwined with the rest of the world as never before. International human rights conventions—still a relatively new idea when I came to the bench in 1959—have created mutual obligations that are accepted throughout the world. As we approach the 100th anniversary of *The Paquete Habana,* then, it perhaps is appropriate to remind ourselves that the United States is part of the global community, that "[i]nternational law *is* part of our law," and that courts should construe our statutes, our treaties, and our Constitution, where possible, consistently with "the customs and usages of civilized nations."[72] Although the recent decisions of the Supreme Court do not offer much hope for the immediate future, I look forward to the day when the majority of the Supreme Court will inform almost all of its decisions almost all of the time with a decent respect to the opinions of mankind.

CONCLUDING NOTES

1. *Statutes and Customary International Law.* When a treaty conflicts with a statute, the later-in-time doctrine usually resolves the conflict (*see* Chapter 3, Section 6). However, as noted in Section 1 of this chapter, customary international law has not been given the status of "supreme law of

71. LOUIS HENKIN, HOW NATIONS BEHAVE 47 (2d ed. 1979).

72. *The Paquete Habana*, 175 U.S. 677, 700 (1900) (emphasis added).

the land" by the Constitution, despite some supportive rhetoric. Thus, customary international law may be ousted for purposes of litigation in U.S. courts by an inconsistent statute. The question may arise most frequently in the kind of jurisdictional context found in *Yousef* because the United States has historically taken a relatively aggressive view of its jurisdiction and the relevant international law is often customary in character. *See* L. Littlejohn & Co. v. United States, 270 U.S. 215, 226–27, 46 S.Ct. 244, 70 L.Ed. 553 (1926) (affirming the power of Congress to make laws permitting the seizure of enemy ships even in contravention of recognized international law). Cases like *Yousef* make the superiority of (constitutional) statutes unequivocal, and irrespective of the enactment's relative timing, but note that Section 115 of the *Restatement (Third)* says only that "[a]n act of Congress supersedes an *earlier* rule of international law" (emphasis added). *See also* United States v. Georgescu, 723 F.Supp. 912, 921 (E.D.N.Y. 1989) (upholding jurisdiction over defendant who committed sexual assault on airplane based on controlling domestic legislation enacted subsequent to arguably conflicting obligations arising under customary international law and Tokyo Convention; "[w]hile the courts must make a fair effort to interpret domestic law in a way consistent with international obligations ... in the event of irreconcilable conflict, the courts are bound to apply domestic law if it was passed more recently").

2. *The President and Customary International Law*. The President may be confronted with a norm of customary international law in many different ways; constraints imposed by human rights law and the laws of war are touched on in remaining sections of this chapter. In still other instances, customary international law is just part of the overall context. Customary international law may appear to temper the exercise of presidential authority under a statute, for example. In still other instances, customary international law is entangled with treaty-related obligations. For instance, an extremely important norm of customary international law is the rule of *pacta sunt servanda* (agreements must be kept); indeed, some view that norm as central to the functioning of the international legal system. *Pacta sunt servanda* has been incorporated into the Vienna Convention on the Law of Treaties, May 23, 1969, 1155 U.N.T.S. 331. While the United States has not yet joined that convention, it does regard *pacta sunt servanda* as a rule of customary international law. If an international tribunal decides that the United States must undertake a certain action as part of its obligation under a treaty, there would appear to be obligations for the United States arising under both treaty law and customary international law. Is the President entitled, or even authorized, to see that these obligations are given effect? How may he do so? Does he have the power to instruct state or federal courts to comply with such decisions? Can he refuse to give effect to such obligations?

This issue squarely arose in a series of cases in the late 1990s and early 2000s involving foreign nationals who had been sentenced to death by various U.S. state courts, in apparent violation of the Vienna Convention on Consular Relations (as construed by the International Court of Justice). *See* Chapter 6, Section 8.

3. *The Courts and Customary International Law*. The excerpt above from Justice Blackmun seems to present a cautiously optimistic acceptance of

the law of nations in modern jurisprudence. The historical record shows that some U.S. judges have tended to employ international legal norms to leaven judgments which might have come out the same way had the international legal component been deleted. Even the landmark decision in *The Paquete Habana* could have been decided simply on a narrow interpretation of the applicable presidential proclamation, without direct recourse to the law of nations. How do you see U.S. courts treating customary international law? Should it be viewed as judges merely bolstering an argument that would have come out the same way in the absence of customary international law? Is it simply a sly tribute to the judge's broad scholarship and erudition? Is it a significant reflection of broad judicial vision that international law should be allowed to flourish by planting some of its roots in fertile American jurisprudential soil?

SECTION 4. USE OF INTERNATIONAL CUSTOM FOR CONSTITUTIONAL INTERPRETATION

INTRODUCTORY NOTE

To what extent should Congress, the President, or U.S. courts use customary international law when interpreting the U.S. Constitution? If there is an open-textured term in the Constitution, one that appears to invite reasoning based on broad notions of justice, equity, or humanity, is it appropriate to look to the norms that regulate relations among countries? Or is it wholly inappropriate to use the views of other countries to inform our understanding of an instrument drafted by Americans to govern Americans—given that the Constitution is not only hierarchically superior to customary international law, but also to decisions by the political branches that U.S. courts have held may themselves trump international law?

HARRY A. BLACKMUN, THE SUPREME COURT AND THE LAW OF NATIONS

104 Yale L.J. 39, 45–49 (1994).

III. RESPECT FOR THE LAW OF NATIONS IN CONSTITUTIONAL LAW

Although questions of international law typically arise before the Court in cases involving the construction of international conventions, the law of nations is implicated in Supreme Court jurisprudence in other situations as well. International law can and should inform the interpretation of various clauses of the Constitution, notably the Due Process Clause and the Eighth Amendment prohibition against cruel and unusual punishments. I thus turn to a second area where the Court has failed to inform its decisions with a "decent respect to the opinions of mankind": the execution of juvenile offenders.

For nearly half a century, the Supreme Court has acknowledged that the Eighth Amendment's Cruel and Unusual Punishments Clause "must draw its meaning from evolving standards of decency that mark the progress of a maturing society."[43] The drafters of the Amendment were concerned, at root, with "the dignity of man,"[44] and understood that "evolving standards of decency" should be measured, in part, against international norms. Thus, in cases striking down the death penalty as a punishment for rape[45] or for unintentional killings,[46] the Court has looked to both domestic custom and the "climate of international opinion" to determine what punishments are cruel and unusual.[47]

Taking international law seriously where the death penalty is concerned, of course, draws into question the United States' entire capital punishment enterprise. According to Amnesty International, more than fifty countries (including almost all of Western Europe) have abolished the death penalty entirely, and thirty-seven others either have ceased imposing it or have limited its imposition to extraordinary crimes.[48] Even those countries that continue to impose the death penalty almost universally condemn the execution of juvenile offenders.[49] They do so in recognition of the fact that juveniles are too young, and too capable of growth and development, to act with the culpability necessary to justify society's ultimate punishment. The United States, however, persistently has defended its "right" to sentence juvenile offenders to death.

. . . .

Refusing to consider international practice in construing the Eighth Amendment is convenient for a Court that wishes to avoid conflict between the death penalty and the Constitution. But it is not consistent with this Court's established construction of the Eighth Amendment. If the substance of the Eighth Amendment is to turn on the "evolving standards of decency" of the civilized world, there can be no justification for limiting judicial inquiry to the opinions of the United States. Under the principles set forth in *The Paquete Habana,* interpretation of the Eighth Amendment, no less than interpretations of treaties and statutes, should be informed by a decent respect for the global opinions of mankind.

I am confident, however, that at some point the courts and the country will come to appreciate that the execution of juvenile offenders—and the imposition of the death penalty generally—is no more tolerable than other violations of international law.

ROPER v. SIMMONS

543 U.S. 551, 125 S.Ct. 1183, 161 L.Ed.2d 1 (2005).

JUSTICE KENNEDY delivered the opinion of the Court.

This case requires us to address, for the second time in a decade and a half, whether it is permissible under the Eighth and Fourteenth Amend-

43. *Trop v. Dulles*, 356 U.S. 86, 101 (1958) (plurality opinion).

44. *Id.* at 100.

45. *Coker v. Georgia*, 433 U.S. 584 (1977).

46. *Enmund v. Florida*, 458 U.S. 782 (1982).

47. *Coker*, 433 U.S. at 596 n.10.

48. *See* INTERNATIONAL SECRETARIAT, AMNESTY INT'L, THE DEATH PENALTY: LIST OF ABOLITIONIST AND RETENTIONIST COUNTRIES 1 (1994).

49. *See* INTERNATIONAL SECRETARIAT, AMNESTY, INT'L, OPEN LETTER TO THE PRESIDENT ON THE DEATH PENALTY 8 (1994) [hereinafter OPEN LETTER].

ments to the Constitution of the United States to execute a juvenile offender who was older than 15 but younger than 18 when he committed a capital crime. In *Stanford v. Kentucky*, 492 U.S. 361 (1989), a divided Court rejected the proposition that the Constitution bars capital punishment for juvenile offenders in this age group. We reconsider the question.

I

At the age of 17, when he was still a junior in high school, Christopher Simmons, the respondent here, committed murder. About nine months later, after he had turned 18, he was tried and sentenced to death. There is little doubt that Simmons was the instigator of the crime. Before its commission Simmons said he wanted to murder someone. In chilling, callous terms he talked about his plan, discussing it for the most part with two friends, Charles Benjamin and John Tessmer, then aged 15 and 16 respectively. Simmons proposed to commit burglary and murder by breaking and entering, tying up a victim, and throwing the victim off a bridge. Simmons assured his friends they could "get away with it" because they were minors.

The three met at about 2 a.m. on the night of the murder, but Tessmer left before the other two set out. (The State later charged Tessmer with conspiracy, but dropped the charge in exchange for his testimony against Simmons.) Simmons and Benjamin entered the home of the victim, Shirley Crook, after reaching through an open window and unlocking the back door. Simmons turned on a hallway light. Awakened, Mrs. Crook called out, "Who's there?" In response Simmons entered Mrs. Crook's bedroom, where he recognized her from a previous car accident involving them both. Simmons later admitted this confirmed his resolve to murder her.

Using duct tape to cover her eyes and mouth and bind her hands, the two perpetrators put Mrs. Crook in her minivan and drove to a state park. They reinforced the bindings, covered her head with a towel, and walked her to a railroad trestle spanning the Meramec River. There they tied her hands and feet together with electrical wire, wrapped her whole face in duct tape and threw her from the bridge, drowning her in the waters below.

. . . .

II

. . . .

The prohibition against "cruel and unusual punishments," like other expansive language in the Constitution, must be interpreted according to its text, by considering history, tradition, and precedent, and with due regard for its purpose and function in the constitutional design. To implement this framework we have established the propriety and affirmed the necessity of referring to "the evolving standards of decency that mark the progress of a maturing society" to determine which punishments are so disproportionate as to be cruel and unusual. *Trop v. Dulles*, 356 U.S. 86, 100–101 (1958) (plurality opinion).

In *Thompson v. Oklahoma*, 487 U.S. 815 (1988), a plurality of the Court determined that our standards of decency do not permit the execution of any offender under the age of 16 at the time of the crime. *Id.*, at 818–838 (opinion of STEVENS, J., joined by Brennan, Marshall, and Blackmun, JJ.). The plurality opinion explained that no death penalty State that had given express consideration to a minimum age for the death penalty had set the age lower than 16. *Id.*, at 826–829. The plurality also observed that "[t]he conclusion that it would offend civilized standards of decency to execute a person who was less than 16 years old at the time of his or her offense is consistent with the views that have been expressed by respected professional organizations, by other nations that share our Anglo–American heritage, and by the leading members of the Western European community." *Id.*, at 830. The opinion further noted that juries imposed the death penalty on offenders under 16 with exceeding rarity; the last execution of an offender for a crime committed under the age of 16 had been carried out in 1948, 40 years prior. *Id.*, at 832–833.

Bringing its independent judgment to bear on the permissibility of the death penalty for a 15–year-old offender, the *Thompson* plurality stressed that "[t]he reasons why juveniles are not trusted with the privileges and responsibilities of an adult also explain why their irresponsible conduct is not as morally reprehensible as that of an adult." *Id.*, at 835. According to the plurality, the lesser culpability of offenders under 16 made the death penalty inappropriate as a form of retribution, while the low likelihood that offenders under 16 engaged in "the kind of cost-benefit analysis that attaches any weight to the possibility of execution" made the death penalty ineffective as a means of deterrence. *Id.*, at 836–838. With Justice O'CONNOR concurring in the judgment on narrower grounds, *id.*, at 848–859, the Court set aside the death sentence that had been imposed on the 15–year-old offender.

The next year, in *Stanford v. Kentucky*, 492 U.S. 361 (1989), the Court, over a dissenting opinion joined by four Justices, referred to contemporary standards of decency in this country and concluded the Eighth and Fourteenth Amendments did not proscribe the execution of juvenile offenders over 15 but under 18. The Court noted that 22 of the 37 death penalty States permitted the death penalty for 16–year-old offenders, and, among these 37 States, 25 permitted it for 17–year-old offenders. These numbers, in the Court's view, indicated there was no national consensus "sufficient to label a particular punishment cruel and unusual." *Id.*, at 370–371. . . .

The same day the Court decided *Stanford*, it held that the Eighth Amendment did not mandate a categorical exemption from the death penalty for the mentally retarded. *Penry v. Lynaugh*, 492 U.S. 302 (1989). In reaching this conclusion it stressed that only two States had enacted laws banning the imposition of the death penalty on a mentally retarded person convicted of a capital offense. *Id.*, at 334. According to the Court, "the two state statutes prohibiting execution of the mentally retarded, even when added to the 14 States that have rejected capital punishment completely, [did] not provide sufficient evidence at present of a national consensus." *Ibid.*

Three Terms ago the subject was reconsidered in *Atkins*. We held that standards of decency have evolved since *Penry* and now demonstrate that the execution of the mentally retarded is cruel and unusual punishment. . . .

. . . .

Just as the *Atkins* Court reconsidered the issue decided in *Penry*, we now reconsider the issue decided in *Stanford*. The beginning point is a review of objective indicia of consensus, as expressed in particular by the enactments of legislatures that have addressed the question. These data give us essential instruction. We then must determine, in the exercise of our own independent judgment, whether the death penalty is a disproportionate punishment for juveniles.

III

A

The evidence of national consensus against the death penalty for juveniles is similar, and in some respects parallel, to the evidence *Atkins* held sufficient to demonstrate a national consensus against the death penalty for the mentally retarded. When *Atkins* was decided, 30 States prohibited the death penalty for the mentally retarded. This number comprised 12 that had abandoned the death penalty altogether, and 18 that maintained it but excluded the mentally retarded from its reach. 536 U.S., at 313–315. By a similar calculation in this case, 30 States prohibit the juvenile death penalty, comprising 12 that have rejected the death penalty altogether and 18 that maintain it but, by express provision or judicial interpretation, exclude juveniles from its reach. *Atkins* emphasized that even in the 20 States without formal prohibition, the practice of executing the mentally retarded was infrequent. Since *Penry*, only five States had executed offenders known to have an IQ under 70. 536 U.S., at 316. In the present case, too, even in the 20 States without a formal prohibition on executing juveniles, the practice is infrequent. Since *Stanford*, six States have executed prisoners for crimes committed as juveniles. In the past 10 years, only three have done so: Oklahoma, Texas, and Virginia.

. . . .

Petitioner cannot show national consensus in favor of capital punishment for juveniles but still resists the conclusion that any consensus exists against it. Petitioner supports this position with, in particular, the observation that when the Senate ratified the International Covenant on Civil and Political Rights (ICCPR), Dec. 19, 1966, 999 U.N.T.S. 171 (entered into force Mar. 23, 1976), it did so subject to the President's proposed reservation regarding Article 6(5) of that treaty, which prohibits capital punishment for juveniles. Brief for Petitioner 27. This reservation at best provides only faint support for petitioner's argument. First, the reservation was passed in 1992; since then, five States have abandoned capital punishment for juveniles. Second, Congress considered the issue when enacting the Federal Death Penalty Act in 1994, and determined that the death penalty should not extend to juveniles. See 18 U.S.C. § 3591. The reservation to Article 6(5) of the ICCPR provides minimal evidence that there is not now a national consensus against juvenile executions.

As in *Atkins*, the objective indicia of consensus in this case—the rejection of the juvenile death penalty in the majority of States; the infrequency of its use even where it remains on the books; and the consistency in the trend toward abolition of the practice—provide sufficient evidence that today our society views juveniles, in the words *Atkins* used respecting the mentally retarded, as "categorically less culpable than the average criminal." 536 U.S., at 316.

B

A majority of States have rejected the imposition of the death penalty on juvenile offenders under 18, and we now hold this is required by the Eighth Amendment.

Because the death penalty is the most severe punishment, the Eighth Amendment applies to it with special force. *Thompson*, 487 U.S., at 856 (O'CONNOR, J., concurring in judgment). Capital punishment must be limited to those offenders who commit "a narrow category of the most serious crimes" and whose extreme culpability makes them "the most deserving of execution." *Atkins, supra*, at 319. . . .

Three general differences between juveniles under 18 and adults demonstrate that juvenile offenders cannot with reliability be classified among the worst offenders. First, as any parent knows and as the scientific and sociological studies respondent and his *amici* cite tend to confirm, "[a] lack of maturity and an underdeveloped sense of responsibility are found in youth more often than in adults and are more understandable among the young. These qualities often result in impetuous and ill-considered actions and decisions." *Johnson, supra*, at 367. . . .

The second area of difference is that juveniles are more vulnerable or susceptible to negative influences and outside pressures, including peer pressure. *Eddings, supra*, at 115 ("[Y]outh is more than a chronological fact. . . .")

The third broad difference is that the character of a juvenile is not as well formed as that of an adult. The personality traits of juveniles are more transitory, less fixed. See generally E. Erikson, Identity: Youth and Crisis (1968).

These differences render suspect any conclusion that a juvenile falls among the worst offenders. The susceptibility of juveniles to immature and irresponsible behavior means "their irresponsible conduct is not as morally reprehensible as that of an adult." *Thompson, supra*, at 835 (plurality opinion). Their own vulnerability and comparative lack of control over their immediate surroundings mean juveniles have a greater claim than adults to be forgiven for failing to escape negative influences in their whole environment. See *Stanford*, 492 U.S., at 395 (Brennan, J., dissenting). The reality that juveniles still struggle to define their identity means it is less supportable to conclude that even a heinous crime committed by a juvenile is evidence of irretrievably depraved character. . . .

. . . .

IV

Our determination that the death penalty is disproportionate punishment for offenders under 18 finds confirmation in the stark reality that the United States is the only country in the world that continues to give official sanction to the juvenile death penalty. This reality does not become controlling, for the task of interpreting the Eighth Amendment remains our responsibility. Yet at least from the time of the Court's decision in *Trop*, the Court has referred to the laws of other countries and to international authorities as instructive for its interpretation of the Eighth Amendment's prohibition of "cruel and unusual punishments." 356 U.S., at 102–103 (plurality opinion) ("The civilized nations of the world are in virtual unanimity that statelessness is not to be imposed as punishment for crime"); see also *Atkins, supra*, at 317, n. 21 (recognizing that "within the world community, the imposition of the death penalty for crimes committed by mentally retarded offenders is overwhelmingly disapproved"); *Thompson, supra*, at 830–831, and n. 31 (plurality opinion) (noting the abolition of the juvenile death penalty "by other nations that share our Anglo–American heritage, and by the leading members of the Western European community," and observing that "[w]e have previously recognized the relevance of the views of the international community in determining whether a punishment is cruel and unusual"); *Enmund, supra*, at 796–797, n. 22 (observing that "the doctrine of felony murder has been abolished in England and India, severely restricted in Canada and a number of other Commonwealth countries, and is unknown in continental Europe"); *Coker, supra*, at 596, n. 10 (plurality opinion) ("It is . . . not irrelevant here that out of 60 major nations in the world surveyed in 1965, only 3 retained the death penalty for rape where death did not ensue").

As respondent and a number of *amici* emphasize, Article 37 of the United Nations Convention on the Rights of the Child, which every country in the world has ratified save for the United States and Somalia, contains an express prohibition on capital punishment for crimes committed by juveniles under 18. United Nations Convention on the Rights of the Child, Art. 37, Nov. 20, 1989, 1577 U.N.T.S. 3, 28 I.L.M. 1448, 1468–1470 (entered into force Sept. 2, 1990); Brief for Respondent 48; Brief for European Union et al. as *Amici Curiae* 12–13; Brief for President James Earl Carter, Jr., et al. as *Amici Curiae* 9; Brief for Former U.S. Diplomats Morton Abramowitz et al. as *Amici Curiae* 7; Brief for Human Rights Committee of the Bar of England and Wales et al. as *Amici Curiae* 13–14. No ratifying country has entered a reservation to the provision prohibiting the execution of juvenile offenders. Parallel prohibitions are contained in other significant international covenants. See ICCPR, Art. 6(5), 999 U.N.T.S., at 175 (prohibiting capital punishment for anyone under 18 at the time of offense) (signed and ratified by the United States subject to a reservation regarding Article 6(5), as noted, *supra*); American Convention on Human Rights: Pact of San Jose, Costa Rica, Art. 4(5), Nov. 22, 1969, 1144 U.N.T.S. 146 (entered into force July 19, 1978) (same); African Charter on the Rights and Welfare of the Child, Art. 5(3), OAU Doc. CAB/LEG/ 24.9/49 (1990) (entered into force Nov. 29, 1999) (same).

Respondent and his *amici* have submitted, and petitioner does not contest, that only seven countries other than the United States have executed juvenile offenders since 1990: Iran, Pakistan, Saudi Arabia, Yemen, Nigeria, the Democratic Republic of Congo, and China. Since then each of these countries has either abolished capital punishment for juveniles or made public disavowal of the practice. Brief for Respondent 49–50. In sum, it is fair to say that the United States now stands alone in a world that has turned its face against the juvenile death penalty.

Though the international covenants prohibiting the juvenile death penalty are of more recent date, it is instructive to note that the United Kingdom abolished the juvenile death penalty before these covenants came into being. The United Kingdom's experience bears particular relevance here in light of the historic ties between our countries and in light of the Eighth Amendment's own origins. The Amendment was modeled on a parallel provision in the English Declaration of Rights of 1689, which provided: "[E]xcessive Bail ought not to be required nor excessive Fines imposed; nor cruel and unusual Punishments inflicted." 1 W. & M., ch. 2, § 10, in 3 Eng. Stat. at Large 441 (1770); see also *Trop, supra*, at 100 (plurality opinion). As of now, the United Kingdom has abolished the death penalty in its entirety; but, decades before it took this step, it recognized the disproportionate nature of the juvenile death penalty; and it abolished that penalty as a separate matter. . . .

It is proper that we acknowledge the overwhelming weight of international opinion against the juvenile death penalty, resting in large part on the understanding that the instability and emotional imbalance of young people may often be a factor in the crime. See Brief for Human Rights

Committee of the Bar of England and Wales et al. as *Amici Curiae* 10–11. The opinion of the world community, while not controlling our outcome, does provide respected and significant confirmation for our own conclusions.

Over time, from one generation to the next, the Constitution has come to earn the high respect and even, as Madison dared to hope, the veneration of the American people. See The Federalist No. 49, p. 314 (C. Rossiter ed.1961). The document sets forth, and rests upon, innovative principles original to the American experience, such as federalism; a proven balance in political mechanisms through separation of powers; specific guarantees for the accused in criminal cases; and broad provisions to secure individual freedom and preserve human dignity. These doctrines and guarantees are central to the American experience and remain essential to our present-day self-definition and national identity. Not the least of the reasons we honor the Constitution, then, is because we know it to be our own. It does not lessen our fidelity to the Constitution or our pride in its origins to acknowledge that the express affirmation of certain fundamental rights by other nations and peoples simply underscores the centrality of those same rights within our own heritage of freedom.

* * *

The Eighth and Fourteenth Amendments forbid imposition of the death penalty on offenders who were under the age of 18 when their crimes were committed. The judgment of the Missouri Supreme Court setting aside the sentence of death imposed upon Christopher Simmons is affirmed.

It is so ordered.

. . . .

JUSTICE SCALIA, with whom THE CHIEF JUSTICE and JUSTICE THOMAS join, dissenting.

In urging approval of a constitution that gave life-tenured judges the power to nullify laws enacted by the people's representatives, Alexander Hamilton assured the citizens of New York that there was little risk in this, since "[t]he judiciary . . . ha[s] neither FORCE nor WILL but merely judgment." The Federalist No. 78, p. 465 (C. Rossiter ed.1961). But Hamilton had in mind a traditional judiciary, "bound down by strict rules and precedents which serve to define and point out their duty in every particular case that comes before them." *Id.,* at 471. Bound down, indeed. What a mockery today's opinion makes of Hamilton's expectation, announcing the Court's conclusion that the meaning of our Constitution has changed over the past 15 years—not, mind you, that this Court's decision 15 years ago was *wrong*, but that the Constitution *has changed*. The Court reaches this implausible result by purporting to advert, not to the original meaning of the Eighth Amendment, but to "the evolving standards of decency," *ante* (internal quotation marks omitted), of our national society. It then finds, on the flimsiest of grounds, that a national consensus which could not be perceived in our people's laws barely 15 years ago now solidly exists. Worse still, the Court says in so many words that what our people's laws say about the issue does not, in the last analysis, matter: "[I]n the end our own judgment will be brought to bear on the question of the acceptability of the death penalty under the Eighth Amendment." *Ante* (internal quotation marks omitted). The Court thus proclaims itself sole arbiter of our Nation's moral standards—and in the course of discharging that awesome responsibility purports to take guidance from the views of foreign courts and legislatures. Because I do not believe that the meaning of our Eighth Amendment, any more than the meaning of other provisions of our Constitution, should be determined by the subjective views of five Members of this Court and like-minded foreigners, I dissent.

. . . .

III

Though the views of our own citizens are essentially irrelevant to the Court's decision today, the views of other countries and the so-called international community take center stage.

The Court begins by noting that "Article 37 of the United Nations Convention on the Rights of the Child, [1577 U.N.T.S. 3, 28 I.L.M. 1448, 1468–1470, entered into force Sept. 2, 1990,] which every country in the world has ratified *save for the United States* and Somalia, contains an express prohibition on capital punishment for crimes committed by juveniles under 18." *Ante* (emphasis added). The Court also discusses the International Covenant on Civil and Political Rights (ICCPR), December 19, 1966, 999 U.N.T.S. 175, *ante*, which the Senate ratified only subject to a reservation that reads:

> "The United States reserves the right, subject to its Constitutional constraints, to impose capital punishment on any person (other than a pregnant woman) duly convicted under existing or future laws permitting the imposition of capital punishment, including such punishment for crimes committed by persons below eighteen years of age." Senate Committee on Foreign Relations, International Covenant on Civil and Political Rights, S. Exec. Rep. No. 102–23, 11 (1992).

Unless the Court has added to its arsenal the power to join and ratify treaties on behalf of the United States, I cannot see how this evidence favors, rather than refutes, its position. That the Senate and the President—those actors our Constitution empowers to enter into treaties, see Art. II, § 2—have declined to join and ratify treaties prohibiting execution of under—18 offenders can only suggest that *our country* has either not reached a national consensus on the question, or has reached a consensus contrary to what the Court announces. That the reservation to the ICCPR was made in 1992 does not suggest otherwise, since the reservation still remains in place today. It is also worth noting that, in addition to barring the execution of under—18 offenders, the United Nations Convention on the Rights of the Child prohibits punishing them with life in prison without the possibility of release. If we are truly going to get in line with the international community, then the Court's reassurance that the death penalty is really not needed, since "the punishment of life imprisonment without the possibility of parole is itself a severe sanction," *ante*, gives little comfort.

It is interesting that whereas the Court is not content to accept what the States of our Federal Union *say*, but insists on inquiring into what they *do* (specifically, whether they in fact *apply* the juvenile death penalty that their laws allow), the Court is quite willing to believe that every foreign nation—of whatever tyrannical political makeup and with however subservient or incompetent a court system—in fact *adheres* to a rule of no death penalty for offenders under 18. Nor does the Court inquire into how many of the countries that have the death penalty, but have forsworn (on paper at least) imposing that penalty on offenders under 18, have what no State of this country can constitutionally have: a *mandatory* death penalty for certain crimes, with no possibility of mitigation by the sentencing authority, for youth or any other reason. I suspect it is most of them. See, *e.g.,* R. Simon & D. Blaskovich, A Comparative Analysis of Capital Punishment: Statutes, Policies, Frequencies, and Public Attitudes the World Over 25, 26, 29 (2002). To forbid the death penalty for juveniles under such a system may be a good idea, but it says nothing about our system, in which the sentencing authority, typically a jury, always can, and almost always does, withhold the death penalty from an under—18 offender except, after considering all the circumstances, in the rare cases where it is warranted. The foreign authorities, in other words, do not even speak to the issue before us here.

More fundamentally, however, the basic premise of the Court's argument—that American law should conform to the laws of the rest of the world—ought to be rejected out of hand. In fact the Court itself does not believe it. In many significant respects the laws of most other countries differ from our law—including not only such explicit provisions of our Constitution as the right to jury trial and grand jury indictment, but even many interpretations of the Constitution prescribed by this Court itself. The Court-pronounced exclusionary rule, for example, is distinctively American. When we adopted that rule in *Mapp v. Ohio*, 367 U.S. 643, 655 (1961), it was "unique to American jurisprudence." *Bivens v. Six Unknown Fed. Narcotics Agents*, 403 U.S. 388, 415 (1971) (Burger, C. J., dissenting). Since then a categorical exclusionary rule has been "universally rejected" by other countries, including those with rules prohibiting illegal searches and police misconduct, despite the fact that none of these countries "appears to have any alternative form of discipline for police that is effective in preventing search violations." Bradley, *Mapp* Goes Abroad, 52 Case W. Res. L.Rev. 375, 399–400 (2001). England, for example, rarely excludes evidence found during an illegal search or seizure and has only recently begun excluding evidence from illegally obtained confessions. See C. Slobogin, Criminal Procedure: Regulation of Police Investigation 550 (3d ed. 2002). Canada rarely excludes evidence and will only do so if admission will "bring the administration of justice into disrepute." *Id.*, at 550–551 (internal quotation marks omitted). The European Court of Human Rights has held that introduction of illegally seized evidence does not violate the "fair trial" requirement in Article 6, § 1, of the European Convention on Human Rights. See Slobogin, *supra*, at 551; Bradley, *supra*, at 377–378.

The Court has been oblivious to the views of other countries when deciding how to interpret our Constitution's requirement that "Congress shall make no law respecting an establishment of religion...." Amdt. 1. Most other countries—including those committed to religious neutrality—do not insist on the degree of separation between church and state that this Court requires. ...

And let us not forget the Court's abortion jurisprudence, which makes us one of only six countries that allow abortion on demand until the point of viability. ...

The Court's special reliance on the laws of the United Kingdom is perhaps the most indefensible part of its opinion. It is of course true that we share a common history with the United Kingdom, and that we often consult English sources when asked to discern the meaning of a constitutional text written against the backdrop of 18th-century English law and legal thought. If we applied that approach today, our task would be an easy one. As we explained in *Harmelin v. Michigan*, 501 U.S. 957, 973–974 (1991), the "Cruell and Unusuall Punishments" provision of the English Declaration of Rights was originally meant to describe those punishments " 'out of [the Judges'] Power' "—that is, those punishments that were not authorized by common law or statute, but that were nonetheless administered by the Crown or the Crown's judges. Under that reasoning, the death penalty for under–18 offenders would easily survive this challenge. The Court has, however—I think wrongly—long rejected a purely originalist approach to our Eighth Amendment, and that is certainly not the approach the Court takes today. Instead, the Court undertakes the majestic task of determining (and thereby prescribing) *our* Nation's *current* standards of decency. It is beyond comprehension why we should look, for that purpose, to a country that has developed, in the centuries since the Revolutionary War—and with increasing speed since the United Kingdom's recent submission to the jurisprudence of European courts dominated by continental jurists—a legal, political, and social culture quite different from our own. If we took the Court's directive seriously, we would also consider relaxing our double jeopardy prohibition, since the British Law Commission recently published a report that would significantly extend the rights of the prosecution to appeal cases where an acquittal was the result of a judge's ruling that was legally incorrect. See Law Commission, Double Jeopardy and Prosecution Appeals, LAW COM No. 267, Cm. 5048, p. 6, ¶ 1.19 (Mar. 2001); J. Spencer, The English System in European Criminal Procedures 142, 204, and n. 239 (M. Delmas-Marty & J. Spencer eds. 2002). We would also curtail our right to jury trial in criminal cases since, despite the jury system's deep roots in our shared common law, England now permits all but the most serious offenders to be tried by magistrates without a jury. See D. Feldman, England and Wales, in Criminal Procedure: A Worldwide Study 91, 114–115 (C. Bradley ed. 1999).

The Court should either profess its willingness to reconsider all these matters in light of the views of foreigners, or else it should cease putting forth foreigners' views as part of the *reasoned basis* of its decisions. To invoke alien law when it agrees with one's own thinking, and ignore it otherwise, is not reasoned decisionmaking, but sophistry.[9]

The Court responds that "[i]t does not lessen our fidelity to the Constitution or our pride in its origins to acknowledge that the express affirmation of certain fundamental rights by other nations and peoples simply underscores the centrality of those same rights within our own heritage of freedom." *Ante*. To begin with, I do not believe that approval by "other nations and peoples" should buttress our commitment to American principles any more than (what should logically follow) disapproval by "other nations and peoples" should weaken that commitment. More importantly, however, the Court's statement flatly misdescribes what is going on here. Foreign sources are cited today, *not* to underscore our "fidelity" to the Constitution, our "pride in its origins," and "our own [American] heritage." To the contrary, they are cited to *set aside* the centuries-old American practice—a practice still engaged in by a large majority of the relevant States—of letting a jury of 12 citizens decide whether, in the particular case, youth should be the basis for withholding the death penalty. What these foreign sources "affirm," rather than repudiate, is the Justices' own notion of how the world ought to be, and their diktat that it shall be so henceforth in America. The Court's parting attempt to downplay the significance of its extensive discussion of foreign law is unconvincing. "Acknowledgment" of foreign approval has no place in the legal opinion of this Court *unless it is part of the basis for the Court's judgment*—which is surely what it parades as today.

---

9. JUSTICE O'CONNOR asserts that the Eighth Amendment has a "special character," in that it "draws its meaning directly from the maturing values of civilized society." *Ante*. Nothing in the text reflects such a distinctive character—and we have certainly applied the "maturing values" rationale to give brave new meaning to other provisions of the Constitution, such as the Due Process Clause and the Equal Protection Clause. See, *e.g., Lawrence v. Texas*, 539 U.S. 558, 571–573 (2003); *United States v. Virginia*, 518 U.S. 515, 532–534 (1996); *Planned Parenthood of Southeastern Pa. v. Casey*, 505 U.S. 833, 847–850 (1992). JUSTICE O'CONNOR asserts that an international consensus can at least "serve to confirm the reasonableness of a consonant and genuine American consensus." *Ante*. Surely not unless it can also demonstrate the *un*reasonableness of such a consensus. Either America's principles are its own, or they follow the world; one cannot have it both ways. Finally, JUSTICE O'CONNOR finds it unnecessary to consult foreign law in the present case because there is "no ... domestic consensus" to be confirmed. *Ibid*. But since she believes that the Justices can announce their own requirements of "moral proportionality" despite the absence of consensus, why would foreign law not be relevant to *that* judgment? If foreign law is powerful enough to supplant the judgment of the American people, surely it is powerful enough to change a personal assessment of moral proportionality.

HAROLD HONGJU KOH, INTERNATIONAL LAW AS PART OF OUR LAW*

98 Am. J. Int'l L. 43 (2004) (some footnotes omitted).

What did the United States Supreme Court mean when it famously said, "International law is part of our law, and must be ascertained and administered by the courts of justice of appropriate jurisdiction, as often as questions of right depending upon it are duly presented for their determination"?[1] Perhaps the Court was suggesting that, in an interdependent world, United States courts should not decide cases without paying "a decent respect to the opinions of mankind," in the memorable words of the Declaration of Independence. The framers and early Justices understood that the global legitimacy of a fledgling nation crucially depended upon the compatibility of its domestic law with the rules of the international system within which it sought acceptance. Their recognition seems both prudent and sensible. Even today, for any nation consciously to ignore global standards not only would ensure constant frictions with the rest of the world, but also would diminish that nation's ability to invoke those international rules that served its own national purposes.

Not surprisingly, the early Supreme Court saw the judicial branch as a central channel for making international law part of U.S. law.[5] The original design and early practice of our courts envisioned that they would not merely accept, but would actively pursue, an understanding and incorporation of international law standards out of a decent respect for the opinions of mankind. When "there is no written law upon the subject," Justice Horace Gray directed, "*the duty still rests upon the judicial tribunals of ascertaining and declaring what the law is*, whenever it becomes necessary to do so, in order to determine the rights of parties to suits regularly brought before them."[6] By so saying, he echoed Chief Justice John Marshall's memorable cadence in *Marbury v. Madison*: "[i]t is emphatically the province and duty of the judicial department to say what the law is,"[7] a directive that nowhere limited the judiciary's law-declaring function to cases involving domestic law.

Thus, many of Marshall's early opinions expressly promoted the implicit or explicit internalization of international law into U.S. domestic law: through statutory construction, direct invocation, and even constitutional interpretation. Within a year after writing *Marbury*, for example, Chief Justice Marshall ruled in *The Charming Betsy* that "an act of Congress ought never to be construed to violate the law of nations if any

1. *The Paquete Habana*, 175 U.S. 677, 700 (1900). . . .

5. See RESTATEMENT (THIRD) OF THE FOREIGN RELATIONS LAW OF THE UNITED STATES § 111 introductory note (1987) ("From the beginning, the law of nations, later referred to as international law, was considered to be incorporated into the law of the United States without the need for any action by Congress or the President, *and the courts, State and federal, have applied it and given it effect as the courts of England had done.*") (emphasis added). . . .

6. *Hilton v. Guyot*, 159 U.S. at 163 (emphasis added).

7. 5 U.S. (1 Cranch) 137, 177 (1803).

other possible construction remains."[8] Eleven years later, he clarified that absent a contrary statute, "the Court is bound by the law of nations which is a part of the law of the land."[9] In *McCulloch v. Maryland*, Chief Justice Marshall suggested that mankind's views are also relevant to the task of constitutional interpretation, noting:

> *If any one proposition could command the universal assent of mankind, we might expect it would be this*—that the government of the Union, though limited in its powers, is supreme within its sphere of action....
>
> ....
>
> ... In considering this question, then, we must never forget, that it is a constitution we are expounding.[10]

Significantly, at the beginning of the Republic, U.S. courts drew no sharp line between international and foreign law, precisely because of the extensive overlap of these two bodies of law. Customary rules like *lex mercatoria* and the criminal prohibition against piracies and felonies on the high seas were both "international," in the sense of governing transboundary transactions, and "foreign," in the sense of being internalized into the domestic law of foreign legal systems, as well as that of the United States. It was thus often difficult to distinguish when American courts were treating "international" or "foreign" law as part of our law. Some rules were inherently "transnational," hence not easily categorized as local or global in nature.

From the beginning, then, American courts regularly took judicial notice of both international law and foreign law (the law and practice of other nations) when construing American law. Given this historical tradition, should United States constitutional interpretation now ignore international law standards and the practices of other countries? Remarkably, some offer reasons why it should. But such an approach would constitute a stunning reversal of history.

When is it appropriate for the Supreme Court to construe our Constitution in light of foreign and international law? History suggests that over the years, the Court has regularly looked to foreign and international precedents as an aid to constitutional interpretation in at least three situations, which for simplicity's sake I will call "parallel rules," "empirical light," and "community standard." First, the Court has noted when American legal rules seem to parallel those of other nations, particularly those with similar legal and social traditions.[13] As the Court has repeatedly recognized, the concept of "ordered liberty" is not uniquely American

8. *Murray v. The Schooner Charming Betsy*, 6 U.S. (2 Cranch) 64, 118 (1804).

9. *The Nereide*, 13 U.S. (9 Cranch) 388, 423 (1815); *see also The Schooner Exchange v. M'Faddon*, 11 U.S. (7 Cranch) 116 (1812) (declaring international rule of absolute foreign sovereign immunity as U.S. law).

10. 17 U.S. (4 Wheat.) 316, 405–07 (1819) (emphasis added).

13. *See, e.g., Reynolds v. United States*, 98 U.S. 145, 164 (1878) (pointing out that "[p]olygamy has always been odious among the northern and western nations of Europe").

but, rather, is "enshrined" in the legal history of "English-speaking peoples," as well as other legal systems.[14]

Second, as Justice Stephen Breyer recently noted, the "Court has long considered as relevant and informative the way in which foreign courts have applied standards roughly comparable to our own constitutional standards in roughly comparable circumstances."[15] In *Printz v. United States*, he elaborated:

> Of course, we are interpreting our own Constitution, not those of other nations, and there may be relevant political and structural differences between their systems and our own. ... *But their experience may nonetheless cast an empirical light* on the consequences of different solutions to a common legal problem—in this case the problem of reconciling central authority with the need to preserve the liberty-enhancing autonomy of a smaller constituent governmental entity.[16]

Third, in addition to situations involving parallel rules and empirical lessons, the Court has looked outside the United States when a U.S. constitutional concept, by its own terms, implicitly refers to a *community standard*—e.g., "cruel and *unusual*," "*due* process of law," "*unreasonable* searches and seizures." In such cases, the Court has long since recognized that the relevant communities to be consulted include those outside our shores. ...

....

[T]he last Supreme Court Term confirms that two distinct approaches now uncomfortably coexist within our own Supreme Court's global jurisprudence. The first is a "nationalist jurisprudence," exemplified by the opinions of Justices Scalia and Clarence Thomas. That jurisprudence is characterized by commitments to territoriality, extreme deference to national executive power and political institutions, and resistance to comity or international law as meaningful constraints on national prerogatives. This line of cases largely refuses to look beyond U.S. national interests when assessing the legality of extraterritorial action. Moreover, these decisions have largely rejected international comity as a reason unilaterally to restrain the scope of U.S. regulation, and dismiss treaty or customary international law rules as meaningful restraints upon U.S. action. To deal with perceived exigencies, these rulings have broadly deferred to federal executive power, largely unchecked by judicial oversight, "clear statement" principles, or claims of individual rights. When advised of foreign legal precedents, these decisions have treated them as irrelevant, or worse yet, an impermissible imposition on the exercise of American sovereignty.

14. *See, e.g., Ingraham v. Wright*, 430 U.S. 651, 673 n.42 (1977)....

15. *Knight v. Florida*, 528 U.S. 990, 997 (1999) (Breyer, J., dissenting from denial of certiorari).

16. 521 U.S. 898, 921 n.11, 977 (1997) (Breyer, J., dissenting) (citations omitted) (emphasis added).

A second, more venerable strand of "transnationalist jurisprudence," [is] now being carried forward by Justices Breyer and Ginsburg. ...

Unlike nationalist jurisprudence, which rejects foreign and international precedents and looks for guidance primarily to national territory, political institutions, and executive power, the transnationalist jurisprudence assumes America's political and economic interdependence with other nations operating within the international legal system. Nor, significantly, do these Justices distinguish sharply between the relevance of foreign and international law, recognizing that one prominent feature of a globalizing world is the emergence of a transnational law, particularly in the area of human rights, that merges the national and the international. Addressing the American Society of International Law, Justice O'Connor noted that, increasingly, foreign and international law issues are coming before U.S. courts "because international law is no longer confined in relevance to a few treaties and business agreements. Rather, it has taken on the character of transnational law—what Philip Jessup has defined as law that regulates actions or events that transcend national frontiers." Similarly, Justice Breyer has noted, time has blurred

> the differences between what my law professors used to call comparative law and public international law. ... Formally speaking, state law is state law, but practically speaking, much of that law is national, if not international, in scope. Analogous developments internationally, including the emergence of regional or specialized international legal bodies, tend similarly to produce *cross-country results that resemble each other more and more, exhibiting common, if not universal, principles in a variety of legal areas*.

In such a transnationalist system, as Justice Breyer has noted, understanding and making reference to foreign constitutional precedents aids U.S. constitutional interpretation, "simply because of the enormous value in any discipline of trying to learn from the similar experience of others." Under this view, domestic courts must play a key role in coordinating U.S. domestic constitutional rules with rules of foreign and international law, not simply to promote American aims, but to advance the broader development of a well-functioning international judicial system. In Justice Blackmun's words, U.S. courts must look beyond narrow U.S. interests to the "mutual interests of all nations in a smoothly functioning international legal regime" and, whenever possible, should "consider if there is a course that furthers, rather than impedes, the development of an ordered international system."

The nationalist justices reject the transnationalist views on the ground that comparative and international analysis is appropriate only to legislative and constitutional *drafting*, not to the task of judicial constitutional *interpretation*. Yet on reflection, this distinction makes no sense. The U.S. Constitution served as a principal inspiration and model for many foreign and international constitutions and covenants, including the Universal Declaration of Human Rights and the International Covenants on Civil and Political Rights and Economic, Social and Cultural Rights. There remains to this day a "vigorous overseas trade in the Bill of Rights, in international and constitutional litigation involving norms derived from American constitutional law." Concepts like liberty, equality, and privacy are not exclusively American constitutional ideas but, rather, part and parcel of the global human rights movement. Nor is the United States the world's only civilized society. By their nature, human rights concepts evolve and "[j]udges in different countries increasingly apply somewhat similar legal phrases to somewhat similar circumstances." Construing U.S. constitutional law by referring to other nations' constitutional drafters, but not their constitutional interpreters, would be akin to operating a building by examining the blueprints of others on which it was modeled, while ignoring all subsequent progress reports on how well those other buildings actually functioned over time.

. . . .

Nationalist academics add a second objection, which one dubs the "international countermajoritarian difficulty": the claim that U.S. constitutional protections that are responsive to "national consensus giving expression to the sovereign will of the American people" cannot "be interpreted to give expression to the international majoritarian impulse to protect the individual from democratic governance." Yet this argument assumes that the job of judges construing the Constitution is to give expression to majoritarian impulses, when their long-settled role (which, of course, gives rise to the *domestic* countermajoritarian difficulty) has been to apply enduring principles of law to evolving circumstance without regard to the will of shifting democratic majorities.[90] In effect, the nationalists claim that unelected federal judges may not interpret the Constitution by applying rules made by foreign governments or the world community at the expense of state prerogatives. But obviously, every court in the United States applies law that was not made by its own polity—including foreign law—whenever the court's own choice of law principles so direct.

Nor is there anything necessarily antidemocratic about construing U.S. constitutional law in light of transnational law. As Justice Breyer recently noted:

> [T]he transnational law that is being created is not simply a product of treaty-writers, legislatures, or courts. We in America know full well that in a democracy, law, perhaps most law, is not decreed from on high but bubbles up from the interested publics, affected groups, specialists, legislatures, and others, all interacting through

---

90. Justice Kennedy made the point eloquently in *Lawrence*:

Had those who drew and ratified the Due Process Clauses of the Fifth Amendment or the Fourteenth Amendment known the components of liberty in its manifold possibilities, they might have been more specific. They did not presume to have this insight. They knew times can blind us to certain truths and later generations can see that laws once thought necessary and proper in fact serve only to oppress. As the Constitution endures, persons in every generation can invoke its principles in their own search for greater freedom.

Lawrence, 123 S.Ct. at 2484.

meetings, journal articles, the popular press, legislative hearings, and in many other ways. *That is the democratic process in action*. Legislation typically comes long after this process has been underway. Judicial decisions, particularly from our Court, work best when they come last, after experience has made the consequences of legislation apparent.

What Justice Breyer describes is what I have elsewhere called "transnational legal process," the process whereby domestic systems incorporate international rules into domestic law through a three-part process of interaction, interpretation, and norm internalization. . . .

In this transnational legal process, the several states, foreign governments, and international bodies do not represent competing sovereigns, all vying for the right to control America's judicial destiny. Rather, a transnationalist jurisprudence suggests, the United States expresses its national sovereignty not by blocking out all foreign influence but by vigorous "participation in the various regimes that regulate and order the international system." The nationalists' suggestion that U.S. courts should disregard the rest of the civilized world by ignoring parallel foreign precedents only invites charges of parochialism, and undermines U.S. influence over the global development of human rights.

Nationalist academics charge that American human rights advocates have used international and foreign legal materials selectively; in one commentator's words, refusing to "take the bitter with the sweet," or in another's view, proposing "international sources . . . for comparison only if they are viewed as rights enhancing." Bizarrely, these scholars assume that United States judges should construe a national bill of rights that the framers thought was the model for the world in light of the world's worst practices. What this claim misunderstands is that those who advocate the use of international and foreign sources in U.S. constitutional interpretation are not urging U.S. courts to defer automatically to some kind of global "nose count." Instead, they are suggesting that the practices of other mature democracies—not those that lag behind developmentally—constitute the most relevant evidence of what Eighth Amendment jurisprudence calls the "evolving standards of decency that mark the progress of a maturing society."

My point is simple: those who advocate the use of international law in U.S. constitutional interpretation are not mere "international majoritarians" who believe that American constitutional liberties should be determined by a worldwide vote. Rather, transnationalists suggest that particular provisions of our Constitution should be construed with decent respect for international and foreign comparative law. When phrases like "due process of law," "equal protection," and "cruel and unusual punishments" are illuminated by parallel rules, empirical evidence, or community standards found in other mature legal systems, that evidence should not simply be ignored. Wise American judges did not do so at the beginning of the Republic, and there is no warrant for them to start now.

CONCLUDING NOTES

1. *International Law Versus Foreign Law.* In reading these excerpts, note the references to "international law," "foreign law," and the law of international courts and tribunals. International law covers matters such as treaties and international custom, whereas foreign law has to do with the domestic laws of foreign countries, including their constitutions, statutes, and case law. Should each of these receive a separate and distinct treatment in U.S. jurisprudence?

2. *Recent Supreme Court Cases.* As reflected in the *Roper v. Simmons* opinions, there has been a heated debate in recent years about the appropriate role for international and foreign jurisprudence in the opinions of U.S. judges. Nevertheless, references to such jurisprudence have been made in various majority and concurring opinions in recent years.

In *Lawrence v. Texas*, 539 U.S. 558, 123 S.Ct. 2472, 156 L.Ed.2d 508 (2003), Justice Kennedy (writing for a 5–3 majority) found that a Texas statute making it a crime for two persons of the same sex to engage in certain intimate sexual conduct was an unconstitutional impingement on the petitioners' right to exercise liberty interests protected by the Constitution. In doing so, he stated: "Other nations, too, have taken action consistent with an affirmation of the protected right of homosexual adults to engage in intimate, consensual conduct. ... The right the petitioners seek in this case has been accepted as an integral part of human freedom in many other countries." 539 U.S. at 577–78.

In *Grutter v. Bollinger*, 539 U.S. 306, 123 S.Ct. 2325, 156 L.Ed.2d 304 (2003), a 5–4 majority of the Court found that the University of Michigan Law School's admissions program, designed to promote the racial diversity of the student body, did not violate the Equal Protection clause of the Fourteenth Amendment because it was narrowly tailored to serve the compelling interest of attaining a diverse student body. At the same time, the Court said that the program must come to logical end-point in twenty-five years. In her concurring opinion, Justice Ginsburg cited decisions of the European Court of Human Rights when stating: "The Court's observation that race-conscious programs 'must have a logical end point' accords with the international understanding of the office of affirmative action." 539 U.S. at 344.

In *Washington v. Glucksberg*, 521 U.S. 702, 117 S.Ct. 2258, 138 L.Ed.2d 772 (1997), an 8–0 majority of the Court found that the State of Washington's ban on physician-assisted suicide did not violate the Constitution because there is no fundamental liberty interest in assisted suicide. Justice Souter stated in his concurring opinion: "Respondents' proposals, as it turns out, sound much like the guidelines now in place in the Netherlands, the only place where experience with physician-assisted suicide and euthanasia has yielded empirical evidence about how such regulations might affect actual practice." 521 U.S. at 785.

In *Graham v. Florida*, 130 S.Ct. 2011, 176 L.Ed.2d 825 (2010), five justices joined in an opinion that cited the fact that only the United States authorized life without parole for juvenile non-homicide offenders and noted that U.S. practice would violate the United Nations Convention on the Rights of the Child, Nov. 20, 1989, 1577 U.N.T.S. 3 (entered into force Sept. 2, 1990), as supporting—but not controlling—the Court's decision that such practice violated the Eighth Amendment. 130 S.Ct. at 2033–34.

For analysis and commentary on these cases, see discussion between Justice Stephen Breyer and Justice Antonin Scalia, "The Constitutional Relevance of Foreign Court Decisions," American University, January 13, 2005, *available at* http://domino.american.edu/AU/media/mediarel.nsf; *see also* Stephen Yeazell, *When and How U.S. Courts Should Cite Foreign Law*, 26 CONST. COMM. 59 (2009); Melissa Waters, *Creeping Monism: The Judicial Trend Toward Interpretive Incorporation of Human Rights Treaties*, 107 COLUM. L. REV. 628 (2007); Sarah H. Cleveland, *Our International Constitution*, 31 YALE J. INT'L 1 (2006); Symposium, *The Debate Over Foreign Law in* Roper v. Simmons, 119 HARV. L. REV. 103 (2005); Symposium, *The United States Constitution and International Law*, 98 AM. J. INT'L L. 42 (2004); Hon. Patricia M. Wald, *The Use of International Law in the American Adjudicative Process*, 27 HARV. J.L. & PUB. POL'Y 431 (2004); Roger P. Alford, *Federal Courts, International Tribunals, and the Continuum of Deference*, 43 VA. J. INT'L L. 675 (2003).

3. *Prohibiting the Use of International/Foreign Law by U.S. Courts.* Would you support adoption of a statute that limits the use by U.S. courts of international or foreign law? As discussed further in Section 7 below, the Military Commissions Act of 2006 provides:

> No foreign or international source of law shall supply a basis for a rule of decision in the courts of the United States in interpreting the prohibitions enumerated in subsection (d) of such section 2441.

Pub. L. No. 109–366, § 6(a)(2), 120 Stat. 2600 (2006). The purpose of that provision (and of § 6 in general) appears to be to preclude U.S. courts from interpreting the meaning of "grave breaches" of the 1949 Geneva Conventions by reference to any foreign or international source of law. Presumably this category includes foreign and international courts' decisions as to the meaning of the Conventions, as well as the Conventions themselves and their negotiating history, and by reference to foreign and state practice. The constitutionality of this provision remains as yet untested.

Similar efforts have been made by Congress in the recent past concerning the use of international and foreign law to interpret the U.S. Constitution, albeit without success. A notable example is the failed "Constitution Restoration Act of 2004," introduced in essentially identical form in the House and Senate on various occasions throughout 2004 and 2005. The bill would have precluded U.S. courts, when engaged in constitutional interpretation, from relying on any legal materials—including constitutions, laws, and judicial decisions—of any foreign state or international organization or agency. Interestingly, English common law in existence at the time of the enactment of the Constitution was excluded from the prohibition. See H.R. 3799, 108th CONG. § 201 (2004); S. 2082, 108th CONG. § 201 (2004); S. 520, 109th CONG. § 201 (2005).

Are these prohibitions constitutional? Or do they improperly intrude upon the judicial function of U.S. courts accorded under Article III of the Constitution? Note that while such efforts have not resulted in any enactments, members of the Senate have become attentive to this issue during confirmation hearings for Supreme Court nominees and, for the most part, have been successful in extracting commitments to refrain from all but the most innocuous practices. *See, e.g.*, Confirmation Hearing on the Nomination of Hon. Sonia Sotomayor, To Be An Associate Justice of the Supreme Court of the United States: Hearing before the S. Comm. on the Judiciary, 111th Cong. 132 (2009).

Similar efforts have made somewhat greater headway in the states. The "Save Our State Amendment," approved by referendum in Oklahoma in late 2010, provides in relevant part that "[t]he courts shall not look to the legal precepts of other nations or cultures" and "[s]pecifically, the courts shall not consider international law or Sharia law." A U.S. district court issued a preliminary injunction barring certification of the referendum based on a claimed violation of the Establishment Clause of the U.S. Constitution. *Awad v. Ziriax*, 754 F. Supp. 2d 1298 (W.D. Ok. 2010). Does the regulation by state voters of state courts pose a different question than the regulation of federal courts by Congress, or the self-regulation of federal courts? As you reflect on the preemption issues posed in Chapter 6, consider whether—putting aside the attempt to regulate consideration of Sharia law and related Establishment Clause issues—the Save Our State Amendment also violates, or vindicates, principles of constitutional federalism.

4. *Next Steps.* The next few sections of this chapter explore the areas where the law of nations has been most frequently applied (or not applied) by U.S. courts. In some of these areas, Congress has defined specific offenses against the law of nations. In others, it has passed laws that simply incorporated undefined "offenses against the law of nations," leaving it to the courts to define them. In still other instances, the courts have acted in the absence of statutory incorporation to bring international customary law into the U.S. law. In addition to general maritime and admiralty matters (see the cases in Section 2 above), U.S. courts have tended to apply the law of nations in four subject areas: the protection of human rights; the punishment of piracy and terrorism; the punishment of war-related crimes; and immunities for states, diplomats, and their property.

SECTION 5. HUMAN RIGHTS

ALIEN TORT STATUTE

28 U.S.C. § 1350 (2006).

The district courts shall have original jurisdiction of any civil action by an alien for a tort only, committed in violation of the law of nations or a treaty of the United States.

RESTATEMENT (THIRD) OF THE FOREIGN RELATIONS LAW OF THE UNITED STATES § 702

(1987).

§ 702. *Customary International Law of Human Rights*

A state violates international law if, as a matter of state policy, it practices, encourages, or condones

(a) genocide,

(b) slavery or slave trade,

(c) the murder or causing the disappearance of individuals,

(d) torture or other cruel, inhuman, or degrading treatment or punishment,

(e) prolonged arbitrary detention,

(f) systematic racial discrimination, or

(g) a consistent pattern of gross violations of internationally recognized human rights.

Comment:

a. *Scope of customary law of human rights.* This section includes as customary law only those human rights whose status as customary law is generally accepted (as of 1987) and whose scope and content are generally agreed. . . . The list is not necessarily complete, and is not closed: human rights not listed in this section may have achieved the status of customary law, and some rights might achieve that status in the future. . . .

b. *State policy as violation of customary law.* In general, a state is responsible for acts of officials or official bodies, national or local, even if the acts were not authorized by or known to the responsible national authorities, indeed even if expressly forbidden by law, decree or instruction. . . . The violations of human rights cited in this section, however, are violations of customary international law only if practiced, encouraged, or condoned by the government of a state as official policy. A state is not responsible under this section for a violation of human rights by an official that was not authorized, encouraged, or condoned by the responsible governmental authorities of the state. . . .

A government may be presumed to have encouraged or condoned acts prohibited by this section if such acts, especially by its officials, have been repeated or notorious and no steps have been taken to prevent them or to punish the perpetrators. That state law prohibits the violation and provides generally effective remedies is strong evidence that the violation is not state policy. A state is not ordinarily responsible under this section for violations of human rights by individuals, such as individual acts of torture or of racial discrimination. A state would be responsible if, as a matter of state policy, it required, encouraged, or condoned such private violations, but mere failure to enact laws prohibiting private violations of human rights would not ordinarily constitute encouragement or condonation. International law requires a state to outlaw genocide, slavery, and the slave trade, and the state would be responsible under this section if it failed to prohibit them or to enforce the prohibition.

Even when a state is not responsible under this section because a violation is not state policy, the state may be responsible under some international agreement that requires the state to prevent the violation. For example, under the Covenant on Civil and Political Rights, a state party is guilty of a violation if any of the acts listed in this section is perpetrated by officials, persons acting under color of law, or other persons for whose acts the state is responsible . . ., even when their acts are contrary to state law or policy.

FILARTIGA v. PENA–IRALA

630 F.2d 876 (2d Cir. 1980).

IRVING R. KAUFMAN, CIRCUIT JUDGE:

Upon ratification of the Constitution, the thirteen former colonies were fused into a single nation, one which, in its relations with foreign states, is bound both to observe and construe the accepted norms of international law, formerly known as the law of nations. Under the Articles of Confederation, the several states had interpreted and applied this body of doctrine as a part of their common law, but with the founding of the "more perfect Union" of 1789, the law of nations became preeminently a federal concern.

Implementing the constitutional mandate for national control over foreign relations, the First Congress established original district court jurisdiction over "all causes where an alien sues for a tort only [committed] in violation of the law of nations." Judiciary Act of 1789, ch. 20, § 9(b), 1 Stat. 73, 77 (1789), *codified at* 28 U.S.C. § 1350. Construing this rarely-invoked provision, we hold that deliberate torture perpetrated under color of official authority violates universally accepted norms of the international law of human rights, regardless of the nationality of the parties. Thus, whenever an alleged torturer is found and served with process by an alien within our borders, § 1350 provides federal jurisdiction. Accordingly, we reverse the judgment of the district court dismissing the complaint for want of federal jurisdiction.

I

The appellants, plaintiffs below, are citizens of the Republic of Paraguay. Dr. Joel Filartiga, a physician, describes himself as a longstanding opponent of the government of President Alfredo Stroessner, which has held power in Paraguay since 1954. His daughter, Dolly Filartiga, arrived in the United States in 1978 under a visitor's visa, and has since applied for permanent political asylum. The Filartigas brought this action in the Eastern District of New York against Americo Norberto Pena–Irala

(Pena), also a citizen of Paraguay, for wrongfully causing the death of Dr. Filartiga's seventeen-year old son, Joelito. Because the district court dismissed the action for want of subject matter jurisdiction, we must accept as true the allegations contained in the Filartigas' complaint and affidavits for purposes of this appeal.

The appellants contend that on March 29, 1976, Joelito Filartiga was kidnapped and tortured to death by Pena, who was then Inspector General of Police in Asuncion, Paraguay. Later that day, the police brought Dolly Filartiga to Pena's home where she was confronted with the body of her brother, which evidenced marks of severe torture. As she fled, horrified, from the house, Pena followed after her shouting, "Here you have what you have been looking for for so long and what you deserve. Now shut up." The Filartigas claim that Joelito was tortured and killed in retaliation for his father's political activities and beliefs.

Shortly thereafter, Dr. Filartiga commenced a criminal action in the Paraguayan courts against Pena and the police for the murder of his son. As a result, Dr. Filartiga's attorney was arrested and brought to police headquarters where, shackled to a wall, Pena threatened him with death. This attorney, it is alleged, has since been disbarred without just cause.

During the course of the Paraguayan criminal proceeding, which is apparently still pending after four years, another man, Hugo Duarte, confessed to the murder. Duarte, who was a member of the Pena household,[1] claimed that he had discovered his wife and Joelito *in flagrante delicto,* and that the crime was one of passion. The Filartigas have submitted a photograph of Joelito's corpse showing injuries they believe refute this claim. Dolly Filartiga, moreover, has stated that she will offer evidence of three independent autopsies demonstrating that her brother's death "was the result of professional methods of torture." Despite his confession, Duarte, we are told, has never been convicted or sentenced in connection with the crime.

In July of 1978, Pena sold his house in Paraguay and entered the United States under a visitor's visa. He was accompanied by Juana Bautista Fernandez Villalba, who had lived with him in Paraguay. The couple remained in the United States beyond the term of their visas, and were living in Brooklyn, New York, when Dolly Filartiga, who was then living in Washington, D.C., learned of their presence. Acting on information provided by Dolly, the Immigration and Naturalization Service arrested Pena and his companion, both of whom were subsequently ordered deported on April 5, 1979 following a hearing. They had then resided in the United States for more than nine months.

Almost immediately, Dolly caused Pena to be served with a summons and civil complaint at the Brooklyn Navy Yard, where he was being held pending deportation. The complaint alleged that Pena had wrongfully caused Joelito's death by torture and sought compensatory and punitive

---

1. Duarte is the son of Pena's companion, Juana Bautista Fernandez Villalba, who later accompanied Pena to the United States.

damages of $10,000,000. The Filartigas also sought to enjoin Pena's deportation to ensure his availability for testimony at trial.[2] The cause of action is stated as arising under "wrongful death statutes; the U.N. Charter; the Universal Declaration on Human Rights; the U.N. Declaration Against Torture; the American Declaration of the Rights and Duties of Man; and other pertinent declarations, documents and practices constituting the customary international law of human rights and the law of nations," as well as 28 U.S.C. § 1350, Article II, sec. 2 and the Supremacy Clause of the U.S. Constitution. Jurisdiction is claimed under the general federal question provision, 28 U.S.C. § 1331 and, principally on this appeal, under the Alien Tort Statute, 28 U.S.C. § 1350.[3]

Judge Nickerson stayed the order of deportation, and Pena immediately moved to dismiss the complaint on the grounds that subject matter jurisdiction was absent and for *forum non conveniens.* On the jurisdictional issue, there has been no suggestion that Pena claims diplomatic immunity from suit. The Filartigas submitted the affidavits of a number of distinguished international legal scholars, who stated unanimously that the law of nations prohibits absolutely the use of torture as alleged in the complaint.[4] Pena, in support of his motion to dismiss on the ground of *forum non conveniens,* submitted the affidavit of his Paraguayan counsel, Jose Emilio Gorostiaga, who averred that Paraguayan law provides a full and adequate civil remedy for the wrong alleged.[5] Dr. Filartiga has not

2. Several officials of the Immigration and Naturalization Service were named as defendants in connection with this portion of the action. Because Pena has now been deported, the federal defendants are no longer parties to this suit, and the claims against them are not before us on this appeal.

3. Jurisdiction was also invoked pursuant to 28 U.S.C. §§ 1651, 2201 & 2202, presumably in connection with appellants' attempt to delay Pena's return to Paraguay.

4. Richard Falk, the Albert G. Milbank Professor of International Law and Practice at Princeton University, and a former Vice President of the American Society of International Law, avers that, in his judgment, "it is now beyond reasonable doubt that torture of a person held in detention that results in severe harm or death is a violation of the law of nations." Thomas Franck, professor of international law at New York University and Director of the New York University Center for International Studies offers his opinion that torture has now been rejected by virtually all nations, although it was once commonly used to extract confessions. Richard Lillich, the Howard W. Smith Professor of Law at the University of Virginia School of Law, concludes, after a lengthy review of the authorities, that officially perpetrated torture is "a violation of international law (formerly called the law of nations)." Finally, Myres MacDougal, a former Sterling Professor of Law at the Yale Law School, and a past President of the American Society of International Law, states that torture is an offense against the law of nations, and that "it has long been recognized that such offenses vitally affect relations between states."

5. The Gorostiaga affidavit states that

> a father whose son has been wrongfully killed may in addition to commencing a criminal proceeding bring a civil action for damages against the person responsible. Accordingly, Mr. Filartiga has the right to commence a civil action against Mr. Duarte and Mr. Pena–Irala since he accuses them both of responsibility for his son's death. He may commence such a civil action either simultaneously with the commencement of the criminal proceeding, during the time that the criminal proceeding lasts, or within a year after the criminal proceeding has terminated. In either event, however, the civil action may not proceed to judgment until the criminal proceeding has been disposed of. If the defendant is found not guilty because he was not the author of the case under investigation in the criminal proceeding, no civil action for indemnity for damages based upon the same deed investigated in the criminal proceeding, can prosper or succeed.

commenced such an action, however, believing that further resort to the courts of his own country would be futile.

Judge Nickerson heard argument on the motion to dismiss on May 14, 1979, and on May 15 dismissed the complaint on jurisdictional grounds.[6] The district judge recognized the strength of appellants' argument that official torture violates an emerging norm of customary international law. Nonetheless, he felt constrained by dicta contained in two recent opinions of this Court, *Dreyfus v. von Finck,* 534 F.2d 24 (2d Cir.), *cert. denied,* 429 U.S. 835 (1976); *IIT v. Vencap, Ltd.,* 519 F.2d 1001 (2d Cir.1975), to construe narrowly "the law of nations," as employed in § 1350, as excluding that law which governs a state's treatment of its own citizens.

The district court continued the stay of deportation for forty-eight hours while appellants applied for further stays. These applications were denied by a panel of this Court on May 22, 1979, and by the Supreme Court two days later. Shortly thereafter, Pena and his companion returned to Paraguay.

II

Appellants rest their principal argument in support of federal jurisdiction upon the Alien Tort Statute, 28 U.S.C. § 1350, which provides: "The district courts shall have original jurisdiction of any civil action by an alien for a tort only, committed in violation of the law of nations or a treaty of the United States." Since appellants do not contend that their action arises directly under a treaty of the United States,[7] a threshold question on the jurisdictional issue is whether the conduct alleged violates the law of nations. In light of the universal condemnation of torture in numerous international agreements, and the renunciation of torture as an instrument of official policy by virtually all of the nations of the world (in principle if not in practice), we find that an act of torture committed by a state official against one held in detention violates established norms of the international law of human rights, and hence the law of nations.

The Supreme Court has enumerated the appropriate sources of international law. The law of nations "may be ascertained by consulting the works of jurists, writing professedly on public law; or by the general usage and practice of nations; or by judicial decisions recognizing and enforcing that law." *United States v. Smith,* 18 U.S. (5 Wheat.) 153, 160–61 (1820); *Lopes v. Reederei Richard Schroder,* 225 F.Supp. 292, 295 (E.D. Pa. 1963). In *Smith,* a statute proscribing "the crime of piracy [on the high seas] as defined by the law of nations," 3 Stat. 510(a) (1819), was held sufficiently determinate in meaning to afford the basis for a death sentence. The *Smith* Court discovered among the works of Lord Bacon, Grotius, Bochard

6. The court below accordingly did not consider the motion to dismiss on *forum non conveniens* grounds, which is not before us on this appeal.

7. Appellants "associate themselves with" the argument of some of the *amici curiae* that their claim arises directly under a treaty of the United States, Brief for Appellants at 23 n.*, but nonetheless primarily rely upon treaties and other international instruments as evidence of an emerging norm of customary international law, rather then independent sources of law.

and other commentators a genuine consensus that rendered the crime "sufficiently and constitutionally defined." *Smith, supra,* 18 U.S. (5 Wheat.) at 162.

The Paquete Habana, 175 U.S. 677 (1900), reaffirmed that

> where there is no treaty, and no controlling executive or legislative act or judicial decision, resort must be had to the customs and usages of civilized nations; and, as evidence of these, to the works of jurists and commentators, who by years of labor, research and experience, have made themselves peculiarly well acquainted with the subjects of which they treat. Such works are resorted to by judicial tribunals, not for the speculations of their authors concerning what the law ought to be, but for trustworthy evidence of what the law really is.

Id. at 700. Modern international sources confirm the propriety of this approach.[8]

Habana is particularly instructive for present purposes, for it held that the traditional prohibition against seizure of an enemy's coastal fishing vessels during wartime, a standard that began as one of comity only, had ripened over the preceding century into "a settled rule of international law" by "the general assent of civilized nations." *Id.* at 694; *accord, id.* at 686. Thus it is clear that courts must interpret international law not as it was in 1789, but as it has evolved and exists among the nations of the world today. *See Ware v. Hylton,* 3 U.S. (3 Dall.) 199 (1796) (distinguishing between "ancient" and "modern" law of nations).

The requirement that a rule command the "general assent of civilized nations" to become binding upon them all is a stringent one. Were this not so, the courts of one nation might feel free to impose idiosyncratic legal rules upon others, in the name of applying international law. Thus, in *Banco Nacional de Cuba v. Sabbatino,* 376 U.S. 398 (1964), the Court declined to pass on the validity of the Cuban government's expropriation of a foreign-owned corporation's assets, noting the sharply conflicting

---

8. The Statute of the International Court of Justice, Arts. 38 & 59, June 26, 1945, 59 Stat. 1055, 1060 (1945) provides:

Art. 38

1. The Court, whose function is to decide in accordance with international law such disputes as are submitted to it, shall apply:

(a) international conventions, whether general or particular, establishing rules expressly recognized by the contesting states;

(b) international custom, as evidence of a general practice accepted as law;

(c) the general principles of law recognized by civilized nations;

(d) subject to the provisions of Article 59, judicial decisions and the teachings of the most highly qualified publicists of the various nations, as subsidiary means for the determination of the rules of law.

2. This provision shall not prejudice the power of the Court to decide a case *ex aequo et bono,* if the parties agree thereto.

Art. 59

The decision of the Court has no binding force except between the parties and in respect of that particular case.

views on the issue propounded by the capital-exporting, capital-importing, socialist and capitalist nations. *Id.* at 428–30.

The case at bar presents us with a situation diametrically opposed to the conflicted state of law that confronted the *Sabbatino* Court. Indeed, to paraphrase that Court's statement, *id.* at 428, there are few, if any, issues in international law today on which opinion seems to be so united as the limitations on a state's power to torture persons held in its custody.

The United Nations Charter (a treaty of the United States, *see* 59 Stat. 1033 (1945)) makes it clear that in this modern age a state's treatment of its own citizens is a matter of international concern. It provides:

> With a view to the creation of conditions of stability and well-being which are necessary for peaceful and friendly relations among nations ... the United Nations shall promote ... universal respect for, and observance of, human rights and fundamental freedoms for all without distinctions as to race, sex, language or religion.

Id. Art. 55. And further:

> All members pledge themselves to take joint and separate action in cooperation with the Organization for the achievement of the purposes set forth in Article 55.

Id. Art. 56.

While this broad mandate has been held not to be wholly self-executing, *Hitai v. Immigration and Naturalization Service,* 343 F.2d 466, 468 (2d Cir. 1965), this observation alone does not end our inquiry.[9] For although there is no universal agreement as to the precise extent of the "human rights and fundamental freedoms" guaranteed to all by the Charter, there is at present no dissent from the view that the guaranties include, at a bare minimum, the right to be free from torture. This prohibition has become part of customary international law, as evidenced and defined by the Universal Declaration of Human Rights, General Assembly Resolution 217 (III)(A) (Dec. 10, 1948) which states, in the plainest of terms, "no one shall be subjected to torture."[10] The General Assembly has declared that the Charter precepts embodied in this Universal Declaration "constitute basic principles of international law." G.A. Res. 2625 (XXV) (Oct. 24, 1970).

Particularly relevant is the Declaration on the Protection of All Persons from Being Subjected to Torture, General Assembly Resolution 3452, 30 U.N. GAOR Supp. (No. 34) 91, U.N.Doc. A/1034 (1975). ... The

9. We observe that this Court has previously utilized the U.N. Charter and the Charter of the Organization of American States, another non-self-executing agreement, as evidence of binding principles of international law. *United States v. Toscanino,* 500 F.2d 267 (2d Cir. 1974). In that case, our government's duty under international law to refrain from kidnapping a criminal defendant from within the borders of another nation, where formal extradition procedures existed, infringed the personal rights of the defendant, whose international law claims were thereupon remanded for a hearing in the district court.

10. Eighteen nations have incorporated the Universal Declaration into their own constitutions. 48 *Revue Internationale de Droit Penal* Nos. 3 & 4, at 211 (1977).

Declaration expressly prohibits any state from permitting the dastardly and totally inhuman act of torture. . . .

These U.N. declarations are significant because they specify with great precision the obligations of member nations under the Charter. Since their adoption, "[m]embers can no longer contend that they do not know what human rights they promised in the Charter to promote." Sohn, "A Short History of United Nations Documents on Human Rights," in *The United Nations and Human Rights, 18th Report of the Commission* (Commission to Study the Organization of Peace ed. 1968). Moreover, a U.N. Declaration is, according to one authoritative definition, "a formal and solemn instrument, suitable for rare occasions when principles of great and lasting importance are being enunciated." 34 U.N. ESCOR, Supp. (No. 8) 15, U.N. Doc. E/cn.4/1/610 (1962) (memorandum of Office of Legal Affairs, U.N. Secretariat). Accordingly, it has been observed that the Universal Declaration of Human Rights "no longer fits into the dichotomy of 'binding treaty' against 'non-binding pronouncement,' but is rather an authoritative statement of the international community." E. Schwelb, *Human Rights and the International Community* 70 (1964). Thus, a Declaration creates an expectation of adherence, and "insofar as the expectation is gradually justified by State practice, a declaration may by custom become recognized as laying down rules binding upon the States." 34 U.N. ESCOR, *supra.* Indeed, several commentators have concluded that the Universal Declaration has become, *in toto,* a part of binding, customary international law. Nayar, *supra,* at 816–17; Waldock, "Human Rights in Contemporary International Law and the Significance of the European Convention," *Int'l & Comp. L.Q.*, Supp. Publ. No. 11 at 15 (1965).

Turning to the act of torture, we have little difficulty discerning its universal renunciation in the modern usage and practice of nations. *Smith, supra,* 18 U.S. (5 Wheat.) at 160–61. The international consensus surrounding torture has found expression in numerous international treaties and accords. *E.g., American Convention on Human Rights,* Art. 5, OAS Treaty Series No. 36 at 1, OAS Off. Rec. OEA/Ser 4 v/II 23, doc. 21, rev. 2 (English ed., 1975) . . .

Having examined the sources from which customary international law is derived—the usage of nations, judicial opinions and the works of jurists[16]—we conclude that official torture is now prohibited by the law of nations. The prohibition is clear and unambiguous, and admits of no distinction between treatment of aliens and citizens. Accordingly, we must conclude that the dictum in *Dreyfus v. von Finck, supra,* 534 F.2d at 31, to the effect that "violations of international law do not occur when the aggrieved parties are nationals of the acting state," is clearly out of tune with the current usage and practice of international law. The treaties and

16. *See* note 4, *supra: see also Ireland v. United Kingdom,* Judgment of Jan. 18, 1978 (European Court of Human Rights), *summarized in* [1978] Yearbook, European Convention on Human Rights 602 (Council of Europe) (holding that Britain's subjection of prisoners to sleep deprivation, hooding, exposure to hissing noise, reduced diet and standing against a wall for hours was "inhuman and degrading," but not "torture" within meaning of European Convention on Human Rights).

accords cited above, as well as the express foreign policy of our own government,[17] all make it clear that international law confers fundamental rights upon all people vis-a-vis their own governments. While the ultimate scope of those rights will be a subject for continuing refinement and elaboration, we hold that the right to be free from torture is now among them. We therefore turn to the question whether the other requirements for jurisdiction are met.

III

Appellee submits that even if the tort alleged is a violation of modern international law, federal jurisdiction may not be exercised consistent with the dictates of Article III of the Constitution. The claim is without merit. Common law courts of general jurisdiction regularly adjudicate transitory tort claims between individuals over whom they exercise personal jurisdiction, wherever the tort occurred. Moreover, as part of an articulated scheme of federal control over external affairs, Congress provided, in the first Judiciary Act, § 9(b), 1 Stat. 73, 77 (1789), for federal jurisdiction over suits by aliens where principles of international law are in issue. The constitutional basis for the Alien Tort Statute is the law of nations, which has always been part of the federal common law.

. . . .

. . . A case properly "aris(es) under the . . . laws of the United States" for Article III purposes if grounded upon statutes enacted by Congress or upon the common law of the United States. *See Illinois v. City of Milwaukee,* 406 U.S. 91, 99–100 (1972); *Ivy Broadcasting Co., Inc. v. American Tel. & Tel. Co.*, 391 F.2d 486, 492 (2d Cir. 1968). The law of nations forms an integral part of the common law, and a review of the history surrounding the adoption of the Constitution demonstrates that it became a part of the common law *of the United States* upon the adoption of the Constitution. Therefore, the enactment of the Alien Tort Statute was authorized by Article III.

. . . .

As ratified, the judiciary article contained no express reference to cases arising under the law of nations. Indeed, the only express reference to that body of law is contained in Article I, sec. 8, cl. 10, which grants to the Congress the power to "define and punish . . . offenses against the law of nations." Appellees seize upon this circumstance and advance the proposition that the law of nations forms a part of the laws of the United States only to the extent that Congress has acted to define it. This extravagant claim is amply refuted by the numerous decisions applying

17. *E.g.,* 22 U.S.C. § 2304(a)(2) ("Except under circumstances specified in this section, no security assistance may be provided to any country the government of which engages in a consistent pattern of gross violations of internationally recognized human rights."); 22 U.S.C. § 2151(a) ("The Congress finds that fundamental political, economic, and technological changes have resulted in the interdependence of nations. The Congress declares that the individual liberties, economic prosperity, and security of the people of the United States are best sustained and enhanced in a community of nations which respect individual civil and economic rights and freedoms").

rules of international law uncodified in any act of Congress. *E. g., Ware v. Hylton*, 3 U.S. (3 Dall.) 199 (1796); *The Paquete Habana, supra*, 175 U.S. 677; *Sabbatino, supra*, 376 U.S. 398 (1964). A similar argument was offered to and rejected by the Supreme Court in *United States v. Smith, supra,* 18 U.S. (5 Wheat.) 153, 158–60, and we reject it today. As John Jay wrote in *The Federalist* No. 3, at 22 (1 Bourne ed. 1901), "Under the national government, treaties and articles of treaties, as well as the laws of nations, will always be expounded in one sense and executed in the same manner, whereas adjudications on the same points and questions in the thirteen states will not always accord or be consistent." Federal jurisdiction over cases involving international law is clear.

Thus, it was hardly a radical initiative for Chief Justice Marshall to state in *The Nereide*, 13 U.S. (9 Cranch) 388, 422 (1815), that in the absence of a congressional enactment,[20] United States courts are "bound by the law of nations, which is a part of the law of the land." These words were echoed in *The Paquete Habana, supra*, 175 U.S. at 700: "(i)nternational law is part of our law, and must be ascertained and administered by the courts of justice of appropriate jurisdiction, as often as questions of right depending upon it are duly presented for their determination."

The Filartigas urge that 28 U.S.C. § 1350 be treated as an exercise of Congress's power to define offenses against the law of nations. While such a reading is possible, *see Lincoln Mills v. Textile Workers*, 353 U.S. 448 (1957) (jurisdictional statute authorizes judicial explication of federal common law), we believe it is sufficient here to construe the Alien Tort Statute, not as granting new rights to aliens, but simply as opening the federal courts for adjudication of the rights already recognized by international law. The statute nonetheless does inform our analysis of Article III, for we recognize that questions of jurisdiction "must be considered part of an organic growth—part of an evolutionary process," and that the history of the judiciary article gives meaning to its pithy phrases. *Romero v. International Terminal Operating Co.*, 358 U.S. 354, 360 (1959). The Framers' overarching concern that control over international affairs be vested in the new national government to safeguard the standing of the United States among the nations of the world therefore reinforces the result we reach today.

Although the Alien Tort Statute has rarely been the basis for jurisdiction during its long history,[21] in light of the foregoing discussion, there can be little doubt that this action is properly brought in federal court.[22]

---

20. The plainest evidence that international law has an existence in the federal courts independent of acts of Congress is the long-standing rule of construction first enunciated by Chief Justice Marshall: "an act of congress ought never to be construed to violate the law of nations, if any other possible construction remains. . . ." *The Charming Betsy*, 6 U.S. (2 Cranch) 64, 67 (1804), *quoted in Lauritzen v. Larsen*, 345 U.S. 571, 578 (1953).

21. Section 1350 afforded the basis for jurisdiction over a child custody suit between aliens in *Adra v. Clift*, 195 F.Supp. 857 (D.Md. 1961), with a falsified passport supplying the requisite international law violation. In *Bolchos v. Darrell*, 3 Fed. Cas. 810 (D.S.C. 1795), the Alien Tort Statute provided an alternative basis of jurisdiction over a suit to determine title to slaves on board an enemy vessel taken on the high seas.

22. We recognize that our reasoning might also sustain jurisdiction under the general federal question provision, 28 U.S.C. § 1331. We prefer, however, to rest our decision upon the Alien

This is undeniably an action by an alien, for a tort only, committed in violation of the law of nations. The paucity of suits successfully maintained under the section is readily attributable to the statute's requirement of alleging a "*violation* of the law of nations" (emphasis supplied) at the jurisdictional threshold. Courts have, accordingly, engaged in a more searching preliminary review of the merits than is required, for example, under the more flexible "arising under" formulation. *Compare O'Reilly De Camara v. Brooke,* 209 U.S. 45, 52 (1907) (question of Alien Tort Statute jurisdiction disposed of "on the merits") (Holmes, J.), *with Bell v. Hood,* 327 U.S. 678 (1946) (general federal question jurisdiction not defeated by the possibility that the averments in the complaint may fail to state a cause of action). Thus, the narrowing construction that the Alien Tort Statute has previously received reflects the fact that earlier cases did not involve such well-established, universally recognized norms of international law that are here at issue.

. . . .

Since federal jurisdiction may properly be exercised over the Filartigas' claim, the action must be remanded for further proceedings.

NOTES ON LITIGATING THE "LEGAL LOHENGRIN"

1. *The Phoenix Arises.* The Alien Tort Statute, or ATS (also known as the Alien Tort Claims Act or ATCA), was a provision of the First Judiciary Act of 1789, ch. 20, § 9, 1 Stat. 73, 77 (1789). Today it is codified at 28 U.S.C. § 1350 (2006). Prior to the *Filartiga* case, the ATS had almost never been invoked. Judge Friendly famously referred to the ATS as "a kind of legal Lohengrin," IIT v. Vencap, Ltd., 519 F.2d 1001 (2d Cir. 1975), meaning that, although it has been with us since the founding of the republic, no one seems to know from whence it came. For efforts to explain its origins, see Anne–Marie Burley, *The Alien Tort Statute and the Judiciary Act of 1789: A Badge of Honor*, 83 AM. J. INT'L L. 461 (1989); William R. Casto, *The Federal Courts' Protective Jurisdiction Over Torts Committed in Violation of the Law of Nations*, 18 CONN. L. REV. 467, 495 (1986); William S. Dodge, *The Historical Origins of the Alien Tort Statute: A Response to the "Originalists"*, 19 HASTINGS INT'L & COMP. L. REV. 221, 232–33 (1996).

The *Filartiga* case infused the ATS with renewed importance, signaling a watershed moment for the human rights movement by raising the possibility of using U.S. courts to bring individuals to account for egregious human rights crimes committed anywhere in the world. Note how in the *Filartiga* case the plaintiffs were aliens, the defendant was an alien, and the conduct at issue occurred abroad. The only direct connection to the United States was that, at the time the case was filed, both the plaintiffs and the defendant were present in the United States. *See The Alien Tort Claims Act: An Analytical Anthology* (Ralph G. Steinhardt & Anthony D'Amato, eds., 1999); Beth

Tort Statute, in light of that provision's close coincidence with the jurisdictional facts presented in this case. *See Romero v. International Terminal Operating Co.*, 358 U.S. 354 (1959).

Stephens & Michael Ratner, *International Human Rights Litigation in U.S. Courts* (1996).

2. *Treaties and Custom under the ATS.* The ATS refers to violations of either treaties or the "law of nations." The *Filartiga* case was filed before the United States ratified the Convention Against Torture and Other Cruel, Inhuman, or Degrading Treatment or Punishment, Dec. 10, 1984, S. Treaty Doc. No. 100–20 (1988), 1465 U.N.T.S. 85. Consequently, the Second Circuit had to determine whether the conduct at issue violated customary international law. Do you think the court engaged in a careful analysis of whether customary international law prohibited state-sponsored torture? Or do you see flaws in the approach? Note the different sources relied upon by the court. Does this provide a template for how U.S. courts can engage in an analysis of customary human rights law? Does it remind you of the Supreme Court's approach in *The Paquete Habana*?

In the two decades following *Filartiga*, dozens of cases followed and some resulted in the award of civil damages. The courts generally required that the international norms alleged to have been violated be specific, universal, and mandatory. The *Restatement (Third)* § 702 provided a good starting point for considering whether a human rights norm is firmly embedded in customary international law (a starting point that did not exist at the time of the *Filartiga* decision). For each of the human rights listed in § 702, it is now possible to find a U.S. court case construing that right under the ATS, including genocide, *see, e.g.*, Kadic v. Karadzic, 70 F.3d 232 (2d Cir. 1995); slavery or forced labor, *see, e.g.*, Doe I v. Unocal Corp., 395 F.3d 932 (9th Cir. 2002), vacated, 395 F.3d 978 (9th Cir. 2003); disappearance of persons, *see, e.g.*, Forti v. Suarez–Mason, 694 F.Supp. 707 (N.D. Cal. 1988); cruel, degrading, or inhuman treatment, *see, e.g.*, Abebe–Jira v. Negewo, 72 F.3d 844 (11th Cir. 1996); and arbitrary detention, *see, e.g.*, Paul v. Avril, 901 F.Supp. 330 (S.D. Fla. 1994). At the same time, the Comment to *Restatement (Third)* § 702 made clear that the "list is not necessarily complete, and is not closed." Hence, it should be no surprise that cases can be found in U.S. courts involving ATS actions for other human rights violations, such as war crimes, *see, e.g.*, Mehinovic v. Vuckovic, 198 F.Supp.2d 1322 (N.D. Ga. 2002), and crimes against humanity, *see, e.g.*, Estate of Cabello v. Fernandez–Larios, 157 F.Supp.2d 1345 (S.D. Fla. 2001).

3. *Government Actor or Private Actor?* Although *Filartiga* involved only the conduct of a government official, U.S. courts have held that ATS claims may sometimes be brought against private actors. For example, in *Kadic v. Karadzic*, 70 F.3d 232 (2d Cir. 1995), the Second Circuit found certain heinous acts to be of such "universal concern" that they constitute violations of customary international law not only when they are committed by state actors, but also when they are committed by private individuals. *Id.* at 239–40. In particular, the Second Circuit determined that acts of piracy, slave trading, war crimes, and genocide violate customary international law regardless of whether they are undertaken by state or private actors, whereas acts of torture and "summary execution" constitute violations of customary international law only when committed by state officials or under color of law. *Id.* at 239–43.

4. *Trouble in Paradise.* In the wake of *Filartiga*, some courts and scholars balked at what they viewed as an objectionable breadth to the resurrected statute. *See, e.g.,* Tel-Oren v. Libyan Arab Republic, 726 F.2d 774 (D.C. Cir. 1984) (per curiam), *cert. denied*, 470 U.S. 1003, 105 S.Ct. 1354, 84 L.Ed.2d 377 (1985); Curtis Bradley, *The Costs of International Human Rights Litigation*, 2 CHI. J. INT'L L. 457 (2001).

Some ATS claims were dismissed prior to adjudication of the merits of the claim. Thus, in some cases the claim was dismissed as time-barred, *see, e.g.,* Iwanowa v. Ford Motor Co., 67 F.Supp.2d 424 (D.N.J. 1999); on grounds of forum non conveniens, *see, e.g.,* Flores v. Southern Peru Copper Corp., 253 F.Supp.2d 510 (S.D.N.Y. 2002); or due to the political question doctrine. *See, e.g.,* United States v. Noriega, 746 F.Supp. 1506 (S.D. Fla. 1990). In other cases, the claim was dismissed due to the Act of State doctrine, where the act in question was in pursuit of a public purpose. *See, e.g.,* Sarei v. Rio Tinto PLC, 221 F.Supp.2d 1116 (C.D.Cal. 2002), *vacated for further consideration*, 487 F.3d 1193 (9th Cir. 2007). If the claim was brought against a foreign diplomat, it was prone to dismissal on grounds of diplomatic immunity. *See, e.g.,* Ahmed v. Hoque, 2002 WL 1964806 (S.D.N.Y. Aug. 23, 2002). If the claim was brought against a foreign government, the claim was often dismissed on grounds of immunity under the Foreign Sovereign Immunities Act. *See, e.g.,* Argentine Republic v. Amerada Hess Shipping Corp., 488 U.S. 428, 109 S.Ct. 683, 102 L.Ed.2d 818 (1989); Hwang Geum Joo v. Japan, 332 F.3d 679 (D.C. Cir. 2003).

If the merits were reached, some claims were rejected on grounds that the alleged norm of customary international law simply did not exist. For example, in *Hamid v. Price Waterhouse*, 51 F.3d 1411 (9th Cir. 1995), the depositors of a failed international bank (BCCI) brought a class action against seventy-seven people, several firms, and a foreign country (Abu Dhaibi), alleging inter alia violation of the ATS. The Ninth Circuit, however, determined that "garden variety" fraud was not a violation of the law of nations:

> The wrongs alleged are in substance fraud, breach of fiduciary duty and misappropriation of funds. Although the conduct was international in scope, no violation of what has traditionally been the subject of international law is claimed. International law includes more than international treaties. *See e.g., Estate of Marcos*, 978 F.2d at 499 (official torture); *Filartiga v. Pena–Irala,* 630 F.2d 876, 880 (2nd Cir. 1980) (same). But looting of a bank by its insiders, and misrepresentations about the bank's financial condition, have never been in the traditional classification of international law. These are garden variety violations of statutes, banking regulations, and common law.

Id. at 1418. Similarly, in *Flores v. Southern Peru Copper Corp.*, 343 F.3d 140 (2d Cir. 2003), the plaintiffs alleged that for forty years the defendant's smelter had engaged in massive pollution, causing loss of life and severe injury to the health of the people of Ilo, Peru. The Second Circuit, however, found that environmental torts are not a violation of customary international law. *Id.* at 172. Spurious claims have been dismissed by the courts as well. *See, e.g.,* Zapata v. Quinn, 707 F.2d 691 (2d Cir. 1983) (rejecting a claim challenging the fairness of state-lottery distribution systems).

Beneath these varying results were fundamental, unresolved questions regarding the scope of the ATS. One issue concerned whether the ATS was solely a jurisdictional statute or whether it also created a private cause of action. For arguments that the ATS was solely jurisdictional and that it was incumbent upon Congress to adopt additional legislation implementing the relevant human rights norm, see Tel-Oren v. Libya, 726 F.2d 774, 798–99 (D.C. Cir. 1984) (Bork, J., concurring); Al Odah v. United States, 321 F.3d 1134, 1145–47 (D.C. Cir. 2003) (Randoph, J., concurring) ("To hold that the [ATS] creates a cause of action ... as the *Filartiga* [line of] decisions indicate[s], would be to grant aliens greater rights in the nation's courts than American citizens enjoy."), rev'd on other grounds, Rasul v. Bush, 542 U.S. 466, 124 S.Ct. 2686, 159 L.Ed.2d 548 (2004). For agreement with the Second Circuit in *Filartiga* that the ATS not only creates a jurisdictional basis but also creates a cause of action, see Abebe-Jira v. Negewo, 72 F.3d 844, 848 (11th Cir. 1996), and Hilao v. Estate of Marcos (In re Estate of Ferdinand Marcos, Human Rights Litig.), 25 F.3d 1467, 1475 (9th Cir. 1994) ("We thus join the Second Circuit in concluding that the [ATCA] creates a cause of action for violations of specific, universal and obligatory international human rights standards[.]").

Assuming that the ATS is solely a jurisdictional statute, a second issue of dispute was whether the "law of nations" as a part of U.S. law could provide such a cause of action. Here a key issue was the effect of the Supreme Court's decision in *Erie R.R. Co. v. Tompkins,* 304 U.S. 64, 58 S.Ct. 817, 82 L.Ed. 1188 (1938), on the "law of nations" in U.S. law. Critics of the ATS noted that in *Erie* the Court denied the existence of any "general" federal common law, and thus maintained that federal courts could apply the law of nations only when properly authorized, such as in the context of federal maritime jurisdiction. *See* Curtis A. Bradley & Jack L. Goldsmith, *Customary International Law as Federal Common Law: A Critique of the Modern Position*, 110 HARV. L. REV. 815 (1997); Curtis Bradley, *The Status of Customary International Law in U.S. Courts—Before and After* Erie, 26 DENV. J. INT'L L. & POL'Y 807 (1998). Others rejected that contention, seeing customary international law as firmly grounded in U.S. law and as one of the areas of federal common law that survived *Erie. See* Harold Hongju Koh, *Is International Law Really State Law?*, 111 HARV. L. REV. 1824 (1998); Gerald L. Neuman, *Sense and Nonsense About Customary International Law: A Response to Professors Bradley and Goldsmith*, 66 FORDHAM L. REV. 371 (1997).

Both issues were addressed by the Supreme Court in 2004.

SOSA v. ALVAREZ-MACHAIN

542 U.S. 692, 124 S.Ct. 2739, 159 L.Ed.2d 718 (2004)
(some footnotes omitted).

[Humberto Alvarez-Machain (Alvarez) was indicted by a federal grand jury for the torture and murder in Mexico of a U.S. Drug Enforcement Administration (DEA) agent. After attempts by the U.S. government to secure the assistance of the Mexican government failed, the DEA arranged for Mexican nationals, including defendant Jose Francisco Sosa, to kidnap and deliver Alvarez to the United States to stand trial. Alvarez was brought to Texas and turned over to DEA agents. In 1992, the Supreme Court rejected Alvarez's argument that the kidnapping violated an extradition treaty between the United States and Mexico, and remanded the case for trial. United States v. Alvarez-Machain, 504 U.S. 655 (1992).

Alvarez was ultimately acquitted in the ensuing criminal trial. Utilizing the Federal Tort Claims Act (FTCA), he subsequently brought suit against the United States. He also brought suit against Sosa for violating the law of nations under the ATS. The district court dismissed the FTCA claim but found for Alvarez on the ATS claim. A three-judge panel of the Ninth Circuit reversed the dismissal of the FTCA claim and affirmed the ATS judgment, 266 F.3d 1045 (9th Cir. 2001), and the court sitting *en banc* agreed, 331 F.3d 604 (9th Cir. 2003). The Supreme Court granted writs of certiorari.]

JUSTICE SOUTER delivered the opinion of the Court.

The two issues are whether respondent Alvarez-Machain's allegation that the Drug Enforcement Administration instigated his abduction from Mexico for criminal trial in the United States supports a claim against the Government under the Federal Tort Claims Act (FTCA or Act), 28 U.S.C. §§ 1346(b)(1), 2671–2680, and whether he may recover under the Alien Tort Statute (ATS), 28 U.S.C. § 1350. We hold that he is not entitled to a remedy under either statute.

. . . .

III

Alvarez has also brought an action under the ATS against petitioner, Sosa, who argues (as does the United States supporting him) that there is no relief under the ATS because the statute does no more than vest federal courts with jurisdiction, neither creating nor authorizing the courts to recognize any particular right of action without further congressional action. Although we agree the statute is in terms only jurisdictional, we think that at the time of enactment the jurisdiction enabled federal courts to hear claims in a very limited category defined by the law of nations and recognized at common law. We do not believe, however, that the limited, implicit sanction to entertain the handful of international law *cum* common law claims understood in 1789 should be taken as authority to recognize the right of action asserted by Alvarez here.

A

Judge Friendly called the ATS a "legal Lohengrin," *IIT v. Vencap, Ltd.*, 519 F.2d 1001, 1015 (2d Cir. 1975); "no one seems to know whence it came," *ibid.*, and for over 170 years after its enactment it provided jurisdiction in only one case. The first Congress passed it as part of the Judiciary Act of 1789, in providing that the new federal district courts "shall also have cognizance, concurrent with the courts of the several States, or the circuit courts, as the case may be, of all causes where an alien sues for a tort only in violation of the law of nations or a treaty of the United States." Act of Sept. 24, 1789, ch. 20, § 9, 1 Stat. 79.[10]

The parties and *amici* here advance radically different historical interpretations of this terse provision. Alvarez says that the ATS was intended not simply as a jurisdictional grant, but as authority for the creation of a new cause of action for torts in violation of international law. We think that reading is implausible. As enacted in 1789, the ATS gave the district courts "cognizance" of certain causes of action, and the term bespoke a grant of jurisdiction, not power to mold substantive law. *See, e.g.,* The Federalist No. 81, pp. 447, 451 (J. Cooke ed. 1961) (A. Hamilton) (using "jurisdiction" interchangeably with "cognizance"). The fact that the ATS was placed in § 9 of the Judiciary Act, a statute otherwise exclusively concerned with federal-court jurisdiction, is itself support for its strictly jurisdictional nature. Nor would the distinction between jurisdiction and cause of action have been elided by the drafters of the Act or those who voted on it. As Fisher Ames put it, "there is a substantial difference between the jurisdiction of courts and rules of decision." 1 Annals of Cong. 807 (Gales ed. 1834). It is unsurprising, then, that an authority on the historical origins of the ATS has written that "section 1350 clearly does not create a statutory cause of action," and that the contrary suggestion is "simply frivolous." Casto, The Federal Courts' Protective Jurisdiction Over Torts Committed in Violation of the Law of Nations, 18 Conn. L. Rev. 467, 479, 480 (1986) (hereinafter Casto, Law of Nations); cf. Dodge, The Constitutionality of the Alien Tort Statute: Some Observations on Text and Context, 42 Va. J. Int'l L. 687, 689 (2002). In sum, we think the statute was intended as jurisdictional in the sense of addressing the power of the courts to entertain cases concerned with a certain subject.

But holding the ATS jurisdictional raises a new question, this one about the interaction between the ATS at the time of its enactment and the ambient law of the era. Sosa would have it that the ATS was stillborn because there could be no claim for relief without a further statute expressly authorizing adoption of causes of action. *Amici* professors of federal jurisdiction and legal history take a different tack, that federal courts could entertain claims once the jurisdictional grant was on the books, because torts in violation of the law of nations would have been recognized within the common law of the time. Brief for Vikram Amar et al. as *Amici Curiae*. We think history and practice give the edge to this latter position.

1

"When the *United States* declared their independence, they were bound to receive the law of nations, in its modern state of purity and

10. The statute has been slightly modified on a number of occasions since its original enactment. It now reads in its entirety: "The district courts shall have original jurisdiction of any civil action by an alien for a tort only, committed in violation of the law of nations or a treaty of the United States." 28 U.S.C. § 1350.

refinement." *Ware v. Hylton,* 3 U.S. (3 Dall.) 199, 281 . . . (1796) (Wilson, J.). In the years of the early Republic, this law of nations comprised two principal elements, the first covering the general norms governing the behavior of national states with each other: *"the science which teaches the rights subsisting between nations or states, and the obligations correspondent to those rights,"* E. de Vattel, The Law of Nations, Preliminaries § 3 (J. Chitty et al. transl. and ed. 1883) (hereinafter Vattel) (footnote omitted), or "that code of public instruction which defines the rights and prescribes the duties of nations, in their intercourse with each other," 1 Kent Commentaries on American Law *1. This aspect of the law of nations thus occupied the executive and legislative domains, not the judicial. *See* 4 W. Blackstone, Commentaries on the Laws of England 68 (1769) (hereinafter Commentaries) ("[O]ffenses against" the law of nations are "principally incident to whole states or nations").

The law of nations included a second, more pedestrian element, however, that did fall within the judicial sphere, as a body of judge-made law regulating the conduct of individuals situated outside domestic boundaries and consequently carrying an international savor. To Blackstone, the law of nations in this sense was implicated "in mercantile questions, such as bills of exchange and the like; in all marine causes, relating to freight, average, demurrage, insurances, bottomry . . . ; [and] in all disputes relating to prizes, to shipwrecks, to hostages, and ransom bills." *Id.,* at 67. The law merchant emerged from the customary practices of international traders and admiralty required its own transnational regulation. And it was the law of nations in this sense that our precursors spoke about when the Court explained the status of coast fishing vessels in wartime grew from "ancient usage among civilized nations, beginning centuries ago, and gradually ripening into a rule of international law. . . ." *The Paquete Habana,* 175 U.S. 677, 686 . . . (1900).

There was, finally, a sphere in which these rules binding individuals for the benefit of other individuals overlapped with the norms of state relationships. Blackstone referred to it when he mentioned three specific offenses against the law of nations addressed by the criminal law of England: violation of safe conducts, infringement of the rights of ambassadors, and piracy. 4 Commentaries 68. An assault against an ambassador, for example, impinged upon the sovereignty of the foreign nation and if not adequately redressed could rise to an issue of war. *See* Vattel 463–464. It was this narrow set of violations of the law of nations, admitting of a judicial remedy and at the same time threatening serious consequences in international affairs, that was probably on [the] minds of the men who drafted the ATS with its reference to tort.

. . . .

3

Although Congress modified the draft of what became the Judiciary Act, *see generally* Warren, New Light on the History of the Federal Judiciary Act of 1789, 37 Harv. L. Rev. 49 (1923), it made hardly any changes to the provisions on aliens, including what became the ATS, *see* Casto, Law of Nations 498. There is no record of congressional discussion about private actions that might be subject to the jurisdictional provision, or about any need for further legislation to create private remedies; there is no record even of debate on the section. Given the poverty of drafting history, modern commentators have necessarily concentrated on the text, remarking on the innovative use of the word "tort," *see, e.g.*, Sweeney, A Tort only in Violation of the Law of Nations, 18 Hastings Int'l & Comp. L. Rev. 445 (1995) (arguing that "tort" refers to the law of prize), and the statute's mixture of terms expansive ("all suits"), *see, e.g.*, Casto, Law of Nations 500, and restrictive ("for a tort only"), *see, e.g.*, Randall, at 28–31 (limiting suits to torts, as opposed to commercial actions, especially by British plaintiffs).[12] The historical scholarship has also placed the ATS within the competition between federalist and antifederalist forces over the national role in foreign relations. *Id.*, at 22–23 (nonexclusiveness of federal jurisdiction under the ATS may reflect compromise). But despite considerable scholarly attention, it is fair to say that a consensus understanding of what Congress intended has proven elusive.

Still, the history does tend to support two propositions. First, there is every reason to suppose that the First Congress did not pass the ATS as a jurisdictional convenience to be placed on the shelf for use by a future Congress or state legislature that might, someday, authorize the creation of causes of action or itself decide to make some element of the law of nations actionable for the benefit of foreigners. The anxieties of the preconstitutional period cannot be ignored easily enough to think that the statute was not meant to have a practical effect. Consider that the principal draftsman of the ATS was apparently Oliver Ellsworth,[13] previously a member of the Continental Congress that had passed the 1781 resolution [calling on the States to enact laws punishing "infractions of the immunities of ambassadors and other public ministers, authorised and received as such by the United States in Congress assembled," targeting in particular "violence offered to their persons, houses, carriages and property," 21 Journal of the Continental Cong. 1136–37 (1784) (G. Hunt ed. 1912),] and a member of the Connecticut Legislature that made good on that congressional request. *See generally* W. Brown, The Life of Oliver Ellsworth (1905). Consider, too, that the First Congress was attentive enough to the law of nations to recognize certain offenses expressly as criminal, including the three mentioned by Blackstone. *See* An Act for the Punishment of Certain Crimes Against the United States, § 8, 1 Stat. 113–114 (murder or robbery, or other capital crimes, punishable as piracy if committed on the high seas), and § 28, *id.*, at 118 (violation of safe

12. The restriction may have served the different purpose of putting foreigners on notice that they would no longer be able to prosecute their own criminal cases in federal court. *Compare, e.g.*, 3 Commentaries 160 (victims could start prosecutions) with the Judiciary Act § 35. (creating the office of the district attorney). *Cf.* 1 Op. Atty. Gen. 41, 42 (1794) (British consul could not himself initiate criminal prosecution, but could provide evidence to the grand jury.)

13. The ATS appears in Ellsworth's handwriting in the original version of the bill in the National Archives. Casto, Law of Nations 498, n. 169.

conducts and assaults against ambassadors punished by imprisonment and fines described as "infract[ions of] the law of nations"). It would have been passing strange for Ellsworth and this very Congress to vest federal courts expressly with jurisdiction to entertain civil causes brought by aliens alleging violations of the law of nations, but to no effect whatever until the Congress should take further action. There is too much in the historical record to believe that Congress would have enacted the ATS only to leave it lying fallow indefinitely.

The second inference to be drawn from the history is that Congress intended the ATS to furnish jurisdiction for a relatively modest set of actions alleging violations of the law of nations. Uppermost in the legislative mind appears to have been offenses against ambassadors, *see id.*, at 118; violations of safe conduct were probably understood to be actionable, *ibid.*, and individual actions arising out of prize captures and piracy may well have also been contemplated, *id.*, at 113–114. But the common law appears to have understood only those three of the hybrid variety as definite and actionable, or at any rate, to have assumed only a very limited set of claims. As Blackstone had put it, "offences against this law [of nations] are principally incident to whole states or nations," and not individuals seeking relief in court. 4 Commentaries 68.

. . . .

In sum, although the ATS is a jurisdictional statute creating no new causes of action, the reasonable inference from the historical materials is that the statute was intended to have practical effect the moment it became law. The jurisdictional grant is best read as having been enacted on the understanding that the common law would provide a cause of action for the modest number of international law violations with a potential for personal liability at the time.

IV

We think it is correct, then, to assume that the First Congress understood that the district courts would recognize private causes of action for certain torts in violation of the law of nations, though we have found no basis to suspect Congress had any examples in mind beyond those torts corresponding to Blackstone's three primary offenses: violation of safe conducts, infringement of the rights of ambassadors, and piracy. We assume, too, that no development in the two centuries from the enactment of § 1350 to the birth of the modern line of cases beginning with *Filartiga v. Pena–Irala,* 630 F.2d 876 (2d Cir. 1980), has categorically precluded federal courts from recognizing a claim under the law of nations as an element of common law; Congress has not in any relevant way amended § 1350 or limited civil common law power by another statute. Still, there are good reasons for a restrained conception of the discretion a federal court should exercise in considering a new cause of action of this kind. Accordingly, we think courts should require any claim based on the present-day law of nations to rest on a norm of international character accepted by the civilized world and defined with a specificity comparable to the features of the 18th-century paradigms we have recognized. This requirement is fatal to Alvarez's claim.

A

A series of reasons argue for judicial caution when considering the kinds of individual claims that might implement the jurisdiction conferred by the early statute. First, the prevailing conception of the common law has changed since 1789 in a way that counsels restraint in judicially applying internationally generated norms. When § 1350 was enacted, the accepted conception was of the common law as "a transcendental body of law outside of any particular State but obligatory within it unless and until changed by statute." *Black and White Taxicab & Transfer Co. v. Brown and Yellow Taxicab & Transfer Co.,* 276 U.S. 518, 533 ... (1928) (Holmes, J., dissenting). Now, however, in most cases where a court is asked to state or formulate a common law principle in a new context, there is a general understanding that the law is not so much found or discovered as it is either made or created. Holmes explained famously in 1881 that

> "in substance the growth of the law is legislative ... [because t]he very considerations which judges most rarely mention, and always with an apology, are the secret root from which the law draws all the juices of life. I mean, of course, considerations of what is expedient for the community concerned." The Common Law 31–32 (Howe ed. 1963).

One need not accept the Holmesian view as far as its ultimate implications to acknowledge that a judge deciding in reliance on an international norm will find a substantial element of discretionary judgment in the decision.

Second, along with, and in part driven by, that conceptual development in understanding common law has come an equally significant rethinking of the role of the federal courts in making it. *Erie R. Co. v. Tompkins,* 304 U.S. 64 ... (1938), was the watershed in which we denied the existence of any federal "general" common law, *id.,* at 78, which largely withdrew to havens of specialty, some of them defined by express congressional authorization to devise a body of law directly, *e.g., Textile Workers v. Lincoln Mills of Ala.,* 353 U.S. 448 ... (1957) (interpretation of collective-bargaining agreements); Fed. Rule Evid. 501 (evidentiary privileges in federal-question cases). Elsewhere, this Court has thought it was in order to create federal common law rules in interstitial areas of particular federal interest. *E.g., United States v. Kimbell Foods, Inc.,* 440 U.S. 715, 726–727 ... (1979).[17] And although we have even assumed competence to make judicial rules of decision of particular importance to foreign relations, such as the act of state doctrine, *see Banco Nacional de Cuba v. Sabbatino,* 376 U.S. 398, 427 ... (1964), the general practice has

---

17. *See generally* R. Fallon, D. Meltzer & D. Shapiro, Hart and Wechsler's The Federal Courts and the Federal System ch. 7 (5th ed. 2003); Friendly, In Praise of *Erie*—and of the New Federal Common Law, 39 N.Y.U. L. Rev. 383, 405–422 (1964).

been to look for legislative guidance before exercising innovative authority over substantive law. It would be remarkable to take a more aggressive role in exercising a jurisdiction that remained largely in shadow for much of the prior two centuries.

Third, this Court has recently and repeatedly said that a decision to create a private right of action is one better left to legislative judgment in the great majority of cases. *Correctional Services Corp. v. Malesko,* 534 U.S. 61, 68 . . . (2001); *Alexander v. Sandoval,* 532 U.S. 275, 286–287 . . . (2001). The creation of a private right of action raises issues beyond the mere consideration whether underlying primary conduct should be allowed or not, entailing, for example, a decision to permit enforcement without the check imposed by prosecutorial discretion. Accordingly, even when Congress has made it clear by statute that a rule applies to purely domestic conduct, we are reluctant to infer intent to provide a private cause of action where the statute does not supply one expressly. While the absence of congressional action addressing private rights of action under an international norm is more equivocal than its failure to provide such a right when it creates a statute, the possible collateral consequences of making international rules privately actionable argue for judicial caution.

Fourth, the subject of those collateral consequences is itself a reason for a high bar to new private causes of action for violating international law, for the potential implications for the foreign relations of the United States of recognizing such causes should make courts particularly wary of impinging on the discretion of the Legislative and Executive Branches in managing foreign affairs. It is one thing for American courts to enforce constitutional limits on our own State and Federal Governments' power, but quite another to consider suits under rules that would go so far as to claim a limit on the power of foreign governments over their own citizens, and to hold that a foreign government or its agent has transgressed those limits. *Cf. Sabbatino, supra,* at 431–432. Yet modern international law is very much concerned with just such questions, and apt to stimulate calls for vindicating private interests in § 1350 cases. Since many attempts by federal courts to craft remedies for the violation of new norms of international law would raise risks of adverse foreign policy consequences, they should be undertaken, if at all, with great caution. *Cf. Tel–Oren v. Libyan Arab Republic,* 726 F.2d 774, 813 (D.C. Cir. 1984) (Bork, J., concurring) (expressing doubt that § 1350 should be read to require "our courts [to] sit in judgment of the conduct of foreign officials in their own countries with respect to their own citizens").

The fifth reason is particularly important in light of the first four. We have no congressional mandate to seek out and define new and debatable violations of the law of nations, and modern indications of congressional understanding of the judicial role in the field have not affirmatively encouraged greater judicial creativity. It is true that a clear mandate appears in the Torture Victim Protection Act of 1991, 106 Stat. 73, providing authority that "establish[es] an unambiguous and modern basis for" federal claims of torture and extrajudicial killing, H.R.Rep. No. 102–

367, pt. 1, p. 3 (1991). But that affirmative authority is confined to specific subject matter, and although the legislative history includes the remark that § 1350 should "remain intact to permit suits based on other norms that already exist or may ripen in the future into rules of customary international law," *id.*, at 4, Congress as a body has done nothing to promote such suits. Several times, indeed, the Senate has expressly declined to give the federal courts the task of interpreting and applying international human rights law, as when its ratification of the International Covenant on Civil and Political Rights declared that the substantive provisions of the document were not self-executing. 138 Cong. Rec. 8071 (1992).

B

These reasons argue for great caution in adapting the law of nations to private rights. Justice SCALIA, *post,* (opinion concurring in part and concurring in judgment) concludes that caution is too hospitable, and a word is in order to summarize where we have come so far and to focus our difference with him on whether some norms of today's law of nations may ever be recognized legitimately by federal courts in the absence of congressional action beyond § 1350. All Members of the Court agree that § 1350 is only jurisdictional. We also agree, or at least Justice SCALIA does not dispute, *post,* that the jurisdiction was originally understood to be available to enforce a small number of international norms that a federal court could properly recognize as within the common law enforceable without further statutory authority. Justice Scalia concludes, however, that two subsequent developments should be understood to preclude federal courts from recognizing any further international norms as judicially enforceable today, absent further congressional action. As described before, we now tend to understand common law not as a discoverable reflection of universal reason but, in a positivistic way, as a product of human choice. And we now adhere to a conception of limited judicial power first expressed in reorienting federal diversity jurisdiction, *see Erie R. Co. v. Tompkins,* 304 U.S. 64 . . . (1938), that federal courts have no authority to derive "general" common law.

Whereas JUSTICE SCALIA sees these developments as sufficient to close the door to further independent judicial recognition of actionable international norms, other considerations persuade us that the judicial power should be exercised on the understanding that the door is still ajar subject to vigilant doorkeeping, and thus open to a narrow class of international norms today. *Erie* did not in terms bar any judicial recognition of new substantive rules, no matter what the circumstances, and post-*Erie* understanding has identified limited enclaves in which federal courts may derive some substantive law in a common law way. For two centuries we have affirmed that the domestic law of the United States recognizes the law of nations. *See, e.g., Sabbatino,* 376 U.S., at 423 ("[I]t is, of course, true that United States courts apply international law as a part of our own in appropriate circumstances");[18] *The Paquete Habana,* 175 U.S., at 700 ("International law is part of our law, and must be ascertained and administered by the courts of justice of appropriate jurisdiction, as often as questions of right depending upon it are duly presented for their determination"); *The Nereide,* 9 Cranch 388, 423 ... (1815) (Marshall, C.J.) ("[T]he Court is bound by the law of nations which is a part of the law of the land"); *see also Texas Industries, Inc. v. Radcliff Materials, Inc.,* 451 U.S. 630, 641 ... (1981) (recognizing that "international disputes implicating ... our relations with foreign nations" are one of the "narrow areas" in which "federal common law" continues to exist). It would take some explaining to say now that federal courts must avert their gaze entirely from any international norm intended to protect individuals.

We think an attempt to justify such a position would be particularly unconvincing in light of what we know about congressional understanding bearing on this issue lying at the intersection of the judicial and legislative powers. The First Congress, which reflected the understanding of the framing generation and included some of the Framers, assumed that federal courts could properly identify some international norms as enforceable in the exercise of § 1350 jurisdiction. We think it would be unreasonable to assume that the First Congress would have expected federal courts to lose all capacity to recognize enforceable international norms simply because the common law might lose some metaphysical cachet on the road to modern realism. Later Congresses seem to have shared our view. The position we take today has been assumed by some federal courts for 24 years, ever since the Second Circuit decided *Filartiga v. Pena–Irala,* 630 F.2d 876 (2d Cir. 1980), and for practical purposes the point of today's disagreement has been focused since the exchange between Judge Edwards and Judge Bork in *Tel-Oren v. Libyan Arab Republic,* 726 F.2d 774 (D.C. Cir. 1984), Congress, however, has not only expressed no disagreement with our view of the proper exercise of the judicial power, but has responded to its most notable instance by enacting legislation supplementing the judicial determination in some detail. *See supra* (discussing the Torture Victim Protection Act).

While we agree with Justice SCALIA to the point that we would welcome any congressional guidance in exercising jurisdiction with such obvious potential to affect foreign relations, nothing Congress has done is a reason for us to shut the door to the law of nations entirely. It is enough to say that Congress may do that at any time (explicitly, or implicitly by treaties or statutes that occupy the field), just as it may modify or cancel any judicial decision so far as it rests on recognizing an international norm as such.[19]

---

18. *Sabbatino* itself did not directly apply international law, *see* 376 U.S., at 421–423, but neither did it question the application of that law in appropriate cases, and it further endorsed the reasoning of a noted commentator who had argued that *Erie* should not preclude the continued application of international law in federal courts. 376 U.S., at 425 (citing Jessup, The Doctrine of Erie Railroad v. Tompkins Applied to International Law, 33 Am. J. Int'l L. 740 (1939)).

19. Our position does not, as Justice SCALIA suggests, imply that every grant of jurisdiction to a federal court carries with it an opportunity to develop common law (so that the grant of federal-

C

We must still, however, derive a standard or set of standards for assessing the particular claim Alvarez raises, and for this action it suffices to look to the historical antecedents. Whatever the ultimate criteria for accepting a cause of action subject to jurisdiction under § 1350, we are persuaded that federal courts should not recognize private claims under federal common law for violations of any international law norm with less definite content and acceptance among civilized nations than the historical paradigms familiar when § 1350 was enacted. *See, e.g., United States v. Smith,* 5 Wheat. 153, 163–180, n. a . . . (1820) (illustrating the specificity with which the law of nations defined piracy). This limit upon judicial recognition is generally consistent with the reasoning of many of the courts and judges who faced the issue before it reached this Court. See *Filartiga, supra,* at 890 ("[F]or purposes of civil liability, the torturer has become—like the pirate and slave trader before him—hostis humani generis, an enemy of all mankind"); *Tel-Oren, supra,* at 781 (Edwards, J., concurring) (suggesting that the "limits of section 1350's reach" be defined by "a handful of heinous actions—each of which violates definable, universal and obligatory norms"); *see also In re Estate of Marcos, Human Rights Litigation,* 25 F.3d 1467, 1475 (9th Cir. 1994) ("Actionable violations of international law must be of a norm that is specific, universal, and obligatory"). And the determination whether a norm is sufficiently definite to support a cause of action[20] should (and, indeed, inevitably must) involve an element of judgment about the practical consequences of making that cause available to litigants in the federal courts.[21]

---

question jurisdiction would be equally as good for our purposes as § 1350), *see post,* n. 1. Section 1350 was enacted on the congressional understanding that courts would exercise jurisdiction by entertaining some common law claims derived from the law of nations; and we know of no reason to think that federal-question jurisdiction was extended subject to any comparable congressional assumption. Further, our holding today is consistent with the division of responsibilities between federal and state courts after *Erie, see supra,* as a more expansive common law power related to 28 U.S.C. § 1331 might not be.

20. A related consideration is whether international law extends the scope of liability for a violation of a given norm to the perpetrator being sued, if the defendant is a private actor such as a corporation or individual. *Compare Tel–Oren v. Libyan Arab Republic,* 726 F.2d 774, 791–795 (D.C. Cir.1984) (Edwards, J., concurring) (insufficient consensus in 1984 that torture by private actors violates international law), with *Kadic v. Karadzic,* 70 F.3d 232, 239–241 (2d Cir. 1995) (sufficient consensus in 1995 that genocide by private actors violates international law).

21. This requirement of clear definition is not meant to be the only principle limiting the availability of relief in the federal courts for violations of customary international law, though it disposes of this case. For example, the European Commission argues as *amicus curiae* that basic principles of international law require that before asserting a claim in a foreign forum, the claimant must have exhausted any remedies available in the domestic legal system, and perhaps in other fora such as international claims tribunals. *See* Brief for European Commission as *Amicus Curiae* 24, n. 54 (citing I. Brownlie, Principles of Public International Law 472–481 (6th ed.2003)); cf. Torture Victim Protection Act of 1991, § 2(b), 106 Stat. 73 (exhaustion requirement). We would certainly consider this requirement in an appropriate case. Another possible limitation that we need not apply here is a policy of case-specific deference to the political branches. For example, there are now pending in federal district court several class actions seeking damages from various corporations alleged to have participated in, or abetted, the regime of apartheid that formerly controlled South Africa. *See In re South African Apartheid Litigation,* 238 F. Supp. 2d 1379 (J.P.M.L. 2002) (granting a motion to transfer the cases to the Southern District of New York). The Government of South Africa has said that these cases interfere with the policy embodied by its Truth and Reconciliation Commission, which "deliberately avoided a

Thus, Alvarez's detention claim must be gauged against the current state of international law, looking to those sources we have long, albeit cautiously, recognized.

> "[W]here there is no treaty, and no controlling executive or legislative act or judicial decision, resort must be had to the customs and usages of civilized nations; and, as evidence of these, to the works of jurists and commentators, who by years of labor, research and experience, have made themselves peculiarly well acquainted with the subjects of which they treat. Such works are resorted to by judicial tribunals, not for the speculations of their authors concerning what the law ought to be, but for trustworthy evidence of what the law really is." *The Paquete Habana,* 175 U.S., at 700.

To begin with, Alvarez cites two well-known international agreements that, despite their moral authority, have little utility under the standard set out in this opinion. He says that his abduction by Sosa was an "arbitrary arrest" within the meaning of the Universal Declaration of Human Rights (Declaration), G.A. Res. 217A (III), U.N. Doc. A/810 (1948). And he traces the rule against arbitrary arrest not only to the Declaration, but also to article nine of the International Covenant on Civil and Political Rights (Covenant), Dec. 16, 1966, 999 U.N.T.S. 171,[22] to which the United States is a party, and to various other conventions to which it is not. But the Declaration does not of its own force impose obligations as a matter of international law. *See* Humphrey, The UN Charter and the Universal Declaration of Human Rights, in The International Protection of Human Rights 39, 50 (E. Luard ed. 1967) (quoting Eleanor Roosevelt calling the Declaration " 'a statement of principles . . . setting up a common standard of achievement for all peoples and all nations' " and " 'not a treaty or international agreement . . . impos[ing] legal obligations' ").[23] And, although the Covenant does bind the United States as a matter of international law, the United States ratified the Covenant on the express understanding that it was not self-executing and so did not itself create obligations enforceable in the federal courts. *See supra.* Accordingly, Alvarez cannot say that the Declaration and Covenant themselves establish the relevant and applicable rule of international law. He instead

'victors' justice' approach to the crimes of apartheid and chose instead one based on confession and absolution, informed by the principles of reconciliation, reconstruction, reparation and goodwill." Declaration of Penuell Mpapa Maduna, Minister of Justice and Constitutional Development, Republic of South Africa, reprinted in App. to Brief for Government of Commonwealth of Australia et al. as Amici Curiae 7a, ¶ 3.2.1 (emphasis deleted). The United States has agreed. *See* Letter of William H. Taft IV, Legal Adviser, U.S. Dept. of State, to Shannen W. Coffin, Deputy Asst. Atty. Gen., Oct. 27, 2003, *reprinted in id.*, at 2a. In such cases, there is a strong argument that federal courts should give serious weight to the Executive Branch's view of the case's impact on foreign policy. . . .

22. Article nine provides that "[n]o one shall be subjected to arbitrary arrest or detention," that "[n]o one shall be deprived of his liberty except on such grounds and in accordance with such procedure as are established by law," and that "[a]nyone who has been the victim of unlawful arrest or detention shall have an enforceable right to compensation." 999 U.N.T. S., at 175–176.

23. It has nevertheless had substantial indirect effect on international law. *See* Brownlie, *supra*, at 535 (calling the Declaration a "good example of an informal prescription given legal significance by the actions of authoritative decision-makers").

attempts to show that prohibition of arbitrary arrest has attained the status of binding customary international law.

Here, it is useful to examine Alvarez's complaint in greater detail. As he presently argues it, the claim does not rest on the cross-border feature of his abduction. Although the District Court granted relief in part on finding a violation of international law in taking Alvarez across the border from Mexico to the United States, the Court of Appeals rejected that ground of liability for failure to identify a norm of requisite force prohibiting a forcible abduction across a border. Instead, it relied on the conclusion that the law of the United States did not authorize Alvarez's arrest, because the DEA lacked extraterritorial authority under 21 U.S.C. § 878, and because Federal Rule of Criminal Procedure 4(d)(2) limited the warrant for Alvarez's arrest to "the jurisdiction of the United States." It is this position that Alvarez takes now: that his arrest was arbitrary and as such forbidden by international law not because it infringed the prerogatives of Mexico, but because no applicable law authorized it.

Alvarez thus invokes a general prohibition of "arbitrary" detention defined as officially sanctioned action exceeding positive authorization to detain under the domestic law of some government, regardless of the circumstances. Whether or not this is an accurate reading of the Covenant, Alvarez cites little authority that a rule so broad has the status of a binding customary norm today.[27] He certainly cites nothing to justify the federal courts in taking his broad rule as the predicate for a federal lawsuit, for its implications would be breathtaking. His rule would support a cause of action in federal court for any arrest, anywhere in the world, unauthorized by the law of the jurisdiction in which it took place, and would create a cause of action for any seizure of an alien in violation of the Fourth Amendment, supplanting the actions under Rev. Stat. § 1979, 42 U.S.C. § 1983, and *Bivens v. Six Unknown Fed. Narcotics Agents*, 403 U.S. 388 ... (1971), that now provide damages remedies for such violations. It would create an action in federal court for arrests by state officers who simply exceed their authority; and for the violation of any limit that the law of any country might place on the authority of its own officers to arrest. And all of this assumes that Alvarez could establish that Sosa was acting on behalf of a government when he made the arrest, for otherwise he would need a rule broader still.

27. Specifically, he relies on a survey of national constitutions, Bassiouni, Human Rights in the Context of Criminal Justice: Identifying International Procedural Protections and Equivalent Protections in National Constitutions, 3 Duke J. Comp. & Int'l L. 235, 260–261 (1993); a case from the International Court of Justice, *United States v. Iran*, 1980 I.C.J. 3, 42; and some authority drawn from the federal courts. None of these suffice. The Bassiouni survey does show that many nations recognize a norm against arbitrary detention, but that consensus is at a high level of generality. The *Iran* case, in which the United States sought relief for the taking of its diplomatic and consular staff as hostages, involved a different set of international norms and mentioned the problem of arbitrary detention only in passing; the detention in that case was, moreover, far longer and harsher than Alvarez's. *See* 1980 I.C. J., at 42, ¶ 91 ("detention of [United States] staff by a group of armed militants" lasted "many months"). And the authority from the federal courts, to the extent it supports Alvarez's position, reflects a more assertive view of federal judicial discretion over claims based on customary international law than the position we take today.

Alvarez's failure to marshal support for his proposed rule is underscored by the Restatement (Third) of Foreign Relations Law of the United States (1986), which says in its discussion of customary international human rights law that a "state violates international law if, as a matter of state policy, it practices, encourages, or condones . . . prolonged arbitrary detention." 2 *Id.*, § 702. Although the Restatement does not explain its requirements of a "state policy" and of "prolonged" detention, the implication is clear. Any credible invocation of a principle against arbitrary detention that the civilized world accepts as binding customary international law requires a factual basis beyond relatively brief detention in excess of positive authority. Even the Restatement's limits are only the beginning of the enquiry, because although it is easy to say that some policies of prolonged arbitrary detentions are so bad that those who enforce them become enemies of the human race, it may be harder to say which policies cross that line with the certainty afforded by Blackstone's three common law offenses. In any event, the label would never fit the reckless policeman who botches his warrant, even though that same officer might pay damages under municipal law. *E.g.*, *Groh v. Ramirez*, 540 U.S. 551 . . . (2004).[28]

Whatever may be said for the broad principle Alvarez advances, in the present, imperfect world, it expresses an aspiration that exceeds any binding customary rule having the specificity we require.[29] Creating a private cause of action to further that aspiration would go beyond any residual common law discretion we think it appropriate to exercise.[30] It is enough to hold that a single illegal detention of less than a day, followed by the transfer of custody to lawful authorities and a prompt arraignment, violates no norm of customary international law so well defined as to support the creation of a federal remedy.

The judgment of the Court of Appeals is

Reversed.

---

28. In this action, Sosa might well have been liable under Mexican law. Alvarez asserted such a claim, but the District Court concluded that the applicable law was the law of California, and that under California law Sosa had been privileged to make a citizen's arrest in Mexico. Whether this was correct is not now before us, though we discern tension between the court's simultaneous conclusions that the detention so lacked any legal basis as to violate international law, yet was privileged by state law against ordinary tort recovery.

29. It is not that violations of a rule logically foreclose the existence of that rule as international law. *Cf. Filartiga v. Pena-Irala,* 630 F.2d 876, 884, n. 15 (2d Cir. 1980) ("The fact that the prohibition of torture is often honored in the breach does not diminish its binding effect as a norm of international law"). Nevertheless, that a rule as stated is as far from full realization as the one Alvarez urges is evidence against its status as binding law; and an even clearer point against the creation by judges of a private cause of action to enforce the aspiration behind the rule claimed.

30. Alvarez also cites Brief for Respondent Alvarez-Machain 49–50, a finding by a United Nations working group that his detention was arbitrary under the Declaration, the Covenant, and customary international law. *See* Report of the United Nations Working Group on Arbitrary Detention, U.N. Doc. E/CN.4/1994/27, pp. 139–140 (Dec. 17, 1993). That finding is not addressed, however, to our demanding standard of definition, which must be met to raise even the possibility of a private cause of action. If Alvarez wishes to seek compensation on the basis of the working group's finding, he must address his request to Congress.

JUSTICE SCALIA, with whom the CHIEF JUSTICE and JUSTICE THOMAS join, concurring in part and concurring in the judgment.

. . . .

III.

The analysis in the Court's opinion departs from my own in this respect: After concluding in Part III that "the ATS is a jurisdictional statute creating no new causes of action," *ante,* the Court addresses at length in Part IV the "good reasons for a restrained conception of the *discretion* a federal court should exercise in considering a new cause of action" under the ATS. *Ibid.* (emphasis added). By framing the issue as one of "discretion," the Court skips over the antecedent question of authority. This neglects the "lesson of *Erie*," that "grants of jurisdiction alone" (which the Court has acknowledged the ATS to be) "are not themselves grants of lawmaking authority." *Meltzer, supra.* On this point, the Court observes only that no development between the enactment of the ATS (in 1789) and the birth of modern international human rights litigation under that statute (in 1980) "has categorically *precluded* federal courts from recognizing a claim under the law of nations as an element of common law." *Ante* (emphasis added). This turns our jurisprudence regarding federal common law on its head. The question is not what case or congressional action *prevents* federal courts from applying the law of nations as part of the general common law; it is what *authorizes* that peculiar exception from *Erie*'s fundamental holding that a general common law *does not exist.*

. . . .

Because today's federal common law is not our Framers' general common law, the question presented by the suggestion of discretionary authority to enforce the law of nations is not whether to extend old-school general-common-law adjudication. Rather, it is whether to create new federal common law. The Court masks the novelty of its approach when it suggests that the difference between us is that I would "close the door to further independent judicial recognition of actionable international norms," whereas the Court would permit the exercise of judicial power "on the understanding that the door is still ajar subject to vigilant doorkeeping." *Ante.* The general common law was the old door. We do not close that door today, for the deed was done in *Erie.* Federal common law is a *new* door. The question is not whether that door will be left ajar, but whether this Court will open it.

. . . .

To be sure, today's opinion does not itself precipitate a direct confrontation with Congress by creating a cause of action that Congress has not. But it invites precisely that action by the lower courts, even while recognizing (1) that Congress understood the difference between granting jurisdiction and creating a federal cause of action in 1789, (2) that Congress understands that difference today, and (3) that the ATS itself supplies only jurisdiction. *Ante.* In holding open the possibility that judges may create rights where Congress has not authorized them to do so, the Court countenances judicial occupation of a domain that belongs to the people's representatives. One does not need a crystal ball to predict that this occupation will not be long in coming, since the Court endorses the reasoning of "many of the courts and judges who faced the issue before it reached this Court," including the Second and Ninth Circuits. *Ante.*

The Ninth Circuit brought us the judgment that the Court reverses today. Perhaps its decision in this particular case, like the decisions of other lower federal courts that receive passing attention in the Court's opinion, "reflects a more assertive view of federal judicial discretion over claims based on customary international law than the position we take today." *Ante.* But the verbal formula it applied is the same verbal formula that the Court explicitly endorses. *Compare ante* (quoting *In re Estate of Marcos, Human Rights Litigation*, 25 F.3d 1467, 1475 (9th Cir. 1994), for the proposition that actionable norms must be " 'specific, universal, and obligatory' "), with 331 F.3d 604, 621 (9th Cir. 2003) (en banc) (finding the norm against arbitrary arrest and detention in this action to be "universal, obligatory, and specific"); *id.*, at 619 ("[A]n actionable claim under the [ATS] requires the showing of a violation of the law of nations that is specific, universal, and obligatory" (internal quotation marks omitted)). Endorsing the very formula that led the Ninth Circuit to its result in this action hardly seems to be a recipe for restraint in the future.

The Second Circuit, which started the Judiciary down the path the Court today tries to hedge in, is a good indicator of where that path leads us: directly into confrontation with the political branches. *Kadic v. Karadzíc*, 70 F.3d 232 (2d Cir. 1995), provides a case in point. One of the norms at issue in that case was a norm against genocide set forth in the Convention on the Prevention and Punishment of the Crime of Genocide, Dec. 9, 1948, 78 U.N.T.S. 278. The Second Circuit held that the norm was actionable under the ATS after applying Circuit case law that the Court today endorses. 70 F.3d, at 238–239, 241–242. The Court of Appeals then did something that is perfectly logical and yet truly remarkable: It dismissed the determination by Congress and the Executive that this norm should *not* give rise to a private cause of action. We *know* that Congress and the Executive made this determination, because Congress inscribed it into the Genocide Convention Implementation Act of 1987, 18 U.S.C. § 1091 *et seq.*, a law signed by the President attaching criminal penalties to the norm against genocide. The Act, Congress said, shall not "be construed as creating any substantive or procedural right enforceable by law by any party in any proceeding." § 1092. Undeterred, the Second Circuit reasoned that this "decision not to create a *new* private remedy" could hardly be construed as *repealing* by implication the cause of action supplied by the ATS. 70 F.3d, at 242 (emphasis added). Does this Court truly wish to encourage the use of a jurisdiction-granting statute with respect to which there is "no record of congressional discussion about private actions that might be subject to the jurisdictional provision, or about any need for further legislation to create private remedies; [and] no record even of debate on the section," *ante,* to override a clear indication from the political branches that a "specific, universal, and obligatory" norm against genocide is *not* to be enforced through a private damages action? Today's opinion leads the lower courts right down that perilous path.

. . . .

We Americans have a method for making the laws that are over us. We elect representatives to two Houses of Congress, each of which must enact the new law and present it for the approval of a President, whom we also elect. For over two decades now, unelected federal judges have been usurping this lawmaking power by converting what they regard as norms of international law into American law. Today's opinion approves that process in principle, though urging the lower courts to be more restrained.

This Court seems incapable of admitting that some matters—*any* matters—are none of its business. *See, e.g., Rasul v. Bush, ante*, 542 U.S. 446 . . . (2004); *INS v. St. Cyr*, 533 U.S. 289 . . . (2001). In today's latest victory for its Never Say Never Jurisprudence, the Court ignores its own conclusion that the ATS provides only jurisdiction, wags a finger at the lower courts for going too far, and then—repeating the same formula the ambitious lower courts *themselves* have used—invites them to try again.

NOTE ON THE DOORS OPENED, AND CLOSED, IN SOSA

1. *The Supreme Court Jumps In*. One key issue that *Sosa* decided was that the ATS is solely a jurisdictional statute; it does not itself provide a cause of action. At the same time, the Court concluded that a cause of action could be found in either treaties or customary international law, notwithstanding *Erie*. Although the Court rejected the plaintiff's claim that he had been subjected to a violation of the law of nations, the Court accepted that the ATS encompassed torts existing under contemporary international law, and cited *Filartiga* favorably in the course of its decision. What standards did the Court set for the type of international norm that must be established by a plaintiff? Is the Court's decision best read as basically articulating an evidentiary standard for ATS cases (*i.e.*, establishing what must be proved to establish an actionable violation of the law of nations)?

Why exactly did Alvarez–Machain lose? Did the Court find that there was no international consensus supporting a norm against arbitrary arrest and detention? Or is the decision limited to a finding of no violation of the law of nations when there is a "single illegal detention of less than a day, followed by a transfer of custody to lawful authorities and a prompt arraignment"? If that is the central finding, then is the discussion of the Universal Declaration of Human Rights and the International Covenant on Civil and Political Rights (ICCPR) dicta? Recall that the *Filartiga* decision cited favorably to and relied upon the Universal Declaration.

Not only is there uncertainty about from whence the ATS came, but, after *Sosa*, there remains some dispute about where the ATS will go. Was the

Supreme Court in *Sosa* right in rejecting the idea that further congressional action was necessary to create causes of action under the ATS? Was the Supreme Court right to accept actionable torts under the law of nations other than Blackstone's three specific offenses? Do you think the Court has properly circumscribed the reach of the law, or do you agree with Justice Scalia that little guidance has been provided? Is its holding—that the law provided a cause of action for a "modest number of international law violations thought to carry personal liability at the time"—consistent with the general thrust of domestic incorporation of the law of nations? Are you worried that the *Sosa* decision leaves too much discretion to federal judges in these cases? Are you concerned that it allows judges to apply as U.S. law norms that were not created through U.S. democratic institutions? For post-*Sosa* examples, see *Taveras v. Taveraz*, 477 F.3d 767 (6th Cir. 2007) (rejecting an ATS claim based on a cross-border parental child abduction, on grounds that the sources of international law upon which plaintiff based his claim are neither specific enough nor widely accepted enough to satisfy the *Sosa* standard), and *Cisneros v. Aragon*, 485 F.3d 1226 (10th Cir. 2007) (rejecting an ATS claim based on the crime of statutory rape, on grounds that it did not meet the *Sosa* standard).

2. *Statutory Fix?* Should the ATS be repealed on the ground that it either means far too much or nothing at all? For a post-*Sosa* proposal for a new statute replacing the ATS, see Ralph G. Steinhardt, *Laying One Bankrupt Critique to Rest:* Sosa v. Alvarez–Machain *and the Future of International Human Rights Litigation*, 57 VANDERBILT L. REV. 2241, 2294 (2004). For a short-lived alternative that articulated a limited number of actionable torts, largely so as increase certainty for U.S.-based multinational corporations, see Alien Tort Statute Reform Act, S. 1874, 109th Cong. (1st Sess. 2005); 151 Cong. Rec. 22,858 (2005).

3. *Corporate Complicity and the ATS.* Commentary—as well as efforts at legislative reform—frequently note that the targets of ATS lawsuits have changed over time. *Filartiga* and *Sosa* considered ATS claims against individuals, neither of whom was serving at the time in an official capacity. Attempts to attach responsibility to government actors typically provoke immunities-based defenses, considered in greater depth in Chapter 7, Section 6. It is unsurprising, then, that plaintiffs would seek to establish the liability of corporate actors for complicity in human rights abuses—in the typical case, when a corporation engages in a joint venture with a foreign government, which in turn commits human rights violations in furtherance of the venture.

For example, in 1996 villagers from Myanmar (Burma) filed a class action lawsuit in U.S. federal court against, inter alia, a U.S. corporation (Unocal), alleging that Unocal was responsible under the ATS for international human rights violations, including forced labor perpetrated by the Burmese military in furtherance of the pipeline portion of a natural gas joint venture with the Myanmar government. The district court initially found that corporations may fall within the ambit of the ATS, *see Doe v. Unocal Corp.*, 963 F.Supp. 880 (C.D. Cal. 1997), but following discovery granted Unocal's motion for summary judgment because—as a factual matter—the corporation was not sufficiently connected to the construction and operation of the gas pipeline to sustain a claim that it engaged in a tort "in violation of the law of nations or a treaty of the United States." Doe v. Unocal Corp., 110 F. Supp. 2d 1294 (C.D. Cal. 2000).

A Ninth Circuit Court of Appeals panel held that the district court erred in requiring that the plaintiffs must show that Unocal controlled the Burmese military's actions in order to establish Unocal's liability. Rather, the plaintiffs needed to show only that Unocal "knowingly assisted" the military in perpetrating the abuses, and they had produced sufficient evidence under this standard for the case to proceed to trial on the forced labor claim (but not for claims of torture). *See* Doe I v. Unocal Corp., 395 F.3d 932 (9th Cir. 2002). Soon thereafter, the Ninth Circuit decided to rehear the appeal before the full eleven-judge court and vacated the decision of the three-judge panel. *See* Doe I v. Unocal Corp., 395 F.3d 978 (9th Cir. 2003). Before the Ninth Circuit could reach a final decision, however, the parties announced a settlement. Although the terms of the settlement were not released publicly, Unocal stated that it would pay the plaintiffs an unspecified amount of money and fund programs to improve the living conditions of people who lived in the region surrounding the pipeline and who may have suffered hardships.

The Second Circuit, home of *Filartiga*, has been especially active in wrestling with the issues posed by corporate liability under the ATS. On one of the issues in the Unocal litigation, aiding and abetting liability, the Second Circuit held that actionable conduct must be done with the intention of violating the law of nations. Presbyterian Church of Sudan v. Talisman Energy, 582 F.3d 244 (2d Cir. 2009). Later, considering the issue of its own accord, another panel held that the ATS does not confer jurisdiction over claims against corporations at all; because corporations were not subject to liability under customary international law, they were not liable under the ATS. Kiobel v. Royal Dutch Petroleum, 621 F.3d 111 (2d Cir. 2010). *But see id.* at 149, 174–76 (Leval, J., concurring in the judgment) (accepting that international law may in theory resolve whether corporations should be held liable for violations of customary international law, but in fact leaves the question to domestic law).

Talisman arguably overshadowed *Kiobel*, given that under *Talisman*'s approach corporate liability would at most have extended to corporations that purposefully involved themselves in genocide or other wrongs satisfying the *Sosa* standard. Kiobel v. Royal Dutch Petroleum, 642 F.3d 268 (2d Cir. 2011) (statement of Jacobs, J., concurring in the denial of panel rehearing). In any event, both decisions looked to customary international law, whether for establishing the standard for aiding-and-abetting liability or for determining whether to recognize corporate liability for violation of customary international law norms. Under *Sosa*, do you think that approach was correct? Would you apply international law to one question, but not the other? Would it be preferable to apply national law, or would it be proper to apply the law of the state where the underlying events occurred? *See* Wiwa v. Royal Dutch Petroleum Co., 226 F.3d 88, 105 n.12 (2d Cir. 2000) (noting ATS cases applying international law, forum state law, and foreign law to address comparable questions); Chimène I. Keitner, *Conceptualizing Complicity in Alien Tort Cases*, 60 HASTINGS L.J. 61 (2008) (distinguishing between conduct-regulating rules, like accomplice liability, that are defined by international law, as opposed to ancillary questions governed by domestic law).

In practice, other post-*Sosa* decisions have divided as to the proper source of law to be applied to aiding-and-abetting questions and, even among those courts drawing on the same source of law, reached different conclusions as to the proper standard. *See, e.g.*, Doe v. Exxon Mobil Corp., 2011 WL 2652384 (D.C. Cir. 2011) (adopting less demanding "knowledge" standard, based on customary international law, but suggesting that "[f]or all practical purposes" the federal common law standard was identical and could be applied); Aziz v. Alcolac, Inc., 2011 WL 434935 (4th Cir. 2011) (adopting purpose standard, following *Talisman*); Doe I v. Unocal Corp., 395 F.3d at 948–51 (Pregerson, J.) (deriving from international law, in vacated panel opinion, less demanding aiding-and-abetting standard of "knowing practical assistance or encouragement which has a substantial effect on the perpetration of the crime"); *id.* at 963–65 (Reinhardt, J., concurring) (applying federal common law to determine aiding-and-abetting standard). They had, prior to *Kiobel*, been more uniform in deciding (or at least assuming) that corporations may be held liable. *See, e.g.*, Romero v. Drummond Co., 552 F.3d 1303, 1315–16 (11th Cir. 2008) (reaffirming that the ATS confers jurisdiction over actions against corporations); *see also Doe v. Exxon Mobil, supra* (rejecting *Kiobel* and upholding corporate liability under ATS). *But see* Doe v. Nestle, S.A., 748 F. Supp. 2d 1057, 1128–29 (C.D. Cal. 2010) (noting contrary district court decisions, but deciding in dicta that there was an insufficient consensus under international law supporting corporate liability). While aiding-and-abetting liability and corporate liability have received the most attention, other issues central to ATS litigation remain mired in fundamental questions relating to the proper choice of law. *See, e.g.,* Sarei v. Rio Tinto, PLC, 550 F.3d 822, 827–32 (9th Cir. 2008) (en banc) (describing prior exhaustion of ATS claims as a "prudential" requirement of domestic law); *id.* at 833, 833-37 (Bea, J., concurring) (describing prior exhaustion as a substantive element of the international law claim); *id.* at 841–46 (Reinhardt, J., dissenting) (suggesting that neither domestic nor international law requires prior exhaustion).

4. *Effects of Ratifying the Convention Against Torture.* After the United States ratified the Convention Against Torture (CAT) in 1994, there was little difficulty in determining that a treaty-based norm prohibiting state-sponsored torture existed in international law and was binding upon the United States. Yet when ratifying the CAT, the United States filed a declaration asserting that the operative provisions of the convention were not "self-executing" in the United States; as you will see, one way to understand that declaration is that the prohibition on state-sponsored torture contained in the CAT could not be relied upon in an ATS action in U.S. court (*see* Chapter 3, Section 4). If so, would an ATS claim, even after U.S. ratification of the CAT, still have to rely upon the prohibition on state-sponsored torture that exists in customary international law? Or did the ATS itself serve as the U.S. statute that allowed the prohibition contained in the CAT to be "executed" in U.S. law for purposes of tort actions by aliens? Consider again the *Sosa* majority's treatment of the ICCPR and Justice Scalia's critique of the Second Circuit's decision in *Kadic v. Karadzic*. *See also* Flomo v. Firestone Natural Rubber Co., 2010 WL 4174583, *8 (S.D. Ind. 2010) (holding that because International Labor Organization convention relating to child "was . . . non-self-executing, it likewise cannot form a basis for an ATS claim was non-self-executing").

5. *Torture Victim Protection Act.* In 1992, Congress adopted the Torture Victim Protection Act, 28 U.S.C. § 1350 note (2006). The TVPA imposes civil liability on any "individual who, under actual or apparent authority, or color of law, of any foreign nation ... subjects an individual to torture ... or ... to extrajudicial killing." TVPA § 2(a). Rather than making a direct cross-reference to the "law of nations," the statute defines torture using language virtually identical to that found in the Convention Against Torture. The TVPA differs from the ATS insofar as it provides that the claim must concern action under the authority of a foreign government, that the claimant need not be an alien, and that, in order to bring a claim under the statute, a claimant must have "exhausted [any] adequate and available remedies in the place in which the conduct giving rise to the claim occurred." *Id.* § 2(b). For further text of the statute, see Chapter 3, Section 3.

The Senate report on the TVPA states that the statute was intended to "establish an unambiguous basis for a cause of action that has been successfully maintained under [the ATS,] ... which permits Federal district courts to hear claims by aliens for torts committed 'in violation of the law of nations.'" S. REP. NO. 102–249, at 4 (1991). The report specifically noted that "[t]he *Filartiga* case has met with general approval." Recognizing that "[a]t least one Federal judge ... has questioned whether [the ATS] can be used by victims of torture committed in foreign nations absent an explicit grant of a cause of action by Congress," *id.* (citing *Tel-Oren*, 726 F.2d at 774 (Bork, J., concurring)), the Senate report concluded that "[t]he TVPA would provide such a grant," *id.* at 5.

Does the TVPA defer to the law of nations as clearly as does the ATS? The case below suggests ways that the TVPA allows customary norms of international law—including norms identified by international courts and tribunals—to be applied as a part of U.S. law, in this instance in the context of norms relating to the important issue of command responsibility.

FORD v. GARCIA

289 F.3d 1283 (11th Cir. 2002) (footnotes omitted).

KRAVITCH, CIRCUIT JUDGE:

The main issue presented in this appeal, one of first impression in the federal courts, is the allocation of the burden of proof in a civil action involving the command responsibility doctrine brought under the Torture Victim Protection Act....

I. BACKGROUND

Three nuns and one layperson (the "churchwomen"), all Americans engaged in missionary and relief work in El Salvador, were abducted, tortured, and murdered in December 1980 by five members of the Salvadoran National Guard (the "Guardsmen"). Approximately three years later, in response to American pressure to punish the responsible parties, the Guardsmen were convicted of the crimes and sentenced to prison terms. In the period before and after this tragic incident, thousands of civilians in El Salvador were victimized by violence during a civil war in which both communist and colonialist forces competed with the government for control of the country. At the time of the murders and directly before, Defendant General Carlos Eugenio Vides Casanova was Director of the Salvadoran National Guard and Defendant General Jose Guillermo Garcia was El Salvador's Minister of Defense. Both defendants currently reside in Florida.

Subsequent to the murders of the churchwomen, Congress passed the Torture Victim Protection Act of 1991 ("TVPA"), Pub. L. No. 102–256, 106 Stat. 73 at Historical and Statutory Notes to 28 U.S.C.A. § 1350. The TVPA allows victims of violations of international law, or those victims' representatives, to bring a civil cause of action in federal district court against commanders under the international law doctrine of command responsibility. This doctrine makes a commander liable for acts of his subordinates, even where the commander did not order those acts, when certain elements are met. Relying on the TVPA, Plaintiffs–Appellants, for and on behalf of the estates of the churchwomen, filed suit against Defendants–Appellees in 1999 seeking to recover damages for the torture and murders. Appellants invoked the doctrine of command responsibility and alleged that the executions at issue were part of a pattern and practice of extrajudicial killings committed by the Salvadoran National Guard under Appellees' command.

At trial, Appellants offered evidence of the great number of atrocities committed against civilians at the hands of the Salvadoran military in the months preceding the churchwomen's deaths. The Generals conceded that they were aware of a pattern of human rights abuses in El Salvador during their tenures as Minister of Defense and Director of the National Guard, but argued that they did not have the ability to control their troops during this period.... After deliberations, the jury returned a verdict for Appellees. Appellants argue on appeal that the jury instructions given at trial contained material misstatements of law....

II. DISCUSSION

....

Appellants contend that the jury instructions in this case contained errors of law which placed on them the burden of establishing elements that they are not required to prove under either the TVPA or the international law which the TVPA has adopted. The instructions required Appellants to prove by a preponderance of the evidence first that the Guardsmen were under Appellees' "effective command," defined as the legal authority and the practical ability of the Generals to control the guilty troops, and second, that the Generals failed to take all reasonable steps to prevent or repress the murders of the churchwomen. Appellants argue that both of these showings are properly affirmative defenses that the Appellees had the burden of proving at trial. Finally, Appellants contend that the district court's instructions erroneously included proximate cause as a required element before liability could be established under the TVPA and command responsibility doctrine.

. . . .

The essential elements of liability under the command responsibility doctrine are: (1) the existence of a superior-subordinate relationship between the commander and the perpetrator of the crime; (2) that the commander knew or should have known, owing to the circumstances at the time, that his subordinates had committed, were committing, or planned to commit acts violative of the law of war; and (3) that the commander failed to prevent the commission of the crimes, or failed to punish the subordinates after the commission of the crimes. Although the TVPA does not explicitly provide for liability of commanders for human rights violations of their troops, legislative history makes clear that Congress intended to adopt the doctrine of command responsibility from international law as part of the Act. Specifically identified in the Senate report is *In re Yamashita*, 327 U.S. 1 (1946), a World War II era case involving the command responsibility doctrine in habeas review of the conviction of a Japanese commander in the Philippines by an American military tribunal. *See* S. Rep. No. 102–249, at 9 (1991). Describing *Yamashita*'s holding, the Senate Report stated that the Supreme Court found a foreign general "responsible for a pervasive pattern of war crimes (1) committed by his officers when (2) he knew or should have known they were going on but (3) failed to prevent or punish them." *Id.* In the years since *Yamashita* and the passage of the TVPA, the International Criminal Tribunals for the Former Yugoslavia and Rwanda have been established, and their statutes contain language providing for imposition of command responsibility on substantively identical grounds to those enunciated in *Yamashita*.

Appellants assert that once a plaintiff has proven these three prima facie elements by a preponderance of the evidence, the burden then shifts to the defendant to establish any affirmative defenses. In Appellants' view, possible affirmative defenses are that the commander did not have effective command over his troops, i.e. the practical ability to control them, or that he took all necessary and reasonable measures to prevent the abuses.... They contend that contrary to the command responsibility instruction given, it is for the defendants to come forward with evidence sufficient to prove that they did not have the practical ability to control their troops or that they took all necessary and reasonable measures to control the troops, either one of which would serve to exonerate them from liability.

Appellants urge that their position that Defendants were required to show their lack of practical ability to control the guilty troops as part of an affirmative defense finds support in the Supreme Court's *In re Yamashita* decision. There the Supreme Court upheld on habeas review the military tribunal's authority to try General Yamashita, as well as its findings and jury instructions. *In re Yamashita*, 327 U.S. at 17, 25. Appellants read the decision as allocating the burden of persuasion to be applied for each issue in future command responsibility cases to whichever party raised that issue in front of the original *Yamashita* tribunal. Appellants maintain that at the military tribunal Yamashita attempted to show his lack of effective control over his troops, and insist that he would not have made this effort had he not carried the burden of persuasion on this matter.

Despite Appellants' assertions that the district court's definition of "effective command" misplaced the burden of persuasion, we find no plain error. *In re Yamashita* did not explicitly address the allocation of the burdens on the elements of command responsibility. Nor is there any indication that the Court there ever considered how to allocate the burdens of production or persuasion in future command responsibility trials. Further, Appellants' contention that Yamashita's raising his lack of effective control before the American military tribunal necessarily implies that he carried the burden of persuasion on that issue is flawed. Yamashita might have raised his lack of effective control because he had the burden of production on the issue, although not the burden of persuasion. Alternatively, he may have believed that his most effective defense lay in pointing out facts that, if believed by the trier of fact, would establish that the prosecution could not carry out its burden of proving the elements of command responsibility.

The recently constituted international tribunals of Rwanda and the former Yugoslavia have applied the doctrine of command responsibility since *In re Yamashita*, and therefore their cases provide insight into how the doctrine should be applied in TVPA cases. Recent international cases consistently have found that effective control of a commander over his troops is required before liability will be imposed under the command responsibility doctrine. The consensus is that "[t]he concept of effective *control* over a subordinate—in the sense of a material ability to prevent or punish criminal conduct, however that control is exercised—is the threshold to be reached in establishing a superior-subordinate relationship...." *Prosecutor v. Delalic* (Appeals Chamber ICTY, Feb. 20, 2001) ¶ 256; *accord id.* at ¶ 266; *Prosecutor v. Aleksovski*, Judgment (Appeals Chamber ICTY, March 24, 2000) ¶ 76; *Prosecutor v. Blaskic*, Judgment (Trial Chamber ICTY, March 3, 2000) ¶ ¶ 295, 302 ("Proof is required that the superior has effective control over the persons committing the violations of international humanitarian law in question, that is, has the material ability to prevent the crimes and to punish the perpetrators thereof."); *Prosecutor v. Kayishema*, Judgment (Trial Chamber ICTR, May 21, 1999) ¶ 229 (stating that the "material ability to control the actions of subordinates is the touchstone of individual responsibility under Article 6(3)"); *Prosecutor v. Delalic*, Judgment (Trial Chamber ICTY, Nov. 16, 1998) ¶¶ 377, 378; *Prosecutor v. Akayesu*, Judgment (Trial Chamber ICTR, Sept. 2, 1998) ¶ 491. Many of these cases dealt with the situation converse to the one presented here, i.e., where a superior without *de jure* command was accused of having *de facto* control over the guilty troops. These cases emphasize, nonetheless, that the command responsibility theory of liability is premised on the actual ability of a superior to control his troops. A reading of the cases suggests that a showing of the defendant's actual ability to control the guilty troops is required as part of the plaintiff's burden under the superior-subordinate prong of command responsibility, whether the plaintiff attempts to assert liability under a theory of *de facto* or *de jure* authority. *Prosecutor v. Delalic* (Appeals Chamber ICTY, Feb. 20, 2001) ¶ 196 ("Effective control has been accepted, including in the jurisprudence of the Tribunal, as a standard for the purposes of determining superior responsibility. ... The showing of effective control is required in cases involving both *de jure* and *de facto* superiors."). Explaining the difference in application of this requirement in *de jure* and *de facto* cases, the same tribunal announced, "In general, the possession of *de jure* power in itself may not suffice for the finding of command responsibility if it does not manifest in effective control, although a court may presume that possession of such power *prima facie* results in effective control unless proof to the contrary is produced." *Id.* at ¶ 197.

Notably, the tribunal said that *de jure* authority over the guilty troops results in only a *presumption* of effective control. In other contexts, this court has held that a presumption shifts the burden of production with respect to the element it concerns, but not the burden of persuasion. *See Walker v. Mortham*, 158 F.3d 1177, 1184 (11th Cir. 1998) (distinguishing between "presumptions" and "inferences"); *see also* Fed. R. Evid. 301 (noting that presumptions create a burden of production for the party against whom the presumption is directed, but do not shift the ultimate burden of persuasion). Put another way, *Delalic* indicates that *de jure* authority of a commander over the troops who perpetrated the underlying crime is *prima facie* evidence of effective control, which accordingly can be rebutted only by the defense putting forth evidence to the finder of fact that the defendant lacked this effective control.... Thus, although we do not decide the issue, we note that nowhere in any international tribunal decision have we found any indication that the ultimate burden of *persuasion* shifts on this issue when the prosecutor—or in TVPA cases, the plaintiff—shows that the defendant possessed de jure power over the guilty troops.

To the contrary, *Delalic* provides a strong suggestion that it is the plaintiff who must establish, in all command responsibility cases, that the defendant had effective control over his troops. That a *de jure* commander bears the burden of production on this issue does not affect the ultimate jury instruction that should be given. We previously have held that jury instructions are to address the ultimate burden of persuasion only, and should not needlessly confuse the jurors with which party held the burden of production at trial. *See Dudley v. Wal–Mart Stores, Inc.*, 166 F.3d 1317, 1321–22 (11th Cir. 1999) (noting that "[a]lthough statements like 'prima facie case' and 'burden of production' faithfully endeavor to track [the law], they create a distinct risk of confusing the jury") (quoting *Cabrera v. Jakabovitz*, 24 F.3d 372, 381 (2d Cir. 1994)). This reasoning recognizes that "the distinction between burden of persuasion and burden of production is not familiar to jurors, and they may easily be misled by hearing the word 'burden' (though referring to a burden of production) used with reference to a defendant in an explanation of that part of the charge that concerns a plaintiff's burden of persuasion." *Id.* (quoting *Cabrera*, 24 F.3d at 381).

In the end, then, there is ample authority contrary to Appellants' argument that Defendants bore the burden of persuasion on effective control....

With regard to the "necessary and reasonable measures" portion of the district court's instruction, which the court included as part of Appellant's necessary showing in establishing the third prong of command responsibility, the governing statutes of both the Rwanda and former Yugoslavia international tribunals use the precise language employed here. *See* Art. 6(3), Statute of the ICTR (Nov. 8, 1994); Art. 7(3), Statute of the ICTY (May 25, 1993). Despite Appellants' claim that the defendant ordinarily bears the burden of persuasion on this element, we have found no international tribunal decision that has addressed this issue. Rather, by not explicitly identifying who possesses the burden on this element, there seems to be a tacit assumption in the tribunal cases that the prosecutor—whose burden replicates the burden of the plaintiff in TVPA command responsibility cases—carries the burden to prove that the defendant failed to take necessary and reasonable measures to prevent the crime or punish the guilty troops. *See e.g., Prosecutor v. Blaskic*, Judgment (Trial Chamber ICTY, March 3, 2000) ¶ 294 ("[P]roof is required that: ... the accused failed to take the necessary and reasonable measures to prevent the crime or punish the perpetrator thereof."). Either way, as with the issue of effective control, we find no plain error where the district court's instruction mirrored the language of the most recent indicia of customary international law on this point, and where no clear case law exists allocating the burden of persuasion to the defendant on whether he took all necessary and reasonable measures to control his troops.

Although case law from recent international tribunals is sufficient to convince us that no plain error occurred here in the giving of the command responsibility instruction, we observe that the statute of the recently ratified International Criminal Court, commonly referred to as the Rome Statute, supports our holding on this matter as well. As the statute addresses the command responsibility doctrine, it provides relevant authority for the required elements in TVPA cases invoking the doctrine....

....

III. CONCLUSION

Based on the foregoing, we find no reversible error on the part of the district court. *Affirmed.*

NOTE ON THE ATS AND TVPA IN THE "WAR ON TERROR"

Several aliens detained as enemy combatants in the "war on terror" have attempted to challenge their detention and treatment by invoking, *inter alia*, the ATS and TVPA. *See, e.g.*, Rasul v. Bush, 215 F.Supp.2d 55 (D.D.C. 2002), *aff'd sub nom*, Al Odah v. United States, 321 F.3d 1134 (D.C. Cir. 2003), *rev'd sub nom.* Rasul v. Bush, 542 U.S. 466, 124 S.Ct. 2686, 159 L.Ed.2d 548 (2004). In *Al Odah*, the D.C. Circuit found that

> Each of the detainees alleges violations of the Constitution, treaties, and laws of the United States. The Alien Tort Act is a "law of the United States" and, the detainees believe, so is some international law. As to the latter, the theories are that federal common law incorporates "customary international law" and that the Alien Tort Act not only provides jurisdiction but also creates a cause of action—theories the Second Circuit promulgated in *Filartiga v. Pena-Irala,* 630 F.2d 876, 885–87 (2d Cir. 1980). But as we have decided, the detainees are in all relevant respects in the same position as the prisoners in *Eisentrager*. They cannot seek release based on violations of the Constitution or treaties or federal law; the courts are not open to them. Whatever other relief the detainees seek, their claims necessarily rest on alleged violations of the same category of laws listed in the habeas corpus statute, and are therefore beyond the jurisdiction of the federal courts.

321 F.3d at 1144–45. On appeal, the Supreme Court disagreed, holding that:

> But in any event, nothing in *Eisentrager* or in any of our other cases categorically excludes aliens detained in military custody outside the United States from the " 'privilege of litigation' " in U.S. courts. 321 F.3d, at 1139. ... And indeed, 28 U.S.C. § 1350 explicitly confers the privilege of suing for an actionable "tort ... committed in violation of the law of nations or a treaty of the United States" on aliens alone. The fact that petitioners in these cases are being held in military custody is immaterial to the question of the District Court's jurisdiction over their nonhabeas statutory claims.

Rasul v. Bush, 542 U.S. at 484–85; *see* Chapter 4, Section 11.

SECTION 6. PIRACY

UNITED STATES v. SMITH

18 U.S. (5 Wheat.) 153, 5 L.Ed. 57 (1820) (footnotes omitted).

[A jury found that, in March 1819, the defendant Thomas Smith and others were part of the crew of a private armed vessel called the *Creollo*. The *Creollo* had been commissioned by the government of Buenos Ayres (a Spanish colony then at war with Spain). While the vessel was lying in the port of Margaritta, the defendant and other crew members mutinied, confined their officer, left the vessel, and seized by violence another private- armed vessel called the *Irresistible*. The mutineers then took the *Irresistible* to sea, where they engaged in the plunder and robbery of a Spanish vessel. The jury determined that such conduct violated a U.S. criminal statute on piracy that was enacted on March 3, 1819 and that referenced the "law of nations."]

MR. JUSTICE STORY delivered the opinion of the court.

The act of Congress upon which this indictment is founded provides, "that if any person or persons whatsoever, shall, upon the high seas, commit the crime of piracy, as defined by the law of nations, and such offender or offenders shall be brought into, or found in the United States, every such offender or offenders shall, upon conviction thereof, & c. be punished with death."

. . . .

It is next to be considered, whether the crime of piracy is defined by the law of nations with reasonable certainty. What the law of nations on this subject is, may be ascertained by consulting the works of jurists, writing professedly on public law; or by the general usage and practice of nations; or by judicial decisions recognising and enforcing that law. There is scarcely a writer on the law of nations, who does not allude to piracy as a crime of a settled and determinate nature; and whatever may be the diversity of definitions, in other respects, all writers concur, in holding, that robbery, or forcible depredations upon the sea, *animo furandi,* is piracy. The same doctrine is held by all the great writers on maritime law, in terms that admit of no reasonable doubt. The common law, too, recognises and punishes piracy as an offence, not against its own municipal code, but as an offence against the law of nations, (which is part of the common law,), as an offence against the universal law of society, a pirate being deemed an enemy of the human race. Indeed, until the statute of 28th of Henry VIII. ch. 15. piracy was punishable in England only in the admiralty as a civil law offence; and that statute, in changing the jurisdiction, has been universally admitted not to have changed the nature of the offence. Sir Charles Hedges, in his charge at the Admiralty sessions, in the case of *Rex v. Dawson*, (5 *State Trials,*) declared in emphatic terms, that "piracy is only a sea term for robbery, piracy being a robbery committed within the jurisdiction of the admiralty." Sir Leoline Jenkins, too, on a like occasion, declared that "a robbery, when committed upon the sea, is what we call piracy;" and he cited the civil law writers, in proof. And it is manifest from the language of Sir William Blackstone, in his comments on piracy, that he considered the common law definition as distinguishable in no essential respect from that of the law of nations. So that, whether we advert to writers on the common law, or the maritime law, or the law of nations, we shall find that they universally treat of piracy as an offence against the law of nations, and that its true definition by that law is robbery upon the sea. And the general practice of all nations in punishing all persons, whether natives or foreigners, who have committed this offence against any person whatsoever, with whom they are in amity, is a conclusive proof that the offence is supposed to depend, not upon the particular provisions of any municipal code, but upon the law of nations, both for its definition and punishment. We have, therefore, no hesitation in declaring, that piracy, by the law of nations, is robbery upon the sea, and that it is sufficiently and constitutionally defined by the fifth section of the act of 1819.

. . . .

It is to be certified to the Circuit Court, that upon the facts stated, the case is piracy, as defined by the law of nations, so as to be punishable under the act of Congress of the 3d of March, 1819.

MR. JUSTICE LIVINGSTON dissented.

In a case affecting life, no apology can be necessary for expressing my dissent from the opinion which has just been delivered.

The only question of any importance in this case is, whether the act of the 3d of March, 1819, be a constitutional exercise of the power delegated to Congress of "defining and punishing piracies?" The act declares, that any person who shall commit on the high seas the crime of piracy as *defined by the law of nations,* shall be punished with death. The special power here given to define piracy, can be attributed to no other cause, than to the uncertainty which it was known existed on this subject in the law of nations, and which it must have been the intention of the framers of the constitution to remove, by conferring on the national legislature the power which has been mentioned. It was well known to the members of the Federal Convention, that in treatises on the law of nations, or in some of them at least, definitions of piracy might be found; but it must have been as well known to them that there was not such a coincidence on this subject, as to render a reference to that code a desirable or safe mode of proceeding in a criminal, and especially in a capital case. If it had been intended to adopt the definition or definitions of this crime, so far as they were to be collected from the different commentators on this code, with all the uncertainty and difficulty attending a research for that purpose, it might as well at once have been adopted as a standard by the constitution itself. The object, therefore, of referring its definition to Congress was, and could have been no other than, to enable that body, to select from sources it might think proper, and then to declare, and with reasonable precision to define, what act or acts should constitute this crime; and having done so, to annex to it such punishment as might be thought proper. Such a mode of proceeding would be consonant with the universal practice in this country, and with those feelings of humanity which are ever opposed to the putting in jeopardy the life of a fellow-being, unless for the contravention of a rule which has been previously prescribed, and in language so plain and explicit as not to be misunderstood by any one. ... [I]t is the duty of Congress to incorporate into their own statutes a definition in *terms,* and not to refer the citizens of the United States for rules of conduct to the statutes or laws of any foreign country, with which it is not to be presumed that they are acquainted. Nor does it make any difference in this case, that the law of nations forms part of the law of every civilized country. This may be the case to a certain extent; but as to criminal cases, and as to the offence of piracy in particular, the law of nations could not be supposed of itself to form a rule of action; and, therefore, a reference to it in this instance, must be regarded in the same light, as a reference to any other foreign code. ... Congress have power to punish offences against the law of nations, and yet it would hardly be deemed a fair and legitimate execution of this authority, to declare, that all offences against the law of nations, without defining any one of them, should be punished with death. Such mode of legislation is but badly calculated to furnish that precise and accurate information in criminal cases, which it is the duty, and ought to be the object, of every legislature to impart.

Upon the whole, my opinion is, that there is not to be found in the act that definition of piracy which the constitution requires, and that, therefore, judgment on the special verdict ought to be rendered for the prisoner.

CONTEMPORARY PIRACY AND PRIVATEERING STATUTES

18 U.S.C. Ch. 81, § 1651–1654 (2006).

§ 1651. Piracy under law of nations

Whoever, on the high seas, commits the crime of piracy as defined by the law of nations, and is afterwards brought into or found in the United States, shall be imprisoned for life.

§ 1652. Citizens as pirates

Whoever, being a citizen of the United States, commits any murder or robbery, or any act of hostility against the United States, or against any citizen thereof, on the high seas, under color of any commission from any foreign prince, or state, or on pretense of authority from any person, is a pirate, and shall be imprisoned for life.

§ 1653. Aliens as pirates

Whoever, being a citizen or subject of any foreign state, is found and taken on the sea making war upon the United States, or cruising against the vessels and property thereof, or of the citizens of the same, contrary to the provisions of any treaty existing between the United States and the state of which the offender is a citizen or subject, when by such treaty such acts are declared to be piracy, is a pirate, and shall be imprisoned for life.

§ 1654. Arming or serving on privateers

Whoever, being a citizen of the United States, without the limits thereof, fits out and arms, or attempts to fit out and arm or is concerned in furnishing, fitting out, or arming any private vessel of war or privateer, with intent that such vessel shall be employed to cruise or commit hostilities upon the citizens of the United States or their property; or

Whoever takes the command of or enters on board of any such vessel with such intent; or

Whoever purchases any interest in any such vessel with a view to share in the profits thereof—

Shall be fined [not more than $10,000] or imprisoned not more than ten years, or both.

SAMUEL PYEATT MENEFEE, "YO HEAVE HO!": UPDATING AMERICA'S PIRACY LAWS

21 Cal. W. Int'l L.J. 151 (1990) (some footnotes omitted).

I. GENERAL BACKGROUND

. . . .

. . . While subsequent years have seen revisions in the *arrangement* of these statutes, their general *content* has remained largely unchanged for over a century and a half! At the same time, this period, particularly the half-century since the Second World War, has seen important changes in occurrences of violence at sea. The 1856 Declaration of Paris, for example, virtually put an end to privateering. While the United States did not accede to this document, it has generally followed its provisions, and the overall disappearance of privateering from international law itself points up the obsolescent nature of much of Chapter 81. As some scholars have pointed out, an *emerging* problem has been the takeover of vessels by passengers for political purposes. The problem of localized piracy, seemingly confined to the Aegean, the South China Sea, and Malay Archipelago after the Caribbean "campaign" of the 1820s and 1930s, has broken out anew in the post-War years. Clusters of piratical activity are found in West Africa, the Malaccan Straits area, the Philippines, and the Caribbean, not to mention in ports such as Santos, Brazil. Often, the objects of the assaults are United States vessels, cargos, or nationals. At the very least, these activities should call for a *review* of Chapter 81, as the issue is not a *theoretical* one, but a contemporary problem affecting American lives and property.

Finally, there are developments undreamed of by the drafters of the Code's piracy statutes. Submarines, offshore platforms, pipelines and cables have widened the sphere of potential maritime operations. Bombs allow for "remote-controlled mayhem," while telephones have opened the floodgates to *threatened* actions. The rise of environmental issues (and, unfortunately, of environmental extremists) have provided new incentives for maritime violence. In the last fifteen years, for example, six whaling vessels have been attacked (and five sunk) in protests against depletion of cetaceans. Sealing, fishing, ocean dumping, and nuclear energy provide lightning-rods for similar potential outbursts. The international law of piracy has been at least *partially* codified in the 1958 Geneva Convention on the High Seas and in its successor, the 1982 Convention on the Law of the Sea.[50] But, during this century and a half of change and development, the United States Code provisions on piracy have remained frozen.

II. CHAPTER 81 AND ITS PROBLEMS

In examining Chapter 81 and its problems, it seems most useful to proceed with a section-by-section review of the law as it now stands. The

---

50. *See* Convention on the High Seas, Apr. 29, 1958, 13 U.S.T. 2312, T.I.A.S. No. 5200; 450 U.N.T.S. 82 (arts. 14–22) [hereinafter Convention on the High Seas]; United Nations Convention on the Law of Sea, Dec. 10, 1982, U.N. Doc. A/CONF.62/122, *reprinted in* UNITED NATIONS CONVENTION ON THE LAW OF THE SEA 1982: A COMMENTARY 206, 248–49 (M. Nordquist ed. 1985) (arts. 100–107) [hereinafter Convention on the Law of the Sea]. . . .

criticisms and comments offered herein do not pretend to be complete, but should indicate some problems with the Code provisions as they exist, and will, hopefully, provide a basis for future discussion.

A. *Section 1651: Piracy Under Law of Nations*

This section is obviously derived from section 5 of the Act of March 3, 1819. The only major difference is that life imprisonment has been substituted for the death penalty. The provision raises two questions. First, if the 1958 Convention on the High Seas and its successor, the 1982 Convention, are judged to be the *complete and exclusive* codification of the intended crime of piracy, section 1651 would *not* cover all cases of piracy "against a ship, aircraft, persons or property in a place outside the jurisdiction of any State."[53] Similarly, the specified high seas nexus might well *omit* some acts "of voluntary participation in the operation of a ship or of an aircraft with knowledge of facts making it a pirate ship or aircraft"[54] or acts "of inciting or of intentionally facilitating" piratical acts.[55]

If the two Conventions are *not* considered to be a definitive codification of the international law of piracy, the question arises as to what constitutes piracy "as defined by the law of nations." . . .

The worst problem with this section appears to be the use of the term "high seas." As used in section 1651, this does not appear to have the jurisdictional meaning which it has acquired in international law, but rather to attach to *any* waters beyond the low water mark.[58] It would therefore seem appropriate for the term to be used in its correct treaty sense or, alternately, to be dropped in any revision of section 1651.

B. *Section 1652: Citizens as Pirates*

This section derives from section 9 of the Act of April 30, 1790. Its purpose was to cover acts of privateering by American citizens, but it has been wrenched out of context and this, plus a number of changes in circumstance, has resulted in several problems. The most obvious is the demise of privateering; people simply do not cruise on the seas "under color of any commission" to commit hostile acts against the United States or its citizens, to murder, or to rob. While politically-motivated crimes by American citizens still occur, the dwindling role of formalities in international law make it desirable to omit specific references to commissions from a revised statute. At the same time, bearing in mind the possibility of ideological crimes which are *non-political* in nature, thought should be given to a more expansive description of the criminal mind-set involved.

53. . . . The quotation comes from Article 101 of the 1982 Convention. . . .

54. *See* Convention on the Law of the Sea, *supra* note 50, art. 101(b); Convention on the High Seas, *supra* note 50, art. 15(2). . . .

55. *See* Convention on the Law of the Sea, art. 101(c), *supra* note 50; Convention on the High Seas, art. 15(3), *supra* note 50. . . .

58. *See United States v. Pirates,* 18 U.S. (5 Wheat.) 184 (1820); *United States v. Wilson*, 28 Fed. Cas. no. 16,731 (S.D.N.Y. 1856); *United States v. Gourlay*, 25 Fed. Cas. no. 15,241 (S.D.N.Y. 1823); *United States v. Ross*, Fed. Cas. no. 16,196 (C.C.R.I. 1813). . . .

Another tangle arises from the reference to "any murder or robbery, or any act of hostility against the United States, or against any citizen thereof." As currently phrased, *all murders or robberies* by U.S. citizens falling under the terms of the statute would be included, but *only those other acts of hostility directed against the United States or its citizens* are covered by this section. The murder or robbery of a British passenger by an American for political purposes would thus appear to be covered by this section of the Code, but *not* his kidnap or torture. A decision should be made as to whether only political crimes by Americans against the United States or fellow citizens should be covered, or whether it is desirable that maritime political crimes against *any* nation or national by an American should fall within the Code's ambit.

There are again questions of jurisdiction. In addition to the problems of terminology, the extension of territorial waters and Exclusive Economic Zones means that fewer crimes will be committed *outside* national jurisdiction. It must therefore be decided whether cases occurring *within* national jurisdiction should be left to the jurisdiction of the coastal state, or whether the United States should preserve at least the *option* of exerting its own jurisdiction. Finally, one must consider whether only *citizens* should be covered by this section, or whether others, such as resident aliens, should be included as well.

C. Section 1653: Aliens as Pirates

Section 1653 is a direct descendent of the Act of March 3, 1847. While its title and positioning suggest that it is intended as a counter-point to section 1652, several differences prevent the two statutes from serving as mirror images. First, the provision that the individual must be "a citizen or subject of [a] foreign state" could allow a *stateless* alien to escape punishment. Next, the requirement that the individual be "found and taken on the sea" disallows any possibility of later capture on land, regardless of whether the national's country assents to extradition, the individual is apprehended in a third county, or capture occurs within the territorial (dry land) confines of the United States itself! Finally, there may (or may not) be a difference between the term "high seas" and "sea."[72]

Again returning to changed concepts, "making war upon the United States, or cruising against the vessels and property thereof, or of the citizens of the same," has a nineteenth- century flavor which has not "kept" well. It would be far more to the point to speak of ideologically or politically motivated actions. Similarly, the *absence* of a bilateral (or multilateral) treaty declaring certain acts to be piracy should not permit the citizens of any particular state to "cruise" with impunity. Following such logic, the term "Barbary pirates" would be an oxymoron! As in prior sections, the *extent* of jurisdiction is also open to question. Should the current "high seas" jurisdiction (assuming that is what is meant by

72. . . . There appears to be no case law discussing this issue, but it is at least arguable that "sea" could refer to *all* waters subject to tidal ebb and flow. . . .

"sea") be retained, or should a different scope of potential jurisdiction be contemplated?

D. Section 1654: Arming or Serving as Privateers

This section is based on section 4 of the Act of 1818. Like section 1652, it deals with the problem of privateering by U.S. nationals under color of a commission, and suffers from similar defects. In addition to problems with "privateering" itself, and the limitation of the section to "citizen[s] of the United States," section 1654, unlike section 1652, does *not* apply within U.S. territorial waters. Thus, some privateering activities by American citizens in American waters would be covered by the Code while *others* would not. The wording of the section, furthermore, makes it illegal to (intentionally) furnish a *vessel* for privateering purposes, but arguably does not cover the furnishing of *armaments*. Similarly, the phrase, "with intent that such vessel shall be employed to cruise or commit hostilities upon the citizens of the United States," is liable to varying interpretations.[84] Nor do the problems end here. "Whoever takes the command of or enters on board of any such vessel with such intent," *could* be taken as referring to an *intent to take command*, rather than an intent to cruise against United States citizens or property. It can also be argued that, as phrased, the purchaser of an interest in a privateer need not buy with *intent* that the boat cruise against American targets to be liable under the penalties of law.

. . . .

CONCLUSION

A general review of the background to 18 U.S.C. Chapter 81 has shown that the laws on piracy do *not* reflect recent developments in maritime law. Additionally, reactions to *prior* developments have resulted in a composite chapter of laws which, as the reviser noted, cry out for "a fundamental reconsideration and complete restatement," including "drastic changes by way of modification and expansion."[131]

Analysis of Chapter 81 as it currently exists reveals problems due to: a) potential discrepancies with international law, b) spatial jurisdiction, c) jurisdiction over individuals, and d) jurisdiction over specific acts, notably over those which no longer constitute problems and over those other practices which have arisen since the 1840s. . . .

It is hoped that this evaluation will serve as a starting point for further discussions, resulting in a "yo heave ho!" of the outdated piracy provisions of the Code and their replacement with a coherent set of laws on the subject, "modified and restated in accordance with the needs of the times."[132]

---

84. . . . In particular, it is unclear whether *specific* intent is called for, or whether a *general* intent would be deemed sufficient to bring an activity under the purview of the statute.

131. *See* [18 U.S.C. Ch. 81 (1988) (Historical and Revision Notes)] and accompanying text.

132. *Id.*

UNITED STATES v. SUERTE

291 F.3d 366 (5th Cir. 2002).

RHESA HAWKINS BARKSDALE, CIRCUIT JUDGE:

At issue is whether, for extraterritorial application of the Maritime Drug Law Enforcement Act, 46 U.S.C.App. § 1901 *et seq.*, the Fifth Amendment's Due Process Clause requires a nexus between a foreign citizen and the United States, where the flag nation for his vessel "has consented or waived objection to the enforcement of United States law by the United States". *Id.* § 1903(c)(1)(C). Requiring such a nexus, the district court dismissed the indictment for lack of jurisdiction. *Vacated* and *remanded.*

I.

Defendant Nestor Suerte, a Philippine national and resident of Colombia, has apparently never entered the United States. The Government alleges the following.

Suerte was captain of a freighter registered in Malta and owned by a member of a Colombian/Venezuelan drug trafficking organization (DTO); he met in Venezuela with DTO members in July and August 2000 to coordinate loading the freighter, off the northern coast of Venezuela, with 4900 kilograms of cocaine for transport to, and distribution in, Europe; the freighter apparently departed Venezuela on 11 August; the next day, an attempt was made, using speed boats, to transport the cocaine to it; after Venezuelan law enforcement detected the boats, they took evasive action....

The DTO telexed Suerte plans for the second attempt, ... however, Venezuelan authorities arrested some of the DTO members, thwarting the second attempt; but, nevertheless, on 17 August, the freighter was at the vicinity of the designated rendezvous point, in international waters.

The United States requested, and received, permission from Malta (the flag nation) to board and search the freighter.... A search by the Coast Guard did not find cocaine.

Approximately a week later, Malta waived objection to the enforcement of United States laws over the freighter and its crew. The Government towed the vessel to the Port of Houston, Texas; on 2 September, it was searched by United States Customs Special Agents; found in Suerte's cabin was a torn copy of the above-referenced telex giving the date, time, and coordinates for the second attempt to load cocaine; and also found was an attache case containing $3500 in $100 bills.

Suerte was arrested and indicted for *conspiracy* (as discussed *infra*) to possess, with intent to distribute, more than five kilograms of cocaine on board a vessel subject to United States jurisdiction, in violation of the Maritime Drug Law Enforcement Act (MDLEA), 46 U.S.C.App. § 1903. The Act provides, in pertinent part:

(a) It is unlawful for any person ... *on board a vessel subject to the jurisdiction of the United States* ... to knowingly or intentionally ... possess with intent to ... distribute[ ] a controlled substance.

....

(c)(1) For purposes of this section, a "vessel subject to the jurisdiction of the United States" includes—

....

(C) a vessel registered in a foreign nation where the *flag nation has consented or waived objection* to the enforcement of United States law by the United States;

....

(j) Any person who attempts or *conspires* to commit any offense defined in this chapter shall be subject to the same penalties as those prescribed for the offense, the commission of which was the object of the attempt or conspiracy.

Id. (emphasis added).

Suerte moved to dismiss the indictment for lack of jurisdiction, claiming that, because he did not have a nexus to the United States, the Constitution does not permit the MDLEA to have extraterritorial effect over him. *See United States v. Suerte*, No. H–00–CR–659–1, slip op. at 3 (S.D. Tex. 7 June 2001). Agreeing with Suerte's position, the district court reviewed international law principles of extraterritorial jurisdiction, which "represent[ed] the different types of nexuses recognized under international law, and thus, inform[ed its] analysis", *id.* at 5 held no nexus existed between Suerte and the United States; and, accordingly, dismissed the indictment.

II.

....

B.

... [S]everal sources of law which, although not dispositive of the present issue, provide us great assurance that, "where the flag nation has consented or waived objection to the enforcement of United States law by the United States", § 1903(c)(1)(C), due process does not require a nexus for the MDLEA's extraterritorial application. Those sources include: the Constitutional Convention debate surrounding the Piracies and Felonies Clause ("The Congress shall have Power ... [t]o define and punish Piracies and Felonies committed on the high Seas, and Offenses against the Law of Nations"); the earliest exercise of Congressional power under the clause; and Supreme Court opinions reviewing that exercise.

1.

Concerning the Piracies and Felonies Clause, the Committee of Detail's draft Constitution, submitted to the Convention on 6 August 1787, would have empowered Congress "[t]o *declare* the law and punishment of piracies and felonies committed on the high seas, and the punishment of counterfeiting the coin of the United States, and of offences against the law of nations". 2 RECORDS OF THE FEDERAL CONVENTION OF 1787 182 (Max Farrand ed., 1999) (emphasis added). Subsequent debate over the clause primarily concerned the propriety of granting the power to both punish *and* declare and whether the latter power should read "declare", "designate", or "define". *See id.* at 315–16.

There was apparently no debate regarding constraints *vel non* on the clause's extraterritorial reach. It would seem that, had they been of concern, the matter would have been discussed, especially because the clause contains "the only specific grant of power to be found in the Constitution for the punishment of offenses outside the territorial limits of the United States". CONGRESSIONAL RESEARCH SERVICE, LIBRARY OF CONGRESS, THE CONSTITUTION OF THE UNITED STATES, ANALYSIS AND INTERPRETATION, S. DOC. NO. 103–6, at 304 (Johnny H. Killian & George A. Costello eds., 1992) (S. DOC. NO. 103–6).

The First Congress promptly enacted far-reaching legislation under the Piracies and Felonies power. In April 1790, approximately seven months *after* proposing the Bill of Rights to the States (25 September 1789), Congress approved An Act for the Punishment of Certain Crimes Against the United States (1790 Act). It provides, in part: in § 8, "[t]hat if *any person or persons* shall commit upon the high seas ... murder or robbery, ... every such offender shall be ... adjudged ... a pirate and felon, and being thereof convicted, shall suffer death"; and, in § 12, "[t]hat if *any* ... *person* shall commit manslaughter upon the high seas, ... such person ... so offending, and being thereof convicted, shall be imprisoned not exceeding three years, and fined not exceeding one thousand dollars". Act of 30 Apr. 1790, ch. 9, 1 Stat. 112, 113–15 (emphasis added).

For purposes of this appeal, perhaps the most striking aspect of the 1790 Act is that many of its provisions regarding crimes on the high seas apply to "*any* person". (Emphasis added.) It is important to note, especially in a case in which at issue is the constitutionality of another exercise of the Piracies and Felonies power, that, at the time it passed the 1790 Act, the First Congress had already drafted the Fifth Amendment and proposed it to the States.

While that Amendment was not ratified until 15 December 1791, during "[t]he debates [in August 1789 for] what became the Fifth Amendment ... there was no hint ... of any intention, by the adoption of that amendment, to deprive Congress of this [Piracies and Felonies] power expressly and uncontroversially granted to it by the Convention". A. Mark Weisburd, *Due Process Limits on Federal Extraterritorial Legislation?*, 35 COLUM. J. TRANSNAT'L L. 379, 421 (1997) (citing 1 ANNALS OF CONG. 753 (Joseph Gales ed., 1789)). In this regard, the First Congress, which drafted the 1790 Act and the Amendment, "included 20 Members who had been delegates to the [Constitutional] Convention". *Bowsher v. Synar*, 478 U.S. 714, 724 n. 3 (1986).

2.

Early Supreme Court opinions addressing extraterritorial applications of the 1790 Act intimate that the Fifth Amendment imposes no nexus requirement on the reach of statutes criminalizing felonious conduct by foreign citizens on the high seas. In *United States v. Palmer*, 16 U.S. (3 Wheat.) 610 (1818), the Court considered, *inter alia,* whether the United States had jurisdiction, pursuant to § 8 of the 1790 Act, to try, and punish, foreign citizens who had, on the high seas, boarded and robbed a foreign-owned vessel manned by a Spanish crew.

In answering "whether th[e] act extends farther than to American citizens, or to persons on board American vessels, or to offences committed against citizens of the United States", *id.* at 630, Chief Justice Marshall stated for the Court:

> *The constitution having conferred on congress the power of defining and punishing piracy,* there can be no doubt of the right of the legislature to enact laws punishing pirates, *although they may be foreigners, and may have committed no particular offence against the United States. The only question is, has the legislature enacted such a law?* Do the words of the act authorize the courts of the Union to inflict its penalties on persons who are not citizens of the United States, nor sailing under their flag, nor offending particularly against them?

Id. at 630–31 (emphasis added).

The Court answered in the negative. After emphasizing the generality of the language employed by the 1790 Act in setting its reach (*e.g.,* "any captain, or mariner of any ship or vessel"; "any seaman"; "any person or persons"), the Court stated: "Every nation provides for such offense[s] the punishment its own policy may dictate, and *no general words of a statute ought to be construed* to embrace them when committed by foreigners against a foreign government". *Id.* at 632–33 (emphasis added). Therefore, the Court concluded that, as a *statutory* matter, "the crime of robbery, committed by a person on the high seas, on board of any ship or vessel belonging exclusively to subjects of a foreign state, on persons within a vessel belonging exclusively to subjects of a foreign state, *is not a piracy within the true intent and meaning of the act*". *Id.* at 633–34 (emphasis added).

Palmer is an illustration of the well-established canon of construction espoused by Chief Justice Marshall in *Murray v. The Schooner Charming Betsy,* 6 U.S. (2 Cranch) 64 (1804): "[A]n act of Congress ought never to be construed to violate the law of nations if any other possible construction remains...." *Id.* at 118. Later, the Court emphasized in *Lauritzen v. Larsen*, 345 U.S. 571 (1953), however, that this canon "is not, as sometimes is implied, any impairment of our own sovereignty, or limitation of the power of Congress". *Id.* at 578.

While the constraints *vel non* imposed by the Fifth Amendment on extraterritorial application of laws enacted pursuant to the Piracies and Felonies Clause may not have been directly at issue in *Palmer*, Chief Justice Marshall's assessment of the relevant inquiry regarding extraterritorial applications—"The constitution having conferred on congress the power of defining and punishing piracy, . . . [t]he only question is, has the legislature enacted such a law?"—arguably removes any doubt that such enactments comport with the Fifth Amendment. And while at issue was Congress' power to define and punish *piracies,* Chief Justice Marshall's assessment should apply with equal weight to *felonies* such as at issue here, a parallel provision within the same constitutional clause.

Other case law interpreting the 1790 Act suggests international law principles are in some way inherent in the Piracies and Felonies Clause. In *United States v. Furlong*, 18 U.S. (5 Wheat.) 184 (1820), the Court considered, in *dictum,* whether Congress could punish a murder, committed upon the high seas, by one foreign crew member against another aboard a foreign vessel. *Id.* at 193–98. Justice Johnson opined for the Court: "I am led to the conclusion, that [§ 8 of the 1790 Act] does not extend the punishment for murder to the case of that offence committed by a foreigner upon a foreigner in a foreign ship. But otherwise as to piracy, *for that is a crime within the acknowledged reach of the punishing power of Congress*". *Id.* at 197 (emphasis added).

Addressing the fact that, in § 8 of the 1790 Act, Congress had declared murder committed upon the high seas to be piracy, Justice Johnson further concluded: "[Murder and piracy] are things so essentially different in their nature, that not even the omnipotence of legislative power can confound or identify them". *Id.* at 198. He continued:

> If, by calling murder *piracy*, it might assert a jurisdiction over that offence committed by a foreigner in a foreign vessel, what offence might not be brought within their power by the same device? *The most offensive interference with the governments of other nations might be defended on the precedent.* Upon the whole, I am satisfied that Congress [did not] intend [ ] to punish murder *in cases with which they had no right to interfere*. . . .

Id. at 198 (first emphasis in original).

In short, it appears Justice Johnson thought Congress' Piracies and Felonies power extends *only so far* as permitted by international law. That position may be at loggerheads, however, with more recent pronouncements by the Court. *See, e.g., Lauritzen,* 345 U.S. at 578 (as discussed *supra,* noting that the canon of construction announced in *The Charming Betsy* "is not, as sometimes is implied, any impairment of our own sovereignty, or limitation of the power of Congress"); *Hartford Fire Ins. Co. v. California*, 509 U.S. 764, 815 (1993) (Scalia, J., dissenting in part) ("*Though it clearly has constitutional authority to do so,* Congress is generally presumed not to have exceeded those customary international-law limits on jurisdiction to prescribe." (Emphasis added.)).

The opinions addressing the reach of the 1790 Act are of significance to our consideration of the MDLEA's reach. Those opinions concern an exercise of power, pursuant to the Piracies and Felonies Clause, by a Congress which, as noted, had some members who had drafted that clause, the 1790 Act, *and* the Fifth Amendment. While none of these cases addresses whether the Fifth Amendment has any applicability to exercises of power under the Piracies and Felonies Clause, neither the Fifth Amendment generally, nor its Due Process Clause specifically, was flagged as an issue in any of them. In fact, in addressing an 1819 law providing for the punishment of piracy on the high seas, the Court noted that, "notwithstanding a series of contested adjudications on [§ 8 of the 1790 Act], *no doubt has hitherto been breathed of its conformity to the constitution*". *United States v. Smith*, 18 U.S. (5 Wheat.) 153, 158 (1820) (emphasis added).

3.

In the light of this rich history, and for the issue at hand, it is not necessary to decide whether the Due Process Clause imposes *no* constraints on the extraterritorial application of the MDLEA. For example, in previously considering whether a predecessor to the MDLEA required a nexus for stateless vessels, our court noted:

> [G]iven the clear authority of Congress in the premises, [citing the Piracies and Felonies Clause], the relevance of international law to the problem at hand is as a reflection of Congressional intent rather than as a limitation on the power of Congress, *at least where, as here, there is no basis for any claim of due process violation.*

United States v. Alvarez–Mena, 765 F.2d 1259, 1266 (5th Cir. 1985) (emphasis added).

Accordingly, we hold that, for the MDLEA issue at hand, and to the extent the Due Process Clause may constrain the MDLEA's extraterritorial reach, that clause does not impose a nexus requirement, in that Congress has acted pursuant to the Piracies and Felonies Clause. Again, that clause is "the only specific grant of power to be found in the Constitution for the punishment of offenses outside the territorial limits of the United States". S. DOC. NO. 103–6, at 304.

C.

Assuming, *arguendo,* that resolution of this issue does require consulting international law, the MDLEA's application to Suerte still passes constitutional muster because, on these facts, international law does not require a nexus.

1.

Malta, under whose flag Suerte's vessel was registered, consented to the boarding and search of his vessel, as well as to the application of

United States law. A flag nation's consent to a seizure on the high seas constitutes a waiver of that nation's rights under international law. *See United States v. Williams,* 617 F.2d 1063, 1090 (5th Cir. 1980) (en banc). "[I]nterference with a ship that would otherwise be unlawful under international law is permissible if the flag state has consented". RESTATEMENT (THIRD) OF FOREIGN RELATIONS LAW OF THE UNITED STATES § 522 cmt. e (1987); *see also Robinson,* 843 F.2d at 4.

Along this line, and as noted, the MDLEA provides: "[A] 'vessel subject to the jurisdiction of the United States' includes ... a vessel registered in a foreign nation where the flag nation has consented or waived objection to the enforcement of United States law by the United States". 46 U.S.C.App. § 1903(c)(1)(C). This codifies the above-described generally accepted principle of international law: a flag nation may consent to another's jurisdiction. *See* RESTATEMENT (THIRD) § 522 reporters note 8 (the MDLEA "*confirmed the practice*" of relying on informal grants of consent by flag nations (emphasis added)); THOMAS J. SCHOENBAUM, ADMIRALTY AND MARITIME LAW § 3–12 n.41 (3d ed. 2001) (the principle that flag-nation consent satisfies international law requirements "is *confirmed* by the MDLEA" (emphasis added)). Such an agreement between the United States and a flag nation to apply United States law on a flag-nation vessel may be made informally. *Robinson,* 843 F.2d at 4; *see also* RESTATEMENT (THIRD) § 301 & cmt. b. (international agreements need not be formalized, nor need they be in writing).

2.

Maintaining that Malta's consent is irrelevant, Suerte asserts that, because no drugs were found on his vessel, he was not in violation of United States law when his vessel "was converted in effect to American territory" by Malta's consent.

A.

This claim has no merit. As noted earlier, we held recently: "The only statutory prerequisite to the district court's jurisdiction under section 1903(c)(1)(C) is that the flag nation consent to the enforcement of United States law *before trial*". *Bustos-Useche*, 273 F.3d at 627 (emphasis added).

B.

Even accepting Suerte's contention, we note he was not charged with drug possession; instead, he was charged with *conspiracy* to possess with intent to distribute. "A conspiracy is 'an agreement by two or more persons to commit one or more unlawful acts and an overt act by one of the conspirators in furtherance of the conspiracy.'" *United States v. Thomas*, 12 F.3d 1350, 1356 (5th Cir.) (quoting *United States v. Romeros*, 600 F.2d 1104, 1106 (5th Cir. 1979), *cert. denied,* 444 U.S. 1077 (1980)), *cert. denied,* 511 U.S. 1114 (1994). "If the totality ... of evidence is adequate to show a concert of action, all the parties working together understandingly, with a single design for the accomplishment of a common purpose[,] then the conspiracy may be found." *United States v. Perez*, 489 F.2d 51, 61 (5th Cir. 1973), *cert. denied*, 417 U.S. 945 (1974).

As alleged by the Government: meetings during which Suerte agreed to receive and transport the cocaine occurred in Venezuela; he was working with others with a single design for a common purpose *at the time the United States requested and received permission from Malta* to board and search his vessel; and, he was then acting in furtherance of that common purpose—he was assisting and awaiting the second attempt to load cocaine by positioning his vessel in the vicinity of the coordinates provided by the telex (found in the search of his cabin) designating the location for that attempt.

In this light, application of the MDLEA to Suerte is permissible; a nexus between his conduct and the United States is not required. Rejecting a nexus requirement will not result in the unrestrained, global law enforcement by the United States decried by Suerte.

Again, the power "to define and punish Piracies and Felonies committed on the high seas, and Offenses against the Law of Nations" is "the *only* specific grant of power to be found in the Constitution for the punishment of offenses outside the territorial limits of the United States". S. DOC. NO. 103–6, at 304 (emphasis added). The MDLEA represents an extremely limited exercise of that power. For certain persons not aboard United States vessels or in United States customs waters, it proscribes drug trafficking only aboard a stateless vessel or, as in the case at hand, a vessel whose flag nation consents to enforcement of United States law.

Enforcement of the MDLEA in these circumstances is neither arbitrary nor fundamentally unfair (the due process standard agreed upon by Suerte and the Government). Those subject to its reach are on notice. In addition to finding "that trafficking in controlled substances aboard vessels . . . presents a specific threat to the security and societal well-being of the United States", Congress has also found that such activity "is a serious *international* problem and is *universally* condemned". 46 U.S.C.App. § 1902 (emphasis added). Along this line, the United Nations Convention Against Illicit Traffic in Narcotic Drugs and Psychotropic Substances, *opened for signature* 20 Dec. 1988, 28 I.L.M. 493, to which Malta and the United States are signatories, provides as its purpose: "to promote cooperation among the Parties so that they may address more effectively the various aspects of illicit traffic in narcotic drugs and psychotropic substances having an international dimension". *Id.* art. 2.

III.

For the foregoing reasons, we *vacate* the dismissal of the indictment in this case and *remand* for further proceedings.

CONCLUDING NOTES

1. *Contemporary Piracy.* In recent years, attacks by pirates against commercial vessels, including U.S.-flagged vessels, have increased, especially

in areas of the world where governmental control is weak and economic conditions are poor. For example, in 2010, at least 219 attacks occurred in the waters off the Horn of Africa, of which 49 resulted in successful hijackings. "Success" usually means taking passengers hostage for ransom, with more than 1,180 persons taken hostage at sea in 2010 (more than any year since records on this issue have been kept). The average ransom per ship is reportedly more than $5 million. *See* Congressional Research Service, *Piracy Off the Horn of Africa*, CRS Rep. R40528 (Apr. 27, 2011).

2. *Attempted Piracy and Evolving International Law.* If the pirates are seized before they succeed in obtaining property or ransom, have they actually committed "piracy"? In other words, does attempted piracy violate the law? In two separate instances, Somali pirates attempted to attack vessels that proved to be U.S. naval warships, and after the attacks were thwarted, the defendants were indicted in the Eastern District of Virginia for violation of 18 U.S.C. § 1651 (2006). In the first of these cases, *United States v. Said*, 757 F.Supp. 2d 554 (E.D. Va. 2010), the district court dismissed the indictment on the basis that section 1651's reference to "the crime of piracy as defined by the law of nations"—informed by *United States v. Smith* (*supra*), and unaltered by subsequent decisions or congressional intervention—limited the statutory offense of piracy to sea robbery (or "robbery or forcible depredations"), and excluded mere armed attacks. The court rejected attempts to invoke contemporary international in support of a broader definition, concluding that such law was insufficiently settled and, if applied, would violate constitutional due process.

In the second case, *United States v. Hasan*, 747 F. Supp. 2d 599 (E.D. Va. 2010), a different judge accepted the U.S. government's contention that section 1651 permitted indictment for violent acts committed on the high seas for private ends, even in the absence of an actual taking. The critical point of departure from *Said* was the *Hasan* court's conclusion that section 1651, understood in light of *Sosa v. Alvarez-Machain* (see Section 5, *supra*) and *United States v. Arjona* (see Section 2, *supra*), should be read "according to the international consensus definition at the time of the alleged offense." *Id.* at 623. On that basis, the court applied the definition of piracy from the 1982 U.N. Convention on the Law of the Sea, to which the United States is not a party—but that, the court stressed, did not mean it failed to state customary international law. The court also observed that the United States generally accepted the 1982 Convention as stating customary international law on traditional uses, and also was a party to the 1958 High Seas Convention, which employed a virtually identical definition. *Id.* at 632–37.

3. *Commentary.* For analysis of contemporary legal issues relating to piracy, see Agora: *Piracy Prosecutions*, 104 AM. J. INT'L L. 397 (2010). For efforts to relate the complex legal history of piracy to contemporary controversies, including the ATS, see Eugene Kontorovich, *The "Define and Punish" Clause and the Limits of Universal Jurisdiction*, 103 NW. U. L. REV. 149 (2009); Eugene Kontorovich, *The Piracy Analogy: Modern Universal Jurisdiction's Hollow Foundation*, 45 HARV. INT'L L.J. 183 (2004); Alfred P. Rubin, *The Law of Piracy* (2d ed.1998).

CHAPTER 3

TREATIES AND OTHER INTERNATIONAL AGREEMENTS

■ ■ ■

SECTION 1. HISTORICAL CONTEXT OF THE TREATY POWER

NOTE: ORIGINS OF THE TREATY-MAKING POWER

Article II, Section 2, of the Constitution states that the President "shall have power, by and with the advice and consent of the Senate, to make treaties, provided two-thirds of the senators present concur...." This note traces the origins of that clause.

British Treaty–Making Power

In founding the American Republic, the framers were also influenced by their former colonizers. As the most successful constitutional system of the time, Great Britain's governmental structure offered examples of both virtues and shortcomings in governmental structure. Alexander Hamilton remarked at the Constitutional Convention in Philadelphia "that the British government was the best in the world," and he "doubted much whether any thing short of it would do in America."[1] Hamilton understood that many Americans saw the necessity of tempering "the vices of democracy" and looked forward to "the time, when others as well as himself would join in the praise bestowed ... on the British Constitution."[2]

A noted authority on British constitutional practice states:

> It is a peculiar function of sovereignty to make treaties, leagues, and alliances with foreign states or princes; and by the law of nations it is essential to the validity of a treaty that it be made by the sovereign power, for then it binds the whole community. In the

---

1. *Debates on the Adoption of the Federal Constitution in the Convention Held at Philadelphia, reprinted in* 5 *The Debates in the Several State Conventions, on the Adoption of the Federal Constitution, as Recommended by the General Convention at Philadelphia, in 1787,* at 202 (Jonathan Elliot ed., 2d ed. 1996) (1891) [hereinafter "5 *Elliot's Debates*"].

2. *Id.*

British empire this sovereign power is vested exclusively in the crown, acting under the advice of its responsible ministers.

Whatever engagements or contracts the sovereign enters into, no other power within the kingdom can legally delay, resist, or annul....[3]

While it is not contended that the treaty-making powers granted to the President were directly drawn from the implied authority of the English Monarch, the treaty-making power, considered a "prerogative of the Crown"[4] in the British System, was conferred upon the American President in partial accordance with Hamilton's oft quoted belief that "[A]s to the executive ... [t]he English model was the only good one...."[5]

Treaty-Making in the U.S. Colonies

Though prior to U.S. independence the treaty-making power resided with Britain, many of the colonies—so distant from London—pursued their own paths in important areas of foreign relations (i.e., trade, fishing rights, access to natural resources, Indian relations, relations with the French or Spanish). At times the colonies concluded their own written agreements, usually with Indian tribes. Colonial action was not only separate from Britain, but separate among the colonies as well. Historian John Ferling writes:

> Indeed, the colonies often had strikingly different interests. Some traded with the Indians to a far greater degree than others. Some had extensive claims to western lands; others had none. Massachusetts at times wished to fight to secure fishing rights off Newfoundland, or coal deposits in Nova Scotia, or timberlands in Maine whose products were essential in its ship construction yards. Those were not burning issues in the Carolinas or Georgia, which were preoccupied with trade with the Indians in the Southern backcountry, while they kept a wary eye on the Spanish in nearby Florida. Nor did every colony always feel threatened, even in the midst of war. Massachusetts, New York, and Connecticut had the misfortune to be hit hard by each of the previous intercolonial wars, but Maryland and New Jersey were hardly scathed, and before the 1740's Virginians were barely aware that the European powers were fighting one another in North America.[6]

The lack of coordination in colonial foreign relations affairs led the London Board of Trade to propose in 1753 that a meeting of representatives of the colonies be held in New York, along with Indian representatives. In particular, the Board (which supervised provincial affairs in the

---

3. Alpheus Todd, 1 *Parliamentary Government in England: Its Origins, Development, and Practical Operation* 132 (1892).

4. William R. Anson, *The Law and Custom of the Constitution* pt. 2, at 279 (Richard H. Leach ed., 1970) (1892).

5. 5 *Elliot's Debates*, *supra* note 1, at 203.

6. John Ferling, *A Leap in the Dark: The Struggle to Create the American Republic* 15–16 (2003).

Americas) was concerned that the French were securing support from the Iroquois, while at the same time, some of the colonies were antagonizing the Iroquois. The meeting would try to resolve any differences among the colonies and, through a single treaty made in the name of the Crown, settle affairs with the Iroquois (rather than by piecemeal agreements between the colonies and the Indians, which might be conflicting). The meeting did conclude a treaty with the tribes represented, but the treaty failed to prevent the outbreak of the French and Indian War in 1756.

Though the 1754 "Albany Congress" was designed to address Indian affairs and trade, several colonial delegations were instructed to investigate a union of the colonies, in part as a means of coordinating better their external relations. Benjamin Franklin (representing Pennsylvania) compiled ideas for a union into a single document, which was adopted by the Albany Congress and referred to the colonial governments and to the Crown. The Albany Plan was rejected by Britain and by the assemblies in several of the colonies, but it presaged the later movement toward independence.[7]

Treaty-Making Under the Articles of Confederation (1777–1789)

The Articles of Confederation were adopted by the Continental Congress in 1777 and ratified by the states in 1781. The Articles conferred upon Congress "the sole and exclusive right and power of ... entering into treaties and alliances." Yet the states were eager to retain the commercial freedom and political control they had gained as a result of the 1776 revolution. They stipulated in article 2 that "each State retains its sovereignty, freedom, and independence, and every power, jurisdiction, and right, which is not by this Confederation expressly delegated to the United States in Congress assembled." Exposed to a constant weighing of multiple states' interests, Congress was obliged to operate in circumstances that were not conducive to formulating a coherent foreign policy designed to promote the welfare of the community as a whole. The problem arose from the fact that the "states" were not "united" and were naturally inclined to pursue distinct objectives.

Not only were the inharmonious goals of the several states an obstacle to foreign affairs, but the governmental instrument required by the nature of a confederation, a congress of many deputies, inhibited efficient administration. Treaty-making proved to be an especially trying exercise for the members of the Continental Congress. They eventually revised the process by introducing measures to ensure smoother management. The creation and strengthening (during Jay's tenure) of the position of Secretary of Foreign Affairs (to be filled by a member of Congress) were the most important. However, relations with foreign governments were not easily controlled by a collective process. By examining the difficulties experienced by the Continental Congress, and the remedial steps subse-

7. *See* Timothy J. Shannon, *Indians and Colonists at the Crossroads of Empire: The Albany Congress of 1754* (2002).

quently taken, one may gain insight into the reasoning of the framers when they wrote the present Constitution's treaty-making provisions.

Problems Resulting From Collective Responsibility for Foreign Relations

As the war of independence drew to a close, the United States found itself with the awesome task of negotiating a multilateral peace settlement. Congress corresponded with its plenipotentiaries at Paris but, in the course of the deliberations of a large chamber, found it difficult to keep information classified. Madison recorded in his diaries of congressional proceedings an instance where this problem made itself manifest:

> The publication of the preliminary articles [of the draft agreement] . . . was not a deliberate act of Congress. A hasty question for enjoining secrecy on certain parts of the despatches, which included those articles, was lost; and copies having been taken by members, and some of them handed to the delegates of Pennsylvania, one of them reached the printer. When the publication appeared, Congress in general regretted it . . . as leading France into suspicions that Congress favored the premature signature of the articles, and were, at least, willing to remove, in the minds of the people, the blame of delaying peace from Great Britain to France.[8]

Events such as this no doubt had an influence on the decision to exclude congressional representatives from any part in treaty-negotiating when the new Constitution was drafted.

Ultimately a peace treaty—the Treaty of Paris—was concluded in September 1783. *See* Definitive Treaty of Peace, Sept. 3, 1783, U.S.-Gr. Brit., *reprinted in* 2 *Treaties and Other International Agreements of the United States of America* 151 (Hunter Miller ed., 1931). Yet the failure of some states to comply with treaty stipulations to which the United States, as represented by ministers commissioned by Congress, had agreed severely impaired the nation's early diplomatic efforts. Included in a report by Secretary Jay in October, 1783, was a letter in which the British Secretary of State for Foreign Affairs, Lord Carmarthen, complained of the refusal of the United States to respect article IV of the Treaty of Peace, which ensured that neither country would enact laws that would prevent the collection of debts:

> The little attention paid to the fulfilling [of] this engagement on the part of the subjects of the United States in general, and the direct breach of it in many particular instances, have already reduced many of the king's subjects to the utmost degree of difficulty and distress. . . .
>
> The engagements entered into by treaty ought to be mutual and equally binding on the respective contracting parties. It would therefore be the height of folly as well as injustice, to suppose one party alone obliged to a strict observance of the publick faith, while the

8. 5 *Elliot's Debates*, *supra* note 1, at 66.

> other might remain free to deviate from its own engagements, as often as convenience might render such deviation necessary, though at the expense of its own national credit and importance.[9]

Congress realized that, in order to restore the waning credibility of the United States, the central government would have to take a more forceful stand. On March 21, 1787, the legislators passed the following resolution:

> *Resolved* That the legislatures of the several States cannot of right pass any act or acts for interpreting, explaining, or construing a national treaty or any part or clause of it; nor for restraining, limiting or in any manner impeding, retarding or counteracting the operation and execution of the same for that on being constitutionally made ratified and published, they become in virtue of the confederation part of the law of the land and are not only independent of the will and power of such legislatures but also binding and obligatory upon them.[10]

The lack of an executive agent came to be perceived as a structural deficiency hindering the Confederation's diplomatic efforts. Hamilton, assessing the ills of the nation, stated:

> Another defect in our system, is want of method and energy in the administration. This has partly resulted from the other defect [the weakness of Congress]; but in a great degree from prejudice, and the want of a proper executive. Congress have kept the power too much in their own hands, and have meddled too much with details of every sort. Congress is, properly, a deliberative corps; and it forgets itself when it attempts to play the executive. It is impossible such a body, numerous as it is, constantly fluctuating, can ever act with sufficient decision, or with system. . . .[11]

Jefferson, too, understood the need for a separate executive:

> I think it very material, to separate, in the hands of Congress, the executive and legislative powers, as the judiciary already are, in some degree. This, I hope, will be done. The want of it has been the source of more evil than we have experienced from any other cause. Nothing is so embarrassing nor so mischievous, in a great assembly, as the details of execution. . . . I have ever viewed the executive details as the greatest cause of evil to us, because they in fact place us as if we had no federal head, by diverting the attention of that head from great to small subjects; and should this division of power not be recommended by the convention, it is my opinion Congress should make it itself, by establishing an executive committee.[12]

---

9. 4 *Secret Journals of the Acts and Proceedings of Congress* 188 (1821).

10. 32 *Journals of the Continental Congress* 124–25 (1787).

11. Letter from Alexander Hamilton to James Duane (Sept. 3, 1780), in 1 *The Works of Alexander Hamilton* 150, 154 (John C. Hamilton ed., 1850).

12. Letter from Thomas Jefferson to Edward Carrington (Aug. 4, 1787), in *The Best Letters of Thomas Jefferson* 30, 31 (J. G. de Roulhac Hamilton ed., 1926).

In response to the exasperating managerial task of conducting foreign relations without the full cooperation of the state governments, Congress was forced to consolidate the control of this function in the Secretary of State, John Jay. A letter from a French diplomat to the French minister, Vergennes, illustrates the need for an executive agent. This power vacuum which resulted in Jay's dominance over members of Congress:

> The little stability of congress, my lord, insensibly gives to the ministers of the different departments a power incompatible with the spirit of liberty and of jealousy which prevails in this country. ... Mr. Jay especially has acquired a peculiar ascendancy over the members of congress. All important business passes through his hands. He makes his report on it, and congress seldom has an opinion different from his. Instead of appointing committees, they will insensibly become accustomed to seeing only through the eyes of Mr. Jay.... [13]

With all of these problems in mind, the delegates went on to the Convention at Philadelphia anxious to revise the *status quo.*

Debates at the Federal Convention of 1787 and Thereafter

The Treaty Clause. The Virginia Resolutions presented by Edmund Randolph were the first proposals made to the Convention. They did not constitute a comprehensive plan and therefore did not specifically mention treaty-making. They did, however, resolve "that a national executive be instituted ... and that, besides a general authority to execute the national laws, it ought to enjoy the executive rights vested in Congress by the Confederation."[14] This provision was designed, *inter alia,* to remedy the problems created by Congress's management of foreign affairs. Charles Pickney next laid before the Convention a different proposal that stipulated that the "Senate shall have the sole and exclusive power to declare war, and to make treaties...."[15]

The Convention began to consider more radical remedies in a speech made by Alexander Hamilton on June 18. At the conclusion of his remarks, he submitted some "amendments which he should probably propose to the plan of Mr. Randolph...."[16] In regard to treaty-making, he suggested that the "supreme executive authority of the United States to be vested in a governor ... have, with the advice and approbation of the senate, the power of making all treaties...."[17]

Given the early tradition of congressional preeminence in foreign affairs, it is not surprising that, until late in the Convention, there was little inclination to alter prior arrangements for the conclusion of treaties. Some preferred to strengthen, rather than alter, these. For example, Mr.

---

13. Letter from Otto to Vergennes (Dec. 25, 1785), in George Bancroft, 1 *History of the Formation of the Constitution of the United States of America* 473, 474 (1882).

14. 5 *Elliot's Debates, supra* note 1, at 128.

15. *Id.* at 131.

16. *Id.* at 205.

17. *Id.*

Wilson of Pennsylvania stressed that the Senate ought "to be made respectable in the eyes of foreign nations"[18] and urged that this be accomplished through longer senatorial terms of office.[19]

On August 6, however, John Mercer began the challenge to the Convention's conventional received wisdom, arguing "that the Senate ought not to have the power of treaties. This power belonged to the executive department...."[20] On August 23, the floor was opened for discussion of the proposed clause: "The Senate ... shall have power to make treaties...."[21] James Madison, stressing the predictable propensity of Senators (who were to be appointed by the state legislatures) to favor local interests, stated "that for this, as well as other obvious reasons, it was proper that the President should be an agent in treaties."[22] Governeur Morris of Pennsylvania "did not know that he should agree to refer the making of treaties to the Senate at all but for the present would move to add, as an amendment ...: 'But no treaty shall be binding on the United States which is not ratified by law.' "[23] At the end of the day Madison, in connection with legislative assent, "hinted, for consideration, whether a distinction might not be made between different sorts of treaties...."[24]

The business of deciding upon this issue was referred to a committee of eleven who reported on September 4 that "The President, by and with the advice and consent of the Senate, shall have power to make treaties.... But no treaty shall be made without the consent of two-thirds of the members present."[25] This wording remained practically unaltered in the final draft.

John Jay, in *The Federalist Papers* No. 64, pointed to "secrecy and dispatch" as the primary reasons for vesting the treaty-making power with the President and Senate:

> It seldom happens in the negotiation of treaties, of whatever nature, but that perfect *secrecy* and immediate *dispatch* are sometimes requisite....
>
> ... So often and so essentially have we heretofore suffered from the want of secrecy and dispatch that the Constitution would have been inexcusably defective if no attention had been paid to those objects.[26]

In proclaiming their dissent, the minority of the Pennsylvania's ratifying convention addressed the Senate's "dangerous mixture of the

---

18. *Id.* at 245.

19. *See id.*

20. *Id.* at 428.

21. *Id.* at 469.

22. *Id.*

23. *Id.*

24. *Id.* at 470.

25. *Id.* at 507.

26. *The Federalist Papers* No. 64, at 392–93 (Jay) (Clinton Rossiter ed., 1961).

powers of government; the same body possessing legislative, executive, and judicial powers." They also predicted "uncorseted corruption" as a result of blurring the delineation between the branches of government in the process of treaty-making. They feared it would "destroy all independency and purity in the executive department,"[27] while Elbridge Gerry of Massachusetts thought it would give the Executive "undue influence over the legislature."[28] Cato, examining the "legislation of treaties,"[29] suspected that a division of powers between the President and the Senate would destroy accountability. He stated: "If treaties are erroneously or wickedly made who is there to punish—the executive can always cover himself with the plea, that he was advised by the senate; and the senate being a collective body are not easily made accountable for mal-administration."[30]

Hamilton, on the other hand, justified the collaborative method:

> With regard to the intermixture of powers, ... the union of the executive with the Senate, in the article of treaties, is no infringement of that rule. I venture to add that the particular nature of the power of making treaties indicates a peculiar propriety in that union. Though several writers on the subject of government place that power in the class of executive authorities, yet this is evidently an arbitrary disposition; for if we attend carefully to its operation it will be found to partake more of the legislative than of the executive character, though it does not seem strictly to fall within the definition of either of them. The essence of the legislative authority is to enact laws, or, in other words, to prescribe rules for the regulation of the society; while the execution of the laws and the employment of the common strength, either for this purpose or for the common defense, seem to comprise all the functions of the executive magistrate. The power of making treaties is, plainly, neither the one nor the other. It relates neither to the execution of the subsisting laws nor to the enaction of new ones; and still less to an exertion of the common strength. Its objects are CONTRACTS with foreign nations which have the force of law, but derive it from the obligations of good faith. They are not rules prescribed by the sovereign to the subject, but agreements between sovereign and sovereign. The power in question seems therefore to form a distinct department, and to belong, properly, neither to the legislative nor to the executive. The qualities elsewhere detailed as indispensable in the management of foreign negotiations point out the executive as the most fit agent in those transactions; while the vast importance of the trust and the operation of treaties as laws

27. *The Address and Reasons of Dissent of the Minority of the Convention of Pennsylvania to Their Constituents* (PENN. PACKET and DAILY ADVERTISER, Dec. 18, 1787), *reprinted in* 3 *The Complete Anti-federalist* 145, 161–62 (Herbert J. Storing ed., 1981) [hereinafter cited as "Storing"].

28. *Hon. Mr. Gerry's objections to signing the National Constitution* (MASS. CENTINEL, Nov. 3, 1787), *reprinted in* 2 Storing, *supra* note 27, at 6–7.

29. Letters of Cato (NEW YORK JOURNAL, Sept. 1787–Jan. 1788), *reprinted in* 2 Storing, *supra* note 27, at 120, 122.

30. *Id.* at 123.

plead strongly for the participation of the whole or a portion of the legislative body in the office of making them.[31]

The Supremacy Clause. On July 17, Luther Martin of Maryland proposed to the federal Convention: "That the legislative acts of the United States, made by virtue and in pursuance of the Articles of Union, and all treaties made and ratified under the authority of the United States, shall be the supreme law of the respective states. . . ."[32] In the prevailing spirit of nationalism, which induced the transfer of power from state to federal government, Mr. Martin's motion passed. This shift in the distribution of legislative authority was facilitated by Madison's insistence that the states, otherwise, would "pass laws which will accomplish their injurious objects before they can be repealed by the general [federal] legislature,"[33] and that "confidence cannot be put in the state tribunals as guardians of the national authority and interests."[34] He urged that federal preeminence in the conduct of foreign relations was essential "to the efficacy and security of the general government."[35]

Martin's resolution remained in essence unaltered in the Convention's final draft. Yet, the "supremacy clause," to many opponents of the adoption of the Constitution, continued to remain an important issue.

George Mason, attending the federal Convention as a deputy from Virginia, opposed the adoption of Martin's formula during the months of debate that followed. He distrusted the exclusion of the House of Representatives from treaty ratification and was not moved by the lessons others purported to derive from the experience of treaty-making during the confederate period. Instead, Mason was primarily concerned with the dangers of an omnipotent central government:

> By declaring all Treaties supreme Laws of the Land, the Executive and the Senate have in many Cases, an exclusive Power of Legislation; which might have been avoided by proper Distinctions with Respect to Treaties, and requiring the Assent of the House of Representatives, where it [could] be done with Safety.[36]

As a critical blow to state sovereignty, the supremacy clause stirred more controversy in the following months. Although some critics, in attacking the measure, focused on the effect of treaties on state power, the crux of the argument centered on the legal validity of a treaty not sanctioned by bicameral promulgation. John Jay, in *The Federalist Papers* No. 64, rebutted this line of attack:

> Some are displeased . . . because, as the treaties, when made, are to have the force of laws, they should be made only by men invested

31. *The Federalist Papers* No. 75, *supra* note 26, at 450–51 (Hamilton).

32. 5 *Elliot's Debates*, *supra* note 1, at 322.

33. *Id.* at 321.

34. *Id.*

35. *Id.*

36. George Mason, *Objections to the Constitution of Government formed by the Convention* (1787), *reprinted in* 2 Storing, *supra* note 27, at 11, 12.

> with legislative authority. These gentlemen seem not to consider that the judgments of our courts, and the commissions constitutionally given by our governor, are as valid and as binding on all persons whom they concern as the laws passed by our legislature.... It surely does not follow that because they have given the power of making laws to the legislature, that therefore they should likewise give them the power to do every other act of sovereignty by which the citizens are to be bound and affected.[37]

Critics remained troubled, however, by the centralization (and division) of treaty-making powers. They continued to argue that, if treaties were to be "law of the land," they should be enacted in accordance with the legislative provisions of the Constitution. The lack of limitations on the content of international agreements provoked another controversy, emanating from suspicion that this power would eventually be abused. The *Federal Farmer* regarded the provision as a loophole for creating unjust laws because "[i]t is not said that these treaties shall be made in pursuance of the Constitution—nor are there any constitutional bounds set to those who shall make them...."[38] An antifederalist using the pseudonym Brutus complained: "I do not find any limitation, or restriction, to the exercise of this power."[39]

Attempts are often made to explain why the framers insisted on a two-thirds majority in the Senate to approve a treaty. The historian, Samuel Bemis, attributes this provision, in part, to dissatisfaction with John Jay's willingness to abandon navigation privileges on the Mississippi River that had been held for thirty years in negotiations with Spain concerning Florida. Bemis says:

> A few months later when the delegates to the Philadelphia Convention of 1787 were drawing up the new Constitution the men from the southern states remembered the dangers, so recently presented to them, of any constitution which would allow a bare majority to ratify a treaty, either with a foreign nation or with Indian tribes. The Jay–Gardoqui negotiations are responsible for that clause in the Constitution of 1787 which requires a two-thirds majority of senators present for the ratification of any treaty.[40]

This may have contributed to the result. However, the two-thirds provision primarily stems from the founding fathers' wish to avoid unnecessary alliances. Washington, in his Farewell Address, gave voice to these concerns when he asked: "Why, by interweaving our own destiny with that of any part of Europe, entangle our peace and prosperity in the toils of European ambition, rivalship, interest, humor, or caprice?"[41]

---

37. *The Federalist Papers* No. 64, *supra* note 26, at 393–94.

38. *Letters from The Federal Farmer* (No. IV: Oct. 12, 1787), *reprinted in* 2 Storing, *supra* note 27, at 245, 246–47.

39. *Essays of Brutus* (No. II: Nov. 1, 1787), *reprinted in* 2 Storing, *supra* note 27, at 372, 377.

40. Samuel F. Bemis, *A Diplomatic History of the United States* 79–80 (1938) (footnotes omitted).

41. Washington's Farewell Address (Sept. 17, 1796), *reprinted in Documents of American History* 169, 174 (Henry Steele Commager ed., 1968).

Treaty-Making Under the Constitution

Since 1789, the United States has concluded thousands of treaties at the bilateral, regional, and global level. Important early treaties ended wars, such as the 1814 Treaty of Ghent (ending the War of 1812 with Great Britain), or secured U.S. boundaries, such as the 1817 Rush–Bagot Treaty (demilitarizing the Great Lakes), the 1819 Adams–Onís Treaty (purchasing Florida from Spain), the 1842 Webster–Ashburton Treaty (settling the boundary with Canada), or the 1867 treaty purchasing Alaska from Russia. Other treaties focused on core interests of the United States in areas of trade and immigration, such as the 1855 U.S.-Canadian Reciprocity Treaty on trade and tariffs, the 1858 U.S.-Japan Treaty of Amity and Commerce, and the 1868 Burlingame Treaty establishing relations with China. By the latter part of the nineteenth century, major multilateral treaties became increasingly important, such as the 1883 Paris Convention for the Protection of Industrial Property and the 1899 Hague Conventions on the laws of war.

Throughout the twentieth century, the United States concluded major multilateral and bilateral treaties covering an increasing wide array of subject matter areas (such as peace and security, dispute settlement, human rights, oceans, environment, criminal law, immunities) and establishing major international organizations (such as the United Nations, the Organization of American States, the World Bank, the International Monetary Fund, and the World Trade Organization). Among the treaties concluded by the United States in this century are those relating to arms control (*e.g.*, Treaty on Measures for the Further Reduction and Limitation of Strategic Offensive Arms, Apr. 8, 2010, U.S.-Russia, Treaty Doc. No. 111–05 (2010)); family law (*e.g.*, Hague Convention on International Recovery of Child Support and Family Maintenance, Nov. 23, 2007, Treaty Doc. No. 110–21 (2009)); and terrorism (*e.g.*, International Convention for Suppression of Acts of Nuclear Terrorism, Treaty Doc. No. 110–4) (2008)).

What exactly is the process for making such treaties and what are the key legal issues in doing so?

SECTION 2. SENATORIAL ADVICE AND CONSENT FUNCTION

INTRODUCTORY NOTE

Article II, Section 2 of the U.S. Constitution provides that the President "shall have Power, by and with the Advice and Consent of the Senate, to make Treaties, provided two thirds of the Senators present concur. . . ." This language, and its inclusion in Article II, makes clear that it is the President, not the Senate, who makes treaties, typically by depositing an instrument of ratification.

At the same time, Section 2 says that before the President "makes" a treaty, the Senate must give its "advice" and "consent," thus suggesting that the Senate is expected to provide counsel to the President in addition to a final stamp of approval. Such counsel may include the involvement of senators or their staff as observers to treaty negotiations or as reviewers of draft treaty language, but usually congressional involvement in negotiations is *de minimis*. Normally, the Executive Branch prefers to keep the Senate out of the process until final consent is needed, unless its involvement at an earlier stage is necessary to secure political support for the treaty.[1] The following excerpt sets forth the basic treaty-making process.

TREATIES AND OTHER INTERNATIONAL AGREEMENTS: THE ROLE OF THE UNITED STATES SENATE

S. Prt. 106–71, at 6–12 (2001) (footnotes omitted).

NEGOTIATION AND CONCLUSION

The first phase of treatymaking, negotiation and conclusion, is widely considered an exclusive prerogative of the President.... The President chooses and instructs the negotiators and decides whether to sign an agreement after its terms have been negotiated. Nevertheless, the Senate or Congress sometimes proposes negotiations and influences them through advice and consultation. In addition, the executive branch is supposed to advise appropriate congressional leaders and committees of the intention to negotiate significant new agreements and consult them as to the form of the agreement.

Steps in the negotiating phase follow.

(1) *Initiation.*—The executive branch formally initiates the negotiations. The original concept or proposal for a treaty on a particular subject, however, may come from Congress.

(2) *Appointment of negotiators.*—The President selects the negotiators of international agreements, but appointments may be subject to the advice and consent of the Senate. Negotiations are often conducted by ambassadors or foreign service officers in a relevant post who have already been confirmed by the Senate.

(3) *Issuance of full powers and instructions.*—The President issues full power documents to the negotiators, authorizing them officially to represent the United States. Similarly, he issues instructions as to the objectives to be sought and positions to be taken. On occasion the Senate participates in setting the objectives during the confirmation process, or Congress contributes to defining the objectives through hearings or resolutions.

---

1. *See* Arthur Bestor, *"Advice" From the Very Beginning, "Consent" When the End Is Achieved*, 83 AM. J. INT'L L. 718 (1989); Marjorie M. Whiteman, 14 *Digest of International Law* 53–55 (1970) (describing the Senate's role).

Chart 1. Steps in the Making of a Treaty

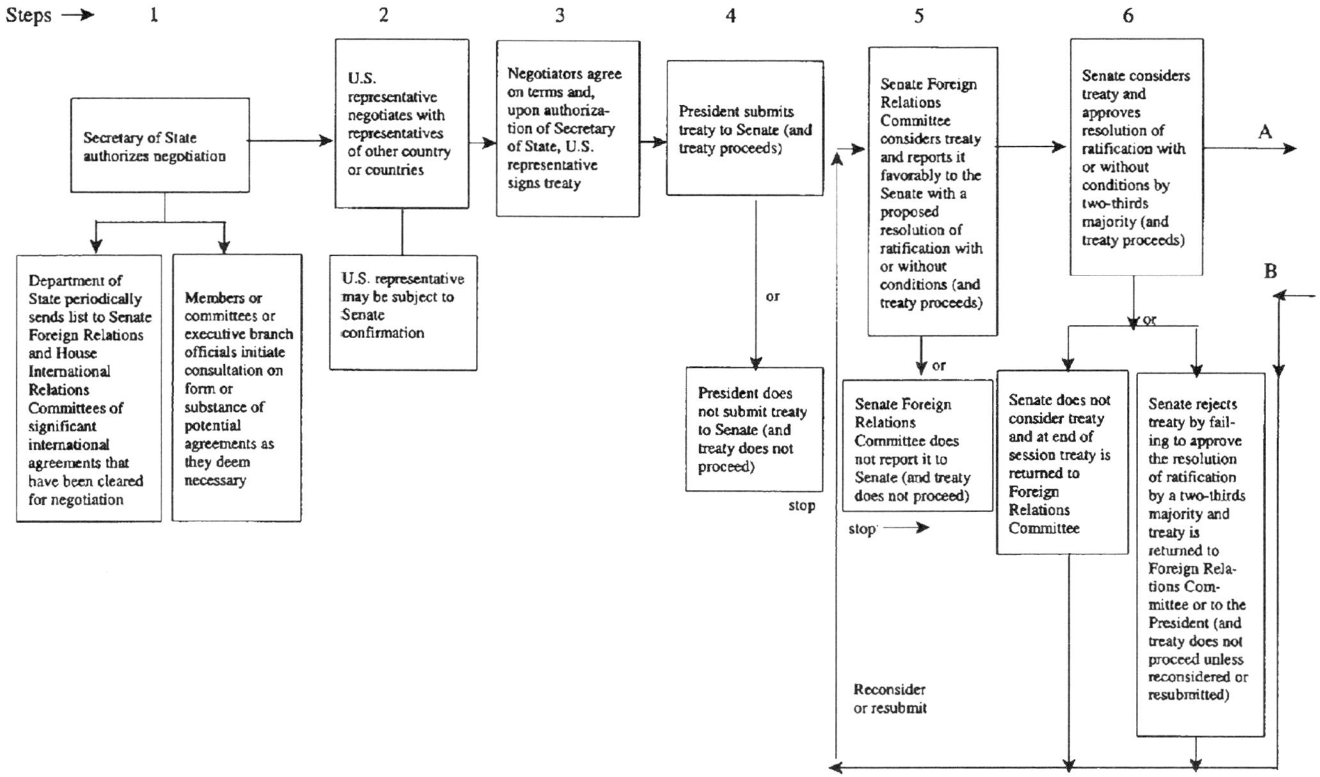

Chart 1. Steps in the Making of a Treaty (continued)

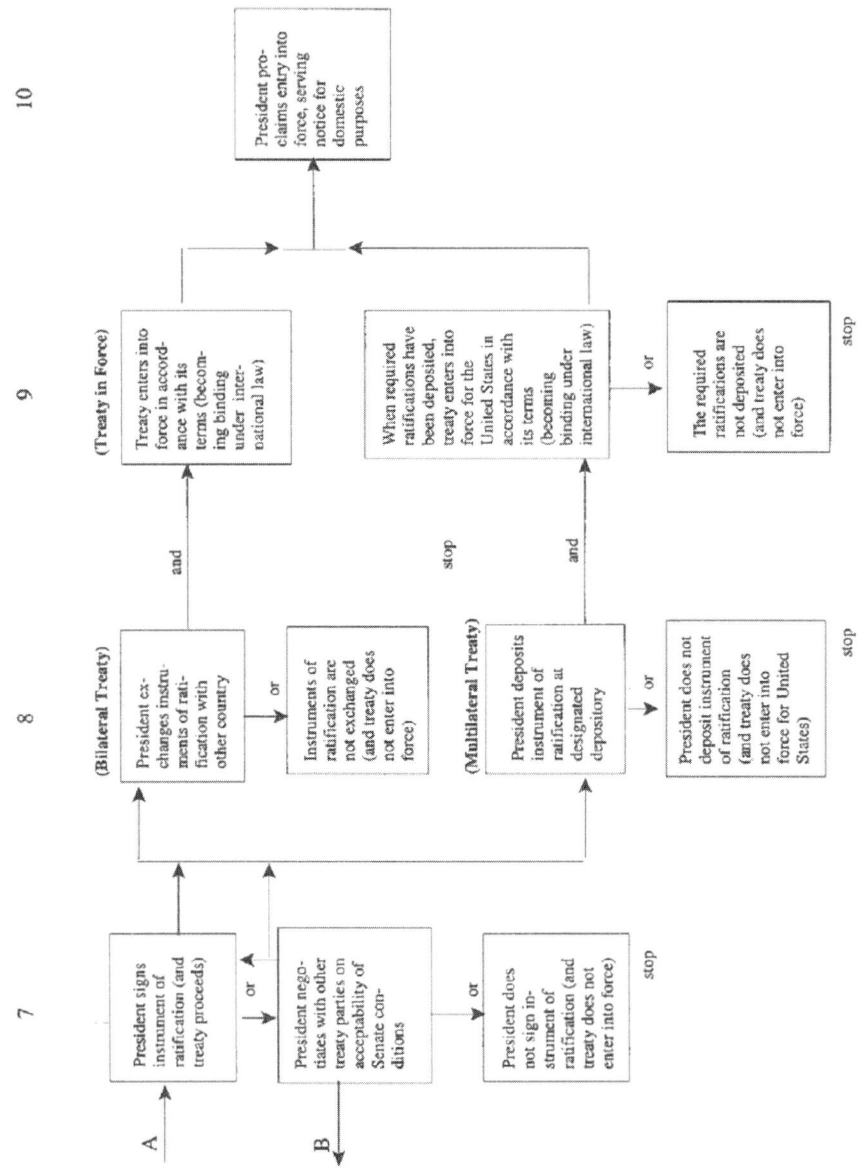

(4) *Negotiation.*—Negotiation is the process by which representatives of the President and other governments concerned agree on the substance, terms, wording, and form of an international agreement. Members of Congress sometimes provide advice through consultations arranged either by Congress or the executive branch, and through their statements and writings. Members of Congress or their staff have served as members or advisers of delegations and as observers at international negotiations.

(5) *Conclusion.*—The conclusion or signing marks the end of the negotiating process and indicates that the negotiators have reached agree-

ment. In the case of a treaty the term "conclusion" is a misnomer in that the agreement does not enter into force until the exchange or deposit of ratifications. In the case of executive agreements, however, the signing and entry into force are frequently simultaneous.

CONSIDERATION BY THE SENATE

A second phase begins when the President transmits a concluded treaty to the Senate and the responsibility moves to the Senate. Following are the main steps during the Senate phase.

(1) *Presidential submission.*—The Secretary of State formally submits treaties to the President for transmittal to the Senate. A considerable time may elapse between signature and submission to the Senate, and on rare occasions a treaty signed on behalf of the United States may never be submitted to the Senate at all and thus never enter into force for the United States. When transmitted to the Senate, treaties are accompanied by a Presidential message consisting of the text of the treaty, a letter of transmittal requesting the advice and consent of the Senate, and the earlier letter of submittal of the Secretary of State which usually contains a detailed description and analysis of the treaty.

(2) *Senate receipt and referral.*—The Parliamentarian transmits the treaty to the Executive Clerk, who assigns it a document number. The Majority Leader then, as in executive session, asks the unanimous consent of the Senate that the injunction of secrecy be removed, that the treaty be considered as having been read the first time, and that it be referred to the Foreign Relations Committee and ordered to be printed. The Presiding Officer then refers the treaty, regardless of its subject matter, to the Foreign Relations Committee in accordance with Rule XXV of the Senate Rules. (Rule XXV makes an exception only for reciprocal trade agreements.) At this point the treaty text is printed and made available to the public.

(3) *Senate Foreign Relations Committee action.*—The treaty is placed on the committee calendar and remains there until the committee reports it to the full Senate. While it is committee practice to allow a treaty to remain pending long enough to receive study and comments from the public, the committee usually considers a treaty within a year or two, holding a hearing and preparing a written report.

The committee recommends Senate advice and consent by reporting a treaty with a proposed resolution of ratification. While most treaties have historically been reported without conditions, the committee may recommend that the Senate approve a treaty subject to conditions incorporated in the resolution of ratification.

(4) *Conditional approval.*—The conditions traditionally have been grouped into categories described in the following way.

— Amendments to a treaty change the text of the treaty and require the consent of the other party or parties. (Note that in Senate debate the term may refer to an amendment of the resolution of ratification, not the treaty itself, and therefore be comprised of some other type of condition.)

— Reservations change U.S. obligations without necessarily changing the text, and they require the acceptance of the other party.

— Understandings are interpretive statements that clarify or elaborate provisions but do not alter them.

— Declarations are statements expressing the Senate's position or opinion on matters relating to issues raised by the treaty rather than to specific provisions.

— Provisos relate to issues of U.S. law or procedure and are not intended to be included in the instruments of ratification to be deposited or exchanged with other countries.

Whatever name a condition is given by the Senate, if a condition alters an international obligation under the treaty, the President is expected to transmit it to the other party. In recent years, the Senate on occasion has explicitly designated that some conditions were to be transmitted to the other party or parties and, in some cases, formally agreed to by them. It has also designated that some conditions need not be formally communicated to the other party, that some conditions were binding on the President, and that some conditions expressed the intent of the Senate.

(5) *Action by the full Senate.*—After a treaty is reported by the Foreign Relations Committee, it is placed on the Senate's Executive Calendar and the Majority Leader arranges for the Senate to consider it. In 1986 the Senate amended Rule XXX of the Senate Rules, which governs its consideration of treaties, to simplify the procedure in this step. Still, under the full procedures of the revised Rule XXX, in the first stage of consideration the treaty would be read a second time and any proposed amendments to the treaty itself would be considered and voted upon by a simple majority. Usually the Majority Leader obtains unanimous consent to abbreviate the procedures, and the Senate proceeds directly to the consideration of the resolution of ratification as recommended by the Foreign Relations Committee.

The Senate then considers amendments to the resolution of ratification, which would incorporate any amendments to the treaty itself that the Senate had agreed to in the first stage, as well as conditions recommended by the Foreign Relations Committee. Senators may then offer reservations, understandings, and other conditions to be placed in the resolution of ratification. Votes on these conditions, as well as other motions, are determined by a simple majority. Finally, the Senate votes on the resolution of ratification, as it has been amended. The final vote on the resolution of ratification requires, for approval, a two-thirds majority of the Senators present. Although the number of Senators who must be present is not specified, the Senate's practice with respect to major treaties is to conduct the final treaty vote at a time when most Senators are available. After approval of a controversial treaty, a Senator may offer a motion to reconsider which is usually laid on the table (defeated). In the case of a treaty that has failed to receive a two-thirds majority, if the motion to reconsider is not taken up, the treaty is returned to the Foreign Relations Committee. . . .

(6) *Return to committee.*—Treaties reported by the committee but neither approved nor formally returned to the President by the Senate are automatically returned to the committee calendar at the end of a Congress; the committee must report them out again in order for the Senate to consider them.

(7) *Return to President or withdrawal.*—The President may request the return of a treaty, or the Foreign Relations Committee may report and the Senate adopt a simple resolution directing the Secretary of the Senate to return a treaty to the President. Otherwise, treaties that do not receive the advice and consent of the Senate remain pending on the committee calendar indefinitely.

Presidential Action After Senate action

After the Senate gives its advice and consent to a treaty, the Senate sends it to the President. He resumes control and decides whether to take further action to complete the treaty.

(1) *Ratification.*—The President ratifies a treaty by signing an instrument of ratification, thus declaring the consent of the United States to be bound. If the Senate has consented with reservations or conditions that the President deems unacceptable, he may at a later date resubmit the original treaty to the Senate for further consideration, or he may renegotiate it with the other parties prior to resubmission. Or the President may decide not to ratify the treaty because of the conditions or for any other reason.

(2) *Exchange or deposit of instruments of ratification and entry into force.*—If he ratifies the treaty, the President then directs the Secretary of State to take any action necessary for the treaty to enter into force. A bilateral treaty usually enters into force when the parties exchange instruments of ratification. A multilateral treaty enters into force when the number of parties specified in the treaty deposit the instruments of ratification at a specified location. Once a treaty enters into force, it is binding in international law on the parties who have ratified it.

(3) *Proclamation.*—When the instruments of ratification have been exchanged or the necessary number deposited, the President issues a proclamation that the treaty has entered into force. Proclamation serves as legal notice for domestic purposes and publicizes the text.

NOTE ON THE FAILURE OF THE SENATE TO GIVE CONSENT

As indicated above, treaties that do not receive the advice and consent of the Senate can remain pending on the committee calendar indefinitely. *See*

Unperfected Treaties of the United States of America, 1776–1976 (Christian L. Wiktor ed., 1976). Should that be the case? After the Senate decisively rejected the Covenant of the League of Nations (by votes in November 1919 and March 1920), Senator Henry Cabot Lodge moved to return it to the President, which the Senate approved by a vote of 47 to 37. *See* Henry Cabot Lodge, *The Senate and the League of Nations* 208 (1925); *see generally* Alan Cranston, *Killing of the Peace* (1945); John Milton Cooper, Jr. *Breaking the Heart of the World: Woodrow Wilson and the Fight for the League of Nations* (2001). By contrast, when the Comprehensive Test Ban Treaty (CTBT) failed to receive the Senate's consent by a vote of 51 to 48, no action was taken to return the treaty to the President, and it remained on the Senate's calendar. Moreover, President Clinton stated that the United States would voluntarily refrain from conducting nuclear tests during the remainder of his term in office. *See* Remarks on Senate Action on the Comprehensive Nuclear Test–Ban Treaty and an Exchange with Reporters, 35 WEEKLY COMP. PRES. DOC. 2026 (Oct. 18, 1999).

While treaties that do not receive Senate consent cannot be ratified, it is important to note that under international treaty law, there is an obligation created upon *signing* the treaty that the prospective state party not defeat the object and purpose of the treaty. *See* Vienna Convention on the Law of Treaties art. 18, May 23, 1969, 1155 U.N.T.S. 331, 336 ("A State is obliged to refrain from acts which would defeat the object and purpose of a treaty when ... [i]t has signed the treaty ... until it shall have made its intention clear not to become a party to the treaty...."). Thus, even before ratification, an obligation arises not to take steps that will make it difficult for the state ultimately to join the treaty. If the Senate refuses to consent to a treaty, should the President inform the depositary of the treaty that the United States has failed to perfect its ratification procedures, so as to avoid any international obligation to uphold the object and purpose of the treaty? Otherwise, has not the President bound the Senate to an element of the treaty without the Senate's consent? For a discussion, see Curtis A. Bradley, *Unratified Treaties, Domestic Politics, and the U.S. Constitution*, 48 HARV. INT'L L. J. 307 (2007); David H. Moore, *The President's Unconstitutional Treatymaking*, 59 U.C.L.A. L. Rev. (forthcoming 2012).

It is certainly possible for a state to notify the depositary that it has no further intention of seeking ratification (sometimes referred to by non-lawyers as "unsigning" a treaty). Just prior to entry into force of the Rome Statute of the International Criminal Court, July 17, 1998, 2187 U.N.T.S. 3, the United States decided that it had no intention of pursuing ratification. Therefore, on May 6, 2002, the Department of State notified the Secretary–General that "the United States does not intend to become a party to the treaty." *See* U.S. Department of State Press Release on International Criminal Court: Letter to UN Secretary–General Kofi Annan (May 6, 2002).

NOTE: CASE STUDY ON SENATORIAL ADVICE AND CONSENT TO THE CONVENTION AGAINST TORTURE

To demonstrate the Senate's advice and consent role, the materials below depict the United States' process for negotiating and ratifying the Convention

Against Torture and Other Cruel, Inhuman or Degrading Treatment or Punishment, Dec. 10, 1984, S. TREATY DOC. NO. 100–20 (1988), 1465 U.N.T.S. 85 (Convention Against Torture, or CAT). The United States voted at the U.N. General Assembly to "adopt" the treaty in 1984 and "signed" the treaty in 1988, yet the treaty only "entered into force" for the United States in 1994. What is the legal significance of these different stages?

The Executive Branch played the main role in the negotiating process for the Convention Against Torture, which largely took place in Geneva at the U.N. Commission on Human Rights. Once the negotiations were over, the United States had to decide whether to join the treaty. What might be done if various aspects of the treaty conflict with U.S. policy preferences, U.S. statutes, or U.S. constitutional law (including powers that traditionally have been left to the several states)? The United States can "swallow hard" and change its policy preferences and even federal statutes, but it may not wish to do so. Further, the United States cannot change the Constitution absent a cumbersome amendment process. Consequently, the advice and consent process for any given treaty may entail the imposition of reservations, understandings, or declarations (referred to as RUDs) on the U.S. ratification as a means of aligning U.S. obligations under the treaty with U.S. policy preferences and national legal requirements. RUDs can be proposed by the President when the treaty is sent to the Senate or may be demanded by the Senate as a condition for its consent. *See* Haver v. Yaker, 76 U.S. (9 Wall.) 32, 35, 19 L.Ed. 571 (1869). As you read these particular materials, imagine that you are the Attorney General or a senator who must decide whether the United States should join the treaty. You might well have concerns about the following issues:

- The United States follows a federal system, where state and local units have important responsibilities for enforcement of criminal law. How should this be taken into account in the process of U.S. adherence to a treaty that calls for punishing certain behavior?
- If the treaty is going to call for punishing persons who commit torture, what is "torture"? What kinds of acts must be criminalized? U.S. law enforcement officers, judges, and others will want to know.
- What should you do if the treaty uses one standard, such as whether "there are substantial grounds for believing" something, but U.S. law historically has used a different standard, such as "it is more likely than not" that something will happen? Or the treaty uses a broad standard, such as "cruel, inhuman, or degrading treatment," which may or may not be consistent with analogous standards in U.S. law?
- Do you want the principal provisions of the treaty to have direct effect as a part of U.S. law (a "self-executing treaty"), or do you want to insist that the treaty only have force of law within the United States when implemented by statute (a "non-self-executing" treaty)? Section 4 of this Chapter will explore in greater detail the phenomenon of the self-executing treaty, but for the time being, note that the Senate can play a critical role in determining whether a treaty is self-executing.

The process of securing the Senate's advice and consent to the CAT was far from a "rubber stamp" on the President's preferred course of action. The initial RUDs proposed by the President were revised due to adverse reactions from various interest groups, including human rights organizations. Some of these changes are attributable to the transition from one presidential administration (under President Ronald Reagan) to another (that of President George H.W. Bush), which highlights political dynamics that can arise over the course of the advice and consent process. Further changes to the RUDs were made on the floor of the Senate to accommodate the views of a senator.

Finally, note how at each stage of the advice and consent process, important statements are made by the Executive Branch or Senate that can assist in understanding the meaning of a treaty or of the RUDs. Thereafter, courts and other decision-makers will typically refer to these statements as interpretive aides when applying the treaty.

CONVENTION AGAINST TORTURE AND OTHER CRUEL, INHUMAN OR DEGRADING TREATMENT OR PUNISHMENT

Dec. 10, 1984, S. Treaty Doc. No. 100–20 (1988), 1465 U.N.T.S. 85 (footnotes omitted).

The States Parties to this Convention,

. . . .

Having regard also to the Declaration ... adopted by the General Assembly on 9 December 1975,

Desiring to make more effective the struggle against torture and other cruel, inhuman or degrading treatment or punishment throughout the world,

Have agreed as follows:

. . . .

Article 1. 1. For the purposes of this Convention, the term "torture" means any act by which severe pain or suffering, whether physical or mental, is intentionally inflicted on a person for such purposes as obtaining from him or a third person information or a confession, punishing him for an act he or a third person has committed or is suspected of having committed, or intimidating or coercing him or a third person, or for any reason based on discrimination of any kind, when such pain or suffering is inflicted by or at the instigation of or with the consent or acquiescence of a public official or other person acting in an official capacity. It does not include pain or suffering arising only from, inherent in or incidental to lawful sanctions.

. . . .

Article 2. 1. Each State Party shall take effective legislative, administrative, judicial or other measures to prevent acts of torture in any territory under its jurisdiction.

2. No exceptional circumstances whatsoever, whether a state of war or a threat of war, internal political instability or any other public emergency, may be invoked as a justification of torture.

. . . .

Article 3. 1. No State Party shall expel, return (*refouler*) or extradite a person to another State where there are substantial grounds for believing that he would be in danger of being subjected to torture.

2. For the purpose of determining whether there are such grounds, the competent authorities shall take into account all relevant considerations including, where applicable, the existence in the State concerned of a consistent pattern of gross, flagrant or mass violations of human rights.

Article 4. 1. Each State Party shall ensure that all acts of torture are offences under its criminal law. The same shall apply to an attempt to commit torture and to an act by any person which constitutes complicity or participation in torture.

2. Each State Party shall make these offences punishable by appropriate penalties which take into account their grave nature.

Article 5. 1. Each State Party shall take such measures as may be necessary to establish its jurisdiction over the offences referred to in article 4 in the following cases:

(a) When the offences are committed in any territory under its jurisdiction or on board a ship or aircraft registered in that State;

(b) When the alleged offender is a national of that State;

(c) When the victim is a national of that State if that State considers it appropriate.

2. Each State Party shall likewise take such measures as may be necessary to establish its jurisdiction over such offences in cases where the alleged offender is present in any territory under its jurisdiction and it does not extradite him. . . . .

. . . .

Article 7. 1. The State Party in the territory under whose jurisdiction a person alleged to have committed any offence referred to in article 4 is found shall in the cases contemplated in article 5, if it does not extradite him, submit the case to its competent authorities for the purpose of prosecution.

. . . .

Article 14. 1. Each State Party shall ensure in its legal system that the victim of an act of torture obtains redress and has an enforceable right to fair and adequate compensation, including the means for as full rehabilitation as possible. . . .

. . . .

Article 16. 1. Each State Party shall undertake to prevent in any territory under its jurisdiction other acts of cruel, inhuman or degrading treatment or punishment which do not amount to torture as defined in article 1, when such acts are committed by or at the instigation of or with the consent or acquiescence of a public official or other person acting in an official capacity....

....

UNITED STATES SIGNS U.N. CONVENTION AGAINST TORTURE

Reuters News Service, Apr. 18, 1988.

UNITED NATIONS, April 18, Reuters—The United States on Monday signed the U.N. Convention against Torture, adopted by the General Assembly in 1984.

U.S. Deputy Secretary of State John Whitehead said at the signing ceremony: "Torture is one of the most serious human rights violations in the world today. Unfortunately, it is also one of the most prevalent."

He said the accord would shortly be sent to the U.S. Senate for ratification, together with some proposed declarations intended to resolve ambiguities in the Convention and safeguard U.S. law enforcement interests.

LETTER OF SUBMITTAL TO THE PRESIDENT FROM SECRETARY OF STATE GEORGE P. SHULTZ (MAY 10, 1988)

S. Treaty Doc. No. 100–20, at v–vi (1988).

DEPARTMENT OF STATE,
Washington, DC, May 10, 1988.

THE PRESIDENT,
The White House.

THE PRESIDENT: I have the honor to submit to you, with a view to its transmission to the Senate for advice and consent to ratification ... the Convention Against Torture.... The Convention was adopted by unanimous agreement of the United Nations General Assembly on December 10, 1984, and entered into force on June 26, 1987. The United States signed it on April 18, 1988.

....

... The attached memorandum contains a summary and discussion of the provisions of the Convention, and the reservations, declarations, and understandings recommended to the Senate by the Departments of State, Justice, and Defense.

....

Respectfully submitted,

GEORGE P. SHULTZ.

U.S. DEPARTMENT OF STATE SUMMARY AND ANALYSIS OF THE CONVENTION AGAINST TORTURE

S. Treaty Doc. No. 100–20, at 2–18 (1988).

Although the terms of the Convention, with the suggested reservations and understandings, are consonant with U.S. law, it is nevertheless preferable to leave any further implementation that may be desired to the domestic legislature and judicial process. The following declaration is therefore recommended, to clarify that the provisions of the Convention would not of themselves become effective as domestic law:

> "The United States declares that the provisions of Articles 1 through 16 are not self-executing."

. . . .

Given the decentralized distribution of police and other governmental authority at federal, state and local levels, it is desirable to make [t]he following federal-state reservation:

> "The United States shall implement the Convention to the extent that the Federal Government exercises legislative and judicial jurisdiction over the matters covered therein; to the extent that constituent units exercise jurisdiction over such matters, the Federal Government shall take appropriate measures to the end that the competent authorities of the constituent units of the United States of America may take appropriate measures for the fulfillment of the Convention."

. . . .

The requirement that torture be an extreme form of cruel and inhuman treatment is expressed in Article 16, which refers to "other acts of cruel, inhuman or degrading treatment or punishment *which do not amount to torture. . . .*" The negotiating history indicates that the underlined portion of this description was adopted in order to emphasize that torture is at the extreme end of cruel, inhuman and degrading treatment or punishment and that Article 1 should be construed with this in mind.

. . . .

The following understandings are recommended to reflect the United States understanding of Article 1 as explained above. These understandings are intended to guard against the improper application of the Convention to legitimate law enforcement actions and thereby would protect U.S. law enforcement interests.

> "The United States understands that, in order to constitute torture, an act must be a deliberate and calculated act of an extremely cruel and inhuman nature, specifically intended to inflict excruciating and agonizing physical or mental pain or suffering."

> "The United States understands that the definition of torture in Article 1 is intended to apply only to acts directed against persons in the offender's custody or physical control."

. . . .

Although no circumstances justify torture, legitimate acts of self-defense or defense of others do not constitute torture as defined by Article 1, since they are not performed with the specific intent to cause excruciating and agonizing pain or suffering. To clarify that Article 2 does not affect the availability of these common-law defenses, the following understanding is recommended:

> "The United States understands that paragraph 2 of Article 2 does not preclude the availability of relevant common law defenses, including but not limited to self-defense and defense of others."

. . . .

Under current U.S. law, an individual may not normally be expelled or returned where his "life or freedom would be threatened ... on account of race, religion, nationality, membership in a particular social group, or political opinion." 8 U.S.C. § 1253(h)(1). The U.S. Supreme Court has interpreted this provision to mean that a person entitled to its protections may not be deported to a country where it is more likely than not that he would be persecuted. *INS v. Stevic*, 467 U.S. 407 (1984). To clarify that Article 3 is not intended to alter this standard of proof, the following understanding is recommended:

> "The United States understands the phrase, 'where there are substantial grounds for believing that he would be in danger of being subjected to torture,' as used in Article 3 of the Convention, to mean 'if it is more likely than not that he would be tortured.' "

. . . .

Article 16 is arguably broader than existing U.S. law. The phrase "cruel, inhuman or degrading treatment or punishment" is a standard formula in international instruments and is found in the Universal Declaration of Human Rights, the International Covenant on Civil and Political Rights, and the European Convention on Human Rights. To the extent the phrase has been interpreted in the context of those agreements, "cruel" and "inhuman" treatment or punishment appears to be roughly equivalent to the treatment or punishment barred in the United States by the Fifth, Eighth and Fourteenth Amendments. "Degrading" treatment or punishment, however, has been interpreted as potentially including treatment that would probably not be prohibited by the U.S. Constitution. *See, e.g.*, European Commission of Human Rights, *Dec. on Adm.*, Dec. 15, 1977, *Case of X v. Federal Republic of Germany* (No. 6694/74), 11 Dec. & Rep. 16 (refusal of authorities to give formal recognition to an individual's change of sex might constitute "degrading" treatment). To make clear that the United States construes the phrase to be coextensive with its constitutional guarantees against cruel, unusual, and inhumane treatment, the following understanding is recommended:

> "The United States understands the term 'cruel, inhuman or degrading treatment or punishment,' as used in Article 16 of the Convention, to mean cruel, unusual, and inhumane treatment or punishment prohibited by the Fifth, Eighth and/or Fourteenth Amendments to the Constitution of the United States."

LETTER OF TRANSMITTAL TO THE SENATE FROM PRESIDENT RONALD REAGAN (MAY 20, 1988)

S. Treaty Doc. No. 100–20, at iii–iv (1988).

THE WHITE HOUSE, *May 20, 1988.*

To the Senate of the United States:

With a view to receiving the advice and consent of the Senate to ratification, subject to certain reservations, understandings, and declarations, I transmit herewith the Convention against Torture.... I also transmit, for the information of the Senate, the report of the Department of State on the Convention.

The United States participated actively and effectively in the negotiation of the Convention. It marks a significant step in the development during this century of international measures against torture and other inhuman treatment or punishment. Ratification of the Convention by the United States will clearly express United States opposition to torture, an abhorrent practice unfortunately still prevalent in the world today.

The core provisions of the Convention establish a regime for international cooperation in the criminal prosecution of torturers relying on so-called "universal jurisdiction." Each State Party is required either to prosecute torturers who are found in its territory or to extradite them to other countries for prosecution.

In view of the large number of States concerned, it was not possible to negotiate a treaty that was acceptable to the United States in all respects. Accordingly, certain reservations, understandings, and declarations have been drafted, which are discussed in the report of the Department of State. With the inclusion of these reservations, understandings, and declarations, I believe there are no constitutional or other legal obstacles to United States ratification. The recommended legislation necessary to implement the Convention will be submitted to the Congress separately.

....

By giving its advice and consent to ratification of this Convention, the Senate of the United States will demonstrate unequivocally our desire to bring an end to the abhorrent practice of torture.

RONALD REAGAN.

LETTER TO SENATOR PELL FROM DEPARTMENT OF STATE ASSISTANT SECRETARY OF LEGISLATIVE AFFAIRS JANET G. MULLINS (DEC. 10, 1989)

S. Exec. Rep. No. 101–30, at 35–36 (1990).

U.S. DEPARTMENT OF STATE
WASHINGTON, DC.,
December 10, 1989.

HON. CLAIBORNE PELL
Chairman, Committee on Foreign Relations
U.S. Senate, Washington, D.C.

DEAR MR. CHAIRMAN: In his message of May 23, 1988, President Reagan transmitted the Convention Against Torture ... to the Senate for its advice and consent to ratification.... Accompanying the transmittal of the Convention to the Senate was the report of the Secretary of State containing a number of proposed reservations, understandings, and declarations.

In your letter to the Secretary of State dated July 24, 1989, you expressed concern that the administration's proposed package faced substantial opposition from human rights groups and other interested parties. In particular, you were concerned with the overall length and breadth of the package, and the understandings concerning the definition of torture. According to critics of the proposed package, the understandings to the definition of torture could be construed to raise "the threshold of pain that an individual must suffer" and to permit "certain circumstances and justifications for torture."

....

... I am pleased to submit herewith the enclosed revised package of reservations, understandings, and declarations for consideration by the Senate. Reflecting our consultations with various interested groups in the private sector, the package now contains a revised understanding to the definition of torture, which would not raise the high threshold of pain already required under international law, clarifies the definition of mental pain and suffering, and maintains our position that specific intent is required for torture. The revised package also eliminates the understanding relating to "common law" defenses, makes it clear that the United States does not regard authorized sanctions that unquestionably violate international law as "lawful sanctions" exempt from the prohibition on torture....

....

JANET G. MULLINS
ASSISTANT SECRETARY, LEGISLATIVE AFFAIRS

CONVENTION AGAINST TORTURE: HEARING ON S. TREATY DOC. 100–20 BEFORE THE SENATE FOREIGN RELATIONS COMMITTEE

101st Cong. 9–18 (Jan. 30, 1990).

PREPARED STATEMENT OF ABRAHAM D. SOFAER, LEGAL ADVISER, U.S. STATE DEPARTMENT

. . . .

[An] important revision we propose concerns the definition of "torture" under Article I. The original package proposed an understanding to the effect that, in order to constitute "torture," an act must be a deliberate and calculated act of an extremely cruel and inhuman nature, specifically intended to inflict excruciating and agonizing physical or mental pain or suffering. This proposal was criticized by some as possibly setting a higher, more difficult evidentiary standard than the Convention required. Substantial concern was expressed that the effect of this understanding might be to undercut the central feature of the Convention, at least as codified in U.S. law, and to encourage other States also to adopt higher domestic standards, thereby limiting the effectiveness of the Convention.

Although no higher standard was intended, we recognized the concern raised by this criticism. At the same time, our colleagues at the Justice Department felt that, since the definition of "torture" will constitute the basis for a criminal punishment under U.S. law, some clarification of the Convention's definition was constitutionally required.

Accordingly, and on the basis of extensive discussions with concerned representatives in the human rights community, we prepared a codified proposal which does not raise the high threshold of pain already required under international law, but clarifies the definition of mental pain and suffering, and maintains the position that specific intent is required for torture.

. . . .

Mr. Chairman, I want to emphasize my firm and considered opinion that the death penalty does not violate international law, nor does international law require abolition of the death penalty. . . .

Moreover, international law could not develop a prohibition against capital punishment applicable to the United States, as long as the United States continues to impose the death penalty and to object to development of such a norm.

Nonetheless, some concerns have been expressed that the United States should take no risks in this regard. To allay these concerns, the administration has decided to propose an additional understanding, addressed explicitly to the death penalty issue. Since the death penalty is clearly not a violation of international law, this in no way derogates from the Convention. . . .

. . . .

The Convention deals primarily with "torture." In Article 16, however, the Parties also undertake to prohibit lesser forms of ill-treatment under the rubric of "cruel, inhuman or degrading treatment or punishment." The revised package retains a statement to the effect that the United States considers itself bound, under Article 16, to prevent "cruel, inhuman or degrading treatment or punishment" not amounting to torture only insofar as those words mean the cruel and unusual punishment prohibited by the Fifth, Eighth and/or Fourteenth Amendments to the Constitution. In fact, the revised package upgrades this point to a reservation from the status of an understanding.

The reason for this reservation is straightforward. The formulation used by Article 16 is ambiguous, particularly its reference to "degrading treatment." Of course, our own 8th Amendment to the Constitution protects against cruel and unusual punishment. Our courts have interpreted this prohibition to protect against a broad range of practices that involve the unnecessary and wanton infliction of pain. . . .

. . . .

. . . [I]t is prudent that the U.S. specify that, because the Constitution of the United States directly addresses this area of the law, and because of the ambiguity of the phrase "degrading," we would limit our obligations under this Convention to the proscriptions already covered in our Constitution.

PREPARED STATEMENT OF MARK RICHARD,
DEPUTY ASSISTANT ATTORNEY GENERAL,
CRIMINAL DIVISION, DEPARTMENT OF JUSTICE

At the outset, I note with some pride that torture, as understood by most persons, committed by public officials does not often occur within this country and when, if it does, the Department of Justice is committed to seeing that appropriate prosecutions are instituted. . . .

Having said such, one might wonder why we found it necessary to propose a number of reservations, understandings, or declarations in regard to a well intended convention against torture. The basic problem with the Torture Convention—one which permeates all our concerns—is its imprecise definition of torture, especially as that term is applied to actions which result solely in mental anguish. This definitional vagueness makes it very doubtful that the United States can, consistent with Constitutional due process constraints, fulfill its obligation under the Convention to adequately engraft the definition of torture into the domestic criminal law of the United States. Further, unless this definitional problem is addressed, the Torture Convention we fear will have the effect of fostering unwarranted litigation in numerous areas of law enforcement.

The potentially adverse impact of the definitional imprecision of the term torture is compounded when considered in the context of the international jurisdiction created by the Convention. The Convention places U.S. law enforcement officials, when traveling overseas, at risk of arrest and prosecution in foreign jurisdictions, or even extradition to a third country, for purported violations committed within the United States. . . .

. . . .

As applied to physical torture, there appears to be some degree of consensus that the concept involves conduct the mere mention of which sends chills down one's spine: the needle under the fingernail, the application of electrical shock to the genital area, the piercing of eyeballs, etc. Techniques which inflict such excruciating and agonizing physical pain are recognized as the essence of torture. Hence, the Convention chose the [word] "severe" to indicate the high level of the pain required to support a finding of torture. Moreover, to constitute torture the action must be done in a deliberate and calculated manner, or, to put it in customary United States legal terminology, it must be done with specific intent to inflict such a high level of pain. Therefore, insofar as physical pain is concerned, the boundaries of torture as defined by the Convention appear to have satisfactory clarity.

It is, however, in regard to the area of mental pain that the definition poses the greatest problem. Mental pain is by its nature subjective. Action that causes one person severe mental suffering may seem inconsequential to another person. Moreover, mental suffering is often transitory, causing no lasting harm.

. . . .

In an effort to overcome [the] unacceptable element of vagueness in Article 1 of the Convention, we have proposed an understanding which defines severe mental pain constituting torture with sufficient specificity to protect innocent persons and meet Constitutional due process requirements. In formulating this understanding, we have drawn on international case law and treaties as well as on international law scholars. Our proposed understanding encompasses conduct calculated to generate severe and prolonged mental suffering of the type which can properly be viewed as rising to the level of torture. As such, it properly condemns as torture intentional acts such as those designed to damage and destroy the human personality. In contrast, it does not encompass the normal legal compulsions which are properly a part of the criminal justice system interrogation, incarceration, prosecution, compelled testimony against a friend, etc.—notwithstanding the fact that they may have the incidental effect of producing a mental strain.

COMMENTS OF THE SENATE COMMITTEE ON FOREIGN RELATIONS

S. Exec. Rep. No. 101–30, at 3–4 (1990).

The committee regards the Convention Against Torture as a major step forward in the international community's efforts to eliminate torture and other cruel, inhuman or degrading treatment or punishment. The Convention codifies international law as it has evolved, particularly in the 1970's, on the subject of torture and takes a comprehensive approach to the problem of combating torture. The strength of the Convention lies in the obligation of States Parties to make torture a crime and to prosecute or extradite alleged torturers found in their territory.

Ratification of the Convention Against Torture will demonstrate clearly and unequivocally U.S. opposition to torture and U.S. determination to take steps to eradicate it. Ratification is a natural follow-on to the active role that the United States played in the negotiating process for the Convention and is consistent with longstanding U.S. efforts to promote and protect basic human rights and fundamental freedoms throughout the world. As a party to the Convention, the United States will be in a stronger position to prosecute alleged torturers and to bring to task those countries in the international arena that continue to engage in this heinous and inhumane practice.

The committee appreciates the efforts of the present administration to address the concerns raised by the human rights community and others, including members of this committee, about the reservations, understandings and declarations submitted by the Reagan administration. Those conditions, in number and substance, created the impression that the United States was not serious in its commitment to end torture worldwide. The conditions proposed by the present administration in large measure eliminate this problem.

SENATE FLOOR DEBATE ON CONVENTION AGAINST TORTURE

136 Cong. Rec. 36193–99 (1990).

Mr. PELL. Mr. President, this convention is the product of some 7 years of intense negotiation in which the United States played an active role. The convention was unanimously adopted by the U.N. General Assembly on December 10, 1984. . . . It has now been ratified by or acceded to by 51 States and signed by 21 others.

The Convention . . . represents a major step forward in the international community's campaign to combat torture because it makes torture a criminally punishable offense and obligates each State party to prosecute alleged torturers or extradite them for prosecution elsewhere.

The Reagan administration submitted the convention to the Senate in May 1988 with 19 proposed U.S. conditions, many of which were of concern to the human rights community, the American Bar Association, and others. After consulting with these groups, the Bush administration substantially reduced and revised the proposed list of conditions. I appreciate and applaud this effort.

The Foreign Relations Committee held a hearing on the treaty on January 30 of this year. On July 19, the committee voted 10 to 0 to report favorably the convention with a resolution of ratification containing the reservations, understandings and declarations proposed by the Bush administration.

In categorizing the treaties pending before the Senate, the administration listed the Convention Against Torture as one for which there is an urgent need for Senate action. At the appropriate time, I will be offering four amendments en bloc on behalf of myself and Senator HELMS. The first three amendments would make changes in the language of the resolution of ratification dealing with the issue of Federal–State relations as it impacts on our obligations under the treaty and the lawful sanctions issue in article 1. These have been worked out with the administration and the administration supports their adoption. The fourth amendment would add a new proviso to the resolution of ratification regarding deposition of the instrument of ratification by the President. This proviso will not be included in the instrument. The administration accepts this amendment. The administration strongly supports ratification of the convention with its proposed conditions, as modified by the committee amendments.

. . . .

Mr. HELMS. Mr. President, I commend the distinguished Senator from Rhode Island for his cooperation and courtesy in working out the problems in developing the proviso package to the convention. He has been unfailingly cooperative and understanding in coordinating the negotiations between our respective staffs and the Department of State. I commend him for his contribution to the negotiation process.

. . . .

THE PRESIDING OFFICER. The question is on agreeing to the amendments, en bloc.

Those in favor of the amendments will rise and stand until counted. (After a pause.) Those opposed will rise and stand until counted.

The amendments . . . were agreed to.

. . . .

THE PRESIDING OFFICER. A division is requested. Senators in favor of the resolution of ratification will rise and stand until counted. (After a pause.) Those opposed will rise and stand until counted.

On a division, two-thirds of the Senators present and voting have voted in the affirmative, the resolution of ratification is agreed to.

The resolution of ratification, as agreed to, is as follows:

Resolved (two-thirds of the Senators present concurring therein), That the Senate advise and consent to the ratification of the Convention Against Torture . . . : *Provided,* That:

I. The Senate's advice and consent is subject to the following reservations:

(1) That the United States considers itself bound by the obligation under Article 16 to prevent "cruel, inhuman or degrading treatment or punishment," only insofar as the term "cruel, inhuman or degrading treatment or punishment" means the cruel, unusual and inhumane treatment or punishment prohibited by the Fifth, Eighth, and/or Fourteenth Amendments to the Constitution of the United States.

. . . .

II. The Senate's advice and consent is subject to the following understandings, which shall apply to the obligations of the United States under this Convention:

(1) (a) That with reference to Article 1, the United States understands that, in order to constitute torture, an act must be specifically intended to inflict severe physical or mental pain or suffering and that mental pain or suffering refers to prolonged mental harm caused by or resulting from: (1) the intentional infliction or threatened infliction of severe physical pain or suffering; (2) the administration or application, or threatened administration or application, of mind altering substances or other procedures calculated to disrupt profoundly the senses or the personality; (3) the threat of imminent death; or (4) the threat that another person will imminently be subjected to death, severe physical pain or suffering, or the administration or application of mind altering substances or other procedures calculated to disrupt profoundly the senses or personality.

(b) That the United States understands that the definition of torture in Article 1 is intended to apply only to acts directed against persons in the offender's custody or physical control.

. . . .

(2) That the United States understands the phrase, "where there are substantial grounds for believing that he would be in danger of being subjected to torture," as used in Article 3 of the Convention, to mean "if it is more likely than not that he would be tortured."

(3) That it is the understanding of the United States that Article 14 requires a State Party to provide a private right of action for damages only for acts of torture committed in territory under the jurisdiction of that State Party.

(4) That the United States understands that international law does not prohibit the death penalty, and does not consider this Convention to restrict or prohibit the United States from applying the death penalty consistent with the Fifth, Eighth and/or Fourteenth Amendments to the

Constitution of the United States, including any constitutional period of confinement prior to the imposition of the death penalty.

(5) That the United States understands that this Convention shall be implemented by the United States Government to the extent that it exercises legislative and judicial jurisdiction over the matters covered by the Convention and otherwise by the state and local governments. Accordingly, in implementing Articles 10–14 and 16, the United States Government shall take measures appropriate to the Federal system to the end that the competent authorities of the constituent units of the United States of America may take appropriate measures for the fulfillment of the Convention.

III. The Senate's advice and consent is subject to the following declarations:

(1) That the United States declares that the provisions of Articles 1 through 16 of the Convention are not self-executing.

. . . .

IV. The Senate's advice and consent is subject to the following proviso, which shall not be included in the instrument of ratification to be deposited by the President:

> The President of the United States shall not deposit the instrument of ratification until such time as he has notified all present and prospective ratifying parties to this Convention that nothing in this Convention requires or authorizes legislation, or other action, by the United States of America prohibited by the Constitution of the United States as interpreted by the United States.

CONCLUDING NOTES ON THE SENATORIAL ADVICE AND CONSENT FUNCTION

1. *Entry Into Force.* On October 21, 1994, President Clinton deposited the U.S. instrument of ratification with the United Nations. The Convention entered into force for the United States one month later. *See* 18 U.N.T.S. 320.

2. *RUDs.* Why do you think the various U.S. conditions were classified as "reservation," "understanding," "declaration," or "proviso"? What was the significance of upgrading one of the conditions from "understanding" to "reservation"? Why include an understanding on a punishment (the death penalty) that the U.S. government regarded as outside the scope of the prohibitions in the Convention? When an originally proposed reservation or understanding that was thought to be important is later dropped (*e.g.*, on common- law defenses) or modified (*e.g.*, on the meaning of "torture"), does it call into question whether all or most of these RUDs are really needed? Is the Justice Department correct that filing a U.S. reservation regarding the meaning of "torture" will have an effect on potential criminal prosecutions of U.S. officials abroad?

The precise effect of RUDs upon U.S. domestic law is sometimes disputed. For example, former executive branch officials John Bolton and John Yoo asserted that any reservations and understandings included in the Senate's resolution approving the New START treaty would not be legally binding because they would not be part of the treaty itself; rather they would be "mere policy statements." *See* John R. Bolton & John Yoo, *Why Rush to Cut Nukes?*, N.Y. TIMES, Nov. 9, 2010, at A35. By contrast, former legal counsel to the Senate Foreign Relations Committee Michael Glennon responded:

> When the Senate approves a treaty, it can condition its consent (by reservation, understanding or whatever—the label doesn't matter) either by requiring the president to get the other party to agree to a change in the treaty's text, or simply by including its condition in the resolution of ratification.
>
> After the Senate acts, the president decides whether to bring the treaty into force. If he wishes to do so, he is constitutionally required to respect the Senate's conditions, regardless of which method the Senate has used. Each is equally binding in international law as well as law of the land, and each has been used on numerous occasions for over 200 years without raising any legal concern.

Michael Glennon, *What the New Arms Treaty Would Do*, N.Y. TIMES, Nov. 16, 2010, at A32.

3. *RUDs by Other States*. Other countries have also filed RUDs to the Convention against Torture (for a complete listing for this and other human rights conventions, see http://www.ohchr.org/english/countries/ratification/9.htm). Consider the following:

- "The Government of the Republic of Botswana considers itself bound by Article 1 of the Convention to the extent that 'torture' means the torture and inhuman or degrading punishment or other treatment prohibited by Section 7 of the Constitution of the Republic of Botswana."
- "Ecuador declares that, in accordance with the provisions of article 42 of its Political Constitution, it will not permit extradition of its nationals."
- Germany: Article 3 "prohibits the transfer of a person directly to a State where this person is exposed to a concrete danger of being subjected to torture. In the opinion of the Federal Republic of Germany, article 3 as well as the other provisions of the Convention exclusively establish State obligations that are met by the Federal Republic of Germany in conformity with the provisions of its domestic law which is in accordance with the Convention."
- "The Government of New Zealand reserves the right to award compensation to torture victims referred to in article 14 of the Convention Against Torture only at the discretion of the Attorney–General of New Zealand."
- Qatar reserves to "[a]ny interpretation of the provisions of the Convention that is incompatible with the precepts of Islamic law and the Islamic religion."

4. *Reaction to U.S. RUDs*. Other countries are also entitled to object to the United States' RUDs and, if they do, to indicate whether (1) the treaty

does not enter into force as between the two states; or (2) the treaty does enter into force, in which case the provision to which the reservation relates drops out of the treaty. Consider the following objection filed on February 26, 1996:

> The Government of the Netherlands considers the reservation made by the United States of America regarding the article 16 of [the Convention] to be incompatible with the object and purpose of the Convention, to which the obligation laid down in article 16 is essential. Moreover, it is not clear how the provisions of the Constitution of the United States of America relate to the obligations under the Convention. The Government of the Kingdom of the Netherlands therefore objects to the said reservation. This objection shall not preclude the entry into force of the Convention between the Kingdom of the Netherlands and the United States of America.
>
> The Government of the Kingdom of the Netherlands considers the following understandings to have no impact on the obligations of the United States of America under the Convention:
>
> II.1 (a) This understanding appears to restrict the scope of the definition of torture under article 1 of the Convention.
>
> . . . .
>
> The Government of the Kingdom of the Netherlands reserves its position with regard to the understandings II. 1b ... and 2 as the contents thereof are insufficiently clear.

1 *Multilateral Treaties Deposited with the Secretary–General* 300, U.N. Doc. ST/LEG/SER.E, 123 (Dec. 31, 2004).

5. *Incorporation of Senate Conditions by Reference.* Must the conditions adopted by the Senate appear in the text of the instrument of ratification, or may they simply be incorporated by reference? In 1976, President Ford submitted the Treaty of Friendship and Cooperation with Spain to the Senate for advice and consent. Treaty of Friendship and Cooperation, Jan. 24, 1976, U.S.-Spain, 27 U.S.T. 3005. The Senate Foreign Relations Committee, concerned about the slow pace of Spanish democratization, appended a five-part "declaration" to its resolution consenting to ratification. The declaration included a statement that the Senate "hopes and intends that this Treaty will serve to support and foster Spain's progress toward free institutions." S. Res. 401, 94th Cong., (1976). The declaration so displeased the Spanish Cortes (Parliament), according to the State Department, that it endangered Spanish ratification. To avoid Spain's rejection of the treaty, the State Department placed the declaration in an annex to the instrument of ratification, which was incorporated by reference in the instrument. According to the State Department, attaching the Senate's declaration to the instrument of ratification by means of an annex was the equivalent of placing the declaration in the instrument itself. Nevertheless, the Spanish government ignored the declaration in its instrument of ratification. *See* U.S. Department of State, *Digest of United States Practice in International Law 1976*, at 216 (E. McDowell ed., 1977); *see also* Michael J. Glennon, *The Senate Role in Treaty Ratification,* 77 AM. J. INT'L L. 257, 259 (1983) (arguing that failure to include the condition in

the instrument itself may evidence that the condition is not part of the treaty). Two years later, when the Senate considered the Panama Canal Treaties, it required that its conditions be included in the instrument of ratification to be exchanged with Panama, expressly to avoid a repetition of the Spanish precedent. *See* S. EXEC. REP. NO. 95–12, at 10–11 (1978) ("That such conditions must be so included is as much a part of customary constitutional law in this country as the right of the Senate to grant conditional consent.").

6. *Invalidity of Senate Condition.* If the Senate imposes a reservation that is essentially unrelated to the bilateral concerns addressed by a treaty, does the reservation become "supreme law of the land," or is it invalid? If invalid, does the failure of the reservation mean that the U.S. ratification is void?

In 1950, the Senate consented to a Treaty on Uses of Waters of Niagara River, Can.-U.S., 1 U.S.T. 694. The Senate conditioned its consent on the right to provide by subsequent law for the development of the U.S. share of the Niagara River waters. S. EXEC. REP. NO. 81–11, at 7 (1950). Thereafter, however, Congress did not adopt any new legislation allocating the U.S. share of the waters. When the New York Power Authority applied for a license to utilize the Niagara River waters, the Federal Power Commission rejected the application, stating that it had to give effect to the Senate's reservation. The New York Power Authority then sued, claiming that the reservation was invalid. The D.C. Circuit Court of Appeals agreed, finding that the reservation, to which the Canadian government had formally agreed, was a mere "expression of domestic policy." Power Auth. v. Federal Power Comm'n, 247 F.2d 538 (D.C. Cir. 1957).

> A true reservation which becomes a part of a treaty is one which alters " 'the effect of the treaty in so far as it may apply in the relations of (the) State with the other State or States which may be parties to the treaty.' " ... It creates " 'a different relationship between' " the parties and varies " 'the obligations of the party proposing it. ...' " ... The purported reservation to the 1950 treaty makes no change in the relationship between the United States and Canada under the treaty and has nothing at all to do with the rights or obligations of either party. To the extent here relevant, the treaty was wholly executed on its effective date. Each party became entitled to divert its half of the agreed quantum of water. Neither party had any interest in how the share of the other would be exploited, nor any obligation to the other as to how it would exploit its own share.

Id. at 541–42. The Supreme Court, however, vacated the D.C. Circuit's decision as moot after Congress adopted the legislation called for by the Senate. Am. Public Power Ass'n v. Power Auth., 355 U.S. 64, 78 S.Ct. 141, 2 L.Ed.2d 107 (1957).

If the D.C. Circuit was correct that the reservation was invalid, and yet Senate consent was conditioned on the reservation, can the treaty still be in force for the United States? In other words, is the reservation severable from the instrument of ratification even though the Senate's consent was predicated on the reservation? The dissenting judge in the D.C. Circuit decision notes that "[i]f it is beyond the power of the Senate, then not just the reservation falls, but the entire treaty. How can it be otherwise when the Senate has made it abundantly clear that without the reservation it would not have consented to the treaty?" 247 F.2d at 546 (Bastian, J., dissenting). *But see* New York Indians v. United States, 170 U.S. 1, 18 S.Ct. 531, 42 L.Ed. 927 (1898); Louis Henkin, *The Treaty Makers and the Law Makers: The Niagara Reservation*, 56 COLUM. L. REV. 1151 (1956).

7. *Prohibition of Reservations*. Some treaties prohibit reservations, such as the U.N. Convention on the Law of the Sea art. 309, Dec. 10, 1982, 1833 U.N.T.S. 3 ("No reservations or exceptions may be made to this Convention unless expressly permitted by other articles of this Convention."), or the Rome Statute for the International Criminal Court art. 120, July 17, 1998, 2187 U.N.T.S. 3 ("No reservations may be made to this Statute."). When this occurs, the Senate is presented with a "take it or leave it" situation; it can either consent to or reject the treaty, but it cannot seek to modify U.S. obligations thereunder. Since this deprives the Senate of an important opportunity in U.S. adherence to international agreements, the Senate Foreign Relations Committee has periodically expressed its view that "no-reservation clauses" are inconsistent with the Senate's "constitutional prerogatives" with respect to treaties. *See, e.g.*, U.S. Department of State, 1 *Digest of United States Practice in International Law, 1991–1999*, at 732 (2005).

8. *Consequences of an Invalid Reservation*. Suppose an international court or some other authoritative body determines that the United States has ratified a treaty, but in doing so included a reservation that was for some reason invalid (such as a reservation that defeats the object and purpose of the treaty). Does that mean that the United States is not a party to the treaty? That it is a party to the treaty, but without the benefit of the reservation? Does it matter what kind of treaty is at issue, such as whether it is an important treaty protective of human rights? Does it matter whether the United States indicated expressly or implicitly, when joining the treaty, what consequences would flow from an invalid reservation?

In 1994, the U.N. Human Rights Committee issued Comment No. 24 which stated, among other things, that a reserving State would remain a party to the International Covenant on Civil and Political Rights without the benefit of its invalid reservation. *See* Human Rights Committee, General Comment No. 24, Issues Relating to Reservations Made Upon Ratification or Accession to the Covenant or the Optional Protocols Thereto, or in Relation to Declarations under Article 41 of the Covenant, 52d Sess., U.N. Doc. CCPR/C/21/Rev.1/Add.6 (Apr. 10, 1994), *reprinted in* 34 I.L.M. 839 (1994). The United States reacted to Comment 24 by asserting that the Human Rights Committee was not empowered to make an authoritative statement on this issue and that, in any event, was wrong as to the consequences of an invalid reservation. *See* Observations by the United States of America on General Comment No. 24, U.N. Doc. A/50/40, annex VI, at 131–59 (1995).

For scholarly commentary, see Ryan Goodman, *Human Rights Treaties, Invalid Reservations, and State Consent*, 96 AM. J. INT'L L. 531 (2002); Jack L. Goldsmith & Eric A. Posner, *The Limits of International Law* 96 (2005); Roberto Baratta, *Should Invalid Reservations to Human Rights Treaties Be*

Disregarded?, *11 EUR. J. INT'L L. 413 (2000); Curtis A. Bradley & Jack L. Goldsmith,* Treaties, Human Rights, and Conditional Consent, *149 U. PA. L. REV. 399 (2000); Catherine Redgwell,* Reservations to Treaties and Human Rights Committee General Comment No. 24, *46 INT'L & COMP. L.Q. 390 (1997).*

SECTION 3. NATIONAL IMPLEMENTATION OF TREATIES BY STATUTES/REGULATIONS

INTRODUCTORY NOTE

When a country ratifies or accedes to a treaty, it may find that the obligations undertaken require no further implementation under national law. Thus, a treaty obliging a country to make periodic reports to an international organization usually may be fulfilled by the country's government without any further enactment under national law.

Many treaties, however, require the states parties to ensure that certain measures are taken under their national legal systems, such as criminalizing or regulating the conduct of persons. When a treaty requires such measures, a country may determine that its existing national law is sufficient to ensure compliance, in which case no further steps are needed. If existing national law is insufficient, there are then two possibilities. First, the country might enact new laws or regulations that allow for compliance with the treaty. Second, the country might regard the new treaty itself as having the force of law within its national legal system (*i.e.*, regard the treaty as "self-executing"). This section considers the first possibility, while Section 4 considers the second.

The following materials illustrate how the United States implemented the Convention Against Torture through existing U.S. laws, new statutes and regulations, interpretations and reinterpretations of the Executive Branch, interpretations by U.S. courts, and, in one instance, a legislative fix to an Executive Branch interpretation. Materials dated after September 2001 should be considered in the context of the United States' detention and interrogation of suspected terrorists, and the tension between the requirements of the Convention and the desire for obtaining information on terrorist networks. As you review these materials, you may wish to revisit some of the materials excerpted in Section 2 relating to the Convention's ratification process.

U.S. DEPARTMENT OF STATE SUMMARY AND ANALYSIS OF THE CONVENTION AGAINST TORTURE (MAY 10, 1988)

S. Treaty Doc. No. 100–20, at 8–10 (1988).

Acts of torture committed in the United States, . . . as well as acts in the United States constituting an attempt or conspiracy to torture, would appear to violate criminal statutes under existing state or federal law. When such acts are subject to state jurisdiction, the offense would presumably be a common crime such as assault or murder. In particular cases, the nature of the activity or persons involved could give rise to a federal offense as well, such as interstate kidnapping or hostage-taking. *See, e.g.*, 18 U.S.C. § 112, § 114, § 115, § 878, § 1201 and § 1203.

Where the acts are subject to federal jurisdiction, similar common crimes are defined under federal criminal law, for example, assault, maiming, murder, manslaughter, attempt to commit murder or manslaughter, and rape. 18 U.S.C. § 113, § 114, § 1111, § 1112, § 1113, and § 2031. Conspiracy to commit the above crimes and being an accessory after the fact are also offenses. 18 U.S.C. § 3, § 371 and § 1117. Moreover, where acts are committed within the special maritime and territorial jurisdiction located within a state, federal law incorporates criminal offenses as defined by state law. 18 U.S.C. § 13.

. . . .

In general, protection against torture is afforded by the Eighth, Fifth and Fourteenth Amendments to the U.S. Constitution. The Eighth Amendment prohibition of cruel and unusual punishment is, of the three, the most limited in scope, as this amendment has consistently been interpreted as protecting only "those convicted of crimes." *Ingraham v. Wright*, 430 U.S. 651, 664 (1977). The Eighth Amendment does, however, afford protection against torture and ill-treatment of persons in prison and similar situations of criminal punishment.

In other situations, the Fifth and Fourteenth Amendments provide protection against torture. Such protection is afforded most generally by substantive due process protection of the right to personal security.... The prohibition against self-incrimination also provides more specific protection against torture being used to coerce a confession. ...

. . . .

... [E]xisting federal and state law appears sufficient to establish jurisdiction when the offense has allegedly been committed in any territory under U.S. jurisdiction or on board a ship or aircraft registered in the United States. *See* 18 U.S.C. § 7; 49 U.S.C. App. §§ 1301(38), 1472. Implementing legislation is therefore needed only to establish Article 5(1)(b) jurisdiction over offenses committed by U.S. nationals outside the United States, and to establish Article 5(2) jurisdiction over foreign offenders committing torture abroad who are later found in territory under U.S. jurisdiction. Recommended legislation will be transmitted to Congress by the Department of Justice. ...

STATUTE CRIMINALIZING TORTURE OUTSIDE THE UNITED STATES

18 U.S.C. §§ 2340, 2340A, & 2340B (2006).

§ 2340. Definitions

As used in this chapter—

(1) "torture" means an act committed by a person acting under the color of law specifically intended to inflict severe physical or mental pain

or suffering (other than pain or suffering incidental to lawful sanctions) upon another person within his custody or physical control;

(2) "severe mental pain or suffering" means the prolonged mental harm caused by or resulting from—

(A) the intentional infliction or threatened infliction of severe physical pain or suffering;

(B) the administration or application, or threatened administration or application, of mind-altering substances or other procedures calculated to disrupt profoundly the senses or the personality;

(C) the threat of imminent death; or

(D) the threat that another person will imminently be subjected to death, severe physical pain or suffering, or the administration or application of mind-altering substances or other procedures calculated to disrupt profoundly the senses or personality; and

(3) "United States" means the several States of the United States, the District of Columbia, and the commonwealths, territories, and possessions of the United States.[1]

§ 2340A. Torture

(a) OFFENSE.—Whoever outside the United States commits or attempts to commit torture shall be fined under this title or imprisoned not more than 20 years, or both, and if death results to any person from conduct prohibited by this subsection, shall be punished by death or imprisoned for any term of years or for life.

(b) JURISDICTION.—There is jurisdiction over the activity prohibited in subsection (a) if—

(1) the alleged offender is a national of the United States; or

(2) the alleged offender is present in the United States, irrespective of the nationality of the victim or alleged offender.

(c) CONSPIRACY.—A person who conspires to commit an offense under this section shall be subject to the same penalties (other than the penalty of death) as the penalties prescribed for the offense, the commission of which was the object of the conspiracy.[2]

§ 2340B. Exclusive remedies

Nothing in this chapter shall be construed as precluding the application of State or local laws on the same subject, nor shall anything in this

---

1. [Authors' Note: Originally, this definition embraced all areas within the U.S. "special maritime and territorial jurisdiction," which includes military bases and buildings abroad. As such, the original statute did not cover torture committed at those facilities since they were not "outside the United States." The definition was changed to the provision shown above by Pub. L. No. 108–375, § 1089, 118 Stat. 1811, 2067 (2004), such that those facilities are now covered by this statute.]

2. [Authors' Note: Subsection (c) was added by the USA Patriot Act, Pub. L. No. 107–56, § 811(g) (2001).]

chapter be construed as creating any substantive or procedural right enforceable by law by any party in any civil proceeding.

TORTURE VICTIM PROTECTION ACT

28 U.S.C. § 1350 note (2006).

[The United States filed an understanding to the Convention Against Torture stating that Article 14 did not require the United States to create a private right of action in U.S. courts for torture occurring outside the United States. Nevertheless, in 1991, Congress enacted the Torture Victim Protection Act (TVPA), which provides for such a right of action, with "torture" defined in a manner similar to that in Article 1 of the Convention Against Torture.]

Section 1. Short Title

This Act may be cited as the "Torture Victim Protection Act of 1991".

Section 2. Establishment of Civil Action

(a) LIABILITY.—An individual who, under actual or apparent authority, or color of law, of any foreign nation—

(1) subjects an individual to torture shall, in a civil action, be liable for damages to that individual; or

(2) subjects an individual to extrajudicial killing shall, in a civil action, be liable for damages to the individual's legal representative, or to any person who may be a claimant in an action for wrongful death.

(b) EXHAUSTION OF REMEDIES.—A court shall decline to hear a claim under this section if the claimant has not exhausted adequate and available remedies in the place in which the conduct giving rise to the claim occurred.

(c) STATUTE OF LIMITATIONS.—No action shall be maintained under this section unless it is commenced within 10 years after the cause of action arose.

Section 3. Definitions

(a) EXTRAJUDICIAL KILLING.—For the purposes of this Act, the term "extrajudicial killing" means a deliberated killing not authorized by a previous judgment pronounced by a regularly constituted court affording all the judicial guarantees which are recognized as indispensable by civilized peoples. Such term, however, does not include any such killing that, under international law, is lawfully carried out under the authority of a foreign nation.

(b) TORTURE.—For the purposes of this Act—

(1) the term "torture" means any act, directed against an individual in the offender's custody or physical control, by which severe

pain or suffering (other than pain or suffering arising only from or inherent in, or incidental to, lawful sanctions), whether physical or mental, is intentionally inflicted on that individual for such purposes as obtaining from that individual or a third person information or a confession, punishing that individual for an act that individual or a third person has committed or is suspected of having committed, intimidating or coercing that individual or a third person, or for any reason based on discrimination of any kind; and

(2) mental pain or suffering refers to prolonged mental harm caused by or resulting from—

(A) the intentional infliction or threatened infliction of severe physical pain or suffering;

(B) the administration or application, or threatened administration or application, of mind altering substances or other procedures calculated to disrupt profoundly the senses or the personality;

(C) the threat of imminent death; or

(D) the threat that another individual will imminently be subjected to death, severe physical pain or suffering, or the administration or application of mind altering substances or other procedures calculated to disrupt profoundly the senses or personality.

NOTE ON INTERROGATION OF GUANTÁNAMO DETAINEES

In late 2001 to 2002, hundreds of suspected Al Qaeda and Taliban operatives were captured by the United States in Afghanistan and elsewhere, and transported to the U.S. Naval Base at Guantánamo in Cuba. The Bush Administration engaged in "enhanced" interrogation techniques in an effort to uncover information about Al Qaeda and its plans for terrorist attacks. Military and intelligence interrogators wished to know what kinds of techniques, if any, were criminalized by 18 U.S.C. §§ 2340–2340A (2006). Consequently, advice was sought from the U.S. Department of Justice Office of the Legal Counsel (OLC). An initial memorandum was issued by OLC in August 2002 advancing a permissive interpretation, which was then walked back in December 2004 and January 2009. Separately, questions were also raised as to whether such techniques ran afoul of the U.S. obligation under Article 16 of the Convention Against Torture to prevent "in any territory under its jurisdiction" conduct not constituting torture, but that is still cruel, inhuman or degrading treatment. If you were asked to "draw the line" for a U.S. interrogator as to what acts were impermissible torture or inhuman treatment, and what acts were not, what advice would you give?

U.S. DEPARTMENT OF JUSTICE OFFICE OF LEGAL COUNSEL 2002 MEMORANDUM ON INTERROGATION

Page 1, 13, 31 (footnotes omitted).

August 1, 2002

Memorandum for Alberto R. Gonzales
Counsel to the President

Re: Standards of Conduct for Interrogation under 18 U.S.C. §§ 2340–2340A

You have asked for our Office's views regarding the standards of conduct under the Convention Against Torture ... as implemented by Sections 2340–2340A of title 18 of the United States Code. As we understand it, this question has arisen in the context of the conduct of interrogations outside of the United States. ...

....

... Each component of the definition [of torture in Section 2340] emphasizes that torture is not the mere infliction of pain or suffering on another, but is instead a step well removed. The victim must experience intense pain or suffering of the kind that is equivalent to the pain that would be associated with serious physical injury so severe that death, organ failure, or permanent damage resulting in a loss of significant body function will likely result. If that pain or suffering is psychological, that suffering must result from one of the acts set forth in the statute. In addition, these acts must cause long-term mental harm. ... In short, reading the definition of torture as a whole, it is plain that the term encompasses only extreme acts.

....

Even if an interrogation method arguably were to violate Section 2340A, the statute would be unconstitutional if it impermissibly encroached on the President's constitutional power to conduct a military campaign. As Commander-in-Chief, the President has the constitutional authority to order interrogations of enemy combatants to gain intelligence information concerning the military plans of the enemy. The demands of the Commander-in-Chief power are especially pronounced in the middle of a war in which the nation has already suffered a direct attack. In such a case, the information gained from interrogations may prevent future attacks by foreign enemies. Any effort to apply Section 2340A in a manner that interferes with the President's direction of such core war matters as the detention and interrogation of enemy combatants thus would be unconstitutional.

....

JAY S. BYBEE
Assistant Attorney General

U.S. DEPARTMENT OF JUSTICE OFFICE OF LEGAL COUNSEL 2004 MEMORANDUM ON INTERROGATION

Page 1–2, 8–10, 17 (footnotes omitted).

December 30, 2004

Memorandum for James B. Comey
Deputy Attorney General

Re: Legal Standards Applicable Under 18 U.S.C. §§ 2340–2340A

Torture is abhorrent both to American law and values and to international norms. This universal repudiation of torture is reflected in our criminal law, for example, 18 U.S.C. §§ 2340–2340A; international agreements, exemplified by the United Nations Convention Against Torture (the "CAT"); customary international law; centuries of Anglo–American law; and the longstanding policy of the United States, repeatedly and recently reaffirmed by the President.

This Office interpreted the federal criminal prohibition against torture—codified at 18 U.S.C. §§ 2340–2340A—in *Standards of Conduct for Interrogation under 18 U.S.C. §§ 2340–2340A* (Aug. 1, 2002) ("August 2002 Memorandum"). The August 2002 Memorandum also addressed a number of issues beyond interpretation of those statutory provisions. . . .

Questions have since been raised, both by this Office and by others, about the appropriateness and relevance of the non-statutory discussion in the August 2002 Memorandum, and also about various aspects of the statutory analysis, in particular the statement that "severe" pain under the statute was limited to pain "equivalent in intensity to the pain accompanying serious physical injury, such as organ failure, impairment of bodily function, or even death." . . . We decided to withdraw the August 2002 Memorandum, a decision you announced in June 2004. . . .

This memorandum supersedes the August 2002 Memorandum in its entirety. . . .

. . . .

Although Congress defined "torture" under sections 2340–2340A to require conduct specifically intended to cause "severe" pain or suffering, we do not believe Congress intended to reach only conduct involving "excruciating and agonizing" pain or suffering. Although there is some support for this formulation in the ratification history of the CAT, a proposed express understanding to that effect was "criticized for setting too high a threshold of pain," S. Exec. Rep. No. 101–30 at 9, and was not adopted. We are not aware of any evidence suggesting that the standard was raised in the statute and we do not believe that it was.

Drawing distinctions among gradations of pain (for example, severe, mild, moderate, substantial, extreme, intense, excruciating, or agonizing) is obviously not an easy task, especially given the lack of any precise, objective scientific criteria for measuring pain. We are, however, aided in this task by judicial interpretations of the Torture Victims Protection Act ("TVPA"), 28 U.S.C. § 1350 note (2000). The TVPA, also enacted to implement the CAT, provides a civil remedy to victims of torture. The TVPA defines "torture" to include:

> any act, directed against an individual in the offender's custody or physical control, by which *severe pain or suffering* ... *whether physical or mental*, is intentionally inflicted. ...

... The emphasized language is similar to section 2340's "severe physical or mental pain or suffering." As the Court of Appeals for the District of Columbia Circuit has explained:

> The severity requirement is crucial to ensuring that the conduct proscribed by the [CAT] and the TVPA is sufficiently extreme and outrageous to warrant the universal condemnation that the term "torture" both connotes and invokes. The drafters of the [CAT], as well as the Reagan Administration that signed it, the Bush Administration that submitted it to Congress, and the Senate that ultimately ratified it, therefore all sought to ensure that "only acts of a certain gravity shall be considered to constitute torture."
>
> The critical issue is the degree of pain and suffering that the alleged torturer intended to, and actually did, inflict upon the victim. The more intense, lasting, or heinous the agony, the more likely it is to be torture.

Price v. Socialist People's Libyan Arab Jamahiriya, 294 F.3d 82, 92–93 (D.C. Cir. 2002) (citations omitted). That court concluded that a complaint that alleged beatings at the hands of police but that did not provide details concerning "the severity of plaintiffs' alleged beatings, including their frequency, duration, the parts of the body at which they were aimed, and the weapons used to carry them out," did not suffice "to ensure that [it] satisf[ied] the TVPA's rigorous definition of torture." *Id.* at 93.

In *Simpson v. Socialist People's Libyan Arab Jamahiriya*, 326 F.3d 230 (D.C. Cir. 2003), the D.C. Circuit again considered the types of acts that constitute torture under the TVPA definition. The plaintiff alleged, among other things, that Libyan authorities had held her incommunicado and threatened to kill her if she tried to leave. *See id.* at 232, 234. The court acknowledged that "these alleged acts certainly reflect a bent toward cruelty on the part of their perpetrators," but, reversing the district court, went on to hold that "they are not in themselves so unusually cruel or sufficiently extreme and outrageous as to constitute torture within the meaning of the [TVPA]." *Id.* at 234. Cases in which courts have found torture suggest the nature of the extreme conduct that falls within the statutory definition. *See, e.g., Hilao v. Estate of Marcos*, 103 F.3d 789, 790–91, 795 (9th Cir. 1996) (concluding that a course of conduct that included, among other things, severe beatings of plaintiff, repeated threats of death and electric shock, sleep deprivation, extended shackling to a cot (at times with a towel over his nose and mouth and water poured down his nostrils), seven months of confinement in a "suffocatingly hot" and cramped cell, and eight years of solitary or near-solitary confinement, constituted torture); *Mehinovic v. Vuckovic*, 198 F.Supp.2d 1332–40, 1345–46 (N.D.Ga.2002) (concluding that a course of conduct that included, among other things, severe beatings to the genitals, head, and other parts of the body with metal pipes, brass knuckles, batons, a baseball bat, and various other items; removal of teeth with pliers; kicking in the face and ribs; breaking of bones and ribs and dislocation of fingers; cutting a figure into the victim's forehead; hanging the victim and beating him; extreme limitations of food and water; and subjection to games of "Russian roulette," constituted torture); *Daliberti v. Republic of Iraq*, 146 F. Supp. 2d 19, 22–23 (D.D.C. 2001) (entering default judgment against Iraq where plaintiffs alleged, among other things, threats of "physical torture, such as cutting off . . . fingers, pulling out . . . fingernails," and electric shocks to the testicles); *Cicippio v. Islamic Republic of Iran*, 18 F. Supp. 2d 62, 64–66 (D.D.C. 1998) (concluding that a course of conduct that included frequent beatings, pistol whipping, threats of imminent death, electric shocks, and attempts to force confessions by playing Russian roulette and pulling the trigger at each denial, constituted torture).

. . . .

DANIEL LEVIN
Acting Assistant Attorney General

U.S. DEPARTMENT OF JUSTICE OFFICE OF LEGAL COUNSEL 2009 MEMORANDUM ON INTERROGATION

Pages 4, 11.

January 15, 2009

Memorandum for the Files

Re: Status of Certain OLC Opinions Issued in the Aftermath of the Terrorist Attacks of September 11, 2001

It is well established that the President has broad authority as Commander in Chief to take military actions in defense of the country. . . .

At the same time, Article I, Section 8 of the Constitution also grants significant war powers to Congress. We recognize that a law that is constitutional in general may still raise serious constitutional issues if applied in particular circumstances to frustrate the President's ability to fulfill his essential responsibilities under Article II. Nevertheless, the sweeping assertions in the [August 1, 2002, as well as other] opinions . . . that the President's Commander in Chief authority categorically precludes Congress from enacting any legislation concerning the detention, interrogation, prosecution, and transfer of enemy combatants are not sustainable.

Congress's power to "define and punish ... Offences against the Law of Nations," U.S. Const., art. I, § 8, cl. 10, provides a basis for Congress to establish the federal crime of torture, in accordance with U.S. treaty obligations under the Convention Against Torture, and the War Crimes Act offenses, in accordance, for example, with the "grave breach" provisions of the Geneva Conventions. This grant of authority also provides a basis for Congress to establish a statutory framework, such as that set forth in the Military Commissions Act of 2006 ("MCA"), for trying and punishing unlawful enemy combatants for violations of the law of war and other hostile acts in support of terrorism....

....

We have advised the Attorney General, the Counsel to the President, the Legal Adviser to the National Security Council, the Principal Deputy General Counsel of the Department of Defense, and appropriate offices within the Department of Justice of these conclusions.

STEVEN G. BRADBURY
Principal Deputy Assistant Attorney General

RESPONSE OF ALBERTO R. GONZALES, U.S. ATTORNEY GENERAL–DESIGNATE, TO A WRITTEN QUESTION OF SENATOR RICHARD J. DURBIN ON THE GEOGRAPHICAL LIMITATION OF TORTURE CONVENTION ARTICLE 16

(January 2005).

[B]ecause of the Senate's reservation to Article 16 of the Convention Against Torture and the jurisdictional and other limitations of Article 16 and of the Fifth, Eighth and Fourteenth Amendments, which have been held not to apply to aliens overseas who are not being punished within the meaning of the Eighth Amendment, Article 16 has a limited reach. However, we also want to be in compliance with the relevant substantive constitutional standard incorporated into Article 16 by virtue of the Senate's reservation, even where it may not be legally required. I have been advised that approved interrogation techniques were analyzed under that standard and satisfied it.

LETTER FROM ABRAHAM D. SOFAER, FORMER STATE DEPARTMENT LEGAL ADVISER, TO SENATOR PATRICK J. LEAHY

(January 21, 2005).

Dear Senator Leahy:

....

... I do not hesitate to say that I disagree with the merits and wisdom of the conclusion reached by the Department of Justice and cited in the response of Judge Gonzales concerning the geographical reach of Article 16 of the Convention Against Torture. ... Article 16 on its face limits the obligation of the United States to undertake to prevent cruel, inhuman, or degrading acts not amounting to torture to "territory under its jurisdiction." Within such territory, the US is obliged to undertake to prevent such "other" acts, even if they do not amount to torture.

... [T]he Senate agreed to ratify the Torture Convention at the urging of the Reagan and Bush Administrations, and one of its reservations was that in applying Article 16 the US government would not be obliged to undertake to enforce its provisions, anywhere, in a manner inconsistent with the US interpretation of its almost identically worded Eighth Amendment prohibiting cruel and unusual punishment. As I testified at the time, in writing and orally, the purpose of this reservation was to prevent any tribunal or state from claiming that the US would have to follow a different and broader meaning of the language of Article 16 than the meaning of those same words in the Eighth Amendment. The words of the reservation support this understanding, in that they relate to the meaning of the terms involved, not their geographic application. ... The Department of Justice at the time characterized this reservation as "modest," and explained its purpose as being to use established meanings under the Eighth Amendment instead of the Treaty's vague terms that had not yet evolved under international law. No evidence of which I am aware indicates that the reservation was intended to enable the US to refuse to enforce Article 16 in any territory "under its jurisdiction."

The Department of Justice contends, as I understand it, that Article 16 has no application outside the territory of the US, because the Supreme Court has interpreted the Eighth Amendment to be inapplicable beyond our territorial limits. The Department reasons that, since the Senate reservation limited enforcement of Article 16 to the US understanding of the Eighth Amendment's language, and since the Supreme Court has concluded that the Eighth Amendment is inapplicable beyond US territory, Article 16 itself is inapplicable beyond US territory. On the basis of my understanding of the purposes of the Convention, and of the purpose of the reservation related to Article 16 and the Eighth Amendment, I disagree with the Department's view and would urge the Attorney General Designate to accept a different view.

....

Sincerely,

ABE SOFAER

SENATOR McCAIN AMENDMENT BARRING CRUEL AND INHUMAN TREATMENT ABROAD

42 U.S.C. 2000dd note (2006).

PROHIBITION ON CRUEL, INHUMAN, OR DEGRADING TREATMENT OR PUNISHMENT OF PERSONS UNDER CUSTODY OR CONTROL OF THE UNITED STATES GOVERNMENT.

(a) IN GENERAL.—No individual in the custody or under the physical control of the United States Government, regardless of nationality or physical location, shall be subject to cruel, inhuman, or degrading treatment or punishment.

(b) CONSTRUCTION.—Nothing in this section shall be construed to impose any geographical limitation on the applicability of the prohibition against cruel, inhuman, or degrading treatment or punishment under this section.

(c) LIMITATION ON SUPERSEDURE.—The provisions of this section shall not be superseded, except by a provision of law enacted after the date of the enactment of this Act which specifically repeals, modifies, or supersedes the provisions of this section.

(d) CRUEL, INHUMAN, OR DEGRADING TREATMENT OR PUNISHMENT DEFINED.—In this section, the term "cruel, inhuman, or degrading treatment or punishment" means the cruel, unusual, and inhumane treatment or punishment prohibited by the Fifth, Eighth, and Fourteenth Amendments to the Constitution of the United States, as defined in the United States Reservations, Declarations and Understandings to the United Nations Convention Against Torture. . . .

NOTE ON DEPORTATION OF ALIENS

Article 3 of the Convention Against Torture requires the United States not to "expel, return (*refouler*) or extradite a person to another State where there are substantial grounds for believing that he would be in danger of being subjected to torture." Recall that in the course of ratifying the Convention, the United States issued an "understanding" regarding the meaning of the phrase "substantial grounds for believing." To implement its obligation, Congress adopted a statute, the Foreign Affairs Reform and Restructuring (FARR) Act, 8 U.S.C. § 1231 note (2006), which addressed both the issue of deportation of aliens and extradition of persons. With respect to deportation of aliens, the FARR Act required the executive branch to adopt implementing regulations, which appear below. In what way do the regulations incorporate the Convention into U.S. law? In what way do they alter the Convention obligation based on the RUDs asserted by the United States? In what way do they help clarify the obligation, providing more detailed guidance to executive and judicial branch officials?

U.S. IMMIGRATION AND NATURALIZATION SERVICE (INS) 1999 REGULATIONS IMPLEMENTING THE FARR ACT

8 C.F.R. §§ 208.16(c) & 208.18 (2010).

§ 208.16 Withholding of removal under section 241(b)(3)(B) of the Act and withholding of removal under the Convention Against Torture

. . . .

(c) *Eligibility for withholding of removal under the Convention Against Torture.* (1) For purposes of regulations under Title II of the [Immigration and Naturalization] Act, "Convention Against Torture" shall refer to the United Nations Convention Against Torture . . . , subject to any reservations, understandings, declarations, and provisos contained in the United States Senate resolution of ratification of the Convention, as implemented by section 2242 of the Foreign Affairs Reform and Restructuring Act of 1998 (Pub. L. 105–277, 112 Stat. 2681, 2681–821). The definition of torture contained in Sec. 208.18(a) of this part shall govern all decisions made under regulations under Title II of the Act about the applicability of Article 3 of the Convention Against Torture.

(2) The burden of proof is on the applicant for withholding of removal under this paragraph to establish that it is more likely than not that he or she would be tortured if removed to the proposed country of removal. The testimony of the applicant, if credible, may be sufficient to sustain the burden of proof without corroboration.

(3) In assessing whether it is more likely than not that an applicant would be tortured in the proposed country of removal, all evidence relevant to the possibility of future torture shall be considered, including, but not limited to:

(i) Evidence of past torture inflicted upon the applicant;

(ii) Evidence that the applicant could relocate to a part of the country of removal where he or she is not likely to be tortured;

(iii) Evidence of gross, flagrant or mass violations of human rights within the country of removal, where applicable; and

(iv) Other relevant information regarding conditions in the country of removal.

(4) In considering an application for withholding of removal under the Convention Against Torture, the immigration judge shall first determine whether the alien is more likely than not to be tortured in the country of removal. If the immigration judge determines that the alien is more likely than not to be tortured in the country of removal, the alien is entitled to protection under the Convention Against Torture. Protection under the Convention Against Torture will be granted either in the form of withholding of removal or in the form of deferral of removal. An alien entitled to such protection shall be granted withholding of removal unless the alien is subject to mandatory denial of withholding of removal. . . .[1]

1. [Authors' Note: If the alien's removal is deferred, various outcomes are possible. The alien may remain in detention in the United States for periods prescribed by regulation (8 C.F.R. § 241.13–14), or he may be removed to a different country where he will not be tortured (8 C.F.R. § 208.17(b)(2)). In addition, the alien may request that the deferral be terminated, or an immigration judge may determine that the alien would no longer likely be tortured if removed, in which case the removal could go forward (8 C.F.R. § 208.17(d)–(e)).]

§ 208.18 Implementation of the Convention Against Torture

(a) *Definitions.* The definitions in this subsection incorporate the definition of torture contained in Article 1 of the Convention Against Torture, subject to the reservations, understandings, declarations, and provisos contained in the United States Senate resolution of ratification of the Convention.

(1) Torture is defined as any act by which severe pain or suffering, whether physical or mental, is intentionally inflicted on a person for such purposes as obtaining from him or her or a third person information or a confession, punishing him or her for an act he or she or a third person has committed or is suspected of having committed, or intimidating or coercing him or her or a third person, or for any reason based on discrimination of any kind, when such pain or suffering is inflicted by or at the instigation of or with the consent or acquiescence of a public official or other person acting in an official capacity.

(2) Torture is an extreme form of cruel and inhuman treatment and does not include lesser forms of cruel, inhuman or degrading treatment or punishment that do not amount to torture.

(3) Torture does not include pain or suffering arising only from, inherent in or incidental to lawful sanctions. Lawful sanctions include judicially imposed sanctions and other enforcement actions authorized by law, including the death penalty, but do not include sanctions that defeat the object and purpose of the Convention Against Torture to prohibit torture.

(4) In order to constitute torture, mental pain or suffering must be prolonged mental harm caused by or resulting from:

(i) The intentional infliction or threatened infliction of severe physical pain or suffering;

(ii) The administration or application, or threatened administration or application, of mind altering substances or other procedures calculated to disrupt profoundly the senses or the personality;

(iii) The threat of imminent death; or

(iv) The threat that another person will imminently be subjected to death, severe physical pain or suffering, or the administration or application of mind altering substances or other procedures calculated to disrupt profoundly the sense or personality.

(5) In order to constitute torture, an act must be specifically intended to inflict severe physical or mental pain or suffering. An act that results in unanticipated or unintended severity of pain and suffering is not torture.

(6) In order to constitute torture an act must be directed against a person in the offender's custody or physical control.

(7) Acquiescence of a public official requires that the public official, prior to the activity constituting torture, have awareness of such activity and thereafter breach his or her legal responsibility to intervene to prevent such activity.

(8) Noncompliance with applicable legal procedural standards does not *per se* constitute torture.

. . . .

(c) *Diplomatic assurances against torture obtained by the Secretary of State.*

(1) The Secretary of State may forward to the Attorney General assurances that the Secretary has obtained from the government of a specific country that an alien would not be tortured there if the alien were removed to that country.

(2) If the Secretary of State forwards assurances described in paragraph (c)(1) of this section to the Attorney General for consideration by the Attorney General or her delegates under this paragraph, the Attorney General shall determine, in consultation with the Secretary of State, whether the assurances are sufficiently reliable to allow the alien's removal to that country consistent with Article 3 of the Convention Against Torture. . . .

(3) Once assurances are provided under paragraph (c)(2) of this section, the alien's claim for protection under the Convention Against Torture shall not be considered further by an immigration judge, the Board of Immigration Appeals, or an asylum officer.

AL-SAHER v. INS

268 F.3d 1143, 1144–48 (9th Cir. 2001).

HUG, CIRCUIT JUDGE:

Mudher Jassim Mohamed Al–Saher, a native and citizen of Iraq, petitions for review of the Board of Immigration Appeals' ("BIA")[1] dismissal of his appeal from the Immigration Judge's ("IJ") denial of his application for asylum and withholding of removal and for protection under the Convention against Torture. . . .

. . . .

Al–Saher arrived at Los Angeles International Airport seeking admission to the United States as a non-immigrant visitor. He presented no valid entry document and the INS issued a Notice to Appear (NTA) charging him with removability as an immigrant not in possession of a valid travel or entry document.

At his hearing he presented the following testimony. He was in the Iraqi military from 1984 until 1992 and thereafter until he left Iraq he

1. [Authors' Note: The BIA is the highest administrative body for interpreting and applying U.S. immigration law. The BIA is a part of the U.S. Department of Justice and consists of eleven board members.]

was a civilian government worker assigned to work with the military. When he initially applied for military service in 1984 he claimed to be a Sunni Muslim from Baghdad even though he was a Shiite Muslim from Al–Bashra. He stated he misrepresented his religion and place of birth because there was discrimination against Shiite Muslims. In 1997, the truth was revealed when his father completed a census form stating that his family was Shiite.

Al–Saher was arrested in 1997 for misrepresenting his religion and place of birth. He was detained, interrogated and beaten for one month. He described the type of beatings he received stating that two people came in, blindfolded him, tied his hands behind his back, [“]and the only thing I felt was getting beaten up. They just kept beating me. . . . It kept on this way somewhere between 10 days to 2 weeks.[”]

He explained that at that time his father was trying to get in contact with high authority so that he would not be beaten up. He stated that he stayed two weeks after the first period of beatings. During that time every three or four days an officer would come in at night and beat him up until his father paid a half million dinar to someone in the office of Saddam Hussein. As he left they told him that he was to tell no one about his experience, stating “if we ever heard anything that you have talked, you're going to come back and do the same thing again. Same room will be reserved for you.” When asked at the hearing what he was being beaten with he stated it was with their hands and feet and a thick electrical cable.

He went back to work on his job and in December he was instructed to take a number of men to construct a fence that was to be built in a sensitive location, somewhere near the president. When he asked exactly where the fence was to be built, he was arrested. He stated that this time the beating was more severe and “had lots of monstrosities in it.” He was again blindfolded with his hands tied behind him and beaten like before. This time they burned him with cigarettes. His parents got a hold of a friend who got him out after 8 to 10 days.

In April 1998 he was arrested again after he was heard talking with friends about how the elite Iraqi eat well while the poor go hungry. He and his friends were detained for 5 or 6 days until they escaped. He stated he found out it was not going to be the last time because anyone who has been accused and suspected twice that's going to be it for him—“it's impossible to let him go.”

. . . .

The BIA addressed Al–Saher's torture claim and concluded that the arrests did not amount to torture as defined in the regulations. Accepting Al–Saher's testimony as true, we must disagree. Al–Saher testified that he was subjected to sustained beatings for a month on the first arrest. On the second arrest he suffered severe beatings and was burned with cigarettes over an 8 to 10 day period. These are not practices “inherent in or incidental to lawful sanction.” These actions were specifically intended by officials to inflict severe physical pain on Al–Saher.

The Country Reports on Human Rights and Practices for 1997 for Iraq tell of the torture routinely administered to those detained or imprisoned.

> The [Iraqi] Constitution prohibits torture, however, the security services routinely tortured detainees. According to former detainees, torture techniques included branding, electric shocks administered to the genitals and other areas, beating, burning with hot irons, suspension from rotating ceiling fans, dripping acid on the skin, rape, breaking of limbs, denial of food and water, and threats to rape or otherwise harm relatives. The security forces killed many of their torture victims and mutilated their bodies before returning them to the victims' families. There are persistent reports that the families are made to pay for the costs of the execution, before the bodies are returned to them. Iraqi refugees arriving in Europe often reported instances of torture to the receiving governments and—as was the case with a group of refugees arriving in Italy in June—displayed scars and mutilations to substantiate their claims.

The BIA must take this into consideration when assessing whether an applicant qualifies under the Convention. . . . Al–Saher was informed that if he told anyone about the beatings he would be arrested again and suffer the same consequences.

When officials detained Al–Saher for the third time based on an imputed political opinion, Al–Saher managed to escape from custody and avoid the possibility of further severe beatings and physical abuse. He then fled the country. If forced to return to Iraq, it is likely that Al–Saher would be tortured again. The Iraqi officials would correctly assume he has told of the beatings in making his claims in this proceeding. Based on these facts, we find that Al–Saher is entitled to withholding of removal under the Convention Against Torture. We grant Al–Saher's petition for review and remand to the BIA for entry of an order granting withholding of removal.

Petition for review GRANTED and case REMANDED.

CONCLUDING NOTES ON STATUTORY IMPLEMENTATION

1. *Implementing Statutes.* As indicated in the materials above, there already existed in the United States various constitutional and statutory provisions at the Federal and state level allowing the United States to implement most of its obligations under the Convention Against Torture. At the same time, the United States decided to enact some new statutes as a means of implementing its obligations. In late 2006, the U.S. Department of Justice for the first time initiated a prosecution under 18 U.S.C. § 2340A (2006), which allows prosecution of anyone involved in torture who is present in the United States, regardless of nationality or location of the crime. The indictment alleged that the son of former Liberian president Charles Taylor used a hot iron, scalding water, and an electrical device to shock and burn one

of his father's political opponents in Liberia in July 2002. After his father's fall from power, the son had attempted to enter the United States using a false passport. In October 2009, Taylor was convicted and sentenced to 97 years in prison, which was upheld on appeal. United States v. Belfast, 611 F.3d 783 (11th Cir. 2010). Among other things, Taylor attacked the statute as an invalid exercise of congressional power because the statute's definition of torture was broader than that of the Convention. The circuit court, however, found that "slight variances between a treaty and its congressional implementing legislation do not make the enactment unconstitutional; identicality is not required." *Id.* at 806; *see* Melissa A. Beckman, *No Longer a Safe Haven for Torturers: The United States Makes Its First Successful Prosecution Under the Torture Statute*, 14 PUB. INT. L. REP. 74 (2008).

2. *Importance of Governmental Interpretation of Treaty Provisions.* The memoranda by the Justice Department's Office of Legal Counsel sought to determine the meaning of "severe pain or suffering, whether physical or mental," through an interpretation of the Convention's ratification history, U.S. implementing legislation, and case law. Notice how the 2002 Memorandum, issued shortly after the September 11, 2001, terrorist attacks, takes a very limited view as to what constitutes "torture." By contrast, the 2004 Memorandum—issued after revelations of abuses by U.S. military personnel at the largest U.S. detention facility in Iraq, Abu Ghraib prison—takes a broader view of acts that amount to "torture." An investigation by the U.S. Central Command concluded in February 2004:

> [B]etween October and December 2003, at the Abu Ghraib Confinement Facility ..., numerous incidents of sadistic, blatant, and wanton criminal abuses were inflicted on several detainees. This systemic and illegal abuse of detainees was intentionally perpetrated by several members of the military police guard force ... of the Abu Ghraib Prison. ... The allegations of abuse were substantiated by detailed witness statements ... and the discovery of extremely graphic photographic evidence.

Article 15–6 Investigation of the 800th Military Police Brigade pt. 1 (*Findings and Recommendations*), ¶ 5, at 16 (commonly referred to as the Taguba Report, after its author, Major General Antonio Taguba); *see generally The Torture Papers: The Road to Abu Ghraib* (Karen J. Greenberg & Joshua T. Dratel eds., 2005). Thereafter, the U.S. Army charged several U.S. military personnel with the physical and sexual abuse of prisoners at Abu Ghraib.

Reports also emerged regarding harsh treatment of persons detained by the U.S. government at Guantánamo Bay Naval Base in Cuba. For example, a Saudi national, Mohammed al-Qahtani, was reportedly treated by U.S. interrogators in late 2001/early 2002 as follows:

> Qahtani had been subjected to a hundred and sixty days of isolation in a pen perpetually flooded with artificial light. He was interrogated on forty-eight of fifty-four days for eighteen to twenty hours at a stretch. He had been stripped naked; straddled by taunting female guards, in an exercise called "invasion of space by a female"; forced to wear women's underwear on his head, and to put on a bra; threatened by dogs; placed on a leash; and told that his mother was a whore. By December, Qahtani had been subjected to a phony kidnapping, deprived of heat, given large

> quantities of intravenous liquids without access to a toilet, and deprived of sleep for three days. . . . Qahtani's heart rate had dropped so precipitately, to thirty-five beats a minute, that he required cardiac monitoring.
>
> . . . .
>
> [By January 2002], Qahtani had been stripped and shaved and told to bark like a dog. He'd been forced to listen to pop music at ear-splitting volume, deprived of sleep, and kept in a painfully cold room. Between confessing to and then recanting various terrorist plots, he had begged to be allowed to commit suicide.

Jane Mayer, *The Memo*, THE NEW YORKER, Feb. 27, 2006, at 32, 34, 37; *see also* Jane Mayer, *The Black Sites*, THE NEW YORKER, Aug. 8, 2007, at 46 (recounting tactics used on Khalid Sheik Mohammad, the alleged mastermind of the September 11 terrorist attacks). Do you view such interrogation tactics as "torture" within the meaning of the Convention Against Torture and the U.S. implementing statute? Within the meaning of either of the Justice Department memoranda? Is there further information you would like to have before deciding? Is it relevant that, in June 2006, three detainees at Guantánamo Bay hanged themselves in an apparent suicide pact, marking the first deaths in custody at the military prison?

In a report to the Committee Against Torture (a group of ten experts established under Article 17 of the Convention), the United States asserted:

> The United States is aware of allegations that detainees held in U.S. custody pursuant to the global war on terrorism have been subject to torture or other mistreatment. The President of the United States . . . has clearly stated that torture is prohibited. When allegations of torture or other unlawful treatment arise, they are investigated and, if substantiated, prosecuted. . . .

Second Periodic Report of the United States of America to the Committee Against Torture, ¶ 10 (May 6, 2005), *available at* http://www.state.gov/g/drl/rls/45738.htm.

3. *Relevance of Reciprocity*. One interesting aspect of the 2004 Memorandum is that it draws upon U.S. case law dealing with how the U.S. courts believe U.S. nationals should be treated by foreign governments when they travel abroad. When thinking about how to interpret and implement U.S. treaty obligations under U.S. law, is it helpful to consider how the United States would like other nations to implement the treaty, especially when the well-being of U.S. nationals is at stake? This section has focused on U.S. implementation, yet other parties to the Convention Against Torture also have adopted laws and decided cases to implement their obligations. Good sources of information on such implementation are the reports submitted periodically by states to the Convention's Committee Against Torture. Those reports typically describe the states' implementing legislation and relevant case law.

Obviously, not all countries (including the United States) live up to the standards of the Convention at all times, but they nevertheless have enacted laws and regulations banning torture and inhuman treatment. For example, to implement the Convention, the United Kingdom adopted the Criminal

Justice Act, 1988, c. 33, §§ 134–38 (Eng.). Among other things, the statute makes it a criminal offense for a public official (or person acting in an official capacity) to commit torture or cruel, inhuman, or degrading treatment or punishment, whatever his nationality and wherever in the world he commits the offense. Likewise, Mexico has adopted laws prohibiting torture. *See* CÓDIGO PENAL FEDERAL, art. 225 (XII) (criminalizing the use of torture by public servants against suspected criminals). In addition, Mexico (unlike the United States) has allowed individuals to bring complaints against it before the Committee Against Torture under Article 22 of the Convention. *See* Decreto promulgatorio de la declaración para el reconocimiento de la competencia del comité contra la tortura, de la Convención contra la Tortura (May 3, 2002).

4. *Extraterritorial Application of CAT Generally.* Does the CAT impose obligations upon the U.S. government with respect to actions taken outside U.S. territory? Article 2 imposes on a state party the obligation to prevent torture "in any territory under its jurisdiction." Does this mean that U.S. authorities are not restricted by the CAT when engaging in interrogations abroad? Article 3 imposes the obligation not to "expel, return or extradite" a person to another state where he might be tortured, but does not expressly state whether this only covers expulsion, return, or extradition from U.S. territory. In *Sale v. Haitian Centers Council, Inc.*, 509 U.S. 155, 187–88, 113 S.Ct. 2549, 125 L.Ed.2d 128 (1993), the Supreme Court held that a comparable *non-refoulement* requirement in Article 33 of the Refugee Convention, July 28, 1951, 189 U.N.T.S. 150, did not apply to the interdiction and return of Haitians apprehended on the high seas prior to their arrival in the United States. (While the United States is not a party to the Refugee Convention, it is derivatively bound to the Convention's core provisions through its adherence to the Protocol. *See* Protocol Relating to the Status of Refugees, Jan. 31, 1967, 19 U.S.T. 6223, 606 U.N.T.S. 267.) Does *Sale* suggest that CAT Article 3 does not apply to actions taken outside U.S. territory?

5. *Extraterritorial Application of CAT Article 16.* The materials above considered whether, in accepting Article 16 of the Convention Against Torture, the United States undertook a legal obligation to refrain from cruel and inhuman treatment outside U.S. territory. According to Attorney General Designate Alberto Gonzales (who was thereafter confirmed as Attorney General), the U.S. understanding filed with respect to that Article limited its scope to conduct within the United States. Former U.S. State Department Legal Adviser Abraham Sofaer, who testified before the Senate Foreign Relations Committee during the advice-and-consent process, disagreed with that interpretation. Rather than let the issue fester, Senator John McCain, a Vietnam veteran who was tortured during several years as a prisoner of war, succeeded in having his amendment adopted by a wide (and veto-proof) margin in both Houses of Congress (90 to 9 in the Senate and 308 to 122 in the House). President George W. Bush, who had resisted passage of the amendment, reluctantly signed it into law. Yet when doing so, the president stated:

> The executive branch shall construe Title X in Division A of the Act, relating to detainees, in a manner consistent with the constitutional authority of the President to supervise the unitary executive branch and

> as Commander in Chief and consistent with the constitutional limitations on the judicial power, which will assist in achieving the shared objective of the Congress and the President, evidenced in Title X, of protecting the American people from further terrorist attacks.

Statement on Signing the Department of Defense, Emergency Supplemental Appropriations to Address Hurricanes in the Gulf of Mexico, and Pandemic Influenza Act, 2006, 41 WEEKLY COMP. PRES. DOC. 1918–19 (Dec. 30, 2005). What do you think this statement means? Does it have any legal significance?

6. *Deportation of Aliens*. The materials above provide a sense of how the Convention Against Torture has been implemented with respect to the deportation (or "removal") of aliens. Article 3 of the Convention has had the most significant day-to-day impact upon U.S. law enforcement activity. According to the Congressional Research Service:

> The requirements of CAT Article 3 take the form of a two-track system requiring the withholding or deferral of the alien's removal to the proposed receiving state if it is more likely than not that he would be tortured there. Reliance on these protections by aliens in removal proceedings has been frequent, though usually unsuccessful. In 2007, for example, immigration courts considered 28,130 claims for CAT-based relief, and granted such relief in 541 cases. [The Department of Homeland Security] has estimated that in the first four years following the implementation of regulations implementing CAT Article 3, approximately 1,700 aliens were granted deferral or withholding of removal based on CAT protections. In 2007, deferral of removal was granted in 92 cases, compared to 173 cases in 2006 and 70 cases in 2005.

Congressional Research Service, The U.N. Convention Against Torture: Overview of U.S. Implementation Policy Concerning the Removal of Aliens, CRS Doc. RL32276, at 7 (Jan. 21, 2009) (footnotes omitted).

Although Al–Saher's petition was granted, the petitions of other aliens have been denied. *See, e.g.*, Ahmed v. Keisler, 504 F.3d 1183, 1200–01 (9th Cir. 2007) (finding insufficient evidence that the petitioner, a Bihari who had been subject to beatings in Bangladesh, would be tortured within the meaning of the Convention if returned); *see also* John T. Parry, *Torture Nation, Torture Law*, 97 GEO. L.J. 1001, 1048–51 (2009).

What if the United States receives assurances from the receiving State that the alien will not be tortured? *See* Jane C. Kim, *Nonrefoulement under the Convention Against Torture: How U.S. Allowances for Diplomatic Assurances Contravene Treaty Obligations and Federal Law*, 32 BROOK. J. INT'L L. 1227 (2007) (discussing how, if the Secretary of State obtains diplomatic assurances that the alien will not be tortured and forwards the assurances to the Attorney General, then the alien may be removed without further administrative review or review by federal courts).

7. *Extradition of Persons*. Article 3 of the Convention Against Torture also imposes an obligation not to extradite persons to a country where they may be tortured. Here, too, the basic U.S. extradition statute, 18 U.S.C. §§ 1384–86 (2006) has been augmented with regulations implementing the Convention's obligation. *See* 22 C.F.R. pt. 95, §§ 95.2–.4 (2010). A key issue in

this area, however, is whether under the "rule of non-inquiry" in extradition law—by which U.S. courts refrain from examining the penal systems of the foreign country and instead defer to the Secretary of State's determination of whether the extradited person will likely be mistreated by the foreign country—has been displaced by the FARR Act and its implementing regulations. Under the new rules, can the detained person challenge in court the Secretary's decision to extradite? *See, e.g.*, Mironescu v. Costner, 480 F.3d 664 (4th Cir. 2007) (holding that, while the rule of non-inquiry does not bar habeas review, the FARR Act itself precludes judicial review of the Secretary's decision); *see also* Trinidad y Garcia v. Benov, 395 F. Appx. 329 (9th Cir. 2010); Prasoprat v. Benov, 622 F. Supp. 2d 980 (C.D. Cal. 2009); Cornejo-Barreto v. Siefert, 379 F.3d 1075, *vacated as moot*, 389 F.3d 1307 (9th Cir. 2004); Garcia v. Benov, 715 F. Supp. 2d 974, 991–94 (C.D. Cal. 2009).

The Supreme Court, as of mid–2011, has not addressed the issue directly. The Court has found, however, that the decision of the executive branch to surrender a detainee held by U.S. forces in Iraq to the Government of Iraq for criminal prosecution, including the decision of the Secretary of State that the detainee was not likely to be tortured, was a matter that should be addressed by the executive branch rather than the courts. *See* Munaf v. Geren, 553 U.S. 674, 128 S.Ct. 2207, 171 L.Ed.2d 1 (2008); *see* Jeffrey H. Fisher, *Detainee Transfers after* Munaf: *Executive Deference and the Convention Against Torture*, 43 GA. L. REV. 953 (2009).

8. *Extraordinary Rendition.* A component of the U.S. response to the September 2001 terrorist attacks has been the practice of "extraordinary rendition," whereby persons suspected of having information about terrorist activities are handed over by the United States to foreign governments for interrogation. Here, too, U.S. laws implementing the Convention Against Torture are of relevance. For example, in January 2004, a Canadian national, Maher Arar, sued various U.S. government officials, alleging that they had detained him in 2002 while he was transiting through JFK Airport in New York for a flight to Canada. The defendants then allegedly sent Arar to Syria for interrogation, because he was suspected of being involved with terrorists. According to Arar, he was held by the Syrian government for ten months, during which time he was subjected to physical and mental torture, which led him to confess to acts (such as training with terrorists) that he did not do. The Syrian officials then allegedly provided the information obtained from Arar to U.S. authorities. According to Arar, since Syria could not separately link Arar to terrorist activity, he was eventually allowed to return to Canada. Thereafter, Arar filed his suit against U.S. government officials, claiming both a violation of the TVPA and a denial of his constitutional right to substantive due process under the Fifth Amendment of the Constitution. Arar's factual assertions were confirmed in September 2006 by a commission established by the Canadian government. *See* Doug Struck, *Canadian Was Falsely Accused, Panel Says*, WASH. POST, Sept. 19, 2006, at A1. Since Canada had provided exaggerated and false information to the United States identifying Arar as a terrorist, the prime minister of Canada apologized to Arar and agreed to pay him $9 million in compensation. *See* Doug Struck, *Tortured Man Gets Apology from Canada*, WASH. POST, Jan. 27, 2007, at A14. The Second Circuit, however, affirmed the dismissal of Arar's complaint, stating that if a civil remedy in

damages is to be created for extraordinary rendition, it must be expressly done by Congress. *See* Arar v. Ashcroft, 585 F.3d 559 (2d Cir. 2009).

SECTION 4. NATIONAL IMPLEMENTATION BY SELF-EXECUTION

FOSTER & ELAM v. NEILSON

27 U.S. (2 Pet.) 253, 299–317, 7 L.Ed. 415 (1829).

MR. CHIEF JUSTICE MARSHALL delivered the opinion of the Court.

This suit was brought by the plaintiffs in error in the court of the United States, for the eastern district of Louisiana, to recover a tract of land lying in that district, about thirty miles east of the Mississippi, and in the possession of the defendant. The plaintiffs claimed under a grant for 40,000 arpents of land, made by the Spanish governor, on the 2d of January 1804, to Jayme Joydra, and ratified by the king of Spain on the 29th of May 1804. The petition and order of survey are dated in September 1803, and the return of the survey itself was made on the 27th of October in the same year. The defendant excepted to the petition of the plaintiffs, alleging that it does not show a title on which they can recover; that the territory, within which the land claimed is situated, had been ceded, before the grant, to France, and by France to the United States; and that the grant is void, being made by persons who had no authority to make it. The court sustained the exception, and dismissed the petition. The cause is brought before this Court by a writ of error.

The case presents this very intricate, and at one time very interesting question: To whom did the country between the Iberville and the Perdido rightfully belong, when the title now asserted by the plaintiffs was acquired?

This question has been repeatedly discussed with great talent and research, by the government of the United States and that of Spain. The United States have perseveringly and earnestly insisted, that by the Treaty of St Ildefonso, made on the 1st of October in the year 1800, Spain ceded the disputed territory as part of Louisiana to France; and that France, by the treaty of Paris, signed on the 30th of April 1803, and ratified on the 21st of October in the same year, ceded it to the United States. Spain has with equal perseverance and earnestness maintained, that her cession to France comprehended that territory only which was at that time denominated Louisiana, consisting of the island of New Orleans, and the country she received from France west of the Mississippi.

[The Court proceeded to decide that it must accept the U.S. government's interpretation that Spain ceded the territory to France in 1800, from which the rights of the parties flowed, unless the United States and Spain had subsequently reached an alternative arrangement.]

A "treaty of amity, settlement, and limits, between the United States of America and the king of Spain," was signed at Washington on the 22d day of February 1819. By the 2d article, "his catholic majesty cedes to the United States in full property and sovereignty, all the territories which belong to him, situated to the eastward of the Mississippi, known by the name of East and West Florida."

The 8th article stipulates, that "all the grants of land made before the 24th of January 1818 by his catholic majesty, or by his lawful authorities, in the said territories ceded by his majesty to the United States, shall be ratified and confirmed to the persons in possession of the lands, to the same extent that the same grants would be valid if the territories had remained under the dominion of his catholic majesty."

. . . .

[W]e think the sound construction of the eighth article will not enable this Court to apply its provisions to the present case. The words of the article are, that "all the grants of land made before the 24th of January 1818, by his catholic majesty, & c. shall be ratified and confirmed to the persons in possession of the lands, to the same extent that the same grants would be valid if the territories had remained under the dominion of his catholic majesty." Do these words act directly on the grants, so as to give validity to those not otherwise valid; or do they pledge the faith of the United States to pass acts which shall ratify and confirm them?

A treaty is in its nature a contract between two nations, not a legislative act. It does not generally effect, of itself, the object to be accomplished, especially so far as its operation is infra-territorial; but is carried into execution by the sovereign power of the respective parties to the instrument.

In the United States a different principle is established. Our constitution declares a treaty to be the law of the land. It is, consequently, to be regarded in courts of justice as equivalent to an act of the legislature, whenever it operates of itself without the aid of any legislative provision. But when the terms of the stipulation import a contract, when either of the parties engages to perform a particular act, the treaty addresses itself to the political, not the judicial department; and the legislature must execute the contract before it can become a rule for the Court.

The article under consideration does not declare that all the grants made by his catholic majesty before the 24th of January 1818, shall be valid to the same extent as if the ceded territories had remained under his dominion. It does not say that those grants are hereby confirmed. Had such been its language, it would have acted directly on the subject, and would have repealed those acts of congress which were repugnant to it; but its language is that those grants shall be ratified and confirmed to the persons in possession, & c. By whom shall they be ratified and confirmed? This seems to be the language of contract; and if it is, the ratification and confirmation which are promised must be the act of the legislature. Until such act shall be passed, the Court is not at liberty to disregard the existing laws on the subject. Congress appears to have understood this article as it is understood by the Court. Boards of commissioners have been appointed for East and West Florida, to receive claims for lands; and on their reports titles to lands not exceeding ______ acres have been confirmed, and to a very large amount. On the 23d of May 1828, an act was passed supplementary to the several acts providing for the settlement and confirmation of private land claims in Florida; the 6th section of which enacts, that [“]all claims to land within the territory of Florida, embraced by the treaty between Spain and the United States of the 22d of February 1819, which shall not be decided and finally settled under the foregoing provisions of this act, containing a greater quantity of land than the commissioners were authorized to decide, and which have not been reported as antedated or forged, & c., shall be received and adjudicated by the judge of the superior court of the district within which the land lies, upon the petition of the claimant,” & c. Provided, that nothing in this section shall be construed to enable the judges to take cognizance of any claim annulled by the said treaty, or the decree ratifying the same by the king of Spain, nor any claim not presented to the commissioners or register and receiver. An appeal is allowed from the decision of the judge of the district to this Court. No such act of confirmation has been extended to grants for lands lying west of the Perdido.

The act of 1804, erecting Louisiana into two territories, . . . annuls all grants for lands in the ceded territories, the title whereof was at the date of the treaty of St Ildefonso in the crown of Spain. The grant in controversy is not brought within any of the exceptions from the enacting clause.

The legislature has passed many subsequent acts previous to the treaty of 1819, the object of which was to adjust the titles to lands in the country acquired by the treaty of 1803.

They cautiously confirm to residents all incomplete titles to lands, for which a warrant or order of survey had been obtained previous to the 1st of October 1800.

. . . .

Congress has reserved to itself the supervision of the titles reported by its commissioners, and has confirmed those which the commissioners have approved, but has passed no law, withdrawing grants generally for lands west of the Perdido from the operation of the . . . act of 1804. . . .

We are of opinion then, that the court committed no error in dismissing the petition of the plaintiff, and that the judgment ought to be affirmed with costs.

HEAD MONEY CASES (EDYE & ANOTHER v. ROBERTSON)

112 U.S. 580, 586–99, 5 S.Ct. 247, 28 L.Ed. 798 (1884).

MR. JUSTICE MILLER delivered the opinion of the court.

. . . .

The suit is brought to recover from Robertson the sum of money received by him, as collector of the port of New York, from plaintiffs, on account of their landing in that port passengers from foreign ports, not citizens of the United States, at the rate of fifty cents for each of such passengers, under the act of Congress of August 3, 1882, entitled "An Act to regulate immigration."

. . . .

An[] objection to the validity of this act of Congress, is that it violates provisions contained in numerous treaties of our government with friendly nations. And several of the articles of these treaties are annexed to the careful brief of counsel. We are not satisfied that this act of Congress violates any of these treaties, on any just construction of them. Though laws similar to this have long been enforced by the State of New York in the great metropolis of foreign trade, where four-fifths of these passengers have been landed, no complaint has been made by any foreign nation to ours, of the violation of treaty obligations by the enforcement of those laws.

. . . .

A treaty is primarily a compact between independent nations. It depends for the enforcement of its provisions on the interest and the honor of the governments which are parties to it. If these fail, its infraction becomes the subject of international negotiations and reclamations, so far as the injured party chooses to seek redress which may in the end, be enforced by actual war. It is obvious that with all this the judicial courts have nothing to do and can give no redress. But a treaty may also contain provisions which confer certain rights upon the citizens or subjects of one of the nations residing in the territorial limits of the other, which partake of the nature of municipal law, and which are capable of enforcement as between private parties in the courts of the country. An illustration of this character is found in treaties, which regulate the mutual rights of citizens and subjects of the contracting nations in regard to rights of property by descent or inheritance, when the individuals concerned are aliens. The Constitution of the United States places such provisions as these in the same category as other laws of Congress by its declaration that "this Constitution and the laws made in pursuance thereof, and all treaties made or which shall be made under authority of the United States, shall be the supreme law of the land." A treaty, then, is a law of the land as an act of Congress is, whenever its provisions prescribe a rule by which the rights of the private citizen or subject may be determined. And when such rights are of a nature to be enforced in a court of justice, that court resorts to the treaty for a rule of decision for the case before it as it would to a statute.

[The Court proceeded to determine that the provisions of the treaty had been superseded by a later-in-time statute. *See infra* Section 6].

ASAKURA v. CITY OF SEATTLE

265 U.S. 332, 339–44, 44 S.Ct. 515, 68 L.Ed. 1041 (1924) (footnote omitted).

MR. JUSTICE BUTLER delivered the opinion of the Court.

Plaintiff in error is a subject of the Emperor of Japan, and, since 1904, has resided in Seattle, Washington. Since July, 1915, he has been engaged in business there as a pawnbroker. The city passed an ordinance, which took effect July 2, 1921, regulating the business of pawnbroker and repealing former ordinances on the same subject. It makes it unlawful for any person to engage in the business unless he shall have a license, and the ordinance provides "that no such license shall be granted unless the applicant be a citizen of the United States." Violations of the ordinance are punishable by fine or imprisonment or both. Plaintiff in error brought this suit in the Superior Court of King County, Washington, against the city, its Comptroller and its Chief of Police to restrain them from enforcing the ordinance against him. He attacked the ordinance on the ground that it violates the treaty between the United States and the Empire of Japan, proclaimed April 5, 1911, 37 Stat. 1504; violates the constitution of the State of Washington, and also the due process and equal protection clauses of the Fourteenth Amendment of the Constitution of the United States. He declared his willingness to comply with any valid ordinance relating to the business of pawnbroker. It was shown that he had about $5,000 invested in his business, which would be broken up and destroyed by the enforcement of the ordinance. The Superior Court granted the relief prayed. On appeal, the Supreme Court of the State held the ordinance valid and reversed the decree. . . .

Does the ordinance violate the treaty? Plaintiff in error invokes and relies upon the following provisions: "The citizens or subjects of each of the High Contracting Parties shall have liberty to enter, travel and reside in the territories of the other to carry on trade, wholesale and retail, to own or lease and occupy houses, manufactories, warehouses and shops, to employ agents of their choice, to lease land for residential and commercial purposes, and generally to do anything incident to or necessary for trade upon the same terms as native citizens or subjects, submitting themselves to the laws and regulations there established. . . . The citizens or subjects of each . . . shall receive, in the territories of the other, the most constant protection and security for their persons and property. . . ."

A treaty made under the authority of the United States "shall be the supreme law of the land; and the judges in every State shall be bound thereby, any thing in the Constitution or laws of any State to the contrary notwithstanding." Constitution, Art. VI, § 2.

The treaty-making power of the United States is not limited by any express provision of the Constitution, and, though it does not extend "so far as to authorize what the Constitution forbids," it does extend to all proper subjects of negotiation between our government and other nations.

De Geofroy v. Riggs, 133 U.S. 258, 266, 267; *In re Ross*, 140 U.S. 453, 463; *Missouri v. Holland*, 252 U.S. 416. The treaty was made to strengthen friendly relations between the two nations. As to the things covered by it, the provision quoted establishes the rule of equality between Japanese subjects while in this country and native citizens. Treaties for the protection of citizens of one country residing in the territory of another are numerous, and make for good understanding between nations. The treaty is binding within the State of Washington. *Baldwin v. Franks*, 120 U.S. 678, 682–683. The rule of equality established by it cannot be rendered nugatory in any part of the United States by municipal ordinances or state laws. It stands on the same footing of supremacy as do the provisions of the Constitution and laws of the United States. It operates of itself without the aid of any legislation, state or national; and it will be applied and given authoritative effect by the courts. *Foster v. Neilson*, 2 Pet. 253, 314; *Head Money Cases*, 112 U.S. 580, 598; *Chew Heong v. United States*, 112 U.S. 536, 540; *Whitney v. Robertson*, 124 U.S. 190, 194; *Maiorano v. Baltimore & Ohio R.R. Co.*, 213 U.S. 268, 272.

The purpose of the ordinance complained of is to regulate, not to prohibit, the business of pawnbroker. But it makes it impossible for aliens to carry on the business. It need not be considered whether the State, if it sees fit, may forbid and destroy the business generally. Such a law would apply equally to aliens and citizens, and no question of conflict with the treaty would arise. The grievance here alleged is that plaintiff in error, in violation of the treaty, is denied equal opportunity.

. . . .

Decree reversed.

MEDELLIN v. TEXAS

552 U.S. 491, 128 S.Ct. 1346, 170 L.Ed.2d 190 (2008)
(footnotes and some citations omitted).

CHIEF JUSTICE ROBERTS delivered the opinion of the Court.

The International Court of Justice (ICJ), located in the Hague, is a tribunal established pursuant to the United Nations Charter to adjudicate disputes between member states. In the *Case Concerning Avena and Other Mexican Nationals* (Mex. v. U.S.), 2004 I.C.J. 12 (Judgment of Mar. 31) (*Avena*), that tribunal considered a claim brought by Mexico against the United States. The ICJ held that, based on violations of the Vienna Convention [on Consular Relations], 51 named Mexican nationals were entitled to review and reconsideration of their state-court convictions and sentences in the United States. This was so regardless of any forfeiture of the right to raise Vienna Convention claims because of a failure to comply with generally applicable state rules governing challenges to criminal convictions.

In *Sanchez-Llamas v. Oregon*, 548 U.S. 331 (2006)—issued after *Avena* but involving individuals who were not named in the *Avena* judgment—we held that, contrary to the ICJ's determination, the Vienna Convention did not preclude the application of state default rules....

Petitioner José Ernesto Medellín, who had been convicted and sentenced in Texas state court for murder, is one of the 51 Mexican nationals named in the *Avena* decision. Relying on the ICJ's decision ..., Medellín filed an application for a writ of *habeas corpus* in state court. The Texas Court of Criminal Appeals dismissed Medellín's application as an abuse of the writ under state law, given Medellín's failure to raise his Vienna Convention claim in a timely manner under state law. We granted certiorari to decide[:] ... is the ICJ's judgment in *Avena* directly enforceable as domestic law in a state court in the United States? ...

I

A

In 1969, the United States, upon the advice and consent of the Senate, ratified the Vienna Convention on Consular Relations (Vienna Convention or Convention), Apr. 24, 1963, and the Optional Protocol Concerning the Compulsory Settlement of Disputes to the Vienna Convention (Optional Protocol or Protocol), Apr. 24, 1963.... Article 36 of the Convention ... provides that if a person detained by a foreign country "so requests, the competent authorities of the receiving State shall, without delay, inform the consular post of the sending State" of such detention, and "inform the [detainee] of his righ[t]" to request assistance from the consul of his own state. Art. 36(1)(b).

The Optional Protocol provides a venue for the resolution of disputes arising out of the interpretation or application of the Vienna Convention. Under the Protocol, such disputes "shall lie within the compulsory jurisdiction of the International Court of Justice" and "may accordingly be brought before the [ICJ] ... by any party to the dispute being a Party to the present Protocol."

The ICJ is "the principal judicial organ of the United Nations." United Nations Charter, Art. 92. It was established in 1945 pursuant to the United Nations Charter. The ICJ Statute—annexed to the U.N. Charter—provides the organizational framework and governing procedures for cases brought before the ICJ. Statute of the International Court of Justice (ICJ Statute).

Under Article 94(1) of the U.N. Charter, "[e]ach Member of the United Nations undertakes to comply with the decision of the [ICJ] in any case to which it is a party." The ICJ's jurisdiction in any particular case, however, is dependent upon the consent of the parties.... By ratifying the Optional Protocol to the Vienna Convention, the United States consented to the specific jurisdiction of the ICJ with respect to claims arising out of the Vienna Convention. On March 7, 2005, subsequent to the ICJ's judgment in *Avena*, the United States gave notice of withdrawal from the Optional Protocol to the Vienna Convention.

B

. . . .

Medellín first raised his Vienna Convention claim in his first application for state post-conviction relief. The state trial court held that the claim was procedurally defaulted because Medellín had failed to raise it at trial or on direct review. . . .

Medellín then filed a *habeas* petition in Federal District Court. The District Court denied relief, holding that Medellín's Vienna Convention claim was procedurally defaulted and that Medellín had failed to show prejudice arising from the Vienna Convention violation.

While Medellín's application for a certificate of appealability was pending in the Fifth Circuit, the ICJ issued its decision in *Avena*. The ICJ held that the United States had violated Article 36(1)(b) of the Vienna Convention by failing to inform the 51 named Mexican nationals, including Medellín, of their Vienna Convention rights. In the ICJ's determination, the United States was obligated "to provide, by means of its own choosing, review and reconsideration of the convictions and sentences of the [affected] Mexican nationals." The ICJ indicated that such review was required without regard to state procedural default rules.

The Fifth Circuit denied a certificate of appealability. *Medellín v. Dretke*, 371 F. 3d 270, 281 (2004). The court concluded that the Vienna Convention did not confer individually enforceable rights. The court further ruled that it was in any event bound by this Court's decision in *Breard v. Greene*, 523 U.S. 371, 375 (1998) (per curiam), which held that Vienna Convention claims are subject to procedural default rules, rather than by the ICJ's contrary decision in *Avena*.

. . . .

II

. . . .

No one disputes that the *Avena* decision—a decision that flows from the treaties through which the United States submitted to ICJ jurisdiction with respect to Vienna Convention disputes—constitutes an international law obligation on the part of the United States. But not all international law obligations automatically constitute binding federal law enforceable in United States courts. The question we confront here is whether the *Avena* judgment has automatic domestic legal effect such that the judgment of its own force applies in state and federal courts.

This Court has long recognized the distinction between treaties that automatically have effect as domestic law, and those that—while they constitute international law commitments—do not by themselves function as binding federal law. The distinction was well explained by Chief Justice Marshall's opinion in *Foster v. Neilson* . . . .

. . . .

Medellín and his *amici* nonetheless contend that the Optional Protocol, United Nations Charter, and ICJ Statute supply the "relevant obligation" to give the *Avena* judgment binding effect in the domestic courts of the United States. Because none of these treaty sources creates binding federal law in the absence of implementing legislation, and because it is uncontested that no such legislation exists, we conclude that the *Avena* judgment is not automatically binding domestic law.

A

. . . .

As a signatory to the Optional Protocol, the United States agreed to submit disputes arising out of the Vienna Convention to the ICJ. . . .

The most natural reading of the Optional Protocol is as a bare grant of jurisdiction. . . . The Protocol says nothing about the effect of an ICJ decision and does not itself commit signatories to comply with an ICJ judgment. The Protocol is similarly silent as to any enforcement mechanism.

The obligation on the part of signatory nations to comply with ICJ judgments derives not from the Optional Protocol, but rather from Article 94 of the United Nations Charter—the provision that specifically addresses the effect of ICJ decisions. Article 94(1) provides that "[e]ach Member of the United Nations undertakes to comply with the decision of the [ICJ] in any case to which it is a party." The Executive Branch contends that the phrase "undertakes to comply" is not "an acknowledgment that an ICJ decision will have immediate legal effect in the courts of U.N. members," but rather "a commitment on the part of U.N. Members to take future action through their political branches to comply with an ICJ decision."

We agree with this construction of Article 94. The Article is not a directive to domestic courts. It does not provide that the United States "shall" or "must" comply with an ICJ decision, nor indicate that the Senate that ratified the U.N. Charter intended to vest ICJ decisions with immediate legal effect in domestic courts. Instead, "[t]he words of Article 94 . . . call upon governments to take certain action." *Committee of United States Citizens Living in Nicaragua v. Reagan*, 859 F. 2d 929, 938 (CADC 1988). . . . *See also Foster.* In other words, the U.N. Charter reads like "a compact between independent nations" that "depends for the enforcement of its provisions on the interest and the honor of the governments which are parties to it." *Head Money Cases*, 112 U.S., at 598.5

The remainder of Article 94 confirms that the U.N. Charter does not contemplate the automatic enforceability of ICJ decisions in domestic courts.6 Article 94(2)—the enforcement provision—provides the sole remedy for noncompliance: referral to the United Nations Security Council by an aggrieved state.

. . . .

This was the understanding of the Executive Branch when the President agreed to the U.N. Charter.... *See, e.g.*, The Charter of the United Nations for the Maintenance of International Peace and Security: Hearings before the Senate Committee on Foreign Relations, 79th Cong., 1st Sess., 124–125 (1945) ("[I]f a state fails to perform its obligations under a judgment of the [ICJ], the other party may have recourse to the Security Council"); *id.*, at 286 (statement of Leo Paslovsky, Special Assistant to the Secretary of State for International Organizations and Security Affairs) ("[W]hen the Court has rendered a judgment and one of the parties refuses to accept it, then the dispute becomes political rather than legal. It is as a political dispute that the matter is referred to the Security Council")....

If ICJ judgments were instead regarded as automatically enforceable domestic law, they would be immediately and directly binding on state and federal courts pursuant to the Supremacy Clause. Mexico or the ICJ would have no need to proceed to the Security Council to enforce the judgment in this case. Noncompliance with an ICJ judgment through exercise of the Security Council veto—always regarded as an option by the Executive and ratifying Senate during and after consideration of the U.N. Charter, Optional Protocol, and ICJ Statute—would no longer be a viable alternative. There would be nothing to veto. In light of the U.N. Charter's remedial scheme, there is no reason to believe that the President and Senate signed up for such a result.

....

The ICJ Statute, incorporated into the U.N. Charter, provides further evidence that the ICJ's judgment in *Avena* does not automatically constitute federal law judicially enforceable in United States courts. To begin with, the ICJ's "principal purpose" is said to be to "arbitrate particular disputes between national governments." *Sanchez-Llamas, supra*, at 355 (citing 59 Stat. 1055). Accordingly, the ICJ can hear disputes only between nations, not individuals. Art. 34(1), 59 Stat. 1059 ("Only states [i.e., countries] may be parties in cases before the [ICJ]"). More important, Article 59 of the statute provides that "[t]he decision of the [ICJ] has no binding force except between the parties and in respect of that particular case." *Id.*, at 1062 (emphasis added). The dissent does not explain how Medellín, an individual, can be a party to the ICJ proceeding.

....

It is, moreover, well settled that the United States' interpretation of a treaty "is entitled to great weight." *Sumitomo Shoji America, Inc. v. Avagliano*, 457 U.S. 176, 184–185 (1982). The Executive Branch has unfailingly adhered to its view that the relevant treaties do not create domestically enforceable federal law.

The pertinent international agreements, therefore, do not provide for implementation of ICJ judgments through direct enforcement in domestic courts, and "where a treaty does not provide a particular remedy, either expressly or implicitly, it is not for the federal courts to impose one on the

States through lawmaking of their own." *Sanchez-Llamas*, 548 U.S., at 347.

B

The dissent faults our analysis because it "looks for the wrong thing (explicit textual expression about self-execution) using the wrong standard (clarity) in the wrong place (the treaty language)." Given our obligation to interpret treaty provisions to determine whether they are self-executing, we have to confess that we do think it rather important to look to the treaty language to see what it has to say about the issue. That is after all what the Senate looks to in deciding whether to approve the treaty.

The interpretive approach employed by the Court today—resorting to the text—is hardly novel. [The Court cites, *inter alia*, to *Foster & Elam v. Neilson*]....

As against this time-honored textual approach, the dissent proposes a multifactor, judgment-by-judgment analysis that would "jettiso[n] relative predictability for the open-ended rough-and-tumble of factors." *Jerome B. Grubart, Inc. v. Great Lakes Dredge & Dock Co.*, 513 U.S. 527, 547 (1995). The dissent's novel approach to deciding which (or, more accurately, when) treaties give rise to directly enforceable federal law is arrestingly indeterminate....

....

The dissent's approach risks the United States' involvement in international agreements. It is hard to believe that the United States would enter into treaties that are sometimes enforceable and sometimes not. Such a treaty would be the equivalent of writing a blank check to the judiciary. Senators could never be quite sure what the treaties on which they were voting meant. Only a judge could say for sure and only at some future date. This uncertainty could hobble the United States' efforts to negotiate and sign international agreements.

....

C

Our conclusion that *Avena* does not by itself constitute binding federal law is confirmed by the "postratification understanding" of signatory nations. There are currently 47 nations that are parties to the Optional Protocol and 171 nations that are parties to the Vienna Convention. Yet neither Medellín nor his *amici* have identified a single nation that treats ICJ judgments as binding in domestic courts....

Our conclusion is further supported by general principles of interpretation. To begin with, ... " 'absent a clear and express statement to the contrary, the procedural rules of the forum State govern the implementation of the treaty in that State.' " 548 U.S., at 351. Given that ICJ judgments may interfere with state procedural rules, one would expect the ratifying parties to the relevant treaties to have clearly stated their intent to give those judgments domestic effect, if they had so intended. Here there is no statement in the Optional Protocol, the U.N. Charter, or the ICJ Statute that supports the notion that ICJ judgments displace state procedural rules.

Moreover, the consequences of Medellín's argument give pause. An ICJ judgment, the argument goes, is not only binding domestic law but is also unassailable. As a result, neither Texas nor this Court may look behind a judgment and quarrel with its reasoning or result.... And there is nothing to prevent the ICJ from ordering state courts to annul criminal convictions and sentences, for any reason deemed sufficient by the ICJ. Indeed, that is precisely the relief Mexico requested.

....

D

....

In addition, Congress is up to the task of implementing non-self-executing treaties, even those involving complex commercial disputes. The judgments of a number of international tribunals enjoy a different status because of implementing legislation enacted by Congress. *See, e.g.*, 22 U.S.C. § 1650a(a) ("An award of an arbitral tribunal rendered pursuant to chapter IV of the [Convention on the Settlement of Investment Disputes] shall create a right arising under a treaty of the United States. The pecuniary obligations imposed by such an award shall be enforced and shall be given the same full faith and credit as if the award were a final judgment of a court of general jurisdiction of one of the several States"); 9 U.S.C. §§ 201–208 ("The [U.N.] Convention on the Recognition and Enforcement of Foreign Arbitral Awards of June 10, 1958, shall be enforced in United States courts in accordance with this chapter," § 201). Such language demonstrates that Congress knows how to accord domestic effect to international obligations when it desires such a result.

....

JUSTICE BREYER, with whom JUSTICE SOUTER and JUSTICE GINSBURG join, dissenting.

....

The critical question here is whether the Supremacy Clause requires Texas to follow, i.e., to enforce, this ICJ judgment. The Court says "no." And it reaches its negative answer by interpreting the labyrinth of treaty provisions as creating a legal obligation that binds the United States internationally, but which, for Supremacy Clause purposes, is not automatically enforceable as domestic law. In the majority's view, the Optional Protocol simply sends the dispute to the ICJ; the ICJ statute says that the ICJ will subsequently reach a judgment; and the U.N. Charter contains no more than a promise to " 'undertak[e] to comply' " with that judgment. Such a promise, the majority says, does not as a domestic law matter (in Chief Justice Marshall's words) "operat[e] of itself without the aid of any legislative provision." *Foster*, 2 Pet., at 314. Rather, here (and presumably in any other ICJ judgment rendered pursuant to any of the approximately 70 U.S. treaties in force that contain similar provisions for submitting treaty-based disputes to the ICJ for decisions that bind the parties) Congress must enact specific legislation before ICJ judgments entered pursuant to our consent to compulsory ICJ jurisdiction can become domestic law.

... The majority places too much weight upon treaty language that says little about the matter. The words "undertak[e] to comply," for example, do not tell us whether an ICJ judgment rendered pursuant to the parties' consent to compulsory ICJ jurisdiction does, or does not, automatically become part of our domestic law. To answer that question we must look instead to our own domestic law, in particular, to the many treaty-related cases interpreting the Supremacy Clause. Those cases, including some written by Justices well aware of the Founders' original intent, lead to the conclusion that the ICJ judgment before us is enforceable as a matter of domestic law without further legislation.

....

The case law provides no simple magic answer to the question whether a particular treaty provision is self-executing. But the case law does make clear that, insofar as today's majority looks for language about "self-execution" in the treaty itself and insofar as it erects "clear statement" presumptions designed to help find an answer, it is misguided.

The many treaty provisions that this Court has found self-executing contain no textual language on the point. Few, if any, of these provisions are clear. Those that displace state law in respect to such quintessential state matters as, say, property, inheritance, or debt repayment, lack the "clea[r] state[ment]" that the Court today apparently requires.... These many Supreme Court cases finding treaty provisions to be self-executing cannot be reconciled with the majority's demand for textual clarity.

Indeed, the majority does not point to a single ratified United States treaty that contains the kind of "clea[r]" or "plai[n]" textual indication for which the majority searches.... Rather, it is because the issue whether further legislative action is required before a treaty provision takes domestic effect in a signatory nation is often a matter of how that Nation's domestic law regards the provision's legal status. And that domestic status-determining law differs markedly from one nation to another. *See generally* Hollis, Comparative Approach to Treaty Law and Practice, in National Treaty Law and Practice 1, 9–50 (D. Hollis, M. Blakeslee, & L. Ederington eds. 2005) (hereinafter Hollis)....

....

The case law also suggests practical, context-specific criteria that this Court has previously used to help determine whether, for Supremacy Clause purposes, a treaty provision is self-executing. The provision's text matters very much. But that is not because it contains language that explicitly refers to self-execution. For reasons I have already explained, one should not expect that kind of textual statement. Drafting history is also relevant. But, again, that is not because it will explicitly address the relevant question. Instead text and history, along with subject matter and related characteristics will help our courts determine whether, as Chief Justice Marshall put it, the treaty provision "addresses itself to the political . . . department[s]" for further action or to "the judicial department" for direct enforcement. *Foster*, 2 Pet., at 314. . . .

In making this determination, this Court has found the provision's subject matter of particular importance. Does the treaty provision declare peace? Does it promise not to engage in hostilities? If so, it addresses itself to the political branches. Alternatively, does it concern the adjudication of traditional private legal rights such as rights to own property, to conduct a business, or to obtain civil tort recovery? If so, it may well address itself to the Judiciary. Enforcing such rights and setting their boundaries is the bread-and-butter work of the courts.

One might also ask whether the treaty provision confers specific, detailed individual legal rights. Does it set forth definite standards that judges can readily enforce? Other things being equal, where rights are specific and readily enforceable, the treaty provision more likely "addresses" the judiciary.

Alternatively, would direct enforcement require the courts to create a new cause of action? Would such enforcement engender constitutional controversy? Would it create constitutionally undesirable conflict with the other branches? In such circumstances, it is not likely that the provision contemplates direct judicial enforcement. *See, e.g., Asakura* (although "not limited by any express provision of the Constitution," the treaty-making power of the United States "does not extend 'so far as to authorize what the Constitution forbids' ").

Such questions, drawn from case law stretching back 200 years, do not create a simple test, let alone a magic formula. But they do help to constitute a practical, context-specific judicial approach, seeking to separate run-of-the-mill judicial matters from other matters, sometimes more politically charged, sometimes more clearly the responsibility of other branches, sometimes lacking those attributes that would permit courts to act on their own without more ado. And such an approach is all that we need to find an answer to the legal question now before us.

. . . .

Applying the approach just described, I would find the relevant treaty provisions self-executing as applied to the ICJ judgment before us (giving that judgment domestic legal effect) for the following reasons, taken together.

First, the language of the relevant treaties strongly supports direct judicial enforceability, at least of judgments of the kind at issue here. The Optional Protocol bears the title "Compulsory Settlement of Disputes," thereby emphasizing the mandatory and binding nature of the procedures it sets forth....

Moreover, in accepting Article 94(1) of the Charter, "[e]ach Member ... undertakes to comply with the decision" of the ICJ "in any case to which it is a party." And the ICJ Statute (part of the U.N. Charter) makes clear that, a decision of the ICJ between parties that have consented to the ICJ's compulsory jurisdiction has "binding force ... between the parties and in respect of that particular case." Enforcement of a court's judgment that has "binding force" involves quintessential judicial activity.

....

The upshot is that treaty language says that an ICJ decision is legally binding, but it leaves the implementation of that binding legal obligation to the domestic law of each signatory nation. In this Nation, the Supremacy Clause, as long and consistently interpreted, indicates that ICJ decisions rendered pursuant to provisions for binding adjudication must be domestically legally binding and enforceable in domestic courts at least sometimes. And for purposes of this argument, that conclusion is all that I need. The remainder of the discussion will explain why, if ICJ judgments sometimes bind domestic courts, then they have that effect here.

Second, the Optional Protocol here applies to a dispute about the meaning of a Vienna Convention provision that is itself self-executing and judicially enforceable. The Convention provision is about an individual's "rights," namely, his right upon being arrested to be informed of his separate right to contact his nation's consul. *See* Art. 36(1)(b), 21 U.S.T., at 101. The provision language is precise. The dispute arises at the intersection of an individual right with ordinary rules of criminal procedure; it consequently concerns the kind of matter with which judges are familiar. The provisions contain judicially enforceable standards. See Art. 36(2), ibid. (providing for exercise of rights "in conformity with the laws and regulations" of the arresting nation provided that the "laws and regulations ... enable full effect to be given to the purposes for which the rights accorded under this Article are intended"). And the judgment itself requires a further hearing of a sort that is typically judicial.

....

Third, logic suggests that a treaty provision providing for "final" and "binding" judgments that "settl[e]" treaty-based disputes is self-executing insofar as the judgment in question concerns the meaning of an underlying treaty provision that is itself self-executing. Imagine that two parties to a contract agree to binding arbitration about whether a contract provision's word "grain" includes rye. They would expect that, if the arbitrator decides that the word "grain" does include rye, the arbitrator will then simply read the relevant provision as if it said "grain including rye." They would also expect the arbitrator to issue a binding award that embodies whatever relief would be appropriate under that circumstance.

Why treat differently the parties' agreement to binding ICJ determination about, e.g., the proper interpretation of the Vienna Convention clauses containing the rights here at issue? Why not simply read the relevant Vienna Convention provisions as if (between the parties and in respect to the 51 individuals at issue) they contain words that encapsulate the ICJ's decision? Why would the ICJ judgment not bind in precisely the same way those words would bind if they appeared in the relevant Vienna Convention provisions—just as the ICJ says, for purposes of this case, that they do?

. . . .

Fourth, the majority's very different approach has seriously negative practical implications. The United States has entered into at least 70 treaties that contain provisions for ICJ dispute settlement similar to the Protocol before us. . . . If the Optional Protocol here, taken together with the U.N. Charter and its annexed ICJ Statute, is insufficient to warrant enforcement of the ICJ judgment before us, it is difficult to see how one could reach a different conclusion in any of these other instances. And the consequence is to undermine longstanding efforts in those treaties to create an effective international system for interpreting and applying many, often commercial, self-executing treaty provisions. . . .

Nor can the majority look to congressional legislation for a quick fix. Congress is unlikely to authorize automatic judicial enforceability of all ICJ judgments, for that could include some politically sensitive judgments and others better suited for enforcement by other branches. . . .

Fifth, other factors, related to the particular judgment here at issue, make that judgment well suited to direct judicial enforcement. The specific issue before the ICJ concerned " 'review and reconsideration' " of the "possible prejudice" caused in each of the 51 affected cases by an arresting State's failure to provide the defendant with rights guaranteed by the Vienna Convention. . . . Judicial standards are readily available for working in this technical area. Legislative standards are not readily available. . . .

Sixth, to find the United States' treaty obligations self-executing as applied to the ICJ judgment (and consequently to find that judgment enforceable) does not threaten constitutional conflict with other branches; it does not require us to engage in nonjudicial activity; and it does not require us to create a new cause of action. The only question before us concerns the application of the ICJ judgment as binding law applicable to the parties in a particular criminal proceeding that Texas law creates independently of the treaty. . . .

Seventh, neither the President nor Congress has expressed concern about direct judicial enforcement of the ICJ decision. . . .

For these seven reasons, I would find that the United States' treaty obligation to comply with the ICJ judgment in *Avena* is enforceable in court in this case without further congressional action beyond Senate ratification of the relevant treaties. The majority reaches a different conclusion because it looks for the wrong thing (explicit textual expression about self-execution) using the wrong standard (clarity) in the wrong place (the treaty language). Hunting for what the text cannot contain, it takes a wrong turn. It threatens to deprive individuals, including businesses, property owners, testamentary beneficiaries, consular officials, and others, of the workable dispute resolution procedures that many treaties, including commercially oriented treaties, provide. In a world where commerce, trade, and travel have become ever more international, that is a step in the wrong direction.

. . . .

For the reasons set forth, I respectfully dissent.

SENATE FOREIGN RELATIONS COMMITTEE REPORT ON EXTRADITION TREATIES WITH THE EUROPEAN UNION

S. Exec. Rep. No. 110–12, at 9–1– (2008).

[As a part of its report in favor of Senate consent to ratification of 49 treaties involving the EU and its member states on extradition and mutual legal assistance, the Senate Foreign Relations Committee stated the following with respect to the multiple resolutions drafted for adoption by the Senate.]

In every resolution of advice and consent, the committee has included a proposed declaration that states that each treaty is self-executing. This declaration is consistent with statements made in the Letters of Submittal from the Secretary of State to the President on each of these instruments and with the historical practice of the committee in approving extradition treaties. Such a statement, while generally included in the documents associated with treaties submitted to the Senate by the executive branch and in committee reports, has not generally been included in Resolutions of advice and consent. The committee, however, proposes making such a declaration in the Resolution of advice and consent in light of the recent Supreme Court decision, *Medellín v. Texas*, 128 S.Ct. 1346 (2008), which has highlighted the utility of a clear statement regarding the self-executing nature of treaty provisions.

The committee believes it is of great importance that the United States complies with the treaty obligations it undertakes. In accordance with the Constitution, all treaties—whether self-executing or not—are the supreme law of the land, and the President shall take care that they be faithfully executed. In general, the committee does not recommend that the Senate give advice and consent to treaties unless it is satisfied that the United States will be able to implement them, either through implementing legislation, the exercise of relevant constitutional authorities, or through the direct application of the treaty itself in U.S. law. While situations may arise that were not contemplated when the treaty was concluded and ratified that raise questions about the authority of the United States to comply, the committee expects that such cases will be rare. Accordingly, in the committee's view, a strong presumption should exist against the conclusion in any particular case that the United States lacks the necessary authority in U.S. law to implement obligations it has assumed under treaties that have received the advice and consent of the Senate.

NOTE ON SELF-EXECUTING TREATIES

1. *Treaties as Supreme Law of the Land.* By reading just the text of the U.S. Constitution, one might have the impression that treaties have the same effect under U.S. law as do statutes. The "supremacy" clause (Article VI of the Constitution) states that "all Treaties made, or which shall be made, under Authority of the United States, shall be the supreme Law of the Land. . . ." Arguably, this means that a treaty negotiated by the President, to which the Senate has consented, and which has been ratified by the President in accordance with Article II, Section 2 of the Constitution, is deemed as effective a method of law-making as is the normal legislative procedure set out in Article I, Section 7, Clause 2. Is that how the framers understood the Constitution? Professor Michael Ramsey writes:

> Both opponents and defenders of the Constitution plainly understood that Article VI's designation of the Constitution and statutes as "supreme Law of the Land" made them judicially enforceable. Further, in general both sides saw Article VI as giving the same effect to treaties, and this became a central point of contention. Former Convention delegate George Mason wrote, "By declaring all Treaties supreme Laws of the land, the Executive & Senate have, in many Cases, an exclusive power of legislation." Antifederalist pamphleteers complained that the "president and two thirds of the Senate have power to make laws in the form of treaties, independent of the legislature itself," and that "there is one of the most important duties [that] may be managed in the senate and executive alone, and to have all the force of the law paramount without the aid or interference of the house of representatives; that is the power of making treaties." The main Federalist response was not to dispute the premise, but to argue that the supermajority rule in the Senate provided sufficient protection.

Michael D. Ramsey, *Toward a Rule of Law in Foreign Affairs*, 106 COLUM. L. REV. 1450, 1470 (2006). This understanding of Article VI may be discerned in the *Asakura* case. The treaty discussed therein was deemed by the Supreme Court to be "self-executing"—which is to say, it was treated by the Court as "supreme law of the land" exactly as if the treaty had been legislated by Congress, presented to the President, and signed by him into statutory law.

In addition to the *Asakura* case, the Supreme Court has on many occasions found a treaty provision to be self-executing, as Justice Breyer pointed out in an annex to his dissent in *Medellín*. *See* Olympic Airways v. Husain, 540 U.S. 644, 649, 657, 124 S.Ct. 1221, 157 L.Ed.2d 1146 (2004) (air carrier liability); El Al Israel Airlines, Ltd. v. Tsui Yuan Tseng, 525 U.S. 155,

161–163, 176, 119 S.Ct. 662, 142 L.Ed.2d 576 (1999) (same); Zicherman v. Korean Air Lines Co., 516 U.S. 217, 221, 231, 116 S.Ct. 629, 133 L.Ed.2d 596 (1996) (same); Société Nationale Industrielle Aérospatiale v. United States Dist. Court for Southern District of Iowa, 482 U.S. 522, 524, 533, 107 S.Ct. 2542, 96 L.Ed.2d 461 (1987) (international discovery rules); Sumitomo Shoji America, Inc. v. Avagliano, 457 U.S. 176, 181, 189–90, 102 S.Ct. 2374, 72 L.Ed.2d 765 (1982) (employment practices); Trans World Airlines, Inc. v. Franklin Mint Corp., 466 U.S. 243, 245, 252, 104 S.Ct. 1776, 80 L.Ed.2d 273 (1984) (air carrier liability); Kolovrat v. Oregon, 366 U.S. 187, n.6, 198, 81 S.Ct. 922, 6 L.Ed.2d 218 (1961) (property rights and inheritance); Clark v. Allen, 331 U.S. 503, 507–08, 517–18, 67 S.Ct. 1431, 91 L.Ed. 1633 (1947) (same); Bacardi Corp. of America v. Domenech, 311 U.S. 150, 161, 61 S.Ct. 219, 85 L.Ed. 98 (1940) (trademark); Todok v. Union State Bank of Harvard, 281 U.S. 449, 453, 455, 50 S.Ct. 363, 74 L.Ed. 956 (1930) (property rights and inheritance); Nielsen v. Johnson, 279 U.S. 47, 50, 58, 49 S.Ct. 223, 73 L.Ed. 607 (1929) (taxation); Jordan v. K. Tashiro, 278 U.S. 123, 128–129, 49 S.Ct. 47, 73 L.Ed. 214 (1928) (trade and commerce); Maiorano v. Baltimore & Ohio R. Co., 213 U.S. 268, 273–74, 29 S.Ct. 424, 53 L.Ed. 792 (1909) (travel, trade, access to courts); Johnson v. Browne, 205 U.S. 309, 317–22, 27 S.Ct. 539, 51 L.Ed. 816 (1907) (extradition); De Geofroy v. Riggs, 133 U.S. 258, 267–68, 273, 10 S.Ct. 295, 33 L.Ed. 642 (1890) (inheritance); Wildenhus's Case, 120 U.S. 1, 11, 17–18, 7 S.Ct. 385, 30 L.Ed. 565 (1887) (criminal jurisdiction); United States v. Rauscher, 119 U.S. 407, 410–11, 429–30, 7 S.Ct. 234, 30 L.Ed. 425 (1886) (extradition); Hauenstein v. Lynham, 100 U.S. 483, 485–86, 490–91, 25 L.Ed. 628 (1880) (property rights and inheritance); American Ins. Co. v. 356 Bales of Cotton, 26 U.S. (1 Pet.) 511, 542 (1828) (property); United States v. Arredondo, 31 U.S. (6 Pet.) 691, 697, 749, 8 L.Ed. 547 (1832) (land ownership); Orr v. Hodgson, 17 U.S. (4 Wheat.) 453, 462–465, 4 L.Ed. 613 (1819) (same); Chirac v. Lessee of Chirac, 15 U.S. (2 Wheat.) 259, 270–271, 274, 275, 4 L.Ed. 234 (1817) (land ownership and inheritance); Martin v. Hunter's Lessee, 14 U.S. (1 Wheat.) 304, 356–357, 4 L.Ed. 97 (1816) (land ownership); Hannay v. Eve, 7 U.S. (3 Cranch) 242, 248, 2 L.Ed. 427 (1806) (monetary debts); Hopkirk v. Bell, 7 U.S. (3 Cranch) 454, 457–458, 2 L.Ed. 497 (1806) (same); Ware v. Hylton, 3 U.S. (3 Dall.) 199, 203–204, 285, 1 L.Ed. 568 (1796) (same); Georgia v. Brailsford, 3 U.S. (3 Dall.) 1, 4, 1 L.Ed. 483 (1794) (same). Many more cases may be found at the circuit court level. *See, e.g.,* In re Premises Located at 840 140th Ave. NE, Bellevue, Wash., 634 F.3d 557, 567–68 (9th Cir. 2011) (mutual legal assistance).

2. *The Doctrine of "Non-Self-Executing" Treaties.* Yet beginning with *Foster & Elam v. Neilson*, the Supreme Court has maintained that some treaties do *not* automatically become the equivalent of statutory law in the sense of being enforceable in courts by the "beneficiaries" of its provisions. The sentiment behind the view seems animated by the language in the *Head Money Cases*, where the Court asserted that a "treaty is primarily a compact between independent nations. It depends for the enforcement of its provisions on the interest and the honor of the governments which are parties to it." 112 U.S. at 598. Under this vision of treaties, which may be seen in the *Medellín* case, treaties are not principally concerned with creating rights or obligations within domestic law. Some treaty provisions do, but whether a treaty provi-

sion becomes "law of the land" in this sense, or requires incorporation into the law by subsequent act of Congress, depends on whether the court finds that the particular provision is "self-executing."

A joint task force of the ABA Section of International Law and the American Society of International Law suggested that the *Medellín* case may:

- only affect the domestic enforceability of International Court of Justice decisions (a narrow interpretation)
- only affect treaty provisions that contemplate future action by states parties and are not specifically addressed to the judiciary (an intermediate interpretation)
- affect all treaties not affirmatively providing for judicial enforceability that might otherwise have been treated as self-executing (a broad interpretation)

See ABA Section of International Law/American Society of International Law Joint Task Force on Treaties in U.S. Law, *Report* (Mar. 16, 2009), *available at* http://www.asil.org/files/TreatiesTaskForceReport.pdf. Which interpretation do you think is correct? Do you discern one of these interpretations as favored by the Senate Foreign Relations Committee?

For analyses of the implications of the *Medellín* case, see David H. Moore, Medellín*, the Alien Tort Statute, and the Domestic Status of International Law*, 50 VA. J. INT'L L. 485 (2010); David H. Moore, *Do U.S. Courts Discriminate Against Treaties?: Equivalence, Duality, and Non–Self–Execution*, 110 COLUM. L. REV. 2228 (2010); A. Mark Weisburd, Medellín, *The President's Foreign Affairs Power and Domestic Law*, 28 PENN ST. INT'L L. REV. 595 (2010); Anthony S. Winer, *An Escape Route from the* Medellín *Maze*, 25 CONN. J. INT'L L. 331 (2010); David H. Moore, *Law (Makers) of the Land: The Doctrine of Treaty Non–Self–Execution*, 122 HARV. L. REV. 32 (2009); Carlos Vázquez, *Treaties as the Law of the Land: The Supremacy Clause and the Judicial Enforcement of Treaties*, 122 HARV. L. REV. 599 (2008); David J. Bederman, Medellín*'s New Paradigm for Treaty Interpretation*, 102 AM. J. INT'L L. 529, 529 (2008); Curtis Bradley, *Self-Execution and Treaty Duality*, 2008 SUP. CT. REV. 131; Curtis A. Bradley, *Intent, Presumptions, and Non–Self–Executing Treaties*, 102 AM. J. INT'L L. 540, 541 (2008); Julian G. Ku, Medellín*'s Clear Statement Rule: A Solution for International Delegations*, 77 FORDHAM L. REV. 609, 615 (2008).

3. *"Oops" Says Justice Marshall.* Ironically, four years after *Foster & Elam* was decided, Justice Marshall changed his position about the 1819 treaty with Spain. In *United States v. Percheman*, 32 U.S. (7 Pet.) 51 (1833), Justice Marshall found that the 1819 treaty with Spain *was* self-executing, since the Spanish version of the treaty should have been translated to read that land grants "shall remain ratified" rather than "shall be ratified."

4. *Factors in Finding a Treaty Self–Executing.* What factors do you think are important to a court when it finds that a treaty provision is not self-executing? Should there be a presumption, one way or the other, as to whether a treaty is self-executing?

Many courts appear to determine whether an agreement is self-executing by examining the intent of the parties. Intent might be discerned from the text of the treaty. Chief Justice Marshall viewed the language of the U.S.–Spain treaty in *Foster & Elam* as signaling an expectation of subsequent implementing legislation. Alternatively, intent may be discerned from statements made by the political branches separate from the treaty itself. For example, in *Cheung v. United States*, the Second Circuit found an agreement between the United States and Hong Kong to be self-executing by reference to statements made by the Executive when transmitting the agreement to Senate, to the effect that "this Agreement will not require implementing legislation." 213 F.3d 82, 95 (2d Cir. 2000).

Conversely, U.S. courts will give weight to a Senate reservation stating that a treaty, or particular provision of a treaty, is not self-executing (recall such a U.S. declaration when ratifying the Convention Against Torture). The Senate has begun reacting to the *Medellín* case, as seen in its treatment of the European Union treaties. In 2008, the Senate inserted declarations concerning the self- or non-self-executing nature for 78 of the 82 treaties to which it provided advice and consent. *See* U.S. Department of State, *Digest of U.S. Practice in International Law, 2008* 154 (Elizabeth Wilcox ed., 2010). Should it be constitutional for the Senate, on the one hand, to consent to ratification of a treaty, thus making it part of the "supreme law of the land," and yet, on the other hand, to assert that the treaty is not self-executing? *Compare* Stefan A. Riesenfeld & Frederick M. Abbott, *The Scope of U.S. Senate Control Over the Conclusion and Operation of Treaties*, 67 CHI.-KENT L. REV. 571, 577 (1991) *with* Curtis A. Bradley & Jack L. Goldsmith, *Treaties, Human Rights, and Conditional Consent*, 149 U. PA. L. REV. 399 (2000); *see also* ICCPR Human Rights Comm., General Comment 24, 52d Sess., 1382 mtg., para. 18, U.N. Doc. CCPR/C/21/Rev.1/Add.6 (1994) (finding that reservations violative of the treaty's object and purpose may be severed from the instrument of ratification, such that the treaty remains "operative for the reserving party without the benefit of the reservation.").

Are factors other than the intent of the U.S. treaty-makers important in determining whether a treaty is self-executing? What "contextual factors" did the majority of the Supreme Court in *Medellín* take into account? What factors did Justice Breyer consider in his dissent? Which side do you find more persuasive?

Do you think that a treaty containing hortatory or indeterminate language may be non-self-executing, whereas a treaty establishing clear standards may be self-executing, such as the treaty in *Asakura* (which simply called for application to Japanese aliens of standards applied to Americans)? What if a treaty sought to regulate a matter over which Congress has the sole competence to legislate (*e.g.*, the appropriation of funds); should it be regarded as self-executing? Sometimes courts seem to confuse the issue of whether a treaty is self-executing (*i.e.*, not in need of implementing legislation) with the issue of whether the treaty creates a private right of action. Treaties, just like statutes, may have full effect as U.S. law, but nevertheless not create a private right of action (*see* Note 6 below). For a discussion of different ways in which the doctrine of self-executing treaties operates in U.S. courts, see Carlos Manuel Vázquez, *The Four Doctrines of Self-Executing Treaties*, 89 AM. J. INT'L L. 695 (1995); Jordan J. Paust, *Self-Executing Treaties*, 82 AM. J. INT'L

L. 760 (1988). For a spirited discussion of whether *any* treaties should be self-executing, see 99 COLUM. L. REV. 1955–2258 (1999).

6. *Private Rights of Action.* Is the issue of whether a treaty is self-executing different from the issue of whether a treaty creates a private right of action? Bear in mind that a treaty might be raised as a defense, such as to establish an immunity. *See, e.g.,* Brzak v. United Nations, 597 F.3d 107 (2d Cir. 2010) (finding the U.N. Convention on Privileges and Immunities to be self-executing). Consider the following position taken by the U.S. government in September 2003 in the case of *McKesson HBOC, Inc. v. Iran* before the District Court for the District of Columbia:

> A treaty is self executing "whenever it operates of itself without the aid of any legislative provision." *Foster v. Neilson.* . . . But that means only that the treaty is "regarded in courts of justice as equivalent to an act of the legislature." *Id.* . . . Thus, a "self-executing" treaty preempts inconsistent state law, can be interpreted by federal courts, and may be relied upon as a defense to a state or federal claim. *See Ford v. United States,* 273 U.S. 593, 602, 611 (1927) (while treaty "creates no offense against the law of the United States" it may still provide a defense to prosecution).
>
> Like an Act of Congress, however, a treaty may establish legal standards or rules of decision in litigation without itself creating a private right of action. Indeed, there is a general presumption that treaty rights are *not* privately enforceable. *See* Goldstar (Panama) S.A. v. United States, 967 F.2d 965, 968 (4th Cir.) ("[i]nternational treaties are not presumed to create rights that are privately enforceable."), *cert. denied,* 506 U.S. 955 (1992). . . . As the Supreme Court said well over 100 years ago in the *Head Money Cases*:
>
>> A treaty is primarily a compact between independent nations. It depends for the enforcement of its provisions on the interest and the honor of the governments which are parties to it.
>
> 112 U.S. 580, 598, 5 S.Ct. 247, 28 L.Ed. 798 (1884). . . .
>
> In line with these governing principles, courts have interpreted various treaties as not providing private rights of action even though they are self-executing. . . . Most relevant here, in *Argentine Republic v. Amerada Hess Shipping Corp.*, 488 U.S. 428 (1989), the Supreme Court ruled that a foreign corporation could not sue Argentina for certain alleged wrongs, explaining that the treaties on which the respondents relied "only set forth substantive rules of conduct and state that compensation shall be paid for certain wrongs. They do not create private rights of action for foreign corporations to recover compensation from foreign states in United States courts." *Id.*, at 442 citing, in support *Head Money Cases*, 112 U.S. at 598–99, and *Foster*, 27 U.S. (2 Pet.) at 314 (footnote omitted). Thus, while the treaties established "substantive rules of conduct," they did not confer private rights of action, and the Court held they therefore did not constitute an express waiver of sovereign immunity for purposes of the Foreign Sovereign Immunities Act. *See* 488 U.S. at 442 (discussing 28 U.S.C. § 1604).

Statement of Interest of the United States, McKesson HBOC, Inc. v. Iran, Civ. Action No. 1:82–cv–00220 (RJL) (D.D.C.) (filed Sept. 29, 2003), *reprinted in part in* U.S. Department of State, *Digest of United States Practice in International Law 2003* at 259–61 (Sally J. Cummins & David P. Stewart eds., 2003). The D.C. Circuit ultimately concluded that the treaty did not provide a private cause of action, stating that it did not overcome "the presumption that international agreements do not create private rights or provide for a private right of action in U.S. courts." *See* McKesson v. Iran, 539 F.3d 485 (D.C. Cir. 2008); *see also* Katel Ltd. Liability Co. v. AT & T Corp., 607 F.3d 60 (2d Cir. 2010).

Thus, U.S. courts generally presume that treaties, as international agreements concluded among sovereign nations, do not create rights that are enforceable by an individual in a U.S. court. This general presumption, however, may be overcome, as has been acknowledged by the Supreme Court. *See* United States v. Alvarez–Machain, 504 U.S. 655, 667–68, 112 S.Ct. 2188, 119 L.Ed.2d 441 (1992).

Might the presumption be overcome by looking at the Senate's consent to the treaty? In its resolutions of advice and consent for nine treaties in 2008, the Senate included a statement that the treaty does not confer private rights enforceable in U.S. courts. *See* U.S. Department of State, *Digest of U.S. Practice in International Law, 2008*, at 154 (Elizabeth Wilcox ed. 2010). For one of those treaties, the Senate Foreign Relations Committee explained that it was making such a declaration "in light of the recent Supreme Court decision, *Medellín v. Texas,* 552 U.S. 491, 128 S.Ct. 1346, 170 L.Ed.2d 190 (2008), which has highlighted the utility of a clear statement regarding the self-executing nature of treaty provisions." *See* S. REP. NO. 110–26, at 9 (2008). If, when consenting to a treaty, the Senate indicates that a treaty is self-executing and either (1) says that it creates a private right of action or (2) is silent on whether it creates a private right of action, then should U.S. courts regard the general presumption as overcome?

Yet why should there be a general presumption that treaty rights are not privately enforceable in U.S. courts? While it is correct that under traditional international law individuals do not have rights under treaties (rather, states do), did not the framers of the Constitution declare treaties to be part of the supreme law of the land precisely to make treaties enforceable by individuals in U.S. courts? *See* Carlos Manuel Vázquez, *Treaty-Based Rights and Remedies of Individuals*, 92 COLUM. L. REV. 1082 (1992).

7. *Human Rights Treaties*. On the whole, U.S. courts have not been receptive to international human-rights and humanitarian treaty provisions as sources of U.S. domestic law. The United States has failed to ratify some of the principal treaties, and those that it has ratified often include U.S. declarations that the treaties are not to be regarded as self-executing. *See, e.g.*, Sosa v. Alvarez–Machain, 542 U.S. 692, 124 S.Ct. 2739, 159 L.Ed.2d 718 (2004) (International Covenant on Civil and Political Rights (ICCPR) is not self-executing); Serra v. Lappin, 600 F.3d 1191 (9th Cir. 2010) (same); Khan v. Holder, 584 F.3d 773 (9th Cir. 2009) (U.N. Protocol Relating to the Status of Refugees is not self-executing); Frolova v. USSR, 761 F.2d 370 (7th Cir. 1985)

(human rights provisions contained in the U.N. Charter and in the Helsinki Accords are not self-executing).

8. *World Trade Organization Agreements*. When adhering to the Uruguay Round Agreements of the World Trade Organization (WTO), Congress enacted a statute stating:

> No person other than the United States—
>
> (A) shall have any cause of action or defense under any of the Uruguay Round Agreements or by virtue of congressional approval of such an agreement, or
>
> (B) may challenge . . . any action or inaction by any department, agency, or any other instrumentality of the United States, any State, or any political subdivision of a State on the ground that such action or inaction is inconsistent with any such agreement.

19 U.S.C. § 3512(c)(1) (2006); *see also* Bronco Wine Co. v. Bureau of Alcohol, Tobacco & Firearms, 168 F.3d 498 (9th Cir. 1999) (finding that section 3512(c) bars private actions relating to the implementation of the Uruguay Round Agreements); Corus Staal BV v. Dept. of Commerce, 395 F.3d 1343 (Fed. Cir. 2005) (finding that the Commerce Department is not obligated to incorporate WTO procedures into its interpretation of U.S. law); ITC Ltd. v. Punchgini, Inc., 482 F.3d 135 (2d Cir. 2007) (finding that the Uruguay Round Agreement on Trade-Related Aspects of Intellectual Property Rights is not self-executing). Does the implementing statute preclude the use WTO agreements for *any* purpose in U.S. courts? For example, should U.S. litigants and courts make use of interpretations of U.S. obligations under WTO agreements issued by WTO dispute resolution panels, on grounds that the *Charming Betsy* principle (*see* Chapter 2, Section 2) calls for construing U.S. statutes in a manner consistent with international law, absent a clear congressional intent to the contrary? *See* Alex O. Canizares, *Is Charming Betsy Losing Her Charm? Interpreting U.S. Statutes Consistently with International Trade Agreements and the Chevron Doctrine*, 20 EMORY INT'L L. REV. 591 (2006).

9. *Practice in Other Countries*. In most common-law countries, the Executive is not obligated to inform or involve Parliament in treaty-making at any point. Nevertheless, Parliament typically remains the ultimate authority for creating national law, and thus often must adopt implementing legislation if the treaty requires certain conduct at the national level. *See* Joanna Harrington, *Scrutiny and Approval: The Role for Westminster–Style Parliaments in Treaty–Making*, 55 I.C.L.Q. 121 (2006) (reviewing the practice of Australia, Canada, South Africa, and the United Kingdom). Yet a study of the law of treaties in nineteen countries worldwide (common law, civil law, and other systems) reveals that many allow for some type of direct effect in national law. Professor Duncan Hollis categorizes these types as follows:

> 1.a. *Direct Effect upon Entry into Force*. Nearly two-thirds of the states surveyed considered treaties to operate directly as domestic law under certain circumstances. For one group of these states, a treaty's status as law turns solely on the completion of the procedures that authorize the executive to join a treaty. The conclusion of a treaty binding under international law provides it with attendant and automatic status as law

within the national legal system. For example, Mexico treats all treaties receiving Senate approval as "law of the land." Similarly, Switzerland views all its treaties as domestically applicable upon their international entry into force. In states that have sanctioned more than one procedure for joining a treaty, the completion of any one of the procedures may provide the treaty with its status as domestic law. Thus, the United States regards all its treaties as the supreme law of the land, whether they were concluded through the Senate advice and consent process, Congressional authorization, or pursuant to the President's own executive authorities.

Some states within this first group may restrict direct legal status to certain treaties or require the completion of additional procedures before some treaties will be treated as a law. On its face, Article 14 of Russia's constitution suggests a universal approach—"international treaties of the Russian Federation shall be an integral part of its legal system." Russia's Supreme Court, however, has interpreted this provision to apply only to those treaties that have received legislative approval. At present, therefore, executive treaties lack the status of law within the Russian Federation. In Germany, a law of approval will not only authorize the executive to join a treaty, but will also transform the treaty into German law. Alternatively, a law of enactment may be required to give other treaties the same effect, although that law would be enacted prior to the treaty's entry into force.

1.b. *Direct Effect Upon Entry into Force and Completion of Additional Steps.* A second group of states recognizes a treaty's direct legal effect, but only upon the completion of domestic procedures separate from those that authorized the formation of the treaty itself. For a few states, the only additional procedure required is publication. Thus, in Egypt, treaties qualify as law so long as they are in force *and* published. The Netherlands has a similar tradition, regarding published treaties as an integral part of the law of the land. For other states, publication must be associated with domestic promulgation of the treaty by the executive. France and Chile give treaties domestic legal status upon publication via a Presidential Decree. Japan follows a similar practice. A few states require separate legislative procedures to give treaties direct legal effect. Thailand allows publication to effectively incorporate its treaties into the internal laws of the Kingdom, but actual legislative enactment into Thai law is also used to transform treaty obligations into Thai law. South Africa more generally relies on legislative enactment to give any of its treaties (whether executive treaties or those subject to Parliamentary approval) the status of law.

Requiring [that] the completion of such separate procedures before a treaty can function as domestic law has several implications. First, it may mean that a treaty will bind the state internationally, but lack domestic legal effect pending publication. At the same time, a state with a publication requirement may not publish all its treaties, thereby depriving certain treaties of any direct status as law. France, for example, only publishes treaties the implementation of which affect[s] the rights or duties of individuals. Japan makes its decision to promulgate based on whether the treaty received the Diet's approval.

1.c. *Indirect Effect through Legislation.* For a third group of states, treaties do not operate in and of themselves as domestic law, regardless of what procedures are put in place. The United Kingdom serves as the leading proponent of this approach, although Canada, India, and Israel identify with it to varying extents. These states only give treaties indirect domestic legal effect through existing legislation or the enactment of new laws to enable compliance with the treaty's requirements. The legislation operates as the law, while the treaty itself has no such status. This means that without legislation, a treaty can have no relationship with the state's internal law whatsoever. For example, although it is a party to the Vienna Convention on Diplomatic Relations, Israel never adopted any implementing legislation for that treaty, leaving it outside of Israel's internal law.

In practice, however, indirect application of a treaty does not necessarily alter the actual legal effect of the treaty on the national legal order. True, in some cases, the treaty's legal effect may turn on the content of the implementing legislation, which may read differently than the treaty's actual text. It is possible, however, for the legislation to simply quote treaty provisions *verbatim*, which effectively converts an indirect effect into a direct one. For example, the United Kingdom enacted the provisions of the Vienna Convention on Diplomatic Relations directly into the Diplomatic Privileges Act of 1964. Thus, even if the treaty cannot be referred to as law, the implementing legislation can serve as its functional equivalent. Moreover, as these states have a practice of enacting any necessary implementing legislation prior to the conclusion of the treaty-making process, this indirect approach may actually result in giving internal validity to treaties faster than those states requiring promulgation or publication after entry into force.

See Duncan B. Hollis, *A Comparative Approach to Treaty Law and Practice,* in *National Treaty Law and Practice* 1, 41–44 (Duncan B. Hollis, Merritt R. Blakeslee, & L. Benjamin Ederington eds., 2005) (footnotes omitted) (published by Brill).

SECTION 5. DYNAMIC TREATY REGIMES

Most treaties create "static" obligations, meaning that the obligation created by the treaty stays the same throughout the life of the treaty. Yet treaties can change over time. One way that treaties change is through the process of interpretation or "reinterpretation"—a process considered in Section 9 below. Another way that treaties change is through the amendment process, where the parties to the treaty agree upon a change and then submit that change to the ratification process in the same way that they did the original treaty.

Certain types of treaty are crafted so that they can change in an even more dynamic way. Instead of changes being made through interpretive or amendment processes, the treaty may provide that certain changes can occur simply by agreement of the representatives of the parties. Such changes might occur at an annual meeting of the parties (often referred to as a "meeting of the parties," or MOP, or a "conference of the parties," or COP). Alternatively, the treaty might provide that changes can occur by an affirmative vote of a particular organ of an international organization. The decision by the MOP, COP, or international organization might require consensus, but examples exist of such decision-making by a simple majority or super-majority vote. States that are in the minority might be given a chance to "opt-out" of the change, but it is also possible for the treaty to bind the minority to the change. Normally, the treaty would not allow extreme changes to be made in this manner (such changes would have to occur through the amendment process), but the treaty would allow changes that are more limited in nature. *See* Annecoos Wiersema, *The New International Law–Makers? Conferences of the Parties to Multilateral Environmental Agreements*, 31 MICH. J. INT'L L. 231 (2009).

These "dynamic" treaty regimes raise interesting and important questions for U.S. foreign relations law. On the one hand, if the Senate has consented to a treaty regime that provides for dynamic changes, then arguably U.S. constitutional requirements have been satisfied. On the other hand, when the President and Senate accord to a MOP, COP, or international organization the power to change legal obligations under a treaty, are they abdicating their constitutional role of "making" treaty obligations for the United States? To the extent that such treaty changes have direct effect under U.S. law (since treaties are part of the "supreme law of the land"), are the U.S. political branches of government unconstitutionally delegating power to other political bodies?

Bear in mind that the whole point in having dynamic treaty regimes is because it is often difficult, with changing technologies, to be constantly changing treaties through the formal amendment process. The reason for wanting those changes to be binding is to avoid having the treaty simply be a constellation of political commitments. States may adhere to those political commitments, but it is typically thought that legal commitments are a stronger normative basis for promoting and compelling compliance. If one state (*e.g.*, the United States) fails to abide by its commitments or declares those commitments to be political in nature, other states may react in kind.

For example, consider the Montreal Protocol on Substances that Deplete the Ozone Layer, Sept. 16, 1987, S. TREATY DOC. 100–10 (1987), 1522 UNTS 3, *reprinted in* 26 ILM 1550 (1987). States that joined the treaty have agreed to the progressive reduction by specified dates of certain types of ozone-depleting chemicals listing in the annexes to the Protocol. There are different ways that the Protocol may be changed.

- *Amendments*. For a new chemical to be listed in an annex, the Protocol requires that the parties *amend* the treaty. Thus, the extreme change of adding an entirely new chemical must be done through the normal ratification processes. If a state does not ratify the amendment, the state incurs no obligation with respect to that chemical. For example, in 1992 an amendment was adopted by the COP adding methyl bromide (a widely used agricultural fumigant) as a covered chemical (part of the "Copenhagen Amendment"). The parties to the Protocol then underwent their normal ratification procedures such that by 2006 about 175 states had ratified this change. The remaining 16 states that had joined the Montreal Protocol but not ratified the amendment incurred no obligation under the amendment.

- *Adjustments*. Once a chemical is added to the treaty, however, the target date for reducing or eliminating the chemical can be changed by an *adjustment*. An adjustment does not require the normal ratification process, but it does require at least a two-thirds vote of the MOP (and preferably consensus), where that two-thirds of states represents at least half of global consumption of the chemical in question. For example, while the Copenhagen Amendment initially provided only that states not exceed their annual levels of consumption and production of methyl bromide using 1991 as a baseline, a subsequent MOP in 1997 decided to *adjust* the obligation to require a complete phase-out of the chemical beginning in January 2005 (called the "London Adjustment"), with some latitude for developing countries.

- *Decisions*. An adjustment may contemplate a further decision by the MOP that would allow a state temporarily to avoid its obligations under the adjustment. For example, the London Adjustment provided that, despite the complete phase-out, the MOP could "decide to permit the level of production or consumption that is necessary to satisfy uses agreed by them to be critical uses." In fact, the MOP issued a decision (called "Decision IX/6") setting general guidelines for when a methyl bromide "critical-use exemption" would be permitted and then issued a decision (called "Decision EX.I/3") granting the United States an exemption from the phase-out for certain amounts of methyl bromide to be used for certain purposes.

Thus, the Montreal Protocol treaty regime is dynamic in the sense that not only may amendments be made to the treaty through the normal ratification process, but further changes may be made simply through adjustments and decisions made within the MOP. Yet since these further changes are not expressly consented to by the U.S. Senate, do they create binding treaty obligations upon the United States? Do they have the effect of binding law within the United States?

NATURAL RESOURCES DEFENSE COUNCIL v. ENVIRONMENTAL PROTECTION AGENCY

464 F.3d 1, 1, 2–11 (D.C. Cir. 2006) (footnotes omitted).

RANDOLPH, CIRCUIT JUDGE.

The United States and other countries entered into the Montreal Protocol on Substances that Deplete the Ozone Layer, Sept. 16, 1987, S. TREATY DOC. NO. 100–10, 1522 U.N.T.S. 29 ("Montreal Protocol"), a treaty in which the signatory nations agreed to reduce the use of certain substances, including methyl bromide, that degrade the stratospheric ozone layer. The Environmental Protection Agency issued a rule implementing "critical use" exemptions from the treaty's general ban on production and consumption of methyl bromide. Protection of Stratospheric Ozone: Process for Exempting Critical Uses From the Phaseout of Methyl Bromide, 69 Fed.Reg. 76,982 (Dec. 23, 2004) (*codified at* 40 C.F.R. pt. 82) ("Final Rule"). . . .

. . . .

Amidst growing international concern about ozone depletion, the United States and twenty-four other nations entered into the Montreal Protocol. The Protocol requires signatory nations—which now number 189—to reduce and eliminate their production and use of ozone-depleting chemicals in accordance with agreed-upon timetables. Montreal Protocol arts. 2–2I. The Senate ratified the treaty in 1988, and Congress incorporated its terms into domestic law through the Clean Air Act Amendments of 1990, Pub.L. No. 101–549, tit. VI, 104 Stat. 2399, 2648. Since then, the United States has reduced its use of methyl bromide to less than 39% of its 1991 baseline.

In 1997, the Parties "adjusted" the Protocol to require developed-country Parties to cease "production" and "consumption" of methyl bromide by 2005. *See* Montreal Protocol art. 2H(5). In response, Congress amended the Clean Air Act to require EPA to "promulgate rules for reductions in, and terminate the production, importation, and consumption of, methyl bromide under a schedule that is in accordance with, but not more stringent than, the phaseout schedule of the Montreal Protocol Treaty as in effect on October 21, 1998." 42 U.S.C. § 7671c(h).

. . . .

In light of methyl bromide's wide use and the lack of comparable substitute pesticides, *see* Final Rule, 69 Fed.Reg. at 76,985, the Protocol allows exemptions from the general ban "to the extent that the Parties decide to permit the level of production or consumption that is necessary to satisfy uses agreed by them to be critical uses." Montreal Protocol art. 2H(5); *see also* 42 U.S.C. § 7671c(d)(6) ("To the extent consistent with the Montreal Protocol, the [EPA] Administrator . . . may exempt the production, importation, and consumption of methyl bromide for critical uses."). The Parties to the Protocol meet annually to "decide to permit the level of production or consumption that is necessary to satisfy uses agreed by them to be critical uses." Montreal Protocol art. 2H(5). At one of these meetings the Parties set general guidelines for implementing the critical-use exemptions, *see Ninth Report*, ... at 26–27 ("Decision IX/6"), and at another the Parties approved exemptions for 2005. The United States formally began the process of establishing its 2005 critical-use exemptions in May 2002, when EPA published a notice in the *Federal Register* seeking applications for 2005 and 2006 critical uses of methyl bromide and the amounts of new production and consumption needed to satisfy those uses. *See* Protection of Stratospheric Ozone: Process for Exempting Critical Uses From the Phaseout of Methyl Bromide, 67 Fed.Reg. 31,798 (May 10, 2002). EPA teams composed of biologists and economists reviewed each application and decided which to include in the aggregate U.S. nomination to the Parties. The final U.S. nomination, submitted to the Montreal Protocol's administrative body (the "Ozone Secretariat") in February 2003, requested a total exemption of about ten-thousand metric tons of methyl bromide for sixteen different uses.

The process then moved to the international stage. Two working groups operating under the auspices of the Ozone Secretariat—the "Methyl Bromide Technical Options Committee" and the "Technology and Economic Assessment Panel"—evaluated each country's nomination and made a recommendation to the Parties at their November 2003 meeting. At that meeting, the Parties deadlocked over the proposed critical-use exemptions and called an "extraordinary meeting" to make the final decisions. *See* U.N. Env't Programme, *Report of the Fifteenth Meeting of the Parties to the Montreal Protocol on Substances that Deplete the Ozone Layer*, U.N. Doc. UNEP/OzL.Pro.15/9, at 8–11, 77–78 (Nov. 11, 2003).

The Parties reached agreement at their First Extraordinary Meeting in March 2004. They granted the United States critical uses in sixteen categories, amounting to 8,942 metric tons of methyl bromide. To satisfy these critical uses, the Parties authorized 7,659 metric tons of new production and consumption, with the remainder (1,283 metric tons) to be made up from existing stocks of methyl bromide. *See* U.N. Env't Programme, *Report of the First Extraordinary Meeting of the Parties to the Montreal Protocol on Substances that Deplete the Ozone Layer*, U.N. Doc. UNEP/OzL.Pro.ExMP/1/3, at 14–15, 26 (Mar. 27, 2004) ("Decision Ex.I/3"). Decision Ex.I/3 noted that "each Party which has an agreed critical use should ensure that the criteria in paragraph 1 of decision IX/6 are applied when ... authorizing the use of methyl bromide and that such procedures take into account available stocks." *Id.* ¶ 5.

With Decision Ex.I/3 in hand, EPA proposed rules to implement the critical-use exemption. *See* Protection of Stratospheric Ozone: Process for Exempting Critical Uses From the Phaseout of Methyl Bromide, 69 Fed.Reg. 52,366 (Aug. 25, 2004). Many parties, including NRDC, submitted comments. The Final Rule, issued in December 2004, authorized new production and consumption up to the limit established in Decision Ex.I/3. Final Rule, 69 Fed.Reg. at 76,990 tbl.1. It also authorized the use of stocks as permitted by the decision, *id.* at 76,986, 76,991 tbl.2, and permitted noncritical users to draw upon existing stocks, *id.* at 76,988.

. . . .

. . . Paragraph 1 of Decision IX/6 directs the Parties to authorize new production and consumption of methyl bromide only if it "is not available in sufficient quantity and quality from existing stocks," Decision IX/6 ¶ 1(b)(ii), and only after "[a]ll technically and economically feasible steps have been taken to minimize the critical use," *id.* ¶ 1(b)(I).

NRDC believes EPA's rule departs from these post-treaty agreements in three respects. First, the rule authorizes 7,659 metric tons of new production and consumption—the maximum agreed upon in Decision Ex.I/3—without offsetting this amount by existing stocks.[1] *See* Final Rule, 69 Fed.Reg. at 76,989. EPA declined to disclose the size of the total nationwide methyl bromide stockpile, *see id.* at 76,990—an action NRDC claims is itself a violation of the Clean Air Act, 42 U.S.C. § 7607(d)(4)(B)(i). Still, the record suggests that the stockpile is at least as large as the United States' total critical-use allocation for 2005. Second, EPA's rule allows noncritical users to draw down existing stocks. *See* Final Rule, 69 Fed.Reg. at 76,987–88. NRDC claims that the "decisions" implicitly reserve the stocks for critical users only. Third, EPA approved 8,942 metric tons of critical uses—again the maximum agreed upon in Decision Ex.I/3—without considering anew whether this was the minimum amount feasible. *Id.* at 76,989. EPA counters that it adhered to the agreed-upon critical-use and new production and consumption levels, and that the remainder of the decisions are "hortatory." *Id.* at 76,987.

NRDC fashions the entirety of its argument around the proposition that the "decisions" under the Protocol are "law." This premise is flawed. The "decisions" of the Parties—post-ratification side agreements reached by consensus among 189 nations—are not "law" within the meaning of the Clean Air Act and are not enforceable in federal court.

The Clean Air Act authorizes EPA to "exempt the production, importation, and consumption of methyl bromide for critical uses" only "[t]o the extent consistent with the Montreal Protocol." 42 U.S.C. § 7671c(d)(6); *see also id.* § 7671m(b). The Protocol bans the production or consumption of methyl bromide after December 31, 2004, except "to the extent that the Parties decide to permit the level of production or consumption that is necessary to satisfy uses agreed by them to be critical uses." Montreal Protocol art. 2H(5). NRDC argues that because the Clean Air Act requires EPA to abide by the Protocol, and because the Protocol authorizes future agreements concerning the scope of the critical-use exemption, those future agreements must "define the scope of EPA's Clean Air Act authority." . . .

NRDC's interpretation raises significant constitutional problems. If the "decisions" are "law"—enforceable in federal court like statutes or

1. [Authors' Note: In other words, the NRDC believed that EPA should first take account of existing methyl bromide stocks before authorizing any further production.]

legislative rules—then Congress either has delegated lawmaking authority to an international body or authorized amendments to a treaty without presidential signature or Senate ratification, in violation of Article II of the Constitution. The Supreme Court has not determined whether decisions of an international body created by treaty are judicially enforceable. But there is a close analogy in this court. The United States is a party to a treaty establishing the International Court of Justice (ICJ). In *Committee of United States Citizens Living in Nicaragua v. Reagan*, 859 F.2d 929 (D.C.Cir.1988), we held that rulings of the ICJ do not provide "substantive legal standards for reviewing agency actions," *id.* at 942, because the rulings, though authorized by the ratified treaty, were not themselves self-executing treaties. *Id.* at 937–38; *see, e.g.*, Medellín v. Dretke, 544 U.S. 660, 682–84. . . . (2005) (O'Connor, J., dissenting).

Although *Committee of United States Citizens* is highly suggestive of the outcome in this case, several features of the Montreal Protocol "decisions" may distinguish them from ICJ "adjudications." For one thing, Congress implemented the Montreal Protocol with a direction to EPA to abide by its terms. *See* 42 U.S.C. §§ 7671c(d)(6), 7671m(b). For another, Montreal Protocol "decisions" are not adjudications between parties; instead, they purport to set rules for implementing ongoing treaty commitments.

The legal status of "decisions" of this sort appears to be a question of first impression. There is significant debate over the constitutionality of assigning lawmaking functions to international bodies. *See, e.g.*, Julian G. Ku, *The Delegation of Federal Power to International Organizations: New Problems with Old Solutions*, 85 MINN. L. REV. 71 (2000); Edward T. Swaine, *The Constitutionality of International Delegations*, 104 COLUM. L. REV. 1492 (2004). A holding that the Parties' post-ratification side agreements were "law" would raise serious constitutional questions in light of the nondelegation doctrine, numerous constitutional procedural requirements for making law, and the separation of powers.

We need not confront the "serious likelihood that the statute will be held unconstitutional." *Almendarez-Torres v. United States*, 523 U.S. 224, 238. . . . (1998); *see also id.* at 250 . . . (Scalia, J., dissenting). It is far more plausible to interpret the Clean Air Act and Montreal Protocol as creating an ongoing international political commitment rather than a delegation of lawmaking authority to annual meetings of the Parties. *Cf. Mistretta v. United States*, 488 U.S. 361, 373 n.7 . . . (1989).

Nowhere does the Protocol suggest that the Parties' post-ratification consensus agreements about how to implement the critical-use exemption are binding in domestic courts. The only pertinent language in Article 2H(5) states that the Parties will "decide to permit" production and consumption necessary to satisfy those uses that they "agree[ ]" to be critical uses. The Protocol is silent on any specific conditions accompanying the critical-use exemption. Post-ratification agreements setting these conditions are not the Protocol.

To illustrate, suppose the President signed and the Senate ratified a treaty with Germany and France to conserve fossil fuel. How this is to be accomplished the treaty does not specify. In a later meeting of representatives of the signatory countries at the United Nations, a consensus is reached to lower the speed limits on all major highways of the signatory nations to a maximum of 45 miles per hour. No one would say that United States law has thus been made.

EPA characterizes the decisions as "subsequent consensus agreements of the Parties that address the interpretation and application of the critical use provision. . . ." Final Rule, 69 Fed.Reg. at 76,985. This may be so. Like any interpretive tool, however, the "decisions" are useful only to the extent they shed light on ambiguous terms in the Protocol. But the details of the critical-use exemption are not ambiguous. They are nonexistent. The "decisions" do not interpret treaty language. They fill in treaty gaps.

Article 2H(5) thus constitutes an "agreement to agree." The parties agree in the Protocol to reach an agreement concerning the types of uses for which new production and consumption will be permitted, and the amounts that will be permitted. "Agreements to agree" are usually not enforceable in contract. *See* 1 Richard A. Lord, *Williston on Contracts* § 3:5, at 223–24 & n.17 (4th ed.1990); *cf. El Al Israel Airlines, Ltd. v. Tsui Yuan Tseng*, 525 U .S. 155, 167 . . . (1999); *Zicherman v. Korean Air Lines Co., Ltd.*, 516 U.S. 217, 226 . . . (1996); *Foster v. Neilson*, 27 U.S. (2 Pet.) 253, 314 (1829) ("A treaty is in its nature a contract between . . . nations."). And the fruits of those agreements are enforceable only to the extent that they themselves are contracts. There is no doubt that the "decisions" are not treaties.

The Parties' post-ratification actions suggest their common understanding that the decisions are international political commitments rather than judicially enforceable domestic law. *See Olympic Airways v. Husain*, 540 U.S. 644, 650 . . . (2004); *Tseng*, 525 U.S. at 167 . . .; *Restatement (Third) of Foreign Relations Law of the United States* § 325(2) (1987) ("Any subsequent . . . practice between the parties in the application of the agreement [is] to be taken into account in its interpretation."). The Parties met to decide the 2006 critical-use exemptions well after EPA's rule went into effect. . . . Yet they did not invoke the Protocol's internal noncompliance procedure against the United States, *see* Montreal Protocol art. 8, nor did they admonish the United States to change its interpretation of the previous decisions. This course of dealing suggests that the Parties intended the side agreements to be enforceable as a political matter at the negotiating table.

Our holding in this case in no way diminishes the power of the Executive to enter into international agreements that constrain its own behavior within the confines of statutory and treaty law. The Executive has the power to implement ongoing collective endeavors with other countries. *See* Louis Henkin, *Foreign Affairs and the Constitution* 219–20

(2d ed.1996). Without congressional action, however, side agreements reached after a treaty has been ratified are not the law of the land; they are enforceable not through the federal courts, but through international negotiations.

. . . .

. . . Because the post-ratification agreements of the parties are not "law," EPA's rule—even if inconsistent with those agreements—is not in violation of any domestic law within the meaning of the Clean Air Act, 42 U.S.C. § 7607(d)(9)(A), the petition for review is denied.

CONCLUDING NOTES ON DYNAMIC TREATY REGIMES

1. *Scope of the Court's Decision.* The D.C. Circuit was explicitly addressing whether "decisions" by the MOP about how to implement the critical-use exemption are binding under U.S. law; it did not have before it the broader issue of the status of all post-ratification changes, such as MOP "adjustments." Indeed, the U.S. government took the position before the court that the Clean Air Act *did* accord legal effect under U.S. law to MOP "adjustments," but not to MOP "decisions." Yet does the reasoning of the court suggest that *no* post-ratification change by the MOP, whether in the form of an "adjustment" or in the form of a "decision" for an exemption from an adjustment, can have the effect of law in the United States and be enforceable in U.S. courts?

2. *MOP Decisions as Political Commitments.* The D.C. Circuit took the position that the Clean Air Act and the Montreal Protocol simply created "an ongoing international political commitment rather than a delegation of law-making authority to annual meetings of the Parties." Further, the court characterizes the adjustments as "side agreements" and the adjustment process as an "agreement to agree." Is that right? The Montreal Protocol provides in Article 2(9)(d) that adjustment "decisions, which shall be binding on all Parties, shall be forthwith communicated to the Parties by the Depositary. Unless otherwise provided in the decisions, they shall enter into force on the expiry of six months from the date of the circulation and communication by the Depositary." As such, it would appear that the Senate consented to a treaty that contained a process within the MOP for creating binding obligations upon the United States as a matter of international treaty law. Since treaties are part of the supreme law of the land and the President is constitutionally obligated to faithfully execute the law, why should MOP decisions be viewed as creating just political commitments? *See* Andrew D. Finkelman, Note, *The Post-Ratification Consensus Agreements of the Parties to the Montreal Protocol: Law or Politics? An Analysis of* Natural Resources Defense Council v. EPA, 93 IOWA L. REV. 665 (2008).

3. *MOP Decisions as a Delegation of Power.* Assuming that the MOP adjustments do create binding obligations upon the United States, does U.S. ratification of the Montreal Protocol constitute an unconstitutional delegation of power? The non-delegation doctrine arises from the "vesting clauses" of the U.S. Constitution, by which the legislative, executive, and judicial powers are vested respectively in the three branches. *See* U.S. CONST. art. I, § 1, art.

II, § 1, & art. III, § 1. The doctrine states that these grants of power may not be reallocated, since doing so would impinge upon the basic checks and balances established under the Constitution, but that the branches can "coordinate" their conduct where there is an "intelligible principle" for doing so. *See* Hampton v. United States, 276 U.S. 394, 409, 48 S.Ct. 348, 72 L.Ed. 624 (1928) (finding that if Congress lays down an "intelligible principle" for allowing the Executive to under take acts in pursuance of Congress's will, then that act is "not a forbidden delegation of legislative power"). Since the 1930's, however, U.S. courts have largely abandoned the practice of striking down statutes on grounds that they unconstitutionally delegate congressional power to the executive. *See, e.g.,* Mistretta v. United States, 488 U.S. 361, 372, 109 S.Ct. 647, 102 L.Ed.2d 714 (1989) (finding that "in our increasingly complex society . . . Congress simply cannot do its job absent an ability to delegate power under broad general directives"); EPA v. American Trucking Ass'n, 531 U.S. 457, 473–75, 121 S.Ct. 903, 149 L.Ed.2d 1 (2001) (stating that the Court has "almost never felt qualified to second guess Congress regarding the permissible degree of policy judgment that can be left to those executing or applying the law"); *see also* Eric A. Posner & Adrian Vermeule, *Interring the Nondelegation Doctrine*, 69 U. CHI. L. REV. 1721 (2002).

Should the doctrine still have vitality when it comes to delegating power to a MOP or COP, or to an international organization? If so, are all areas of U.S. law that turn on decision-making by a MOP or COP best regarded as unconstitutional? *See, e.g.*, 16 U.S.C. § 1538(c)(1) (2006) (criminalizing within U.S. jurisdiction trading any of the species protected under the Convention on the International Trade in Endangered Species (CITES), Mar. 3, 1973, 27 U.S.T. 1087, 993 U.N.T.S. 243, where those species are listed and de-listed based on decisions of the biennial meetings of the CITES parties). Is this process best conceived as U.S. law-making that is being "delegated" to an international entity? Or are those entities engaging in a form of international law-making that cannot be done by the U.S. government, and hence cannot be regarded as vested in the U.S. government?

For commentary, see John O. McGinnis, Medellín *and the Future of International Delegation*, 118 YALE L.J. 1712 (2009); Andrew T. Guzman & Jennifer Landsidle, *The Myth of International Delegation*, 96 CAL. L. REV. 1693 (2008); Curtis A. Bradley & Judith G. Kelley, *The Concept of International Delegation*, 71 LAW & CONTEMP. PROBS. 1 (2008); Laurence R. Helfer, *Nonconsensual International Lawmaking*, 2008 U. ILL. L. REV. 71; Kristina Daugirdas, *International Delegations and Administrative Law*, 66 MD. L. REV. 707 (2007).

4. *MOP Decisions as Non–Self–Executing*. Rather than view such regimes as unconstitutional "delegations" of U.S. power, would it be better to regard them as a permissible exercise of the treaty power, but as involving treaty norms that are not self-executing as a matter of U.S. law (*see supra* Section 4)? Under that approach, there would need to be implementing legislation before the change could have effect in U.S. law. In the case of the adjustment for the phase-out of methyl bromide, the court correctly noted that Congress expressly blessed the methyl bromide adjustment process by statute. It did so by amending the Clean Air Act to require the EPA to "promulgate rules for reductions in, and terminate the production, importation, and consumption of, methyl bromide under a schedule that is in

accordance with, but not more stringent than, the phaseout schedule of the Montreal Protocol Treaty as in effect on October 21, 1998," 42 U.S.C. § 7671c(h) (2006). If you think that the statute cures any "delegation" problem, what exactly is gained by having Congress by statute authorize the EPA to follow decisions of the MOP? What does that add beyond the Senate's original consent to a treaty that contemplated such decision-making by the MOP?

Similarly, perhaps the issue is not whether MOP decisions create binding law (either internationally or nationally) or whether the political branches can delegate their power. Instead, perhaps the real issue is whether a private party may bring an action in federal court to enforce the binding obligation. Would it make a difference if the relevant treaty or implementing statute specifically accorded a right of action in U.S. courts, such as in the language discussed below regarding ICSID awards? Would language along these lines in either the Montreal Protocol or a statute, which spoke of enforcing "MOP decisions," solve the problem?

5. *Other Avenues of Dynamic Decision–Making: International Organizations.* The United States has been actively involved in numerous international organizations that make decisions that have effects within U.S. law. For example, in ratifying the 1944 Chicago Convention, the United States joined an International Civil Aviation Organization (ICAO) charged with creating rules for the safety of civil aviation worldwide. In addition to the rules contained in the Chicago Convention itself, ICAO's principal executive organ (the ICAO Council) adopts further rules (called "annexes" to the Chicago Convention) that bind ICAO's membership. Thus, Article 12 of the Chicago Convention requires that states adopt measures to ensure that aircraft of their nationality flying over the high seas conform with ICAO regulations on the "rules of the air." The United States implements this obligation by stating in the relevant FAA regulations that "[e]ach person operating a civil aircraft of U.S. registry outside of the United States shall . . . [w]hen over the high seas, comply with annex 2 (Rules of the Air) to the Convention on International Civil Aviation. . . ." 14 C.F.R. § 91.703(a) (2006). Further, the regulation states that Annex 2, "to which reference is made in this part, is incorporated into this part and made a part hereof. . . ." 14 C.F.R. § 91.703(b) (2006). Other examples of such direct incorporation include ICAO rules that foreign carriers within the United States conduct their operations in accordance with Annex 6 on the operation of aircraft and rules affirming that the system and procedures for sampling and measuring smoke emissions "shall be as specified by" *See* 14 C.F.R. § 129.11(a) (2006); ICAO annex 16. 40 C.F.R. § 87.82 (2006).

Does this deference to the decision-making of the ICAO Council constitute an unconstitutional delegation of power? Similar examples exist in other areas of regulation by international organizations.

6. *International Tribunal Decisions.* The court analogized to the situation where the United States ratifies a treaty that establishes an international court, and says that decisions by international courts cannot have binding effect within U.S. law. Yet while some international tribunal decisions have

not been enforced, there are situations where such decisions are regarded as creating binding obligations cognizable under U.S. law.

For example, the United States is a party to the Convention on the Settlement of Investment Disputes between States and Nationals of Other States, Mar. 18, 1965, 17 U.S.T. 1270, 575 U.N.T.S. 159 (ICSID Convention). The ICSID Convention allows for the rendering of arbitral awards by panels of arbitrators and provides, in Article 54(1), that each "Contracting State shall recognize an award rendered pursuant to this Convention as binding and enforce the pecuniary obligations imposed by that award within its territories as if it were a final judgment of a court in that State." U.S. implementing legislation instructs U.S. courts to give full faith and credit to ICSID judgments:

> An award of an arbitral tribunal rendered pursuant to chapter IV of the [ICSID] convention shall create a right arising under a treaty of the United States. The pecuniary obligations imposed by such an award shall be enforced and shall be given the same full faith and credit as if the award were a final judgment of a court of general jurisdiction of one of the several States.

22 U.S.C. § 1650a(a) (2006).

Similarly, the Convention on the Recognition and Enforcement of Foreign Arbitral Awards (New York Convention), June 10, 1958, 21 U.S.T. 2517, 330 U.N.T.S. 38, obligates the United States (and some 134 other countries) to enforce a private contract to submit a dispute to arbitration. It further obligates the enforcement of foreign arbitral awards once rendered. For the United States implementing legislation (chapter 2 of the Federal Arbitration Act), see 9 U.S.C. §§ 201–208 (2006). An analogous convention for just Western Hemisphere states, which has also been ratified by the United States, is the Inter–American Convention on International Commercial Arbitration, Jan. 30, 1975, 1438 U.N.T.S. 245, 14 I.L.M. 336 (Panama Convention). The U.N. Convention on the Law of the Sea, which the United States has not yet ratified, states that "decisions of the [Seabed Disputes] Chamber shall be enforceable in the territories of the States Parties in the same manner as judgments or orders of the highest court of the State Party in whose territory the enforcement is sought." U.N. Convention on the Law of the Sea annex VI, art. 39, Dec. 10, 1982, 1833 U.N.T.S. 397, 570.

In the context of the North American Free Trade Agreement (NAFTA), Dec. 8, 1992, 32 I.L.M. 296, the United States has even accepted that an international dispute panel can overturn U.S. administrative decisions concerning antidumping or countervailing duties. Prior to the NAFTA (and its predecessor agreement between just the United States and Canada), final determinations by the U.S. Department of Commerce regarding antidumping and countervailing duty matters against Canada and Mexico were appealed solely within the U.S. national legal system to the U.S. Court of International Trade. Under NAFTA Chapter 19, those decisions may now be appealed by either Canada or Mexico to arbitral panels constituted under the NAFTA, which are charged with deciding whether the U.S. final determination was consistent with U.S. law. The panel "may uphold a final determination, or remand it for action not inconsistent with the panel's decision" (NAFTA art. 1904(8)). Further, the decision "shall be binding on the involved Parties with respect to the particular matter between the Parties that is before the panel" (NAFTA art. 1904(9)). For example, in a case concerning Canadian softwood lumber products, a NAFTA panel in August 2004 ordered the Department of Commerce's International Trade Commission (ITC) to revoke its "threat of material injury" finding in antidumping and countervailing duty cases on Canadian softwood lumber. *Certain Softwood Lumber Products from Canada: Final Affirmative Threat of Injury Determination* (NAFTA Ch. 19 Panel. Aug. 31, 2004). In September 2004, the ITC revoked its finding.

To the extent that the United States joins such conventions, and enacts implementing legislation, are these unconstitutional delegations of power? Or is an inexorable process of "globalization" placing the United States in a position where such "delegation" must occur if the United States is to coordinate decision-making with other states in an effective manner?

7. *A Hypothetical Fossil Fuels Treaty.* The court in *NRDC v. EPA* hypothesized the conclusion of a treaty among France, Germany, and the United States that might result in lower speed limits on highways. To make the court's hypothetical truly analogous, one should postulate that the fossil fuels treaty specifically contemplates that the MOP may regulate on the issue of motor speed limits (that would be analogous to the Montreal Protocol specifically authorizing the MOP to regulate on the issue of methyl bromide consumption and production levels). Thus, the Senate would have expressly consented to a treaty that, by its terms, accorded to the MOP the ability to adjust motor speed limits, presumably because it was in the interest of the United States to have such a mechanism to help reduce fossil fuel consumption. When the MOP then decides that all parties are bound under the treaty to lower their speed limits to a maximum of 45 miles per hour, the D.C. Circuit says that "[n]o one would say that United States law has thus been made." Do you agree? Would you agree if there were also a federal statute directing the Department of Transportation to promulgate federal regulations consistent with the decisions of the MOP?

8. *Further Reading. See Delegating State Powers: The Effect of Treaty Regimes on Democracy and Sovereignty* (Thomas M. Franck ed., 2000); Julian G. Ku, *The Delegation of Federal Power to International Organizations: New Problems with Old Solutions*, 85 MINN. L. REV. 71 (2000); Curtis A. Bradley, *International Delegations, the Structural Constitution, and Non-Self-Execution*, 55 STAN. L. REV. 1557 (2003); David Golove, *The New Confederalism: Treaty Delegations of Legislative, Executive, and Judicial Authority*, 55 STAN. L. REV. 1697 (2003); Ernest A. Young, *The Trouble with Global Constitutionalism*, 38 TEX. INT'L L.J. 527 (2003); Edward T. Swaine, *The Constitutionality of International Delegations*, 104 COLUM. L. REV. 1492 (2004); Oona A. Hathaway, *International Delegation and State Sovereignty*, 71 L. & CONTEMP. PROB. 115 (2008).

SECTION 6. SCOPE AND HIERARCHICAL STATUS OF TREATIES IN U.S. LAW

INTRODUCTORY NOTE ON THE SCOPE OF THE TREATY POWER

Are there any substantive limitations on the scope of the treaty power? Can a treaty be concluded on any topic the President and Senate so desire? Must treaties only relate to things that are in some sense "external" to the United States or can they relate to matters that are largely internal, such as the treatment by the U.S. or state governments of U.S. nationals in the United States? Can the President and the Senate legislate by treaty on all matters falling *within* the scope of Article I, even though doing so cuts the House of Representatives out of the process? Could a treaty make a structural change to the operation of the U.S. government under the Constitution, such as delegating to the President the power to declare war in certain situations?

Ratification Debates. Concern about the scope of the treaty power dates back to the founding. John Jay argued in *The Federalist Papers* No. 64 that concerns about a broad scope of the treaty power should be allayed because of the political process that requires approval of a treaty:

> As all the States are equally represented in the Senate, and by men the most able and the most willing to promote the interests of their constituents, they will all have an equal degree of influence in that body, especially while they continue to be careful in appointing proper persons, and to insist on their punctual attendance. In proportion as the United States assume a national form and a national character, so will the good of the whole be more and more an object of attention, and the government must be a weak one indeed if it should forget that the good of the whole can only be promoted by advancing the good of each of the parts or members which compose the whole. It will not be in the power of the President and the Senate to make any treaties by which they and their families and estates will not be equally bound and affected with the rest of the community; and, having no private interests distinct from that of the nation, they will be under no temptations to neglect the latter.[1]

Such assurances, however, did not satisfy opponents of the Constitution. In Virginia's Convention on whether to ratify the U.S. Constitution, opponents expressed concern that the treaty power would be used by the federal government to affect important rights, such as ceding the territory west of the Mississippi to a foreign power, or granting aliens a right to own real property in Virginia, even though Virginia common law denied aliens such a right. Patrick Henry and George Mason led those who denounced such a treaty power. Henry's intervention is recorded as follows:

> Mr. HENRY begged gentlemen to consider the condition this country would be in if two thirds of a quorum should be empowered to make a treaty: they might relinquish and alienate territorial rights, and our most valuable commercial advantages. In short, if any thing should be left us,

1. *The Federalist Papers* No. 64, at 395 (Jay) (Clinton Rossiter ed., 1961).

it would be because the President and senators were pleased to admit it. The power of making treaties, by this Constitution, ill-guarded as it is, extended farther than it did in any country in the world. ... Treaties rest, says [Madison], on the laws and usages of nations. To say [under the proposed Constitution] that they are municipal is, to me, a doctrine totally novel. To make them paramount to the Constitution and laws of the states, is unprecedented.[2]

George Mason also opposed ratification, stating that if any such power existed, there should be certain subject-matter limitations placed upon it:

Will any gentleman say that they may not make a treaty [under the proposed Constitution], whereby the subjects of France, England, and other powers, may buy what lands they please in this country? This would violate those principles which we have received from the mother country. The indiscriminate admission of all foreigners to the first rights of citizenship, without any permanent security for their attachment to the country, is repugnant to every principle of prudence and good policy. The President and Senate can make any treaty whatsoever. We wish not to refuse, but to guard, this power, as it is done in England. The empire there cannot be dismembered without the consent of the national Parliament. We wish an express and explicit declaration, in [the proposed Constitution], that the power which can make other treaties cannot, without the consent of the national Parliament—the national legislature—dismember the empire. The Senate alone ought not to have this power; much less ought a few states to have it. No treaty to dismember the empire ought to be made without the consent of three fourths of the legislature in all its branches. Nor ought such a treaty be made but in case of the most urgent and unavoidable necessity.[3]

Since Henry and Mason ultimately lost, do their comments suggest that the treaty power as drafted in Article II has no subject-matter limits? Virginia Governor Edmund Randolph and James Madison responded in support of ratification. In assuring their opponents that their fears were unfounded, do Randolph and Madison's comments establish that there are limits to the treaty power? Randolph asserted:

Mr. Chairman, I conceive that neither the life nor property of any citizen, nor the particular right of any state, can be affected by a treaty. The lives and properties of European subjects are not affected by treaties, which are binding on the aggregate community in its political, social capacity.

The honorable gentleman says that, if you place treaties on the same footing here as they are in England, he will consent to the power, because the king is restrained in making treaties. Will not the President and Senate be restrained? Being creatures of that Constitution, can they destroy it? Can any particular body, instituted for a particular purpose, destroy the existence of the society for whose benefit it is created?[4]

2. *The Debates in the Several State Conventions, on the Adoption of the Federal Constitution, As Recommended by the General Convention at Philadelphia, in 1787,* at 500 (Jonathan Elliot ed., 2d ed. 1996) (1891) [hereinafter "3 *Elliot's Debates*"]

3. *Id.* at 509.

4. *Id.* at 504.

Meanwhile, Madison maintained:

> Does it follow, because this [treaty] power is given to Congress, that it is absolute and unlimited? I do not conceive that power is given to the President and Senate to dismember the empire, or to alienate any great, essential right. I do not think the whole legislative authority have this power. The exercise of the power must be consistent with the object of the delegation.
>
> . . . The object of treaties is the regulation of intercourse with foreign nations, and is external. I do not think it possible to enumerate all the cases in which such external regulations would be necessary. Would it be right to define all the cases in which Congress could exercise this authority? The definition might, and probably would, be defective. They might be restrained, by such a definition, from exercising the authority where it would be essential to the interest and safety of the community. It is most safe, therefore, to leave it to be exercised as contingencies may arise.[5]

The Jay Treaty. The scope of the treaty power remained an issue of contention for the early American Republic. In 1794, John Jay negotiated with Great Britain a treaty for settling several outstanding disputes and regularizing commerce. Article IX of the Jay Treaty provided:

> that British Subjects who now hold Lands in the Territories of the United States . . . shall continue to hold them according to the nature and Tenure of their respective Estates and Titles therein, and may grant Sell or Devise the same to whom they please, in like manner as if they were Natives. . . .[6]

This provision conflicted with the common law of most of the states, which denied the right of aliens to own real property. The Jay Treaty sparked an extensive controversy between the emerging Federalist and Democratic–Republican parties, which in part concerned the scope of the treaty power.

Robert Livingston wrote a series of essays under the pseudonym Cato arguing that treaties could not address subjects that Article I of the Constitution had assigned to Congress, unless the House of Representatives approved. Nor could treaties interfere in subjects not assigned to Congress, since those subjects were left to the states, unless the states agreed otherwise. Therefore, since Congress had not been accorded any power to regulate alien ownership of real property in the several states, that power was left to the states, which had not consented to it being addressed by treaty.[7]

The response of Federalists to such claims is best seen in a series of essays crafted by Alexander Hamilton in 1795–96 called *The Defence.* Hamilton asserted:

> It was impossible for words more comprehensive to be used than those which grant the power to make treaties. They are such as would

5. *Id.* at 514–15.

6. The Jay Treaty, U.S.-Gr. Brit., art. IX, Nov. 19, 1794, *reprinted in* 2 *Treaties and Other International Acts of the United States of America* 245, 253–54 (Hunter Miller ed., 1931).

7. *See* Robert Livingston, CATO No. XVI, *reprinted in* 3 *American Remembrancer* 63 (Mathew Carey ed., 1795).

> naturally be employed to confer a *plenipotentiary* authority. A power "to make Treaties," granted in these indefinite terms, extends to all kinds of treaties and with all the latitude which such a power under any form of Government can possess. ... With regard to the objects of the Treaty, there being no specification, there is of course a *charte blanche.* The general proposition must therefore be that whatever is a proper subject of compact between Nation & Nation may be embraced by a Treaty. ...[8]

For Hamilton, the breadth of the Supremacy Clause was meant to ensure that the federal government did not have to rely on the states to pursue and secure compliance with U.S. treaty obligations.

Hamilton's position prevailed. After receiving the consent of the Senate, President Washington ratified the treaty, and even the House of Representatives voted to support it. Thereafter, a case came before the Supreme Court addressing the effect of the Jay Treaty on states rights. In *Fairfax Devisee v. Hunter's Lessee,* the Supreme Court (per Justice Story) upheld the Jay Treaty against Virginia state law, finding that Article IX, "being the supreme law of the land, confirmed the title to [a British subject, Denny Martin Fairfax], his heirs and assigns, and protected him from any forfeiture by reason of alienage."[9] Interestingly, one of the lawyers involved in this protracted litigation in support of Fairfax's title was none other than John Marshall, who became Chief Justice by the time of *Fairfax Devisee* and therefore did not sit in the case.

Jefferson's Manual. Nevertheless, states-rights advocates continued to lament the scope of the treaty power. After the Democratic–Republicans experienced considerable losses in the election of 1796 to the Federalists, Thomas Jefferson wrote a *Manual of Parliamentary Practice* while serving as Vice President and presiding officer in the Senate. Published just prior to Jefferson's ascension to the Presidency in 1801, the *Manual* states in part:

> By the Constitution of the United States, this department of legislation [*i.e.,* treaty-making] is confined to two branches only of the ordinary Legislature—the President originating, and the Senate having a negative. To what subject this power extends, has not been defined in detail by the Constitution; nor are we entirely agreed among ourselves. 1. It is admitted that it must concern the foreign nation, party to the contract, or it would be a mere nullity, *res inter alias acta.* 2. By the general power to make treaties, the Constitution must have intended to comprehend only those objects which are usually regulated by treaty, and cannot be otherwise regulated. 3. It must have meant to except out of these the rights reserved to the States; for surely the President and Senate cannot do by treaty what the whole government is interdicted from doing in any way. 4. And also to except those subjects of legislation in which it gave a participation to the House of Representatives. This last exception is denied by some, on the ground that it would leave very little matter for the treaty power to work on. The less the better, say others.[10]

---

8. Alexander Hamilton, *The Defence* No. XXXVI (Jan. 2, 1796), *reprinted in* 20 *The Papers of Alexander Hamilton* 3, 6 (Harold C. Syrett ed., 1974).

9. 11 U.S. (7 Cranch) 603, 627, 3 L.Ed. 453 (1812).

10. Thomas Jefferson, *A Manual of Parliamentary Practice* § 52 (1801), *reprinted in* 2 *The Writings of Thomas Jefferson* 335, 442 (Albert Ellery Bergh ed., 1904).

Does Jefferson's *Manual* evoke the same arguments as that of the earlier Cato? If Jefferson (and Cato) are correct, and treaties may not address subjects within the scope of Congress's power or outside the scope of the federal government as a whole, then what is left of the treaty power?

Further, did Jefferson stay true to his views when, as President, he used the treaty power to acquire vast new territory in the form of the 1803 Louisiana Purchase and to incorporate its inhabitants into the United States? The power of the U.S. government to purchase or otherwise acquire territory is not enumerated in Article I of the Constitution, and yet it would be odd to regard it as reserved to the several states. So does it fall within the limited zone for treaties envisaged in Jefferson's *Manual*?[11]

SANTOVINCENZO v. EGAN

284 U.S. 30, 40, 52 S.Ct. 81, 76 L.Ed. 151 (1931).

[An 1878 U.S.-Italy consular convention provided that when an Italian national died intestate in the United States, the proceeds would be paid to the Italian Consul for distribution in accordance with Italian law (and vice versa for U.S. nationals in Italy). By contrast, New York law provided that the proceeds would escheat to the state. Upon the death intestate of an Italian national, the Italy's Consul General in New York sought the proceeds, but New York's Attorney General contested the claim. The U.S. Supreme Court found for the Consul General. In doing so, the Court discussed the scope of the treaty power.]

There can be no question as to the power of the Government of the United States to make the Treaty. . . . The treaty-making power is broad enough to cover all subjects that properly pertain to our foreign relations, and agreement with respect to the rights and privileges of citizens of the United States in foreign countries, and of the nationals of such countries within the United States, and the disposition of the property of aliens dying within the territory of the respective parties, is within the scope of the power, and any conflicting law of the State must yield. . . .

NOTES: ARE THERE LIMITS TO THE SCOPE OF THE TREATY POWER?

1. *Commentary*. Commentators cannot agree on the exact scope of the treaty power and controversies occasionally resurface. Indeed, the issue was raised in the first volume of the AMERICAN JOURNAL OF INTERNATIONAL LAW. *See* Chandler P. Anderson, *The Extent and Limitations of the Treaty-Making Power Under the Constitution*, 1 AM. J. INT'L L. 636 (1907); *see also* Comment,

---

11. *See* American Ins. Co. v. Canter, 26 U.S. (1 Pet.) 511, 542, 7 L.Ed. 242 (1828) (Chief Justice Marshall finding that the "Constitution confers absolutely on the government of the Union, the powers of making war, and of making treaties; consequently, that government possesses the power of acquiring territory, either by conquest or by treaty"). On Jefferson's willingness to bend the Constitution to support his presidential initiative, see IV Dumas Malone, *Jefferson and His Time [Jefferson the President: First Term, 1801–1805]*, at 311–332 (1970). Jefferson wrote to Secretary of State James Madison: "I infer that the less we say about constitutional difficulties respecting Louisiana the better, and that what is necessary for surmounting them must be done sub silentio." *Id.* at 316.

Constitutional Law: The Treaty Making Power and the Constitution, 6 CORNELL L.Q. 91 (1920); Comment, *Treaty-Making Power as Support for Federal Legislation,* 29 YALE L.J. 445 (1920); Note, *The Power to Make Treaties,* 20 COLUM. L. REV. 692 (1920); Comment, *Constitutional Law: Encroachment by Treaty Upon the Reserve Powers of the States,* 8 CAL. L. REV. 177 (1920).

Not surprisingly the issue re-emerged with the decisions in *United States v. Pink*, 315 U.S. 203, 62 S.Ct. 552, 86 L.Ed. 796 (1942) and *United States v. Belmont* (this Chapter, Section 7), which upheld the U.S.-USSR Litvinov Assignment over challenges based on the takings clause of the Fifth Amendment and state laws governing the assignment of claims. The Litvinov Assignment was part of an executive agreement providing that Soviet claims to Russian assets in the United States would be assigned to the U.S. government and used to settle claims of American creditors resulting from Soviet nationalization decrees. Settlement was a precondition to establishing diplomatic relations with the Soviet government. *See, e.g.*, D. Barlow Burke, *Federal Treaties and State Sovereignty,* 46 DICK. L. REV. 246 (1942); Henry S. Fraser, *The Constitutional Scope of Treaties and Executive Agreements,* 31 A.B.A. J. 286 (1941); J. Mervyn Jones, *Constitutional Limitations on the Treaty-Making Power,* 35 AM. J. INT'L L. 462 (1941).

2. *U.S. Treaty Practice and the Several States.* Various bilateral and multilateral treaties now address subjects that had once been the preserve of state regulation. In *Santovincenzo*, a New York inheritance statute fell in the face of a consular treaty. Some of these treaties operate alone, while others operate in conjunction with federal implementing legislation. Consider the following:

- Numerous treaties grant foreign nationals the right to practice certain professions or provide certain services in the United States (and grant U.S. nationals reciprocal rights abroad) even though state governments regulate the specified professions or services. *See, e.g.*, Treaty of Friendship, Commerce and Consular Rights, U.S.–Hond., art. I, Dec. 7, 1927, T.S. No. 764, 87 L.N.T.S. 421; Treaty of Friendship, Commerce and Navigation, U.S.–Italy, art. I, Feb. 2, 1948, T.I.A.S. No. 1965, 79 U.N.T.S. 171; North American Free Trade Agreement, U.S.–Can.–Mex., chs. 12 (cross-border trade in services) & 14 (financial services), Dec. 17, 1992, 32 I.L.M. 289 & 605 (1993).
- Various treaties accord privileges and immunities to foreign nationals that must be respected by the several states, such as exemption from state criminal prosecution or from the payment of state taxes. *See, e.g.*, Treaty of Friendship, Commerce and Consular Rights, U.S.-Austria, art. XV, June 19, 1928, T.S. No. 838, 118 L.N.T.S. 241; Vienna Convention on Diplomatic Relations, Apr. 18, 1961, 23 U.S.T. 3227, 500 U.N.T.S. 95.
- Several treaties regulate areas of "private international law," which deals with both private business and family-relations matters. For example, the Convention on the Recognition and Enforcement of Foreign Arbitral Awards, done at New York June 10, 1958, 21 U.S.T. 2517, 330 U.N.T.S. 38, obligates U.S. courts (with limited exceptions) to enforce certain private contracts that provide for the submission of

disputes to arbitration and enforcement of the arbitral award once rendered, regardless of conflicting state laws. *See, e.g.*, Lim v. Offshore Specialty Fabricators, Inc., 404 F.3d 898 (5th Cir. 2005) (preempting Louisiana law).

- Various treaties require the enactment of U.S. criminal statutes on issues such as narcotics, terrorism, or organized crime, which in turn preempt state law. *See, e.g.*, United Nations Convention Against the Illicit Traffic in Narcotic Drugs and Psychotropic Substances, Dec. 20, 1988, S. TREATY DOC. NO. 101–4 (1989), 1582 U.N.T.S. 95; International Convention for the Suppression of Terrorist Bombings, G.A. Res. 52/164, annex (Dec. 15, 1997); United Nations Convention against Transnational Organized Crime (TOC Convention), Nov. 15, 2000, S. TREATY DOC. NO. 108–16 (2003), G.A. Res. 55/25, annexes I (main convention), II (protocol on trafficking in persons), & III (protocol on smuggling migrants) (Nov. 15, 2000).

3. *Drafting Around the Problem.* Are there ways the political branches might craft U.S. treaty obligations to avoid intruding upon core state functions? Consider the following reservation that was placed by the United States when it ratified the U.N. Convention Against Transnational Organized Crime, Nov. 15, 2000, S. TREATY DOC. NO. 108–16 (2003):

> The United States of America reserves the right to assume obligations under the Convention in a manner consistent with its fundamental principles of federalism, pursuant to which both federal and state criminal laws must be considered in relation to the conduct addressed in the Convention. U.S. federal criminal law, which regulates conduct based on its effect on interstate or foreign commerce, or another federal interest, serves as the principal legal regime within the United States for combating organized crime, and is broadly effective for this purpose. Federal criminal law does not apply in the rare case where such criminal conduct does not so involve interstate or foreign commerce, or another federal interest. There are a small number of conceivable situations involving such rare offenses of a purely local character where U.S. federal and state criminal law may not be entirely adequate to satisfy an obligation under the Convention. The United States of America therefore reserves to the obligations set forth in the Convention to the extent they address conduct which would fall within this narrow category of highly localized activity. This reservation does not affect in any respect the ability of the United States to provide international cooperation to other Parties as contemplated in the Convention.

See http://www.unodc.org/unodc/crime_cicp_signatures_convention.html. Does this suggest a theory for embracing international obligations while being sensitive to issues of federalism?

NOTE ON THE HIERARCHICAL STATUS OF TREATIES IN U.S. LAW

How exactly do treaties (assuming that they are self-executing) fit into the hierarchy of U.S. law to the extent that conflicts arise? As you read the following materials, consider the following possibilities:

- Treaties are of an equivalent legal status to the U.S. Constitution. The Supremacy Clause in Article VI says that three things are "the supreme law of the Land": (1) the Constitution; (2) laws "made in Pursuance" of the Constitution; and (3) treaties made "under the Authority of the United States." Arguably, this means that laws enacted by Congress must conform to the Constitution, but treaties may not. So long as treaties are made in accordance with Article II and are properly authorized, they can act essentially as amendments to the Constitution.
- Treaties are equivalent in legal status to a federal statute. A treaty that is inconsistent with the Constitution is invalid as a matter of U.S. law. A constitutionally valid treaty can repeal a pre-existing conflicting statute, and always supersede conflicting federal common law or state law.
- Treaties are inferior to the Constitution and to federal statutes, since the latter—by involving both houses of Congress—are a more democratic form of legislation. Thus, a treaty does not repeal a conflicting pre-existing statute. Nevertheless, treaties are superior to inconsistent federal common law or state law.

Based solely on your reading of Article VI, which of these possibilities do you favor? As a practical matter, does one of these possibilities commend itself?

MISSOURI v. HOLLAND

252 U.S. 416, 430–35, 40 S.Ct. 382, 64 L.Ed. 641 (1920).

MR. JUSTICE HOLMES delivered the opinion of the Court.

This is a bill in equity brought by the State of Missouri to prevent a game warden of the United States from attempting to enforce the Migratory Bird Treaty Act of July 3, 1918, c. 128, 40 Stat. 755, and the regulations made by the Secretary of Agriculture in pursuance of the same. The ground of the bill is that the statute is an unconstitutional interference with the rights reserved to the States by the Tenth Amendment, and that the acts of the defendant done and threatened under that authority invade the sovereign right of the State and contravene its will manifested in statutes. The State also alleges a pecuniary interest, as owner of the wild birds within its borders and otherwise. . . . A motion to dismiss was sustained by the District Court on the ground that the Act of Congress is constitutional. . . . The State appeals.

On December 8, 1916, a treaty between the United States and Great Britain was proclaimed by the President. It recited that many species of birds in their annual migrations traversed many parts of the United States and of Canada, that they were of great value as a source of food and in destroying insects injurious to vegetation, but were in danger of extermination through lack of adequate protection. It therefore provided for specified close[d] seasons and protection in other forms, and agreed that the two powers would take or propose to their law-making bodies the necessary measures for carrying the treaty out. 39 Stat. 1702. The above mentioned act of July 3, 1918, ... [gave] effect to the convention, prohibited the killing, capturing or selling any of the migratory birds included in the terms of the treaty except as permitted by regulations compatible with those terms, to be made by the Secretary of Agriculture. Regulations were proclaimed on July 31, and October 25, 1918. 40 Stat. 1812, 1863. It is unnecessary to go into any details, because, as we have said, the question raised is the general one whether the treaty and statute are void as an interference with the rights reserved to the States.

To answer this question it is not enough to refer to the Tenth Amendment, reserving the powers not delegated to the United States, because by Article II, § 2, the power to make treaties is delegated expressly [to the federal government], and by Article VI treaties made under the authority of the United States, along with the Constitution and laws of the United States made in pursuance thereof, are declared the supreme law of the land. If the treaty is valid there can be no dispute about the validity of the statute under Article I, § 8, as a necessary and proper means to execute the powers of the Government. The language of the Constitution as to the supremacy of treaties being general, the question before us is narrowed to an inquiry into the ground upon which the present supposed exception is placed.

It is said that a treaty cannot be valid if it infringes the Constitution, that there are limits, therefore, to the treaty-making power, and that one such limit is that what an act of Congress could not do unaided, in derogation of the powers reserved to the States, a treaty cannot do. An earlier [1913] act of Congress that attempted by itself and not in pursuance of a treaty to regulate the killing of migratory birds within the States had been held bad in the District Court. *United States v. Shauver*, 214 Fed. Rep. 154. *United States v. McCullagh*, 221 Fed. Rep. 288. Those decisions were supported by arguments that migratory birds were owned by the States in their sovereign capacity for the benefit of their people, and that under cases like *Geer v. Connecticut*, 161 U.S. 519, this control was one that Congress had no power to displace. The same argument is supposed to apply now with equal force.

Whether the two cases cited were decided rightly or not they cannot be accepted as a test of the treaty power. Acts of Congress are the supreme law of the land only when made in pursuance of the Constitution, while treaties are declared to be so when made under the authority of the United States. It is open to question whether the authority of the United States means more than the formal acts prescribed to make the convention. We do not mean to imply that there are no qualifications to the treaty-making power; but they must be ascertained in a different way. It is obvious that there may be matters of the sharpest exigency for the national well being that an act of Congress could not deal with but that a treaty followed by such an act could, and it is not lightly to be assumed that, in matters requiring national action, "a power which must belong to and somewhere reside in every civilized government" is not to be found. *Andrews v. Andrews*, 188 U.S. 14, 33. What was said in that case with regard to the powers of the States applies with equal force to the powers of the nation in cases where the States individually are incompetent to act. We are not yet discussing the particular case before us but only are considering the validity of the test proposed. With regard to that we may add that when we are dealing with words that also are a constituent act, like the Constitution of the United States, we must realize that they have called into life a being the development of which could not have been foreseen completely by the most gifted of its begetters. It was enough for them to realize or to hope that they had created an organism; it has taken a century and has cost their successors much sweat and blood to prove that they created a nation. The case before us must be considered in the light of our whole experience and not merely in that of what was said a hundred years ago. The treaty in question does not contravene any prohibitory words to be found in the Constitution. The only question is whether it is forbidden by some invisible radiation from the general terms of the Tenth Amendment. We must consider what this country has become in deciding what that Amendment has reserved.

The State as we have intimated founds its claim of exclusive authority upon an assertion of title to migratory birds, an assertion that is embodied in statute. No doubt it is true that as between a State and its inhabitants the State may regulate the killing and sale of such birds, but it does not follow that its authority is exclusive of paramount powers. To put the claim of the State upon title is to lean upon a slender reed. Wild birds are not in the possession of anyone; and possession is the beginning of ownership. The whole foundation of the State's rights is the presence within their jurisdiction of birds that yesterday had not arrived, tomorrow may be in another State and in a week a thousand miles away. If we are to be accurate we cannot put the case of the State upon higher ground than that the treaty deals with creatures that for the moment are within the state borders, that it must be carried out by officers of the United States within the same territory, and that but for the treaty the State would be free to regulate this subject itself.

As most of the laws of the United States are carried out within the States and as many of them deal with matters which in the silence of such laws the State might regulate, such general grounds are not enough to support Missouri's claim. Valid treaties of course "are as binding within the territorial limits of the States as they are elsewhere throughout the dominion of the United States." *Baldwin v. Franks*, 120 U.S. 678, 683. No doubt the great body of private relations usually fall within the control of the State, but a treaty may override its power. We do not have to invoke the later developments of constitutional law for this proposition; it was recognized as early as *Hopkirk v. Bell*, 3 Cranch, 454, with regard to statutes of limitation, and even earlier, as to confiscation, in *Ware v. Hylton*, 3 Dall. 199. It was assumed by Chief Justice Marshall with regard to the escheat of land to the State in *Chirac v. Chirac*, 2 Wheat. 259, 275; *Hauenstein v. Lynham*, 100 U.S. 483; *De Geofroy v. Riggs*, 133 U.S. 258; *Blythe v. Hinckley*, 180 U.S. 333, 340. So as to a limited jurisdiction of foreign consuls within a State. *Wildenhus' Case*, 120 U.S. 1. *See Ross v. McIntyre*, 140 U.S. 453. Further illustration seems unnecessary, and it only remains to consider the application of established rules to the present case.

Here a national interest of very nearly the first magnitude is involved. It can be protected only by national action in concert with that of another power. The subject-matter is only transitorily within the State and has no permanent habitat therein. But for the treaty and the statute there soon might be no birds for any powers to deal with. We see nothing in the Constitution that compels the Government to sit by while a food supply is cut off and the protectors of our forests and our crops are destroyed. It is not sufficient to rely upon the States. The reliance is vain, and were it otherwise, the question is whether the United States is forbidden to act. We are of opinion that the treaty and statute must be upheld. . . .

Decree affirmed.

REID v. COVERT

354 U.S. 1, 3–19, 77 S.Ct. 1222, 1 L.Ed.2d 1148 (1957) (some footnotes omitted).

[Two spouses of U.S. soldiers, one in the United Kingdom (Clarice Covert) and one in Japan (Dorothy Smith), murdered their husbands. The United States was accorded jurisdiction over the spouses pursuant to bilateral agreements: Executive Agreement, U.S.-U.K., July 27, 1942, 57 Stat. 1193; Administrative Agreement, U.S.-Japan, Feb. 28, 1952, T.I.A.S. 2492, 3 U.S.T. 3341. Although the spouses were not members of the U.S. armed services, they were tried and convicted by court martial under the Uniform Code of Military Justice (UCMJ), which, among other things, did not provide for an indictment by a grand jury or a trial by jury. The spouses challenged the convictions as violating their rights under Article III, Section 2 and the Fifth and Sixth Amendments of the U.S. Constitution.]

MR. JUSTICE BLACK announced the judgment of the Court and delivered an opinion, in which THE CHIEF JUSTICE, MR. JUSTICE DOUGLAS, and MR. JUSTICE BRENNAN join.

These cases raise basic constitutional issues of the utmost concern. They call into question the role of the military under our system of government. They involve the power of Congress to expose civilians to trial by military tribunals, under military regulations and procedures, for offenses against the United States thereby depriving them of trial in civilian courts, under civilian laws and procedures and with all the safeguards of the Bill of Rights. . . .

. . . .

At the beginning we reject the idea that when the United States acts against citizens abroad it can do so free of the Bill of Rights. The United States is entirely a creature of the Constitution. Its power and authority have no other source. It can only act in accordance with all the limitations imposed by the Constitution. When the Government reaches out to punish a citizen who is abroad, the shield which the Bill of Rights and other parts of the Constitution provide to protect his life and liberty should not be stripped away just because he happens to be in another land. . . .

. . . .

At the time of Mrs. Covert's alleged offense, an executive agreement was in effect between the United States and Great Britain which permitted United States' military courts to exercise exclusive jurisdiction over offenses committed in Great Britain by American servicemen or their dependents. For its part, the United States agreed that these military courts would be willing and able to try and to punish all offenses against the laws of Great Britain by such persons. In all material respects, the same situation existed in Japan when Mrs. Smith killed her husband. Even though a court-martial does not give an accused trial by jury and other Bill of Rights protections, the Government contends that Art. 2 (11) of the UCMJ, insofar as it provides for the military trial of dependents accompanying the armed forces in Great Britain and Japan, can be sustained as legislation which is necessary and proper to carry out the United States' obligations under the international agreements made with those countries. The obvious and decisive answer to this, of course, is that no agreement with a foreign nation can confer power on the Congress, or on any other branch of Government, which is free from the restraints of the Constitution.

Article VI, the Supremacy Clause of the Constitution, declares:

> "This Constitution, and the Laws of the United States which shall be made in Pursuance thereof; and all Treaties made, or which shall be made, under the Authority of the United States, shall be the supreme Law of the Land; . . ."

There is nothing in this language which intimates that treaties and laws enacted pursuant to them do not have to comply with the provisions of the Constitution. Nor is there anything in the debates which accompanied the drafting and ratification of the Constitution which even suggests such a result. These debates as well as the history that surrounds the adoption of the treaty provision in Article VI make it clear that the reason treaties were not limited to those made in "pursuance" of the Constitution was so that agreements made by the United States under the Articles of Confederation, including the important peace treaties which concluded the Revolutionary War, would remain in effect. It would be manifestly contrary to the objectives of those who created the Constitution, as well as those who were responsible for the Bill of Rights—let alone alien to our entire constitutional history and tradition—to construe Article VI as permitting the United States to exercise power under an international agreement without observing constitutional prohibitions. In effect, such construction would permit amendment of that document in a manner not sanctioned by Article V. The prohibitions of the Constitution were designed to apply to all branches of the National Government and they cannot be nullified by the Executive or by the Executive and the Senate combined.

There is nothing new or unique about what we say here. This Court has regularly and uniformly recognized the supremacy of the Constitution over a treaty.[33] For example, *de Geofroy v. Riggs*, 133 U.S. 258, 267, it declared:

> "The treaty power, as expressed in the Constitution, is in terms unlimited except by those restraints which are found in that instrument against the action of the government or of its departments, and those arising from the nature of the government itself and of that of the States. It would not be contended that it extends so far as to authorize what the Constitution forbids, or a change in the character of the government or in that of one of the States, or a cession of any portion of the territory of the latter without its consent."

. . . .

There is nothing in *Missouri v. Holland*, 252 U.S. 416, which is contrary to the position taken here. There the Court carefully noted that the treaty involved was not inconsistent with any specific provision of the Constitution. The Court was concerned with the Tenth Amendment which reserves to the States or the people all power not delegated to the National Government. To the extent that the United States can validly make treaties, the people and the States have delegated their power to the National Government and the Tenth Amendment is no barrier.

In summary, we conclude that the Constitution in its entirety applied to the trials of Mrs. Smith and Mrs. Covert. . . . [The plurality decision further found that the necessary and proper clause of Article 1, Section 8, could not be stretched to validate military jurisdiction over a person not a member of the class described in Clause 14, *i.e.*, "land and naval Forces."]

NOTE: CAN TREATIES "TRUMP" THE CONSTITUTION?

1. *The Bricker Amendment.* In the 1950s, a conservative Ohio Republican, Senator John W. Bricker, sponsored an amendment to the Constitution declaring that no treaty could be made by the United States that: (1) conflicted with the U.S. Constitution; (2) was self-executing; or (3) granted Congress legislative powers beyond those enumerated in the Constitution. The amendment also limited the President's power to enter into executive agreements. (Over the years the amendment evolved in various formulae. For its initial formulation, see *Treaties and Executive Agreements: Hearing on S.J. Res. 130 Before a Subcomm. of the S. Comm. on the Judiciary*, 82d Cong. 21 (1952)).

For Bricker and his colleagues, Holmes's dictum in *Missouri v. Holland* (suggesting that treaties are not bound by constitutional limitations), combined with the ability of treaties to be self-executing, seriously threatened states rights. These concerns increased after a California court invalidated a

---

33. *E.g., United States v. Minnesota*, 270 U.S. 181, 207–08; *Holden v. Joy*, 17 Wall. 211, 242–243; *The Cherokee Tobacco*, 11 Wall. 616, 620–621; *Doe v. Braden*, 16 How. 635, 657. *Cf. Marbury v. Madison*, 1 Cranch 137, 176–180. We recognize that executive agreements are involved here but it cannot be contended that such an agreement rises to greater stature than a treaty.

discriminatory state alien land law on the ground that it violated the U.N. Charter. *See* Fujii v. State, 217 P.2d 481 (Cal. Ct. App. 1950). The California Supreme Court, however, later found that the relevant U.N. Charter provisions were not self-executing, striking down the land law on other grounds. *See* Sei Fujii v. California, 38 Cal.2d 718, 722–25, 242 P.2d 617 (1952).

Senator Bricker claimed that his constitutional amendment would "prohibit the use of the treaty as an instrument of domestic legislation," and would "prevent its use as a vehicle for surrendering national sovereignty." Indeed, he wished to "plug" the "loophole" of *Missouri v. Holland. See Treaties and Executive Agreements: Hearing on S.J. Res. 1 Before the Subcomm. on Constitutional Amendments of the S. Comm. on the Judiciary*, 84th Cong. 19 (1955). The proposed amendment attracted considerable support (including that of the American Bar Association), with the debate raging in Congress, in the media, and among constitutional lawyers. *See, e.g.*, Arthur E. Sutherland, Jr., *Restricting the Treaty Power,* 65 HARV. L. REV. 1305 (1952); Arthur H. Dean, *Amending the Treaty Power,* 6 STAN. L. REV. 589 (1954). In February 1954, a floor vote was taken (on Senator George's substitute), resulting in a tally of 60 to 31 in favor, one vote short of the two-thirds requirement. The operative language of the defeated amendment read:

> Section 1. A provision of a treaty or other international agreement which conflicts with this Constitution shall not be of any force or effect.
>
> Section 2. An international agreement other than a treaty shall become effective as internal law in the United States only by an act of the Congress.

See 100 CONG. REC. 853 (1954) (proposal of the substitute); 100 CONG. REC. 2358 (1954) (replacement of the committee text with the substitute); 100 CONG. REC. 2374–75 (1954) (defeat of the proposed amendment). Afterwards, the effort flagged, especially in the wake of the Supreme Court's finding in *Reid v. Covert* that a treaty may not operate in a manner inconsistent with the U.S. Constitution.

2. *The Basic Principle. Reid* indicates that international agreements must be consistent with the Constitution, but the judgment was announced as a plurality decision; only four justices joined in its legal reasoning. Does this undermine the precedential value of *Reid*? Justice Frankfurter and Justice Harlan's concurring opinions did not question or challenge the Court's reasoning as it related to the relationship of international agreements to the U.S. Constitution. Rather, they focused on whether, in some circumstances, it would be permissible for civilian dependents of members of the armed forces to be tried overseas by court martial based on Congress's power under Article I, Section 8, Clause 14, to "make Rules for the Government and Regulation of the land and naval Forces." Thus, neither the plurality nor Justices Frankfurter and Harlan regarded international agreements as being supreme over the Constitution. Relying upon *Reid*, the *Restatement (Third) on the Foreign Relations Law of the United States*, § 302(2) (1987) states: "No provision of an agreement may contravene any of the prohibitions or limitations of the Constitution applicable to the exercise of authority by the United States"; *see also, id.*, Reporters' Note 1.

3. *Constitutional Prohibitions.* In light of *Reid*, it is generally accepted that a treaty that contravenes the first eight amendments of the Bill of Rights (safeguarding individual rights), the Eleventh Amendment (limiting suits against the several states), or the Fourteenth Amendment (applying Bill of Rights protections to the states) would be invalid as a matter of U.S. law (though it may still bind the United States under international law). Likewise, a treaty that sought to reallocate Constitutional power (*e.g.*, transferring the power to declare war from Congress to the President) likely would be struck down by U.S. courts.

4. *Limiting* Reid *to Executive Agreements?* Technically, the international agreements at issue in *Reid* were "executive agreements" (*see* Section 7 *infra*), not "treaties." They were agreements concluded by the President without congressional involvement based on legal authority emanating from pre-existing treaties. Does that fact weaken *Reid* as a precedent that *treaties* concluded under Article II, Section 2, cannot contravene the Constitution? The *Reid* plurality saw no significance in the fact that the agreements before the Court were executive agreements and asserted that, in many cases, such as *De Geofroy v. Riggs*, 133 U.S. 258, 10 S.Ct. 295, 33 L.Ed. 642 (1890), the Court had declared the supremacy of the Constitution over a treaty. Even in *Missouri v. Holland,* which is often read as announcing a broad treaty power for the federal government, Justice Holmes stated that a treaty cannot stand in the face of "prohibitory words" contained in the Constitution.

5. *Post-*Reid *Developments.* The reason Clarice Covert and Dorothy Smith were prosecuted before a military court was that, at the time, there was no alternative jurisdiction available under U.S. law. State criminal laws in the United States typically only cover crimes committed in each state, not crimes committed elsewhere. Further, federal law at the time of *Covert* did not criminalize murder abroad. In part to solve this problem, Congress enacted in 2000 the Military Extraterritorial Jurisdiction Act (MEJA), 18 U.S.C. §§ 3261–67 (2006). MEJA creates federal jurisdiction over crimes committed abroad by civilians who are "accompanying or employed by" U.S. military forces. Thus, all civilian employees of the military, civilian contractors and subcontractors, and dependents are covered, and they may be prosecuted in federal courts for federal crimes they commit abroad. MEJA does not create new substantive offenses, but incorporates by reference existing federal crimes on murder, manslaughter, assault, and sexual abuse.

6. *Relationship to Treaty Ratification.* Since the basic principle of *Reid* indicates that the Constitution "trumps," or supercedes, treaties, the U.S. government is wary of joining treaties that will obligate the United States internationally but cannot be fulfilled as a matter of U.S. constitutional law, a situation that especially arises with respect to human-rights treaties. Thus, the United States has declined to join certain treaties, such as the Convention on the Rights of the Child, Nov. 20, 1989, 1577 U.N.T.S. 3, arguing that doing so would intrude inappropriately into core matters of family law that are constitutionally reserved to the several states. Further, even when the United States has joined treaties, it has filed reservations, understandings, or declarations (RUDs) designed to protect existing constitutional rights or state prerogatives. Many of the RUDs filed by the United States when ratifying the Convention Against Torture may be seen in this light (*see supra*, Section 2).

Similar RUDs were made when the United States ratified the International Covenant on Civil and Political Rights (ICCPR), Dec. 16, 1966, 999 U.N.T.S. 171, and the International Convention on the Elimination of All Forms of Racial Discrimination (CERD), Dec. 21, 1965, 660 U.N.T.S. 195. For both the ICCPR and CERD, the United States declared that the treaty's substantive rights were not self-executing. For both, the United States included an understanding that recognized the role of federalism in U.S. law. For the ICCPR, the federalism understanding read that

> the United States understands that this Covenant shall be implemented by the Federal Government to the extent that it exercises legislative and judicial jurisdiction over matters covered therein, and otherwise by the state and local governments; to the extent that the state and local governments exercise jurisdiction over such matters, the Federal Government shall take measures appropriate to the Federal system to the end that the competent authorities of the state or local governments may take appropriate measures for the fulfillment of the Covenant.

138 CONG. REC. 8071 (1992).

7. *Treaties and Religious Freedom.* In the Religious Freedom Restoration Act (RFRA), Congress prohibited the federal government from substantially burdening a person's exercise of religion "even if the burden results from a rule of general applicability," 42 U.S.C. § 2000bb–1(a) (2006), except when the Government can "demonstrat[e] that application of the burden to the person (1) [furthers] a compelling government interest; and (2) is the least restrictive means of furthering that ... interest," § 2000bb–1(b) (2000). In *Gonzales v. O Centro Espirita Beneficiente Uniao do Vegetal*, 546 U.S. 418, 126 S.Ct. 1211, 163 L.Ed.2d 1017 (2006), the Supreme Court considered whether the U.S. government could regulate the use of hallucinogenic tea by an American branch of a religious sect based in the Amazon rainforest. Members of the church (UDV) receive communion by drinking a sacramental tea brewed from plants unique to the rainforest, which are called hoasca (pronounced "wass-ca"). The U.S. government maintained that the tea, which contains an illegal drug called dimethyltryptamine (DMT), violated U.S. narcotics laws as well as U.S. obligations under the U.N. Convention on Psychotropic Substances, which prohibit importation of DMT. The Supreme Court considered whether the Convention could be regarded as supporting a "compelling interest" of the U.S. government to regulate this aspect of religious liberty. Chief Justice Roberts wrote for the Court:

> Before the District Court, the Government ... asserted an interest in compliance with the 1971 United Nations Convention on Psychotropic Substances, Feb. 21, 1971, [1979–1980], 32 U.S.T. 543, T.I.A.S. No. 9725. The Convention, signed by the United States and implemented by the Controlled Substances Act, calls on signatories to prohibit the use of hallucinogens, including DMT. The Government argues that it has a compelling interest in meeting its international obligations by complying with the Convention.
>
> . . . .
>
> The fact that hoasca is covered by the Convention, however, does not automatically mean that the Government has demonstrated a compelling

interest in applying the Controlled Substances Act, which implements the Convention, to the UDV's sacramental use of the tea. At the present stage, it suffices to observe that the Government did not even submit evidence addressing the international consequences of granting an exemption for the UDV. The Government simply submitted two affidavits by State Department officials attesting to the general importance of honoring international obligations and of maintaining the leadership position of the United States in the international war on drugs. . . . We do not doubt the validity of these interests, any more than we doubt the general interest in promoting public health and safety by enforcing the Controlled Substances Act, but under RFRA invocation of such general interests, standing alone, is not enough.

126 S. Ct. at 1224–25.

8. *Altering Constitutional Allocation of Power.* Can an international agreement really not alter the allocation of power set forth in the Constitution? Consider that question in the context of international panels created by treaty to review domestic administrative decisions, which occurred first under the U.S.-Canada Free Trade Agreement, Can.-U.S., Jan. 2, 1988, 27 I.L.M. 281 (1988) [hereinafter FTA] and then in its successor agreement, the North American Free Trade Agreement, U.S.-Can.-Mex., Dec. 17, 1992, 32 I.L.M. 289 & 605 [hereinafter NAFTA]. Article III of the Constitution vests judicial power in federal courts subject to the regulation of Congress, and those courts normally review decisions taken by U.S. administrative agencies. May the President enter into an international agreement instead, vesting binding review of certain U.S. administrative decisions in an international tribunal?

The FTA and NAFTA were international agreements in the form of "congressional-executive agreements" (thus authorized by a majority vote of both Houses of Congress rather than by a two-thirds majority of just the Senate; *see infra* Section 7). To alleviate concerns about bias in national courts, Chapter Nineteen of the FTA and the NAFTA provides for international panels of arbitrators to make binding decisions about final determinations relating to antidumping and countervailing duties made by administrative agencies of each country (in the United States, such orders are made by the Department of Commerce and the U.S. International Trade Commission; in Canada, such orders are made by the Canada Border Services Agency and the Canadian International Trade Tribunal; in Mexico, such orders are made by the Secretaría de Economía, Unidad de Prácticas Comerciales Internacionales).

When Chapter Nineteen was first proposed for the FTA, some members of Congress saw it as constitutionally suspect. They pointed to a denial of due-process rights and infringements on executive, congressional, and judicial power in the following features of the Chapter Nineteen process: (1) the unique "supranational" nature of the international panels; (2) the procedure for appointing the panelists; (3) the panels' ability to interpret national law and precedent; and (4) the panels' authority to make binding, nonreviewable determinations. *See United States–Canada Free–Trade Agreement: Hearing Before the Senate Comm. on the Judiciary*, 100th Cong. (1988); H.R. REP. NO. 100–816, pt. 4 (1988). Ultimately, Congress approved the FTA in legislation that preserved the jurisdiction of Article III courts to review constitutional questions not addressed by a panel. The House Committee on the Judiciary made the following report:

> After an extensive review of the FTA and the constitutional and legal issues, the Committee has concluded that the binational panel mechanism of the FTA and its implementing legislation is constitutional. The FTA and implementing legislation are the product of extensive discussions and dialogue between the legislative and executive branches, and thus carries more than the usual presumption of constitutionality. Where federal courts are faced with fundamental constitutional questions, concerning the FTA it is likely that the shared responsibility for regulating foreign commerce and foreign affairs possessed by these two branches will place the FTA "on strong constitutional ground." It is in large part the international context of this Agreement—impinging on the regulation of both foreign affairs and foreign commerce—that makes the binational panel review process constitutional.
>
> Article III of the Constitution grants Congress general authority to affect federal court jurisdiction. In the case of the FTA—involving adjudication of government-created "public rights"—that Congressional authority permits the removal of statutory claims from ordinary judicial review mechanisms. This is particularly true where, as here, the review function will be performed by an international body applying international law.
>
> Substitution of panel review for the preexisting system of judicial review does not deprive anyone of due process. The binational panel process contemplates the selection of five panelists: two from the United States, two from Canada and a fifth selected either by agreement or in the case of disagreement, by lot. The panelists are charged with a duty to apply the law and precedent of the relevant country. The panels will use the basic rules of appellate procedure as they exist in the United States and Canada, respectively. In addition, the panelists will be subject to a strict code of ethics and will be subject to peremptory challenges by each government. Finally, the FTA provides for a review mechanism of aberrant panel decisions through the use of extraordinary challenge committees. Thus, the binational panel process meets any requirements for a fundamentally fair process. To the extent that the Constitution requires a judicial forum for the adjudication of constitutional claims—both facial and as applied—the implementing legislation accomplishes that goal.
>
> As Professor Andreas Lowenfeld put it:
>
> > While some aspects of the [FTA] are unique . . . overall it fits within the traditions of the foreign relations law of the United States, both with respect to dispute settlement and with respect to legislation concerning international trade.

H.R. REP. NO. 100–816, pt. 4, at 4–5 (1988) (footnotes omitted).

After the FTA entered into force on January 1, 1989, several binational panels convened to resolve disputes concerning U.S. final antidumping and countervailing duty orders. *See, e.g.*, In the Matter of Fresh, Chilled, and Frozen Pork from Canada, 12 I.T.R.D. (BNA) 2299 (Binational Panel 1990);

Replacement Parts for Self–Propelled Bituminous Paving Equipment from Canada, 12 I.T.R.D. (BNA) 1297 (Binational Panel 1990). Similarly, after the NAFTA entered into force on January 1, 1994, several such panels also issued decisions. *See, e.g.*, Certain Corrosion–Resistant Carbon Steel Flat Products from Canada, Full Sunset Review (NAFTA Ch. 19 Panel Oct. 19, 2004). For an analysis that finds such adjudication constitutionally permissible, see Henry Paul Monaghan, *Article III and Supranational Review*, 107 COLUM. L. REV. 833 (2007).

9. Missouri*'s Continued Vitality*. Despite recent Supreme Court cases protective of state sovereignty, the Supreme Court has evinced no desire to alter the robust position taken by *Missouri v. Holland* with respect to the breadth of the treaty power. In 1999, the Supreme Court quoted *Missouri* approvingly when considering whether a U.S. treaty with an Indian tribe could grant the tribe hunting and fishing privileges on state land, preempting conflicting state law or policy. The Court found: "Although States have important interests in regulating wildlife and natural resources within their borders, this authority is shared with the Federal Government when the Federal Government exercises one of its enumerated constitutional powers, such as treaty making. U.S. CONST., Art. VI, cl. 2. *See, e.g., Missouri v. Holland*, 252 U.S. 416, 40 S.Ct. 382, 64 L.Ed. 641 (1920). . . ." Minnesota v. Mille Lacs Band of Chippewa Indians, 526 U.S. 172, 204, 119 S.Ct. 1187, 143 L.Ed.2d 270 (1999). In 2004, the Supreme Court cited *Missouri* favorably for the proposition that the treaty power (in conjunction with the Indian Commerce Clause) provided Congress plenary power to regulate the exercise of criminal jurisdiction by Indian tribes. Among other things, Justice Breyer noted that the treaty power authorized Congress to implement matters that it could not otherwise legislate under Article I. *See* United States v. Lara, 541 U.S. 193, 201, 124 S.Ct. 1628, 158 L.Ed.2d 420 (2004). Overall, as of 2006, members of the Court had cited *Missouri* in thirty-four opinions, none of which overturned it. *See* Duncan B. Hollis, *Executive Federalism: Forging New Federalist Constraints on the Treaty Power*, 79 S. CAL. L. REV. 1327, 1353 (2006). Professor Hollis suggests that a close reading of the Court's decisions indicates five reasons that the Court "is unlikely to re-examine *Missouri* any time soon: (i) support for *Missouri* on the Court; (ii) judicial reluctance to review treaties; (iii) renewed deference to the foreign affairs power; (iv) re-emergence of broader conceptions of Congress' legislative powers; and (v) Executive interpretations of the treaty power's scope." *Id.* at 1352–60; *see also* Peter J. Spiro, *Resurrecting* Missouri v. Holland, 73 MO. L. REV. 1029 (2008).

10. *What About Treaties Versus Statutes*? If the Constitution always prevails in the event of a conflict with a treaty, what about when a treaty conflicts with a Federal statute?

WHITNEY v. ROBERTSON

124 U.S. 190–95, 8 S.Ct. 456, 31 L.Ed. 386 (1888).

MR. JUSTICE FIELD delivered the opinion of the court.

The plaintiffs are merchants, doing business in the city of New York, and in August, 1882, they imported a large quantity of "centrifugal and molasses sugars," the produce and manufacture of the island of San Domingo.[1] These goods were similar in kind to sugars produced in the Hawaiian Islands, which are admitted free of duty under the treaty with the king of those islands, and the act of Congress, passed to carry the treaty into effect. They were duly entered at the custom house at the port of New York, the plaintiffs claiming that by the treaty with the Republic of San Domingo the goods should be admitted on the same terms, that is, free of duty, as similar articles, the produce and manufacture of the Hawaiian Islands. The defendant, who was at the time collector of the port, refused to allow this claim, treated the goods as dutiable articles under the acts of Congress, and exacted duties on them to the amount of $21,936. The plaintiffs appealed from the collector's decision to the Secretary of the Treasury, by whom the appeal was denied. They then paid under protest the duties exacted, and brought the present action to recover the amount.

... The defendant demurred to the complaint, the demurrer was sustained, and final judgment was entered in his favor; to review which the case is brought here.

The treaty with the king of the Hawaiian Islands provides for the importation into the United States, free of duty, of various articles, the produce and manufacture of those islands, in consideration, among other things, of like exemption from duty, on the importation into that country, of sundry specified articles which are the produce and manufacture of the United States. 19 Stat. 625. The language of the first two articles of the treaty, which recite the reciprocal engagements of the two countries, declares that they are made in consideration "of the rights and privileges" and "as an equivalent therefor," which one concedes to the other.

The plaintiffs rely for a like exemption of the sugars imported by them from San Domingo upon the ninth article of the treaty with the Dominican Republic, which is as follows: "No higher or other duty shall be imposed on the importation into the United States of any article the growth, produce, or manufacture of the Dominican Republic, or of her fisheries; and no higher or other duty shall be imposed on the importation into the Dominican Republic of any article, the growth, produce, or manufacture of the United States, or their fisheries, than are or shall be payable on the like articles, the growth, produce, or manufacture of any other foreign country, or its fisheries." 15 St. 473, 478.

. . . .

... The act of Congress under which the duties were collected, authorized their exaction. It is of general application, making no exception in favor of goods of any country. It was passed after the treaty with the Dominican Republic, and, if there be any conflict between the stipulations

---

1. [Authors' Note: The island of Hispaniola lies west of Puerto Rico and east of Cuba. In 1697, Spain recognized French dominion over the western third of the island, which in 1804 became Haiti. The remainder of the island, known as "Santo Domingo" or "San Domingo," was conquered by Haiti in 1821. In 1844, it attained independence as the "Dominican Republic," with a capital named "Santo Domingo."]

of the treaty and the requirements of the law, the latter must control. A treaty is primarily a contract between two or more independent nations, and is so regarded by writers on public law. For the infraction of its provisions a remedy must be sought by the injured party through reclamations upon the other. When the stipulations are not self-executing they can only be enforced pursuant to legislation to carry them into effect, and such legislation is as much subject to modification and repeal by Congress as legislation upon any other subject. If the treaty contains stipulations which are self-executing, that is, require no legislation to make them operative, to that extent they have the force and effect of a legislative enactment. Congress may modify such provisions, so far as they bind the United States, or supersede them altogether. By the Constitution a treaty is placed on the same footing, and made of like obligation, with an act of legislation. Both are declared by that instrument to be the supreme law of the land, and no superior efficacy is given to either over the other. When the two relate to the same subject, the courts will always endeavor to construe them so as to give effect to both, if that can be done without violating the language of either; but if the two are inconsistent, the one last in date will control the other, provided always the stipulation of the treaty on the subject is self-executing. If the country with which the treaty is made is dissatisfied with the action of the legislative department, it may present its complaint to the executive head of the government, and take such other measures as it may deem essential for the protection of its interests. The courts can afford no redress. . . .

. . . The duty of the courts is to construe and give effect to the latest expression of the sovereign will. In *Head-Money Cases*, 112 U.S. 580 . . ., it was objected to an act of Congress that it violated provisions contained in treaties with foreign nations, but the court replied that so far as the provisions of the act were in conflict with any treaty, they must prevail in all the courts of the country; and, after a full and elaborate consideration of the subject, it held that "so far as a treaty made by the United States with any foreign nation can be the subject of judicial cognizance in the courts of this country, it is subject to such acts as Congress may pass for its enforcement, modification, or repeal."

Judgment affirmed.

NOTES ON THE "LATER-IN-TIME" DOCTRINE FOR TREATIES AND STATUTES

1. *The Basic Doctrine. Whitney v. Robertson* articulates the "later-in-time" doctrine, which is based on a reading of the Supremacy Clause that views treaty law on the same footing (neither higher nor lower) as federal statutory law. Thus, either may repeal the other. An early case establishing the "last-in-time" doctrine is *The Cherokee Tobacco,* 78 U.S. (11 Wall.) 616, 20 L.Ed. 227 (1871). In that case the Supreme Court was faced with a conflict between an 1866 U.S.–Cherokee Nation treaty and the Internal Revenue Act of July 20, 1868. The Court said: "Undoubtedly one or the other must yield. The repugnancy is clear and cannot stand together. . . . The effect of treaties

and acts of Congress, when in conflict, is not settled by the Constitution. But the question is not involved in any doubt as to its proper solution. A treaty may supersede a prior act of Congress, and an act of Congress may supersede a prior treaty." *Id.* at 620–21 (footnote omitted). For a contemporary formulation, see the *Restatement (Third) of the Foreign Relations Law of the United States* §§ 114, 115 (1987) (reproduced in Chapter 2, Section 3).

2. *Head Money Cases*. As noted in *Whitney v. Robertson*, the doctrine was also considered in the *Head Money Cases* (*supra* Section 4). Those cases dealt with the enforcement against the shipping company by the collector of the port of New York of a levy of fifty cents per passenger for each non-citizen brought to these shores. The statutory authorization for this alien transport tax was in a law passed by Congress on August 3, 1882, shortly before the case was filed. In its decision, the Supreme Court confirmed that so far as the provisions in an act "may be found to be in conflict with any treaty with a foreign nation, they must prevail in all the judicial courts of this country." 112 U.S. 580, at 597. Even as to self-executing clauses of a treaty, the "Constitution of the United States places such provisions as these in the same category as other laws of Congress. ... The Constitution gives [them] no superiority over an act of Congress in this respect, which may be repealed or modified by an act of a later date." *Id.* at 598–99.

3. *Chinese Exclusion Case*. The "Chinese Exclusion" case (Chae Chan Ping v. United States, 130 U.S. 581, 9 S.Ct. 623, 32 L.Ed. 1068 (1889)) (*see* Chapter 1, Section 1) held that the fact that treaties with China were violated by the Chinese Exclusion Act of 1888 is no objection to the later statute's validity. That law had been enacted by Congress to prevent Chinese immigration at the time of the gold rush. As explained by the Court, "They," the Chinese, "were generally industrious and frugal. Not being accompanied by families, except in rare instances, their expenses were small; and they were content with the simplest fare, such as would not suffice for our laborers and artisans. The competition between them and our people was for this reason altogether in their favor, and the consequent irritation, proportionately deep and bitter, was followed, in many cases, by open conflicts, to the great disturbance of the public peace." 130 U.S. at 595. The 1888 Act did not merely stanch immigration; it also denied re-entry to any Chinese laborers who were outside the United States at the time of the passage of the law, and precluded subsequent departure and return. It was thus assailed as a "Chinese expulsion act," since most of the laborers would be expected to return to China to visit their families. The Supreme Court said, in part:

> It must be conceded that the act of 1888 is in contravention of express stipulations of the treaty of 1868 and of the supplemental treaty of 1880, but it is not on that account invalid, or to be restricted in its enforcement. The treaties were of no greater legal obligation than the act of Congress. By the Constitution, laws made in pursuance thereof and treaties made under the authority of the United States are both declared to be the supreme law of the land, and no paramount authority is given to one over the other. A treaty, it is true, is in its nature a contract between nations and is often merely promissory in its character, requiring legislation to carry its stipulations into effect. Such legislation will be open to future repeal or amendment. If the treaty operates by its own force, and relates

> to a subject within the power of Congress, it can be deemed in that particular only the equivalent of a legislative act, to be repealed or modified at the pleasure of Congress. In either case the last expression of the sovereign will must control.

130 U.S. at 600.

4. *Relationship to Constitutional Supremacy.* Interestingly, the Supreme Court in *Reid v. Covert* relied upon its holding in *Whitney* to support the proposition that the Constitution was supreme over treaties. The *Reid* Court stated:

> This Court has also repeatedly taken the position that an Act of Congress which must comply with the Constitution, is on a full parity with a treaty, and that when a statute which is subsequent in time is inconsistent with a treaty, the statute to the extent of a conflict renders the treaty null.[34] It would be completely anomalous to say that a treaty need not comply with the Constitution when such an agreement can be overridden by a statute that must conform to that instrument.

354 U.S. at 18.

5. *Interpreting Statutes and Treaties so as to Avoid a Conflict.* In *Whitney v. Robertson*, the Court stated that "the courts will always endeavor to construe [a potentially conflicting statute and treaty] so as to give effect to both, if that can be done without violating the language of either...." Yet how creative may a court be when construing such instruments? Consider the following incident, where a U.S. anti-terrorism statute seemed to conflict with an earlier-in-time treaty between the United States and the United Nations.

In 1947, the United States and the United Nations concluded an Agreement Regarding the Headquarters of the United Nations, July 26, 1947, 61 Stat. 3416, 11 U.N.T.S. 11 ("Headquarters Agreement"). In essence, the agreement established a U.N. headquarters district in New York as an international enclave. The United States is obligated to permit unimpeded transit, entry and access to the U.N. headquarters district for representatives of members to the United Nations and others persons invited by the United Nations. Invited persons include permanent observers. In 1974, the Palestine Liberation Organization (PLO) was designated as permanent observer and was allowed to establish a permanent observer Mission in New York. *See* U.S. Department of State, *1974 Digest of United States Practice in International Law* 27–29; U.S. Department of State, *1976 Digest of United States Practice in International Law* 74–75; B'nai B'rith v. Kissinger, No. 74 Civ. 1545 (E.D.N.Y. November 1, 1974) (upholding the PLO's right of access to the United Nations under the Headquarters Agreement).

In 1987, Congress enacted an Anti–Terrorism Act (ATA), which was designed, in part, to force the closure of all PLO offices located in the United

34. In *Whitney v. Robertson*, 124 U.S. 190, the Court stated, at p. 194: "By the Constitution a treaty is placed on the same footing, and made of like obligation, with an act of legislation. Both are declared by that instrument to be the supreme law of the land, and no superior efficacy is given to either over the other. ... [I]f the two are inconsistent, the one last in date will control the other. ..." *Head Money Cases*, 112 U.S. 580; *Botiller v. Dominguez*, 130 U.S. 238; *Chae Chan Ping v. United States*, 130 U.S. 581. See *Clark v. Allen*, 331 U.S. 503, 509–510; *Moser v. United States*, 341 U.S. 41, 45.

States. The ATA determined that the PLO was "a terrorist organization and a threat to the interests of the United States, its allies, and to international law and should not benefit from operating in the United States." 22 U.S.C. § 5201(b) (2006). Consequently, the ATA provided that

> It shall be unlawful, if the purpose be to further the interests of the Palestinian Liberation Organization ... notwithstanding any provision of law to the contrary, to establish or maintain an office, headquarters, premises, or other facilities or establishments within the jurisdiction of the United States at the behest or direction of, or with funds provided by the Palestinian Liberation Organization.

22 U.S.C. § 5202 (2006).

As a consequence of the statute, the U.S. government sought to close the PLO Mission in New York. The PLO maintained that doing so violated the Headquarters Agreement. In *United States v. Palestine Liberation Organization,* 695 F.Supp. 1456 (S.D.N.Y. 1988), the district court found the ATA inapplicable to the PLO Mission because of the "long standing and well-established position of the Mission at the United Nations, sustained by international agreement," and the lack of a "clear legislative intent that the Congress was directing the Attorney General, the State Department or this Court to act in contravention of the Headquarters Agreement." *Id.* at 1464. The court analyzed the ATA's text and legislative history as follows:

> First, neither the Mission nor the Headquarters Agreement is mentioned in the ATA itself. Such an inclusion would have left no doubt as to Congress' intent on a matter which had been raised repeatedly with respect to this act, and its absence here reflects equivocation and avoidance, leaving the court without clear interpretive guidance in the language of the act. Second, while the section of the ATA prohibiting the maintenance of an office applies "notwithstanding any provision of law to the contrary," 22 U.S.C. § 5202(3), it does not purport to apply notwithstanding any *treaty*. The absence of that interpretive instruction is especially relevant because elsewhere in the same legislation Congress expressly referred to "United States law (including any treaty)." 101 Stat. at 1343. Thus Congress failed, in the text of the ATA, to provide guidance for the interpretation of the act, where it became repeatedly apparent before its passage that the prospect of an interpretive problem was inevitable. Third, no member of Congress expressed a clear and unequivocal intent to supersede the Headquarters Agreement by passage of the ATA. In contrast, most who addressed the subject of conflict denied that there would be a conflict: in their view, the Headquarters Agreement did not provide the PLO with any right to maintain an office. Here again, Congress provided no guidance for the interpretation of the ATA in the event of a conflict which was clearly foreseeable. And Senator Claiborne Pell, Chairman of the Senate Foreign Relations Committee, who voted for the bill, raised the possibility that the Headquarters Agreement would take precedence over the ATA in the event of a conflict between the two. His suggestion was neither opposed nor debated, even though it came in the final minutes before passage of the ATA.

Id. at 1468–69 (footnote omitted). Is the language of the ATA really "equivocal"? Was the court doing a standard statutory analysis, or was it really trying to prevent the United States from taking a step that would violate its treaty obligations? If the latter, should courts be pressing fidelity to international commitments when the political branches have decided otherwise? Does it affect your analysis to know that the Executive Branch strongly opposed this ATA provision, but not enough to veto the enactment of the ATA as a whole?

Since the Headquarters Agreement provides that, when disputes arise, the matter shall be resolved through arbitration, the United Nations sought to arbitrate the threatened closure of the PLO Mission with the United States. When the United States declined to do so, the General Assembly requested an advisory opinion from the International Court of Justice. The Court unanimously found that the United States of America was obligated to arbitrate the matter. *See Applicability of the Obligation to Arbitrate Under Section 21 of the United Nations Headquarters Agreement of 26 June 1947,* 1988 I.C.J. 12 (Apr. 26). After the district court's interpretation of the ATA, however, the U.S. government decided not to appeal the decision and not to pursue further the closure of the PLO Mission. Congress did not react. The dispute quietly ended.

6. *Questioning the Doctrine.* Do you think the later-in-time doctrine is a good one? Some commentators have questioned the rule, expressing displeasure that federal statutes can be subsequently overturned by treaties. Professor Akhil Reed Amar writes:

> By allowing federal treaties to repeal federal statutes and, symmetrically, statutes to repeal treaties, the modern judiciary has paid insufficient heed to the text of Article VI itself, ignoring the apparent legal hierarchy implicit in that text. In *Marbury v. Madison*, Chief Justice Marshall, in emphasizing the legal priority of the Constitution, deemed it "not entirely unworthy of observation" that the Article VI supremacy clause listed the Constitution *first*. Isn't it likewise worthy of notice that this very same clause listed federal statutes *ahead of* federal treaties, thereby implying a rank order between the two? . . .
>
> . . . [T]he Constitution deserved priority over lesser laws because of its superior democratic pedigree. A similar argument would seem to support the priority of federal statutes over federal treaties. After all, treaties cut the House of Representatives out of the loop.

Akhil Reed Amar, *America's Constitution: A Biography* 303 (2005) (footnotes omitted). Other commentators, however, have expressed displeasure that treaties can be subsequently overturned by federal statutes. Professor Louis Henkin writes:

> [O]ne might well argue . . . that a treaty should prevail as law even in the face of a subsequent statute. The international obligations of the United States are the responsibility of the treaty-makers. The Senate was given a part in the process, but the House, and Congress as a whole, were purposely denied any voice in it. Congress . . . has a constitutional obligation to implement the treaties which the President and the Senate make; it is anomalous to accord it power to disregard a treaty obligation, compel its violation, and put the United States in default. Particularly as

> regards multilateral treaties of general applicability which establish universal standards—on human rights, international trade or finance, the law of the sea, protection of intellectual property (trademarks, copyrights, patents)—inconsistent legislation by Congress not only violates international obligations but ruptures international consensus which the President-and-Senate helped achieve. . . .

Louis Henkin, *Foreign Affairs and the Constitution* 210–11 (2d ed. 1996).

7. *Practice of Other Countries*. In some countries, such as France and the Netherlands, treaties are paramount even with respect to subsequent legislation. For example, the French Constitution provides: "Duly ratified or approved treaties or agreements shall, upon their publication, override laws, subject, for each agreement or treaty, to its application by the other party." CONSTITUTION OF FRANCE, art. 55 (1958). Similarly, the Dutch Constitution provides: "Statutory regulations in force within the Kingdom shall not be applicable if such application is in conflict with provisions of treaties that are binding on all persons or of resolutions by international institutions." GRONDWET [CONSTITUTION OF THE KINGDOM OF THE NETHERLANDS], art. 94 (1983).

NOTE: CAN A LATER-IN-TIME CUSTOMARY INTERNATIONAL LAW RULE "TRUMP" A TREATY OR STATUTE?

If a treaty that is later-in-time to a U.S. statute can "trump" the statute as a matter of U.S. law, does a later-in-time rule of customary international law have the same effect on either a treaty or a statute? In other words, if it appears that a rule of customary international law has crystallized in recent years, and the United States has not persistently objected to the rule, can it have the effect of superseding earlier U.S. treaties or statutes under U.S. law?

Consider the following example. In 1961, the United States ratified the Convention on the Territorial Sea and Contiguous Zone, Apr. 29, 1958, 15 U.S.T. 1606, 516 U.N.T.S. 205. Article 24(2) of that Convention provides that a state's contiguous zone (a zone outside the territorial sea in which the coastal state can enforce certain types of its laws, such as on customs) may not extend beyond twelve miles from the coast. Thus, the treaty precluded the United States from declaring a contiguous zone beyond twelve miles from U.S. shores. The 1982 Law of the Sea Convention, to which the United States is not a party, permits the contiguous zone to be as much as twenty-four nautical miles from the coast, and many states (either as parties or non-parties) began claiming a contiguous zone of that distance.

In 1989, the U.S. Department of State Office of the Legal Adviser determined that an international consensus had emerged that a twenty-four nautical-mile contiguous zone was now permitted under customary international law. Further, the Office of the Legal Adviser assessed the repercussions of the emergence of this new customary rule on the U.S. obligations under the conflicting 1958 treaty. The memorandum was transmitted to the U.S. Department of Justice Office of Legal Counsel, which in 1991 responded that it deferred to the Department of State on this matter. *See* Letter of John O. McGinnis, Deputy Assistant Attorney General, U.S. Department of Justice, to Allen Kreczko, Deputy Legal Adviser, U.S. Department of State (July 1, 1991).

As you read the memorandum, consider two issues. First, much of the State Department's analysis turns on the President's power to terminate treaties, which is discussed in greater depth *infra* Section 10. Second, does this analysis support the idea that a sole executive agreement (an agreement based solely on the Executive's power, without any form of consent from Congress) can also alter an existing treaty?

MEMORANDUM OF THE U.S. DEPARTMENT OF STATE OFFICE OF THE LEGAL ADVISER REGARDING THE TERRITORIAL SEA CONVENTION

(Apr. 5, 1989) available at http://www.state.gov/s/l/65626.htm.

As a general matter, the President has "the power to determine how far this country will claim territorial rights in the marginal sea as against other nations." *United States v. Louisiana*, 363 U.S. 1, 35 (1960); *see also* Proclamation 5928, December 27, 1988 (extending the U.S. territorial sea to 12 nautical miles). *A fortiori*, the President has the power to extend a maritime jurisdiction under international law which is less than full sovereignty, such as the contiguous zone. This has been done by Presidential action with respect to the exclusive economic zone. Proclamation 5030, March 10, 1983.

The question has been raised, however, whether Article 24(2) of the 1958 Territorial Sea Convention limits the President's authority to extend the contiguous zone beyond 12 nautical miles. That it does not do so in present circumstances flows from two constitutional considerations: first, the President may unilaterally determine for the United States that Article 24(2) no longer binds the United States as a matter of international law; and second, a treaty provision's force in domestic law is generally no greater than its international law force.

A. PRESIDENTIAL AUTHORITY TO ACT ON THE INTERNATIONAL PLANE

It is well-established that the President is "the sole organ of the federal government in the field of international relations." *United States v. Curtiss-Wright Export Corp.*, 299 U.S. 304, 320 (1936); *see also* 10 *Annals of Congress* 613 (1800) (Representative John Marshall) (President "the sole organ of the nation in its external relations, and its sole representative with foreign nations"), *rpt. in* 18 U.S. (5 Wheat.) Appendix note 1, at 26.

The President's constitutional authority to act for the United States in international relations includes the power to engage in state practice that contributes to or dissents from the establishment of customary norms, as well as the power to assess the customary norms relevant to United States action. As a leading scholar has stated,

> "It is principally the President, 'sole organ' of the United States in its international relations, who is responsible for the behavior of the United States in regard to international law, and who participates on her behalf in the indefinable process by which customary internation-

al law is made, unmade, remade. He makes legal claims for the United States and reacts to the claims of others; he performs acts reflecting views on legal questions and justifies them under the law, in diplomatic exchange, in judicial or arbitral proceedings, in international organizations or in the public forum."

L. Henkin, *Foreign Affairs and the Constitution* 188 (1972). His constitutional authority also includes significant power with relation to the operation of treaties. As Alexander Hamilton stated:

> "[The President's] power of determining virtually upon the operation of national treaties, as a consequence of the power to receive public ministers, is an important instance of the right of the executive to decide upon the obligations of the country with regard to foreign nations. Hence ..., treaties can only be made by the President and Senate jointly, but their activity may be continued or suspended by the President alone."

A. Hamilton, *Letters of Pacificus and Helvidius on the Proclamation of Neutrality of 1793*, at 12–13 (Gideon ed. 1845). *But cf. Taylor v. Morton*, 23 Fed. Cas. 784, 786 (C.C. Mass. 1855); 4 Moore, *Digest of International Law* 321 (1906) (quoting Jan. 2, 1791, letter of James Madison intimating that Senate must participate in decision to declare a treaty void).

At the extreme, it is often asserted that a President has the general authority to terminate treaties on behalf of the United States. *See* L. Henkin, *supra*, at 168–69 and notes; 2 C. Hyde, *International Law Chiefly as Interpreted and Applied by the United States* 1519–20 (2d ed. 1945); *Restatement (Third) of the Foreign Relations Law of the United States*, § 115, Reporters' Note 3; *cf. Goldwater v. Carter*, 617 F.2d 697 (D.C. Cir.)(en banc)(President has power to terminate treaty in order to recognize foreign state), *vacated on other grounds*, 444 U.S. 996 (1979). While this has never been specifically approved by the courts, there are numerous instances in which the President has terminated a treaty unilaterally. *See* Declaration of Arthur Rovine, *Goldwater v. Carter*, Civ. No. 78–2412 (D.D.C. 1979)(of 25 instances of Presidential actions to terminate treaties, in twelve cases the President acted unilaterally), *rpt. in U.S. Foreign Relations Law: Documents and Sources* 513 (M. Glennon & T. Franck eds. 1980).

Acts in exercise of the foreign relations power may contribute to the modification or termination of a treaty provision. For example, when another party acts inconsistently with a treaty provision, it is the President who must determine whether it constitutes a material breach. Since such breach renders a treaty voidable but not void, a decision must also be made on the appropriate response under international law, *e.g.*, suspension or termination of the agreement in whole or in part or acquiescence or waiver on behalf of the United States. It is settled that the President has the power to waive the right of the United States to terminate a treaty for breach by another party. *Charlton v. Kelly*, 229 U.S. 447, 474–76 (1913) ("The executive department having thus elected to waive any right to free itself from the obligation to deliver up its own citizens, it is the plain duty of this court to recognize the obligation to surrender the appellant. . . ."). Implicit in this is the view that the executive can exercise the U.S. right rather than waive it. *But cf. Taylor v. Morton*, 23 Fed. Cas. 784, 786 (C.C. Mass. 1855) stating in dicta that "no body other than congress possesses [the power of repealing treaties operating as part of municipal law]". If he acquiesces in general violations of the treaty by the other parties, this can have the effect of terminating the treaty obligation. *See* 5 Hackworth, *Digest of International Law* 340–41; 14 M. Whiteman, *Digest of International Law* 441 (1970).

> "The President is, of course, without authority, except by and with the advice and consent of the Senate, to modify a treaty provision. There are, however, instances in which he, acting through the Secretary of State, has tacitly acquiesced in action by foreign governments which had the effect of modifying stipulations in our treaties."

Memorandum of the Solicitor for the Department of State (Hackworth), Feb. 28, 1931, *quoted in* 5 Hackworth, *supra*, at 340.

The Court has also deferred to the executive branch in determining whether a treaty was abrogated due to the outbreak of war, *Clark v. Allen*, 331 U.S. 503, 508–09 (1947) (although the outbreak of war does not "necessarily suspend or abrogate treaty provisions," the executive may formulate a national policy "inconsistent with the enforcement of a treaty in whole or in part"), or was abrogated by the operation of law, due to the absorption of the other party into another state, *Terlinden v. Ames*, 184 U.S. 270 (1902) (Court was without power to review the validity of a treaty if the practice of the parties indicated that they recognized the treaty as in force). Similarly, during World War II, the Attorney General ruled that the President had the authority to suspend or declare inoperative a peacetime treaty on the grounds of *rebus sic stantibus*. 40 *Op. Att'y Gen.* 119 (1941). As the Attorney General stated:

> "Attention to the observance of treaties is an executive responsibility. . . . The facts which bring into operation the right to declare the convention inoperative or suspended, are within the knowledge of and can be promptly and adequately appraised by the executive department; and it is proper that the President, as 'the sole organ of the nation in its external relations,' should speak for the nation in announcing action which international law clearly permits."

Id. at 123.

Another relevant and more routinely exercised aspect of the President's foreign affairs power is that the President has the initial and primary responsibility to interpret and apply treaty provisions. The President has submitted treaty construction issues to the Senate only in exceptional instances. S. Crandall, *Treaties, Their Making and Enforcement* 369 (2d ed. 1916). While courts may interpret treaty provisions in the context of cases properly before them, they have traditionally given great weight to the interpretations of the Executive Branch. *See Sullivan v. Kidd*, 254 U.S. 433 (1921); *Charlton v. Kelly*, 229 U.S. 447, 468 (1913); *Whitney v. Robertson*, 124 U.S. 190, 194–95 (1888); *Restatement* 326; L. Henkin, *supra*, at 167. Were the issue to arise before our courts, substantial deference would be given to the Executive Branch view that the 1958 Territorial Sea Convention was adopted as a law-stating treaty and was not intended to constitute a special regime, particularly given that no contrary interpretation was presented to the Senate during the ratification process. *See* Four Conventions and an Optional Protocol Formulated at the United Nations Conference on the Law of the Sea, Message of the President, Exec. J–N, 86th Cong. 2d Sess. (1959) (Conventions were mixture of codification of existing law and progressive development); Law of the Sea Conventions, Rpt. of the Senate Comm. on For. Rel., Exec. Rpt. No. 5, 86th Cong. 2d Sess. (1960); Conventions on the Law of the Sea, Hearings before the Senate Comm. on For. Rel., 86th Cong. 2d Sess. (1960) (testimony of Arthur Dean, head of U.S. delegation to UN Law of Sea Conference).

Thus, in the context of the contiguous zone extension, the President, as the "sole organ of the United States in its external relations," has the constitutional authority (1) to determine that customary international law now permits a 24 nautical mile Contiguous zone, (2) to assess the intent of the 1958 Convention parties regarding the preservation of Article 24(2) as a special regime, (3) to acquiesce in conduct by other parties inconsistent with the wording of the 1958 Territorial Sea Convention, thereby leading to the termination of Article 24(2) by estoppel and (4) to decide that Article 24(2) no longer is operative under international law for the United States.

B. TREATIES AS DOMESTIC LAW

Article VI of the Constitution declares that treaties are among the "supreme law of the land." Although this provision appears largely to have been intended to ensure that the states abide by federal treaty obligations, *see* S. Crandall, *Treaties, Their Making and Enforcement* 153 (2d ed. 1916); L. Henkin, *supra*, at 129, treaties are viewed as on a par with statute, and, if self-executing, can be given direct effect by U.S. courts. Moreover, treaties are among the laws that the President must "faithfully execute." U.S. Constitution, Art. II, sec. 2; *see Restatement (Third)*, at § 111, comment c ("That international law and agreements of the United States are law of the United States means ... that the President has the obligation and the necessary authority to take care that they be faithfully executed.").

The status of treaties as law of the land, however, does not mean that they are in all respects equivalent to statutes. Treaties are, at root, compacts among sovereigns. *Head Money Cases*, 112 U.S. 580, 598 (1884); *Federalist* No. 75. They become the law of the land through the combined action of the President and Senate—the "fourth branch of government" as Hamilton called it. *See* L. Henkin, *supra*, at 130. More importantly, their status as "law of the land" depends on their status as international law. Except perhaps with respect to treaties that create vested rights, "[a] rule of international law or an international agreement has no status as law of the United States if the United States is not in fact bound by it: for example, ... a provision in a treaty that is invalid or has been terminated or suspended." *Restatement (*Third*)*, at § 111, comment b; *see also id.* at § 339, Reporters' Note 1; L. Henkin, *supra*, at 160 ("The status of a treaty as law of the land derives from and depends on its status as a valid, living treaty of the United States. ... It is not law of the land if it is not an effective treaty of the United States internationally because it is not binding, or is invalid under international law, or because it has expired, or has been terminated or destroyed by breach, whether by the United States or the other party."); *cf.* S. Crandall, *supra,* at 446 (if rights vested under treaty, these rights not terminated by treaty termination); *Society for Propagation of the Gospel v. Town of New Haven*, 21 U.S.(8 Wheat.) 464, 491 (1823) (termination of treaty, like repeal of municipal law, does not divest property rights vested under it).

Based on these principles, it follows that, if Article 24(2) of the 1958 Territorial Sea Convention has been superseded on the international plane by a new rule of customary international law permitting a 24 nautical mile contiguous zone, then Article 24(2) no longer has effect as a law of the United States and need not be "faithfully executed" by the President. Henkin, *supra*, at 168 *note* (President's duty to see that treaties are faithfully executed ceases to apply if President terminates the treaty pursuant to his foreign affairs powers).

It is important to note that to reach this conclusion one need not reach the question of whether customary international law will supersede a statute. *See Paquete Habana*, 175 U.S. 677, 700 (1900) (only resort to customary international law if there is "no controlling executive or legislative act"). Treaty and custom both operate on the international plane and, on that plane, the customary norm can supersede the treaty norm; this terminates the domestic legal effects of the treaty because those effects are derivative of the treaty's status as binding under international law. In contrast, statutes derive their effect from independent action of domestic institutions. The effect of changed custom on an earlier statute involves a different constitutional question, whether domestic and customary international law have the same status or whether they stand in a hierarchical relationship.

While it has not been authoritatively determined that the emergence of a new rule of customary international law which supersedes a treaty provision on the international plane also has the effect of superseding the treaty provision as a matter of domestic law, there seems, not surprisingly, to be no authority for the contrary proposition. It would be anomalous to have our domestic law on the obligations of the United States vis-a-vis other nations derive from but become more restrictive than our international law obligations. Where (i) the treaty has not created vested rights, (ii) the new rule of customary international law is clearly recognized as internationally controlling by the executive and (iii) there were no contrary assurances on which the Senate relied in granting advice and consent, there is no good reason to adopt a constitutional rule creating such an anomaly. Because treaties are, at root, compacts among sovereigns, it is appropriate that the President, "sole organ" of the United States in its foreign relations, have wider powers with respect to treaties than statutes.

C. CONCLUSION

In light of the international legal considerations set forth in the first section of this memorandum, Article 24(2) has lost its controlling effect internationally for the United States.

The Constitution does not provide Article 24(2) with independent continuing legal force and, therefore, does not require the President to refrain from exercising his foreign affairs power to extend the contiguous zone of the United States beyond the 12 nautical mile limited stated in that Article.

SECTION 7. EXECUTIVE AGREEMENTS

NOTE: ORIGINS OF THE EXECUTIVE AGREEMENT

The Constitution nowhere makes provision for the President to conclude international agreements other than by treaty, with the advice and consent of two-thirds of the Senate. The Constitution does recognize (Article I, Section 10) the right of a state of the Union to enter into an "agreement or compact with another State or with a foreign power" if it has obtained the consent of Congress, while prohibiting absolutely any state from entering into a "treaty, alliance, or confederation. . . ." (*See* Chapter 6, Section 7). From this it may be argued either:

(1) that the drafters knew the distinction between "treaties" and "agreements" and deliberately chose not to create a federal "agreement" power distinct from the treaty power, or;

(2) that the drafters could not reasonably be assumed to have denied to the federal government a power which, within restrictions, was residually accorded to states of the Union.[1]

While the Constitution may be ambiguous, the Executive's right to enter into agreements even without the advice and consent of the Senate has long been recognized both in practice and by the courts.[2] Indeed, the "executive agreement" has come to occupy a prominent place in the arsenal of diplomatic tools of the U.S. government. This note sketches the emergence of the executive agreement in U.S. history.

---

1. *See* 14 Marjorie M. Whiteman, *Digest of International Law* 193–216 (1970); Myres McDougal & Asher Lans, *Treaties and Congressional-Executive or Presidential Agreements: Interchangeable Instruments of National Policy,* 54 YALE L.J. 181–351 (1945).

2. *See* Edwin S. Corwin, *The Constitution of the United States of America, Analysis and Interpretation*, S. DOC. NO. 82–170, at 433 (1953).

Colonial Practice

The earliest American executives were, primarily, the colonial Governors commissioned by the British Government. The discharge of their duties was subject to royal approval and, in particular, North American inter-colonial relations were supposed to be referred back to the mother country. Nevertheless, as the interests of the colonies often differed from their colonizers, the colonies often entered into engagements with other sovereign entities and with Indian tribes without formal approval from London. Thus, even in this period, many agreements were concluded by means other than formal treaty, which would have required royal assent and been too cumbersome a process. This pragmatic solution foreshadowed the development of the "executive agreement" in modern American politics.

The majority of the inter-colonial agreements established reciprocal trading privileges. One of the earliest involved New England and New Netherland:

> [T]he Dutch governor of New Amsterdam, Peter Minuit, wrote to the Governor of New Plymouth in March, 1627, proposing the establishment of a mutual trade between the two colonies. Governor William Bradford replied that the offer of trade was acceptable. . . .[3]

Despite boundary disputes and political clashes between the mother countries in Europe, "[t]he convenience of an intercolonial trade encouraged the English to accept the Dutch proposal, and an informal alliance for mutual defense and trade was established."[4]

Practice under the Articles of Confederation

The same men who ran the revolutionary government and the government under the Articles of Confederation were also mainly responsible for the formation of the Constitution of 1787. During the period of the Articles, it appears that the founders also employed the executive agreement as an instrument of diplomacy. McClure notes that, although there was no "executive" under the Articles of Confederation, "[a] pre-Constitution international act not formally ratified may reasonably be regarded as an executive agreement."[5] He adds: "[I]t is appropriate that the executive agreement system should have been substantially inaugurated with the armistice which brought to an end the war of the American Revolution."[6] He then recounts three instances in which an international agreement was concluded without the use of a "treaty", including a commercial accord with France, providing for unconditional most-favored-nation treatment, and a ship-signal arrangement with Morocco.

---

3. Max Savelle, *The Origins of American Diplomacy: The International History of Angloamerica 1492–1763*, at 159 (1968).

4. *Id.*

5. Wallace McClure, *International Executive Agreements: Democratic Procedure Under the Constitution of the United States* 35 (1941) (footnote omitted) [hereinafter "*McClure*"].

6. *Id.*

Early Practice Under the Constitution

On April 22, 1793, President Washington issued a proclamation that stated the U.S. policy of neutrality in the recently begun war between Great Britain and France. The proclamation was not itself an executive agreement; it was merely a formalized policy declaration indicating that the United States would "pursue a course friendly and impartial to both belligerent powers."[7] Nevertheless, the power of the President to establish an instrument, without congressional approval, that affected U.S. rights and obligations internationally had important implications for the authority to enter into executive agreements. In a series of articles which that appeared in *The Gazette of the United States,* Alexander Hamilton, under the pseudonym "Pacificus," defended the proclamation against critics who saw the declaration of neutrality as beyond the President's competence. Hamilton's forceful arguments influenced the shape of the President's role in foreign affairs.[8] Hamilton inquired as to "what department of our government is the proper one to make a declaration of neutrality." Insisting that a "correct mind will discern at once that it ... must belong to the executive," he argued:

> The Legislative Department is not the *organ* of intercourse between the UStates and foreign Nations. It is charged neither with *making* nor *interpreting* Treaties. It is therefore not naturally that Organ of the Government which is to pronounce the existing condition of the Nation, with regard to foreign Powers. ...

Embedded in this broad executive power appears to be the ability to engage in "executive agreements" with foreign nations. The earliest executive agreements under the Constitution were the "Postal Acts of the Washington Administration."[9] These agreements were later authorized by Congress but are, nonetheless, significant because they indicated the possibility of concluding international engagements while bypassing the formal treaty-making process.

Early executive agreements, however, were not limited to routine or inconsequential matters. McClure points out an 1817 executive agreement between Great Britain and the United States entered into for determining the naval armaments which should be maintained by the respective parties on the Great Lakes and Lake Champlain. The agreement was promptly made operative. John Quincy Adams, then Secretary of State, records the fact that some months later British Foreign Minister Charles Bagot asked him whether it was the intention of the President to communicate to Congress the notes in question which constituted "a sort of treaty." Mr. Adams spoke to the President, "who did not think it necessary that they should be communicated."

---

7. *Id.* at 37.

8. The quotations that follow are taken from the article dated June 29, 1793, *reprinted in* 15 *The Papers of Alexander Hamilton* 33–43 (Harold C. Syrett ed., 1969).

9. *McClure, supra* note 5, at 38.

Nevertheless, in April, 1818, he did send the agreement to the Senate, which duly accorded thereto advice and consent; since that time it has been in force as a treaty.[10]

As with so many historical precedents, this one can be read in several ways. Does it illustrate the power of the President to enter into an agreement without any congressional participation? Or does it, on the contrary, argue that Monroe ultimately repented and acknowledged the need to regularize his agreement by securing the imprimatur of the Senate?

Frequency of Executive Agreements

Whatever meaning may be drawn from such precedents, the reality is that the vast majority of international agreements that have been concluded by the United States since the early American republic have been done *without* securing a two-thirds vote of consent by the U.S. Senate. *See* Glen S. Krutz and Jeffrey S. Peake, *Treaty Politics and the Rise of Executive Agreements: International Commitments in a System of Shared Powers* (2009). The following tables are drawn from *Treaties and Other International Agreements: The Role of the United States Senate*, S. Prt. 106–71, at 39 (2001).

TREATIES AND EXECUTIVE AGREEMENTS CONCLUDED BY THE UNITED STATES, 1789–1989

Period	Number of Treaties	Number of Executive Agreements
1789–1839	60	27
1839–1889	215	238
1889–1939	524	917
1939–1989	702	11,698
Total	1,501	12,880

10. *Id.* at 31 (footnote omitted).

TREATIES AND EXECUTIVE AGREEMENTS CONCLUDED BY THE UNITED STATES 1990–1999

Year	Number of Treaties	Number of Executive Agreements
1990	20	398
1991	11	286
1992	21	303
1993	17	257
1994	24	338
1995	17	300
1996	48	260
1997	40	257
1998	25	259
1999	26	199
Total	249	2,857

The extensive practice of the Executive Branch in concluding executive agreements ultimately resulted in the adoption of two important regulatory instruments. First, the Department of State adopted a "Circular 175" Procedure, which is designed to ensure that the Department consider carefully whether an agreement should be concluded as a treaty and, if not, the exact legal basis for concluding the agreement as an executive agreement. Second, the Case–Zablocki Act requires that all executive agreements be transmitted to Congress upon their completion, thereby allowing Congress to monitor the use of executive agreements by the Executive Branch. Below are the salient provisions of the Circular 175 Procedure and the Case–Zablocki Act. Following the Case–Zablocki Act is an example of an internal memorandum at the Department of State whereby the Office of the Legal Adviser determines whether certain specific executive agreements may be negotiated and concluded. As you read these materials, consider whether they provide sufficient guidance to the Executive Branch regarding the use of executive agreements and whether Congress has preserved an ability to effectively monitor such practice.

U.S. DEPARTMENT OF STATE CIRCULAR 175 PROCEDURE

11 Foreign Affairs Manual (FAM) 721–726 (May 26, 2006).

11 FAM 723.2 Constitutional Requirements

. . . .

There are two procedures under the Constitution through which the United States becomes a party to an international agreement. Those procedures and the constitutional parameters of each are:

11 FAM 723.2–1 Treaties

. . . .

International agreements (regardless of their title, designation, or form) whose entry into force with respect to the United States takes places only after the Senate has given its advice and consent are "treaties." The President, with the advice and consent of two-thirds of the Senators present, may enter into an international agreement on any subject of concern in foreign relations, so long as the agreement does not contravene the United States Constitution; and

11 FAM 723.2–2 International Agreements Other Than Treaties

. . . .

International Agreements brought into force with respect to the United States on a constitutional basis other than with the advice and consent of the Senate are "international agreements other than treaties." (The term "sole executive agreement" is appropriately reserved for agreements made solely on the basis of the constitutional authority of the President.) There are three constitutional bases for international agreements other than treaties as set forth below. An international agreement may be concluded pursuant to one or more of these constitutional bases:

11 FAM 723.2–2(A) Agreements Pursuant to Treaty

. . . .

The President may conclude an international agreement pursuant to a treaty brought into force with the advice and consent of the Senate, the provisions of which constitute authorization for the agreement by the Executive without subsequent action by the Congress;

11 FAM 723.2–2(B) Agreements Pursuant to Legislation

. . . .

The President may conclude an international agreement on the basis of existing legislation, or subject to legislation to be adopted by the Congress, or upon the failure of Congress to adopt a disapproving joint or concurrent resolution within designated time periods; and

11 FAM 723.2–2(C) Agreements Pursuant to the Constitutional Authority of the President

. . . .

The President may conclude an international agreement on any subject within his constitutional authority so long as the agreement is not inconsistent with legislation enacted by the Congress in the exercise of its constitutional authority. The constitutional sources of authority for the President to conclude international agreements include:

(1) The President's authority as Chief Executive to represent the nation in foreign affairs;

(2) The President's authority to receive ambassadors and other public ministers;

(3) The President's authority as "Commander-in-Chief"; and

(4) The President's authority to "take care that the laws be faithfully executed."

11 FAM 723.3 Considerations for Selecting Among Constitutionally Authorized Procedures

. . . .

In determining a question as to the procedure which should be followed for any particular international agreement, due consideration is given to the following factors along with those in 11 FAM 723.2:

(1) The extent to which the agreement involves commitments or risks affecting the nation as a whole;

(2) Whether the agreement is intended to affect state laws;

(3) Whether the agreement can be given effect without the enactment of subsequent legislation by the Congress;

(4) Past U.S. practice as to similar agreements;

(5) The preference of the Congress as to a particular type of agreement;

(6) The degree of formality desired for an agreement;

(7) The proposed duration of the agreement, the need for prompt conclusion of an agreement, and the desirability of concluding a routine or short-term agreement; and

(8) The general international practice as to similar agreements.

In determining whether an international agreement should be brought into force as a treaty or as an international agreement other than a treaty, the utmost care is to be exercised to avoid any invasion or compromise of the constitutional powers of the President, the Senate, and the Congress as a whole.

. . . .

11 FAM 724.3 Request for Authorization to Negotiation and/or Sign Action Memorandum

. . . .

a. A request for authorization to negotiate and/or conclude a treaty or other international agreement takes the form of an action memorandum addressed to the Secretary or other principal to whom such authority has been delegated, as appropriate, and cleared with the Office of the Legal Adviser. . . .

. . . .

h. The action memorandum is accompanied by: (1) the U.S. draft, if available, of any agreement or other instrument intended to be negotiated; or (2) the text of any agreement and related exchange of notes, agreed minutes, or other document to be signed . . .; and (3) a memorandum of law prepared in the Office of the Legal Adviser.

. . . .

11 FAM 726 Transmission of International Agreements Other than Treaties to Congress: Compliance with the Case–Zablocki Act

. . . .

All officers will be especially diligent in cooperating to assure compliance with Public Law 92–403 "An Act to require that international agreements other than treaties, hereafter entered into by the United States, be transmitted to the Congress within sixty days after the execution thereof." . . .

CASE-ZABLOCKI ACT

1 U.S.C. § 112b (2006).

(a) The Secretary of State shall transmit to the Congress the text of any international agreement (including the text of any oral international agreement, which agreement shall be reduced to writing), other than a treaty, to which the United States is a party as soon as practicable after such agreement has entered into force with respect to the United States but in no event later than sixty days thereafter. However, any such agreement the immediate public disclosure of which would, in the opinion of the President, be prejudicial to the national security of the United States shall not be so transmitted to the Congress but shall be transmitted to the Committee on Foreign Relations of the Senate and the Committee on International Relations of the House of Representatives under an appropriate injunction of secrecy to be removed only upon due notice from the President. Any department or agency of the United States Government which enters into any international agreement on behalf of the United States shall transmit to the Department of State the text of such agreement not later than twenty days after such agreement has been signed.

(b) Not later than March 1, 1979, and at yearly intervals thereafter, the President shall, under his own signature, transmit to the Speaker of the House of Representatives and the chairman of the Committee on Foreign Relations of the Senate a report with respect to each international agreement which, during the preceding year, was transmitted to the Congress after the expiration of the 60–day period referred to in the first sentence of subsection (a), describing fully and completely the reasons for the late transmittal.

(c) Notwithstanding any other provision of law, an international agreement may not be signed or otherwise concluded on behalf of the United States without prior consultation with the Secretary of State. Such consultation may encompass a class of agreements rather than a particular agreement.

(d)(1) The Secretary of State shall annually submit to Congress a report that contains an index of all international agreements, listed by country, date, title, and summary of each such agreement (including a description of the duration of activities under the agreement and the agreement itself), that the United States—

(A) has signed, proclaimed, or with reference to which any other final formality has been executed, or that has been extended or otherwise modified, during the preceding calendar year; and

(B) has not been published, or is not proposed to be published, in the compilation entitled "United States Treaties and Other International Agreements".

(2) The report described in paragraph (1) may be submitted in classified form.

(e)(1) Subject to paragraph (2), the Secretary of State shall determine for and within the executive branch whether an arrangement constitutes an international agreement within the meaning of this section. . . .

DEPARTMENT OF STATE CIRCULAR 175 LEGAL MEMORANDUM REGARDING A REQUEST FOR USAID TO NEGOTIATE AND CONCLUDE CERTAIN INTERNATIONAL AGREEMENTS

(August 15, 2002), available at http://www.usaid.gov/policy/ads/300/349maa.pdf.

[In accordance with the Circular 175 procedure, the Secretary of State or his designee each year approves dozens of authorizations to negotiate or conclude international agreements. For example, on August 15, 2002, Secretary Colin Powell approved a request from the Administrator of the U.S. Agency for International Development (USAID) for "blanket" authority (*i.e.*, authority not specific to any particular country) to negotiate and conclude certain bilateral agreements with countries that are recipients of U.S. foreign aid. Attached at Tab 2 of the "action memo" from USAID to the Secretary requesting such authority was a memorandum of law prepared by the Office of the Legal Adviser addressing the legal authority for concluding such agreements.]

Memorandum of Law

SUBJECT: *Circular 175: U.S. Agency for International Development ("USAID") Request for Blanket Authorization to Negotiate and Conclude Certain International Agreements*

In accordance with the Circular 175 procedure, 11 FAM 700 *et seq.*, the accompanying action memorandum requests blanket authority for USAID to negotiate and conclude certain classes of international agreements for its foreign assistance and food aid programs. . . .

USAID is currently operating under a blanket authorization from the Secretary [of State] issued on July 27, 1956, to USAID's predecessor agency, the International Cooperation Agency. The present C–175 request is designed to address the extensive changes to the format, scope and content of USAID agreements and to be more consistent with current

USAID operations, for example with respect to privileges and immunities as well as fiscal privileges granted the USAID mission and its personnel.

The agreements subject to the accompanying Circular 175 authority fall into two broad categories: (a) framework agreements that establish the USAID Mission as a special mission in another country, where the other party commits to provide the mission with specific privileges and immunities for USAID, USAID personnel, contractors and recipients, as well as USAID-financed supplies and services; and (b) implementing agreements that govern the provision of foreign assistance, in the form of a particular grant or a program to the other party.

The framework agreement generally involves unilateral non-reciprocal commitments by the other government to the United States. It contains no ongoing USG commitments to provide foreign assistance, in any form (*e.g.*, either by grants or program activities); but rather apply to such assistance as may be given subject to U.S. law. The implementing agreements may apply to grants of amounts stated therein. They are carefully and appropriately caveated that the provision of any assistance generally be subject to U.S. law, including that the provision in specified amounts be subject to the availability of funds to USAID for this purpose. Such assistance funds are appropriated in annual Foreign Operations, Export Financing and Related Programs Appropriations Acts.

Accordingly, the authority to negotiate and conclude such agreements is derived from the President's Constitutional Powers (Article II), including his authority to represent the nation in foreign affairs, as delegated to the Secretary of State on a day–to–day basis (22 U.S.C. 2656). Furthermore, additional authority exists under the Foreign Assistance Act and the Agricultural Trade Development and Assistance Act of 1954—the statutes pursuant to which USAID conducts its foreign assistance and food aid programs, respectively—for the President to enter into agreements concerning the provision of foreign assistance. Specifically, section 635(b) of the Foreign Assistance Act of 1961, as amended, ("FAA"), 22 U.S.C. § 2151 *et seq.* provides legal authority for the negotiation and conclusion of executive agreements. Section 635 (b) provides:

> The President may make loans, advances, and grants to, make and perform agreements and contracts with, or enter into other transactions with, any individual, corporation, or other body of persons, friendly government or government agency, whether within or without the United States, and international organizations in furtherance of the purposes and within the limitations of this Act.

This authority was delegated to the Secretary of State in Executive Order 12163, as amended (March 31, 1999). The Secretary specifically delegated to the Administrator of USAID in Delegation of Authority No. 145 the authority to negotiate, sign and terminate international agreements for USAID programs, subject to the Circular 175 procedure.

Similarly, Titles II and III of the Agricultural Trade Development and Assistance Act of 1954, as amended, ("P.L. 480"), 7 U.S.C. § 1691 *et seq.*

authorize the President in Sections 201 and 202 of Title II, to "establish a program to provide agricultural commodities to foreign countries"; to provide emergency assistance "through governments and public or private agencies, including intergovernmental organizations"; and to provide non-emergency assistance through intergovernmental organizations. 7 U.S.C §§ 1721 and 1722. To this end, section 301(b) of Title III, 7 U.S.C. § 1727 (b) provides that the Administrator of USAID "may negotiate and execute agreements with less developed countries to provide commodities to such countries on a grant basis."

The authority to implement Titles II and III of P.L. 480 is delegated to the Administrator of USAID by the President in Executive Order 12752 (February 25, 1991).

Only implementing agreements involving specific grants of assistance greater than $25 million are considered subject to the accompanying Circular 175 request. The Department has taken the position that grant agreements involving less than $25 million are not considered international agreements and has stated the following in its regulations concerning Circular 175 procedures:

> Finally, it should be noted that United States agencies frequently enter into contracts and similar arrangements with other governments that the Department of State does not consider constitute international agreements under the criteria established in the Department's regulations, 22 C.F.R. 181.2. These include ... such arrangements as bilateral agreements extending grants of $25 million or less by the Agency for International Development to foreign governments and P.L. 480 agreements under which the United States sells food commodities to foreign governments. The Department of State does not publish such arrangements, as it considers them not to be international agreements within the meaning of the Case Act.

60 Fed. Reg. 54320 (Oct. 23, 1995).

At the same time, framework agreements and implementing agreements in excess of $25 million will generally be considered international agreements, within the meaning established in 22 C.F.R. 181.2. As such, USAID will transmit these agreements to the Department as they are concluded so that they can be reported to Congress consistent with the requirements of the Case Act, 1 U.S.C. 112b. Finally, as noted in the action memorandum, agreements relating to assistance or less than $25 million may be considered international agreements if they present issues of a non-routine nature (*e.g.*, political), and hence any such non-routine agreements, regardless of the value of the assistance with which they are associated, shall be considered international agreements requiring a separate Circular 175 authorization. The Office of General Counsel at USAID has advised that there are no legal impediments to concluding such agreements.

On the basis of these considerations, I conclude that there are no legal objections to granting USAID blanket authorization to negotiate and conclude the framework and implementing agreements described in the accompanying action memo and its attachments.

CAROL SCHWAB
ASSISTANT LEGAL ADVISER FOR
POLITICAL & MILITARY AFFAIRS

NOTES ON TYPES OF EXECUTIVE AGREEMENTS

1. *Nomenclature.* Although their names used may vary, the Circular 175 Procedure makes clear that there are three different types of executive agreement, which derive their authority from different sources:

- *Presidential-executive agreements.* These executive agreements are entered into by the President solely in pursuance of the exercise of his plenary powers. To the extent textual authority has been marshaled, it has derived from the "vesting" of the executive power in the President and from extrapolations of the enumerated presidential powers as chief executive (Article II, Section 1), the commander-in-chief power (Article II, Section 2), presidential powers pertaining to the nomination (Article II, Section 2) and receiving (Article II, Section 3) of ambassadors, and the President's authority to "take care that the laws be faithfully executed" (Article II, Section 3).
- *Treaty-based executive agreements.* These executive agreements are entered into by the President solely on the basis of authorization contained in an existing treaty. For example, in *Wilson v. Girard,* 354 U.S. 524 (1957), the Court based the validity of an agreement defining jurisdiction over offenses committed by U.S. military personnel in Japan on the authorization of such an agreement in Security Treaty, Sept. 8, 1951, U.S.-Jap., Art. III, 3 U.S.T. 3329, T.I.A.S. No. 2491.

Chart 2. Steps in the Making of an Executive Agreement

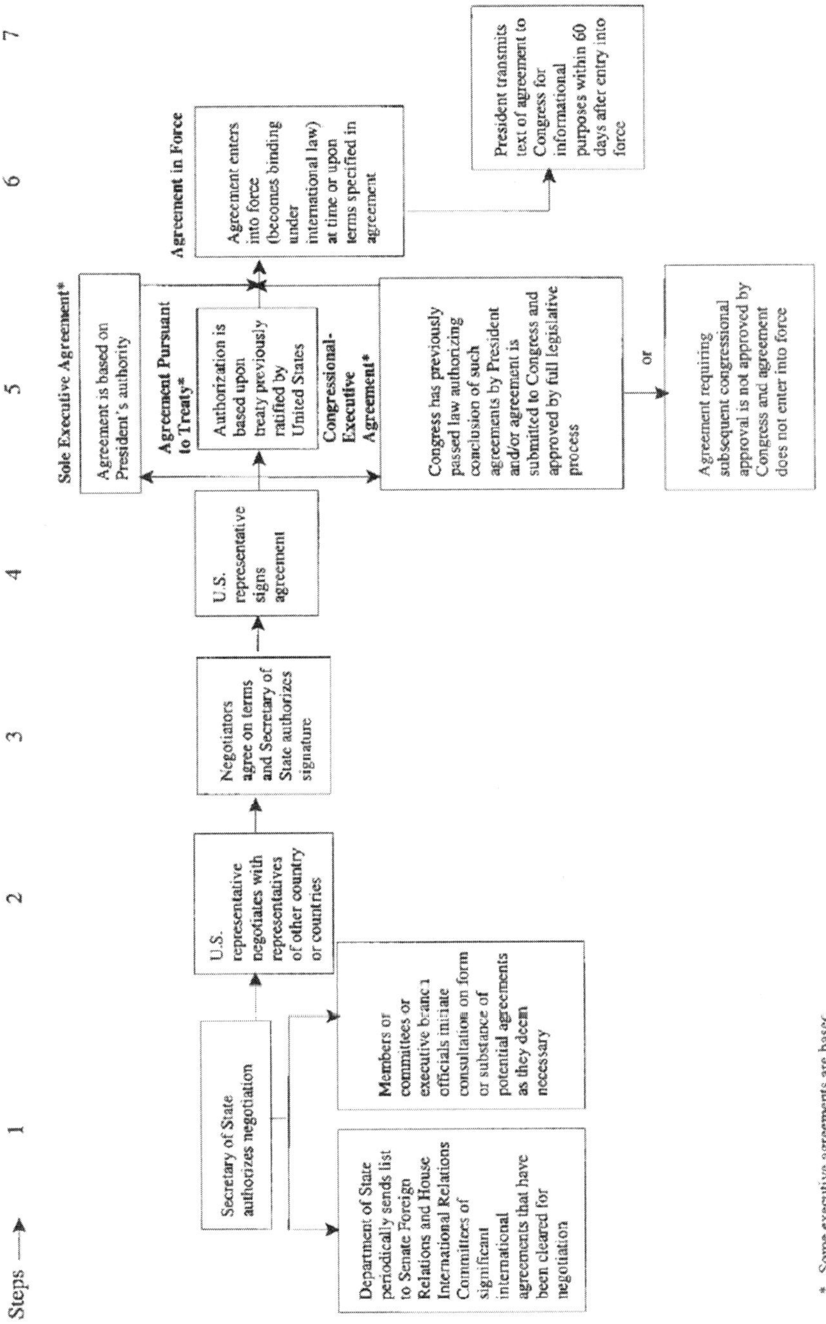

* Some executive agreements are based on more than one type of authority.

- *Congressional-executive agreements.* These executive agreements are entered into by the President solely on the basis of authorization from a simple majority vote of *both* houses of Congress. Such authorization may arise from a standing statute authorizing the President to conclude an entire class of agreements, typically subject to certain conditions. Alternatively, the authorization may arise after the President completes negotiation of the agreement, by the President submitting the agreement for approval to both houses of Congress.

These labels are not used consistently by scholars, officials, or judges. Therefore, students of the subject should observe closely exactly which kind of "executive agreement" is being discussed in any given situation. As you read the materials below, try to determine which type of executive agreement is at stake.

2. *AID Agreements.* Which of the three types of authority is the basis for the AID agreements? Suppose that in the course of negotiating one of the AID agreements, the foreign country insists upon reciprocity, such that any of its foreign aid personnel operating in the United States obtain the same privileges and immunities. Could the U.S. negotiators agree?

3. *A Further Threshold.* This Section is focused on how certain international agreements do not qualify as "treaties" under U.S. constitutional law but, rather, may be based on authority other than the Treaty Clause. Section (e) of the Case-Zablocki Act, however, indicates that a threshold must be met before an instrument will be regarded as an "international agreement" at all (either as a treaty or as an executive agreement). In short, it is left to the Secretary of State to determine whether an instrument (or "arrangement") rises to the level of being an international agreement. When will that be the case? Obviously an instrument or arrangement that has no legally binding effect will not be regarded as an international agreement (*see infra* Section 8). Yet the memorandum of law on the AID agreements suggests that certain instruments concluded by the United States with a foreign country might not qualify as an international agreements even though they are legally binding. Thus, a grant agreement involving less than $25 million is not considered an international agreement., but is instead in the nature of a contract. Do you think that this ability to carve out certain agreements from the field of "treaties or executive agreements" is appropriate as a matter of expediency? Or do you worry that it represents a further diminishment of the treaty power?

4. *Practice Abroad.* Some countries, such as Colombia, do not allow any executive agreements; all international agreements must be concluded as treaties, thus requiring approval by Colombia's Congress. Most countries, however, appear to allow for the conclusion of executive agreements of one kind or another. Thus, Germany and South Africa allow executive agreements so long as they only relate only to minor technical or administrative matters. Canada and Switzerland allow executive agreements so long as they are based on the Executive's sole constitutional authority. China, Egypt, France, and Russia allow executive agreements so long as they fall outside of specific

categories that require legislative approval. Japan allows executive agreements so long as they have been authorized by a prior law or treaty. The United Kingdom and many of the Commonwealth countries impose no constraints on the ability of the Executive to enter into international agreements, including executive agreements. However, such agreements do not have the force of domestic law until such time as implemented by the legislature. Thus, the U.K. Prime Minister has the ability to bind the United Kingdom internationally, but typically will not do so unless the international commitment requires no domestic implementation or can be fulfilled through existing legislative authorization. *See* Duncan B. Hollis, *A Comparative Approach to Treaty Law and Practice, in National Treaty Law and Practice* 1, 24–26 (Duncan B. Hollis, Merritt R. Blakeslee, & L. Benjamin Ederington eds., 2005).

UNITED STATES v. BELMONT

301 U.S. 324–32, 57 S.Ct. 758, 81 L.Ed. 1134 (1937).

MR. JUSTICE SUTHERLAND delivered the opinion of the Court.

This is an action at law brought by petitioner against respondents in a federal district court to recover a sum of money deposited by a Russian corporation (Petrograd Metal Works) with August Belmont, a private banker doing business in New York City under the name of August Belmont & Co. August Belmont died in 1924; and respondents are the duly-appointed executors of his will. A motion to dismiss the complaint for failure to state facts sufficient to constitute a cause of action was sustained by the district court, and its judgment was affirmed by the court below. 85 F.(2d) 542. The facts alleged, so far as necessary to be stated, follow.

The corporation had deposited with Belmont, prior to 1918, the sum of money which petitioner seeks to recover. In 1918, the Soviet Government duly enacted a decree by which it dissolved, terminated and liquidated the corporation (together with others), and nationalized and appropriated all of its property and assets of every kind and wherever situated, including the deposit account with Belmont. As a result, the deposit became the property of the Soviet Government, and so remained until November 16, 1933, at which time the Soviet Government released and assigned to petitioner all amounts due to that government from American nationals, including the deposit account of the corporation with Belmont. Respondents failed and refused to pay the amount upon demand duly made by petitioner.

The assignment was effected by an exchange of diplomatic correspondence between the Soviet Government and the United States. The purpose was to bring about a final settlement of the claims and counterclaims between the Soviet Government and the United States; and it was agreed that the Soviet Government would take no steps to enforce claims against American nationals; but all such claims were released and assigned to the United States, with the understanding that the Soviet Government was to be duly notified of all amounts realized by the United States from such release and assignment. The assignment and requirement for notice are parts of the larger plan to bring about a settlement of the rival claims of the high contracting parties. The continuing and definite interest of the Soviet Government in the collection of assigned claims is evident; and the case, therefore, presents a question of public concern, the determination of which well might involve the good faith of the United States in the eyes of a foreign government. The court below held that the assignment thus effected embraced the claim here in question; and with that we agree.

That court, however, took the view that the situs of the bank deposit was within the state of New York; that in no sense could it be regarded as an intangible property right within Soviet territory; and that the nationalization decree, if enforced, would put into effect an act of confiscation. And it held that a judgment for the United States could not be had, because, in view of that result, it would be contrary to the controlling public policy of the state of New York. The further contention is made by respondents that the public policy of the United States would likewise be infringed by such a judgment. The two questions thus presented are the only ones necessary to be considered.

First. We do not pause to inquire whether in fact there was any policy of the state of New York to be infringed, since we are of opinion that no state policy can prevail against the international compact here involved.

. . . .

We take judicial notice of the fact that coincident with the assignment set forth in the complaint, the President recognized the Soviet Government, and normal diplomatic relations were established between that government and the government of the United States, followed by an exchange of ambassadors. The effect of this was to validate, so far as this country is concerned, all acts of the Soviet Government here involved from the commencement of its existence. The recognition, establishment of diplomatic relations, the assignment, and agreements with respect thereto, were all parts of one transaction, resulting in an international compact between the two governments. That the negotiations, acceptance of the assignment and agreements and understandings in respect thereof were within the competence of the President may not be doubted. Governmental power over internal affairs is distributed between the national government and the several states. Governmental power over external affairs is not distributed, but is vested exclusively in the national government. And in respect of what was done here, the Executive had authority to speak as the sole organ of that government. The assignment and the agreements in connection therewith did not, as in the case of treaties, as that term is used in the treaty making clause of the Constitution (Art. II, § 2), require the advice and consent of the Senate.

A treaty signifies "a compact made between two or more independent nations, with a view to the public welfare." *Altman & Co. v. United States*, 224 U.S. 583, 600. But an international compact, as this was, is not always a treaty which requires the participation of the Senate. There are many such compacts, of which a protocol, a modus vivendi, a postal convention, and agreements like that now under consideration are illustrations. *See* 5 Moore, Int. Law Digest, 210–221. The distinction was pointed out by this court in the *Altman* case, *supra*, which arose under § 3 of the Tariff Act of 1897, authorizing the President to conclude commercial agreements with foreign countries in certain specified matters. We held that although this might not be a treaty requiring ratification by the Senate, it was a compact negotiated and proclaimed under the authority of the President, and as such was a "treaty" within the meaning of the Circuit Court of Appeals Act, the construction of which might be reviewed upon direct appeal to this court.

Plainly, the external powers of the United States are to be exercised without regard to state laws or policies. The supremacy of a treaty in this respect has been recognized from the beginning. Mr. Madison, in the Virginia Convention, said that if a treaty does not supersede existing state laws, as far as they contravene its operation, the treaty would be ineffective. "To counteract it by the supremacy of the state laws, would bring on the Union the just charge of national perfidy, and involve us in war." 3 Elliot's Debates 515. And *see Ware v. Hylton*, 3 Dall. 199, 236–237. And while this rule in respect of treaties is established by the express language of cl. 2, Art. VI, of the Constitution, the same rule would result in the case of all international compacts and agreements from the very fact that complete power over international affairs is in the national government and is not and cannot be subject to any curtailment or interference on the part of the several states. *Compare United States v. Curtiss–Wright Export Corp.*, 299 U.S. 304, 316 *et seq*. In respect of all international negotiations and compacts, and in respect of our foreign relations generally, state lines disappear. As to such purposes the State of New York does not exist. Within the field of its powers, whatever the United States rightfully undertakes, it necessarily has warrant to consummate. And when judicial authority is invoked in aid of such consummation, state constitutions, state laws, and state policies are irrelevant to the inquiry and decision. It is inconceivable that any of them can be interposed as an obstacle to the effective operation of a federal constitutional power. *Cf. Missouri v. Holland*, 252 U.S. 416; *Asakura v. Seattle*, 265 U.S. 332, 341.

Second. The public policy of the United States relied upon as a bar to the action is that declared by the Constitution, namely, that private property shall not be taken without just compensation. But the answer is that our Constitution, laws, and policies have no extraterritorial operation, unless in respect of our own citizens. *Compare United States v. Curtiss–Wright Export Corp.*, *supra*, 299 U.S. 304, at p. 318. What another country has done in the way of taking over property of its nationals, and especially of its corporations, is not a matter for judicial consideration here. Such nationals must look to their own government for any redress to which they may be entitled. So far as the record shows, only the rights of the Russian corporation have been affected by what has been done; and it will be time enough to consider the rights of our nationals when, if ever, by proper judicial proceeding, it shall be made to appear that they are so affected as to entitle them to judicial relief. The substantive right to the moneys, as now disclosed, became vested in the Soviet Government as the successor to the corporation; and this right that government has passed to the United States. It does not appear that respondents have any interest in the matter beyond that of a custodian. Thus far no question under the Fifth Amendment is involved.

It results that the complaint states a cause of action and that the judgment of the court below to the contrary is erroneous. In so holding, we deal only with the case as now presented and with the parties now before us. We do not consider the status of adverse claims, if there be any, of others not parties to this action. And nothing we have said is to be construed as foreclosing the assertion of any such claim to the fund involved, by intervention or other appropriate proceeding. We decide only that the complaint alleges facts sufficient to constitute a cause of action against the respondents.

Judgment reversed.

DAMES & MOORE v. REGAN

453 U.S. 654, 659–90, 101 S.Ct. 2972, 69 L.Ed.2d 918 (1981) (some footnotes and citations omitted).

JUSTICE REHNQUIST delivered the opinion of the Court.

. . . .

. . . We are confined to a resolution of the dispute presented to us. That dispute involves various Executive Orders and regulations by which the President nullified attachments and liens on Iranian assets in the United States, directed that these assets be transferred to Iran, and suspended claims against Iran that may be presented to an International Claims Tribunal. This action was taken in an effort to comply with an Executive Agreement between the United States and Iran. . . .

I

On November 4, 1979, the American Embassy in Tehran was seized and our diplomatic personnel were captured and held hostage. In response to that crisis, President Carter, acting pursuant to the International Emergency Economic Powers Act, 91 Stat. 1626, 50 U.S.C. §§ 1701–1706 (1976 ed., Supp. III) (hereinafter IEEPA), declared a national emergency on November 14, 1979,[1] and blocked the removal or transfer of "all property and interests in property of the Government of Iran, its instru-

1. Title 50 U.S.C. § 1701(a) (1976 ed., Supp. III) states that the President's authority under the Act "may be exercised to deal with any unusual and extraordinary threat, which has its source in whole or substantial part outside the United States, to the national security, foreign policy, or economy of the United States, if the President declares a national emergency with respect to such threat." Petitioner does not challenge President Carter's declaration of a national emergency.

mentalities and controlled entities and the Central Bank of Iran which are or become subject to the jurisdiction of the United States. ..." Exec. Order No. 12170, 3 CFR 457 (1980), note following 50 U.S.C. § 1701 (1976 ed., Supp. III).[2] President Carter authorized the Secretary of the Treasury to promulgate regulations carrying out the blocking order. On November 15, 1979, the Treasury Department's Office of Foreign Assets Control issued a regulation providing that "[u]nless licensed or authorized ... any attachment, judgment, decree, lien, execution, garnishment, or other judicial process is null and void with respect to any property in which on or since [November 14, 1979] there existed an interest of Iran." 31 CFR § 535.203(e) (1980). The regulations also made clear that any licenses or authorizations granted could be "amended, modified, or revoked at any time." § 535.805.[3]

On November 26, 1979, the President granted a general license authorizing certain judicial proceedings against Iran but which did not allow the "entry of any judgment or of any decree or order of similar or analogous effect. ..." § 535.504(a). On December 19, 1979, a clarifying regulation was issued stating that "the general authorization for judicial proceedings contained in § 535.504(a) includes pre-judgment attachment." § 535.418.

....

On January 20, 1981, the Americans held hostage were released by Iran pursuant to an Agreement entered into the day before and embodied in two Declarations of the Democratic and Popular Republic of Algeria[:]. Declaration of the Government of the Democratic and Popular Republic of Algeria, and Declaration of the Government of the Democratic and Popular Republic of Algeria Concerning the Settlement of Claims by the Government of the United States of America and the Government of the Islamic Republic of Iran. The Agreement stated that "[i]t is the purpose of [the United States and Iran] ... to terminate all litigation as between the Government of each party and the nationals of the other, and to bring about the settlement and termination of all such claims through binding arbitration." In furtherance of this goal, the Agreement called for the establishment of an Iran–United States Claims Tribunal which would arbitrate any claims not settled within six months. Awards of the Claims Tribunal are to be "final and binding" and "enforceable ... in the courts of any nation in accordance with its laws." Under the Agreement, the United States is obligated

2. Title 50 U.S.C. § 1702(a)(1)(B) (1976 ed., Supp. III) empowers the President to

"investigate, regulate, direct and compel, nullify, void, prevent or prohibit, any acquisition, holding, withholding, use, transfer, withdrawal, transportation, importation or exportation of, or dealing in, or exercising any right, power, or privilege with respect to, or transactions involving, any property in which any foreign country or a national thereof has any interest...."

3. Title 31 CFR § 535.805 (1980) provides in full:

"The provisions of this part and any rulings, licenses, authorizations, instructions, orders, or forms issued thereunder may be amended, modified, or revoked at any time."

> "to terminate all legal proceedings in United States courts involving claims of United States persons and institutions against Iran and its state enterprises, to nullify all attachments and judgments obtained therein, to prohibit all further litigation based on such claims, and to bring about the termination of such claims through binding arbitration."

In addition, the United States must "act to bring about the transfer" by July 19, 1981, of all Iranian assets held in this country by American banks. One billion dollars of these assets will be deposited in a security account in the Bank of England, to the account of the Algerian Central Bank, and used to satisfy awards rendered against Iran by the Claims Tribunal.

On January 19, 1981, President Carter issued a series of Executive Orders implementing the terms of the agreement. Exec. Orders Nos. 12276–12285, 46 Fed.Reg. 7913–7932. . . .

. . . .

[Petitioner brought a claim in U.S. court against the government of Iran for its failure to pay for services rendered under a contract prior to its termination by Iran. Petitioner secured a pre-judgment attachment of certain Iranian assets and obtained a U.S. court judgment against Iran, but was prohibited from enforcing the judgment by the President's Executive Orders and the Treasury Department regulations.]

On April 28, 1981, petitioner filed this action in the District Court for declaratory and injunctive relief against the United States and the Secretary of the Treasury, seeking to prevent enforcement of the Executive Orders and Treasury Department regulations implementing the Agreement with Iran. In its complaint, petitioner alleged that the actions of the President and the Secretary of the Treasury implementing the Agreement with Iran were beyond their statutory and constitutional powers and, in any event, were unconstitutional to the extent they adversely affect petitioner's final judgment against the Government of Iran and the Atomic Energy Organization, its execution of that judgment in the State of Washington, its prejudgment attachments, and its ability to continue to litigate against the Iranian banks. On May 28, 1981, the District Court denied petitioner's motion for a preliminary injunction and dismissed petitioner's complaint for failure to state a claim upon which relief could be granted. . . .

. . . .

II

The parties and the lower courts, confronted with the instant questions, have all agreed that much relevant analysis is contained in *Youngstown Sheet & Tube Co. v. Sawyer,* 343 U.S. 579 (1952). Justice Black's opinion for the Court in that case, involving the validity of President Truman's effort to seize the country's steel mills in the wake of a nationwide strike, recognized that "[t]he President's power, if any, to issue the order must stem either from an act of Congress or from the Constitution itself." *Id.*, at 585. . . .

. . . .

III

In nullifying post-November 14, 1979, attachments and directing those persons holding blocked Iranian funds and securities to transfer them to the Federal Reserve Bank of New York for ultimate transfer to Iran, President Carter cited five sources of express or inherent power. The Government, however, has principally relied on § 203 of the IEEPA as authorization for these actions. . . .

. . . .

IV

Although we have concluded that the IEEPA constitutes specific congressional authorization to the President to nullify the attachments and order the transfer of Iranian assets, there remains the question of the President's authority to suspend claims pending in American courts. Such claims have, of course, an existence apart from the attachments which accompanied them. In terminating these claims through Executive Order No. 12294, the President purported to act under authority of both the IEEPA and 22 U.S.C. § 1732, the so-called "Hostage Act." 46 Fed. Reg. 14111 (1981).

We conclude that although the IEEPA authorized the nullification of the attachments, it cannot be read to authorize the suspension of the claims. The claims of American citizens against Iran are not in themselves transactions involving Iranian property or efforts to exercise any rights with respect to such property. An *in personam* lawsuit, although it might eventually be reduced to judgment and that judgment might be executed upon, is an effort to establish liability and fix damages and does not focus on any particular property within the jurisdiction. The terms of the IEEPA therefore do not authorize the President to suspend claims in American courts. . . .

. . . .

Although we have declined to conclude that the IEEPA or the Hostage Act directly authorizes the President's suspension of claims for the reasons noted, we cannot ignore the general tenor of Congress' legislation in this area in trying to determine whether the President is acting alone or at least with the acceptance of Congress. As we have noted, Congress cannot anticipate and legislate with regard to every possible action the President may find it necessary to take or every possible situation in which he might act. Such failure of Congress specifically to delegate authority does not, "especially . . . in the areas of foreign policy and national security," imply "congressional disapproval" of action taken by the Executive. *Haig v. Agee*, [453 U.S. 280,] 291. On the contrary, the enactment of legislation closely related to the question of the President's authority in a particular case which evinces legislative intent to accord the President broad discretion may be considered to "invite" "measures on independent presidential responsibility," *Youngstown,* 343 U.S., at 637 (Jackson, J., concurring). At least this is so where there is no contrary indication of legislative intent and when, as here, there is a history of congressional acquiescence in conduct of the sort engaged in by the President. It is to that history which we now turn.

Not infrequently in affairs between nations, outstanding claims by nationals of one country against the government of another country are "sources of friction" between the two sovereigns. *United States v. Pink,* 315 U.S. 203, 225.[1] To resolve these difficulties, nations have often entered into agreements settling the claims of their respective nationals. As one treatise writer puts it, international agreements settling claims by nationals of one state against the government of another "are established international practice reflecting traditional international theory." L. Henkin, *Foreign Affairs and the Constitution* 262 (1972). Consistent with that principle, the United States has repeatedly exercised its sovereign authority to settle the claims of its nationals against foreign countries. Though those settlements have sometimes been made by treaty, there has also been a longstanding practice of settling such claims by executive agreement without the advice and consent of the Senate.[8] Under such agreements, the President has agreed to renounce or extinguish claims of United States nationals against foreign governments in return for lump-sum payments or the establishment of arbitration procedures. To be sure, many of these settlements were encouraged by the United States claimants themselves, since a claimant's only hope of obtaining any payment at all might lie in having his Government negotiate a diplomatic settlement on his behalf. But it is also undisputed that the "United States has sometimes disposed of the claims of its citizens without their consent, or even without consultation with them, usually without exclusive regard for their interests, as distinguished from those of the nation as a whole." Henkin, *supra,* at 262–263. Accord, *Restatement (Second) of Foreign Relations Law of the United States* § 213 (1965) (President "may waive or settle a claim against a foreign state . . . [even] without the consent of the [injured] national"). It is clear that the practice of settling claims continues today. Since 1952, the President has entered into at least 10 binding

---

1. [Authors' Note: *United States v. Pink*, 315 U.S. 203 (1942), entailed the same basic facts as occurred in *Belmont*, but involved the U.S. government suing the New York State Superintendent of Insurance to obtain assets acquired pursuant to the Litvinov assignment—assets that might otherwise have gone to persons whose property was expropriated by the Soviet Union. The Supreme Court again upheld the President's power to conclude the executive agreement as an incident to recognition of the Soviet Union. Among other things, the Court said that the "Fifth Amendment does not stand in the way of giving full force and effect to the Litinov Assignment." *Id.* at 228.]

8. At least since the case of the "Wilmington Packet" in 1799, Presidents have exercised the power to settle claims of United States nationals by executive agreement. *See* Lillich, *The Gravel Amendment to the Trade Reform Act of 1974*, 69 Am.J.Int'l L. 837, 844 (1975). In fact, during the period of 1817–1917, "no fewer than eighty executive agreements were entered into by the United States looking toward the liquidation of claims of its citizens." W. McClure, International Executive Agreements 53 (1941). *See also* 14 M. Whiteman, *Digest of International Law* 247 (1970).

settlements with foreign nations, including an $80 million settlement with the People's Republic of China.[9]

Crucial to our decision today is the conclusion that Congress has implicitly approved the practice of claim settlement by executive agreement. This is best demonstrated by Congress' enactment of the International Claims Settlement Act of 1949, 64 Stat. 13, as amended, 22 U.S.C. § 1621 *et seq.* (1976 ed. and Supp. IV). The Act had two purposes: (1) to allocate to United States nationals funds received in the course of an executive claims settlement with Yugoslavia, and (2) to provide a procedure whereby funds resulting from future settlements could be distributed. To achieve these ends Congress created the International Claims Commission, now the Foreign Claims Settlement Commission, and gave it jurisdiction to make final and binding decisions with respect to claims by United States nationals against settlement funds. 22 U.S.C. § 1623(a). By creating a procedure to implement future settlement agreements, Congress placed its stamp of approval on such agreements. Indeed, the legislative history of the Act observed that the United States was seeking settlements with countries other than Yugoslavia and that the bill contemplated settlements of a similar nature in the future. H.R.Rep. No. 770, 81st Cong., 1st Sess., 4, 8 (1949).

Over the years Congress has frequently amended the International Claims Settlement Act to provide for particular problems arising out of settlement agreements, thus demonstrating Congress' continuing acceptance of the President's claim settlement authority. ... Finally, the legislative history of the IEEPA further reveals that Congress has accepted the authority of the Executive to enter into settlement agreements. Though the IEEPA was enacted to provide for some limitation on the President's emergency powers, Congress stressed that "[n]othing in this act is intended ... to interfere with the authority of the President to [block assets], or to impede the settlement of claims of U.S. citizens against foreign countries." S.Rep. No. 95–466, p. 6 (1977); 50 U.S.C. § 1706(a)(1) (1976 ed., Supp. III).[10]

---

9. Those agreements are [1979] 30 U.S.T. 1957 (People's Republic of China); [1976] 27 U.S.T. 3933 (Peru); [1976] 27 U.S.T. 4214 (Egypt); [1974] 25 U.S.T. 227 (Peru); [1973] 24 U.S.T. 522 (Hungary); [1969] 20 U.S.T. 2654 (Japan); [1965] 16 U.S.T. 1 (Yugoslavia); [1963] 14 U.S.T. 969 (Bulgaria); [1960] 11 U.S.T. 1953 (Poland); [1960] 11 U.S.T. 317 (Rumania).

10. Indeed, Congress has consistently failed to object to this longstanding practice of claim settlement by executive agreement, even when it has had an opportunity to do so. In 1972, Congress entertained legislation relating to congressional oversight of such agreements. But Congress took only limited action, requiring that the text of significant executive agreements be transmitted to Congress. 1 U.S.C. § 112b. In *Haig v. Agee,* [453 U.S. 280], we noted that "[d]espite the longstanding and officially promulgated view that the Executive has the power to withhold passports for reasons of national security and foreign policy, Congress in 1978, 'though it once again enacted legislation relating to passports, left completely untouched the broad rule-making authority granted in the earlier Act.' " [*Id.*], at 301, quoting *Zemel v. Rusk,* 381 U.S. 1, 12 (1965). Likewise in this case, Congress, though legislating in the area has left "untouched" the authority of the President to enter into settlement agreements.

The legislative history of 1 U.S.C. § 112b further reveals that Congress has accepted the President's authority to settle claims. During the hearings on the bill, Senator Case, the sponsor of the Act, stated with respect to executive claim settlements:

In addition to congressional acquiescence in the President's power to settle claims, prior cases of this Court have also recognized that the President does have some measure of power to enter into executive agreements without obtaining the advice and consent of the Senate. In *United States v. Pink,* 315 U.S. 203 (1942), for example, the Court upheld the validity of the Litvinov Assignment, which was part of an Executive Agreement whereby the Soviet Union assigned to the United States amounts owed to it by American nationals so that outstanding claims of other American nationals could be paid. The Court explained that the resolution of such claims was integrally connected with normalizing United States' relations with a foreign state:

> "Power to remove such obstacles to full recognition as settlement of claims of our nationals . . . certainly is a modest implied power of the President. . . . No such obstacle can be placed in the way of rehabilitation of relations between this country and another nation, unless the historic conception of the powers and responsibilities . . . is to be drastically revised." *Id.,* at 229–230.

. . . .

In light of all of the foregoing—the inferences to be drawn from the character of the legislation Congress has enacted in the area, such as the IEEPA and the Hostage Act, and from the history of acquiescence in executive claims settlement—we conclude that the President was authorized to suspend pending claims pursuant to Executive Order No. 12294. As Justice Frankfurter pointed out in *Youngstown,* 343 U.S., at 610–611, "a systematic, unbroken, executive practice, long pursued to the knowledge of the Congress and never before questioned . . . may be treated as a gloss on 'Executive Power' vested in the President by § 1 of Art. II." Past practice does not, by itself, create power, but "long-continued practice, known to and acquiesced in by Congress, would raise a presumption that the [action] had been [taken] in pursuance of its consent. . . ." *United States v. Midwest Oil Co.,* 236 U.S. 459, 474 (1915). *See Haig v. Agee,* [453 U.S.], at 291, 292. Such practice is present here and such a presumption is also appropriate. In light of the fact that Congress may be considered to have consented to the President's action in suspending claims, we cannot say that action exceeded the President's powers.

Our conclusion is buttressed by the fact that the means chosen by the President to settle the claims of American nationals provided an alternative forum, the Claims Tribunal, which is capable of providing meaningful relief. The Solicitor General also suggests that the provision of the Claims Tribunal will actually *enhance* the opportunity for claimants to recover their claims, in that the Agreement removes a number of jurisdictional and procedural impediments faced by claimants in United States courts.

"I think it is a most interesting [area] in which we have accepted the right of the President, one individual, acting through his diplomatic force, to adjudicate and settle claims of American nationals against foreign countries. But that is a fact." Transmittal of Executive Agreements to Congress: Hearings on S. 596 before the Senate Committee on Foreign Relations, 92d Cong., 1st Sess., 74 (1971).

Although being overly sanguine about the chances of United States claimants before the Claims Tribunal would require a degree of naiveté which should not be demanded even of judges, the Solicitor General's point cannot be discounted. Moreover, it is important to remember that we have already held that the President has the *statutory* authority to nullify attachments and to transfer the assets out of the country. The President's power to do so does not depend on his provision of a forum whereby claimants can recover on those claims. The fact that the President has provided such a forum here means that the claimants are receiving something in return for the suspension of their claims, namely, access to an international tribunal before which they may well recover something on their claims. Because there does appear to be a real "settlement" here, this case is more easily analogized to the more traditional claim settlement cases of the past.

Just as importantly, Congress has not disapproved of the action taken here. Though Congress has held hearings on the Iranian Agreement itself, Congress has not enacted legislation, or even passed a resolution, indicating its displeasure with the Agreement. Quite the contrary, the relevant Senate Committee has stated that the establishment of the Tribunal is "of vital importance to the United States." S.Rep. No. 97–71, p. 5 (1981).[13] We are thus clearly not confronted with a situation in which Congress has in some way resisted the exercise of Presidential authority.

Finally, we re-emphasize the narrowness of our decision. We do not decide that the President possesses plenary power to settle claims, even as against foreign governmental entities. As the Court of Appeals for the First Circuit stressed, "[t]he sheer magnitude of such a power, considered against the background of the diversity and complexity of modern international trade, cautions against any broader construction of authority than is necessary." *Chas. T. Main Int'l, Inc. v. Khuzestan Water & Power Authority,* 651 F. 2d, at 814. But where, as here, the settlement of claims has been determined to be a necessary incident to the resolution of a major foreign policy dispute between our country and another, and where, as here, we can conclude that Congress acquiesced in the President's action, we are not prepared to say that the President lacks the power to settle such claims.

. . . .

The judgment of the District Court is accordingly affirmed, and the mandate shall issue forthwith.

It is so ordered.

---

13. Contrast congressional reaction to the Iranian Agreements with congressional reaction to a 1973 Executive Agreement with Czechoslovakia. There the President sought to settle over $105 million in claims against Czechoslovakia for $20.5 million. Congress quickly demonstrated its displeasure by enacting legislation requiring that the Agreement be renegotiated. *See* Lillich, *supra,* n. 8, at 839–840. Though Congress has shown itself capable of objecting to executive agreements, it has rarely done so and has not done so in this case.

NOTES ON TAKING OF PROPERTY BY EXECUTIVE AGREEMENT

1. *Congressional Authorization/Accommodation*. Do *Belmont* and *Dames & Moore* support the proposition that there is a freestanding presidential power to make sole presidential executive agreements with the force of federal law? If so, does this power circumvent key political and procedural safeguards embedded in the Constitution? Might these precedents be construed more narrowly so as to accommodate the U.S. constitutional scheme? *See* Bradford Clark, *Domesticating Sole Executive Agreements*, 93 VA. L. REV. 1573 (2007). The executive power to affect rights of citizens by the operation of an executive agreement usually does not present itself in stark form. Some color of explicit legislative authorization, or implicit legislative accommodation, is usually present to buttress the exercise of pure presidential power in making the agreement. It may also be unclear whether an actual property "right" has been affected by the operation of the executive agreement.

2. *Implications of* Dames & Moore. *Dames & Moore v. Regan* has been criticized for striving to find implied congressional authorization for the President to suspend claims by removing them from the jurisdiction of U.S. courts, and doing so on the basis of legislative silence only. *See* Lee R. Marks & John C. Grabow, *The President's Foreign Economic Powers After* Dames & Moore v. Regan: *Legislation by Acquiescence,* 68 CORNELL L. REV. 68, 102–03 (1982). The authors of that article claim "this rule effectively obliterates the rights of American claimants against Iran and creates an unwieldy standard of congressional delegation by acquiescence." *Id.* at 103. The authors also interpret the *Dames & Moore* decision as holding that the President "possesses no plenary power to make such a settlement. . . ." *Id.* If this is correct, could Congress prevent the President's action, as the authors suggest, "with an unambiguous expression of contrary intent"? *Id.*

3. *Iranian Claims Redux*. *Dames & Moore* accepted that the President could suspend claims in U.S. courts in favor of an international arbitral forum, the Iran–U.S. Claims Tribunal based in the Hague. What if the Tribunal determined that it had no jurisdiction over a claim? The company Foremost–McKesson initially pursued in U.S. court a claim for unpaid cash dividends and expropriation. In light of the President's Executive Order and the Treasury Department regulations, the U.S. court suspended the claim and Foremost pursued the claim before the Tribunal. In April 1986, the Tribunal issued an award in favor of Foremost for the unpaid cash dividends, but it dismissed the expropriation claim, saying that any expropriation had not ripened as of January 1981, the cut-off date for the Tribunal's jurisdiction. Foremost Tehran v. Iran, 10 Iran–U.S. Cl. Trib. Rep. 228 (1986). At Foremost's request, the U.S. district court reactivated the expropriation claim in U.S. court, and allowed Foremost to amend its complaint to allege an expropriation ripening in April 1982. The court then determined that such an expropriation had occurred. McKesson Corp. v. Iran, No. Civ. A. 82–220, 1997 WL 361177 (D.D.C. June 23, 1997). For the Tribunal's consideration of this U.S. process for suspending/reactivating claims in U.S. courts, see *Iran v. United States*, Partial Award No. 590–A15(IV)–A/24–FT (Dec. 28, 1998).

4. *Shanghai Power Case*. The U.S. Court of Claims in *Shanghai Power v. United States,* 4 Cl.Ct. 237 (1983), considered the question of whether an unsatisfied (and, perhaps, unsatisfiable) claim by a U.S. citizen against a

foreign government constitutes "property," making it subject to the protection of the Fifth Amendment of the Constitution. There, an executive agreement entered into by President Carter settled plaintiff's claim against the People's Republic of China as part of a general settlement of unsatisfied claims going back to the fall of the Nationalist regime and its replacement by the Communists. The settlement would have entitled the plaintiff to a mere fraction of the face value of the aggregate claims of this and other U.S. citizens. The court first found that the plaintiff's claim was "property" for purposes of the "just compensation clause." Nevertheless, the court then found that there was no "taking" of that property by the executive agreement. The opinion explains that every "U.S. national who trades in foreign commerce is a potential beneficiary of the President's authority to settle claims" and "it is frequently entirely fortuitous who will benefit and who will suffer from any such presidential action." *Id.* at 247.

5. *Later-in-Time Doctrine.* As we have seen, treaties later in time can amend or repeal inconsistent earlier statutes. Do executive agreements have the same status? The issue seldom arises starkly since courts (and even Congress) strive to avoid a collision. In *Weinberger v. Rossi*, 456 U.S. 25, 102 S.Ct. 1510, 71 L.Ed.2d 715 (1982), Justice Rehnquist found that a congressional-executive military-base agreement made by the President with the Philippines and a subsequently negotiated presidential-executive agreement giving employment preferences to locals were not inconsistent with a U.S. statute prohibiting discriminatory hiring by the Department of Defense because of the "treaty" exception in that statute. The "treaty" exception was thus interpreted to permit an executive agreement to preclude application of the statutory nondiscrimination provision. However, this was achieved by harmonizing the statute and the agreement, not by deciding between them. To similar effect, see *Collins v. Weinberger,* 707 F.2d 1518 (D.C. Cir. 1983).

Should a congressional-executive agreement "trump" an earlier-in-time statute? Note that both Houses of Congress are involved in the making of such an agreement. Should a presidential-executive agreement "trump" an earlier-in-time statute? Note that both Houses of Congress are *not* involved in the making of such an agreement. According to the *Restatement (Third),* executive agreements authorized by a federal statute or treaty have the same normative rank as the statute or treaty on which they are based, with the later-in-time having precedence. Presidential-executive agreements supersede inconsistent state laws, but may not prevail against a conflicting prior federal statute. *See* 1 *Restatement (Third),* § 115 Reporters' Note 5.

6. *Constitution versus Executive Agreement.* As for executive agreements that are inconsistent with the Constitution, it would be natural to assume that if treaties cannot abridge constitutional rights, neither can presidential-executive agreements or congressional-executive agreements. *See* Reid v. Covert (*supra* Section 6); Holmes v. Laird, 459 F.2d 1211, 1217 (D.C. Cir. 1972). In the case of *Ozonoff v. Berzak,* 744 F.2d 224 (1st Cir. 1984), the First Circuit considered a "loyalty-screening" executive agreement concluded by the U.S. government with the World Health Organization (WHO) in 1953. Under such an agreement (which the United States concluded with several international organizations), the WHO agreed not to hire a U.S. national until the United States first investigated the "loyalty" of the U.S. national to the

U.S. government. The loyalty checks were undertaken pursuant to Executive Order No. 10422, 18 Fed. Reg. 239 (1953) (*reprinted as amended at* 22 U.S.C. § 287 (2006)). The plaintiff, an American physician, sued the U.S. government on grounds that the loyalty check violated his First Amendment rights. The U.S. government responded, in part, that the executive agreement validated such an exercise of presidential investigatory power. The First Circuit held for the plaintiff, finding that the existence of the executive agreement did not support the President's action.

> Giving full accord to the President's unique foreign policy role, the Executive still must bear some burden of justification when depriving citizens of basic free speech and associational rights. ... It has not met that burden here, for it has not identified any tangible harm that might occur to United States security or foreign policy concerns if persons such as Dr. Ozonoff are not subjected to sweeping, undirected inquiries of this type.

744 F.2d at 233. Had you been counsel for the U.S. government, could you have identified potential "tangible harm that might occur"?

7. *Executive Agreements That Alter Treaties.* Can a congressional-executive agreement substantially modify the obligations that the United States would otherwise have under an existing treaty? In 1996, the U.S. Department of Justice Office of Legal Counsel reasoned that since a later-in-time statute can alter a treaty obligation (as a matter of U.S. law), then a later-in-time executive agreement authorized by Congress should be able to do the same: "Accordingly, it lies within the power of Congress to modify the substantive obligations that a treaty imposed upon the United States, or to authorize the President to modify those obligations, insofar as those treaty obligations are binding as a matter of domestic or municipal law. The advice and consent of the Senate are not necessary to achieve this outcome." *See* Memorandum for Alan J. Kreczko, Special Assistant to the President and Legal Adviser to the National Security Council, at pt. II (Nov. 25, 1996), *available at* http://www.usdoj.gov/olc/treaty.top.htm. Should a presidential-executive agreement also be able to alter a treaty obligation as a matter of U.S. law?

8. *Trade Agreements.* The Constitution gives Congress the authority to regulate foreign commerce, art. I, § 8, cl. 3, and to "lay and collect Taxes, Duties, Imposts and Excises," art. I, § 8, cl. 1. But the President has exercised, in practice, a great deal of control over international trade, asserting the Executive's inherent power to conduct foreign relations, and the President's express constitutional power to make treaties, art. II, § 2. Trade legislation authorizing the Executive to conduct international trade agreements minimizes potential friction, but conflicts can arise if the Executive acts outside the scope of such legislation. *See* Consumers Union of the United States, Inc. v. Kissinger, 421 U.S. 1004, 95 S.Ct. 2406, 44 L.Ed.2d 673 (1975).

Since the 1980's, the Executive has relied on "fast-track" or "trade-promotion" procedures to conduct international trade negotiations. Initially enacted in the Trade Act of 1974, and modified and renewed thereafter, "trade-promotion" authority permits expedited congressional treatment for international trade agreements negotiated by the Executive that harmonize, reduce, or eliminate barriers to trade. When an agreement reaches Congress, it is guaranteed, within a set time period, automatic discharge from committee, limited floor debate, and an up-or-down vote without amendment. In exchange for Congress's accelerated treatment, the President is required: (1) to consult with the House Ways and Means Committee and the Senate Finance Committee for sixty days before notifying Congress of an intent to enter an agreement; and (2) to notify these same Committees at least ninety days before entering an agreement. During these periods either Committee may object to the negotiations, derailing the agreement from fast-track consideration. Congress is also free to set time limits on negotiations, specify negotiation objectives, and require executive consultation with congressional and private trade experts.

Fast track was used for the United States–Israel Free Trade Agreement, Apr. 22, 1985, 50 Fed. Reg. 35, 172 (1985), the United States–Canada Free–Trade Agreement, Jan. 2, 1988, 27 I.L.M. 281 (1988), and the United States–Canada–Mexico North American Free Trade Agreement (NAFTA), Dec. 17, 1992, 32 I.L.M. 289 & 605 (1993).

Some commentators have questioned whether the House Ways and Means and Senate Finance Committees' ability to derail executive negotiations by a single committee's objection amounts to an informal "legislative veto" of the kind declared unconstitutional in *I.N.S. v. Chadha* (*supra* Chapter 1, Section 2) (Powell, J. concurring) ("The Court's decision ... apparently will invalidate every use of the legislative veto."). *See generally* Harold Hongju Koh, *Congressional Controls on Presidential Trade Policymaking After* I.N.S. v. Chadha, 18 N.Y.U. J. INT'L L. & POLITICS 1191 (1986); Harold Hongju Koh, *The Legal Markets of International Trade: A Perspective on the Proposed United States–Canada Free Trade Agreement,* 12 YALE J. INT'L L. 193 (1987).

SECTION 8. CHOICE OF INSTRUMENTS

As is clear from the prior sections of this Chapter, an international agreement might be concluded as a "treaty" within the meaning of the U.S. Constitution, in which case it is submitted to the U.S. Senate for advice and consent by means of a two-thirds majority vote. Thereafter, further international agreements might be concluded in implementation of the treaty without additional approval by Congress. Alternatively, an international agreement might be concluded as a congressional-executive agreement, in which case it must be supported by a majority vote in both houses of Congress, which may occur in advance of or after negotiation of the agreement. Finally, an international agreement may be concluded as a presidential-executive agreement, based solely on the President's own constitutional authority.

Is the President free to choose whichever of these alternatives he or she finds most suitable? Obviously, if an international agreement cannot be supported solely by the President's own constitutional authority, then the alternative of using a presidential-executive agreement will not be available. But is it within the President's discretion to submit an international agreement as a treaty (hence to just the Senate for a super-majority vote) or as a congressional-executive agreement (hence to both houses for simple majority votes)? Recall that the Circular 175 Procedure excerpted above in Section 7 sets forth certain "considerations" when deciding how to proceed (*see* 11 FAM 723.3). The circular, however, does not actually indicate which method of making an international agreement is favored after analyzing those considerations. Moreover, Circular 175 is an internal State Department administrative provision, not a source of law binding upon the President.

There may be situations when the President thinks that the agreement will not obtain majority approval in the House, but can secure a two-thirds vote in the Senate. There may be other situations when the President thinks that the agreement cannot obtain a super-majority vote in the Senate, but can achieve a simple majority in both houses. Is the President allowed to choose whichever route he or she regards as politically feasible? Answering that question may require some reflection on the original purposes of the Senate and the House, and of the requirement for a super-majority vote for treaties. Does allowing presidential discretion in this area trample certain important allocations of power established in the U.S. constitutional scheme?

The treatment of trade agreements in U.S. law provides a prism for considering this issue. Though early trade agreements were concluded by the United States as treaties, by the 1930's most trade agreements were being approved as congressional-executive agreements. By the 1980s, the multilateral trade system began expanding dramatically to cover not just trade in goods, but trade in services, intellectual property, and investment, areas of considerable importance for economic activity at all levels of the U.S. economy. Treaties such as the North American Free Trade Agreement (NAFTA) and the Uruguay Round Agreements (establishing the World Trade Organization and amending the General Agreement on Tariffs and Trade (GATT)) came under considerable fire on policy grounds, and prompted many legal analysts to reconsider whether trade agreements should be concluded as congressional-executive agreements. Prominent academics, such as Professor Lawrence Tribe of Harvard Law School, asserted that such agreements had to be concluded as treaties. Such attacks prompted the Justice Department's Office of the Legal Counsel to defend the practice.

LAURENCE H. TRIBE, PREPARED STATEMENT BEFORE THE SENATE COMMITTEE ON COMMERCE, SCIENCE AND TRANSPORTATION

HEARING ON S. 2467, GATT IMPLEMENTING LEGISLATION, S. Hrg. 103–623, at 298–310 (1994).

Although it is remarkable that such basic constitutional argument need even be made, I begin by defending the view that the Constitution provides that certain agreements with foreign nations may be entered into only "with the Advice and Consent of the Senate," culminating in approval by two-thirds of those Senators present. U.S. Const., Art. II, § 2, cl. 2. Contrary to the claims of some scholars and political leaders, the Constitution's requirement of Senate supermajority approval of treaties is not simply an alternative procedure to be followed only if the President and Senate find it expedient to do so. Rather, the Treaty Clause provides an exclusive procedure for treaty approval.

The Constitution certainly does not mandate that all international agreements be subject to the requirements of the Treaty Clause. The Constitution uses an array of terms to describe a variety of international agreements, including "Agreement[s]," "Compact[s]," and "Treat[ies]," Art. I, § 10, cl. 1, 3. The Constitution makes absolutely clear that these are not completely interchangeable terms, but represent discrete categories of agreements subject to distinct constitutional requirements. For example, although each of the fifty states may, with congressional approval, enter into "agreements" and "compacts" with foreign countries, *see* Art. I, § 10, cl. 3, no state may enter a "treaty" with a foreign nation under any circumstances, *see* Art. I, § 10, cl. 1. The federal government, however, may enter into treaties—but only with the advice of the Senate and the consent of two-thirds of Senators present. *See* Art. 2, § 2, cl. 2.

In countering the claims of those who argue that congressional-executive agreements and treaties are wholly interchangeable, I find support in a variety of sources:

- In the leading Supreme Court case on treaties, *Missouri v. Holland*, 252 U.S. 416 (1920), the Court made clear—as everyone understands—that the treaty power and Congress's legislative power are not coextensive. The Constitution permits treaties to accomplish things that cannot be achieved through mere legislation. *See id.* at 433. It necessarily follows that the treaty form and the congressional-executive agreement are not wholly interchangeable.
- The United States Supreme Court has noted that, "[u]nder the Constitution ... the word 'treaty' has a far more restrictive meaning" than it does under international law, *Weinberger v. Rossi*, 456 U.S. 25, 29 (1982), and has spoken of agreements "possessing the dignity of one requiring ratification by the Senate," *B. Altman & Co. v. United States*, 224 U.S. 583, 601 (1912) (emphasis added).
- Controversy over the Senate Foreign Relations Committee's one-time insistence that the term "treaties" in the Vienna Convention on the Law of Treaties be equated with the constitutional treaty category has been a primary reason for the Senate's failure to approve the Convention. *See id.* at 146 n. 4.
- The notes to the *Restatement (3d) of Foreign Relations Law of the United States* indicate that United States law differs from international law in that, under United States law, 'treaties' constitute one category of international agreement that constitutionally requires a particular process and has a particular status. ...

- The State Department has issued guidelines for deciding whether a particular agreement should properly be negotiated and approved as a treaty. *See* 11 *Foreign Affairs Manual*, Chapter 700, § 721.3 (codifying State Department Circular 175, December 13, 1955, as amended).

All these sources support a conclusion that should be obvious from the mere existence of the Treaty Clause: the content and import of certain international agreements require that they be approved by two-thirds of Senators present. . . .

. . . .

The paragraph of the Constitution that contains the Treaty Clause provides for the "Advice and Consent of the Senate" for both treaty-making and certain federal appointments, but there is a striking and telling difference between the Treaty Clause and the adjacent Appointments Clause, for only the Appointments Clause permits alternative procedures. *See* Art. II, § 2, cl. 2. The Appointments Clause provides for Senate majority approval of both principal and inferior officers, but specifically allows Congress to remove the requirement of Senate approval for inferior officers. The Supreme Court's interpretation of the Appointments Clause makes clear that the Constitution's senatorial advice and consent requirement may be replaced with alternative approval methods only where the Constitution specifically so provides. Principal officers, for example, must be confirmed by the Senate, even though the phrase of the Constitution providing for Senate confirmation does not include the word "only." *See Weiss v. United States*, 114 S. Ct. 752, 767 (1994) (Souter, J. concurring). It is inconceivable that the Constitution would permit or the Senate would agree to the Senate's surrender of its unique role in confirming Supreme Court Justices, for example, to allow the House of Representatives alone or perhaps even a committee of the House or Senate to confirm or reject presidential appointments of Supreme Court Justices. The Constitution's affirmative grant of permission to Congress to alter the procedures for appointing inferior officers indicates that the Constitution is explicit when prescribed methods of confirmation or approval are not exclusive. The Treaty Clause's provision for Senate ratification by supermajority must thus be understood as exclusive.

Some have argued, however, that Congress's broad powers under the Interstate and Foreign Commerce Clause and the Necessary and Proper Clause provide ample authority for the use of congressional-executive agreements to effect any change that a treaty might accomplish. This argument is flawed for two basic reasons. First, it begs the central question at issue here. The Necessary and Proper Clause authorizes Congress "[t]o make all Laws" necessary to execute its powers, but it does not mention treaties. Art. I, § 8, cl. 18. The Necessary and Proper Clause, then, cannot be read to authorize bicameral legislative adoption of measures that properly fall within the Constitution's "treaty" category. Second, the function of the Necessary and Proper Clause, which extends congressional power over all fields fairly related to Congress's enumerated powers, does not speak at all to the structural or procedural requirements for passage of measures. In *INS v. Chadha*, 462 U.S. 919 (1983), the Supreme Court's historic decision to invalidate federal legislative veto provisions, the Court made clear that Congress may not abandon the Constitution's prescribed structural and procedural requirements even to regulate a field properly within the legislative power of Congress. The Necessary and Proper Clause no more provides a circuitous route for the approval of treaties than it authorizes a legislative veto in violation of the Constitution's requirements of bicameralism and presentment.

. . . .

What the text of the Treaty Clause will not permit cannot be validated by so-called congressional "precedent." The *Chadha* case provides strong support for the proposition that congressional practice alone cannot justify abandonment of the Constitution's structural provisions. The Supreme Court was willing to invalidate the legislative veto in *Chadha* even though such provisions had been inserted in hundreds of statutes since 1932. As the Supreme Court has often recognized, congressional "precedent" is most persuasive as an argument for the constitutionality of a practice when the practice extends back to our nation's earliest days under the Constitution. *See, e.g.*, *Field v. Clark*, 143 U.S. 649, 683 (1892). Late-breaking developments, however, can easily be signs of unconstitutional innovation. . . . [T]he adoption of important congressional-executive agreements after World War II was part of a "constitutional transformation." Despite the attempts of some in the 1930s and 1940s to demonstrate that other forms of international agreements had been interchangeable with the treaty form since the early days of our Republic, . . . the widespread use of the congressional-executive agreement for certain types of accords represented an important shift in national practice.

. . . [T]he Supreme Court cases that are sometimes trotted out for the proposition that any executive agreement can become "the supreme Law of the Land" through majority approval of the House and Senate in fact establish no such thing. . . . These cases often deal with the very different issues of unilateral presidential settlement or suspension of claims against foreign nations, *see, e.g.*, *United States v. Pink*, 315 U.S. 203 (1942); *United States v. Belmont*, 301 U.S. 324 (1937), or proclamation statutes, by which Congress authorizes the President to take certain actions upon making particular findings, *see, e.g.*, *United States v. Curtis–Wright*, 299 U.S. 304 (1936); *Field v. Clark*, 143 U.S. 649 (1892). The Supreme Court has never addressed directly the constitutionality of using the congressional-executive agreement to deal with matters that fall within the Constitution's "treaty" category. On the contrary, . . . at least prior to World War II, there really was no congressional or Supreme Court precedent for any attempt to read the Treaty Clause as purely optional and to regard congressionally approved executive agreements as fully interchangeable with Senate-ratified treaties.

Indeed, in the aftermath of World War II, with memories of the demise of the League of Nations still fresh in the national memory, there was considerable concern that the requirements of the Treaty Clause might be an impediment to the establishment of world peace. In this context, the House of Representatives approved a proposed constitutional amendment that provided for treaty approval by majority vote in both houses. As the Senate sought to maintain its distinctive constitutional role, the Executive Branch engineered a compromise by submitting the Bretton Woods Agreement establishing the World Bank and the International Monetary Fund as a congressional-executive agreement and submitting the more important United Nations Charter as a treaty. After the Senate gave in with respect to Bretton Woods, efforts to amend the Constitution's Treaty Clause faded. Nevertheless, the Senate's acquiescence regarding such a prominent international agreement as Bretton Woods could always be looked to as an excuse not to submit the next significant international agreement as a treaty.

There is an important lesson to be learned from this piece of history. Because the Senate essentially ducked the Treaty Clause issue with respect to Bretton Woods, it opened the door to complete evisceration of the Treaty Clause altogether. The Uruguay Round presents the Senate with an opportunity either to repeat or to avoid the mistakes of the past. If political considerations lead the Senate to abdicate its constitutional role "just this once," its practice with regard to an agreement whose ardent supporters call the most significant international trade agreement ever will forever be cited as support for the proposition that no treaty need be submitted for supermajority approval by the Senate. The issue may seem practically unimportant to some Senators now that the Presidency and both Houses of Congress are controlled by the same political party. But as the balance of power shifts throughout our nation's history, it is the Constitution's structural framework that best protects our most enduring national values.

. . . .

The Constitution's structural safeguards were specially designed to provide states, citizens, and each branch of the federal government with ongoing protection from aggrandizement of power or neglect of constitutional responsibilities by those who temporarily hold public office—even when such aggrandizement or abdication seems wise as a matter of policy. The need for such constitutional protections lies in the tendency of seemingly benign departures from constitutional requirements to provide the momentum for permanent departures that will eventually result in the very harms that the constitutional structure was designed to prevent.

This is the situation that the Uruguay Round presents. The fact that the exigencies of war convinced the Senate fifty years ago to accede to demands for bicameral majoritarian approval of an arguably treaty-like agreement (Bretton Woods), and the further fact that political convenience may have extended such practice in the decades that followed, cannot justify continued departure from structural constitutional requirements when the very purposes served by such requirements (such as protecting state sovereignty) are seriously implicated by a proposed international agreement. To transform political leaders' casual approach to the Constitution into constitutional law goes against the fundamental rule-of-law basis of a constitutional form of government.

. . . .

When I first entered this national debate, it was to add a perspective that I felt was missing: the Uruguay Round's impositions on state sovereignty are so serious as to require the protection of states as equal sovereigns that is embodied in the Treaty Clause's provision for supermajority Senate approval. ... [S]uch impositions on state sovereignty so deeply implicate the normal lawmaking process of our political system that they are impermissible if the safeguards of the Treaty Clause are not followed.

The Uruguay Round's establishment of the World Trade Organization and its dispute resolution mechanisms represents a significant departure from prior versions of GATT. Under the Uruguay Round, the United States will commit itself to "ensure the conformity of its laws, regulations and administrative procedures with its obligations as provided" in the Uruguay Round agreements. Agreement Establishing the World Trade Organizations (WTO Agreement), Art. XVI, ¶ 4. This commitment applies not only to those laws directed related to trade, but to any measure with even an indirect impact on trade that would be inconsistent with the provision of the Uruguay Round. Under the Uruguay Round, any nation's complaint against a United States law or regulation could require the United States to submit to the authority of the WTO's Dispute Settlement Body or Appellate Body. Were a panel of the DSB (or the Appellate Body on appeal) to find a United States law "GATT illegal," the United States would be bound by that decision unless it could persuade the entire GATT membership by consensus to overturn the adverse decision. The United States would then be faced with the choice of either changing the challenged law to bring it into conformity with the panel or Appellate Body decision, or accepting the imposition of trade sanctions. With the commitment of the United States to confirm its every law and administrative regulation to GATT, with more than 120 member nations entitled to challenge American law, and with the United States deprived of any veto power over the decisions of the dispute settlement bodies, our participation in the WTO makes very real the prospect of serious economic sanctions imposed in accord with an international regime that will be binding on the United States—sanctions, therefore, against which we will not be in a position to retaliate lawfully.

This prospect seems an inevitability when one considers that the Uruguay Round establishes that its provisions and dispute resolution mechanisms will apply not only to federal laws and regulations, but to all state and local measures as well. See WTO Agreement, Annex 2, Understanding on Rules and Procedures Governing the Settlement of Disputes (Dispute Settlement Understanding), Art. 22, ¶ 9. Like the federal government, states must also bring their laws into conformity with the Uruguay Round agreements. They too must submit to the authority of the WTO dispute resolution system.

The position of the states under the Uruguay Round, however, is decidedly more precarious than that of the federal government. Whereas Congress may choose between a GATT-illegal federal law and WTO-imposed sanctions, a state whose law has been found in violation of GATT provisions will know that if it does not change its law, one of the following will occur: Congress may preempt the offending state law; the Executive Branch may bring an action against the state and persuade a court to strike the law down under GATT; or the nation as a whole will be subject to retaliatory sanctions. If the state does not wish to change its law, the consequences are left to federal officials and to other nations.

This imposes upon states considerable new burdens and vulnerabilities—vulnerabilities that are exacerbated by the secretive dispute resolution procedures of the WTO, in which states may not participate directly. In the dispute resolution process, states to a significant degree will be forced to place their fates under the Uruguay Round in the hands of the Executive Branch, which may have incentives counter to those of particular states in the context of particular disputes. Because even the beneficial aspects of the WTO dispute resolution process offer nations incentives to challenge state laws or impose sanctions against state-based industries, state efforts—perfectly legal under United States law—to experiment with non-uniform laws, rules and regulations may be placed in jeopardy. Because approval of the Uruguay Round will powerfully curtail state sovereignty and shift power from the states to the federal government, this trade agreement calls for the precautions of the Treaty Clause to be followed.

. . . .

Although I do not offer a comprehensive set of criteria for defining the boundary between treaties and other international agreements, it is clear to me that, whatever the precise contours of the treaty category, an agreement warrants the high level of consensus mandated by the Treaty Clause and may not escape classification as a treaty if it (1) creates a governing entity with a "legal personality" and legal powers capable of affecting the lives of all United States citizens by affecting state and federal lawmaking efforts; (2) provides for ongoing cooperation and reciprocal commitments among more than 120 nations; (3) accedes to the more than theoretical possibility of the United States being subjected to substantial international sanctions against which the United States cannot retaliate without placing itself in violation of the agreement; and (4) accordingly contemplates wide-reaching effects on the legal, economic, and political life of every state.

The combination of these factors in a single agreement would seem to compel the conclusion that the agreement warrants the high level of deliberation and consensus that the formal requirements of the Treaty Clause guarantee. This agreement will help shape the future of American trade with nearly every nation on earth and will likely have a significant impact on the efforts of state to regulate their own industries, environment and public safety. The very idea that the creation of a World Trade Organization—an international governance body with real powers—would not require approval as a treaty is remarkable, to say the least.

MEMORANDUM FROM THE OFFICE OF LEGAL COUNSEL, U.S. DEPARTMENT OF JUSTICE, TO AMBASSADOR MICHAEL KANTOR, U.S. TRADE REPRESENTATIVE

(Nov. 22, 1994), available at http://www.usdoj.gov/olc/gatt.htm.

I. THE TREATY CLAUSE

. . . .

Like Professor Tribe, we find that neither the text of the Constitution, nor the materials surrounding its drafting and ratification, nor subsequent Supreme Court case law interpreting it, provide clear-cut tests for deciding when an international agreement must be regarded as a "treaty" in the constitutional sense, and submitted to the Senate for its "Advice and Consent" under the Treaty Clause, U.S. Const. art. II, § 2, cl. 2. In such circumstances, a significant guide to the interpretation of the Constitution's requirements is the practical construction placed on it by the Executive and Legislative Branches acting together. *See, e.g., The Pocket Veto Case*, 279 U.S. 655, 689–90 (1929) ("[l]ong settled and established practice is a consideration of great weight in a proper interpretation of constitutional provisions of this character. *Compare* . . . *State v. South Norwalk*, 77 Conn. 257, 264 [(1904)], in which the court said that a practice of at least twenty years duration 'on the part of the executive department, acquiesced in by the legislative department, while not absolutely binding on the judicial department, is entitled to great regard in determining the true construction of a constitutional provision the phraseology of which is in any respect of doubtful meaning.' "); *Youngstown Sheet & Tube Co. v. Sawyer*, 343 U.S. 579, 610 (1952) (Frankfurter, J., concurring) ("The Constitution is a framework for government. Therefore the way the framework has consistently operated fairly establishes that it has operated according to its true nature."). Indeed, the Court has been particularly willing to rely on the practical statesmanship of the political branches when considering constitutional questions that involve foreign relations. *See, e.g., United States v. Verdugo–Urquidez*, 494 U.S. 259, 273 (1990); *Dames & Moore v. Regan*, 453 U.S. 654, 686 (1981). . . .

Such practical construction has long established (and Professor Tribe acknowledges) that "there are many classes of agreements with foreign countries which are not required to be formulated as treaties" for constitutional purposes. Most pertinently here, practice under the Constitution has established that the United States can assume major international trade obligations such as those found in the Uruguay Round Agreements when they are negotiated by the President and approved and implemented by Act of Congress pursuant to procedures such as those set forth in 19 U.S.C. §§ 2902 & 2903. In following these procedures, Congress acts under its broad Foreign Commerce Clause powers, and the President acts pursuant to his constitutional responsibility for conducting the Nation's foreign affairs. The use of these procedures, in which both political branches deploy sweeping constitutional powers, fully satisfies the Constitution's requirements; the Treaty Clause's provision for concurrence by two-thirds of the Senators present is not constitutionally mandatory for international agreements of this kind.

Professor Tribe recognizes the existence of these decades-old practices, which have resulted in the approval of such fundamental trade pacts as the North American Free Trade Agreement (the "NAFTA"). But he disparages the use of Congressional–Executive agreements as merely a matter of "political leaders' casual approach to the Constitution." This dismissive characterization gives virtually no weight to the considered constitutional judgments of the political branches. We believe that that approach is mistaken. Disagreements and uncertainties surrounding the scope of the Treaty Clause—including its interaction with Congress's power to regulate commerce—are two centuries old. ... Congress's Foreign Commerce Clause authority and the President's responsibility for foreign affairs are unquestionably broad. In such circumstances, the political branches can fairly conclude—and have in fact concluded—that even major trade agreements such as the Uruguay Round Agreements may be approved and implemented by Acts of Congress, rather than ratified as treaties. Indeed, Professor Tribe himself wrote in 1988 that "it does appear settled that a hybrid form of international agreement—that in which the President is supported by a Joint Resolution of Congress—*is coextensive with the treaty power*. Such Congressional–Executive agreements are the law of the land, superseding inconsistent state or federal laws." Laurence H. Tribe, *American Constitutional Law* 228 n.18 (2d ed. 1988) (emphasis added).

Historically, the scope of the Treaty Clause, and its interplay with other constitutional clauses, have provoked controversies of several different kinds. The persistence of these controversies (which trace back to the eighteenth century), and the nearly complete absence of judicial decisions resolving them, underscore the necessity of relying on congressional precedent to *interpret* the relevant constitutional provisions. No one could deny that "congressional practice alone cannot justify abandonment of the Constitution's structural provisions," but it begs the question to assume that the treaty ratification process *is* structurally required by the Constitution in cases such as this. Like other "great ordinances of the Constitution," the Treaty Clause "do[es] not establish and divide fields of black and white." *Springer v. Government of the Philippine Islands*, 277 U.S. 189, 209 (1928) (Holmes, J., joined by Brandeis, J., dissenting).

One recurring kind of dispute over the Treaty Clause has been whether international agreements could be given effect by Executive action alone, or whether they required submission to the Senate for its concurrence. *See, e.g.*, 2 *Messages and Papers of the Presidents* 33 (James D. Richardson ed., 1896) (President Monroe's message to the Senate of April 6, 1818, expressing uncertainty whether the Executive alone could make an international agreement for the naval disarmament of the Great Lakes, or whether Senate advice and consent was required). A second type of recurring dispute, more pertinent here, centered on the respective powers of the Senate and the House of Representatives in such areas as the regulation of foreign trade, where different clauses of the Constitution assign responsibilities either to one House alone or to both Houses together. . . .

Intra-branch disputes over the Treaty Clause can be traced as far back as 1796, when Representative Albert Gallatin argued that the "[t]reaty-making power . . . may be considered as clashing" with Congress's "authority of regulating trade," and that "[a] difference of opinion may exist as to the proper construction of the several articles of the Constitution, so as to reconcile those apparently contradictory provisions." 5 Annals of Cong. 437 (1796); *see also id.* at 466–74 (arguing that Foreign Commerce Clause limits Treaty Clause). . . .

. . . .

From time to time, the House of Representatives has also insisted that a treaty be made dependent on the consent of both Houses of Congress. This has occurred when, for example, the House's power over appropriations has been at issue, as in the Gadsden purchase treaty of 1853 and the Alaskan purchase treaty of 1867. In 1880, the House asserted that the negotiation of a commercial treaty that fixed duties on foreign imports would be an unconstitutional invasion of its prerogatives over the origination of revenues; in 1883, it demanded, in connection with a proposed commercial treaty with Mexico, to have a voice in treaties affecting revenue.

In 1898, the United States annexed Hawaii by joint resolution, Joint Res. 55, 30 Stat. 750 (1898), even though the Senate had previously rejected an annexation treaty, and even though opponents of the measure argued strenuously both in Congress and in the press that such an annexation could by accomplished only by treaty, and not by a simple legislative act.

. . . .

In general, these inter- and intra-branch disputes over the scope of the Treaty Clause have been resolved through the political process, occasionally with marked departures from prior practices. *See Goldwater v. Carter*, 444 U.S. 996, 1004 n.1 (1979) (Rehnquist, J., concurring in judgment); John O. McGinnis, *Constitutional Review by the Executive in Foreign Affairs and War Powers: A Consequence of Rational Choice in the Separation of Powers*, 56 Law & Contemp. Probs. 293, 305–08 (Autumn 1993). For example, after the House of Representatives objected to the concentration of power over Indian affairs in the hands of the Senate through the Treaty Clause, Congress in 1871 enacted a rider to an Indian appropriation bill declaring that no fresh treaties were to be made with the Indian nations. 16 Stat. 544, 566 (1871). Although the United States had been making Indian treaties for almost a century before that enactment, *see United States v. Kagama*, 118 U.S. 375, 382 (1886), after 1871 "the federal government continued to make agreements with Indian tribes, many similar to treaties, that were approved by both Senate and House," but "the House's action sounded the death knell for treaty making." Felix S. Cohen, *Handbook of Federal Indian Law* 107 & n.370 (1982 ed.). The policy of the 1871 enactment remains in effect. *See* 25 U.S.C. § 71. We are uncertain whether this longstanding legislation would be constitutional by Professor Tribe's lights.

The existence of such recurring disputes over the scope and meaning of the Treaty Clause undermines any dogmatic claim that a major trade agreement such as the Uruguay Round Agreements, which stands at the intersection of the foreign affairs, revenue raising and commerce powers, *must* be ratified as a treaty and *cannot* be implemented by the action of both Houses of Congress. The distinctions between the Federal government's treaty power and the other constitutional powers in play are simply too fluid and dynamic to dictate the conclusion that one method must be followed to the complete exclusion of the other. . . .

Finally, Professor Tribe's newly-crafted account of the treaty power entails that the Federal Government may diminish State sovereignty by employing the Treaty Clause to ratify an international agreement, but not by using any other constitutional procedure for giving such an agreement effect. Basic to Professor Tribe's analysis is the assumption that *some* "set of intrusions on state sovereignty is sufficiently grave to trigger the requirements of the Treaty Clause." . . . On this view, the Federal Government is not constitutionally prohibited from curtailing State sovereignty to a certain degree, but it may not accomplish such a curtailment by the ordinary Article I process of legislation. We find that conclusion odd and unconvincing. If the Federal Government may not trespass on State sovereignty beyond certain limits, then the attempt to do so by making a treaty would not remove the constitutional infirmity: it is by now well-established that treaties may not violate basic constitutional ordinances, including the principles of federalism. *See, e.g., Reid v. Covert*, 354 U.S. 1 (1957); *see also* Laurence H. Tribe, *American Constitutional Law* at 228. On the other hand, if it *does* lie within the Federal Government's power to curtail State sovereignty under an international agreement, we see no reason why the Government may not invoke Article I procedures for giving effect to that agreement. In short, if the Uruguay Round Agreements unduly invade State sovereignty, ratification as a treaty will not save them from unconstitutionality; if they are not an undue invasion, they can be given effect by Act of Congress.

II. THE URUGUAY ROUND AGREEMENTS AND PRESIDENTIAL POWER

In considering Professor Tribe's critique of the Uruguay Round Agreements—which focuses on the asserted impairment that the agreement causes to State sovereignty—it should be borne in mind that judicial decisions have treated GATT as effectively a "Treat[y]," and hence "supreme Law," within the meaning of the Supremacy Clause, U.S. Const., art. VI, § 2, and have held provisions of State law to be superseded by the GATT when in conflict with it. It is also important to remember that the existing GATT arrangements include dispute resolution procedures, which often involve referring disputes to panels of individuals, who act in an individual and not a governmental capacity. Professor Tribe does not contend that the existing version of GATT or the dispute resolution procedures that have developed under it are unconstitutional as applied to the Federal or State governments of this country; rather, he alleges that "[t]he Uruguay Round's establishment of the World Trade Organization [the WTO] and its dispute resolution mechanisms represents a [constitutionally] significant departure from prior versions of GATT." ...

Under existing GATT practice, "the Contracting Parties, acting jointly as a whole, have jurisdiction over the final disposition of the dispute procedure." Although decisions on adoption of panel reports have always been made by consensus, the existing GATT permits a vote on these matters. Thus, while the United States, in practice, can exercise a "veto" over any adverse panel decision, this could be changed under existing GATT rules. The Uruguay Round Agreements would alter this procedure by making the panel's or Appellate Body's report final unless the WTO States "decide[] by consensus not to adopt the [panel or] Appellate Body report" within a set period. Professor Tribe appears to take this procedural alteration—the loss of the *de facto* "veto"—as constitutionally decisive. When one asks why that should be so, it appears that his answer is that under the new dispute resolution process, "states to a significant degree will be forced to place their fates under the Uruguay Round in the hands of the Executive Branch, which may have incentives counter to those of particular states in the context of particular disputes. ... [T]he Executive Branch, not Congress, ... would determine the fate of *state* laws found to be in violation of GATT. If a state chose not to alter a measure found by the WTO to be GATT-illegal, the United States Trade Representative could choose to bring an action against the state in a federal court, *see* S. 2467, 103d Cong., 2d Sess. § 102(b)(2) (1994) ...—even if Congress had chosen to allow the state's measure to remain in effect and to accept trade sanctions on behalf of the entire nation rather than preempt the offending state law."

We do not understand why Professor Tribe finds constitutional significance in the Uruguay Round's "reverse consensus" requirement. Under the *current* version of GATT, the States could equally well be said to be "in the hands of the Executive," for the simple reason that the President, as the sole constitutional actor who may represent the United States abroad, alone speaks for the United States in the GATT organization. Thus, the *President*, through his delegate, possesses the "veto" over the outcome of a dispute resolution under existing GATT practice, and *may refuse to exercise it*. In other words, State laws may, even under the current version of GATT, be finally determined to be "GATT-illegal" unless the Executive Branch takes affirmative action to prevent that result.

Moreover, it is misleading to suggest that the WTO procedures of the Uruguay Round Agreements place State law "at the mercy of the Executive Branch and the Trade Representative." As Professor Tribe himself explains, even if the Executive Branch decides to bring an action against a State for the purpose of having a State law declared invalid for inconsistency with the Uruguay Round Agreements, the implementing legislation explicitly precludes the WTO panel's (or Appellate Body's) report from being considered "binding or otherwise accorded deference" by the court that hears the case. *See* S. 2467, § 102(b)(2)(B)(i). Thus, the State law cannot be declared invalid by the Executive Branch acting unilaterally, even if the Executive is armed with a WTO report that has found the State law GATT-illegal; rather, the independent action of another branch of the government—the courts—is required.

Furthermore, given the breadth of the joint authority of Congress and the President in the field of foreign relations, it would be the truly extraordinary case indeed in which Presidential action in that area, when supported by an Act of Congress, could amount to an unconstitutional invasion of State sovereignty. *See Youngstown Sheet & Tube Co. v. Sawyer*, 343 U.S. at 635 (Jackson, J., concurring) (Presidential power in such cases is "at its maximum"). The Supreme Court has held that even *unilateral* Executive action, relying on the President's inherent constitutional powers alone, may constitute a "treaty" for purposes of the Supremacy Clause, and hence supersede contrary State law. Thus, in *United States v. Belmont*, 301 U.S. 324, 331–32 (1937), the Court upheld a unilateral Executive agreement in the face of contrary State law. . . .

In *United States v. Pink*, 315 U.S. 203, 233 (1942), the Court, again upholding a unilateral Executive agreement over State law, reaffirmed that "[p]ower over external affairs is not shared by the States; it is vested in the national government exclusively. It need not be so exercised as to conform to state laws or state policies, whether they be expressed in constitutions, statutes, or judicial decrees." Again, in *Zschernig v. Miller*, 389 U.S. 429, 432, 434 (1968), the Court struck down a State probate statute requiring an inquiry into "the type of governments that obtain in particular foreign nations" as "an intrusion by the State into the field of foreign affairs which the Constitution entrusts to the President and the Congress." And in *Hines v. Davidowitz*, 312 U.S. 52, 68 (1941), the Court stated that the field of international relations is "the one aspect of our government that from the first has been most generally conceded imperatively to demand broad national authority." ...

Accordingly, we cannot agree that the powers assigned to the President by the Uruguay Round Agreements and their implementing legislation would be unconstitutional (unless the agreement were ratified as a treaty) because they might be exercised in a manner that persuaded the courts to rule that State laws were superseded. Against the massive powers of Congress and the President, acting together, to control the Nation's foreign policy and commerce, the claims of State sovereignty have little force.

III. THE WORLD TRADE ORGANIZATION

Professor Tribe has also argued that the Uruguay Round Agreements must be ratified as a treaty because its WTO dispute settlement procedures undermines State sovereignty *directly*, rather than by vesting the power to do so in the President. Unfortunately, Professor Tribe's description of the WTO's powers, scope and functions is mistaken. The proposed arrangements for the WTO do *not* represent an invasion of State sovereignty that can be cured only if the Uruguay Round Agreements are ratified as a treaty; rather, the Uruguay Round Agreements are similar in kind to earlier, Congressionally-approved trade pacts, including NAFTA and the Tokyo Round Codes, that were not, and that did not have to be, ratified as treaties.

In Professor Tribe's view, the "basic thrust" of the Uruguay Round Agreements is "that it would empower international tribunals effectively to override state laws." Hence, he argues, approval by two-thirds of the Senators present is required, because "[t]he Senate ... remains the principal body in which the States *qua* States are represented in our National Government." However, as the court has recently found in *Public Citizen v. Kantor*, No. 94–1148, 1994 WL 549498 at *5 (D.D.C. Oct. 5, 1994),

> the resolution mechanisms contained in the [Uruguay Round] trade agreement permit disputes to be settled without altering domestic law. If a domestic law is found to violate the agreement, the defending party may implement the decision, negotiate a solution, or pay compensation.

Neither the WTO, nor any dispute settlement panels, will have the authority to enter injunctions or impose monetary sanctions against member countries. Nor will they be able to order any member country that has a federal system to change its component governments' laws. While a WTO dispute settlement may opine on whether a law is inconsistent with a member's obligations under the Uruguay Round Agreements, it is up to the parties to decide how to resolve the situation. The complaining country may suspend reciprocal trade concessions if alternative forms of settlement—*e.g.*, compensation in the form of additional trade concessions, or a change in the defending country's domestic law—

are not made. The suspension of trade concessions by a complaining country is likely to mean a temporary increase in the tariffs it imposes on the defending country's goods. No suspension of trade concessions can exceed the amount of the trade injury. Because our foreign trading partners would be able to increase tariffs on American goods even more easily in the absence of a trade agreement, it is hard to see how the attempt in the Uruguay Round Agreements to resolve trade disputes between member countries and to prevent the unilateral imposition of retaliatory tariffs could amount to an unconstitutional invasion of State or local sovereignty.

Professor Tribe objects that it is "no answer that the United States might choose to pay whatever fine is levied by the WTO rather than sacrifice the sovereignty of one of the fifty States, for that makes each State's sovereignty a hostage to the Federal Government's willingness to impose a tax burden on the Nation as a whole. It also puts each State in the dilemma of either accepting the tax burden on its citizens entailed by having the United States pay a WTO fine, or protecting its citizens from that burden by lobbying against the fine and urging instead that the offending State be brought to heel." Setting apart the factual error of assuming that the WTO has the power to "lev[y]" a "fine," Professor Tribe's argument buries the critical point that it is only *the United States*, not the WTO, that would wield the power to limit or displace State law. Even if United States participation in the WTO's dispute resolution procedure might create incentives that would otherwise not exist to set aside some State laws, Congress can certainly structure the range of its future choices in a way that tends to have that effect. There is in such a decision no "meaningful shift of control over state sovereignty to foreign tribunals."

CONCLUSION

We remain persuaded that, in deciding not to submit the Uruguay Round Agreements to the Senate for the concurrence of two-thirds of the Senators present, the President is acting in a wholly proper and constitutional manner. Like other recent trade agreements, including NAFTA, the United States–Canada Free Trade Agreement, the United States–Israel Free Trade Agreement and the Tokyo Round Agreement, the Uruguay Round Agreements may constitutionally be executed by the President and approved and implemented by Act of Congress.

WALTER DELLINGER
Assistant Attorney General

NOTES: POTENTIAL CIRCUMVENTION OF ANY CONGRESSIONAL INVOLVEMENT

1. *Professor Tribe versus the Justice Department.* Who has the better position? For Professor Tribe's further views, see Lawrence H. Tribe, *Taking Text and Structure Seriously: Reflections on Free-Form Method in Constitutional Interpretation*, 108 HARV. L. REV. 1221 (1995); *see also* Bruce Ackerman

& David Golove, *Is Nafta Constitutional*? (1995); Bruce Ackerman & David Golove, *Is NAFTA Constitutional?* 108 HARV. L. REV. 799 (1995). Why not insist that *all* agreements be done by congressional-executive agreement; would that make U.S. engagement with international law more sensible, effective, and democratic? *See* Oona Hathaway, *Treaties' End: The Past, Present, and Future of International Lawmaking in the United States*, 117 YALE L.J. 1236 (2008).

2. *Agreements on Status of U.S. Personnel Abroad.* When U.S. military and civilian personnel are deployed abroad, an agreement is often concluded with the host government concerning the status of those forces within the country. Such "status of forces agreements" (SOFAs) typically address issues such as privileges and immunities of the personnel, the ability to import and export goods and services in support of the personnel, exemptions from local taxation for the force component, and similar matters. In the context of the Bush administration concluding a SOFA in 2008 with the government of Iraq on the presence of U.S. forces, controversy arose as to whether the agreement required congressional approval. The SOFA included provisions on Iraqi consent to U.S. military operations (Article 4(1)), on supervision by a Joint Military Operations Coordination Committee of U.S.-Iraqi cooperation on military operations (Article 4(2)), and on a deadline that all "United States Forces shall withdraw from all Iraqi territory no later than December 31, 2011" (Article 24(1)). *See* Agreement On the Withdrawal of United States Forces from Iraq and the Organization of Their Activities during Their Temporary Presence in Iraq, U.S.-Iraq, Nov. 17, 2008, *available at* http://www.state.gov/documents/organization/122074.pdf.

After the signing of the SOFA, it was submitted to the Iraqi Parliament and the Iraqi Presidency Council for approval. It was not submitted to the U.S. Senate or to both houses of the U.S. Congress. Professor Hathaway argued:

> The Administration intends to conclude the agreement with Iraq as a "sole executive agreement," without seeking the approval of Congress or of the Senate. This agreement, however, includes commitments that reach far beyond any made in any prior sole executive agreement and move far beyond anything that is constitutionally permissible without the consent of Congress or the Senate.
>
> . . . .
>
> The Administration has asserted that the bilateral agreement with Iraq is simply a status of forces agreement (SOFA), more than a hundred of which have been concluded as sole executive agreements. That is incorrect. Although it has been called a SOFA, it includes provisions that have never been a part of any prior SOFA—most notably, provisions granting the authority for U.S. troops to engage in military operations, the grant of power over military operations to a joint U.S.-Iraq Committee, and a specification of timetables for military operations. These commitments go beyond the President's own constitutional authority and must be approved by Congress.

Statement of Professor Oona A. Hathaway, University of California, Berkeley, School of Law Before the House Committee on Foreign Affairs Subcommittee on International Organizations, Human Rights, and Oversight, at 2 (Nov. 18, 2008). Do you agree?

3. *Choosing to Commit by Other Means.* As the President considers his choices for the type of agreement he will use, can his choices also include: (1) avoiding ratification of an international agreement simply by declaring that the agreement reflects customary international law?; (2) declaring that the United States will adhere to an international agreement *as a political matter*, perhaps in the period prior to consent by the Senate or after expiration of a treaty previously consented to?; or (3) completely avoiding the negotiation and ratification of an international agreement by instead using a non-legally binding instrument, even if the instrument addresses rights and obligations? The remainder of these Notes considers each possibility in turn.

4. *Using Customary International Law.* The President might seek to avoid the burden of ever soliciting Senate advice and consent by simply declaring all or part of the provisions of a new international agreement to be declaratory of customary international law. For example, a comprehensive treaty on the law of the sea—the U.N. Convention on the Law of the Sea, 1833 U.N.T.S. 3—was adopted in 1982 by a vote of 130 states in favor, 4 against, and 17 abstentions. *See* 82 DEP'T STATE BULL. NO. 2067, at 48 (1982). The U.S. Executive Branch took the position that the United States would not ratify the treaty principally because of a few unacceptable provisions relating to seabed mining, but it also asserted that there were many things in the treaty which restated or clarified customary law, or which were useful and acceptable developments. *See* President's Statement on United States Oceans Policy, 19 WEEKLY COMP. PRES. DOC. 383–84 (March 14, 1983). Is such a position an unconstitutional evasion of the role of the Senate under Article II, Section 2? Is this an offer extended to other states for the United States to be bound by almost all parts of the treaty, except those applicable to seabed mining (to which the United States objects), so long as those states reciprocate?

5. *Politically Committing to a Legally Binding Agreement.* Given that there will be a lag time between the date negotiations are concluded on a treaty and the date the United States ratifies the treaty, the President might commit the United States to abide by the treaty right away in the hope that Senate approval ultimately will be forthcoming. For example, in March 2002, the United States concluded an agreement with South Pacific states and entities to extend the operation of a 1987 multilateral fisheries treaty and to make certain amendments to the treaty. When concluding the negotiations, the Executive Branch entered into a "Memorandum of Understanding" (MOU) that provisionally applied all but one of the amendments pending ratification. According to the State Department:

> This MOU is an important political commitment that will allow the U.S., among other things, to ensure that as of June, 2003, U.S. longline vessels will be able to fish in the high seas portions of the Treaty Area and that the waters of the Solomon Islands will be open even if every Party has not yet approved those amendments. Both of these issues have long been goals for the U.S. industry.

S. TREATY DOC. NO. 108–2 at VIII (2003); *see also* U.S. Department of State, 2 *Digest of United States Practice in International Law, 1991–1999*, at 1571 &

1744 (Sally Cummins & David Stewart eds. (2005)). Similarly, when President Obama and Russian President Medvedev signed the "New START" Treaty on April 8, 2010, they also signed a protocol which provided that "[u]ntil entry into force of the Treaty, the provisions of the Treaty and this Protocol, listed in this Part, shall apply provisionally from the date of signature of the Treaty." *See* Treaty on Measures for the Further Reduction and Limitation of Strategic Offensive Arms, U.S.-Russ., Apr. 8, 2010, S. TREATY DOC. NO. 111–5, at Protocol, pt. 8 (2010); *see generally* Congressional Research Service, *The New START Treaty: Central Limits and Key Provisions,* CRS Rep. R41219 (Apr. 21, 2011). The international agreement itself may contain an article that anticipates provisional application by signatories, as was the case for the 1994 agreement relating to implementation of the 1982 Law of the Sea Convention. *See id.;* U.S. Department of State, 1 *Digest of United States Practice in International Law, 1991–1999,* at 700. Similarly, the President might commit the United States to continue to abide by the provisions of a treaty that has expired, contingent on a reciprocal commitment by the other party or parties.

Such "parallel unilateral policy declarations" operate by having the President (or Secretary of State) issue a statement or adhere to a memorandum that the United States will do something, or not do something, so long as state X acts in the same fashion. The leader of state X may make an identical statement. Congress (or the Senate) does not participate. Yet such unilateral statements may be binding in international law. *See* Nuclear Tests Case (N.Z. v. Fr.) 1974 I.C.J. 457 (1974). Is such a statement or memorandum the "law of the land" in the United States? Is the making of such a statement, assuming it is binding in international law, a constitutional exercise of a presidential prerogative? *See* Michael J. Glennon, *The Senate Role in Treaty Ratification,* 77 AM. J. INT'L L. 257, 267–79 (1983); Duncan Hollis & Joshua Newcomer, *Political Commitments and the Constitution,* 49 VA. J. INT'L L. 507 (2009).

6. *Opting for a Political Agreement.* The President might decide to adhere to an instrument that he regards as not legally binding, even though it may contain language addressing rights and duties. As the Department of State has noted:

> It has long been recognized in international practice that governments may agree on joint statements of policy or intention that do not establish legal obligations. In recent decades, this has become a common means of announcing the results of diplomatic exchanges, stating common positions on policy issues, recording their intended course of action on matters of mutual concern, or making political commitments to one another.
>
> These documents are sometimes referred to as non-binding agreements, gentlemen's agreements, joint statements or declarations. The title of the document is not determinative as to whether it establishes legal obligations, but rather the intent of the parties, as reflected in the language and context of the document, the circumstances of its conclusion, and the explanations given by the parties.

Robert E. Dalton, Assistant Legal Adviser for Treaty Affairs, U.S. Department of State, *Memorandum on International Documents of a Non–Legally Binding Character*, 88 AM. J. INT'L L. 515 (1994).

For example, consider the following Warsaw Declaration, which was adhered to by the Clinton Administration in 2000 along with more than 100 other countries. What legal force does such a declaration have? Do you think such a declaration should be handled as a treaty or executive agreement, or are you comfortable with such matters being handled as political or moral statements? Note that the Warsaw Declaration was not submitted for congressional or Senate approval, nor reported to Congress under the Case Act.

FINAL WARSAW DECLARATION: TOWARD A COMMUNITY OF DEMOCRACIES (JUNE 27, 2000)

available at http://www.state.gov/g/drl/rls/26811.htm.

We the participants ... in the Community of Democracies Ministerial Meeting ... [h]ereby agree to respect and uphold the following core democratic principles and practices:

- The will of the people shall be the basis of the authority of government, as expressed by exercise of the right and civic duties of citizens to choose their representatives through regular, free and fair elections with universal and equal suffrage, open to multiple parties, conducted by secret ballot, monitored by independent electoral authorities, and free of fraud and intimidation.
- The right of every person to equal access to public service and to take part in the conduct of public affairs, directly or through freely chosen representatives.

....

- The right of the press to collect, report and disseminate information, news and opinions, subject only to restrictions necessary in a democratic society and prescribed by law, while bearing in mind evolving international practices in this field.

....

- The right of every person to freedom of peaceful assembly and association, including to establish or join their own political parties, civic groups, trade unions or other organizations with the necessary legal guarantees to allow them to operate freely on a basis of equal treatment before the law.

....

- That the aforementioned rights, which are essential to full and effective participation in a democratic society, be enforced by a competent, independent and impartial judiciary open to the public, established and protected by law.

SECTION 9. TREATY INTERPRETATION

NOTE: THE VIENNA CONVENTION ON THE LAW OF TREATIES

As the preceding sections have indicated, the U.S. Constitution and constitutional practice recognize the existence of two categories of "contracts" between sovereign states or their subsidiary entities: treaties and executive agreements. While there is a lack of precision in defining their respective roles in constitutional practice, there is little disagreement that both forms constitute international agreements which can bind the parties. Only treaties, however, require the "advice and consent" of two-thirds of the Senate under Article II, Section 2, of the Constitution.

While the U.S. constitutional law thus distinguishes between the two categories of agreement, international law does not. The Vienna Convention on the Law of Treaties, May 23, 1969, 1155 U.N.T.S. 331, provides in Article 2 that a "treaty" is an international agreement concluded between States in written form and governed by international law, whether embodied in a single instrument or in two or more related instruments and whatever its particular designation. Article 2 defines its terms "without prejudice to the use of those terms or to the meanings which may be given them in the internal law of any State."

The Vienna Convention entered into force on January 27, 1980. As of mid-2011, it has 111 state parties. The United States signed the Vienna Convention on April 24, 1970, but has not ratified it. The failure to ratify arises from several factors. An initial problem was that the Senate Foreign Relations Committee

> sought to equate "treaties" as used in the Convention with "treaties" in the United States Constitution, and to declare that every agreement that is a "treaty" under the Convention can be concluded by the United States only by the process prescribed for "treaties" in the Constitution. That position has been rejected by the Executive Branch. . . .[1]

More recently, the failure to ratify the Convention may be attributed to a more general resistance of the United States to entering into wide-ranging multilateral instruments and the desire of the Executive Branch to focus on more high-profile agreements.

Despite the failure to ratify, the Executive Branch has repeatedly taken the position that the Vienna Convention "is already generally recognized as the authoritative guide to current treaty law and practice."[2] The Department has also specifically referred to certain articles of the Convention as illustrating its view of the Convention "as reflecting generally accepted norms of international law."[3] This view has been accepted by the Supreme Court in *Weinberger v. Rossi*, 456 U.S. 25, 29 n. 5, 102 S.Ct. 1510, 71 L.Ed.2d 715

1. *Restatement (Third) of the Foreign Relations Law of the United States*, pt. III, Introductory Note 146 n. 4 (1987).

2. Letter of Submittal, S. EXEC. REP., NO. 92–L, at 1 (1971).

3. U.S. Department of State, 1979 *Digest of United States Practice of International Law* 692–93, 703–05, 767, 769 (1983).

(1982) (referring to Article 2 of the Vienna Convention as denying international importance to the distinction between treaties and other international agreements), and followed by lower courts.

One important component of the Vienna Convention concerns treaty interpretation, which is addressed in Articles 31–33. To the extent that such articles are reflective of customary international law, and to the extent that customary international law is a part of U.S. law (per *Paquete Habana*, *supra* Chapter 2, Section 2), then should U.S. courts apply the treaty interpretation rules of the Vienna Convention when presented with a case concerning a treaty? If not, what is or should be the methodology employed by U.S. courts?

VIENNA CONVENTION ON THE LAW OF TREATIES, ARTICLES 31–33

May 23, 1969, 1155 U.N.T.S. 331.

ARTICLE 31

General rule of interpretation

1. A treaty shall be interpreted in good faith in accordance with the ordinary meaning to be given to the terms of the treaty in their context and in the light of its object and purpose.

2. The context for the purpose of the interpretation of a treaty shall comprise, in addition to the text, including its preamble and annexes:

(a) any agreement relating to the treaty which was made between all the parties in connection with the conclusion of the treaty;

(b) any instrument which was made by one or more parties in connection with the conclusion of the treaty and accepted by the other parties as an instrument related to the treaty.

3. There shall be taken into account, together with the context:

(a) any subsequent agreement between the parties regarding the interpretation of the treaty or the application of its provisions;

(b) any subsequent practice in the application of the treaty which establishes the agreement of the parties regarding its interpretation;

(c) any relevant rules of international law applicable in the relations between the parties.

4. A special meaning shall be given to a term if it is established that the parties so intended.

ARTICLE 32

Supplementary means of interpretation

Recourse may be had to supplementary means of interpretation, including the preparatory work of the treaty and the circumstances of its conclusion, in order to confirm the meaning resulting from the application of article 31, or to determine the meaning when the interpretation according to article 31:

(a) leaves the meaning ambiguous or obscure; or

(b) leads to a result which is manifestly absurd or unreasonable.

ARTICLE 33

Interpretation of treaties authenticated in two or more languages

1. When a treaty has been authenticated in two or more languages, the text is equally authoritative in each language, unless the treaty provides or the parties agree that, in case of divergence, a particular text shall prevail.

2. A version of the treaty in a language other than one of those in which the text was authenticated shall be considered an authentic text only if the treaty so provides or the parties so agree.

3. The terms of the treaty are presumed to have the same meaning in each authentic text.

4. Except where a particular text prevails in accordance with paragraph 1, when a comparison of the authentic texts discloses a difference of meaning which the application of articles 31 and 32 does not remove, the meaning which best reconciles the texts, having regard to the object and purpose of the treaty, shall be adopted.

NOTE: TREATY INTERPRETATION BY U.S. COURTS

Article 31(1) of the Vienna Convention points to different elements of treaty interpretation. First, it calls for focusing on the "ordinary meaning" of treaty provision, something that U.S. lawyers might refer to as the "plain meaning" when engaged in statutory interpretation. Second, it calls for considering that ordinary meaning "in context" which, as Article 31(2) indicates, requires reference to other provisions of the treaty, its preamble, and annexes. Third, it calls for the interpretation to be done in light of the "object and purpose" of the treaty. Article 31(3) appears to favor consideration of subsequent practice of the treaty parties, while resort to the negotiating history (often referred to as the "travaux préparatoires") appears to have a secondary status in Article 32.

Does this approach comport with your sense of how U.S. courts normally interpret a constitutional provision? A statutory provision? A contract? In interpreting those different types of provisions, to what degree do you think U.S. courts follow a theory of textualism (focusing closely on just the text), a theory of originalism (focusing on original intent of the drafters of the text), or a theory of teleology (focusing on achieving the purposes underlying the text)? With an eye to the Vienna Convention on the Law of Treaties, Detlev Vagts suggests that:

> None of these theories in fact represent the practice of the Supreme Court in interpreting the Constitution. A more modest claim would be that cases tend to follow a hierarchy of indicia, starting, as does the Vienna Convention, with the ordinary meaning and moving to evidence of intent and historical meaning, and then to teleology. In addition the

> Supreme Court places an emphasis on previous case-law, which is an approach that international courts do not and cannot share, given their light case load.

Detlev Vagts, *Treaty Interpretation and the New American Ways of Law Reading*, 4 EUR. J. INT'L L. 472, 493–95 (1993).

To the extent that it is difficult to identify the exact theory by which U.S. courts approach interpreting text that is national in origin, the same difficulty arises with respect to their approach to treaty interpretation. U.S. courts do not habitually invoke the methodological approach of the Vienna Convention on the Law of Treaties, though it would be perfectly plausible to do so: (1) as a matter of convenience; (2) out of a desire to promote uniformity with other national courts that also engage in interpreting the same treaty; (3) out of a desire to promote conformity of U.S. law with international law, per the *Charming Betsy* doctrine (*see* Chapter 2, Section 2); or (4) as a matter of law, if the Vienna Convention rules, as customary international law, are received into federal common law.

As you read the next case consider the following:

- Is the U.S. Supreme Court using a textualist, originalist, or teleological approach to treaty interpretation? Some combination of the three? Does any one approach tend to dominate? Is the Court emphasizing different approaches in different cases to achieve outcomes preferred by the Court or outcomes that favor Americans or disfavor foreigners?
- Should the Court approach treaty interpretation just as it would contract interpretation or does the treaty device merit special treatment? If given special treatment, should treaties be construed more cautiously (since it is a matter of inter-governmental relations) or more liberally (so as to help advance transnational relations)? Should the Court be guided by a principle of good faith towards U.S. treaty partners?
- To the extent that the Court is interested in practice prior to and after the conclusion of a treaty, what kind of practice is deemed relevant?
- To what extent is the Court interested in the interpretations reached by the Executive Branch? Interpretations reached by foreign courts?
- Article 33 of the Vienna Convention is sensitive to the fact that treaties may be authenticated in multiple languages. Is the Supreme Court sensitive to that fact as well?

OLYMPIC AIRWAYS v. HUSAIN

540 U.S. 644, 124 S.Ct. 1221, 157 L.Ed.2d 1146 (2004)
(some footnotes and citations omitted).

JUSTICE THOMAS delivered the opinion of the Court.

Article 17 of the Warsaw Convention (Convention) imposes liability on an air carrier for a passenger's death or bodily injury caused by an "accident" that occurred in connection with an international flight. In *Air France v. Saks*, 470 U.S. 392 (1985), the Court explained that the term "accident" in the Convention refers to an "unexpected or unusual event or happening that is external to the passenger," and not to "the passenger's own internal reaction to the usual, normal, and expected operation of the aircraft." *Id.*, at 405, 406. The issue we must decide is whether the "accident" condition precedent to air carrier liability under Article 17 is satisfied when the carrier's unusual and unexpected refusal to assist a passenger is a link in a chain of causation resulting in a passenger's pre-existing medical condition being aggravated by exposure to a normal condition in the aircraft cabin. We conclude that it is.

I

The following facts are taken from the District Court's findings, which, being unchallenged by either party, we accept as true. In December 1997, Dr. Abid Hanson and his wife, Rubina Husain (hereinafter respondent), traveled with their children and another family from San Francisco to Athens and Cairo for a family vacation. During a stopover in New York, Dr. Hanson learned for the first time that petitioner allowed its passengers to smoke on international flights. Because Dr. Hanson had suffered from asthma and was sensitive to secondhand smoke, respondent requested and obtained seats away from the smoking section. Dr. Hanson experienced no problems on the flights to Cairo.

For the return flights, Dr. Hanson and respondent arrived early at the Cairo airport in order to request non-smoking seats. Respondent showed the check-in agent a physician's letter explaining that Dr. Hanson "has [a] history of recurrent anaphylactic reactions," and asked the agent to ensure that their seats were in the non-smoking section. The flight to Athens was uneventful.

After boarding the plane for the flight to San Francisco, Dr. Hanson and respondent discovered that their seats were located only three rows in front of the economy-class smoking section. Respondent advised Maria Leptourgou, a flight attendant for petitioner, that Dr. Hanson could not sit in a smoking area, and said, " 'You have to move him.' " The flight attendant told her to " 'have a seat.' " After all the passengers had boarded but prior to takeoff, respondent again asked Ms. Leptourgou to move Dr. Hanson, explaining that he was " 'allergic to smoke.' " Ms. Leptourgou replied that she could not reseat Dr. Hanson because the plane was " 'totally full' " and she was "too busy" to help.

Shortly after takeoff, passengers in the smoking section began to smoke, and Dr. Hanson was soon surrounded by ambient cigarette smoke. Respondent spoke with Ms. Leptourgou a third time, stating, " 'You have to move my husband from here.' " Ms. Leptourgou again refused, stating that the plane was full. Ms. Leptourgou told respondent that Dr. Hanson could switch seats with another passenger, but that respondent would have to ask other passengers herself, without the flight crew's assistance. Respondent told Ms. Leptourgou that Dr. Hanson had to move even if the only available seat was in the cockpit or in business class, but Ms. Leptourgou refused to provide any assistance.

About two hours into the flight, the smoking noticeably increased in the rows behind Dr. Hanson. Dr. Hanson asked respondent for a new inhaler because the one he had been using was empty. Dr. Hanson then moved toward the front of the plane to get some fresher air. While he was leaning against a chair near the galley area, Dr. Hanson gestured to respondent to get his emergency kit. Respondent returned with it and gave him a shot of epinephrine. She then awoke Dr. Umesh Sabharwal, an allergist, with whom Dr. Hanson and respondent had been traveling. Dr. Sabharwal gave Dr. Hanson another shot of epinephrine and began to administer CPR and oxygen. Dr. Hanson died shortly thereafter.

Respondents filed a wrongful-death suit in California state court. Petitioner removed the case to federal court, and the District Court found petitioner liable for Dr. Hanson's death. The District Court held that Ms. Leptourgou's refusal to reseat Dr. Hanson constituted an "accident" within the meaning of Article 17. Applying Saks' definition of that term, the court reasoned that the flight attendant's conduct was external to Dr. Hanson and, because it was in "blatant disregard of industry standards and airline policies," was not expected or usual.

The Ninth Circuit affirmed. . . . We granted certiorari, 538 U.S. 1056 (2003), and now affirm.

II

A

. . . .

Neither party here contests *Saks*' definition of the term "accident" under Article 17 of the Convention. Rather, the parties differ as to which event should be the focus of the "accident" inquiry. The Court's reasoning in *Saks* sheds light on whether the flight attendant's refusal to assist a passenger in a medical crisis is the proper focus of the "accident" inquiry.

. . . .

The Court [in *Saks*] focused its analysis on determining "what causes can be considered accidents," and observed that Article 17 "embraces causes of injuries" that are "unexpected or unusual." The Court did not suggest that only one event could constitute the "accident," recognizing that "[a]ny injury is the product of a chain of causes." Thus, for purposes of the "accident" inquiry, the Court stated that a plaintiff need only be able to prove that "some link in the chain was an unusual or unexpected event external to the passenger."

B

Petitioner argues that the "accident" inquiry should focus on the "injury producing event," which, according to petitioner, was the presence of ambient cigarette smoke in the aircraft's cabin. Because petitioner's policies permitted smoking on international flights, petitioner contends that Dr. Hanson's death resulted from his own internal reaction—namely, an asthma attack—to the normal operation of the aircraft. Petitioner also argues that the flight attendant's failure to move Dr. Hanson was inaction, whereas Article 17 requires an action that causes the injury.

We disagree. As an initial matter, we note that petitioner did not challenge in the Court of Appeals the District Court's finding that the flight attendant's conduct in three times refusing to move Dr. Hanson was unusual or unexpected in light of the relevant industry standard or petitioner's own company policy. Petitioner instead argued that the flight attendant's conduct was irrelevant for purposes of the "accident" inquiry and that the only relevant event was the presence of the ambient cigarette smoke in the aircraft's cabin. Consequently, we need not dispositively determine whether the flight attendant's conduct qualified as "unusual or unexpected" under Saks, but may assume that it was for purposes of this opinion.

Petitioner's focus on the ambient cigarette smoke as the injury producing event is misplaced. We do not doubt that the presence of ambient cigarette smoke in the aircraft's cabin during an international flight might have been "normal" at the time of the flight in question. But petitioner's "injury producing event" inquiry—which looks to "the precise factual 'event' that caused the injury"—neglects the reality that there are often multiple interrelated factual events that combine to cause any given injury. In *Saks*, the Court recognized that any one of these factual events or happenings may be a link in the chain of causes and—so long as it is unusual or unexpected—could constitute an "accident" under Article 17. Indeed, the very fact that multiple events will necessarily combine and interrelate to cause any particular injury makes it difficult to define, in any coherent or non-question-begging way, any single event as the "injury producing event."

. . . .

And petitioner's argument that the flight attendant's failure to act cannot constitute an "accident" because only affirmative acts are "event[s] or happening[s]" under *Saks* is unavailing. The distinction between action and inaction, as petitioner uses these terms, would perhaps be relevant were this a tort law negligence case. But respondents do not advocate, and petitioner vigorously rejects, that a negligence regime applies under Article 17 of the Convention. The relevant "accident" inquiry under Saks is whether there is "an unexpected or unusual event or happening." The rejection of an explicit request for assistance would be an "event" or "happening" under the ordinary and usual definitions of these terms. See *American Heritage Dictionary* 635 (3d ed. 1992) ("event": "[s]omething that takes place; an occurrence"); *Black's Law Dictionary* 554–555 (6th ed. 1990) ("event": "Something that happens"); *Webster's New International Dictionary* 885 (2d ed. 1957) ("event": "The fact of taking place or occurring; occurrence" or "[t]hat which comes, arrives, or happens").[9]

---

9. The dissent cites two cases from our sister signatories United Kingdom and Australia—*Deep Vein Thrombosis and Air Travel Group Litigation*, [2003] EWCA Civ. 1005, 2003 WL

. . . .

Confirming this interpretation, other provisions of the Convention suggest that there is often no distinction between action and inaction on the issue of ultimate liability. For example, Article 25 provides that Article 22's liability cap does not apply in the event of "wilful misconduct or . . . such default on [the carrier's] part as, in accordance with the law of the court to which the case is submitted, is considered to be equivalent to wilful misconduct." 49 Stat. 3020 (emphasis added).[11] Because liability can be imposed for death or bodily injury only in the case of an Article 17 "accident" and Article 25 only lifts the caps once liability has been found, these provisions read together tend to show that inaction can give rise to liability. Moreover, Article 20(1) makes clear that the "due care" defense is unavailable when a carrier has failed to take "all necessary measures to avoid the damage." These provisions suggest that an air carrier's inaction can be the basis for liability.

. . . .

For the foregoing reasons, we conclude that the conduct here constitutes an "accident" under Article 17 of the Warsaw Convention. Accordingly, the judgment of the Court of Appeals is affirmed.

It is so ordered.

JUSTICE SCALIA, with whom JUSTICE O'CONNOR joins . . . dissenting.

When we interpret a treaty, we accord the judgments of our sister signatories " 'considerable weight.' " *Air France v. Saks*, 470 U.S. 392, 404

21353471, *650 (July 3, 2003), and *Qantas Ltd. v. Povey*, [2003] VSCA 227, ¶ 17, 2003 WL 23000692, ¶ 17 (Dec. 23, 2003) (Ormiston, J. A.), respectively—and suggests that we should simply defer to their judgment on the matter. But our conclusion is not inconsistent with *Deep Vein Thrombosis and Air Travel Litigation*, where the United Kingdom Court of Appeals commented on the District Court and Court of Appeals opinions in this case, and agreed that Dr. Hanson's death had resulted from an accident. The United Kingdom court reasoned: "The refusal of the flight attendant to move Dr. Hanson cannot properly be considered as mere inertia, or a non-event. It was a refusal to provide an alternative seat which formed part of a more complex incident, whereby Dr. Hanson was exposed to smoke in circumstances that can properly be described as unusual and unexpected." EWCA Civ. 1005, ¶ 50, 2003 WL 21353471, at *664, ¶ 50.

To the extent that the precise reasoning used by the courts in *Deep Vein Thrombosis and Air Travel Group Litigation* and *Povey* is inconsistent with our reasoning, we reject the analysis of those cases for the reasons stated in the body of this opinion. In such a circumstance, we are hesitant to "follo[w]" the opinions of intermediate appellate courts of our sister signatories, *post*, at 2 (Scalia, J., dissenting). This is especially true where there are substantial factual distinctions between these cases, see EWCA Civ. 1005, ¶ 29, 2003 WL 21353471, at *659, ¶ 29 (confronting allegations of a "failure to warn of the risk of [deep-vein thrombosis], or to advise on precautions which would avoid or minimize that risk"); VSCA 227, ¶ 3, 2003 WL 23000692, ¶ 3 (noting plaintiff alleged a failure to provide "any information or warning about the risk of [deep-vein thrombosis] or of any measures to reduce the risk"), and where the respective courts of last resort—the House of Lords and High Court of Australia—have yet to speak.

11. The Montreal Protocol No. 4 to Amend the Convention for the Unification of Certain Rules relating to International Carriage by Air (1975) amends Article 25 by replacing "wilful misconduct" with the language "done with intent to cause damage or recklessly and with knowledge that damage would probably result," as long as the airline's employee or agent was acting "within the scope of his employment." S. Exec. Rep. No. 105–20, p. 29 (1998). In 1998, the United States gave its advice and consent to ratification of the protocol, and it entered into force in the United States on March 4, 1999. *See El Al Israel Airlines, Ltd. v. Tsui Yuan Tseng*, 525 U.S. 155, 174, n. 14 (1999). Because the facts here took place in 1997–1998, Montreal Protocol No. 4 does not apply.

. . . (1985). True to that canon, our previous Warsaw Convention opinions have carefully considered foreign case law. *See, e.g.*, *El Al Israel Airlines, Ltd. v. Tsui Yuan Tseng*, 525 U.S. 155, 173–174 . . . (1999); *Eastern Airlines, Inc. v. Floyd*, 499 U.S. 530, 550–551 . . . (1991); *Saks, supra*, at 404. . . . Today's decision stands out for its failure to give any serious consideration to how the courts of our treaty partners have resolved the legal issues before us.

This sudden insularity is striking, since the Court in recent years has canvassed the prevailing law in other nations (at least Western European nations) to determine the meaning of an American Constitution that those nations had no part in framing and that those nations' courts have no role in enforcing. *See Atkins v. Virginia*, 536 U.S. 304, 316–317, n.21 . . . (2002) (whether the Eighth Amendment prohibits execution of the mentally retarded); *Lawrence v. Texas*, . . . [539 U.S. 558, 578] . . . (2003) (whether the Fourteenth Amendment prohibits the criminalization of homosexual conduct). One would have thought that foreign courts' interpretations of a treaty that their governments adopted jointly with ours, and that they have an actual role in applying, would be (to put it mildly) all the more relevant.

The Court's new abstemiousness with regard to foreign fare is not without consequence: Within the past year, appellate courts in both England and Australia have rendered decisions squarely at odds with today's holding. . . .

. . . .

. . . In *Deep Vein Thrombosis and Air Travel Group Litigation*, [2003] EWCA Civ. 1005, 2003 WL 21353471 (July 3, 2003), England's Court of Appeal, in an opinion by the Master of the Rolls that relied heavily on *Abramson v. Japan Airlines Co.*, 739 F.2d 130 (C.A.3 1984), and analyzed more than a half-dozen other non-English decisions, held as follows:

> "A critical issue in this appeal is whether a failure to act, or an omission, can constitute an accident for the purposes of Article 17. Often a failure to act results in an accident, or forms part of a series of acts and omissions which together constitute an accident. In such circumstances it may not be easy to distinguish between acts and omissions. I cannot see, however, how inaction itself can ever properly be described as an accident. It is not an event; it is a non-event. Inaction is the antithesis of an accident." [2003] EWCA Civ. 1005, ¶ 25, 2003 WL 21353471 (Lord Phillips, M. R.).

Six months later, the appellate division of the Supreme Court of Victoria, Australia, in an opinion that likewise gave extensive consideration to American and other foreign decisions, agreed:

> "The allegations in substance do no more than state a failure to do something, and this cannot be characterised as an event or happening, whatever be the concomitant background to that failure to warn

or advise. . . ." *Qantas Ltd. v. Povey*, [2003] VSCA 227, ¶ 17, 2003 WL 23000692 (Dec. 23, 2003) (Ormiston, J. A.).

We can, and should, look to decisions of other signatories when we interpret treaty provisions. Foreign constructions are evidence of the original shared understanding of the contracting parties. Moreover, it is reasonable to impute to the parties an intent that their respective courts strive to interpret the treaty consistently. (The Warsaw Convention's preamble specifically acknowledges "the advantage of regulating *in a uniform manner* the conditions of ... the liability of the carrier." 49 Stat. 3014 (emphasis added).) Finally, even if we disagree, we surely owe the conclusions reached by appellate courts of other signatories the courtesy of respectful consideration.

. . . .

Tragic though Dr. Hanson's death may have been, it does not justify the Court's putting us in needless conflict with other signatories to the Warsaw Convention. I respectfully dissent.

CONCLUDING NOTES ON TREATY INTERPRETATION BY U.S. COURTS

1. *Supreme Court and Treaty Interpretation*. In light of *Olympic Airways*, how would you answer the questions posed at the beginning of this Section?

2. *Good Faith Principle*. In *Chew Heong v. United States*, the Supreme Court stated: " 'Treaties of every kind ... are to receive a fair and liberal interpretation, according to the intention of the contracting parties, and are to be kept in the most scrupulous good faith....' [T]he court cannot be unmindful of the fact that the honor of the government and people of the United States is involved in every inquiry whether rights secured by [treaty] stipulations shall be recognized and protected." 112 U.S. at 540 (citation omitted). Is this an operative principle upon which U.S. courts should interpret treaties and, if so, what consequences should flow from it? *See* Michael P. Van Alstine, *The Death of Good Faith in Treaty Jurisprudence and a Call for Resurrection*, 93 GEO. L.J. 1885 (2005).

3. *Use of International Court Decisions When Interpreting Treaties*. Should U.S. courts follow the interpretations placed upon treaties by international courts (as opposed to foreign courts operating in national legal systems)? The International Court of Justice (ICJ) in the period prior to the *Medellín* case, *supra* Section 4, interpreted the Vienna Convention on Consular Relations as precluding the application of State "procedural default" rules to claims brought under Article 36 of the Convention. While the U.S. Supreme Court stated that the International Court's treaty interpretation deserved "respectful consideration," in *Sanchez-Llamas v. Oregon*, 548 U.S. 331, 165 L.Ed.2d 557 (2006), the Supreme Court declined to adopt that interpretation.

> Under our Constitution, "[t]he judicial Power of the United States" is "vested in one supreme Court, and in such inferior Courts as the Congress may from time to time ordain and establish." Art. III, § 1. That "judicial Power ... extend[s] to ... Treaties." *Id.*, § 2. And, as Chief

Justice Marshall famously explained, that judicial power includes the duty "to say what the law is." *Marbury v. Madison*, 1 Cranch 137, 177 ... (1803). If treaties are to be given effect as federal law under our legal system, determining their meaning as a matter of federal law "is emphatically the province and duty of the judicial department," headed by the "one supreme Court" established by the Constitution. *Ibid.*; *see also Williams v. Taylor*, 529 U.S. 362, 378–379 ... (2000) (opinion of STEVENS, J.) ("At the core of [the judicial] power is the federal courts' independent responsibility—independent from its coequal branches in the Federal Government, and independent from the separate authority of the several States—to interpret federal law"). It is against this background that the United States ratified, and the Senate gave its advice and consent to, the various agreements that govern referral of Vienna Convention disputes to the ICJ.

Nothing in the structure or purpose of the ICJ suggests that its interpretations were intended to be conclusive on our courts. The ICJ's decisions have "*no binding force* except between the parties and in respect of that particular case," Statute of the International Court of Justice, Art. 59, 59 Stat. 1062, T. S. No. 993 (1945) (emphasis added). Any interpretation of law the ICJ renders in the course of resolving particular disputes is thus not binding precedent *even as to the ICJ itself*; there is accordingly little reason to think that such interpretations were intended to be controlling on our courts. The ICJ's principal purpose is to arbitrate particular disputes between national governments. *Id.*, at 1055 (ICJ is "the principal judicial organ of the United Nations"); *see also* Art. 34, *id.*, at 1059 ("Only states [*i.e.*, countries] may be parties in cases before the Court"). While each member of the United Nations has agreed to comply with decisions of the ICJ "in any case to which it is a party," United Nations Charter, Art. 94(1), 59 Stat. 1051, T. S. No. 933 (1945), the Charter's procedure for noncompliance—referral to the Security Council by the aggrieved state—contemplates quintessentially *international* remedies, Art. 94(2), *ibid.*

NOTE ON TREATY INTERPRETATION BY THE EXECUTIVE BRANCH

Of course, interpretation of treaties is often undertaken by the Executive Branch in the course of its day-to-day implementation of treaties without the matter ending up before a U.S. court. *See, e.g.,* U.S. Department of State, *Digest of United States Practice in International Law 2001*, at 219 (Sally J. Cummins & David P. Stewart eds., 2001). Typically, Executive Branch interpretations raise no particular concerns. *See, e.g.*, Abbott v. Abbott, 130 S.Ct. 1983, 1993, 176 L.Ed.2d 789 (2010) ("This Court's conclusion that Mr. Abbott possesses a right of custody under the Convention is supported and informed by the State Department's view on the issue.... It is well settled that the Executive Branch's interpretation of a treaty 'is entitled to great weight.' There is no reason to doubt that this well-established canon of deference is appropriate here.") (citations omitted).

At the same time, U.S. courts do no always defer to the executive branch's interpretation of a treaty. Deborah N Pearlstein notes that

> the Court has invoked a *Marbury*-based insistence on asserting its own formal interpretive authority.... [I]n a series of decisions involving national security, the Court has been anything but deferential to the executive's interpretation of the relevant statute or treaty. In *Rasul v. Bush*, *Hamdi v. Rumsfeld*, *Hamdan v. Rumsfeld*, and *Boumediene v. Bush*, the Court has swept aside vigorous arguments by the executive that it refrain from engagement on abstention or political question grounds. Moreover, the Court has scarcely noted any doctrinal tradition of interpretive "deference" on the meaning of the laws.

Deborah N. Pearlstein, *After Deference: Formalizing the Judicial Power for Foreign Relations Law*, 159 U. PA. L. REV. 783, 793–801 (2011); *see also* Scott M. Sullivan, *Rethinking Treaty Interpretation*, 86 TEX. L. REV. 777 (2008) (finding that, when deciding how much deference to give to an executive interpretation of the treaty, "executive self-interest" should be one of the factors considered); Edward T. Swaine, *Taking Care of Treaties*, 108 COLUM. L. REV. 331 (2008) (concluding that, if *Chevron*-type deference is to be allowed with respect to executive branch treaty administration, "checks on self-aggrandizement" (i.e., executive self-interest) would need to be developed).

Should Congress defer to the executive branch as to the interpretation of a treaty? What if that interpretation is one that at least some members of Congress regard as inconsistent with the meaning of the treaty? Some deference presumably needs to be paid to the Executive Branch, but must Congress defer if it believes that a "reinterpretation" is occurring that, in effect, is altering the treaty from that consented to by Senate?

This issue came to a head in the mid–1980s over the Executive Branch's interpretation of the 1972 Anti–Ballistic Missile Treaty (ABM Treaty). *See* Treaty on the Limitation of Anti–Ballistic Missile Systems, May 26, 1972, U.S.-U.S.S.R., 23 U.S.T. 3435. For the first decade of its existence, the ABM Treaty had been interpreted as imposing a blanket prohibition on the development of anti-ballistic missile systems, except for very limited land-based systems, on a theory that neither the United States nor the Soviet Union would initiate a nuclear attack if it were unable to defend itself against the retaliation that almost certainly would ensue. Thus, the Treaty was interpreted "narrowly," allowing only very limited exceptions.

In March 1983, however, President Ronald Reagan announced his intention to pursue a "Strategic Defense Initiative" (also known as "SDI," or "Star Wars"), which would be a ground-based and space-based system to protect the United States from attack by strategic nuclear ballistic missiles. Pursuing SDI meant engaging in development and testing that, under the "narrow" interpretation of the ABM Treaty, would not be permitted. Consequently, the Reagan Administration offered an alternative interpretation of the ABM Treaty—a "broad" interpretation—that would allow such development and testing, but not deployment. In advancing such an interpretation, the Reagan Administration relied in part on information contained in a secret negotiating record that was not provided to the Senate at the time of its advice and consent to ratification.

On March 11, 1987, the Senate Foreign Relations Committee and the Senate Judiciary Committee began a series of joint hearings on this effort to "reinterpret" the ABM Treaty. Democratic Senator Joseph Biden introduced Senate Resolution 167 (reprinted below), which reasserted the propriety of the narrow interpretation and made certain findings concerning pertinent constitutional principles. It is the dispute concerning these principles, rather than the dispute concerning the merits of the "narrow" versus the "broad" interpretation, that the following materials address.

Three central issues emerge. First, at what point does a "reinterpretation" of a treaty represent an amendment—or even a new treaty? Second, in resolving this issue, what weight is to be accorded to the negotiating record of a treaty—and what difference does it make if that record was not transmitted to the Senate at the time it approved the treaty? Third, when the negotiating record is not transmitted (most are not), what weight is to be accorded the Senate's *implicit* understanding concerning the meaning of a treaty—to be gleaned, for example, from statements made by senators during committee hearings or on the Senate floor—as opposed to *explicit* Senate reservation, understandings, or declarations made by the Senate upon its consent to a treaty?

THE ABM TREATY AND THE CONSTITUTION: JOINT HEARINGS ON SENATE RESOLUTION 167 BEFORE THE SENATE COMMITTEE ON FOREIGN RELATIONS AND THE SENATE COMMITTEE ON THE JUDICIARY

100th Cong. at 229–31, 236–37, 317–20, 355–64, 415–19 (1987).

. . . .

Concerning constitutional principles pertinent to the making of treaties, and further concerning the interpretation of the Treaty Between the United States of America and the Union of Soviet Socialist Republics on the Limitation of Anti–Ballistic Missile Systems.

Resolved, That this resolution may be referred to as the "ABM Treaty Interpretation Resolution".

THE TREATY POWER

SEC. 2. The Senate finds as follows:

(1) (A) Article II, section 2, clause 2 of the United States Constitution provides that the President "shall have power, by and with the advice and consent of the Senate, to make treaties, provided two-thirds of the Senators present concur".

(B) If, following Senate advice and consent, the President proceeds to ratify a treaty, the President may ratify only the treaty to which the Senate advised and consented.

(2) (A) Under the United States Constitution, during the period in which a treaty is in force, the meaning of that treaty is what the Senate understands the treaty to mean when it gives its advice and consent, a meaning which is informed by reference to expressions of

intent by the Senate as well as Senate acquiescence in any interpretation communicated by the Executive.

(B) In the absence of any evidence concerning how the Senate understands such treaty, it is properly interpreted by reference to its text, as reasonably construed, in light of its context and object and purpose.

(C) To the extent the meaning of a treaty is clear under subparagraphs (A) and (B), anything not transmitted to the Senate at such time, including the negotiating record, is not relevant to the meaning of the treaty.

(3) The President may not amend a treaty without the agreement of the Parties and the advice and consent of the Senate.

(4) (A) Under Article II, section 3, clause 4 of the Constitution, the President is required to "take care that the laws be faithfully executed".

(B) For purposes of such provision, during the period in which a treaty is in force, it constitutes a law.

(C) The President is required to take care that each such treaty be faithfully executed.

. . . .

DECLARATION OF POLICY

SEC. 8. The Senate therefore declares that—

(1) under the Constitution, a treaty made by the United States is a treaty to which the Senate advised and consented, and is properly interpreted by reference to the text placed before the Senate, subject to any relevant and material Executive communications to the Senate during its consideration of the treaty and any interpretation expressed by the Senate in advising and consenting to ratification;

(2) the development, testing, or deployment of any sea-based, air-based, space-based, or mobile land-based ABM systems or components for the purpose of countering strategic ballistic missiles or their elements in flight trajectory, including ABM systems or components involving technologies not in existence when the Treaty was ratified, would be inconsistent with the provisions of the Treaty and would require an amendment to the Treaty; and

(3) no amendment to the ABM Treaty may occur without the agreement of the Parties and the advice and consent of the Senate.

PREPARED STATEMENT OF PROFESSOR LOUIS HENKIN TO THE SENATE FOREIGN RELATIONS COMMITTEE

(Mar. 11, 1987).

The Constitution, in Article II, section 2, provides that the President "shall have power, by and with the advice and consent of the Senate, to make treaties, provided two-thirds of the Senators present concur." Unlike some other clauses in the Constitution, those 25 words have not been a source of serious controversy during the two centuries of our national life under the Constitution. There has been some uncertainty, and perhaps some change from what was contemplated, as to the "advice" which the Senate may give to the President in relation to treaties; there has been some uncertainty as to the relation between advice and consent. There has been significant development in the Senate's view of its consent role, particularly as to the amendments or reservations which the Senate may propose as the condition of its consent to a treaty.

Little of that history need concern us here. For present purposes, one may reduce the Constitutional provision to a simple proposition: the President can make a treaty if the Senate has consented to it. Of course, the President can only make the treaty to which the Senate consented; he cannot make a treaty other than the one to which the Senate consented. Therefore, the President cannot make a treaty with a text different from the one to which the Senate consented; he cannot make a treaty with a meaning different from the one to which the Senate consented.

In considering treaties for possible consent, the Senate has on numerous occasions expressed itself on the meaning of one provision or another. Sometimes the Senate has made sure that the meaning it gave to a treaty provision would prevail, by insisting that the United States enter a reservation reflecting the Senate's interpretation. If the Senate does so, the President can make the treaty for the United States only subject to such a reservation. Sometimes the Senate has refrained from proposing a reservation but has expressed its understanding of a provision. Again, the President can make the treaty only subject to the Senate's understanding. He must make the Senate's understanding the United States' understanding, and a condition of United States adherence to the treaty.

The principles I have articulated and the practice I have described have not been disputed in the past and are not controversial today. They govern, I believe, the draft resolution before your committees. The President can only make a treaty that means what the Senate understood the treaty to mean when the Senate gave its consent. That is indisputable when the Senate has made its understanding plain in the form of a proposed reservation or an explicit understanding. The same principle governs when the Senate's understanding of a treaty provision is not expressed in a formal resolution but is apparent from the Senate's deliberations leading to its expression of consent. The Senate's understanding of the treaty to which it consents is binding on the President. He can make the treaty only as so understood. He cannot make the treaty and insist that it means something else.

The principle that the President can only make a treaty as it is understood by the Senate would govern even if the Senate had given no indication of its understanding of the treaty. In that event, it must be assumed—in the absence of any evidence to the contrary—that the Senate understood the treaty to mean what it would be understood to mean by reasonable people, reading the text of the treaty in good faith in accordance with the ordinary meaning to be given to the terms of the treaty, in their context and in the light of their object and purpose. That understanding must be assumed to have been the interpretation given to the treaty by the Senate; that interpretation, therefore, is the interpretation which the President must adopt for the United States when he makes the treaty.

The principles I have articulated seem to me the indisputable implications of the treaty provision in Article II, section 2, of the Constitution.

Let it be clear. I am not suggesting any special prerogative for a later Senate to interpret a treaty made by a President with the consent of an earlier Senate. *See Fourteen Diamond Rings v. United States*, 183 U.S. 176 (1901). I am not suggesting even that the Senate today can determine, finally and exclusively, the understanding of the Senate that gave consent to a treaty in the more or less distant past, though such a determination by the Senate today, if made after careful study, would deserve to be given great weight. Nor am I addressing the extent to which, as a matter of international law, the Senate's understanding of a treaty, if not communicated to other states parties to the treaty, is binding on those other states.

But for our own Constitutional purposes, the only treaty which the President can make (Article II, section 2), the only treaty that is a treaty made under the authority of the United States for purposes of federal jurisdiction (Article III, section 2), the only treaty that is the supreme law of the land (Article VI, clause 2), is the treaty made by the President with the consent of the Senate, as understood by the Senate when it gave its consent.

PREPARED STATEMENT OF U.S. STATE DEPARTMENT LEGAL ADVISER ABRAHAM D. SOFAER TO THE SENATE FOREIGN RELATIONS COMMITTEE

(Mar. 26, 1987).

In my remarks today I thought I could be most helpful by focusing on the proposed Resolution of March 11, 1987, submitted by the Senator from Delaware. That Resolution proposes rules for the interpretation of treaties generally, and then offers specific conclusions as to the ABM Treaty in particular. My study will deal with the conclusions suggested for the ABM Treaty. I can appropriately comment, however, at this time, on the general principles the Resolution proposes.

Let me say, at the outset, that I fully agree with the proposition expressed in Section 2(1)(B) that "the President may ratify only the treaty to which the Senate advised and consented." The treaty power is a special aspect of our Constitution. But it is similar to other aspects of the Constitution that reflect the Framers' intention to have government of shared or mixed powers. The Senate and the President are partners in the treaty-making process, each having its own roles, but each needing the other's concurrence to act effectively. The statement by Professor Henkin in this connection—that the President can only ratify the treaty to which the Senate consents—is unobjectionable. The issue, always, in the context of our international obligations, is: What is that treaty to which the Senate advised and consented?

The key question posed by the Resolution is by what standards should the President, or the Senate, determine the meaning of a treaty ratified years before the issue of interpretation arises. Likewise, the Resolution properly states that a treaty is a law, and that the President must take care that all laws, including treaties, be faithfully executed under Article II, section 3, clause 4 of the Constitution. Once again, however, the question remains what is the treaty, that is the law, that the President must faithfully execute? How is its meaning determined?

The Resolution before these Committees proposes several rules by which it would require such determinations to be made. Some of these rules are traditional standards, such as the proposition that the meaning of a treaty "is informed by reference to expressions of intent by the Senate. ..." If anything, that language is an understatement. The Senate's power over the meaning of a treaty, during the process of advice and consent, is enormous—its decisions and directions can be authoritative, when it chooses to exercise its power for that purpose.

The Resolution misstates the law, however, in at least two important respects. It is wrong, first, in the special weight it seeks to accord to what it defines as "Senate acquiescence in any interpretation communicated by the Executive." It is also wrong in attempting to mandate that, "to the extent the meaning of a treaty is clear" from how the Senate understands it and from the treaty's text, "anything not transmitted to the Senate" during the process of advice and consent, "including the negotiating record, is not relevant to the meaning of the treaty." These standards are inconsistent with established practice, and their adoption could have no effect internationally other than occasionally to bind the United States to standards of conduct which our treaty partners are free to ignore. Moreover, while these standards may appear to protect the prerogatives of the Senate, they would seriously undermine the Constitution's real purpose in assigning to the Senate the power of advice and consent.

The effect of ratification proceedings on the international obligations of the United States can be, and was intended to be, profound. The Senate is able, in a variety of ways, to have a powerful—even decisive—impact on the international obligations of the United States. The Senate has the power to decide in each instance just how far it wishes to go in establishing the meaning of a treaty on any question of interest to the Senate. In each instance, the Senate acts, not merely to protect its own prerogatives, but as a partner with the President in forming an international contract. A treaty is a law, and in some respects it has purely domestic effects that lead to its being applied in the way any law is applied. But a treaty is also more than a law. It is an international contract, and the Senate is as responsible as the President for making sure that the contracts made in behalf of the U.S. are mutually enforceable and do not create unilateral duties.

In implementing its important powers, therefore, over the meaning of treaties, the Senate has developed a set of practices to ensure that the Senate's determinations and opinions have the same degree of binding effect on our treaty partners as they do upon the United States. Thus, the Senate acts to incorporate its proposed interpretations as amendments, reservations, understandings, or other conditions in the Senate's resolution of ratification. The resolution of ratification is the document by which the Senate formally grants advice and consent, and it typically requires the President to take appropriate action in connection with ratification to ensure that the other party is officially informed of the Senate's input on the terms of the international contract, and is mutually bound.

In the case of a bilateral treaty, the practice of the Executive Branch has generally been to seek the express agreement of the other party to all the conditions in the Senate's resolution of ratification which affect the rights and obligations of the parties. The Executive then incorporates all such conditions into the U.S. instrument of ratification. The Senate is well aware of the importance of this process, and has occasionally concerned itself in great detail with the precise manner in which the Executive Branch would ensure that our treaty partners are legally bound with respect to the Senate's understandings or conditions.

In the case of the Panama Treaties, for example, the Senate conditioned its advice and consent on a series of amendments, reservations, understandings and other conditions, some of which addressed the meaning of treaty provisions. The Senate's resolutions of ratification required that the President include in the U.S. instruments of ratification all of the conditions in the Senate's resolutions, and that certain of these conditions be included in both the U.S. and Panamanian instruments, or in a bilateral agreement called a protocol of exchange to be signed by the two parties at the time of ratification.

In considering the SALT II Treaty, the Senate Foreign Relations Committee decided that the Senate should specify explicitly what was required by the President for all conditions. It proposed a three-part resolution of ratification: first, provisions that did not require formal notice to or agreement by the Soviet Union, including a few interpretive statements and a number of internal instructions to the Executive Branch; second, provisions that would be formally communicated to the

Soviet Union prior to ratification as the official position of the United States, including a number of interpretive statements; and third, provisions that would require the explicit agreement of the Soviet Union prior to ratification, concerning the legal status of certain associated documents.

The Committee report indicated that the President would be bound vis-a-vis the Senate with respect to the conditions in all three categories, but that the three categories differed with regard to their effect on the Soviet Union. With respect to the third category, the Committee recognized that even the formal inclusion of the conditions in the U.S. instrument of ratification might be insufficient to bind the Soviet Union, and that the Senate should therefore require the President to obtain express Soviet agreement.

These examples and others from the practice of the two branches illustrate that the Senate may, through its resolution of ratification, oblige the President to act to ensure that the other party is legally bound to an interpretation of treaty terms. They also show that the Senate is fully aware that the proper and effective way to bind treaty partners is to secure their express written agreement to conditions or other terms. In the absence of express agreement, some degree of doubt will always exist as to whether the other party is legally bound to an interpretation, even when it is contained in the Senate's resolution and the U.S. instrument of ratification. Finally, this practice reflects that, by implication, our treaty partners are not bound by interpretations as to which they are not given formal notice prior to ratification.

The fundamental importance given to the Senate's explicit, formally communicated understandings is also clearly supported in law. The Vienna Convention on the Law of Treaties provides that treaties must be interpreted "in good faith in accordance with the ordinary meaning to be given to the terms of the treaty in their context and in light of its object and purpose." Senate additions to a ratification instrument often constitute the terms of a treaty; at times, the Senate rewrites a treaty's terms to make it acceptable. Where the U.S. formally communicates the Senate's conditions, reservations, or understandings, which are not "terms" strictly speaking, they clearly constitute an important part of the "context" in which the treaty's terms must be construed and its purposes ascertained.

In sharp contrast to Senate actions that are contained in the resolution of ratification and formally communicated to treaty partners, interpretations of a treaty merely discussed before, or presented by Executive witnesses to, the Senate in general have far less weight in the process of treaty interpretation. This does not mean that such interpretive statements have no probative value on the issue of the treaty's international meaning and effect.

Their probative value for this purpose, however, is far less certain than statements placed in ratification resolutions, and depends upon a variety of factors, including the degree to which the Senate evidenced an intent to adopt the interpretation as a condition to its assent to the treaty, whether and the manner in which the treaty partner is put officially on notice of such statements, and the extent and manner in which the treaty partner responds.

How the record of internal ratification proceedings fits into the scheme of the Vienna Convention on Treaties is unclear. The internal ratification proceedings of one of the parties to a treaty may shed light on that party's understanding of the meaning intended by its terms and the object and purpose of the treaty. Standing alone, however, such proceedings would not appear to be part of the context of a treaty, or the materials cited in Article 31. Such evidence might, however, qualify under Article 32 as "supplementary materials", and appear to have been treated as such by various scholars. Assuming that internal ratification records are, at best, "supplementary" means of interpretation, they are therefore no higher in status in the interpretation of treaties for international purposes than the negotiating record.

The Convention does not indicate what relative probative weight should be given to ratification proceedings; presumably this would depend on their content, significance, and all other relevant circumstances. But the content of such proceedings must always be considered with caution, in that they reflect the views expressed in the internal processes of only one of the parties.

NOTE: "FULL OF SOUND AND FURY, SIGNIFYING . . ."

1. *Denouement to the ABM Treaty Confrontation.* On May 19, 1987, the Senate Foreign Relations Committee voted to recommend favorably Senate Resolution 167, but the resolution was never brought for consideration by the Senate as a whole. Subsequently, Congress sought to limit SDI funding to programs that the Congress and Executive had determined to be within the "original interpretation" of the Treaty. The Reagan Administration decided that it would not violate the boundaries of the "original interpretation" as a matter of policy, while maintaining that it did not feel compelled as a matter of law. The United States withdrew from the ABM Treaty in 2002.

2. *"Living Tree" Treaties.* Are some treaties of a nature that they must be allowed to be interpreted and reinterpreted in an organic way over time because they were meant to evolve? Consider the following position by Professor Thomas Franck regarding the nature of the U.N. Charter:

> What emerges from the vast legacy of recorded debates and decisions of the principal political organs is that they tend to treat the Charter not as a static formula, but as a constitutive instrument capable of organic growth. Borrowing a phrase coined by the Imperial Privy Council speaking of the Canadian constitution, the Charter is "a living tree."
>
> Ordinary treaties are not "living trees" but international contracts to be construed in strict accord with the black-letter text. Not so the Charter. The Charter also differs from most treaties not only in enumerating rights and duties but also in elaborating institutions to carry them into effect. Two political organs (the General Assembly and the Security

> Council) were given Charter-implementing powers: Chapters IV and V, respectively. An independent civil service, the Secretariat, headed by a Secretary–General, enjoys autonomous, Charter-based power to construe and apply the Charter and decisions of the political organs.
>
> Further, the Charter makes allowance for its interpretation through state practice....
>
> Each principal organ and the members thus continuously interpret the Charter and do so in accordance with the requisites of ever-changing circumstances. This necessarily means that the Charter text is always evolving.

Thomas M. Franck, *Recourse to Force: State Action against Threats and Armed Attacks* 6–7 (2002). If this is correct, does it make sense for the Senate's original understanding of the meaning of a treaty to govern the Executive thereafter? Does it matter whether at the time of ratification it is understood that the treaty will be a "living tree"? What other types of treaties should be regarded as evolving in their meaning? Human-rights treaties? Environmental treaties? Would it also be possible for parts of treaties to be interpreted as regressing (rather than progressing), such as an Executive Branch interpretation that certain laws of war treaties contain provisions that are now "quaint" and of no further relevance to contemporary conflicts?

3. *Commentary*. For commentary on the ABM dispute, see Joseph R. Biden & John B. Ritch, III, *The Treaty Power: Upholding a Constitutional Partnership,* 137 U. PA. L. REV. 1529 (1989); Lawrence J. Block, Lee A. Casey & David B. Rivkin, *The Senate's Pie-in-the-Sky Treaty Interpretation: Power and the Quest for Legislative Supremacy,* 137 U. PA. L. REV. 1481 (1989); Abram Chayes & Antonia H. Chayes, *Testing and Development of "Exotic" Systems Under the ABM Treaty: The Great Reinterpretation Caper,* 99 HARV. L. REV. 1956 (1986); Michael J. Glennon, *Interpreting "Interpretation": The President, the Senate, and When Treaty Interpretation Becomes Treaty Making,* 20 U.C. DAVIS L. REV. 913 (1987); Kevin C. Kennedy, *Treaty Interpretation by the Executive Branch: The ABM Treaty and "Star Wars" Testing and Development,* 80 AM. J. INT'L L. 854 (1986); David A. Koplow, *Constitutional Bait and Switch: Executive Reinterpretation of Arms Control Treaties,* 137 U. PA. L. REV. 1353 (1989); Eugene V. Rostow, *The Reinterpretation Debate and Constitutional Law,* 137 U. PA. L. REV. 1451 (1989); Abraham D. Sofaer, *The ABM Treaty and the Strategic Defense Initiative,* 99 HARV. L. REV. 1972 (1986).

SECTION 10. TREATY TERMINATION

NOTE ON CONGRESSIONAL "PARTICIPATION" IN TERMINATION

Obviously Congress has a role in U.S. adherence to most international agreements, either through the Senate alone (a treaty) or through both Houses acting together (a "congressional-executive agreement"). Yet if the President wishes to terminate (or perhaps suspend) an international agreement to which Congress has assented, must he obtain congressional consent to do so?

In *Van Der Weyde v. Ocean Transp. Co.*, 297 U.S. 114, 56 S.Ct. 392, 80 L.Ed. 515 (1936), the Supreme Court examined section 16 of the Seamen's Act of March 4, 1915 (38 Stat. 1164, 1184). This section expressed "the judgment of Congress" that treaty provisions in conflict with the provisions of the Act "ought to be terminated." It further "requested and directed" the President to give notice to that effect to the several governments concerned within ninety days after the passage of the Act. In consequence, notice was given, and a large number of treaties were terminated in whole or in part. Suppose the President, after signing the bill, had asked you, his counsel, for advice as to whether he was constitutionally required to implement Congress's direction to him concerning the treaties. How would you have advised? What legal consequences would his refusal entail? In the *Van Der Weyde* case, the Supreme Court explicitly refused to consider whether the President could have terminated the inconsistent treaties, or treaty-provisions, had Congress not specifically authorized him to do so, because that issue "is not here involved." *Id.* at 117. However, it is precisely this issue that was involved in the following case brought by Senator Goldwater.

SENSE OF CONGRESS RESOLUTION ON MUTUAL DEFENSE TREATY WITH CHINA, 1978

22 U.S.C. § 2151 (2006).

(a) The Congress finds that—

(1) the continued security and stability of East Asia is a matter of major strategic interest to the United States;

(2) the United States and the Republic of China have for a period of twenty-four years been linked together by the Mutual Defense Treaty of 1954;

(3) the Republic of China has during that twenty-four-year period faithfully and continually carried out its duties and obligations under that treaty; and

(4) it is the responsibility of the Senate to give its advice and consent to treaties entered into by the United States.

(b) It is the sense of the Congress that there should be prior consultation between the Congress and the executive branch on any proposed policy changes affecting the continuation in force of the Mutual Defense Treaty of 1954.

GOLDWATER v. CARTER

481 F.Supp. 949, 950–65 (D.D.C. 1979) (footnotes omitted).

[In 1979, as a precondition to the arrangements for U.S. recognition of the communist government of the People's Republic of China (located in Beijing), President Jimmy Carter unilaterally terminated a 25–year-old mutual defense treaty with the Republic of China, whose nationalist government was based in Taiwan. President Carter did so without obtaining congressional consent. Eight senators, one former senator, and sixteen

House members sued the President, claiming that they were being denied their constitutional role under the Treaty Clause.]

MEMORANDUM

GASCH, DISTRICT JUDGE.

. . . .

Since the first treaty to which the United States was a party was terminated in 1798 by an act of Congress, a variety of means have been used to terminate treaties: by statute directing the President to deliver notice of termination; by the President acting pursuant to a joint resolution of Congress or otherwise acting with the concurrence of both houses of Congress; by the President acting with senatorial consent; and by the President acting alone. The final method of termination is of particular relevance here, but the precedents involving unilateral executive action are of only marginal utility. None of these examples involves a mutual defense treaty, nor any treaty whose national and international significance approaches that of the 1954 Mutual Defense Treaty. Virtually all of them, moreover, can be readily distinguished on the basis of some triggering factor not present here.

The great majority of the historical precedents involve some form of mutual action, whereby the President's notice of termination receives the affirmative approval of the Senate or the entire Congress. Taken as a whole, the historical precedents support rather than detract from the position that the power to terminate treaties is a power shared by the political branches of this government.

A.

Defendants' argument that the President has authority to terminate unilaterally the Mutual Defense Treaty is premised on the executive power over foreign affairs. This authority derives from the enumerated Article II powers, including those that authorize the President to make treaties with the advice and consent of the Senate and to receive representatives of foreign nations.

Because the President has been termed "the sole organ of the federal government in the field of international relations," defendants argue that construing the Constitution to require that the Senate or the Congress also has a right to participate in treaty termination would be inconsistent with the President's constitutional authority over foreign affairs. They further urge that the Senate's role of advising and consenting in the making of treaties is not an independent source of legislative power, but only a limitation upon the treaty-making power of the President. Such limitations, they conclude, must be strictly construed and not extended by implication. *See Myers v. United States,* 272 U.S. 52, 164 . . . (1926).

An attempt to justify a unilateral presidential power to terminate treaties by analogy to the Supreme Court's treatment of the removal power in *Myers* is unpersuasive. The power to remove executive personnel cannot be compared with the power to terminate an important international treaty. The removal power is restricted in its exercise to "purely executive officers" charged with a duty unrelated to the legislative or judicial power. It concerns the President's administrative control over his subordinates and flows from the President's obligations to see that the laws are faithfully executed. By contrast, treaty termination impacts upon the substantial role of Congress in foreign affairs—especially in the context of a mutual defense pact involving the potential exercise of congressional war powers—and is a contradiction rather than a corollary of the Executive's enforcement obligation. The same separation of powers principles that dictate presidential independence and control within the executive establishment preclude the President from exerting an overriding influence in the sphere of constitutional powers that is shared with the legislative branch. A power to terminate treaties that are made "by and with the Advice and Consent of the Senate" simply does not fall within the limited scope of the *Myers* rationale.

Nor, for reasons more fully set forth below, can the President's status as the nation's spokesman and representative in foreign affairs serve as the basis for exclusive executive power over the entire process of treaty termination. While the President may be the sole organ of communication with foreign governments, he is clearly not the sole maker of foreign policy. In short, the conduct of foreign relations is not a plenary executive power.

. . . .

B.

The termination of a treaty is not a single act entrusted by the Constitution to one or the other of our political branches. Like treaty formation, treaty termination is comprised of a series of acts that seek to maintain a constitutional balance. Initially, a policy determination must be made concerning whether the treaty should be terminated and the appropriate negotiations to effect termination undertaken. Such actions are clearly within the competency of the executive branch. Similarly, the communication of the message terminating a treaty, as here by delivery of formal notice to the other party pursuant to the terms of the agreement, is committed to the President as the sole representative of our country in foreign affairs.

But these purely executive functions are not the only elements involved in treaty termination. Termination of a treaty also involves a repeal of the "law of the land" established by the agreement. It is in this area that congressional participation is required under the present circumstances. The mere fact that the President has the authority to make an initial policy determination regarding the exercise of an option to terminate, and to notify the foreign state of termination, does not vest him with the unilateral power to complete the termination process and thereby effect the abrogation of the treaty. As two scholars have recently noted, "[i]t is inherently inconceivable that . . . a constitutional policy requiring joint action for external agreement and internal legislation could allow that agreement and law to be terminated by the president alone, against the intentions of the legislature."

This conclusion is dictated by several constitutional factors: the status of treaties as the supreme law of the land, together with the obligation of the President to faithfully execute those laws; the implications to be derived from the constitutionally delineated role of the Senate in treaty formation; and the fundamental doctrine of separation of powers. It is further bolstered by the historical experience represented by constitutional interpretation and practice.

Article VI of the Constitution provides:

> This Constitution, and the Laws of the United States which shall be made in Pursuance thereof; and all Treaties made, or which shall be made, under the Authority of the United States, shall be the supreme Law of the Land. . . .

U.S.Const. art. VI, cl. 2. Defendants argue, however, that the 1954 Mutual Defense Treaty is not a "law of the land" for supremacy clause purposes. They assert that only those treaties that are self-executing, and thus become effective as domestic law at the time the agreement goes into effect, constitute the supreme law of the land. Careful consideration of the provisions of the Mutual Defense Treaty establishes that a number of its provisions are self-executing and that still others have been implemented by subsequent legislation. In light of the terms and conditions of the Treaty, as well as the acts subsequently taken by the Congress and the President which have fixed and defined the nation's responsibilities under it, it is now far too late to assert that this Treaty fails to have the status of the supreme law of the land under Article VI. Moreover, none of the factors that would impair that status are involved here.

Article II, section three of the Constitution requires that the President "shall take care that the Laws be faithfully executed." This constitutional responsibility clearly extends to all laws of the land, including in this instance the Mutual Defense Treaty. The President cannot faithfully execute that treaty by abrogating it any more than he can faithfully execute by failing to administer. He alone cannot effect the repeal of a law of the land which was formed by joint action of the executive and legislative branches, whether that law be a statute or a treaty. The limits upon his authority are in no way altered by the inclusion of a termination provision in Article X of the Mutual Defense Treaty, allowing either party to terminate upon one year notice. The President's powers of administering the Treaty do not include the power to terminate in accordance with the provisions of Article X. The "party" to which the termination provision refers is the United States, not the President alone, and such termination can only be effectuated in accordance with United States constitutional processes.

The requirements imposed by the Supremacy Clause and the President's responsibility to faithfully execute the laws are further supported by the doctrine of separation of powers and its corollary concept of checks and balances, which lies at the heart of our constitutional system. In the treaty formation process, the Constitution expressly limits the Executive's role by requiring the advice and consent of two-thirds of the Senate. This constitutional requirement reflects the concern of the Founding Fathers that neither political branch possess unchecked power.

A judicial determination that the President enjoys unilateral authority to terminate treaties would raise the same fears and present the same possibility of abuse. It would be incompatible with our system of checks and balances if the executive power in the area of foreign affairs were construed to encompass a unilateral power to terminate treaties. It is undisputed that the President is without power to amend the terms of a treaty. Any such amendment must be submitted to the Senate for its advice and consent. If the lesser power to amend treaties is denied the President, *a fortiori,* the greater power to annul should also be denied. In the present situation the President may very well be carrying out the wishes of the American people but because the legislative branch has not participated in the treaty termination process, there is no way to ascertain this fact. As Justice Frankfurter stated in *Youngstown Sheet & Tube Co. v. Sawyer,* 343 U.S. 579 ... (1952): "The accretion of dangerous power does not come in a day. It does come, however slowly, from the generative force of unchecked disregard of the restrictions that fence in even the most disinterested assertion of authority."

The predominate United States' practice in terminating treaties, including those containing notice provisions, has involved mutual action by the executive and legislative branches. In most instances, the President's notice of termination has received the affirmative approval of either the Senate or the entire Congress. Although no one constitutional interpretation has been accepted, nor has a definitive procedure emerged, the weight of historical precedent clearly supports the view that some form of congressional concurrence is required. Support can be found for requiring either of two alternatives: 1) the approval of a majority of both houses of Congress, or 2) the consent of two-thirds of the Senate. The latter is of course the most analogous to the treaty-making power, while the former is based primarily on congressional authority to repeal a law of the land.

When faced with an apparent gap in the Constitutional allocation of powers, the Court must refer to the fundamental design of the entire document and determine how its purposes would be best served in the gap area. The Court believes that either of these two alternative procedures for congressional participation is a constitutionally sound means of terminating treaties. The important point is that treaty termination generally is a shared power, which cannot be exercised by the President acting alone. Neither the executive nor legislative branch has exclusive power to terminate treaties. At least under the circumstances of this case—involving a significant mutual defense treaty with a faithful ally, who has not violated the terms of the agreement, and the validity of which has not otherwise been destroyed—any decision of the United States to terminate that treaty must be made with the advice and consent of the Senate or the approval of both houses of Congress. That decision cannot be made by the President alone.

In view of the foregoing, it is the declaration of this Court that the President's notice of termination must receive the approval of two-thirds of the United States Senate or a majority of both houses of Congress for it to be effective under our Constitution to terminate the Mutual Defense Treaty of 1954. It is further ordered that the Secretary of State and his subordinate officers are hereby enjoined from taking any action to implement the President's notice of termination unless and until that notice is so approved.

GOLDWATER v. CARTER

617 F.2d 697, 699–716 (D.C. Cir. 1979) (footnotes omitted).

PER CURIAM:

The court *en banc* has before it for review the judgment of the District Court that the notice of termination given by the President pursuant to the terms of the Mutual Defense Treaty with the Republic of China is ineffective absent either (1) a manifestation of the consent of the Senate to such termination by a two-thirds vote or (2) an approving majority vote therefor by both houses of Congress. The preliminary questions we confront are, first, whether the District Court was without jurisdiction because appellees lacked standing, and, second, whether it should in any event have declined to exercise jurisdiction by reason of the political nature of the question it was called upon to decide. Since a majority of the court does not exist to dispose of the appeal on either of these bases, we reach the merits and reverse.

In doing so, however, we think it important at the outset to stress that the Treaty, as it was presented to the Senate in 1954 and consented to by it, contained an explicit provision for termination by either party on one year's notice. The Senate, in the course of giving its consent, exhibited no purpose and took no action to reserve a role for itself—by amendment, reservation, or condition—in the effectuation of this provision. Neither has the Senate, since the giving of the notice of termination, purported to take any final or decisive action with respect to it, either by way of approval or disapproval. The constitutional issue we face, therefore, is solely and simply the one of whether the President in these precise circumstances is, on behalf of the United States, empowered to terminate the Treaty in accordance with its terms. It is our view that he is, and that the limitations which the District Court purported to place on his action in this regard have no foundation in the Constitution.

. . . .

3. The constitutional institution of advice and consent of the Senate, provided two-thirds of the Senators concur, is a special and extraordinary condition of the exercise by the President of certain specified powers

under Article II. It is not lightly to be extended in instances not set forth in the Constitution. Such an extension by implication is not proper unless that implication is unmistakably clear.

The District Court's absolutist extension of this limitation to termination of treaties, irrespective of the particular circumstances involved, is not sound. The making of a treaty has the consequences of an entangling alliance for the nation. Similarly, the amending of a treaty merely continues such entangling alliances, changing only their character, and therefore also requires the advice and consent of the Senate. It does not follow, however, that a constitutional provision for a special concurrence (two-thirds of the Senators) prior to entry into an entangling alliance necessarily applies to its termination in accordance with its terms.

4. The Constitution specifically confers no power of treaty termination on either the Congress or the Executive. We note, however, that the powers conferred upon Congress in Article I of the Constitution are specific, detailed, and limited, while the powers conferred upon the President by Article II are generalized in a manner that bespeaks no such limitation upon foreign affairs powers. "Section 1. The executive Power shall be vested in a President. . . ." Although specific powers are listed in Section 2 and Section 3, these are in many instances not powers necessary to an Executive, while "The executive Power" referred to in Section 1 is nowhere defined. There is no required two-thirds vote of the Senate conditioning the exercise of any power in Section 1.

In some instances this difference is reflective of the origin of the particular power in question. In general, the powers of the federal government arise out of specific grants of authority delegated by the states—hence the enumerated powers of Congress in Article I, Section 8. The foreign affairs powers, however, proceed directly from the sovereignty of the Union. "[I]f they had never been mentioned in the Constitution, [they] would have vested in the federal government as necessary concomitants of nationality." *United States v. Curtiss–Wright Export Corp.*, 299 U.S. 304, 318 . . . (1936).

The President is the constitutional representative of the United States with respect to external affairs. It is significant that the treaty power appears in Article II of the Constitution, relating to the executive branch, and not in Article I, setting forth the powers of the legislative branch. It is the President as Chief Executive who is given the constitutional authority to enter into a treaty; and even after he has obtained the consent of the Senate it is for him to decide whether to ratify a treaty and put it into effect. Senatorial confirmation of a treaty concededly does not obligate the President to go forward with a treaty if he concludes that it is not in the public interest to do so.

Thus, in contrast to the lawmaking power, the constitutional initiative in the treaty-making field is in the President, not Congress. It would take an unprecedented feat of judicial construction to read into the Constitution an absolute condition precedent of congressional or Senate approval for termination of all treaties, similar to the specific one relating to initial approval. And it would unalterably affect the balance of power between the two Branches laid down in Articles I and II.

5. Ultimately, what must be recognized is that a treaty is *sui generis*. It is not just another law. It is an international compact, a solemn obligation of the United States and a "supreme Law" that supersedes state policies and prior federal laws. For clarity of analysis, it is thus well to distinguish between treaty-making as an international act and the consequences which flow domestically from such act. In one realm the Constitution has conferred the primary role upon the President; in the other, Congress retains its primary role as lawmaker. The fact that the Constitution, statutes, and treaties are all listed in the Supremacy Clause as being superior to any form of state law does not mean that the making and unmaking of treaties can be analogized to the making and unmaking of domestic statutes any more than it can be analogized to the making or unmaking of a constitutional amendment.

The recognized powers of Congress to implement (or fail to implement) a treaty by an appropriation or other law essential to its effectuation, or to supersede for all practical purposes the effect of a treaty on domestic law, are legislative powers, not treaty-making or treaty termination powers. The issue here, however, is not Congress' legislative powers to supersede or affect the domestic impact of a treaty; the issue is whether the Senate (or Congress) must in this case give its prior consent to discontinue a treaty which the President thinks it desirable to terminate in the national interest and pursuant to a provision in the treaty itself. The existence, in practical terms, of one power does not imply the existence, in constitutional terms, of the other.

6. If we were to hold that under the Constitution a treaty could only be terminated by exactly the same process by which it was made, we would be locking the United States into all of its international obligations, even if the President and two-thirds of the Senate minus one firmly believed that the proper course for the United States was to terminate a treaty. Many of our treaties in force, such as mutual defense treaties, carry potentially dangerous obligations. These obligations are terminable under international law upon breach by the other party or change in circumstances that frustrates the purpose of the treaty. In many of these situations the President must take immediate action. The creation of a constitutionally obligatory role in all cases for a two-thirds consent by the Senate would give to one-third plus one of the Senate the power to deny the President the authority necessary to conduct our foreign policy in a rational and effective manner.

7. Even as to the formal termination of treaties, as the District Court pointed out, "a variety of means have been used to terminate treaties." There is much debate among the historians and scholars as to whether in some instances the legislature has been involved at all; they are agreed that, when involved, that involvement with the President has

taken many different forms. It appears moreover that the Senate may wish to continue to determine the nature of its involvement on a case by case basis. 125 Cong.Rec. S16683–S16692 (daily ed. Nov. 15, 1979).

The District Court concluded that the diversity of historical precedents left an inconclusive basis on which to decide the issue of whether the President's power to terminate a treaty must always be "shared" in some way by the Senate or Congress. We agree. Yet we think it is not without significance that out of all the historical precedents brought to our attention, in no situation has a treaty been continued in force over the opposition of the President.

There is on the other hand widespread agreement that the President has the power as Chief Executive under many circumstances to exercise functions regarding treaties which have the effect of either terminating or continuing their vitality. Prominent among these is the authority of the President as Chief Executive (1) to determine whether a treaty has terminated because of a breach, *Charlton v. Kelly,* 229 U.S. 447, 473–476 . . . (1913); and (2) to determine whether a treaty is at an end due to changed circumstances.

In short, the determination of the conduct of the United States in regard to treaties is an instance of what has broadly been called the "foreign affairs power" of the President. We have no occasion to define that term, but we do take account of its vitality. The *Curtiss-Wright* opinion, written by a Justice who had served in the United States Senate, declares in oft-repeated language that the President is "the sole organ of the federal government in the field of international relations." That status is not confined to the service of the President as a channel of communication, as the District Court suggested, but embraces an active policy determination as to the conduct of the United States in regard to a treaty in response to numerous problems and circumstances as they arise.

8. How the vital functions of the President in implementing treaties and in deciding on their viability in response to changing events can or should interact with Congress' legitimate concerns and powers in relating to foreign affairs is an area into which we should not and do not prematurely intrude. History shows us that there are too many variables to lay down any hard and fast constitutional rules.

We cannot find an implied role in the Constitution for the Senate in treaty termination for some but not all treaties in terms of their relative importance. There is no judicially ascertainable and manageable method of making any distinction among treaties on the basis of their substance, the magnitude of the risk involved, the degree of controversy which their termination would engender, or by any other standards. We know of no standards to apply in making such distinctions. The facts on which such distinctions might be drawn may be difficult of ascertainment; and the resolution of such inevitable disputes between the two Branches would be an improper and unnecessary role for the courts. To decide whether there was a breach or changed circumstances, for example, would involve a court in making fundamental decisions of foreign policy and would create insuperable problems of evidentiary proof. This is beyond the acceptable judicial role. All we decide today is that two-thirds Senate consent or majority consent in both houses is not necessary to terminate this treaty in the circumstances before us now.

9. The circumstances involved in the termination of the Mutual Defense Treaty with the Republic of China include a number of material and unique elements. Prominent is assertion by the officials of both the Republic of China and the People's Republic of China that each of them is the government of China, intending the term China to comprehend both the mainland of China and the island of Taiwan. In the 1972 Shanghai Communique, the United States acknowledged that position and did not challenge it. It is in this context that the recent Joint Communique set forth as of January 1, 1979 that the United States recognizes the People's Republic of China as "the sole legal government of China." This action made reference to "the people of Taiwan," stating that the peoples of the United States and Taiwan "will maintain cultural, commercial and other unofficial relations." This formulation was confirmed by the Taiwan Relations Act.

It is undisputed that the Constitution gave the President full constitutional authority to recognize the PRC and to derecognize the ROC. What the United States has evolved for Taiwan is a novel and somewhat indefinite relationship, namely, of unofficial relations with the people of Taiwan. The subtleties involved in maintaining amorphous relationships are often the very stuff of diplomacy—a field in which the President, not Congress, has responsibility under our Constitution. The President makes a responsible claim that he has authority as Chief Executive to determine that there is no meaningful vitality to a mutual defense treaty when there is no recognized state. That is not to say that the recognition power automatically gives the President authority to take any action that is required or requested by the state being recognized. We do not need to reach this question. Nevertheless, it remains an important ingredient in the case at bar that the President has determined that circumstances have changed so as to preclude continuation of the Mutual Defense Treaty with the ROC; diplomatic recognition of the ROC came to an end on January 1, 1979, and now there exists only "cultural, commercial and other unofficial relations" with the "people on Taiwan."

10. Finally, and of central significance, the treaty here at issue contains a termination clause. The existence of Article X of the ROC treaty, permitting termination by either party on one year's notice, is an overarching factor in this case, which in effect enables all of the other considerations to be knit together.

Without derogating from the executive power of the President to decide to act contrary to the wording of a treaty—for example, because of a breach by the other party (*Charlton v. Kelly, supra*), or because of a doctrine of fundamental change of circumstances (*rebus sic stantibus*)—

the President's authority as Chief Executive is at its zenith when the Senate has consented to a treaty that expressly provides for termination on one year's notice, and the President's action is the giving of notice of termination.

As already noted, we have no occasion to decide whether this factor would be determinative in a case lacking other factors identified above, *e. g.*, under a notice of withdrawal from the NATO treaty unaccompanied by derecognition of the other signatories. No specific restriction or condition on the President's action is found within the Constitution or this treaty itself. The termination clause is without conditions and without designation as to who shall act to terminate it. No specific role is spelled out in either the Constitution or this treaty for the Senate or the Congress as a whole. That power consequently devolves upon the President, and there is no basis for a court to imply a restriction on the President's power to terminate not contained in the Constitution, in this treaty, or in any other authoritative source.

While under the termination clause of this and similar treaties the power of the President to terminate may appear theoretically absolute, to think that this is so would be to ignore all historical practices in treaty termination and past and current reciprocal relationships between the Chief Executive and Congress. The wide variety of roles played by the Executive and the Congress (or the Senate alone) in the past termination of treaties teaches us nothing conclusive as to constitutional theory, but it instructs us as to what may fairly be contemplated as to the President's future exercise of the treaty termination power. Treaty termination is a political act, but political acts are not customarily taken without political support. Even if formal advice and consent is not constitutionally required as a prerequisite to termination, it might be sought. If the Congress is completely ignored, it has its arsenal of weapons, as previous Chief Executives have on occasion been sharply reminded.

Thus, the court is not to be taken as minimizing the role of the legislature in foreign affairs. The legislature's powers, including prominently its dominant status in the provision of funds, and its authority to investigate the Executive's functioning, establish authority for appropriate legislative participation in foreign affairs. The question of whether the Senate may be able to reserve to itself in particular treaties, at the time of their original submission, a specific role in their termination is not presented by the record in this appeal and we decide nothing with respect to it. The matter before us is solely one of whether the Constitution nullifies the procedure followed by the President in this instance. We find the President did not exceed his authority when he took action to withdraw from the ROC treaty, by giving notice under Article X of the Treaty, without the consent of the Senate or other legislative concurrences.

GOLDWATER v. CARTER

444 U.S. 996, 996–1007, 100 S.Ct. 533, 62 L.Ed.2d 428 (1979) (footnotes omitted).

Certiorari granted, judgment vacated, and case remanded with directions to dismiss the complaint. MR. JUSTICE MARSHALL concurs in the result. MR. JUSTICE POWELL concurs in the judgment and filed a statement. MR. JUSTICE REHNQUIST concurs in the judgment and filed a statement in which THE CHIEF JUSTICE, MR. JUSTICE STEWART, and MR. JUSTICE STEVENS join. MR. JUSTICE WHITE and MR. JUSTICE BLACKMUN join in the grant of the petition for a writ of certiorari but would set the case for argument and give it plenary consideration. MR. JUSTICE BLACKMUN filed a statement in which MR. JUSTICE WHITE joins. MR. JUSTICE BRENNAN would grant the petition for writ of certiorari and affirm the judgment of the Court of Appeals and filed a statement. . . .

MR. JUSTICE POWELL, concurring in the judgment.

Although I agree with the result reached by the Court, I would dismiss the complaint as not ripe for judicial review.

I

This Court has recognized that an issue should not be decided if it is not ripe for judicial review. *Buckley v. Valeo,* 424 U.S. 1, 113–114 (*per curiam*). Prudential considerations persuade me that a dispute between Congress and the President is not ready for judicial review unless and until each branch has taken action asserting its constitutional authority. Differences between the President and the Congress are commonplace under our system. The differences should, and almost invariably do, turn on political rather than legal considerations. The Judicial Branch should not decide issues affecting the allocation of power between the President and Congress until the political branches reach a constitutional impasse. Otherwise, we would encourage small groups or even individual Members of Congress to seek judicial resolution of issues before the normal political process has the opportunity to resolve the conflict.

In this case, a few Members of Congress claim that the President's action in terminating the treaty with Taiwan has deprived them of their constitutional role with respect to a change in the supreme law of the land. Congress has taken no official action. In the present posture of this case, we do not know whether there ever will be an actual confrontation between the Legislative and Executive Branches. Although the Senate has considered a resolution declaring that Senate approval is necessary for the termination of any mutual defense treaty, *see* 125 Cong. Rec. 13672, 13695–13697 (1979), no final vote has been taken on the resolution. *See id.*, at 32522–32531. Moreover, it is unclear whether the resolution would have retroactive effect. *See id.*, at 13711–13721; *id.*, at 15210. It cannot be said that either the Senate or the House has rejected the President's claim. If the Congress chooses not to confront the President, it is not our task to do so. I therefore concur in the dismissal of this case.

II

MR. JUSTICE REHNQUIST suggests, however, that the issue presented by this case is a nonjusticiable political question which can never be considered by this Court. I cannot agree. In my view, reliance upon the political-question doctrine is inconsistent with our precedents. As set forth in the seminal case of *Baker v. Carr,* 369 U.S. 186, 217 (1962), the doctrine incorporates three inquiries: (i) Does the issue involve resolution of questions committed by the text of the Constitution to a coordinate branch of Government? (ii) Would resolution of the question demand that a court move beyond areas of judicial expertise? (iii) Do prudential considerations counsel against judicial intervention? In my opinion the answer to each of these inquiries would require us to decide this case if it were ready for review.

First, the existence of "a textually demonstrable constitutional commitment of the issue to a coordinate political department," *ibid.,* turns on an examination of the constitutional provisions governing the exercise of the power in question. *Powell v. McCormack,* 395 U.S. 486, 519 (1969). No constitutional provision explicitly confers upon the President the power to terminate treaties. Further, Art. II, § 2, of the Constitution authorizes the President to make treaties with the advice and consent of the Senate. Article VI provides that treaties shall be a part of the supreme law of the land. These provisions add support to the view that the text of the Constitution does not unquestionably commit the power to terminate treaties to the President alone. *Cf. Gilligan v. Morgan,* 413 U.S. 1, 6 (1973); *Luther v. Borden,* 7 How. 1, 42 (1849).

Second, there is no "lack of judicially discoverable and manageable standards for resolving" this case; nor is a decision impossible "without an initial policy determination of a kind clearly for nonjudicial discretion." *Baker v. Carr, supra,* at 217. We are asked to decide whether the President may terminate a treaty under the Constitution without congressional approval. Resolution of the question may not be easy, but it only requires us to apply normal principles of interpretation to the constitutional provisions at issue. *See Powell v. McCormack, supra,* at 548–549. The present case involves neither review of the President's activities as Commander in Chief nor impermissible interference in the field of foreign affairs. Such a case would arise if we were asked to decide, for example, whether a treaty required the President to order troops into a foreign country. But "it is error to suppose that every case or controversy which touches foreign relations lies beyond judicial cognizance." *Baker v. Carr, supra,* at 211. This case "touches" foreign relations, but the question presented to us concerns only the constitutional division of power between Congress and the President.

A simple hypothetical demonstrates the confusion that I find inherent in MR. JUSTICE REHNQUIST'S opinion concurring in the judgment. Assume that the President signed a mutual defense treaty with a foreign country and announced that it would go into effect despite its rejection by the

Senate. Under MR. JUSTICE REHNQUIST'S analysis that situation would present a political question even though Art. II, § 2, clearly would resolve the dispute. Although the answer to the hypothetical case seems self-evident because it demands textual rather than interstitial analysis, the nature of the legal issue presented is no different from the issue presented in the case before us. In both cases, the Court would interpret the Constitution to decide whether congressional approval is necessary to give a Presidential decision on the validity of a treaty the force of law. Such an inquiry demands no special competence or information beyond the reach of the Judiciary. *Cf. Chicago & Southern Air Lines v. Waterman S.S. Corp.,* 333 U.S. 103, 111 (1948).

Finally, the political-question doctrine rests in part on prudential concerns calling for mutual respect among the three branches of Government. Thus, the Judicial Branch should avoid "the potentiality of embarrassment [that would result] from multifarious pronouncements by various departments on one question." Similarly, the doctrine restrains judicial action where there is an "unusual need for unquestioning adherence to a political decision already made." *Baker v. Carr, supra,* at 217.

If this case were ripe for judicial review, *see* Part I *supra,* none of these prudential considerations would be present. Interpretation of the Constitution does not imply lack of respect for a coordinate branch. *Powell v. McCormack, supra,* at 548. If the President and the Congress had reached irreconcilable positions, final disposition of the question presented by this case would eliminate, rather than create, multiple constitutional interpretations. The specter of the Federal Government brought to a halt because of the mutual intransigence of the President and the Congress would require this Court to provide a resolution pursuant to our duty " 'to say what the law is.' " *United States v. Nixon,* 418 U.S. 683, 703 (1974), quoting *Marbury v. Madison,* 1 Cranch 137, 177 (1803).

III

In my view, the suggestion that this case presents a political question is incompatible with this Court's willingness on previous occasions to decide whether one branch of our Government has impinged upon the power of another. *See Buckley v. Valeo,* 424 U.S., at 138; *United States v. Nixon, supra,* at 707; *The Pocket Veto Case,* 279 U.S. 655, 676–678 (1929); *Myers v. United States,* 272 U.S. 52 (1926). Under the criteria enunciated in *Baker v. Carr,* we have the responsibility to decide whether both the Executive and Legislative Branches have constitutional roles to play in termination of a treaty. If the Congress, by appropriate formal action, had challenged the President's authority to terminate the treaty with Taiwan, the resulting uncertainty could have serious consequences for our country. In that situation, it would be the duty of this Court to resolve the issue.

MR. JUSTICE REHNQUIST, with whom THE CHIEF JUSTICE, MR. JUSTICE STEWART, and MR. JUSTICE STEVENS join, concurring in the judgment.

I am of the view that the basic question presented by the petitioners in this case is "political" and therefore nonjusticiable because it involves the authority of the President in the conduct of our country's foreign relations and the extent to which the Senate or the Congress is authorized to negate the action of the President. In *Coleman v. Miller,* 307 U.S. 433 (1939), a case in which members of the Kansas Legislature brought an action attacking a vote of the State Senate in favor of the ratification of the Child Labor Amendment, Mr. Chief Justice Hughes wrote in what is referred to as the "Opinion of the Court":

> "We think that ... the question of the efficacy of ratifications by state legislatures, in the light of previous rejection or attempted withdrawal, should be regarded as a political question pertaining to the political departments, with the ultimate authority in the Congress in the exercise of its control over the promulgation of the adoption of the Amendment.
>
> "The precise question as now raised is whether, when the legislature of the State, as we have found, has actually ratified the proposed amendment, the Court should restrain the state officers from certifying the ratification to the Secretary of State, because of an earlier rejection, and thus prevent the question from coming before the political departments. We find no basis in either Constitution or statute for such judicial action. Article V, speaking solely of ratification, contains no provision as to rejection. ..." *Id.,* at 450.

Thus, Mr. Chief Justice Hughes' opinion concluded that "Congress in controlling the promulgation of the adoption of a constitutional amendment has the final determination of the question whether by lapse of time its proposal of the amendment had lost its vitality prior to the required ratifications." *Id.,* at 456.

I believe it follows *a fortiori* from *Coleman* that the controversy in the instant case is a nonjusticiable political dispute that should be left for resolution by the Executive and Legislative Branches of the Government. Here, while the Constitution is express as to the manner in which the Senate shall participate in the ratification of a treaty, it is silent as to that body's participation in the abrogation of a treaty. In this respect the case is directly analogous to *Coleman, supra.* As stated in *Dyer v. Blair,* 390 F. Supp. 1291, 1302 (ND Ill. 1975) (three-judge court):

> "A question that might be answered in different ways for different amendments must surely be controlled by political standards rather than standards easily characterized as judicially manageable."

In light of the absence of any constitutional provision governing the termination of a treaty, and the fact that different termination procedures may be appropriate for different treaties (*see, e. g.,* n. 1, *infra*), the instant case in my view also "must surely be controlled by political standards."

I think that the justifications for concluding that the question here is political in nature are even more compelling than in *Coleman* because it involves foreign relations—specifically a treaty commitment to use military force in the defense of a foreign government if attacked. In *United States v. Curtiss-Wright Corp.,* 299 U.S. 304 (1936), this Court said:

> "Whether, if the Joint Resolution had related solely to internal affairs it would be open to the challenge that it constituted an unlawful delegation of legislative power to the Executive, we find it unnecessary to determine. The whole aim of the resolution is to affect a situation entirely external to the United States, and falling within the category of foreign affairs. . . ." *Id.,* at 315.

The present case differs in several important respects from *Youngstown Sheet & Tube Co. v. Sawyer,* 343 U.S. 579 (1952), cited by petitioners as authority both for reaching the merits of this dispute and for reversing the Court of Appeals. In *Youngstown,* private litigants brought a suit contesting the President's authority under his war powers to seize the Nation's steel industry, an action of profound and demonstrable domestic impact. Here, by contrast, we are asked to settle a dispute between coequal branches of our Government, each of which has resources available to protect and assert its interests, resources not available to private litigants outside the judicial forum. Moreover, as in *Curtiss-Wright,* the effect of this action, as far as we can tell, is "entirely external to the United States, and [falls] within the category of foreign affairs." Finally, as already noted, the situation presented here is closely akin to that presented in *Coleman,* where the Constitution spoke only to the procedure for ratification of an amendment, not to its rejection.

Having decided that the question presented in this action is nonjusticiable, I believe that the appropriate disposition is for this Court to vacate the decision of the Court of Appeals and remand with instructions for the District Court to dismiss the complaint. This procedure derives support from our practice in disposing of moot actions in federal courts. For more than 30 years, we have instructed lower courts to vacate any decision on the merits of an action that has become moot prior to a resolution of the case in this Court. *United States v. Munsingwear, Inc.,* 340 U.S. 36 (1950). The Court has required such decisions to be vacated in order to "prevent a judgment, unreviewable because of mootness, from spawning any legal consequences." *Id.,* at 41. It is even more imperative that this Court invoke this procedure to ensure that resolution of a "political question," which should not have been decided by a lower court, does not "spawn any legal consequences." An Art. III court's resolution of a question that is "political" in character can create far more disruption among the three coequal branches of Government than the resolution of a question presented in a moot controversy. Since the political nature of the questions presented should have precluded the lower courts from considering or deciding the merits of the controversy, the prior proceedings in the federal courts must be vacated, and the complaint dismissed.

MR. JUSTICE BLACKMUN, with whom MR. JUSTICE WHITE joins, dissenting in part.

In my view, the time factor and its importance are illusory; if the President does not have the power to terminate the treaty (a substantial issue that we should address only after briefing and oral argument), the notice of intention to terminate surely has no legal effect. It is also indefensible, without further study, to pass on the issue of justiciability or on the issues of standing or ripeness. While I therefore join in the grant of the petition for certiorari, I would set the case for oral argument and give it the plenary consideration it so obviously deserves.

MR. JUSTICE BRENNAN, dissenting.

I respectfully dissent from the order directing the District Court to dismiss this case, and would affirm the judgment of the Court of Appeals insofar as it rests upon the President's well-established authority to recognize, and withdraw recognition from, foreign governments. App. to Pet. for Cert. 27A–29A.

In stating that this case presents a nonjusticiable "political question," MR. JUSTICE REHNQUIST, in my view, profoundly misapprehends the political-question principle as it applies to matters of foreign relations. Properly understood, the political-question doctrine restrains courts from reviewing an exercise of foreign policy judgment by the coordinate political branch to which authority to make that judgment has been "constitutional[ly] commit[ted]." *Baker v. Carr,* 369 U.S. 186, 211–213, 217 (1962). But the doctrine does not pertain when a court is faced with the *antecedent* question whether a particular branch has been constitutionally designated as the repository of political decisionmaking power. *Cf. Powell v. McCormack,* 395 U.S. 486, 519–521 (1969). The issue of decisionmaking authority must be resolved as a matter of constitutional law, not political discretion; accordingly, it falls within the competence of the courts.

The constitutional question raised here is prudently answered in narrow terms. Abrogation of the defense treaty with Taiwan was a necessary incident to Executive recognition of the Peking Government, because the defense treaty was predicated upon the now-abandoned view that the Taiwan Government was the only legitimate political authority in China. Our cases firmly establish that the Constitution commits to the President alone the power to recognize, and withdraw recognition from, foreign regimes. *See Banco Nacional de Cuba v. Sabbatino,* 376 U.S. 398, 410 (1964); *Baker v. Carr, supra,* at 212; *United States v. Pink,* 315 U.S. 203, 228–230 (1942). That mandate being clear, our judicial inquiry into the treaty rupture can go no further. *See Baker v. Carr, supra,* at 212; *United States v. Pink, supra,* at 229.

CONCLUDING NOTES

1. Goldwater's *Legacy*. In the case of *Kucinich v. Bush*, 236 F. Supp. 2d 1 (D.D.C. 2002), District Court Judge John Bates assessed the Supreme Court's decision in *Goldwater* as follows:

> The Court's ruling resulted in four opinions, two concurring in the judgment and two dissenting. Four Justices in the majority—Justices

Rehnquist, Stevens and Stewart, and Chief Justice Burger—concluded that the case should be dismissed because the issue presented a nonjusticiable political question that was inappropriate for resolution by the courts. Justice Powell concurred, finding that the issue was "not ripe for judicial review" because neither Congress nor the President had asserted their constitutional authority to the point of political impasse. Justice Marshall simply concurred in the result.

Three Justices dissented from the Court's order to remand for dismissal. Without reaching the merits, Justices Blackmun and White stated only that the case should be set for oral argument and considered fully. Justice Brennan disagreed that the issue was nonjusticiable and concluded that the President had a constitutional right to withdraw from the treaty, without congressional consent, given "the President's well-established authority to recognize, and withdraw recognition from, foreign governments." ...

None of the opinions in *Goldwater* obtained a majority of votes, and hence no single rationale controls. To be sure, six Justices voted for dismissal on jurisdictional grounds, but only four expressly agreed that the issue was a nonjusticiable political question. As a result, there is no obviously binding holding in *Goldwater.*

Does Judge Bates's analysis in *Kucinich v. Bush* help explain what the Supreme Court "decided" in the *Goldwater v. Carter* case? Does it suggest that, at present, we do not have firm guidance from the Supreme Court on this issue? Are there circumstances under which you think it might well be possible for the Supreme Court to reach the merits of this issue, and even possible for the Court to find against the President? For example, recall that the circuit court in *Goldwater* said that it was not deciding "whether the Senate may be able to reserve to itself in particular treaties, at the time of their original submission, a specific role in their termination. ..."

The *Goldwater* case spawned a cottage industry of commentary. *See, e.g.*, Louis Henkin, *Litigating the President's Power to Terminate Treaties,* 73 AM. J. INT'L L. 647 (1979); David J. Scheffer, Comment, *The Law of Treaty Termination as Applied to the United States De-Recognition of the Republic of China,* 19 HARV. INT'L L.J. 931 (1978); Jonathan Y. Thomas, *The Abuse of History: A Refutation of the State Department Analysis of Alleged Instances of Independent Presidential Treaty Termination,* 6 YALE STUDIES IN WORLD PUB. ORDER 27 (1979); Michael J. Glennon, *Treaty Process Reform: Saving Constitutionalism Without Destroying Diplomacy,* 52 CINN. L. REV. 84 (1983). For early historical practice, see Samuel B. Crandall, *Treaties, Their Making and Enforcement* 423 (2d ed. 1916).

2. *Restatement (Third).* The *Restatement (Third) of the Foreign Relations Law of the United States* § 339 (1987) states that the President has the power to:

(a) to suspend or terminate an agreement in accordance with its terms;

(b) to make the determination that would justify the United States in terminating or suspending an agreement because of its violation by another party or because of supervening events, and to proceed to terminate or suspend the agreement on behalf of the United States; or

(c) to elect in a particular case not to suspend or terminate an agreement.

3. *Termination of Treaties Since* Goldwater. From 1980 to 2002, the President terminated about thirty bilateral and multilateral treaties without the Senate's consent. *See* U.S. Department of State, *Digest of United States Practice in International Law 2002* (Sally J. Cummins & David P. Stewart eds., 2003). As noted in *Kucinich*, a high-profile bilateral treaty that was terminated was the Treaty of Friendship, Commerce, and Navigation, U.S.-Nicar., Jan. 21, 1956, 9 U.S.T. 449, T.I.A.S. No. 4024. On May 1, 1985, the Department of State gave one year's notice to Nicaragua that the United States would be terminating the treaty as of May 1, 1986. *See* Beacon Prods Corp. v. Reagan, 633 F.Supp. 1191, 1199 (D.Mass. 1986), *aff'd,* 814 F.2d 1 (1st Cir. 1987) (dismissing challenge to administration's unilateral termination of treaty with Nicaragua).

Some terminations of multilateral treaties took the form of withdrawal from the constituent instruments of international organizations. In 1983, the United States withdrew from U.S. membership in the U.N. Educational, Scientific and Cultural Organization (UNESCO). *See* Letter from Secretary of State George P. Shultz to Director–General of UNESCO Amadou Mahtar M'Bow (Dec. 28, 1983), 23 I.L.M. 220 (1984). In 2003, however, the United States resumed its membership. In December 1996, the United States withdrew from both the Statute of the World Tourism Organization, Sept. 27, 1970, 27 U.S.T. 2211, and the Constitution of the U.N. Industrial Development Organization, Apr. 8, 1979, S. TREATY DOC. NO. 97–19 (1981). In none of these instances did the Senate provide its consent.

The United States has also withdrawn its acceptance of the jurisdiction of the International Court of Justice over certain types of cases. In one instance, such withdrawal entailed terminating a treaty protocol to which the U.S. Senate had consented. On March 7, 2005, the U.S. Government informed the U.N. Secretary–General that it had terminated its adherence to the Optional Protocol Concerning Compulsory Settlement of Disputes to the Vienna Convention on Consular Relations, Apr. 24, 1963, 21 U.S.T. 325, 596 U.N.T.S. 487. *See* Journal of the United Nations: Programme of Meetings and Agenda, No. 2005/48, at 13 (Mar. 12, 2005) (reporting receipt of the withdrawal on Mar. 7); *see* Charles Lane, *U.S. Quits Pact Used in Capital Cases*, WASH. POST, Mar. 10, 2005, at A1. In another instance, the U.S. withdrawal entailed first a notice of modification and then of termination of a U.S. declaration accepting the Court's compulsory jurisdiction, which had been consented to by the U.S. Senate in 1946. *See* Letter from Secretary of State George P. Shultz to Secretary–General of the United Nations Javier Perez de Cuellar (Apr. 6, 1984), 23 I.L.M. 670 (1984) (modifying the 1946 U.S. declaration accepting the Court's compulsory jurisdiction); Letter from Secretary of State George P. Shultz to Secretary–General of the United Nations Javier Perez de Cuellar (Oct. 7, 1985), 24 I.L.M. 1742 (1985) (terminating the declaration). Should the Senate have been involved in such decisions?

4. *Terminating a Treaty Outside Its Terms.* Does the *Restatement* and subsequent Executive Branch practice suggest that *Goldwater v. Carter* stands for the proposition that the President has the power to terminate (or modify) treaties regardless of whether the treaty permits such action? The 1954 mutual defense treaty with nationalist China was terminated by President Carter in 1979 by giving one year's notice *as required by the termination clause of the treaty*. (This created an anomalous situation because the United States was obliged to defend Taiwan for twelve months after recognition had been withdrawn from the nationalist regime and switched to the regime in Beijing.) The decision to proceed by notice, rather than by immediate termination, was obviously taken deliberately. Why might this have been the preferred method of termination? Would the outcome of the *Goldwater v. Carter* litigation have been any different had the President decided to terminate the treaty instantly, in violation of its notice requirement? In short, may the President, on his own authority, terminate a treaty in violation of it?

Consider the following positions. The U.S. Department of Justice Office of Legal Counsel (OLC) issued opinions in 2001 and 2002 addressing whether the President could decide, on his own, that the 1949 Geneva Conventions were suspended with respect to the armed conflict in Afghanistan, especially as they might relate to the detention and trial of members of Al Qaeda and the Taliban militia. OLC asserted that the President, under U.S. law, has unconstrained discretion to suspend U.S. treaty obligations at any time and for any reason as an aspect of the "executive Power" vested in him by the Constitution. *See* Memorandum for John B. Bellinger III, Legal Adviser to the National Security Council, from John C. Yoo, Deputy Assistant Attorney General, and Robert J. Delahunty, Special Counsel, Office of Legal Counsel, *Re: Authority of the President to Suspend Certain Provisions of the ABM Treaty* at 12,13 (Nov. 15, 2001) ("11/15/01 ABM Suspension Opinion") ("The President's power to suspend treaties is wholly discretionary, and may be exercised whenever he determines that it is in the national interest to do so. While the President will ordinarily take international law into account when deciding whether to suspend a treaty in whole or in part, his constitutional authority to suspend a treaty provision does not hinge on whether such suspension is or is not consistent with international law."); Memorandum for Alberto R. Gonzales, Counsel to the President, and William J. Haynes II, General Counsel, Department of Defense, from Jay S. Bybee, Assistant Attorney General, Office of Legal Counsel, *Re: Application of Treaties and Laws to al Qaeda and Taliban Detainees* at 11–13 (Jan. 22, 2002) ("1/22/02 Treaties Opinion") (reasoning that the President has "unrestricted discretion, as a matter of domestic law, in suspending treaties").

Reacting to such opinions, Professor Michael Ramsey argued that they:

> fail to make a key distinction. Many treaties contain express provisions allowing them to be terminated or suspended in certain circumstances, such as by giving advance notice, or upon the occurrence of certain events. Moreover, the international law of treaties allows signatories to suspend or withdraw from treaties under certain circumstances, and that background rule is presumably an implied term in every treaty, unless stated otherwise. As a result, it is quite possible, and indeed routine, for a nation to suspend or terminate a treaty *in accordance with* the express or

implied terms of the treaty. On the other hand, it is obviously possible that a withdrawal or suspension might occur *in violation of* the treaty's express or implied terms.

Yoo and Delahunty plainly mean to claim both powers for the President, and do not distinguish between them in any meaningful way.

Michael D. Ramsey, *Torturing Executive Power*, 93 GEO. L.J. 1213, 1229–1232 (2005) (footnotes omitted).

In 2009, after the assumption of office by President Barack Obama, OLC issued a new memorandum, indicating that

> Presidents have traditionally suspended treaties where authorized by Congress or where suspension was authorized by the terms of the treaty or under recognized principles of international law, such as where another party has materially breached the treaty or where there has been a fundamental change in circumstances. . . . [The relevant portions of the 2001 and 2002 OLC opinions] do not reflect the current views of this Office and should not be treated as authoritative, and . . . appropriate caution should be exercised before relying upon these opinions in other respects.

Memorandum from Steven G. Bradbury, Principal Deputy Assistant Attorney General, *Re: Status of Certain OLC Opinions Issued in the Aftermath of the Terrorist Attacks of September 11, 2001* at 8–9 (Jan. 15, 2009).

Do you think that the President can either suspend or terminate a treaty without the consent of the Senate, even if it is done outside the terms of the treaty and for a reason not sanctioned by international treaty law?

CHAPTER 4

THE WAR POWER

■ ■ ■

SECTION 1. CONSTITUTIONAL ORIGINS

INTRODUCTORY NOTE

Though it is not the most commonly invoked power in the field of foreign relations law (thankfully), the war power is of extraordinary importance. With the strongest military in the world, the United States is capable of unleashing tremendous firepower by land, sea, and air across the globe in a matter of minutes. That power may be used to protect the American homeland, to assist an endangered ally, or to help quell civil unrest in troubled lands. Exercise of the war power often raises the most turbulent of policy debates. What American values and interests merit endangering American soldiers? When have diplomatic efforts proven ineffective? To what extent should allies be enlisted in the recourse to force? To what extent should the support of the United Nations or regional organizations be secured before acting? Rarely does use of the war power find unanimous support from the American polity; usually there are strong views on both sides.

In tandem with disagreements over policy, there is also often disagreement over the constitutional allocation of the war power. What exactly is Congress's role in "declaring war" or in "supporting" the army and "providing" the navy? What exactly is the President's role as "Commander in Chief"? Did the founding fathers seek to mimic the royal prerogatives of the King in this area or did they choose a different path? Regardless of what path they chose in the Constitution, in what direction has the course of American history taken the war power? Is it a course well-chosen or is there something amiss that should be corrected? If the latter, how should any change be accomplished?

The Constitution addresses the war power in two sets of provisions. The first (under Article I) relates to congressional power; the second (under Article II) relates to executive power. Based on the text of the Constitution, which war powers appear to be plenary? Where do Congress and the President seem to share concurrent war powers? What were the views of the founders regarding these powers? What were they trying to accomplish?

LOUIS FISHER, PRESIDENTIAL WAR POWER

4–5 (2d ed. rev. 2004) (footnotes omitted).*

On numerous occasions the delegates to the constitutional convention emphasized that the power of peace and war associated with monarchy would not be given to the President. On June 1, 1787, Charles Pinckney said he was for "a vigorous Executive but was afraid the Executive powers of <the existing> Congress might extend to peace & war & c which would render the Executive a Monarchy, of the worst kind, towit an elective one." John Rutledge wanted the executive power placed in a single person, "tho' he was not for giving him the power of war and peace." Roger Sherman considered "the Executive magistracy as nothing more than an institution for carrying the will of the Legislature into effect." James Wilson also preferred a single executive but "did not consider the Prerogatives of the British Monarch as a proper guide in defining the Executive powers. Some of these prerogatives were of a Legislative nature. Among others that of war & peace & c."

Edmund Randolph worried about executive power, calling it "the foetus of monarchy." The delegates to the Philadelphia convention, he said, had "no motive to be governed by the British Governmt. as our prototype." If the United States had no other choice he might adopt the British model, but "the fixt genius of the people of America required a different form of Government." Wilson agreed that the British model "was inapplicable to the situation of this Country; the extent of which was so great, and the manners so republican, that nothing but a great confederated Republic would do for it."

In a lengthy speech on June 18, Alexander Hamilton set forth his principles of government. Although later associated with vigorous and independent presidential power, he too jettisoned the British model of executive prerogatives in foreign affairs and the war power. Explaining that in his "private opinion he had no scruple in declaring ... that the British Govt. was the best in the world," he nonetheless discarded the Blackstonian and Lockean models. He proposed that the President would have "with the advice and approbation of the Senate" the power of making treaties, the Senate would have the "sole power of declaring war," and the President would be authorized to have "the direction of war when authorized or begun."

THE CONSTITUTION OF THE UNITED STATES

ARTICLE I

. . . .

Section 8. [1] The Congress shall have Power to lay and collect Taxes, Duties, Imposts and Excises, to pay the Debts and provide for the Common Defence and general Welfare of the United States; but all Duties, Imposts and Excises shall be uniform throughout the United States;

. . . .

[10] To define and punish Piracies and Felonies committed on the High Seas, and Offenses against the Law of Nations;

[11] To declare War, grant Letters of Marque and Reprisal, and make Rules concerning Captures on Land and Water;

[12] To raise and support Armies, but no Appropriation of Money to that Use shall be for a longer Term than two Years;

[13] To provide and maintain a Navy;

[14] To make Rules for the Government and Regulation of the land and naval Forces;

[15] To provide for calling forth the Militia to execute the Laws of the Union, suppress Insurrections and repel Invasions;

[16] To provide for organizing, arming, and disciplining, the Militia, and for governing such Part of them as may be employed in the Service of the United States, reserving to the States respectively, the Appointment of the Officers, and the Authority of training the Militia according to the discipline prescribed by Congress; [and]

. . . .

[18] To make all Laws which shall be necessary and proper for carrying into Execution the foregoing Powers, and all other Powers vested by this Constitution in the Government of the United States, or in any Department or Officer thereof.

. . . .

ARTICLE II

Section 1. [1] The executive Power shall be vested in a President of the United States of America. . . .

. . . .

[7] Before he enter on the Execution of his Office, he shall take the following Oath or Affirmation: "I do solemnly swear (or affirm) that I will faithfully execute the Office of President of the United States, and will to the best of my Ability, preserve, protect and defend the Constitution of the United States."

Section 2. [1] The President shall be Commander in Chief of the Army and Navy of the United States, and of the Militia of the several States, when called into the actual Service of the United States; he may require the Opinion, in writing, of the principal Officer in each of the executive Departments, upon any Subject relating to the Duties of their respective Offices, and he shall have Power to grant Reprieves and Pardons for Offenses against the United States, except in Cases of Impeachment.

THE FEDERALIST PAPERS NO. 69 (HAMILTON)

(Clinton Rossiter ed., 1961).

The President is to be the "commander-in-chief of the army and navy of the United States, and of the militia of the several States, when called into the actual service of the United States...." In most of these particulars, the power of the President will resemble equally that of the king of Great Britain and of the governor of New York. The most material points of difference are these:—*First*. The President will have only the occasional command of such part of the militia of the nation as by legislative provision may be called into the actual service of the Union. The king of Great Britain and the governor of New York have at all times the entire command of all the militia within their several jurisdictions. In this article, therefore, the power of the President would be inferior to that of either the monarch or the governor. *Second*. The President is to be commander-in-chief of the army and navy of the United States. In this respect his authority would be nominally the same with that of the king of Great Britain, but in substance much inferior to it. It would amount to nothing more than the supreme command and direction of the military and naval forces, as first general and admiral of the Confederacy; while that of the British king extends to the *declaring* of war and to the *raising* and *regulating* of fleets and armies—all which, by the Constitution under consideration, would appertain to the legislature. The governor of New York, on the other hand, is by the constitution of the State vested only with the command of its militia and navy. But the constitutions of several of the States expressly declare their governors to be commanders-in-chief, as well of the army as navy; and it may well be a question whether those of New Hampshire and Massachusetts, in particular, do not, in this instance, confer larger powers upon their respective governors than could be claimed by a President of the United States....

SECTION 2. EARLY CASE LAW

INTRODUCTORY NOTE TO BAS V. TINGY

The undeclared naval war fought with France in 1798–1800 raised for the first time the question whether Congress could authorize hostilities falling short of all-out war. International law had long drawn a distinction between "perfect" and "imperfect" war; did the domestic separation-of-powers reflect this distinction? By granting Congress the power to "declare" perfect war, did the Constitution implicitly leave to the President the power to use military force in "imperfect" wars, when war was not formally declared? Can Congress authorize the use of force without formally declaring war? If Congress authorizes limited, "imperfect" war, is the President bound by those limits?

BAS v. TINGY

4 U.S. (4 Dall.) 37, 1 L.Ed. 731 (1800).

In error from the Circuit Court for the district of *Pennsylvania.* On the return of the record it appeared, by a case stated, that the defendant, in error, had filed a libel in the District Court, as commander of the public armed ship the *Ganges,* for himself and others against the ship *Eliza, John Bas, master,* her cargo, & c. in which he set forth that the said ship and cargo belonged to citizens of the *United States*; that they were taken on the high seas by a *French* privateer, on the 31st of *March,* 1799; and that they were re-taken by the libellant, on the 21st of *April* following, after having been above ninety-six hours in possession of the captors. The libel prayed for salvage conformably to the acts of congress; and the facts being admitted by the answer of the respondents, the District Court decreed to the libellants one half of the whole value of ship and cargo. This decree was affirmed in the Circuit Court without argument, and by consent of the parties, in order to expedite a final decision on the present writ of error.

The controversy involved a consideration of the following sections in two acts of congress: By an act of the 28th of *June* 1798, (4 *vol. p.* 154, *s.* 2.) it is declared, "That whenever any vessel the property of, or employed by, any citizen of the *United States,* or person resident therein, or any goods or effects belonging to any such citizen, or resident, shall be re-captured by any public armed vessel of the *United States,* the same shall be restored to the former owner, or owners, upon due proof, he or they paying and allowing, as and for salvage to the re-captors, one-eighth part of the value of such vessel, goods and effects, free from all deduction and expenses."

By an act of the 2d of *March,* 1799 (4 *vol. p.* 472) it is declared, "That for the ships or goods belonging to the citizens of the *United States,* or to the citizens, or subjects, of any nation in amity with the *United States,* if re-taken from *the enemy* within twenty-four hours, the owners are to allow one-eighth part of the whole value for salvage, & c. and if above ninety-six hours one-half, all of which is to be paid without any deduction whatsoever, & c." And, by the 9th section of the same act it is declared, "That all the money accruing, *or which has already accrued from the sale of prizes,* shall be and remain forever a fund for the payment of the half-pay to the officers and seamen, who may be entitled to receive the same."

The case was argued by *Lewis,* and *E. Tilghman,* for the plaintiff in error, and by *Rawle,* and *W. Tilghman,* for the defendant; and the argument turned, principally, upon two inquiries: 1st. Whether the act of *March* 1799, applied only to the event of a future general war? 2d. Whether France was *an enemy* of the *United States,* within the meaning of the law?

. . . .

The JUDGES delivered their opinions *seriatim* in the following manner:

. . . .

WASHINGTON, *Justice*. It is admitted, on all hands, that the defendant in error is entitled to some compensation; but the plaintiff in error contends, that the compensation should be regulated by the act of the 28th *June* 1798, (4 *vol. p.* 154, *s.* 2.) which allows only one-eighth for salvage; while the defendant in error refers his claim to the act of the 2d *March,* (*ibid.* 456. *s.* 7.) which makes an allowance of one-half, upon a re-capture from *the enemy,* after an adverse possession of ninety-six hours.

If the defendant's claim is well founded, it follows, that the latter law must virtually have worked a repeal of the former; but this has been denied, for a variety of reasons:

1st. Because the former law relates to re-captures from *the French,* and the latter law relates to re-captures from *the enemy*; and, it is said, that "*the enemy*" is not descriptive of *France,* or of her armed vessels, according to the correct and technical understanding of the word.

The decision of this question must depend upon another; which is, whether, at the time of passing the act of congress of the 2d of *March* 1799, there subsisted a state of war between the two nations? It may, I believe, be safely laid down, that every contention by force between two nations, in external matters, under the authority of their respective governments, is not only war, but public war. If it be declared in form, it is called *solemn,* and is of the perfect kind; because one whole nation is at war with another whole nation; and *all* the members of the nation declaring war, are authorised to commit hostilities against all the members of the other, in every place, and under every circumstance. In such a war all the members act under a general authority, and all the rights and consequences of war attach to their condition.

But hostilities may subsist between two nations more confined in its nature and extent; being limited as to places, persons, and things; and this is more properly termed *imperfect war*; because not solemn, and because those who are authorised to commit hostilities, act under special authority, and can go no farther than to the extent of their commission. Still, however, it is *public war,* because it is an external contention by force, between some of the members of the two nations, authorised by the legitimate powers. It is a war between the two nations, though all the members are not authorised to commit hostilities such as in a solemn war, where the government restrain the general power.

Now, if this be the true definition of war, let us see what was the situation of the *United States* in relation to *France.* In *March* 1799, congress had raised an army; stopped all intercourse with *France*; dissolved our treaty; built and equipt ships of war; and commissioned private armed ships; enjoining the former, and authorising the latter, to defend themselves against the armed ships of *France,* to attack them on the high seas, to subdue and take them as prize, and to re-capture armed vessels found in their possession. Here, then, let me ask, what were the technical characters of an *American* and *French* armed vessel, combating on the high seas, with a view the one to subdue the other, and to make prize of his property? They certainly were not friends, because there was a contention by force; nor were they private enemies, because the contention was external, and authorised by the legitimate authority of the two governments. If they were not our enemies, I know not what constitutes an enemy.

2d. But, secondly, it is said, that a war of the imperfect kind, is more properly called acts of hostility, or reprizal, and that congress did not mean to consider the hostility subsisting between *France* and the *United States,* as constituting a state of war.

In support of this position, it has been observed, that in no law prior to *March* 1799, is *France* styled our enemy, nor are we said to be at war. This is true; but neither of these things were necessary to be done: because as to *France,* she was sufficiently described by the title of the *French* republic; and as to *America,* the degree of hostility meant to be carried on, was sufficiently described without declaring war, or declaring that we were at war. Such a declaration by congress, might have constituted a perfect state of war, which was not intended by the government.

3d. It has, likewise, been said, that the 7th section of the act of *March* 1799, embraces cases which, according to pre-existing laws, could not then take place, because no authority had been given to re-capture friendly vessels from the *French*; and this argument was strongly and forcibly pressed.

But, because every case provided for by this law was not then existing, it does not follow, that the law should not operate upon such as did exist, and upon the rest whenever they should arise. It is a permanent law, embracing a variety of subjects, not made in relation to the present war with *France* only, but in relation to any future war with her, or with any other nation. It might then very properly allow salvage for recapturing of *American* vessels from *France,* which had previously been authorised by law, though it could not immediately apply to the vessels of friends: and whenever such a war should exist between the *United States* and *France,* or any other nation, as according to the law of nations, or special authority, would justify the re-capture of friendly vessels, it might on that event, with similar propriety, apply to them; which furnishes, I think, the true construction of the act.

The opinion which I delivered at *New-York,* in *Talbot v. Seaman,* was, that although an *American* vessel could not justify the re-taking of a neutral vessel from the *French,* because neither the sort of war that subsisted, nor the special commission under which the *American* acted, authorised the proceeding; yet, that the 7th sect. of the act of 1799, applied to re-captures from *France as an enemy,* in all cases authorised by congress. And on both points, my opinion remains unshaken....

What then is the evidence of legislative will? In fact and in law we are at war: an *American* vessel fighting with a *French* vessel, to subdue and make her prize, is fighting with an enemy accurately and technically speaking: and if this be not sufficient evidence of the legislative mind, it is explained in the same law. . . .

. . . .

CHASE, JUSTICE. . . . Congress is empowered to declare a general war, or congress may wage a limited war; limited in place, in objects, and in time. If a general war is declared, its extent and operations are only restricted and regulated by the *jus belli,* forming a part of the law of nations; but if a partial war is waged, its extent and operation depend on our municipal laws.

What, then, is the nature of the contest subsisting between *America* and *France*? In my judgment, it is a limited, partial, war. Congress has not declared war in general terms; but congress has authorised hostilities on the high seas by certain persons in certain cases. There is no authority given to commit hostilities on land; to capture unarmed *French* vessels, nor even to capture *French* armed vessels lying in a *French* port; and the authority is not given, indiscriminately, to every citizen of *America,* against every citizen of *France*; but only to citizens appointed by commissions, or exposed to immediate outrage and violence. So far it is, unquestionably, a partial war; but, nevertheless, it is a public war, on account of the public authority from which it emanates.

. . . .

BY the COURT: Let the decree of the Circuit Court be affirmed.

LITTLE v. BARREME

6 U.S. (2 Cranch) 170, 2 L.Ed. 243 (1804).

[Review again this decision, which appears in Chapter 1, Section 2].

BROWN v. UNITED STATES

12 U.S. (8 Cranch) 110, 3 L.Ed. 504 (1814).

[Review again this decision, which appears in Chapter 2, Section 8].

ABRAHAM D. SOFAER, WAR, FOREIGN AFFAIRS AND CONSTITUTIONAL POWER: THE ORIGINS*

145–66, 274–75 (1976) (some footnotes omitted).

Soon [after *Bas v. Tingy*] the Court was presented—in *Talbot v. Seeman*—with a case in which an American commander was denied salvage for rescuing a vessel owned by citizens of a neutral nation. The Court agreed that no salvage could be paid for an unlawful recapture, but

* Reprinted with permission from Ballinger Publishing Company.

concluded that the recapture was lawful because authorized by Congress. "The whole powers of war being, by the constitution of the United States, vested in congress," wrote Chief Justice Marshall, "the acts of that body can alone be resorted to as our guides in this enquiry." No one denied that Congress could authorize general or limited hostilities; the issue was whether the limited hostilities authorized included the recapture of a neutral vessel, and Marshall found that they did.

In *Little v. Barreme* the Court faced a more difficult controversy—whether a seizure pursuant to an executive instruction was invalid because the instruction exceeded the power delegated by Congress. ...

....

The decision [in *Little v. Barreme*] may reflect the Court's desire to protect the rights of neutral vessels, an understandable concern in light of the nation's persistent assertion of neutral rights. More plausibly, though, the decision rests on the notion, articulated in both *Bas v. Tingy* and *Talbot v. Seeman,* that declared war involved a delegation to the executive and all citizens of general authority to commit hostilities against the enemy, while the conduct of undeclared or "imperfect" war was limited to those actions authorized by Congress. As Justice Washington expressed it, in an "imperfect" war "those who are authorized to commit hostilities ... can go no further than to the extent of their commission." *Little v. Barreme* did not explicitly discuss the President's inherent authority; the commanders seem not to have raised the issue. Nor did the decision directly pertain to whether Congress could, if it chose, delegate broadly the power to conduct an undeclared war (or control more closely the conduct of a declared war). The Court did clearly hold, however, that government agents could not successfully defend themselves on the basis of executive orders, issued during an undeclared war, that authorized actions outside the scope of a specific legislative delegation. Congress's authorization to seize vessels sailing *to* French ports was read implicitly to deny the power to seize vessels sailing *from* such ports. The decision strongly suggests, therefore, that the Justices assumed Congress could lawfully have directed the executive not to seize such vessels, and thereby control the conduct of an undeclared war at least to that extent.

....

The Supreme Court made clear that it regarded Congress as the ultimate source of authority on whether and how the nation would make war. It granted relief against a seizure that exceeded the limits of authority implied by a statute, strongly suggesting that Congress has power to control the conduct of war, even over a subject—the seizure of American merchant vessels trading with an enemy—that Chief Justice Marshall suggested might well have come within the President's authority, in the absence of any legislative regulation. Both branches could act, in other words, but Congress had the final say.

....

One limited but significant restraint on executive power to act under broad delegations was imposed by the Supreme Court in *Brown v. United States*. After war against Britain was formally declared, an attorney for the United States seized some British owned timber landed in Massachusetts before the declaration of war. The local United States Attorney relied on the declaration of war as authority for the seizure, and in at least one prior case the Court had suggested that a declaration allowed any and all acts of hostility. But the Court ruled this seizure unauthorized. The Constitution was a document imbued with moderation, concluded the majority, and should be read to require the legislature more specifically to authorize a measure in conflict with the law of nations. The express grant to Congress of power to "make rules concerning captures on land and water" was read to apply to domestic captures as well as those abroad, and required Congress to promulgate the rules more specifically. That Congress had frequently legislated with specificity concerning enemy individuals and property, the majority found, was evidence supporting its decision. Justice Story dissented vigorously, contending that the executive could seize an enemy alien's property when war was generally declared, though not moneys owed him; Story agreed, however, that Congress could have limited and regulated the President's authority in pursuing a general war.

NOTES ON CONTEMPORARY IMPLICATIONS OF THE MARSHALL COURT CASES

1. *The Meaning of "War"*. What application do these early Marshall Court cases concerning the war power have to contemporary armed conflicts? Is Congress's power to declare "war" limited to a power to establish a formal state of "war" within the meaning of international law (sometimes referred to as "perfect" war) or does it encompass all types of military coercion, formal or informal (sometimes referred to as "imperfect" war)? *See* Michael J. Glennon, *Go Big? Go Long? Go Back To Congress*, WASH. POST, Dec. 7, 2006:

> Since its earliest days, the Supreme Court has recognized a president's obligation to respect congressional restrictions when Congress has authorized "imperfect war"—a war fought for limited purposes. In an imperfect war, Justice Bushrod Washington said in *Bas v. Tingy* (1800), those "who are authorized to commit hostilities ... can go no farther than to the extent of their commission." The following year, in *Talbot v. Seeman* (1801), Chief Justice John Marshall wrote that "[t]he whole powers of war being, by the Constitution of the United States, vested in congress, the acts of that body can alone be resorted to as our guides in this enquiry."
>
> Congress in 2002 authorized imperfect war in approving the use of force in Iraq for specific, limited objectives. As those objectives are achieved, or different ones are pursued, legislative reauthorization will be required. Absent congressional approval, the president cannot use force in Iraq to pursue new objectives, beyond the protection of forces being withdrawn.

For a revisionist view on the meaning of the constitutional allocation of power, see John Yoo, *The Powers of War and Peace: The Constitution and Foreign Affairs After 9/11*, 143–60 (2005). According to Professor Yoo, Congress's role in declaring war was meant to be limited to formal declarations of war, since only formal declarations triggered significant consequences for the United States under the law of nations. As such, the resort to less formal uses of force could be undertaken by the President without congressional approval.

2. *The Effects of Launching an "Imperfect" War*. Assuming that Congress initiates military action that falls short of a formal declaration of war, what consequences flow from that action, given the reasoning in *Brown v. United States*? Must Congress be more specific about the effects of a declaration of informal/imperfect war than would be the case for a formal declaration of war? Compare the recent opinions of the Supreme Court in *Hamdan v. Rumsfeld*, 548 U.S. 557, 126 S.Ct. 2749, 165 L.Ed.2d 723 (2006), and *Hamdi v. Rumsfeld*, 542 U.S. 507, 124 S.Ct. 2633, 159 L.Ed.2d 578 (2004), construing the breadth of presidential authority conferred by the Authorization to Use Military Force statute (all found *supra*, Chapter 1, Section 3). Should the same principles of construction apply to a declaration of war and authorization to prosecute an "imperfect" war? Consider, in this connection, the opinion of a three-judge panel of the U.S. Court of Appeals in *Al-Marri v. Wright*, 487 F.3d 160, 188–89 (4th Cir. 2007):

> Finally, we note that the AUMF itself contains nothing that transforms a civilian into a combatant subject to indefinite military detention. Indeed, the AUMF contains only a broad grant of war powers and lacks any specific language authorizing detention. For this reason, the *Hamdi* plurality explained that its opinion "only finds legislative authority to detain under the AUMF once it is sufficiently clear that the individual *is*, in fact, an enemy combatant." *Hamdi*, 542 U.S. at 523 (emphasis added). Although the military detention of enemy combatants like Hamdi is certainly "a fundamental incident of waging war," *id.* at 519, the military detention of civilians like al-Marri just as certainly is not. Notably, even the Government does not contend that the AUMF transforms civilians into combatants or authorizes the President to classify civilians as enemy combatants and so detain them in military custody.
>
> Moreover, assuming the Constitution permitted Congress to grant the President such an awesome and unprecedented power, if Congress intended to grant this authority it could and would have said so explicitly. The AUMF lacks the particularly clear statement from Congress that would, at a minimum, be necessary to authorize the classification and indefinite military detention of *civilians* as "enemy combatants." *See, e.g., Greene v. McElroy*, 360 U.S. 474, 508 (1959) (rejecting Government argument that Executive Orders and statutes permitted deprivation of liberty rights absent "explicit authorization" in them); *Duncan v. Kahanamoku*, 327 U.S. 304, 324 (1946) (rejecting Government argument that statute authorized trial of civilians by military tribunals because Congress could not have intended "to exceed the boundaries between military and civilian power, in which our people have always believed"); *Ex Parte Endo*, 323 U.S. 283, 300 (1944) (rejecting Government argument that a "wartime" executive order and statute permitted detention of citizen of

Japanese heritage when neither "use[d] the language of detention"); *Brown v. United States*, 12 U.S. (8 Cranch) 110, 128–29 (1814) (rejecting Government argument that declaration of war authorized confiscation of enemy property because it did not clearly "declare[]" the legislature's "will"). We are exceedingly reluctant to infer a grant of authority that is so far afield from anything recognized by precedent or law-of-war principles, especially given the serious constitutional concerns it would raise.

3. *Justice Story*. Justice Story was not just an influential member of the Supreme Court, but an outstanding constitutional and private law scholar. Consider the following excerpt from his classic treatise on the U.S. Constitution:

> The power of declaring war is not only the highest sovereign prerogative; . . . it is in its own nature and effects so critical and calamitous, that it requires the utmost deliberation, and the successive review of all the councils of the nations. War, in its best estate, never fails to impose upon the people the most burdensome taxes, and personal sufferings. It is always injurious, and sometimes subversive of the great commercial, manufacturing, and agricultural interests. Nay, it always involves the prosperity, and not infrequently the existence, of a nation. It is sometimes fatal to public liberty itself, by introducing a spirit of military glory, which is ready to follow, wherever a successful commander will lead; . . . It should therefore be difficult in a republic to declare war; but not to make peace. . . . The cooperation of all the branches of the legislative power ought, upon principle, to be required in this the highest act of legislation.

Joseph Story, *Commentaries on the Constitution of the United States* 60–61 (1833).

4. *Further Reading*. For further reading, see Clarence A. Berdahl, *War Powers of the Executive in the United States* (1921); *The President's War Powers* (Demetrios Caraley ed., 1984); Edward S. Corwin, *Total War and the Constitution* (1947); Jacob K. Javits, *Who Makes War: The President Versus Congress* (1973); Charles A. Lofgren, *War Making Under the Constitution: The Original Understanding*, 81 YALE L.J. 672 (1972); Merlo J. Pusey, *The Way We Go to War* (1969); W. Taylor Reveley, *War Powers of the President and Congress: Who Holds the Arrows and Olive Branch* (1981); Martin S. Sheffer, *The Judicial Development of Presidential War Powers* (1999); *The U.S. Constitution and the Power to Go to War* (Gary M. Stern & Morton H. Halperin eds., 1994); Ann Van Wynen Thomas & A.J. Thomas Jr., *The War–Making Powers of the President: Constitutional and International Law Aspects* (1982); Donald L. Westerfield, *War Powers: The President, the Congress, and the Question of War* (1996); Francis P. Wormuth & Edwin B. Firmage, *To Chain the Dog of War: The War Powers of Congress in History and Law* (1986).

DURAND v. HOLLINS

8 F.Cas. 111 (C.C.S.D.N.Y. 1860) (No. 4,186).

[In 1854, following an incident in which a bottle was thrown at an American diplomat in Greytown, Nicaragua, the Secretary of the Navy ordered the *Cyane* to bombard the town. It did, inflicting heavy damage. Among the property damaged was a building owned by Durand, an American citizen, who sued Hollins, the commander of the *Cyane,* in an action that ultimately reached the Supreme Court. It has been argued that the facts presented "no question of emergency intervention to save American citizens; it was rather a calculated retaliation after the fact." A. Schlesinger, *The Imperial Presidency* 55–57 (1973).]

This was an action of trespass, brought to recover damages for the destruction by the defendant [George N. Hollins] of property at San Juan del Norte, Nicaragua, otherwise called Greytown, on the 13th of July, 1854. The defendant, among other defences, pleaded that he was a commander in the navy of the United States, and, as such, commanded a vessel of war called the *Cyane*, and was bound to obey the orders of the president of the United States, and of the secretary of the navy; and that, by virtue of lawful and public orders of the president and secretary, he did cause the place called Greytown, by the naval force of the United States to be bombarded and set fire to, and which are the same alleged trespasses set forth in the declaration. There was, also, a plea setting forth, in addition to the facts above stated, that the community at Greytown had forcibly usurped the possession of the place, and erected an independent government, not recognized by the United States, and had perpetrated acts of violence against the citizens of the United States and their property, and had, on demand for redress, refused it, and that the defendant, under public orders from the president and secretary, as a commander in the navy, and then in command of the *Cyane*, did cause the place to be bombarded and set on fire, as he lawfully might for the cause aforesaid. To these pleas the plaintiff [Calvin Durand] demurred, and the defendant joined in demurrer.

. . . .

NELSON, CIRCUIT JUSTICE. The principal ground of objection to the pleas, as a defence of the action, is, that neither the president nor the secretary of the navy had authority to give the orders relied on to the defendant, and, hence, that they afford no ground of justification.

The executive power, under the constitution, is vested in the president of the United States (article 2, § 1). He is commander-in-chief of the army and navy, (Id. § 2), and has imposed upon him the duty to "take care that the laws be faithfully executed" (Id. § 3). In organizing a government under the constitution, an executive department, called the "Department of Foreign Affairs," was established, and a principal officer, called the "Secretary for the Department of Foreign Affairs," placed at its head, to "execute such duties as shall, from time to time, be enjoined on or intrusted to him by the president of the United States, agreeable to the constitution, relative to correspondences, commissions, or instructions to or with public ministers or consuls from the United States, or to negotiations with public ministers from foreign states or princes, or to memorials or other applications from foreign public ministers or other foreigners, or to such other matters respecting foreign affairs as the president of the United States shall assign to the said department; and, furthermore, that the said principal officer shall conduct the business of the said department in such manner as the president of the United States shall from time to time order or instruct." Act Cong. July 27, 1789, § 1 (1 Stat. 28). By a subsequent act, this department has been denominated the "Department of State," and the head of it the "Secretary of State." There was also established another executive department, denominated the "Department of the Navy," the chief officer of which is called the "Secretary of the Navy," "whose duty it shall be to execute such orders as he shall receive from the president of the United States, relative to the procurement of naval stores and materials, and the construction, armament, equipment and employment of vessels of war, as well as all other matters connected with the naval establishment of the United States." Act Cong. April 30, 1798, § 1 (1 Stat. 553).

As the executive head of the nation, the president is made the only legitimate organ of the general government, to open and carry on correspondence or negotiations with foreign nations, in matters concerning the interests of the country or of its citizens. It is to him, also, the citizens abroad must look for protection of person and of property, and for the faithful execution of the laws existing and intended for their protection. For this purpose, the whole executive power of the country is placed in his hands, under the constitution, and the laws passed in pursuance thereof; and different departments of government have been organized, through which this power may be most conveniently executed, whether by negotiation or by force—a department of state and a department of the navy.

Now, as it respects the interposition of the executive abroad, for the protection of the lives or property of the citizen, the duty must, of necessity, rest in the discretion of the president. Acts of lawless violence, or of threatened violence to the citizen or his property, cannot be anticipated and provided for; and the protection, to be effectual or of any avail, may, not unfrequently, require the most prompt and decided action. Under our system of government, the citizen abroad is as much entitled to protection as the citizen at home. The great object and duty of government is the protection of the lives, liberty, and property of the people composing it, whether abroad or at home; and any government failing in the accomplishment of the object, or the performance of the duty, is not worth preserving.

I have said, that the interposition of the president abroad, for the protection of the citizen, must necessarily rest in his discretion; and it is quite clear that, in all cases where a public act or order rests in executive discretion neither he nor his authorized agent is personally civilly responsible for the consequences. As was observed by Chief Justice Marshall, in *Marbury v. Madison*, 1 Cranch [5 U.S.] 165: "By the constitution of the United States, the president is invested with certain important political powers, in the exercise of which he is to use his own discretion, and is accountable only to his country in his political character, and to his own conscience. To aid him in the performance of these duties, he is authorized to appoint certain officers, who act by his authority, and in conformity with his orders. In such cases, their acts are his acts, and, whatever opinion may be entertained of the manner in which executive discretion may be used, still there exists, and can exist, no power to control that discretion. The subjects are political. They respect the nation, not individual rights, and, being intrusted to the executive, the decision of the executive is conclusive." This is a sound principle, and governs the present case. The question whether it was the duty of the president to interpose for the protection of the citizens at Greytown against an irresponsible and marauding community that had established itself there, was a public political question, in which the government, as well as the citizens whose interests were involved, was concerned, and which belonged to the executive to determine; and his decision is final and conclusive, and justified the defendant in the execution of his orders given through the secretary of the navy.

Judgment for defendant.

INTRODUCTORY NOTE TO THE PRIZE CASES

Professor John Hart Ely wrote as follows: "President Lincoln's actions at the outset of the Civil War are sometimes cited as precedent for presidential military ventures. Although Lincoln did engage in a number of unconstitutional acts during this period, . . . usurpation of the war power was not among them. The important fact is not that Congress retroactively authorized what Lincoln had done (since that shouldn't count) but rather that for constitutional purposes a domestic rebellion is quite different from a foreign war. Article II provides that the President 'shall take Care that the Laws be faithfully executed,' . . . and beyond that, though it shouldn't be necessary, congressional acts of 1795 and 1807 had empowered him to use the military to suppress insurrection against the government of the United States." John Hart Ely, *Suppose Congress Wanted a War Powers Act that Worked,* 88 COLUM. L. REV. 1379, 1390 n. 34 (1988); *see also* John Hart Ely, *War and Responsibility: Constitutional Lessons of Vietnam and its Aftermath* (1993).

THE PRIZE CASES

67 U.S. (2 Black) 365 (1862).

These were cases in which the vessels named, together with their cargoes, were severally captured and brought in as prizes by public ships of the United States. The libels were filed by the proper District Attorneys, on behalf of the United States and on behalf of the officers and crews of the ships, by which the captures were respectively made. In each case the District Court pronounced a decree of condemnation, from which the claimants took an appeal.

. . . .

Mr. JUSTICE GRIER. . . .

. . . Had the President a right to institute a blockade of ports in possession of persons in armed rebellion against the Government, on the principles of international law, as known and acknowledged among civilized States?

. . . .

. . . Neutrals have a right to challenge the existence of a blockade *de facto,* and also the authority of the party exercising the right to institute it. They have a right to enter the ports of a friendly nation for the purposes of trade and commerce, but are bound to recognize the rights of a belligerent engaged in actual war, to use this mode of coercion, for the purpose of subduing the enemy.

That a blockade *de facto* actually existed, and was formally declared and notified by the President on the 27th and 30th of April, 1861, is an admitted fact in these cases.

That the President, as the Executive Chief of the Government and Commander-in-chief of the Army and Navy, was the proper person to make such notification, has not been, and cannot be disputed.

The right of prize and capture has its origin in the "*jus belli,*" and is governed and adjudged under the law of nations. To legitimate the capture of a neutral vessel or property on the high seas, a war must exist *de facto,* and the neutral must have a knowledge or notice of the intention of one of the parties belligerent to use this mode of coercion against a port, city, or territory, in possession of the other.

Let us enquire whether, at the time this blockade was instituted, a state of war existed which would justify a resort to these means of subduing the hostile force.

War has been well defined to be, "That state in which a nation prosecutes its right by force."

The parties belligerent in a public war are independent nations. But it is not necessary to constitute war, that both parties should be acknowledged as independent nations or sovereign States. A war may exist where one of the belligerents, claims sovereign rights as against the other.

Insurrection against a government may or may not culminate in an organized rebellion, but a civil war always begins by insurrection against the lawful authority of the Government. A civil war is never solemnly declared; it becomes such by its accidents—the number, power, and organization of the persons who originate and carry it on. When the party in rebellion occupy and hold in a hostile manner a certain portion of territory; have declared their independence; have cast off their allegiance;

have organized armies; have commenced hostilities against their former sovereign, the world acknowledges them as belligerents, and the contest a *war. They* claim to be in arms to establish their liberty and independence, in order to become a sovereign State, while the sovereign party treats them as insurgents and rebels who owe allegiance, and who should be punished with death for their treason.

The laws of war, as established among nations, have their foundation in reason, and all tend to mitigate the cruelties and misery produced by the scourge of war. Hence the parties to a civil war usually concede to each other belligerent rights. They exchange prisoners, and adopt the other courtesies and rules common to public or national wars.

"A civil war," says Vattel, "breaks the bands of society and government, or at least suspends their force and effect; it produces in the nation two independent parties, who consider each other as enemies, and acknowledge no common judge. Those two parties, therefore, must necessarily be considered as constituting, at least for a time, two separate bodies, two distinct societies. Having no common superior to judge between them, they stand in precisely the same predicament as two nations who engage in a contest and have recourse to arms."

"This being the case, it is very evident that the common laws of war—those maxims of humanity, moderation, and honor—ought to be observed by both parties in every civil war. Should the sovereign conceive he has a right to hang up his prisoners as rebels, the opposite party will make reprisals, & c., & c.; the war will become cruel, horrible, and every day more destructive to the nation."

As a civil war is never publicly proclaimed, *eo nomine* against insurgents, its actual existence is a fact in our domestic history which the Court is bound to notice and to know.

The true test of its existence, as found in the writings of the sages of the common law, may be thus summarily stated: "When the regular course of justice is interrupted by revolt, rebellion, or insurrection, so that the Courts of Justice cannot be kept open, *civil war exists* and hostilities may be prosecuted on the same footing as if those opposing the Government were foreign enemies invading the land."

By the Constitution, Congress alone has the power to declare a national or foreign war. It cannot declare war against a State, or any number of States, by virtue of any clause in the Constitution. The Constitution confers on the President the whole Executive power. He is bound to take care that the laws be faithfully executed. He is Commander-in-chief of the Army and Navy of the United States, and of the militia of the several States when called into the actual service of the United States. He has no power to initiate or declare a war either against a foreign nation or a domestic State. But by the Acts of Congress of February 28th, 1795, and 3d of March, 1807, he is authorized to called out the militia and use the military and naval forces of the United States in case of invasion by foreign nations, and to suppress insurrection against the government of a State or of the United States.

If a war be made by invasion of a foreign nation, the President is not only authorized but bound to resist force by force. He does not initiate the war, but is bound to accept the challenge without waiting for any special legislative authority. And whether the hostile party be a foreign invader, or States organized in rebellion, it is none the less a war, although the declaration of it be "*unilateral.*" Lord Stowell (1 Dodson, 247) observes, "It is not the less a war on *that account,* for war may exist without a declaration on either side. It is so laid down by the best writers on the law of nations. A declaration of war by one country only, is not a mere challenge to be accepted or refused at pleasure by the other."

The battles of Palo Alto and Resaca de la Palma had been fought before the passage of the Act of Congress of May 13th, 1846, which recognized "*a state of war as existing by the act of the Republic of Mexico.*" This act not only provided for the future prosecution of the war, but was itself a vindication and ratification of the Act of the President in accepting the challenge without a previous formal declaration of war by Congress.

This greatest of civil wars was not gradually developed by popular commotion, tumultuous assemblies, or local unorganized insurrections. However long may have been its previous conception, it nevertheless sprung forth suddenly from the parent brain, a Minerva in the full panoply of *war.* The President was bound to meet it in the shape it presented itself, without waiting for Congress to baptize it with a name; and no name given to it by him or them could change the fact.

It is not the less a civil war, with belligerent parties in hostile array, because it may be called an "insurrection" by one side, and the insurgents be considered as rebels or traitors. It is not necessary that the independence of the revolted province or State be acknowledged in order to constitute it a party belligerent in a war according to the law of nations. Foreign nations acknowledge it as war by a declaration of neutrality. The condition of neutrality cannot exist unless there be two belligerent parties. In the case of the *Santissima Trinidad,* (7 Wheaton, 337,) this Court say: "The Government of the United States has recognized the existence of a civil war between Spain and her colonies, and has avowed her determination to remain neutral between the parties. Each party is therefore deemed by us a belligerent nation, having, so far as concerns us, the sovereign rights of war." . . .

As soon as the news of the attack on Fort Sumter, and the organization of a government by the seceding States, assuming to act as belligerents, could become known in Europe, to wit, on the 13th of May, 1861, the Queen of England issued her proclamation of neutrality, "recognizing hostilities as existing between the Government of the United States of America and *certain States* styling themselves the Confederate States of America." This was immediately followed by similar declarations or silent acquiescence by other nations.

After such an official recognition by the sovereign, a citizen of a foreign State is estopped to deny the existence of a war with all its consequences as regards neutrals. They cannot ask a Court to affect a technical ignorance of the existence of a war, which all the world acknowledges to be the greatest civil war known in the history of the human race, and thus cripple the arm of the Government and paralyze its power by subtle definitions and ingenious sophisms.

The law of nations is also called the law of nature; it is founded on the common consent as well as the common sense of the world. It contains no such anomalous doctrine as that which this Court are now for the first time desired to pronounce, to wit: That insurgents who have risen in rebellion against their sovereign, expelled her Courts, established a revolutionary government, organized armies, and commenced hostilities, are not *enemies* because they are *traitors;* and a war levied on the Government by traitors, in order to dismember and destroy it, is not a *war* because it is an "insurrection."

Whether the President in fulfilling his duties, as Commander-in-chief, in suppressing an insurrection, has met with such armed hostile resistance, and a civil war of such alarming proportions as will compel him to accord to them the character of belligerents, is a question to be decided *by him,* and this Court must be governed by the decisions and acts of the political department of the Government to which this power was entrusted. "He must determine what degree of force the crisis demands." The proclamation of blockade is itself official and conclusive evidence to the Court that a state of war existed which demanded and authorized a recourse to such a measure, under the circumstances peculiar to the case.

The correspondence of Lord Lyons with the Secretary of State admits the fact and concludes the question.

If it were necessary to the technical existence of a war, that it should have a legislative sanction, we find it in almost every act passed at the extraordinary session of the Legislature of 1861, which was wholly employed in enacting laws to enable the Government to prosecute the war with vigor and efficiency. And finally, in 1861, we find Congress "*ex majore cautela*" and in anticipation of such astute objections, passing an act "approving, legalizing, and making valid all the acts, proclamations, and orders of the President, & c., as if they had been *issued and done under the previous express authority* and direction of the Congress of the United States."

Without admitting that such an act was necessary under the circumstances, it is plain that if the President had in any manner assumed powers which it was necessary should have the authority or sanction of Congress, that on the well known principle of law, "*omnis ratihabitio retrotrahitur et mandato equiparatur,*" this ratification has operated to perfectly cure the defect. In the case of *Brown vs. United States,* (8 Cr., 131, 132, 133,) Mr. Justice Story treats of this subject, and cites numerous authorities to which we may refer to prove this position, and concludes, "I am perfectly satisfied that no subject can commence hostilities or capture property of an enemy, when the sovereign has prohibited it. But suppose he did, I would ask if the sovereign may not ratify his proceedings, and thus by a retroactive operation give validity to them?"

Although Mr. Justice Story dissented from the majority of the Court on the whole case, the doctrine stated by him on this point is correct and fully substantiated by authority.

The objection made to this act of ratification, that it is *expost facto,* and therefore unconstitutional and void, might possibly have some weight on the trial of an indictment in a criminal Court. But precedents from that source cannot be received as authoritative in a tribunal administering public and international law.

On this first question therefore we are of the opinion that the President had a right, *jure belli,* to institute a blockade of ports in possession of the States in rebellion, which neutrals are bound to regard.

. . . .

MR. JUSTICE NELSON, dissenting. . . .

. . . .

The proclamation, after certain recitals, not material in this branch of the case, provides as follows: the President has "deemed it advisable to set on foot a blockade of the ports within the States aforesaid, (the States referred to in the recitals,) in pursuance of the laws of the United States and of the law of nations, in such case made and provided." "If, therefore, with a view to violate such blockade, a vessel shall approach or shall attempt to leave either of said ports, she will be duly warned by the commander of one of the blockading vessels, who will endorse on her register the fact and date of such warning, and if the same vessel shall again attempt to enter or leave the blockaded port, she will be captured and sent to the nearest convenient port for such proceedings against her and her cargo, as prize, as may be deemed advisable."

. . . .

It has been said that the proclamation, among other grounds, as stated on its face, is founded on the "law of nations," and hence draws after it the law of blockade as found in that code, and that a warning is dispensed with in all cases where the vessel is chargeable with previous notice or knowledge that the port is blockaded. But the obvious answer to the suggestion is, that there is no necessary connection between the authority upon which the proclamation is issued and the terms prescribed as the condition of its penalties or enforcement, and, besides, if founded upon the law of nations, surely it was competent for the President to mitigate the rigors of that code and apply to neutrals the more lenient and friendly principles of international law. We do not doubt but that considerations of this character influenced the President in prescribing these favorable terms in respect to neutrals; for, in his message a few months later to Congress, (4th of July,) he observes: "a proclamation was issued for closing the ports of the insurrectionary districts" (not by blockade, but) "by proceedings *in the nature of a blockade.*"

. . . .

Another objection taken to the seizure of this vessel and cargo is, that there was no existing war between the United States and the States in insurrection within the meaning of the law of nations, which drew after it the consequences of a public or civil war. A contest by force between independent sovereign States is called a public war; and, when duly commenced by proclamation or otherwise, it entitles both of the belligerent parties to all the rights of war against each other, and as respects neutral nations. Chancellor Kent observes, "Though a solemn declaration, or previous notice to the enemy, be now laid aside, it is essential that some formal public act, proceeding directly from the competent source, should announce to the people at home their new relations and duties growing out of a state of war, and which should equally apprize neutral nations of the fact, to enable them to conform their conduct to the rights belonging to the new state of things." "Such an official act operates from its date to legalize all hostile acts, in like manner as a treaty of peace operates from its date to annul them." He further observes, "as war cannot lawfully be commenced on the part of the United States without an act of Congress, such act is, of course, a formal notice to all the world, and equivalent to the most solemn declaration."

The legal consequences resulting from a state of war between two countries at this day are well understood, and will be found described in every approved work on the subject of international law. The people of the two countries become immediately the enemies of each other—all intercourse commercial or otherwise between them unlawful—all contracts existing at the commencement of the war suspended, and all made during its existence utterly void. The insurance of enemies' property, the drawing of bills of exchange or purchase on the enemies' country, the remission of bills or money to it are illegal and void. Existing partnerships between citizens or subjects of the two countries are dissolved, and, in fine, interdiction of trade and intercourse direct or indirect is absolute and complete by the mere force and effect of war itself. All the property of the people of the two countries on land or sea are subject to capture and confiscation by the adverse party as enemies' property, with certain qualifications as it respects property on land, (*Brown vs. United States,* 8 Cranch, 110,) all treaties between the belligerent parties are annulled; The ports of the respective countries may be blockaded, and letters of marque and reprisal granted as rights of war, and the law of prizes as defined by the law of nations comes into full and complete operation, resulting from maritime captures *jure belli.* War also effects a change in the mutual relations of all States or countries, not directly, as in the case of the belligerents, but immediately and indirectly, though they take no part in the contest, but remain neutral.

This great and pervading change in the existing condition of a country, and in the relations of all her citizens or subjects, external and internal, from a state of peace, is the immediate effect and result of a state of war: and hence the same code which has annexed to the existence of a war all these disturbing consequences has declared that the right of making war belongs exclusively to the supreme or sovereign power of the State.

This power in all civilized nations is regulated by the fundamental laws or municipal constitution of the country.

By our Constitution this power is lodged in Congress. Congress shall have power "to declare war, grant letters of marque and reprisal, and make rules concerning captures on land and water."

We have thus far been considering the status of the citizens or subjects of a country at the breaking out of a public war when recognized or declared by the competent power.

In the case of a rebellion or resistance of a portion of the people of a country against the established government, there is no doubt, if in its progress and enlargement the government thus sought to be overthrown sees fit, it may by the competent power recognize or declare the existence of a state of civil war, which will draw after it all the consequences and rights of war between the contending parties as in the case of a public war. Mr. Wheaton observes, speaking of civil war, "But the general usage of nations regards such a war as entitling both the contending parties to all the rights of war as against each other, and even as respects neutral nations." It is not to be denied, therefore, that if a civil war existed between that portion of the people in organized insurrection to overthrow this Government at the time this vessel and cargo were seized, and if she was guilty of a violation of the blockade, she would be lawful prize of war. But before this insurrection against the established Government can be dealt with on the footing of a civil war, within the meaning of the law of nations and the Constitution of the United States, and which will draw after it belligerent rights, it must be recognized or declared by the war-making power of the Government. No power short of this can change the legal status of the Government or the relations of its citizens from that of peace to a state of war, or bring into existence all those duties and obligations of neutral third parties growing out of a state of war. The war power of the Government must be exercised before this changed condition of the Government and people and of neutral third parties can be admitted. There is no difference in this respect between a civil or a public war.

. . . .

Now, in one sense, no doubt this is war, and may be a war of the most extensive and threatening dimensions and effects, but it is a statement simply of its existence in a material sense, and has no relevancy or weight when the question is what constitutes war in a legal sense, in the sense of the law of nations, and of the Constitution of the United States? For it must be a war in this sense to attach to it all the consequences that belong to belligerent rights. Instead, therefore, of inquiring after armies and navies, and victories lost and won, or organized rebellion against the general Government, the inquiry should be into the law of nations and into the municipal fundamental laws of the Government. For we find there that to constitute a civil war in the sense in which we are speaking, before it can exist, in contemplation of law, it must be recognized or declared by the sovereign power of the State, and which sovereign power by our Constitution is lodged in the Congress of the United States—civil war, therefore, under our system of government, can exist only by an act of Congress, which requires the assent of two of the great departments of the Government, the Executive and Legislative.

We have thus far been speaking of the war power under the Constitution of the United States, and as known and recognized by the law of nations. But we are asked, what would become of the peace and integrity of the Union in case of an insurrection at home or invasion from abroad if this power could not be exercised by the President in the recess of Congress, and until that body could be assembled?

The framers of the Constitution fully comprehended this question, and provided for the contingency. Indeed, it would have been surprising if they had not, as a rebellion had occurred in the State of Massachusetts while the Convention was in session, and which had become so general that it was quelled only by calling upon the military power of the State. The Constitution declares that Congress shall have power "to provide for calling forth the militia to execute the laws of the Union, suppress insurrections, and repel invasions." Another clause, "that the President shall be Commander-in-chief of the Army and Navy of the United States, and of the militia of the several States when called into the actual service of the United States;" and, again, "He shall take care that the laws shall be faithfully executed." . . .

The last Act provided that whenever the United States shall be invaded or be in imminent danger of invasion from a foreign nation, it shall be lawful for the President to call forth such number of the militia most convenient to the place of danger, and in case of insurrection in any State against the Government thereof, it shall be lawful for the President, on the application of the Legislature of such State, if in session, or if not, of the Executive of the State, to call forth such number of militia of any other State or States as he may judge sufficient to suppress such insurrection.

The 2d section provides, that when the laws of the United States shall be opposed, or the execution obstructed in any State by combinations too powerful to be suppressed by the course of judicial proceedings, it shall be lawful for the President to call forth the militia of such State, or of any other State or States as may be necessary to suppress such combinations; and by the Act 3 March, 1807, (2 U.S. Laws, 443,) it is provided that in case of insurrection or obstruction of the laws, either in the United States or of any State or Territory, where it is lawful for the President to call forth the militia for the purpose of suppressing such insurrection, and causing the laws to be executed, it shall be lawful to employ for the same purpose such part of the land and naval forces of the United States as shall be judged necessary.

It will be seen, therefore, that ample provision has been made under the Constitution and laws against any sudden and unexpected disturbance of the public peace from insurrection at home or invasion from abroad. The whole military and naval power of the country is put under the control of the President to meet the emergency. He may call out a force in proportion to its necessities, one regiment or fifty, one ship-of-war or any number at his discretion. If, like the insurrection in the State of Pennsylvania in 1793, the disturbance is confined to a small district of country, a few regiments of the militia may be sufficient to suppress it. If of the dimension of the present, when it first broke out, a much larger force would be required. But whatever its numbers, whether great or small, that may be required, ample provision is here made; and whether great or small, the nature of the power is the same. It is the exercise of a power under the municipal laws of the country and not under the law of nations; and, as we see, furnishes the most ample means of repelling attacks from abroad or suppressing disturbances at home until the assembling of Congress, who can, if it be deemed necessary, bring into operation the war power, and thus change the nature and character of the contest. Then, instead of being carried on under the municipal law of 1795, it would be under the law of nations, and the Acts of Congress as war measures with all the rights of war.

It has been argued that the authority conferred on the President by the Act of 1795 invests him with the war power. But the obvious answer is, that it proceeds from a different clause in the Constitution and which is given for different purposes and objects, namely, to execute the laws and preserve the public order and tranquillity of the country in a time of peace by preventing or suppressing any public disorder or disturbance by foreign or domestic enemies. Certainly, if there is any force in this argument, then we are in a state of war with all the rights of war, and all the penal consequences attending it every time this power is exercised by calling out a military force to execute the laws or to suppress insurrection or rebellion; for the nature of the power cannot depend upon the numbers called out. If so, what numbers will constitute war and what numbers will not? It has also been argued that this power of the President from necessity should be construed as vesting him with the war power, or the Republic might greatly suffer or be in danger from the attacks of the hostile party before the assembling of Congress. But we have seen that the whole military and naval force are in his hands under the municipal laws of the country. He can meet the adversary upon land and water with all the forces of the Government. The truth is, this idea of the existence of any necessity for clothing the President with the war power, under the Act of 1795, is simply a monstrous exaggeration; for, besides having the command of the whole of the army and navy, Congress can be assembled within any thirty days, if the safety of the country requires that the war power shall be brought into operation.

The Acts of 1795 and 1807 did not, and could not under the Constitution, confer on the President the power of declaring war against a State of this Union, or of deciding that war existed, and upon that ground authorize the capture and confiscation of the property of every citizen of the State whenever it was found on the waters. The laws of war, whether the war be civil or *inter gentes,* as we have seen, convert every citizen of the hostile State into a public enemy, and treat him accordingly, whatever may have been his previous conduct. This great power over the business and property of the citizen is reserved to the legislative department by the express words of the Constitution. It cannot be delegated or surrendered to the Executive. Congress alone can determine whether war exists or should be declared; and until they have acted, no citizen of the State can be punished in his person or property, unless he has committed some offence against a law of Congress passed before the act was committed, which made it a crime, and defined the punishment. The penalty of confiscation for the acts of others with which he had no concern cannot lawfully be inflicted.

. . . .

Down to this period the only enemy recognized by the Government was the persons engaged in the rebellion, all others were peaceful citizens, entitled to all the privileges of citizens under the Constitution. Certainly it cannot rightfully be said that the President has the power to convert a loyal citizen into a belligerent enemy or confiscate his property as enemy's property.

Congress assembled on the call for an extra session the 4th of July, 1861, and among the first acts passed was one in which the President was authorized by proclamation to interdict all trade and intercourse between all the inhabitants of States in insurrection and the rest of the United States, subjecting vessel and cargo to capture and condemnation as prize, and also to direct the capture of any ship or vessel belonging in whole or in part to any inhabitant of a State whose inhabitants are declared by the proclamation to be in a state of insurrection, found at sea or in any part of the rest of the United States. Act of Congress of 13th of July, 1861, secs. 5, 6. The 4th section also authorized the President to close any port in a Collection District obstructed so that the revenue could not be collected and provided for the capture and condemnation of any vessel attempting to enter.

The President's Proclamation was issued on the 16th of August following, and embraced Georgia, North and South Carolina, part of Virginia, Tennessee, Alabama, Louisiana, Texas, Arkansas, Mississippi and Florida.

This Act of Congress, we think, recognized a state of civil war between the Government and the Confederate States, and made it territorial....

....

... I am compelled to the conclusion that no civil war existed between this Government and the States in insurrection till recognized by the Act of Congress 13th of July, 1861; that the President does not possess the power under the Constitution to declare war or recognize its existence within the meaning of the law of nations, which carries with it belligerent rights, and thus change the country and all its citizens from a state of peace to a state of war; that this power belongs exclusively to the Congress of the United States, and, consequently, that the President had no power to set on foot a blockade under the law of nations, and that the capture of the vessel and cargo in this case, and in all cases before us in which the capture occurred before the 13th of July, 1861, for breach of blockade, or as enemies' property, are illegal and void, and that the decrees of condemnation should be reversed and the vessel and cargo restored.

MR. CHIEF JUSTICE TANEY, MR. JUSTICE CATRON and MR. JUSTICE CLIFFORD, concurred in the dissenting opinion of MR. JUSTICE NELSON.

NOTE ON IN RE NEAGLE

In 1889, the U.S. Attorney–General assigned Deputy U.S. Marshal David Neagle to protect Circuit Judge Stephen J. Field while the judge rode circuit in California. On August 14 of that year, a disappointed litigant before the judge, David S. Terry, burst into a room where Neagle and Judge Field were having breakfast, and proceeded to assault the Judge. Neagle shot Terry twice with his revolver, killing him instantly.

Later that day, the Sheriff of San Joaquin County, California, arrested Neagle on charges of murder. The U.S. government filed a writ of *habeas corpus* in an effort to have Neagle released. Among other things, Neagle argued that "in killing Terry under the circumstances [he was acting] in the discharge of his duty as an officer of the United States." Congress, however, had never actually enacted a statute authorizing such protection. In deciding for Neagle, Justice Samuel F. Miller wrote:

> Is [the President's duty to "take care that the laws be faithfully executed"] limited to the enforcement of acts of Congress or of treaties of the United States according to their *express terms*, or does it include the rights, duties and obligations growing out of the Constitution itself, our international relations, and all the protection implied by the nature of the government under the Constitution?
>
> One of the most remarkable episodes in the history of our foreign relations, and which has become an attractive historical incident, is the case of Martin Koszta, a native of Hungary, who, though not fully a naturalized citizen of the United States, had in due form of law made his declaration of intention to become a citizen. While in Smyrna he was seized by command of the Austrian consul general at that place, and

carried on board the *Hussar*, an Austrian vessel, where he was held in close confinement. Captain Ingraham, in command of the American sloop of war *St. Louis*, arriving in port at that critical period, and ascertaining that Koszta had with him his naturalization papers, demanded his surrender to him, and was compelled to train his guns upon the Austrian vessel before his demands were complied with. It was, however, to prevent bloodshed, agreed that Koszta should be placed in the hands of the French consul subject to the result of diplomatic negotiations between Austria and the United States. The celebrated correspondence between Mr. Marcy, Secretary of State, and Chevalier Hulsemann, the Austrian minister at Washington, which arose out of this affair, and resulted in the release and restoration to liberty of Koszta, attracted a great deal of public attention, and the position assumed by Mr. Marcy met the approval of the country and of Congress, who voted a gold medal to Captain Ingraham for his conduct in the affair. Upon what act of Congress then existing can any one lay his finger in support of the action of our government in this matter?

In Re Neagle, 135 U.S. 1, 10 S.Ct. 658, 34 L.Ed. 55 (1890). Are Justice Miller's statements on the Koszta Affair part of the holding or are they dicta? Do they have precedential significance?

SECTION 3. HISTORICAL PRACTICE

INTRODUCTORY NOTE

What does historical practice suggest about the allocation of war powers between Congress and the President? Over the hundreds of instances in which U.S. armed forces have been deployed abroad, Congress has declared war only eleven times—most recently against Romania in 1942. At the same time, Congress has authorized most major post-World War II conflicts by statute, including the recent deployment of U.S. forces to Afghanistan in 2001 and Iraq in 2003. Does the history suggest a settled view that congressional approval is constitutionally required for all uses of U.S. military force? For only uses of U.S. military force that rise above a certain threshold level of significance? Can the President act on his own authority when necessary to respond to a sudden threat to U.S. national security?

CONGRESSIONAL RESEARCH SERVICE, INSTANCES OF USE OF UNITED STATES ARMED FORCES ABROAD, 1798–2009

CRS Rep. RL32170 (Jan. 27, 2010) (footnotes omitted)
at http://opencrs.cdt.org/document/RL32170.

The following list reviews hundreds of instances in which the United States has utilized military forces abroad in situations of military conflict or potential conflict to protect U.S. citizens or promote U.S. interests. The list does not include covert actions or numerous instances in which U.S. forces have been stationed abroad since World War II in occupation forces or for participation in mutual security organizations, base agreements, or routine military assistance or training operations. Because of differing judgments over the actions to be included, other lists may include more or fewer instances.

The instances vary greatly in size of operation, legal authorization, and significance. The number of troops involved range from a few sailors or Marines landed to protect American lives and property to hundreds of thousands in Korea and Vietnam and millions in World War II. Some actions were of short duration and some lasted a number of years. In some instances a military officer acted without authorization; some actions were conducted solely under the President's powers as Chief Executive or Commander in Chief; other instances were authorized by Congress in some fashion; In eleven separate cases (listed in bold-face type) the United States formally declared war against foreign nations. For most of the instances listed, however, the status of the action under domestic or international law has not been addressed. Most instances listed since 1980, are summaries of U.S. military deployments reported to Congress by the President as a result of the War Powers Resolution. Several of these Presidential reports are summaries of activities related to an on-going operation previously reported. It is important to note that inclusion in this list does not connote either legality or level of significance of the instance described. . . .

1798–1800—*Undeclared Naval War with France*. This contest included land actions, such as that in the Dominican Republic, city of Puerto Plata, where marines captured a French privateer under the guns of the forts. . . .

1801–05—*Tripoli*. The First Barbary War, including the U.S.S. *George Washington* and *Philadelphia* affairs and the Eaton expedition, during which a few marines landed with United States Agent William Eaton to raise a force against Tripoli in an effort to free the crew of the *Philadelphia*. Tripoli declared war but not the United States. . . .

1806—*Mexico (Spanish territory)*. Capt. Z. M. Pike, with a platoon of troops, invaded Spanish territory at the headwaters of the Rio Grande on orders from Gen. James Wilkinson. He was made prisoner without resistance at a fort he constructed in present day Colorado, taken to Mexico, later released after seizure of his papers.

1806–10—*Gulf of Mexico*. American gunboats operated from New Orleans against Spanish and French privateers, off the Mississippi Delta, chiefly under Capt. John Shaw and Master Commandant David Porter.

1810—*West Florida (Spanish territory)*. Gov. Claiborne of Louisiana, on orders of the President, occupied with troops territory in dispute east of Mississippi River as far as the Pearl River, later the eastern boundary of Louisiana. He was authorized to seize as far east as the Perdido River.

1812—*Amelia Island and other parts of eastern Florida, then under Spain*. Temporary possession was authorized by President Madison and by Congress, to prevent occupation by any other power; but possession was obtained by Gen. George Matthews in so irregular a manner that his measures were disavowed by the President.

1812–15—War of 1812. On June 18, 1812, the United States declared war between the United States and the United Kingdom of Great Britain and Ireland. . . .

1813—*West Florida (Spanish territory).* On authority given by Congress, General Wilkinson seized Mobile Bay in April with 600 soldiers. A small Spanish garrison gave way. The U.S. advanced into disputed territory to the Perdido River, as projected in 1810. No fighting.

1813–14—*Marquesas Islands.* U.S. forces built a fort on island of Nukahiva to protect three prize ships which had been captured from the British.

1814—*Spanish Florida.* Gen. Andrew Jackson took Pensacola and drove out the British with whom the United States was at war.

1814–25—*Caribbean.* Engagements between pirates and American ships or squadrons took place repeatedly especially ashore and offshore about Cuba, Puerto Rico, Santo Domingo, and Yucatan. Three thousand pirate attacks on merchantmen were reported between 1815 and 1823. In 1822 Commodore James Biddle employed a squadron of two frigates, four sloops of war, two brigs, four schooners, and two gunboats in the West Indies.

1815—*Algier.* The second Barbary War was declared against the United States by the Dey of Algiers of the Barbary States, an act no reciprocated by the United States. Congress did authorize a military expedition by statutes. A large fleet under Decatur attacked Algiers and obtained indemnities.

1815—*Tripoli.* After securing an agreement from Algiers, Decatur demonstrated with his squadron at Tunis and Tripoli, where he secured indemnities for offenses during the War of 1812.

1816—*Spanish Florida.* United States forces destroyed Nicholls Fort, called also Negro Fort, which harbored raiders making forays into United States territory.

1816–18—*Spanish Florida–First Seminole War.* The Seminole Indians, whose area was a haven for escaped slaves and border ruffians, were attacked by troops under Generals Jackson and Gaines and pursued into northern Florida. Spanish posts were attacked and occupied, British citizens executed. . . .

1817—*Amelia Island (Spanish territory off Florida).* Under orders of President Monroe, United States forces landed and expelled a group of smugglers, adventurers, and freebooters.

1818—*Oregon.* The U.S.S. *Ontario*, dispatched from Washington, landed at the Columbia River and in August took possession of Oregon territory. Britain had conceded sovereignty but Russia and Spain asserted claims to the area.

1820–23—*Africa.* Naval units raided the slave traffic pursuant to the 1819 act of Congress.

1822—*Cuba.* United States naval forces suppressing piracy landed on the northwest coast of Cuba and burned a private station.

1823—*Cuba.* Brief landings in pursuit of pirates occurred April 8 near Escondido; April 16 near Cayo Blanco; July 11 at Siquapa Bay; July 21 at Cape Cruz; and October 23 at Camrioca.

[Authors' Note: The list continues with hundreds of similar incidents from 1824 to 2006, which are excluded here in the interest of brevity.]

. . . .

2007—*Terrorism threat/Kosovo/Afghanistan.* On June 15, 2007, the President sent to Congress "consistent" with the War Powers Resolution, a consolidated report giving details of ongoing United States military deployments and operations "in support of the war on terror," and in support of the NATO-led Kosovo Force (KFOR). The President reported that various U.S. "combat-equipped and combat-support forces" were deployed to "a number of locations in the Central, Pacific, European (KFOR), and Southern Command areas of operation" and were engaged in combat operations against al-Qaida terrorists and their supporters. The U.S. is currently "pursuing and engaging remnant al-Qaida and Taliban fighters in Afghanistan." U.S. forces in Afghanistan currently total approximately 25,945. Of this total, "approximately 14,340 are assigned to the International Security Assistance Force (ISAF) in Afghanistan." The U.S. military continues to support peacekeeping operations in Kosovo, specifically, the NATO-led Kosovo Force (KFOR). Currently, the U.S. contribution to KFOR in Kosovo is approximately 1,584 military personnel.

2007—*Terrorism threat/Kosovo/Afghanistan.* On December 14, 2007, the President sent to Congress "consistent with the War Powers Resolution," a consolidated report giving details of ongoing United States military deployments and operations "in support of the war on terror," and in support of the NATO-led Kosovo Force (KFOR). The President reported that various U.S. "combat-equipped and combat-support forces" were deployed to "a number of locations in the Central, Pacific, European, and Southern Command areas of operation" and were engaged in combat operations against al-Qaida terrorists and their supporters. The U.S. is currently "pursuing and engaging remnant al-Qaida and Taliban fighters in Afghanistan." U.S. forces in Afghanistan currently total approximately 25,900. Of this total, "approximately 15,180 are assigned to the International Security Assistance Force (ISAF) in Afghanistan." The U.S. military continues to support peacekeeping operations in Kosovo, specifically, the NATO-led Kosovo Force (KFOR). Currently, the U.S. contribution to KFOR in Kosovo is approximately 1,498 military personnel.

2008—*Terrorism threat/Kosovo/Afghanistan.* On June 13, 2008, the President sent to Congress "consistent with the War Powers Resolution," a consolidated report giving details of ongoing United States military deployments and operations "in support of the war on terror," and in support of the NATO-led Kosovo Force (KFOR). The President reported that various U.S. "combat-equipped and combat-support forces" were deployed to "a number of locations in the Central, Pacific, European, and Southern Command areas of operation" and were engaged in combat operations against al-Qaida terrorists and their supporters. The U.S. is actively "pursuing and engaging remnant al-Qaida and Taliban fighters in Afghanistan." U.S. forces in Afghanistan currently total approximately 31122. Of this total, "approximately 14,275 are assigned to the International Security Assistance Force (ISAF) in Afghanistan." The U.S. military continues to support peacekeeping operations in Kosovo, specifically, the NATO-led Kosovo Force (KFOR). Currently, the U.S. contribution to KFOR in Kosovo is approximately 1,500 military personnel.

2008—*Terrorism threat/Kosovo/Afghanistan*. On December 16, 2008, the President sent to Congress "consistent with the War Powers Resolution," a consolidated report giving details of ongoing United States military deployments and operations "in support of the war on terror," and in support of the NATO-led Kosovo Force (KFOR). The President reported that various U.S. "combat-equipped and combat-support forces" were deployed to "a number of locations in the Central, Pacific, European, Southern, and Africa Command areas of operation" and were engaged in combat operations against al-Qaida and their supporters. The United States is "actively pursuing and engaging remnant al-Qaida and Taliban fighters in Afghanistan." U.S. forces in Afghanistan total approximately 31, 000. Of this total, "approximately 13, 000 are assigned to the International Security Assistance Force (ISAF) in Afghanistan." The U.S. military continues to support peacekeeping operations in Kosovo, specifically the NATO-led Kosovo Force (KFOR). The current U.S. contribution to KFOR in Kosovo is about 1,500 military personnel.

2009—*Terrorism threat/Afghanistan/Iraq/Kosovo*. On June 15, 2009, the President sent to Congress "consistent with the War Powers Resolution," a supplemental consolidated report, giving details of "ongoing contingency operations overseas." The report noted that the total number of U.S. forces in Afghanistan was "approximately 58,000," of which approximately 20,000 are assigned to the International Security Assistance Force (ISAF) in Afghanistan. The United States continues to pursue and engage "remaining al-Qa'ida and Taliban forces in Afghanistan." The U.S. also continues to deploy military forces in support of the Multinational Force (MNF) in Iraq. The current U.S. contribution to this effort is "approximately 138,000 U.S. military personnel." U.S. military operations continue in Kosovo, as part of the NATO-led Kosovo Force (KFOR). Presently the United States contributes approximately 1,400 U.S. military personnel to KFOR. In addition, the United states continues to deploy "U.S. combat-equipped forces to help enhance the counterterrorism capabilities of our friends and allies" not only in the Horn of Africa region, but globally through "maritime interception operations on the high seas" aimed at blocking the "movement, arming and financing of international terrorists."

2009—*Terrorism threat/Afghanistan/Iraq/Kosovo*. On December 5, 2009, the President sent to Congress "consistent with the War Powers Resolution," a consolidated report, giving details of "global deployments of U.S. Armed Forces equipped for combat." The report detailed "ongoing U.S. contingency operations overseas." The report noted that the total number of U.S. forces in Afghanistan was "approximately 68,000," of which approximately 34,000 are assigned to the International Security Assistance Force (ISAF) in Afghanistan. The United States continues to pursue and engage "remaining al-Qa'ida and Taliban forces in Afghanistan." The United States has deployed "various combat-equipped forces to a number of locations in the Central, Pacific, European, Southern and African Command areas of operation" in support of anti-terrorist and anti-al-Qa'ida actions. The United States also continues to deploy military forces in Iraq to "maintain security and stability" there. These Iraqi operations continue pursuant to the terms of a bilateral agreement between the United States and Iraq, which entered into force on January 1, 2009. The current U.S. force level in Iraq is "approximately 116,000 U.S. military personnel." U.S. military operations continue in Kosovo, as part of the NATO-led Kosovo Force (KFOR). Presently the United States contributes approximately 1,475 U.S. military personnel to KFOR. In addition, the United States continues to deploy "U.S. combat-equipped forces to assist in enhancing the counterterrorism capabilities of our friends and allies" not only in the Horn of Africa region, but globally through "maritime interception operations on the high seas" aimed at blocking the "movement, arming and financing of international terrorists."

NOTES ON OVERVIEW OF HISTORICAL PRECEDENTS

1. *Reading the Tea Leaves*. What significance do the incidents described above have in shaping the contours of executive and congressional war powers? How relevant is it that Congress has declared war only eleven times? Do the incidents above represent, in Justice Frankfurter's words, ". . . a gloss on executive power vested in the President," meaning that they show a robust ability of the president to engage in uses of military force without formal approval from Congress? Or are they simply, as Jules Lobel argued during a district court hearing in *Dellums v. Bush*, ". . . very minor uses of force to chase out some mobs [and] to protect some citizens. . . .", which should not be regarded as relevant when considering the power to deploy military forces on a large-scale? *See infra*, Section 4.

2. *Practical Consequences*. Are there any practical consequences that flow from the President acting pursuant to a "declaration of war," pursuant to an "authorization to use military force," or without any Congressional action? Consider the following:

> With respect to domestic law, a declaration of war automatically triggers many standby statutory authorities conferring special powers on

the President with respect to the military, foreign trade, transportation, communications, manufacturing, alien enemies, etc. In contrast, no standby authorities appear to be triggered automatically by an authorization for the use of force, although the executive branch has argued, with varying success, that the authorization to use force in response to the terrorist attacks of 2001 provided a statutory exception to certain statutory prohibitions.

Most statutory standby authorities do not expressly require a declaration of war to be actualized but can be triggered by a declaration of national emergency or simply by the existence of a state of war; however, courts have sometimes construed the word "war" in a statute as implying a formal declaration, leading Congress to enact clarifying amendments in two cases. Declarations of war and authorizations for the use of force waive the time limitations otherwise applicable to the use of force imposed by the War Powers Resolution.

CRS Report, Declarations of War and Authorizations for the Use of Military Force: Historical Background and Legal Implications, Rep. 31133 (Mar. 17, 2011).

3. *Looking Ahead.* Consider the use of U.S. armed forces to combat terrorism threats following 9/11. Does the contemporary expansiveness of operations (e.g., Afghanistan, Djibouti, Eritrea, Ethiopia, Georgia, Iraq, Pakistan, the Philippines, Kenya, Yemen, etc.) represent a departure from past precedent? Does it suggest a need for the President to act on his own in subtle, careful, and expeditious ways? Or does it suggest that even small combat operations have an important overall effect on U.S. national security, including the potential for inflaming terrorism or antagonizing U.S. allies, such that Congress must play a role in approving deployments?

4. *Covert Operations.* Note that the introduction to the CRS report stipulates that the list of incidents ". . . does not include covert actions or numerous instances in which U.S. forces have been stationed abroad since World War II in occupation forces or for participation in mutual security organizations, base agreements, or routine military assistance or training operations." What bearing do such actions have in assessing customary war powers practice?

SECTION 4. RECENT MAJOR INCIDENTS

INTRODUCTORY NOTE ON THE FIRST GULF WAR (1990–1991)

On August 2, 1990, Iraqi forces under Saddam Hussein invaded Kuwait and swiftly overwhelmed the Kuwaiti military. Thereafter, Iraq declared that it had annexed Kuwait. The same day, the U.N. Security Council adopted Resolution 660 (Aug. 2, 1990) condemning the invasion and demanding that Iraq withdraw immediately and unconditionally. On August 6, 1990, U.S. Secretary of Defense Dick Cheney met with King Fahd bin Abdul Aziz Al Saud in Riyadh to pledge that the United States would defend Saudi Arabia in the event of an attack by Iraq. King Fahd agreed to the deployment of American and allied troops in Saudi Arabia under what became known as

Operation Desert Shield. By early 1991, the allied multinational force had swollen to nearly 500,000 soldiers.

Diplomatic efforts through the fall of 1990, including a series of increasingly stringent Security Council resolutions, failed to secure an Iraqi withdrawal. In November 1990, the Security Council adopted Resolution 678 authorizing states cooperating with Kuwait to "use all necessary means to uphold and implement" the Security Council's resolutions, unless Iraq complied by January 15, 1991.

In late 1990, President Bush made a number of statements suggesting that congressional authority was not necessary to authorize U.S. military intervention to expel Iraq from Kuwait. Based on the Constitution, early case law, and historical practice, do you agree with that position?

U.N. SECURITY COUNCIL RESOLUTION 678

(Nov. 29, 1990).

The Security Council,

. . . .

Acting under Chapter VII of the Charter,

1. *Demands* that Iraq comply fully with resolution 660 (1990) [demanding immediate and unconditional withdrawal of forces from Kuwait] and all subsequent relevant resolutions, and decides, while maintaining all its decisions, to allow Iraq one final opportunity, as a pause of goodwill, to do so;

2. *Authorizes* Member States co-operating with the Government of Kuwait, unless Iraq on or before 15 January 1991 fully implements, as set forth in paragraph 1 above, the above-mentioned resolutions, to use all necessary means to uphold and implement resolution 660 (1990) and all subsequent relevant resolutions and to restore international peace and security in the area;

3. *Requests* all States to provide appropriate support for the actions undertaken in pursuance of paragraph 2 above;

4. *Requests* the States concerned to keep the Security Council regularly informed on the progress of actions undertaken pursuant to paragraphs 2 and 3 above;

5. *Decides* to remain seized of the matter.

TRANSCRIPT OF HEARING BEFORE JUDGE HAROLD H. GREENE IN *DELLUMS v. BUSH*

Transcript at 37–54 (D.D.C. Dec. 4, 1990).

MR. (JULES) LOBEL [CENTER FOR CONSTITUTIONAL RIGHTS]: Your Honor, the question before this court is straightforward: can the President initiate a war against Iraq for the purpose of driving it from Kuwait without first obtaining the prior authorization of Congress. The President says he can; the Constitution says he cannot.

Here the threat that an explicit constitutional provision will be violated is clear. The President has repeatedly threatened Iraq with attack unless it withdraws from Kuwait. Just yesterday, Secretary Cheney said, "We cannot wait for sanctions to work. We must have the option to use force."

Secondly, we are putting into place all of the means for driving Iraq out of Kuwait. We have sent close to 400,000 troops to the Persian Gulf in order to, in the President's words, "develop an adequate offensive military option."

We have traversed the globe and obtained United Nations authority to use force. In short, we have done everything necessary to put into place an offensive military action against Iraq except for one thing, and that is obtained the necessary congressional authority under our Constitution.

. . . .

THE COURT: How does this situation differ from the fighting in Korea?

MR. LOBEL: Your Honor, it may very well be that the Korean War was unconstitutional. It is a position that I will take, that I have written about, and most legal scholars and most people who have thought about the issue would say it was unconstitutional.

However, even in that situation, there is some distinction. There, the President was responding to a surprise attack by North Korea which threatened immediately to totally overwhelm South Korea. There was some time urgency. Here there is no time urgency.

Secondly, that unconstitutional war was not challenged prior to its initiation. [Within weeks] Congress met, and they approved budgetary authorizations, and therefore the question became different. Your Honor, we are here faced with a situation where the plaintiffs are coming in prior to the initiation of war, and saying, we must vote on it before war begins.

THE COURT: I take it you're not conceding that budgetary authorization is the equivalent of a declaration of war.

MR. LOBEL: I certainly am not. It's precisely for that reason, and precisely for what this court said in *Mitchell v. Laird* that every schoolboy knows, that once we are in war there is tremendous pressure on Congress to fund the troops who are out there fighting and dying, that this court must act now before we get into war and before Congress is faced, and this country is faced, and the courts will be faced with that impossible dilemma. It is that reason that the Constitution grants Congress the power to decide whether to go to war prior to its initiation.

Now, the defendant here doesn't like the way the Constitution reads. He would rather the Constitution read, the President can go to war subject to whatever after-the-fact ratification that Congress wants to address. But fortunately, I think for our country and for our history and for our constitutional government, the framers thought otherwise, and this court should act to affirm the explicit command of the Constitution.

We are not talking here about constitutional silence. This case does not raise the question of the silences of the Constitution in the areas of overlapping jurisdiction on foreign affairs. This case raises an explicit constitutional command, which every one of the framers knew what it meant, and that is we cannot go to war without congressional authorization.

. . . .

. . . The Constitution requires an affirmative vote of Congress before we go to war. Therefore, if Congress is silent, the Constitution tells us we cannot go to war for whatever reason: Congress may be divided, Congress may be uncertain, Congress may not want to move. The explicit command of the Constitution is that absent affirmative authorization, the nation cannot be put in a state of war.

Secondly, here there is no question that plaintiffs' dispute is not with their fellow Congress people. In 1973, Congress passed by overwhelming majorities the War Powers Resolution. Section 2(C) of the War Powers Resolution states that the President cannot introduce troops into hostilities unless (1), there is a congressional declaration of war; (2), there is other explicit congressional authorization, which does not include budgetary authorization; or (3), there is an attack on U.S. troops or U.S. territory. None of these three things have occurred here. It is therefore clear that Congress has spoken and has passed a law which is still the law of the land.

THE COURT: Of course, a number of presidents have ignored that.

MR. LOBEL: Exactly. That is why we have a confrontation before you today. Congress has spoken, the Constitution has clearly spoken; the President has ignored what the Constitution says and what Congress has said. The President says, I have my own view of the Constitution. I don't care what you say; the courts have no power to say anything—that's what they tell us today . . . —and I will do what I want.

. . . .

. . . We are not talking about some minor use of force. We are not talking about something that could be argued about. We are talking about, in the words of the Chairman of the Joint Chiefs of Staff, a war, a substantial war, a war which will be coordinated by land, sea, and air forces, designed to drive the fourth largest army in the world out of territory it now occupies.

I don't see how there can be any argument, by any reasonable person, that that decision is for Congress to make. I think the President is simply snubbing his nose at Congress, and I think that the court must say he cannot continue to do so.

. . . .

MR. GERSON [U.S. DEPT. OF JUSTICE]: Needless to say, I view Constitutional language and Constitutional history somewhat differently than my brother. Disputes of the sort that are embodied in this lawsuit are far from novel and were well within the compass of understanding and address of the Constitution's framers. From the earliest days of the republic, which saw Washington's pursuit of the undeclared Indian wars, and Jefferson's campaign against the Barbary Pirates, to McKinley's unilateral dispatch of troops to China to help put down the Boxer Rebellion, to Franklin D. Roosevelt's deviations from Congressional neutrality policy to aid those fighting Hitler before war was declared, to events relating to the military conduct of all nine of the Presidents since then, there have been disputes growing out of the tension between the President's powers as commander in chief and director of the nation's foreign affairs and—

THE COURT: Are you suggesting that the War Power's clause at Article I, Section 8, Clause 11, I think it is, means nothing?

MR. GERSON: No, I'm not suggesting that at all.

THE COURT: When does it apply?

MR. GERSON: Well, what the framers did in Article I, Section 8, which was understood then and now in the context of the vast international expectations and consequences, both internationally and domestic civil rights and the like of [what] a declared war constitutes, they set forth covalent powers, which to declare a war and carry one out had to be jointly exercised. Under this formulation, each branch might advance its conduct in support of belligerency ahead of the other: the President undertaking it, Congress in declaring it. But each could check the other, Congress securing its position through the power of the purse.

Moreover, the framers, and those in government since the framers, envisioned self-initiated military action—that is what these plaintiffs would call offensive military action—but short of war and its profound domestic and international consequences. Perhaps the best evidence, while it has some Constitutional problems that are not relevant here, and I read the literal language significantly differently from Mr. Lobel, is the so-called war powers resolution itself, which clearly envisions, by its literal terms, the introduction of troops into hostility before a declaration of war.

The Congress, which spoke in 1973, had the same understanding that the framers had that has been had since the early days of this country. A declared war means plenty. It's extremely consequential. One need only look to what has gone on during declared wars and how hard it is to get out of one once one starts. International law questions are raised. That's understood.

. . . .

[T]he congress has an ultimate check. . . . While the president is commander in chief, besides being the leader of foreign affairs, it's the congress under Article I, Section 8 which not only declares war but which maintains the armies and navies and which funds them.

THE COURT: Of course then the provision for declaring war is superfluous because Congress has the power to cut off funds anyway.

MR. GERSON: Well, I suggested earlier that the provision for declaring war is not superfluous, that a declared war always has been going back, really, to the 16th century, and before it, but in terms of the development of modern law, been understood to carry grave consequence. Title 50 of the United States Code consists of five or six volumes that are full of the consequences to the application of domestic law and sovereign immunity that occur during a declared war.

Internationally the consequences are grave. What was understood internationally, both at the time of the framers and ever since, is when both political branches of the government are acting in synchronization going forward exercising the declaring war power, the war-making power, the raising and support armies and navies, the power of the purse and the diplomatic power, that the entire fortune of the nation, and, indeed, its existence has been pledged. Just as the risk is the same on the other side, the juridical consequences of a declared war are immense. The term means a great deal.

. . . .

THE COURT: Isn't there some historical evidence, legislative history, so to speak, indicating that one reason for this clause was to make certain that one person does not get the country involved in a war? . . .

. . . .

MR. GERSON: Well, I wish I could say, with absolute certainty, that we could know the answer to that, but let me tell you what I think the evidence is and, in doing so, rebut some of the points that the plaintiffs make about it. They cite Madison and his offering of an amendment to change making war to declaring war, declare war ultimately getting into the Constitution.

What they neglect to point out is following Madison's offering it and reciting a rationale that's very much the same as what your Honor described, that the Convention didn't support him, that they voted it down. It was only at a later time when I believe Rufus King raised a similarly worded provision but advanced the argument that it was the President who should carry out this form of activity—in other words, the individual—that the amendment passed and the language got into the Constitution. At the least, it's not at all certain, and I believe I am accurately quoting the history.

What we can say, and I believe that this runs true all the way through, the conduct of belligerency without a declaration of war was well-known to the framers. It existed for a long period of time throughout history. The events which followed the Constitution are so repetitive, where a vast majority of the Presidents have undertaken activities of this kind, that it vindicates what the framers said and did.

This was well within the compass of their expectation and understanding. They differentiated a declared war from the conduct of a number of kinds of activities, including offensive ones. There are checks in there. There are ways that a Congress could withdraw and paralyze the executive from acting, and that was well understood.

Again, I think that since the plaintiffs cited the source, they ought to have to live with it. If they believe that the War Powers Resolution is authority for any position that they are stating here, they well ought to look at its literal language which allows for the introduction of troops into hostilities. In other words, the conduct of offensive military action, without a war being declared. A number of requirements are then set out in the War Powers Resolution, some of them, as I say, posing significant legal and constitutional difficulty. But nevertheless, it was well within the compass of the understanding of the Congress in general that passed the act that you could have lawful offensive hostilities without a declaration of war. It then came Congress's time to decide whether or not one would be declared, which raises another point.

One can safely say, since the Constitution says it, that it is the role of the Congress to declare war, but in analyzing the right to vote of these plaintiffs, let's note that there is nothing in the Constitution that says when that vote has to take place or when that declaration has to take place. Again, I want to address your point of the consequence and the significance of the declaration. There just isn't any. The Constitution does not say war must be declared in advance of hostilities.

As I say, the historical understanding was otherwise. The historical experience since then has been otherwise. The understanding of Congress within the last few decades is different from that.

DELLUMS v. BUSH

752 F.Supp. 1141, 1143–45 (D.D.C. 1990) (footnotes omitted).

HAROLD H. GREENE, DISTRICT JUDGE.

This is a lawsuit by a number of members of Congress who request an injunction directed to the President of the United States to prevent him from initiating an offensive attack against Iraq without first securing a declaration of war or other explicit congressional authorization for such action.

I.

The factual background is, briefly, as follows. On August 2, 1990, Iraq invaded the neighboring country of Kuwait. President George Bush almost immediately sent United States military forces to the Persian Gulf area to deter Iraqi aggression and to preserve the integrity of Saudi Arabia. The United States, generally by presidential order and at times with congressional concurrence, also took other steps, including a blockade of Iraq, which were approved by the United Nations Security Council, and participated in by a great many other nations.

On November 8, 1990, President Bush announced a substantial increase in the Persian Gulf military deployment, raising the troop level significantly above the 230,000 then present in the area. At the same time, the President stated that the objective was to provide "an adequate offensive military option" should that be necessary to achieve such goals as the withdrawal of Iraqi forces from Kuwait. Secretary of Defense Richard Cheney likewise referred to the ability of the additional military forces "to conduct *offensive* military operations."

The House of Representatives and the Senate have in various ways expressed their support for the President's past and present actions in the Persian Gulf. However, the Congress was not asked for, and it did not take, action pursuant to Article I, Section 8, Clause 11 of the Constitution "to declare war" on Iraq. On November 19, 1990, the congressional plaintiffs brought this action, which proceeds on the premise that the initiation of offensive United States military action is imminent, that such action would be unlawful in the absence of a declaration of war by the Congress, and that a war without concurrence by the Congress would deprive the congressional plaintiffs of the voice to which they are entitled under the Constitution. The Department of Justice, acting on behalf of the President, is opposing the motion for preliminary injunction, and it has also moved to dismiss. Plaintiffs thereafter moved for summary judgment.

. . . .

II. POLITICAL QUESTION

It is appropriate first to sketch out briefly the constitutional and legal framework in which the current controversy arises. Article I, Section 8, Clause 11 of the Constitution grants to the Congress the power "To declare War." To the extent that this unambiguous direction requires construction or explanation, it is provided by the framers' comments that they felt it to be unwise to entrust the momentous power to involve the nation in a war to the President alone; Jefferson explained that he desired "an effectual check to the Dog of war"; James Wilson similarly expressed the expectation that this system would guard against hostilities being initiated by a single man. Even Abraham Lincoln, while a Congressman, said more than half a century later that "*no one man* should hold the power of bringing" war upon us.

The congressional power to declare war does not stand alone, however, but it is accompanied by powers granted to the President. Article II, Section 1, Clause 1 and Section 2 provide that "[t]he executive powers shall be vested in a President of the United States of America," and that "[t]he President shall be Commander in Chief of the Army and Navy. . . ."

It is the position of the Department of Justice on behalf of the President that the simultaneous existence of all these provisions renders it impossible to isolate the war-declaring power. The Department further argues that the design of the Constitution is to have the various war-and military-related provisions construed and acting together, and that their harmonization is a political rather than a legal question. In short, the Department relies on the political question doctrine.

. . . .

This claim on behalf of the Executive is far too sweeping to be accepted by the courts. If the Executive had the sole power to determine that any particular offensive military operation, no matter how vast, does not constitute war-making but only an offensive military attack, the congressional power to declare war will be at the mercy of a semantic decision by the Executive. Such an "interpretation" would evade the plain language of the Constitution, and it cannot stand.

That is not to say that, assuming that the issue is factually close or ambiguous or fraught with intricate technical military and diplomatic baggage, the courts would not defer to the political branches to determine whether or not particular hostilities might qualify as a "war." However, here the forces involved are of such magnitude and significance as to present no serious claim that a war would not ensue if they became engaged in combat, and it is therefore clear that congressional approval is required if Congress desires to become involved.

CONGRESSIONAL DEBATE ON THE AUTHORIZATION FOR USE OF MILITARY FORCE AGAINST IRAQ

102nd Cong., 1st Sess., 137 Cong. Rec. S110, S146, S365, H180 (daily ed. Jan. 10, 1991 and Jan. 12, 1991).

[SENATOR MOYNIHAN]: ... The President told a press conference on November 30, when asked, "What do you think your responsibilities are to Congress and the people that elect them," he said, "Full consultation." Nothing more. When asked on December 28 by David Frost, "Don't you need an authorization from Congress, in effect, for war?" He said, "We have used military force 200 times in history. I think there have been five declarations of war." In effect, he claimed that he did not need congressional support to do what, clearly, the Constitution requires of him.

This is an idea—that Congress decides whether to go to war—that simply eroded in the cold war with the prospect of nuclear confrontation, permitting no time for reflection and consultation. The New York Times wrote this morning, very ably, I think, that Congress' constitutional warmaking authority fell into disuse during the cold war, so much that we can scarcely even remember the number of times that we have declared war. There is a notion that we declared war once during World War II. We declared war three times against six different countries in one form or another.

In the aftermath of the cold war, what we find is a kind of time warp in which we are acting in an old mode in response to a new situation.

. . . .

[SENATOR EXON]: I believe that any objective reading of article I, section 8 of the Constitution yields the conclusion that the architects of that document—the supreme law of our land—gave Congress the power to declare war.

For those who find inconsistency between such an interpretation and the powers afforded the President as Commander in Chief of the military in article II, section 2, the historical record of the Constitutional Convention of 1787 and the Federalist Papers unambiguously document the intentions of our Founding Fathers and affirm the Congress' crucial role.

The Presidents, as Commander in Chief, have sent U.S. forces into combat or potential combat over 200 times in our Nation's history. Only five times has the Executive action been accompanied by a congressional declaration of war. The prevalence of warmaking without a decree has led many in the present day to conclude that the President, therefore, has de facto power to declare war. To the contrary, repeated violation of the constitutional separation of powers is not synonymous with an invalidation or rewriting of the Constitution. If historically the executive branch has exceeded its powers in this respect, so must the Congress share responsibility. As John Hart Ely, a law professor at Stanford University, writes:

> A Congress that lets the President call the shots on war and peace, and devotes itself instead to the construction of private political bomb shelters, is not what the Framers of the Constitution had in mind in vesting the war power in the legislative process.

The voice of Congress must be heard before January 15.

. . . .

[SENATOR INOUYE]: Mr. President, I have read the arguments regarding the inherent powers of the Commander in Chief and I know there have been instances when Presidents have committed U.S. forces to combat without first receiving the assent of Congress. Most frequently these lapses have occurred when U.S. forces in the field were reeling under the armed assault of a foreign foe and were, in fact, already at war. I believe, however, that these were exceptional circumstances which in no way negate or diminish the authority of this body nor its responsibility to the people of the United States. It may be that our predecessors were not sufficiently vigilant in defending the constitutional authority of the Congress to declare war. There is no reason, however, why we in this Chamber today must repeat the errors of the past. To meet our responsibilities, we must insist that the Congress must give its explicit authorization for the use of force before the President can enter into battle.

. . . .

[REP. FIELDS]: Our real power is in the ability to authorize and appropriate moneys. But if you look at the precedents since 1789, there have been 218 instances of foreign involvement by U.S. troops. Congress, by joint resolution with Presidential signature affixed, has formally declared war only five times. In all other instances the President, utilizing his constitutional authority, deployed American forces without the specific approval of Congress.

Now, the first two instances of such use were by President John Adams in the undeclared war with France between 1798 and 1800, and Thomas Jefferson in the war with Tripoli between 1801 and 1805.

I certainly think John Adams and Thomas Jefferson knew the intent of the Framers of our Constitution.

History and practice have never held that the war declaration clause of the Constitution is a restraint on the Executive to utilize Armed Forces abroad. I am not afraid to let my constituents know how I plan to vote.

I plan to support the President as our Commander in Chief. I think he has identified a clear purpose that has a national security interest of this country affixed.

AUTHORIZATION FOR USE OF MILITARY FORCE AGAINST IRAQ

H.J. Res. 77, Pub. L. No. 102–1, 105 Stat. 3 (Jan. 14, 1991).

JOINT RESOLUTION

To authorize the use of United States Armed Forces pursuant to United Nations Security Council Resolution 678.

Whereas the Government of Iraq without provocation invaded and occupied the territory of Kuwait on August 2, 1990;

Whereas both the House of Representatives (in H.J. Res. 658 of the 101st Congress) and the Senate (in S. Con. Res. 147 of the 101st Congress) have condemned Iraq's invasion of Kuwait and declared their support for international action to reverse Iraq's aggression;

Whereas, Iraq's conventional, chemical, biological, and nuclear weapons and ballistic missile programs and its demonstrated willingness to use weapons of mass destruction pose a grave threat to world peace;

Whereas the international community has demanded that Iraq withdraw unconditionally and immediately from Kuwait and that Kuwait's independence and legitimate government be restored;

Whereas the United Nations Security Council repeatedly affirmed the inherent right of individual or collective self-defense in response to the armed attack by Iraq against Kuwait in accordance with Article 51 of the United Nations Charter;

Whereas, in the absence of full compliance by Iraq with its resolutions, the United Nations Security Council in Resolution 678 has authorized member states of the United Nations to use all necessary means, after January 15, 1991, to uphold and implement all relevant Security Council resolutions and to restore international peace and security in the area; and

Whereas Iraq has persisted in its illegal occupation of, and brutal aggression against Kuwait:

Now, therefore, be it

Resolved by the Senate and House of Representatives of the United States of America in Congress assembled,

SEC. 1. SHORT TITLE.

This joint resolution may be cited as the "Authorization for Use of Military Force Against Iraq Resolution".

SEC. 2. AUTHORIZATION FOR USE OF UNITED STATES ARMED FORCES.

(a) AUTHORIZATION.—The President is authorized, subject to subsection (b), to use United States Armed Forces pursuant to United Nations Security Council Resolution 678 (1990) in order to achieve implementation of Security Council Resolutions 660, 661, 662, 664, 665, 666, 667, 669, 670, 674, and 677.

(b) REQUIREMENT FOR DETERMINATION THAT USE OF MILITARY FORCE IS NECESSARY.—Before exercising the authority granted in subsection (a), the President shall make available to the Speaker of the House of Representatives and the President pro tempore of the Senate his determination that—

(1) the United States has used all appropriate diplomatic and other peaceful means to obtain compliance by Iraq with the United Nations Security Council resolutions cited in subsection (a); and

(2) that those efforts have not been and would not be successful in obtaining such compliance.

(c) WAR POWERS RESOLUTION REQUIREMENTS.—

(1) SPECIFIC STATUTORY AUTHORIZATION.—Consistent with section 8(a)(1) of the War Powers Resolution, the Congress declares that this section is intended to constitute specific statutory authorization within the meaning of section 5(b) of the War Powers Resolution.

(2) APPLICABILITY OF OTHER REQUIREMENTS.—Nothing in this resolution supersedes any requirement of the War Powers Resolution.

SEC. 3. REPORTS TO CONGRESS.

At least once every 60 days, the President shall submit to the Congress a summary on the status of efforts to obtain compliance by Iraq with the resolutions adopted by the United Nations Security Council in response to Iraq's aggression.

MICHAEL J. GLENNON, THE GULF WAR AND THE CONSTITUTION

70 Foreign Affairs 84, 84–90 (Spring 1991) (some footnotes omitted).

During the January 1991 debate on whether to go to war in the Persian Gulf, many members of Congress were delighted at the legislature's response. "The Constitution, the American people and the cause of freedom have been served well," House minority leader Robert Michel (R–Ill.) said. Senator Strom Thurmond (R–S.C.) commented, "We have demonstrated to the world the meaning of democracy." Senator Sam Nunn (D–Ga.) rose to "commend President Bush for recognizing Congress' constitutional role." And House Foreign Affairs Committee Chairman Dante Fascell (D–Fla.) exclaimed: "He [the president] acknowledged the principle! ... This is very important. By specific language, Congress authorized the war!" After four months of controversy about the allocation of the power to make war, it seemed easy to conclude, as did Representative Richard Durbin (D–Ill.), that "the United States Constitution had prevailed."

Easy, but wrong.

Starting from President Bush's unilateral commitment to defend Saudi Arabia and proceeding to Congress' jury-rigged approval, the episode represented a textbook example of how an audacious executive, acquiescent legislature and deferential judiciary have pushed the Constitution's system of separation of powers steadily backwards toward the monopolistic system of King George III. When President Bush finally requested legislative approval in a letter to Congress January 8, 1991, he never acknowledged that statutory authorization was constitutionally required. In fact, the president said that he still believed he had the authority to act without legislative authorization. "I don't think I need it," he said the next day, and White House aides hinted that the administration had the right to defy any restrictions that Congress might impose.

. . . .

The congressional debate on explicit authorization for the Gulf War was effectively over long before it began. It should have begun on August 7, 1990, the day after Secretary of Defense Dick Cheney announced the U.S. commitment to defend Saudi Arabia in the event of an attack by Iraq, which had overrun Kuwait four days earlier. John Kelly, assistant secretary of state for near eastern and south Asian affairs, had previously reminded a House Foreign Affairs subcommittee that the United States had no mutual security treaty with Kuwait, and the same applied to other gulf states.

The commitment was thus made as a sole executive agreement—an agreement more sweeping in its terms than any of the seven mutual security treaties to which the United States is party, for none of those contains an ironclad commitment to go to war. The administration could have easily, and probably successfully, sought congressional approval for sending troops to the gulf. Congress was in session and was willing and able to act quickly. In fact, each house adopted measures condemning the August 2 invasion on the very day it occurred.

The train was set in motion, therefore, by a promise of dubious constitutionality. Alexander Hamilton spoke for many of the Founding Fathers when he described the requirement of Senate advice and consent to a treaty as one of the "best digested and unexceptional parts of the plan," since it was "unsafe and improper to entrust that power to an elective magistrate of four years' duration." "The history of human conduct," Hamilton believed, "does not warrant that exalted opinion of human virtue which would make it wise in a nation to commit interests of so delicate and momentous a kind as those which concern its intercourse with the rest of the world to the sole disposal of a magistrate, created and circumstanced, as would be a president of the United States." Time-honored custom reinforced the proposition that a mutual security commitment could be made only with the advice and consent of two-thirds of the Senate—a requirement that cannot be dispensed with by calling a treaty something other than a treaty.

But nary a word was heard from Congress. It mattered naught that the United States was now committed to defend a feudal monarchy where women could not drive cars, adulterers were stoned and American chaplains would be forced to cover their religious insignia and conduct services clandestinely. Instead, members had nothing but praise for the president's bold response. When on August 5 President Bush announced—again with no congressional consultation, let alone approval—that Iraq's invasion of Kuwait "will not stand," members of Congress applauded. Few then cared how this invasion would be undone, or when and even whether Congress might be asked to approve its undoing. David Boren (D–Okla.), chairman of the Senate Intelligence Committee, was asked on September 12 whether the president should have at least consulted Congress before sending troops to the gulf. "No, I think the president should be supported on that point," he said. "It is extremely important that we project absolute unity." Only on November 8, when the president claimed the need for an "adequate offensive military option" and decided to double to nearly half a million the number of U.S. troops in Saudi Arabia, did congressional voices ask from what source the chief executive drew this extraordinary authority to place the nation at war without legislative approval.

The Bush administration, like its predecessor, had on other issues curiously purported to find constitutional insight in "the intent of the framers." Yet once the intent was inconveniently unsupportive, that interest vanished. And there can be no doubt that it was unsupportive....

....

[The] observations of the framers are familiar. That their judgment retains wisdom for contemporary policymakers is suggested by the functional attributes of the two branches. One obvious advantage that Congress brings to the decision to go to war is diversity of opinion. Lincoln knew the value of diverse opinion and legislative deliberation. He said:

> In a certain sense, and to a certain extent, [the president] is the representative of the people. He is elected by them, as well as Congress is. But can he, in the nature [of] things, know the wants of the people, as well as three hundred other men, coming from all the various localities of the nation? If so, where is the propriety of having a Congress?[3]

The safety and well-being of the U.S. forces engaged in combat are enhanced if adversaries as well as allies understand that the American public is resolutely behind them. It has been said often but is worth repeating: if a war—or any other foreign policy—cannot be sold to Congress, it cannot be sold to the American people. The national interest is ill served when a president embarks on a military initiative that lacks public support and, for political reasons, must be curtailed.

Congressional participation in a decision to use offensive force against Iraq would of course not preclude error. Congress is not immune to war-making blunders, nor is it necessarily more disinclined to use force; indeed, Capitol Hill is not territory foreign to hawkish hysteria. Yet history has provided little reason for heavier reliance on presidential judgment in war-powers matters. Lincoln said:

> The provision of the Constitution giving the war-making power to Congress, was dictated, as I understand it, by the following reasons. Kings had always been involving and impoverishing their people in wars, pretending generally, if not always, that the good of the people was the object. This our convention understood to be the most oppressive of all kingly oppressions; and they resolved to so frame the Constitution that no one man should hold the power of bringing this oppression upon us.[4]

Counterposed against these considerations are the advantages of sole presidential control over the decision to go to war. Few would contest the proposition that the presidency is institutionally better suited than Congress to respond to emergencies. But no emergency confronted the nation when President Bush announced the November buildup in Saudi Arabia. Whatever exigency may have attended the initial deployment of forces to that region had ended.

The administration's legal rationale for claiming sole executive power to make war was never spelled out. Its pleadings filed in *Dellums v. Bush* (1990) did not reach the merits, and argued merely that the court should not hear the case. The administration offered Congress no legal analysis, and no congressional committee demanded any. The fullest justification consisted of remarks by Secretary of State James Baker and Defense

3. R. Basler, *The Collected Works of Abraham Lincoln*, vol. 1, 1953. . . .

4. *Ibid.*

Secretary Cheney, the gist of which was that past presidents had used armed force more than 200 times, and that war had been declared only five times.

In principle, custom surely does affect the Constitution's meaning and allocation of power. The president's power to recognize foreign governments, for example, like the Senate's power to condition its consent to treaties, derives largely from unquestioned practice tracing to the earliest days of the republic. But not all practice is of constitutional moment. A practice of constitutional dimension is regarded by *both* political branches as a juridical norm; the incidents comprising the practice are accepted, or at least acquiesced in, by the other branch. In many of the precedents Baker and Cheney cited, Congress objected. Furthermore, the precedents must be on point. Here, they clearly were not: nearly all involved fights with pirates, clashes with cattle rustlers, trivial naval engagements and other minor uses of force not directed at significant adversaries, or risking substantial casualties or large-scale hostilities over a prolonged duration.

CONCLUDING NOTES ON THE FIRST GULF WAR

1. *Form of Congressional Approval.* As indicated above, in January 1991 Congress engaged in a spirited debate about whether the United States should resort to war against Iraq, and ultimately authorized the President to use force to implement the Security Council's resolutions. When Iraq failed to withdraw from Kuwait by the deadline, allied forces began an air campaign against Iraq code—named *Operation Desert Storm.* On February 27, after Iraqi forces had been driven from Kuwait in a ground war lasting less than 100 hours, President Bush declared a cease-fire. Since the Congress did not formally declare war, was the President's resort to war lawful?

2. *Lack of Congressional Approval.* The congressional vote authorizing the President to act was 52–47 in the Senate and 250–183 in the House—the closest margin in authorizing force by the Congress since the War of 1812. What if the vote had fallen short and Congress never enacted H.J. Res. 77: could President Bush have ordered air strikes against Iraq? If so, under what authority? Perhaps Security Council Resolution 678, in conjunction with the U.N. Charter? Compare President Truman's conduct during the Korean War. *See infra*, Section 5. Would it make a difference if Congress adopted an alternative joint resolution prohibiting the President from acting?

3. *The Slippery Slope.* Should it be permissible for the Executive to undertake the sort of pledge made by Secretary of Defense Cheney to King Fahd on August 6, 1990? How is Cheney's pledge distinguished from more formal mutual security pacts entered into by the United States over the past 50 years? Are such formal "guarantees" any more binding under U.S. law? *See infra*, Section 7. Separate from any such pledge, should it be permissible for the Executive to deploy a half a million soldiers across the globe prior to obtaining any congressional authorization? Do such acts at some point make it extremely difficult for Congress to say "no" to military action and, if so, should Congress be expected to step up to the plate at some point early in the

process? How can Congress act early in the process when it is unclear how events, including diplomacy, will unfold?

INTRODUCTORY NOTE TO THE "GLOBAL WAR ON TERRORISM" (2001–PRESENT)

On September 11, 2001, nineteen men affiliated with the terrorist group Al Qaeda hijacked four passenger aircraft, crashing two into New York's World Trade Center and one into the Pentagon (the fourth crashed in the Pennsylvania countryside). Almost 3,000 people died in the attack, making 9/11 the deadliest foreign attack on U.S. soil in American history.

In response to 9/11, President George W. Bush addressed a joint session of Congress on September 20, 2001. "Our war on terror begins with Al Qaeda," he declared, "but it does not end there. It will not end until every terrorist group of global reach has been found, stopped and defeated." On October 7, 2001, *Operation Enduring Freedom* commenced in Afghanistan, a longtime sanctuary for Al Qaeda. By spring 2002, most elements of the ruling Taliban regime had been driven from power. Additional counterterrorism operations—both overt and clandestine—have followed in the Philippines and the Horn of Africa, among other locations.

AUTHORIZATION FOR USE OF MILITARY FORCE AGAINST PERPETRATORS OF 9/11

S.J. Res. 23, Pub. L. No. 107–40, 115 Stat. 224 (Sept. 18, 2001).

Joint Resolution

To authorize the use of United States Armed Forces against those responsible for the recent attacks launched against the United States.

Whereas, on September 11, 2001, acts of treacherous violence were committed against the United States and its citizens; and

Whereas, such acts render it both necessary and appropriate that the United States exercise its rights to self-defense and to protect United States citizens both at home and abroad; and

Whereas, in light of the threat to the national security and foreign policy of the United States posed by these grave acts of violence; and

Whereas, such acts continue to pose an unusual and extraordinary threat to the national security and foreign policy of the United States; and

Whereas, the President has authority under the Constitution to take action to deter and prevent acts of international terrorism against the United States:

Now, therefore, be it

Resolved by the Senate and House of Representatives of the United States of America in Congress assembled,

SEC. 1. SHORT TITLE.

This joint resolution may be cited as the "Authorization for Use of Military Force".

SEC. 2. AUTHORIZATION FOR USE OF UNITED STATES ARMED FORCES.

(a) IN GENERAL.—That the President is authorized to use all necessary and appropriate force against those nations, organizations, or persons he determines planned, authorized, committed, or aided the terrorist attacks that occurred on September 11, 2001, or harbored such organizations or persons, in order to prevent any future acts of international terrorism against the United States by such nations, organizations or persons.

(b) WAR POWERS RESOLUTION REQUIREMENTS.—

(1) SPECIFIC STATUTORY AUTHORIZATION.—Consistent with section 8(a)(1) of the War Powers Resolution, the Congress declares that this section is intended to constitute specific statutory authorization within the meaning of section 5(b) of the War Powers Resolution.

(2) APPLICABILITY OF OTHER REQUIREMENTS.—Nothing in this resolution supercedes any requirement of the War Powers Resolution.

U.S. DEPARTMENT OF JUSTICE OFFICE OF LEGAL COUNSEL, THE PRESIDENT'S CONSTITUTIONAL AUTHORITY TO CONDUCT MILITARY OPERATIONS AGAINST TERRORISTS AND NATIONS SUPPORTING THEM

Available at http://www.usdoj.gov/olc/warpowers925.htm (footnotes and citations omitted).

September 25, 2001

MEMORANDUM OPINION FOR THE DEPUTY COUNSEL TO THE PRESIDENT

You have asked for our opinion as to the scope of the President's authority to take military action in response to the terrorist attacks on the United States on September 11, 2001. We conclude that the President has broad constitutional power to use military force. Congress has acknowledged this inherent executive power in both the War Powers Resolution (the "WPR"), and in the Joint Resolution passed by Congress on September 14, 2001. Further, the President has the constitutional power not only to retaliate against any person, organization, or State suspected of involvement in terrorist attacks on the United States, but also against foreign States suspected of harboring or supporting such organizations. Finally, the President may deploy military force preemptively against terrorist organizations or the States that harbor or support them, whether or not they can be linked to the specific terrorist incidents of September 11.

Our analysis falls into four parts. First, we examine the Constitution's text and structure. We conclude that the Constitution vests the President with the plenary authority, as Commander in Chief and the sole organ of the Nation in its foreign relations, to use military force abroad—especially in response to grave national emergencies created by sudden, unforeseen attacks on the people and territory of the United States. Second, we confirm that conclusion by reviewing the executive and judicial statements and decisions interpreting the Constitution and the President's powers under it. Third, we analyze the relevant practice of the United States, including recent history, that supports the view that the President has the authority to deploy military force in response to emergency conditions such as those created by the September 11, 2001, terrorist attacks. Finally, we discuss congressional enactments that, in our view, acknowledge the President's plenary authority to use force to respond to the terrorist attack on the United States.

Our review establishes that all three branches of the Federal Government—Congress, the Executive, and the Judiciary—agree that the President has broad authority to use military force abroad, including the ability to deter future attacks.

I.

. . . .

Constitutional Text. The text, structure and history of the Constitution establish that the Founders entrusted the President with the primary responsibility, and therefore the power, to use military force in situations of emergency. Article II, Section 2 states that the "President shall be Commander in Chief of the Army and Navy of the United States, and of the Militia of the several States, when called into the actual Service of the United States." U.S. Const. art. II, § 2, cl. 1. He is further vested with all of "the executive Power" and the duty to execute the laws. U.S. Const. art. II, § 1. These powers give the President broad constitutional authority to use military force in response to threats to the national security and foreign policy of the United States. During the period leading up to the Constitution's ratification, the power to initiate hostilities and to control the escalation of conflict had been long understood to rest in the hands of the executive branch.

. . . .

Constitutional Structure. Our reading of the text is reinforced by analysis of the constitutional structure. . . . [I]t is clear that the Constitution secures all federal executive power in the President to ensure a unity in purpose and energy in action. "Decision, activity, secrecy, and dispatch will generally characterize the proceedings of one man in a much more eminent degree than the proceedings of any greater number." *The Federalist* No. 70, at 392 (Alexander Hamilton). The centralization of authority in the President alone is particularly crucial in matters of national defense, war, and foreign policy, where a unitary executive can evaluate threats, consider policy choices, and mobilize national resources with a speed and energy that is far superior to any other branch. . . .

. . . .

II.

Executive Branch Construction and Practice. The position we take here has long represented the view of the executive branch and of the Department of Justice. . . .

. . . .

In *Overview of the War Powers Resolution*, 8 Op. O.L.C. 271, 275 (1984), we noted that "[t]he President's authority to deploy armed forces has been exercised in a broad range of circumstances [in] our history."

In *Presidential Power to Use the Armed Forces Abroad Without Statutory Authorization*, 4A Op. O.L.C. 185, 187 (1980), we stated that:

> "[o]ur history is replete with instances of presidential uses of military force abroad in the absence of prior congressional approval. This pattern of presidential initiative and congressional acquiescence may be said to reflect the implicit advantage held by the executive over the legislature under our constitutional scheme in situations calling for immediate action. Thus, constitutional practice over two centuries, supported by the nature of the functions exercised and by the few legal benchmarks that exist, evidences the existence of broad constitutional power."

. . . .

III.

. . . .

The historical record demonstrates that the power to initiate military hostilities, particularly in response to the threat of an armed attack, rests exclusively with the President. As the Supreme Court has observed, "[t]he United States frequently employs Armed Forces outside this country—over 200 times in our history—for the protection of American citizens or national security." *United States v. Verdugo–Urquidez*, 494 U.S. 259, 273 (1990). On at least 125 such occasions, the President acted without prior express authorization from Congress. Such deployments, based on the President's constitutional authority alone, have occurred since the Administration of George Washington. *See* David P. Currie, *The Constitution in Congress: Substantive Issues in the First Congress, 1789–1791*, 61 U. Chi. L. Rev. 775, 816 (1994) ("[B]oth Secretary [of War] Knox and [President] Washington himself seemed to think that this [Commander in Chief] authority extended to offensive operations taken in retaliation for Indian atrocities."). Perhaps the most significant deployment without specific statutory authorization took place at the time of the Korean War, when President Truman, without prior authorization from Congress, deployed United States troops in a war that lasted for over three years and caused over 142,000 American casualties.

Recent deployments ordered solely on the basis of the President's constitutional authority have also been extremely large, representing a substantial commitment of the Nation's military personnel, diplomatic prestige, and financial resources. On at least one occasion, such a unilateral deployment has constituted full-scale war. On March 24, 1999, without any prior statutory authorization and in the absence of an attack on the United States, President Clinton ordered hostilities to be initiated against the Republic of Yugoslavia. The President informed Congress that, in the initial wave of air strikes, "United States and NATO forces have targeted the [Yugoslavian] government's integrated air defense system, military and security police command and control elements, and military and security police facilities and infrastructure.... I have taken these actions pursuant to my constitutional authority to conduct U.S. foreign relations and as Commander in Chief and Chief Executive." Bombing attacks against targets in both Kosovo and Serbia ended on June 10, 1999, seventy-nine days after the war began. More than 30,000 United States military personnel participated in the operations; some 800 U.S. aircraft flew more than 20,000 sorties; more than 23,000 bombs and missiles were used. As part of the peace settlement, NATO deployed some 50,000 troops into Kosovo, 7,000 of them American. In a News Briefing on June 10, 1999, Secretary of Defense William S. Cohen summarized the effects of the campaign by saying,

> [t]hree months ago Yugoslavia was a heavily armed country with a significant air defense system. We reduced that defense system threat by destroying over 80 percent of Yugoslavia's modern aircraft fighters and strategic surface-to-air missiles. NATO destroyed a significant share of the infrastructure Yugoslavia used to support its military with, we reduced his capacity to make ammunition by two-thirds, and we eliminated all of its oil refining capacity and more than 40 percent of its military fuel supplies. Most important, we severely crippled the military forces in Kosovo by destroying more than 50 percent of the artillery and more than one-third of the armored vehicles.

General Shelton of the Joint Chiefs of Staff reported that "about half of [Yugoslavia's] defense industry has either been damaged or destroyed.... [A]viation, 70 percent; armored vehicle production, 40 [percent]; petroleum refineries, 100 percent down; explosive production, about 50 percent; and 65 percent of his ammunition.... For the most part Belgrade is a city that's got about probably 70 percent without [electrical] power." A report by General Ryan, Air Force Chief of Staff, on June 8, 1999, stated that

> Serbia's air force is essentially useless and its air defenses are dangerous but ineffective. Military armament production is destroyed. Military supply areas are under siege. Oil refinement has ceased and petroleum storage is systematically being destroyed. Electricity is sporadic, at best. Major transportation routes are cut. NATO aircraft are attacking with impunity throughout the country.

Estimates near the time placed the number of Yugoslav military casualties at between five and ten thousand. In recent decades, no President has unilaterally deployed so much force abroad.

Other recent unilateral deployments have also been significant in military, foreign policy, and financial terms. Several such deployments occurred in the Balkans in the mid–1990s. In December 1995, President Clinton ordered the deployment of 20,000 United States troops to Bosnia to implement a peace settlement. In February 1994, sixty United States warplanes conducted airstrikes against Yugoslav targets. In 1993, United

States warplanes were sent to enforce a no-fly zone over Bosnia; in the same year, the President despatched United States troops to Macedonia as part of a United Nations peacekeeping operation.

Major recent deployments have also taken place in Central America and in the Persian Gulf. In 1994, President Clinton ordered some 20,000 United States troops to be deployed into Haiti, again without prior statutory authorization from Congress, in reliance solely upon his Article II authority. On August 8, 1990, in response to the Iraqi invasion of Kuwait and the consequent threat to Saudi Arabia, President Bush ordered the deployment of substantial forces into Saudi Arabia in Operation Desert Shield. The forces were equipped for combat and included two squadrons of F–15 aircraft and a brigade of the 82d Airborne Division; the deployment eventually grew to several hundred thousand. The President informed Congress that he had taken these actions "pursuant to my constitutional authority to conduct our foreign relations and as Commander in Chief." President Bush also deployed some 15,000 troops into Panama in December, 1990, for the purpose (among others) of protecting Americans living in Panama.

Further, when Congress has in fact authorized deployments of troops in hostilities, past Presidents have taken the position that such legislation, although welcome, was not constitutionally necessary. For example, in signing Pub. L. No. 102–01, 105 Stat. 3 (1991), authorizing the use of military force in Operation Desert Storm against Iraq, President Bush stated that "my request for congressional support did not, and my signing this resolution does not, constitute any change in the longstanding positions of the executive branch on either the President's constitutional authority to use the Armed Forces to defend vital U.S. interests or the constitutionality of the War Powers Resolution." Similarly, President John F. Kennedy stated on September 13, 1962, that congressional authorization for a naval blockade of Cuba was unnecessary, maintaining that "I have full authority now to take such action." And in a Report to the American People on October 22, 1962, President Kennedy asserted that he had ordered the blockade "under the authority entrusted to me by the Constitution *as endorsed by* the resolution of the Congress." (emphasis added). Thus, there is abundant precedent, much of it from recent Administrations, for the deployment of military force abroad, including the waging of war, on the basis of the President's sole constitutional authority.

Several recent precedents stand out as particularly relevant to the situation at hand, where the conflict is with terrorists. The first and most relevant precedent is also the most recent: the military actions that President William J. Clinton ordered on August 20, 1998, against terrorist sites in Afghanistan and Sudan. The second is the strike on Iraqi Intelligence Headquarters that President Clinton ordered on June 26, 1993. The third is President Ronald Reagan's action on April 14, 1986, ordering United States armed forces to attack selected targets at Tripoli and Benghazi, Libya.

. . . .

Like the two unilateral Presidential actions [by President Clinton], President Reagan's decision to use armed force in response to a terrorist attack on United States military personnel illustrates that the President has independent constitutional authority to use such force in the present circumstances.

IV.

Our analysis to this point has surveyed the views and practice of the executive and judicial branches. In two enactments, the War Powers Resolution and the recent Joint Resolution, Congress has also addressed the scope of the President's independent constitutional authority. We think these two statutes demonstrate Congress's acceptance of the President's unilateral war powers in an emergency situation like that created by the September 11 incidents.

. . . .

. . . Congress's support for the President's power suggests no limits on the Executive's judgment whether to use military force in response to the national emergency created by those incidents. Section 2(c)(3) [of the War Powers Resolution] leaves undisturbed the President's constitutional authority to determine both when a "national emergency" arising out of an "attack against the United States" exists, and what types and levels of force are necessary or appropriate to respond to that emergency. Because the statute itself supplies no definition of these terms, their interpretation must depend on longstanding constitutional practices and understandings. As we have shown in Parts I–III of this memorandum, constitutional text, structure and practice demonstrate that the President is vested with the plenary power to use military force, especially in the case of a direct attack on the United States. Section 2(c)(3) recognizes the President's broad authority and discretion in this area.

JOHN C. YOO
Deputy Assistant Attorney General
Office of Legal Counsel

CONCLUDING NOTES ON THE "GLOBAL WAR ON TERRORISM"

1. *Is It Really a "War"?* In his September 20, 2001 address to a joint session of Congress, President Bush referred to the September 11 attacks as an "act of war," laying the rhetorical groundwork for what would become known as the "global war on terrorism" (GWOT). Is this really a "war" in the constitutional sense? Is it a "war" in the international law sense? Do the answers to those questions matter when considering the role of Congress and the application of treaties, such as the 1949 Geneva Conventions?

2. *The Scope of the AUMF.* The AUMF was clearly intended to authorize the President to use military force to invade Afghanistan and neutralize any

further threats from Al Qaeda. How much broader is the scope of the statute? In Chapter 1, Section 4, and in this Chapter, Section 11, the breadth of the statute for addressing the detention and prosecution of both aliens and U.S. nationals is considered. Could the statute support the President invading any country where the President believes Al Qaeda operatives are located? Must the President first determine that the country is harboring or supporting those operatives?

3. *The Killing of Osama Bin Laden.* On May 1, 2011, the founder of Al Qaeda, Osama bin Laden, was shot and killed inside a private residential compound in Abbottabad, Pakistan, by U.S. Navy SEALs and CIA operatives. Abbottabad is a city fully under the control of the government of Pakistan; indeed, it hosts a military facility for the training of new recruits. By most accounts, the government of Pakistan was unaware of bin Laden's presence in Abbottabad. The covert operation was ordered by President Barack Obama without consulting or obtaining the consent of the government of Pakistan, apparently to avoid any possibility of Al Qaeda learning of the planned operation. Was there any need for the President to obtain special congressional authorization for the operation? Any need for the President to determine that Pakistan was harboring or supporting bin Laden? Is such a killing consistent with international law? In a blog posting on the web site *Opinio Juris*, the U.S. Department of State Legal Adviser, Harold Koh, stated the following:

> Given bin Laden's unquestioned leadership position within al Qaeda and his clear continuing operational role, there can be no question that he was the leader of an enemy force and a legitimate target in our armed conflict with al Qaeda. In addition, bin Laden continued to pose an imminent threat to the United States that engaged our right to use force, a threat that materials seized during the raid have only further documented. Under these circumstances, there is no question that he presented a lawful target for the use of lethal force. By enacting the [Authorization for Use of Military Force statute (AUMF)], Congress expressly authorized the President to use military force "against ... *persons* [such as bin Laden, whom the President] determines planned, authorized, committed, or aided the terrorist attacks that occurred on September 11, 2001 ... in order to prevent any future acts of international terrorism against the United States by such ... persons" (emphasis added). Moreover, the manner in which the U.S. operation was conducted—taking great pains both to distinguish between legitimate military objectives and civilians and to avoid excessive incidental injury to the latter—followed the principles of distinction and proportionality described above, and was designed specifically to preserve those principles, even if it meant putting U.S. forces in harm's way. Finally, consistent with the laws of armed conflict and U.S. military doctrine, the U.S. forces were prepared to capture bin Laden if he had surrendered in a way that they could safely accept.

Harold Hongju Koh, *The Lawfulness of the U.S. Operation Against Osama bin Laden*, Opinio Juris (May 19, 2011), *available at* http://opiniojuris.org.

4. *The Relevance of the AUMF.* To what extent is the AUMF even needed? Does the memorandum by Deputy Assistant Attorney General John Yoo suggest that the President already has plenary authority to act, with or without the statute? If so, what are the broader implications of Yoo's analysis, even beyond the "war on terrorism"? Can Congress ever limit the President's war-making by statute; does it even have a role in declaring or ending war? Do you think the incidents cited by Yoo constitute "evidence" that the "power to initiate military hostilities ... rests exclusively with the President"?

INTRODUCTORY NOTE ON THE SECOND GULF WAR (2003—2010)

Twelve years after his father took the United States to war against Iraq, President George W. Bush ordered the commencement of Operation Iraqi Freedom on March 20, 2003. Massive explosions erupted over Baghdad as allied coalition forces (the vast majority American) stormed across the border into Iraq. Within a little over a month, President Bush announced "the end of major combat operations" aboard the U.S.S. *Abraham Lincoln.*

The Bush Administration justified intervention in Iraq mainly on the ground that Saddam Hussein's government had been pursuing weapons of mass destruction (WMD) in violation of multiple U.N. Security Council resolutions. Such weapons, it was argued, might ultimately fall into the hands of terrorist groups like Al Qaeda. In actuality, WMD were never discovered in Iraq. And despite early military triumphs, the United States soon found itself faced with a spiraling sectarian conflict.

In 2007, in what became known as the "surge," President Bush increased U.S. force levels in key areas of Iraq in order to combat sectarian violence and provide an atmosphere in which the Iraqi political process could move forward. Over the next few years, violence declined and the political process did move forward, though, as of mid-2011, it still faced significant hurdles.

On August 31, 2010, President Obama announced the end of United States combat operations in Iraq. Six conventional brigades and 4,500 special operations forces remained in Iraq to train Iraqi troops. Under a bilateral agreement between the United States and Iraq, all U.S. forces are required to leave Iraq by the end of 2011. As of 2011, more than 4,425 U.S. soldiers had died in the Second Gulf War, making it the deadliest U.S. conflict since the war in Vietnam.

AUTHORIZATION FOR USE OF MILITARY FORCE AGAINST IRAQ RESOLUTION OF 2002

H.J. Res. 114, Pub. L. No. 107-243, 116 Stat. 1498 (Oct. 16, 2002).

Joint Resolution

To authorize the use of United States Armed Forces against Iraq.

Whereas in 1990 in response to Iraq's war of aggression against and illegal occupation of Kuwait, the United States forged a coalition of nations to liberate Kuwait and its people in order to defend the national security of the United States and enforce United Nations Security Council resolutions relating to Iraq;

Whereas after the liberation of Kuwait in 1991, Iraq entered into a United Nations sponsored cease-fire agreement pursuant to which Iraq unequivocally agreed, among other things, to eliminate its nuclear, biological, and chemical weapons programs and the means to deliver and develop them, and to end its support for international terrorism;

Whereas the efforts of international weapons inspectors, United States intelligence agencies, and Iraqi defectors led to the discovery that Iraq had large stockpiles of chemical weapons and a large scale biological weapons program, and that Iraq had an advanced nuclear weapons development program that was much closer to producing a nuclear weapon than intelligence reporting had previously indicated;

Whereas Iraq, in direct and flagrant violation of the cease-fire, attempted to thwart the efforts of weapons inspectors to identify and destroy Iraq's weapons of mass destruction stockpiles and development capabilities, which finally resulted in the withdrawal of inspectors from Iraq on October 31, 1998;

Whereas in Public Law 105–235 (August 14, 1998), Congress concluded that Iraq's continuing weapons of mass destruction programs threatened vital United States interests and international peace and security, declared Iraq to be in "material and unacceptable breach of its international obligations" and urged the President "to take appropriate action, in accordance with the Constitution and relevant laws of the United States, to bring Iraq into compliance with its international obligations";

Whereas Iraq both poses a continuing threat to the national security of the United States and international peace and security in the Persian Gulf region and remains in material and unacceptable breach of its international obligations by, among other things, continuing to possess and develop a significant chemical and biological weapons capability, actively seeking a nuclear weapons capability, and supporting and harboring terrorist organizations;

Whereas Iraq persists in violating resolutions of the United Nations Security Council by continuing to engage in brutal repression of its civilian population thereby threatening international peace and security in the region, by refusing to release, repatriate, or account for non-Iraqi citizens wrongfully detained by Iraq, including an American serviceman, and by failing to return property wrongfully seized by Iraq from Kuwait;

Whereas the current Iraqi regime has demonstrated its capability and willingness to use weapons of mass destruction against other nations and its own people;

Whereas the current Iraqi regime has demonstrated its continuing hostility toward, and willingness to attack, the United States, including by attempting in 1993 to assassinate former President Bush and by firing on many thousands of occasions on United States and Coalition Armed

Forces engaged in enforcing the resolutions of the United Nations Security Council;

Whereas members of al Qaida, an organization bearing responsibility for attacks on the United States, its citizens, and interests, including the attacks that occurred on September 11, 2001, are known to be in Iraq;

Whereas Iraq continues to aid and harbor other international terrorist organizations, including organizations that threaten the lives and safety of American citizens;

Whereas the attacks on the United States of September 11, 2001, underscored the gravity of the threat posed by the acquisition of weapons of mass destruction by international terrorist organizations;

Whereas Iraq's demonstrated capability and willingness to use weapons of mass destruction, the risk that the current Iraqi regime will either employ those weapons to launch a surprise attack against the United States or its Armed Forces or provide them to international terrorists who would do so, and the extreme magnitude of harm that would result to the United States and its citizens from such an attack, combine to justify action by the United States to defend itself;

Whereas United Nations Security Council Resolution 678 (1990) authorizes the use of all necessary means to enforce United Nations Security Council Resolution 660 (1990) and subsequent relevant resolutions and to compel Iraq to cease certain activities that threaten international peace and security, including the development of weapons of mass destruction and refusal or obstruction of United Nations weapons inspections in violation of United Nations Security Council Resolution 687 (1991), repression of its civilian population in violation of United Nations Security Council Resolution 688 (1991), and threatening its neighbors or United Nations operations in Iraq in violation of United Nations Security Council Resolution 949 (1994);

Whereas in the Authorization for Use of Military Force Against Iraq Resolution (Public Law 102–1), Congress has authorized the President "to use United States Armed Forces pursuant to United Nations Security Council Resolution 678 (1990) in order to achieve implementation of Security Council Resolutions 660, 661, 662, 664, 665, 666, 667, 669, 670, 674, and 677";

Whereas in December 1991, Congress expressed its sense that it "supports the use of all necessary means to achieve the goals of United Nations Security Council Resolution 687 as being consistent with the Authorization of Use of Military Force Against Iraq Resolution (Public Law 102–1)," that Iraq's repression of its civilian population violates United Nations Security Council Resolution 688 and "constitutes a continuing threat to the peace, security, and stability of the Persian Gulf region," and that Congress, "supports the use of all necessary means to achieve the goals of United Nations Security Council Resolution 688";

Whereas the Iraq Liberation Act of 1998 (Public Law 105–338) expressed the sense of Congress that it should be the policy of the United States to support efforts to remove from power the current Iraqi regime and promote the emergence of a democratic government to replace that regime;

Whereas on September 12, 2002, President Bush committed the United States to "work with the United Nations Security Council to meet our common challenge" posed by Iraq and to "work for the necessary resolutions," while also making clear that "the Security Council resolutions will be enforced, and the just demands of peace and security will be met, or action will be unavoidable";

Whereas the United States is determined to prosecute the war on terrorism and Iraq's ongoing support for international terrorist groups combined with its development of weapons of mass destruction in direct violation of its obligations under the 1991 cease-fire and other United Nations Security Council resolutions make clear that it is in the national security interests of the United States and in furtherance of the war on terrorism that all relevant United Nations Security Council resolutions be enforced, including through the use of force if necessary;

Whereas Congress has taken steps to pursue vigorously the war on terrorism through the provision of authorities and funding requested by the President to take the necessary actions against international terrorists and terrorist organizations, including those nations, organizations, or persons who planned, authorized, committed, or aided the terrorist attacks that occurred on September 11, 2001, or harbored such persons or organizations;

Whereas the President and Congress are determined to continue to take all appropriate actions against international terrorists and terrorist organizations, including those nations, organizations, or persons who planned, authorized, committed, or aided the terrorist attacks that occurred on September 11, 2001, or harbored such persons or organizations;

Whereas the President has authority under the Constitution to take action in order to deter and prevent acts of international terrorism against the United States, as Congress recognized in the joint resolution on Authorization for Use of Military Force (Public Law 107–40); and

Whereas it is in the national security of the United States to restore international peace and security to the Persian Gulf region: Now, therefore, be it

Resolved by the Senate and House of Representatives of the United States of America in Congress assembled,

SECTION 1. SHORT TITLE.

This joint resolution may be cited as the "Authorization for Use of Military Force Against Iraq Resolution of 2002".

SEC. 2. SUPPORT FOR UNITED STATES DIPLOMATIC EFFORTS.

The Congress of the United States supports the efforts by the President to—

(1) strictly enforce through the United Nations Security Council all relevant Security Council resolutions regarding Iraq and encourages him in those efforts; and

(2) obtain prompt and decisive action by the Security Council to ensure that Iraq abandons its strategy of delay, evasion and noncompliance and promptly and strictly complies with all relevant Security Council resolutions regarding Iraq.

SEC. 3. AUTHORIZATION FOR USE OF UNITED STATES ARMED FORCES.

(a) AUTHORIZATION.—The President is authorized to use the Armed Forces of the United States as he determines to be necessary and appropriate in order to—

(1) defend the national security of the United States against the continuing threat posed by Iraq; and

(2) enforce all relevant United Nations Security Council resolutions regarding Iraq.

(b) PRESIDENTIAL DETERMINATION.—In connection with the exercise of the authority granted in subsection (a) to use force the President shall, prior to such exercise or as soon thereafter as may be feasible, but no later than 48 hours after exercising such authority, make available to the Speaker of the House of Representatives and the President pro tempore of the Senate his determination that—

(1) reliance by the United States on further diplomatic or other peaceful means alone either (A) will not adequately protect the national security of the United States against the continuing threat posed by Iraq or (B) is not likely to lead to enforcement of all relevant United Nations Security Council resolutions regarding Iraq; and

(2) acting pursuant to this resolution is consistent with the United States and other countries continuing to take the necessary actions against international terrorists and terrorist organizations, including those nations, organizations, or persons who planned, authorized, committed or aided the terrorist attacks that occurred on September 11, 2001.

(c) WAR POWERS RESOLUTION REQUIREMENTS.—

(1) SPECIFIC STATUTORY AUTHORIZATION.—Consistent with section 8(a)(1) of the War Powers Resolution, the Congress declares that this section is intended to constitute specific statutory authorization within the meaning of section 5(b) of the War Powers Resolution.

(2) APPLICABILITY OF OTHER REQUIREMENTS.—Nothing in this joint resolution supersedes any requirement of the War Powers Resolution.

SEC. 4. REPORTS TO CONGRESS.

(a) REPORTS.—The President shall, at least once every 60 days, submit to the Congress a report on matters relevant to this joint resolution, including actions taken pursuant to the exercise of authority granted in section 3 and the status of planning for efforts that are expected to be required after such actions are completed, including those actions described in section 7 of the Iraq Liberation Act of 1998 (Public Law 105–338).

(b) SINGLE CONSOLIDATED REPORT.—To the extent that the submission of any report described in subsection (a) coincides with the submission of any other report on matters relevant to this joint resolution otherwise required to be submitted to Congress pursuant to the reporting requirements of the War Powers Resolution (Public Law 93–148), all such reports may be submitted as a single consolidated report to the Congress.

(c) RULE OF CONSTRUCTION.—To the extent that the information required by section 3 of the Authorization for Use of Military Force Against Iraq Resolution (Public Law 102–1) is included in the report required by this section, such report shall be considered as meeting the requirements of section 3 of such resolution.

U.N. SECURITY COUNCIL RES. 1441

(Nov. 8, 2002).

The Security Council,

. . . .

Acting under Chapter VII of the Charter,

1. *Decides* that Iraq has been and remains in material breach of its obligations under relevant resolutions, including resolution 687 (1991), in particular through Iraq's failure to cooperate with United Nations inspectors and the IAEA, and to complete the actions required under paragraphs 8 to 13 of resolution 687 (1991);

2. *Decides,* while acknowledging paragraph 1 above, to afford Iraq, by this resolution, a final opportunity to comply with its disarmament obligations under relevant resolutions of the Council; and accordingly decides to set up an enhanced inspection regime with the aim of bringing to full and verified completion the disarmament process established by resolution 687 (1991) and subsequent resolutions of the Council;

3. *Decides* that, in order to begin to comply with its disarmament obligations, in addition to submitting the required biannual declarations, the Government of Iraq shall provide to UNMOVIC, the IAEA, and the Council, not later than 30 days form the date of this resolution, a currently accurate, full, and complete declaration of all aspects of its programmes to develop chemical, biological, and nuclear weapons, ballistic missiles, and other delivery systems such as unmanned aerial vehicles and

dispersal systems designed for use on aircraft, including any holdings and precise locations of such weapons, components, sub-components, stocks of agents, and related material and equipment, the locations and work of its research, development and production facilities, as well as all other chemical, biological, and nuclear programmes, including any which it claims are for purposes not related to weapon production or material;

4. *Decides* that false statements or omissions in the declarations submitted by Iraq pursuant to this resolution and failure by Iraq at any time to comply with, and cooperate fully in the implementation of, this resolution shall constitute a further material breach of Iraq's obligations. . . .

LORI FISLER DAMROSCH, WAR AND UNCERTAINTY

114 Yale L.J. 1405, 1408, 1414 (2005) (footnotes omitted).

Only nine times has Congress acted with bright-line clarity to authorize initiation of major combat. . . . Of these nine authorizations, four recite factual premises that in hindsight appear to have been questionable. Two out of five declarations of war (Mexican–American and Spanish–American) and two out of four statutory authorizations functionally equivalent to congressional approval of war (Tonkin Gulf and Iraq 2002) proceeded on the basis of congressional acceptance of unproven, unsupported, or even patently misleading executive representations about the facts of the matter.

. . . .

Congress has not had a good track record in establishing forensic truth at the times that it has authorized the President to proceed with military action. The disabilities under which Congress labors include a reliance on the executive branch for most of the information on which judgments about a military situation are based, an absence of procedures (adversarial or otherwise) to test the reliability of that information, and a tendency to accept the Executive's assertions about the need for urgent action. Even if Congress could improve its fact-finding capabilities—for example, by seeking alternative sources of information from outside the executive branch, through subpoena powers if appropriate; by subjecting executive representations to processes analogous to cross-examination instead of accepting them at face value; or by deliberating at a length appropriate to the gravity of the matter instead of yielding to the Executive's view on urgency—Congress is still not institutionally well suited to becoming a retrospective trier of fact and can hardly be expected to succeed at a task so far from its own institutional competence. The facts it ought to concentrate on developing (in war-and-peace decisions even more than in ordinary legislative enactments) are those that have relevance and salience for the charting of future policy directions.

JIDE NZELIBE & JOHN YOO, RATIONAL WAR AND CONSTITUTIONAL DESIGN

115 Yale L.J. 2512, 2514, 2517–19 (2006) (footnotes omitted).

The issue of war powers, more specifically the question of whether the President or Congress holds the power to initiate military hostilities, remains one of the most controversial and unsettled areas of constitutional law. ... In 1973, Congress enacted a War Powers Resolution that sought to place a sixty-day limit on military intervention, but Congress has never enforced it. ...

....

Much of the war powers literature focuses on the concern that the United States might erroneously enter a war in which the expected costs outweigh the expected benefits. Statisticians usually label such errors of commission Type I errors. However, the other side of the coin is just as important. Errors of omission, when the United States does not enter a conflict whose expected benefits outweigh the costs, are called Type II errors and may be just as undesirable as Type I errors. ...

We must compare the impact of Type I and Type II errors under a Congress-first system with the results of a President-first approach. Presidents may cause the United States to begin wars that appear unnecessary or unwise initially; however, some of these conflicts may look better in hindsight. ...

... We do not claim that the empirical record shows that a President-first approach is always superior. We argue that the Congress-first approach is based on unproven and questionable assumptions, and that as a matter of theory an approach that allows the President to choose whether to seek congressional support for war will be superior.

PAUL F. DIEHL & TOM GINSBURG, IRRATIONAL WAR AND CONSTITUTIONAL DESIGN: A REPLY TO PROFESSORS NZELIBE AND YOO

27 Mich. J. Int'l L. 1239, 1239–48 (2006) (footnotes omitted).

In their recent paper, *Rational War and Constitutional Design*, Professors Jide Nzelibe and John Yoo develop a functional account of the constitutional allocation of war powers. Eschewing the long debate over the actual meaning of the relevant provisions of the United States Constitution, they instead ask what constitutional scheme would best serve the national interest. Drawing together principal-agent theory, institutional analysis, and international relations literature, they seek to demonstrate that a rational constitutional structure of war-making would balance democratic representation with an ability to signal information to other international actors. They argue that an executive-centered system of war powers does better on both accounts and is therefore likely to lead to more legitimate, "better" wars, at least with respect to certain enemies.

. . . .

Nzelibe and Yoo begin by reviewing much of the historical debate—in which Yoo has recently been a central participant—on war powers as delineated by the Constitution. This debate has pitted those who cite the Constitution's Article I, Section 8 Declaration of War Clause in advocating extensive congressional involvement in initiating hostilities, against advocates of executive flexibility who read Article II as providing for a unitary executive with very broad powers—in foreign affairs generally and war making in particular. Nzelibe and Yoo sidestep this debate by concluding (accurately in our view) that much of the evidence invoked in support of these positions is indeterminate, and functional considerations might thus be relevant.

In examining the functions that might be served by various constitutional interpretations, Nzelibe and Yoo introduce the idea that a system of war-making is to be evaluated not only by its ability to prevent "bad" wars (avoiding what they characterize as Type I errors), but also by its ability to authorize "good" wars (avoiding Type II errors). Here they hint at the possibility that the current system, at least as articulated by most constitutional lawyers, has not generated enough war. They use this framework to consider whether a Congress-centered or president-centered approach would be optimal.

To a certain extent, the use of "Congress-centered" and "president-centered" by participants in the debate is misleading. The only issue at stake is whether *ex ante* congressional approval of major hostilities will produce better policies. As the authors acknowledge, Congress is always free to disapprove of actions by cutting funding *ex post*. So the issue is not really allocating powers among alternative agents but determining the sequence and timing of policymaking among multiple agents.

In considering whether a Congress-centered or president-centered regime would produce better war policy, Nzelibe and Yoo argue that the empirical evidence from American history may be "too difficult to analyze." Because the mechanisms of authorization have shifted across different conflicts and different periods of American history, Nzelibe and Yoo argue that there is no clear conclusion to be drawn. They criticize wars authorized by formal congressional declarations of war, such as the Mexican–American and Spanish–American wars, as well as those that involved no such formality, such as Iraq and Vietnam. However, while they indicate that (presumably "good") wars have proceeded without legislative involvement, they do not mention notorious examples of "bad" conflicts initiated without legislative approval, such as the Bay of Pigs incident of 1961 or the funding of the Nicaraguan Contras through weapons sales to Iran in the 1980s. The thrust of their claim is that pro-Congress scholars have not produced data showing *ex ante* congressional authorization results in better war policy, and in this way they subtly seek to shift the burden of proof to those scholars who believe that executive centrality is *not* superior.

. . . .

Nzelibe and Yoo's second justification for making the president the center of the war-making scheme is a common one: the president has better access to information than does Congress. The principal-agent model assumes that an agent has the informational advantage over the principal. When considering which agent among several to assign a particular task, the public should be inclined to choose the agent with the best information. Most scholars assume that the president is the domestic actor with superior information, given her access to a vast array of diplomatic, military, and intelligence information resources that Congress does not control.

Nzelibe and Yoo use the lead up to the Iraq war to illustrate this information advantage. As they note, "Congress based its decision to authorize the use of force against Iraq on the intelligence and analysis presented by the Bush administration." Yet in the same paragraph, they note that this intelligence and analysis were "all wrong." Even if one believes the debatable proposition that poor quality information caused the Iraq misadventure, this point undermines rather than supports the argument of the essay. The risk that presidents may act on the basis of inaccurate information can be reduced by a requirement that another actor evaluate the information *ex ante*. Congressional deliberation and involvement in decisionmaking should therefore reduce Type I error. That it did not do so in this case speaks more to the partisan dominance of a single party and a president committed to attacking Iraq at all costs than to the general institutional competencies of Congress.

Indeed, one normative conclusion that could be drawn from the Nzelibe–Yoo analysis is that congressional information-gathering abilities should be enhanced. Even if the president has structural advantages in this area, a case could be made for improving the independent fact-gathering abilities of Congress so as to reduce the information asymmetry vis-a-vis the executive. One proposal might be to follow the 9/11 Commission's recommendations to streamline legislative organization, minimizing redundant committee structures. Congressional investigative capacity could be enhanced as well.

Congressional involvement in the budgeting and policy evaluation processes illustrates how one might buttress legislative intelligence gathering. Distrustful of executive control over budget information, Congress set up the Congressional Budget Office in 1974 to provide objective information on government budgeting and spending. Congress had earlier expanded its control of the General Accounting Office (now the Government Accountability Office), which was initially set up as an independent auditing and evaluation agency. By analogy, there may be reason to think about special congressional research and analysis capacities in the national security area. Enhanced information ought to ensure that Congress can fulfill its constitutional duty of oversight.

Ultimately, Nzelibe and Yoo do not explain why the current information asymmetry ought to be accepted and sustained, rather than redressed. Though the authors might respond that the national security area is distinctive because it requires secrecy, Congress does hold closed sessions for particularly sensitive topics. Closed-door sessions offer the advantage of deliberation over policy without compromising security or undermining any valuable signals of resolve.

Nzelibe and Yoo imply that the Iraq war resulted from intelligence failures. A different conclusion is that the war stemmed not from intelligence failure but from a classic form of agency problem: executive manipulation of information to exaggerate a threat, not unlike that which led to the Gulf of Tonkin Resolution in 1964. This alternative interpretation illustrates how access to information is not the only consideration when choosing among multiple possible agents. Quality must be balanced against slack: the information advantage of a particular agent must be weighed against the possibility that the agent will pursue her own interests rather than those of the principal. Our own intuition is that greater congressional involvement in approving the use of force abroad can exploit the president's informational advantages while reducing slack, but we need not make the positive case here, for other scholars have done so. For now, we merely point out that the Nzelibe–Yoo analysis is incomplete and conclusory.

NOTES ON THE WAR IN IRAQ

1. *Intelligence and the War Power*. The United States now has a total of sixteen executive branch intelligence agencies under the umbrella of the Directorate of National Intelligence (DNI). To what extent should Congress take a more proactive role in providing oversight of the U.S. intelligence community given the importance of reliable information when resorting to war? What form should any additional oversight take? In 1977, the Carter Administration proposed setting up a "crisis consultative committee," consisting of the leadership of each house. A similar suggestion was made in 1988 by Senators Byrd, Nunn, Warner, and Mitchell in proposing to amend the War Powers Resolution. See Michael J. Glennon, *Constitutional Diplomacy* 307–313 (1990). What are some of the advantages and disadvantages to such proposals? How much authority could a "crisis consultative committee" exercise after *Chadha* (*see infra*, this chapter, section 9)? Is Congress institutionally qualified to judge the reliability of intelligence estimates or is it better suited, as Professor Lori Damrosh writes, to "clarify the policy context" in which intelligence is analyzed?

2. *Errors of Commission/Omission*. Professors Nzelibe and Yoo make a distinction between errors of commission (Type I) and errors of omission (Type II). When it comes to the use of force, is one type of error less desirable than another? Which type of error is Congress more likely to commit? The President? Has the United States committed any major Type II errors in the post-World War II period?

CHAPTER 6

FEDERALISM

■ ■ ■

SECTION 1. THE RELEVANCE OF FEDERALISM TO FOREIGN AFFAIRS

THE FEDERALIST PAPERS NO. 44 (MADISON)

(Clinton Rossiter ed., 1961).

"This Constitution and the laws of the United States which shall be made in pursuance thereof, and all treaties made, or which shall be made, under the authority of the United States, shall be the supreme law of the land, and the judges in every State shall be bound thereby, anything in the constitution or laws of any State to the contrary notwithstanding."[1]

The indiscreet zeal of the adversaries to the Constitution has betrayed them into an attack on this part of it . . ., without which it would have been evidently and radically defective. To be fully sensible of this, we need only to suppose for a moment that the supremacy of the State constitutions had been left complete by a saving clause in their favor.

In the first place, as these constitutions invest the State legislatures with absolute sovereignty in all cases not excepted by the existing Articles of Confederation, all the authorities contained in the proposed Constitution, so far as they exceed those enumerated in the Confederation, would have been annulled, and the new Congress would have been reduced to the same impotent condition with their predecessors.

In the next place, as the constitutions of some of the States do not even expressly and fully recognize the existing powers of the Confederacy, an express saving of the supremacy of the former would, in such States, have brought into question every power contained in the proposed Constitution.

In the third place, as the constitutions of the States differ much from each other, it might happen that a treaty or national law of great and equal importance to the States would interfere with some and not with

1. [Authors' Note: *See* U.S. CONST. art. VI, cl. 2.]

other constitutions, and would consequently be valid in some of the States at the same that it would have no effect in others.

In fine, the world would have seen, for the first time, a system of government founded on an inversion of the fundamental principles of all government; it would have seen the authority of the whole society everywhere subordinate to the authority of the parts; it would have seen a monster, in which the head was under the direction of the members.

INTRODUCTORY NOTE: THE STATUS OF FOREIGN AFFAIRS FEDERALISM

"Federalism" is concerned with the proper allocation of authority between the federal and state governments. Consequently, the materials in this chapter deal with the constitutional propriety of actions by state and local governmental units affecting foreign relations. Federalist No. 44, *supra*, imagines how the United States might have functioned had state constitutions been held out of the Supremacy Clause. Given that they were not exempted, some have contended that the U.S. Constitution vested plenary and exclusive power concerning foreign relations with the national government, as may be seen in the *Curtiss-Wright* case (Chapter 1, Section 1). Yet neither vision (complete state independence or exclusive federal control) seems borne out in practice; the reality lies somewhere in between.

First, while the federal government is the focal point of U.S. foreign policy, a significant amount of activity relating to foreign affairs occurs at the state and local levels without overt opposition from the federal government. Such activities may take many different forms. State legislatures have enacted laws, state courts have issued decisions, and state governors have used their executive powers to implement U.S. treaty obligations and customary international law.[1] Further, the adoption and amendment of state constitutions have been influenced by developments in the field of international law, such as human rights law.[2] In this way, state-level activity may be seen as reinforcing and assisting in the foreign-relations activities of the federal government.

Further, in situations where the federal government has declined to adopt an international standard, some states or cities have chosen to do so on their own. Thus, San Francisco passed legislation in 1998 implementing portions of the Convention on the Elimination of All Forms of Discrimination Against Women (CEDAW),[3] even though the U.S. Senate has been unwilling to consent to U.S. ratification of CEDAW.[4] Likewise, even though the U.S.

1. *See* Earl H. Fry, *The Expanding Role of State and Local Governments in U.S. Foreign Affairs* (1998); Julian G. Ku, *Gubernatorial Foreign Policy*, 115 YALE L.J. 2380 (2006); Julian G. Ku, *The State of New York Does Exist: How the States Control Compliance with International Law*, 82 N.C. L. REV. 457 (2004); Edward T. Swaine, *Negotiating Federalism: State Bargaining and the Dormant Treaty Power*, 49 DUKE L.J. 1127 (2000).

2. *See* Vicki Jackson, *Constitutional Dialogue and Human Dignity: States and Transnational Constitutional Discourse*, 65 MONT. L. REV. 15, 21–27 (2004); Martha F. Davis, *The Spirit of Our Times: State Constitutions and International Human Rights*, 30 N.Y.U. REV. L. & SOC. CHANGE 359 (2006).

3. Dec. 18, 1979, 1249 U.N.T.S. 13.

4. *See* Stacy Laira Lozner, *Diffusion of Local Regulatory Innovations: The San Francisco CEDAW Ordinance and the New York City Human Rights Initiative*, 104 COLUM. L. REV. 768 (2004); *see also* Elizabeth M. Schneider, *Transnational Law as a Domestic Resource: Thoughts on* government chose not to join the Kyoto Protocol to the United Nations Framework Convention on Climate Change,[5] some 185 cities have implemented or modeled local laws on the Protocol. Indeed, in 2004 nine Northeastern states initiated a state-level emissions capping and trading program modeled after the Kyoto Protocol. Among other things, the program requires electric power generators in participating states to reduce carbon dioxide emissions.[6] Similarly, in 2006 five governors from Western states agreed on a plan to cut emissions of greenhouse gases by their states, including through a regional carbon-trading system.[7]

States and cities also have adopted measures that conflict with federal law and policy. For example, more than one hundred cities passed resolutions opposing the U.S. military intervention in Iraq in March 2003 and calling for the expeditious withdrawal of U.S. forces. Similarly, in late 2005 the Massachusetts government and Venezuela's state-owned oil company entered into an agreement for Venezuela to supply oil at highly subsidized prices to low-income Massachusetts families and organizations serving low income communities. This agreement took place even though Venezuelan President Hugo Chavez was a major critic of the Bush Administration's foreign policies, was very friendly with Cuba, and was peddling "21st century socialism" as an alternative model to U.S. "free market" policies. The unusual agreement (involving a developing country providing aid to U.S. citizens) was negotiated with Chavez by Congressman William Delahunt, and was viewed by some as an effort by Chavez to embarrass the Bush administration. *See* Justin Blum, *Chavez Pushes Petro–Diplomacy*, WASH. POST, Nov. 22, 2005, at A22.

Second, when a federal challenge is brought against state laws (or other measures) relating to the field of foreign affairs, the state law might be struck down on a variety of theories. The state law or measure might be invalidated because of an express prohibition in the U.S. Constitution, such as the prohibitions in Article I, Section 10 against states entering into any treaty or, without the consent of Congress, any "Agreement or Compact" with a "foreign Power." (While states have been allowed to enter into agreements with foreign nations or sub-national units on certain local issues (*e.g.*, on the building of transboundary bridges or highways), a state would not be permitted to conclude a peace treaty with another country.[8]) Alternatively, a state law or measure might be preempted by a federal statute, such as with respect to the imposition of sanctions on a foreign nation, or by a treaty concluded by the President with the advice and consent of the Senate under Article II, Section 2. Even if there is no affirmative measure taken at the federal level, a state law might be struck down as running afoul of the "dormant" foreign commerce power found in Article I, Section 8 or based on what is sometimes

---

the Case of Women's Rights, 38 NEW ENG. L. REV. 689, 721 n. 201 (2004) (listing other cities that urged national ratification of CEDAW). For the San Francisco ordinance, see San Francisco, Cal., Administrative Code, ch. 12K (2001).

5. Dec. 10, 1997, 37 I.L.M. 22 (1998).

6. *See* Juliet Eilperin, *Cities, States Aren't Waiting for U.S. Action on Climate*, WASH. POST, Aug. 11, 2006, at A1; Eli Sanders, *Rebuffing Bush, 132 Mayors Embrace Kyoto Rules*, N.Y. TIMES, May 14, 2005, at A9; Regional Greenhouse Gas Initiative, at http://www.rggi.org.

7. *See* Juliet Eilperin, *Western States Agree to Cut Greenhouse Gases*, WASH. POST, Feb. 27, 2007, at A8.

8. *See infra* Section 7 on the Compact Clause.

referred to as the "dormant" foreign affairs power. Since customary international law is a part of federal common law, in theory it too can preempt conflicting state law. The Supremacy Clause (Article VI, Clause 2), however, does not expressly include customary international law. *See supra* Chapter 2, Section 2.

Third, as seen in the materials below, federal power in this area is routinely (although not unfailingly) upheld. Often, courts make reference to the importance of the nation speaking with "one voice" in foreign policy matters.[9] While "uniformity" in foreign relations is widely regarded as desirable, are there some situations where states and cities should be allowed to experiment with different ways of handling transnational matters? In other words, are there some questions about whether it is better to "let a thousand flowers bloom," to allow states and cities to lay the groundwork simultaneously for alternative, possibly antithetical, policies to those of the federal government? And who is empowered to answer that question? Congress? The President? The President acting in conjunction with the Senate? Federal courts? The several states? As you proceed through the following sections, note that the United States itself rarely initiates a legal challenge to state authority. Rather, litigation is usually brought by private parties who prefer the substance of the federal policy (or inaction) to the substance of state policies, and who are only derivatively concerned with the underlying constitutional principles. Does that affect your appraisal?

Fourth, although the focus in this chapter is on current U.S. doctrine, federalism issues can be placed in a somewhat broader context. Numerous other federal systems—including Australia, Brazil, Canada, Germany, India, Malaysia, Nigeria, Russia, and Switzerland—have grappled with the distribution of law-making between the center and quasi-autonomous regions. One common challenge has been the increased use of multilateral conventions to address human rights, criminal law, copyright, air pollution, and other subjects, which has often moved into the federal domain issues previously within the purview of the states or provinces. In some countries (*e.g.*, Australia, Switzerland, and the United States), treaties or their implementing statutes may upset authority previously exercised by the states or provinces, yet this is not true of all nations. In Canada, for instance, the federal treaty-implementing power is limited to those areas in which the central government can legislate absent a treaty, such that adoption of some treaties by the federal government may require concurrent action by provincial legislatures; the federal authorities may not simply proceed on their own. A useful compendium is *National Treaty Law and Practice* (Duncan B. Hollis et al. eds., 2005), which analyzes the law and practice of nineteen nations, several of which have federal systems.

The historical context is also important. Since the ratification of the U.S. Constitution, the power of the federal government to regulate on matters traditionally left to the states has increased dramatically, particularly since the New Deal in the 1930s. Congress's power under the Commerce Clause has supported extensive federal regulation in domestic matters once regarded as

9. *See, e.g.*, Holmes v. Jennison, 39 U.S. (14 Pet.) 540, 575, 10 L.Ed. 579 (1840) (finding that it "was one of the main objects of the Constitution to make us, so far as regarded our foreign relations, one people and one nation. . . .").

quintessentially local in nature, as witnessed by the Civil Rights Act of 1964. Contemporaneously, the U.S. emergence as a superpower in World War II has expanded national activity in the field of foreign affairs.

From the late 1930s to the early 1990s, the courts imposed few limits on the federal power to preempt state laws under the Commerce Clause. *See, e.g.*, Garcia v. San Antonio Metropolitan Transit Authority, 469 U.S. 528, 105 S.Ct. 1005, 83 L.Ed.2d 1016 (1985) (overruling National League of Cities v. Usery, 426 U.S. 833, 96 S.Ct. 2465, 49 L.Ed.2d 245 (1976)). However, more recent Supreme Court cases establish that there are some limits to federal power—in effect, Congress cannot regulate matters that are "truly local." Thus, the Court found that Congress lacked the power to criminalize the "purely intrastate" possession of a gun near a school, since the matter was noneconomic in nature and not part of a larger regulation of economic activity, and since the statute contained no jurisdictional element that would ensure a case-by-case inquiry into whether a particular firearm possession affected interstate commerce. *See* United States v. Lopez, 514 U.S. 549, 115 S.Ct. 1624, 131 L.Ed.2d 626 (1995). Under similar reasoning, a federal civil remedy for gender-motivated crimes was struck down. *See* United States v. Morrison, 529 U.S. 598, 120 S.Ct. 1740, 146 L.Ed.2d 658 (2000). The Court also found that Congress lacks the power under the Commerce Clause to abrogate a state's constitutional immunity from suit under the Eleventh Amendment. *See* Seminole Tribe of Florida v. Florida, 517 U.S. 44, 116 S.Ct. 1114, 134 L.Ed.2d 252 (1996). Further, Congress is limited in its ability to restrict a state's freedom to enforce a federal statute on religious freedom by means the state deems most appropriate. *See* City of Boerne v. Flores, 521 U.S. 507, 117 S.Ct. 2157, 138 L.Ed.2d 624 (1997). On the other hand, Congress may criminalize the purely local cultivation, possession, and use of marijuana for medicinal purposes—even in the face of a California statute allowing such conduct—since failure to do so would undercut congressional regulation of the interstate market. *See* Gonzales v. Raich, 545 U.S. 1, 125 S.Ct. 2195, 162 L.Ed.2d 1 (2005). Further, Congress can abrogate a state's immunity if it is acting to enforce the Fourteenth Amendment. *See* Fitzpatrick v. Bitzer, 427 U.S. 445, 456, 96 S.Ct. 2666, 49 L.Ed.2d 614 (1976).

To date, the Supreme Court has not found that these decisions have direct implications for federalism in the field of foreign relations. When Congress passes a statute purportedly on a matter of foreign relations, or the federal government ratifies an international agreement, is the matter *ipso facto* not "truly local"? Put another way, are such acts *ipso facto* part of a broader scheme of regulation that falls within the realm of federal constitutional power? Interest in whether the Court's recent jurisprudence suggests limits on the federal foreign relations power has given rise to a veritable cottage industry of scholarship. For a sampling, see Martin S. Flaherty, *Are We to Be a Nation?: Federal Power vs. "States' Rights" in Foreign Affairs*, 70 U. COLO. L. REV. 1277 (1999); Michael D. Ramsey, *The Power of the States in Foreign Affairs: The Original Understanding of Foreign Policy Federalism*, 75 NOTRE DAME L. REV. 341 (1999).

SECTION 2. PREEMPTION OF STATE LAW BY FEDERAL STATUTE

TARBLE'S CASE

80 U.S. (13 Wall.) 397, 401–09, 20 L.Ed. 597 (1871).

[Edward Tarble was a U.S. soldier being held in military custody. Tarble's father claimed that his son had enlisted in the U.S. army before his eighteenth birthday without the father's consent. A Wisconsin state court commissioner issued a writ of habeas corpus directing the army to release Tarble. The army produced Tarble, but protested that the commissioner had no jurisdiction to issue the writ. According to the army, Tarble had enlisted as a U.S. soldier for a period of five years and had taken the oath required by the law and regulations of the army. Further, the army maintained that Tarble deserted, but was captured and confined pending trial by the proper military authorities. Upon appeal, the Wisconsin Supreme Court upheld the commissioner's writ.]

MR. JUSTICE FIELD . . . delivered the opinion of the court, as follows:

. . . .

. . . There are within the territorial limits of each State two governments [*i.e.*, the U.S. government and the state government], restricted in their spheres of action, but independent of each other, and supreme within their respective spheres. Each has its separate departments; each has its distinct laws, and each has its own tribunals for their enforcement. Neither government can intrude within the jurisdiction, or authorize any interference therein by its judicial officers with the action of the other. The two governments in each State stand in their respective spheres of action in the same independent relation to each other, except in one particular, that they would if their authority embraced distinct territories. That particular consists in the supremacy of the authority of the United States when any conflict arises between the two governments. The Constitution and the laws passed in pursuance of it, are declared by the Constitution itself to be the supreme law of the land, and the judges of every State are bound thereby, "anything in the constitution or laws of any State to the contrary notwithstanding." Whenever, therefore, any conflict arises between the enactments of the two sovereignties, or in the enforcement of their asserted authorities, those of the National government must have supremacy until the validity of the different enactments and authorities can be finally determined by the tribunals of the United States. This temporary supremacy until judicial decision by the National tribunals, and the ultimate determination of the conflict by such decision, are essential to the preservation of order and peace, and the avoidance of forcible collision between the two governments. "The Constitution," as said by Mr. Chief Justice Taney, "was not framed merely to guard the States against danger from abroad, but chiefly to secure union and harmony at home; and to accomplish this end it was deemed necessary, when the Constitution was framed, that many of the rights of sovereignty which the States then possessed should be ceded to the General government; and that in the sphere of action assigned to it, it should be supreme and strong enough to execute its own laws by its own tribunals, without interruption from a State, or from State authorities." And the judicial power conferred extends to all cases arising under the Constitution, and thus embraces every legislative act of Congress, whether passed in pursuance of it, or in disregard of its provisions. The Constitution is under the view of the tribunals of the United States when any act of Congress is brought before them for consideration.

Such being the distinct and independent character of the two governments, within their respective spheres of action, it follows that neither can intrude with its judicial process into the domain of the other, except so far as such intrusion may be necessary on the part of the National government to preserve its rightful supremacy in cases of conflict of authority. In their laws, and mode of enforcement, neither is responsible to the other. How their respective laws shall be enacted; how they shall be carried into execution; and in what tribunals, or by what officers; and how much discretion, or whether any at all shall be vested in their officers, are matters subject to their own control, and in the regulation of which neither can interfere with the other.

Now, among the powers assigned to the National government, is the power "to raise and support armies," and the power "to provide for the government and regulation of the land and naval forces." The execution of these powers falls within the line of its duties; and its control over the subject is plenary and exclusive. It can determine, without question from any State authority, how the armies shall be raised, whether by voluntary enlistment or forced draft, the age at which the soldier shall be received, and the period for which he shall be taken, the compensation he shall be allowed, and the service to which he shall be assigned. And it can provide the rules for the government and regulation of the forces after they are raised, define what shall constitute military offences, and prescribe their punishment. No interference with the execution of this power of the National government in the formation, organization, and government of its armies by any State officials could be permitted without greatly impairing the efficiency, if it did not utterly destroy, this branch of the public service. . . . It is manifest that the powers of the National government could not be exercised with energy and efficiency at all times, if its acts could be interfered with and controlled for any period by officers or tribunals of another sovereignty.

. . . .

The conclusion we have reached renders it unnecessary to consider how far the declaration of the prisoner as to his age, in the oath of enlistment, is to be deemed conclusive evidence on that point on the return to the writ.

Judgment reversed.

TOLL v. MORENO

458 U.S. 1, 3–17, 102 S.Ct. 2977, 73 L.Ed.2d 563 (1982) (footnotes omitted).

JUSTICE BRENNAN delivered the opinion of the Court.

The state-operated University of Maryland grants preferential treatment for purposes of tuition and fees to students with "in-state" status. Although citizens and immigrant aliens may obtain in-state status upon a showing of domicile within the State, nonimmigrant aliens, even if domiciled, are not eligible for such status. The question in this case is whether the University's in-state policy is invalid under the Supremacy Clause of the Constitution, insofar as the policy categorically denies in-state status to domiciled nonimmigrant aliens who hold G–4 visas.

. . . .

. . . Such visas are issued to nonimmigrant aliens who are officers or employees of certain international organizations, and to members of their immediate families. . . .

. . . .

. . . For the reasons that follow, we hold that the University of Maryland's in-state policy, as applied to G–4 aliens and their dependents, violates the Supremacy Clause of the Constitution, and on that ground affirm the judgment of the Court of Appeals. We therefore have no occasion to consider whether the policy violates the Due Process or Equal Protection Clauses.

II

Our cases have long recognized the preeminent role of the Federal Government with respect to the regulation of aliens within our borders. *See, e.g., Mathews v. Diaz*, 426 U.S. 67 (1976); *Graham v. Richardson*, 403 U.S. 365, 377–380 (1971); *Takahashi v. Fish & Game Comm'n*, 334 U.S. 410, 418–420 (1948); *Hines v. Davidowitz*, 312 U.S. 52, 62–68 (1941); *Truax v. Raich*, 239 U.S. 33, 42 (1915). Federal authority to regulate the status of aliens derives from various sources, including the Federal Government's power "[t]o establish [a] uniform Rule of Naturalization," U.S.Const., Art. I, § 8, cl. 4, its power "[t]o regulate Commerce with foreign Nations," *id.*, cl. 3, and its broad authority over foreign affairs, *see United States v. Curtiss-Wright Export Corp.*, 299 U.S. 304, 318 (1936). . . .

Not surprisingly, therefore, our cases have also been at pains to note the substantial limitations upon the authority of the States in making classifications based upon alienage. In *Takahashi v. Fish & Game Comm'n, supra*, we considered a California statute that precluded aliens who were "ineligible for citizenship under federal law" from obtaining commercial fishing licenses, even though they "met all other state requirements" and were lawful inhabitants of the State. 334 U.S., at 414. In seeking to defend the statute, the State argued that it had "simply followed the Federal Government's lead" in classifying certain persons as "ineligible for citizenship." *Id.*, at 418. We rejected the argument, stressing the delicate nature of the federal-state relationship in regulating aliens:

> "The Federal Government has broad constitutional powers in determining what aliens shall be admitted to the United States, the period they may remain, regulation of their conduct before naturalization, and the terms and conditions of their naturalization. Under the Constitution the states are granted no such powers; they can neither add to nor take from the conditions lawfully imposed by Congress upon admission, naturalization and residence of aliens in the United States or the several states. *State laws which impose discriminatory burdens upon the entrance or residence of aliens lawfully within the United States conflict with this constitutionally derived federal power to regulate immigration, and have accordingly been held invalid.*" *Id.*, at 419 (emphasis added) (citation and footnote omitted).

. . . .

The Immigration and Nationality Act of 1952, 66 Stat. 163, as amended, 8 U.S.C. § 1101 *et seq.* (1976 ed. and Supp. IV), represents "a comprehensive and complete code covering all aspects of admission of aliens to this country, whether for business or pleasure, or as immigrants seeking to become permanent residents." *Elkins v. Moreno*, 435 U.S., at 664. The Act recognizes two basic classes of aliens, immigrant and nonimmigrant. With respect to the nonimmigrant class, the Act establishes various categories, the G–4 category among them. For many of these nonimmigrant categories, Congress has precluded the covered alien from establishing domicile in the United States. *Id.*, at 665. But significantly, Congress has allowed G–4 aliens—employees of various international organizations, and their immediate families—to enter the country on terms permitting the establishment of domicile in the United States. *Id.*, at 666.[1] In light of Congress' explicit decision not to bar G–4 aliens from acquiring domicile, the State's decision to deny "in-state" status to G–4 aliens, *solely* on account of the G–4 alien's federal immigration status, surely amounts to an ancillary "burden not contemplated by Congress" in admitting these aliens to the United States. We need not rely, however, simply on Congress' decision to permit the G–4 alien to establish domicile in this country; the Federal Government has also taken the additional affirmative step of conferring special tax privileges on G–4 aliens.

. . . .

1. [Authors' Note: Under U.S. immigration law, persons admitted temporarily to the United States with non-immigrant status visas have difficulty becoming permanent residents or U.S. citizens. By allowing non-immigrant aliens with G–4 visas to obtain domicile, Congress determined that it was not a violation of U.S. law for such aliens to develop a subjective intent to stay in the United States indefinitely. Moreover, although a G–4 visa lapses on termination of employment with an international organization, a G–4 alien does not necessarily have to leave the United States. Absent an adverse factor (*e.g.*, commission of a crime), such aliens who have been present in the United States for several years usually can have their status adjusted to permanent resident without difficulty.]

In sum, the Federal Government has not merely admitted G–4 aliens into the country; it has also permitted them to establish domicile and afforded significant tax exemptions. . . . In such circumstances, we cannot conclude that Congress ever contemplated that a State, in the operation of a university, might impose discriminatory tuition charges and fees solely on account of the federal immigration classification. We therefore conclude that insofar as it bars domiciled G–4 aliens (and their dependents) from acquiring in-state status, the University's policy violates the Supremacy Clause.

CROSBY v. NATIONAL FOREIGN TRADE COUNCIL

530 U.S. 363, 366–88, 120 S.Ct. 2288, 147 L.Ed.2d 352 (2000) (footnotes omitted).

JUSTICE SOUTER delivered the opinion of the Court.

The issue is whether the Burma law of the Commonwealth of Massachusetts, restricting the authority of its agencies to purchase goods or services from companies doing business with Burma, is invalid under the Supremacy Clause of the National Constitution owing to its threat of frustrating federal statutory objectives. We hold that it is.

I

In June 1996, Massachusetts adopted "An Act Regulating State Contracts with Companies Doing Business with or in Burma (Myanmar)," 1996 Mass. Acts 239, ch. 130 (codified at Mass. Gen. Laws §§ 7:22G–7:22M, 40 F. 1/2 (1997)). The statute generally bars state entities from buying goods or services from any person (defined to include a business organization) identified on a "restricted purchase list" of those doing business with Burma. §§ 7:22H(a), 7:22J. Although the statute has no general provision for waiver or termination of its ban, it does exempt from boycott any entities present in Burma solely to report the news, § 7:22H(e), or to provide international telecommunication goods or services, *ibid.*, or medical supplies, § 7:22I.

. . . .

In September 1996, three months after the Massachusetts law was enacted, Congress passed a statute imposing a set of mandatory and conditional sanctions on Burma. *See* Foreign Operations, Export Financing, and Related Programs Appropriations Act, 1997, § 570, 110 Stat. 3009–166 to 3009–167 (enacted by the Omnibus Consolidated Appropriations Act, 1997, § 101(c), 110 Stat. 3009–121 to 3009–172). The federal Act has five basic parts, three substantive and two procedural.

First, it imposes three sanctions directly on Burma. It bans all aid to the Burmese Government except for humanitarian assistance, counternarcotics efforts, and promotion of human rights and democracy. § 570(a)(1). The statute instructs United States representatives to international financial institutions to vote against loans or other assistance to or for Burma, § 570(a)(2), and it provides that no entry visa shall be issued to any

Burmese Government official unless required by treaty or to staff the Burmese mission to the United Nations, § 570(a)(3). These restrictions are to remain in effect "[u]ntil such time as the President determines and certifies to Congress that Burma has made measurable and substantial progress in improving human rights practices and implementing democratic government." § 570(a).

Second, the federal Act authorizes the President to impose further sanctions subject to certain conditions. He may prohibit "United States persons" from "new investment" in Burma, and shall do so if he determines and certifies to Congress that the Burmese Government has physically harmed, rearrested, or exiled Daw Aung San Suu Kyi (the opposition leader selected to receive the Nobel Peace Prize), or has committed "large-scale repression of or violence against the Democratic opposition." § 570(b). "New investment" is defined as entry into a contract that would favor the "economical development of resources located in Burma," or would provide ownership interests in or benefits from such development, § 570(f)(2), but the term specifically excludes (and thus excludes from any Presidential prohibition) "entry into, performance of, or financing of a contract to sell or purchase goods, services, or technology," *ibid.*

Third, the statute directs the President to work to develop "a comprehensive, multilateral strategy to bring democracy to and improve human rights practices and the quality of life in Burma." § 570(c). He is instructed to cooperate with members of the Association of Southeast Asian Nations (ASEAN) and with other countries having major trade and investment interests in Burma to devise such an approach, and to pursue the additional objective of fostering dialogue between the ruling State Law and Order Restoration Council (SLORC) and democratic opposition groups. *Ibid.*

As for the procedural provisions of the federal statute, the fourth section requires the President to report periodically to certain congressional committee chairmen on the progress toward democratization and better living conditions in Burma as well as on the development of the required strategy. § 570(d). And the fifth part of the federal Act authorizes the President "to waive, temporarily or permanently, any sanction [under the federal Act] . . . if he determines and certifies to Congress that the application of such sanction would be contrary to the national security interests of the United States." § 570(e).

On May 20, 1997, the President issued the Burma Executive Order, Exec. Order No. 13047, 3 CFR 202 (1997 Comp.). He certified for purposes of § 570(b) that the Government of Burma had "committed large-scale repression of the democratic opposition in Burma" and found that the Burmese Government's actions and policies constituted "an unusual and extraordinary threat to the national security and foreign policy of the United States," a threat characterized as a national emergency. The President then prohibited new investment in Burma "by United States persons," Exec. Order No. 13047, § 1, any approval or facilitation by a

United States person of such new investment by foreign persons, § 2(a), and any transaction meant to evade or avoid the ban, § 2(b). The order generally incorporated the exceptions and exemptions addressed in the statute. §§ 3, 4. Finally, the President delegated to the Secretary of State the tasks of working with ASEAN and other countries to develop a strategy for democracy, human rights, and the quality of life in Burma, and of making the required congressional reports. § 5.

II

Respondent National Foreign Trade Council (Council) is a nonprofit corporation representing companies engaged in foreign commerce; 34 of its members were on the Massachusetts restricted purchase list in 1998. . . . Three withdrew from Burma after the passage of the state Act, and one member had its bid for a procurement contract increased by 10 percent under the provision of the state law allowing acceptance of a low bid from a listed bidder only if the next-to-lowest bid is more than 10 percent higher. *Ibid.*

In April 1998, the Council filed suit in the United States District Court for the District of Massachusetts, seeking declaratory and injunctive relief against the petitioner state officials charged with administering and enforcing the state Act (whom we will refer to simply as the State). . . .

. . . .

III

A fundamental principle of the Constitution is that Congress has the power to preempt state law. Art. VI, cl. 2; *Gibbons v. Ogden*, 9 Wheat. 1, 211 (1824); *Savage v. Jones*, 225 U.S. 501, 533 (1912); *California v. ARC America Corp.*, 490 U.S. 93, 101 (1989). Even without an express provision for preemption, we have found that state law must yield to a congressional Act in at least two circumstances. When Congress intends federal law to "occupy the field," state law in that area is preempted. *Id.*, at 100; *cf. United States v. Locke,* 529 U.S. 89, 115 (2000) (citing *Charleston & Western Carolina R. Co. v. Varnville Furniture Co.*, 237 U.S. 597, 604 (1915)). And even if Congress has not occupied the field, state law is naturally preempted to the extent of any conflict with a federal statute. *Hines v. Davidowitz*, 312 U.S. 52, 66–67 (1941); *ARC America Corp., supra,* at 100–101; *Locke, supra,* at 109. We will find preemption where it is impossible for a private party to comply with both state and federal law, *see, e.g., Florida Lime & Avocado Growers, Inc. v. Paul*, 373 U.S. 132, 142–43 (1963), and where "under the circumstances of [a] particular case, [the challenged state law] stands as an obstacle to the accomplishment and execution of the full purposes and objectives of Congress." *Hines, supra,* at 67. What is a sufficient obstacle is a matter of judgment, to be informed by examining the federal statute as a whole and identifying its purpose and intended effects. . . .

Applying this standard, we see the state Burma law as an obstacle to the accomplishment of Congress's full objectives under the federal Act. We find that the state law undermines the intended purpose and "natural effect" of at least three provisions of the federal Act, that is, its delegation of effective discretion to the President to control economic sanctions against Burma, its limitation of sanctions solely to United States persons and new investment, and its directive to the President to proceed diplomatically in developing a comprehensive, multilateral strategy toward Burma.

A

First, Congress clearly intended the federal Act to provide the President with flexible and effective authority over economic sanctions against Burma. Although Congress immediately put in place a set of initial sanctions (prohibiting bilateral aid, § 570(a)(1), support for international financial assistance, § 570(a)(2), and entry by Burmese officials into the United States, § 570(a)(3)), it authorized the President to terminate any and all of those measures upon determining and certifying that there had been progress in human rights and democracy in Burma. § 570(a). It invested the President with the further power to ban new investment by United States persons, dependent only on specific Presidential findings of repression in Burma. § 570(b). And, most significantly, Congress empowered the President "to waive, temporarily or permanently, any sanction [under the federal Act] ... if he determines and certifies to Congress that the application of such sanction would be contrary to the national security interests of the United States." § 570(e).

This express investiture of the President with statutory authority to act for the United States in imposing sanctions with respect to the Government of Burma, augmented by the flexibility to respond to change by suspending sanctions in the interest of national security, recalls Justice Jackson's observation in *Youngstown Sheet & Tube Co. v. Sawyer*, 343 U.S. 579, 635 (1952): "When the President acts pursuant to an express or implied authorization of Congress, his authority is at its maximum, for it includes all that he possesses in his own right plus all that Congress can delegate." ... Within the sphere defined by Congress, then, the statute has placed the President in a position with as much discretion to exercise economic leverage against Burma, with an eye toward national security, as our law will admit. And it is just this plenitude of Executive authority that we think controls the issue of preemption here. The President has been given this authority not merely to make a political statement but to achieve a political result, and the fullness of his authority shows the importance in the congressional mind of reaching that result. It is simply implausible that Congress would have gone to such lengths to empower the President if it had been willing to compromise his effectiveness by deference to every provision of state statute or local ordinance that might, if enforced, blunt the consequences of discretionary Presidential action.

....

B

Congress manifestly intended to limit economic pressure against the Burmese Government to a specific range. The federal Act confines its reach to United States persons, § 570(b), imposes limited immediate sanctions, § 570(a), places only a conditional ban on a carefully defined area of "new investment," § 570(f)(2), and pointedly exempts contracts to sell or purchase goods, services, or technology, § 570(f)(2). These detailed provisions show that Congress's calibrated Burma policy is a deliberate effort "to steer a middle path,". . . .

The State has set a different course, and its statute conflicts with federal law at a number of points by penalizing individuals and conduct that Congress has explicitly exempted or excluded from sanctions. . . .

. . . .

C

Finally, the state Act is at odds with the President's intended authority to speak for the United States among the world's nations in developing a "comprehensive, multilateral strategy to bring democracy to and improve human rights practices and the quality of life in Burma." § 570(c). Congress called for Presidential cooperation with members of ASEAN and other countries in developing such a strategy, *ibid.*, directed the President to encourage a dialogue between the Government of Burma and the democratic opposition, *ibid.*, and required him to report to the Congress on the progress of his diplomatic efforts, § 570(d). As with Congress's explicit delegation to the President of power over economic sanctions, Congress's express command to the President to take the initiative for the United States among the international community invested him with the maximum authority of the National Government, *cf. Youngstown Sheet & Tube Co.*, 343 U.S., at 635, in harmony with the President's own constitutional powers, U.S. Const., Art. II, § 2, cl. 2 ("[The President] shall have Power, by and with the Advice and Consent of the Senate, to make Treaties" and "shall appoint Ambassadors, other public Ministers and Consuls"); § 3 ("[The President] shall receive Ambassadors and other public Ministers"). This clear mandate and invocation of exclusively national power belies any suggestion that Congress intended the President's effective voice to be obscured by state or local action.

. . . .

V

Because the state Act's provisions conflict with Congress's specific delegation to the President of flexible discretion, with limitation of sanctions to a limited scope of actions and actors, and with direction to develop a comprehensive, multilateral strategy under the federal Act, it is preempted, and its application is unconstitutional, under the Supremacy Clause.

NOTES: PREEMPTION OF STATE LAW BY FEDERAL STATUTE

1. *Constitutional Bases for Federal Enactments.* Federal statutes and regulations in the field of foreign affairs must rest, of course, on the constitutional powers accorded to the federal government. In *Tarble*, the military laws and regulations rested upon Congress's power to raise and regulate an army. In *Toll v. Moreno*, the immigration statute rested largely upon Congress's power to regulate immigration and foreign commerce. In *Crosby*, the statute imposing sanctions on Burma (Myanmar) rested principally upon Congress's power to regulate foreign commerce and the President's power to engage in foreign diplomacy. So long as the federal law or regulation is constitutional, it preempts conflicting state law under the Supremacy Clause.

2. *Varieties of Preemption.* When a state's exercise of its police power is challenged under the Supremacy Clause, the Supreme Court has stated that preemption may be either express or implied.

Express preemption involves an explicit direction from Congress that state authority is being ousted. *See, e.g.*, War and National Defense Act, Pub. L. 96–72, § 8, Sept. 29, 1979, 93 Stat. 521, *codified at* 50 U.S.C. app. § 2407(c) (2006) (providing that the statutory section and implementing regulations "shall preempt any law, rule, or regulation of any of the several States or the District of Columbia, or any of the territories or possessions of the United States, or of any governmental subdivision thereof, which law, rule, or regulation pertains to participation in, compliance with, implementation of, or the furnishing of information regarding restrictive trade practices or boycotts fostered or imposed by foreign countries against other countries"). Does the fact that express preemption is relatively unusual in the foreign affairs context suggest anything?

Implied preemption can occur in one of two ways: (1) *conflict preemption* (where compliance with both the federal and state statute is impossible, or "state law 'stands as an obstacle to the accomplishment and execution of the full purposes and objectives of Congress.' "); or (2) *field preemption* (where the federal scheme is so pervasive as to make reasonable the inference that Congress has preempted state law). Gade v. Nat'l Solid Wastes Mgmt. Ass'n, 505 U.S. 88, 98, 112 S.Ct. 2374, 120 L.Ed.2d 73 (1992).

3. *Presumptions About Preemption.* If the information before the court is ambiguous, should the court employ a presumption either against implied preemption or in favor of it? The Supreme Court normally begins with a presumption that Congress has *not* intended to preempt state law. *See* Medtronic, Inc. v. Lohr, 518 U.S. 470, 485, 116 S.Ct. 2240, 135 L.Ed.2d 700 (1996); Rice v. Santa Fe Elevator Corp., 331 U.S. 218, 230, 67 S.Ct. 1146, 91 L.Ed. 1447 (1947). However, in *United States v. Locke*, the Supreme Court stated that such a presumption was inappropriate in the context of considering state law restrictions affecting international maritime commerce, since this was an area in which historically Congress had had a significant presence. *See* United States v. Locke, 529 U.S. 89, 108–10, 120 S.Ct. 1135, 146 L.Ed.2d 69 (2000). When statutes concern foreign relations matters, should courts begin with a presumption that Congress has intended to preempt state law?

See Erwin Chemerinsky, *Empowering States When It Matters: A Different Approach to Preemption*, 69 BROOK. L. REV. 1313 (2004) (arguing against a presumption of preemption); *see also* Jack Goldsmith, *Statutory Foreign Affairs Preemption*, 2000 SUP. CT. REV. 175; Harold G. Maier, *Preemption of State Law: A Recommended Analysis*, 83 AM. J. INT'L L. 832 (1989).

Although the Massachusetts statute in *Crosby* preceded the federal statute by three months, the federal statute contained no reference to existing state or local measures directed against Burma. Thus, Congress did not expressly preempt the Massachusetts statute. Massachusetts argued that Congress's silence should be read as implicit acceptance of the state law, and that the state law could supplement and assist the federal sanctions program. Nevertheless, the Massachusetts statute was found to be preempted. Had the Supreme Court not found Massachusetts' law preempted, the President might have been in a position of being able to waive federal sanctions against Burma (to reward good behavior), but not those of Massachusetts. In *Crosby*, the Court stated that the conflict between the state and federal law was so clear that it would "leave for another day a consideration in this context of a presumption against preemption." 530 U.S. at 374 n. 8.

4. *Statutory Authorization*. What about the opposite of statutory preemption—statutory authorization for states to engage in foreign relations matters? Notwithstanding *Toll v. Moreno*, it is clear that not all state measures that favor or disfavor aliens are preempted by federal immigration laws, and even those bearing on education require nuanced analysis. *See, e.g.*, Equal Access Educ. v. Merten, 305 F. Supp. 2d 585 (E.D. Va. 2004) (Virginia policy denying post-secondary school admission to illegal aliens was not preempted by federal authority to regulate immigration and did not violate the dormant foreign commerce clause); Martinez v. Regents of Univ. of Cal., 50 Cal.4th 1277, 117 Cal.Rptr.3d 359, 241 P.3d 855 (Cal. 2010) (upholding California law exempting certain nonresident aliens, including unlawful aliens, from paying nonresident tuition, notwithstanding federal statutory provision prohibiting extending postsecondary education benefits to such aliens on the basis of in-state residency, on the basis that nonresident benefits were keyed to non-residential criteria).

Sometimes the limits to explicit federal preemption shade into authorization. In 2011, the Supreme Court reviewed a deeply controversial Arizona law providing for the suspension or revocation of licenses of state employers that knowingly or intentionally employ unauthorized aliens, and which requires that state employers use an internet-based system for checking the work authorization status of their employees. Chamber of Commerce v. Whiting, 131 S.Ct. 1968, 179 L.Ed.2d 1031 (2011). Business and civil rights organizations challenged the compatibility of the Arizona law with the Immigration Reform and Control Act (IRCA), which makes it unlawful for employers and other entities "to hire, or to recruit or refer for a fee, for employment in the United States an alien knowing the alien is an unauthorized alien." 8 U.S.C. § 1324a(a)(1)(A). At the same time, IRCA also restricts the ability of States to combat employment of unauthorized workers; the Act expressly preempts "any State or local law imposing civil or criminal sanctions (other than through licensing and similar laws) upon those who employ, or recruit or refer for a fee for employment, unauthorized aliens." § 1324a(h)(2).

Once the Supreme Court determined that the Arizona law was not expressly preempted (since it was styled as a licensing law), a plurality of the justices further rejected the argument that the law was impliedly preempted on the ground that "Arizona's procedures simply implement the sanctions that Congress expressly allowed Arizona to pursue through licensing laws. Given that Congress specifically preserved such authority for the States, it stands to reason that Congress did not intend to prevent the States from using appropriate tools to exercise that authority." 131 S.Ct. at 1981 (Roberts, C.J.) (plurality op.). An exemption from express preemption, in other words, served equally as an exemption from implied preemption.

Can statutory authorization do more than insulate states from statutory preemption? In 2007, Congress enacted the Sudan Accountability and Divestment Act of 2007, Pub. L. No. 110–174, 121 Stat. 2516 (2007) (codified as amended at 15 U.S.C. § 80a–13, 50 U.S.C. § 1701), which among other things permitted states and municipalities to adopt and enforce measures that divested state and local government assets or prohibited the investment of state and local government assets from certain business operations in the Sudan. How completely does this immunize states and localities from claims that the states are intruding on foreign prerogatives? Would it matter if the federal government established the list of implicated business operations in Sudan? If the federal government left it to the states to determine those operations?

President George W. Bush issued a signing statement providing that:

> This Act purports to authorize State and local governments to divest from companies doing business in named sectors in Sudan and thus risks being interpreted as insulating from Federal oversight State and local divestment actions that could interfere with implementation of national foreign policy. However, as the Constitution vests the exclusive authority to conduct foreign relations with the Federal Government, the executive branch shall construe and enforce this legislation in a manner that does not conflict with that authority.

Statement on Signing the Sudan Accountability and Divestment Act of 2007, 43 Weekly Comp. Pres. Doc. (Dec. 31, 2007). Was President Bush's concern well founded? You may be best positioned to evaluate this at the close of this chapter, after contemplating the scope of the dormant foreign affairs power.

5. *Relevance of Foreign Protests to State Laws*. In considering whether the Massachusetts statute conflicted with the federal statute's objective, the Supreme Court noted that protests against the Massachusetts statute had been made to the United States by Japan, the Association of Southeast Asian Nations (ASEAN), and the European Community. Further, the Court noted that the European Community and Japan had filed complaints with the World Trade Organization. For the Court, these protests demonstrated that the Massachusetts law had "complicated [the federal government's] dealings with foreign sovereigns and proven an impediment to accomplishing objectives assigned it by Congress." 530 U.S. at 383. Such language might be read as simply reinforcing the explicit basis for the decision in *Crosby*—preemption by a statute. Yet is the Court really limiting itself to preemption by statute, or is there an "extra-statutory solicitude for formal diplomatic interaction with

foreign powers, and for the President's presumptively exclusive ability to engage in it"? Edward T. Swaine, *Crosby as Foreign Relations Law*, 41 VA. J. INT'L L. 481, 502 (2001); *see* Carlos Manuel Vázquez, *W(h)ither Zschernig?*, 46 VILL. L. REV. 1259, 1287–1304 (2001) (arguing that the Court's approach in *Crosby* would have led to preemption even in the absence of a federal statute); Sarah H. Cleveland, *Crosby and the "One-Voice" Myth in U.S. Foreign Relations*, 46 VILL. L. REV. 975, 976 (2001) (arguing that the Court's use of the "one voice" doctrine in statutory preemption analysis "contravened the federal government's longstanding deference to the states in this area.").

6. *Relevance of a Treaty Regime to Statutory Preemption.* The *Crosby* decision referred to the Court's earlier decision in *United States v. Locke*, 529 U.S. 89, 120 S.Ct. 1135, 146 L.Ed.2d 69 (2000). In that case, an association of tanker owners asked a federal court to strike down a regulatory regime of the State of Washington that was aimed at preventing, and providing remedies for, oil spills by oceangoing oil tankers. The Supreme Court found that the federal government's overall regulation in this area clearly invalidated various regulations of the State of Washington due to "field preemption." In doing so, the Court did not find it necessary to decide whether international treaties and instruments had a direct preemptive effect on the state regulatory scheme. The Court noted, however, that the "existence of the treaties and agreements on standards of shipping is of relevance, of course, for these agreements give force to the longstanding rule that the enactment of a uniform federal scheme displaces state law, and the treaties indicate Congress will have demanded national uniformity regarding maritime commerce." *Id.* at 103.

7. *Other Forms of Preemption.* Preemption in the area of foreign-relations law does not only occur by statute. In *Moreno*, the Court noted various treaties that obligated the United States to accord privileges and immunities to aliens (or their families) employed by international organizations. *See* 458 U.S. at 14–16. The next section considers the issue of preemption of state law by international agreement.

SECTION 3. PREEMPTION OF STATE LAW BY INTERNATIONAL AGREEMENT

THE FEDERALIST PAPERS NO. 22 (HAMILTON)

(Clinton Rossiter ed., 1961).

The treaties of the United States under the present [Articles of Confederation] are liable to the infractions of thirteen different legislatures, and as many different courts of final jurisdiction, acting under the authority of those legislatures. The faith, the reputation, the peace of the whole Union are thus continually at the mercy of the prejudices, the passions, and the interests of every member of which it is composed. Is it possible that foreign nations can either respect or confide in such a government? Is it possible that the people of America will longer consent to trust their honor, their happiness, their safety, on so precarious a foundation?

WARE v. HYLTON

3 U.S. (3 Dall.) 199, 220–77, 1 L.Ed. 568 (1796) (footnote omitted).

[The 1783 Treaty of Paris, which ended the American Revolution, provided that British creditors would "meet with no lawful Impediment to the Recovery" of their debts, and would be paid not in state currency but in the equivalent of gold. *See* Definitive Treaty of Peace, art. IV, Sept. 3, 1783, U.S.-Gr. Brit., *reprinted in* 2 *Treaties and Other International Acts of the United States of America* 151 (Hunter Miller ed., 1931) (Treaty of Paris). After the U.S. Constitution took effect in 1788, a Virginian refused to pay a debt owed to a British subject. An administrator acting on behalf of the British subject sued in U.S. federal court to recover the debt. Virginia state law, enacted in 1777, provided for the confiscation of debts owed to enemy aliens. Consequently, the case presented the question of whether, under the new Constitution, the Treaty of Paris could override an otherwise valid state law. The Supreme Court reached a unanimous holding. Justice Samuel Chase wrote the lead opinion, and the other justices wrote separately, following the British custom of the day.]

CHASE, JUSTICE . . . .

. . . .

. . . If the legislature of Virginia could not, by ordinary acts of legislation, do these things, yet, possessing the supreme sovereign power of the state, she certainly could do them, by a treaty of peace; if she had not parted with the power of making such treaty. If Virginia had such power, before she delegated it to congress [under the Articles of Confederation], it follows, that afterwards, that body possessed it. Whether Virginia parted with the power of making treaties of peace, will be seen by a perusal of the 9th article of the [Articles of Confederation] (ratified by all the states, on the first of March 1781), in which it was declared, "that the United States in congress assembled, shall have the sole and exclusive right and power of determining on peace or war, except in the two cases mentioned in the 6th article; and of entering into treaties and alliances, with a proviso, when made, respecting commerce." This grant has no restriction, nor is there any limitation on the power in any part of the confederation. A right to make peace, necessarily includes the power of determining on what terms peace shall be made. A power to make treaties must, of necessity, imply a power to decide the terms on which they shall be made: a war between two nations can only be concluded by treaty.

Surely, the sacrificing [of] public or private property, to obtain peace, cannot be the cases in which a treaty would be void. . . . It seems to me, that treaties made by congress, according to the confederation, were superior to the laws of the states; because the confederation made them obligatory on all the states. They were so declared by congress on the 13th of April 1787; were so admitted by the legislatures and executives of most of the states; and were so decided by the judiciary of the general government, and by the judiciaries of some of the state governments.

If doubts could exist, before the establishment of the present national government, they must be entirely removed by the 6th article of the constitution, which provides "That all treaties made, or which shall be made, under the authority of the United States, shall be the supreme law of the land; and the judges in every state shall be bound thereby, anything in the constitution or laws of any state to the contrary notwithstanding." There can be no limitation on the power of the people of the United States. By their authority, the state constitutions were made, and by their authority the constitution of the United States was established; and they had the power to change or abolish the state constitutions, or to make them yield to the general government, and to treaties made by their authority. A treaty cannot be the supreme law of the land, that is, of all the United States, if any act of a state legislature can stand in its way. If the constitution of a state (which is the fundamental law of the state, and paramount to its legislature) must give way to a treaty, and fall before it; can it be questioned, whether the less power, an act of the state legislature, must not be prostrate? It is the declared will of the people of the United States, that every treaty made by the authority of the United States, shall be superior to the constitution and laws of any individual state; and their will alone is to decide. If a law of a state, contrary to a treaty, is not void, but voidable only, by a repeal, or nullification by a state legislature, this certain consequence follows, that the will of a small part of the United States may control or defeat the will of the whole. . . .

. . . .

IREDELL, JUSTICE. . . .

. . . .

The opinion I have long entertained and still do entertain . . . [is] that the stipulation in favor of creditors, so as to enable them to bring suits, and recover the full value of their debts, could not, at that time [of the Articles of Confederation], be carried into effect, in any other manner, than by a repeal of the statutes of the different states, constituting the impediments to their recovery, and the passing of such other acts as might be necessary to give the recovery entire efficacy, in execution of the treaty. . . .

. . . .

. . . Requisitions formerly [by Congress, under the Articles of Confederation,] were made binding in point of moral obligation, (so far as the amount of money was concerned, of which congress was the constitutional judge,) but the right and the power being separated, it was found often impracticable to make them act in conjunction. To obviate this difficulty, which every one knows had been the means of greatly distressing the Union, and injuring its public credit, a power was given [under the U.S. Constitution] to the representatives of the whole Union to raise taxes, by their own authority, for the good of the whole. Similar embarrassments had been found about the treaty [power]: this was binding in moral obligation, but could not be constitutionally carried into effect (at least in the opinion of many), so far as acts of legislation then in being constituted an impediment, but by a repeal. The extreme inconveniences felt from such a system dictated the remedy which the constitution has now provided, "that all treaties made or which shall be made under the authority of the United States, shall be the supreme law of the land; and that the judges in every state shall be bound thereby, anything in the constitution or laws of any state to the contrary notwithstanding." Under this constitution, therefore, so far as a treaty constitutionally is binding, upon principles of moral obligation, it is also, by the vigor of its own authority, to be executed in fact. It would not otherwise be the supreme law, in the new sense provided for, and it was so before, in a moral sense.

The provision extends to subsisting as well as to future treaties. I consider, therefore, that when this constitution was ratified, the case as to the treaty in question stood upon the same footing, as if every act constituting an impediment to a creditor's recovery had been expressly repealed, and any further act passed, which the public obligation had before required, if a repeal alone would not have been sufficient.

NOTE ON ORIGINAL MEANING OF TREATIES AS SUPREME LAW

Justices Chase and Iredell in *Ware v. Hylton* agreed that the Treaty of Peace was a self-executing obligation that, under the U.S. Constitution, superseded the conflicting Virginia state law. While they differed over whether treaties under the Articles of Confederation were similarly self-executing, it is generally accepted that one of the problems with the Articles of Confederation was the inability of Congress to compel the several states to comply with treaties. *See* Carlos Manuel Vázquez, *Treaty-Based Rights and Remedies of Individuals*, 92 COLUM. L. REV. 1082, 1101–04 (1992). That is why Hamilton in *The Federalist Papers* No. 22 and Madison in *The Federalist Papers* No. 42 (*see* Chapter 1, Section 1) heralded the need for a new treaty power, one that would not allow treaties to "be substantially frustrated by regulations of the States." *Ware v. Hilton* was the first case to establish federal judicial review of state laws, and preceded *Marbury v. Madison* (establishing federal judicial review of federal statutes and executive acts) by seven years.

As was discussed in Chapter 3, the scope of the treaty power has been regarded by the Supreme Court as quite broad, resulting in the preemption of various state laws. In the case of *Missouri v. Holland*, 252 U.S. 416, 40 S.Ct. 382, 64 L.Ed. 641 (1920) (*see* Chapter 3, Section 6), the Supreme Court endorsed the proposition that the President and the Senate together may achieve via the treaty power what Congress and the President cannot do by statute under Article I, Section 8 of the Constitution. In that case, the Supreme Court found that even if Congress could not by a statute, enacted solely under Article I, impose restrictions on the several states regarding the hunting of migratory birds, such restrictions could be imposed by a statute that implemented a treaty (in that case, the U.S.-U.K. Migratory Bird Treaty). Thereafter, similar preemption of state law has occurred. Note, however, that in each of the following cases—like *Ware* but unlike *Missouri v. Holland*—the

Supreme Court explicitly or implicitly established that the treaty was self-executing and preempted state law without the assistance of a statute.

ASAKURA v. CITY OF SEATTLE

265 U.S. 332, 339–41, 44 S.Ct. 515, 68 L.Ed. 1041 (1924) (footnote omitted).

[Seattle adopted a municipal ordinance that excluded aliens from engaging in business as pawnbrokers. A Japanese national sued on the ground that a U.S.-Japan treaty of commerce and friendship provided that citizens of one country may engage in commerce in the other country on the same terms as local citizens. Seattle argued that since Congress could not regulate on such a matter, the treaty unconstitutionally intruded upon rights left to the states under the Tenth Amendment. For more detail, see Chapter 3, Section 4.]

MR. JUSTICE BUTLER delivered the opinion of the Court.

. . . .

The treaty-making power of the United States is not limited by any express provision of the Constitution, and, though it does not extend "so far as to authorize what the Constitution forbids," it does extend to all proper subjects of negotiation between our government and other nations. . . . The treaty was made to strengthen friendly relations between the two nations. . . . Treaties for the protection of citizens of one country residing in the territory of another are numerous, and make for good understanding between nations. The treaty is binding within the State of Washington. . . . It stands on the same footing of supremacy as do the provisions of the Constitution and the laws of the United States. . . .

KOLOVRAT v. OREGON

366 U.S. 187, 190–98, 81 S.Ct. 922, 6 L.Ed.2d 218 (1961) (footnotes omitted).

[A national and resident of communist Yugoslavia sought to collect an inheritance in Oregon. The state courts denied his claim under an Oregon probate statute that required him to show that he would enjoy the inheritance "without confiscation" and that U.S. nationals had a reciprocal ability to inherit property in the claimant's country. The Oregon Supreme Court found that reciprocity did not exist because Yugoslavian law gave discretion to Yugoslavian authorities to control foreign exchange payments in a way that might prevent Americans from receiving the full value of Yugoslavian inheritances.]

MR. JUSTICE BLACK delivered the opinion of the Court.

. . . .

[R]ecognizing quite properly that state policies as to the rights of aliens to inherit must give way under our Constitution's Supremacy Clause to "overriding" federal treaties and conflicting arrangements, the state court considered petitioners' contention, supported in this Court by the Government as *amicus curiae*, that petitioners were entitled to inherit this personal property because of an 1881 Treaty between the United States and Serbia, which country is now a part of Yugoslavia. The state court rejected this contention on the basis of its interpretation of the Treaty although it correctly recognized that the Treaty is still in effect between the United States and Yugoslavia. The state court also rejected petitioners' contention that their claims could not be defeated solely because of the possible effect of the Yugoslavian Foreign Exchange Laws and Regulations since those laws and regulations admittedly meet the requirements of the Bretton Woods Agreement of 1945, to which both Yugoslavia and the United States are signatories. We granted certiorari because the cases involve important rights asserted in reliance upon federal treaty obligations. . . .

. . . .

The 1881 Treaty clearly declares its basic purpose to bring about "reciprocally full and entire liberty of commerce and navigation" between the two signatory nations so that their citizens "shall be at liberty to establish themselves freely in each other's territory." Their citizens are also to be free to receive, hold and dispose of property by trading, donation, marriage, inheritance or any other manner "under the same conditions as the subjects of the most favored nation." Thus, both paragraphs of Art. II of the Treaty which have pertinence here contain a "most favored nation" clause with regard to "acquiring, possessing or disposing of every kind of property." This clause means that each signatory grants to the other the broadest rights and privileges which it accords to any other nation in other treaties it has made or will make. . . .

. . . .

The International Monetary Fund (Bretton Woods) Agreement of 1945, *supra*, to which Yugoslavia and the United States are signatories, comprehensively obligates participating countries to maintain only such monetary controls as are consistent with the terms of that Agreement. The Agreement's broad purpose, as shown by Art. IV, § 4, is "to promote exchange stability, to maintain orderly exchange arrangements with other members, and to avoid competitive exchange alterations." Article VI, § 3, forbids any participating country from exercising controls over international capital movements "in a manner which will restrict payments for current transactions or which will unduly delay transfers of funds in settlement of commitments. . . ." Article 8 of the Yugoslavian laws regulating payment transactions with other countries expressly recognizes the authority of "the provisions of agreements with foreign countries which are concerned with payments." In addition to all of this, an Agreement of 1948 between our country and Yugoslavia obligated Yugoslavia, in the words of the Senate Report on the Agreement, "to continue to grant most-favored-nation treatment to Americans in ownership and acquisition of assets in Yugoslavia . . . [and] Yugoslavia is required, by article 10, to authorize persons in Yugoslavia to pay debts to United States nationals, firms, or agencies, and, so far as feasible, to permit dollar transfers for such purpose."

These treaties and agreements show that this Nation has adopted programs deemed desirable in bringing about, so far as can be done, stability and uniformity in the difficult field of world monetary controls and exchange. These arrangements have not purported to achieve a sufficiently rigid valuation of moneys to guarantee that foreign exchange payments will at all times, at all places and under all circumstances be based on a "definitely ascertainable" valuation measured by the diverse currencies of the world. Doubtless these agreements may fall short of that goal. But our National Government's powers have been exercised so far as deemed desirable and feasible toward that end, and the power to make policy with regard to such matters is a national one from the compulsion of both necessity and our Constitution. After the proper governmental agencies have selected the policy of foreign exchange for the country as a whole, Oregon of course cannot refuse to give foreign nationals their treaty rights because of fear that valid international agreements might possibly not work completely to the satisfaction of state authorities. Our National Government's assent to these international agreements, coupled with its continuing adherence to the 1881 Treaty, precludes any State from deciding that Yugoslavian laws meeting the standards of those agreements can be the basis for defeating rights conferred by the 1881 Treaty.

The judgment of the Supreme Court of Oregon is reversed and the cause remanded for proceedings not inconsistent with this opinion.

Reversed and remanded.

NOTE ON DRAFTING TREATIES TO AVOID FEDERAL-STATE CONFLICTS

Although the federal government may be able to trump states rights by use of the treaty power, the federal government has generally proceeded with treaty negotiations aware of the *political* need to conform U.S. international obligations with the existing balance of federal-state relations. As you will recall from Chapter 3, Section 6, this concern has a long pedigree, including an attempt in the U.S. Senate to amend the Constitution so as to prevent the treaty power from expanding congressional power beyond that conferred (otherwise) by the Constitution to Congress. In practice, just as federal statutes may be drafted to avoid encroaching on state prerogatives, so may treaties. Consider the approach to treaty negotiation described in the following Department of State memorandum.

U.S. DEPARTMENT OF STATE OFFICE OF THE LEGAL ADVISER MEMORANDUM SUMMARIZING U.S. VIEWS AND PRACTICE IN ADDRESSING FEDERALISM ISSUES IN TREATIES

(Nov. 8, 2002), available at http://www.state.gov/s/l/38637.htm.

As a matter of law, the Supreme Court has refused to interpret the 10th Amendment as a limitation on the exercise of the Treaty Power. In practice, therefore, the United States has not traditionally taken advantage of so-called "federalism clauses" [contained in some treaties] that allow federal states to modify their obligations under a treaty because of the legal division of competencies between a federal government and its constituent units.

As a matter of policy, however, the United States has, on occasion, sought to tailor certain international obligations to maintain the existing balance of federal-state relations with respect to the treaty's subject matter. These federalism concerns have emerged with increased frequency in recent years as the subject-matter of treaties has broadened beyond transnational issues to areas traditionally regulated by U.S. states.

The mechanisms by which the United States has sought to limit or clarify its treaty obligations because of federalism policy concerns have varied:

- It has sought to negotiate provisions that are consistent with the federal government's traditional authorities (i.e., avoiding federalism concerns where possible);
- It has attached understandings as part of its adherence to certain treaties that clarify the U.S. understanding that the treaty's obligations do not require action beyond existing federal authorities;
- In the context of certain human rights treaties, it has attached reservations or understandings that accept all of the treaty's obligations, but clarify that they will be implemented at the appropriate government level—federal, state or local;
- It has sought to negotiate new versions of a "federalism clause" that the United States could invoke as a matter of policy, rather than as a matter of law; and
- It has taken reservations to treaties to modify U.S. obligations to a level that the federal government is willing to assume.

. . . .

Survey of Past Practice with Respect to
Federalism Issues in U.S. Treaties

I. Examples of Federalism Clauses/Reservations *Used* by the United States

- *1948 OAS Charter*: The U.S. instrument of ratification included a reservation that none of the Charter's provisions "shall be considered as enlarging the powers of the Federal Government of the United States or limiting the powers of the several states of the Federal Union with respect to any matters recognized under the Constitution as being within the reserved powers of the several states.["][1]
- *Instrument for Amendment of the Constitution of the International Labor Organization*: Article 19(7) provides:

> (b) in respect of Conventions and Recommendations which the Federal Government regards as appropriate under its constitutional system, in whole or in part, for action by the constituent States ... rather than for federal action, the Federal Government shall—
>
> > (i) make, in accordance with its Constitution and the Constitutions of the States ... concerned, effective arrangements for the reference of such Conventions and Recommendations not later than eighteen months from the closing of the session ... to the appropriate federal [or] State ... authorities for the enactment of legislation or other action;
> >
> > (ii) arrange, subject to the concurrence of the State ..., for periodical consultations between the Federal and the State ... authorities with a view to promoting within the federal State coordinated action to give effect to the provisions of such Conventions and Recommendations;
> >
> > (iii) inform the Director General of the International Labour Office of the measures taken in accordance with this article to bring such Conventions and Recommendations before the appropriate federal [or] State ... authorities with particulars of the authorities regarded as appropriate and of the action taken by them;
> >
> > (iv) in respect of each such Convention which it has not ratified, report to the Director–General of the International Labour Office ... the position of the law and practice of the federation and its constituent States ..., showing the extent to which effect has been ... or is proposed to be given, to any of the provisions of the Convention ...;
> >
> > (v) in respect of each such Recommendation, report to the Director–General of the International Labour Office ... the position of the law and practice of the federation and its constituent States ..., showing the extent to which effect has been ... or is proposed to be given, to the provisions of the Recommendation

1. At the time, the United States reservation had to be accepted by all other states parties, which it was, although Mexico accepted the U.S. reservation on a reciprocal basis, but pointed out that it does not constitute a precedent, inasmuch as reservations of this nature pose the delicate problem of the fulfillment—on the part of the federal states—of obligations arising from international instruments. Uruguay communicated that it objects in principle to federalism reservations but would accept this one, given the unusual circumstances.

and such modifications of these provisions as have been found or may be found necessary in adopting or applying them.

- *1967 Protocol to the Convention Relating to the Status of Refugees*: Article VI incorporates the provisions of Article 41 of the 1951 Convention Relating to the Status of Refugees, 189 UNTS 150, which reads as follows:

  In the case of a Federal or non-unitary State, the following provisions shall apply:

  (b) With respect to those articles of this Convention that come within the legislative jurisdiction of constituent States, provinces or cantons which are not, under the constitutional system of the Federation, bound to take legislative action, the Federal Government shall bring such articles with a favourable recommendation to the notice of the appropriate authorities of States, provinces or cantons at the earliest possible moment.

  (c) A Federal State Party to this Convention shall, at the request of any other Contracting State transmitted through the Secretary–General of the United Nations, supply a statement of the law and practice of the Federation and its constituent units in regard to any particular provision of the Convention showing the extent to which effect has been given to that provision by legislative or other action.

  The Secretary of State's Report (July 25, 1968) that accompanied the President's transmittal of the Protocol to the Senate described the effect of Article VI:

  By virtue of Article VI of the Protocol, the United States would assume obligations only in respect of matters that come within the legislative jurisdiction of the Federal Government. State laws would not be superseded by any provision of the Convention. With respect to any articles of the Convention that may come within the legislative jurisdiction of the states under our constitutional system, the Federal Government is obligated to bring such articles to the notice of the appropriate state authorities with a favorable recommendation.

- *1966 International Covenant on Civil and Political Rights*: the 1992 U.S. instrument of ratification contained a reservation, indicating that the Convention's provisions:

  ["S]hall be implemented by the federal government to the extent that it exercises legislative and judicial jurisdiction over the matters covered therein, and otherwise by state and local governments. The Federal Government shall take measures appropriate to the Federal system to the end that the competent authorities of the state ... may take appropriate measures for the fulfillment of the Covenant."

This was in response to a clause in Article 50 of the Convention providing that the "provisions of the present Covenant shall extend to all parts of federal states without any limitations or exceptions." That Article had been inserted into the Covenant after the United States had proposed a federal-state clause, but then indicated in 1953 that the United States would not ratify the Covenants. A similar reservation was attached to the U.S. instrument of ratification to the International Covenant on the Elimination of All Forms of Racial Discrimination.

. . . .

- *Council of Europe Corruption Convention (transmittal to Senate pending)*: The Convention requires Parties to criminalize "at the national level" various types of bribery. At the final negotiating session, negotiators agreed to a U.S. request to include in the official Explanatory Report a statement that Parties assume obligations under the Convention "only to the extent consistent with their Constitution and the fundamental principles of their legal system, including, where appropriate, the principles of federalism." As an authoritative expression of the intentions of the Convention's negotiators, the United States is relying on this statement as the basis for implementing the Convention obligations solely at the federal level through federal law.
- *Council of Europe Cybercrime Convention* [Authors' Note: The Senate consented to this treaty and in 2007 it entered into force for the United States.]: The Convention requires parties to criminalize certain conduct related to computer systems, to ensure that procedures are available to investigate cybercrime offenses, and to provide broad international cooperation in investigating such crimes and obtaining evidence. Since the United States traditionally regulates conduct based on its effects on interstate or foreign commerce, while matters of minimal or purely local concern are regulated by the states, the United States decided as a policy matter to pursue a provision in the text allowing it to take a federalism reservation. In the absence of the reservation, there would be a narrow category of conduct regulated by U.S. state, but not federal, law that the United States would be required to criminalize. The United States successfully negotiated such a clause just prior to the Convention's adoption, despite the initial objection of several nations, notably France. Article 41 now reads as follows:

  1. A federal State may reserve the right to assume obligations under Chapter II of this Convention consistent with its fundamental principles governing the relationship between its central government and constituent States ... provided that it is still able to co-operate under Chapter II.

  2. When making a reservation under paragraph 1, a federal State may not apply the terms of such reservation to exclude or substantially diminish its obligations to provide for measures set forth

in Chapter II. Overall, it shall provide for a broad and effective law enforcement capability with respect to those measures.

3. With regard to the provisions of this Convention, the application of which comes under the jurisdiction of constituent States or other similar territorial entities, that are not obliged by the constitutional system of the federation to take legislative measures, the federal government shall inform the competent authorities of such States of the said provisions with its favourable opinion encouraging them to take appropriate action to give them effect.

II. Examples of Federalism Clauses *Not Invoked* by the United States

- *1958 UN Convention on the Recognition and Enforcement of Foreign Arbitral Awards*: Article XI is identical to Article VI of the Refugee Protocol (see above). The article-by-article analysis that accompanied the transmittal of the Convention to the Senate described the effect of this provision:

  This article recognizes the special situation with respect to jurisdiction in federal or nonunitary States and attempts to accommodate such States. It would, however, run counter to the express provisions of the article for the United States to seek to take advantage of its provisions with respect to foreign arbitral awards arising out of commercial relationships. The Federal Arbitration Act of 1925 (9 U.S.C. 1–14) and the decisions of U.S. Courts relating thereto show that legislation on arbitration is clearly within the competence of the Federal Government.[2]

. . . .

NOTE ON PREEMPTION OF STATE LAW BY EXECUTIVE AGREEMENT

Chapter 3, Section 7, noted that many international agreements concluded by the United States are not done in the form of a "treaty" as that term is understood in the U.S. Constitution. Some agreements are concluded by the President based on authorization from a majority of both Houses of Congress (congressional-executive agreements) or based solely on the President's own constitutional powers (presidential-executive agreements). In *United States v. Belmont*, 301 U.S. 324, 57 S.Ct. 758, 81 L.Ed. 1134 (1937) and *Dames & Moore v. Regan*, 453 U.S. 654, 101 S.Ct. 2972, 69 L.Ed.2d 918 (1981), the Supreme Court upheld the constitutionality of such agreements even in the face of contrary state laws or rules. In *Belmont*, the President had concluded an executive agreement that, among other things, recognized Soviet ownership rights in expropriated property and transferred those rights to the U.S.

---

2. The SFRC Report (Sen. Executive Rept. 10, 90th Cong., 2d Session) contains the testimony of Amb. Richard D. Kearney of State/L. Amb. Kearney's testimony points out that the effect of the Convention on the laws of U.S. States is mitigated by the gradual adoption by states of uniform laws on arbitration procedures and widespread support of Courts and the bar that will enable the Convention to be enforceable in a growing majority of U.S. States. To a query whether the Convention would extend Federal jurisdiction into new areas, Kearney replied that the Federal Arbitration Act already provided more than is required by the Convention.

government. If the Supreme Court had applied New York law in *Belmont,* certain creditors would have had priority to the property rather than the federal government (the state of New York had refused to recognize the validity of the Soviet expropriation). Instead, the Court looked to the executive agreement as the controlling law, and therefore found that the U.S. government and not the creditors were entitled to the property. *Dames & Moore* upheld the President's authority under a sole-executive agreement to transfer claims pending in both U.S. federal and state courts to an international arbitral tribunal, notwithstanding any state laws or rules to the contrary. In *American Insurance Ass'n v. Garamendi*, 539 U.S. 396, 416, 123 S.Ct. 2374, 156 L.Ed.2d 376 (2003) (excerpted in Section 5 below), the Supreme Court stated that "valid executive agreements are fit to preempt state law, just as treaties are. . . ."

These cases have led most authorities to conclude that executive agreements supersede state law in the same manner as treaties. *See, e.g.*, 1 *Restatement (Third) of the Foreign Relations Law of the United States* § 302(d) (1987); Bruce Ackerman & David Golove, *Is NAFTA Constitutional?*, 108 HARV. L. REV. 799 (1995). Nevertheless, at least one commentator maintains that legislative-executive agreements must remain within the scope of Congress's enumerated powers, see John C. Yoo, *Laws as Treaties?: The Constitutionality of Congressional–Executive Agreements*, 99 MICH. L. REV. 757 (2001), others contend that sole-executive agreements should not be allowed to supersede state law, see Michael D. Ramsey, *Executive Agreements and the (Non)Treaty Power*, 77 N.C. L. REV. 133 (1998), while still others maintain that sole-executive agreements should only be allowed to supercede state law in particular areas, such as claims settlements, see Bradford R. Clark, *Domesticating Sole Executive Agreements*, 93 VA. L. REV. 1573 (2007). Thus far, U.S. courts have not adopted these theories. Do you think they should?

SECTION 4. PREEMPTION OF STATE LAW BY THE DORMANT FOREIGN COMMERCE CLAUSE

INTRODUCTORY NOTE

U.S. Constitution, Article I, Section 8, Clause 3 provides: "The Congress shall have Power . . . To regulate Commerce with foreign Nations, and among the several states, and with the Indian Tribes. . . ." U.S. courts have found that the Commerce Clause and the Foreign Commerce Clause are not only "positive" grants of power to Congress, but are also "negative" constraints upon the several states. In other words, U.S. courts have developed a doctrine of the "dormant" Commerce Clause and dormant Foreign Commerce Clause, which can have the effect of striking down state regulation even in situations where Congress has not expressly or implicitly preempted the state. What is "dormant" is the congressional exercise of the power (not the clauses themselves). The dormant Foreign Commerce Clause may be implicated include state taxation of foreign business and restrictions by states on their governments or companies from doing business with foreign nations. The U.S.

Supreme Court has addressed this issue on more than one occasion in the context of state taxation of foreign business.

As you read *Japan Line*, which concerns a state property tax, and *Barclays Bank PLC*, which concerns a corporate franchise tax, consider the following questions. What four requirements must be met for a state tax law to survive a Commerce Clause challenge? What two additional requirements must be met for a state tax law to survive a Foreign Commerce Clause challenge? Why have those additional requirements? Why was the state law in *Japan Line* struck down, while the state law in *Barclays Bank PLC* was upheld? In the *Natsios* case, what standard is applied when reviewing a state law that imposes a sanction on foreign commerce?

JAPAN LINE, LTD. v. COUNTY OF LOS ANGELES

441 U.S. 434, 435–54, 99 S.Ct. 1813, 60 L.Ed.2d 336 (1979) (footnotes omitted).

MR. JUSTICE BLACKMUN delivered the opinion of the Court.

This case presents the question whether a State, consistently with the Commerce Clause of the Constitution, may impose a nondiscriminatory ad valorem property tax on foreign-owned instrumentalities (cargo containers) of international commerce.

. . . .

Appellants are six Japanese shipping companies; they are incorporated under the laws of Japan, and they have their principal places of business and commercial domiciles in that country. . . . Appellants operate vessels used exclusively in foreign commerce; these vessels are registered in Japan and have their home ports there. . . . The vessels are specifically designed and constructed to accommodate large cargo shipping containers. The containers, like the ships, are owned by appellants, have their home ports in Japan, and are used exclusively for hire in the transportation of cargo in foreign commerce. . . . Each container is in constant transit save for time spent undergoing repair or awaiting loading and unloading of cargo. All appellants' containers are subject to property tax in Japan and, in fact, are taxed there.

Appellees are political subdivisions of the State of California. Appellants' containers, in the course of their international journeys, pass through appellees' jurisdictions intermittently. Although none of appellants' containers stays permanently in California, some are there at any given time; a container's average stay in the State is less than three weeks. . . . The containers engage in no intrastate or interstate transportation of cargo except as continuations of international voyages. . . . Any movements or periods of nonmovement of containers in appellees' jurisdictions are essential to, and inseparable from, the containers' efficient use as instrumentalities of foreign commerce. . . .

Property present in California on March 1 (the "lien date" under California law) of any year is subject to ad valorem property tax. Cal. Rev. & Tax. Code Ann. §§ 117, 405, 2192 (West 1970 and Supp. 1979). A number of appellants' containers were physically present in appellees' jurisdictions on the lien dates in 1970, 1971, and 1972. ... Appellees levied property taxes in excess of $550,000 on the assessed value of the containers present on March 1 of the three years in question. ...

. . . .

Appellees contend that cargo shipping containers, like other vehicles of commercial transport, are subject to property taxation. ... The containers, they argue, have a "substantial nexus" with California because some of them are present in that State at all times. ... The tax, moreover, is "fairly apportioned," since it is levied only on the containers' "average presence" in California. The tax "does not discriminate," thirdly, since it falls evenhandedly on all personal property in the State; indeed, as an ad valorem tax of general application, it is of necessity nondiscriminatory. The tax, finally, is "fairly related to the services provided by" California, services that include not only police and fire protection, but also the benefits of a trained work force and the advantages of a civilized society.

... The premise of appellees' argument is that the Commerce Clause analysis is identical, regardless of whether interstate or foreign commerce is involved. This premise, we have concluded, must be rejected. When construing Congress' power to "regulate Commerce with foreign Nations," a more extensive constitutional inquiry is required.

When a State seeks to tax the instrumentalities of foreign commerce, two additional considerations ... come into play. The first is the enhanced risk of multiple taxation. It is a commonplace of constitutional jurisprudence that multiple taxation may well be offensive to the Commerce Clause. ...

. . . .

Second, a state tax on the instrumentalities of foreign commerce may impair federal uniformity in an area where federal uniformity is essential. Foreign commerce is pre-eminently a matter of national concern. "In international relations and with respect to foreign intercourse and trade the people of the United States act through a single government with unified and adequate national power." *Board of Trustees v. United States,* 289 U.S. 48, 59 (1933). Although the Constitution, Art. I, § 8, cl. 3, grants Congress power to regulate commerce "with foreign Nations" and "among the several States" in parallel phrases, there is evidence that the Founders intended the scope of the foreign commerce power to be the greater. Cases of this Court, stressing the need for uniformity in treating with other nations, echo this distinction. In approving state taxes on the instrumentalities of interstate commerce, the Court consistently has distinguished oceangoing traffic ...; these cases reflect an awareness that the taxation of foreign commerce may necessitate a uniform national rule. Indeed, in *Pullman's Palace,* the Court wrote that the " 'vehicles of commerce by water being instruments of intercommunication with other nations, the regulation of them is assumed by the national legislature.' " 141 U.S., at 24, [q]uoting *Railroad Co. v. Maryland*, 21 Wall. 456, 470 (1875). Finally, in discussing the Import–Export Clause, this Court, in *Michelin Tire Corp. v. Wages*, 423 U.S. 276, 285 (1976), spoke of the Framers' overriding concern that "the Federal Government must speak with one voice when regulating commercial relations with foreign governments." The need for federal uniformity is no less paramount in ascertaining the negative implications of Congress' power to "regulate Commerce with foreign Nations" under the Commerce Clause.

A state tax on instrumentalities of foreign commerce may frustrate the achievement of federal uniformity in several ways. If the State imposes an apportioned tax, international disputes over reconciling apportionment formulae may arise. If a novel state tax creates an asymmetry in the international tax structure, foreign nations disadvantaged by the levy may retaliate against American-owned instrumentalities present in their jurisdictions. Such retaliation of necessity would be directed at American transportation equipment in general, not just that of the taxing State, so that the Nation as a whole would suffer. If other States followed the taxing State's example, various instrumentalities of commerce could be subjected to varying degrees of multiple taxation, a result that would plainly prevent this Nation from "speaking with one voice" in regulating foreign commerce.

... If a state tax contravenes either of these precepts, it is unconstitutional under the Commerce Clause.

....

Analysis of California's tax under these principles dictates that the tax, as applied to appellants' containers, is impermissible. ...

First, California's tax results in multiple taxation of the instrumentalities of foreign commerce. By stipulation, appellants' containers are owned, based, and registered in Japan; they are used exclusively in international commerce; and they remain outside Japan only so long as needed to complete their international missions. Under these circumstances, Japan has the right and the power to tax the containers in full. California's tax, however, creates more than the *risk* of multiple taxation; it produces multiple taxation in fact. Appellants' containers not only "are subject to property tax ... in Japan," ... but, as the trial court found, "are, in fact, taxed in Japan." ... Thus, if appellees' levies were sustained, appellants "would be paying a double tax." ...

Second, California's tax prevents this Nation from "speaking with one voice" in regulating foreign trade. The desirability of uniform treatment of containers used exclusively in foreign commerce is evidenced by the Customs Convention on Containers, which the United States and Japan have signed. ... Under this Convention, containers temporarily imported are admitted free of "all duties and taxes whatsoever chargeable by reason of importation." ... The Convention reflects a national policy to remove impediments to the use of containers as "instruments of international traffic." 19 U.S.C. § 1322(a). California's tax, however, will frustrate attainment of federal uniformity. It is stipulated that American-owned containers are not taxed in Japan. ... California's tax thus creates an asymmetry in international maritime taxation operating to Japan's disadvantage. The risk of retaliation by Japan, under these circumstances, is acute, and such retaliation of necessity would be felt by the Nation as a whole. If other States follow California's example (Oregon already has done so), foreign-owned containers will be subjected to various degrees of multiple taxation, depending on which American ports they enter. This result, obviously, would make "speaking with one voice" impossible. California, by its unilateral act, cannot be permitted to place these impediments before this Nation's conduct of its foreign relations and its foreign trade.

Because California's ad valorem tax, as applied to appellants' containers, results in multiple taxation of the instrumentalities of foreign commerce, and because it prevents the Federal Government from "speaking with one voice" in international trade, the tax is inconsistent with Congress' power to "regulate Commerce with foreign Nations." We hold the tax, as applied, unconstitutional under the Commerce Clause.

BARCLAYS BANK PLC v. FRANCHISE TAX BOARD

512 U.S. 298, 301–31, 114 S.Ct. 2268, 129 L.Ed.2d 244 (1994) (footnotes omitted).

JUSTICE GINSBURG delivered the opinion of the Court.

Eleven years ago, in *Container Corp. of America v. Franchise Tax Bd.*, 463 U.S. 159 (1983), this Court upheld California's income-based corporate franchise tax, as applied to a multinational enterprise, against a comprehensive challenge made under the Due Process and Commerce Clauses of the Federal Constitution. *Container Corp.* involved a corporate taxpayer domiciled and headquartered in the United States; in addition to its stateside components, the taxpayer had a number of overseas subsidiaries incorporated in the countries in which they operated. The Court's decision in *Container Corp.* did not address the constitutionality of California's taxing scheme as applied to "domestic corporations with foreign parents or [to] foreign corporations with either foreign parents or foreign subsidiaries." *Id.*, at 189, n. 26. In the consolidated cases before us, we return to the taxing scheme earlier considered in *Container Corp.* and resolve matters left open in that case.

The petitioner in No. 92–1384, Barclays Bank PLC (Barclays), is a United Kingdom corporation in the Barclays Group, a multinational banking enterprise. The petitioner in No. 92–1839, Colgate–Palmolive Co. (Colgate), is the United States-based parent of a multinational manufacturing and sales enterprise. Each enterprise has operations in California. During the years here at issue, California determined the state corporate franchise tax due for these operations under a method known as "worldwide combined reporting." California's scheme first looked to the worldwide income of the multinational enterprise, and then attributed a portion of that income (equal to the average of the proportions of worldwide payroll, property, and sales located in California) to the California operations. The State imposed its tax on the income thus attributed to Barclays' and Colgate's California business.

Barclays urges that California's tax system distinctively burdens foreign-based multinationals and results in double international taxation, in violation of the Commerce and Due Process Clauses. Both Barclays and Colgate contend that the scheme offends the Commerce Clause by frustrating the Federal Government's ability to "speak with one voice when regulating commercial relations with foreign governments." *Japan Line, Ltd. v. County of Los Angeles*, 441 U.S. 434, 449 (1979) (internal quotation marks omitted). . . .

. . . .

The Commerce Clause expressly gives Congress power "[t]o regulate Commerce with foreign Nations, and among the several States." U.S. Const., Art. I, 8, cl. 3. It has long been understood, as well, to provide "protection from state legislation inimical to the national commerce [even] where Congress has not acted. . . ." . . . The Clause does not shield interstate (or foreign) commerce from its "fair share of the state tax burden." . . . Absent congressional approval, however, a state tax on such commerce will not survive Commerce Clause scrutiny if the taxpayer demonstrates that the tax (1) applies to an activity lacking a substantial nexus to the taxing State; (2) is not fairly apportioned; (3) discriminates against interstate commerce; *or* (4) is not fairly related to the services provided by the State. *Complete Auto Transit, Inc. v. Brady*, 430 U.S. 274, 279 (1977).

In "the unique context of foreign commerce," a State's power is further constrained because of "the special need for federal uniformity." *Wardair Canada, Inc. v. Florida Dept. of Revenue*, 477 U.S. 1, 8 (1986). " 'In international relations and with respect to foreign intercourse and trade the people of the United States act through a single government with unified and adequate national power.' " *Japan Line, Ltd. v. County of Los Angeles*, 441 U.S., at 448. . . . A tax affecting *foreign* commerce therefore raises two concerns in addition to the four delineated in *Complete Auto*. The first is prompted by "the enhanced risk of multiple taxation." *Container Corp.*, 463 U.S., at 185. The second relates to the Federal Government's capacity to " 'speak with one voice when regulating commercial relations with foreign governments.' " *Japan Line*, 441 U.S., at 449, quoting *Michelin Tire Corp. v. Wages*, 423 U.S. 276, 285 (1976).

. . . .

Satisfied that California's corporate franchise tax is "proper and fair" as tested under *Complete Auto*'s guides, . . . we proceed to the "additional scrutiny" required when a State seeks to tax *foreign* commerce. . . . First of the two additional considerations is "the enhanced risk of multiple taxation." . . .

In *Container Corp.*, we upheld application of California's combined reporting obligation to "foreign subsidiaries of *domestic* corporations," . . .

against a charge that such application unconstitutionally exposed those subsidiaries to a risk of multiple international taxation. . . .

. . . .

Container Corp.'s holding on multiple taxation relied on two considerations: first, that multiple taxation was not the "inevitable result" of the California tax; and, second, that the "alternativ[e] reasonably available to the taxing State" (*i.e.*, some version of the separate accounting/"arm's length" approach),[1] . . . "could not eliminate the risk of double taxation" and might in some cases enhance that risk. . . . We underscored that "even though most nations have adopted the arm's-length approach in its general outlines, the precise rules under which they reallocate income among affiliated corporations often differ substantially, and *whenever that difference exists, the possibility of double taxation also exists.*" . . .

. . . .

We turn, finally, to the question ultimately and most energetically presented: Did California's worldwide combined reporting requirement, as applied to Barcal, BBI, and Colgate, "impair federal uniformity in an area where federal uniformity is essential," *Japan Line*, 441 U.S., at 448; in particular, did the State's taxing scheme "preven[t] the Federal Government from 'speaking with one voice' in international trade"? . . .

. . . .

Two decisions principally inform our judgment: first, this Court's 1983 determination in *Container Corp.*; and second, our decision three years later in *Wardair Canada, Inc. v. Florida Dept. of Revenue*, 477 U.S. 1 (1986). *Container Corp.* held that California's worldwide combined reporting requirement, as applied to domestic corporations with foreign subsidiaries, did not violate the "one voice" standard. *Container Corp.* bears on Colgate's case, but not Barclays' or BBI's, to this extent: "[T]he tax [in *Container Corp.*] was imposed not on a foreign entity . . . , but on a domestic corporation." 463 U.S., at 195. Other factors emphasized in *Container Corp.*, however, are relevant to the complaints of all three taxpayers in the consolidated cases now before us. Most significantly, the Court found no "specific indications of congressional intent" to preempt California's tax. . . .

. . . .

The Court again confronted a "one voice" argument in *Wardair Canada, Inc. v. Florida Dept. of Revenue*, 477 U.S. 1 (1986), and there rejected a Commerce Clause challenge to Florida's tax on the sale of fuel

1. [Authors' Note: Under a "separate accounting/arm's-length" approach to taxation, the taxing state treats each corporate entity within a conglomerate separately for the purpose of determining income tax liability (rather than trying to look at the range of related local and foreign corporate entities). The risk in separate accounting is that the conglomerate may manipulate transfers of value among its corporate entities to minimize its total tax liability (*i.e.*, use accounting techniques to move profits to the jurisdiction where taxes are the lowest). To prevent such manipulation, transactions between affiliated corporations need to be scrutinized to ensure that they are reported on an "arm's-length" basis, *i.e.*, at a price reflecting their true market value. California chose not to follow this approach.]

to common carriers, including airlines. Air carriers were taxed on all aviation fuel purchased in Florida, without regard to the amount the carrier consumed within the State or the amount of its in-state business. The carrier in *Wardair*, a Canadian airline that operated charter flights to and from the United States, conceded that the challenged tax satisfied the *Complete Auto* criteria and entailed no threat of multiple international taxation. Joined by the United States as *amicus curiae*, however, the carrier urged that Florida's tax "threaten[ed] the ability of the Federal Government to 'speak with one voice.' " 477 U.S., at 9. There is "a federal policy," the carrier asserted, "of reciprocal tax exemptions for aircraft, equipment, and supplies, including aviation fuel, that constitute the instrumentalities of international air traffic"; this policy, the carrier argued, "represents the statement that the 'one voice' of the Federal Government wishes to make," a statement "threatened by [Florida's tax]." *Ibid.*

This Court disagreed, observing that the proffered evidence disclosed no federal policy of the kind described, and indeed demonstrated that the Federal Government intended to *permit* the States to impose sales taxes on aviation fuel. The international convention and resolution and more than 70 bilateral treaties on which the carrier relied to show a United States policy of tax exemption for the instrumentalities of international air traffic, the Court explained, in fact indicated far less: "[W]hile there appears to be an international *aspiration* on the one hand to eliminate all impediments to foreign air travel—including taxation of fuel—the *law* as it presently stands acquiesces in taxation of the sale of that fuel by political subdivisions of countries." *Id.*, at 10 (emphasis in original). . . .

. . . .

As in *Container Corp.* and *Wardair*, we discern no "specific indications of congressional intent" to bar the state action here challenged. Our decision upholding California's franchise tax in *Container Corp.* left the ball in Congress' court; had Congress, the branch responsible for the regulation of foreign commerce, *see* U.S. Const., Art. I, § 8, cl. 3, considered nationally uniform use of separate accounting "essential," *Japan Line*, 441 U.S., at 448, it could have enacted legislation prohibiting the States from taxing corporate income based on the worldwide combined reporting method. In the 11 years that have elapsed since our decision in *Container Corp.*, Congress has failed to enact such legislation.

. . . .

The Constitution does " 'not make the judiciary the overseer of our government.' " *Dames & Moore v. Regan*, 453 U.S. 654, 660 (1981). . . . Having determined that the taxpayers before us had an adequate nexus with the State, that worldwide combined reporting led to taxation which was fairly apportioned, nondiscriminatory, fairly related to the services provided by the State, and that its imposition did not result inevitably in multiple taxation, we leave it to Congress—whose voice, in this area, is the Nation's—to evaluate whether the national interest is best served by tax uniformity, or state autonomy. Accordingly, the judgments of the California Court of Appeal are

Affirmed.

NATIONAL FOREIGN TRADE COUNCIL v. NATSIOS

181 F.3d 38, 44–67 (1st Cir. 1999).

LYNCH, CIRCUIT JUDGE.

. . . .

[In *Crosby v. National Foreign Trade Council* (excerpted *supra* Section 2), the U.S. Supreme Court found that a Massachusetts statute imposing sanctions on Burma (Myanmar) was directly preempted by a federal statute. The Court did not reach the issue of whether the Massachusetts statute was also invalid under the dormant Foreign Commerce Clause. The First Circuit Court of Appeals, however, had reached that issue (the case name changed on appeal to the Supreme Court).]

Massachusetts puts forth two arguments to support its claim that its law does not violate the Foreign Commerce Clause. First, Massachusetts contends that the law does not discriminate between domestic and foreign companies. Second, Massachusetts argues that its law does not impair the federal government's ability to speak with one voice regarding foreign commerce. Under standard Commerce Clause analysis, a statute that facially discriminates against interstate or foreign commerce will, in most cases, be found unconstitutional. *See, e.g., Oregon Waste Systems, Inc. v. Department of Environmental Quality*, 511 U.S. 93, 99 . . . (1994) ("If a restriction on commerce is discriminatory, it is virtually *per se* invalid. By contrast, nondiscriminatory regulations that have only incidental effects on interstate commerce are valid unless 'the burden imposed on such commerce is clearly excessive in relation to the putative local benefits.' " . . . (emphasis in original) (citation omitted)). Even under that analysis, we find that the [Massachusetts] law is discriminatory and violates the Foreign Commerce Clause. Although the law does not discriminate against foreign companies, it does discriminate against foreign commerce. Also, the law impedes the federal government's ability to speak with one voice in foreign affairs, and amounts to an attempt to regulate conduct outside of Massachusetts and outside of this country's borders. For these three reasons, we hold that the Massachusetts law violates the Foreign Commerce Clause.

CONCLUDING NOTE: PREEMPTION OF STATE LAW BY THE DORMANT FOREIGN COMMERCE CLAUSE

Clearly the U.S. Constitution does not prohibit every state law or measure that has an effect on interstate or foreign commerce. Analysis under the dormant Commerce Clause and the dormant Foreign Commerce Clause seeks to identify situations where state action is so burdensome on commerce that it should be struck down, even in the absence of a conflicting federal law. As indicated in *Japan Line*, *Barclays Bank PLC*, and *Natsios*, a threshold issue is whether the state law discriminates against interstate or foreign commerce (either facially or by substantial effects). In the particular situation of a state tax, the courts focus on whether the tax: (1) applies to an activity with a substantial nexus to the taxing state; (2) is fairly apportioned; and (3) is fairly related to the services provided by the state. In the context of foreign commerce cases, however, the Supreme Court imposes an additional layer of scrutiny: whether the state law prevents the federal government from "speaking with one voice" in international trade. For tax cases, such scrutiny includes whether there is an enhanced risk of multiple taxation.

Why was the outcome different in *Japan Line* than in *Barclays Bank PLC*? Was the same scrutiny applied to different facts, or did the standard of scrutiny change? When the Court says that the federal government must be allowed to "speak with one voice," whose voice is the Court referring to? Since these cases address a situation where the federal government has *not* spoken through statute or treaty, are courts free to strike down a state law affecting foreign commerce to preserve uniformity in U.S. policy? Alternatively, should courts uphold the state law since the federal government could have spoken but chose not to (thus tacitly accepting the state law)? Should courts have such discretion?

SECTION 5. PREEMPTION OF STATE LAW UNDER THE DORMANT FOREIGN AFFAIRS POWER

ZSCHERNIG v. MILLER

389 U.S. 429, 430–41, 88 S.Ct. 664, 19 L.Ed.2d 683 (1968) (some footnotes omitted).

MR. JUSTICE DOUGLAS delivered the opinion of the Court.

This case concerns the disposition of the estate of a resident of Oregon who died there intestate in 1962. Appellants are decedent's sole heirs and they are residents of East Germany. Appellees include members of the [Oregon] State Land Board that petitioned the Oregon probate court for the escheat of the net proceeds of the estate under the provisions of Ore. Rev. Stat. § 111.070 (1957), which provides for escheat in cases where a nonresident alien claims real or personal property unless three requirements are satisfied:

> (1) the existence of a reciprocal right of a United States citizen to take property on the same terms as a citizen or inhabitant of the foreign country;
>
> (2) the right of United States citizens to receive payment here of funds from estates in the foreign country; and
>
> (3) the right of the foreign heirs to receive the proceeds of Oregon estates "without confiscation."

. . . .

[W]e conclude that the history and operation of this Oregon statute make clear that § 111.070 is an intrusion by the State into the field of foreign affairs which the Constitution entrusts to the President and the Congress. *See Hines v. Davidowitz*, 312 U.S. 52, 63.

As already noted, one of the conditions of inheritance under the Oregon statute requires "proof that such foreign heirs, distributees, devisees or legatees may receive the benefit, use or control of money or property from estates of persons dying in this state without confiscation, in whole or in part, by the governments of such foreign countries," the burden being on the nonresident alien to establish that fact.

This provision came into Oregon's law in 1951. Prior to that time the rights of aliens under the Oregon statute were defined in general terms of reciprocity, similar to the California Act which we had before us in *Clark v. Allen*, 331 U.S., at 506, n. 1.

We held in *Clark v. Allen* that a general reciprocity clause did not on its face intrude on the federal domain. 331 U.S., at 516–517. We noted that the California statute, then a recent enactment, would have only "some incidental or indirect effect in foreign countries." *Id.*, at 517.[5]

Had that case appeared in the posture of the present one, a different result would have obtained. We were there concerned with the words of a statute on its face, not the manner of its application. State courts, of course, must frequently read, construe, and apply laws of foreign nations. It has never been seriously suggested that state courts are precluded from performing that function, albeit there is a remote possibility that any holding may disturb a foreign nation—whether the matter involves commercial cases, tort cases, or some other type of controversy. At the time *Clark v. Allen* was decided, the case seemed to involve no more than a routine reading of foreign laws. It now appears that in this reciprocity area under inheritance statutes, the probate courts of various States have launched inquiries into the type of governments that obtain in particular foreign nations—whether aliens under their law have enforceable rights, whether the so-called "rights" are merely dispensations turning upon the whim or caprice of government officials, whether the representation of consuls, ambassadors, and other representatives of foreign nations is credible or made in good faith, whether there is in the actual administration in the particular foreign system of law any element of confiscation.

5. In *Clark v. Allen*, 331 U.S. 503, the District Court had held the California reciprocity statute unconstitutional because of legislative history indicating that the purpose of the statute was to prevent American assets from reaching hostile nations preparing for wars on this country. *Crowley v. Allen*, 52 F. Supp. 850, 853 (D. C. N. D. Calif.). But when the case reached this Court, petitioner contended that the statute was invalid, not because of the legislature's motive, but because on its face the statute constituted "an invasion of the exclusively Federal field of control over our foreign relations." In discussing how the statute was applied, petitioner noted that a California court had accepted as conclusive proof of reciprocity the statement of a foreign ambassador that reciprocal rights existed in his nation. Brief for petitioner in *Clark v. Allen*, No. 626, October Term 1946, pp. 73–74. Thus we had no reason to suspect that the California statute in *Clark v. Allen* was to be applied as anything other than a general reciprocity provision requiring just matching of laws. Had we been reviewing the later California decision of *Estate of Gogabashvele*, ... 16 Cal. Rptr. 77, *see* n. 6, *infra*, the additional problems we now find with the Oregon provision would have been presented.

In a California case, involving a reciprocity provision, the United States made the following representation:

> "The operation and effect of the statute is inextricably enmeshed in international affairs and matters of foreign policy. The statute does not work disinheritance of, or affect ownership of property in California by, any group or class, but on the contrary operates in fields exclusively for, and preempted by, the United States; namely, the control of the international transmission of property, funds, and credits, and the capture of enemy property. The statute is not an inheritance statute, but a statute of confiscation and retaliation." *In re Bevilacqua's Estate*, 161 P. 2d 589, 593 (Dist. Ct. App. Cal.), superseded by . . . 191 P. 2d 752.

In its brief *amicus curiae*, the Department of Justice states that: "The government does not . . . contend that the application of the Oregon escheat statute in the circumstances of this case unduly interferes with the United States' conduct of foreign relations."

The Government's acquiescence in the ruling of *Clark v. Allen* certainly does not justify extending the principle of that case, as we would be required to do here to uphold the Oregon statute as applied; for it has more than "some incidental or indirect effect in foreign countries," and its great potential for disruption or embarrassment makes us hesitate to place it in the category of a diplomatic bagatelle.

As we read the decisions that followed in the wake of *Clark v. Allen*, we find that they radiate some of the attitudes of the "cold war," where the search is for the "democracy quotient" of a foreign regime as opposed to the Marxist theory.[6] The Oregon statute introduces the concept of "confiscation," which is of course opposed to the Just Compensation Clause of the Fifth Amendment. And this has led into minute inquiries concerning the actual administration of foreign law, into the credibility of foreign diplomatic statements, and into speculation whether the fact that some received delivery of funds should "not preclude wonderment as to how many may have been denied 'the right to receive'. . . ." *See State Land Board v. Kolovrat*, . . . 349 P. 2d 255, 262, *rev'd sub nom. Kolovrat v. Oregon*, 366 U.S. 187, on other grounds.

That kind of state involvement in foreign affairs and international relations—matters which the Constitution entrusts solely to the Federal

6. *See Estate of Gogabashvele*, . . . 16 Cal. Rptr. 77, *disapproved in Estate of Larkin*, . . . 416 P. 2d 473, and *Estate of Chichernea*, . . . 424 P. 2d 687. One commentator has described the *Gogabashvele* decision in the following manner:

> "The court analyzed the general nature of rights in the Soviet system instead of examining whether Russian inheritance rights were granted equally to aliens and residents. The court found Russia had no separation of powers, too much control in the hands of the Communist Party, no independent judiciary, confused legislation, unpublished statutes, and unrepealed obsolete statutes. Before stating its holding of no reciprocity, the court also noted Stalin's crimes, the Beria trial, the doctrine of crime by analogy, Soviet xenophobia, and demonstrations at the American Embassy in Moscow unhindered by the police. The court concluded that a leading Soviet jurist's construction of article 8 of the law enacting the R. S. F. S. R. Civil Code seemed modeled after Humpty Dumpty, who said, 'When I use a word . . ., it means just what I choose it to mean—neither more nor less.' " Note, 55 Calif. L. Rev. 592, 594–595, n. 10 (1967).

Government—is not sanctioned by *Clark v. Allen*. Yet such forbidden state activity has infected each of the three provisions of § 111.070, as applied by Oregon.

In *State Land Board v. Pekarek*, ... 378 P.2d 734, the Oregon Supreme Court in ruling against a Czech claimant because he had failed to prove the "benefit" requirement of subsection (1)(c) of the statute said:

> "Assuming, without deciding, that all of the evidence offered by the legatees was admissible, it can be given relatively little weight. The statements of Czechoslovakian officials must be judged in light of the interest which they had in the acquisition of funds for their government. Moreover, in judging the credibility of these witnesses we are entitled to take into consideration the fact that declarations of government officials in communist-controlled countries as to the state of affairs existing within their borders do not always comport with the actual facts." ... 378 P.2d, at 738.

Yet in *State Land Board v. Schwabe*, ... 400 P.2d 10, where the certificate of the Polish Ambassador was tendered against the claim that the inheritance would be confiscated abroad, the Oregon court, appraising the current attitude of Washington, D.C., toward Warsaw, accepted the certificate as true. ... 400 P.2d at 11.

. . . .

As one reads the Oregon decisions, it seems that foreign policy attitudes, the freezing or thawing of the "cold war," and the like are the real desiderata.[8] Yet they of course are matters for the Federal Government, not for local probate courts.

This is as true of (1) (a) of § 111.070 as it is of (1) (b) and (1) (c). In *Clostermann v. Schmidt*, ... 332 P. 2d 1036, the court—applying the predecessor of (1) (a)—held that not only must the foreign law give inheritance rights to Americans, but the political body making the law must have "membership in the family of nations" (... 332 P.2d, at 1041), because the purpose of the Oregon provision was to serve as "an inducement to foreign nations to so frame the inheritance laws of their respective countries in a manner which would insure to Oregonians the same

8. Such attitudes are not confined to the Oregon courts. Representative samples from other States would include statements in the New York courts, such as "This court would consider sending money out of this country and into Hungary tantamount to putting funds within the grasp of the Communists," and "If this money were turned over to the Russian authorities, it would be used to kill our boys and innocent people in Southeast Asia. ..." Heyman, The Nonresident Alien's Right to Succession Under the "Iron Curtain Rule," 52 Nw. U. L. Rev. 221, 234 (1957). In Pennsylvania, a judge stated at the trial of a case involving a Soviet claimant that "If you want to say that I'm prejudiced, you can, because when it comes to Communism I'm a bigoted anti-Communist." And another judge exclaimed, "I am not going to send money to Russia where it can go into making bullets which may one day be used against my son." A California judge, upon being asked if he would hear argument on the law, replied, "No, I won't send any money to Russia." The judge took "judicial notice that Russia kicks the United States in the teeth all the time," and told counsel for the Soviet claimant that "I would think your firm would feel it honor bound to withdraw as representing the Russian government. No American can make it too strong." Berman, Soviet Heirs in American Courts, 62 Col. L. Rev. 257, and n. 3 (1962).

. . . .

opportunities to inherit and take personal property abroad that they enjoy in the state of Oregon." ... 332 P.2d, at 1042.

....

In short, it would seem that Oregon judges in construing § 111.070 seek to ascertain whether "rights" protected by foreign law are the same "rights" that citizens of Oregon enjoy. If, as in the *Rogers* case, the alleged foreign "right" may be vindicated only through Communist-controlled state agencies, then there is no "right" of the type § 111.070 requires. The same seems to be true if enforcement may require approval of a Fascist dictator. ... The statute as construed seems to make unavoidable judicial criticism of nations established on a more authoritarian basis than our own.

It seems inescapable that the type of probate law that Oregon enforces affects international relations in a persistent and subtle way. The practice of state courts in withholding remittances to legatees residing in Communist countries or in preventing them from assigning them is notorious. The several States, of course, have traditionally regulated the descent and distribution of estates. But those regulations must give way if they impair the effective exercise of the Nation's foreign policy. *See* Miller, The Corporation as a Private Government in the World Community, 46 Va. L. Rev. 1539, 1542–1549 (1960). Where those laws conflict with a treaty, they must bow to the superior federal policy. *See Kolovrat v. Oregon*, 366 U.S. 187. Yet, even in absence of a treaty, a State's policy may disturb foreign relations. As we stated in *Hines v. Davidowitz, supra,* at 64: "Experience has shown that international controversies of the gravest moment, sometimes even leading to war, may arise from real or imagined wrongs to another's subjects inflicted, or permitted, by a government." Certainly a State could not deny admission to a traveler from East Germany nor bar its citizens from going there. *Passenger Cases*, 7 How. 283; *cf. Crandall v. Nevada*, 6 Wall. 35; *Kent v. Dulles*, 357 U.S. 116. If there are to be such restraints, they must be provided by the Federal Government. The present Oregon law is not as gross an intrusion in the federal domain as those others might be. Yet, as we have said, it has a direct impact upon foreign relations and may well adversely affect the power of the central government to deal with those problems.

The Oregon law does, indeed, illustrate the dangers which are involved if each State, speaking through its probate courts, is permitted to establish its own foreign policy.

Reversed.

AMERICAN INSURANCE ASSOCIATION v. GARAMENDI

539 U.S. 396, 401–27, 123 S.Ct. 2374, 156 L.Ed.2d 376 (2003) (footnotes omitted).

JUSTICE SOUTER delivered the opinion of the Court.

California's Holocaust Victim Insurance Relief Act of 1999 (HVIRA or Act), Cal. Ins. Code Ann. §§ 13800–13807 (West Cum. Supp. 2003), requires any insurer doing business in that State to disclose information about all policies sold in Europe between 1920 and 1945 by the company itself or any one "related" to it. The issue here is whether HVIRA interferes with the National Government's conduct of foreign relations. We hold that it does, with the consequence that the state statute is preempted.

. . . .

The Nazi Government of Germany engaged not only in genocide and enslavement but theft of Jewish assets, including the value of insurance policies, and in particular policies of life insurance, a form of savings held by many Jews in Europe before the Second World War. Early on in the Nazi era, loss of livelihood forced Jews to cash in life insurance policies prematurely, only to have the government seize the proceeds of the repurchase, and many who tried to emigrate from Germany were forced to liquidate insurance policies to pay the steep "flight taxes" and other levies imposed by the Third Reich to keep Jewish assets from leaving the country. . . . Before long, the Reich began simply seizing the remaining policies outright. . . . After the war, even a policy that had escaped confiscation was likely to be dishonored, whether because insurers denied its existence or claimed it had lapsed from unpaid premiums during the persecution, or because the government would not provide heirs with documentation of the policyholder's death. . . . Responsibility as between the government and insurance companies is disputed, but at the end of the day, the fact is that the value or proceeds of many insurance policies issued to Jews before and during the war were paid to the Reich or never paid at all.

These confiscations and frustrations of claims fell within the subject of reparations, which became a principal object of Allied diplomacy soon after the war. At the Potsdam Conference, the United States, Britain, and the Soviet Union took reparations for wartime losses by seizing industrial assets from their respective occupation zones, putting into effect the plan originally envisioned at the Yalta Conference months before. . . . A year later, the United States was among the parties to an agreement to share seized assets with other western allies as settlement, as to each signatory nation, of "all its claims and those of its nationals against the former German Government and its Agencies, of a governmental or private nature, arising out of the war." Agreement on Reparation from Germany, on the Establishment of Inter-Allied Reparation Agency and Restitution of Monetary Gold, 61 Stat. 3163, Art. 2(A), T. I. A. S. No. 1655 (hereinafter Paris Agreement).

The effect of the Paris Agreement was curtailed, however, and attention to reparations intentionally deferred, when the western allies moved to end their occupation and reestablish a sovereign Germany as a buffer against Soviet expansion. They worried that continued reparations would cripple the new Federal Republic of Germany economically, and so decided in the London Debt Agreement to put off "[c]onsideration of claims arising out of the second World War by countries which were at war with or were occupied by Germany during that war, and by nationals of such countries, against the Reich and agencies of the Reich ... until the final settlement of the problem of reparation." Agreement on German External Debts, Feb. 27, 1953, 4 U. S. T. 443, 449, T. I. A. S. No. 2792. ...

In the meantime, the western allies placed the obligation to provide restitution to victims of Nazi persecution on the new West German Government. ... West Germany enacted its own restitution laws in 1953 and 1956, ... and signed agreements with 16 countries for the compensation of their nationals. ... Despite a payout of more than 100 billion deutsch marks as of 2000, ... these measures left out many claimants and certain types of claims, and when the agreement reunifying East and West Germany ... was read by the German courts as lifting the London Debt Agreement's moratorium on Holocaust claims by foreign nationals, class-action lawsuits for restitution poured into United States courts against companies doing business in Germany during the Nazi era. ...

These suits generated much protest by the defendant companies and their governments, to the point that the Government of the United States took action to try to resolve "the last great compensation related negotiation arising out of World War II." ... From the beginning, the Government's position ... stressed mediated settlement "as an alternative to endless litigation" promising little relief to aging Holocaust survivors. ... Ensuing negotiations at the national level produced the German Foundation Agreement, signed by President Clinton and German Chancellor Schröeder in July 2000, in which Germany agreed to enact legislation establishing a foundation funded with 10 billion deutsch marks contributed equally by the German Government and German companies, to be used to compensate all those "who suffered at the hands of German companies during the National Socialist era." Agreement Concerning the Foundation "Remembrance, Responsibility and the Future," 39 Int'l Legal Materials 1298 (2000).

The willingness of the Germans to create a voluntary compensation fund was conditioned on some expectation of security from lawsuits in United States courts, and after extended dickering President Clinton put his weight behind two specific measures toward that end. ... First, the Government agreed that whenever a German company was sued on a Holocaust-era claim in an American court, the Government of the United States would submit a statement that "it would be in the foreign policy interests of the United States for the Foundation to be the exclusive forum and remedy for the resolution of all asserted claims against German companies arising from their involvement in the National Socialist era and World War II." 39 Int'l Legal Materials, at 1303. Though unwilling to guarantee that its foreign policy interests would "in themselves provide an independent legal basis for dismissal," that being an issue for the courts, the Government agreed to tell courts "that U.S. policy interests favor dismissal on any valid legal ground." *Id.*, at 1304. On top of that undertaking, the Government promised to use its "best efforts, in a manner it considers appropriate," to get state and local governments to respect the foundation as the exclusive mechanism. *Id.*, at 1300.

As for insurance claims specifically, both countries agreed that the German Foundation would work with the International Commission on Holocaust Era Insurance Claims (ICHEIC), a voluntary organization formed in 1998 by several European insurance companies, the State of Israel, Jewish and Holocaust survivor associations, and the National Association of Insurance Commissioners, the organization of American state insurance commissioners. The job of the ICHEIC, chaired by former Secretary of State Eagleburger, includes negotiation with European insurers to provide information about unpaid insurance policies issued to Holocaust victims and settlement of claims brought under them. It has thus set up procedures for handling demands against participating insurers, including "a reasonable review ... of the participating companies' files" for production of unpaid policies, "an investigatory process to determine the current status" of insurance policies for which claims are filed, and a "claims and valuation process to settle and pay individual claims," employing "relaxed standards of proof." ...

....

The German Foundation pact has served as a model for similar [U.S. executive] agreements with Austria and France, and the United States Government continues to pursue comparable agreements with other countries. ...

....

While these international efforts were underway, California's Department of Insurance began its own enquiry into the issue of unpaid claims under Nazi-era insurance policies, prompting state legislation designed to force payment by defaulting insurers. In 1998, the state legislature made it an unfair business practice for any insurer operating in the State to "fai[l] to pay any valid claim from Holocaust survivors." Cal. Ins. Code Ann. § 790.15(a) (West Cum. Supp. 2003). The legislature placed "an affirmative duty" on the Department of Insurance "to play an independent role in representing the interests of Holocaust survivors," including an obligation to "gather, review, and analyze the archives of insurers ... to provide for research and investigation" into unpaid insurance claims. §§ 12967(a)(1), (2).

State legislative efforts culminated the next year with passage of Assembly Bill No. 600, 1999 Cal. Stats. ch. 827, the first section of which amended the State's Code of Civil Procedure to allow state residents to sue in state court on insurance claims based on acts perpetrated in the Holocaust and extended the governing statute of limitations to December 31, 2010. Cal. Civ. Proc. Code Ann. § 354.5 (West Cum. Supp. 2003). The section of the bill codified as HVIRA, at issue here, requires "[a]ny insurer currently doing business in the state" to disclose the details of "life, property, liability, health, annuities, dowry, educational, or casualty insurance policies" issued "to persons in Europe, which were in effect between

1920 and 1945." Cal. Ins. Code Ann. § 13804(a) (West Cum. Supp. 2003). ... The mandatory penalty for default is suspension of the company's license to do business in the State, § 13806, and there are misdemeanor criminal sanctions for falsehood in certain required representations about whether and to whom the proceeds of each policy have been distributed, § 13804(b).

....

[S]everal American and European insurance companies and the American Insurance Association (a national trade association), filed suit for injunctive relief against respondent insurance commissioner of California, challenging the constitutionality of HVIRA. ...

....

The principal argument for preemption made by petitioners and the United States as *amicus curiae* is that HVIRA interferes with foreign policy of the Executive Branch, as expressed principally in the executive agreements with Germany, Austria, and France. The major premises of the argument, at least, are beyond dispute. There is, of course, no question that at some point an exercise of state power that touches on foreign relations must yield to the National Government's policy, given the "concern for uniformity in this country's dealings with foreign nations" that animated the Constitution's allocation of the foreign relations power to the National Government in the first place. *Banco Nacional de Cuba v. Sabbatino*, 376 U.S. 398, 427, n. 25 (1964); *see Crosby v. National Foreign Trade Council*, 530 U.S. 363, 381–382, n. 16 (2000) (" '[T]he peace of the WHOLE ought not to be left at the disposal of a PART' " (quoting *The Federalist* No. 80, pp. 535–536 (J. Cooke ed. 1961) (A. Hamilton))); *Id.*, No. 44, p. 299 (J. Madison) (emphasizing "the advantage of uniformity in all points which relate to foreign powers"); *Id.*, No. 42, p. 279 (J. Madison) ("If we are to be one nation in any respect, it clearly ought to be in respect to other nations"); *see also First Nat. City Bank v. Banco Nacional de Cuba*, 406 U.S. 759, 769 (1972) (plurality opinion) (act of state doctrine was "fashioned because of fear that adjudication would interfere with the conduct of foreign relations"); *Japan Line, Ltd. v. County of Los Angeles*, 441 U.S. 434, 449 (1979) (negative Foreign Commerce Clause protects the National Government's ability to speak with "one voice" in regulating commerce with foreign countries (internal quotation marks omitted)).

Nor is there any question generally that there is executive authority to decide what that policy should be. Although the source of the President's power to act in foreign affairs does not enjoy any textual detail, the historical gloss on the "executive Power" vested in Article II of the Constitution has recognized the President's "vast share of responsibility for the conduct of our foreign relations." *Youngstown Sheet & Tube Co. v. Sawyer*, 343 U.S. 579, 610–611 (1952) (Frankfurter, J., concurring). While Congress holds express authority to regulate public and private dealings with other nations in its war and foreign commerce powers, in foreign affairs the President has a degree of independent authority to act. ...

. . . .

Generally, ... valid executive agreements are fit to preempt state law, just as treaties are, and if the agreements here had expressly preempted laws like HVIRA, the issue would be straightforward. ... But petitioners and the United States as *amicus curiae* both have to acknowledge that the agreements include no preemption clause, and so leave their claim of preemption to rest on asserted interference with the foreign policy those agreements embody. Reliance is placed on our decision in *Zschernig v. Miller*, 389 U.S. 429 (1968).

. . . .

The *Zschernig* majority relied on statements in a number of previous cases open to the reading that state action with more than incidental effect on foreign affairs is preempted, even absent any affirmative federal activity in the subject area of the state law, and hence without any showing of conflict. The Court cited the pronouncement in *Hines v. Davidowitz*, 312 U.S. 52, 63, 61 S.Ct. 399, 85 L.Ed. 581 (1941), that "[o]ur system of government is such that the interest of the cities, counties and states, no less than the interest of the people of the whole nation, imperatively requires that federal power in the field affecting foreign relations be left entirely free from local interference." *See* 389 U.S., at 432, 88 S.Ct. 664; *id.*, at 442–443, 88 S.Ct. 664 (Stewart, J., concurring) (setting out the foregoing quotation). Likewise, Justice Stewart's concurring opinion viewed the Oregon statute as intruding "into a domain of exclusively federal competence." *Id.*, at 442, 88 S.Ct. 664; *see also Belmont*, 301 U.S., at 331, 57 S.Ct. 758 ("[C]omplete power over international affairs is in the national government and is not and cannot be subject to any curtailment or interference on the part of the several states" (citing *Curtiss–Wright Export Corp.*, 299 U.S., at 316, 57 S.Ct. 216 et seq.)).

Justice Harlan, joined substantially by Justice White, disagreed with the *Zschernig* majority on this point, arguing that its implication of preemption of the entire field of foreign affairs was at odds with some other cases suggesting that in the absence of positive federal action "the States may legislate in areas of their traditional competence even though their statutes may have an incidental effect on foreign relations." 389 U.S., at 459, 88 S.Ct. 664 (opinion concurring in result) (citing cases); see *id.*, at 462, 88 S.Ct. 664 (White, J., dissenting). Thus, for Justice Harlan it was crucial that the challenge to the Oregon statute presented no evidence of a "specific interest of the Federal Government which might be interfered with" by the law. *Id.*, at 459, 88 S.Ct. 664 (opinion concurring in result); see *id.*, at 461, 88 S.Ct. 664 (finding "no evidence of adverse effect in the record"). He would, however, have found preemption in a case of "conflicting federal policy," see *id.*, at 458–459, 88 S.Ct. 664, and on this point the majority and Justices Harlan and White basically agreed: state laws "must give way if they impair the effective exercise of the Nation's foreign policy," *id.*, at 440, 88 S.Ct. 664 (opinion of the Court). *See also Pink*, 315 U.S., at 230–231, 62 S.Ct. 552 ("[S]tate law must yield when it is inconsistent with, or impairs ... the superior Federal policy evidenced by a treaty or international compact or agreement"); *id.*, at 240, 62 S.Ct. 552 (Frankfurter, J., concurring) (state law may not be allowed to "interfer[e] with the conduct of our foreign relations by the Executive").

It is a fair question whether respect for the executive foreign relations power requires a categorical choice between the contrasting theories of field and conflict preemption evident in the *Zschernig* opinions,[12] but the question requires no answer here. For even on Justice Harlan's view, the likelihood that state legislation will produce something more than incidental effect in conflict with express foreign policy of the National Government would require preemption of the state law. And since on his view it is legislation within "areas of ... traditional competence" that gives a State any claim to prevail, 389 U.S., at 459, 88 S.Ct. 664, it would be reasonable to consider the strength of the state interest, judged by standards of traditional practice, when deciding how serious a conflict must be shown before declaring the state law preempted. *Cf. Southern Pacific Co. v. Arizona ex rel. Sullivan*, 325 U.S. 761, 768–769, 65 S.Ct. 1515, 89 L.Ed. 1915 (1945) (under negative Commerce Clause, "reconciliation of the conflicting claims of state and national power is to be attained only by some appraisal and accommodation of the competing demands of the state and national interests involved"); Henkin, Foreign Affairs and the United States Constitution, at 164 (suggesting a test that "balance[s] the state's interest in a regulation against the impact on U.S. foreign relations"); Maier, Preemption of State Law: A Recommended Analysis, 83 Am. J. Int'l L. 832, 834 (1989) (similar). Judged by these standards, we think petitioners and the Government have demonstrated a sufficiently clear conflict to require finding preemption here.

. . . .

To begin with, resolving Holocaust-era insurance claims that may be held by residents of this country is a matter well within the Executive's responsibility for foreign affairs. Since claims remaining in the aftermath of hostilities may be "sources of friction" acting as an "impediment to resumption of friendly relations" between the countries involved, ... there is a "longstanding practice" of the national Executive to settle them

12. The two positions can be seen as complementary. If a State were simply to take a position on a matter of foreign policy with no serious claim to be addressing a traditional state responsibility, field preemption might be the appropriate doctrine, whether the National Government had acted and, if it had, without reference to the degree of any conflict, the principle having been established that the Constitution entrusts foreign policy exclusively to the National Government. *See, e.g., Hines v. Davidowitz*, 312 U.S. 52, 63, 61 S.Ct. 399, 85 L.Ed. 581 (1941). Where, however, a State has acted within what Justice Harlan called its "traditional competence," 389 U.S., at 459, 88 S.Ct. 664, but in a way that affects foreign relations, it might make good sense to require a conflict, of a clarity or substantiality that would vary with the strength or the traditional importance of the state concern asserted. Whether the strength of the federal foreign policy interest should itself be weighed is, of course, a further question. *Cf. Rice v. Santa Fe Elevator Corp.*, 331 U.S. 218, 230, 67 S.Ct. 1146, 91 L.Ed. 1447 (1947) (congressional occupation of the field is not to be presumed "in a field which the States have traditionally occupied"); *Boyle v. United Technologies Corp.*, 487 U.S. 500, 507–508, 108 S.Ct. 2510, 101 L.Ed.2d 442 (1988) ("In an area of uniquely federal interest," "[t]he conflict with federal policy need not be as sharp as that which must exist for ordinary pre-emption").

in discharging its responsibility to maintain the Nation's relationships with other countries. . . .

The exercise of the federal executive authority means that state law must give way where, as here, there is evidence of clear conflict between the policies adopted by the two. The foregoing account of negotiations toward the three settlement agreements is enough to illustrate that the consistent Presidential foreign policy has been to encourage European governments and companies to volunteer settlement funds in preference to litigation or coercive sanctions. . . . As for insurance claims in particular, the national position, expressed unmistakably in the executive agreements signed by the President with Germany and Austria, has been to encourage European insurers to work with the ICHEIC to develop acceptable claim procedures, including procedures governing disclosure of policy information. . . . This position, of which the agreements are exemplars, has also been consistently supported in the high levels of the Executive Branch. . . . The approach taken serves to resolve the several competing matters of national concern apparent in the German Foundation Agreement: the national interest in maintaining amicable relationships with current European allies; survivors' interests in a "fair and prompt" but nonadversarial resolution of their claims so as to "bring some measure of justice . . . in their lifetimes"; and the companies' interest in securing "legal peace" when they settle claims in this fashion. 39 Int'l Legal Materials, at 1304. . . .

California has taken a different tack of providing regulatory sanctions to compel disclosure and payment, supplemented by a new cause of action for Holocaust survivors if the other sanctions should fail. The situation created by the California legislation calls to mind the impact of the Massachusetts Burma law on the effective exercise of the President's power, as recounted in the statutory preemption case, *Crosby v. National Foreign Trade Council*, 530 U.S. 363 (2000). HVIRA's economic compulsion to make public disclosure, of far more information about far more policies than ICHEIC rules require, employs "a different, state system of economic pressure," and in doing so undercuts the President's diplomatic discretion and the choice he has made exercising it. *Id.*, at 376. . . .

. . . .

The basic fact is that California seeks to use an iron fist where the President has consistently chosen kid gloves. We have heard powerful arguments that the iron fist would work better, and it may be that if the matter of compensation were considered in isolation from all other issues involving the European allies, the iron fist would be the preferable policy. But our thoughts on the efficacy of the one approach versus the other are beside the point, since our business is not to judge the wisdom of the National Government's policy; dissatisfaction should be addressed to the President or, perhaps, Congress. The question relevant to preemption in this case is conflict, and the evidence here is "more than sufficient to demonstrate that the state Act stands in the way of [the President's] diplomatic objectives." *Crosby*, *supra*, at 386.

NOTES: ZSCHERNIG'S *STAYING POWER*

1. Zschernig*'s Dormant Foreign Affairs Power*. In *Zschernig*, there was no federal statute either directly preempting the state statute or occupying the field. A national and resident of communist East Germany sought to collect an inheritance, but Oregon state courts denied his claim under the same Oregon probate statute at issue in *Kolovrat v. Oregon* (*see supra* Section 3). This time, however, there was no treaty precluding operation of the state statute, at least as it applied to personal property. So, in striking down the state statute, the Court relied simply on what might be called a "dormant foreign affairs power," meaning a power not actually exercised by the federal government, but which nevertheless precludes state action.

The dormant foreign affairs power in *Zschernig* has been regarded as a form of federal common law. Prior to *Garamendi*, some commentators speculated that the *Zschernig* doctrine of preemption by a dormant foreign affairs power was on its way out, since the Supreme Court had not returned to it despite opportunities to do so. *See, e.g.*, Peter J. Spiro, *Foreign Relations Federalism*, 70 U. COLO. L. REV. 1223 (1999). For critics of *Zschernig,* although the Constitution expressly excludes the states from certain activities relating to foreign affairs, it allows them to continue others. As such, there is a more valid basis under the U.S. Constitution for preemption by statute (or even by the dormant foreign commerce clause) than there is for preemption by an unenumerated, dormant foreign affairs power. Instead, preemption should only occur where there is an express prohibition on the states in the Constitution, or an affirmative decision by the political branches to preempt; it should not be left to unelected judges to decide whether state action conflicts with U.S. foreign policy. *See, e.g.*, Jack L. Goldsmith, *Federal Courts, Foreign Affairs, and Federalism*, 83 VA. L. REV. 1617 (1997); Michael D. Ramsey, *The Power of States in Foreign Affairs: The Original Understanding of Foreign Policy Federalism*, 75 NOTRE DAME L. REV. 341, 392–93 (1999).

Given the extensive activity of states relating to foreign relations and the globalization of all manner of activities, how might states know when they have "crossed the line" and violated the dormant foreign affairs power? One commentator argues that the Court should narrow the *Zschernig* doctrine to the following proposition: "[S]tate sanctions that single out foreign states (or their citizens or those who do business with them) for unfavorable treatment are categorically forbidden unless affirmatively authorized by Congress." Carlos Manuel Vázquez, *W(h)ither* Zschernig?, 46 VILL. L. REV. 1259, 1316 (2001). Does this standard capture what *Zschernig* and its progeny seek to accomplish? Alternatively, one commentator favors shifting to a "dormant treaty power." *See* Edward T. Swaine, *Negotiating Federalism: State Bargaining and the Dormant Treaty Power*, 49 DUKE L.J. 1127 (2000). A dormant treaty power would preclude states from bargaining with, or applying measures contingent on the behavior of, foreign governments, except in limited circumstances (*e.g.*, when such action is deemed unobjectionable by the federal government).

2. *Relevance of the Executive Branch's Views.* In an earlier case, *Clark v. Allen*, 331 U.S. 503, 67 S.Ct. 1431, 91 L.Ed. 1633 (1947), the Court upheld a similar California probate statute. Why the difference in *Zschernig*? (Only four of the eight Justices participating in *Zschernig* were confident that the Court's results could be reconciled). *Compare Zschernig*, 389 U.S. at 433–35 (refusing the invitation to reexamine the Court's ruling in *Clark v. Allen*), *with id.* at 443 (Stewart, J., concurring, joined by Brennan, J.) ("To the extent that *Clark v. Allen* is inconsistent with these views, I would overrule that decision."), and *id.* at 458 (Harlan, J., concurring) ("It seems to me impossible to distinguish the present case from *Clark v. Allen* in this respect in any convincing way."), and *id.* at 462 (White, J., dissenting) (indicating agreement with the relevant portion of Justice Harlan's concurrence). How much was the Court engaging in speculation about the effects of state action on foreign affairs? To the extent that the Court was engaging in speculative reasoning, do you think that it would be best for the Court to defer to the political branches on such matters? As noted in the Court's decision, the Executive Branch in *Zschernig* filed an amicus brief that stated: "The government does not . . . contend that the application of the Oregon escheat statute in the circumstances of this case unduly interferes with the United States' conduct of foreign relations." 539 U.S. at 434. Should the Court have regarded that position as dispositive on the issue of undue effects on U.S. foreign affairs? Or did the Court go too far in *Garamendi* in crediting the Executive Branch's views?

3. *Foreign Policymaking and the Dormant Foreign Affairs Power.* Whatever credence may be given to Executive Branch submissions in the course of litigation, the hallmark of the dormant foreign affairs power is the absence of any conflicts arising from formal federal lawmaking. The Court's opinion in *Garamendi*, which appeared reluctant to rely on *Zschernig* overtly, straddled the line in this regard. On the one hand, the case involved no statute or international agreement preempting state law (and did not turn on application of the dormant foreign commerce power). At the same time, the Court relied on conflict with a foreign policy established by the Executive Branch, as "embod[ied]" in executive agreements that merely lacked preemption clauses, thus arguably occupying space somewhere between a dormant foreign affairs power and preemption by lawmaking. Indeed, the Court seemed to distinguish circumstances involving "field preemption" arising regardless "whether the National Government had acted and, if it had, without reference to the degree of any conflict." 539 U.S. at 420 n.11, 123 S.Ct. 2374.

The reference to field preemption was confusing, insofar as it is variously employed in the case law, see *Crosby v. National Foreign Trade Council*, 530 U.S. 363, 372 n.6, 120 S.Ct. 2288, 2294, 147 L.Ed.2d 352 (2000), and post-*Garamendi* courts have been unclear as to whether and why it matters that the federal government is in fact pursuing some foreign policy with which state activities may interfere. In *Von Saher v. Norton Simon Museum of Art at Pasadena*, 592 F.3d 954 (9th Cir. 2010), the court of appeals held that a California statute addressing the recovery of art looted by the Nazis was preempted, agreeing with the district court's conclusion that the statute "intrudes on the power to make and resolve war." *Id.* at 965–66. In reaching this conclusion, which followed *Garamendi*'s invitation to apply a field preemption analysis, *id.* at 965, the court found its conclusion "buttressed by the documented history of federal action addressing the subject of Nazi-looted art" which was "so comprehensive and pervasive as to leave no room for state legislation." *Id.* at 966. In contrast, the same court of appeals upheld against a preemption challenge a California statute that extended the statute of limitations for claims arising out of life insurance policies issued to victims of the Armenian genocide. Movsesian v. Victoria Versicherung AG, 629 F.3d 901 (9th Cir. 2010). That decision found that there was no "clear, express federal policy" that prohibited California from referring to an "Armenian Genocide" and, having made that determination for purposes of a conflict preemption analysis, did not directly consider its relevance to its very brief field preemption analysis. *Id.* at 907–08. A dissenting judge faulted the majority for requiring clear federal policy as a condition for *Garamendi*-type field preemption—though the judge appeared to be citing an inapposite portion of the majority opinion, and himself cited the tension between the California statute and presidential policy choices. *Id.* at 911–12 (Thompson, J., dissenting). *See also* Museum of Fine Arts Boston v. Seger–Thomschitz, 623 F.3d 1, 12–13 (1st Cir. 2010) (upholding against dormant foreign affairs challenge a Massachusetts statute of limitations applicable to Nazi-era artwork claim in part on the basis that, in contrast to *Garamendi*, there is "no comparably express federal policy bearing on the issues"). Should some form of federal activity—at least as concrete as the Cold War policies pursued in *Zschernig*—be a prerequisite for preemption?

4. *"Traditional State Responsibility" and the Dormant Foreign Affairs Power.* In trying to reconcile the majority opinion in *Zschernig* with the views expressed by Justice Harlan in that case, the Court in *Garamendi* made whether the state was acting in an area of traditional state competence relevant in at least two regards—first, "[i]f a State were simply to take a position on a matter of foreign policy with no serious claim to be addressing a traditional state responsibility, field preemption might be the appropriate doctrine" regardless of whether the federal government had acted and, if it had, without regard to the degree of any conflict (539 U.S. at 419 n.11); second, where there was a conflict with "express foreign policy" (albeit not in the form of a preemptive law), "the strength of the state interest, judged by standards of traditional practice," was relevant when "deciding how serious a conflict must be shown before declaring the state law preempted" (*id.* at 420). The former, at least, suggests a difficult threshold inquiry in dormant foreign affairs power cases. *Compare, e.g.*, *Garamendi*, 539 U.S. at 425–27 (explaining the distinction between "a generally applicable 'blue sky' law" and the California policy focusing solely on "policies issued by European companies, in Europe, to European residents, at least 55 years ago"), and *Von Saher*, 592 F.3d 964–65 (emphasizing effect of statute of limitations in allowing suit against out-of-state museums or galleries as excluding it from an area of traditional state responsibility), *with Movsesian*, 629 F.3d at 907–08 (determining that regulation of insurance, notwithstanding focus solely on claims arising from Armenian genocide during 1915 to 1923, did fall within area of traditional state responsibility).

SECTION 6. PREEMPTION OF STATE LAW BY CUSTOMARY INTERNATIONAL LAW

Chapter 2 discussed in detail the manner in which the "law of nations," or customary international law, is a part of U.S. law. For purposes of this chapter, we return briefly to the issue so as to focus on whether customary international law can preempt state law. To the extent that customary international law is regarded as a part of federal common law, *see Sosa v. Alvarez-Machain* (Chapter 2, Section 5), it seems appropriate that customary international law would preempt conflicting state law. Note, however, that the U.S. Constitution does not expressly provide for such preemption. Article VI, Section 2 (the Supremacy Clause) specifically states that "treaties" are supreme over state law, but there is no reference to the "law of nations" (even though elsewhere in the Constitution, in Article I, Section 8, the "law of nations" is contemplated). Since the "Laws of the United States" referred to in the Supremacy Clause are those "made in Pursuance" of the Constitution, viewing customary international law (which is made, or results from, the practice of nations) as falling within that portion of the Supremacy Clause is problematic.

Nevertheless, there is reason to think that the framers expected the law of nations to preempt state law. In *The Federalist Papers* No. 80, Alexander Hamilton spoke about the need for the federal judicial power to extend to application of the law of nations, because "the peace of the WHOLE ought not to be left at the disposal of a PART"—warranting jurisdiction over cases in which foreign citizens were concerned, at least for "cases arising upon treaties and the law of nations." *The Federalist Papers,* No. 80, at 475–78 (Hamilton) (Clinton Rossiter ed., 1961). Likewise, John Jay in *The Federalist Papers* No. 3 saw a need for federal courts to apply the law of nations to avoid inconsistencies by the several states. *The Federalist Papers, supra*, No. 3, at 43 (Jay).

But if the framers intended to allow the law of nations to supersede state law, why was it not made express in the Supremacy Clause? Professor Louis Henkin offered the following explanation:

> [T]here is nothing to suggest that the Framers intended higher constitutional status for treaties than for customary law, and much to suggest that they expected the United States to honor both scrupulously. Their commitment was to "the law of nations" which for them was essentially customary law, including, notably, a state's obligation under customary law to carry out treaties. Their reticence about customary international law in contrast to the several references to treaties did not bespeak a judgment as to their comparative constitutional significances, but had other explanation. The Constitution had to determine who could make treaties for the United States; it sought to deny any treaty power to the states. The Framers wrote treaties explicitly into the Supremacy Clause because the supremacy of trea-

> ties to state law was a major issue that had to be resolved, and accepted by the states. Cases arising under treaties were declared to be within the judicial power of the United States because such cases were to be expected; the Framers probably did not anticipate cases or controversies arising under international law until Congress defined offenses under that law or enacted other legislation to implement international law, and cases arising under international law would then be cases arising under the laws of the United States.

Louis Henkin, *Foreign Affairs and the U.S. Constitution* 237–38 (2d ed. 1996). Thus, Henkin asserted that the framers chose not to write "the law of nations" into the Supremacy Clause because they likely assumed that such law would first be reduced to legislation by Congress, at which point it would qualify as "Laws of the United States." If this is right, then should the Constitution be read as only allowing the "law of nations" to supersede state law in situations where Congress has legislated on the matter? This would be acceptable to many critics of the so-called "modern position." (*See supra*, Chapter 2, Section 2.) Note that in establishing the jurisdiction of federal courts in Article III, the framers did not assume that certain important matters associated with the law of nations (admiralty and maritime issues) would necessarily fall within the scope of the "Laws of the United States." If they took the trouble in Article III to make sure federal courts could hear some matters relating to the law of nations, even if not reduced to federal legislation, why did they not address the law of nations in the Supremacy Clause?

There are no cases squarely addressing whether state law is preempted by customary international law, although U.S. courts have referred to the practice of foreign nations in the course of preempting state law as inconsistent with the U.S. Constitution. *See* Chapter 2, Section 4.

SECTION 7. THE COMPACT CLAUSE

INTRODUCTORY NOTE

Article I, Section 10, clause 1, of the U.S. Constitution prohibits states from entering "into any Treaty, Alliance, or Confederation." At the same time, Clause 3 (the "Compact Clause") provides that "No state shall, without the consent of Congress, ... enter into any Agreement or Compact with another State, or with a foreign Power. ..." Thus, the Constitution provides that states may not enter into a "treaty," but may enter into an "agreement" or "compact" with a "foreign power" if so authorized by Congress.

Despite the language of the Compact Clause, the U.S. Supreme Court has stated that certain compacts may be concluded among the several states ("inter-state compacts") without the approval of Congress. *See* Virginia v. Tennessee, 148 U.S. 504, 13 S.Ct. 728, 37 L.Ed. 537 (1893). In that case, Justice Field said that the test is whether the agreement tends to increase the political power of the states such that it encroaches upon or interferes with the just supremacy of the United States.

If there are certain compacts that the several states may conclude among themselves without any congressional authorization, do the same conditions apply for compacts concluded with foreign countries or their political sub-divisions ("state-foreign country compacts")? The only Supreme Court case addressing state-foreign country compacts is *Holmes v. Jennison*, 39 U.S. (14 Pet.) 540, 10 L.Ed. 579 (1840). In that case, the Court (per Justice Taney) struck down a Vermont governor's agreement with Canada regarding the extradition of an individual because the agreement had not been approved by Congress. Yet, in light of the Supreme Court's decision in *Virginia v. Tennessee*, at least one state court has found that a state-foreign country compact was permissible even without congressional consent. *See* McHenry County v. Brady, 37 N.D. 59, 163 N.W. 540 (1917).

More recently, the Supreme Court has maintained the position it took in *Virginia v. Tennessee*. *See* United States Steel Corp. v. Multistate Tax Commission, 434 U.S. 452, 473, 98 S.Ct. 799, 54 L.Ed.2d 682 (1978); Northeast Bancorp Inc. v. Board of Governors of Fed. Res. Sys., 472 U.S. 159, 105 S.Ct. 2545, 86 L.Ed.2d 112 (1985). However, in *Multistate Tax Commission*, the Court underlined that Justice Field's statement in *Virginia v. Tennessee* was in the context of a state-state agreement and not a state-foreign country agreement. Nevertheless, several states have entered into agreements with foreign countries or their political sub-divisions without seeking the consent of Congress. Is this constitutional?

As one example, consider the memorandum of understanding of January 25, 2001, between the State of Missouri and the Canadian province of Manitoba. As background, you should know that for about 800 years, Devils Lake in North Dakota has had no natural outlet. Consequently, its waters have continually risen, resulting in periodic flooding of the surrounding areas. In the early 2000s, North Dakota began constructing a fourteen-mile open channel and pipeline to drain water from Devils Lake to the Sheyenne River. From there, the water would flow into the Red River, which flows north into Canada.

The flood-mitigation project was strongly opposed by Canada, which believed that North Dakota had not adequately studied the project's environmental impact, including the possibility of introducing invasive species and pollutants (such as phosphorous) into Canada's Hudson Bay watershed in Manitoba province. Fierce lobbying broke out in Washington, D.C., with Canada trying to convince the federal government to have the project reviewed by a U.S.-Canadian boundary water commission. Canada sought to secure allies among various states operating within the same water basin, including Minnesota, Ohio, and Missouri. For background, see Joseph M. Flanders, *Transboundary Water Disputes on an International and State Platform: A Controversial Resolution to North Dakota's Devils Lake Dilemma*, 82 N.D. L. REV. 997 (2006). Upon the conclusion of a Memorandum of Understanding (MOU) between Manitoba and Missouri, U.S. Senator Byron L. Dorgan (of North Dakota) wrote to the U.S. Department of State Legal Adviser, expressing the position that the MOU was inconsistent with the Constitution and soliciting a reaction. The Legal Adviser's reply follows.

LETTER OF U.S. DEPARTMENT OF STATE LEGAL ADVISER TO U.S. SENATOR BYRON DORGAN

(Nov. 20, 2001) (footnotes omitted).

Dear Senator Dorgan:

This is in response to your February 14, 2001 letter requesting the Department of State's views on the Memorandum of Understanding (MOU) signed by the State of Missouri and the Province of Manitoba. . . . As described in the attached memorandum, the Constitution does not assign to the Executive Branch the responsibility for interpreting or enforcing the Compact Clause. However, the way this clause is applied has obvious effects on Executive Branch interests in the field of foreign affairs, and it is not uncommon for states of the United States to consult with the Department of State when they are considering entering into arrangements with a foreign power that may engage these interests. In the case of the MOU you have brought to our attention we were not consulted prior to its signature. The attached memorandum describes some of the considerations that we would have raised if we had been consulted.

I trust that you will find the attached Memorandum responsive to your inquiry.

Sincerely,

WILLIAM H. TAFT, IV
Legal Adviser, U.S. Department of State

MEMORANDUM

This memorandum sets forth Department of State comments on the January 25, 2001 Memorandum of Understanding between the State of Missouri and the Province of Manitoba ("MOU") in light of relevant provisions of the U.S. Constitution.

In the MOU, Missouri and Manitoba agree "to work cooperatively to the fullest extent possible consistent with law and existing treaties . . . in their efforts to oppose water transfers" between the Missouri River watershed (Missouri's water supply) and the Hudson Bay watershed (Manitoba's water supply).The MOU includes commitments to exchange information; to mutually support opposition to inter-basin transfers, including related incremental works; and to communicate concerns about such transfers to their respective national governments.

There appear to be three constitutional doctrines implicated by the MOU: (a) the Compact Clause; (b) the Supremacy Clause by which federal law may preempt state action; and (c) the Foreign Affairs Power generally.

THE MOU AND THE COMPACT CLAUSE

The question has been raised whether the MOU, given that it has not been approved by Congress, is consistent with the Compact Clause of the

Constitution. Article 1, Section 10, Clause 3 of the Constitution provides that "[n]o State shall, without the Consent of Congress ... enter into any Agreement or Compact with another State, or with a foreign Power...." The Constitution does not specifically assign responsibility for interpretation or enforcement of this clause to the Executive branch of the federal government. In practice, however, it is not uncommon for states of the United States to consult with the Department of State when they are considering entering into an arrangement with a foreign power for advice as to the consistency of that arrangement with the Compact Clause. In the first instance, responsibility for fidelity to the requirements of the Compact Clause lies with the states themselves, pursuant to the Supremacy Clause of the Constitution. Should they submit a proposed compact to the Congress, it is the prerogative of the Congress to approve or disapprove the compact, or to require modifications. Ultimately, issues concerning the Compact Clause or a particular arrangement by a state with a foreign power may need to be resolved in the courts, either state or federal.

The Department of State has not been consulted by the state authorities of either North Dakota or Missouri concerning the MOU at issue here, and thus is not aware of whether there is an intention to bring the MOU before the Congress or the courts. However, in accordance with the Department's normal practice, this memorandum identifies the kinds of considerations that the Department would raise about an MOU like this.

THE SCOPE OF THE COMPACT CLAUSE

The Department ordinarily looks to *Virginia v. Tennessee*, 148 U.S. 503 (1893), in assessing whether an agreement involving a U.S. state would constitute a "Compact ... with a foreign Power," although that case did not involve a compact with a foreign power. The only Supreme Court case actually to review a potential state compact with a foreign power, *Holmes v. Jennison*, [39 U.S. 540, 572–79 (1840),] resulted in a divided court. The case involved the question of whether the Governor of Vermont had entered into an agreement with Canadian authorities to extradite a fugitive back to Canada. Chief Justice Taney, speaking for three other justices, took the view that "every agreement, written or verbal, formal or informal, positive or implied, by the mutual understanding of the parties" falls within the Compact Clause's ambit. Taney was particularly concerned about the ability of a U.S. state to extradite fugitives to a country when it was the policy of the federal government not to extradite persons. In Taney's view, the only permissible way for Vermont to make such a hand-over would be if Congress consented, since that would make the agreement subject to federal supervision. In contrast, the other justices found either that the Supreme Court had no jurisdiction to hear the case or that no agreement could be inferred.

In general, the notion articulated by Chief Justice Taney that all U.S. state agreements constitute compacts that require congressional consent has not been widely supported. In *Virginia v. Tennessee*, the Supreme Court, in reviewing an interstate compact delineating a boundary line, concluded that despite the Constitution's general language, its prohibition on compacts without congressional consent was not absolute. Specifically, the Court reasoned the Clause should only extend to those compacts that involved "the formation of any combination tending to the increase of political power in the states, which may encroach upon or interfere with the just supremacy of the United States." Subsequent Supreme Court case law has affirmed that, at least with respect to interstate compacts that would increase the political power of the states in such a way as to interfere with the supremacy of the federal government require congressional consent.

Although it is not a settled question that the *Virginia* standard applies to state compacts with foreign powers, at least one state court, the Department of State and numerous scholars have assumed that it does. In *McHenry County v. Brady*, [37 N.D. 59 (1917),] the Supreme Court of North Dakota declined to enjoin construction and maintenance of a drain from North Dakota into Canada called for by a contract between U.S. and Canadian municipal entities as a violation of the Compact Clause. In so ruling, the court declined to adopt the "sweeping language" of *Jennison* since the subject matter of that case (extradition) involved a national power, and instead relied on *Virginia* and its progeny in light of the local context in which the contract was concluded. In a similar 1981 case regarding a proposed international water district involving areas of both Vermont and Quebec, the Department of State took the view that such an arrangement did not implicate the Compact Clause because federal permitting procedures would still apply and the district's activities would be limited to traditionally local functions (e.g., water service) rather than political functions.

In practice, Congress has been asked to consent to only a few foreign compacts involving U.S. states, leaving uncertain Congress' view of the scope of the Compact Clause. However, we are aware of no compacts approved by Congress that involved local interference with national policy. Among the most well-known examples of congressionally-approved compacts are a 1956 New York–Canada agreement to establish a port authority for a bridge across the Niagara river; a 1958 Minnesota–Manitoba highway agreement; 1949 and 1952 Northeastern Interstate Forest Fire Protection Compacts; and various compacts authorized under the 1972 International Bridge Act. In one case involving water rights, Congress consented in 1968 to a Great Lake Basin Compact. Originally intended to include all U.S. states and Canadian provinces bordering the Great Lakes, the compact was to establish a Commission with the goal of promoting the use, development and conservation of the water resources of the Great Lakes. In giving its consent, however, Congress refused to approve certain compact provisions, including those that allowed Canadian provinces to join as members, in light of Department of State concerns about such participation and the potential overlap between the compact and the mechanisms established under the 1909 U.S.-Canadian Boundary Waters Treaty.

At the same time, the Department of State is aware that U.S. states often conclude various arrangements with foreign powers without congressional consent. It appears that such arrangements principally involve matters of common local interest, e.g., coordination on roads, police cooperation, border control, local trade cooperation initiatives, education exchanges, local conservation measures, and similar matters. When they are called to the Department's attention, such arrangements have generally been analyzed under the *Virginia* standard, with particular attention to whether such texts would interfere with the President's foreign relations responsibilities.

THE MOU AND THE COMPACT CLAUSE

Turning to the MOU, it appears that two questions need to be asked to determine whether it triggers the Compact Clause's requirement for congressional approval. First, is the MOU a "compact or agreement" for constitutional purposes? Second, if so, does it belong to that class of agreements that the Supreme Court has determined require congressional consent?

As for the first question, to qualify as a "compact or agreement" the Department traditionally has looked to whether the text in question is intended to be legally binding. The form and the content of this MOU suggest that Missouri and Manitoba likely intended to conclude such a legal agreement. The MOU is structured as an agreement with a title, preamble, specific commitments and a signature block. The terminology used (e.g., "agree" and "ensure") is consistent with legally binding intent. . . .

The fact that the two parties condition their cooperation on existing law and treaties does not preclude a finding that the MOU is intended to be legally binding. The United States has concluded a number of treaties and other international agreements in which a particular provision or the agreement as a whole is subject to the parties' laws or international commitments. In such circumstances, although the parties can avoid their obligations based on an existing law or treaty, they may not avoid such obligations simply because, from a policy perspective, they no longer desire to comply with them.

Ultimately, however, the legal status of an instrument such as the MOU may not itself be determinative of whether the document qualifies as a compact. As the Supreme Court reasoned in *U.S. Steel Corp.* "the mere form of the interstate agreement cannot be dispositive." [*U.S. Steel Corp. v. Multistate Tax Comm.*, 434 U.S. 452, 470 (1978).] In other words, even in the absence of a legally binding agreement, the Compact Clause may be implicated. In *Northeast Bancorp, Inc.*, for example, the Court undertook a Compact Clause analysis of reciprocal state banking legislation even where there was no evidence of a legal agreement between the states to enact such legislation. Instead, the Court looked for "several of the classic indicia" of a Compact: e.g., establishment of a joint organization or a body; some restriction on the state's ability to withdraw from the arrangements by repealing or modifying its law unilaterally; or a requirement that limitations on state action are reciprocal. [*Northeast Bancorp, Inc. v. Board of Governors of the Fed. Reserve System*, 472 U.S. 159, 175 (1985)]. Although these factors seem particularly relevant where a court has to determine if independent state statutes constitute a compact, the Court has not to our knowledge addressed whether such indicia are also required where in fact a legal agreement exists. At a minimum, however, assuming that the same indicia applicable to interstate compacts apply to state compacts with foreign powers, these indicia are useful in evaluating the MOU.

Whether the "indicia" cited in *Northeast Bancorp, Inc.* are present in the MOU is not immediately apparent. Missouri and Manitoba have had at least one meeting "under" the MOU, but it is not clear if such meetings would constitute the "joint organization" referred to by the Supreme Court. Another question is whether Manitoba could argue that Missouri had violated the MOU if Missouri announced that it supported inter-basin water transfer (à la a repeal in legislation). Similarly, *Northeast Bancorp, Inc.* would ask whether the obligation of Missouri to cooperate in opposing inter-basin water-transfers is contingent on Manitoba's performance of similar obligations. Firm answers to such questions would require further factual development of what actions the parties understood as being required by their agreement "to work cooperatively to the fullest possible extent consistent with law and existing treaties . . . to oppose [inter-basin] water transfers."

Assuming for purposes of analysis that the MOU constitutes a "compact or agreement," the next question is whether it is the sort of compact or agreement for which congressional consent is required. As stated above, the Department traditionally applies the standard laid out in *Virginia*—i.e., whether a compact is "directed to the formation of any combination tending to the increase of political power in the states, which may encroach upon or interfere with the just supremacy of the United States." Evidence of an actual impact on the federal government's supremacy has traditionally not been required; it is the potential impact of the compact that has led the Department to point out the need for congressional consent.

Examining the MOU in light of *Virginia* and its progeny, the Department would look to whether the MOU (a) impacts other U.S. states; (b) interferes with the federal government's interests in inter-basin water transfers; (c) deals solely with local matters; or (d) involves activities that could be carried out by Missouri even in the absence of the MOU. The following discussion briefly reviews each of these factors.

First, with respect to the effects on other states, the water in the Missouri and Hudson Bay watersheds that is the subject of the MOU borders or supplies water for numerous states. Missouri and Manitoba are therefore not the only parties interested in how those watersheds are treated. Missouri's alliance with Manitoba to support each other's effort to oppose inter-basin water-transfers could affect the interest of other states both as to the outcome and the process leading to decisions on how these waters are managed.

Second, in terms of the federal government's role, Congress has indicated an express interest in the inter-basin transfers at issue in the MOU. Two statutes—the Dakota Waters Resources Act of 2000 ("DWRA"), which amended the Garrison Diversion Reformulation Act of 1986 ("Garrison Act") and the Garrison Act itself—address inter-basin water transfer directly. ... The DWRA provides a comprehensive set of procedures for the Secretary of the Interior to follow in order to study and possibly construct projects involving inter-basin transfers in the Red River Valley (part of the Hudson Bay watershed), with both federal and state involvement in the review process. Ultimately, the DWRA reserves to Congress the final decision on whether a transfer will be authorized, but any such transfers are limited to those that the Executive branch determines comport with 1909 U.S.-Canada Boundary Waters Treaty's restrictions on activities that might pollute or otherwise affect the level or flow of boundary waters.

Given such federal interest, applications of the *Virginia* standard would require an analysis of whether the MOU encroaches on the political power of the federal government to address inter-basin water-transfers. It is not enough to show simply that the federal government has competence over these matters. Rather, one must ask whether Missouri's enlistment of Manitoba's support in the MOU to oppose particular transfers potentially operates to the legal detriment of the federal government by interfering with the decision-making scheme set out in the federal legislation or, where decisions have been made, in their effective implementation. A secondary question is whether the MOU could interfere with administration of the Boundary Waters Treaty. That Treaty affords the United States and Canada, not Missouri or Manitoba, the right to interpret and apply the Treaty as well as to refer matters to the International Joint Commission.

As indicated above, a third factor the Department would customarily examine is the question of whether the MOU deals only with matters of local policy. Some state arrangements with foreign powers dealing with water use issues have been deemed to be solely of local interest for Compact Clause purposes. This was true of the drainage basin at issue in *McHenry County* and the Vermont–Quebec International Water District, which had "no political function." The MOU in this case, in contrast, addresses cooperation between a U.S. state and a Canadian province to work together to oppose the possibility of inter-basin water transfers that could affect other states of the United States and which are to be considered pursuant to federal statute.

Fourth, the Department would assess the implications of the Supreme Court's decision in *Multistate Tax Commission*, which highlighted that congressional consent to an interstate compact is not required so long as the state is free to undertake the contemplated activities in the absence of the MOU, on a proposed arrangement. Thus, if one could show in this case that activities contemplated under the MOU—i.e., sharing information on actions contemplated under the DWRA, opposing inter-basin water transfers and communicating concerns about such transfers to the federal government—are actions that Missouri has the authority to carry out irrespective of an MOU, it would argue against applying the Compact Clause.

A key inquiry for this purpose is the extent to which the MOU calls for "mutually supportive" cooperation which might be understood as cooperation that cannot occur without another party. This would pose two issues: first, the extent to which such activities are possible even in the absence of the MOU, and secondly, whether this kind of activity impinges upon the "exclusive foreign relations power expressly reserved to the federal government," and therefore falls outside the *Multistate Tax Commission* authorization for interstate compacts to be concluded without Congressional approval.

Finally, in addition to these four factors, evidence of agreement on concrete actions by the parties undertaken pursuant to the MOU could assist in ascertaining whether the MOU impacts our federal structure. The MOU, however, is not so specific as to require either party to cooperate in ways that must physically manifest themselves (i.e., constructing a facility, etc.) nor does it appear to require them to enact any reciprocal obligations into law. This is presumably because the objects and purpose of the MOU seems to be to commit Missouri and Manitoba to oppose the actions of others; i.e., to oppose what the federal government is studying, and in some cases, doing, with respect to inter-basin water transfers. Thus, any interference that the MOU might cause to the federal government's supremacy would likely be procedural rather that substantive in nature. For example, if the MOU requires Missouri to operate not only on its own behalf, but also on Manitoba's behalf, in attempting to influence federal water management policy, would that interfere with the federal government's ability to implement the DWRA, the Garrison Act and the 1909 Boundary Waters Treaty? As discussed below, in the event Missouri sought to undertake concrete actions with respect to such water management issues, a strong argument can be made that such actions would be pre-empted by the DWRA, the Garrison Act, and the 1909 Boundary Waters Treaty.

Because of the expressions of federal policy, in addition to Compact Clause considerations, the MOU also potentially implicates the more general constitutional issues of federal preemption and the foreign affairs powers of the federal government. This memorandum therefore provides some additional background on these separate constitutional issues.

THE MOU, THE SUPREMACY CLAUSE AND THE FOREIGN AFFAIRS POWER

The Supreme Court decision in *Crosby v. National Foreign Trade Council*, [530 U.S. 363 (2000)] illustrates the Court's most recent views on federal preemption in a foreign affairs context. In *Crosby*, the Court held unanimously that Massachusetts law imposing sanctions on Burma was invalid under the Supremacy Clause of the Constitution "owing to its threat of frustrating federal statutory objectives." . . .

. . . .

In examining the issue, the Court emphasized that "[I]t is simply implausible that Congress would have gone to such lengths to empower the President had it been willing to compromise the effectiveness by deference to every provision of state statute or local ordinance that might, if enforced, blunt the consequences of discretionary Presidential action." Referring to the foreign affairs context of the statute, the Court also stressed that Massachusetts' independent actions threatened the ability of the United States to speak effectively with one voice on the international plane, noting that "the President's maximum power to persuade rest[s] on his capacity to bargain for the benefits of access to the entire national economy without exception for enclaves fenced off willy-nilly by inconsistent political tactics."

As far as the Department is aware the courts have not had occasion to consider the applicability of these principles to a state agreement with a foreign power, rather than a state statute. It would seem, however, that the logic of *Crosby* would prohibit states from accomplishing, via agreement with foreign states, what they are not able to accomplish by their own statutes. Therefore, it would appear relevant to assess the MOU's operation in light of federal preemption principles.

The central issue would be the MOU's compatibility with the federal statutory scheme for addressing the inter-basin water issue covered by the MOU. The NAWS project, for example, will involve such a transfer and has already been approved by the federal government in accordance with the terms of the Garrison Act. As for the DWRA, it is as comprehensive, if not more so, than the federal sanctions at issue in *Crosby*. Under the DWRA, the Secretary of Interior is charged with preparing a comprehensive report for Congress studying the Red River Valley's water needs and options for fulfilling them. The Secretary is required to solicit input from states that may be impacted by possible options. Environmental impact assessments of all feasible options are mandated by the statute. Within the statutory scheme, the Secretary of Interior is given some responsibility for selecting among potential projects, with the notable exception that any project that would require transfer of water from the Missouri River or its tributaries must be submitted to Congress for specific approval by an Act of Congress.

Given this comprehensive scheme, it is plain that Congress intended, in enacting the DWRA, to ensure that the decision making process about water allocation to the Red River Valley be centrally coordinated at the federal level. State input is recognized by the DWRA as an important piece of the process, but it is clearly subsumed into a federal decision-making process that reserves all final decision-making authority to the federal government. ... As such, the statute appears to be designed to "occupy the field" when it comes to major decisions impacting certain water resources across several states.

Analogizing to the logic in *Crosby*, it is difficult to believe that Congress would have enacted the DWRA "had it been willing to compromise the effectiveness by deference to every provision of state statute or legal ordinance" that might, if enforced, interfere with [the] overall purpose of the scheme. Any concrete actions by Missouri to oppose inter-basin water transfers outside of this scheme would likely be preempted in that they would interfere with federal policies and programs. On the other hand, Missouri is not precluded from expressing its own viewpoint on the resolution of federal water management issues; to the contrary, the DWRA explicitly allows Missouri such a role. Thus, the question under *Crosby* is whether through the MOU Missouri is seeking to afford a surrogate voice for Manitoba in the federal government's decision-making and implementation process that would interfere with the scheme envisioned by Congress.

Besides such principles of federal preemption, the courts have also confirmed the exclusive assignment of foreign affairs responsibilities to the federal government under the U.S. Constitution. Although the Court in *Crosby* did not reach the question of whether the Massachusetts statute unconstitutionally interfered in foreign affairs, both the district court and the appeals court held that it did, based on the decision by the Supreme Court in *Zschernig v. Miller*. The appellate court opined that "*Zschernig* stands for the principle that there is a threshold level of involvement in and impact on foreign affairs which the states may not exceed." The court held that while the boundaries of *Zschernig* were unclear, the Massachusetts law was clearly inconsistent with the principle in *Zschernig*. The court rejected arguments by Massachusetts to the effect that courts must balance the interests in a unified foreign policy against the particular interests of an individual state. Rather, quoting from *Zschernig*, the court reiterated that "[state] regulations must give away if they impair the effective exercise of the nation's foreign policy." A similar ruling was recently issued by the U.S. District Court for the Northern District of California. In that case, the Court found *Zschernig* applicable where a state was conducting its own foreign policy.

Thus, depending on the extent of its actual interference with U.S. foreign policy efforts in managing the water resources of the Hudson Bay watershed shared with Canada, the Missouri–Manitoba MOU would need to be evaluated for whether it constitutes an unconstitutional disruption of the federal government's foreign affairs power.

CONCLUSION

In light of the DWRA, the Garrison Act, the Boundary Waters Treaty and relevant practice, the Missouri–Manitoba MOU potentially implicates several constitutional doctrines. First, if the MOU is intended to be an instrument that could interfere with the just supremacy of the federal government, issues are raised as to the necessity for congressional consent under the Compact Clause. Given Congress's occupation of the field of inter-basin water transfers by statute (e.g., the DWRA), there are further issues under *Crosby* which set out the standards for determining when a state statute is preempted under the Supremacy Clause. Finally, to the extent the MOU may potentially interfere with the foreign affairs power more generally it would need to be evaluated for its consistency with principles set out in *Zschernig*.

CONCLUDING NOTES

1. *Post-Script.* In August 2005, North Dakota, Minnesota, Manitoba and the U.S. and Canadian federal governments reached an accord on guidelines allowing North Dakota to operate the new outlet. The agreement, which was not legally binding, provided that the two federal governments would design and build a filtration system for the diverted waters. *See* U.S. Dep't of State, Joint Press Statement on Devils Lake Flooding and Ecological Protection by the United States and Canada, North Dakota, Minnesota and Manitoba (Aug. 5, 2005).

2. *Great Lakes Compact to Limit Water Diversion.* In December 2005, the governors of eight U.S. states in the Great Lakes region (Illinois, Indiana, Michigan, Minnesota, New York, Ohio, Pennsylvania, and Wisconsin) and the premiers of two Canadian provinces (Ontario and Quebec) entered into an agreement that severely limited diversions of water to areas outside the Great Lakes–St. Lawrence River basin. The agreement, called The Great Lakes–St. Lawrence River Basin Sustainable Water Resources Agreement, says that the states and provinces "agree" to adopt and implement various measures necessary to limit water diversion. Article 700(2) of the Agreement states: "This Agreement is not intended to infringe upon the treaty power of the United States of America, nor shall any term hereof be construed to alter or amend any treaty or term thereof that has been or may hereafter be executed by the United States of America." Does Article 700(2) satisfy completely any constitutional concerns about the agreement?

SECTION 8. CASE STUDY: THE CONSULAR CONVENTION, THE DEATH PENALTY, AND FEDERALISM

INTRODUCTORY NOTE

From 1998 to 2004, the International Court of Justice considered three cases filed against the United States by Paraguay (the *Breard* case), Germany (the *LaGrand* case), and Mexico (the *Avena* case) concerning the treatment of aliens on death row in the United States. A central issue in these cases was that U.S. law enforcement personnel repeatedly failed to advise aliens upon their arrest of the right to have their consulate notified, a right contained in Article 36 of the Vienna Convention on Consular Relations (VCCR). That failure is perhaps not surprising given the distribution of law enforcement authority in the United States, which is predominantly exercised at the state and local level. A further issue was whether, as a remedy for violation of the VCCR, state courts should review and reconsider the death sentences, to determine whether the lack of consular access prejudiced the aliens (i.e., whether the inability to have consular assistance impaired the alien from undertaking a strong defense). One problem that many aliens faced was that they only became aware of the protections contained in the VCCR after the trial stage and were therefore bared under the "procedural default rule" contained in many state laws from raising the issue for the first time in state appellate proceedings or collateral federal proceedings.

These cases posed an unprecedented challenge to the United States as a litigant before the ICJ—and, because the ICJ concluded that the United States was violating its international obligations under the Consular Convention, to the incorporation of international law and the appropriate remedies for its violation in our federal system. Chapter 3, Section 4 considered one important aspect of this latter question: the Supreme Court's decision in *Medellín v. Texas*, 552 U.S. 491, 128 S.Ct. 1346, 170 L.Ed.2d 190 (2008), that the obligation to comply with the ICJ judgment in *Avena* was not self-executing. Understanding that decision is critical to this case study, but the materials that follow focus on two additional questions, one analytically prior to the issue of self-execution in *Medellín* and the second arising only in the event that the ICJ judgment in *Avena* was not self-executing (as the Supreme Court in fact held in *Medellín*). First, how should courts ensure the implementation of U.S. obligations under the Consular Convention itself (as opposed to obligations under the U.N. Charter or the Optional Protocol relating to the obligation to follow the ICJ), given state law governing procedural default, remedies for violation of a defendant's treaty-based rights, and the death penalty? Second, assuming that federal law does not otherwise require states to abide by the ICJ's interpretation of the Consular Convention, may the President order them to do so? These two questions are addressed following this introductory material.

In all three consular convention cases, the International Court ordered provisionally that the United States "take all measures at its disposal to ensure" (*Breard*, *LaGrand*) or "all measures necessary to ensure" (*Avena*) that the relevant aliens not be executed pending a final decision by the Court. Vienna Convention on Consular Relations (Para. v. U.S.), Provisional Measures, 1998 I.C.J. 248 (Apr. 9); *LaGrand Case* (F.R.G. v. U.S.), Provisional Measures, 1999 I.C.J. 9 (Mar. 3); Case Concerning Avena and Other Mexican Nationals (Mex. v. U.S.), Provisional Measures, 2003 I.C.J. 6 (Feb. 5) (*Avena*), *reprinted in* 42 I.L.M. 309 (2003). The position of the U.S. government in the *Breard* and *LaGrand* cases, however, was that such I.C.J. provisional orders were not binding upon the United States under the U.N. Charter, I.C.J. Statute, or VCCR optional protocol.

After the provisional-measures order was issued in *Breard*, the U.S. Secretary of State sent a letter to the governor of Virginia (where Breard was on death row). The Secretary requested that the governor stay Breard's execution since the

> execution of Mr. Breard in the face of the Court's April 9 action could be seen as a denial by the United States of the significance of international law and the Court's processes in its international relations and thereby limit our ability to ensure that Americans are protected when living or traveling abroad.

Letter from Madeleine K. Albright, U.S. Sec'y of State, to James S. Gilmore III, Gov. of Virginia (Apr. 13, 1998), *partially reprinted in* 92 AM. J. INT'L L. 671–72 (1998). In declining to intervene in the case, the U.S. Supreme Court stated that it was "clear that Breard procedurally defaulted his claim, if any, under the Vienna Convention by failing to raise that claim in the state courts." Breard v. Greene, 523 U.S. 371, 375, 118 S.Ct. 1352, 140 L.Ed.2d 529 (1998). Further, the Court stated:

> [W]hile we should give respectful consideration to the interpretation of an international treaty rendered by an international court with jurisdiction to interpret such, it has been recognized in international law that, absent a clear and express statement to the contrary, the procedural rules of the forum State govern the implementation of the treaty in that State.

Id. Thereafter, the governor of Virginia decided not to stay the execution, and Breard was executed.

After the provisional-measures order was issued in *LaGrand*, the U.S. government transmitted the order to the governor of Arizona (where LaGrand was on death row). Again, the U.S. Supreme Court declined to intervene, *Federal Republic of Germany v. United States*, 526 U.S. 111, 119 S.Ct. 1016, 143 L.Ed.2d 192 (1999), and the governor of Arizona decided not to stay LaGrand's execution.

After Breard was executed, Paraguay withdrew its case from the International Court. Germany, however, continued its case even after LaGrand was executed. In a judgment on the merits, the Court found that by not immediately informing LaGrand (and his brother who was executed prior to the I.C.J.'s provisional-measures order) of the right of consular notification, the United States breached its obligations under the Vienna Convention. The U.S. failure to provide judicial review of the conviction and sentence in light of the lack of notification constituted a further breach. The Court also found that its provisional orders are binding on states and that the United States violated the Court's provisional order by failing to take all measures at its disposal to ensure that LaGrand was not executed pending a final decision by the Court.

Noting the steps already taken by the United States to improve implementation of its Vienna Convention obligations, the Court did not order it to provide a general assurance of nonrepetition (Germany did not request reparation in the form of compensation). The Court did find, however, that "should nationals of the Federal Republic of Germany nonetheless be sentenced to severe penalties" without their right to consular notification having been respected, the United States, "by means of its own choosing, shall allow the review and reconsideration of the conviction and sentence by taking account of the violation of the rights set forth" in the Vienna Convention. *LaGrand* (F.R.G. v. U.S.), 2001 I.C.J. 466, 516, ¶ 128(7) (June 27). In a declaration filed separate from the Court's judgment, the President of the Court commented on this finding:

This subparagraph represents a response to certain submissions by Germany and hence rules only on the obligations of the United States in cases of severe penalties imposed upon German nationals.

Thus, subparagraph (7) does not address the position of nationals of other countries or that of individuals sentenced to penalties that are not of a severe nature.

LaGrand (F.R.G. v. U.S.), 2001 I.C.J. 466, 517 (June 27) (declaration of President Guillaume).

In the *Avena* case, Mexico also pursued a decision on the merits, this time on behalf of more than fifty Mexicans on death row.

VIENNA CONVENTION ON CONSULAR RELATIONS, ARTICLE 36

Apr. 24, 1963, 21 U.S.T. 77, 596 U.N.T.S. 261.

COMMUNICATION AND CONTACT WITH NATIONALS OF THE SENDING STATE

1. With a view to facilitating the exercise of consular functions relating to nationals of the sending State:

(a) consular officers shall be free to communicate with nationals of the sending State and to have access to them. Nationals of the sending State shall have the same freedom with respect to communication with and access to consular officers of the sending State;

(b) if he so requests, the competent authorities of the receiving State shall, without delay, inform the consular post of the sending State if, within its consular district, a national of that State is arrested or committed to prison or to custody pending trial or is detained in any other manner. Any communication addressed to the consular post by the person arrested, in prison, custody or detention shall also be forwarded by the said authorities without delay. The said authorities shall inform the person concerned without delay of his rights under this sub-paragraph;

(c) consular officers shall have the right to visit a national of the sending State who is in prison, custody or detention, to converse and correspond with him and to arrange for his legal representation. They shall also have the right to visit any national of the sending State who is in prison, custody or detention in their district in pursuance of a judgment. Nevertheless, consular officers shall refrain from taking action on behalf of a national who is in prison, custody or detention if he expressly opposes such action.

2. The rights referred to in paragraph 1 of this article shall be exercised in conformity with the laws and regulations of the receiving State, subject to the proviso, however, that the said laws and regulations must enable full effect to be given to the purposes for which the rights accorded under this article are intended.

OPTIONAL PROTOCOL TO THE VIENNA CONVENTION ON CONSULAR RELATIONS CONCERNING THE COMPULSORY SETTLEMENT OF DISPUTES, ARTICLE I

Apr. 24, 1963, 21 U.S.T. 325, 596 U.N.T.S. 487.

Disputes arising out of the interpretation or application of the Convention shall lie within the compulsory jurisdiction of the International Court of Justice and may accordingly be brought before the Court by an application made by any party to the dispute being a Party to the present Protocol.

UNITED NATIONS CHARTER, ARTICLE 94

June 26, 1945, 59 Stat. 1031, T.S. No. 993.

1. Each Member of the United Nations undertakes to comply with the decision of the International Court of Justice in any case to which it is a party.

2. If any party to a case fails to perform the obligations incumbent upon it under a judgment rendered by the Court, the other party may have recourse to the Security Council, which may, if it deems necessary, make recommendations or decide upon measures to be taken to give effect to the judgment.

CASE CONCERNING AVENA AND OTHER MEXICAN NATIONALS (MEX. v. U.S.)

2004 I.C.J. 12 (Mar. 31).

1. On 9 January 2003 the United Mexican States (hereinafter referred to as "Mexico") filed in the Registry of the Court an Application instituting proceedings against the United States of America (hereinafter referred to as the "United States") for "violations of the Vienna Convention on Consular Relations" of 24 April 1963 (hereinafter referred to as the "Vienna Convention") allegedly committed by the United States.

In its Application, Mexico based the jurisdiction of the Court on Article 36, paragraph 1, of the Statute of the Court and on Article I of the Optional Protocol concerning the Compulsory Settlement of Disputes, which accompanies the Vienna Convention (hereinafter referred to as the "Optional Protocol").

. . . .

19. The underlying facts alleged by Mexico may be briefly described as follows: some are conceded by the United States, and some disputed. Mexico states that all the individuals the subject of its claims were Mexican nationals at the time of their arrest. It further contends that the United States authorities that arrested and interrogated these individuals

had sufficient information at their disposal to be aware of the foreign nationality of those individuals. According to Mexico's account, in 50 of the specified cases, Mexican nationals were never informed by the competent United States authorities of their rights under Article 36, paragraph 1 *(b)*, of the Vienna Convention and, in the two remaining cases, such information was not provided "without delay", as required by that provision. Mexico has indicated that in 29 of the 52 cases its consular authorities learned of the detention of the Mexican nationals only after death sentences had been handed down. In the 23 remaining cases, Mexico contends that it learned of the cases through means other than notification to the consular post by the competent United States authorities under Article 36, paragraph 1 *(b)*. It explains that in five cases this was too late to affect the trials, that in 15 cases the defendants had already made incriminating statements, and that it became aware of the other three cases only after considerable delay.

. . . .

111. The "procedural default" rule in United States law has already been brought to the attention of the Court in the *LaGrand* case. The following brief definition of the rule was provided by Mexico in its Memorial in this case and has not been challenged by the United States: "a defendant who could have raised, but fails to raise, a legal issue at trial will generally not be permitted to raise it in future proceedings, on appeal or in a petition for a writ of *habeas corpus*". The rule requires exhaustion of remedies, *inter alia*, at the state level and before a *habeas corpus* motion can be filed with federal courts. In the *LaGrand* case, the rule in question was applied by United States federal courts; in the present case, Mexico also complains of the application of the rule in certain state courts of criminal appeal.

. . . .

115. Having concluded that in most of the cases brought before the Court by Mexico in the 52 instances, there has been a failure to observe the obligations prescribed by Article 36, paragraph 1 *(b)*, of the Vienna Convention, the Court now proceeds to the examination of the legal consequences of such a breach and of what legal remedies should be considered for the breach.

. . . .

131. In stating in its Judgment in the *LaGrand* case that "the United States of America, *by means of its own choosing*, shall allow the review and reconsideration of the conviction and sentence" (*I.C.J. Reports 2001*, p. 516, para. 128; emphasis added), the Court acknowledged that the concrete modalities for such review and reconsideration should be left primarily to the United States. It should be underlined, however, that this freedom in the choice of means for such review and reconsideration is not without qualification: as the passage of the Judgment quoted above makes abundantly clear, such review and reconsideration has to be carried out "by taking account of the violation of the rights set forth in the Conven-

tion" (*I.C.J. Reports 2001*, p. 514, para. 125), including, in particular, the question of the legal consequences of the violation upon the criminal proceedings that have followed the violation.

. . . .

133. However, the Court wishes to point out that the current situation in the United States criminal procedure, as explained by the Agent at the hearings, is that "If the defendant alleged at trial that *a failure of consular information resulted in harm to a particular right essential to a fair trial*, an appeals court can *review how the lower court handled that claim of prejudice*", but that "*If the foreign national did not raise his Article 36 claim at trial, he may face procedural constraints* [i.e., the application of the procedural default rule] on raising that particular claim in direct or collateral judicial appeals" (emphasis added). As a result, a claim based on the violation of Article 36, paragraph 1, of the Vienna Convention, however meritorious in itself, could be barred in the courts of the United States by the operation of the procedural default rule (see paragraph 111 above).

. . . .

138. The Court would emphasize that the "review and reconsideration" prescribed by it in the *LaGrand* case should be effective. Thus it should "tak[e] account of the violation of the rights set forth in [the] Convention" (*I.C.J. Reports 2001*, p. 516, para. 128 (7)) and guarantee that the violation and the possible prejudice caused by that violation will be fully examined and taken into account in the review and reconsideration process. Lastly, review and reconsideration should be both of the sentence and of the conviction.

139. Accordingly, in a situation of the violation of rights under Article 36, paragraph 1, of the Vienna Convention, the defendant raises his claim in this respect not as a case of "harm to a particular right essential to a fair trial"—a concept relevant to the enjoyment of due process rights under the United States Constitution—but as a case involving the infringement of his rights under Article 36, paragraph 1. The rights guaranteed under the Vienna Convention are treaty rights which the United States has undertaken to comply with in relation to the individual concerned, irrespective of the due process rights under United States constitutional law. In this regard, the Court would point out that what is crucial in the review and reconsideration process is the existence of a procedure which guarantees that full weight is given to the violation of the rights set forth in the Vienna Convention, whatever may be the actual outcome of such review and reconsideration.

140. . . . [T]he Court is of the view that, in cases where the breach of the individual rights of Mexican nationals under Article 36, paragraph 1 *(b)*, of the Convention has resulted, in the sequence of judicial proceedings that has followed, in the individuals concerned being subjected to prolonged detention or convicted and sentenced to severe penalties, the legal consequences of this breach have to be examined and taken into account

in the course of review and reconsideration. The Court considers that it is the judicial process that is suited to this task.

141. The Court in the *LaGrand* case left to the United States the choice of means as to how review and reconsideration should be achieved, especially in the light of the procedural default rule. Nevertheless, the premise on which the Court proceeded in that case was that the process of review and reconsideration should occur within the overall judicial proceedings relating to the individual defendant concerned.

. . . .

[The United States had informed the Court that it was focusing on clemency proceedings as the best route for "review and reconsideration" because the U.S. government saw clemency as effective and as not hampered by legal constraints such as the procedural default rule.]

143. It may be true, as the United States argues, that in a number of cases "clemency in fact results in pardons of convictions as well as commutations of sentences". In that sense and to that extent, it might be argued that the facts demonstrated by the United States testify to a degree of effectiveness of the clemency procedures as a means of relieving defendants on death row from execution. The Court notes, however, that the clemency process, as currently practised within the United States criminal justice system, does not appear to meet the requirements described in paragraph 138 above and that it is therefore not sufficient in itself to serve as an appropriate means of "review and reconsideration" as envisaged by the Court in the *LaGrand* case. The Court considers nevertheless that appropriate clemency procedures can supplement judicial review and reconsideration, in particular where the judicial system has failed to take due account of the violation of the rights set forth in the Vienna Convention.

. . . .

153. For these reasons,

THE COURT,

. . . .

(4) By fourteen votes to one,

Finds that, by not informing, without delay upon their detention, the 51 Mexican nationals referred to in paragraph 106(1) above of their rights under Article 36, paragraph 1(b), of the Vienna Convention on Consular Relations of 24 April 1963, the United States of America breached the obligations incumbent upon it under that subparagraph;

. . . .

(5) By fourteen votes to one,

Finds that, by not notifying the appropriate Mexican consular post without delay of the detention of the 49 Mexican nationals referred to in paragraph 106(2) above and thereby depriving the United Mexican States of the right, in a timely fashion, to render the assistance provided for by the Vienna Convention to the individuals concerned, the United States of America breached the obligations incumbent upon it under Article 36, paragraph 1(b);

. . . .

(6) By fourteen votes to one,

Finds that, in relation to the 49 Mexican nationals referred to in paragraph 106(3) above, the United States of America deprived the United Mexican States of the right, in a timely fashion, to communicate with and have access to those nationals and to visit them in detention, and thereby breached the obligations incumbent upon it under Article 36, paragraph 1(a) and (c), of the Convention;

(7) By fourteen votes to one,

Finds that, in relation to the 34 Mexican nationals referred to in paragraph 106(4) above, the United States of America deprived the United Mexican States of the right, in a timely fashion, to arrange for legal representation of those nationals, and thereby breached the obligations incumbent upon it under Article 36, paragraph 1(c), of the Convention;

. . . .

(8) By fourteen votes to one,

Finds that, by not permitting the review and reconsideration, in the light of the rights set forth in the Convention, of the conviction and sentences of Mr. César Roberto Fierro Reyna, Mr. Roberto Moreno Ramos and Mr. Osvaldo Torres Aguilera, after the violations referred to in subparagraph (4) above had been established in respect of those individuals, the United States of America breached the obligations incumbent upon it under Article 36, paragraph 2, of the Convention;

. . . .

(9) By fourteen votes to one,

Finds that the appropriate reparation in this case consists in the obligation of the United States of America to provide, by means of its own choosing, review and reconsideration of the convictions and sentences of the Mexican nationals referred to in subparagraphs (4), (5), (6) and (7) above, by taking account both of the violation of the rights set forth in Article 36 of the Convention and of paragraphs 138 to 141 of this Judgment;

. . . .

(10) Unanimously,

Takes note of the commitment undertaken by the United States of America to ensure implementation of the specific measures adopted in performance of its obligations under Article 36, paragraph 1 (b), of the Vienna Convention; and *finds* that this commitment must be regarded as meeting the request by the United Mexican States for guarantees and assurances of non-repetition;

(11) Unanimously,

Finds that, should Mexican nationals nonetheless be sentenced to severe penalties, without their rights under Article 36, paragraph 1 (b), of the Convention having been respected, the United States of America shall provide, by means of its own choosing, review and reconsideration of the conviction and sentence, so as to allow full weight to be given to the violation of the rights set forth in the Convention, taking account of paragraphs 138 to 141 of this Judgment.

*NOTE ON POST-*AVENA *REMEDIES*

After issuance of *Avena*, aliens on death row in the United States sought to use the decision to obtain review and reconsideration of their death sentences. For example, Osbaldo Torres, one of the fifty-one Mexican nationals at issue in *Avena*, had been scheduled for execution on May 18, 2004. After issuance of the I.C.J.'s *Avena* decision, Torres filed a new request for post-conviction relief in the Oklahoma Court of Criminal Appeals and a stay of his execution. On May 13, the court granted the stay and remanded the case to a lower court for an evidentiary hearing. *See* Torres v. Oklahoma, No. PCD–04–442, 2004 WL 3711623 (Okla. Crim. App. May 13, 2004), *reprinted in* 43 I.L.M. 1227 (2004). In doing so, one of the judges stated in an unpublished concurrence that "we are bound to give full faith and credit to the *Avena* decision." *Id.* at 1229 (Chapel, J., specially concurring). Among other things, Judge Chapel noted:

> I am not suggesting that the International Court of Justice has jurisdiction over this Court—far from it. However, in these unusual circumstances the issue of whether this Court must abide by that court's opinion in Torres's case is not ours to determine. The United States Senate and the President have made that decision for us. The Optional Protocol . . . provides that the International Court of Justice is the forum for resolution of disputes under the Vienna Convention.

Id. (footnote omitted).

On a separate track, the U.S. Department of State Legal Adviser on May 11, 2004, wrote a letter to the governor of Oklahoma describing and transmitting a copy of the I.C.J.'s decision in *Avena*. The letter to the governor requested "that in your review of the case you give careful consideration to the pending clemency request of Mr. Torres, including by considering the failure to provide Mr. Torres with consular information and notification pursuant to Article 36 of the VCCR and whether that failure should be regarded as having ultimately led to his conviction and sentence." Letter from Department of State Legal Adviser William H. Taft, IV, to Governor of Oklahoma Brad Henry, at 2 (May 11, 2004). On May 13, the governor of Oklahoma commuted Torres's penalty to life without parole, thus ending the matter. For background, see Janet Koven Levit, *A Tale of International Law in the Heartland: Torres and the Role of State Courts in Transnational Legal*

Conversation, 12 TULSA J. COMP. & INT'L L. 163 (2004–2005); *see also* Torres v. State of Oklahoma, 120 P.3d 1184 (Ct. of Crim. App. 2005).

Other courts, however, did not see the *Avena* decision as altering the alien's rights in U.S. courts, including in the case of a Mexican national named José Ernesto Medellín. *See* Medellín v. Dretke, 371 F.3d 270 (5th Cir. 2004). After the Supreme Court granted certiorari to consider the effects of *Avena* in the *Medellín* case, the Bush Administration moved to alter the terms of the debate by issuance of a presidential memorandum (reproduced below) designed to implement the *Avena* decision for the Mexican nationals implicated by that decision. The Supreme Court then remanded the *Medellín* case back to Texas state courts for consideration of the President's memorandum.

In the meantime, the Supreme Court considered the relevance of the I.C.J.'s decision in the *Avena* case for aliens not directly addressed by that decision—either because they were not sentenced to death, or because they were not Mexican nationals—but who nonetheless invoked Avena as support for their claims for relief under the Consular Convention. That case, *Sanchez-Llamas v. Oregon* (reproduced below), noted the President's memorandum, though it too did not directly apply to the defendants at issue in *Sanchez–Llamas*. In reading *Sanchez-Llamas*, observe that the Supreme Court assumes for purposes of its analysis that Article 36 of the Consular Convention is self-executing, a position that had found favor in the lower courts—and which was not unsettled by the Supreme Court's subsequent determination in *Medellín* that the obligation to comply with ICJ judgments, which arose from different treaty provisions, was for its part non-self-executing.

Medellín, of course, continued to percolate through the courts. The Texas Court of Criminal Appeals, the authoritative body on criminal matters in the state court system, rejected Medellín's attempt to secure reconsideration based either on the ICJ's decision in *Avena* itself or the President's memorandum. *See* Ex Parte Medellín, 223 S.W.3d 315 (Tex. Crim. App. 2006). The Supreme Court, continuing its remarkable engagement in Consular Convention issues, granted Medellín's petition for a writ of certiorari and affirmed. The part of its opinion addressing the self-execution of U.S. treaty obligations to comply with *Avena* was reproduced in Chapter 3, Section 4, and warrants review; the portion of its opinion addressing the President's memorandum is reproduced below, after *Sanchez-Llamas*.

MEMORANDUM OF PRESIDENT GEORGE W. BUSH TO THE U.S. ATTORNEY GENERAL ALBERTO GONZALES

44 I.L.M. 950 (2005).

SUBJECT: Compliance with the Decision of the International Court of Justice in *Avena*

The United States is a party to the Vienna Convention on Consular Relations (the "Convention") and the Convention's Optional Protocol Concerning the Compulsory Settlement of Disputes (Optional Protocol), which gives the International Court of Justice (ICJ) jurisdiction to decide disputes concerning the "interpretation and application" of the Convention.

I have determined, pursuant to the authority vested in me as President by the Constitution and the laws of the United States of America, that the United States will discharge its international obligations under the decision of the International Court of Justice in the *Case Concerning Avena and Other Mexican Nationals (Mexico v. United States of America) (Avena)*, 2004 ICJ 128 (Mar. 31), by having State courts give effect to the decision in accordance with general principles of comity in cases filed by the 51 Mexican nationals addressed in that decision.

GEORGE BUSH

SANCHEZ-LLAMAS v. OREGON

548 U.S. 331, 126 S.Ct. 2669, 165 L.Ed.2d 557 (2006) (footnotes omitted).

CHIEF JUSTICE ROBERTS delivered the opinion of the Court.

Article 36 of the Vienna Convention on Consular Relations (Vienna Convention or Convention), Apr. 24, 1963, [1970] 21 U. S. T. 77, 100–101, T. I. A. S. No. 6820, addresses communication between an individual and his consular officers when the individual is detained by authorities in a foreign country. These consolidated cases concern the availability of judicial relief for violations of Article 36. We are confronted with three questions. *First*, does Article 36 create rights that defendants may invoke against the detaining authorities in a criminal trial or in a postconviction proceeding? *Second*, does a violation of Article 36 require suppression of a defendant's statements to police? *Third*, may a State, in a postconviction proceeding, treat a defendant's Article 36 claim as defaulted because he failed to raise the claim at trial? We conclude, even assuming the Convention creates judicially enforceable rights, that suppression is not an appropriate remedy for a violation of Article 36, and that a State may apply its regular rules of procedural default to Article 36 claims. We therefore affirm the decisions below.

I

. . . .

Petitioner Moises Sanchez–Llamas is a Mexican national. In December 1999, he was involved in an exchange of gunfire with police in which one officer suffered a gunshot wound in the leg. Police arrested Sanchez–Llamas and gave him warnings under *Miranda v. Arizona*, 384 U.S. 436 (1966) . . ., in both English and Spanish. At no time, however, did they inform him that he could ask to have the Mexican Consulate notified of his detention.

Shortly after the arrest and *Miranda* warnings, police interrogated Sanchez–Llamas with the assistance of an interpreter. In the course of the interrogation, Sanchez–Llamas made several incriminating statements regarding the shootout with police. He was charged with attempted aggravated murder, attempted murder, and several other offenses. Before trial, Sanchez–Llamas moved to suppress the statements he made to police. He argued that suppression was warranted because the statements were made involuntarily and because the authorities had failed to comply with Article 36 of the Vienna Convention. The trial court denied the motion. The case proceeded to trial, and Sanchez–Llamas was convicted and sentenced to 20 1/2 years in prison.

He appealed, again arguing that the Vienna Convention violation required suppression of his statements. The Oregon Court of Appeals affirmed. ... The Oregon Supreme Court also affirmed, concluding that Article 36 "does not create rights to consular access or notification that are enforceable by detained individuals in a judicial proceeding." ... 108 P. 3d 573, 578 (2005) (en banc). We granted certiorari. ...

. . . .

Petitioner Mario Bustillo, a Honduran national, was with several other men at a restaurant in Springfield, Virginia, on the night of December 10, 1997. That evening, outside the restaurant, James Merry was struck in the head with a baseball bat as he stood smoking a cigarette. He died several days later. Several witnesses at the scene identified Bustillo as the assailant. Police arrested Bustillo the morning after the attack and eventually charged him with murder. Authorities never informed him that he could request to have the Honduran Consulate notified of his detention.

At trial, the defense pursued a theory that another man, known as "Sirena," was responsible for the attack. ... A jury convicted Bustillo of first-degree murder, and he was sentenced to 30 years in prison. His conviction and sentence were affirmed on appeal.

After his conviction became final, Bustillo filed a petition for a writ of habeas corpus in state court. There, for the first time, he argued that authorities had violated his right to consular notification under Article 36 of the Vienna Convention. He claimed that if he had been advised of his right to confer with the Honduran Consulate, he "would have done so without delay." ... Moreover, the Honduran Consulate executed an affidavit stating that "it would have endeavoured to help Mr. Bustillo in his defense" had it learned of his detention prior to trial. ... Bustillo insisted that the consulate could have helped him locate Sirena prior to trial. His habeas petition also argued, as part of a claim of ineffective assistance of counsel, that his attorney should have advised him of his right to notify the Honduran Consulate of his arrest and detention.

The state habeas court dismissed Bustillo's Vienna Convention claim as "procedurally barred" because he had failed to raise the issue at trial or on appeal. ... The court also denied Bustillo's claim of ineffective assistance of counsel, ruling that his belated claim that counsel should have informed him of his Vienna Convention rights was barred by the applicable statute of limitations and also meritless under *Strickland v. Washington*, 466 U.S. 668 ... (1984). ... In an order refusing Bustillo's petition for appeal, the Supreme Court of Virginia found "no reversible error" in the habeas court's dismissal of the Vienna Convention claim. ...

II

. . . .

As a predicate to their claims for relief, Sanchez–Llamas and Bustillo each argue that Article 36 grants them an individually enforceable right to request that their consular officers be notified of their detention, and an accompanying right to be informed by authorities of the availability of consular notification. Respondents and the United States, as *amicus curiae*, strongly dispute this contention. They argue that "there is a presumption that a treaty will be enforced through political and diplomatic channels, rather than through the courts." Brief for United States 11 ... (quoting *Head Money Cases*, 112 U.S. 580, 598 ... (1884) (a treaty " 'is primarily a compact between independent nations,' " and " 'depends for the enforcement of its provisions on the interest and the honor of the governments which are parties to it' ")). Because we conclude that Sanchez–Llamas and Bustillo are not in any event entitled to relief on their claims, we find it unnecessary to resolve the question whether the Vienna Convention grants individuals enforceable rights. Therefore, for purposes of addressing petitioners' claims, we assume, without deciding, that Article 36 does grant Bustillo and Sanchez–Llamas such rights.

A

Sanchez–Llamas argues that the trial court was required to suppress his statements to police because authorities never told him of his rights under Article 36. He refrains, however, from arguing that the Vienna Convention itself mandates suppression. We think this a wise concession. The Convention does not prescribe specific remedies for violations of Article 36. Rather, it expressly leaves the implementation of Article 36 to domestic law: Rights under Article 36 are to "be exercised in conformity with the laws and regulations of the receiving State." Art. 36(2), 21 U. S. T., at 101. As far as the text of the Convention is concerned, the question of the availability of the exclusionary rule for Article 36 violations is a matter of domestic law.

It would be startling if the Convention were read to require suppression. The exclusionary rule as we know it is an entirely American legal creation. *See Bivens v. Six Unknown Fed. Narcotics Agents*, 403 U.S. 388, 415 ... (1971) (Burger, C. J., dissenting) (the exclusionary rule "is unique to American jurisprudence"). ... There is no reason to suppose that Sanchez–Llamas would be afforded the relief he seeks here in any of the other 169 countries party to the Vienna Convention.

For good reason then, Sanchez–Llamas argues only that suppression is required because it is the appropriate remedy for an Article 36 violation under United States law, and urges us to require suppression for Article 36 violations as a matter of our "authority to develop remedies for the enforcement of federal law in state-court criminal proceedings." ...

For their part, the State of Oregon and the United States, as *amicus curiae*, contend that we lack any such authority over state-court proceedings. They argue that our cases suppressing evidence obtained in violation of federal statutes are grounded in our supervisory authority over the federal courts—an authority that does not extend to state-court proceedings. ... Unless required to do so by the Convention itself, they argue, we cannot direct Oregon courts to exclude Sanchez–Llamas' statements from his criminal trial.

To the extent Sanchez–Llamas argues that we should invoke our supervisory authority, the law is clear: "It is beyond dispute that we do not hold a supervisory power over the courts of the several States." *Dickerson v. United States*, 530 U.S. 428, 438 ... (2000); *see also Smith v. Phillips*, 455 U.S. 209, 221 ("Federal courts hold no supervisory authority over state court judicial proceedings and may intervene only to correct wrongs of a constitutional dimension"). The cases on which Sanchez–Llamas principally relies are inapplicable in light of the limited reach of our supervisory powers. ...

We also agree with the State of Oregon and the United States that our authority to create a judicial remedy applicable in state court must lie, if anywhere, in the treaty itself. Under the Constitution, the President has the power, "by and with the Advice and Consent of the Senate, to make Treaties." Art. II, § 2, cl. 2. The United States ratified the Convention with the expectation that it would be interpreted according to its terms. *See Restatement (Third) of Foreign Relations Law of the United States* § 325(1) (1986) ("An international agreement is to be interpreted in good faith in accordance with the ordinary meaning to be given to its terms in their context and in the light of its object and purpose"). If we were to require suppression for Article 36 violations without some authority in the Convention, we would in effect be supplementing those terms by enlarging the obligations of the United States under the Convention. This is entirely inconsistent with the judicial function. *Cf. The Amiable Isabella*, 6 Wheat. 1, 71 ... (1821) (Story, J.) ("[T]o alter, amend, or add to any treaty, by inserting any clause, whether small or great, important or trivial, would be on our part an usurpation of power, and not an exercise of judicial functions. It would be to make, and not to construe a treaty").

Of course, it is well established that a self-executing treaty binds the States pursuant to the Supremacy Clause, and that the States therefore must recognize the force of the treaty in the course of adjudicating the rights of litigants. *See, e.g., Hauenstein v. Lynham*, 100 U.S. 483 ... (1880). And where a treaty provides for a particular judicial remedy, there is no issue of intruding on the constitutional prerogatives of the States or the other federal branches. Courts must apply the remedy as a requirement of federal law. *Cf.* 18 U.S.C. § 2515; *United States v. Giordano*, 416 U.S. 505, 524–525 ... (1974). But where a treaty does not provide a particular remedy, either expressly or implicitly, it is not for the federal courts to impose one on the States through lawmaking of their own.

Sanchez–Llamas argues that the language of the Convention implicitly requires a judicial remedy because it states that the laws and regulations governing the exercise of Article 36 rights "must enable *full effect* to be given to the purposes for which the rights ... are intended," Art. 36(2), 21 U. S. T., at 101 (emphasis added). In his view, although "full effect" may not automatically require an exclusionary rule, it does require an appropriate judicial remedy of some kind. There is reason to doubt this interpretation. In particular, there is little indication that other parties to the Convention have interpreted Article 36 to require a judicial remedy in the context of criminal prosecutions. *See* Department of State Answers to Questions Posed by the First Circuit in *United States v. Nai Fook Li*, No. 97–2034 etc., p. A–9 ... (Oct. 15, 1999) ("We are unaware of any country party to the [Vienna Convention] that provides remedies for violations of consular notification through its domestic criminal justice system").

Nevertheless, even if Sanchez–Llamas is correct that Article 36 implicitly requires a judicial remedy, the Convention equally states that Article 36 rights "shall be exercised in conformity with the laws and regulations of the receiving State." Art. 36(2), 21 U. S. T., at 101. Under our domestic law, the exclusionary rule is not a remedy we apply lightly. "[O]ur cases have repeatedly emphasized that the rule's 'costly toll' upon truth-seeking and law enforcement objectives presents a high obstacle for those urging application of the rule." *Pennsylvania Bd. of Probation and Parole v. Scott*, 524 U.S. 357, 364–365 ... (1998). Because the rule's social costs are considerable, suppression is warranted only where the rule's " 'remedial objectives are thought most efficaciously served.' " *United States v. Leon*, 468 U.S. 897, 908 (1984) (quoting *United States v. Calandra*, 414 U.S. 338, 348 ... (1974)).

We have applied the exclusionary rule primarily to deter constitutional violations. In particular, we have ruled that the Constitution requires the exclusion of evidence obtained by certain violations of the Fourth Amendment, *see Taylor v. Alabama*, 457 U.S. 687, 694 ... (1982) (arrests in violation of the Fourth Amendment); *Mapp v. Ohio*, 367 U.S. 643, 655–657 ... (1961) (unconstitutional searches and seizures), and confessions exacted by police in violation of the right against compelled self-incrimination or due process, *see Dickerson*, 530 U.S., at 435 ... (failure to give *Miranda* warnings); *Payne v. Arkansas*, 356 U.S. 560, 568 ... (1958) (involuntary confessions).

The few cases in which we have suppressed evidence for statutory violations do not help Sanchez–Llamas. In those cases, the excluded evidence arose directly out of statutory violations that implicated important Fourth and Fifth Amendment interests. ...

The violation of the right to consular notification, in contrast, is at best remotely connected to the gathering of evidence. Article 36 has nothing whatsoever to do with searches or interrogations. Indeed, Article 36 does not guarantee defendants any assistance at all. The provision secures only a right of foreign nationals to have their consulate *informed* of their arrest or detention—not to have their consulate intervene, or to have law enforcement authorities cease their investigation pending any such notice or intervention. In most circumstances, there is likely to be little connection between an Article 36 violation and evidence or statements obtained by police.

Moreover, the reasons we often require suppression for Fourth and Fifth Amendment violations are entirely absent from the consular notification context. We require exclusion of coerced confessions both because we disapprove of such coercion and because such confessions tend to be unreliable. *Watkins v. Sowders*, 449 U.S. 341, 347 . . . (1981). We exclude the fruits of unreasonable searches on the theory that without a strong deterrent, the constraints of the Fourth Amendment might be too easily disregarded by law enforcement. *Elkins v. United States*, 364 U.S. 206, 217 . . . (1960). The situation here is quite different. The failure to inform a defendant of his Article 36 rights is unlikely, with any frequency, to produce unreliable confessions. And unlike the search-and-seizure context—where the need to obtain valuable evidence may tempt authorities to transgress Fourth Amendment limitations—police win little, if any, practical advantage from violating Article 36. Suppression would be a vastly disproportionate remedy for an Article 36 violation.

Sanchez–Llamas counters that the failure to inform defendants of their right to consular notification gives them "a misleadingly incomplete picture of [their] legal options," . . . and that suppression will give authorities an incentive to abide by Article 36.

Leaving aside the suggestion that it is the role of police generally to advise defendants of their legal options, we think other constitutional and statutory requirements effectively protect the interests served, in Sanchez–Llamas' view, by Article 36. A foreign national detained on suspicion of crime, like anyone else in our country, enjoys under our system the protections of the Due Process Clause. Among other things, he is entitled to an attorney, and is protected against compelled self-incrimination. *See Wong Wing v. United States*, 163 U.S. 228, 238 . . . (1896) ("[A]ll persons within the territory of the United States are entitled to the protection guaranteed by" the Fifth and Sixth Amendments). Article 36 adds little to these "legal options," and we think it unnecessary to apply the exclusionary rule where other constitutional and statutory protections—many of them already enforced by the exclusionary rule—safeguard the same interests Sanchez–Llamas claims are advanced by Article 36.

Finally, suppression is not the only means of vindicating Vienna Convention rights. A defendant can raise an Article 36 claim as part of a broader challenge to the voluntariness of his statements to police. If he raises an Article 36 violation at trial, a court can make appropriate accommodations to ensure that the defendant secures, to the extent possible, the benefits of consular assistance. Of course, diplomatic avenues—the primary means of enforcing the Convention—also remain open.

In sum, neither the Vienna Convention itself nor our precedents applying the exclusionary rule support suppression of Sanchez–Llamas' statements to police.

B

The Virginia courts denied petitioner Bustillo's Article 36 claim on the ground that he failed to raise it at trial or on direct appeal. The general rule in federal habeas cases is that a defendant who fails to raise a claim on direct appeal is barred from raising the claim on collateral review. *See Massaro v. United States*, 538 U.S. 500, 504 ... (2003); *Bousley v. United States*, 523 U.S. 614, 621 ... (1998). There is an exception if a defendant can demonstrate both "cause" for not raising the claim at trial, and "prejudice" from not having done so. *Massaro, supra*, at 504. ... Like many States, Virginia applies a similar rule in state postconviction proceedings, and did so here to bar Bustillo's Vienna Convention claim. Normally, in our review of state-court judgments, such rules constitute an adequate and independent state-law ground preventing us from reviewing the federal claim. *Coleman v. Thompson*, 501 U.S. 722, 729 ... (1991). Bustillo contends, however, that state procedural default rules cannot apply to Article 36 claims. He argues that the Convention requires that Article 36 rights be given " 'full effect' " and that Virginia's procedural default rules "prevented any effect (much less 'full effect') from being given to" those rights. ...

This is not the first time we have been asked to set aside procedural default rules for a Vienna Convention claim. Respondent Johnson and the United States persuasively argue that this question is controlled by our decision in *Breard v. Greene*, 523 U.S. 371 ... (1998) (*per curiam*). In *Breard*, the petitioner failed to raise an Article 36 claim in state court—at trial or on collateral review—and then sought to have the claim heard in a subsequent federal habeas proceeding. *Id.*, at 375. ... He argued that "the Convention is the 'supreme law of the land' and thus trumps the procedural default doctrine." *Ibid.* We rejected this argument as "plainly incorrect," for two reasons. *Ibid.* First, we observed, "it has been recognized in international law that, absent a clear and express statement to the contrary, the procedural rules of the forum State govern the implementation of the treaty in that State." *Ibid.* Furthermore, we reasoned that while treaty protections such as Article 36 may constitute supreme federal law, this is "no less true of provisions of the Constitution itself, to which rules of procedural default apply." *Id.*, at 376. ... In light of *Breard*'s holding, Bustillo faces an uphill task in arguing that the Convention requires States to set aside their procedural default rules for Article 36 claims.

....

Bustillo argues that *LaGrand* and *Avena* warrant revisiting the procedural default holding of *Breard*. In a similar vein, several amici contend that "the United States is *obligated* to comply with the Convention, *as interpreted by the ICJ*." ... We disagree. Although the ICJ's interpretation deserves "respectful consideration," *Breard, supra*, at 375 ..., we conclude that it does not compel us to reconsider our understanding of the Convention in *Breard*.

Under our Constitution, "[t]he judicial Power of the United States" is "vested in one supreme Court, and in such inferior Courts as the Congress may from time to time ordain and establish." Art. III, § 1. That "judicial Power ... extend[s] to ... Treaties." *Id.*, § 2. And, as Chief Justice Marshall famously explained, that judicial power includes the duty "to say what the law is." *Marbury v. Madison*, 1 Cranch 137, 177 ... (1803). If treaties are to be given effect as federal law under our legal system, determining their meaning as a matter of federal law "is emphatically the province and duty of the judicial department," headed by the "one supreme Court" established by the Constitution. *Ibid.*; *see also Williams v. Taylor*, 529 U.S. 362, 378–379 ... (2000) (opinion of STEVENS, J.) ("At the core of [the judicial] power is the federal courts' independent responsibility—independent from its coequal branches in the Federal Government, and independent from the separate authority of the several States—to interpret federal law"). It is against this background that the United States ratified, and the Senate gave its advice and consent to, the various agreements that govern referral of Vienna Convention disputes to the ICJ.

Nothing in the structure or purpose of the ICJ suggests that its interpretations were intended to be conclusive on our courts. The ICJ's decisions have "*no binding force* except between the parties and in respect of that particular case," Statute of the International Court of Justice, Art. 59, 59 Stat. 1062, T. S. No. 993 (1945) (emphasis added). Any interpretation of law the ICJ renders in the course of resolving particular disputes is thus not binding precedent *even as to the ICJ itself*; there is accordingly little reason to think that such interpretations were intended to be controlling on our courts. The ICJ's principal purpose is to arbitrate particular disputes between national governments. *Id.*, at 1055 (ICJ is "the principal judicial organ of the United Nations"); *see also* Art. 34, *id.*, at 1059 ("Only states [*i.e.*, countries] may be parties in cases before the Court"). While each member of the United Nations has agreed to comply with decisions of the ICJ "in any case to which it is a party," United Nations Charter, Art. 94(1), 59 Stat. 1051, T. S. No. 933 (1945), the Charter's procedure for noncompliance—referral to the Security Council by the aggrieved state—contemplates quintessentially *international* remedies, Art. 94(2), *ibid.*

In addition, "[w]hile courts interpret treaties for themselves, the meaning given them by the departments of government particularly charged with their negotiation and enforcement is given great weight." *Kolovrat v. Oregon*, 366 U.S. 187, 194 ... (1961). Although the United States has agreed to "discharge its international obligations" in having state courts give effect to the decision in *Avena*, it has not taken the view that the ICJ's interpretation of Article 36 is binding on our courts. President Bush, Memorandum for the Attorney General (Feb. 28, 2005), App. to Brief for United States as *Amicus Curiae* in *Medellin v. Dretke*, O. T. 2004, No. 04–5928, p. 9a. Moreover, shortly after *Avena*, the United States withdrew from the Optional Protocol concerning Vienna Convention disputes. Whatever the effect of *Avena* and *LaGrand* before this withdrawal, it is doubtful that our courts should give decisive weight to the interpretation of a tribunal whose jurisdiction in this area is no longer recognized by the United States.

LaGrand and *Avena* are therefore entitled only to the "respectful consideration" due an interpretation of an international agreement by an international court. *Breard*, 523 U.S., at 375. ... Even according such consideration, the ICJ's interpretation cannot overcome the plain import of Article 36. As we explained in *Breard*, the procedural rules of domestic law generally govern the implementation of an international treaty. *Ibid.* In addition, Article 36 makes clear that the rights it provides "shall be exercised in conformity with the laws and regulations of the receiving State" provided that "full effect ... be given to the purposes for which the rights accorded under this Article are intended." Art. 36(2), 21 U. S. T., at 101. In the United States, this means that the rule of procedural default—which applies even to claimed violations of our Constitution, *see Engle v. Isaac*, 456 U.S. 107, 129 ... (1982)—applies also to Vienna Convention claims. Bustillo points to nothing in the drafting history of Article 36 or in the contemporary practice of other signatories that undermines this conclusion.

The ICJ concluded that where a defendant was not notified of his rights under Article 36, application of the procedural default rule failed to give "full effect" to the purposes of Article 36 because it prevented courts from attaching "legal significance" to the Article 36 violation. *LaGrand*, 2001 I.C.J., at 497–498, ¶¶ 90–91. This reasoning overlooks the importance of procedural default rules in an adversary system, which relies chiefly on the *parties* to raise significant issues and present them to the courts in the appropriate manner at the appropriate time for adjudication. *See Castro v. United States*, 540 U.S. 375, 386 ... (2003) (SCALIA, J., concurring in part and concurring in judgment) ("Our adversary system is designed around the premise that the parties know what is best for them, and are responsible for advancing the facts and arguments entitling them to relief"). Procedural default rules are designed to encourage parties to raise their claims promptly and to vindicate "the law's important interest in the finality of judgments." *Massaro*, 538 U.S., at 504. ... The consequence of failing to raise a claim for adjudication at the proper time is generally forfeiture of that claim. As a result, rules such as procedural default routinely deny "legal significance"—in the *Avena* and *LaGrand* sense—to otherwise viable legal claims.

Procedural default rules generally take on greater importance in an adversary system such as ours than in the sort of magistrate-directed, inquisitorial legal system characteristic of many of the other countries that are signatories to the Vienna Convention. "What makes a system adversarial rather than inquisitorial is the presence of a judge who does not (as an inquisitor does) conduct the factual and legal investigation himself, but instead decides on the basis of facts and arguments pro and con adduced by the parties." *McNeil v. Wisconsin*, 501 U.S. 171, n. 2 ... (1991). In an inquisitorial system, the failure to raise a legal error can in part be attributed to the magistrate, and thus to the state itself. In our system, however, the responsibility for failing to raise an issue generally rests with the parties themselves.

The ICJ's interpretation of Article 36 is inconsistent with the basic framework of an adversary system. Under the ICJ's reading of "full effect," Article 36 claims could trump not only procedural default rules, but any number of other rules requiring parties to present their legal claims at the appropriate time for adjudication. If the State's failure to inform the defendant of his Article 36 rights generally excuses the defendant's failure to comply with relevant procedural rules, then presumably rules such as statutes of limitations and prohibitions against filing successive habeas petitions must also yield in the face of Article 36 claims. This sweeps too broadly, for it reads the "full effect" proviso in a way that leaves little room for Article 36's clear instruction that Article 36 rights "shall be exercised in conformity with the laws and regulations of the receiving State." Art. 36(2), 21 U. S. T., at 101.

Much as Sanchez–Llamas cannot show that suppression is an appropriate remedy for Article 36 violations under domestic law principles, so too Bustillo cannot show that normally applicable procedural default rules should be suspended in light of the type of right he claims. In this regard, a comparison of Article 36 and a suspect's rights under *Miranda* disposes of Bustillo's claim. Bustillo contends that applying procedural default rules to Article 36 rights denies such rights "full effect" because the violation itself—*i.e.*, the failure to inform defendants of their right to consular notification—prevents them from becoming aware of their Article 36 rights and asserting them at trial. Of course, precisely the same thing is true of rights under *Miranda*. Police are required to advise suspects that they have a right to remain silent and a right to an attorney. *See Miranda*, 384 U.S., at 479 . . . ; *see also Dickerson*, 530 U.S., at 435. . . . If police do not give such warnings, and counsel fails to object, it is equally true that a suspect may not be "aware he even *had* such rights until well after his trial had concluded." . . . Nevertheless, it is well established that where a defendant fails to raise a *Miranda* claim at trial, procedural default rules may bar him from raising the claim in a subsequent postconviction proceeding. *Wainwright v. Sykes*, 433 U.S. 72, 87 . . . (1977).

. . . .

We therefore conclude, as we did in *Breard*, that claims under Article 36 of the Vienna Convention may be subjected to the same procedural default rules that apply generally to other federal-law claims.

. . . .

Although these cases involve the delicate question of the application of an international treaty, the issues in many ways turn on established principles of domestic law. Our holding in no way disparages the importance of the Vienna Convention. The relief petitioners request is, by any measure, extraordinary. Sanchez–Llamas seeks a suppression remedy for an asserted right with little if any connection to the gathering of evidence; Bustillo requests an exception to procedural rules that is accorded to almost no other right, including many of our most fundamental constitutional protections. It is no slight to the Convention to deny petitioners' claims under the same principles we would apply to an Act of Congress, or to the Constitution itself.

The judgments of the Supreme Court of Oregon and the Supreme Court of Virginia are affirmed.

. . . .

JUSTICE BREYER . . . dissenting.

. . . .

Unlike the majority, I would decide the first question and answer it affirmatively. A criminal defendant may, at trial or in a postconviction proceeding, raise the claim that state authorities violated the Convention in his case. My answer to the second question is that *sometimes* state procedural default rules must yield to the Convention's insistence that domestic laws "enable full effect to be given to the purposes for which" Article 36's "rights . . . are intended." Art. 36(2), 21 U. S. T., at 101. And my answer to the third question is that suppression may *sometimes* provide an appropriate remedy. After answering these questions, I would remand these cases, thereby permitting the States to apply their procedural and remedial laws, but with the understanding that the Federal Constitution requires that the application of those laws be consistent with the Convention's demand for an effective remedy for an Article 36 violation. *See* U.S. Const., Art. VI, cl. 2 ("[A]ll Treaties made . . . under the Authority of the United States, shall be the supreme Law of the Land; and the Judges in every State shall be bound thereby.")

MEDELLIN v. TEXAS

552 U.S. 491, 128 S.Ct. 1346, 170 L.Ed.2d 190 (2008).

[For a brief summary of the facts and excerpts from Parts I and II of the majority opinion, as well as relevant portions of the dissent, see Chapter 3, Section 4.]

CHIEF JUSTICE ROBERTS delivered the opinion of the Court.

. . . .

III

Medellín next argues that the ICJ's judgment in *Avena* is binding on state courts by virtue of the President's February 28, 2005 Memorandum. The United States contends that while the *Avena* judgment does not of its own force require domestic courts to set aside ordinary rules of procedural default, that judgment became the law of the land with precisely that effect pursuant to the President's Memorandum and his power "to establish binding rules of decision that preempt contrary state law." Brief for

United States as *Amicus Curiae* 5. Accordingly, we must decide whether the President's declaration alters our conclusion that the *Avena* judgment is not a rule of domestic law binding in state and federal courts.[13]

A

The United States maintains that the President's constitutional role "uniquely qualifies" him to resolve the sensitive foreign policy decisions that bear on compliance with an ICJ decision and "to do so expeditiously." Brief for United States as *Amicus Curiae* 11, 12. We do not question these propositions. . . . In this case, the President seeks to vindicate United States interests in ensuring the reciprocal observance of the Vienna Convention, protecting relations with foreign governments, and demonstrating commitment to the role of international law. These interests are plainly compelling.

Such considerations, however, do not allow us to set aside first principles. The President's authority to act, as with the exercise of any governmental power, "must stem either from an act of Congress or from the Constitution itself." *Youngstown, supra,* at 585, 72 S.Ct. 863; *Dames & Moore v. Regan,* 453 U.S. 654, 668, 101 S.Ct. 2972, 69 L.Ed.2d 918 (1981).

Justice Jackson's familiar tripartite scheme provides the accepted framework for evaluating executive action in this area. First, "[w]hen the President acts pursuant to an express or implied authorization of Congress, his authority is at its maximum, for it includes all that he possesses in his own right plus all that Congress can delegate." *Youngstown,* 343 U.S., at 635, 72 S.Ct. 863 (Jackson, J., concurring). Second, "[w]hen the President acts in absence of either a congressional grant or denial of authority, he can only rely upon his own independent powers, but there is a zone of twilight in which he and Congress may have concurrent authority, or in which its distribution is uncertain." *Id.*, at 637, 72 S.Ct. 863. In this circumstance, Presidential authority can derive support from "congressional inertia, indifference or quiescence." *Ibid.* Finally, "[w]hen the President takes measures incompatible with the expressed or implied will of Congress, his power is at its lowest ebb," and the Court can sustain his actions "only by disabling the Congress from acting upon the subject." *Id.,* at 637–638, 72 S.Ct. 863.

B

The United States marshals two principal arguments in favor of the President's authority "to establish binding rules of decision that preempt contrary state law." Brief for United States as *Amicus Curiae* 5. The

---

13. The dissent refrains from deciding the issue, but finds it "difficult to believe that in the exercise of his Article II powers pursuant to a ratified treaty, the President can *never* take action that would result in setting aside state law." *Post,* at 1390. We agree. The questions here are the far more limited ones of whether he may unilaterally create federal law by giving effect to the judgment of this international tribunal pursuant to this non-self-executing treaty, and, if not, whether he may rely on other authority under the Constitution to support the action taken in this particular case. Those are the only questions we decide.

Solicitor General first argues that the relevant treaties give the President the authority to implement the *Avena* judgment and that Congress has acquiesced in the exercise of such authority. The United States also relies upon an "independent" international dispute-resolution power wholly apart from the asserted authority based on the pertinent treaties. Medellín adds the additional argument that the President's Memorandum is a valid exercise of his power to take care that the laws be faithfully executed.

1

The United States maintains that the President's Memorandum is authorized by the Optional Protocol and the U.N. Charter. Brief for United States as *Amicus Curiae* 9. That is, because the relevant treaties "create an obligation to comply with *Avena*," they "*implicitly* give the President authority to implement that treaty-based obligation." *Id.*, at 11 (emphasis added). As a result, the President's Memorandum is well grounded in the first category of the *Youngstown* framework.

We disagree. The President has an array of political and diplomatic means available to enforce international obligations, but unilaterally converting a non-self-executing treaty into a self-executing one is not among them. The responsibility for transforming an international obligation arising from a non-self-executing treaty into domestic law falls to Congress. *Foster,* 2 Pet., at 315; *Whitney,* 124 U.S., at 194, 8 S.Ct. 456; *Igartua-De La Rosa,* 417 F.3d, at 150. As this Court has explained, when treaty stipulations are "not self-executing they can only be enforced pursuant to legislation to carry them into effect." *Whitney, supra,* at 194, 8 S.Ct. 456. Moreover, "[u]ntil such act shall be passed, the Court is not at liberty to disregard the existing laws on the subject." *Foster, supra,* at 315.

The requirement that Congress, rather than the President, implement a non-self-executing treaty derives from the text of the Constitution, which divides the treaty-making power between the President and the Senate. The Constitution vests the President with the authority to "make" a treaty. Art. II, § 2. If the Executive determines that a treaty should have domestic effect of its own force, that determination may be implemented "in mak[ing]" the treaty, by ensuring that it contains language plainly providing for domestic enforceability. If the treaty is to be self-executing in this respect, the Senate must consent to the treaty by the requisite two-thirds vote, *ibid.,* consistent with all other constitutional restraints.

Once a treaty is ratified without provisions clearly according it domestic effect, however, whether the treaty will ever have such effect is governed by the fundamental constitutional principle that " '[t]he power to make the necessary laws is in Congress; the power to execute in the President.' " *Hamdan v. Rumsfeld,* 548 U.S. 557, 591, 126 S.Ct. 2749, 165 L.Ed.2d 723 (2006) (quoting *Ex parte Milligan,* 4 Wall. 2, 139, 18 L.Ed. 281 (1866) (opinion of Chase, C. J.)); *see* U.S. Const., Art. I, § 1 ("All legislative Powers herein granted shall be vested in a Congress of the

United States"). As already noted, the terms of a non-self-executing treaty can become domestic law only in the same way as any other law-through passage of legislation by both Houses of Congress, combined with either the President's signature or a congressional override of a Presidential veto. *See* Art. I, § 7. Indeed, "the President's power to see that the laws are faithfully executed refutes the idea that he is to be a lawmaker." *Youngstown,* 343 U.S., at 587, 72 S.Ct. 863.

A non-self-executing treaty, by definition, is one that was ratified with the understanding that it is not to have domestic effect of its own force. That understanding precludes the assertion that Congress has implicitly authorized the President—acting on his own—to achieve precisely the same result. We therefore conclude, given the absence of congressional legislation, that the non-self-executing treaties at issue here did not "express[ly] or implied[ly]" vest the President with the unilateral authority to make them self-executing. *See id.,* at 635, 72 S.Ct. 863 (Jackson, J., concurring). Accordingly, the President's Memorandum does not fall within the first category of the *Youngstown* framework.

Indeed, the preceding discussion should make clear that the non-self-executing character of the relevant treaties not only refutes the notion that the ratifying parties vested the President with the authority to unilaterally make treaty obligations binding on domestic courts, but also implicitly prohibits him from doing so. When the President asserts the power to "enforce" a non-self-executing treaty by unilaterally creating domestic law, he acts in conflict with the implicit understanding of the ratifying Senate. His assertion of authority, insofar as it is based on the pertinent non-self-executing treaties, is therefore within Justice Jackson's third category, not the first or even the second. *See id.,* at 637–638, 72 S.Ct. 863.

Each of the two means described above for giving domestic effect to an international treaty obligation under the Constitution-for making law-requires joint action by the Executive and Legislative Branches: The Senate can ratify a self-executing treaty "ma[de]" by the Executive, or, if the ratified treaty is not self-executing, Congress can enact implementing legislation approved by the President. It should not be surprising that our Constitution does not contemplate vesting such power in the Executive alone. As Madison explained in The Federalist No. 47, under our constitutional system of checks and balances, "[t]he magistrate in whom the whole executive power resides cannot of himself make a law." J. Cooke ed., p. 326 (1961). That would, however, seem an apt description of the asserted executive authority unilaterally to give the effect of domestic law to obligations under a non-self-executing treaty.

The United States nonetheless maintains that the President's Memorandum should be given effect as domestic law because "this case involves a valid Presidential action in the context of Congressional 'acquiescence'." Brief for United States as *Amicus Curiae* 11, n. 2. Under the *Youngstown* tripartite framework, congressional acquiescence is pertinent when the

President's action falls within the second category—that is, when he "acts in absence of either a congressional grant or denial of authority." 343 U.S., at 637, 72 S.Ct. 863 (Jackson, J., concurring). Here, however, as we have explained, the President's effort to accord domestic effect to the *Avena* judgment does not meet that prerequisite.

In any event, even if we were persuaded that congressional acquiescence could support the President's asserted authority to create domestic law pursuant to a non-self-executing treaty, such acquiescence does not exist here. The United States first locates congressional acquiescence in Congress's failure to act following the President's resolution of prior ICJ controversies. A review of the Executive's actions in those prior cases, however, cannot support the claim that Congress acquiesced in this particular exercise of Presidential authority, for none of them remotely involved transforming an international obligation into domestic law and thereby displacing state law.[14]

The United States also directs us to the President's "related" statutory responsibilities and to his "established role" in litigating foreign policy concerns as support for the President's asserted authority to give the ICJ's decision in *Avena* the force of domestic law. Brief for United States as *Amicus Curiae* 16–19. Congress has indeed authorized the President to represent the United States before the United Nations, the ICJ, and the Security Council, 22 U.S.C. § 287, but the authority of the President to represent the United States before such bodies speaks to the President's *international* responsibilities, not any unilateral authority to create domestic law. The authority expressly conferred by Congress in the international realm cannot be said to "invite" the Presidential action at issue here. *See Youngstown, supra,* at 637, 72 S.Ct. 863 (Jackson, J., concur-

14. Rather, in the *Case Concerning Military and Paramilitary Activities in and Against Nicaragua* (*Nicar. v. U.S.*), 1986 I.C.J. 14 (Judgment of June 27), the President determined that the United States would *not* comply with the ICJ's conclusion that the United States owed reparations to Nicaragua. In the *Case Concerning Delimitation of the Maritime Boundary in the Gulf of Maine Area* (*Can.v.U.S.*), 1984 I.C.J. 246 (Judgment of Oct. 12), a federal agency-the National Oceanic and Atmospheric Administration-issued a final rule which complied with the ICJ's boundary determination. The *Case Concerning Rights of Nationals of the United States of America in Morocco* (*Fr.v.U.S.*), 1952 I.C.J. 176 (Judgment of Aug. 27), concerned the legal status of United States citizens living in Morocco; it was not enforced in United States courts.

The final two cases arose under the Vienna Convention. In the *Lagrand Case* (*F.R. G.v.U.S.*), 2001 I.C.J. 466 (Judgment of June 27), the ICJ ordered the review and reconsideration of convictions and sentences of German nationals denied consular notification. In response, the State Department sent letters to the States "encouraging" them to consider the Vienna Convention in the clemency process. Brief for United States as *Amicus Curiae* 20–21. Such encouragement did not give the ICJ judgment direct effect as domestic law; thus, it cannot serve as precedent for doing so in which Congress might be said to have acquiesced. In the *Case Concerning the Vienna Convention on Consular Relations* (*Para.v.U.S.*), 1998 I.C.J. 248 (Judgment of Apr. 9), the ICJ issued a provisional order, directing the United States to "*take all measures at its disposal* to ensure that [Breard] is not executed pending the final decision in [the ICJ's] proceedings." *Breard,* 523 U.S., at 374, 118 S.Ct. 1352 (internal quotation marks omitted). In response, the Secretary of State sent a letter to the Governor of Virginia requesting that he stay Breard's execution. *Id.*, at 378, 118 S.Ct. 1352. When Paraguay sought a stay of execution from this Court, the United States argued that it had taken every measure at its disposal: because "our federal system imposes limits on the federal government's ability to interfere with the criminal justice systems of the States," those measures included "only persuasion," not "legal compulsion." Brief for United States as *Amicus Curiae,* O.T.1997, No. 97–8214, p. 51. This of course is precedent contrary to the proposition asserted by the Solicitor General in this case.

ring). At bottom, none of the sources of authority identified by the United States supports the President's claim that Congress has acquiesced in his asserted power to establish on his own federal law or to override state law.

None of this is to say, however, that the combination of a non-self-executing treaty and the lack of implementing legislation precludes the President from acting to comply with an international treaty obligation. It is only to say that the Executive cannot unilaterally execute a non-self-executing treaty by giving it domestic effect. That is, the non-self-executing character of a treaty constrains the President's ability to comply with treaty commitments by unilaterally making the treaty binding on domestic courts. The President may comply with the treaty's obligations by some other means, so long as they are consistent with the Constitution. But he may not rely upon a non-self-executing treaty to "establish binding rules of decision that preempt contrary state law." Brief for United States as *Amicus Curiae* 5.

2

We thus turn to the United States' claim that—independent of the United States' treaty obligations—the Memorandum is a valid exercise of the President's foreign affairs authority to resolve claims disputes with foreign nations. *Id.*, at 12–16. The United States relies on a series of cases in which this Court has upheld the authority of the President to settle foreign claims pursuant to an executive agreement. *See Garamendi,* 539 U.S., at 415, 123 S.Ct. 2374; *Dames & Moore,* 453 U.S., at 679–680, 101 S.Ct. 2972; *United States v. Pink,* 315 U.S. 203, 229, 62 S.Ct. 552, 86 L.Ed. 796 (1942); *United States v. Belmont,* 301 U.S. 324, 330, 57 S.Ct. 758, 81 L.Ed. 1134 (1937). In these cases this Court has explained that, if pervasive enough, a history of congressional acquiescence can be treated as a "gloss on 'Executive Power' vested in the President by § 1 of Art. II." *Dames & Moore, supra,* at 686, 101 S.Ct. 2972 (some internal quotation marks omitted).

This argument is of a different nature than the one rejected above. Rather than relying on the United States' treaty obligations, the President relies on an independent source of authority in ordering Texas to put aside its procedural bar to successive habeas petitions. Nevertheless, we find that our claims-settlement cases do not support the authority that the President asserts in this case.

The claims-settlement cases involve a narrow set of circumstances: the making of executive agreements to settle civil claims between American citizens and foreign governments or foreign nationals. *See, e.g., Belmont, supra,* at 327, 57 S.Ct. 758. They are based on the view that "a systematic, unbroken, executive practice, long pursued to the knowledge of the Congress and never before questioned," can "raise a presumption that the [action] had been [taken] in pursuance of its consent." *Dames & Moore, supra,* at 686, 101 S.Ct. 2972 (some internal quotation marks omitted). . . .

Even still, the limitations on this source of executive power are clearly set forth and the Court has been careful to note that "[p]ast practice does not, by itself, create power." *Dames & Moore, supra,* at 686, 101 S.Ct. 2972.

The President's Memorandum is not supported by a "particularly longstanding practice" of congressional acquiescence, see *Garamendi, supra,* at 415, 123 S.Ct. 2374, but rather is what the United States itself has described as "unprecedented action," Brief for United States as *Amicus Curiae* in *Sanchez-Llamas,* O.T.2005, Nos. 05–51 and 04–10566, pp. 29–30. Indeed, the Government has not identified a single instance in which the President has attempted (or Congress has acquiesced in) a Presidential directive issued to state courts, much less one that reaches deep into the heart of the State's police powers and compels state courts to reopen final criminal judgments and set aside neutrally applicable state laws. . . .

3

Medellín argues that the President's Memorandum is a valid exercise of his "Take Care" power. Brief for Petitioner 28. The United States, however, does not rely upon the President's responsibility to "take Care that the Laws be faithfully executed." U.S. Const., Art. II, § 3. We think this a wise concession. This authority allows the President to execute the laws, not make them. For the reasons we have stated, the *Avena* judgment is not domestic law; accordingly, the President cannot rely on his Take Care powers here.

. . . .

JUSTICE STEVENS, concurring in the judgment.

[Justice Stevens concurred in the judgment; in relevant part, his opinion suggested that it was Texas' responsibility to comply, and in view of developments in the case of Osbaldo Torres, one of the Mexican nationals involved in the *Avena* judgment (*see supra*), he remarked that this "minimal" cost is one "that the State of Oklahoma unhesitatingly assumed."]

Justice BREYER, with whom Justice SOUTER and Justice GINSBURG join, dissenting

. . . .

III

Because the majority concludes that the Nation's international legal obligation to enforce the ICJ's decision is not automatically a domestic legal obligation, it must then determine whether the President has the constitutional authority to enforce it. And the majority finds that he does not. *See* Part III, *ante*.

In my view, that second conclusion has broader implications than the majority suggests. The President here seeks to implement treaty provisions in which the United States agrees that the ICJ judgment is binding with respect to the *Avena* parties. Consequently, his actions draw upon his constitutional authority in the area of foreign affairs. In this case, his exercise of that power falls within that middle range of Presidential authority where Congress has neither specifically authorized nor specifically forbidden the Presidential action in question. *See Youngstown Sheet & Tube Co. v. Sawyer,* 343 U.S. 579, 637, 72 S.Ct. 863, 96 L.Ed. 1153 (1952) (Jackson, J., concurring). At the same time, if the President were to have the authority he asserts here, it would require setting aside a state procedural law.

It is difficult to believe that in the exercise of his Article II powers pursuant to a ratified treaty, the President can *never* take action that would result in setting aside state law. *Cf. United States v. Pink,* 315 U.S. 203, 233, 62 S.Ct. 552, 86 L.Ed. 796 (1942) ("No State can rewrite our foreign policy to conform to its own domestic policies"). Suppose that the President believes it necessary that he implement a treaty provision requiring a prisoner exchange involving someone in state custody in order to avoid a proven military threat. *Cf. Ware,* 3 Dall., at 205. Or suppose he believes it necessary to secure a foreign consul's treaty-based rights to move freely or to contact an arrested foreign national. *Cf.* Vienna Convention, Art. 34, 21 U.S.T., at 98. Does the Constitution require the President in each and every such instance to obtain a special statute authorizing his action? On the other hand, the Constitution must impose significant restrictions upon the President's ability, by invoking Article II treaty-implementation authority, to circumvent ordinary legislative processes and to pre-empt state law as he does so.

Previously this Court has said little about this question. It has held that the President has a fair amount of authority to make and to implement executive agreements, at least in respect to international claims settlement, and that this authority can require contrary state law to be set aside. *See, e.g.,Pink, supra,* at 223, 230–231, 233–234, 62 S.Ct. 552; *United States v. Belmont,* 301 U.S. 324, 326–327, 57 S.Ct. 758, 81 L.Ed. 1134 (1937). It has made clear that principles of foreign sovereign immunity trump state law and that the Executive, operating without explicit legislative authority, can assert those principles in state court. *See Ex parte Peru,* 318 U.S. 578, 588, 63 S.Ct. 793, 87 L.Ed. 1014 (1943). It has also made clear that the Executive has inherent power to bring a lawsuit "to carry out treaty obligations." *Sanitary Dist. of Chicago v. United States,* 266 U.S. 405, 425, 426, 45 S.Ct. 176, 69 L.Ed. 352 (1925). But it has reserved judgment as to "the scope of the President's power to preempt state law pursuant to authority delegated by ... a ratified treaty"-a fact that helps to explain the majority's inability to find support in precedent for its own conclusions. *Barclays Bank PLC v. Franchise Tax Bd. of Cal.,* 512 U.S. 298, 329, 114 S.Ct. 2268, 129 L.Ed.2d 244 (1994).

Given the Court's comparative lack of expertise in foreign affairs; given the importance of the Nation's foreign relations; given the difficulty of finding the proper constitutional balance among state and federal, executive and legislative, powers in such matters; and given the likely future importance of this Court's efforts to do so, I would very much hesitate before concluding that the Constitution implicitly sets forth broad prohibitions (or permissions) in this area. *Cf. ante,* at 1367, n. 13 (stating that the Court's holding is "limited" by the facts that (1) this treaty is non-self-executing and (2) the judgment of an international tribunal is involved).

I would thus be content to leave the matter in the constitutional shade from which it has emerged. Given my view of this case, I need not answer the question. And I shall not try to do so. That silence, however, cannot be taken as agreement with the majority's Part III conclusion.

NOTES ON THE JUDICIAL AND PRESIDENTIAL POWER TO PREEMPT

1. *Authority for Judicial Intervention.* In *Sanchez-Llamas v. Oregon,* the Supreme Court rejected the claim that suppression was the appropriate remedy for an Article 36 violation: while the Consular Convention provides that the laws and regulations governing the exercise of Article 36 rights "must enable *full effect* to be given to the purposes for which the rights ... are intended," it also provided that such rights "shall be exercised in conformity with the laws and regulations of the receiving State." Art. 36(2), 21 U. S. T., at 101 Art. 36(2), 21 U. S. T., at 101 (emphasis added). Because the remedy was derived from U.S. law (in the absence of any contention that the Consular Convention itself contemplated suppression), the Court emphasized its traditional reluctance in other U.S. contexts to apply the exclusionary rule as an entailment of its judicial authority. Did the Court's analysis take adequate account of the special standing owed treaty rights? Given its reluctance even to assume that Article 36 contemplated judicial remedies of some kind, was the Court mindful of the role accorded federal and state courts under the Supremacy Clause?

The request for relief from procedural default in that case was particularly ticklish, given the Court's prior *per curiam* decision in *Breard v. Greene,* 523 U.S. 371, 375, 118 S.Ct. 1352, 140 L.Ed.2d 529 (1998). Did the Court genuinely accord "respectful consideration" to the contrary view of the ICJ? Is that the right balance of relative authority in the first place? For example, does it sufficiently anticipate the complications continued disagreements over treaty interpretation may pose for the President, as the voice for the United States in international relations? Note in this connection that following *Avena,* which evidently disagreed with *Breard,* the U.S. government informed the U.N. Secretary–General that it was terminating its adherence to the VCCR optional protocol, thereby limiting the potential for future I.C.J. cases against the United States based on the Consular Convention.

2. *Authority for the President's Memorandum.* What exactly is the constitutional basis for the President's memorandum? Consider the strengths and weaknesses of the various grounds reviewed by the Supreme Court, both from the President's perspective and as a matter of dispassionate constitutional analysis. For example, one ground urged by Medellín—but not by the executive branch—was that the President's memorandum effectuated his

responsibility to "take Care that the Laws be faithfully executed." U.S. Const., Art. II, § 3. From the President's perspective, such an argument had definite drawbacks; can you imagine what they are? Do they bear any relation to the Court's analysis? For contemporaneous commentary on the strengths and weaknesses of the arguments considered in *Medellín*, see Margaret E. McGuinness, *Medellin, Norm Portals, and the Horizontal Integration of International Human Rights*, 82 NOTRE DAME L. REV. 755 (2006); Edward T. Swaine, *Taking Care of Treaties*, 108 COLUM. L. REV. 331 (2008); Michael P. Van Alstine, *Executive Aggrandizement in Foreign Affairs Lawmaking*, 54 U.C.L.A. L. REV. 309 (2006).

One of the Court's most important conclusions, one bearing on all the potential bases for presidential authority was its understanding of the implications of non-self-execution: namely, that only congressional legislation could implement a non-self-executing treaty, and that for this reason, the conclusion that a treaty was non-self-executing implicitly negated presidential authority, leaving it to be analyzed within the third tier of Justice Jackson's *Youngstown* framework. Do you think this accords with the meaning of non-self-execution preceding *Medellín*? For a criticism, see Edward T. Swaine, *The Political Economy of* Youngstown, *83 S. CAL. L. REV. 263, 329–33 (2010). When the Supreme Court insists that its view does not deprive the executive branch of the authority to direct compliance with the international obligations of the United States, what might it mean?*

Yet more broadly, some have speculated that the result in *Medellín* undermines the broader language relating to preemptive executive branch authority in *American Ins. Ass'n v. Garamendi*. A. Mark Weisburd, *Medellín, the President's Foreign Affairs Power and Domestic Law,* 28 PENN ST. INT'L L.REV. 595, 625 (2010). *But cf.* Museum of Fine Arts Boston v. Seger–Thomschitz, 623 F.3d 1, 12 n.12 (1st Cir. 2010) (distinguishing *Garamendi* on other grounds, and noting post-*Medellín* case applying broad understanding of *Garamendi).*

3. *Alternative Remedies*. Commandments by the Supreme Court or the President are not the only possible means of remedying a treaty violation. As noted earlier, both Oklahoma's courts and its governor proved receptive on at least one occasion to the claims that Article 36 violations should bear upon an alien's conviction and sentence; in other instances pleas from the President went essentially unheeded. Following President Bush's February 2005 memorandum, a Virginia state court judge decided to grant a motion to prohibit the application of the death penalty in the case of *Virginia v. Dinh Pham*, Crim. No. K105537 (19th Jud. Cir. Va. Jan. 3, 2006), based on the need to respect the Consular Convention and the ICJ's decision in *Avena*. However, the Supreme Court of Virginia in January 2006 overruled that decision by issuing a rare writ of mandamus directing the judge to permit the prosecutor to ask the jury to impose the death penalty based upon concerns the judge had interfered with the discretion vested by state law in the prosecutor to determine which charges to file and which penalties to seek. *See* In re Horan, 271 Va. 258, 634 S.E.2d 675 (2006). In July 2006, the defendant entered a guilty plea, leading to a life sentence without parole.

Another avenue, of course, is Congress. There have been several attempts to generate congressional interest in legislating a remedy to Article 36 violations in general or to *Avena* in particular. In late spring 2011, Senator Leahy introduced a bill backed by the Obama Administration, entitled the "Consular Notification Compliance Act of 2011," that implements the Article 36 obligation as a matter of federal law and provides federal jurisdiction to the review the merits of petitions alleging Article 36 violations that caused actual prejudice to a criminal conviction or sentence. The bill generally afforded one year for filing a petition of review alleging such violations and, while not generally relieving petitioners of the rules for federal habeas petitions, effectively relieved procedural limitations that would have inhibited petitioners whose applications would otherwise have been due before or shortly after enactment. S. 1194, 112th Cong., 157 Cong. Rec. S3779 (daily ed. June 14, 2011). If such legislation is adopted, would it vindicate the Supreme Court's approach in *Medellín*? And would it vindicate or condemn the litigation strategy by Texas?

Last, but not least, should an alien who is not notified of his right to contact his consulate be able to sue state law enforcement officials for damages? Lower courts disagreed. *Compare, e.g.*, Cornejo v. San Diego, 504 F.3d 853 (9th Cir. 2007) (finding that Vienna Convention does not create judicially enforceable private rights pursuant to 42 U.S.C. § 1983), *with* Jogi v. Voges, 425 F.3d 367 (7th Cir. 2005) (holding that Vienna Convention on Consular Relations provides implied right of action for damages). The issue clearly implicates the question, still unresolved after *Sanchez-Llamas*, of whether the Consular Convention confers individually enforceable rights. How does *Medellín* affect that analysis?

CHAPTER 7

THE JUDICIARY

■ ■ ■

Many issues in U.S. foreign relations law are addressed, if not completely resolved, by the judiciary, and the foregoing chapters illustrate the courts' ongoing struggle to say what the law is while respecting the function of other actors in the constitutional system—not to mention international actors.

While the relative capacity and expertise of courts comes up frequently in the foreign relations and national security law doctrines considered elsewhere in this text, questions of justiciability—essentially, a set of doctrines designed to ensure that Article III courts in the United States only hear "cases or controversies"—arise distinctly in judicial proceedings. Various discrete concepts operate within the realm of justiciability, such as the political question doctrine, ripeness, mootness, and standing (including, in the foreign relations context, whether a foreign government that has not been "recognized" by the U.S. government has standing to sue or be sued).

Justiciability issues have frequently barred U.S. courts from reaching the merits of foreign relations and national security cases, and the materials in the first five sections of this chapter analyze this phenomenon, with a particular focus on how these hurdles differ in this field. The remaining sections then address two additional issues, immunities and the act of state doctrine, that have undoubtedly had a substantial influence on the functioning of courts in these areas.

SECTION 1. POLITICAL QUESTION DOCTRINE GENERALLY

INTRODUCTORY NOTE ON THE POLITICAL QUESTION DOCTRINE AND FOREIGN AFFAIRS

When a U.S. court is confronted with a case concerning foreign affairs, the court sometimes will declare that the issue in controversy is a "political question" about which the court is unwilling to rule. When this occurs, the court dismisses the case. At other times, however, the court will proceed to adjudicate the matter on the merits. The cases and materials in this section address the use of the political question doctrine in cases that touch upon foreign relations and national security.

The two cases below, which were both decided by the D.C. Circuit Court of Appeals, concern allegedly wrongful conduct by the U.S. government abroad that seriously affected the rights of individuals. In the first case, *Ramirez de Arellano v. Weinberger*, 745 F.2d 1500 (D.C. Cir. 1984), the majority found that the political question doctrine was *not* a basis for dismissal of the case, even though important issues of U.S. foreign policy and national security were at stake. Judge Tamm, writing in dissent, strongly disagreed. In the second case, *Schneider v. Kissinger*, 412 F.3d 190 (D.C. Cir. 2005), the majority found that the political question doctrine *was* a basis for dismissal.

As you read the cases, ask yourself the following questions. How would you have decided these cases if you were a judge on the D.C. Circuit Court of Appeals? Who has the better argument in *Ramirez de Arellano*: the majority or Judge Tamm? Is there a way of harmonizing the majority opinions in *Ramirez de Arellano* and in *Schneider v. Kissinger* or is the same circuit court simply going in different directions in comparable cases? Is there a clear theory in these opinions about when the political question doctrine is properly invoked in a foreign relations case or does the reasoning seem muddled and confused? What factors do the judges seem to find important? Unimportant?

RAMIREZ de ARELLANO v. WEINBERGER

745 F.2d 1500, 1506–50 (D.C. Cir. 1984) (some footnotes and citations omitted).

WILKEY, Circuit Judge:

. . . .

Plaintiff Ramirez is a citizen of the United States. He is the sole beneficial owner, the general manager, and the chief executive officer of a large agricultural-industrial complex in the northern region of Honduras. Plaintiff Ramirez is a businessman and was a founding member of the Lion's Club of Trujillo, Honduras, as well as the founder of the Association for the Defense of the Free Enterprise System in San Juan, Puerto Rico. Ramirez has engaged in numerous civic and community services in Puerto Rico and in Central America, including assisting the United States government in a meat distribution program for Puerto Rico. Ramirez conducts his business operations through six corporations which he owns and controls. Two of these corporate plaintiffs are United States nationals and four are incorporated in Honduras. Together they form a chain of title through which plaintiff Ramirez holds his interest in the land and property at issue.

Plaintiff Ramirez acquired his large tract of land in Honduras more than 20 years ago, when it was raw, undeveloped jungle. Since then he has transformed the land into a 14,000-acre cattle ranch, meat-packing operation and shrimp-packing plant. According to Ramirez's sworn declaration filed with the court, he "supervised the clearing of this land, planting feed grass, constructing fences, farmroads, cattle pens, cattle treatment facilities, warehouses and numerous other buildings, water ponds and reservoirs, and housing for [his] employees and their families." The business operation employs approximately 500 workers and is the single largest employer in the Department of Colon, Honduras. The plaintiffs' initial total investment in the property has increased from approximately $700,000 to more than $13,000,000.

Still assuming the truth of the plaintiffs' factual allegations, the plaintiffs' property was occupied by the defendants without permission in 1983. In March of that year, the United States Department of Defense decided to establish a Regional Military Training Center for the United States to train soldiers from the army of El Salvador. Because of Congress's unwillingness to increase the number of military advisers in El Salvador itself, the Defense Department decided not to locate the military training center there. Instead, after reportedly considering several other countries, the Defense Department chose Honduras as the location for the RMTC. Newspaper articles in the United States at the time reported that the Honduran government was resisting the Defense Department's placement of the military center in Honduras and that a United States Army spokesman said that Honduras did not have anywhere to locate the training center.

Nonetheless, officials of the United States Department of Defense began a survey of land in the vicinity of Ramirez's property, and in April of 1983 they picked a specific site in Honduras for the Regional Military Training Center. Unknown to Ramirez, the chosen site was his cattle ranch. Officers of the Army Corps of Engineers immediately started planning the construction of a 1,000-man tent camp and training facility on the plaintiffs' property, and by May 1983, they had drawn up blueprints for the military center.

In this same month, plaintiff Ramirez discovered the United States plans. The First Secretary of the United States Embassy in Honduras was visiting Ramirez's home and "casually mentioned that a training base for Salvadoran soldiers was going to be built in the area." When Ramirez asked its location, the official pointed to property across the bay. Ramirez instantly realized that the official was pointing to his privately owned cattle ranch and he immediately informed his guest and other officials of the United States Embassy that the intended site for the RMTC was his land.

Construction of the military camp proceeded apace. Work crews from Litton Industries, under the supervision of the United States Army Corps of Engineers, began bulldozing the ranch in early June 1983. The crews constructed a 1,000-man tent camp for housing Salvadoran soldiers as well as an unspecified number of buildings on the ranch. The Army Corps of Engineers also built an ammunition storage facility and a firing range on the private land. In addition, plans were drawn up for mortar and other long distance firing ranges on the plaintiffs' property.

Next, according to the plaintiffs' allegations, United States military training personnel moved in. Over 100 United States Army Special Forces Soldiers began training over 1,000 soldiers on the plaintiffs' pastures, conducting training exercises all over the ranch using live ammunition.

As a result of the construction and the military operations, plaintiffs allege that they have suffered numerous injuries. Prime grazing land and fences have been bulldozed. The flow of water to the plaintiffs' meat-packing plant has been interrupted by the soldiers' diversion of substantial quantities of water for their own use. Cattle have been shot by stray bullets. "Large numbers of armed soldiers and trainees roaming around [the] ranch and the area of [the] meat-packing plant" have frightened Ramirez's family and his employees. Ranch employees, fearing for their lives, have refused to tend cattle near the military operations, causing the livestock to become undernourished.... Over half of the ranch's 14,000 acres and nearly 90% of the year-round grazing land has been seized by soldiers of the Regional Military Training Center. The operations are destroying the plaintiffs' investment and Ramirez's life's work.

The plaintiffs claim that the land on which their operations are based is irreplaceable. Land in other areas of Honduras is either too arid, too mountainous or too inaccessible for the integrated agro-industrial enterprise. The only other land in Honduras suitable for cattle ranching is neighboring property, which is privately owned.

The plaintiffs allege that in May 1983, the *Washington Post* reported an announcement by officials of the Departments of State and Defense pertaining to the establishment of the RMTC. One month later, the National Congress of Honduras entered a decree which authorized "the admission of military instructors and students, coming from friendly countries" to the Military Training Center. According to Ramirez, however, "the site for the RMTC was neither presented to, nor decided by the Honduran legislature." In the summer of 1983, Honduran military officials discussed expropriation of a small portion of the ranch with Ramirez, but this discussion, Ramirez alleges, only pertained to a 1,500–2,000 acre section of the ranch called the "Designated Area." These discussions did not result in any expropriation of the Designated Area and the training activities spilled over onto the majority of the ranch's acreage.

Meanwhile, according to the complaint, plaintiff Ramirez made numerous efforts to resolve his dispute with officials of the United States Embassy in Honduras and the Departments of State and Defense in Washington, D.C., but these efforts were unproductive or rebuffed. The plaintiffs have not received any compensation for the seizure nor has any hearing on the dispute been held. The plaintiffs do not know from day to day what is going to happen on their ranch.

. . . .

... The district court dismissed the complaint on the ground that the case presented a nonjusticiable political question. It determined that the case was a direct challenge to the propriety of the United States military presence in Central America, and having so characterized the complaint, it held that the dispute was nonjusticiable. The district court found that the case presented all of the three criteria identified by the Supreme Court in *Baker v. Carr*[33] for nonjusticiable political questions. The panel opinion by Judge Scalia (later vacated for en banc) found unanimously that the trial court was in error in relying on this ground. On this point our en banc disposition is in accord with the panel opinion.

The factors for identifying political questions were recently summarized by Justice Powell in his concurrence in *Goldwater v. Carter.* The doctrine incorporates three inquiries:

> (i) Does the issue involve resolution of questions committed by the text of the Constitution to a coordinate branch of Government? (ii) Would resolution of the question demand that a court move beyond areas of judicial expertise? (iii) Do prudential considerations counsel against judicial intervention?[34]

The first of these formulations requires the court to determine whether the text of the Constitution implicitly or explicitly commits the stated claim to the political branches. According to the Supreme Court, this necessitates a close textual analysis of specific provisions of the Constitution. The Supreme Court determined, for example, that certain suits brought pursuant to the Constitution's guarantee of a republican form of government in article IV are nonjusticiable political questions textually committed for resolution to Congress, not the Judiciary, because the Constitution gives Congress the exclusive power to determine whether a particular state government should be recognized.[35] In addition, certain disputes over internal procedures in Congress may be textually committed for resolution to Congress by article I, section 5, clause 2, which provides that "[e]ach House may determine the Rules of its Proceedings."[36]

In the area of foreign affairs, some broad challenges to the Executive's conducting of foreign relations have been found nonjusticiable because formulation of foreign policy is constitutionally committed to the political branches. In *Johnson v. Eisentrager,* for example, the Supreme Court refused to adjudicate claims by enemy aliens who were convicted of violating laws of war in China after Germany had surrendered. The aliens' claims were found to be committed to resolution by the political branches because they fundamentally challenged the propriety of United States military activities in China. There, the Court stated: "[I]t is not the function of the Judiciary to entertain private litigation ... which chal-

33. 369 U.S. 186 (1962).

34. 444 U.S. 996, 998 (1979) (Powell, J., concurring).

35. *See, e.g., Luther v. Borden,* 48 U.S. (7 How.) 1, 12 L.Ed. 581 (1849).

36. *See, e.g., Metzenbaum v. FERC,* 675 F.2d 1282, 1287 (D.C. Cir. 1982).

lenges the legality, the wisdom, or the propriety of the Commander-in-Chief in sending our armed forces abroad or to any particular region."[37]

Not every issue related to foreign relations, however, is constitutionally committed for resolution by the Executive. *Baker v. Carr* states that "it is error to suppose that every case or controversy which touches foreign relations lies beyond judicial cognizance."[38] Issues which are not at base sweeping challenges to the Executive's foreign policy typically are adjudicated by the courts because they do not involve judicial usurpation of the Executive's constitutional powers to manage foreign affairs.

A careful analysis of the plaintiffs' case shows that their claims are not exclusively committed for resolution to the political branches. Unlike the claim addressed by the Court in *Johnson v. Eisentrager,* the plaintiffs do not seek to adjudicate the lawfulness of the United States military presence abroad. Instead, they seek adjudication of the narrow issue whether the United States defendants may run military exercises throughout the plaintiff's private pastures when their land has not been lawfully expropriated. They do not challenge the United States military presence in Honduras or in Central America, nor do they object to United States sponsorship of a Regional Military Training Center in Honduras. Plaintiffs' claim, properly understood, is narrowly focused on the lawfulness of the United States defendants' occupation and use of the plaintiffs' cattle ranch.

This is a paradigmatic issue for resolution by the Judiciary. The federal courts historically have resolved disputes over land, even when the United States military is occupying the property at issue.[39] Furthermore, certain disputes over property rights to land located abroad are appropriately resolved by the federal courts,[40] as are property disputes involving the Executive Branch and foreign affairs. In *Youngstown,* for example, the Supreme Court adjudicated the claim that the President had unlawfully seized most of the nation's steel mills, even though the case arose in the context of the nation's military involvement in Korea.[41] The issues in the instant case are well within the traditional bounds of justiciability by the federal Judiciary.

Secondly, it cannot be said on review of this dismissal that resolution of the case will require the court to move outside of its areas of expertise. On the basis of the complaint and affidavits, it appears that adjudication of the defendants' constitutional authority to occupy and use the plaintiffs' property will necessitate interpretations of the Constitution and of federal statutes—which are quintessential tasks of the federal Judiciary.[42]

---

37. 339 U.S. 763, 789 (1950).

38. 369 U.S. at 211.

39. *See, e.g., Meigs v. McClung's Lessee,* 13 U.S. (9 Cranch) 11 (1815).

40. *See, e.g., United States v. Caltex (Philippines), Inc.,* 344 U.S. 149 (1952).

41. 343 U.S. 579 (1952).

42. *See Powell v. McCormack,* 395 U.S. 486, 548–49 (1969) (requirements of nonjusticiability not met when court is called upon merely to interpret the Constitution); *Consumer Energy*

The complaint does not reveal that expertise beyond the capacity of the Judiciary is essential to a resolution of the claims.

The district court found, however, that adjudication of the plaintiffs' claims would be unmanageable because reaching "the heart of this matter would necessarily involve sensitive and confidential communications between the highest members of the Executive branch and officials of a foreign power that are not judicially discoverable."[43] We disagree. It is premature to conclude that essential evidence is undiscoverable merely on the basis of the complaint and related declarations in this case. Evidentiary privileges turn on facts, such as the harm that might flow from disclosure of particular communications,[44] which are not yet part of the record in the instant case. In *Attorney General v. The Irish People, Inc.*, this court held that dismissal of a complaint is not proper "when information which *'might'* be relevant to a ... claim is unavailable for discovery."[45] That case applies squarely to the instant appeal. If it turns out that essential evidence is undiscoverable due to Executive privilege, the district court can take appropriate action at that time. Speculation about Executive privilege in this case cannot justify squelching the plaintiffs' complaint prior to any factfinding.

Finally, the district court erred by holding that prudential considerations compel dismissal of the complaint. *Baker v. Carr* identifies four circumstances in which prudential considerations may bar adjudication of a claim. These are:

> [T]he impossibility of deciding without an initial policy determination of a kind clearly for nonjudicial discretion; or the impossibility of a court's undertaking independent resolution without expressing lack of the respect due coordinate branches of government; or an unusual need for unquestioning adherence to a political decision already made; or the potentiality of embarrassment from multifarious pronouncements by various departments on one question.[46]

None of these circumstances is necessarily presented by the plaintiffs' complaint and related declarations.

The plaintiffs do not seek judicial monitoring of foreign policy in Central America nor do they challenge United States relations with any foreign country. The case does not raise the specter of judicial control and management of United States foreign policy. As such, the issues in the instant case are qualitatively different from those posed in several recent cases which were dismissed as nonjusticiable political questions. In *Dickson v. Ford* the Fifth Circuit upheld the dismissal of a taxpayer's challenge

---

Council of America v. FERC, 673 F.2d 425, 452 (D.C. Cir. 1982), *affirmed mem. sub nom. Process Gas Consumer Group v. Consumers Energy Council of America,* [463 U.S. 1216] (1983).

43. 568 F. Supp. at 1239 (footnote omitted).

44. *See Halkin v. Helms,* 690 F.2d 977, 990 (D.C. Cir. 1982).

45. 684 F.2d 928, 951 (D.C. Cir. 1982), *cert. denied,* 459 U.S. 1172 (1983).

46. 369 U.S. at 217.

to military and economic assistance to Israel.[47] Likewise, in *Crockett v. Reagan* a panel of this circuit upheld the dismissal of a suit brought by members of Congress challenging the legality of United States military aid to El Salvador.[48] If adjudicated, those broadside attacks on fundamental foreign policy decisions might have resulted in conflicting pronouncements from the Judiciary and the political branches over the basic tenets of United States relations with foreign states.

By contrast, those factors which have permitted adjudication in other cases implicating foreign affairs are present here. Private United States litigants seek a determination of the lawfulness of the Executive's deprivation of their private property.[49] The prudential, separation-of-powers concerns presented by the instant case are certainly not greater than those underlying the wartime seizure of an entire industry by the Executive in *Youngstown*. Ramirez's dispute with the United States military over land in Honduras does not require unquestioning adherence to a political decision by the Executive. The complaint does not present any of the criteria used by the Supreme Court to identify nonjusticiable political questions.

The political question doctrine is a tempting refuge from the adjudication of difficult constitutional claims. Its shifting contours and uncertain underpinnings make it susceptible to indiscriminate and overbroad application to claims properly before the federal courts. Recent cases raise doubts about the contours and vitality of the political question doctrine, which continues to be the subject of scathing scholarly attack.[50] We need not, however, announce the demise of the political question doctrine by our holding in this case. Despite confusion over whether a retreat to the political question doctrine is proper in particular cases,[51] it is clear that the doctrine is, at best, a narrow one. *Baker v. Carr* admonishes that "[t]he doctrine ... is one of 'political question,' not one of 'political cases.' "[52] For similar reasons we fundamentally disagree with Judge Tamm's dissenting suggestion that granting these plaintiffs their day in court will "intolerably" impinge and intrude upon the Executive's con-

47. 521 F.2d 234 (5th Cir. 1975), *cert. denied,* 424 U.S. 954 (1975).

48. 720 F.2d 1355 (D.C. Cir. 1983) (per curiam), *cert. denied,* [467 U.S. 1251] (1984).

49. *See Goldwater v. Carter,* 444 U.S. 996, 1004 (1979) (Rehnquist, J., concurring) (Justice Rehnquist noted that the claim in *Youngstown* was *not* a nonjusticiable political question because "[i]n *Youngstown,* private litigants brought a suit contesting the President's authority under his war powers to seize the Nation's steel industry.").

50. *See Tel-Oren v. Libyan Arab Republic,* 726 F.2d 774, 796–98 (D.C. Cir. 1984) (Edwards, J., concurring); *id.* at 803 n. 8 (Bork, J., concurring) ("That the contours of the doctrine are murky and unsettled is shown by the lack of consensus about its meaning among the members of the Supreme Court...."); *Vander Jagt v. O'Neill,* 699 F.2d 1166, 1173–74 (D.C. Cir. 1982), *cert. denied,* [464 U.S. 823] (1983); McGowan, *Congressmen in Court: The New Plaintiffs,* 15 Ga. L. Rev. 241, 256–60 (1981). Professor Louis Henkin suggested in his influential article debunking the political question doctrine that the leading cases foreswearing judicial review on the ground that the issue posed was a political question might instead be understood as determinations that the challenged actions were in fact constitutional. *See* Henkin, *Is There A "Political Question" Doctrine?,* 85 Yale L.J. 597 (1976).

51. *See, e.g., Goldwater v. Carter,* 444 U.S. 996 (1979).

52. 369 U.S. 186, 217 (1962).

ducting of foreign affairs. This dissent relies heavily on *United States v. Curtiss–Wright Export Corp.,*[53] to establish the existence of a "realm" of Executive power in the foreign relations area which courts should not curtail. But this same decision reviewed, *on the merits,* a constitutional challenge to certain laws granting foreign affairs power to the President.[54] The possibility that the laws would not withstand constitutional scrutiny, with the concomitant embarrassment to the President who had relied on those laws in prohibiting arms sales to specific foreign countries, did not deter the Court from finding the controversy to be justiciable.

The Executive's power to conduct foreign relations free from the unwarranted supervision of the Judiciary cannot give the Executive *carte blanche* to trample the most fundamental liberty and property rights of this country's citizenry. The Executive's foreign relations prerogatives are subject to constitutional limitation,[55] no agreement with a foreign country can confer upon the Executive Branch any power greater than those bounded by the Constitution.[56] We recognize that review by the Judiciary may not always be appropriate. But unlike *Curtiss-Wright,*[57] the government has not relied on a specific legislative grant of authority to conduct the challenged activities. Moreover, this is not a case like *Chicago & Southern Airlines, Inc. v. Waterman Steamship Corp.,*[58] in which the plaintiffs, who were denied review of an Executive order, were at least granted some process through which their contention could be heard *prior* to the Executive decision. Indeed, if the dissent's approach were adopted by all judicial forums, then no ordinary process at all could be offered.[59] We must be most reluctant to withhold judicial scrutiny in these circumstances.

Every act taken by the Executive having an effect beyond this country's borders may be described as political, with a potential or actual impact on our foreign relations. Affirmance of this dismissal on the ground that plaintiffs' claims are political questions or an improper challenge to foreign affairs powers would mean that virtually *anything*

---

53. 299 U.S. 304 (1936).

54. After reviewing the series of statutes relevant to the exercise of Executive power, the Supreme Court concluded that "this court may not, and should not hesitate to declare acts of Congress, however many times repeated, to be unconstitutional if beyond all rational doubt it finds them to be so." *Id.* at 327.

55. *Id.* at 319.

56. *Reid v. Covert,* 354 U.S. 1, 16 (1957).

57. 299 U.S. 304 (1936).

58. 333 U.S. 103 (1948).

59. The theory proposed by the dissent is equally applicable to other forums. Thus it is seriously doubtful whether any judicial remedy for the asserted taking would be available. *See, e.g., Langenegger v. United States,* 5 Cl. Ct. 229 (1984) (denying review on alternative theory of impermissible inquiry into foreign affairs when plaintiff's claim was unavoidably predicated upon a challenge to the intrusive manner in which the United States conducted its foreign policy). Judge Tamm's apparent assumption that a remedy would exist in the Claims Court under the Tucker Act may be incorrect. Dissenting Opinion of Tamm, J., at 1550. Of course, the possibility of a private bill of relief may theoretically be available. *But see* P. BATOR, P. MISHKIN, D. SHAPIRO & H. WECHSLER, HART & WECHSLER'S FEDERAL COURTS IN THE FEDERAL SYSTEM 1326–31 (2d ed. 1973) (original purpose of Tucker Act to end the plague of private relief bills dogging Congress).

done by United States officials to United States citizens on foreign soil is nonjusticiable. This is not the law. A proper application of the political question doctrine to the plaintiffs' case shows that dismissal on this ground was erroneous.

. . . .

TAMM, CIRCUIT JUDGE, dissenting:

. . . .

Because any judicial action in this case would potentially hinder the executive's exercise of a foreign policy judgment, I agree that the controversy is nonjusticiable. I therefore respectfully dissent from the majority's decision.

. . . .

The critical importance of preserving the proper allocation of power among the three branches of government guides my analysis in this case. The conduct of foreign affairs and the proper disposition of military power are, without question, subjects committed to the exclusive authority of the political branches of government. U.S. Const. art. I, § 8; *id.* art. 2, § 2. *Oetjen v. Central Leather Co.,* 246 U.S. 297, 302 (1918) ("[t]he conduct of the foreign relations of our Government is committed by the Constitution to the Executive and Legislative—'the political'—Departments. . . ."). *See Johnson v. Eisentrager,* 339 U.S. 763, 788–89 (1950); *Chicago & Southern Air Lines, Inc. v. Waterman Steamship Corp.,* 333 U.S. 103, 113–14 (1948); *Luftig v. McNamara,* 373 F.2d 664, 665–66 (D.C. Cir.) (per curiam), *cert. denied,* 387 U.S. 945 (1967); *Atlee v. Laird,* 347 F. Supp. 689, 704–05 (E.D. Pa. 1972) (three-judge court), *aff'd sub nom. mem. Atlee v. Richardson,* 411 U.S. 911 (1973). In my view, granting plaintiffs' requested relief will necessarily result in an intolerable judicial intrusion into the conduct of foreign affairs. I therefore conclude that adjudicating this case would be inconsistent with our system of separation of powers. Accordingly, I believe that the controversy presented here is nonjusticiable.

A

The Supreme Court has acknowledged that cases involving foreign affairs are often nonjusticiable. Such cases frequently turn on standards that defy judicial application, involve the exercise of a discretion demonstrably committed to the executive or legislature, or demand a single-voiced statement of the Government's views. *Baker v. Carr,* 369 U.S. 186, 211 (1962). The nonjusticiability of cases involving foreign affairs, however, is "primarily a function of the separation of powers." *Baker,* 369 U.S. at 210. This fundamental principle, which constitutes the very basis of our system of government, requires courts to refrain from infringing on the powers reserved to the legislative and executive branches of government. Indeed, judicial power exists "only when adjudication is 'consistent with a system of separated powers. . . .' " *Allen v. Wright,* [468 U.S. 737, 750] (1984) (quoting *Flast v. Cohen,* 392 U.S. 83, 97 (1968)).

Impermissible judicial encroachment upon the power of the political branches can occur not only from the act of resolving a question whose nature is political, but also from the consequences that flow from judicial action. Indeed, in *Atlee v. Laird,* 347 F. Supp. 689 (E.D. Pa. 1972), *aff'd sub nom. mem. Atlee v. Richardson,* 411 U.S. 911 (1973), a three-judge district court concluded that the *consequence* of resolving a controversy involving foreign affairs is of paramount concern in determining justiciability. 347 F. Supp. at 702. A court's initial task, therefore, when faced with a case involving foreign affairs, is to scrutinize the claims not only in terms of their historical management by the political branches and their susceptibility to judicial handling, but also in terms *"of the possible consequences of judicial action." Baker,* 369 U.S. at 211–12 (emphasis added).[5]

An important element in assessing the consequences of judicial action is, of course, the effect of granting the relief sought. In *Gilligan v. Morgan,* 413 U.S. 1, 5–10 (1973), for example, the Supreme Court held the controversy at bar nonjusticiable at least in part because the injunctive relief requested intruded into the power committed to the political branches. Similarly, in this case, the intrusive nature of the relief requested leads me to conclude this controversy is nonjusticiable.

B

I recognize that the complaint here is not styled as a facial challenge to the executive's foreign policy decision to locate a military training center in Honduras. The stated claim alleges only that the United States defendants may not lawfully run a military operation on plaintiffs' land when that land has not been expropriated. As the majority characterizes it, therefore, the case is a simple dispute over land—an issue that is traditionally subject to judicial review. To focus only on the narrow issue immediately presented for review, however, overlooks the serious intrusion on the conduct of foreign policy that will result from granting the requested relief. A complaint need not purport to challenge a fundamental executive branch policy to implicate separation of powers concerns.[6]

5. In *Baker v. Carr,* 369 U.S. 186 (1962), the Court was primarily concerned with outlining the characteristics of issues nonjusticiable under the political question doctrine. The political question doctrine, in the strict sense, may pertain only to the nature of the *question* presented, and not to the effect of granting the relief requested. The same separation of powers concerns that give rise to the political question doctrine, however, are implicated where the effect of resolving a dispute infringes on the executive's conduct of foreign policy. *See Tel–Oren v. Libyan Arab Republic,* 726 F.2d 774, 804 (D.C. Cir. 1984) (Bork, J., concurring), *petition for cert. filed,* 52 U.S.L.W. 3922 (U.S. June 14, 1984) (No. 83–2052). Just as a court must refrain from resolving a question whose nature is political, so must it refrain from adjudicating a claim where the relief sought would intrude on the independence of the political branches.

6. In *Chicago & Southern Air Lines, Inc. v. Waterman Steamship Corp.,* 333 U.S. 103 (1948), for example, the Court declined to review an administrative order, approved by the President, regarding assignment of foreign air routes. Although the complaint did not directly question a political judgment, the Court observed that assignment of foreign air routes raised issues concerning the conduct of foreign relations and national defense. Because the complaint indirectly, yet no less intrusively, challenged an executive judgment on foreign affairs, the Court held the order nonreviewable. 333 U.S. at 111–14.

Injunctive relief might take two forms in this case. First, the scope of the Regional Military Training Center could be restricted to the designated 1500–2000 acres to which Ramirez originally agreed. Second, the construction and operation of the center on plaintiffs' land could be enjoined.[7] Both of these alternatives would essentially dictate to the executive branch the proper situs or scope of a Central American military training facility and severely restrict the executive's authority to determine the use and disposition of military operations.

A judicial ruling may also hinder the executive's conduct of foreign affairs by detrimentally affecting our relations with Honduras. The plaintiffs' own declarations indicate at least that Honduran officials knew about, and acquiesced in, the construction and operation of the training center. If Hondurans are involved in the challenged activity in any way, even if only to the extent that they have knowledge of United States activities, any injunctive or declaratory relief implicitly questions Honduran sovereignty. The potential for disruption of our relations with Honduras is not altered by the fact that the action is brought only against the United States officials. The court could end up embroiled in sensitive diplomatic matters.

This is not to say, of course, that all claims touching on foreign affairs in which injunctive relief is sought are nonjusticiable. In *Youngstown Sheet & Tube Co. v. Sawyer,* 343 U.S. 579 (1952), the Supreme Court affirmed a district court order enjoining the seizure of privately owned domestic steel mills. The President ordered the seizure to avoid a labor strike that he believed would jeopardize national defense during the Korean War. The Court concluded that the seizure of private property to avoid a domestic labor dispute was not authorized as an exercise of the President's military power. 343 U.S. at 587–89.

The circumstances in *Youngstown* differ significantly from those in the instant case. Although the seizure in *Youngstown* may have been related to military operations abroad, its primary effect was on domestic, and not foreign, affairs. As Justice Jackson recognized, there is an important distinction between the President's "largely uncontrolled" power to conduct foreign affairs and his more limited power to master domestic affairs, even when those domestic affairs may affect a foreign venture. 343 U.S. at 635–36 n. 2, 642, 644–45 (Jackson, J., concurring). The Court has long emphasized that the executive's discretion to manage foreign affairs is considerably greater than his power to control domestic matters.

> Not only ... is the federal power over external affairs in origin and essential character different from that over internal affairs, but participation in the exercise of the power is significantly limited. In this vast external realm, with its important, complicated, delicate, and

7. Plaintiffs assert that they do not seek to enjoin generally the operation of a United States military facility but only the military activities on their land so long as that land has not been lawfully acquired. In either case, however, an injunction would have the same effect: halting the operation of a United States military facility in Central America, at least for a time.

manifold problems, the President alone has the power to speak or listen as a representative of the nation.

United States v. Curtiss–Wright Export Corp., 299 U.S. 304, 319 (1936).

The Court in *Youngstown* was therefore concerned with whether injunctive relief may appropriately issue to restrain the executive's unlawful action with respect to domestic affairs where the domestic problem might have a secondary effect on foreign affairs. *Youngstown* does not imply that judicial action is appropriate where resolution of a controversy will directly impinge on the executive's conduct of foreign affairs.

In this case, the injunctive relief sought would directly limit the executive's discretion in conducting military affairs and diplomatic relations in Honduras. In contrast to the domestic setting of the seizure in *Youngstown,* the dispute here arises out of the operation of a military base, located within the borders of a foreign nation, created to train yet another foreign nation's soldiers. Judicial action here would be tantamount to oversight of the executive's military and diplomatic policy decisions in a foreign country. Separation of powers principles bar such an intrusion by the judiciary and render this controversy nonjusticiable.[8]

. . . .

. . . Courts have often recognized the importance of our government's speaking with one voice on matters pertaining to foreign affairs. *Baker,* 369 U.S. at 211. A judgment declaring the executive's construction and operation of the Honduran military center unlawful while leaving open the possibility of further judicial enforcement could inject uncertainty into our foreign affairs in Honduras. The consequence of such an abstract judicial statement on the propriety of our foreign military operations is, of course, impossible to predict. Embarrassment, confusion, and decreased confidence in the United States' capacity to speak with one voice in foreign relations, however, are sufficiently likely to weigh heavily against granting the discretionary declaratory relief sought here.[10]

---

8. The majority states that there is a "long line" of cases permitting judicial relief for unlawful action by United States officials in the context of military and foreign affairs. Maj. op. at 1530. In determining that the instant case is nonjusticiable, I do not conclude that courts can never adjudicate claims involving the conduct of foreign affairs. *See supra* at 1548–1549. Where, however, the consequence of judicial action intrudes directly upon the executive's ability to exercise discretion in foreign policy matters, the court must stay its hand. Significantly, the cases cited by the majority are either "just compensation" cases, in which the consequences of judicial action in no way impeded the exercise of executive discretion with respect to foreign affairs, *e.g., United States v. Caltex* (Philippines), *Inc.,* 344 U.S. 149 (1952); *Mitchell v. Harmony,* 54 U.S. (13 How.) 115 (1852); or arose in the domestic context, *e.g., Gilligan v. Morgan,* 413 U.S. 1 (1973); *Youngstown Sheet & Tube Co. v. Sawyer,* 343 U.S. 579 (1952); *Duncan v. Kahanamoku,* 327 U.S. 304 (1946); *Sterling v. Constantin,* 287 U.S. 378 (1932).

10. The original panel opinion in this case expressed similar separation of powers concerns with respect to the requested relief. *Ramirez de Arellano v. Weinberger,* 724 F.2d 143 (D.C. Cir. 1983), *vacated,* F.2d (1984). The panel's analysis, however, rested on the traditional discretion of courts to grant or deny injunctive relief depending on the relative equities of the parties' positions. The panel concluded that injunctive relief could not issue because intrusion into foreign affairs coupled with the possibility of impugning foreign law and the problems of monitoring compliance "establish a formidable obstacle which the equities of plaintiffs' case cannot overcome." 724 F.2d at 150.

NOTE ON AFTERMATH OF RAMIREZ DE ARELLANO

In your view, who has the better argument in *Ramirez de Arellano*: the majority or Judge Tamm?

While the case was on appeal to the Supreme Court, Congress passed a law prohibiting funding of the Regional Military Training Center until the President certified to Congress that the Honduran Government recognized "the need to compensate as required by international law the United States citizen who claims injury from the establishment and operation of the existing Center." Foreign Assistance and Related Programs Appropriations Act, 1985, Pub. L. No. 98–473, 98 Stat. 1884, 1893–94 (1984). Thereafter, the Supreme Court vacated the judgment and remanded the case to the circuit court "for reconsideration of its opinion and judgment in light of the [statute] and other events occurring since October 5, 1984." Weinberger v. Ramirez de Arellano, 471 U.S. 1113, 105 S.Ct. 2353, 86 L.Ed.2d 255 (1985). Do you think that by vacating the decision, the Supreme Court was expressing disagreement on the merits with the circuit court's opinion (see *Schneider v. Kissinger* below)?

On remand, the D.C. Circuit reversed the district court's decision and remanded with instructions that the complaint be dismissed. According to the circuit court, since the United States had discontinued its participation in the military center, plaintiff's request for injunctive relief was no longer equitable for it "would not halt an asserted, ongoing violation but would merely forestall a potential violation." De Arellano v. Weinberger, 788 F.2d 762 (D.C. Cir. 1986). In other words, the plaintiff's action had become too attenuated to justify the extraordinary relief that was being sought through equitable intervention.

Meanwhile, in light of the new statute, Honduras accepted that it had a responsibility to compensate Ramirez, although its exact offer was not divulged. *See* Associated Press, *Hondurans Agree to Pay American in Land Case*, N.Y. TIMES, Jan. 10, 1985, at A9. Congress proceeded to block $38.5 million in funds in 1985 for the training center to be built on Ramirez's ranch until the President certified that the Honduran Government had taken steps to discharge its obligations to compensate Ramirez. In October 1985, Ramirez agreed with the Honduran government to nonbinding fact-finding in a Honduran court, but he rejected the fact finder's report. In 1987, Congress applied more pressure: suspending $20 million in economic assistance for Honduras;

I cannot agree with the panel's reasoning. The panel's reliance on traditional principles of equity implies that were the plaintiffs' case more compelling, equitable relief might be appropriate. The panel's decision to affirm the dismissal, therefore, was not compelled by separation of powers principles but resulted from the court's exercise of its traditional equitable discretion. When there is a danger of a federal court exceeding its limited authority, constitutional principles of separation of powers, not a subjective assessment of the relative equities, should control a court's decision whether to resolve a controversy. *See Vander Jagt v. O'Neill,* 699 F.2d 1166, 1184–85 (D.C. Cir.) (Bork, J., concurring), *cert. denied,* [464 U.S. 823] (1983).

. . . .

[B]alancing the equities in this case could require the court to evaluate the necessity and urgency of operating the Center in its current location. Such an evaluation is properly and practically better left to the political branches. I would thus dismiss plaintiffs' claim, not because of its adequate equitable support, but because it would carry the judiciary into matters reserved to the coordinate branches.

appointing a new, independent fact finder; and setting November 30, 1987, as a deadline for final settlement between the Honduran government and Ramirez, after which the parties were obligated to submit the dispute to binding international arbitration. In December 1987, Ramirez rejected the fact finder's report and proposed offer, and the parties failed to submit the matter to international arbitration.

Congress responded in 1989 by urging Ramirez to accept the proposed offer and released $5 million of the aid to Honduras because of the Government's good faith efforts, with the proviso that the remaining funds would be available when a final settlement was reached. Later, another $5 million was released. Finally, on June 28, 1990, the United States and the Honduran Government signed an agreement under which Honduras paid $7.8 million to the U.S. Government in final settlement of all claims of the United States and its nationals that had been blocking the economic assistance. On July 5, 1990, the State Department transferred the entire amount to Ramirez, who released his rights to the ranch.

SCHNEIDER v. KISSINGER

412 F.3d 190, 191–98 (D.C. Cir. 2005) (some citations omitted).

SENTELLE, CIRCUIT JUDGE.

René and Raúl Schneider, surviving sons of deceased Chilean General René Schneider, together with José Pertierra, personal representative of the estate of General Schneider, brought this action in United States District Court for the District of Columbia against the United States and Henry Kissinger, who at the time of the relevant events was the National Security Advisor to the President of the United States. The complaint alleged in nine counts, all of them directed against both defendants, that Kissinger and the United States had caused, in conjunction with Chilean persons not named as defendants, the kidnapping, torture, and death of Plaintiffs–Appellants' decedent. The District Court granted the motion of Defendants–Appellees to dismiss Appellants' complaint ... for lack of jurisdiction and failure to state a claim upon which relief could be granted. Plaintiffs filed this appeal. Because we agree with the District Court that the courts lack jurisdiction over nonjusticiable questions raised by the complaint, we affirm the grant of dismissal....[1]

I. BACKGROUND

Appellants filed their original complaint on September 10, 2001, identifying their relationship to the deceased general and claiming against Kissinger, the United States, and Richard Helms (former Director of the CIA). That complaint alleged that in 1970 the leader of the Chilean leftist coalition, Dr. Salvador Allende, won a slight plurality of the vote (36.3%) in Chile's presidential election, and that this victory on his part created

1. [Authors' Note: In a similar case involving Henry Kissinger's role in formulating U.S. policy toward the Chilean coup and its aftermath, the D.C. Circuit also dismissed the suit as nonjusticiable under the political question doctrine. *See Gonzalez–Vera v. Kissinger*, 449 F.3d 1260 (D.C. Cir. 2006).]

the expectation that he would, in the following months, be ratified by the Chilean congress as the first socialist president of the country. According to the complaint, "[k]ey United States policymakers" opposed the choice of Allende as president of Chile and on September 8, 1970, "policymakers" began the process of assessing "the pros and cons and problems and prospects involved should a Chilean military coup be organized ... with U.S. assistance." After receiving further information, on September 15, 1970, defendants Kissinger, Helms, and Attorney General John Mitchell met with President Nixon. The President ordered that steps be taken to prevent Allende from becoming president, and specifically, that the CIA was to "play a direct role in organizing a military coup d'etat in Chile" and do quickly whatever was possible to prevent the seating of a possible socialist president. The President expressed that he was "not concerned" about any risks involved, authorized $10 million in funds to effect such a coup, and required a plan of action be drafted within 48 hours.

The complaint further alleged that efforts to prevent Allende from achieving the presidency proceeded on two tracks. "Track I" was a covert political, economic, and propaganda campaign approved by a subcabinet level body of the executive established to exercise political control over covert operations abroad. "Track II" activities were undertaken in direct response to the President's September 15 order and were directed "towards actively promoting and encouraging the Chilean military to move against Allende." In the following months, the tracks moved together. The United States Ambassador to Chile was authorized to encourage a military coup and to intensify contacts with Chilean military officers in order to ascertain their willingness to support such a coup. The Ambassador was also authorized to make contacts in the Chilean military aware that the military would receive no military assistance from the United States if Allende became president of Chile. The Ambassador reported back that General Schneider would be an impediment to achieving the goals outlined in the President's directive, and that he would have to be neutralized. The complaint went on to allege particular acts undertaken in furtherance of the goal of establishing a military coup and claims for relief based on those actions, including the kidnapping, torture, and killing of General Schneider. In all, the complaint alleged seven claims: (1) summary execution; (2) torture; (3) cruel, inhumane, or degrading treatment; (4) arbitrary detention; (5) wrongful death; (6) assault and battery; and (7) intentional infliction of emotional distress.

. . . .

II. THE POLITICAL QUESTION DOCTRINE

The principle that the courts lack jurisdiction over political decisions that are by their nature "committed to the political branches to the exclusion of the judiciary" is as old as the fundamental principle of judicial review. *Antolok v. United States,* 873 F.2d 369, 379 (D.C. Cir. 1989) (separate opinion of Sentelle, J.). In the venerable case of *Marbury v. Madison,* 5 U.S. (1 Cranch) 137 (1803), Chief Justice Marshall first expressed the recognition by the judiciary of the existence of a class of cases constituting "political act[s], belonging to the executive department alone, for the performance of which entire confidence is placed by our Constitution in the supreme executive; and for any misconduct respecting which, the injured individual has no remedy." *Id.* at 164. In a continuing line beginning with Chief Justice Marshall's analysis in *Marbury v. Madison,* this doctrine has evolved as a limitation of the jurisdiction of the courts particularly applicable to foreign relations. *See Oetjen v. Cent. Leather Co.,* 246 U.S. 297, 302–03 (1918). Chief Justice Marshall, writing again in *United States v. Palmer,* 16 U.S. (3 Wheat.) 610 (1818), described questions of foreign policy as "belong[ing] more properly to those . . . who can place the nation in such a position with respect to foreign powers as to their own judgment shall appear wise; *to whom are entrusted all its foreign relations;* then to that tribunal whose power as well as duty is confined to the application of the rule which the legislature may prescribe for it." *Id.* at 634 (emphasis added).

Contemporary application of the Political Question Doctrine, as recognized by the District Court, draws on the analysis set forth in *Baker v. Carr,* 369 U.S. 186 (1962). The *Baker* Court first recognized that "the political question doctrine is 'primarily a function of the separation of powers.' " *Schneider v. Kissinger,* 310 F. Supp. 2d at 258 (quoting *Baker,* 369 U.S. at 210). In *Baker,* the Supreme Court enumerated six factors that may render a case nonjusticiable under the Political Question Doctrine:

> Prominent on the surface of any case held to involve a political question is found a [1] textually demonstrable constitutional commitment of the issue to a coordinate political department; or [2] a lack of judicially discoverable and manageable standards for resolving it; or [3] the impossibility of deciding without an initial policy determination of a kind clearly for nonjudicial discretion; or [4] the impossibility of a court's undertaking independent resolution without expressing lack of respect due coordinate branches of government; or [5] an unusual need for unquestioning adherence to a political decision already made; or [6] the potentiality of embarrassment of multifarious pronouncements by various departments on one question.

Baker, 369 U.S. at 217. The *Baker* analysis lists the six factors in the disjunctive, not the conjunctive. To find a political question, we need only conclude that one factor is present, not all. Nonetheless, we note that most of the factors counsel against the exercise of jurisdiction over the controversy that Plaintiff–Appellants bring to the court.

1. *Textually demonstrable constitutional commitment to other branches*

First, the lawsuit raises policy questions that are textually committed to a coordinate branch of government. As the Supreme Court suggested in *Marbury* and made clear in later cases, "The conduct of the foreign relations of our Government is committed by the Constitution to the Executive and Legislative—'the political'—Departments of the Government, and the propriety of what may be done in the exercise of this political power is not subject to judicial inquiry or decision." *Oetjen,* 246 U.S. at 302. Otherwise put, "foreign policy decisions are the subject of just such a textual commitment," as contemplated in *Baker v. Carr. Comm. of United States Citizens v. Reagan,* 859 F.2d 929, 933–34 (D.C. Cir. 1988).

Absent precedent, there could still be no doubt that decision-making in the fields of foreign policy and national security is textually committed to the political branches of government. Article I, Section 8 of the Constitution provides an enumeration of powers of the legislature. That article is richly laden with delegation of foreign policy and national security powers. Direct allocation of such power is found in Section 8, Clause 1, "the Congress shall have the Power To ... provide for the Common Defence ..."; Clause 3, "To regulate commerce with foreign nations"; Clause 10, "To define and punish Piracies and Felonies committed on the High Seas and Offenses against the Law of Nations"; Clause 11, "To declare War, grant Letters of Marque and Reprisal, and make Rules concerning Captures on Land and Water"; Clause 12, "To raise and support Armies ..."; Clause 13, "To provide and maintain a Navy"; Clause 14, "to make Rules for the Government and Regulation of the land and naval Forces"; Clause 15, "To provide for calling forth the Militia to ... repel Invasions"; Clause 16, "To provide for organizing, arming, and disciplining, the Militia, and for governing such Part of them as may be employed in the Service of the United States."

In addition to these direct allocations to the Congress of these foreign relations and national security powers, other sections and clauses of Article I bear on the subject to provide further weight to the conclusion of contextual allocation. For example, Section 9 of Article I provides for the suspension of the writ of habeas corpus "when in cases of ... invasion the public safety may require it." Section 10 allocates to the Congress the authority to provide consent to individual states, without which they may not "enter into any Agreement or Compact with ... a foreign Power, or engage in War...." This is not to mention the perhaps less direct but undeniably real connection between national security and other powers of Congress, such as that under Article I, Section 8, Clause 1, to "lay and collect Taxes," and Clause 2, to "borrow money on the credit of the United States."

Just as Article I of the Constitution evinces a clear textual allocation to the legislative branch, Article II likewise provides allocation of foreign relations and national security powers to the President, the unitary chief executive. Article II, Section 2 provides, *inter alia,* that "the President shall be Commander in Chief of the Army and Navy of the United States, and of the Militia of the several States, when called into the actual Service of the United States...." That same section further provides that the President "shall have Power, by and with the Advice and Consent of the Senate, to make Treaties, ... [and to] appoint Ambassadors, other public Ministers and Consuls." Section 3 of Article II provides that "he shall receive Ambassadors and other public Ministers ... and shall Commission all the Officers of the United States," including obviously the officers of the military.

While the language of textual commitment of the President is not as extensive as that relating to the legislative branch, nonetheless it is plain that that commitment is real. Indeed, the Supreme Court has described the President as possessing "plenary and exclusive power" in the international arena and "as the sole organ of the federal government in the field of international relations. . . ." *United States v. Curtiss–Wright Export Corp.,* 299 U.S. 304, 320 (1936).

By contrast, in Article III defining the judicial power of the United States the closest there is to a reference to foreign relations is the extension of jurisdiction to "Cases affecting Ambassadors, other public Ministers and Consuls." U.S. CONST., Art. III, § 1. Obviously all this provides is jurisdiction for adjudication of cases against those officers. It provides no authority for policymaking in the realm of foreign relations or provision of national security. It cannot then be denied that decision-making in the areas of foreign policy and national security is textually committed to the political branches.

Neither can it be gainsaid that the subject matter of the instant case involves the foreign policy decisions of the United States. In 1970, at the height of the Cold War, officials of the executive branch, performing their delegated functions concerning national security and foreign relations, determined that it was in the best interest of the United States to take such steps as they deemed necessary to prevent the establishment of a government in a Western Hemisphere nation that in the view of those officials could lead to the establishment or spread of communism as a governing force in the Americas. This decision may have been unwise, or it may have been wise. The political branches may have since rejected the approach, or not. In any event, that decision was classically within the province of the political branches, not the courts. As the Supreme Court has repeatedly reminded us, "[t]he political question doctrine excludes from judicial review those controversies which revolve around policy choices and value determinations constitutionally committed for resolution to the halls of Congress or the confines of the Executive Branch." *Japan Whaling Ass'n v. Am. Cetacean Soc'y,* 478 U.S. 221, 230 (1986). This is so because "[t]he Judiciary is particularly ill suited to make such decisions, as 'courts are fundamentally underequipped to formulate national policies or develop standards for matters not legal in nature.' " *Id.* (quoting *United States ex rel. Joseph v. Cannon,* 642 F.2d 1373, 1379 (D.C. Cir. 1981)).

2. *No judicially discoverable and manageable standards*

The second criterion of the *Baker* six brings under the nonjusticiable umbrella of political question any case as to which there is "a lack of judicially discoverable and manageable standards for resolving it." 369 U.S. at 217. This factor, even taken apart from the first factor, supports the District Court's conclusion that this case must be dismissed under

Rule 12(b)(1). As the District Court well understood, for a court to adjudicate this case would be for that court to undertake the determination of whether, 35 years ago, at the height of the Cold War between the United States and the western powers on the one hand and the expanding communist empire on the other, "it was proper for an Executive Branch official ... to support covert actions against" a committed Marxist who was set to take power in a Latin American country. *Schneider,* 310 F. Supp. 2d at 261–62. Unlike the executive, the judiciary has no covert agents, no intelligence sources, and no policy advisors. The courts are therefore ill-suited to displace the political branches in such decision-making.

As we have said before of other security considerations in another context, "it is within the role of the executive to acquire and exercise the expertise of protecting national security. It is not within the role of the courts to second-guess executive judgments made in furtherance of that branch's proper role." *Center for Nat'l Sec. Studies v. Dep't of Justice,* 331 F.3d 918, 932 (D.C. Cir. 2003).

Appellants claim that the District Court erred in holding that no standards exist for determining whether "it was proper for an Executive Branch official ... to support covert actions against an undesirable figure who was set to take power in a foreign nation." *Schneider,* 310 F. Supp. 2d at 261–62. They assert that the District Court "misconstrued Plaintiffs' claims by framing the issue as an attack on policy." However, it is not at all clear to us why Appellants believe their suit to be anything other than such an attack. They claim that "the D.C. Circuit has held that courts should not invoke the political question doctrine to avoid adjudication of a violation of basic rights." However, the only case from this court which they offer for that proposition is *Ramirez de Arellano v. Weinberger,* 745 F.2d 1500 (D.C. Cir. 1984). In fact, that case stands for nothing at all, as it was vacated by the Supreme Court in *Weinberger v. Ramirez de Arellano,* 471 U.S. 1113 (1985). After the remand, this Court reversed and sent the case back to the District Court for dismissal, with no reinstatement of the original opinion ever occurring. *See Ramirez De Arellano v. Weinberger,* 788 F.2d 762 (D.C. Cir. 1986).

In the District Court, though not expressly before us, Appellants had urged that " 'the standards for evaluating wrongful death are well established' ... and that the 'Court need not depart from these in managing the instant action.' " *Schneider,* 310 F. Supp. 2d at 261. We agree with the District Court that this formulation of the issues is no help. As the District Court stated, "[r]esolving the present lawsuit would compel the court, at a minimum, to determine whether actions or omissions by an Executive Branch officer in the area of foreign relations and national security were 'wrongful' under tort law." *Id.* at 262. We agree with the District Court and the Eleventh Circuit in *Aktepe v. United States,* 105 F.3d 1400, 1404 (11th Cir. 1997), that recasting foreign policy and national security questions in tort terms does not provide standards for making or reviewing foreign policy judgments. In *Aktepe,* the Eleventh Circuit considered a case brought by Turkish sailors alleging injuries and wrongful death suffered as a result of missiles fired by a United States Navy vessel during North Atlantic Treaty Organization training exercises. In holding that the action was barred, *inter alia,* by the second *Baker* political question factor, that Circuit noted that "in order to determine whether the Navy conducted the missile-firing drill in a negligent manner, a court would have to determine how a reasonable military force would have conducted the drill." *Id.* The *Aktepe* court went on to observe "[a]s the Supreme Court noted in a related context, 'it is difficult to conceive of an area of governmental activity in which the courts have less competence.' " *Id.* (quoting *Gilligan v. Morgan,* 413 U.S. 1, 10 (1973)). Similarly here, in order to determine whether the covert operations which allegedly led to the tragic death of General Schneider were wrongful, the court would have to define the standard for the government's use of covert operations in conjunction with political turmoil in another country. There are no justiciably discoverable and manageable standards for the resolution of such a claim.

3. *Judicial resolution would require an initial policy determination of a kind clearly for nonjudicial discretion*

Without rehashing the constitutional separation of powers concerns raised by the two *Baker* factors already discussed, we note that the same sort of problems raise the third factor as well. The District Court well stated the matter:

> [P]laintiffs contend that "the Court is not here asked to pass judgment on any perceived value or danger of the Allende government to United States interests and need not make any policy determination[.]" While the plaintiffs are correct that the Court might be able to avoid evaluating the merits of a potential Allende Government in 1970, it would nonetheless be forced to pass judgment on the means used by the United States to keep that government from taking power.

Schneider, 310 F. Supp. 2d at 263. While we are not at all convinced that we would be able to avoid evaluating the merits of the potential Allende government in 1970, we are completely in agreement with the District Court that we would be forced to pass judgment on the policy-based decision of the executive to use covert action to prevent that government from taking power. Allying United States intelligence operatives with dissidents in another country to kidnap a national of that country may be a drastic measure. To determine whether drastic measures should be taken in matters of foreign policy and national security is not the stuff of adjudication, but of policymaking. As the Supreme Court has emphasized, "the 'nuances' of 'the foreign policy of the United States ... are much more the province of the Executive Branch and Congress than of this Court.' " *Crosby v. Nat'l Foreign Trade Council,* 530 U.S. 363, 386 (2000) (quoting *Container Corp. of Am. v. Franchise Tax Bd.,* 463 U.S. 159, 196 (1983)).

Thus, we agree with the District Court that the third *Baker* factor also counsels against jurisdiction over this case.

4. *The court could not proceed without expressing a lack of respect to coordinate branches of government*

From what we have concluded as to the first three *Baker* factors, it seems apparent to us that we could not determine Appellants' claims without passing judgment on the decision of the executive branch to participate in the alleged covert operations-participation in which, we note from the record, has already been the subject of congressional investigation. We therefore affirm the conclusion of the District Court that "[a] court should refrain from entertaining a suit if it would be unable to do so without expressing a lack of respect due to its coequal Branches of Government." 310 F. Supp. 2d at 264 (citing *Baker v. Carr,* 369 U.S. at 217) (other citations omitted).

5. *Summary*

For the reasons set forth above, we conclude that at least the first four of the six *Baker* factors compel a determination that this case raises political questions committed to the political branches and therefore is beyond the jurisdiction of the courts. Appellants counter the government's political question arguments by asserting that this case does not fall within the Political Question Doctrine because "there is a difference between policy and the implementation of policy, and . . . the latter is within the realm of the judiciary to oversee." For this proposition, they cite *DKT Memorial Fund Ltd. v. Agency for Int'l Dev.,* 810 F.2d 1236 (D.C. Cir. 1987), which stated, "whereas attacks on foreign policymaking are nonjusticiable, claims alleging non-compliance with the law are justiciable, even though the limited review that the court undertakes may have an effect on foreign affairs." 810 F.2d at 1238.

Appellants are indeed correct that the *DKT Memorial* opinion so stated. However, it did so on a record immediately distinguishable from the controversy raised by the present litigation. *DKT Memorial* concerned not the executive's making of a policy decision and implementing that decision, but rather a challenge to the constitutionality of the manner in which an agency sought to implement an earlier policy pronouncement by the President. Indeed, after the jurisdictional decision in *DKT Memorial* had ordered the matter remanded to the District Court, the District Court's decision on remand came before this Court in a second appeal. We then made plain the narrowness of our original jurisdictional holding:

> In the present case, where the President acted under a congressional grant of discretion as broadly worded as any we are likely to see, and where the exercise of that discretion occurs in the area of foreign affairs, we cannot disturb his decision simply because some might find it unwise or because it differs from the policies pursued by previous administrations.

DKT Memorial Fund Ltd. v. Agency for Int'l Development, 887 F.2d 275, 281–82 (D.C. Cir. 1989). Thus, our ultimate disposition of the *DKT Memorial* question supports rather than undermines the District Court's holding that the present case falls within the realm of nonjusticiable political questions first recognized in *Marbury v. Madison* and delineated in *Baker v. Carr.*

NOTES ON THE POLITICAL QUESTION DOCTRINE IN THEORY AND PRACTICE

1. *Political Question Doctrine in Theory.* What is the exact nature of the political question doctrine? In one formulation, the doctrine is a finding by the court that the question before it has been constitutionally allocated exclusively to one or both of the other branches of the federal government, i.e., the political branches. In this sense, the court does not assert nonjusticiability but, employing the appropriate level of judicial review, implicitly reaches the merits and decides that the government has acted constitutionally. In another formulation, the doctrine is a finding by the court that the question before it, while normally within the scope of its review, will nevertheless not be adjudicated due to a lack of judicial capacity or out of prudence. In this sense, the court is extraordinarily asserting nonjusticiability. Unlike a determination of lack of standing, which only affects the individual litigants, a finding of a political question preempts all future judicial inquiry into the subject matter. The court is thus eschewing its pervasive role to "say what the law is." Marbury v. Madison, 5 U.S. (1 Cranch) 137, 176, 2 L.Ed. 60 (1803).

Both interpretations of the political question doctrine have received scholarly support. Arguing for the constitutionally-allocated position, Herbert Wechsler wrote that "the only proper judgment that may lead to an abstention from decision is that the Constitution has committed the determination of the issue to another agency of government than the courts," a judgment he described as completely "different from a broad discretion to abstain or intervene." Herbert Wechsler, *Toward Neutral Principles of Constitutional Law,* 73 HARV. L. REV. 1, 9 (1959).

In response, Alexander Bickel argued for the prudential position:

> Such is the basis of the political-question doctrine: the court's sense of lack of capacity, compounded in unequal parts of the strangeness of the issue and the suspicion that it will have to yield more often and more substantially to expediency than to principle; the sheer momentousness of it, which unbalances judgment and prevents one from subsuming the normal calculations of probabilities; the anxiety not so much that judicial judgment will be ignored, as that perhaps it should be, but won't; finally and in sum ("in a mature democracy"), the inner vulnerability of an institution which is electorally irresponsible and has no earth to draw strength from.

Alexander M. Bickel, *The Supreme Court, 1960 Term—Foreword: The Passive Virtues,* 75 HARV. L. REV. 40, 75 (1961).

Some academics have urged the elimination of the doctrine or tried to redesign its application. Louis Henkin, rejecting the prudential formulation and viewing the constitutionally-allocated formulation as congruent with the normal scope of judicial review, suggested scrapping the doctrine—to the extent it really existed at all. *See* Louis Henkin, *Is There a "Political Question" Doctrine?*, 85 YALE L.J. 597 (1976). In its place, he discerned discrete components now mixed in the doctrine: ordinary judicial respect for the coordinate branches of government, discretionary refusal of a court of equity to issue relief, and lack of a private cause of action.

Finding Henkin's position too extreme, Linda Champlin and Alan Schwarz argued that, correctly understood, the political question doctrine results from a judicial assumption of validity dictated by an overwhelming need for finality. Linda Champlin & Alan Schwarz, *Political Question Doctrine and Allocation of the Foreign Affairs Power,* 13 HOFSTRA L. REV. 215 (1985). According to them, such a need arises only in the context of foreign affairs and only when the political branches have acted jointly. If the two branches dispute the allocation of foreign affairs power, the judiciary should decide the matter. Champlin and Schwarz maintain that preservation of order is the underlying rationale of the political question doctrine and that this goal is not furthered by inter-branch battles left unresolved by judicial abstention.

Others have defended the doctrine. Peter Mulhern argued that the political question doctrine is a useful tool for demarcating the responsibility to interpret the Constitution that is shared by the courts and the political branches. He claimed that criticism of the doctrine relies on the invalid assumptions that the judiciary has a "monopoly" on constitutional interpretation and that limiting this monopoly would undermine the rule of law. J. Peter Mulhern, *In Defense of the Political Question Doctrine,* 137 U. PA. L. REV. 97 (1988); *see also* Jesse H. Choper, *The Political Question Doctrine: Suggested Criteria*, 54 DUKE L.J. 1457 (2005).

2. *Political Question Doctrine in Practice.* In practice, the Supreme Court only rarely has disposed of litigation solely on the basis of the political question doctrine—with its most common application being to the guarantee clause (the article IV, section 4 requirement that "[t]he United States shall guarantee to every State in this Union a Republican Form of Government") or similar questions that are literally political in character. *See, e.g.*, Luther v. Borden, 48 U.S. (7 How.) 1, 12 L.Ed. 581 (1849) (dismissing as a political question a dispute as to which government of Rhode Island was the legitimate government during the Dorr rebellion); Pacific States Telephone & Telegraph Co. v. Oregon, 223 U.S. 118, 32 S.Ct. 224, 56 L.Ed. 377 (1912) (dismissing as a political question a dispute concerning whether direct popular initiatives and referenda violated the guarantee clause); Coleman v. Miller, 307 U.S. 433, 59 S.Ct. 972, 83 L.Ed. 1385 (1939) (efficacy of state ratification of proposed constitutional amendment a political question).

In the case most commonly cited as having set out the standard for the political question doctrine, *Baker v. Carr,* 369 U.S. 186, 82 S.Ct. 691, 7 L.Ed.2d 663 (1962), the Court actually managed to reach the merits of a voting district case and, in effect, reversed *Colegrove v. Green*, 328 U.S. 549, 66 S.Ct. 1198, 90 L.Ed. 1432 (1946). The Court rested its decision on its duty to give effect to the equal protection clause, insisting that a claim based solely on the guarantee clause would have presented a political question. Later cases continued to apply the doctrine warily. For instance, in *Powell v. McCormack,* the Court avoided application of the political question doctrine in a case involving the refusal of the House of Representatives to seat Adam Clayton Powell. Powell v. McCormack, 395 U.S. 486, 518–49, 89 S.Ct. 1944, 23 L.Ed.2d 491 (1969) (concluding that, despite claims that the decision whether to seat an elected member was constitutionally allocated to the House under article I, section 5, only refusals premised on the criteria of article I, section 2 (i.e., age, citizenship, and residence) would be a political question); *see also* Davis v. Bandemer, 478 U.S. 109, 118–27, 106 S.Ct. 2797, 92 L.Ed.2d 85 (1986) (refusing to apply the political question doctrine to political gerrymandering claims); United States v. Munoz–Flores, 495 U.S. 385, 389–96, 110 S.Ct. 1964, 109 L.Ed.2d 384 (1990) (holding that a lawsuit seeking to invalidate a law on Origination Clause grounds presents no political question). *But see* Gilligan v. Morgan, 413 U.S. 1, 93 S.Ct. 2440, 37 L.Ed.2d 407 (1973) (finding that evaluation of the training, procedures and weaponry of the Ohio National Guard was a political question).

Given the dearth of cases accepting political question objections, some academics have begun writing its obituary. *See* Rachel E. Barkow, *More Supreme Than Court? The Fall of the Political Question Doctrine and the Rise of Judicial Supremacy*, 102 COLUM. L. REV. 237, 273–317 (2002); Martin H. Redish, *Judicial Review and the "Political Question"*, 79 NW. L. REV. 1031 (1985); Mark Tushnet, *Law and Prudence in the Law of Justiciability: The Transformation and Disappearance of the Political Question Doctrine*, 80 N.C. L. REV. 1203, 1230–31 (2002).

3. *Political Question Doctrine and Foreign Affairs*. In the context of foreign affairs, the political question doctrine has displayed some greater vitality, particularly among the lower federal courts—some of these cases are excerpted below. Both concepts of the doctrine have been employed: that the handling of foreign affairs is allocated to the political branches of the government, and that judicial meddling into foreign affairs could involve determining issues controlled by judicially unassessable facts or making determinations which might be of great detrimental consequence to the United States in its foreign relations. For commentary, see, e.g., Harold Hongju Koh, *Why the President (Almost) Always Wins in Foreign Affairs: Lessons of the Iran–Contra Affair,* 97 YALE L.J. 1255 (1988); Lisa Rudikoff Price, *Banishing the Specter of Judicial Foreign Policymaking: A Competence–Based Approach to the Political Question Doctrine*, 38 N.Y.U. J. INT'L L. & POL. 323 (2005–2006).

The Supreme Court has endorsed these premises in *dicta*. In *Oetjen v. Central Leather Co.*, the Court stated: "The conduct of the foreign relations of our Government is committed by the Constitution to the Executive and Legislative—'the political'—Departments of the Government, and the propriety of what may be done in the exercise of this political power is not subject to judicial inquiry or decision." 246 U.S. 297, 302, 38 S.Ct. 309, 62 L.Ed. 726 (1918). In *United States v. Curtiss–Wright Export Corp.,* 299 U.S. 304, 57 S.Ct. 216, 81 L.Ed. 255 (1936), Justice Sutherland, for the Court, announced the expansive *dicta* which has so often been cited to advance the prudential abstention of the judiciary in foreign affairs-based cases: "In this vast external realm, with its important, complicated, delicate and manifold problems, the President alone has the power to speak or listen as a representative of the nation." *Id.* at 319. The Court further spoke of the "very delicate, plenary and exclusive power of the President as the sole organ of the federal government in the field of international relations" even though the very exercise of "plenary" power under consideration was one as to which Congress had already legislated without constitutional challenge. *Id.* at 319–20. In *Chicago & S. Air Lines, Inc. v. Waterman S.S. Corp.*, Justice Jackson again articulated the Court's reluctance to decide issues involving foreign policy:

> Such decisions are wholly confided by our Constitution to the political departments of the government, Executive and Legislative. They are delicate, complex, and involve large elements of prophecy. They are and should be undertaken only by those directly responsible to the people whose welfare they advance or imperil. They are decisions of a kind for which the Judiciary has neither aptitude, facilities nor responsibility and which has long been held to belong in the domain of political power not subject to judicial intrusion or inquiry.

333 U.S. 103, 111, 68 S.Ct. 431, 92 L.Ed. 568 (1948) (citations omitted).

In *Baker v. Carr*, Justice Brennan also referred to the unique nature of foreign affairs issues. "Not only does resolution of such issues frequently turn on standards that defy judicial application, or involve the exercise of a discretion demonstrably committed to the executive or legislature," he said, "but many such questions uniquely demand single-voiced statement of the Government's views." 369 U.S. 186, 211, 82 S.Ct. 691, 7 L.Ed.2d 663 (1962). Yet, significantly, he went on to caution that "it is error to suppose that every case or controversy which touches foreign relations lies beyond judicial cognizance." *Id.* Brennan then arrived at his classic formulation of what factors give rise to political questions.

Aside from the "prominent" inquiry into textual constitutional allocation, is the Brennan catalogue troublesome? For example, pointing to "a lack of judicially discoverable and manageable standards" seems anomolous given the Supreme Court's past ability to itself provide standards to make judicially manageable such broad principles as due process, equal protection, and free speech. What about fear of "expressing lack of the respect due coordinate branches"? Does that mean complete judicial abdication in each instance of conflict with congressional or presidential exercise of constitutionally-based power? As for the possibility of "multifarious pronouncements by various departments on one question," might not judicial intervention prevent as often as aggravate such confusion by resolving a dispute between the Congress and the Executive? For contrasting views, compare Thomas M. Franck, *Political Questions/Judicial Answers: Does the Rule of Law Apply to Foreign Affairs* 10–30 (1992), with Jide Nzelibe, *The Uniqueness of Foreign Affairs*, 89 IOWA L.REV. 941, 966–1009 (2004).

Since *Baker*, the Supreme Court has adjudicated several issues that touch upon foreign affairs issues. In *Japan Whaling Ass'n v. American Cetacean Society*, 478 U.S. 221, 106 S.Ct. 2860, 92 L.Ed.2d 166 (1986) (cited above in *Schneider v. Kissinger*), several wildlife conservation groups claimed that congressional amendments required the Secretary of Commerce, upon certain findings of fact, to certify that Japan's whaling practices "diminish the effectiveness" of the International Convention for the Regulation of Whaling

(ICRW) because Japan's annual harvest exceeded quotas established under the Convention. Under the law, such a finding would have triggered U.S. import restrictions. Prior to the suit, the Secretary had negotiated an executive agreement with Japan that provided for reduced whaling harvests but did not bring Japan into immediate compliance. Nevertheless, the President refused to certify noncompliance. The district court ordered the Secretary to certify to the President that Japan was in violation of the ICRW quota. 604 F.Supp. 1398 (D.D.C. 1985). The Court of Appeals affirmed. 768 F.2d 426 (D.C. Cir. 1985). But the Supreme Court reversed on the merits. Writing for the majority, Justice White determined that the Secretary's decision to secure Japan's gradual compliance with the ICRW with an executive agreement rather than certification was a "reasonable construction" of the amendments. 478 U.S. at 223. However, regarding the Japanese petitioners' claim that a federal court lacks the judicial power to command the Secretary to repudiate the executive agreement with Japan because to do so might create "embarrassment from multifarious pronouncements by various departments on one question," *id.* at 229 (quoting *Baker v. Carr,* 369 U.S. at 217), the Court responded:

> The political question doctrine excludes from judicial review those controversies which revolve around policy choices and value determinations constitutionally committed for resolution to the halls of Congress or the confines of the Executive Branch. The Judiciary is particularly ill suited to make such decisions, as "courts are fundamentally underequipped to formulate national policies or develop standards for matters not legal in nature." . . .
>
> As *Baker* plainly held, however, the courts have the authority to construe treaties and executive agreements, and it goes without saying that interpreting congressional legislation is a recurring and accepted task for the federal courts. It is also evident that the challenge to the Secretary's decision not to certify Japan for harvesting whales in excess of IWC quotas presents a purely legal question of statutory interpretation. The Court must first determine the nature and scope of the duty imposed upon the Secretary by the Amendments, a decision which calls for applying no more than the traditional rules of statutory construction, and then applying this analysis to the particular set of facts presented below. We are cognizant of the interplay between these Amendments and the conduct of this Nation's foreign relations, and we recognize the premier role which both Congress and the Executive play in this field. But under the Constitution, one of the Judiciary's characteristic roles is to interpret statutes, and we cannot shirk this responsibility merely because our decision may have significant political overtones.

478 U.S. at 229–30 (footnote omitted). Does *Japan Whaling* suggest that courts must always retain the power to interpret the legality of executive policy when there is a statute or treaty to guide the exercise of executive discretion? Does this limit the political question doctrine to cases in which the Executive is acting under a constitutional authority unfettered by statute or treaty? What if the statute or treaty conflicts with an "inherent" presidential power?

Following *Baker*, the Supreme Court has also invoked the political question doctrine to dismiss two foreign affairs controversies. In *Gilligan v. Morgan*, 413 U.S. 1, 93 S.Ct. 2440, 37 L.Ed.2d 407 (1973), the Court applied the political question doctrine to dismiss a constitutional challenge to the training regimen of a National Guard unit. In *Goldwater v. Carter,* 444 U.S. 996, 100 S.Ct. 533, 62 L.Ed.2d 428 (1979), a plurality of the Court invoked the doctrine to dismiss a challenge to the President's authority to terminate a treaty without Senate ratification. In *Goldwater*, Justice Powell redefined judicial inquiry as limited to three questions:

> (i) Does the issue involve resolution of questions committed by the text of the Constitution to a coordinate branch of Government? (ii) Would resolution of the question demand that a court move beyond areas of judicial expertise? (iii) Do prudential considerations counsel against judicial intervention?

444 U.S. at 998. Is this an improvement on the inquiry as framed by Justice Brennan in *Baker*?

4. *Legislating the Political Question Doctrine.* Whether Congress may circumscribe the courts' recourse to the political question doctrine depends on the basis of the doctrine. If the doctrine is an interpretation of the Constitution's allocation of powers, then legislation seeking to alter or repeal an aspect of it would be unconstitutional. If the "prudential" formulation is correct—that is, if the doctrine is merely an instance of the courts' recourse to what Alexander Bickel has called "the passive virtues"—then legislation might compel justiciability. One article suggested that the Hickenlooper Amendment to the Foreign Assistance Act of 1961—which requires courts to decide claims alleging foreign expropriation of U.S.-owned assets "on the merits giving effect to the principles of international law," 22 U.S.C. § 2370(e)(2) (2006), thus limiting the act of state doctrine—suggests that Congress might require the adjudication of cases otherwise falling within the political question doctrine. Thomas M. Franck & Clifford A. Bob, *The Return of Humpty–Dumpty: Foreign Relations Law After the* Chadha *Case*, 79 AM. J. INT'L L. 912, 957–59 (1985); *see* Banco Nacional de Cuba v. Farr, 383 F.2d 166, 181 n.18 (2d Cir. 1967) (leaving open "whether there might be a constitutional compulsion that the courts accept the direction of Congress even as to issues the Court has held to be nonjusticiable because they are 'political questions.' "), *cert. denied,* 390 U.S. 956, 88 S.Ct. 1038, 19 L.Ed.2d 1151, *reh'g denied*, 390 U.S. 1037, 88 S.Ct. 1406, 20 L.Ed.2d 298 (1968).

SECTION 2. POLITICAL QUESTION DOCTRINE AND THE WAR POWER

NOTE: POLITICAL QUESTION AND THE VIETNAM WAR CASES

U.S. involvement in the Vietnam War in the 1960s and early 1970s, and the lack of a formal declaration of war by Congress, prompted various legal challenges in U.S. courts, which in turn produced several distinct theories as to the basis for, and extent of, the political question doctrine.

When the Circuit Court for the District of Columbia was first seized of the matter, it refused even to analyze the threshold question of whether congressional approval of American military involvement in Vietnam was constitutionally required. Luftig v. McNamara, 373 F.2d 664, 665–66 (D.C. Cir.) (per curiam) (citations omitted), *cert. denied*, 387 U.S. 945, 87 S.Ct. 2078, 18 L.Ed.2d 1332 (1967); *see also* Mora v. McNamara, 387 F.2d 862 (D.C. Cir.) (per curiam), *cert. denied*, 389 U.S. 934, 88 S.Ct. 282, 19 L.Ed.2d 287 (1967). In effect, this position allowed that the President was unilaterally conducting a war. If that impinged constitutional powers of the Congress, the courts reasoned, it was for Congress to retaliate. The judges refused to umpire that dispute.

The Second Circuit in *Orlando v. Laird* rejected that position, determined that congressional participation was necessary to sanction the Vietnam war, and found that congressional authorization had in fact been extended. 443 F.2d 1039 (2d Cir. 1971), *cert. denied,* 404 U.S. 869, 92 S.Ct. 94, 30 L.Ed.2d 113 (1971). Nevertheless, a political question still remained. A court would adjudicate whether "some" mutual participation between the Congress and the President existed, but would not adjudicate the sufficiency of the means by which congressional authorization was made. For example, whether defense appropriations were a constitutionally correct means to convey congressional approval was a political question. Accordingly, the Second Circuit found that the repeal of the Gulf of Tonkin Resolution left the result of *Orlando* unchanged; "some" congressional approval remained, such as the draft extension and budget appropriations. DaCosta v. Laird (I), 448 F.2d 1368 (2d Cir. 1971), *cert. denied,* 405 U.S. 979, 92 S.Ct. 1193, 31 L.Ed.2d 255 (1972) (hereinafter *DaCosta (I)*). The court would not define or demand "particular means of collaboration" between the Congress and the Executive. 448 F.2d at 1370.

Other courts reached the issue and examined the collaborative means. In a remarkable turnabout from *Luftig,* the D.C. Circuit found that defense appropriations and draft extensions did not add up to "valid assent to the Vietnam war" by Congress. Mitchell v. Laird, 488 F.2d 611 (D.C. Cir. 1973). In *Mottola v. Nixon,* Judge Sweigert, while not deciding the merits, maintained:

> a strong case can be made that compliance with the Constitution of the United States and its plain provision that the power to declare war lies, not in the President, but in the Congress, should be made to rest upon something better than the ambivalences of congressional inaction or mere defense legislation, appropriations and questionable resolutions; that such compliance calls for nothing less than what the Constitution plainly says—a declaration of war by the Congress or at least an equally explicit congressional expression....

318 F.Supp. 538 (N.D. Cal. 1970), *rev'd*, 464 F.2d 178 (9th Cir. 1972). Judge Sweigert's demand was unique; even the *Mitchell* court accepted that, in general, the sufficiency of the form that congressional consent had taken was itself a political question.

Plaintiffs encountered yet another political question when they argued that new U.S. military undertakings had so fundamentally altered U.S. involvement in Indo-China that further congressional consent was needed. Dictum in *DaCosta (I)* helped spawn this argument: "If the Executive were now escalating the prolonged struggle instead of decreasing it, additional supporting action by the Legislative Branch over what is presently afforded, might well be required." 448 F.2d at 1370. DaCosta pursued this line of argument following the 1972 mining of North Vietnamese ports that was combined with intensified aerial bombardment. DaCosta v. Laird (II), 471 F.2d 1146 (2d Cir. 1973). The Second Circuit responded that a "lack of discoverable and manageable judicial standards" made this issue a political question and prevented the court from determining "whether a specific military operation constitutes an 'escalation' of the war or is merely a new tactical approach within a continuing strategic plan." 471 F.2d at 1155. Judge Kaufman added, "we specifically do not pass on the point urged by appellant whether a radical change in the character of war operations—as by an intentional policy of indiscriminate bombing of civilians without any military objective—might be sufficiently measurable judicially to warrant a court's consideration, i.e., might contain a standard which we seek in this record and do not find." *Id.* at 1156. In *Holtzman v. Schlesinger,* 361 F.Supp. 553 (E.D.N.Y. 1973), plaintiffs argued that the 1973 bombing of Cambodia amounted to such a "radical change." Reversing the district court decision, the Second Circuit again found that a lack of manageable standards precluded adjudication. Holtzman v. Schlesinger, 484 F.2d 1307 (2d Cir. 1973).

Throughout this period, the Supreme Court successfully evaded the issue of the constitutionality of the Vietnam war. It denied certiorari to the appeals of *Luftig*, *Mora*, *Orlando*, *DaCosta* (I) and *Holtzman.* Justice Douglas often dissented and supported granting certiorari. He had previously noted in his *Baker v. Carr* concurrence that "[t]he category of the 'political' question is, in my view, narrower than the decided cases indicate." 369 U.S. 186, 246 n. 3, 82 S.Ct. 691, 7 L.Ed.2d 663 (1962). His dissents followed that spirit. Douglas succinctly restated his position in his dissent from the denial of *certiorari* in *DaCosta (I)*:

> This Court, of course, should give deference to the coordinate branches of the Government. But we did not defer in the *Prize Cases*, 2 Black 635, 17 L.Ed. 459, when the issue was presidential power as Commander in Chief to order a blockade. We did not defer in the *Steel Seizure Case,* when the issue was presidential power, in time of armed international conflict, to order the seizure of domestic steel mills. Nor should we defer here, when the issue is presidential power to seize, not steel, but people. See *Mass. I, supra*, at 891–900.
>
> The Constitution gives Congress the power "To declare War," Art. I, § 8; and it is argued that the Constitution gives to Congress the *exclusive* power to determine when it has declared war. But if there is such a "textually demonstrable constitutional commitment," *Baker v. Carr,* 369 U.S. 186, 217, 82 S.Ct. 691, 7 L.Ed.2d 663, it is for this Court to determine its scope. *Powell v. McCormack,* 395 U.S. 486, 521, 89 S.Ct. 1944, 23 L.Ed.2d 491. See *Mass. I, supra*, at 892.
>
> While we debate whether to decide the constitutionality of this war, our countrymen are daily compelled to undergo the physical and psychological tortures of armed combat on foreign soil. Families and careers are

> disrupted; young men maimed and disfigured; lives lost. The issues are large; they are precisely framed; we should decide them.

405 U.S. 979, 979–81, 92 S.Ct. 1193, 31 L.Ed.2d 255 (1972) (footnotes omitted).

In *Massachusetts v. Laird,* the Court denied the Commonwealth of Massachusetts leave to file a complaint against the Secretary of State seeking adjudication of the constitutionality of the Vietnam War. Justice Douglas, applying the *Baker v. Carr* tests, concluded that no political question existed. 400 U.S. 886, 91 S.Ct. 128, 27 L.Ed.2d 140 (1970) (Douglas, J., dissenting). Justices Stewart and Harlan separately dissented without opinion. *Id.* Stewart had also joined Douglas's dissent in *Mora v. McNamara* in addition to writing his own. 389 U.S. 934, 88 S.Ct. 282, 19 L.Ed.2d 287 (1967). Stewart revealed, through a posthumously released interview, that he had serious doubts over the constitutionality of U.S. participation in Vietnam. Edwin Yoder, *A Judge and the War,* WASH. POST, Dec. 10, 1985, at A21, col. 5.

For contemporaneous articles on the Vietnam War, see Louis Henkin, *Vietnam in the Courts of the United States: "Political Questions",* 63 AM. J. INT'L L. 284 (1969); John Norton Moore, *The Justiciability of Challenges to the Use of Military Forces Abroad,* 10 VA. J. INT'L L. 85 (1969); Warren F. Schwartz & Wayne McCormack, *The Justiciability of Legal Objections to the American Military Effort in Vietnam,* 46 TEX. L. REV. 1033 (1968); Robert P. Sugarman, *Judicial Decisions Concerning the Constitutionality of United States Military Activity in Indo-China: A Bibliography of Court Decisions,* 13 COLUM. J. TRANSNAT'L L. 470 (1974); Michael E. Tigar, *Judicial Power, the "Political Question Doctrine," and Foreign Relations,* 17 UCLA L. REV. 1135 (1970); Lawrence R. Velvel, *The War in Vietnam: Unconstitutional, Justiciable, and Jurisdictionally Attackable,* 16 KAN. L. REV. 449 (1968). For a thoughtful reflection on the period, see John Hart Ely, *War and Responsibility: Constitutional Lessons of Vietnam and Its Aftermath* (1993).

NOTE: THE IRAN-IRAQ WAR OF THE 1980'S

In 1980, Iraq invaded Iran, commencing a protracted and bloody war that would continue through most of the decade. Though ostensibly neutral, the United States in fact favored Iraq over the newly-installed, hostile regime of Ayatollah Khomeini, under whose leadership the Iranian hostage crisis transpired.

The belligerents frequently engaged in military incidents in the Persian Gulf—an important conduit for oil tankers providing much of the world's supply of oil—resulting in an increase in attacks on commercial vessels. As a result, in 1986 Kuwaiti oil tankers sailing in the Gulf requested protection from the U.S. Navy. In 1987, under a policy promulgated by President Reagan, the United States began reflagging Kuwaiti oil tankers under the U.S. flag and escorting them with U.S. Navy warships. One such reflagged ship struck a mine in the Gulf; several months thereafter, U.S. naval forces encountered an Iranian ship laying such mines in the Gulf and fired on the ship, engaging a fire fight. Less than a month later, a missile alleged to belong to Iran hit a reflagged Kuwaiti ship.

Lowry v. Reagan was a suit brought by members of Congress to enforce the War Powers Resolution in this so-called "tanker war," charging that U.S. involvement constituted military actions that must be approved by Congress. (Note that an initial charge by plaintiffs protesting the legality of the reflagging operation was dropped before the District Court decided the case.) Before reading this case, revisit the War Powers Resolution, 50 U.S.C. §§ 1541–1548, reprinted in Chapter 4, Section 5. The War Powers Resolution was a joint resolution passed by Congress over President Nixon's veto in 1973, in the wake of the Vietnam War. The Resolution addressed the issue of declaration of war by other means, enacting a framework for congressional involvement and approval of the use of force initiated unilaterally by the President. Some of Nixon's successors as president have also objected to the Resolution; its constitutionality and effectiveness remain a source of heated debate.

LOWRY v. REAGAN

676 F.Supp. 333 (D.D.C. 1987) (some footnotes omitted).

REVERCOMB, District Judge.

This matter came before the Court on plaintiffs' Motion for Summary Judgment, defendant's Opposition, defendant's Motion to Dismiss, plaintiffs' Opposition and Reply, and defendant's Reply. A brief in support of defendant's Motion to Dismiss was submitted by *amicus curiae* Representative Howard L. Berman. Both parties filed Replies. Oral argument was heard on November 10, 1987.

Plaintiffs, 110 members of the House of Representatives,[1] contend that the reporting requirement of section 4(a)(1) of the War Powers Resolution, 50 U.S.C. sec. 1543(a)(1) (1982), was triggered by the July 22, 1987 initiation of United States escort operations in the Persian Gulf and by the September 21, 1987 attack on an Iranian Navy ship laying mines in the Persian Gulf. Specifically, plaintiffs contend that United States Armed Forces have been introduced, without a declaration of war, "into hostilities or into situations where imminent involvement in hostilities is clearly indicated by the circumstances." 50 U.S.C. sec. 1543(a)(1). Plaintiffs petition this Court to declare that the President was required to file reports concerning both the July and September incidents and to order the President to submit a report concerning continued use of United States Armed Forces in the Persian Gulf within forty-eight hours of the order in this case. For the reasons stated below, the Court declines to accept jurisdiction and DISMISSES this action.

. . . .

II. FACTS

The current case concerns the application of the War Powers Resolution to recent activities of United States Armed Forces in the Persian

1. The three Senators originally identified as plaintiffs in this lawsuit have withdrawn from the action.

Gulf. The Persian Gulf, a body of water partly bounded by Iran and Iraq, has become the site of numerous military incidents in the ongoing war between these two belligerents.[13] In response to an increase in attacks on commercial shipping during 1986, Kuwait requested the United States to provide protection for Kuwaiti petroleum tankers passing through the Persian Gulf. The United States responded affirmatively on March 7, 1987, and the first reflagged tankers, escorted by United States Navy warships, entered the Persian Gulf by way of the Strait of Hormuz on July 22, 1987. Two days later a reflagged tanker, the S.S. Bridgeton, was seriously damaged when it struck a mine. On September 21, 1987, United States naval forces fired at an Iranian Navy ship that was laying mines in the Persian Gulf.

The executive and legislative branches gave prompt consideration to the applicability of the War Powers Resolution to these events. In the first of several official communications to Congress on the Persian Gulf situation, the President described the September 21, 1987 incident and stated his belief that the War Powers Resolution was unconstitutional.[20] Moreover, the Administration has stated that the War Powers Resolution does not apply to the escort operation in the Persian Gulf. Legislative debate on this topic is reflected in the introduction of several bills to invoke the War Powers Resolution with regard to the situation in the Persian Gulf.[22] Recently, the Senate rejected Senator Brock Adams' bill to authorize the escort operations under the War Powers Resolution but moved to set new rules for handling future war powers disputes. Congress also debated the question of whether the War Powers Resolution should be amended or

13. Iran and Iraq have been in a state of war since September 1980. *See* Declaration of Richard L. Armitage at Par. 12. The United States is neutral in this war. C. Weinberger, *A Report to the Congress on security arrangements in the Persian Gulf* 2 (June 15, 1987).

20. *Communication From The President of the United States Transmitting A Report On The September 21, 1987 Engagement of United States Armed Forces and Iranian Minelaying Craft In the Persian Gulf*, H. Doc. No. 110–112, 100th Cong., 1st Sess. 1–2 (1987).

The other presidential communications, submitted in October 1987, did not reiterate the President's views on the constitutionality of the Resolution but were filed "consistent with the War Powers Resolution." *See Communication from the President of the United States Transmitting A Report On The October 8, 1987 Engagement Between United States Armed Forces and Iranian Naval Vessels In the Persian Gulf*, H. Doc. No. 110–113, 100th Cong., 1st Sess. 2 (1987). *See also Communication From The President of the United States Transmitting A Report On The October 19, 1987 Actions By U.S. Armed Forces In the Persian Gulf*, H.Doc. No. 100–120, 100th Cong., 1st Sess. 1 (1987).

Representative Howard Berman argues in his brief *amicus curiae* that these presidential communications satisfy the section 4(a)(1) reporting requirement and that the automatic sixty-day withdrawal provision therefore has been triggered. Defendant opposes Representative Berman's claim on the grounds that it is non-justiciable. Defendant's Response to Brief Amicus Curiae of Representative Howard Berman. Plaintiff opposes Representative Berman's argument on the grounds that the presidential communications do not comply with the requirements for a War Powers Resolution report because they discuss neither the circumstances necessitating United States intervention nor the estimated scope and duration of the intervention. *See* Plaintiffs' Memorandum In Reply to Brief of Amicus Curiae Representative Howard Berman at 1–2.

22. *See e.g.* H.J. Res. 310, 100th Cong., 1st Sess. (1987); S. 1343, 100th Cong. 1st Sess. (1987); H.J. Res. 295, 100th Cong. 1st Sess. (1987).

even repealed.[24] Last summer, 110 Members of the House of Representatives and 3 Senators filed the initial complaint in this action. An amended complaint was filed on September 29, 1987. In the amended complaint, plaintiffs dropped their claims against the Secretary of Defense and the Secretary of Transportation regarding the legality of the reflagging operation and retained only their claim against the President under the War Powers Resolution.

III. ANALYSIS

[First the court invoked the remedial discretion doctrine—described here as the "equitable discretion doctrine" because the plaintiffs were seeking equitable relief, a threshold evaluation for separation of powers issues in congressional plaintiff cases. The doctrine counsels judicial restraint in granting relief when challenges concern congressional action or inaction regarding legislation. After reviewing legislation pertaining to the Persian Gulf crisis, the court concluded: "[a]lthough styled as a dispute between the legislative and executive branches of government, this lawsuit evidences and indeed is a by-product of political disputes within Congress regarding the applicability of the War Powers Resolution to the Persian Gulf situation." The court refused to "impose a consensus on Congress," but conceded that judicial review of the constitutionality of the War Powers Resolution would be available in the event of a "true confrontation between the Executive and a unified Congress, as evidenced by its passage of legislation to enforce the Resolution." For further discussion of the equitable discretion doctrine, see Notes on the Equitable Discretion Doctrine, *infra*, Section 5.]

. . . .

B. The Political Question Doctrine

The profusion of relevant congressional activity also indicates that this case must be dismissed as a prudential matter under the political question doctrine. In a now-classic catalogue of conditions to which the political question doctrine applies, Mr. Justice Brennan stated in *Baker v. Carr* that:

> [p]rominent on the surface of any case held to involve a political question is found a textually demonstrable constitutional commitment of the issue to a coordinate political department; or a lack of judicially discoverable and manageable standards for resolving it; or the impossibility of deciding without an initial policy determination of a kind clearly for non-judicial discretion; or the impossibility of a court's

24. Senator John Warner proposed the creation of a bipartisan commission to revise the War Powers Resolution. Washington Post, Oct. 6, 1987 at A8, col. 1. Bills to strengthen and repeal the War Powers Resolution also were introduced. *See* H.R. 508, 100th Cong. 1st Sess. (1987) (strengthening War Powers Resolution); H.R. 2520, 100th Cong. 1st Sess. Sec. 2(a) (1987) (repealing War Powers Resolution); H.R. 2525, 100th Cong., 1st Sess. (1987) (repealing War Powers Resolution).

Finally, the Byrd–Warner Amendment, which did not directly refer to the War Powers Resolution, provided alternate procedures for congressional action regarding the Persian Gulf. Am. No. 952 to Am. No. 951 to S.J. Res. 194, 100th Cong., 1st Sess. 133 Cong. Rec. S14018 (daily ed. Oct. 9, 1987). The Byrd–Warner Amendment provided for automatic congressional approval of the President's actions in the Persian Gulf absent congressional passage of a joint resolution to the contrary within thirty days of the President's submission of a report. *Id.*

undertaking independent resolution without expressing lack of respect due coordinate branches of government; or an unusual need for unquestioning adherence to a political decision already made; or the potentiality of embarrassment from multifarious pronouncements by various departments on one question.

Mr. Justice Brennan also stated, with regard to cases concerning foreign relations, that these matters often "lie beyond judicial cognizance" due the need for a "single-voiced statement of the Government's views." Mr. Justice Brennan noted, however, that it would be error to presume that all such cases are nonjusticiable absent "a discriminating analysis of the question posed."

Having analyzed the question in this case, the Court concludes that plaintiffs' request for declaratory relief presents a nonjusticiable political question. If the Court were to grant or deny declaratory relief, and decide whether United States Armed Forces stationed in the Persian Gulf are engaged in "hostilities or . . . [in] situations where imminent involvement in hostilities is clearly indicated by the circumstances,"[48] the Court would risk "the potentiality of embarrassment [that would result] from multifarious pronouncements by various departments on one question." Indeed, such a declaration necessarily would contradict legislative pronouncements on one side or the other of this issue.[50] Moreover, a declaration of "hostilities" by this Court could impact on statements by the Executive that the United States is neutral in the Iran–Iraq war and, moreover, might create doubts in the international community regarding the resolve of the United States to adhere to this position.[51] Because this Court concludes that the volatile situation in the Persian Gulf demands, in the words of Baker v. Carr, a "single-voiced statement of the Government's

48. 48 50 U.S.C. sec. 1543(a)(1).

50. *See supra* notes 22–24 and accompanying text. The Court is not persuaded by plaintiffs' suggestion that the drafters of the War Powers Resolution recognized and, indeed, accepted the risk of multifarious pronouncements by different branches of government, including the judiciary, regarding the existence of hostilities. The drafters did not condone a divided government; if anything, they intended the War Powers Resolution to provide a fixed mechanism by which the executive and legislative branches could make decisions on matters related to war. See 50 U.S.C. sec. 1541(a). The only risk Congress appears to have addressed in its debates is the risk associated with the military and international consequences of the automatic sixty-day withdrawal provision. See e.g., 119 Cong. Rec. 24,660 (1973) (statement of Rep. Frelinghuysen); 119 Cong.Rec. 36,212 (1973) (statement of Rep. Brown).

51. The Court notes that, in an earlier action to enforce the War Powers Resolution with regard to U.S. intervention in El Salvador, Judge Joyce Green of this Court stated that the foreign policy prong of the political question doctrine is not implicated by lawsuits to enforce the War Powers Resolution. *Crockett v. Reagan, supra* note 31, 558 F. Supp. at 898. Judge Green reasoned that the equitable relief granted in such a case would not "dictate foreign policy but rather [would] enforce existing law concerning the procedures for decision-making." *Id.*

The current case is distinguishable from *Crockett*. First, the situation in the Persian Gulf is both more volatile and more critical to U.S. economic interests than the situation in El Salvador. This volatility compels the Court to conclude that, although a decision on declaratory relief admittedly would not dictate foreign policy, an affirmative order might well have international ramifications that could affect U.S. policy in the Persian Gulf. Second, in the current case, Congress has debated and voted on the subject of this lawsuit, but in *Crockett* "Congress [had] taken absolutely no action." *Crockett, supra* note 31, 558 F. Supp. at 899. Therefore, the risk of multifarious pronouncements on a sensitive matter of foreign policy is significantly higher in this case than in Crockett.

views," the Court refrains from joining the debate on the question of whether "hostilities" exist in that region.[53]

The Court nonetheless notes that, had the constitutionality of the War Powers Resolution been squarely presented, "these prudential considerations would [not have been relevant.]"[54] Indeed, if Congress had enacted a joint resolution stating that "hostilities" existed in the Persian Gulf for purposes of section 4(a)(1) of the War Powers Resolution, but if the President still refused to file a section 4(a) report, this Court would have been presented with an issue ripe for judicial review. The Court's task then would have been to analyze the constitutional division of powers rather than to evaluate the seriousness of military activities. The former is within the purview of the judiciary.

IV. CONCLUSION

This Court will not take jurisdiction of this suit to enforce the War Powers Resolution because of the constraints of the equitable discretion and political question doctrines. The constitutionality of the War Powers Resolution is not before the Court. Although adjudication of constitutional questions should not be encouraged, the courts nonetheless would have the responsibility of resolving the constitutionality of this provision if it were properly presented.

Therefore, defendant's Motion to Dismiss is GRANTED and this case is DISMISSED.

NOTES ON LOWRY

1. Lowry *on Appeal*. On appeal, the district court's dismissal in the *Lowry* case was affirmed. In finding that the case presented a non-justiciable political question, the Court of Appeals stated:

---

53. Even if this Court were inclined to add its voice to the debate, this case might well present a non-justiciable political question due to the lack of "judicially discoverable and manageable standards." *Baker v. Carr, supra* note 45, 369 U.S. at 217....

Plaintiffs argue that, although the War Powers Resolution does not define "hostilities or ... situations where imminent involvement in hostilities is clearly indicated by the circumstances", legislative history indicates that Congress intended these terms to be broad and thus to encompass even "relatively minor action[s]." Plaintiffs' Memorandum In Support of Motion for Summary Judgment 22 (quoting H.R. Rep. No. 93–287, 93rd Cong., 1st Sess. (1973)). The intent behind these provisions, plaintiff argues, was to involve Congress in the decision-making process at a relatively early stage of United States military involvement abroad. *Id.* at 22–23.

If one were to take this discussion at face value, it might be possible to make a common-sense determination regarding the existence of hostilities. However, two considerations compel the Court to question this approach. First, and most importantly, the very absence of a definitional section in the Resolution, coupled with debate suggesting that determinations of "hostilities" were intended to be political decisions made by the President and Congress, suggest to this Court that fixed legal standards were deliberately omitted from this statutory scheme. Second, the factual evaluation of "hostilities [and] ... situations where imminent involvement in hostilities is clearly indicated by the circumstances" is always hampered, to some degree, by a Court's lack of access to intelligence information and other pertinent expertise. This is exacerbated by the ever-changing intensity of "hostilities," especially when they are in their early stages. The President must have flexibility in executing military and foreign policy on a day to day basis. Thus, this Court is inclined to conclude that this case does not present judicially manageable standards.

54. *Goldwater v. Carter*, supra note 43, 444 U.S. at 1000–1001.

> Appellants' first claim, that United States Armed Forces are currently involved in present or imminent hostilities in the Persian Gulf, presents a nonjusticiable political question. The claim is in essence that hostilities remain present or imminent because the Gulf cease-fire is unstable. An assessment of the cease-fire's stability, however, would require an inquiry into the likely intentions of the Iranian and Iraqi governments. Although we express no view as to the justiciability of other claims under § 4(a)(1), we hold that an inquiry of this sort is beyond the judicial competence.

Lowry v. Reagan, No. 87–5426 (D.C. Cir. Oct. 1, 1988) (per curiam) (order dismissing appeal). Does the circuit court have a narrower view of the political question doctrine than the district court? Does it matter that equitable discretion was not discussed in the dismissal order? Can you imagine circumstances in which courts could hear challenges under the War Powers Resolution to presidential warmaking? Would it matter if there had been a resolution passed by one or both Houses of Congress declaring that "hostilities" exist or are "imminent"?

2. *Commentary*. For discussion and commentary on the *Lowry* decision, see Glen Lavy, *Constitutional Law: Judicial Restraint and the War Powers Resolution—Lowry v. Reagan*, 11 HARV. J.L. & PUB. POL'Y 849 (1987); Michael J. Glennon, *Foreign Affairs and the Political Question Doctrine,* 83 AM. J. INT'L L. 814 (1989).

3. *Suit at the International Court of Justice*. In two separate incidents during the Iran–Iraq War, the United States made retaliatory attacks against Iranian oil platforms: in October 1987, in response to the missile attack on a reflagged Kuwaiti vessel, and in April 1988, several days after a U.S. warship struck a mine in the Persian Gulf. In 1992 Iran filed suit in the International Court of Justice against the United States over these incidents, claiming they breached a 1955 Treaty of Amity between the two countries. The United States succeeded in challenging two of the three treaty provisions pled by Iran, but a third provision—concerning freedom of navigation and commerce—was accepted by the Court as potentially providing jurisdiction. *See* Case Concerning Oil Platforms (Iran v. U.S.), 1996 I.C.J. 902 (Dec. 12, 1996). The United States filed a counterclaim against Iran asserting that Iran's attacks on U.S. shipping and commerce in the Gulf violated the same treaty provision. Ultimately, the Court found that the evidence presented by both sides was insufficient to establish that the conduct of either side violated a right of freedom of commerce and navigation. The complex decision rendered by the Court can be found at *Case Concerning Oil Platforms (Iran v. U.S.)*, 2003 I.C.J. 90 (Nov. 6, 2003). Although the Court found that the United States had not violated the Treaty of Amity, the Court proceeded to engage in an extensive analysis of why the U.S. attacks on the oil platforms violated international law on the use of force, an analysis thereafter questioned by the U.S. Department of State legal adviser. *See* William H. Taft, IV, *Self-Defense and the* Oil Platforms *Decision*, 29 YALE J. INT'L L. 295 (2004); *see also* James A. Green, *The Oil Platforms Case: An Error in Judgment?*, 9 J. CONFLICT & SECURITY L. 357 (2004).

CAMPBELL v. CLINTON

203 F.3d 19 (D.C. Cir. 2000) (some footnotes omitted).

SILBERMAN, CIRCUIT JUDGE:

A number of congressmen, led by Tom Campbell of California, filed suit claiming that the President violated the War Powers Resolution and the War Powers Clause of the Constitution by directing U.S. forces' participation in the recent NATO campaign in Yugoslavia. The district court dismissed for lack of standing. We agree with the district court and therefore affirm.

I.

On March 24, 1999, President Clinton announced the commencement of NATO air and cruise missile attacks on Yugoslav targets. Two days later he submitted to Congress a report, "consistent with the War Powers Resolution," detailing the circumstances necessitating the use of armed forces, the deployment's scope and expected duration, and asserting that he had "taken these actions pursuant to [his] authority ... as Commander in Chief and Chief Executive." On April 28, Congress voted on four resolutions related to the Yugoslav conflict: It voted down a declaration of war 427 to 2 and an "authorization" of the air strikes 213 to 213, but it also voted against requiring the President to immediately end U.S. participation in the NATO operation and voted to fund that involvement. The conflict between NATO and Yugoslavia continued for 79 days, ending on June 10 with Yugoslavia's agreement to withdraw its forces from Kosovo and allow deployment of a NATO-led peacekeeping force. Throughout this period Pentagon, State Department, and NATO spokesmen informed the public on a frequent basis of developments in the fighting.

Appellants, 31 congressmen opposed to U.S. involvement in the Kosovo intervention, filed suit prior to termination of that conflict seeking a declaratory judgment that the President's use of American forces against Yugoslavia was unlawful under both the War Powers Clause of the Constitution and the War Powers Resolution ("the WPR"). *See* 50 U.S.C. § 1541 *et seq.* The WPR requires the President to submit a report within 48 hours "in any case in which United States Armed Forces are introduced ... into hostilities or into situations where imminent involvement in hostilities is clearly indicated by the circumstances," and to "terminate any use of United States Armed Forces with respect to which a report was submitted (or required to be submitted), unless the Congress ... has declared war or has enacted a specific authorization for such use of United States Armed Forces" within 60 days. Appellants claim that the President did submit a report sufficient to trigger the WPR on March 26, or in any event was required to submit a report by that date, but nonetheless failed to end U.S. involvement in the hostilities after 60 days. The district court granted the President's motion to dismiss, *see Campbell v. Clinton*, 52 F. Supp. 2d 34 (D.D.C. 1999), and this appeal followed.

II.

The government does not respond to appellants' claim on the merits. Instead the government challenges the jurisdiction of the federal courts to adjudicate this claim on three separate grounds: the case is moot; appellants lack standing, as the district court concluded; and the case is nonjusticiable. Since we agree with the district court that the congressmen lack standing it is not necessary to decide whether there are other jurisdictional defects. [For the Court's analysis of the standing issue, see *infra* Section 5 of this Chapter.]

. . . .

Accordingly, the district court is affirmed; appellants lack standing.

SILBERMAN, CIRCUIT JUDGE, concurring:

Appellants argued that we should consider in our standing analysis that if congressmen lack standing only military personnel might be able to challenge a President's arguably unlawful use of force, and it would be undesirable to put the armed forces in such a position. Although that is not a consideration that bears on standing, *see Schlesinger v. Reservists Comm. to Stop the War*, 418 U.S. 208, 227 (1974), that argument leads me to observe that, in my view, no one is able to bring this challenge because the two claims are not justiciable. We lack "judicially discoverable and manageable standards" for addressing them, and the War Powers Clause claim implicates the political question doctrine. *See Baker v. Carr*, 369 U.S. 186, 217 (1962).

Prior litigation under the WPR has turned on the threshold test whether U.S. forces are engaged in hostilities or are in imminent danger of hostilities. But the question posed by appellants—whether the President's refusal to discontinue American activities in Yugoslavia violates the WPR—necessarily depends on the statute having been triggered in the first place. It has been held that the statutory threshold standard is not precise enough and too obviously calls for a political judgment to be one suitable for judicial determinations. *See, e.g., Sanchez–Espinoza v. Reagan*, 770 F.2d 202, 209 (D.C. Cir. 1985) (aid to Contras); *Crockett v. Reagan*, 720 F.2d 1355, 1356–57 (D.C. Cir. 1983) (U.S. advisors in El Salvador); *see also Ange v. Bush,* 752 F. Supp. 509, 514 (D.D.C. 1990) (pre-Gulf War buildup); *Lowry v. Reagan,* 676 F. Supp. 333, 340 n. 53 (D.D.C. 1987) (reflagging operations in the Persian Gulf). I think that is correct. Appellants point to a House Report suggesting that hostilities for purposes of the WPR include all situations "where there is a reasonable expectation that American military personnel will be subject to hostile fire." See H.R. REP. NO. 287, 93rd Cong., 1st Sess. 7 (1973). That elaboration hardly helps. It could reasonably be thought that anytime American soldiers are confronted by armed or potentially armed forces of a non-ally there is a reasonable expectation that they will be subject to hostile fire. Certainly any competent military leader will assume that to be so.

Appellants argue that here there is no real problem of definition because this air war was so overwhelming and indisputable. It is asserted that the President implicitly conceded the applicability of the WPR by sending the report to Congress. In truth, the President only said the report was "consistent" with the WPR. In any event, I do not think it matters how clear it is in any particular case that "hostilities" were initiated if the statutory standard is one generally unsuited to judicial resolution.

Nor is the constitutional claim justiciable. Appellants contend this case is governed by *Mitchell v. Laird*, 488 F.2d 611, 614 (D.C. Cir. 1973), where we said that "[t]here would be no insuperable difficulty in a court determining whether" the Vietnam conflict constituted a war in the Constitutional sense. *See also Dellums v. Bush,* 752 F. Supp. 1141, 1146 (D.D.C. 1990) ("[T]he Court has no hesitation in concluding that an offensive entry into Iraq by several hundred thousand United States servicemen ... could be described as a 'war' within the meaning ... of the Constitution."). But a careful reading of both cases reveals that the language upon which appellants rely is only dicta. (In *Laird* the Court ultimately held that the resolution of the issues was a political question. *See* 488 F.2d at 616.).[1]

Appellants cannot point to any constitutional test for what is war. *See, e.g., Holtzman v. Schlesinger*, 414 U.S. 1316 (1973) (Justice Douglas, in chambers, vacating order of Court of Appeals granting stay of district court's injunction against bombing of Cambodia), 414 U.S. at 1321 (1973) (Justice Marshall, in chambers, granting stay the same day with the concurrence of the other Justices); *Holtzman v. Schlesinger,* 484 F.2d 1307 (2d Cir. 1973) (holding legality of Cambodia bombing nonjusticiable because courts lack expertise to determine import of various military actions). Instead, appellants offer a rough definition of war provided in 1994 by an Assistant Attorney General to four Senators with respect to a planned intervention in Haiti, as well as a number of law review articles each containing its own definition of war. I do not think any of these sources, however, offers a coherent test for judges to apply to the question what constitutes war, a point only accentuated by the variances, for instance, between the numerous law review articles. For that reason, I disagree with Judge Tatel's assertion that we can decide appellants' constitutional claim because it is somehow obvious in this case that our country fought a war.... *Baker v. Carr* speaks of a case involving "a lack of judicially discoverable and manageable standards for resolving" the issue presented, *see* 369 U.S. at 217, not just a case the facts of which are

1. The additional cases upon which Judge Tatel relies with respect to this point were also held to present political questions. *See Massachusetts v. Laird,* 451 F.2d 26, 34 (1st Cir. 1971) ("All we hold here is that in a situation of prolonged but undeclared hostilities, where the executive continues to act not only in the absence of any conflicting congressional claim of authority but with steady congressional support, the Constitution has not been breached."); *Orlando v. Laird,* 443 F.2d 1039, 1043 (2d Cir. 1971) (whether Vietnam conflict required a declaration of war was a political question); *Berk v. Laird,* 429 F.2d 302 (2d Cir. 1970) (denying a preliminary injunction against dispatch of soldier to Vietnam because whether Congress had authorized conflict was a political question).

obscure; the focus is on the standards. Even if this court knows all there is to know about the Kosovo conflict, we still do not know what standards to apply to those facts.

Judge Tatel points to numerous cases in which a court has determined that our nation was at war, but none of these cases involved the question whether the President had "declared war" in violation of the Constitution. For instance, in *Bas v. Tingy*, 4 U.S. (4 Dall.) 37 (1800), the question whether there was a "war" was only relevant to determining whether France was an "enemy" within the meaning of a prize statute. *See id.* at 37 ("[T]he argument turned, principally, upon two inquiries: 1st. Whether the Act of March 1799, applied only to the event of a future general war? 2d. Whether France was *an enemy* of the United States, within the meaning of the law?"). Indeed, Justice Washington's opinion in that case, upon which Judge Tatel principally relies, suggests that whether there was a war in the constitutional sense was irrelevant. *See id.* at 42 ("Besides, it may be asked, why should the rate of salvage be different in such a war as the present, from the salvage in a war more solemn [*i.e.* a declared war] or general?"). It is similarly irrelevant that courts have determined the existence of a war in cases involving insurance policies and other contracts, the Federal Tort Claims Act, and provisions of the military criminal code applicable in "time of war." *See infra* ... (Tatel, J., concurring). None of these cases asked whether there was a war as the Constitution uses that word, but only whether a particular statutory or contractual provision was triggered by some instance of fighting. Comparing *Bas v. Tingy*'s lengthy discussion whether our quarrel with France constituted a solemn or imperfect, general or limited war, *see* 4 U.S. at 40–41, with today's propensity to label any widespread conflict an undifferentiated war, it would not be surprising if an insurance contract's "war" provisions, or even a statute's for that matter, were triggered before the Constitution's.

Even assuming a court could determine what "war" is, it is important to remember that the Constitution grants Congress the power to declare war, which is not necessarily the same as the power to determine whether U.S. forces will fight in a war. This distinction was drawn in the *Prize Cases*, 67 U.S. (2 Black) 635 (1862). There, petitioners challenged the authority of the President to impose a blockade on the secessionist States, an act of war, where Congress had not declared war against the Confederacy. The Court, while recognizing that the President "has no power to initiate or declare a war," observed that "war may exist without a declaration on either side." *Id.* at 668. In instances where war is declared against the United States by the actions of another country, the President "does not initiate the war, but is bound to accept the challenge without waiting for any special legislative authority." *Id.* Importantly, the Court made clear that it would not dispute the President on measures necessary to repel foreign aggression. The President alone

> must determine what degree of force the crisis demands. The proclamation of blockade is itself official and conclusive evidence to the

> Court that a state of war existed which demanded and authorized a recourse to such a measure, under the circumstances peculiar to the case.

Id. at 670.[2] And, to confirm the independent authority of the President to meet foreign aggression, the Court noted that while Congress had authorized the war, it may not have been required to: "*If* it were necessary to the technical existence of a war, that it should have a legislative sanction, we find it...." *Id.* (emphasis added).

I read the *Prize Cases* to stand for the proposition that the President has independent authority to repel aggressive acts by third parties even without specific congressional authorization, and courts may not review the level of force selected. *See* Geoffrey Corn, *Presidential War Power: Do the Courts Offer Any Answers?,* 157 MIL. L. REV. 180, 214 (1998); J. Gregory Sidak, *To Declare War,* 41 DUKE L.J. 27, 54 (1991); Cyrus R. Vance, *Striking the Balance: Congress and the President Under the War Powers Resolution*, 133 U. PA. L. REV. 79, 85 (1984). Therefore, I assume, *arguendo*, that appellants are correct and only Congress has authority to *initiate* "war." If the President may direct U.S. forces in response to third-party initiated war, then the question any plaintiff who challenges the constitutionality of a war must answer is, who started it? The question of who is responsible for a conflict is, as history reveals, rather difficult to answer, and we lack judicial standards for resolving it. *See, e.g.*, *Greenham Women Against Cruise Missiles v. Reagan*, 591 F. Supp. 1332, 1337–38 (S.D.N.Y. 1984) (court lacked judicially manageable standards to decide if placement of U.S. cruise missiles in England was a war-like, "aggressive" act). Then there is the problem of actually discovering the necessary information to answer the question, when such information may be unavailable to the U.S. or its allies, or unavailable to courts due to its sensitivity. *See id.* at 1338. Perhaps Yugoslavia did pose a threat to a much wider region of Europe and to U.S. civilian and military interests and personnel there.

Judge Tatel does not take into account the *Prize Cases* when he concludes that the President was not exercising his independent authority to respond to foreign aggression because "in fact, the Kosovo issue had been festering for years." *See infra* ... (Tatel, J., concurring). As quoted above the President alone "must determine what degree of force the crisis demands." *See* 67 U.S. at 670. Judge Tatel would substitute our judgment

2. Judge Tatel's reliance on the *Prize Cases* as an example of the Court concluding a war exists is misplaced because the Court itself did not label the Civil War such, but instead deferred to the President's determination that the country was at war. *See* 67 U.S. (2 Black) at 670 ("Whether the President in fulfilling his duties, as Commander-in-chief ... has met with such armed hostile resistance ... as will compel him to accord to them the character of belligerents, is a question to be decided by *him*, and this Court must be governed by the decisions and acts of the political department of the Government to which this power was entrusted") (emphasis in original). Therefore, the Court's assertion that "it is bound to notice and to know" the war, *see id.* at 667, provides no support for the proposition that a court itself may decide when in fact there is one. The *Prize Cases* thus refute the suggestion in *Talbot v. Seeman,* 5 U.S. (1 Cranch) 1, 28 (1801), that only acts of Congress are evidence of the existence of a war. *See infra* ... (Tatel, J., concurring).

for the President's as to the point at which an intervention for reasons of national security is justified, after which point—when the crisis is no longer acute—the President must obtain a declaration of war. One should bear in mind that Kosovo's tensions antedate the creation of this republic.

In most cases this will also be an issue of the greatest sensitivity for our foreign relations. Here, the President claimed on national television that our country needed to respond to Yugoslav aggression to protect our trading interests in Europe, and to prevent a replay of World War I. A pronouncement by another branch of the U.S. government that U.S. participation in Kosovo was "unjustified" would no doubt cause strains within NATO. *Cf. United States v. New*, 50 M.J. 729, 739–40 (Army Ct. Crim. App.1999) (lawfulness of U.N. peacekeeping operation in Macedonia was a political question).

In sum, there are no standards to determine either the statutory or constitutional questions raised in this case, and the question of whether the President has intruded on the war-declaring authority of Congress fits squarely within the political question doctrine. We therefore have another basis for our affirming the district court's dismissal of appellants' case.

. . . .

TATEL, CIRCUIT JUDGE, concurring:

Although I agree with Judge Silberman that *Raines v. Byrd*, 521 U.S. 811 (1997), as interpreted by this court in *Chenoweth v. Clinton*, 181 F.3d 112 (D.C. Cir. 1999), deprives plaintiffs of standing to bring this action, I do not share his view that the case poses a nonjusticiable political question. *See supra* (Silberman, J., concurring). In my view, were this case brought by plaintiffs with standing, we could determine whether the President, in undertaking the air campaign in Yugoslavia, exceeded his authority under the Constitution or the War Powers Resolution.

To begin with, I do not agree that courts lack judicially discoverable and manageable standards for "determining the existence of a 'war.'" Brief of Appellee at 36. *See also supra* ... (Silberman, J., concurring). Whether the military activity in Yugoslavia amounted to "war" within the meaning of the Declare War Clause, U.S. CONST. art. I, § 8, cl. 11, is no more standardless than any other question regarding the constitutionality of government action. Precisely what police conduct violates the Fourth Amendment guarantee "against unreasonable searches and seizures?" When does government action amount to "an establishment of religion" prohibited by the First Amendment? When is an election district so bizarrely shaped as to violate the Fourteenth Amendment guarantee of "equal protection of the laws?" Because such constitutional terms are not self-defining, standards for answering these questions have evolved, as legal standards always do, through years of judicial decisionmaking. Courts have proven no less capable of developing standards to resolve war powers challenges.

Since the earliest years of the nation, courts have not hesitated to determine when military action constitutes "war." In *Bas v. Tingy*, 4 U.S. (4 Dall.) 37 (1800), the Supreme Court had to decide whether hostilities between France and the United States amounted to a state of war in order to resolve disputes over captured ships. Because outright war had not been declared, the justices examined both the facts of the conflict ("the scene of bloodshed, depredation and confiscation, which has unhappily occurred," id. at 39) and the acts of Congress that had authorized limited military action:

> In March 1799, congress had raised an army; stopped all intercourse with France; dissolved our treaty; built and equipt ships of war; and commissioned private armed ships; enjoining the former, and authorising the latter, to defend themselves against the armed ships of France, to attack them on the high seas, to subdue and take them as prize, and to re-capture armed vessels found in their possession.

Id. at 41. Given these events, Justice Bushrod Washington concluded that France and the United States were at war both "[i]n fact and in law." *Id.* at 42. "If they were not our enemies," he said, "I know not what constitutes an enemy." *Id.* at 41. One year later, Chief Justice Marshall, focusing on the same conflict with France, said: "The whole powers of war being, by the constitution of the United States, vested in congress, the acts of that body can alone be resorted to as our guides in this enquiry.... To determine the real situation of America in regard to France, the acts of congress are to be inspected." *Talbot v. Seeman*, 5 U.S. (1 Cranch) 1, 28 (1801).

Half a century later, in *The Prize Cases*, 67 U.S. (2 Black) 635, 666 (1862), the Court had to determine whether a state of war, though undeclared, existed "*de facto*" between the United States and the confederacy, and if so, whether it justified the U.S. naval blockade of confederate ports. "As a civil war is never publicly proclaimed, ... its actual existence is a fact in our domestic history which the Court is bound to notice and to know." *Id.* at 667. There was no formal declaration of war, the Court explained, because the Constitution does not permit Congress to "declare war against a State, or any number of States." *Id.* at 668. Yet the Court, guided by the definition of war as "[t]hat state in which a nation prosecutes its right by force," *id.* at 666, determined that a state of war actually existed.

> A civil war is never solemnly declared; it becomes such by its accidents—the number, power, and organization of the persons who originate and carry it on. When the party in rebellion occupy and hold in a hostile manner a certain portion of territory; have declared their independence; have cast off their allegiance; have organized armies; have commenced hostilities against their former sovereign, the world acknowledges them as belligerents, and the contest *a war*.

Id. at 666–67. In making this determination, the Court looked to the facts of the conflict, *id.*, to the acts of foreign governments recognizing the war and declaring their neutrality, *id.* at 669, and to congressional action authorizing the President's use of force, *id.* at 670–71. Given these facts, the Court refused "to affect a technical ignorance of the existence of a war, which all the world acknowledges to be the greatest civil war known in the history of the human race." *Id.* at 669.

More recent cases have also recognized the competence of courts to determine whether a state of war exists. Responding to a challenge to the constitutionality of the Vietnam War, this circuit confronted "the critical question ... whether the hostilities in Indo–China constitute *in the Constitutional sense* a 'war,' both within and beyond the meaning of that term in Article I, Section 8, Clause 11." *Mitchell v. Laird,* 488 F.2d 611, 614 (D.C. Cir. 1973) (emphasis added). The court found "no insuperable difficulty in a court determining whether," given the extent of the hostilities, "there has been a war in Indo–China." *Id.* Once the war was recognized as such, the court saw no problem in "facing up to the question as to whether because of the war's duration and magnitude the President is or was without power to continue the war without Congressional approval," or "whether Congress has given, in a Constitutionally satisfactory form, the approval requisite for a war of considerable duration and magnitude." *Id.* Nor did the court hesitate to determine that once the Gulf of Tonkin resolution had been repealed, later congressional actions appropriating funds for the war and extending the draft were insufficient to "serve as a valid assent to the Vietnam war." *Id.* at 615. Given this absence of congressional approval for the war's continuation, the President had a duty to try "in good faith and to the best of his ability, to bring the war to an end as promptly as was consistent with the safety of those fighting and with a profound concern for the durable interests of the nation—its defense, its honor, its morality." *Id.* at 616. Although the court ultimately declined to answer the question whether President Nixon was in fact fulfilling his duty to end the Vietnam War, *see id.*, it nonetheless made clear that courts are competent to adjudge the existence of war and the allocation of war powers between the President and Congress. Regardless of whether this language is dicta, *see supra* ... (Silberman, J., concurring), *Mitchell* supports my view that this court could resolve the war powers claims presented here. *See also, e.g., Massachusetts v. Laird,* 451 F.2d 26, 34 (1st Cir. 1971) ("The war in Vietnam is a product of the jointly supportive actions of the two branches to whom the congeries of the war powers have been committed. Because the branches are not in opposition, there is no necessity of determining boundaries. Should either branch be opposed to the continuance of hostilities, however, and present the issue in clear terms, a court might well take a different view."); *Orlando v. Laird,* 443 F.2d 1039, 1042 (2d Cir. 1971) ("[T]he constitutional delegation of the war-declaring power to the Congress contains a discoverable and manageable standard imposing on the Congress a duty of mutual participation in the prosecution of war. Judicial scrutiny of that duty, therefore, is not foreclosed by the political question doctrine."); *Berk v. Laird*, 429 F.2d 302, 305 (2d Cir. 1970) ("History makes clear that the congressional power 'to declare War' conferred by Article I, section 8, of the Constitution was intended as an explicit restriction upon the power of the Executive to initiate war on his own prerogative which was enjoyed by the British sovereign.... [E]xecutive officers are under a threshold constitutional duty which can be judicially identified and its breach judicially determined.") (internal quotation marks and brackets omitted).

Without undue difficulty, courts have also determined whether hostilities amount to "war" in other contexts. These have included insurance policies and other contracts, *see, e.g., Western Reserve Life Ins. Co. v. Meadows,* 152 Tex. 559, 567, 261 S.W.2d 554, 559 (1953) ("We are unwilling in deciding this case to shut our eyes to what everyone knows, that there has been ... actually and in reality a war in Korea in which the United States has been seriously engaged."); *Pan Am. World Airways, Inc. v. Aetna Casualty & Sur. Co.,* 505 F.2d 989, 1012–15 (2d Cir. 1974); *Navios Corp. v. The Ulysses II,* 161 F. Supp. 932 (D. Md. 1958), *aff'd,* 260 F.2d 959 (4th Cir. 1958), the Federal Tort Claims Act, *see, e.g., Koohi v. United States,* 976 F.2d 1328 (9th Cir. 1992) (noting that even absent a formal declaration, "no one can doubt that a state of war existed when our armed forces marched first into Kuwait and then into Iraq"); *Rotko v. Abrams,* 338 F. Supp. 46, 47–48 (D. Conn. 1971), *aff'd,* 455 F.2d 992 (2d Cir. 1972), and provisions of military criminal law applicable "in time of war," *see, e.g., United States v. Anderson,* 17 U.S.C.M.A. 588, 1968 WL 5425 (1968); *United States v. Ayers,* 4 U.S.C.M.A. 220, 1954 WL 2280 (1954).

Although courts have thus determined the existence of war as defined by the Constitution, statutes, and contracts, in this case plaintiffs' War Powers Resolution claim would not even require that we do so. We would need to ask only whether, and at what time, "United States Armed Forces [were] introduced into hostilities or into situations where imminent involvement in hostilities [was] clearly indicated by the circumstances." 50 U.S.C. § 1543(a)(1). On this question, the record is clear. In his report to the Speaker of the House and the President pro tempore of the Senate, transmitted "consistent with the War Powers Resolution," President Clinton stated: "on March 24, 1999, U.S. military forces, at my direction ... began a series of air strikes in the Federal Republic of Yugoslavia...." 35 Weekly Comp. Pres. Doc. 527 (March 26, 1999), available at 1999 WL 12654381. Pursuant to the priority procedures of the War Powers Resolution, 50 U.S.C. §§ 1545–46, both houses of Congress responded by expediting consideration of resolutions to declare war, H.J. Res 44, to authorize airstrikes, S.J. Res. 20, and to withdraw troops, H. Con. Res. 82. Defense Secretary William Cohen told the Senate Armed Services Committee: "We're certainly engaged in hostilities, we're engaged in combat." Hearing on Kosovo, Senate Armed Services Comm., 106th Cong., April 15, 1999, 1999 WL 221637 (testimony of William Cohen, Secretary of Defense). President Clinton issued an Executive Order designating the region a U.S. combat zone and March 24 as "the date of the commencement of combatant activities in such zone." Exec. Order No. 13,119, 64 Fed. Reg. 18797 (Apr. 13, 1999).

The undisputed facts of this case are equally compelling with respect to plaintiffs' constitutional claim. If in 1799 the Supreme Court could recognize that sporadic battles between American and French vessels amounted to a state of war, and if in 1862 it could examine the record of hostilities and conclude that a state of war existed with the confederacy, then surely we, looking to similar evidence, could determine whether months of daily airstrikes involving 800 U.S. aircraft flying more than 20,000 sorties and causing thousands of enemy casualties amounted to "war" within the meaning of Article I, section 8, clause 11.

Determining whether a state of war exists would certainly be more difficult in situations involving more limited military force over a shorter period of time. But just as we never shrink from deciding a First Amendment case simply because we can imagine a more difficult one, the fact that a challenge to a different military action might present a closer question would not justify abdicating our responsibility to construe the law and apply it to the facts of this case.

Nor is the question nonjusticiable because the President, as Commander in Chief, possesses emergency authority to use military force to defend the nation from attack without obtaining prior congressional approval. Judge Silberman's suggestion notwithstanding, *see supra.* (Silberman, J., concurring), President Clinton does not claim that the air campaign was necessary to protect the nation from imminent attack. In his report to Congress, the President explained that the military action was "in response to the FRY government's continued campaign of violence and repression against the ethnic Albanian population in Kosovo." 35 Weekly Comp. Pres. Doc. 527 (Mar. 26, 1999), available at 1999 WL 12654381. Although the President also said that military action would prevent an expanded war in Europe, *see* Radio Address of the President to the Nation, March 27, 1999, available at 1999 WL 170552, he never claimed that an emergency required him to act without congressional authorization; in fact, the Kosovo issue had been festering for years. . . .

The government also claims that this case is nonjusticiable because it "requires a political, not a judicial, judgment." The government has it backwards. Resolving the issue in this case would require us to decide not whether the air campaign was wise—a "policy choice[] and value determination [] constitutionally committed for resolution to the halls of Congress or the confines of the Executive Branch," *Japan Whaling Ass'n v. American Cetacean Soc'y*, 478 U.S. 221, 230 (1986)—but whether the President possessed legal authority to conduct the military operation. Did the President exceed his constitutional authority as Commander in Chief? Did he intrude on Congress's power to declare war? Did he violate the War Powers Resolution? Presenting purely legal issues, these questions call on us to perform one of the most important functions of Article III courts: determining the proper constitutional allocation of power among the branches of government. Although our answer could well have political implications, "the presence of constitutional issues with significant political overtones does not automatically invoke the political question doctrine. Resolution of litigation challenging the constitutional authority of one of the three branches cannot be evaded by courts because the issues have political implications. . . ." *INS v. Chadha,* 462 U.S. 919, 942–43 (1983). *See also Baker v. Carr,* 369 U.S. 186, 217 (1962) ("The doctrine . . . is one of 'political questions,' not one of 'political cases.' The courts cannot reject as 'no law suit' a bona fide controversy as to whether some action denominated 'political' exceeds constitutional authority."). This is so even where, as here (and as in the other cases discussed above), the issue relates to foreign policy. *See Baker,* 369 U.S. at 211 ("[I]t is error to suppose that every case or controversy which touches foreign relations lies beyond judicial cognizance"). If "we cannot shirk [our] responsibility" to decide whether an Act of Congress requires the President to impose economic sanctions on a foreign nation for diminishing the effectiveness of an international treaty, a question rife with "political overtones," *Japan Whaling Ass'n,* 478 U.S. at 230, then surely we cannot shirk our responsibility to decide whether the President exceeded his constitutional or statutory authority by conducting the air campaign in Yugoslavia.

The Government's final argument—that entertaining a war powers challenge risks the government speaking with "multifarious voices" on a delicate issue of foreign policy—fails for similar reasons. Because courts are the final arbiters of the constitutionality of the President's actions, "there is no possibility of 'multifarious pronouncements' on this question." *Chadha,* 462 U.S. at 942. Any short-term confusion that judicial action might instill in the mind of an authoritarian enemy, or even an ally, is but a small price to pay for preserving the constitutional separation of powers and protecting the bedrock constitutional principle that "[i]t is emphatically the province and duty of the judicial department to say what the law is." *Marbury v. Madison,* 5 U.S. (1 Cranch) 137 (1803).

CONCLUDING NOTES

1. *Suing to Avoid Military Deployment.* As discussed in greater detail in Chapter 4, Section 4, in March 2003 the United States and allied countries invaded Iraq. The Bush Administration justified the intervention mainly on the ground that Saddam Hussein's government had been pursuing weapons of mass destruction (WMD) in violation of multiple U.N. Security Council resolutions. U.S. Army First Lieutenant Ehren Watada became the first commissioned officer to refuse to be deployed to Iraq. He was court-martialed by the Army in 2006. He said he believed the war was illegal and immoral and that he had a duty to disobey his deployment order. In January 2007, Judge Lt. Col. John Head ruled that Watada would not be permitted to present a defense based on the illegality of the Iraq war: "Applying the law to the facts of this case, the issue of whether the Iraq war is lawful is a nonjusticiable political question." Ruling of the Court: Defense Request for Hearing for Nuernberg Defense, United States v. Watada (U.S. Army Trial Judiciary, 4th

Jud. Cir. Jan. 16, 2007). In early February, Judge Head declared a mistrial for reasons related to Watada's stipulation of facts as to his refusal to deploy with his unit.

2. *Suing to Challenge Uses of Force That Violate International Law.* Can a suit (or a defensive claim) be brought in U.S. court challenging whether the federal government is violating international law in resorting to the use of armed force? For example, should the judiciary entertain complaints rising from U.S. Armed Forces' negligent exercise of police protection during occupation of a foreign territory? *See* Industria Panificadora v. United States, 763 F.Supp. 1154, 1159–61 (D.D.C. 1991) (dismissing as political question suit by Panamanian corporations to recover for damage to property, which was looted or destroyed by Panamanian civilians during the American military operation to remove General Noriega); *see also* Nejad v. United States, 724 F.Supp. 753, 755 (C.D. Cal. 1989) (dismissing as political question suit by families and dependents of passengers who died aboard Iranian airliner shot down by missile from U.S.S. *Vincennes*); Chaser Shipping Corp. v. United States, 649 F.Supp. 736, 737–40 (S.D.N.Y. 1986), *aff'd mem.,* 819 F.2d 1129 (2d Cir. 1987), *cert. denied,* 484 U.S. 1004, 108 S.Ct. 695, 98 L.Ed.2d 647 (1988) (dismissing as political question suit by shipowners whose vessels were damaged by U.S. mines in Nicaraguan port).

As a part of the defense in his criminal trial in U.S. court, deposed Panamanian leader Manuel Noriega sought to argue that the U.S. invasion of Panama in 1989 was unlawful. The court responded:

> Noriega does not, and legally cannot, allege that President Bush exceeded his powers as Commander–in–Chief in ordering the invasion of Panama. Rather, he asks this Court to find that the deaths of innocent civilians and destruction of private property is "shocking to the conscience and in violation of the laws and norms of humanity." At bottom, then, Noriega's complaint is a challenge to the very morality of war itself. This is a political question in its most paradigmatic and pristine form. It raises the specter of judicial management and control of foreign policy and challenges in a most sweeping fashion the wisdom, propriety, and morality of sending armed forces into combat—a decision which is constitutionally committed to the executive and legislative branches and hence beyond judicial review. Questions such as under what circumstances armed conflict is immoral, or whether it is always so, are not ones for the courts, but must be resolved by the political branches entrusted by the Constitution with the awesome responsibility of committing this country to battle.

United States v. Noriega, 746 F.Supp. 1506, 1538–39 (S.D. Fla. 1990), *aff'd,* 117 F.3d 1206 (11th Cir. 1997).

3. *Suing Against U.S. Military Goals, Directives, or Tactics.* In general, courts refuse to hear challenges to the military establishment, its goals, directives, or tactics. *See* Gilligan v. Morgan, 413 U.S. 1, 5–12, 93 S.Ct. 2440, 37 L.Ed.2d 407 (1973) (congressional and executive authority to prescribe and regulate training, weaponry, programs, and standing orders of the National Guard precludes any form of judicial regulation). In other cases nearly unreviewable discretion is found vested in the political branches. *See, e.g.,*

Chappell v. Wallace, 462 U.S. 296, 300, 103 S.Ct. 2362, 76 L.Ed.2d 586 (1983) (Court refuses to entertain suit to recover damages by enlisted military personnel against a superior officer for alleged constitutional violations since the special nature of the military requires two systems of justice and the judiciary is ill-equipped to regulate military discipline); Parker v. Levy, 417 U.S. 733, 749–56, 94 S.Ct. 2547, 41 L.Ed.2d 439 (1974) (special nature and needs that differentiate military society from civil society barred court consideration of legality of more encompassing regulations defining criminal conduct and restricting First Amendment rights in the military); Orloff v. Willoughby, 345 U.S. 83, 90, 73 S.Ct. 534, 97 L.Ed. 842 (1953) (commissioning of officers in Army is matter of discretion within the province of the President over which the courts have no control); Bancoult v. McNamara, 445 F.3d 427 (D.C. Cir. 2006) (forced depopulation of an island in the Chagos archipelago in the Indian Ocean for construction of a U.S. naval base is a nonreviewable political question).

In 2006, the D.C. Circuit refused to entertain a petition for a writ of habeas corpus by a U.S. servicemember who was convicted by a court-martial for violating an order to add the U.N. insignia to his uniform when he was deployed as part of a peacekeeping force in Macedonia, a mission he viewed as unlawful. The decision conveyed a willingness to defer broadly to a military court's application of the political doctrine question:

> Two of the canonical factors from *Baker v. Carr,* 369 U.S. 186, 217 (1962), "an unusual need for unquestioning adherence to a political decision already made," 369 U.S. at 217, and "the potentiality of embarrassment from multifarious pronouncements by various departments on one question," *id.,* are uniquely powerful when the context is a soldier's use of the "self-help remedy of disobedience." Also supporting a broader sweep to the political question doctrine in military trials is the point made by Judge Effron in his concurring opinion-that the doctrine "ensur[es] that courts-martial do not become a vehicle for altering the traditional relationship between the armed forces and the civilian policy-making branches of government" by adjudicating the legality of political decisions. *Id.* at 110. Thus we find no defect in the Court of Appeals' application of the political question doctrine, even though that application might be highly contestable in another context. Compare *Campbell v. Clinton,* 203 F.3d 19, 24–28 (D.C. Cir. 2000) (Silberman, J., concurring) (finding that no "judicially discoverable and manageable standards" exist for application of the Constitution's war powers clause or the War Powers Resolution, 50 U.S.C. § 1541 *et seq.*), with *id.* at 37–41 (Tatel, J., concurring) (concluding that such standards do exist). Given the threat to military discipline, see Court–Martial Transcript at 433, we have no difficulty accepting the military courts' reliance on the doctrine.

United States ex rel. New v. Rumsfeld, 448 F.3d 403, 411 (D.C. Cir. 2006).

At the same time, a challenge by press members to media pool regulations promulgated by armed forces overseas during the First Gulf War did not present a political question. Nation Magazine v. United States Department of Defense, 762 F.Supp. 1558, 1566–68 (S.D.N.Y. 1991). The central issues involved press access and inequality of treatment, which have only an incidental relationship to American foreign policy; they raise claims judicially enforceable under the First and Fifth Amendments. For commentary, see Tom Dienes, *When the First Amendment Is Not Preferred: The Military and Other "Special Contexts,"* 56 U. CINN. L. REV. 779 (1988); Note, *Judicial Review of Constitutional Claims against the Military,* 84 COLUM. L. REV. 387 (1984); Note, *Judicial Review and Soldiers' Rights: Is the Principle of Deference a Standard of Review?,* 17 HOFSTRA L. REV. 465 (1989).

4. *Suing for Wrongful Acts of Foreign Forces.* Should the political question analysis be affected if the alleged misconduct was committed by another country's armed forces? *See* In re Korean Air Lines Disaster, 597 F.Supp. 613, 616–17 (D.D.C. 1984) (dismissing as political question suits arising from deaths of passengers aboard a Korean airliner allegedly shot down by Soviet military aircraft). A key problem in bringing such a suit is not just justiciability, but sovereign immunity as well. *See, e.g.,* Argentine Republic v. Amerada Hess Shipping Corp., 488 U.S. 428, 109 S.Ct. 683, 102 L.Ed.2d 818 (1989) (dismissing for lack of subject matter jurisdiction suit by shipowners whose oil tanker was damaged by Argentine military aircraft during the war over the Malvinas or Falkland Islands; the Court stated that the Foreign Sovereign Immunity Act provides the exclusive basis for federal jurisdiction over suits against foreign states and the suit did not fall within any exception to the rule that a foreign state is immune from the jurisdiction of U.S. courts).

5. *Commentary.* For further commentary, *see* David Cole, *Challenging Covert War: The Politics of the Political Question Doctrine,* 26 HARV. INT'L L.J. 155 (1985); Michael Ratner & David Cole, *The Force of Law: Judicial Enforcement of the War Powers Resolution,* 17 LOY. L.A.L. REV. 715 (1984); Patrick Robbins, *The War Powers Resolution After Fifteen Years: A Reassessment,* 38 AM. U.L. REV. 141 (1988); Note, *Covert Wars and Presidential Power: Judicial Complicity in a Realignment of Constitutional Power,* 14 HASTINGS CONST. L.Q. 683 (1987); Jonathan L. Entin, *The Dog That Rarely Barks: Why the Courts Won't Resolve the War Powers Debate,* 47 CASE W. RES. L. REV. 1305 (1997); John C. Yoo, *Judicial Review and the War on Terrorism,* 72 GEO. WASH. L. REV. 427 (2003).

SECTION 3. POLITICAL QUESTION DOCTRINE WHEN PROTECTING RIGHTS OF INDIVIDUALS

QUINN v. ROBINSON

783 F.2d 776, 781–90 (9th Cir. 1986) (some citations omitted).

REINHARDT, Circuit Judge:

Pursuant to 18 U.S.C. § 3184 (1982) and the governing treaty between the United States and the United Kingdom of Great Britain and Northern Ireland ("United Kingdom"), Extradition Treaty of June 8, 1972, United States—United Kingdom, 28 U.S.T. 227, T.I.A.S. No. 8468 [hereinafter cited as *Treaty*], the United Kingdom seeks the extradition of William Joseph Quinn, a member of the Irish Republican Army ("IRA"), in order to try him for the commission of a murder in 1975 and for conspiring to cause explosions in London in 1974 and 1975. After a United States magistrate found Quinn extraditable, Quinn filed a petition for a writ of habeas corpus. The district court determined that Quinn cannot be extradited because a long-standing principle of international law which has been incorporated in the extradition treaty at issue—the political offense exception—bars extradition for the charged offenses. The United States government, on behalf of the United Kingdom, appeals.

. . . .

II. JURISDICTION TO CONSIDER THE POLITICAL OFFENSE EXCEPTION

. . . .

B. The Political Question Doctrine

The government next argues that because three of the factors enumerated in *Baker v. Carr*, 369 U.S. 186, 217 (1962), are present in this case, the judiciary should abstain, under the political question doctrine, from determining whether the political offense exception applies. The government contends that determining whether the exception applies requires a policy determination of a kind clearly inappropriate for the exercise of judicial discretion, that different pronouncements from the executive and judiciary on matters necessary to a determination of the applicability of the exception could embarrass the government, and that the issue does not lend itself to resolution through judicially discoverable manageable standards. Other circuit courts have considered and rejected the precise arguments advanced by the government in this case. *See Mackin,* 668 F.2d at 132–37; *Eain,* 641 F.2d at 513–18; *cf. Tel–Oren v. Libyan Arab Republic*, 726 F.2d 774, 796–98 (D.C. Cir. 1984) (Edwards, J., concurring) (political question doctrine is a very limited basis for nonjusticiability and does not bar review of a tort claim for damages consequent to terrorist activities), *cert. denied*, 470 U.S. 1003, 105 S.Ct. 1354 (1985). *But see id.* at 826 (Robb, J., concurring) ("[T]here is simply 'no justiciable standard to the political offense.' ") (quoting *Extradition Reform Act of 1981: Hearings on H.R. 5227 Before the Subcommittee on Crime of the House Committee on the Judiciary,* 97th Cong., 2d Sess. 24–25 (testimony of Roger Olson, Deputy Assistant Attorney General, Criminal Division, U.S. Department of Justice)). Like these courts, we recognize the executive branch's interest in matters that touch on foreign policy. However, as did Judge Friendly in *Mackin*, 668 F.2d at 134, we also recognize the individual liberty concerns at stake in cases of this nature and note the Supreme Court's long accepted conclusion that "extradition without an unbiased hearing before an independent judiciary ... [is] highly dangerous to liberty, and ought never to be allowed in this country." *In re Kaine*, 55 U.S. (14 How.) 103, 112 (1852).

In identifying the specific *Baker v. Carr* factors that it claims are present in this case, the government begins by noting that in order to consider whether the political offense exception applies, a court must determine whether a political uprising was in progress in the foreign land when the offense occurred ..... The government contends that such a factual finding requires a policy determination. We disagree. We need not determine whether the uprising was "justified" or was motivated by political forces of which we approve.[6] Rather, we must determine simply whether an uprising was in progress. "The existence of a violent political uprising is an issue of past fact: either there was demonstrable, violent activity tied to political causes or there was not." *Eain,* 641 F.2d at 514. Furthermore, like the Seventh Circuit, we believe that even if unique, sensitive information that is available to the State Department bears on this factual issue, there are adequate mechanisms—such as *in camera* disclosure—for ensuring that the material can be produced for judicial consideration. *See id.* at 514–15.

The government also contends that the presence of a second factor enumerated in *Baker v. Carr* counsels judicial abstention. The government argues that a judicial determination that Quinn's extradition is precluded by the political offense exception would "recognize" political terrorists and would thus constitute a potentially embarrassing pronouncement different than the pronouncements of the executive branch. Like the Seventh Circuit, *see Eain*, 641 F.2d at 515, we do not believe the executive branch has refused to recognize the existence of terrorists. Rather, in some cases, it may have refused to recognize the *legitimacy* of these groups. We fail to see why a judicial acknowledgment that terrorist groups exist would constitute a "recognition" of those groups in the sense of legitimizing their actions. *Cf. Tel–Oren*, 726 F.2d at 822 (Bork, J., concurring) (noting that judicial acknowledgment of effect of PLO on the foreign relations of the United States does not grant the PLO any form of "official recognition" and is similar to the executive branch's commenting on the subject of the PLO while continuing to maintain that the group is not deserving of recognition).

Far from embarrassing the executive branch, assigning to the judiciary the responsibility for determining when the exception applies actually affords a degree of protection to the executive branch. As a political branch, the executive could face undue pressure when public and international opposition to the activities of an unpopular group create conflicts with the treaty obligation created by the political offense exception. *See* Epps, [*The Validity of the Political Offender Exception in Extradition Treaties in Anglo–American Jurisprudence*, 20 Harv. Int'l L.J. 61, 84 (1979)], ("[T]he requesting state is much more likely to be irate if a court deems the fugitive extradictable but the executive reverses that decision."); *cf. Eain,* 641 F.2d at 513 (assignment of this determination to judiciary allows executive branch to avoid risk of political and economic sanctions that could result from discretionary executive refusal to extra-

---

6. Clearly, if application of the exception required us to approve of the political goals of an uprising group, executive discretion in granting protection from extradition would be more appropriate than judicial review. *See, e.g.*, Note, *Terrorist Extradition and the Political Offense Exception: An Administrative Solution,* 21 Va. J. Int'l L. 163, 182 (1980).

dite). By assigning the initial determination of when the exception applies to the impartial judiciary—particularly life-tenured Article III judges—Congress has substantially lessened the risk that majoritarian consensus or favor due or not due to the country seeking extradition will interfere with individual liberty. *See* C. Van den Wijngaert, *The Political Offense Exception to Extradition* 100 (1980) ("[A]dministrative decisions with respect to extradition are much more likely to be influenced by political elements than the decisions of the courts."). The treaty's assignment to the judiciary of the task of determining the applicability of the political offense exception "reflects a congressional judgment that that decision not be made on the basis of what may be the current view of any one political administration." *In re Doherty,* 599 F. Supp. 270, 277 n. 6 (S.D.N.Y. 1984).[7]

Nor does the assignment to the judiciary of the initial determination of the applicability of the political offense exception deprive the executive branch of all discretion to determine that a person claiming the protection of that exception should not be extradited. The executive branch has the ultimate authority to decide whether to extradite the accused after a judicial determination that the individual is, in fact, extraditable. Although the Secretary of State's authority to refuse extradition is presumably constrained by our treaty obligations, the contours of executive branch discretion in this area have never been expressly delineated. Nevertheless, it is clear that the Secretary of State has sole discretion to determine whether a request for extradition should be denied because it is a subterfuge made for the purpose of punishing the accused for a political crime, or to refuse extradition on humanitarian grounds because of the procedures or treatment that await a surrendered fugitive.

Finally, the government points out the difficulty of defining which offenses are of a political character. It suggests that this difficulty demonstrates an absence of judicially discoverable manageable standards, another factor that, according to *Baker v. Carr,* counsels for judicial abstention. As in many areas of the law, and as we discuss further in the remainder of this opinion, there has always been debate about the precise contours of the political offense exception. But the absence of perfect predictive ability in discerning whether a given act falls within the exception is not synonymous with an absence of manageable standards. Rather, as with other complex legal problems, the basic standards that guide us in deciding whether the exception applies are refined on a case-by-case basis as new situations arise. The determination whether there was a violent political disturbance in the requesting country at the time of the alleged

7. We note that since this case was argued, Congress has enacted the 1984 Act to Combat International Terrorism, Pub. L. 98–533, 98 Stat. 2706 (to be codified in scattered sections of 18 U.S.C., 22 U.S.C., & 41 U.S.C.). Section 201(a) of that Act, 98 Stat. 2709, urges the President "to seek more effective international cooperation in combating international terrorism, including ... extradition of all terrorists." This mandate supports some of the substantive conclusions we reach below.... However, it does not assign to the executive initial responsibility for determining when the exception applies or suggest that the relationship between the United States and the requesting nation should be considered when a judicial determination is made regarding whether the exception applies.

acts and whether the acts were incidental to the disturbance, are mixed questions of law and fact, that do not require a political judgment. We fail to see how the judicial construction of 18 U.S.C. § 3184 and the applicable treaty, and the application of these laws to the facts of a given case, differs from all other judicial decisionmaking.

As the Supreme Court noted in *Baker v. Carr*, "it is error to suppose that every case or controversy which touches foreign relations lies beyond judicial cognizance." 369 U.S. at 211.[8] The magistrate properly considered the applicability of the political offense exception to the offenses charged against Quinn, and we as well have a responsibility to construe the treaty and to determine whether "it provides the answer." *Id.* at 212.

[Authors' Note: On the merits, the Ninth Circuit found the political offense exception inapplicable.]

SAREI v. RIO TINTO PLC

487 F.3d 1193, 1197–1208 (9th Cir. 2007).

FISHER, CIRCUIT JUDGE:

This appeal presents questions of justiciability and exhaustion in the context of the Alien Tort Claims Act, 28 U.S.C. § 1350 ("ATCA"). Plaintiffs are current or former residents of Bougainville, Papua New Guinea ("PNG"), who allege that they or their family members were the victims of numerous violations of international law as a result of defendant mining corporation Rio Tinto, PLC's ("Rio Tinto") Bougainville mining operations and the 10–year civil conflict that followed an uprising at the Rio Tinto mine.[1] The plaintiffs appeal the district court's dismissal of their lawsuit seeking redress under the ATCA, which provides that "[t]he district courts shall have original jurisdiction of any civil action by an alien for a tort only, committed in violation of the law of nations or a treaty of the United States." 28 U.S.C. § 1350.

Although several different doctrines of justiciability are at issue here—the political question doctrine, the act of state doctrine and the doctrine of international comity—all in effect provide different ways of asking one central question: are United States courts the appropriate forum for resolving the plaintiffs' claims? The answer to this question

8. Whether the political offense exception applies in a particular case requires an inquiry not unrelated to and somewhat less intrusive than that required to determine if the Attorney General is prohibited from deporting or returning an alien to a country if "such alien's life or freedom would be threatened in such country on account of ... political opinion," 8 U.S.C. § 1253(h) (1982). *See Bolanos–Hernandez v. INS,* 767 F.2d 1277, 1283 (9th Cir. 1984) (evaluating whether threatened persecution is based on political opinion). We note that, rather than considering such a determination as one properly left to the executive branch, Congress has recently amended this section of the Immigration and Nationality Act to *remove* the Attorney General's discretion in making the determination that an alien is likely to be persecuted on the basis of political opinion. *See INS v. Stevic,* 467 U.S. 407, 421 n. 15 (1984) (discussing effect of section 203(e) of the Refugee Act of 1980, Pub. L. No. 96–212, 94 Stat. 102, which amended 8 U.S.C. § 1253(h)).

1. The plaintiffs, who appear as appellants and cross-appellees in this appeal, will be referred to as "plaintiffs" throughout.

turns in part on the weight to be given to a statement of interest submitted by the United States Department of State ("State Department") asserting that continuation of the lawsuit "would risk a potentially serious adverse impact ... on the conduct of [United States] foreign relations." Rio Tinto's cross-appeal also argues that the ATCA requires exhaustion of local remedies—yet another way of questioning whether there is a different and more appropriate forum to develop and try these claims.

We conclude that most of the plaintiffs' claims may be tried in the United States. We hold that the district court erred in dismissing all of the plaintiffs' claims as presenting nonjusticiable political questions, and in dismissing the plaintiffs' racial discrimination claim under the act of state doctrine....

I. BACKGROUND

....

If plaintiffs' allegations are believed, the defendant Rio Tinto, an international mining company, with the assistance of the PNG Government, committed various egregious violations of jus cogens norms and customary international law including racial discrimination, environmental devastation, war crimes and crimes against humanity, with severe repercussions for many citizens of PNG.[2]

A. *The Bougainville Civil Uprising*

Rio Tinto is an international mining group headquartered in London. During the 1960s, Rio Tinto sought to build a mine in the village of Panguna on Bougainville, an island province of PNG. Rio Tinto offered the PNG government 19.1 percent of the mine's profits to obtain its assistance in this venture.

Operations commenced in 1972. Each day, approximately 300,000 tons of ore and waste rock were blasted, excavated and removed from the mine, producing 180,000 tons of copper concentrate and 400,000 ounces of gold annually. The resulting waste products from the mine polluted Bougainville's waterways and atmosphere and undermined the physical and mental health of the island's residents. In addition, the islanders who worked for Rio Tinto, all of whom were black, were paid lower wages than the white workers recruited off island and lived in "slave-like" conditions.

In November 1988, Bougainvilleans engaged in acts of sabotage that forced the mine to close. Rio Tinto sought the assistance of the PNG government to quell the uprising and reopen the mine. The PNG army mounted an attack on February 14, 1990, killing many civilians. In

---

2. A jus cogens norm "is a norm accepted and recognized by the international community of states as a whole as a norm from which no derogation is permitted and which can be modified only by a subsequent norm of general international law having the same character." *Siderman de Blake v. Republic of Argentina,* 965 F.2d 699, 714 (9th Cir. 1992) (quoting Vienna Convention on the Law of Treaties, art. 53, May 23, 1969, 1155 U.N.T.S. 332, 8 I.L.M. 679).

response, Bougainvilleans called for secession from PNG, and 10 years of civil war ensued.

During the 10–year struggle, PNG allegedly committed atrocious human rights abuses and war crimes at the behest of Rio Tinto, including a blockade, aerial bombardment of civilian targets, burning of villages, rape and pillage. Plaintiffs assert that the war has ravaged the island and devastated its inhabitants. Thousands of Bougainville's residents have died; those who survived suffer health problems, are internally displaced and live in care centers or refugee camps or have fled the island.

The plaintiffs filed suit in federal district court seeking compensatory, punitive and exemplary damages, as well as equitable and injunctive relief on environmental contamination and medical monitoring claims, and attorney's fees and costs. They also seek disgorgement of all profits earned from the mine.

B. The State Department's Statement of Interest

After Rio Tinto moved to dismiss the first amended complaint, the district court, by letter dated August 30, 2001, sought guidance from the State Department "as to the effect, if any, that adjudication of this suit may have on the foreign policy of the United States."

On November 5, 2001, the State Department filed a statement of interest ("SOI"). After noting that the district court had not asked the United States to comment on the act of state and political question doctrines, the State Department reported that "in our judgment, continued adjudication of the claims ... would risk a potentially serious adverse impact on the peace process, and hence on the conduct of our foreign relations," and that PNG, a "friendly foreign state," had "perceive[d] the potential impact of this litigation on U.S.-PNG relations, and wider regional interests, to be 'very grave.' " Attached to the SOI was the PNG government's communique stating that the case "has potentially very serious social, economic, legal, political and security implications for" PNG, including adverse effects on PNG's international relations, "especially its relations with the United States."

The plaintiffs responded by submitting as offers of proof declarations from peace agreement participants stating that the agreement would not be affected by the litigation, and in fact would be strengthened. The plaintiffs later asked the State Department to "clarify" its submission to the court. The State Department on May 20, 2002 informed the district court that it "did not intend to file another statement of interest" in response.

. . . .

III. DISCUSSION

A. The Political Question Doctrine

The district court dismissed all of the plaintiffs' claims on the ground that they presented nonjusticiable political questions. We have recently observed that this inquiry "proceeds from the age-old observation of Chief Justice Marshall that 'questions, in their nature political, or which are, by the constitution and laws, submitted to the executive, can never be made in this court.' " *Alperin v. Vatican Bank,* 410 F.3d 532, 544 (9th Cir. 2005) (quoting *Marbury v. Madison,* 1 Cranch 137, 5 U.S. 137, 170 (1803)).

Courts considering the political question doctrine begin with the Supreme Court's elaboration of the appropriate analysis in *Baker v. Carr,* 369 U.S. 186 (1962), where the Court described the doctrine as a function of the separation of powers, and set forth six factors that require the dismissal of a suit under the political question doctrine if any one of them is "inextricable from the case at bar." 369 U.S. at 217. Four are at issue here:

> 1. "a textually demonstrable constitutional commitment of the issue to a coordinate political department";
>
> . . . .
>
> 4. "the impossibility of a court's undertaking independent resolution without expressing lack of the respect due coordinate branches of government";
>
> 5. "an unusual need for unquestioning adherence to a political decision already made"; or
>
> 6. "the potentiality of embarrassment from multifarious pronouncements by various departments on one question."[8]

Id. In the context of foreign relations, "[n]ot only does resolution of such issues frequently turn on standards that defy judicial application, or involve the exercise of a discretion demonstrably committed to the executive or legislature; but many such questions uniquely demand single-voiced statement of the Government's views." *Id.* at 211.

The district court dismissed all of the plaintiffs' claims because it concluded that the fourth and sixth *Baker* factors were present. *Sarei,* 221 F. Supp. 2d at 1197–98. Rio Tinto asserts that the first and fifth *Baker* factors are also present; the plaintiffs claim that none are present. We will address each in turn.

1. Factor One: Constitutional Commitment to Another Branch

In *Alvarez-Machain v. United States,* 331 F.3d 604 (9th Cir. 2003), *rev'd on other grounds, Sosa v. Alvarez–Machain,* 542 U.S. 692 (2004), we adopted the Second Circuit's holding that the resolution of claims brought under the ATCA has been constitutionally entrusted to the judiciary. *Alvarez-Machain,* 331 F.3d at 615 n. 7 (citing and quoting *Kadic,* 70 F.3d at 249 ("The department to whom this [tort suit] has been constitutionally committed is none other than our own-the Judiciary.")); *see also Klinghoffer v. S.N.C. Achille Lauro,* 937 F.2d 44, 48 (2d Cir. 1991) (same); *Tel-Oren,* 726 F.2d at 797 (Edwards, J., concurring) ("[I]n implementing

8. We do not address the second and third *Baker* factors, as Rio Tinto does not contend they are applicable.

section 1350, courts merely carry out the existing view of the legislature that federal courts should entertain certain actions that implicate the law of nations."); Restatement (Third) of the Foreign Relations Law of the United States § 111(2) (1987) [hereinafter Foreign Relations Law Restatement] (cases arising under international law are within the judicial power of the United States).

When the Supreme Court reversed our en banc decision in *Sosa,* it did not question our conclusion that ATCA suits are constitutionally entrusted to the judiciary; it simply determined that the specific claim at issue was not cognizable under the ATCA. To the extent that Rio Tinto seeks to argue that the first *Baker* factor is satisfied as to *all* ATCA claims, or relies on a logic that itself derives from such a view, the argument fails. Given that plaintiffs have properly alleged cognizable ATCA claims, it is not tenable to insist that the claims themselves are not entrusted to the judiciary.

2. Factors Four, Five and Six: Interference With A Coordinate Branch

The fourth, fifth and sixth *Baker* factors are relevant in an ATCA case "if judicial resolution of a question would contradict prior decisions taken by a political branch in those limited contexts where such contradiction would seriously interfere with important governmental interests." *Kadic,* 70 F.3d at 249. To determine whether these factors are present, we must first decide how much weight to give the State Department's statement of interest, which provided the basis for the district court's determination that the fourth and six factors were present.

a. Treatment of SOIs by Other Courts

The Second Circuit has stated that "an assertion of the political question doctrine by the Executive Branch, entitled to respectful consideration, would not necessarily preclude adjudication." *Kadic,* 70 F.3d at 250.[9] As for exactly how much weight to give such statements, two Second Circuit cases suggest that the executive statements should be reviewed for "arbitrariness." In *National Petrochemical Co. of Iran v. M/T Stolt Sheaf,* 860 F.2d 551, 555 (2d Cir.1988), the court found there was "no indication

9. As discussed *infra,* the act of state doctrine also involves a determination of the political repercussions of judicial action, and in that context courts have held that statements of interest, although entitled to respect, are not conclusive. *See Allied Bank Int'l v. Banco Credito Agricola de Cartago,* 757 F.2d 516, 521 n. 2 (2d Cir. 1985) ("This estimation [of the applicability of the act of state doctrine] may be guided but not controlled by the position, if any, articulated by the executive as to the applicability *vel non* of the doctrine to a particular set of facts. Whether to invoke the act of state doctrine is ultimately and always a judicial question."); *Environmental Tectonics v. W.S. Kirkpatrick, Inc.,* 847 F.2d 1052, 1062 (3d Cir. 1988) (holding that the State Department's legal conclusions "are not controlling on the courts," but that its "factual assessment of whether fulfillment of its responsibilities will be prejudiced by the course of civil litigation is entitled to substantial respect"). The Supreme Court also recently stated in the context of assertions of foreign sovereign immunity that "should the State Department choose to express its opinion on the implications of asserting jurisdiction over particular petitioners in connection with their alleged conduct, the opinion might well be entitled to deference as the considered judgment of the Executive on a particular question of foreign policy." *Altmann,* 541 U.S. at 702 (emphasis in original omitted).

that [the SOI] is an arbitrary or ad hoc directive." Following *Petrochemical,* the court in *Matimak Trading Co. v. Khalily,* 118 F.3d 76 (2d Cir. 1997), *abrogated on other grounds by JPMorgan Chase Bank v. Traffic Stream,* 536 U.S. 88 (2002), recognized that an "unexplained change in stance ... might under different circumstances require further inquiry of its ulterior motives," but that "no reason is apparent ... for refusing to defer to the State Department in this case." 118 F.3d at 82 (citing *Petrochemical* for proposition that "court might boggle at 'ad hoc, pro hac vice' directive of the government").

More recently, in *Ungaro-Benages v. Dresdner Bank AG,* the Eleventh Circuit found an ATCA suit justiciable despite a SOI from the government disapproving of the suit, and noted, "This statement of interest from the executive is entitled to deference.... A statement of nation interest alone, however, does not take the present litigation outside of the competence of the judiciary." 379 F.3d 1227, 1236 (11th Cir. 2004).[10] And we recently stated that if "the State Department express[es] a view [on whether a case presents a political question,] that fact would certainly weigh" in the court's determination. *Vatican Bank,* 410 F.3d at 556.

The Supreme Court in *Sosa* stated that "there is a strong argument that federal courts should give serious weight to the Executive Branch's view of the case's impact on foreign policy," *Sosa,* 542 U.S. at 733 n. 21, and prior to *Sosa,* some courts found a nonjusticiable political question where the State Department had indicated that a judicial decision would impinge upon important foreign policy interests. *See, e.g., 767 Third Ave. Assocs. v. Consulate General (Yugo.),* 218 F.3d 152, 160–61 (2d Cir. 2000); *Occidental of Umm Al Qaywayn, Inc. v. A Certain Cargo of Petroleum,* 577 F.2d 1196, 1204 (5th Cir. 1978); *see also In re Nazi Era Cases Against German Defs. Litig.,* 129 F. Supp. 2d 370, 380–83 (D.N.J. 2001); *Burger-Fischer v. Degussa AG,* 65 F. Supp. 2d 248, 281–85 (D.N.J. 1999).

Guided by separation of powers principles, as well as the cases discussed above, we conclude that although we will give the view in the SOI "serious weight," *Sosa,* 542 U.S. at 733 n. 21, it is not controlling on our determination of whether the fourth through sixth *Baker* factors are present. Ultimately, it is our responsibility to determine whether a political question is present, rather than to dismiss on that ground simply because the Executive Branch expresses some hesitancy about a case proceeding.

b. The 2001 State Department SOI in this Case

Although it is a close question, we conclude that the SOI submitted in this case, even when given serious weight, does not establish that any of the final three *Baker* factors is "inextricable from the case," *Baker,* 369 U.S. at 217.

The SOI begins by noting that the State Department has not been "invited" to comment on the applicability of the political question doctrine

10. In *Ungaro-Benages,* the court ultimately dismissed the claims on comity grounds. *Id.* at 1240.

itself. It next states that "[i]n our judgment, continued adjudication of the claims ... would risk a potentially serious adverse impact on the peace process, and hence on the conduct of our foreign relations."[11] The SOI concludes with the observation that "[t]he Government of Papua New Guinea ... has stated its objection to these proceedings in the strongest terms," and that PNG "perceives the potential impact of this litigation on U.S.-PNG relations, and wider regional interests, to be 'very grave.' "[12]

We first observe that without the SOI, there would be little reason to dismiss this case on political question grounds, and therefore that the SOI must carry the primary burden of establishing a political question. There is no independent reason why the claims presented to us raise any warning flags as infringing on the prerogatives of our Executive Branch. As such, these claims can be distinguished from cases in which the claims by their very nature present political questions requiring dismissal. *See, e.g., Vatican Bank,* 410 F.3d at 562 (identifying nonjusticiable political question presented by claims regarding alleged war crimes of an enemy of the United States committed during World War II). The Supreme Court has been clear that "it is error to suppose that every case or controversy which touches foreign relations lies beyond judicial cognizance," and that the doctrine "is one of 'political questions,' not of 'political cases'." *Baker,* 369 U.S. at 211, 217. Without the SOI, this case presents claims that relate to a foreign conflict in which the United States had little involvement (so far as the record demonstrates), and therefore that merely "touch[ ] foreign relations." *Id.* at 211.[13]

When we take the SOI into consideration and give it "serious weight," we still conclude that a political question is not presented. Even if the continued adjudication of this case does present some risk to the Bougainville peace process, that is not sufficient to implicate the final three *Baker* factors, which require "the impossibility of a court's undertaking independent resolution without expressing lack of the respect due coordinate branches of government," "an unusual need for unquestioning adherence to a political decision already made" or "the potentiality of embarrassment from multifarious pronouncements by various departments on one question." *Baker,* 369 U.S. at 217. The State Department explicitly did *not* request that we dismiss this suit on political question grounds, and we are confident that proceeding does not express any disrespect for the executive, even if it would prefer that the suit disappear.[14] Nor do we see any "unusual need for unquestioning adherence" to

11. The SOI adds that "[c]ountries participating in the multilateral peace process have raised this concern" as well.

12. The D.C. Circuit recently confronted a similarly equivocal SOI and, citing our earlier opinion in this appeal, denied an ATCA defendant's petition for a writ of mandamus invoking the political question doctrine. *See Doe v. Exxon Mobil Corp.,* 473 F.3d 345, 354–55 (D.C. Cir. 2007) (interpreting the SOI at issue "not as an unqualified opinion that this suit must be dismissed, but rather as a word of caution to the district court alerting it to the State Department's concerns").

13. We address below the separate question of whether the act of state or international comity doctrines warrant dismissal due to a balancing of the interests of PNG and the United States.

14. We need not determine whether a refusal to honor an explicit request to dismiss would constitute sufficient "disrespect" to warrant dismissal under this factor, although we note the Second Circuit's conclusion in *Kadic* that it would not. *Kadic,* 70 F.3d at 250.

the SOI's nonspecific invocations of risks to the peace process. And finally, given the guarded nature of the SOI, we see no "embarrassment" that would follow from fulfilling our independent duty to determine whether the case should proceed. We are mindful of *Sosa's* instruction to give "serious weight" to the views of the executive, but we cannot uphold the dismissal of this lawsuit solely on the basis of the SOI.[15]

. . . .

We hold that none of the plaintiffs' claims present nonjusticiable political questions. The district court's dismissal on that ground must be reversed.

[The panel opinion was later reheard en banc and remanded to the district court so that it might determine whether to require the exhaustion of local remedies. In doing so, the Ninth Circuit explained that, "[a]s a prudential matter, in this case there is a certain logic to considering exhaustion before considering threshold grounds that may 'deny[ ] audience to a case on the merits' ", such as the political question doctrine. 550 F.3d 822 (9th Cir. 2008) (quoting *Sinochem Int'l Co. v. Malaysia Int'l Shipping Corp.*, 549 U.S. 422, 431, 127 S.Ct. 1184, 1191, 167 L.Ed.2d 15 (2007)).]

We also note that after we issued our original opinion in this appeal the United States filed an amicus brief in support of Rio Tinto's Petition For Panel Rehearing and for Rehearing En Banc. The brief, which was signed both by officials from the State Department and the Department of Justice, does not take issue with our understanding of the SOI, but instead agrees that the "statement did not recommend a specific disposition of any of the legal issues presented" in this case. Brief for the United States as Amicus Curiae Supporting Panel Rehearing or Rehearing En Banc at 14 n. 3.

Indeed, after noting that the SOI was based on concerns in 2001 "which are different from the interests and circumstances that exist today" the government expressly declines to endorse a dismissal of this case based on the SOI. *See id.* ("[T]he United States is not here seeking dismissal of the litigation based on purely case-specific foreign policy concerns." (citing *Sosa*, 542 U.S. at 733 n. 21)).

15. The plaintiffs have submitted recent letters from members of PNG's government urging that the suit will *not* harm or affect the ongoing Bougainville peace process. The Chief Secretary to the Government of PNG, Joseph Kalinoe, wrote to the United States Ambassador to PNG on March 30, 2005 that "the [PNG Government] does not see the case presently before the U.S. courts in the U.S. affecting diplomatic and bilateral relations between our two countries nor does it see it affecting the peace process on the island of Bougainville." And on January 8, 2005, John Momis, the Interim Bougainville Provincial Governor, wrote to the State Department's legal advisor under whose name the SOI was written, "urg[ing] the Government of the United States to support the Prime Minister's position to permit the case to proceed in the courts of America, and to explain that the people of Bougainville strongly desire the case to proceed in America. . . ." Momis' letter includes detail about the current state of the Bougainville peace process, and about how "the litigation has not hindered or in any way adversely affected the peace negotiations." Indeed, the letter adds that "the *Sarei* litigation has helped facilitate the process as it is viewed as another source of rectifying the historic injustices perpetrated against the people of Bougainville." Finally, the letter asserts that "the only way that the litigation will impact [U.S./PNG] foreign relations is if the litigation is discontinued."

Whether these letters are properly authenticated is in dispute. But if they are authentic and their authors accurately describe the current state of affairs in PNG, that would seriously undercut the State Department's concerns expressed in its November 5, 2001 SOI—which itself depended on assessments by local government officials, including Joseph Kalinoe's predecessor as Chief Secretary to the Government of PNG. For whatever reason, the State Department has declined to update the SOI. Under these circumstances, we do not rely on the letters' substantive representations. But the letters, by suggesting there exists today a different reality in PNG from that portrayed in the SOI, illustrate why it is inappropriate to give the SOI final and conclusive weight as establishing a political question under Baker.

CONCLUDING NOTES

1. *The Distinct Treatment of Individual and Constitutional Rights.* As the *Quinn*, *Sarei*, and *Ramirez* cases (Section 1, *supra*) demonstrate, some complaints alleging violations of individual or constitutional rights by government action have been found appropriate for judicial review, even though they implicate the conduct of foreign relations. Chief Justice Marshall first made this distinction in *Marbury v. Madison,* qualifying his assertion of absolute executive discretion in political subjects:

> It follows then that the question, whether the legality of an act of the head of a department be examinable in a court of justice or not, must always depend on the nature of that act.
>
> If some acts be examinable, and others not, there must be some rule of law to guide the court in the exercise of its jurisdiction.
>
> In some instances there may be difficulty in applying the rule to particular cases; but there cannot, it is believed, be much difficulty in laying down the rule.
>
> By the constitution of the United States, the President is invested with certain important political powers, in the exercise of which he is to use his own discretion, and is accountable only to his country in his political character, and to his own conscience. To aid him in the performance of these duties, he is authorized to appoint certain officers, who act by his authority and in conformity with his orders.
>
> In such cases, their acts are his acts; and whatever opinion may be entertained of the manner in which executive discretion may be used, still there exists, and can exist, no power to control that discretion. The subjects are political. They respect the nation, not individual rights, and being entrusted to the executive, the decision of the executive is conclusive. The application of this remark will be perceived by adverting to the act of congress for establishing the department of foreign affairs. This officer, as his duties were prescribed by that act, is to conform precisely to the will of the President. He is the mere organ by whom that will is communicated. The acts of such an officer, as an officer, can never be examinable by the courts.
>
> But when the legislature proceeds to impose on that officer other duties; when he is directed peremptorily to perform certain acts; when the rights of individuals are dependent on the performance of those acts; he is so far the officer of the law; is amenable to the laws for his conduct; and cannot at his discretion sport away the vested rights of others.

1 Cranch (5 U.S.) 137, 165–66, 2 L.Ed. 60 (1803). Is it fair to say that "there cannot . . . be much difficulty in laying down the rule," insofar as it depends on the presence or absence of the rights of individuals? How narrowly, or broadly, should we construe Marshall's reference to "the act of congress for establishing the department of foreign affairs"?

Although it is hazardous to generalize, it would appear that courts have been more reluctant to embrace the political question doctrine in cases involving alleged constitutional violations. *See, e.g.* Lamont v. Woods, 948 F.2d 825, 831–34 (2d Cir. 1991) (Walker, J., concurring in the result) (permitting federal taxpayers' Establishment Clause challenge to the appropriation and expenditure of public funds by the United States for the construction, maintenance and operation of foreign religious schools); Ukrainian–American Bar Ass'n v. Baker, 893 F.2d 1374, 1380 (D.C. Cir. 1990) (permitting claim by organization seeking to integrate persons of Ukrainian descent into the United States that it has a First Amendment right to provide counsel to aliens from Soviet or Eastern Bloc countries seeking asylum); Planned Parenthood Fed'n, Inc. v. AID, 838 F.2d 649, 653–54 (2d Cir. 1988) (permitting First Amendment challenge to clause inserted by the executive branch in family planning grants barring federal assistance to foreign nongovernmental organizations that perform abortions). For a case reminiscent of *Ramirez,* see *Langenegger v. United States,* 756 F.2d 1565, 1568–70 (Fed. Cir.), *cert. denied,* 474 U.S. 824, 106 S.Ct. 78, 88 L.Ed.2d 64 (1985), in which the court held that it was able to determine whether the United States had effected an illegal taking of a citizen's coffee plantation in El Salvador by prompting expropriation of the plantation by the Government of El Salvador—reasoning that the claim concerned whether there had been a taking requiring compensation, and did not challenge the sovereignty of the El Salvador government, the validity of the expropriation, nor executive authority to encourage such an expropriation.

At the same time, "[t]he political question doctrine bars ... review of claims that, regardless of how they are styled, call into question the prudence of the political branches in matters of foreign policy or national security committed to their discretion"—suggesting that the mere fact that a case involves individual rights, even those of private citizens, should not be dispositive. El-Shifa Pharmaceutical Indus. v. United States, 607 F.3d 836, 842 (D.C. Cir. 2010), *cert. denied,* 131 S.Ct. 997, 178 L.Ed.2d 826. El-Shifa stemmed from an American cruise missile strike on a Sudanese pharmaceutical plant that the United States believe to be associated with Osama bin Laden. The plaintiffs, the company owning the plant and its individual owner, sued under the Federal Tort Claims Act seeking compensation for the plant's destruction and for retraction of associated allegations that they were involved in terrorism. The en banc majority held that whether compensation was due because the plant's destruction was " 'mistaken and not justified'," and whether the government's justifications for the attack were false and defamatory, ultimately called into question the decision to launch a military strike abroad and posed nonjusticiable political questions. *Id.* at 844–49. Did the court err? Three judges concurred in the judgment on the ground that the plaintiffs' claims were so legally insubstantial as to deprive the federal courts of subject matter jurisdiction. As to the political question analysis, however, they stressed that the complaint had not alleged the violation of constitutional rights, but only "that the Executive Branch violated congressionally enacted statutes that purportedly constraint the Executive," and that "[t]he Supreme Court has never applied the political question doctrine in cases involving statutory claims of this kind." *Id.* at 852, 855 (Kavanaugh, J., concurring in the judgment). As the opinion explained, applying the political question doctrine under such circumstances would at least implicitly decide that

Congress was without capacity to constrain the executive branch and "would systematically favor the Executive Branch over the Legislative Branch—without the courts' acknowledging as much or grappling with the critical separation of powers and Article II issues." *Id.* at 857. Do you find this position persuasive, both in its distinction of statutory rights and its interrogation of the result? Would the concurrence's dismissal for lack of subject matter jurisdiction, which the majority critiqued as expanding that avenue considerably (*id.* at 849–50), accomplish the same thing under a different guise?

2. *The Distinct Character of Alien Tort Statute Cases*. As the discussion in *Sarei* suggests, the political question doctrine arises with some frequency in ATS cases. Like many claims that potentially present political questions, these cases typically involve conduct by foreign governments overseas; beyond that, they implicate a wariness toward claims predicated on customary international law, and the Supreme Court's suggestion—not formalized, or tied directly to the political question doctrine—of a possible limitation consisting of "case-specific deference to the political branches." Sosa v. Alvarez–Machain, 542 U.S. 692, 733 n.21, 124 S.Ct. 2739, 159 L.Ed.2d 718 (2004); *see* Chapter 2, Section 5.

Before and after *Sosa*, the lower courts have struggled to distinguish and apply these objections to adjudicating ATS claims. *See, e.g.*, Gonzalez–Vera v. Kissinger, 449 F.3d 1260, 1262–64 (D.C. Cir. 2006) (dismissing on political question grounds claims brought, inter alia, under the ATS, against the former Secretary of State and National Security Adviser based on human rights abuses allegedly carried out by Chilean government) (citing *Schneider v. Kissinger, supra* Section 1); In re XE Services Alien Tort Litigation, 665 F. Supp. 2d 569, 601–02 (E.D. Va. 2009) (declining to dismiss on political question grounds action brought by Iraqi nationals against eleven business entities under, inter alia, the ATS, in part because while the defendants allegedly killed or seriously injured the plaintiffs while providing security services for United States government, adjudication of the claims would not require "second-guessing the battlefield procedures, plans, or decisions of the United States Armed Forces, or of any government entity"); Lizarbe v. Rondon, 642 F. Supp. 2d 473, 485–87 (D. Md. 2009) (declining to dismiss on political question grounds action brought against a former Peruvian Army officer under, inter alia, the ATS, because allegations of extrajudicial killing, torture, and war crimes arising out of a massacre in a Peruvian village during a civil war did not relate to any policy decision of the United States or any conduct of U.S. armed forces), *aff'd on other grounds,* 402 Fed. Appx. 834 (4th Cir. 2010) (unpublished op.); In re South African Apartheid Litigation, 617 F. Supp. 2d 228, 283–85 (S.D.N.Y. 2009) (declining to dismiss on political question action brought on behalf of individuals who suffered damages as result of crimes of apartheid in South Africa).

Some courts have indicated that the political question doctrine is less germane because separation of powers principles are not implicated when actions are brought against private parties—at least so long as the private parties were not carrying out policies of the United States. Indeed, the private party may have been acting contrary to those policies. Al-Quraishi v. Nakhla, 728 F. Supp. 2d 702, 726–32 (D. Md. 2010) (declining to dismiss on political question grounds action by Iraqi citizens formerly detained at various military prisons in Iraq against military contractor under, inter alia, the ATS, and discussing comparable cases). Of course, determining whether the complained-of acts were within the scope of U.S. policy may be difficult and sensitive. *See, e.g.*, Corrie v. Caterpillar, Inc., 503 F.3d 974, 979–84 (9th Cir. 2007) (dismissing on political question grounds claims against U.S. manufacturer of bulldozers used by Israeli Defense Forces to demolish homes in the Palestinian Territories and financed by Foreign Military Financing program adopted by Congress and administered by the executive branch).

Other courts have been guided by statements of interest filed by the executive branch that support dismissal, *see, e.g.*, Matar v. Dichter, 500 F. Supp. 2d 284, 293–96 (S.D.N.Y. 2007) (holding nonjusticiable as political question a class action brought by citizens injured or killed in bombing of Gaza apartment building against former head of Israeli General Security Service (GSS) under, inter alia, the ATS, because the claims implicated anti-terrorism policies and diplomacy and "elicited request for dismissal from Department of State and Israel"), *aff'd on other grounds*, 563 F.3d 9 (2nd Cir. 2009); Mujica v. Occidental Petroleum Corp., 381 F. Supp. 2d 1164 (C.D. Cal. 2005) (dismissing on political question grounds action brought, inter alia, under the ATS, by Colombian citizens against oil company and private security firm based on bombing of village by Colombian military, in part because the United States had already expressed its disapproval of Colombian military's actions by ending military assistance to unit involved in bombing and the State Department submitted that litigation would interfere with its approach to encouraging protection of human rights in Colombia), *vacated and remanded on other grounds*, 564 F.3d 1190 (9th Cir. 2009), or by statements of interest that declined to support dismissal on political question grounds or appeared equivocal. *See, e.g.*, Kadic v. Karadzic, 70 F.3d 232, 248–50 (2d Cir. 1995) (declining to dismiss on political question grounds action against self-proclaimed president of unrecognized Bosnian–Serb entity under, inter alia, Alien Tort Statute, and noting that the State Department's statement of interest expressly disclaimed suggesting the political question doctrine should be invoked).

One interesting borderline case was *Doe v. Exxon–Mobil*, 473 F.3d 345 (D.C. Cir. 2007), *cert. denied*, 554 U.S. 909, 128 S.Ct. 2931, 171 L.Ed.2d 876 (2008), which involved a suit by Indonesian villagers who claimed that Exxon had employed as its security forces Indonesian military members who subjected the villagers to various human rights abuses. The district court solicited a letter from the State Department's Legal Adviser as to whether adjudication of plaintiffs' claims would adversely impact U.S. foreign policy interests. The Legal Adviser subsequently advised that the litigation "would in fact risk a potentially serious adverse impact on significant interests of the United States," principally by harming U.S. relations with Indonesia and discouraging foreign investment in Indonesia; however, the letter cautioned that these potential effects on U.S.-Indonesian relations "cannot be determined with certainty." 473 F.3d at 347. When the lower court refused to dismiss the plaintiffs' common law tort claims as raising non-justiciable political questions, 393 F. Supp. 2d 20 (D.D.C. 2005), Exxon–Mobil filed an interlocutory appeal. The D.C. Circuit Court of Appeals found that the district court's decision was not an immediately appealable collateral order, and that Exxon could not be granted its requested writ of mandamus because the district court had not clearly and indisputably exceeded its jurisdiction by refusing dismissal on political question grounds, explaining that:

> We interpret the State Department's letter not as an unqualified opinion that this suit must be dismissed, but rather as a word of caution to the district court alerting it to the State Department's concerns. Indeed, the fact that the letter refers to "how the case might unfold in the course of the litigation" shows that the State Department did not necessarily expect the district court to immediately dismiss the case in its entirety. Thus, we need not decide what level of deference would be owed to a letter from the State Department that *unambiguously* requests that the district court dismiss a case as a non-justiciable political question. *See Sosa v. Alvarez–Machain,* 542 U.S. 692, 733 n. 21, 124 S.Ct. 2739, 159 L.Ed.2d 718 (2004) (suggesting that when the State Department files a statement of interest "there is a strong argument that federal courts should give serious weight to the Executive Branch's view of the case's impact on foreign policy"). Of course, if we have misinterpreted this letter, or if the State Department has additional concerns about this litigation, it is free to file further letters or briefs with the district court expressing its views. *Cf. Republic of Austria v. Altmann,* 541 U.S. 677, 701, 124 S.Ct. 2240, 159 L.Ed.2d 1 (2004) (noting that "nothing in our holding prevents the State Department from filing statements of interest suggesting that courts decline to exercise jurisdiction in particular cases implicating foreign sovereign immunity"). But given the letter before us in the record, we cannot say it is "indisputable" that the district court erroneously failed to dismiss the plaintiffs' claims under the political question doctrine, no matter what level of deference is owed to the State Department's letter.

Id. at 354.

If the State Department's letter was an unqualified opinion that the suit must be dismissed, should a federal court be bound to defer to that opinion? (And would it matter if the letter cited as a basis the political question doctrine, or the *Sosa* footnote concerning "case-specific deference to the political branches"?) Should a court be bound by a letter that is an unqualified opinion that the suit must go forward? Would it matter if the U.S. government were a party in the case? Should a letter sent to the court on behalf of Congress calling either for or against dismissal also be given deference? What if the political branches are in conflict?

In reviewing the issue subsequent to its decision on interlocutory appeal, the D.C. Circuit stood by its analysis and refused to dismiss on political question grounds. The court noted not only the qualified statement by the U.S. Department of State, but also: (1) a subsequent amicus brief by the United States on petition for writ of certiorari that also refrained from seeking dismissal; (2) the Department's failure to file any later statement of interest; and (3) the Department's acknowledgement in other proceedings that it would explicitly seek dismissal when appropriate. The court, however, again invited the Department to assert an unambiguous position, which might be a basis for dismissal. Doe v. Exxon Mobil Corp., 2011 WL 2652384 (D.C. Cir. 2011).

2. *The Distinct Character of Political Question Determinations.* Although courts may be reluctant to deem nonjusticiable cases involving individual and constitutional rights, decisions on the merits often give considerable deference to government explanations for challenged governmental conduct. *See* Haig v. Agee, 453 U.S. 280, 101 S.Ct. 2766, 69 L.Ed.2d 640 (1981) (President, through Secretary of State, has authority to revoke passport in order to restrict holder's ability to travel to foreign countries where his activities may damage national security or foreign policy of the United States). The courts' reasoning often reflects traditional political question concerns. In the context of immigration and naturalization, the Supreme Court has stated that "any policy toward aliens is vitally and intricately interwoven with contemporaneous policies in regard to the conduct of foreign relations, the war power, and the maintenance of a republican form of government. Such matters are so exclusively trusted to the political branches of government as to be largely immune from judicial inquiry or interference." Harisiades v. Shaughnessy, 342 U.S. 580, 588–89, 72 S.Ct. 512, 96 L.Ed. 586 (1952). *See also* Mathews v. Diaz, 426 U.S. 67, 81, 96 S.Ct. 1883, 48 L.Ed.2d 478 (1976) (in cases involving rights of aliens courts should use a narrow standard of review to allow for "flexibility in policy choices rather than the rigidity often characteristic of constitutional adjudication"). One Supreme Court case suggested in a footnote that it was an open question "whether there may be actions of the Congress with respect to aliens that are so essentially political in character as to be non-justiciable." Fiallo v. Bell, 430 U.S. 787, 793 n. 5, 97 S.Ct. 1473, 52 L.Ed.2d 50 (1977).

Just as some merits decisions may conceal political question concerns, cases nominally decided on political question grounds may just as easily be depicted as involving the merits. *See, e.g.*, Smith v. Reagan, 844 F.2d 195, 198–200 (4th Cir. 1988) (dismissing as political question a challenge to the adequacy of the President's efforts, required by the Hostage Act, to secure release of American citizens who remain in captivity in Southeast Asia).

An important recent decision, *Zivotofsky v. Sec'y of State*, 571 F.3d 1227 (D.C. Cir. July 10, 2009), presents this choice sharply. The Foreign Relations Authorization Act for 2003 challenged—as Congress has, repeatedly—the executive branch's refusal to recognize Jerusalem as the capital of Israel. Section 214(d) (Pub. L. No. 107–228, 116 Stat. 1350 (2002) (codified at 22 U.S.C. § 2651 note (2006))) provides that in issuing a passport (among other things) the Secretary of State "shall, upon the request of the citizen or the citizen's legal guardian, record the place of birth as Israel." President Bush issued a signing statement indicating that he regarded section 214 as advisory only, explaining that dictating the United States' position on the status of Jerusalem would "impermissibly interfere with the President's constitutional authority to formulate the position of the United States, speak for the Nation in international affairs, and determine the terms on which recognition is given to foreign states." President George W. Bush, Statement on Signing the Foreign Relations Authorization Act, 38 WEEKLY COMP. PRES. DOC. 1659 (2002).

When the mother of a child of U.S. citizens born in Jerusalem sought a passport and report of birth identifying his birthplace as "Jerusalem, Israel," the U.S. Consulate in Jerusalem followed State Department guidelines and instead listed "Jerusalem" only. After the child and parents sued, the district court initially dismissed on standing grounds and, following reversal (Zivotofsky v. Sec'y of State, 444 F.3d 614 (D.C. Cir. 2006)), dismissed instead on the basis that the action presented a political question—which was upheld on appeal. The panel majority took the view that the issue was "whether the State Department can lawfully refuse to record his place of birth as 'Israel' in the face of a statute that directs it to do so," rather than (as a concurrence by Judge Edwards put it) "[w]hether § 214(d) ... is a constitutionally valid enactment." 571 F.3d at 1230. Thus refusing the invitation "to order the State Department to mark official government documents in a manner that would directly contravene the President's policy ... [and] call into question the President's exercise of the recognition power," the majority held that "Zivotofsky's claim presents a nonjusticiable political question because it trenches upon the President's constitutionally committed recognition power." *Id.* at 1232.

Judge Edwards concurred with the panel majority on the basis that that Section 214(d) infringed on the President's exclusive recognition power. *Id.* at 1233, 1244–45 (Edwards, J., concurring). However, his concurrence criticized the majority's reliance on the political question doctrine, and he summed his argument anew in an opinion issued in connection with the denial of rehearing en banc. 610 F.3d 84, 84 (D.C. Cir. 2010) (Edwards, J., statement regarding the denial of en banc review). Judge Edwards argued that "the court has effectively conflated the distinction between cases involving justiciable separation of powers issues and nonjusticiable political questions"; by his lights, the two questions before the court were "(1) whether the Executive's passport policy reflects an action taken within the President's exclusive power to recognize foreign sovereigns; and, if so, (2) whether Congress' enactment of § 214(d) impermissibly intrudes on the President's exclusive power to recognize foreign sovereigns," and both were "constitutionally committed to the Judicial Branch to decide." *Id.* at 85–86. Put differently:

> In a case of this sort, the political question doctrine would bar judicial review only if the precise matter to be decided has been constitutionally committed to the exclusive authority of one of the political branches of government. ... Because there is nothing in the Constitution that gives either political branch the exclusive authority to determine whether the Executive has acted pursuant to the recognition power or whether a congressional enactment has infringed the Executive's power, the court must resolve the issues.

Id. at 87–88. The Supreme Court granted certiorari, not only on the political question issue presented by the petition but also on whether Section 214 "impermissibly infringes the President's power to recognize foreign sovereigns." M.B.Z. ex rel. Zivotofsky v. Clinton, 131 S.Ct. 2897, 179 L.Ed.2d 1187 (2011) (Nos. 10–699, 10A227). Which of these two bases would be a better means for resolving the controversy? For commentary, see Robert J. Reinstein, *Recognition: A Case Study on the Original Understanding of Executive Power*, 45 U. RICHMOND L. REV. 801 (2011).

3. *Detainees, Habeas, and the Political Question Doctrine.* Many cases in the "War on Terror" hinge on the justiciability of habeas corpus petitions, both statutory and constitutional. In cases such as *Hamdi*, *Hamdan* and *Rasul* (*see* Chapter 2, Section 7), the Supreme Court has remained remarkably silent on the issue of justiciability, including the political question doctrine. One case overtly addressing the political question doctrine in this context was *Omar v. Harvey*, 479 F.3d 1 (D.C. Cir. 2007), which confronted a petition for a writ of habeas corpus from a dual American–Jordanian citizen arrested in Iraq and held at first at various military detention facilities there. The petitioner challenged his detention, on the ground that it violated the U.S. Constitution, federal law, Army regulations, and international law; he also challenged plans to transfer him to Iraqi custody, arguing that the military lacked statutory or treaty authorization to do so and that transferring him to a government likely to torture him would violate the Constitution. The court of appeals concluded that both claims were justiciable. As to detention, it relied primarily on *Hamdi*, acknowledging that *Hamdi* did not directly involve a political question issue. As to transfer, the court held that whether the executive branch possessed the necessary statutory or treaty authorization, or needed it, presented difficult questions of constitutional law that could be "resolve[d] without making any judgments about foreign policy or the war in Iraq."

The Supreme Court later vacated the court of appeals decision. Munaf v. Geren, 553 U.S. 674, 128 S.Ct. 2207, 171 L.Ed.2d 1 (2008). The Court concluded that jurisdiction was properly exercised over habeas corpus petitions by U.S. citizens challenging their detention by multinational forces operating under the direction of U.S. military leaders in Iraq. *Id.* at 685–88 (distinguishing Hirota v. MacArthur, 338 U.S. 197, 69 S.Ct. 197, 93 L.Ed. 1902 (1948)). However, it also held that this jurisdiction was not properly exercised to enjoin the U.S. military from "transferring individuals detained within another sovereign's territory to that sovereign's government for criminal prosecution," bearing in mind both the need to avoid intruding on executive branch authority in military and national security matters and the respect owed Iraq's right to punish criminal offenses committed within its territory. *Id.* at 689, 692–700. Regarding the claim that the transferees would be mistreated, the Court noted that the U.S. government had not determined there to be a likelihood of torture and that second-guessing that conclusion would undermine the capacity of the United States to speak with one voice in foreign affairs. *Id.* at 702–03. At bottom, did the Supreme Court's emphasis on separation of power considerations and the need to defer to the executive branch differ so radically from accepting a political question defense to the transfer claim?

SECTION 4. RIPENESS AND MOOTNESS

In the context of foreign affairs litigation, the concepts of ripeness and mootness also sometimes come into play. For example, in 1990, while President George H.W. Bush was deploying armed forces in preparation for the Gulf War between the United States and Iraq, fifty-three representatives and one senator brought an action on the premise that an initiation of offensive military action was imminent and that such action would be unlawful in the absence of a declaration of war by Congress. The government argued that it was impermissible for the judiciary to question the President's conduct because it was impossible for the court to isolate responsibility for the war-declaring power; there were no judicially discoverable and manageable standards to determine whether the United States was at war; and resolution of the suit would represent an intrusion by the judiciary into foreign affairs, an area constitutionally committed to the political branches.

In *Dellums v. Bush* (also extracted in Chapter 4, Section 4), the District Court for the District of Columbia responded:

> While the Constitution grants to the political branches, and in particular to the Executive, responsibility for conducting the nation's foreign affairs, it does not follow that the judicial power is excluded from the resolution of cases merely because they may touch upon such affairs. The court must instead look at "the particular question posed" in the case. *Baker v. Carr,* 369 U.S. at 211. In fact, courts are routinely deciding cases that touch upon or even have a substantial impact on foreign and defense policy. *Japan Whaling Assn. v. American Cetacean Soc.,* 478 U.S. 221, 106 S.Ct. 2860, 92 L.Ed.2d 166 (1986); *Dames & Moore v. Regan*, 453 U.S. 654, 101 S.Ct. 2972, 69 L.Ed.2d 918 (1981); *Youngstown Sheet & Tube Co. v. Sawyer*, 343 U.S. 579, 72 S.Ct. 863, 96 L.Ed. 1153 (1952); *United States v. Curtiss–Wright Export Corp.*, 299 U.S. 304, 57 S.Ct. 216, 81 L.Ed. 255 (1936).
>
> The Department's argument also ignores the fact that courts have historically made determinations about whether this country was at war for many other purposes—the construction of treaties, statutes, and even insurance contracts. These judicial determinations of a de facto state of war have occurred even in the absence of a congressional declaration.
>
> Plaintiffs allege in their complaint that 230,000 American troops are currently deployed in Saudi Arabia and the Persian Gulf area, and that by the end of this month the number of American troops in the region will reach 380,000. They also allege, in light of the President's obtaining the support of the United Nations Security Council in a resolution allowing for the use of force against Iraq, that he is planning for an offensive military attack on Iraqi forces.
>
> Given these factual allegations and the legal principles outlined above, the Court has no hesitation in concluding that an offensive entry into Iraq by several hundred thousand United States servicemen under the conditions described above could be described as a "war" within the meaning of Article I, Section 8, Clause 11, of the Constitution. To put it another way: the Court is not prepared to read out of the Constitution the clause granting to the Congress, and to it alone, the authority "to declare war."

Dellums v. Bush, 752 F.Supp. 1141, 1146 (D.D.C. 1990) (footnotes omitted).

The claim was held non-justiciable, however, because it lacked ripeness, not because of the nature of the claim. According to the court, as of the time the suit was filed: "No one knows the position of the Legislative Branch on the issue of war or peace with Iraq; certainly no one, including this Court, is able to ascertain the congressional position on that issue on the basis of this lawsuit brought by fifty-three members of the House of Representatives and one member of the U.S. Senate." *Id.* at 1149 (footnote omitted). The court argued that its position was consistent with Justice Powell's concurrence in *Goldwater v. Carter,* 444 U.S. 996, 997–1002, 100 S.Ct. 533, 62 L.Ed.2d 428 (1979). "[A] dispute between Congress and the President is not ready for judicial review unless and until each branch has taken action asserting its constitutional authority." *Id.* at 997.

Is ripeness a better rationale for non-justiciability than the political question doctrine in the context of delimiting constitutional responsibility for war-making? What practical obstacles are likely to arise to block judicial review once the "ripeness" test has been met?

DOE v. BUSH

323 F.3d 133, 134–39 (1st Cir. 2003).

LYNCH, CIRCUIT JUDGE.

Plaintiffs are active-duty members of the military, parents of military personnel, and members of the U.S. House of Representatives.[1] They filed a complaint in district court seeking a preliminary injunction to prevent the defendants, President George W. Bush and Secretary of Defense Donald Rumsfeld, from initiating a war against Iraq. They assert that such an action would violate the Constitution. The district court dismissed the suit, and plaintiffs appeal. We affirm the dismissal.

In October 2002, Congress passed the Authorization for Use of Military Force Against Iraq Resolution of 2002 (the "October Resolution"), Pub L. No. 107–243, 116 Stat. 1498. Plaintiffs argue that the October Resolution is constitutionally inadequate to authorize the military offensive that defendants are now planning against Iraq. *See* U.S. Const. art. I, § 8, cl. 11 (granting Congress the power "[t]o declare war"). They base this argument on two theories. They argue that Congress and the President are in collision—that the President is about to act in violation of the October Resolution. They also argue that Congress and the President are in collusion—that Congress has handed over to the President its exclusive power to declare war.

---

1. The military personnel and some of the parents are proceeding under pseudonyms, pursuant to an order by the district court that is not before us. The members of the House of Representatives are John Conyers, Dennis Kucinich, Jesse Jackson, Jr., Sheila Jackson Lee, Jim McDermott, José E. Serrano, Danny K. Davis, Maurice D. Hinchey, Carolyn Kilpatrick, Pete Stark, Diane Watson, and Lynn C. Woolsey. We also acknowledge the assistance provided by amicus curiae on behalf of the plaintiffs.

In either case, plaintiffs argue, judicial intervention is necessary to preserve the principle of separation of powers which undergirds our constitutional structure. Only the judiciary, they argue, has the constitutionally assigned role and the institutional competence to police the boundaries of the constitutional mandates given to the other branches: Congress alone has the authority to declare war and the President alone has the authority to make war.

The plaintiffs argue that important and increasingly vital interests are served by the requirement that it be Congress which decides whether to declare war. Quoting Thomas Jefferson, they argue that congressional involvement will slow the "dogs of war"; that Congress, the voice of the people, should make this momentous decision, one which will cost lives; and that congressional support is needed to ensure that the country is behind the war, a key element in any victory. They also argue that, absent an attack on this country or our allies, congressional involvement must come prior to war, because once war has started, Congress is in an uncomfortable default position where the use of its appropriations powers to cut short any war is an inadequate remedy.

The defendants are equally eloquent about the impropriety of judicial intrusion into the "extraordinarily delicate foreign affairs and military calculus, one that could be fatally upset by judicial interference." Such intervention would be all the worse here, defendants say, because Congress and the President are in accord as to the threat to the nation and the legitimacy of a military response to that threat.

The case before us is a somber and weighty one. We have considered these important concerns carefully, and we have concluded that the circumstances call for judicial restraint. The theory of collision between the legislative and executive branches is not suitable for judicial review, because there is not a ripe dispute concerning the President's acts and the requirements of the October Resolution passed by Congress. By contrast, the theory of collusion, by its nature, assumes no conflict between the political branches, but rather a willing abdication of congressional power to an emboldened and enlarged presidency. That theory is not fit for judicial review for a different, but related, reason: Plaintiffs' claim that Congress and the President have transgressed the boundaries of their shared war powers, as demarcated by the Constitution, is presently insufficient to present a justiciable issue. Common to both is our assessment that, before courts adjudicate a case involving the war powers allocated to the two political branches, they must be presented with a case or controversy that clearly raises the specter of undermining the constitutional structure.[2]

---

2. We do not reach all the issues concerning the justiciability of the case, including the question of the parties' standing. There is no required sequence to the consideration of the various non-merits issues presented here. *See Ruhrgas AG v. Marathon Oil Co.*, 526 U.S. 574, 584–85 (1999); *In re Middlesex Power Equip. & Marine, Inc.*, 292 F.3d 61, 66 n. 1 (1st Cir. 2002).

I.

Tensions between the United States and Iraq have been high at least since Iraq invaded neighboring Kuwait in 1990. In 1991, the United States led an international coalition in the Persian Gulf War, which drove Iraqi forces from Kuwait. Before that conflict, Congress passed a resolution quite similar to the October Resolution. *See* Pub. L. No. 102–1, 105 Stat. 3 (1991). As part of the ceasefire ending the Gulf War, Iraq agreed to United Nations Security Council Resolution 687, which required that Iraq end the development of nuclear, biological, and chemical weapons, destroy all existing weapons of this sort and their delivery systems, and allow United Nations weapons inspections to confirm its compliance with these terms. *See* S.C. Res. 687, U.N. SCOR, 46th Sess., 2981st mtg., U.N. Doc. S/RES/687 (1991). Since that time, Iraq has repeatedly been in breach of this agreement by, among other things, blocking inspections and hiding banned weapons. Iraq ended cooperation with the weapons inspection program in 1998. Since 1991, the United States and other nations have enforced a no-fly zone near the Kuwaiti border and on several occasions have launched missile strikes against Iraq.

Congress has been engaged in the American response to Iraqi non-compliance throughout this period. It was well-informed about ongoing American military activities, enforcement of the no-fly zone, and the missile strikes. In 1998, Congress passed a joint resolution which chronicled Iraqi noncompliance and declared that "the Government of Iraq is in material and unacceptable breach of its international obligations, and therefore the President is urged to take appropriate action, in accordance with the Constitution and relevant laws of the United States, to bring Iraq into compliance with its international obligations." Pub. L. No. 105–235, 112 Stat. 1538, 1541 (1998). Later that year, Congress also passed the Iraq Liberation Act of 1998, Pub. L. No. 105–338, 112 Stat. 3178. This statute authorized assistance, including military equipment and training, for "Iraqi democratic opposition organizations," and declared that it should be United States policy to remove Iraqi leader Saddam Hussein from power. *Id.* §§ 3, 4, 112 Stat. at 3179.[3]

The United Nations has also remained engaged in the dispute ever since the Persian Gulf War. It supervised weapons inspections, supported economic sanctions against Iraq, and, through the Security Council, repeatedly passed resolutions declaring that Iraq was not fulfilling the conditions of Resolution 687. On September 12, 2002, President Bush addressed the United Nations General Assembly. There he called for a renewed effort to demand Iraqi disarmament and indicated that he thought military force would be necessary if diplomacy continued to fail. In response, Iraq agreed to allow inspectors back into the country, but it has failed to comply fully with the earlier Security Council resolutions.

3. Another provision of the Iraq Liberation Act stated that, other than the military assistance provision in § 4(a)(2), the Act should not "be construed to authorize or otherwise speak to the use of United States Armed Forces." § 8, 112 Stat. at 3181. Nonetheless, this statute provides important context.

The week after his September 12 speech at the United Nations, President Bush proposed language for a congressional resolution supporting the use of force against Iraq. Detailed and lengthy negotiations between and among congressional leaders and the Administration hammered out a revised and much narrower version of the resolution. The House of Representatives passed this measure by a vote of 296 to 133 on October 10, 2002; the Senate followed suit on October 11 by a vote of 77 to 23. The full text of the October Resolution is attached as an appendix to this opinion.

On November 8, 2002, the Security Council passed Resolution 1441, which declared that Iraq remained in material breach of its obligations and offered "a final opportunity to comply with its disarmament obligations." S.C. Res. 1441, U.N. SCOR, 57th Sess., 4644th mtg., U.N. Doc. S/RES/1441 (2002). It also noted that "the Council has repeatedly warned Iraq that it will face serious consequences as a result of its continued violations of its obligations." *Id.* In diplomatic parlance, the phrase "serious consequences" generally refers to military action. More than 200,000 United States troops are now deployed around Iraq, preparing for the possibility of an invasion.

The complaint was filed, along with motions for preliminary injunction and expedited hearing, on February 13, 2003. The district court heard oral argument on February 24 and denied the motion in an order issued that day. The court released a more detailed written opinion on February 27. *See Doe v. Bush,* 240 F. Supp. 2d 95 (D. Mass. 2003). Plaintiffs appealed and this court expedited consideration, hearing oral argument on March 4, 2003 and receiving additional briefing on March 11. Because the case was dismissed on a pretrial motion, we independently review the claims afresh.

II.

The Constitution reserves the war powers to the legislative and executive branches. This court has declined the invitation to become involved in such matters once before. Over thirty years ago, the First Circuit addressed a war powers case challenging the constitutionality of the Vietnam War on the basis that Congress had not declared war. *Massachusetts v. Laird*, 451 F.2d 26 (1st Cir. 1971). The court found that other actions by Congress, such as continued appropriations to fund the war over the course of six years, *id.* at 34, provided enough indication of congressional approval to put the question beyond the reach of judicial review:

> The war in Vietnam is a product of the jointly supportive actions of the two branches to whom the congeries of the war powers have been committed. Because the branches are not in opposition, there is no necessity of determining boundaries. Should either branch be opposed to the continuance of hostilities, however, and present the issue in clear terms, a court might well take a different view. This question we do not face.

Id. Applying this precedent to the case at hand today, the district court concluded, "[T]here is a day to day fluidity in the situation that does not amount to resolute conflict between the branches—but that does argue against an uninformed judicial intervention," *Doe*, 240 F. Supp. 2d at 96. *See Drinan v. Nixon*, 364 F. Supp. 854, 858 (D. Mass. 1973); *see also DaCosta v. Laird,* 471 F.2d 1146, 1157 (2d Cir. 1973); *Orlando v. Laird,* 443 F.2d 1039, 1043 (2d Cir. 1971); *cf. United States v. Kin–Hong*, 110 F.3d 103, 111 (1st Cir. 1997) (drawing support from political question doctrine in case where "questions involve an evaluation of contingent political events").

The lack of a fully developed dispute between the two elected branches, and the consequent lack of a clearly defined issue, is exactly the type of concern which causes courts to find a case unripe. In his concurring opinion in *Goldwater v. Carter*, 444 U.S. 996 (1979), Justice Powell stated that courts should decline, on ripeness grounds, to decide "issues affecting the allocation of power between the President and Congress until the political branches reach a constitutional impasse." *Id.* at 997 (Powell, J., concurring). A number of courts have adopted Justice Powell's ripeness reasoning in cases involving military powers. *See Greenham Women Against Cruise Missiles v. Reagan*, 755 F.2d 34, 37 (2d Cir. 1985) (per curiam); *Dellums v. Bush,* 752 F.Supp. 1141, 1150 & nn. 23–25 (D.D.C. 1990); *see also Sanchez–Espinoza v. Reagan,* 770 F.2d 202, 210–11 (D.C. Cir. 1985) (R. Ginsburg, J., concurring).

Ripeness doctrine involves more than simply the timing of the case. It mixes various mutually reinforcing constitutional and prudential considerations. *See Mangual v. Rotger–Sabat*, 317 F.3d 45, 59 (1st Cir. 2003). One such consideration is the need "to prevent the courts, through avoidance of premature adjudication, from entangling themselves in abstract disagreements." *Abbott Labs. v. Gardner*, 387 U.S. 136, 148 (1967). Another is to avoid unnecessary constitutional decisions. *Reg'l Rail Reorganization Act Cases,* 419 U.S. 102, 138 (1974). A third is the recognition that, by waiting until a case is fully developed before deciding it, courts benefit from a focus sharpened by particular facts. *See Ohio Forestry Ass'n v. Sierra Club,* 523 U.S. 726, 736 (1998). The case before us raises all three of these concerns.

These rationales spring, in part, from the recognition that the scope of judicial power is bounded by the Constitution. "It is a principle of first importance that the federal courts are courts of limited jurisdiction." C.A. Wright & M.K. Kane, *Law of Federal Courts* 27 (6th ed. 2002). Article III of the Constitution limits jurisdiction to "cases" and "controversies," and prudential doctrines may counsel additional restraint.

The ripeness of a dispute is determined de novo. *Stern v. U.S. Dist. Court,* 214 F.3d 4, 10 (1st Cir. 2000). Ripeness is dependent on the circumstances of a particular case. *See Ernst & Young v. Depositors Econ. Prot. Corp.*, 45 F.3d 530, 535 (1st Cir. 1995) ("[T]he various integers that enter into the ripeness equation play out quite differently from case to case. . . ."). Two factors are used to evaluate ripeness: "the fitness of the issues for judicial decision and the hardship to the parties of withholding court consideration." *Abbott Labs.,* 387 U.S. at 149. Ordinarily, both factors must be present. *Ernst & Young,* 45 F.3d at 535.

The hardship prong of this test is most likely satisfied here; the current mobilization already imposes difficulties on the plaintiff soldiers and family members, so that they suffer "present injury from a future contemplated event." *McInnis-Misenor v. Me. Med. Ctr.*, 319 F.3d 63, 70 (1st Cir. 2003). Plaintiffs also lack a realistic opportunity to secure comparable relief by bringing the action at a later time. *See Ohio Forestry,* 523 U.S. at 734.[4]

The fitness inquiry here presents a greater obstacle. Fitness "typically involves subsidiary queries concerning finality, definiteness, and the extent to which resolution of the challenge depends upon facts that may not yet be sufficiently developed." *Ernst & Young*, 45 F.3d at 535. The baseline question is whether allowing more time for development of events would "significantly advance our ability to deal with the legal issues presented [or] aid us in their resolution." *Duke Power Co. v. Carolina Envtl. Study Group*, 438 U.S. 59, 82 (1978); *see Ohio Forestry*, 523 U.S. at 737; *Regional Rail,* 419 U.S. at 144–45; *Gun Owners' Action League v. Swift,* 284 F.3d 198, 208–09 (1st Cir. 2002); *R.I. Ass'n of Realtors v. Whitehouse*, 199 F.3d 26, 34 (1st Cir. 1999). "[T]he question of fitness does not pivot solely on whether a court is capable of resolving a claim intelligently, but also involves an assessment of whether it is appropriate for the court to undertake the task." *Ernst & Young,* 45 F.3d at 537. These prudential considerations are particularly strong in this case, which presents a politically-charged controversy involving momentous issues, both substantively (war and peace) and constitutionally (the powers of coequal branches). *See Dellums*, 752 F. Supp. at 1149.

One thrust of the plaintiffs' argument is that the October Resolution only permits actions sanctioned by the Security Council.[5] In plaintiffs' view, the Resolution's authorization is so narrow that, even with Security Council approval of military force, Congress would need to pass a new resolution before United States participation in an attack on Iraq would be constitutional. At a minimum, according to plaintiffs, the October Resolution authorizes no military action "outside of a United Nations coalition."

---

4. Defendants, citing *Ange v. Bush,* 752 F.Supp. at 515, assert that no claim can ever be ripe until an attack has actually occurred. We would be reluctant to accept this assertion; it would seem to say that a case cannot be ripe on the basis of reasonably predictable future injury. This is not the law. "[T]he doctrine of ripeness . . . asks whether an injury that has not yet happened is sufficiently likely to happen to warrant judicial review." *Gun Owners' Action League v. Swift,* 284 F.3d 198, 205 (1st Cir. 2002) (internal quotation omitted).

5. Plaintiffs argue that § 3(a) of the October Resolution, which authorizes use of force to "defend the national security of the United States . . . and . . . enforce all relevant United Nations Security Council resolutions," 116 Stat. at 1501, excludes any action that is not called for by a Security Council resolution. They support their reading by reference to the October Resolution's preamble and to legislative history.

For various reasons, this issue is not fit now for judicial review. For example, should there be an attack, Congress may take some action immediately. The purported conflict between the political branches may disappear. "[T]hat the future event may never come to pass augurs against a finding of fitness." *McInnis-Misenor,* 319 F.3d at 72.

Many important questions remain unanswered about whether there will be a war, and, if so, under what conditions. Diplomatic negotiations, in particular, fluctuate daily. The President has emphasized repeatedly that hostilities still may be averted if Iraq takes certain actions. The Security Council is now debating the possibility of passing a new resolution that sets a final deadline for Iraqi compliance. United Nations weapons inspectors continue their investigations inside Iraq. Other countries ranging from Canada to Cameroon have reportedly pursued their own proposals to broker a compromise. As events unfold, it may become clear that diplomacy has either succeeded or failed decisively. The Security Council, now divided on the issue, may reach a consensus. To evaluate this claim now, the court would need to pile one hypothesis on top of another. We would need to assume that the Security Council will not authorize war, and that the President will proceed nonetheless. *See id.* at 72–73 (outlining chain of uncertain events necessary to make case ripe); *Ernst & Young,* 45 F.3d at 538 (same).

Thus, even assuming that plaintiffs correctly interpret the commands of the legislative branch, it is impossible to say yet whether or not those commands will be obeyed. As was the situation in *Goldwater*, "[i]n the present posture of this case, we do not know whether there will ever be an actual confrontation between the Legislative and Executive Branches." 444 U.S. at 998 (Powell, J., concurring).

Dismissal of the complaint is *affirmed.*

NOTES ON RIPENESS AND MOOTNESS

1. *The Ripeness Analysis in* Doe v. Bush. Do you find the court's decision in *Doe v. Bush* convincing? Is it not better for a court to contemplate the legality of the resort to war in a setting where an attack is *not* imminent, in order to provide suitable time for briefing by the parties and careful deliberation by the court? If the bombers are about to take off and the ballistic missiles are being warmed up, is it not a bit late for judicial intervention? Or is the court right that it would be premature to act before that point, since perhaps the rumor of war will prove only to be a rumor?

The plaintiffs' second claim in *Doe v. Bush* stated that Congress and the President were in "collusion" to effect a "willing abdication of congressional power to an emboldened and enlarged presidency." This the court refused to entertain on justiciability grounds, though it did not explicitly invoke the political question doctrine:

> In this zone of shared congressional and presidential responsibility, courts should intervene only when the dispute is clearly framed. . . .

> . . . .
>
> . . . Questions about the structure of congressional power can be justiciable under the proper circumstances. But courts are rightly hesitant to second-guess the form or means by which the coequal political branches choose to exercise their textually committed constitutional powers. As the circumstances presented here do not warrant judicial intervention, the appropriate recourse for those who oppose war with Iraq lies with the political branches.

323 F.3d at 143–44 (internal citations omitted). Plaintiffs' subsequent petition for a rehearing based on intervening events was dismissed on March 18. The court found that "the case continues not to be fit for judicial review." John Doe I v. Bush, 322 F.3d 109, 110 (1st Cir. 2003).

2. *Mootness Meets Ripeness.* Section 2 above contained excerpts from the case of *Campbell v. Clinton*, 203 F.3d 19 (D.C. Cir. 2000), with respect to the political question doctrine. Recall that in *Campbell*, certain members of Congress argued that a presidential decision to conduct airstrikes against Yugoslavia conflicted with the War Powers Resolution. Although the D.C. Circuit dismissed the case on the basis of the political question doctrine, the U.S. government argued in the alternative that it should be dismissed on grounds of mootness. Judge Randolph in his concurring opinion addressed that argument.

> The amended complaint, filed on May 19, 1999, sought a declaratory judgment "that no later than May 25, 1999, the President must terminate the involvement of the United States Armed Forces in such hostilities unless Congress declares war, or enacts other explicit authorization, or has extended the sixty day period." Amended Complaint at 12; *see* 50 U.S.C. § 1544(b)(1)–(2). All agree that the "hostilities" ended by June 21, 1999, after NATO's Secretary General announced the official termination of the air campaign and Secretary of Defense Cohen announced the redeployment of more than 300 U.S. aircraft back to their home bases.
>
> To save their case from mootness, plaintiffs therefore invoke the rule regarding issues "capable of repetition, yet evading review." *Southern Pacific Terminal Co. v. ICC*, 219 U.S. 498, 515, 31 S.Ct. 279, 55 L.Ed. 310 (1911); *Christian Knights of the Ku Klux Klan v. District of Columbia*, 972 F.2d 365, 369–71 (D.C. Cir. 1992). Plaintiffs must, but cannot, satisfy both elements to prevail. Their constitutional and statutory claims are at cross purposes.
>
> The "evading review" part of the formulation is temporal. How quickly must an activity begin and end to evade judicial review? This depends on which court does the reviewing. The Supreme Court has treated the matter in terms of itself. Hence evading review means evading Supreme Court review, *see Christian Knights,* 972 F.2d at 369, which can be (though usually is not) swift review. *See, e.g., New York Times Co. v. United States*, 403 U.S. 713 (1971); *Buckley v. Valeo*, 424 U.S. 1 (1976). Some undeclared wars, or in the euphemism of the day, "hostilities," are over quickly; others, like the Korean War and the war in Vietnam, last for years. Circuit precedent requires us to determine whether the activity challenged is "inherently" of a sort that evades review; circuit precedent

> also holds that "offensive wars initiated without congressional approval" are not in that category. *Conyers v. Reagan*, 765 F.2d 1124, 1128 (D.C. Cir. 1985). That holding, which remains the law of the circuit, means that we must treat plaintiffs' claims as moot.
>
> Plaintiffs' statutory claim—that President Clinton continued the war for more than 60 days without congressional authorization, in violation of the War Powers Resolution—also may not satisfy the "capable of repetition" element. There is an aspect of probability involved here. "By 'capable of repetition' the Supreme Court means 'a reasonable expectation that the same complaining party would be subject to the same action again.' " *Christian Knights*, 972 F.2d at 370 (quoting *Weinstein v. Bradford*, 423 U.S. 147, 149 (1975) (per curiam)).[14] This introduces some complications. Who should be considered the "same complaining parties"? And what is the "same action again"?
>
> The same "complaining parties" must refer to the individual Members of Congress who brought this suit. They have sued in their official capacity and, as in *Karcher v. May*, 484 U.S. 72, 79–81 (1987), the injury they allege relates to their conduct as legislators. Thus, in assessing the likelihood of a recurrence of "the same action," the inquiry must be restricted only to the period in which these Congressmen would likely remain in office. As to the "same action," this refers to President Clinton's alleged violation of the War Powers Resolution by continuing hostilities for more than 60 days without Congress's affirmative approval. How likely is that to recur? Not very, if history is any guide. The War Powers Resolution has been in effect for a quarter of a century. Yet President Clinton is the first President who arguably violated the 60–day provision. In order to show why their claims will "evade review," plaintiffs tell us that, in modern times, United States attacks on foreign nations will be over quickly, by which they mean less than 60 days.[15] Accepting that prediction as accurate dooms their case. It means that the likelihood of this President, or some other, violating the 60–day provision of the War Powers Resolution is remote, not only because we can expect other Presidents to obtain congressional approval for wars lasting more than 60 days, but also because most military actions in the future (as plaintiffs agree) will be over before the 60–day limit for undeclared or unauthorized wars has been exceeded.

203 F.3d 19, 33–34 (D.C. Cir. 2000) (Randolph, J., concurring). Does the pairing of ripeness and mootness alter the appeal of one or the other? Should

---

14. The Supreme Court recently stated that "a defendant claiming that its voluntary compliance moots a case bears the formidable burden of showing that it is absolutely clear the allegedly wrongful behavior could not reasonably be expected to recur." *Friends of the Earth*, 528 U.S. at 190, 120 S.Ct. at 709 (citing *United States v. Concentrated Phosphate Export Ass'n*, 393 U.S. 199, 203, 89 S.Ct. 361, 21 L.Ed.2d 344 (1968)). The President's cessation of the attack on Yugoslavia was not "voluntary" within the Court's meaning; the war ended because the United States won, not because the President sought to avoid litigation.

15. "The 1998 air attack against Afghanistan and Sudan, the December 1998 air attacks against Iraq, the 1995 air assault against the Bosnian Serbs, the 1994 Haitian invasion, the 1991 Persian Gulf War, the 1989 Panama invasion, the 1986 air attack against Libya, the 1983 Grenada attack were all completed in less than 60 days." Reply Brief for Plaintiffs–Appellants at 5–6.

those doctrines be managed so as to ensure an adequate opportunity for review?

SECTION 5. STANDING

INTRODUCTORY NOTE

The concept of "standing" encompasses both constitutional doctrine and prudential concerns. To meet the minimum requirements of article III, a litigant must

> show [1] that he personally has suffered some actual or threatened injury as a result of the putatively illegal conduct of the defendant, and that the injury [2] fairly can be traced to the challenged action and [3] is likely to be redressed by a favorable decision.

Valley Forge Christian College v. Americans United for Separation of Church & State, Inc., 454 U.S. 464, 472, 102 S.Ct. 752, 70 L.Ed.2d 700 (1982) (citations and internal quotations omitted); *see also* Lujan v. Defenders of Wildlife, 504 U.S. 555, 112 S.Ct. 2130, 119 L.Ed.2d 351 (1992); Massachusetts v. EPA, 549 U.S. 497, 127 S.Ct. 1438, 167 L.Ed.2d 248 (2007). The prudential limits self-imposed by the judiciary in this area include a "general prohibition on a litigant's raising another person's legal rights, the rule barring adjudication of generalized grievances more appropriately addressed in the representative branches, and the requirement that a plaintiff's complaint fall within the zone of interests protected by the law invoked." Allen v. Wright, 468 U.S. 737, 751, 104 S.Ct. 3315, 82 L.Ed.2d 556 (1984).

These requirements make judicial enforcement of non-individualized, abstract rights problematic. To take a domestic example, what if the President, by executive order, created titles of nobility, and bestowed knighthood upon some favored cronies? The Constitution, art. I, § 9, cl. 8, directly forbids this action; Hamilton termed this prohibition a "Cornerstone of Republican government." *Federalist Papers* No. 84, at 512 (Clinton Rossiter ed., 1961). Nonetheless, would any potential litigant have suffered the requisite particularized injury to have standing to challenge the action? If no one has standing, is the ostensible constitutional prohibition only precatory? Would it make any difference if the plaintiff was a member of Congress or a private individual?

Unlike the political question doctrine, a dismissal based on standing merely indicates that the suit could not be brought by that particular plaintiff, rather than a general determination that the court could not adjudicate the merits of such a case. In this sense, it is a narrower doctrine. Nonetheless, it can have very significant implications for the ability of plaintiffs to bring suit regarding foreign affairs issues. Plaintiffs who bring suit against the government in matters of foreign policy tend to fall into three main categories: (1) members of the U.S. Congress; (2) U.S. servicemembers and their families; and (3) concerned citizens. In the last few decades, members of Congress have regularly requested judicial relief for alleged harms to them in their official capacities. Some of the cases discussed below do not involve foreign affairs, but congressional plaintiffs in those instances of domestic litigation are asserting similar institutional rights and face the same standing difficulties as do those who sue to alter foreign policy.

The Supreme Court first addressed the standing of legislators in *Coleman v. Miller,* 307 U.S. 433, 59 S.Ct. 972, 83 L.Ed. 1385 (1939), which concerned the standing of Kansas state legislators. When the Kansas State Senate voted twenty for and twenty against the Child Labor Amendment, the Lieutenant Governor, the presiding officer of the Senate, broke the deadlock and voted for it. The twenty senators who voted against (along with another senator and three members of the House of Representatives) contested, *inter alia,* this procedure, demanding a court ruling that the resolution concerning the Amendment had not been effectively passed. On appeal from the Kansas Supreme Court, the U.S. Supreme Court divided into three positions. Chief Justice Hughes, joined by Justices Stone and Reed, granted the plaintiffs standing but then held the political question doctrine prevented judicial examination of the merits. Justices Butler and McReynolds granted standing but dissented, arguing on other grounds that the resolution was invalid. Justice Frankfurter, joined by Justices Roberts, Black and Douglas, argued that standing should not be granted. Chief Justice Hughes, in support of granting standing, wrote:

> Here, the plaintiffs include twenty senators, whose votes against ratification have been overridden and virtually held for naught although if they are right in their contentions their votes would have been sufficient to defeat ratification. We think that these senators have a plain, direct and adequate interest in maintaining the effectiveness of their votes.

307 U.S. at 438. Justice Frankfurter responded:

> [T]hese Kansas legislators must have standing in this Court. What is their distinctive claim to be here, not possessed by every Kansan? What is it that they complain of, which could not be complained of here by all their fellow citizens? . . .
>
> . . . The fact that these legislators are part of the ratifying mechanism while the ordinary citizen of Kansas is not, is wholly irrelevant to this issue. . . .

Id. at 464 (Frankfurter, J., concurring). Frankfurter supported the English tradition of leaving "intra-parliamentary controversies to parliaments and outside the scrutiny of law courts." *Id.* at 469.

In 1997, the Supreme Court again addressed legislator standing, dismissing a suit brought by six members of Congress for lack of standing. Raines v. Byrd, 521 U.S. 811, 117 S.Ct. 2312, 138 L.Ed.2d 849 (1997). In *Raines*, the six members had voted against passage of the Line Item Veto Act, and brought suit alleging that the Act was an unconstitutional expansion of the President's powers in violation of Article I of the Constitution. The members claimed that they had been injured "directly and concretely . . . in their official capacities." *Id.* at 816. Justice Rehnquist, writing for the Court, found that, unlike in *Coleman,* the votes of the legislators in *Raines* had not been "completely nullified."

> In the vote on the Act, their votes were given full effect. They simply lost that vote. . . .

> . . . .
>
> . . . There is a vast difference between the level of vote nullification at issue in *Coleman* and the abstract dilution of institutional legislative power that is alleged here. To uphold standing here would require a drastic extension of *Coleman*. We are unwilling to take that step.
>
> . . . .
>
> We therefore hold that these individual members of Congress do not have a sufficient "personal stake" in this dispute and have not alleged a sufficiently concrete injury to have established Article III standing. The judgment of the District Court is vacated, and the case is remanded with instructions to dismiss the complaint for lack of jurisdiction.

521 U.S. at 824–30 (footnotes omitted). *See also* Neal Devins & Michael A. Fitts, *The Triumph of Timing:* Raines v. Byrd *and the Modern Supreme Court's Attempts to Control Constitutional Confrontations*, 86 GEO. L.J. 351 (1997). Subsequently, when the President exercised his line-item authority, different plaintiffs directly affected by the President's cancellation decisions—the City of New York, hospitals and hospital associations, unions, farmers and a farmer's cooperative—were held to have standing, and the Supreme Court further held that the authority violated the Presentment Clause of the Constitution (Art. I, § 7, cl. 2). Clinton v. City of New York, 524 U.S. 417, 118 S.Ct. 2091, 141 L.Ed.2d 393 (1998).

Since 1997, the District Court for the District of Columbia has invoked *Raines* in dismissing for lack of standing various suits brought by members of Congress. For example, in *Kucinich v. Bush*, 236 F. Supp. 2d 1 (D.D.C. 2002), the court dismissed an action brought by members of Congress over the President's unilateral withdrawal from the Anti-Ballistic Missile Treaty. At the same time, courts have often been generous in their grants of standing when simultaneously anticipating the deployment of other judicial doctrines that will prevent them reaching the merits, such as the doctrine of "equitable discretion" discussed below.

GOLDWATER v. CARTER

617 F.2d 697 (D.C. Cir.1979) (some footnotes omitted), vacated on other grounds, 444 U.S. 996, 100 S.Ct. 533, 62 L.Ed.2d 428 (1979).

[The *Goldwater v. Carter* case is recounted in greater detail in Chapter 3, Section 10. For present purposes, recall that in 1979, as a precondition to the arrangements for U.S. recognition of the communist government of the People's Republic of China (located in Beijing), President Jimmy Carter unilaterally terminated a 25-year-old mutual defense treaty with the Republic of China, whose nationalist government was based in Taiwan. President Carter did so without obtaining congressional consent. Eight senators, one former senator, and sixteen House members sued the President, claiming that they were being denied their constitutional role under the Treaty Clause.

The district court found that the plaintiffs had standing and further agreed with them that termination of the treaty must receive the approval of two-thirds of the United States Senate or a majority of both Houses of Congress for it to be effective. The D.C. Circuit found that the plaintiffs had standing, but determined that the President did not exceed his authority when he took action to withdraw from the ROC treaty, and therefore reversed the district court's decision. The extracts below evince disagreement between the circuit court majority and minority as to whether the plaintiffs had standing.]

PER CURIAM:

. . . .

For purposes of the standing issue, we accept, as we must, appellees' pleaded theories as valid. A majority of the court is of the view that, at least as their principal theory has evolved—that the Senate has a constitutional right to vote on the President's proposed treaty termination and to block such termination with a one-third plus one vote—the appellee Senators have standing.

If there is merit to their allegations, such Senators have suffered injury in fact from the President's action terminating the Treaty without Senate consent. This action has deprived the Senate of the opportunity—which appellees assert to be constitutionally prescribed—to vote whether to prevent the termination of this treaty. By excluding the Senate from the treaty termination process, the President has deprived each individual Senator of his alleged right to cast a vote that will have binding effect on whether the Treaty can be terminated. The President has thus nullified the right that each appellee Senator claims under the Constitution to be able to block the termination of this treaty by voting, in conjunction with one-third of his colleagues, against it.

In our decisions on congressional standing this court has carefully drawn a distinction between (1) a diminution in congressional influence resulting from an Executive action that nullifies a specific congressional vote or opportunity to vote, in an objectively verifiable manner—which, we have found, constitutes injury in fact; and (2) a diminution in a legislator's effectiveness, subjectively judged by him or her, resulting from Executive action withholding information or failing to obey a statute enacted through the legislator's vote, where the plaintiff-legislator still has power to act through the legislative process to remedy the alleged abuses—in which situations we do not find injury in fact. To be cognizable for standing purposes, the alleged diminution in congressional influence must amount to a disenfranchisement, a complete nullification or withdrawal of a voting opportunity; and the plaintiff must point to an objective standard in the Constitution, statutes or congressional house rules, by which disenfranchisement can be shown.

In the present case, appellees plead an objective standard in the Constitution as giving them a right to vote on treaty termination. They further allege disenfranchisement in the context of a specific measure, *i.e.*, the proposed termination of the Mutual Defense Treaty. Whether the President's action amounts to a complete disenfranchisement depends on whether appellees have left to them any legislative means to vote in the way they claim is their right. In other words, do they have effective power to block the termination of this treaty despite the President's action? This is the crucial issue, and the focus of our disagreement with the concurring opinion.

The crucial fact is that, on the record before us, there is no conceivable senatorial action that could likely prevent termination of the Treaty. A congressional resolution or statute might at most have persuasive effect with the President; it could not block termination if he persisted in his present interpretation of the Constitution giving him unilateral power to terminate. That appellee Senators have no power to enact a remedy is especially clear in light of the nature of their constitutional claim. They claim the right to block termination with only one-third plus one of their colleagues. There is no way that such a minority can even force a resolution to the floor, let alone pass it. To pretend that effective remedies are open to appellees is to ignore that, first, their alleged right would enable them to block termination with a minority, and, second, that even if they could muster a majority, any legislative action they might take under the present circumstances could well be futile. The only way the Senate can effectively vote on a treaty termination, with the burden on termination proponents to secure a two-thirds majority, is for the President to submit the proposed treaty termination to the Senate as he would a proposed treaty. This is the concrete remedy appellees seek. For the court to require of them some other legislative action before allowing them standing to pursue this claim would be to require a useless act.

Since the President has not afforded an opportunity for an up-or-down vote as appellees request, we do not know whether the Senate would actually block the President's action if given the opportunity. Yet courts consistently vindicate the right to vote without first demanding that the votes when cast will achieve their intended end. A live controversy exists in appellees' claim of an opportunity to cast a binding vote. The President's action has deprived them of this opportunity completely, in the sense that they have no legislative power to exercise an equivalent voting opportunity. Therefore, appellee Senators have standing.

. . . .

WRIGHT, CHIEF JUDGE, with whom TAMM, CIRCUIT JUDGE, joins, concurring in the result:

We agree that the judgment and opinion of the District Court must be vacated and that appellees' complaint must be dismissed. Because we believe the appellees lack standing, we reach no other issue.

. . . .

Appellees gain no particular stake simply by being members of Congress. This court has made clear that a legislator "receives no special consideration in the standing inquiry." *Reuss v. Balles,* 189 U.S. App. D.C. 303, 308, 584 F.2d 461, 466 (D.C. Cir.), *cert. denied,* 439 U.S. 997 (1978).

The interests of an elected representative do not necessarily differ from those of his constituents. In fact, courts could logically afford legislators even *less* consideration on standing than they afford other citizens, since the legislator's position gives him special access to the political process through which general constitutional grievances should find redress. *See Schlesinger v. Reservists Committee to Stop the War,* 418 U.S. 208, 220–227 (1974). Thus, to sustain their lawsuit plaintiff senators and congressmen must demonstrate a "distinct and palpable injury" to themselves. *See Warth v. Seldin, supra,* 422 U.S. at 501.

. . . .

. . . The most distinct injury alleged is that the President has prevented the appellees from voting on treaty termination.[2]

. . . .

. . . Under the paradigm of injury emerging from *Kennedy [v. Sampson],*[1] if the legislature manifests its will through final legislative action, and if the Executive nullifies the effect of that legislative action, a legislator whose vote contributed to the legislative action will have standing. The injury derives from the injury to the legislature, and becomes personal to the individual congressman-plaintiff.

[W]e have declined the occasion to confer standing where a legislator alleges injury to an *opportunity* to cast a specific *future* vote. *See [Harrington v. Bush,* 180 U.S. App. D.C.] at 66, 553 F.2d at 211; *Reuss v. Balles, supra,* 189 U.S. App. D.C. at 308–310, 584 F.2d at 466–468. We have required the plaintiff legislator to show that the challenged Executive action has *nullified* a vote already taken by preventing it from ever taking its intended legal effect.

The Supreme Court's pronouncements on standing compel this view. As we have noted, where a legislator alleges Executive impairment of the effectiveness of his vote, his injury can only be derivative. He cannot suffer injury in fact unless Congress has suffered injury in fact. Congress suffers no injury unless the Executive has thwarted its will; and there is no such will to thwart unless a majority of Congress has spoken unequivocally.[6] Unless Congress has taken all final action in its power to exercise

---

2. The complaint implies two other injuries. One which appellees do not press on appeal is the injury to their "sworn duty to preserve, protect and defend the Constitutional allocation of powers to the Executive and Legislative branches of the federal government." Complaint at 3. Since this injury is nothing more than a general grievance about alleged illegal conduct, it affords no basis for standing. The other injury is that alleged by Senator Thurmond and former Senator Curtis—the alleged nullification of their original 1955 votes to consent to ratification of the Treaty. The District Court rejected standing on that ground, and we agree. The 25-year life of the Treaty has given substantial effect to those 1955 votes, and so the President cannot be said to have rendered them "a direct and immediate nullity, as if [they] had not cast the vote at all." *Harrington v. Bush,* 180 U.S. App. D.C. 45, 66, 553 F.2d 190, 211 (D.C. Cir. 1977).

The allegation that the President has impaired Congress' right to be *consulted* on the treaty termination is really inseparable from the allegation of injury to opportunity to vote.

1. [Authors' Note: In *Kennedy v. Sampson,* 511 F.2d 430 (D.C. Cir. 1974), the D.C. Circuit held that a single United States Senator had standing to challenge an unconstitutional pocket veto on the ground that it had nullified his original vote in favor of the legislation in question.]

6. One other possible basis of standing has no application here—where a majority of Congress approves a lawsuit by expressly authorizing a member or a committee to represent it in the its constitutional prerogative, any injury an individual legislator suffers may find its source not in the President, but in his colleagues in Congress. Where Congress itself, and not the Executive, renders an individual legislator's vote ineffective, the courts have no role. *Harrington v. Bush, supra,* 180 U.S. App. D.C. at 69, 553 F.2d at 214; *Holtzman v. Schlesinger,* 484 F.2d 1307, 1311 (2d Cir. 1973), *cert. denied,* 416 U.S. 936 (1974).

In this case, neither House has ever taken final action to voice disapproval of the termination of the Treaty. In holding that appellees had standing, the District Court accepted their argument that congressional action on the termination effectively amounted to a confrontation with the President. The majority now asserts that Congress has done all it can practically do—short of obtaining judicial relief—to prevent the President from unilaterally terminating the Treaty. But the actual sequence of events in Congress belies these positions.... Congress was well aware of strong legislative measures within its means for expressing disapproval of the termination. It simply did not take those measures.

....

... Thus the President himself has not nullified the effect of any vote appellees have actually cast, nor has he thwarted the will of Congress in the special sense our cases demand. Congress has not suffered the requisite injury, and so neither have appellees. Any harm they have suffered can be "fairly traced" to their minority position in the legislature, and to the vagaries of politics. Surely courts cannot be expected to manage the calendar of the United States Senate.

....

The issue here is whether or in what manner Congress and the President share the power to terminate treaties. For over 200 years, through bargaining, compromise, and accommodation, these popularly elected branches of our government have in fact shared the task, without the help or need of the courts. There has never been a single, settled method of termination. 5 *G. Hackworth, Digest of International Law* 330 (1943). Plaintiffs and defendants here have offered competing interpretations of how the long sequence of treaty terminations in our history was accomplished. Whether or not the historical record supports either party's substantive constitutional argument—and we express no views on this—it does show that when Congress wants to participate directly in a treaty termination it can find the means to do so. Thus Congress had initiated the termination of treaties by directing or requiring the President to give notice of termination, without any prior presidential request. Congress has annulled treaties without any presidential notice. It has conferred on the President the power to terminate a particular treaty, and it has enacted statutes practically nullifying the domestic effects of a treaty and thus caused the President to carry out termination. If Congress can do

---

courts. *See United States v. American Telephone & Telegraph Co.,* 179 U.S. App. D.C. 198, 205, 551 F.2d 384, 391 (D.C. Cir. 1976); *Senate Select Committee on Presidential Campaign Activities v. Nixon,* 162 U.S. App. D.C. 183, 185, 498 F.2d 725, 727 (D.C. Cir. 1974).

this, it can pass a resolution objecting to termination of a treaty if it wishes to do so. A President is likely to pay heed to such disapproval, in which event no court need intervene.[25]

Moreover, Congress has a variety of powerful tools for influencing foreign policy decisions that bear on treaty matters. Under Article I, Section 8 of the Constitution, it can regulate commerce with foreign nations, raise and support armies, and declare war. It has power over the appointment of ambassadors and the funding of embassies and consulates. Congress thus retains a strong influence over the President's conduct in treaty matters.

As our political history demonstrates, treaty creation and termination are complex phenomena rooted in the dynamic relationship between the two political branches of our government. We thus should decline the invitation to set in concrete a particular constitutionally acceptable arrangement by which the President and Congress are to share treaty termination. This principle of prudence especially counsels against judicial intervention in a case like this, where Congress has taken no final action to make known its views on the termination of a particular treaty. Were a President to attempt to unilaterally break a treaty vital to the interests of the nation, without sound reason and against the wishes of the great majority of citizens, congressional representatives, by any means they have already used or by those they may yet design, can ensure that the voice of that majority reaches the President.

III

Managing the foreign relations of a great nation is an intensely political undertaking calling for the greatest skills and the exercise of the most informed judgments, for the stakes are high. It is an area in which judges have no special competence or experience. Unless a case or controversy fully satisfying the constitutional command is presented for adjudication, a court should stay its hand. Since the constitutional command is not satisfied in this case, in our judgment it is appropriate that the court dismiss it without more. We would do so. To come to the same result after a journey through an uncharted judicial wilderness, dropping hints or attempting to set in concrete how future foreign relations cases might be

---

25. As the majority concedes, the heart of its reasoning is that even if Congress does take a final vote disapproving treaty termination, the President might well ignore it and persist in carrying out the termination. Thus, the majority asserts, the appellees' injury is already manifest.

Even if the President does now take such a stand, the perspective of this 200–year–old, continuing political controversy suggests that we view that stand as a bargaining position which cannot confer standing where it would not otherwise exist. Since there has been no definitive congressional vote disapproving termination, a large enough number of congressmen may well *agree* with the President's view of the constitutional issue as to prevent any legal controversy. Similarly, no matter how resolute the President's position appears, we cannot know if he would maintain it in the face of an unequivocal vote of disapproval by Congress.

Thus we see how the standing issue in this case may be cast as a *ripeness* issue. The President's alleged position may *portend* a true legal controversy, but it remains part of a chain of contingency too attenuated to confer standing. *Compare Abbott Laboratories v. Gardner,* 387 U.S. 136 (1967).

decided, invites additional unnecessary, and potentially dangerous, judicial incursions into the area.

NOTES ON THE EQUITABLE DISCRETION DOCTRINE

1. *The Birth of the Equitable Discretion Doctrine.* On appeal, the U.S. Supreme Court found the matter nonjusticiable and vacated the D.C. Circuit's decision. 444 U.S. 996, 100 S.Ct. 533, 62 L.Ed.2d 428 (1979). The Supreme Court's failure even to discuss standing in *Goldwater* prompted the D.C. Circuit to re-assess its analysis of congressional standing rules. It said soon after:

> If, as the ultimate disposition of *Goldwater v. Carter* suggests, the Supreme Court does not believe that the standing doctrine is capable of reflecting the prudential concerns raised by congressional plaintiff suits, this court ought not persist in the attempt to make it do so. The doctrinal difficulties presented by an attempt to reconcile our denial of congressional standing in the *Public Citizen, Harrington,* and *Reuss* cases, on the one hand, with our conferral of legislator standing in the *Kennedy* and *Goldwater* cases, on the other, suggest that . . . "its day may have passed insofar as these lawsuits are concerned."

Riegle v. Federal Open Market Committee, 656 F.2d 873, 880 (D.C. Cir. 1981) (quoting Carl McGowan, *Congressmen In Court: The New Plaintiffs,* 15 GA. L. REV. 241 (1981)). In *Riegle,* a panel of the D.C. Circuit, tracking an argument promulgated by the Circuit's Chief Judge, Carl McGowan, rejected the *Kennedy–Harrington–Goldwater* approach and launched a new analysis: the equitable discretion doctrine.

Riegle involved an attack on the composition of the Federal Open Market Committee ("FOMC"), a part of the Federal Reserve System. While seven members of FOMC are appointed by the President and confirmed by the Senate, its other five members are elected by the boards of directors of the Federal Reserve Banks and thereby evade Senate review. 12 U.S.C. §§ 241, 263(2) (2006). Senator Riegle alleged these appointments infringed upon the exercise of his institutional rights under the Appointments Clause of the Constitution, art. II, § 2, cl. 2. *See also* Reuss v. Balles, 584 F.2d 461 (D.C. Cir.), *cert. denied,* 439 U.S. 997, 99 S.Ct. 598, 58 L.Ed.2d 670 (1978).

The *Riegle* court repeated McGowan's conclusion that

> there can be no peaceful coexistence between, on the one hand, the notion that legislators are treated like any other plaintiff for standing purposes, and, on the other, the idea that courts should rigorously scrutinize whether the congressional plaintiff's true quarrel is with his colleagues, rather than the executive. There is no general requirement that a private litigant employ self-help before seeking judicial relief.

656 F.2d at 877–78 (quoting McGowan at 254). Accordingly, the court divorced these two concepts and only applied "traditional standing tests for non-congressional plaintiffs." 656 F.2d at 878. Finding "Riegle's inability to exercise his right under the Appointments Clause of the Constitution is an

injury sufficiently personal to constitute an injury-in-fact," the court granted standing. *Id.* at 879.

Now, however, what had been the second prong of the congressional plaintiff standing test, a prong motivated by separation of power concerns, became the focus of a new and separate inquiry. According to the court, "The most satisfactory means of translating our separation-of-powers concerns into principled decisionmaking is through a doctrine of circumscribed equitable discretion." *Id.* at 881. As precedent, McGowan cited Justice Rutledge's concurrence in *Colegrove v. Green,* 328 U.S. 549, 564, 66 S.Ct. 1198, 90 L.Ed. 1432 (1946). McGowan at 262. Rutledge preferred dismissing that vote redistricting case for want of equity, not as presenting a political question.

Applying separation-of-powers concerns to the case at hand, the *Riegle* court said: "Where a congressional plaintiff could obtain substantial relief from his fellow legislators through the enactment, repeal, or amendment of a statute, this court should exercise its equitable discretion to dismiss the legislator's action." 656 F.2d at 881. By contrast, because a "private plaintiff's suit would not raise separation-of-powers concerns, the court would be obliged to reach the merits of the claim. In this case, for example, although prudential considerations warrant the dismissal of Senator Riegle's claim, one can easily conceive of a private plaintiff who could acquire standing to bring a similar claim." *Id.* The court summarized its holding: "In short, our standard would counsel dismissal of congressional plaintiff actions only in cases in which (i) the plaintiff lacks standing under the traditional tests, or (ii) the plaintiff has standing but could get legislative redress and a similar action could be brought by a private plaintiff". *Id.* at 882.

2. *Practice Under the Doctrine. Riegle* set a recurrent, if not invariable, pattern: standing granted but equitable discretion found to prevent reaching the merits. *See, e.g.,* Vander Jagt v. O'Neill, 699 F.2d 1166 (D.C. Cir. 1982), *cert. denied,* 464 U.S. 823, 104 S.Ct. 91, 78 L.Ed.2d 98 (1983) (equitable discretion exercised to withhold relief in suit by Republican representatives alleging the compositions of House committees were unfairly partisan); Moore v. United States House of Representatives, 733 F.2d 946 (D.C. Cir. 1984), *cert. denied,* 469 U.S. 1106, 105 S.Ct. 779, 83 L.Ed.2d 775 (1985) (equitable discretion exercised to withhold relief in suit by eighteen representatives alleging that tax bill had unconstitutionally originated in the Senate); Gregg v. Barrett, 771 F.2d 539 (D.C. Cir. 1985) (equitable discretion exercised to withhold relief in suit by three congressmen alleging that the congressional record was not properly prepared).

3. *The Critics Strike Back.* Judge Bork and, prior to his appointment to the Supreme Court, then-Judge Scalia vigorously criticized the equitable discretion doctrine and urged that separation-of-powers concerns be re-injected into standing analysis. Judge Bork originally argued only for a return to the vote nullification standard of *Kennedy v. Sampson* and *Goldwater v. Carter.* Vander Jagt v. O'Neill, 699 F.2d 1166, 1177 (D.C. Cir. 1982) (Bork, J., concurring), *cert. denied,* 464 U.S. 823, 104 S.Ct. 91, 78 L.Ed.2d 98 (1983). In *Moore v. United States House of Representatives,* Judge Scalia took the more extreme position that congressmen *qua* congressmen could not have standing. 733 F.2d 946, 958–59 (D.C. Cir. 1984) (Scalia, J., concurring), *cert. denied,* 469

U.S. 1106, 105 S.Ct. 779, 83 L.Ed.2d 775 (1985). For Scalia's position on individual standing, see Antonin Scalia, *The Doctrine of Standing as an Essential Element of the Separation of Powers,* 17 SUFFOLK U.L. REV. 881 (1983).

Judge Bork gravitated towards Scalia's view in *Barnes v. Kline,* 759 F.2d 21 (D.C.Cir. 1985). Like *Kennedy*, *Barnes* involved a challenge to a presidential pocket veto. The bill presented to the President renewed the human rights certification requirements of the International Security and Development Cooperation Act of 1981, which included the requirement that the President certify, semi-annually, that the El Salvadoran government had progressed in its protection of human rights. In *Barnes,* however, the President was putatively unable to return the bill due to an intersession adjournment, not an intrasession Christmas recess as in *Kennedy.* Unlike Senator Kennedy's individual action, the *Barnes* plaintiffs were thirty-three representatives, the Senate itself (pursuant to S. Res. 313, 98th Cong., 1st Sess., 130 CONG. REC. 5223–24 (daily ed. Jan. 26, 1984)) and the Speaker and bipartisan leadership of the House. Judge Carl McGowan, who wrote the majority opinion, upheld standing, reasoning that "the thirty-three individual Representatives allege an injury identical to that of the individual lawmaker in *Kennedy v. Sampson,*" and "[t]he House Bipartisan Leadership Group and the United States Senate assert an injury of the second, more direct type described in that opinion, that is, an injury to the lawmaking powers of the two houses of Congress" (*id.* at 26). The *Barnes* decision matched the author of the equitable discretion doctrine, Judge McGowan, against Judge Bork's thirty page dissent. The Supreme Court never opined, since on appeal it vacated the circuit court's decision as moot. *See* Burke v. Barnes, 479 U.S. 361, 107 S.Ct. 734, 93 L.Ed.2d 732 (1987).

Within the D.C. Circuit, the equitable discretion doctrine remains good law, but its continuing influence seems doubtful—if it ever affected outcomes at all. Chenoweth v. Clinton, 181 F.3d 112, 114–15 (D.C. Cir. 1999) (noting that "[w]ith one exception ... every decision in which we applied the doctrine of equitable discretion was either reversed upon another jurisdictional ground by the Supreme Court ... or reached the same result that would have obtained had we treated separation of powers concerns as part of our inquiry into the plaintiff's standing"). Instead, informed by the Supreme Court's decision in *Raines v. Byrd*, the court of appeals appears to have reverted to a standing test particularized to congressional challenges, as cases like *Campbell v. Clinton* demonstrate.

CAMPBELL v. CLINTON

203 F.3d 19 (D.C. Cir. 2000).

SILBERMAN, CIRCUIT JUDGE:

A number of congressmen, led by Tom Campbell of California, filed suit claiming that the President violated the War Powers Resolution and the War Powers Clause of the Constitution by directing U.S. forces' participation in the recent NATO campaign in Yugoslavia. The district court dismissed for lack of standing. We agree with the district court and therefore affirm.

. . . .

[For additional facts on this case, see *supra* Section 2].

The question whether congressmen have standing in federal court to challenge the lawfulness of actions of the executive was answered, at least in large part, in the Supreme Court's recent decision in *Raines v. Byrd*, 521 U.S. 811 (1997). *Raines* involved a constitutional challenge to the President's authority under the short-lived Line Item Veto Act. Individual congressmen claimed that under that Act a President could veto (unconstitutionally) only part of a law and thereby diminish the institutional power of Congress. Observing it had never held that congressmen have standing to assert an institutional injury as against the executive, *see id.* at 821,[2] the Court held that petitioners in the case lacked "legislative standing" to challenge the Act. The Court noted that petitioners already possessed an adequate political remedy, since they could vote to have the Line Item Veto Act repealed, or to provide individual spending bills with a statutory exemption. See id. at 829.

Thereafter in *Chenoweth v. Clinton,* 181 F.3d 112, 115 (D.C. Cir. 1999), emphasizing the separation-of-powers problems inherent in legislative standing, we held that congressmen had no standing to challenge the President's introduction of a program through executive order rather than statute. As in *Raines*, appellants contended that the President's action inflicted an institutional injury upon Congress, in this case by circumventing its legislative authority, but, we said,

> It is uncontested that the Congress could terminate the [contested program] were a sufficient number in each House so inclined. Because the parties' dispute is therefore fully susceptible to political resolution, we would [under circuit precedent] dismiss the complaint to avoid "meddl[ing] in the internal affairs of the legislative branch." Applying *Raines*, we would reach the same conclusion.

Id. at 116 (citation omitted).

There remains, however, a soft spot in the legal barrier against congressional legal challenges to executive action, and it is a soft spot that appellants sought to penetrate. In 1939 the Supreme Court in *Coleman v. Miller* voted 5–4 to recognize the standing of Kansas State legislators in the Supreme Court to challenge the actions of the Kansas Secretary of State and the Secretary of the State Senate. *See* 307 U.S. 433 (1939). That case arose out of a State Senate vote on the ratification of a constitutional amendment, the Child Labor Amendment, proposed by Congress in 1924. The State Senate split 20 to 20, and the Lieutenant Governor, the presiding officer of the Senate, then cast a deciding vote in favor. The

2. The Court noted that it had found standing for a congressman in *Powell v. McCormack,* 395 U.S. 486 (1969), where he was unconstitutionally excluded from Congress, thus depriving him of a salary and the House seat he was constitutionally due, both personal injuries. The Court did not decide whether congressmen would have standing to challenge actions of Congress which diminished their institutional role. *Cf. Michel v. Anderson,* 14 F.3d 623 (D.C. Cir. 1994) (congressmen had standing to challenge House rule which diluted their vote in Committee of the Whole).

State House subsequently also passed a ratification resolution. Thereupon the twenty State Senators who voted against ratification plus one more (who presumably had voted for the resolution) brought a mandamus action in the State Supreme Court challenging the Lieutenant Governor's right to vote.[3] They sought an order compelling the Secretary of the Senate to erase the endorsement on the resolution and restraining the Secretary of State from authenticating the resolution and passing it on to the Governor. The Supreme Court of Kansas entertained the action but ruled against the plaintiffs on the merits. Granting certiorari, the United States Supreme Court determined that "at least the twenty senators whose votes, if their contention were sustained, would have been sufficient to defeat the resolution ... have an interest ... sufficient to give the Court jurisdiction," *id.* at 446, because they have a legal interest "in maintaining the effectiveness of their votes." *Id.* at 438.

In *Raines* the plaintiff congressmen had relied on *Coleman* to argue that they had standing because the presidential veto had undermined the "effectiveness of their votes." The Supreme Court noted that *Coleman* might be distinguished on grounds that the federal constitutional separation of powers concerns that underlay its decision in *Raines* (and which we emphasized in *Chenoweth*) were not present, or that if the Court in *Coleman* had not taken the case a question of federal law—the ratification *vel non* by the Kansas Legislature—would remain as decided by the Kansas Court. *But cf. Coleman,* 307 U.S. at 465–66 (opinion of Frankfurter, J.). But the Court thought it unnecessary to cabin *Coleman* on those grounds. *See Raines*, 521 U.S. at 824 n. 8. Instead, the Court emphasized that the congressmen were not asserting that their votes had been "completely nullified":

> They have not alleged that they voted for a specific bill, that there were sufficient votes to pass the bill, and that the bill was nonetheless deemed defeated....
>
> Nor can they allege that the Act will nullify their votes in the future in the same way that the votes of the *Coleman* legislators had been nullified ...
>
> In addition, a majority of Senators and Congressmen can vote to repeal the Act, or to exempt a given appropriations bill....

Id. at 824.

Here the plaintiff congressmen, by specifically defeating the War Powers Resolution authorization by a tie vote and by defeating a declaration of war, sought to fit within the *Coleman* exception to the *Raines* rule. This parliamentary tactic led to an extensive argument before us as to

---

3. The government also challenges the congressmen's standing on the basis that they do not constitute a majority of the Congress. In *Raines* the Supreme Court did "attach some importance to the fact that appellees have not been authorized to represent their respective Houses of Congress in this action," but it declined to say how much importance. *Raines,* 521 U.S. at 829–30. Because we find that appellants lack standing for another reason, we need not discuss that issue.

exactly what the Supreme Court meant by a claim that a legislator's vote was completely "nullified."

It is, to be sure, not readily apparent what the Supreme Court meant by that word. It would seem the Court used nullify to mean treating a vote that did not pass as if it had, or vice versa. The "nullification" alleged in this case therefore differs from *Coleman* in a significant respect. In that case state officials endorsed a defeated ratification, treating it as approved, while the President here did not claim to be acting pursuant to the defeated declaration of war or a statutory authorization, but instead "pursuant to [his] constitutional authority to conduct U.S. foreign relations and as Commander-in-Chief and Chief Executive." *See* Letter to Congressional Leaders Reporting on Airstrikes Against Serbian Targets in the Federal Republic of Yugoslavia (Serbia and Montenegro), 35 Weekly Comp. Pres. Doc. 528 (March 26, 1999). The Court did not suggest in *Raines* that the President "nullifies" a congressional vote and thus legislators have standing whenever the government does something Congress voted against, still less that congressmen would have standing anytime a President allegedly acts in excess of statutory authority. As the government correctly observes, appellants' statutory argument, although cast in terms of the nullification of a recent vote, essentially is that the President violated the quarter-century old War Powers Resolution. Similarly, their constitutional argument is that the President has acted illegally—in excess of his authority—because he waged war in the constitutional sense without a congressional delegation. Neither claim is analogous to a *Coleman* nullification.

We think the key to understanding the Court's treatment of *Coleman* and its use of the word nullification is its implicit recognition that a ratification vote on a constitutional amendment is an unusual situation. It is not at all clear whether once the amendment was "deemed ratified," *see Raines*, 521 U.S. at 822, the Kansas Senate could have done anything to reverse that position.[4] We think that must be what the Supreme Court implied when it said the *Raines* plaintiffs could not allege that the "[Line Item Veto Act] would nullify their votes *in the future*," and that, after all, a majority of senators and congressmen could always repeal the Line Item Veto Act. *Id.* at 824 (emphasis added). The *Coleman* senators, by contrast, may well have been powerless to rescind a ratification of a constitutional amendment that they claimed had been defeated. In other words, they had no legislative remedy. Under that reading—which we think explains the very narrow possible *Coleman* exception to *Raines*—appellants fail because they continued, after the votes, to enjoy ample legislative power to have stopped prosecution of the "war."

In this case, Congress certainly could have passed a law forbidding the use of U.S. forces in the Yugoslav campaign; indeed, there was a measure—albeit only a concurrent resolution—introduced to require the

---

4. *See Coleman,* 307 U.S. at 450 ("[T]he question of the efficacy of ratifications of state legislatures, in the light of ... attempted withdrawal, should be regarded as a political question....").

President to withdraw U.S. troops. Unfortunately, however, for those congressmen who, like appellants, desired an end to U.S. involvement in Yugoslavia, this measure was *defeated* by a 139 to 290 vote. Of course, Congress always retains appropriations authority and could have cut off funds for the American role in the conflict. Again there was an effort to do so but it failed; appropriations were authorized. And there always remains the possibility of impeachment should a President act in disregard of Congress' authority on these matters.

. . . .

Appellants' constitutional claim stands on no firmer footing. Appellants argue that the War Powers Clause of the Constitution proscribes a President from using military force except as is necessary to repel a sudden attack. But they also argue that the WPR "implements" or channels congressional authority under the Constitution. It may well be then that since we have determined that appellants lack standing to enforce the WPR there is nothing left of their constitutional claim. Assuming, however, that appellants' constitutional claim should be considered separately, the same logic dictates they do not have standing to bring such a challenge. That is to say Congress has a broad range of legislative authority it can use to stop a President's war making, *see generally* John C. Yoo, *The Continuation of Politics by Other Means: The Original Understanding of War Powers*, 84 CAL. L. REV. 167 (1996), and therefore under *Raines* congressmen may not challenge the President's war-making powers in federal court.

Judge Randolph asserts that appellants lack standing because they do not claim that the President violated various statutes that depend on the existence of a war or the *imminence* of war. But that position sidesteps appellants' basic claim that the President unconstitutionally conducted a war without authority, and the logic of Judge Randolph's reasoning ("There is no suggestion that despite the vote, President Clinton *invaded* Yugoslavia by land or took some other action authorized only during a declared war.") is that if there had been a "war" appellants would have had standing. *See infra* at 31 (Randolph, J., concurring).[5] He therefore presents as an alternate reason for denying standing that the President did not "nullify" the vote against the declaration of war because he did not take any actions that constitute "war" in the constitutional sense. *See id.* at 29–31. That analysis, however, conflates standing with the merits. At the standing stage we must take as correct appellants' claim that the President violated the Constitution simply by ordering U.S. forces to attack Yugoslavia.

In our view Judge Randolph's criticism of our analysis does not give sufficient attention to *Raines*' focus on the political self-help available to congressmen. *See infra* at 22 (Randolph, J., concurring). Even though the

---

5. It is certainly not logically necessary for appellants to assert a violation of the statutes (three of which do not even depend on a declaration of war) relied upon by the concurrence in order to make their constitutional claim.

congressmen in *Raines* sought review before the Court of what was soon after determined in *Clinton v. City of New York,* 524 U.S. 417 (1998), to be an unconstitutional statute, the Court denied them standing as congressmen because they possessed political tools with which to remedy their purported injury. Our colleague notes a distinction drawn by *Raines* between "the right to vote in the future [and] the nullification of a vote in the past," *see infra* at 22 (Randolph, J., concurring), and asserts that the former does not remedy the latter. But *Raines* rejected this argument, which is why the congressmen in *Raines* lacked standing whereas petitioners in *New York* were allowed to contest the President's "nullification" of particular appropriations line items. Indeed, *Raines* explicitly rejected Judge Randolph's argument that legislators should not be required to turn to politics instead of the courts for their remedy. Although the plaintiff legislators in *Raines* had already failed to stop passage of the Line Item Veto Act, the Court's response was the equivalent of "if at first you don't succeed, try and try again"—either work for repeal of the Act, or seek to have individual spending bills made exempt. *See Raines*, 521 U.S. at 824–25, 825 n. 9, 830. Judge Randolph overlooks this key portion of *Raines* when he disagrees with our conclusion that plaintiffs lack standing because they may "fight again tomorrow." *Infra* at 22 (Randolph, J., concurring).[6]

. . . .

RANDOLPH, CIRCUIT JUDGE, concurring in the judgment:

The majority opinion does not, I believe, correctly analyze plaintiffs' standing to sue. It misconceives the holding of *Raines v. Byrd,* 521 U.S. 811 (1997), and conflicts with the law of this circuit. I believe plaintiffs lack standing, at least to litigate their constitutional claim, but for reasons the majority opinion neglects. I also believe that the case is moot, an optional disposition of the appeal.[1] The serious questions about the

6. Judge Randolph also contends that our opinion is in conflict with *Chenoweth v. Clinton*, 181 F.3d 112, 116–17 (D.C. Cir. 1999). But as we have already described that opinion, *see supra* at 21, it too focused on the political options available to congressmen when denying them standing. *Chenoweth* did not hold, as Judge Randolph would have it, that *Kennedy v. Sampson*, 511 F.2d 430 (D.C. Cir. 1974), survived *Raines*. Instead, we stressed the increased emphasis placed by such post-*Kennedy* cases as *Raines* on separation of powers concerns. *See Chenoweth*, 181 F.3d at 113–15. Although appellants' injury in *Chenoweth* was "precisely the harm we held in ... *Kennedy* to be cognizable under Article III," it was also "identical to the injury the Court in *Raines* deprecated as 'widely dispersed' and 'abstract,'" and therefore we affirmed the district court's dismissal for lack of standing. *Id.* We only suggested tentatively that "*Kennedy may* remain good law ... as a peculiar application of the narrow rule announced in" *Coleman*. *See id.* at 116 (emphasis added). Indeed, Judge Tatel understandably read our opinion to "essentially overrule[ ] the theory of legislative standing recognized in *Kennedy*...." *See id.* at 117 (Tatel, J., concurring). In any event, *Chenoweth's* discussion of *Kennedy's* fate after *Raines* was dicta, and we need not decide for purposes of this case if *Kennedy,* which involved the special question of a pocket veto, survived *Raines*.

1. While we may be required to decide jurisdictional issues before disposing of a case on the merits, we are not required to decide jurisdictional questions in any particular order. *See Arizonans for Official English v. Arizona,* 520 U.S. 43, 66–67 (1997); *Galvan v. Federal Prison Indus., Inc.,* 199 F.3d 461 (D.C. Cir. 1999) (citing *Steel Co. v. Citizens for a Better Environment,* 523 U.S. 83, 94–95 (1998); *Ruhrgas A.G. v. Marathon Oil Co.*, 526 U.S. 574 (1999)). Specifically, we may assume standing when dismissing a case as moot. *See Friends of the Earth, Inc. v.*

constitutionality of the War Powers Resolution[2] must therefore be put off for still another day.

I. STANDING

The Constitution reserves the power to declare "war"[3] to Congress and delegates the power to conduct war to the President. *Compare* U.S. CONST. art. I, § 8, cl. 11, *with id.* art. II, § 2. When President Clinton committed armed forces to the attack on the Federal Republic of Yugoslavia, he did so without a declaration of war from Congress. On April 28, 1999, after air operations and missile strikes were underway, the House of Representatives voted 427 to 2 against a declaration of war. *See* H.R.J. Res. 44, 106th Cong. (1999); 126 CONG. REC. H2440–41 (daily ed. Apr. 28, 1999).

The War Powers Resolution, passed over President Nixon's veto in 1973, implements Congress's power to declare war under the Constitution. *See* 50 U.S.C. § 1541(a)–(b). It commands the President to "terminate any use of United States Armed Forces" within sixty days "unless the Congress (1) has declared war or has enacted a specific authorization for such use of United States Armed Forces, (2) has extended by law such sixty-day period, or (3) is physically unable to meet as a result of an armed attack upon the United States." 50 U.S.C. § 1544(b). The Senate, on March 23, 1999, passed a concurrent resolution providing that "the President of the United States is authorized to conduct military air operations and missile strikes in cooperation with our NATO allies against the Federal Republic of Yugoslavia." S. Con. Res. 21, 106th Cong. (1999); 145 CONG. REC. S3118 (daily ed. Mar. 23, 1999). The House rejected that measure by a tie vote on April 28, 1999. *See* 126 CONG. REC. H2451–52 (daily ed. Apr. 28, 1999).

The Members of Congress appearing as plaintiffs contend that President Clinton violated the Constitution and the War Powers Resolution and that they are entitled to a judicial declaration so stating. They have standing, they say, because President Clinton's prosecution of the war "completely nullified" their votes against declaring war and against authorizing a continuation of the hostilities. *See* Amended Complaint ¶ 18; Brief for Plaintiffs–Appellants at 8, 16.

Laidlaw Envtl. Servs., 528 U.S. at 180, 120 S.Ct. 693, 703–04 (2000) (citing *Arizonans,* 520 U.S. at 66–67).

2. I include as an Addendum to this opinion President Nixon's 1973 message to the House of Representatives explaining why he vetoed the War Powers Resolution on the grounds of its unconstitutionality.

3. *War* may be defined [as] the exercise of violence under sovereign command against withstanders; force, authority and resistance being the essential parts thereof. Violence, limited by authority, is sufficiently distinguished from robbery, and like outrages; yet consisting in relation towards others, it necessarily requires a supposition of resistance, whereby the force of *war* becomes different from the violence inflicted upon slaves or yielding malefactors.

SAMUEL JOHNSON, A DICTIONARY OF THE ENGLISH LANGUAGE (facsimile ed., Times Books, Ltd., London 1978) (1755). *See United States v. Bajakajian,* 524 U.S. 321, 335 (1998) (citing *Johnson*); *Nixon v. United States,* 506 U.S. 224, 229–30 (1993) (same); *see also Bas v. Tingy,* 4 U.S. (4 Dall.) 37 (1800) (relying on Blackstone and other commentators to distinguish between perfect and imperfect wars).

A.

The quoted phrase—"completely nullified"—is from *Raines v. Byrd,* 521 U.S. 811, 823 (1997), giving the Court's appraisal of the rule in *Coleman v. Miller*, 307 U.S. 433 (1939). The majority opinion in our case seems to assume that the only thing left of legislative standing is whatever *Raines* preserves. I will not quarrel with the assumption, at least for cases in which a legislator is claiming that his vote has been illegally nullified.[4] The heart of the *Raines* decision is this: "legislators whose votes would have been sufficient to defeat (or enact) a specific legislative act have standing to sue if that legislative action goes into effect (or does not go into effect), on the ground that their votes have been completely nullified." 521 U.S. at 823.[5]

Here, plaintiffs had the votes "sufficient to defeat" "a specific legislative action"—they defeated a declaration of war (their constitutional claim) and they blocked a resolution approving the President's continuation of the war (their statutory claim). To follow precisely the formulation in *Raines*, they would have standing only if the legislative actions they defeated went "into effect." Obviously, this did not happen: war was not declared, and the President never maintained that he was prosecuting the war with the House's approval.

Plaintiffs' reply is that the President's military action against Yugoslavia without congressional authorization had the effect of completely nullifying their votes, of making their votes worthless. With respect to their vote against declaring war, that clearly is not true. A congressional declaration of war carries with it profound consequences.[6] The United States Code is thick with laws expanding executive power "in time of war." *See* OFFICE OF THE JUDGE ADVOCATE GENERAL, UNITED STATES AIR FORCE, DIGEST OF WAR AND EMERGENCY LEGISLATION AFFECTING THE DEPARTMENT OF DEFENSE 171–84 (1996) (listing statutes "effective in time of war"); *cf. id.* at 185–91 (listing statutes "effective in time of national emergency declared by the President"); id. at 192–98 (listing statutes "effective in time

4. The Court has "recognized that state legislators have standing to contest a decision holding a state statute unconstitutional if state law authorizes legislators to represent the State's interests," *Arizonans*, 520 U.S. at 65 (citing *Karcher v. May*, 484 U.S. 72, 82 (1987)). Compare *INS v. Chadha*, 462 U.S. 919, 930 n. 5, 939–40 (1983), in which the "Court held Congress to be a proper party to defend [a] measure's validity where both Houses, by resolution, had authorized intervention in the lawsuit," and the executive branch refused to defend the one-House veto provision. 520 U.S. at 65 n. 20.

5. A vote is "completely nullified" when it is "deprived of all validity," *Raines*, 521 U.S. at 822, "overridden and virtually held for naught," *id.* at 822–23, or "stripped of its validity," *id.* at 824 n. 7.

6. Although the United States has committed its armed forces into combat more than a hundred times, Congress has declared war only five times: the War of 1812, the Mexican–American War of 1848, the Spanish–American War of 1898, World War I, and World War II. *See* CONGRESSIONAL RESEARCH SERVICE, INSTANCES OF USE OF UNITED STATES ARMED FORCES ABROAD, 1789–1989 (Ellen C. Collier ed., 1989), *reprinted in* THOMAS M. FRANCK & MICHAEL J. GLENNON, FOREIGN RELATIONS AND NATIONAL SECURITY LAW 650 (2d ed.1993); OFFICE OF THE LEGAL ADVISER, U.S. DEPARTMENT OF STATE, THE LEGALITY OF UNITED STATES PARTICIPATION IN THE DEFENSE OF VIETNAM (1966), *reprinted in* 1 THE VIETNAM WAR AND INTERNATIONAL LAW 583, 597 (Richard A. Falk ed., 1968) (listing 125 incidents prior to the Vietnam Conflict).

of national emergency declared by Congress").[7] Under these laws, the President's authority over industries, the use of land, and the terms and conditions of military employment is greatly enhanced.[8] A declaration of war may also have the effect of decreasing commercial choices and curtailing civil liberties.[9] *See* WILLIAM H. REHNQUIST, ALL THE LAWS BUT ONE: CIVIL LIBERTIES IN WARTIME 218–19 (1998) ("Without question the government's authority to engage in conduct that infringes civil liberty is greatest in time of declared war—the *Schenck* and *Hirabayashi* opinions make this clear.... [B]ut from the point of view of governmental authority under the Constitution, it is clear that the President may do many things in carrying out a congressional directive that he may not be able to do on his own.").

The vote of the House on April 28, 1999, deprived President Clinton of these powers. The vote against declaring war followed immediately upon the vote not to require immediate withdrawal. Those who voted against a declaration of war did so to deprive the President of the authority to expand hostilities beyond the bombing campaign and, specifically, to deprive him of the authority to introduce ground troops into the conflict. *See* 145 CONG. REC. H2427–41 (daily ed. Apr. 28, 1999). There is no suggestion that despite the vote, President Clinton invaded Yugoslavia by land or took some other action authorized only during a declared war. It follows that plaintiffs' votes against declaring war were not for naught. For that reason, plaintiffs do not have standing to sue on their constitutional claim.

---

7. In the early days of the Republic, the power of the executive in time of war was constrained by an absence of legislation. For example, in *Brown v. United States*, 12 U.S. (8 Cranch) 110 (1814), the Court rejected the argument that the President had the authority to confiscate enemy property found within the United States without explicit statutory authority even during a declared war. See id. at 129. The same reasoning was applied to the taking of ships on the high seas in *Little v. Barreme*, 6 U.S. (2 Cranch) 170 (1804). Even in the wake of World War II, after Congress passed a large number of war-related measures, the Court strictly construed the President's authority. The most notable example, of course, is *Youngstown Sheet & Tube Co. v. Sawyer*, 343 U.S. 579, 585 (1952) ("The President's power, if any, to issue the order must stem either from an act of Congress or from the Constitution itself."); *cf. also Dames & Moore v. Regan,* 453 U.S. 654 (1981).

8. *See, e.g.,* 10 U.S.C. § 2538 (authorizing the President to "take immediate possession of any plant that is equipped to manufacture, or that ... is capable of manufacturing" war material "in time of war or when war is imminent"); 10 U.S.C. § 2644 ("In time of war, the President, through the Secretary of Defense, may take possession and assume control of all or part of any system of transportation to transport troops, war material, and equipment, or for other purposes related to the emergency."); 10 U.S.C. § 2663(b) ("In time of war or when war is imminent, the United States may, immediately upon the filing of a petition for condemnation under subsection (a), take and use the land to the extent of the interest sought to be acquired."); 50 U.S.C. § 1829 ("Notwithstanding any other provision of law, the President, through the Attorney General, may authorize physical searches without a court order ... to acquire foreign intelligence information for a period not to exceed 15 calendar days following a declaration of war by the Congress.").

9. *See, e.g.,* 18 U.S.C. § 2388(a) ("Whoever, when the United States is at war, willfully causes or attempts to cause insubordination, disloyalty, mutiny, or refusal of duty, in the military or naval forces of the United States, or willfully obstructs the recruiting or enlistment service of the United States, to the injury of the service or the United States, or attempts to do so—Shall be fined under this title or imprisoned not more than twenty years, or both."); 18 U.S.C. § 3287 (tolling statute of limitations for any offense involving fraud against the property of the United States until three years after the termination of hostilities).

As to their claim under the War Powers Resolution, the beauty of this measure, or one of its defects (see the Addendum to this opinion), is in its automatic operation: unless a majority of both Houses declares war, or approves continuation of hostilities beyond 60 days, or Congress is "physically unable to meet as a result of an armed attack upon the United States," the Resolution requires the President to withdraw the troops. 50 U.S.C. § 1544(b). The President has nothing to veto. Congress may allow the time to run without taking any vote, or it may—as the House did here—take a vote and fail to muster a majority in favor of continuing the hostilities.

To put the matter in terms of *Raines* once again, plaintiffs had the votes "sufficient to defeat" "a specific legislative action"—they blocked a resolution authorizing the President's continuation of the war with Yugoslavia—but it is not true, in the language of *Raines*, that this "legislative action" nevertheless went "into effect." Congressional authorization simply did not occur. The President may have acted as if he had Congress's approval, or he may have acted as if he did not need it. Either way, plaintiffs' real complaint is not that the President ignored their votes; it is that he ignored the War Powers Resolution, and hence the votes of an earlier Congress, which enacted the law over President Nixon's veto. It is hard for me to see that this amounts to anything more than saying: "We, the members of Congress, have standing because the President violated one of our laws." To hold that Members of Congress may litigate on such a basis strikes me as highly problematic, not only because the principle is unconfined but also because it raises very serious separation-of-powers concerns. *See Raines*, 521 U.S. at 825 n. 8; *Barnes v. Kline*, 759 F.2d 21, 41 (D.C. Cir. 1985) (Bork, J., dissenting), *vacated as moot*, 479 U.S. 361 (1987). But because the case is moot, I need say no more.

B.

The majority opinion analyzes standing rather differently than I do. It says plaintiffs lack standing to pursue their statutory claim because "they continued, after the votes, to enjoy ample legislative power to have stopped prosecution of the 'war.'" Maj. op. at 23. For specifics, the opinion points out that Congress defeated House Concurrent Resolution 82, a resolution requiring immediate disengagement from the conflict in Yugoslavia; that "Congress always retains appropriations authority and could have cut off funds for the American role in the conflict";[10] and that

10. The majority attaches some importance to Congress's decision to authorize funding for Operation Allied Force and argues that Congress could have denied funding if it wished to end the war. However, in *Mitchell v. Laird,* 488 F.2d 611, 616 (D.C. Cir.1 973), we held that, as "every schoolboy knows," Congress may pass such legislation, not because it is in favor of continuing the hostilities, but because it does not want to endanger soldiers in the field. The War Powers Resolution itself makes the same point: "Authority to introduce United States Armed Forces into hostilities or into situations wherein involvement in hostilities is clearly indicated by the circumstances *shall not be inferred* ... from any provision of law (whether or not in effect before November 7, 1973), *including any provision contained in any appropriation Act*, unless such provision specifically authorizes the introduction of United States Armed Forces into hostilities or into such situations and states that it is intended to constitute specific statutory authorization within the meaning of this chapter." 50 U.S.C. § 1547(a)(1) (emphasis added). Those portions of

"there always remains the possibility of impeachment." *Id.*[11] The same reason—the possibility of future legislative action—is used to defeat plaintiffs' standing with respect to their constitutional claim. *Id.* at 23.

The majority has, I believe, confused the right to vote in the future with the nullification of a vote in the past, a distinction *Raines* clearly made. See 521 U.S. at 824. To say that your vote was not nullified because you can vote for other legislation in the future is like saying you did not lose yesterday's battle because you can fight again tomorrow. The Supreme Court did not engage in such illogic. When the Court in *Raines* mentioned the possibility of future legislation, it was addressing the argument that "the [Line Item Veto] Act will nullify the [Congressmen's] votes in the future...." *Id.* This part of the Court's opinion, which the majority adopts here, is quite beside the point to our case. No one is claiming that their votes on future legislation will be impaired or nullified or rendered ineffective.

Besides, as long as Congress and the Constitution exist, Members will always be able to vote for legislation. And so the majority's decision is tantamount to a decision abolishing legislative standing. I have two problems with this. First, if we are going to get rid of legislative standing altogether, we ought to do so openly and not under the cover of an interpretation, or rather misinterpretation, of a phrase in *Raines*. If the Supreme Court had meant to do away with legislative standing, it would have said so and it would have given reasons for taking that step.

My second problem is just as serious, perhaps more so: the majority's decision conflicts with this court's latest legislative standing decision. In *Chenoweth v. Clinton,* 181 F.3d 112, 116–17 (D.C. Cir. 1999), we interpreted *Raines* consistently with my analysis in this case and concluded that a previous legislative standing decision of this court—*Kennedy v. Sampson,* 511 F.2d 430 (D.C. Cir. 1974)—upholding legislative standing to challenge the legality of a pocket veto was still good law. The plaintiff in *Kennedy* had standing under the proper interpretation of *Raines*, we held, because the "pocket veto challenged in that case had made ineffective a bill that both houses of the Congress had approved. Because it was the President's veto—not a lack of legislative support—that prevented the bill from becoming law (either directly or by the Congress voting to override the President's veto), those in the majority could plausibly describe the President's action as a complete nullification of their votes." 181 F.3d at 116–17. If *Chenoweth* is correct, the majority opinion in this case must be wrong. If *Chenoweth* is correct, it is no answer to say—as the majority

the Emergency Supplemental Appropriations Act, Pub. L. No. 106–31, 113 Stat. 57, relating to the attacks on Yugoslavia specified the limited purpose for the emergency appropriations, but contained no language even roughly approximating that required by the War Powers Resolution. *See id.,* ch. 3, 113 Stat. 76–83.

11. These are not the only possibilities. "It has been thought that Congress could constitutionally cut the President's salary in half and auction off the White House, reduce the President's staff to one secretary, and limit her or him to answering personal correspondence." A. Raymond Randolph, *Introduction-Disciplining Congress: The Boundaries of Legislative Power*, 13 J.L. & POL. 585, 586 (1997).

says in this case—that standing is lacking because, despite the pocket veto, Congress could pass the same law again, or it could retaliate by cutting off appropriations for the White House or it could impeach the President.

C.

My position, the majority complains, "sidesteps" plaintiffs' merits "claim that the President unconstitutionally conducted a war without authority," Maj. op. at 23. This is meant to be criticism? A properly-conducted standing analysis almost always avoids—sidesteps—a decision on the merits.[12] In the next breath, the majority turns around and contradicts itself, proclaiming that my analysis "conflates standing with the merits." *Id.* I am familiar with what I have written. I do not recall having rendered a judgment about whether the President violated the Constitution. The careful reader will, I think, agree with me. Nor do I present "as an alternative reason for denying standing that the President did not ... take any actions constituting war in the constitutional sense." *Id.* The majority's sentence is doubly misleading. Here is my alternative reason for denying standing, pure and simple: regardless whether President Clinton waged a "war," plaintiffs never claimed that he exercised statutory authority reserved to him only when Congress has declared a war; and so their votes against declaring war cannot be considered a nullity. Thus, one, I have taken no position on whether the President engaged in a "war," and two, I say only that plaintiffs never *alleged* that the President utilized these statutory powers. Too often a strategy in legal argumentation is to pretend to answer an argument by misstating it.[13] My argument remains unanswered. All the majority has done is to misstate it almost as badly as it has misread *Raines*.

Concluding Notes

1. *Standing Cases in the Vietnam War Era.* Challenges to the constitutionality of the Vietnam War frequently encountered two justiciability hurdles: standing and the political question doctrine. *See supra,* Section 2. For individual litigants, standing was usually granted only to a party "under orders to fight in the combat in which he objects." Holtzman v. Schlesinger, 484 F.2d 1307, 1315 (2d Cir. 1973), *cert. denied,* 416 U.S. 936, 94 S.Ct. 1935, 40 L.Ed.2d 286 (1974). *See* Berk v. Laird, 429 F.2d 302 (2d Cir. 1970); Massachusetts v. Laird, 451 F.2d 26 (1st Cir. 1971). As the Second Circuit explained, being a draftee or draft registrant was insufficient:

---

12. The majority drops this footnote: "It is certainly not logically necessary for appellants to assert a violation of the statutes ... relied upon by the concurrence in order to make their constitutional claim." Maj. op. at 23 n.5. How strange a statement. I refer to the statutes not in the context of plaintiffs' making their constitutional claim, but in regard to their standing to litigate that claim. It is as if the majority had made this brow-furrowing statement: "in order to make out their constitutional claim, it is not logically necessary for plaintiffs to assert that their votes were nullified within the meaning of *Raines*."

13. See also the sentence attributing to me the "argument that legislators should not be required to turn to politics instead of the courts for their remedy." Maj. op. at 24. There are other examples not worth mentioning.

> Regardless of the proof that appellant might present to demonstrate the correlation between the Selective Service and our nation's efforts in Vietnam, as a matter of law the congressional power "to raise and support armies" and "to provide and maintain a navy" is a matter quite distinct from the use which the Executive makes of those who have been found qualified and who have been inducted into the Armed Forces.

United States v. Mitchell, 369 F.2d 323, 324 (2d Cir. 1966), *cert. denied,* 386 U.S. 972, 87 S.Ct. 1162, 18 L.Ed.2d 132 (1967). *See also* Ashton v. United States, 404 F.2d 95 (8th Cir. 1968), *cert. denied,* 394 U.S. 960, 89 S.Ct. 1308, 22 L.Ed.2d 561 (1969); United States v. Battaglia, 410 F.2d 279 (7th Cir. 1969); United States v. Rehfield, 416 F.2d 273 (9th Cir.1969), *cert. denied,* 397 U.S. 996, 90 S.Ct. 1137, 25 L.Ed.2d 405 (1970); Mottola v. Nixon, 464 F.2d 178 (9th Cir. 1972). *But see* United States v. Sisson, 294 F.Supp. 511 (D. Mass. 1968) (draftee granted standing).

While many suits challenging the Vietnam War were brought by service-members, United States congressmen also brought suits to protect their institutional rights in response to the Vietnam War. *See, e.g.,* Mitchell v. Laird, 488 F.2d 611 (D.C. Cir. 1973) (Court, *sua sponte,* proposed a very weak test for congressional standing; plaintiffs, though granted standing, were precluded from adjudication on basis of political question doctrine); Holtzman v. Schlesinger, 484 F.2d 1307, 1315 (2d Cir. 1973), *cert. denied,* 416 U.S. 936, 94 S.Ct. 1935, 40 L.Ed.2d 286 (1974) (Congresswoman Holtzman, among others, having asked that the bombing of Cambodia be enjoined, was denied standing); Harrington v. Schlesinger, 528 F.2d 455 (4th Cir. 1975) (plaintiffs denied standing).

Attempts by citizen-taxpayers to litigate the constitutionality of the Vietnam war were unsuccessful. In *Velvel v. Nixon,* the Tenth Circuit examined a law school professor's complaint in terms of *Flast v. Cohen*, 392 U.S. 83, 88 S.Ct. 1942, 20 L.Ed.2d 947 (1968), then the leading Supreme Court case on taxpayer standing:

> . . . the first requirement of *Flast* is that the taxpayer challenge "exercises of congressional power under the taxing and spending clause. . . ." 392 U.S. at 102. Since congressional appropriations for the war are made under authority of the powers "to raise and support Armies" and "to provide and maintain a Navy," such expenditures are not exercises of the power to spend for the general welfare, but rather, represent exercises of power under the later enumerated powers, powers which are separate and distinct from the grant of authority to tax and spend for the general welfare. *United States v. Butler,* 297 U.S. 1, 65, 56 S.Ct. 312, 80 L.Ed. 477 (1936). It follows then that appellant has not satisfied the first criterion of *Flast* and therefore lacks standing to sue.
>
> Even if we were to assume that the first criterion for standing had been met, the Court's discussion of *Frothingham v. Mellon* would still require a finding that the appellant must fail. The Court in *Flast* noted that although the taxpayer in *Frothingham* complied with the first criterion by attacking a federal spending program, she nonetheless lacked standing because her constitutional complaint was not based on an allegation that Congress had breached a *specific* limitation upon its taxing

> and spending power. Instead, the taxpayer alleged essentially that Congress in enacting the challenged program, had exceeded the general powers delegated to it by Art. I, § 8, and thereby invaded the legislative province of the states. Similarly, in the case at bar the appellant is attempting to assert the congressional interest in its legislative prerogatives, and just as was the case of the taxpayer in *Frothingham*, this is "not a federal taxpayer's interest in being free of taxing and spending in contravention of specific constitutional limitations imposed upon Congress' taxing and spending power." Thus, the appellant will not be permitted "to employ a federal court as a forum in which to air his generalized grievances about the conduct of government or the allocation of power in the Federal System." 392 U.S. at 106.

Velvel v. Nixon, 415 F.2d 236, 239 (10th Cir. 1969), *cert. denied*, 396 U.S. 1042, 90 S.Ct. 684, 24 L.Ed.2d 686 (1970). *See also* Kalish v. United States, 411 F.2d 606 (9th Cir. 1969); Pietsch v. President of the United States, 434 F.2d 861 (2d Cir. 1970), *cert. denied,* 403 U.S. 920, 91 S.Ct. 2236, 29 L.Ed.2d 698 (1971). As to whether a state has standing, representing its citizens as *parens patriae,* see *Massachusetts v. Laird,* 400 U.S. 886, 91 S.Ct. 128, 27 L.Ed.2d 140 (1970) (Douglas, J., dissenting); *Massachusetts v. Laird,* 451 F.2d 26 (1st Cir. 1971).

2. *Further Reading*. For further analysis of the doctrine of standing, see David J. Weiner, *The New Law of Legislative Standing*, 54 STAN. L. REV. 205 (2001); John O. McGinnis, *Constitutional Review by the Executive in Foreign Affairs and War Powers: a Consequence of Rational Choice in the Separation of Powers*, 56 LAW. & CONTEMP. PROBS. 293, 319–320 (1993); Carlin Meyer, *Imbalance of Powers: Can Congressional Lawsuits Serve as Counterweight?*, 54 U. PITT. L. REV. 63 (1992); Theodore Y. Blumoff, *Judicial Review, Foreign Affairs and Legislative Standing,* 25 GA. L. REV. 227 (1991); R. Lawrence Dessem, *Congressional Standing to Sue: Whose Vote Is This Anyway?,* 62 NOTRE DAME L. REV. 1 (1986); Note, *The Burger Court's Unified Approach to Standing And Its Impact on Congressional Plaintiffs*, 60 NOTRE DAME L. REV. 1187 (1985); Note, *The Justiciability of Congressional–Plaintiff Suits*, 82 COLUM. L. REV. 526 (1982); Note, *Congressional Access to the Federal Courts,* 90 HARV. L. REV. 1632 (1977).

SECTION 6. UNRECOGNIZED GOVERNMENTS IN U.S. COURTS

RUSSIAN SOCIALIST FEDERATED SOVIET REPUBLIC v. CIBRARIO

235 N.Y. 255, 260–65, 139 N.E. 259 (1923).

ANDREWS, J. . . .

[Established in 1917 after the Bolshevik revolution in Russia, the Russian Soviet Federated Socialist Republic (RSFSR) was the largest and most populous of the fifteen Soviet republics, which became part of the Soviet

Union in 1922. The United States initially refused to recognize the new communist regime as the lawful government in Russia (eventually U.S. recognition and opening of diplomatic relations occurred in 1933). In this case, the RSFSR sought to bring an action in New York state court against an individual.]

Does any rule of comity then require us to permit a suit by an unrecognized power? In view of the attitude of our government should we permit an action to be brought by the Soviet government? To both queries we must give a negative answer.

We may state at the outset that we find no precedent that a power not recognized by the United States may seek relief in our courts. Such intimations as exist are to the contrary....

What then is the meaning and effect of recognition in its relation to comity? It is difficult to find a clear discussion of this question, either in reports or in textbooks. Where a new government has seized power "no official intercourse is possible between the powers refusing recognition and the state concerned." "Through recognition the other states declare that they are ready to negotiate with such individual (a new ruler) as the highest organ of his state." *(Oppenheim International Law* [3d ed.], vol. 1, sections 77, 342.) Speaking of the recognition of a new state Wheaton (*International Law* [2d ed.], p. 39) says: "So long, indeed, as the new state confines its action to its own citizens and to the limits of its own territory, it may well dispense with such recognition. But if it desires to enter into the great society of nations, all the members of which recognize rights to which they are mutually entitled, and duties which they may be called upon reciprocally to fulfil, such recognition becomes essentially necessary to the complete participation of the new state in all the advantages of this society.... The new state becomes entitled to the exercise of its external sovereignty as to those states only by whom that sovereignty has been recognized." In Hyde's *International Law* (Vol. 1, sec. 37) is the statement that "the mode of recognition is not material, provided there be an unequivocal act indicating clearly that the new state is dealt with as such and is deemed to be entitled to exercise the privileges of statehood in the society of nations."

More assistance may be found in the reasons underlying various decisions of the courts as to the effect to be given to the acts of foreign governments. This effect depends upon our acknowledgment of the comity of nations. "The principle that the conduct of one independent government cannot be successfully questioned in the courts of another is as applicable to a case involving the title to property brought within the custody of a court such as we have here, as it was held to be to the cases cited, in which claims for damages were based upon acts done in a foreign country, for it rests at last upon the highest considerations of international comity and expediency." (*Oetjen v. Central Leather Co.*, 246 U.S. 297, 303....) Therefore, where comity exists between two nations and no question of public policy arises this rule is invariable. Yet in specific cases the question of recognition is thought controlling—recognition existing at the time the alleged wrongful act was done, or recognition later which relates back to that time. *Oetjen v. Central Leather Co.*, supra. . . .

We reach the conclusion, therefore, that a foreign power brings an action in our courts not as a matter of right. Its power to do so is the creature of comity. Until such government is recognized by the United States no such comity exists. The plaintiff concededly has not been so recognized. There is, therefore, no proper party before us. We may add that recognition and consequently the existence of comity is purely a matter for the determination of the legislative or executive departments of the government. Who is the sovereign of a territory is a political question. In any case where that question is in dispute the courts are bound by the decision reached by those departments. (*Jones v. U.S.*, 137 U.S. 202; *Luther v. Sagor*, [3 K.B. 1921 532], 556). It is not for the courts to say whether the present governments of Russia or Mexico or Great Britain should or should not be recognized. They are or they are not. That is as far as we may inquire. Nor is anything here decided inconsistent with *Wulfsohn v. Soviet Republic*, (supra). Upon the facts in that case, if the defendant was not an existing government it might not be sued. There was no party before the court. If it were, as was alleged and admitted, the same result followed not because of comity, but because an independent government is not answerable for its acts to our courts.

We are the more ready to reach this conclusion because to hold otherwise might tend to nullify the rule that public policy must always prevail over comity. More than once during the last seventy years our relations with one or another existing but unrecognized government have been of so critical a character that to permit it to recover in our courts funds which might strengthen it or which might even be used against our interests would be unwise. We should do nothing to thwart the policy which the United States has adopted. Yet unless recognition is the test of the right to sue we do not see why Maximilian as emperor of Mexico might not have maintained an action here.

With regard to the present Russian government the case is still stronger, even did comity not depend on recognition. We not only refuse to recognize it. Our State Department gives the reasons. Secretary Colby has stated them in an official note, dated August 10, 1920. He begins by saying that our government will not participate in any plan for the expansion of the armistice negotiations between Russia and Poland into a general European conference, "which would in all probability involve two results, from both of which this country strongly recoils, viz.: The recognition of the Bolshevist régime and a settlement of the Russian problem almost inevitably upon the basis of a dismemberment of Russia." He continues:

> "We are unwilling that while it is helpless in the grip of a nonrepresentative government whose only sanction is brutal force, Russia shall be weakened still further by a policy of dismemberment, conceived in other than Russian interests. . . . The Bolsheviki, although in number

an inconsiderable minority of the people, by force and cunning seized the powers and machinery of government, and have continued to use them with savage oppression to maintain themselves in power.... It is not possible for the government of the United States to recognize the present rulers of Russia as a government with which the relations common to friendly governments can be maintained.... The existing régime in Russia is based upon the negation of every principle of honor and good faith, and every usage and convention, underlying the whole structure of international law, the negation, in short, of every principle upon which it is possible to base harmonious and trustful relations, whether of nations or of individuals. The responsible leaders of the régime have frequently and openly boasted that they are willing to sign agreements and undertakings with foreign powers while not having the slightest intention of observing such undertakings or carrying out such agreements.... They have made it quite plain that they intend to use every means ... to promote revolutionary movements in other countries.... In the view of this government, there cannot be any common ground upon which it can stand with a power whose conceptions of international relations are so entirely alien to its own, so utterly repugnant to its moral sense. There can be no mutual confidence or trust, no respect even, if pledges are to be given and agreements made with a cynical repudiation of their obligations already in the mind of one of the parties. We cannot recognize, hold official relations with, or give friendly reception to the agents of a government which is determined and bound to conspire against our institutions, whose diplomats will be the agitators of dangerous revolt, whose spokesmen say that they sign agreements with no intention of keeping them."

....

The judgment appealed from should be affirmed, with costs.

BANCO NACIONAL de CUBA v. SABBATINO

376 U.S. 398, 410–412, 84 S.Ct. 923, 11 L.Ed.2d 804 (1964) (footnote omitted).

[As discussed in greater depth *infra*, Section 7, in this case an instrumentality of the Cuban government brought suit in U.S. court against a commodities broker for conversion of bills of lading and against a receiver for certain injunctive relief. The defendants responded in part by challenging the ability of the Cuban government (or its instrumentalities) to appear in U.S. court, since there were no diplomatic relations between the United States and Cuba. Although no such relations existed, the United States did recognize Cuba as a sovereign state and did recognize the government of Fidel Castro as the government of Cuba.]

Respondents, pointing to the severance of diplomatic relations, commercial embargo, and freezing of Cuban assets in this country, contend that relations between the United States and Cuba manifest such animosity that unfriendliness is clear, and that the courts should be closed to the Cuban Government. We do not agree. This Court would hardly be competent to undertake assessments of varying degrees of friendliness or its absence, and, lacking some definite touchstone for determination, we are constrained to consider any relationship, short of war, with a recognized sovereign power as embracing the privilege of resorting to United States courts. Although the severance of diplomatic relations is an overt act with objective significance in the dealings of sovereign states, we are unwilling to say that it should inevitably result in the withdrawal of the privilege of bringing suit. Severance may take place for any number of political reasons, its duration is unpredictable, and whatever expression of animosity it may imply does not approach that implicit in a declaration of war.

It is perhaps true that nonrecognition of a government in certain circumstances may reflect no greater unfriendliness than the severance of diplomatic relations with a recognized government, but the refusal to recognize has a unique legal aspect. It signifies this country's unwillingness to acknowledge that the government in question speaks as the sovereign authority for the territory it purports to control, see *Russian Republic v. Cibrario*, ... 235 N.Y. at 260–263. Political recognition is exclusively a function of the Executive. The possible incongruity of judicial "recognition," by permitting suit, of a government not recognized by the Executive is completely absent when merely diplomatic relations are broken.[12]

The view that the existing situation between the United States and Cuba should not lead to a denial of status to sue is buttressed by the circumstance that none of the acts of our Government have been aimed at closing the courts of this country to Cuba, and more particularly by the fact that the Government has come to the support of Cuba's "act of state" claim in this very litigation.

Respondents further urge that reciprocity of treatment is an essential ingredient of comity generally, and, therefore, of the privilege of foreign states to bring suit here. Although *Hilton v. Guyot*, 159 U.S. 113, contains some broad language about the relationship of reciprocity to comity, the case in fact imposed a requirement of reciprocity only in regard to conclusiveness of judgments, and even then only in limited circumstances. *Id.*, at 170–171. In *Direction der Disconto-Gesellschaft v. United States Steel Corp.*, 300 F. 741, 747 (D.C.S.D.N.Y.), Judge Learned Hand pointed

12. The doctrine that nonrecognition precludes suit by the foreign government in every circumstance has been the subject of discussion and criticism. See, *e.g.*, Hervey, The Legal Effects of Recognition in International Law (1928) 112–119; Jaffe, Judicial Aspects of Foreign Relations (1933) 148–156; Borchard, The Unrecognized Government in American Courts, 26 Am. J. Int'l L. 261 (1932); Dickinson, The Unrecognized Government or State in English and American Law, 22 Mich. L. Rev. 118 (1923); Fraenkel, The Juristic Status of Foreign States, Their Property and Their Acts, 25 Col. L. Rev. 544, 547–552 (1925); Lubman, The Unrecognized Government in American Courts: Upright v. Mercury Business Machines, 62 Col. L. Rev. 275 (1962). In this litigation we need intimate no view on the possibility of access by an unrecognized government to United States courts, except to point out that even the most inhospitable attitude on the matter does not dictate denial of standing here.

out that the doctrine of reciprocity has apparently been confined to foreign judgments.

There are good reasons for declining to extend the principle to the question of standing of sovereign states to sue. Whether a foreign sovereign will be permitted to sue involves a problem more sensitive politically than whether the judgments of its courts may be re-examined, and the possibility of embarrassment to the Executive Branch in handling foreign relations is substantially more acute. Re-examination of judgments, in principle, reduces rather than enhances the possibility of injustice being done in a particular case; refusal to allow suit makes it impossible for a court to see that a particular dispute is fairly resolved. The freezing of Cuban assets exemplifies the capacity of the political branches to assure, through a variety of techniques . . ., that the national interest is protected against a country which is thought to be improperly denying the rights of United States citizens.

Furthermore, the question whether a country gives *res judicata* effect to United States judgments presents a relatively simple inquiry. The precise status of the United States Government and its nationals before foreign courts is much more difficult to determine. To make such an investigation significant, a court would have to discover not only what is provided by the formal structure of the foreign judicial system, but also what the practical possibilities of fair treatment are. The courts, whose powers to further the national interest in foreign affairs are necessarily circumscribed as compared with those of the political branches, can best serve the rule of law by not excluding otherwise proper suitors because of deficiencies in their legal systems.

We hold that this petitioner is not barred from access to the federal courts.

PFIZER INC. v. INDIA

434 U.S. 308, 318–20, 98 S.Ct. 584, 54 L.Ed.2d 563 (1978) (footnote omitted).

[In this case, the governments of several foreign countries, as purchasers of antibiotics, brought antitrust treble damage suits against major pharmaceutical firms in the United States. The Eighth Circuit Court of Appeals found that the governments had standing to pursue the claim and the case was appealed.]

. . . This Court has long recognized the rule that a foreign nation is generally entitled to prosecute any civil claim in the courts of the United States upon the same basis as a domestic corporation or individual might do. "To deny him this privilege would manifest a want of comity and friendly feeling." *The Sapphire,* 11 Wall. 164, 167; *Monaco v. Mississippi,* 292 U.S. 313, 323 n.2; *Banco Nacional de Cuba v. Sabbatino,* 376 U.S. 398, 408–409; see U.S. Const., Art. III, § 2, cl. 1.[19] To allow a foreign sovereign

19. Congress has explicitly conferred jurisdiction upon the federal courts to entertain such suits:

to sue in our courts for treble damages to the same extent as any other person injured by an antitrust violation is thus no more than a specific application of a long-settled general rule. To exclude foreign nations from the protections of our antitrust laws would, on the other hand, create a conspicuous exception to this rule, an exception that could not be justified in the absence of clear legislative intent.

[T]he result we reach does not require the Judiciary in any way to interfere in sensitive matters of foreign policy.[20] It has long been established that only governments recognized by the United States and at peace with us are entitled to access to our courts, and that it is within the exclusive power of the Executive Branch to determine which nations are entitled to sue. *Jones v. United States,* 137 U.S. 202, 212; *Guaranty Trust Co. v. United States*, 304 U.S. 126, 137–138; *Banco Nacional de Cuba v. Sabbatino, supra*, at 408–412. Nothing we decide today qualifies this established rule of complete judicial deference to the Executive Branch.

We hold today only that a foreign nation otherwise entitled to sue in our courts is entitled to sue for treble damages under the antitrust laws to the same extent as any other plaintiff. Neither the fact that the respondents are foreign nor the fact that they are sovereign is reason to deny them the remedy of treble damages Congress afforded to "any person" victimized by violations of the antitrust laws.

Accordingly, the judgment of the Court of Appeals is

Affirmed.

NOTES ON THE CONSTITUTIONAL AND INTERNATIONAL LAW DIMENSIONS OF RECOGNITION

1. *The Basic Issues*. A government's capacity to sue or be sued in U.S. courts would appear to depend on whether its existence is "recognized." But recognized by whom? The Department of State? The majority of the world's governments? The courts applying objective standards about whether an entity is the legitimate representative of the citizens of a country, or about whether an entity exercises control over those citizens?

It seems obvious that the political branches of the U.S. government will make recognition determinations for their own purposes, as will foreign

"The district courts shall have original jurisdiction of all civil actions where the matter in controversy exceeds the sum or value of $10,000, exclusive of interest and costs, and is between—

. . . .

"(4) a foreign state . . . as plaintiff and citizens of a State or of different States." 28 U.S.C. § 1332(a)(4) (1976 ed.).

. . . .

20. In a letter that was presented to the Court of Appeals when it reconsidered this case en banc, the Legal Adviser of the Department of State advised "that the Department of State would not anticipate any foreign policy problems if . . . foreign governments [were held to be] 'persons' within the meaning of Clayton Act § 4." A copy of this letter is contained in the Memorandum for the United States as *Amicus Curiae* in opposition to the petition for a writ of certiorari filed in this Court.

governments, but it is less obvious that these determinations should be outcome-determinative for the many contexts in which recognition might matter in judicial proceedings. If a foreign government obviously is "in charge" but has not been recognized by the United States for diplomatic reasons—for example, to bring pressure on it to adhere to basic human rights standards in the treatment of minorities or dissidents—is it necessary, or useful, for U.S. courts to defer to this policy by barring the unrecognized government from its precincts, even in ordinary commercial suits? Should the U.S. government speak, in such matters, with a single voice? Or is such consistency, as Ralph Waldo Emerson wrote, "the hobgoblin of little minds, adored by little statesmen and philosophers and divines. With consistency a great soul has simply nothing to do."? *Self-Reliance,* in *The Selected Writings of Ralph Waldo Emerson* 152 (B. Atkinson ed., 1950).

Perhaps the answer also varies by the context in which a court encounters recognition issues. We may regard the "right" to sue as a sort of privilege—and thus consider this the strongest case for deferring to an executive branch determination that seeks to disadvantage the unrecognized state or government—but can the same be said of the "right" to be sued? If not, should the two concepts be severed? In other words, if a recognized government has the right to sue a person in U.S. court, should it follow that the person be able to sue the recognized government in U.S. court? Conversely, if a government cannot sue in U.S. court because it is not recognized as being a government, does that mean it also cannot claim governmental immunity from being sued in U.S. court? (Note that prior to deciding the *Cibrario* case, the New York Court of Appeals decided that the unrecognized RSFSR *was immune* from suit in U.S. court, where the plaintiff sought to hold the RSFSR accountable for governmental acts committed within the RSFSR's jurisdiction. *See* Wulfsohn v. Russian Socialist Federated Soviet Republic, 234 N.Y. 372, 138 N.E. 24 (1923).) If nonrecognition bears on the capacity to sue and/or be sued, does it also affect the legal status of the unrecognized government's acts?

As this discussion suggests, U.S. courts generally encounter the issue of recognition in three contexts:

> (1) cases where the foreign government (or its instrumentality) appears as a plaintiff in a suit, usually for purposes of vindicating a contract right or claiming state assets located in the United States;
>
> (2) cases where the foreign government is sued as a defendant and wishes to claim immunity from suit, an issue that is now governed by the Foreign Sovereign Immunities Act; and
>
> (3) cases where the foreign government itself does not appear in a U.S. court but its acts or laws are at issue with respect to persons or chattels before the court. In each of these kinds of cases the court must ask whether the foreign government is an entity entitled to standing or entitled to acceptance of its acts as a sovereign government.

Mary Beth West & Sean D. Murphy, *The Impact on U.S. Litigation of Non-Recognition of Foreign Governments,* 26 STAN. J. INT'L L. 435, 440 (1990).

2. *International Legal Theory*. Recognition in U.S. courts is distinct from recognition on the international plane, but understanding the international context is important. In international legal theory, three concepts need to be distinguished: (1) recognition of a state, (2) recognition of a government, and (3) establishment of diplomatic relations. Initially, the three terms need to be understood as indicating distinct functions. Put at its simplest, *recognition of a state* is the affirmation, usually by the government of another state, that a new nation has come into existence which, at least as far as the recognizer is concerned, is subject to all the rights and duties of a state in international law. *Recognition of a government* is the affirmation, by the government of an existing state, of a regime's entitlement to the rights and duties accruing to governments under international law. A form of recognition may also be extended by an international organization when it admits a state to membership, and again, when it accepts the credentials of the representatives of the member state. The *establishing of diplomatic relations* is accomplished by accrediting an ambassador or lower level diplomat who is received by the government of the state to whom he or she is accredited, and, usually, by establishing a diplomatic mission, often on a reciprocal basis, at the seat of the recognized government. Note, however, that an ambassador may be accredited to several (usually small, neighboring) states and that one embassy may serve several capitals.

These three different events—recognition of state, recognition of government, and establishment of diplomatic relations—often occur simultaneously. There is no inherent reason, however, why this should be so. The coming into existence of a new state, in theory, could be recognized even though there are several contenders for its leadership. In such circumstances, recognition of government may be withheld until the outcome of the civil contest is clarified by events. The overthrow of the recognized government of an established state may cause other governments for a time to withhold recognition of the usurpers for various reasons, including plain pique, while still recognizing the state itself. Logically and practically, however, it is not possible to recognize more than one government at a time in one state. (Nevertheless, the United States did manage to have a defense treaty with the nationalist regime on Taiwan for one year after it had switched recognition from that regime to the one in Beijing. *See* Chapter 3, Section 10.) In the past, some states have recognized the existence of a government *de facto* and another *de jure*. This can arise when a formerly acknowledged government has been replaced by a successful usurper under circumstances eliciting special sympathy for the former.

There is no legal requirement that any government must maintain diplomatic relations with any other, even one it has recognized. That the United States does not have formal diplomatic relations with the Castro regime in Havana in no way diminishes Washington's recognition of that government and of the Cuban state. On the other hand, the establishing of diplomatic relations does, of course, presume recognition.

3. *U.S. Constitutional Doctrine*. Once the distinctions between these three acts—recognition of state, recognition of government, and establishment of diplomatic relations—are clear, it may appear odd that the Constitution does not specifically assign responsibility for the first two, either to the

President or Congress. Article II, section 3 is concerned solely with the third category, providing that the President "shall receive Ambassadors and other public Ministers...." It was in defense of this prerogative that Jefferson refused to receive an exequator of citizen Genet when he presented himself as consul of the French Republic, because his commission was addressed to the Congress of the United States. The President pointed out that he was "the only channel of communication between the United States and foreign nations." J.B. Moore, 4 *International Law Digest* 680–81 (1906).

It is a considerable step from such presidential exercise of the constitutionally-stipulated diplomatic function to the contemporary practice, which gives to the President virtually uncontested authority to recognize, or refuse recognition to, foreign states and governments. Nevertheless, the claim to such a broader function was already laid by Jefferson in 1790, when he asserted that "the transaction of business with foreign nations is Executive altogether. It belongs, then, to the head of that department, except to such portions of it as are specially submitted to the Senate. Exceptions are to be construed strictly." *Opinion on the Question Whether the Senate Has the Right to Negative the Grade of Persons Appointed by the Executive to Fill Foreign Missions* (April 24, 1790), in S. Padover, *The Complete Jefferson* 138 (1943). Madison, however, was of quite another view, seeing in the reception clause nothing more than a designation of "the department of the government, most proper for the ceremony of admitting public ministers, of examining their credentials, and of authenticating their title to the privileges annexed to their character by the law of nations. This being the apparent design of the constitution," he concluded, "it would be highly improper to magnify the function into an important prerogative, even when no rights of other departments could be affected by it." *The Federalist* 444 (1852 ed.) (containing the Letters of Pacificus and Helvidius).

Writing as Pacificus, Hamilton early acknowledged that the key, the real locus of power, was not reception of ambassadors but recognition. He thought, however, that the lesser encompassed the greater, being essentially in the nature of an example of wider presidential power. "The right of the executive to receive ambassadors and other public ministers," he stated, "may serve to illustrate the relative duties of the executive and legislative departments. This right includes that of judging, in the case of a revolution of government in a foreign country, whether the new rulers are competent organs of the national will, and ought to be recognized, or not; which, where a treaty antecedently exists between the United States and such nation, involves the power of continuing or suspending its operation.... This power ... is an important instance of the right of the executive, to decide upon the obligations of the country with regard to foreign nations." *Id.* at 405.

That the issue was not at once laid to rest for all time is suggested by Congress's "recognition" of the independence of Cuba in 1898, although even this can be reconciled with prevailing practice by the exceptional circumstance that it did so by adding the recognition as an appendage to the declaration of war against Spain. See 31 CONG. REC. 3984 (1898) (statement of Senator Nelson (Minn.)). In any event, except for an occasional exercise of the power of the purse, the ability of Congress nowadays to exercise a function in this area appears to have lapsed, and this seems to have been recognized even by Congress. *See, e.g.,* S. Doc. No. 56, 54th Cong., 2d Sess. 20–22 (1897).

4. *The Role of the Judiciary.* While the Congress and President may have struggled from time to time over control of the recognition power, a third party, the judiciary, has also been involved in the question of who speaks for the United States. In reading the cases in this chapter, it should be observed that the stakes in this struggle are far from esoteric. On the contrary, in U.S. domestic law, the recognition power may have important, even dispositive, effects on the legal interests of foreign nations, individuals, states of the union, and other legal entities. While Madison, Hamilton, Jefferson and Washington may have been concerned primarily with the question of the relative powers of Congress and the Executive, currently, the question primarily appears in terms of the extent to which U.S. courts should defer to the Executive in such matters.

The conduct of diplomatic relations and the recognition of new states, and of new governments, is often said to fall squarely within the political discretion of the Executive Branch. *See, e.g.,* Americans United for Separation of Church and State v. Reagan, 786 F.2d 194 (3d Cir.), *cert. denied,* 479 U.S. 914, 107 S.Ct. 314, 93 L.Ed.2d 288 (1986) (dismissing as a political question a challenge to the establishment of an embassy to the Vatican); Freiberg v. Muskie, 651 F.2d 608 (8th Cir. 1981) (dismissing as political question action to compel State Department to intervene on behalf of the plaintiff with the West German government). Indeed, courts are reluctant to enter the foreign relations "thicket" because judges have tended to accept a theory of separation of powers that accords unique primacy to the Executive Branch in that area. United States v. Curtiss–Wright Export Corp., 299 U.S. 304, 57 S.Ct. 216, 81 L.Ed. 255 (1936). Moreover, courts are evidently ill-equipped to make close, informed judgment-calls on such fact-grounded issues as which one of several rival claimant "governments" speaks for a nation which is in the throes of a civil war. Both considerations admonish the judiciary to defer to the views of the President (*viz.* the State Department). Yet, disputes do come before the courts that make it difficult to heed these admonitions. As you read the cases that follow, consider whether they suggest a somewhat greater degree of judicial independence than might have been forecast by the dicta about executive supremacy so liberally sprinkled by Justice Sutherland around the pages of the *Curtiss–Wright* case.

5. *Executive Communication to the Judiciary.* The method by which courts learn the Executive Branch's official recognition policy has changed from independent judicial determinations to specific State Department instructions. In the first half of the 20th century, courts usually took "judicial notice" of official policy. Given the public nature of recognition, discerning the position of the Executive was not difficult. The Supreme Court sanctioned this method when it took judicial notice of U.S. recognition of the Mexican Carranza government. Oetjen v. Central Leather Co., 246 U.S. 297, 301, 38 S.Ct. 309, 62 L.Ed. 726 (1918). The New York *Cibrario* court (extracted above) quoted public pronouncements concerning U.S. nonrecognition of the Soviet Union by the Secretary of State. When two ambassadors vied for judicial recognition, the courts accepted the one to whom the Executive had issued official credentials. *See, e.g.,* Agency of Canadian Car & Foundry Co. v.

American Can Co., 258 Fed. 363, 368 (2d Cir. 1919). Other courts have looked to letters submitted directly to the court by the Executive. *See, e.g.,* Russian Volunteer Fleet v. United States, 282 U.S. 481, 51 S.Ct. 229, 75 L.Ed. 473 (1931) (government brief included a letter from the Secretary of State expressly informing the Court of official U.S. policy). In *Guaranty Trust Co. of New York v. United States,* the State Department reaffirmed the diplomatic status of a Kerensky official at the time crucial for purposes of the litigation. 304 U.S. 126, 138 n. 4, 58 S.Ct. 785, 82 L.Ed. 1224 (1938).

After World War II, perhaps to ensure that executive and judicial positions did not diverge, the State Department often issued specific "suggestions" or instructions to courts, frequently prompted by the requests of individual litigants. Courts sometimes compared these State Department submissions to public pronouncements (not made with a particular litigation in mind) to see whether they were congruent. Latvian State Cargo & Passenger S.S. Line v. McGrath, 188 F.2d 1000, 1003 (D.C. Cir. 1951).

Most cases, however, have relied on the Department's "suggestions" whenever these have been forthcoming. This is in part due to the fact that U.S. policy has shifted away from formal recognition after a change in government. In 1977, the State Department announced that it would thenceforth focus on the existence of diplomatic relations with new governments, rather than on formal recognition or non-recognition of those governments—a gesture that can be particularly freighted when a government that is non-democratic or authoritarian comes to power. 77 DEP'T ST. BULL. 462 (1977). Similarly, very few putative states today are identified by the State Department as unrecognized. The most notable exception is Taiwan; in that case, the State Department has stated that "With the establishment of diplomatic relations with China on January 1, 1979, the US Government recognized the People's Republic of China as the sole legal government of China and acknowledged the Chinese position that there is only one China and that Taiwan is part of China." *U.S Department of State, Fact Sheet: Independent States in the World*, April 13, 2011, *available at* http://www.state.gov/s/inr/rls/4250.htm. Other entities claiming statehood that are not recognized by the United States include, for example, the Turkish Republic of Cyprus; Palestine; Abkhazia (a separatist region of Georgia); and Republika Srpska (a region of Bosnia and Herzegovina).

The diminished interest in formal recognition or non-recognition has caused courts to rely increasingly on interventions by the State Department on a case-by-case basis. *See* West & Murphy, *supra* note 4, at 456.

At times, the Department has acted to instruct the court on its own initiative, relaying its views through the Department of Justice. *See, e.g.,* Republic of Vietnam v. Pfizer, Inc., 556 F.2d 892, 895 n. 4 (8th Cir. 1977). More often, individual litigants have requested the Department to provide information. *See, e.g.,* Japanese Government v. Commercial Cas. Ins. Co., 101 F.Supp. 243, 250 (S.D.N.Y. 1951). Courts themselves have also solicited State Department positions. *See* P & E Shipping Corp. v. Banco Para El Comercio Exterior De Cuba, 307 F.2d 415 (1st Cir. 1962) (remanding case in order for lower court to procure State Department position on the effect of breaking diplomatic relations with Cuba); Sarei v. Rio Tinto, 487 F.3d 1193 (9th Cir. 2007) (*supra* Section 3).

6. *On Fictions and Interventions.* Unsurprisingly, some cases potentially decided on the basis of nonrecognition have found other ways of categorizing the parties in interest—at least where the entity in question is the plaintiff. Cases such as *Upright v. Mercury Business Machines Co.*, 13 A.D.2d 36, 213 N.Y.S.2d 417 (App. Div. 1961), turn on a quasi-fiction: that the plaintiff is not an agency of an unrecognized government (there, the German Democratic Republic), but merely an assignee for value—albeit a corporation created by the state. The court explained:

> In a time in which governments with established control over territories may be denied recognition for many reasons, it does not mean that the denizens of such territories or the corporate creatures of such powers do not have the juridical capacity to trade, transfer title, or collect the price for the merchandise they sell to outsiders, even in the courts of nonrecognizing nations.

Id. at 41. Is this a useful distinction?

Useful or not, it does have some jurisprudential pedigree. *See, e.g.*, Russian Volunteer Fleet v. United States, 282 U.S. 481, 482, 51 S.Ct. 229, 75 L.Ed. 473 (1931) (permitting, notwithstanding nonrecognition of the Soviet regime by the U.S. government—and the submission to the Supreme Court of a letter by the State Department emphasizing that fact—a shipowning corporation organized under U.S.S.R. laws to sue the U.S. government under statutory scheme compensating for vessels requisitioned by the United States); Amtorg Trading Corp. v. United States, 71 F.2d 524, 527–28 (C.P.A. 1934) (permitting, again prior to the recognition of the Soviet regime by the United States, a wholly-owned agency of the Soviet government to sue because, being organized under the laws of the State of New York where it was domiciled, it was a "person" with the rights of New York "citizenship").

Why should a judge decide such a case in conformity with executive recognition policy when the U.S. government, by its inaction, has permitted the unrecognized foreign state entity to enter the American market? If there is no executive policy against such market entry, why should the courts deny the foreign entity the rights it would otherwise enjoy in accordance with due process of law? Or does this overestimate the Executive Branch's capacity to control entry?

In some instances, the Executive Branch has itself taken the initiative to see that the courts do not decide a case in conformity with its own nonrecognition policy. *See* Transportes Aereos de Angola v. Ronair, Inc., 544 F.Supp. 858, 863 (D. Del. 1982).

7. *Federal Diversity Cases.* The "diversity" jurisdiction clause of the U.S. Constitution, art. III, § 2, gives federal courts jurisdiction over all cases in law and equity "between a State, or the Citizens thereof, and foreign States, Citizens or Subjects." What constitutes a foreign state—and, consequently whether a citizen or subject is of a foreign state—thus has important implications for litigants. The tendency in these, as in the preceding cases, is for the courts to declare that a foreign entity's sovereign statehood is a matter

for determination by the Executive. In some of these cases, however, the courts seem to make their own determination based on collaterally-ascertained facts and "common sense." Compare Klausner v. Levy, 83 F.Supp. 599 (E.D. Va. 1949) with Murarka v. Bachrack Bros., Inc., 215 F.2d 547 (2d Cir. 1954) (Harlan, J.). *See also* Iran Handicraft & Carpet Export Center v. Marjan Int'l Corp., 655 F.Supp. 1275 (S.D.N.Y. 1987) (interpreting "foreign state" for the purpose of diversity jurisdiction to mean recognition by the U.S. government as an "international jurisdicial person"). An interesting borderline case is the status of a corporation incorporated in what was then the Crown Colony of Hong Kong. For two judicial views on that status, see *Windert Watch Co., Inc. v. Remex Electronics Ltd.,* 468 F.Supp. 1242 (S.D.N.Y. 1979) and *Tetra Finance (HK) Ltd. v. Shaheen,* 584 F.Supp. 847 (S.D.N.Y. 1984). *See also* Matimak Trading Co. v. Khalily, 118 F.3d 76 (2d Cir. 1997) (recognition of foreign governments for the purposes of alienage jurisdiction under 28 U.S.C. § 1332 is a matter of executive determination to which courts must defer; here, the State Department indicated that Hong Kong had not been accorded such status).

8. *Further Reading.* In general see Jonathan L. Alder, *The Unrecognized Government in the Courts of the United States,* 5 VA. J. INT'L L. 36 (1964); Thomas M. Franck, *The Courts, The State Department and National Policy: A Criterion for Judicial Abdication,* 44 MINN. L. REV. 1101 (1959–60); Stanley Lubman, *The Unrecognized Government in American Courts:* Upright v. Mercury Business Machines, 62 COLUM. L. REV. 275 (1962); Note, *Out from the Precarious Orbit of Politics: Reconsidering Recognition and the Standing of Foreign Governments to Sue in U.S. Courts,* 29 VA. J. INT'L L. 473 (1989); Note, Transportes Aereos de Angola v. Ronair, Inc.: *Nonaccess to U.S. Courts by Unrecognized Governments—A New Exception?,* 8 N.C.J. INT'L L. & COM. REG . 225 (1983); Michael E. Field, Liberia v. Bickford: *The Continuing Problem of Recognition of Governments and Civil Litigation in the United States*, 18 MD. J. INT'L L. & TRADE 113 (1994).

NATIONAL PETROCHEMICAL COMPANY OF IRAN v. M/T STOLT SHEAF

860 F.2d 551 (2d Cir. 1988).

CARDAMONE, CIRCUIT JUDGE:

The sole question presented on this appeal is whether National Petrochemical Company of Iran (NPC), a foreign corporation wholly owned by the government of Iran, is entitled to bring suit as a plaintiff in a diversity action in federal court. To answer such a question in this shoalstrewn area of the law, it is wise for courts to have in mind, like doctors taking the Hippocratic oath, that they must "first, do no harm." For the reasons that follow, we hold that NPC may maintain its action in the courts of the United States.

I

A brief background is necessary. In November of 1979 militants loyal to the Ayatollah Khomeini seized the United States Embassy in Tehran and took 52 American diplomatic personnel hostage. With the embassy and its personnel still in the militants' hands, on April 7, 1980 President Carter severed diplomatic relations with Iran and issued Executive Order No. 12,205, 45 Fed.Reg. 24,099 (1980), barring the sale to it of American products. As a result, NPC—which is a subsidiary of the National Iranian Oil Company that in turn is wholly owned by the government of Iran—found itself unable to procure essential chemicals such as ethylhexanol, orthoxylene, and ethylene dichloride from its usual sources in the United States. NPC's attempts to circumvent President Carter's trade embargo resulted in the transactions that brought about the instant litigation.

In the spring of 1980, NPC agreed to buy the needed chemicals from Monnris Enterprises (Monnris) of Dubai, United Arab Emirates. Monnris arranged to purchase them from Rotexchemie Brunst & Co. of Hamburg (Rotex), which contracted with United States sellers through its Geneva affiliate, Formula, S.A. (Formula). Rotex and Formula apparently fabricated shipping documents that concealed both the origin of the chemical cargo and its destination, and by such illegal methods were able to draw on the letters of credit issued by NPC before the cargoes were even shipped.

In August, 1980 Rotex chartered the defendant M/T Stolt Sheaf from the Liberian defendant Parcel Tankers, Inc. to carry the chemicals from Houston, Texas to Iran, via Barcelona, Spain. The remaining defendants are United States and Norwegian companies affiliated with Parcel Tankers and the M/T Stolt Sheaf. Rotex planned to deliver the embargoed goods to NPC in Iran, but when war broke out between Iran and Iraq in September, 1980 the chemicals were diverted to Taiwan, where Rotex resold them.

NPC thereupon instituted civil and criminal suits against the middlemen in Hamburg and Rotterdam to recover the losses it incurred in its scheme to skirt the American trade embargo. Because these suits were unsuccessful, plaintiff filed a complaint on September 30, 1986 in the United States District Court for the Southern District of New York (Owen, J.) alleging that the above named defendants had participated with the middlemen in fraud, conversion, falsifying bills of lading, all in breach of their duties and obligations under the bills of lading and the law. In a published decision, 671 F. Supp. 1009 (S.D.N.Y. 1987), Judge Owen concluded—based upon a United States State Department letter written in connection with an unrelated case, *Iran Handicraft & Carpet Export Center v. Marjan Int'l Corp.*, 655 F. Supp. 1275 (S.D.N.Y. 1987)—that the United States has not recognized the Khomeini government of Iran. The district court therefore held that because NPC is a wholly-owned entity of an unrecognized foreign government, it is not entitled to bring suit in the courts of the United States. It dismissed NPC's complaint with prejudice. 671 F.Supp. at 1010.

On NPC's appeal from dismissal of its complaint, the United States has, for the first time, entered the litigation, submitting a brief as Amicus

Curiae signed by attorneys from the Justice and State Departments, urging that NPC be granted access to the courts of the United States in this case.

II

We turn to an analysis of the law. Article III of the United States Constitution extends the federal judicial power to "all Cases ... between a State, or the Citizens thereof, and foreign States, Citizens or Subjects." U.S. Const., art. III, § 2, cl. 1. To effectuate this power, the United States Judicial Code provides diversity jurisdiction over any civil action arising between "a foreign state ... as plaintiff and citizens of a State or of different States." 28 U.S.C. § 1332(a)(4) (1982).

To determine whether NPC as a wholly-owned entity of the Khomeini government of Iran should be granted access to federal court under § 1332(a)(4), it is helpful to review several well-established rules in this area of the law. In order to take advantage of diversity jurisdiction, a foreign state and the government representing it must be "recognized" by the United States. *See Pfizer Inc. v. India,* 434 U.S. 308, 319–20 (1978); *Calderone v. Naviera Vacuba S/A,* 325 F.2d 76, 77 (2d Cir. 1963); *Land Oberoesterreich v. Gude,* 109 F.2d 635, 637 (2d Cir.), *cert. denied,* 311 U.S. 670 (1940). As an incident to the President's express constitutional powers to appoint, U.S. Const., art. II, § 2, and to receive ambassadors, *id.* § 3, and to his implied power to maintain international relations, *United States v. Curtiss–Wright Export Corp.,* 299 U.S. 304, 318–20 (1936), the Supreme Court has acknowledged the President's exclusive authority to recognize or refuse to recognize a foreign state or government and to establish or refuse to establish diplomatic relations with it. *See Banco Nacional de Cuba v. Sabbatino,* 376 U.S. 398, 410 (1964); *Guaranty Trust Co. v. United States,* 304 U.S. 126, 137 (1938); *see also Restatement (Third) of the Foreign Relations Law of the United States* § 204 (1987) (*Restatement 3d*).

For our purposes in this case, we also note that, under international law, a "state" is generally defined as "an entity that has a defined territory and a permanent population, under the control of its own government, and that engages in, or has the capacity to engage in, formal relations with other such entities." *Restatement 3d* § 201; *see Texas v. White,* 74 U.S. (7 Wall.) 700, 720 (1868). Although international law purports to require recognition of "states" that satisfy the elements of this definition, recognition of the particular government in control of another state is not mandatory. Further, a state *derecognizes* a governmental regime when it recognizes another regime as the legitimate government of that state. For example, when the United States recognized the People's Republic of China it derecognized the regime of the Taiwanese "Republic of China" which the United States had previously treated as the Chinese government. *See Restatement 3d* § 203, Comment f.

A break in diplomatic relations with another government does not automatically signify denial of access to federal courts. *See Sabbatino*, 376 U.S. 408–12. As the Supreme Court has observed, courts are hardly competent to assess how friendly or unfriendly our relationship with a foreign government is at any given moment, and absent some "definite touchstone for determination, we are constrained to consider any relationship, short of war, with a recognized sovereign power as embracing the privilege of resorting to United States courts." *Id.* at 410; *see Pfizer Inc.*, 434 U.S. at 319–20. With these general rules in mind, we consider the circumstance of the instant case.

III

A. Recognition For Purposes of Federal Diversity Jurisdiction

The United States, as noted, severed diplomatic relations with Iran in 1980. In addition, NPC and Amicus concede that the President has never formally recognized the Khomeini government of Iran. The district court relied on a letter from the Assistant Legal Advisor for Management of the Department of State clarifying Iran's diplomatic status in connection with *Iran Handicraft & Carpet Export Center v. Marjan Int'l Corp.*, 655 F. Supp. 1275 (S.D.N.Y. 1987). The letter, dated December 26, 1985, stated in part:

> In response to your letter of December 13, 1985, the questions you posed and the answers of the State Department are as follows:
>
> "1. Has the United States recognized the Khomeini government of the Islamic Republic of Iran?"
>
> Answer: No.

Id. at 1280 n. 4. Amicus contends that this response referred merely to the absence of formal recognition and was not intended to foreclose courts from entertaining suits by the Khomeini regime. NPC and Amicus argue that the Executive Branch has not prohibited the Khomeini regime's access to federal courts, and that the Executive Branch may recognize a government for the purposes of bringing suit despite the absence of formal recognition.

Appellees assert, to the contrary, that unlike diplomatic relations, the President's formal statement of recognition of a foreign government is a necessary condition to permitting it to sue in federal court. Certain language in the Supreme Court's decisions arguably supports such a requirement. *See, e.g., Sabbatino*, 376 U.S. at 410 ("[T]he refusal to recognize has a unique legal aspect. It signifies this country's unwillingness to acknowledge that the government in question speaks ... for the territory it purports to control.") (citations omitted); *Guaranty Trust*, 304 U.S. at 137 ("[I]n conformity to generally accepted principles, the Soviet Government could not maintain a suit in our courts before its recognition by the political department of the Government."). Thus, appellees urge that NPC must be denied access to federal court based on the President's failure to extend formal recognition to the Khomeini government. We disagree and hold that the absence of formal recognition does not necessarily result in a foreign government being barred from access to United States courts.

Two reasons support this holding. First, as this century draws to a close, the practice of extending formal recognition to new governments has altered: The United States Department of State has sometimes refrained from announcing recognition of a new government because grants of recognition have been misinterpreted as pronouncements of approval. *See* *77 State Dep't Bull.* 462–63 (Oct. 10, 1977) ("In recent years, U.S. practice has been to deemphasize and avoid the use of recognition in cases of changes of governments...."); *Restatement 3d* § 203, reporter's note 1 (commenting on recent deemphasis of formal recognition). As a result, the absence of formal recognition cannot serve as the touchstone for determining whether the Executive Branch has "recognized" a foreign nation for the purpose of granting that government access to United States courts.

Second, the power to deal with foreign nations outside the bounds of formal recognition is essential to a president's implied power to maintain international relations. *Cf. United States v. Curtiss–Wright Export Corp.*, 299 U.S. 304, 318–20 (1936). As part of this power, the Executive Branch must have the latitude to permit a foreign nation access to U.S. courts, even if that nation is not formally recognized by the U.S. government. This is because the president alone—as the constitutional guardian of foreign policy—knows what action is necessary to effectuate American relations with foreign governments. *Cf. Sabbatino*, 376 U.S. at 411 n. 12 (citing criticisms of any policy which would mandate formal recognition before a foreign nation could sue in U.S. courts).

This case serves as an excellent example. Relations between the United States and Iran over the past eight years have been less than friendly. Yet, the status of that relationship has not been unchanging. There have been periods of improvement, for example, release of the embassy hostages, and periods of worsening relations, most recently occasioned by the unfortunate downing of an Iranian civilian airliner by the U.S.S. Vincennes. It is evident that in today's topsy-turvy world governments can topple and relationships can change in a moment. The Executive Branch must therefore have broad, unfettered discretion in matters involving such sensitive, fast-changing, and complex foreign relationships. *See Guaranty Trust*, 304 U.S. at 137 ("What government is to be regarded here as representative of a foreign sovereign state is a political rather than a judicial question, and is to be determined by the political department of the government."); *Sabbatino*, 376 U.S. at 410 ("This Court would hardly be competent to undertake assessments of varying degrees of friendliness or its absence...."); *Curtiss–Wright,* 299 U.S. at 319 ("In this vast external realm, with its important, complicated, delicate and manifold problems, the President alone has the power to speak or listen as a representative of the nation.").

B. Deference to the Executive Branch

Determining that formal recognition is not necessary for Iran to gain access to U.S. courts does not end our inquiry. We must also consider whether the Executive Branch—despite its withholding of formal recognition—has evinced a willingness to permit Iran to litigate its claims in the U.S. forum. Several facts persuasively indicate such a willingness. For example, Iran and the United States entered into the Algerian Accords to resolve the embassy personnel hostage crisis; an ongoing Iran–United States Claims Tribunal at the Hague continues to adjudicate disputes between the two countries; and the 1955 Treaty of Amity, Economic Relations and Consular Rights between the United States and Iran remains in full force and effect. Standing alone, none of these indicia of Executive Branch willingness to allow Iran to proceed as a plaintiff in the United States courts would necessarily persuade us to reverse the district court and grant access. Considering these factors in the aggregate, and not in isolation, as integral components of the United States overall relationship to Iran, the above recited connections strongly suggest that the Executive Branch has evinced an implicit willingness to permit the government of Iran to avail itself of a federal forum.

It is unnecessary to go further in examining other treaties, documents, or ties in order to ascertain the Executive Branch's intentions regarding Iran's access to the federal courts. The United States has submitted a Statement of Interest pursuant to 28 U.S.C. § 517 (1982) stating that "it is the position of the Executive Branch that the Iranian government and its instrumentality should be afforded access to our courts for purposes of resolution of the instant dispute." Because this Statement was not filed with Judge Owen, he was not apprised of the Executive Branch's position prior to ruling.

Appellees protest that for us to defer to what they term an "*ad hoc, pro hac vice*" directive to allow NPC's suit will encourage arbitrary and unpredictable pronouncements on the status of foreign governments, but we need not reach that question here because there is no indication that this is an arbitrary or *ad hoc* directive. This is not a case where the Executive Branch is attempting to prohibit a formally recognized government from bringing a single suit in the United States courts, nor is it a case where the Executive is arbitrarily allowing some suits by an unrecognized nation while disallowing others. Rather, here the Executive Branch—after entering into treaties with Iran, after establishing a claims tribunal to adjudicate disputes between the two countries, and after complying with U.S.–Iran agreements—expressly entered this case as Amicus requesting that Iran be given access to our courts. Under such circumstances, and as the sole branch authorized to conduct relations with foreign countries, the Executive clearly did not act arbitrarily. Accordingly, we hold that, for all the reasons stated, NPC must be permitted to proceed with its diversity suit in the Southern District of New York.

NOTE ON SOVEREIGN IMMUNITY OF UNRECOGNIZED GOVERNMENTS

A recognized foreign government is entitled to immunity from judicial process in U.S. courts for certain of its public (or sovereign) acts. *See infra*

Section 7; Foreign Sovereign Immunities Act of 1976, 28 U.S.C. § 1604 (2006). Is this immunity available to unrecognized regimes? There are some indications that in immunity cases, as in cases turning on an unrecognized government's right to sue, courts do not invariably follow the President's lead.

In *Wulfsohn v. Russian Socialist Federated Soviet Republic,* 234 N.Y. 372, 138 N.E. 24 (1923), the Court of Appeals of New York held that the Soviet government's existence "whenever it becomes material may probably be proved in other ways" than by reference to the State Department's recognition policy. *Id.* at 375. The court's result "depends upon more basic considerations than recognition or nonrecognition by the United States. Whether or not a government exists clothed with the power to enforce its authority within its own territory, obeyed by the people over whom it rules, capable of performing the duties and fulfilling the obligations of an independent power, able to enforce its claims by military force, is a fact, not a theory." *Id.* The plaintiff "may not bring a foreign sovereign before our bar, not because of comity, but because he has not submitted himself to our laws. Without his consent he is not subject to them. Concededly that is so as to a foreign government that has received recognition.... But whether recognized or not, the evil of such an attempt would be the same." *Id.* at 376 (citations omitted). Consider the court's reasoning about this "evil." It said that it would "vex the peace of nations" and "the hands of the State Department would be tied." *Id.* Why? Does it matter that in *Wulfsohn* the property, which plaintiff alleged had been wrongfully seized by the Soviet government, was in territory under its control? If the court had reached the conclusion that the Soviet defendant, being unrecognized, was not entitled to immunity, would that have made it an entity capable of being sued? In passing, the court says of the question at issue: "Here, however, we need no proof. The fact is conceded. We have an existing government sovereign within its own territories." *Id.* Who conceded this? Why would the plaintiff make such a concession in light of the Executive's nonrecognition policy and his own litigating strategy? *See also* Nankivel v. Omsk All Russian Government, 237 N.Y. 150, 142 N.E. 569 (1923). In *Voevodine v. Government of the Commander-in-Chief of the Armed Forces in the South of Russia,* 232 A.D. 204, 249 N.Y.S. 644 (App. Div.), *aff'd,* 257 N.Y. 557, 178 N.E. 793 (1931), the immunity of an unrecognized regime appears to have been extended even to a suit based on its mere commercial transaction.

KNOX v. PALESTINE LIBERATION ORGANIZATION

306 F. Supp. 2d 424 (S.D.N.Y. 2004).

MARRERO, DISTRICT JUDGE.

....

I. BACKGROUND

A. Facts and Issues Presented

On the night of January 17, 2002, [Aharon] Ellis, an American citizen then 31 years old, was performing as a singer before approximately 180 relatives and guests celebrating the Bat Mitzvah of twelve-year-old Nina

Kardoshova ("Nina") at the David's Palace banquet hall in Hadera, Israel. At approximately 10:45 p.m., random violence struck. While Nina, her family and guests were dancing, [Abdel Salam Sadek] Hassuna, a named defendant in this case though now deceased,[3] arrived at the banquet hall, burst through the door and, using a machine gun, opened fire into the crowd of celebrants. Six people were killed in the attack, including Ellis, and over 30 were wounded....

Plaintiffs seek damages from Defendants, claiming that [Hassuna] and the other individually named and unnamed defendants were employees, agents and/or co-conspirators of the PLO and PA and, as such, planned and carried out the attack acting in concert with or under instructions or inducements or with the assistance or material support and resources provided by the PLO, the PA, Arafat and the other individual defendants.

The issues the parties' arguments and rebuttals present to the Court, however, far transcend the tragedy that ended Ellis's life and the compensation his heirs seek from Defendants. As framed in its larger dimensions, the dispute the parties portray implicates several other far-reaching questions. Is Palestine a state? Is the Israeli military occupation of Palestinian territories an illegal hostile act under international law, or a reality that bears on the validity of Palestine's claim to statehood? Are the PLO and PA constituted governmental entities of a state of Palestine entitled to sovereign immunity, or incubators and agents of international terrorism? Was the violent attack underlying this action carried out with the active knowledge, assistance or participation of Arafat and other high ranking PLO and PA officials? Are Defendants entitled to claim any form of state or governmental immunity to shield them from any further inquiry here into Plaintiffs' allegations? Does this Court possess authority to exercise jurisdiction over the subject matter or over any individual Defendants to permit discovery and further consideration of the merits of Plaintiffs' claims?

....

The parties actually do agree, albeit tacitly, on a point that their polemics then proceed to ignore: that this litigation cannot serve to transform this Court into another public platform used for the parties to reenact struggles over what, at bottom, present ancillary political issues, intractable questions that are neither before the Court in the legal dispute at hand, nor are readily susceptible of judicial resolution....

....

That said, the Court is mindful that, enveloped beneath and through the smoke generated by the parties' adjunct rhetorical fray, there are issues that have tangential bearing on the Court's determination of the motion at hand: for example, whether, given the character and scope of Israel's occupation of the Palestinian territories and of Israel's relation-

3. The complaint does not specify the circumstances of Hassuna's death.

ship with the PLO, the PA and Palestinian leaders—as described by Defendants themselves and supported by the rebuttal documents upon which Plaintiffs rely—Defendants' claim of sovereign immunity deriving from the alleged statehood of Palestine can reasonably be validated for the purposes of defeating the application of the ATA in this case. On this point, this Court finds the record before it ample enough to warrant a conclusion that Defendants' invocation of immunity must fail on two separate grounds.

First, the Court is not persuaded that Defendants have compellingly established that Palestine is a state as defined by the governing standard applicable here: that articulated in § 201 of the Restatement (Third) of the Foreign Relations Law of the United States (the "Restatement (Third)") (1987). For, in the final analysis, Defendants' claim of statehood for Palestine reduces to an intense, enduring aspiration that, however devoutly wished, apparently still seems more boosted by impassioned protestations and pretensions than affirmed by the juridically recognized ensigns of a sovereign nation. Second, whatever the status of Palestine in the view of other countries, even if it were widely considered an independent state elsewhere, Palestine is not a foreign entity politically recognized by the United States, and therefore, is not one entitled in our courts to be accorded all the privileges and immunities of sovereign states to which this country, acting through the executive branch, does confer formal recognition.

II. DISCUSSION

. . . .

B. Unrecognized State

Even assuming for the sake of argument that, as Defendants contend, there exists a sovereign "State of Palestine under international law" (Def. Mem. at 13), it does not follow that Defendants are entitled to the immunity they seek from the exercise of this Court's subject matter jurisdiction. Defendants have presented no evidence, and the Court is not aware of any, establishing that Palestine, whatever its status in other jurisdictions, has been recognized, or otherwise treated as a sovereign state, by the United States. Nor is there any indication that the United States has conferred upon the PLO and PA recognition as official representatives of the government of the purported Palestinian state, thereby entitling them to assert the privileges and immunities ordinarily accorded to specified officials and agents of sovereign entities. These circumstances thus raise a question concerning the extent to which this Court is bound to give effect to Defendants' invocation of foreign state immunity of a purported unrecognized state.

In *Kadic* [*v. Karadzic*], the Second Circuit observed that "[r]ecognized states enjoy certain privileges and immunities relevant to judicial proceedings," such as access to United States courts and head-of-state immunity. 70 F.3d at 244 (citing *Banco Nacional de Cuba v. Sabbatino,* 376 U.S. 398,

408–12 (1964) and *Lafontant v. Aristide,* 844 F. Supp. 128, 131 (E.D.N.Y. 1994)). The Circuit Court also noted, however, that "an unrecognized state is not a juridical nullity" and that "[o]ur courts have regularly given effect to the 'state' action of unrecognized states." *Id.*

The scope of whatever effect United States courts give to the state actions or privileges and immunities of an unrecognized state is a matter ultimately determined not by juridical right or rule of law, but by whether, by application of the doctrine of comity or as a matter of public policy, it is warranted for a court, under the circumstances of a particular case, to accord any measure of respect to the asserted acts or protections of the foreign entity or government in question. The Supreme Court has defined international comity as "the recognition which one nation allows within its territory to the legislative, executive, or judicial acts of another nation, having due regard both to international duty and convenience, and to the rights of [its] or citizens, or of other persons who are under the protection of its laws." *Hilton v. Guyot,* 159 U.S. 113, 164 (1895). Elaborating on several prerequisites to be considered in applying comity to an action or decision of a foreign government, the Second Circuit required among them a showing that "the laws and public policy of the forum state and the rights of its residents will not be violated." *Cunard S.S. Co. Ltd. v. Salen Reefer Servs. AB,* 773 F.2d 452, 457 (2d Cir. 1985).

But comity developed as a principle generally applicable to certain interactions between sovereign states and governments that maintain some relations. "[C]omity is often associated with the existence of friendly relations between states. . . ." *Sabbatino,* 376 U.S. at 409; *Russian Socialist Federated Soviet Republic v. Cibrario,* 235 N.Y. 255, 139 N.E. 259, 260 (1923) (noting that comity "presupposes friendship"). Thus, the degree of friendliness that characterizes the relations between particular states and that typically is embodied in the act of mutual recognition, ordinarily defines the types of sovereign acts and the range of privileges and immunities to which comity may be conferred in judicial proceedings in this country. Conversely, as the Supreme Court observed in *Sabbatino:* "[T]he refusal to recognize has a unique legal aspect. It signifies this country's unwillingness to acknowledge that the Government in question speaks . . . for the territory it purports to control." 376 U.S. at 410 (citations omitted).

Moreover, because comity is often a function of recognition, matters concerning who is recognized as the sovereign or government of a particular territory, and whether and to what extent comity is accorded to its acts and officials, are political questions uniquely within the domain and prerogatives of the executive branch. Thus comity "may . . . not be demanded as a right. It is yielded as a favor." *Cibrario,* 139 N.E. at 260. Most significant for the purposes of the inquiry now before the Court, " '[i]t is not the comity of the Courts, but the comity of the nation which is administered, and ascertained in the same way. . . .' " *Bank of Augusta v. Earle,* 38 U.S. (13 Pet.) 519, 589 (1839) (quoting Joseph Story, *Conflict of Laws* 37 (1834)); *Guaranty Trust,* 58 S.Ct. at 791 ("What government is to be regarded here as representative of a foreign sovereign state is a political rather than a judicial question, and is to be determined by the political department of the government."); *see also Sabbatino,* 376 U.S. at 410 (noting that "[p]olitical recognition is exclusively a function of the Executive" and that the Court "would hardly be competent to undertake assessments of varying degrees of friendliness or its absence"); *United States v. Curtiss–Wright Export Corp.,* 299 U.S. 304, 319–20 (1936) (noting that in the realm of external relations "the President alone has the power to speak or listen as a representative of the nation" and to determine when, how and upon what subjects to negotiate with foreign states); *National Petrochemical Co. v. M/T Stolt Sheaf,* 860 F.2d 551, 555 (2d Cir. 1988).

Recognition of a foreign entity of a sovereign state, or of a regime as the government of a state, may be effectuated by express declaration of the executive branch, by bilateral agreement with the foreign state, by the presentation of credentials by the United States to the authorities of the state and by the United States receiving the credentials of the diplomatic representatives of the foreign state. *See KMW Int'l v. Chase Manh. Bank, N.A.,* 606 F.2d 10, 17 n. 5 (2d Cir. 1979); Restatement (Third) § 204 Rptrs. n. 2. Recognition may also be found to be implied, for example, through a vote by the United States to admit a foreign entity to membership in an international body open only to sovereign states. *See id.; see also id.* at § 201 cmt. h. While recognition is a matter of which courts may take judicial notice, *see KMW Int'l,* 606 F.2d at 17 n. 5 (citing *United States v. Belmont,* 301 U.S. 324, 330 (1937)), the "possible incongruity of judicial 'recognition'," *Sabbatino,* 376 U.S. at 410–11, would constitute an unwarranted arrogation of power. This constraint on judicial authority is especially compelling because the political discretion to recognize foreign states and governments carries with it "the power to determine the policy which is to govern the question of recognition." *United States v. Pink,* 315 U.S. 203, 229 (1942). Hence, "recognition is not always absolute; it is sometimes conditional." *Id.* Accordingly, the manner, means and timing that define the terms of any such conditions of recognition of a purported sovereign or its representatives are matters clearly beyond the realm of judicial competence.

By the same token, the effects of political nonrecognition are whatever the states involved intend the consequences to be. *See, e.g., Latvian State Cargo & Passenger S.S. Line v. McGrath,* 188 F.2d 1000, 1003 (D.C. Cir. 1951); *The Maret,* 145 F.2d 431, 442 (3d Cir. 1944); *Transportes Aereos de Angola v. Ronair, Inc.,* 544 F.Supp. 858, 863–64 (D. Del. 1982); *Bank of China v. Wells Fargo Bank & Union Trust Co.,* 104 F. Supp. 59, 64 (N.D. Cal. 1952), *rev'd on other grounds,* 209 F.2d 467 (9th Cir. 1953); *see generally* Crawford, *supra,* at 120–21. In addressing claims of sovereign or governmental immunity or disputes concerning the legitimacy of the actions of unrecognized foreign states, courts have taken divergent approaches. Some have enunciated as a categorical rule that "[i]n the absence of recognition no comity exists." *Cibrario,* 139 N.E. at 262 (holding that a government not recognized by the United States is not entitled to bring suit in courts in this country); *see also Guaranty Trust Co.,* 304 U.S. at 137 ("It is not denied that, in conformity to generally accepted principles, the Soviet Government could not maintain a suit in our courts before its recognition by the political department of the government."); *The Maret,* 145 F.2d at 442 ("When the fact of nonrecognition of a foreign sovereign and nonrecognition of its decrees by our Executive is demonstrated . . . the courts of this country may not examine the effect of decrees of the unrecognized foreign sovereign and determine rights in property . . . upon the basis of these decrees."); *The Gul Djemal,* 296 F. 563, 564 (S.D.N.Y. 1920), *aff'd,* 264 U.S. 90, 95 (1924); Restatement (Third) § 204; *see generally* Stanley Lubman, *The Unrecognized Government in American Courts:* Upright v. Mercury Business Machines, 62 Col. L. Rev. 275 (1962); Edwin M. Borchard, *The Unrecognized Government in American Courts,* 26 Am. J. Int'l L. 261 (1932).

This proposition is grounded on the premise that actual recognition serves as a prerequisite for a United States court to exercise jurisdiction over a claim concerning the existence of a foreign state or the legitimacy of an act of such a state. Thus, following this course, the executive branch's decision to withhold or reject recognition would be dispositive of the judicial proceeding; regardless of the nature of the dispute, the court would not venture beyond the status of the foreign entity as an unrecognized state. In *Republic of China v. Merchants' Fire Assur. Corp.,* for example, a suit commenced by a foreign government prior to its recognition by the United States was dismissed and later ordered reinstated when recognition was conferred while the case was pending at the Court of Appeals. 30 F.2d 278, 279 (9th Cir. 1929). In reversing the judgment of dismissal, the Ninth Circuit stated: "[I]nasmuch as there had been no such recognition of the National Government of China at the time of the trial in the court below, it would seem to follow that that government had no existence in contemplation of law and no legal capacity to sue in the courts of this country." *Id.; The Maret,* 145 F.2d at 442; *see also Russian Reinsurance Co. v. Stoddard,* 240 N.Y. 149, 147 N.E. 703, 705 (1925) (noting that in considering claims arising out of the actions of unrecognized states, "[u]ntil the State Department has recognized the new establishment, the court may not pass upon the [foreign state's] legitimacy or ascribe to its decrees all the effect which inheres in the laws or orders of a sovereign"); *Sokoloff v. National City Bank,* 239 N.Y. 158, 145 N.E. 917, 918 (1024) ("Juridically, a government that is unrecognized may be viewed as no government at all, if the power withholding recognition chooses thus to view it.").

More specifically, according to this doctrine, nonrecognition may result in denial of access to courts in this country. *See Pfizer Inc. v. India,* 434 U.S. 308, 319–20 (1978) ("It has long been established that only governments recognized by the United States and at peace with us are entitled to access to our courts, and that it is within the exclusive power of the Executive Branch to determine which nations are entitled to sue.");

Guaranty Trust Co., 304 U.S. at 137; *Federal Republic of Germany v. Elicofon,* 358 F. Supp. 747, 752 (E.D.N.Y. 1970). Similarly, recognition may be decisive in determining entitlement to property of the foreign entity in the United States. *See Republic of Panama v. Republic Nat'l Bank of New York,* 681 F. Supp. 1066, 1070 (S.D.N.Y. 1988) (rejecting a claim to funds in a bank account of a foreign state whose regime the United States did not recognize as the country's legitimate government); *see also The Maret,* 145 F.2d at 442. The extent to which other privileges and immunities traditionally associated with national sovereignty are conferred may also turn directly on recognition. *See, e.g., United States v. Lumumba,* 741 F.2d 12, 15 (2d Cir. 1984) (noting that the assertion of diplomatic and sovereign immunity is precluded where there is no recognition of the purported foreign state); *see also The Gul Djemal,* 296 F. at 564; *Cibrario,* 139 N.E. at 262; Restatement (Third) § 205.

Under another approach, other courts have not been beholden solely to the status of nonrecognition and, without relying only on the executive branch's ultimate determination in that regard, have not categorically nullified the official actions or disregarded the sovereignty claims of unrecognized entities. *See Kadic,* 70 F.3d at 244. Rather, in adjudicating these questions they generally have endeavored to draw certain pragmatic distinctions. First, these courts take cognizance of the difference between recognition of the existence of a particular unrecognized foreign state and the scope of any privileges and immunities that may be conferred upon it in a given case, including the treatment accorded to the purported government and representatives of the entity. Hence, while as a factual and juridical matter an unrecognized foreign entity may satisfy the criteria for statehood under the Restatement (Third)'s definition in a specific judicial proceeding, it does not follow that all of the privileges and immunities that ordinarily accompany sovereign status will necessarily be extended to the entity or its designated rulers. *See, e.g., Kadic,* 70 F.3d at 247–48 (rejecting claims of sovereign and diplomatic immunity asserted by the president of an unrecognized state even though the entity theoretically met the prerequisites of statehood); *Russian Gov't v. Lehigh Valley R.R. Co.,* 293 F. 135, 137 (S.D.N.Y. 1923) (acknowledging that Russia as a sovereign state existed and was the real party in interest in the action before the court even if the United States did not recognize Russia's government).

Second, the unrecognized foreign state is accorded *de facto* existence with respect to adjudications of strictly commercial transactions, adjustments of private rights, and effectuation of juridical and ministerial acts properly taken by it within the ambit of its territory incidental to sovereign or governmental functions that are deemed judicially cognizable; however, no such presumptive effect is generally given to circumstances involving political questions that fundamentally implicate the status of the foreign entity in its formal relations with the United States and that thus necessarily demand an expression from the executive branch concerning the United States foreign policy consequences of a legal determination regarding the matter at issue. *See United States v. Insurance Cos.,* 89 U.S. (22 Wall.) 99, 101–03 (1875); *Texas v. White,* 74 U.S. (7 Wall.) 700, 733 (1868); *Carl Zeiss Stiftung v. VEB Carl Zeiss Jena,* 433 F.2d 686, 699 (2d Cir. 1970), *cert. denied,* 403 U.S. 905 (1971); *see also Sabbatino,* 376 U.S. at 409–10.

A third approach adopted by the courts in some unrecognized state case is to defer to an expression of United States foreign policy with regard to the appropriateness of entertaining the assertion of immunity or giving effect to the foreign act in question. *See Sabbatino,* 376 U.S. at 410. (permitting access to United States courts to a foreign entity where the executive had clearly expressed its support for the granting of such privilege); *National Petrochemical,* 860 F.2d at 555 (same); *Lehigh Valley,* 293 F. at 137.

Fourth, in some cases where the executive branch has not interposed any suggestion of foreign policy interest in the prosecution of an action involving an unrecognized state, the courts have exercised jurisdiction to consider the matter if adjudication of the controversy would not violate domestic public policy or otherwise conflict with the interests of justice. *See, e.g., Banque de France v. Equitable Trust Co.,* 33 F.2d 202, 206 (S.D.N.Y. 1929) ("Justice requires that effect should be given by our courts, even though we do not recognize the Russian Government, to those acts in Russia upon which the rights of our citizens depend, provided that in doing so our judicial department does not encroach upon or interfere with the political branch of our government."); *Wulfsohn v. Russian Socialist Federated Soviet Republic,* 234 N.Y. 372, 138 N.E. 24, 25–26 (1923), *appeal dismissed,* 266 U.S. 580 (1924) (reversing an exercise of jurisdiction over the nonrecognized government of Soviet Russian Republic where plaintiff had conceded that there was "an existing government, sovereign within its own territories."); *Upright v. Mercury Business Mach. Co.,* 13 A.D.2d 36, 213 N.Y.S.2d 417, 419 (1st Dep't 1961); *cf. Sokoloff,* 145 N.E. at 919 (noting that "a body or group which has vindicated by the course of events its pretensions to sovereign power, but which has forfeited by its conduct the privileges or immunities of sovereignty, may gain for its acts and decrees a validity quasi-governmental, if violence to fundamental principles of justice or to our own public policy might otherwise be done").

Whatever doctrinal differences may distinguish the courts' treatment of rights and duties asserted in claims by or against unrecognized states or governments, a reconciling principle may be discerned threading through the various approaches, either expressed or implied, about which there appears to be no judicial dispute. When the executive branch, either by word or deed, does manifest its political determination that the courts' exercise of jurisdiction over a particular matter involving actions or privileges and immunities of unrecognized states or governments would be inimical to United States foreign policy interests or relations with the unrecognized sovereign, or when the court on its own, from demonstrable matters of public record, may readily ascertain such fundamental conflict with public policy were it to give effect to the invocation of sovereign status of the unrecognized state or government, the courts generally accept as conclusive such declared or ascertained expression of United States international relations policy. As the District of Columbia Circuit has remarked:

> [W]hen the executive branch ... has determined upon a foreign policy, which can be and is ascertained, and the non-recognition of specific foreign decrees is deliberate and is shown to be part of that policy, such non-recognition must be given effect by the courts. The rule applicable in such circumstances is the same rule applicable to an act of recognition. Any other treatment of a deliberate policy and act of non-recognition would reduce the effective control over foreign affairs by the executive branch to a mere effectiveness of acts of recognition. The control of the executive branch over foreign affairs must necessarily be broader than that.

McGrath, 188 F.2d at 1003; *see also The Maret,* 145 F.2d at 442 ("Nonrecognition of a foreign sovereign ... [is] to be deemed to be as essential a part of the power confided by the Constitution to the Executive for the conduct of foreign affairs as recognition.... A policy of nonrecognition when demonstrated by the Executive must be deemed to be as affirmative and positive in effect as a policy of recognition."); *Ronair,* 544 F. Supp. at 863–64 ("[W]here the executive branch, either by its actions or words, evinces a definite desire to remove the impediment to a suit brought by an unrecognized government, or an instrumentality thereof, that determination necessarily frees this Court from any strictures placed on the exercise of its jurisdiction."); *Bank of China,* 104 F. Supp. at 66 ("It is not a proper function of a domestic court of the United States to attempt to judge which government best represents the interests of the Chinese State in the Bank of China. In this situation, the Court should justly accept, as the representative of the Chinese State, that government which our executive deems best able to further the mutual interests of China and the United States.").

The courts have also declared, in a doctrine especially germane to the issues at hand, that an unrecognized state cannot assert its sovereign status to immunize its acts or its representatives from exercise of "jurisdiction in [actions] alleging violations of basic human rights or international law." *See Kadic,* 70 F.3d at 245 (holding that customary international law of human rights "applies to states without distinction between recognized and unrecognized states"); *Klinghoffer,* 937 F.2d at 49 (noting that "there is no bar to suit where an unrecognized regime is brought into court as a defendant"); *see also* Shaw, *supra,* at 262 ("[A]n unrecognized state must be deemed subject to the rules of international law. It cannot consider itself free from restraints as to aggressive behaviour....").

In *Kadic,* the Second Circuit found that plaintiffs' allegations concerning the existence of a state of Srpska, a self-proclaimed Bosnian–Serb republic that emerged from the collapse of the former Yugoslavia, were sufficient to satisfy the criteria for a state under international law. The Circuit Court nonetheless allowed plaintiffs' action brought under the Alien Tort Claims Act and the Torture Victim Protection Act to proceed against defendant Radovan Karadzic, president of Srpska, an entity not recognized by the United States even if it may have qualified for treatment as a sovereign under the standard definition of statehood. The Circuit Court rejected Karadzic's various claims of sovereign and diplomatic immunity. *See* 70 F.3d at 247–48. It concluded that, at bottom "[t]he inquiry ... is whether a person purporting to wield official power has exceeded internationally recognized standards of civilized conduct, not whether statehood in all its formal aspects exists." *Id.* at 245.

Applying the preceding principles here, even if Defendants presented sufficient evidence that Palestine and the PA and PLO regime satisfy the criteria for statehood, this Court would decline to give effect to the foreign state and governmental immunities Defendants invoke as a shield from application of the Antiterrorism Act.

First, there is nothing in the ATA or the FSIA to suggest that by carving out a foreign state exclusion from the application of those statutes Congress intended to disturb the traditional rules of comity. In particular, the exceptions do not evince any Congressional purpose to directly confer sovereign privileges and immunities, in matters uniquely fraught with foreign policy implications, upon any unrecognized foreign entity which satisfied the prerequisites of statehood, even before the executive branch had occasion to assess whether or not to extend any degree of comity to the sovereignty claims of such unrecognized state or its government. Because the scope of this country's relations with foreign states is a subject solely within the purview of the executive branch to determine in the first instance, to construe the foreign state exemption of the FSIA and the ATA to effectuate such immunities automatically upon an invocation of sovereignty by any unrecognized state, thereby effectively preempting assessment by the executive branch of the appropriateness of granting such exception as regards particular foreign entities or policy concerns, would necessarily engender potential conflict of constitutional dimension between the powers of Congress and the prerogatives of the president in the sphere of external affairs. *See, e.g., Sabbatino,* 376 U.S. at 410; *Guaranty Trust,* 58 S.Ct. at 791; *Curtiss-Wright,* 299 U.S. at 319–20.

Thus, while Congress could properly legislate to exempt foreign states from the courts' jurisdiction pertaining to specific subject matters, such categorical exclusions must presuppose applicability to sovereign entities that the United States has formally recognized, and thereby presumptively "determine[d] the policy which is to govern the question of recognition," *Pink,* 315 U.S. at 229, including the bounds of the privileges and immunities that the foreign states may properly assert by virtue of comity or international agreements. Otherwise, any jurisdictional bar may apply only to an unrecognized state to which, on an exceptional basis, the executive branch has expressly or implicitly chosen to extend some degree of comity in the form of any of the customary perquisites of sovereignty.

See, e.g., *Kadic*, 70 F.3d at 245; *Klinghoffer*, 937 F.2d at 49; *National Petrochemical*, 860 F.2d at 555. Or else, absent such executive branch expression, the Court could allow the exemption invoked if it determines that honoring the unrecognized foreign state's assertion of sovereignty would not otherwise violate United States public policy and the interests of justice. *See Banque de France*, 33 F.2d at 206; *Sokoloff*, 145 N.E. at 919.

Second, the Court notes, as mentioned above, that the same issue of Palestinian statehood as a basis for immunity of these Defendants from the subject matter jurisdiction of this Court has arisen in several other recent actions pending in other federal courts. There is no indication that the government's executive branch has expressed a view in any of these actions suggesting that Defendants possess any form of immunity from the exercise of the courts' jurisdiction, or that the status of relations between the United States and Defendants would render the prosecution of such litigation in our courts inimical to current United States foreign policy interests, or to this country's relations with Defendants. The Court notes that in other cases where the executive branch has made these assessments as regards unrecognized states, it has taken affirmative steps to convey its position to the courts. *See, e.g.*, *Sabbatino*, 376 U.S. at 410; *National Petrochemical*, 860 F.2d at 555; *Republic of Panama*, 681 F. Supp. at 1069; *Lehigh Valley*, 293 F. at 135.

Absent any contrary formal expression as regards a foreign relations issue of such great moment entailing extensive controversy and public debate as that surrounding United States policy concerning the purported Palestinian state, the Court construes the silence of the executive branch here as manifesting a view that at this time it has no compelling interest in suggesting that there are issues implicating current United States foreign policy as to why this litigation should not proceed in this Court. On this basis, the Court is not prepared to find sovereign immunity where none may exist. *See Kadic* 70 F.3d at 248 ("[I]t is the duty of the courts, in a matter so intimately associated with our foreign policy . . ., not to enlarge an immunity to an extent which the government . . . has not seen fit to recognize.") (citing *Mexico v. Hoffman*, 324 U.S. 30, 35 (1945)); Borchard, *supra*, at 264 ("There are occasions when reference to the executive is appropriate, *e.g.*, to determine the real and diplomatic status of a foreign potentate . . . claiming jurisdictional immunity as sovereign or public, boundary questions. . . .").

As the parties invoking foreign state immunity, Defendants have the burden of establishing its existence under the FSIA, or, given the conflict with prevailing United States public policy discussed above, of otherwise producing an authoritative expression of the executive branch's view of the protection they seek from the exercise of the Court's jurisdiction in this matter. *See Virtual Countries, Inc. v. Republic of South Africa*, 300 F.3d 230, 241 (2d Cir. 2002) (noting that under the FSIA a foreign entity asserting immunity must present a prima facie case that it is a foreign sovereign and has the " 'ultimate burden of persuasion' " in establishing its claim of sovereignty) (quoting *Cargill Int'l S.A. v. M/T Pavel Dybenko*,

991 F.2d 1012, 1016 (2d Cir. 1993)); *accord Ungar II* 2003 WL 21254790, at *1; *International Ins. Co. v. Caja Nacional De Ahorro Y Seguro,* 293 F.3d 392, 397 (7th Cir. 2002); *Keller v. Central Bank of Nigeria,* 277 F.3d 811, 815 (6th Cir. 2002). Defendants have not met this burden here. Should they do so at any later stage of this litigation, the Court will of course reexamine its ruling in the light of the then controlling circumstances.

Third, even absent any intervention from the executive branch, the Court notes that its granting the immunities Defendants seek would in fact conflict with declared United States public policy regarding the Defendants. Though the PLO has declared Palestine's statehood and several other nations have apparently recognized that status, the United States has yet to recognize a Palestinian state. *Cf. Belmont,* 301 U.S. at 330 (noting that courts may take judicial notice of recognition). In fact, it is a matter of public record that the United States affirmatively opposes the notion that a sovereign Palestine presently exists....

....

As discussed above, in determining questions of international comity inherent in the issue of sovereign immunity, courts must be mindful that their decisions not conflict with the laws and express public policies of the United States and that the rights of its residents are not violated. *See Cunard,* 773 F.2d at 457. The executive branch, not the judiciary, is uniquely empowered to delineate the bounds of international comity. In this connection, Defendants cannot escape a reality that compels this Court's assessment of their assertion of jurisdictional immunity. The United States has not recognized their declaration of statehood for Palestine or their claim that they constitute the legitimate "government ... [that] speaks as the sovereign authority for the territory it purports to control." *Sabbatino,* 376 U.S. at 410. Nor has this country defined, in any authoritative way called to the attention of this Court, "the policy which is to govern the question of [such] recognition." *Pink,* 315 U.S. at 229.

A ruling by this Court construing the foreign state exception in the FSIA and ATA as giving warrant to Defendants' claims of jurisdictional immunity on the basis of Defendants' own assertion that they represent the sovereign nation and government of a purported state of Palestine would essentially imply a judicial validation of Defendants' claim of legitimacy as the sovereign and representatives of the people they purport to govern, and that Defendants are thus entitled to be accorded in this country legal privileges and protections that derive solely by virtue of the factual existence of that alleged sovereignty—the very assertion of legitimacy that United States foreign policy has deliberately denied or withheld. Consequently, such a ruling not only would have constitutive effect imbued with domestic legal consequences, but run directly counter to the executive branch's declared public policy of nonrecognition of Palestine and the PLO. *See The Maret,* 145 F.2d at 442 ("A policy of nonrecognition when demonstrated by the Executive must be deemed as affirmative and positive in effect as a policy of recognition."). Thus, the application of the statutes that Defendants seek would serve to create potential congressional and judicial encroachments upon the president's unique powers in the domain of external affairs. *See Ronair,* 544 F. Supp. at 862; *Elicofon,* 358 F. Supp. at 752. For, to indirectly invest the PLO and PA, before the executive branch has formally articulated relevant foreign policies, with the mantle of sovereignty and its concomitant privilege of immunity from the jurisdiction of this Court, may be deemed tantamount to an incongruous act of "judicial 'recognition' " of a government not recognized by the United States. *Sabbatino,* 376 U.S. at 410; *see also National Petrochemical,* 860 F.2d at 554–55 ("The power to deal with foreign nations outside the bounds of formal recognition is essential to a president's implied power to maintain international relations.").

. . . .

III. ORDER

For the reasons discussed above, it is hereby

Ordered that the motion of defendants to dismiss the claims asserted by plaintiffs in this action as against the Palestinian Authority and the Palestine Liberation Organization on the ground that the Court lacks subject matter jurisdiction is *denied*. . .

CONCLUDING NOTES

1. *Respecting Executive Branch Nonrecognition Determinations.* There is considerable variation in how courts deal with the fact of nonrecognition in deciding whether to give effect to acts of the unrecognized governments. Courts seem sometimes to give effect to unrecognized governments' decrees on various grounds, among them the perceived compatibility of so doing with the purposes behind the Executive's policy of nonrecognition. Conversely, among the reasons given by courts for *not* giving effect to such decrees is the incompatibility of doing so with the perceived intent of the Executive's nonrecognition policy. How do the courts know whether a presidential policy of nonrecognition would or would not be frustrated by giving effect to any particular decree of the foreign regime? If the courts, as they constantly protest in these cases, are unequipped to make foreign policy, what equips them to determine whether a particular policy would be helped or hindered by departing from, or applying, the strict letter of that policy in a particular case? In some instances, the State Department will attempt to provide the courts with information as to whether its nonrecognition policy should be applied to the circumstances of a case. *See* The Rogdai, 278 Fed. 294 (N.D. Cal. 1920). Or the courts may take "judicial notice" of the actions of the Executive which seem controlling, even if only a general press release. *See* The Penza, 277 Fed. 91 (E.D.N.Y. 1921). Particularly "when the executive branch of the Government has determined upon a foreign policy, which can be and is ascertained, and the non-recognition of specific foreign decrees is deliberate and is shown to be part of that policy, such non-recognition must be given effect by the courts." Latvian State Cargo & Passenger S.S. Line v. McGrath, 188 F.2d

1000 (D.C. Cir. 1951) (refusing to recognize confiscations effectuated by nationalization decrees of Latvia in light of affidavits by the Secretary of State addressing both nonrecognition in general and the decrees in particular).

Suppose the State Department, having withheld recognition from a government, nevertheless sends a suggestion that effect be given to its expropriation of property owned by a U.S. national—not because to do so would constitute no interference with the general purposes of nonrecognition, but because the unrecognized regime was engaged in a delicate negotiation for the release of a U.S. hostage being held by terrorists in a third country. How should the court treat such a suggestion? Would it matter whether the property in question, at the time it was seized, was in the territory of the state ruled by the expropriating government? Would it matter if there were still a recognized regime engaged in civil war and still controlling some territory of the state which had done the expropriating? Are there constitutional limits to the exercise of foreign relations power by the Executive through the instrumentality of U.S. courts in such cases? Must the Executive give reasons for its advice to a U.S. court? *See* Spacil v. Crowe, 489 F.2d 614 (5th Cir. 1974) and discussion thereon in 68 AM. J. INT'L L. 541 (1974).

2. *Giving Effect to Certain Acts of Unrecognized Governments*. Should some acts that are less politically significant or that do not offend public policy be given effect? Is it practical or appropriate to withhold effect for certain types of private rights and acts, such as government-sanctioned marriages or divorces?

In *Sokoloff v. National City Bank,* 239 N.Y. 158, 145 N.E. 917 (1924), the Court of Appeals of New York (Cardozo, J.) stated that a plaintiff who paid money into the defendant U.S. bank to open an account at its branch in Petrograd could recover the deposit even though the Petrograd branch and its accounts had been expropriated by the unrecognized Soviet government. The court said, in part:

> We think the case at hand is not so governed by authority but that it may be dealt with upon principle.
>
> Juridically, a government that is unrecognized may be viewed as no government at all, if the power withholding recognition chooses thus to view it. In practice, however, since juridical conceptions are seldom, if ever, carried to the limit of their logic, the equivalence is not absolute, but is subject to self-imposed limitations of common sense and fairness, as we learned in litigations following our Civil War. In those litigations acts or decrees of the rebellious governments, which, of course, had not been recognized as governments de facto, were held to be nullities when they worked injustice to citizens of the Union, or were in conflict with its public policy. Williams v. Bruffy, 96 U.S. 176, 187. On the other hand, acts or decrees that were just in operation and consistent with public policy, were sustained not infrequently to the same extent as if the governments were lawful. U.S. v. Insurance Companies, 22 Wall. 99; Sprott v. U.S., 20 Wall. 459; Texas v. White, 7 Wall. 700, 733; Mauran v. Alliance Ins. Co., 6 Wall. 1; Baldy v. Hunter, 171 U.S. 388; cf. Dickinson, Unrecognized Governments, 22 Mich. L. R. 29, 42. These analogies suggest the thought that, subject to like restrictions, effect may at times

be due to the ordinances of foreign governments which, though formally unrecognized, have notoriously an existence as governments de facto. Consequences appropriate enough when recognition is withheld on the ground that rival factions are still contending for the mastery, may be in need of readjustment before they can be fitted to the practice, now a growing one, of withholding recognition whenever it is thought that a government, functioning unhampered, is unworthy of a place in the society of nations. Limitations upon the general rule may be appropriate for the protection of one who has been the victim of spoliation though they would be refused to the spoliator or to others claiming under him. We leave these questions open. At the utmost, they suggest the possibility that a body or group which has vindicated by the course of events its pretensions to sovereign power, but which has forfeited by its conduct the privileges or immunities of sovereignty, may gain for its acts and decrees a validity quasi-governmental, if violence to fundamental principles of justice or to our own public policy might otherwise be done.

... The res belonging to the plaintiff was not a physical object committed to the defendant's keeping, but an intangible right, a chose in action, the right to receive rubles in the future under an executory contract. This contract the defendant has not performed, yet it refuses to return the dollars that were paid to it by the plaintiff upon its promise of performance. Two acts that must be kept distinct in thought are said to justify this refusal. One is the decree nationalizing the banks of Russia with the accompanying seizure of their assets. The other is the later decree confiscating the accounts of the depositors as a "revolutionary tax."

The defendant's liability was unaffected by the attempt to terminate its existence and the seizure of its assets. A government of Russia could not terminate its existence either by dissolution or by merger, for it was a corporation formed under our laws, and its corporate life continued until the law of its creation declared that it should end. What a Russian government could do was to deprive it of the privilege of doing business upon Russian soil. But the ending of its Russian business was not the ending of its duty to make restitution for benefits received without requital. . . .

239 N.Y. at 165–67.

SECTION 7. IMMUNITIES

INTRODUCTORY NOTE ON INTERNATIONAL IMMUNITIES FOR PERSONS

Justiciability questions do not exhaust the kinds of issues posed directly to the judiciary. A longstanding feature of the international legal system is the immunity of foreign diplomatic, consular, and other personnel and property from proceedings before national courts or other authorities. Such immunity contributes to friendly relations among states by allowing state officials to perform their functions without the risk of being exposed to national proceedings, which in some instances might be a form of harassment or retaliation.

The contours of these immunities, and the kinds of law from which they derive, depend on the type of official concerned.

Diplomatic Immunities. In general, once a government (the "sending state") accredits a person as a diplomat to another government (the "receiving state"), that person is immune with respect to acts or omissions in the exercise of his or her official functions and in other circumstances in which lack of immunity would be inconsistent with diplomatic status. The diplomat is also immune from criminal process and most civil process in the receiving state. *See Restatement (Third) of the Foreign Relations Law of the United States* § 464 (1987).

Customary international law governing the treatment of diplomats and diplomatic property is now codified in the Vienna Convention on Diplomatic Relations (VCDR), Apr. 18, 1961, 23 U.S.T. 3227, 500 U.N.T.S. 95. The VCDR has been ratified by 187 states as of mid-2011, including the United States. Under the VCDR, the "person" of the diplomat is inviolable, and the receiving state has an affirmative duty to protect each diplomat from an attack "on his person, freedom or dignity." *Id.*, art. 29. The receiving state may neither arrest nor detain the diplomat, and the diplomat is immune from criminal laws as well as from civil and administrative jurisdiction. *Id.*, art. 31(1). Diplomats may not be compelled to give evidence, and they are immune from personal service, most taxes, social security provisions, and customs duties and inspections. *Id.*, arts. 31(2), 33–36. Diplomatic immunity also extends to the diplomat's family members. *Id.*, art. 37. *See generally* Eileen Denza, *Diplomatic Law: Commentary on the Vienna Convention on Diplomatic Relations* (2d ed. 1998); Grant V. McClanahan, *Diplomatic Immunity: Principles, Practices, Problems* (1989).

For the role of the President in the provision of such immunities, see Section 4 of the Diplomatic Relations Act of 1978, 22 U.S.C. § 254c (2006). Section 4 provides that the "President may, on the basis of reciprocity and under such terms and conditions as he may determine, specify privileges and immunities for members of the mission, their families, and the diplomatic couriers of any sending state which results in more favorable treatment or less favorable treatment than is provided under the Vienna Convention."

Consular Immunities. Customary international law governing the treatment of consular officers and consulates is codified in the Vienna Convention on Consular Relations (VCCR), Apr. 24, 1963, 21 U.S.T. 77, 596 U.N.T.S. 261. The VCCR has been ratified by 173 states as of mid-2011, including the United States. It prohibits the arrest or detention of consular officers except for grave crimes and under court order. *Id.*, art. 41. Consular officers are not subject to judicial jurisdiction "in respect of acts performed in the exercise of consular functions," although they may be required to give evidence, and their privileges may be waived by the sending state. *Id.*, arts. 43–45; *see Restatement (Third)*, § 465; Luke T. Lee, *Consular Law and Practice* (2d ed. 1991).

The VCCR also obligates states, when they arrest a foreign national, to notify the national of a right to have his or her consulate informed. The failure to notify foreigners of this right has been used to challenge their convictions and sentences in U.S. court, in the Inter–American Commission on Human Rights, and in cases before the International Court of Justice.

International Civil Servant Immunities. Civil servants employed by international organizations typically enjoy a variety of immunities. They are usually exempted from alien registration acts and generally have personal immunities similar to those accorded diplomats and consuls. For the United Nations, the relevant multilateral treaty is the General Convention on the Privileges and Immunities of the United Nations, Feb. 13, 1946, 21 U.S.T. 1418, 1 U.N.T.S. 15. The General Convention provides for immunity from personal arrest and protects papers, documents, and courier bags. Further, since the U.N. headquarters is in the United States, certain privileges and immunities are accorded U.N. personnel pursuant to a bilateral U.S.-U.N. Headquarters Agreement, June 26, 1947, 61 Stat. 3416, 11 U.N.T.S. 11.

The United States implements many of its obligations toward international civil servants via the International Organizations Immunities Act (IOIA), Pub. L. No. 79–291, 59 Stat. 669 (1945) (codified at 22 U.S.C. §§ 288–288k (2006)). The statute grants to presidentially-designated international organizations the same immunity enjoyed by foreign governments. *Id.* § 288a(b). (The scope of foreign government immunity, as opposed to foreign *official* immunity, is considered later in this section.) The statute also provides to persons designated by foreign governments as their representatives and the officers and employees of those organizations (and their immediate families, other than U.S. nationals) the same privileges, exemptions, and immunities enjoyed by officers and employees of foreign governments (and their families) in relation to entry, departure, and registration requirements. More important, it provides representatives, officers, and employees "immunity from suit and legal process relating to acts performed by them in their official capacity and falling within their functions ... except insofar as such immunity may be waived by the foreign government or international organization concerned." *Id.* § 288d.

Head-of-State Immunity. Separate from the immunities accorded to diplomats, consular officials, and international civil servants, international law has developed the concept of "head-of-state" immunity. Since there is no multilateral treaty addressing this type of immunity, head-of-state immunity in the United States is a part of federal common law derived from customary international law.

As the cases below indicate, when foreign officials are sued or prosecuted in U.S. courts, they will often raise head-of-state immunity as a defense. Sometimes immunity is granted, whereas other times it is rejected. For rejections, see *United States v. Noriega*, 117 F.3d 1206, 1212 (11th Cir. 1997) (rejecting head-of-state immunity for Panamanian military leader being prosecuted on drug charges) and *Kadic v. Karadzic*, 70 F.3d 232, 248 (2d Cir. 1995) (rejecting head-of-state immunity for civilian leader of Serbs in Bosnia). Moreover, such immunity may be waived by an individual's government. *See, e.g.*, Doe v. United States, 860 F.2d 40, 44–46 (2d Cir. 1988) (finding no head-of-state immunity for former Philippine leader and his wife in light of waiver by the Philippine government).

When reading these cases, consider the role that customary international law is playing in this area. If the relevant touchstone is customary international law, should U.S. courts typically defer to the Executive Branch in determining whether head-of-state immunity should be accorded? Is deference being granted because the President is best placed to interpret international law or for some other reason?

MOTIONS OR SUGGESTIONS OF IMMUNITY

22 U.S.C. § 254d (2006).

Dismissal on motion of action against individual entitled to immunity

Any action or proceeding brought against an individual who is entitled to immunity with respect to such action or proceeding under the Vienna Convention on Diplomatic Relations . . . or under any other laws extending diplomatic privileges and immunities, shall be dismissed. Such immunity may be established upon motion or suggestion by or on behalf of the individual, or as otherwise permitted by law or applicable rules of procedure.

LAFONTANT v. ARISTIDE

844 F.Supp. 128 (E.D.N.Y. 1994).

WEINSTEIN, SENIOR DISTRICT JUDGE:

. . . .

Plaintiff, a resident of Queens, New York, seeks compensation in money damages for the killing of her husband, Dr. Roger Lafontant, by Haitian soldiers acting on the specific order of the then and present President of Haiti, Jean Bertrand Aristide. She bases jurisdiction on 28 U.S.C. §§ 1331, 1350 note, § 2(a), 1651, 2201 and 2202 and the doctrine of pendent jurisdiction. Her cause of action is predicated on: Article 2, § 2, Clause 1 and Article 6, Clause 2 of the Constitution of the United States; 28 U.S.C. § 1350 (Alien Tort Statute); 28 U.S.C. § 1350 note, § 2(a) (Torture Victim Protection Act); 28 U.S.C. §§ 2201 and 2202, 8 U.S.C. § 1252(c), "the wrongful death statutes"; the United Nations Charter; the Universal Declaration of the Rights and Duties of Man; and customary international law.

Defendant submitted a suggestion of immunity under 22 U.S.C. § 254d claiming that President Aristide is immune from suit because of his status as the head-of-state of the Republic of Haiti. He asks the court to quash service of process and dismiss the action.

The Court requested the view of the United States government. The State Department then submitted a suggestion of immunity letter, filed with the Court by the Justice Department pursuant to 28 U.S.C. § 517. Section 517 provides, in pertinent part:

any officer of the Department of Justice may be sent by the Attorney General to ... any district in the United States to attend to the interests of the United States in a suit pending in a court in the United States.

A final judgment, quashing service of process on President Jean–Bertrand Aristide and dismissing the action was promptly entered. This memorandum explains why this result is required.

I. FACTS

According to the complaint, on January 7, 1991, Dr. Roger Lafontant, along with others, attempted a coup d'etat to prevent Haitian president-elect, Jean–Bertrand Aristide, from taking office. The next day, the coup was thwarted. Lafontant had been a central figure in Haitian politics for many years; he had held the position of Secretary of the Interior, Secretary of Defense and other positions in former Haitian governments. He was arrested and jailed for his participation in the failed coup and sentenced to life imprisonment on July 29, 1991.

President Aristide then, it is alleged, instructed Captain Stagne Doura, a member of the Armed Forces of Haiti, to execute Lafontant. These orders were carried-out by Private First Class Sincere Leus who shot and killed Lafontant in a Haitian prison at midnight September 29, 1991. President Aristide's conduct, it is alleged, under color of law of the Republic of Haiti, constituted a criminal act and tort that was not officially sanctioned or in furtherance of the defendant's official function as President.

Two days after this killing, President Aristide was exiled from Haiti following a successful military coup. He has since been living in the United States.

The United States government has consistently recognized Jean–Bertrand Aristide as the current lawful head-of-state of the Republic of Haiti. When President Bush received the credentials of President Aristide's designated ambassador, Jean Casimir, he publicly stated that "the United States continues to recognize President Aristide as the duly elected President of Haiti." *Statement of President Bush* (Oct. 1, 1991). In a speech by Secretary of State James Baker on October 2, 1991 before the Organization of American States he declared, "we [the United States government] will not recognize this outlaw regime." *Address Before Organization of American States (OAS), Washington, D.C. (Oct. 2, 1991)*. ...

In reply to defendant's suggestion of immunity, plaintiff submitted what purports to be a letter signed by President Aristide on September 30, 1991, relinquishing his title as President of the Republic of Haiti. She also relies on the fact that on October 6, 1991, the parliament of Haiti applied Article 149 of the Constitution of Haiti which governs succession in the event of a presidential vacancy. On October 8, 1991 a judge of the Supreme Court of Haiti, Joseph Nerette, was sworn in as temporary President of Haiti. Mr. Nerette chose Jean Jacques Honorat as Prime

Minister on October 11, 1991. On October 16 the new government was approved by the parliament. This government functioned in Haiti until June 19, 1992, when President Nerette stepped aside. An agreement was signed between the defendant and Lieutenant General Raoul Cedras allowing President Aristide to return to Haiti by October 30, 1993 (the Governor's Island Agreement). President Aristide did not return to Haiti by that date and has remained continuously outside Haiti since the coup d'etat.

Defendant questions the assertion that the agreement "permits" President Aristide to return to Haiti. He claims that the agreement provides for the nomination of a Prime Minister, commander-in-chief of the Armed Forces, and the granting of an amnesty, all to be undertaken "by the President of the Republic." It is his contention that the "President of the Republic" refers to President Aristide.

Plaintiff has also submitted a copy of an arrest warrant dated November 6, 1991, issued for President Aristide's arrest by a criminal court in Haiti. This warrant charges President Aristide with the assassination of plaintiff's husband, Dr. Lafontant.

The Justice Department submitted a suggestion of immunity letter. It states in pertinent part:

> The United States has an interest and concern in this action against President Aristide insofar as the action involves the question of immunity from the Court's jurisdiction of the head-of-state of a friendly foreign state. The United States' interest arises from a determination by the Executive Branch of the Government of the United States, in the implementation of its foreign policy and in the conduct of its international relations, that permitting this action to proceed against President Aristide would be incompatible with the United States' foreign policy interests.

II. LAW

A. Common Law Head-of-State Immunity

A head-of-state recognized by the United States government is absolutely immune from personal jurisdiction in United States courts unless that immunity has been waived by statute or by the foreign government recognized by the United States. A visiting head-of-state is generally immune from the jurisdiction of a foreign state's courts. *See, e.g. Mr. Saltany v. Reagan*, 702 F.Supp.319 (D.D.C. 1988), *order aff'd in part, reversed in part (on other grounds),* 886 F.2d 438 (D.C. Cir. 1989), *cert. denied,* 495 U.S. 932 ... (1990) (granting head-of-state immunity to Prime Minister of England in suit alleging violations of international law); *Kilroy v. Windsor*, Civ. No. C–78–291 (N.D. Ohio 1978), (Prince Charles, The Prince of Wales, granted immunity from suit alleging human rights violations in Northern Ireland), excerpted in 1978 Dig. U.S. Prac. Int'l L. 641–43; *Psinakis v. Marcos*, Civ. No. C–75–1725 (N.D. Cal. 1975), excerpted in 1975 Dig. U.S. Prac. Int'l L. 344–45 (immunity granted to then-

President Marcos following suggestion of immunity by the Executive Branch); *Kendall v. Saudi Arabia*, 65 Adm. 885 (S.D.N.Y. 1965), reported in 1977 Dig. U.S. Prac. Int'l L. 1017, 1053–34.

Head-of-state immunity, like foreign sovereign immunity, is premised on the concept that a state and its ruler are one for purposes of immunity. As early as 1812 the Supreme Court embraced the notion, grounded in customary international law, that a head-of-state is absolutely "exempted" from the jurisdiction of the receiving state's courts. *Schooner Exchange v. M'Faddon*, 11 U.S. (7 Cranch) 116 ... (1812).

This absolute form of immunity is based on the notion that all states are equal and that no one state may exercise judicial authority over another. The foreign head-of-state, as representative of his nation, enjoys extraterritorial status when travelling abroad because he would not intend "to subject himself to a jurisdiction incompatible with his dignity, and the dignity of his nation." *Id.* at 137; *see also* L. Henkin, *International Law* 893 (2d Ed. 1987).

Head-of-state immunity is also supported by the doctrine of comity-that is to say, each state protects the immunity concept so that its own head-of-state will be protected when he or she is abroad. Comity has been described as:

> neither a matter of absolute obligation ... nor of mere courtesy and good will ... [b]ut it is the recognition which one nation allows within its territory to the legislative, executive or judicial acts of another nation, having due regard both to international duty and convenience, and to the rights of its own citizens or of other persons who are under the protection of its laws.

Hilton v. Guyot, 159 U.S. 113, 163–64 ... (1895). This concept of doing to others as you would have them do to you is the principal rationale for a number of important doctrines of international law. *See, e.g., Mitsubishi Motors Corp. v. Soler Chrysler–Plymouth, Inc.,* 473 U.S. 614 ... (1985) (rationale for enforcing arbitration agreements in international contracts rests on comity); *The Bremen v. Zapata Off–Shore Co.,* 407 U.S. 1 ... (1972) (rationale for enforcing forum selection clauses in international contracts rests on comity); *First Nat'l City Bank v. Banco National de Cuba*, 406 U.S. 759, 762 ... (1972) (Act of State rule based on comity).

Like the related doctrine of diplomatic immunity, head-of-state immunity is required to safeguard mutual respect among nations. *See,* Restatement (Third) of Foreign Relations Law of the United States (1986) §§ 464, 455 (diplomatic immunity). Heads of state must be able to freely perform their duties at home and abroad without the threat of civil and criminal liability in a foreign legal system. *See,* Note, *Resolving the Confusion Over Head of State Immunity: The Defined Rights of Kings*, 86 Colum. L. Rev. 169 (1986).

The immunity extends only to the person the United States government acknowledges as the official head-of-state. Recognition of a government and its officers is the exclusive function of the Executive Branch. Whether the recognized head-of-state has *de facto* control of the government is irrelevant; the courts must defer to the Executive determination. *Banco Nacional de Cuba v. Sabbatino*, 376 U.S. 398, 410 ... (1964) (Act of State doctrine premised on Executive Branch's recognition of state in question). Presidential decisions to recognize a government are binding on the courts, and the courts must give them legal effect. *United States v. Pink*, 315 U.S. 203, 230 ... (1942) (Executive Branch's determination that recognition of Soviet Union required settlement of claims is binding on the courts).

Since determination of who qualifies as a head-of-state is made by the Executive Branch, it is not a factual issue to be determined by the courts. No judicial hearing or factual determination aside from receipt of the State Department's communication is warranted.

In *United States v. Noriega,* 746 F.Supp.1506 (S.D. Fla. 1990), General Noriega, prosecuted criminally in this country, challenged jurisdiction, arguing that he was entitled to head-of-state immunity. Noriega had never been officially recognized by the United States as the head-of-state of Panama. Instead, the United States had recognized President Eric Arturo Delvalle, even though General Noriega held *de facto* power in Panama and was dealt with as if he were head-of-state by United States officials. General Noriega argued that because he was the *de facto* ruler of Panama, he was entitled to head-of-state immunity. *Noriega*, 746 F.Supp.at 1520. This argument was rejected because the grant of immunity is a privilege which the United States may withhold from any claimant. The fact that Noriega controlled Panama did not entitle him to head-of-state immunity absent explicit recognition from the United States. *Id.* at 1520. The court noted that if Noriega's argument that he was entitled to head-of-state immunity were accepted, "illegitimate dictators [would be granted] the benefit of their unscrupulous and possibly brutal seizures of power." *Id.* at 1521.

In *Saltany v. Reagan,* 702 F.Supp.319 (D.D.C. 1988), residents of Libya brought suit against Prime Minister Margaret Thatcher of the United Kingdom, for alleged violations of international law. Pursuant to 28 U.S.C. § 517 the State Department submitted an immunity letter, suggesting that the court grant Prime Minister Thatcher immunity as the head of government of a friendly foreign state. The court accepted the State Department's suggestion as conclusive, and granted immunity. *Saltany,* 702 F.Supp. at 320. *See also*, Restatement (Second) of Foreign Relations Law of the United States (1962) § 66 (defining head-of-state as either the head-of-state or head of government, thus both Queen and Prime Minister are considered the head-of-state); *Kilroy v. Windsor (Prince Charles, The Prince of Wales),* Civ. No. C–78–291 (N.D. Ohio 1978), excerpted in 1978 Dig. U.S. Prac. Int'l L. 641–43, (holding Prince Charles as heir apparent to the throne is head-of-state in accordance with State Department suggestion of immunity).

The government of a foreign state which is recognized by the Executive Branch may waive its head-of-state immunity. In *In re Grand Jury Proceedings*, 817 F.2d 1108 (4th Cir. 1987), *cert. denied,* 484 U.S. 890 ... (1987), Ferdinand and Imelda Marcos, the former leaders of the Philippines, were found civilly liable for failing to comply with federal grand jury subpoenas. The court held that the doctrine of head-of-state immunity is not an individual right but an "attribute of state sovereignty," a privilege that can be revoked by the foreign state. Corazon Aquino was recognized by the United States as the then head-of-state of the Philippines. The Aquino government waived Mr. and Mrs. Marcos' residual head-of-state or diplomatic immunity in a note to the United States government. The court honored President Aquino's waiver, holding that application of head-of-state immunity to the Marcoses would "clearly offend the present Philippine government, and would therefore undermine the international comity that the head-of-state immunity doctrine is designed to promote." *Id.* at 1111; *see also Mr. and Mrs. Doe v. United States*, 860 F.2d 40 (2nd Cir. 1988).

Similarly, the court held that the foreign government waived immunity in *Paul v. Avril,* 812 F.Supp. 207 (S.D. Fla. 1993). Prosper Avril, the ex-Lieutenant–General of the Armed Forces of Haiti and former military ruler of Haiti was sued for alleged violations of international law. Defendant moved to dismiss, claiming head-of-state immunity. The government of Haiti waived any immunity enjoyed by Mr. Avril. Mr. Avril argued that by following Haiti's suggestion of waiver the court would "encourage countries to disavow those former leaders who do not curry favor with the new government." *Paul*, 812 F.Supp. at 210. The court held that the Haitian government then recognized by the United States could waive head-of-state immunity of the former head of military government, and that waiver extends to whatever "residual" head-of-state immunity defendant possessed. *Id.*

Waiver of head-of-state immunity is analogous to waiver provisions in the Vienna Convention of Diplomatic Relations, April 18, 1961, 23 U.S.T. 3227, T.I.A.S. No. 7502, 500 U.N.T.S. 95, Articles 31(a), 31(2), and 29, which provide that the immunity of diplomatic agents may be waived by the sending state. Such waiver must be explicit. *See Libra Bank Ltd. v. Banco Nacional de Costa Rica*, 676 F.2d 47, 49 (2d Cir. 1982) (requirement of explicit waiver of foreign sovereign immunity prevents "inadvertent, implied or constructive waiver in cases where the intent of the foreign state is equivocal or ambiguous").

B. Application of Common Law Immunity to Facts

President Aristide is the head-of-state of the Republic of Haiti who is recognized by the U.S. government. He enjoys head-of-state immunity unless there has been a waiver of immunity.

Plaintiff contends that the Republic of Haiti has waived President Aristide's immunity. She argues that the failure of the military rulers of Haiti to comply with the terms of the Governor's Island Agreement constitutes an implied waiver of President Aristide's right to legally govern Haiti and claim head-of-state immunity.

This argument is invalid for several reasons. First, the terms of the Governor's Island agreement do not explicitly or implicitly condition President Aristide's status as President of Haiti on his return to Haiti. Second, even if the agreement did provide for the forfeiture of President Aristide's status, recognition of a head-of-state by courts of the United States is an issue for resolution by the Executive Branch of the United States government. A court may not make an independent inquiry into the facts underlying our government's decision. *See United States v. Pink*, 315 U.S. 203 ... (1942).

The warrant for President Aristide's arrest issued by a Haitian court and a personal note allegedly signed by President Aristide that purports to declare his renunciation of the Presidential office are without effect on the issue of immunity. Assuming without deciding that these documents are valid, they cannot affect the court's treatment of the suggestion of immunity. The court must rely on the Executive's determination of who is a lawful head-of-state.

Here there has been no explicit waiver of President Aristide's immunity recognized as a waiver by the United States. Unlike *In re Mr. and Mrs. Doe*, 860 F.2d 40 (2nd Cir. 1988), where the recognized Philippines government specifically waived the Marcoses' head-of-state immunity, the unrecognized *de facto* rulers of Haiti have no power to and have not undertaken any action accepted by our government as an implicit waiver of immunity. While not decisive, we note that the recognized Ambassador of Haiti to the United States has submitted a letter stating affirmatively that President Aristide is the head-of-state of the Republic of Haiti, and that the embassy does not waive any of the sovereign, head-of-state, or diplomatic immunities that he may enjoy.

The United States government does not recognize the *de facto* military rulers of Haiti. It has repeatedly condemned their regime. The United Nations has also severely criticized their illegal seizure of power. *See, The Situation of Democracy and Human Rights in Haiti: Report of the Secretary General,* U.N. GAOR, 47th Sess., Agenda Item 22, U.N. Doc. A/47/975 (July 12, 1993). Because the United States does not recognize the *de facto* government, that government does not have the power to waive President Aristide's immunity.

Granting President Aristide head-of-state immunity will further the goals of comity. The State Department, in its suggestion of immunity letter, states that "permitting this action to proceed against President Aristide would be incompatible with the United States' foreign policy interests."

The United States foreign policy goal of encouraging democratic elections is strengthened by recognizing President Aristide as the democratically elected head of Haiti. Numerous Executive Orders supporting

President Aristide establish that the Republic of Haiti is a "friendly foreign state."

Even, however, if the goal of the United States were less lofty, it would make no difference. In this matter the courts are bound by executive decision.

C. Lack of Statutory Modification of Immunity Law

No statute has modified the long standing rule of international and common law. [The court then discussed why neither the Foreign Sovereign Immunities Act nor the Torture Victim Protection Act modified the rule on head- of- state immunity.]

. . . .

III. CONCLUSION

. . . .

This court has subject matter jurisdiction, but it cannot exercise in personam jurisdiction over defendant because of his head-of-state immunity.

The case is dismissed. . . .

YE v. ZEMIN

383 F.3d 620 (7th Cir. 2004) (some footnotes omitted).

MANION, CIRCUIT JUDGE.

The appellants are practitioners of Falun Gong, a spiritual movement of Chinese origin. Most of the appellants are current or past residents of the People's Republic of China. In addition, two of the appellants are United States citizens and a third is an alien resident of Illinois. The appellants appeal from a decision of the United States District Court for the Northern District of Illinois dismissing their lawsuit against the former President of China, Jiang Zemin, and an office of the Chinese Communist Party (the "Party") allegedly established by Jiang for the purpose of suppressing Falun Gong. We affirm.

I.

Jiang Zemin served as President of China for approximately ten years, from March 1993 to March 15, 2003. During part of his tenure as President, he also served as the Secretary General of the Central Committee of the Chinese Communist Party (the head of the Party). President Jiang stepped down as head of the Party on November 15, 2002.

Beginning in 1999, the Chinese government and the Party took steps to crack down on Falun Gong. Falun Gong, formed in 1992 by a former Chinese soldier, Li Hongzhi, "combin[es] traditional Buddhist teachings and predictions about the end of the world with meditation and martial arts discipline as a prescription for physical and spiritual well-being. Falun

Gong teaches that illness stems from evil and that by following the principles of 'truth, compassion and forbearance,' one can attain clairvoyance and other preternatural faculties."[2] The Chinese government and the Party see things differently. They have denounced the movement as a cult and have accused it of seeking to subvert or overthrow the government and the Party's grip on power. According to at least one news report, President Jiang himself declared that suppressing Falun Gong was one of the " 'three major political struggles' of 1999."[4]

To that end, on June 10, 1999, President Jiang established, as part of the Party's apparatus, the Falun Gong Control Office. The Office is known as "Office 6/10" after the date of its creation. In July 1999, President Jiang issued an edict outlawing Falun Gong. This edict was followed by mass arrests, allegedly farcical trials, torture, forced labor, "re-education," and the killing of members.

The appellants filed this lawsuit against President Jiang and Office 6/10 on October 18, 2002. The appellants' complaint, recites, *inter alia*, claims of torture, genocide, arbitrary arrest and imprisonment, as well as other claims related to the appellants' freedom of conscience, movement, and religion. The appellants argued that the district court had jurisdiction to hear their case pursuant to the Alien Tort Claim Act, 28 U.S.C. § 1350, as well as, in part, 28 U.S.C. §§ 1343(4) and 1331.

Because President Jiang was scheduled to be in Chicago on October 22 and 23 on his way to visit with United States President George W. Bush in Washington, D.C., the appellants moved *ex parte* for leave from the district court to effect service on President Jiang (and by extension Office 6/10) while he was in Chicago. The district court granted this motion and entered an order permitting service by delivery of a copy of the summons and complaint "to any of the security agents or hotel staff helping to guard" President Jiang. The appellants contend that service was complete when they delivered a copy of these documents to a Chicago police officer and agents of the United States Secret Service detail stationed at the hotel at which President Jiang was staying in Chicago.

Neither President Jiang nor a representative of the Chinese government or Office 6/10 responded to the complaint, and the appellants moved for an entry of default. The United States, however, intervened pursuant to 28 U.S.C. § 517 and moved to vacate the service order or, in the alternative, to assert head-of-state immunity for President Jiang. The United States further argued that President Jiang was personally inviolable and, therefore, incapable of being served in any capacity. Specifically, the government argued that President Jiang could not be served as an agent of Office 6/10.

---

2. John Pomfret and Michael Laris, "China Outlaws Nonconformist Spiritual Sect; Group Had Organized Protests Across Nation," *Wash. Post,* July 23, 1999, at A1.

4. John Pomfret, "China Girds for a Battle of the Spirit; Ruling Party Fears Religious Challenge," *Wash. Post,* Jan. 10, 2000, at A1.

The district court accepted the United States' assertion of head-of-state immunity on behalf of President Jiang and dismissed the appellants' claims against him. The district court rejected, however, the government's argument of personal inviolability. Instead, the district court found that service of process on Office 6/10 could not be achieved through President Jiang because the appellants had not shown that President Jiang was either an agent or an officer of Office 6/10. Further, the district court held that, even assuming service of process on Office 6/10 could be effectuated through President Jiang, it lacked personal jurisdiction to hear claims against it. The district court, therefore, dismissed the appellants' complaint in its entirety. This appeal followed.

II.

The appellants raise three issues on appeal. First, they argue that the district court erred when it accepted, as controlling, the United States' assertion of head-of-state immunity on behalf of President Jiang. Second, the appellants argue that the district court erred when it determined that President Jiang could not be served as an agent of Office 6/10. Finally, the appellants argue that the district court erred when it held that it lacked personal jurisdiction over Office 6/10.

. . . .

B. The Present Case

In this case the Executive Branch entered a suggestion of immunity. The appellants argue, however, that the Executive Branch has no power to immunize a head of state (or any person for that matter) for acts that violate *jus cogens* norms of international law. We have explained *jus cogens* norms before:

> A *jus cogens* norm is a special type of customary international law. A *jus cogens* norm " 'is a norm accepted and recognized by the international community of states as a whole as a norm from which no derogation is permitted and which can be modified only by a subsequent norm of general international law having the same character.' " *See Siderman de Blake v. Republic of Argentina,* 965 F.2d 699, 714 (9th Cir. 1992) (*quoting* Vienna Convention on the Law of Treaties, art. 53, May 23, 1969, 1155 U.N.T.S. 332, 8 I.L.M. 679). Most famously, *jus cogens* norms supported the prosecutions in the Nuremberg trials. *See Siderman,* 965 F.2d at 715 (9th Cir. 1992) ("The universal and fundamental rights of human beings identified by Nuremberg—rights against genocide, enslavement, and other inhumane acts . . .—are the direct ancestors of the universal and fundamental norms recognized as jus cogens.").

Sampson v. Federal Republic of Germany, 250 F.3d 1145, 1149–50 (7th Cir. 2001).

The appellants' position, therefore, is that, in at least a particular class of cases (those involving *jus cogens* norms), a court cannot defer to the position of the Executive Branch with respect to immunity for heads of states. The Supreme Court has held, however, that the Executive Branch's suggestion of immunity is conclusive and not subject to judicial inquiry. *See Ex Parte Republic of Peru*, 318 U.S. 578, 589 ... (1943) ("The certification and the request that the vessel be declared immune *must be accepted by the courts as a conclusive determination* by the political arm of the Government that the continued retention of the vessel interferes with the proper conduct of our foreign relations.") (emphasis added); *Compañia Española de Navegacion Maritima, S.A. v. The Navemar*, 303 U.S. 68, 74 ... (1938) ("If [a claim of immunity by a foreign government] is recognized and allowed by the Executive Branch of the government, *it is then the duty of the courts* to release the vessel upon appropriate suggestion by the Attorney General of the United States, or other officer acting under his discretion.") (emphasis added); *see also Spacil v. Crowe*, 489 F.2d 614, 617 (5th Cir. 1974) ("The precedents are overwhelming. For more than 160 years American courts have consistently applied the doctrine of sovereign immunity when requested to do so by the executive branch. Moreover, they have done so with no further review of the executive's determination."); *Isbrandtsen Tankers, Inc. v. President of India*, 446 F.2d 1198, 1201 (2d Cir. 1971) ("The State Department is to make [an immunity determination] in light of the potential consequences to our own international position. Hence once the State Department has ruled in a matter of this nature, the judiciary will not interfere."); *Rich v. Naviera Vacuba S.A.*, 295 F.2d 24, 26 (4th Cir. 1961) ("[W]e conclude that the certificate and grant of immunity issued by the Department of State should be accepted by the court without further inquiry. We think that the doctrine of the separation of powers under our Constitution requires us to assume that all pertinent considerations have been taken into account by the Secretary of State in reaching his conclusion.") (internal citations omitted).

The appellants present their argument as one of international law—under customary international law, a state cannot provide immunity to a defendant accused of violating *jus cogens* norms. Our first concern, however, is to ascertain the proper relationship between the Executive and Judicial Branches insofar as the immunity of foreign leaders is concerned. The obligation of the Judicial Branch is clear—a determination by the Executive Branch that a foreign head of state is immune from suit is conclusive and a court must accept such a determination without reference to the underlying claims of a plaintiff. *See Spacil*, 489 F.2d at 618 ("[W]e are analyzing here the proper allocation of functions of the branches of government in the scheme of the United States. We are not analyzing the proper scope of sovereign immunity under international law.").

Our deference to the Executive Branch is motivated by the caution we believe appropriate of the Judicial Branch when the conduct of foreign affairs is involved. *Cf. Republic of Mexico v. Hoffman*, 324 U.S. 30, 35 ... (1945) ("[I]t is a guiding principle in determining whether a court should [recognize a suggestion of immunity] in such cases, that the courts should not so act as to embarrass the executive arm in its conduct of foreign affairs. 'In such cases the judicial department of this government follows the action of the political branch, and will not embarrass the latter by assuming an antagonistic jurisdiction.' ") (quoting *United States v. Lee*, 106 U.S. 196, 209 ... (1882)); *Spacil,* 489 F.2d at 619 ("Separation-of-powers principles impel a reluctance in the judiciary to interfere with or embarrass the executive in its constitutional role as the nation's primary organ of international policy."). The determination to grant (or not grant) immunity can have significant implications for this country's relationship with other nations. A court is ill-prepared to assess these implications and resolve the competing concerns the Executive Branch is faced with in determining whether to immunize a head of state. *Spacil*, 489 F.2d at 619 ("[T]he degree to which granting or denying a claim of immunity may be important to foreign policy is a question on which the judiciary is particularly ill-equipped to second-guess the executive. The executive's institutional resources and expertise in foreign affairs far outstrip those of the judiciary.").

Although our decision in *Sampson* was one of statutory interpretation, we believe it is also instructive here. In *Sampson* we held that the [Foreign Sovereign Immunities Act of 1976, 28 U.S.C. §§ 1602 et seq. (2000) (FSIA)] did not include an implied exception to its general grant of sovereign immunity to foreign states where a foreign state was accused of violating *jus cogens* norms. [250 F.3d] at 1156. Because the FSIA contained no such exception, Germany was immune from suit brought by a survivor of Auschwitz in the Northern District of Illinois.

Our interpretation of the FSIA confirmed that Congress could grant immunity to a foreign state for acts that amounted to violations of *jus cogens* norms. Just as the FSIA is the Legislative Branch's determination that a nation should be immune from suit in the courts of this country, the immunity of foreign leaders remains the province of the Executive Branch. The Executive Branch's determination that a foreign leader should be immune from suit even when the leader is accused of acts that violate *jus cogens* norms is established by a suggestion of immunity. We are no more free to ignore the Executive Branch's determination than we are free to ignore a legislative determination concerning a foreign state. *Cf. Hoffman*, 324 U.S. at 35 ... (1945) ("It is ... not for the courts to deny an immunity which our government has seen fit to allow, or to allow an immunity on new grounds which the government has not seen fit to recognize."). Pursuant to their respective authorities, Congress or the Executive Branch can create exceptions to blanket immunity. In such cases the courts would be obliged to respect such exceptions. In the present case the Executive Branch has recognized the immunity of President Jiang from the appellants' suit. The district court was correct to accept this recognition as conclusive.

C. Service of Process on President Jiang to Reach Third Parties

We turn next to Office 6/10. The appellants maintain that service on Office 6/10 was complete when President Jiang was served during his stay in Chicago. As recounted above, the United States argues that President Jiang's immunity extends to service aimed not at him, but at a third party.

The district court rejected the United States' immunity argument but, nonetheless, held that service on President Jiang was insufficient to reach Office 6/10 because the appellants had provided only conclusory evidence that President Jiang was, at the time of service, an officer or agent of Office 6/10. The district court also held that "even if Jiang was an agent or officer of Office 6/10 and thus capable of receiving service on its behalf, such service was insufficient to confer personal jurisdiction over Office 6/10 because the Office is not subject to the jurisdiction of Illinois courts."

Although the district court reached the correct result, it erred when it rejected the United States' argument concerning the scope of President Jiang's immunity. Because the Executive Branch has recognized President Jiang's immunity from suit, President Jiang could not be used as an involuntary agent of the appellants to effect service on Office 6/10. We need not therefore consider whether President Jiang was acting as an agent or officer of Office 6/10 or whether the district court had personal jurisdiction over Office 6/10.

We agree with the Executive Branch that its power to recognize the immunity of a foreign head of state includes the power to preclude service of process in that same suit on the head of state even where that service is intended to reach third parties.

Recognizing the immunity of a head of state and precluding service of process on a head of state are motivated by the same concern for the effective conduct of this nation's foreign affairs. As emphasized above, this responsibility is left to the political branches of this government. The Executive Branch has represented to this court that permitting service of process is often viewed by foreign governments and their heads of state "as an affront to the dignity of both the leader and the state." The Executive Branch has also indicated that "the potential for insult is the same, regardless of whether the service relates to the visiting head of state himself, or to service on the visiting leader in some purported representational or agency capacity." Finally, the Executive Branch has indicated that "[s]uch attacks on the dignity of a visiting head of state can easily frustrate our President's ability to reach this Nation's diplomatic objectives. ..." The deference we extend the Executive Branch with regard to its determination of immunity, *see supra,* is equally appropriate here. The Executive Branch is better equipped than this court or the district court to assess the consequences for our foreign policy of permitting service of process on visiting heads of state, and it is the Executive Branch in its dealings with China that will confront, in the first instance, the consequences of that determination. *Cf. Hellenic Lines, Ltd. v. Moore,* 345 F.2d

978, 980–81 (D.C. Cir. 1965) (holding that the Ambassador of Tunisia was not properly subject to service directed to Tunisia after the State Department informed the court that "service would prejudice the United States foreign relations and would probably impair the performance of diplomatic functions."); *see also Spacil,* 489 F.2d at 619 ("[I]n the chess game that is diplomacy only the executive has a view of the entire board and an understanding of the relationship between isolated moves. Will granting immunity serve as a bargaining counter in complex diplomatic negotiations? Will it preclude a significant diplomatic advance; perhaps a detente between this country and one with whom we are not on the best speaking terms? These are questions for the executive, not the judiciary.") (internal citation omitted).

Also important to our decision is the treatment accorded the President of the United States in his travels abroad. The Executive Branch has stated that it would be a "great offense if foreign states and their courts were to encourage process servers to hound our President when he is abroad to conduct important negotiations with his foreign counterparts." Such concerns must weigh heavily in our determination that service of process should not be permitted on foreign heads of state visiting this country in the circumstances of this case.

. . . .

The district court is correct that there are exceptions to the immunity a head of state (as well as a foreign nation) is granted in this country's courts. As we have discussed above, however, and the district court recognized elsewhere in its opinion, the determination that these exceptions apply to a head of state is left to the Executive Branch. Likewise, the determination that service in the circumstances of this case would be detrimental to the Nation's foreign policy should be left to the Executive Branch.

III.

In this case the Executive Branch has recognized President Jiang's immunity from the appellants' suit. We are required to defer to the decision of the Executive Branch. The Executive Branch has also determined that service of process by the appellants on President Jiang in order to reach an intended co-defendant in the same suit could frustrate this Nation's diplomatic objectives. It is appropriate to defer to that decision as well. Because we do so, service on Office 6/10 could not be effectuated through President Jiang. We need not reach, therefore, the question of whether President Jiang was, at the time of service, an officer or agent of Office 6/10 or whether the district court had personal jurisdiction over Office 6/10.

We conclude by stating that we are not unsympathetic to the appellants' claims. For the reasons stated above, however, we cannot permit this suit to go forward. The Executive Branch has stated it is working to persuade the government of China to put an end to the human rights violations it has inflicted on its people for more than half a century. Success depends on diplomacy, not United States courts.

Affirmed

NOTES ON HEAD OF STATE AND RELATED IMMUNITIES

1. *Immunity for Heads of State.* The scope of head-of-state immunity was clarified somewhat by the International Court of Justice (ICJ) in a case involving an arrest warrant issued by a Belgian court for the detention of the then-foreign affairs minister of the Democratic Republic of the Congo (DRC). The minister was accused of committing war crimes and crimes against humanity—acts committed prior to assuming his post, which he held at the time of the issuance of the warrant but which he relinquished prior to the announcement of the ICJ's judgment—by making speeches that incited the massacre of civilians. Belgium asserted that the exercise of its national criminal law over such conduct was permissible under international law because of the principle of "universal jurisdiction."

Without speaking to the issue of whether such jurisdiction was permissible under international law, the Court asserted "that in international law it is firmly established that, as also diplomatic and consular agents, certain holders of high-ranking office in a State, such as the Head of State, Head of Government and Minister for Foreign Affairs, enjoy immunities from jurisdiction in other States, both civil and criminal." Arrest Warrant of 11 April 2000 (Congo v. Belgium), 2002 I.C.J. 3, 20–21 (Feb. 14). As such, the ICJ held that Belgium's warrant violated customary international law, because it failed to respect the incumbent minister's inviolability and immunity from criminal jurisdiction.

2. *Breadth of Head of State Immunity.* The ICJ found that a sitting foreign minister warranted absolute immunity, as would a sitting head of state. Similar immunity has been accorded by U.S. courts. *See, e.g.*, Chong Boon Kim v. Kim Yong Shik (Hawaii Cir. Ct. 1963), *excerpted in* 58 Am. J. Int'l L. 186–87 (1964) (dismissing suit against South Korean foreign minister, in accordance with State Department suggestion of immunity); Tachiona v. Mugabe, 169 F.Supp.2d 259, 296–97 (S.D.N.Y. 2001) (dismissing case against a Zimbabwe foreign minister, in accordance with State Department suggestion of immunity), *aff'd in part on other grounds, rev'd in part,* 386 F.3d 205 (2d Cir. 2004). Yet precisely which other government officials are to be accorded immunity is not clear. Certainly other officials have had immunity suggested on their behalf by the executive branch and recognized by U.S. courts. *See, e.g.*, Kilroy v. Windsor (Prince Charles, The Prince of Wales), Civ. No. C–78–291 (N.D.Ohio 1978), *excerpted in* U.S. Dept. of State, *Digest of United States Practice in International Law* 641–43 (1978) (dismissing suit against Prince Charles, in accordance with State Department suggestion of immunity); Philippines v. Marcos, 665 F.Supp. 793, 799 (N.D.Cal.1987) (dismissing suit against Philippines solicitor general, in accordance with State Department suggestion of immunity). If you were a lawyer for the U.S. government, which officials would you regard as being entitled to head of state immunity?

3. *Special Missions Immunity.* Foreign officials (other than accredited diplomats) who are engaged in diplomatic activities are sometimes described as serving "special missions" in their host states. Those missions may be entitled to "special missions" immunity under customary international law or pursuant to the Convention on the Prevention and Punishment of Crimes Against Internationally Protected Persons including Diplomatic Agents, Dec. 14, 1973, 28 U.S.T. 1975, 1035 U.N.T.S. 167. Although not a party to that convention, the U.S. government has effectively recognized instances of special mission immunity. Cases like *Kilroy v. Windsor*, *Chong Boon Kim v. Kim Yong Shik*, *Tachiona v. Mugabe*, and *Republic of Philippines v. Marcos*, *supra*, involved suggestions of immunity for officials who not only held high office, but who were present in the United States and served with process while performing diplomatic or other similar official functions.

For example, a visiting Chinese Commerce Minister was recently served with process for actions he took as a provincial governor. As such, his status both when he acted and when he was served was not that of a head of state (or foreign minister), nor was he an accredited diplomat. Nonetheless, the State Department suggested immunity on the ground that the minister was serving as a diplomatic envoy at the time process was served. The district court agreed and dismissed the action. Weixum v. Xilai, 568 F.Supp.2d 35 (D.D.C. 2008).

4. *Former Heads of State.* In the *Arrest Warrant* case, the ICJ found that the issuance of an arrest warrant against a then-incumbent foreign minister violated Belgium's international legal obligations. Because the "head of state" immunity to which a foreign minister was entitled was absolute in character, it protected against "any act of authority of another State which would hinder him or her in the performance of his or her duties." 2002 I.C.J. at 22. It was irrelevant, then, whether the warrant related to acts undertaken by the minister in an official or private capacity, whether those acts occurred before the minister even assumed office, or whether the acts were especially severe or heinous under international law. *Id.*

At the same time, the Court emphasized that the minister would potentially be vulnerable to prosecution under other circumstances. The DRC could choose itself to prosecute him or to waive immunity so as to enable prosecution by another state. The minister might also be subject to prosecution by certain international criminal tribunals with jurisdiction over the matter. Last, but not least, absolute immunity was effective only for the period in which the minister held office: afterward, he might be prosecuted by Belgium or another state for acts committed prior or subsequent to the minister's period of office, as well as for private acts committed during his or her tenure, so long as the prosecuting state's asserted jurisdiction was consistent with international law. *Id.* at 26–27.

Without precisely embracing the ICJ's approach, the executive branch has asserted that it may suggest immunity on behalf of former heads of state (and like officials) for official acts. *See, e.g.*, Matar v. Dichter, 563 F.3d 9, 13–14 (2d Cir. 2009) (dismissing suit against former director of security and intelligence service, in accordance with State Department suggestion of immunity). On remand following the Supreme Court's decision in *Samantar v. Yousuf*, 130

S.Ct. 2278, 176 L.Ed.2d 1047 (2010) (discussed *supra*), the question arose whether a former Somali vice president, minister of defense, and prime minister was entitled to immunity from civil suit for acts he asserted had been taken in an official capacity. The State Department filed a statement of interest determining that the official in question did not enjoy immunity, emphasizing in particular that because the United States did not recognize a government of Somalia, there was no government to assert immunity on the official's behalf or to express a position as to whether the acts concerned were taken in an official capacity. Further, the Department argued that the defendant official was now a resident of the United States. Statement of Interest of the United States of America, Yousuf v. Samantar, No. 1:04 CV 1360 (LMV) (E.D. Va.). The district court promptly dismissed the defendant's common law official immunity defense. Order, Yousuf v. Samantar, No. 1:04 CV 1360 (LMV) (E.D. Va. Feb. 15, 2011).

The U.S. government's brief in the earlier Supreme Court proceedings in *Samantar* had listed further considerations bearing on its immunity decision, other than the issue of recognition of the Somali government. Those other considerations included "issues of reciprocity, customary international law and state practice, the immunity of the state itself, and, when appropriate, domestic precedents" and, as to the nature of the acts in question, not only whether they were taken in an official capacity, but also whether plaintiffs relied on a statutory cause of action (like the TVPA) or (merely) a federal common law cause of action (like the ATS). Brief for the United States as Amicus Curiae at 24–25, Samantar v. Yousuf, 130 S.Ct. 2278, 176 L.Ed.2d 1047 (2010). The clear predicate, in all events, is that the U.S. government continues to assert the right to determine whether a foreign official is protected by immunity for official acts, even after the period in office has come to a close.

5. *The Role of the Courts.* Should U.S. courts rely conclusively on the judgment of the State Department as to whether a foreign government official is to be accorded immunity? Note that the executive branch's view might turn on several different factors: whether the person in question is the head of state (or other high-ranking official) of a government; whether that government is recognized by the United States; whether that official because of his or her position qualities for head-of-state immunity; whether that official because of his or work qualifies for special mission immunity; and whether, if that immunity only extends to acts undertaken in an official capacity, the acts in question were of that nature. Should conclusive effect be given by U.S. courts for all or just some of those factors? For criticism of the judiciary's reliance on executive branch determinations, see Ingrid B. Wuerth, *Foreign Official Immunity Determinations in U.S. Courts: The Case Against the State Department*, 51 VA. J. INT'L L. 915 (2011).

For example, should the judiciary exercise any greater degree of independent judgment with respect the claims of special mission immunity than is the case for head-of-state immunity? Is it troubling to depart from an approach that limits immunity to only a relatively small number of high-level officials (head of state immunity) to a different approach (special missions immunity) that potentially immunizes a wide range of individuals at the wholesale discretion of the executive branch? Or is it preferable to focus less on the position of the person and more on whether diplomatic activity is being performed, a matter best left to executive scrutiny?

If U.S. courts are not to accord conclusive effect to judgments of the State Department on all or some of these factors, or if the State Department fails to provide any guidance, are the courts really able to draw lines in this area?

NOTE ON THE PROTECTION OF DIPLOMATS VERSUS FREE SPEECH

18 U.S.C. § 112 (2006) subjects to criminal punishment willful acts or attempts to "intimidate, coerce, threaten, or harass a foreign official or an official guest or obstruct a foreign official in the performance of his duties." Can this statute be used to preclude persons from picketing foreign embassies in the United States, since protesting the policies of foreign countries constitutes a form of "harassment"?

In *CISPES v. Federal Bureau of Investigation,* 770 F.2d 468 (5th Cir. 1985), the Fifth Circuit Court of Appeals upheld the constitutionality of that statute against a challenge by the Committee in Solidarity with the People of El Salvador (CISPES), which had sought a confrontation with the Honduran Consul in New Orleans, including a picket line in front of the main entrance to the consulate. The FBI had ordered the picket dissolved on the basis of the statute. The court found that the law "is a legislative effort to implement various international obligations of the United States government." *Id.* at 472. These obligations were found to include the norms established by the Convention to Prevent and Punish the Acts of Terrorism Taking the Form of Crimes against Persons and Related Extortion That Are of International Significance, adopted by the Organization of American States, and the Convention on the Prevention and Punishment of Crimes against Internationally Protected Persons, adopted by the United Nations. *Id.* at 472 n. 5. Since peaceful picketing is normally regarded as an activity protected by the First Amendment, is the court demonstrating a willingness to tolerate what amounts to prior restraint on such activity because of the government's interest in upholding its international legal obligations?

In *Concerned Jewish Youth v. McGuire,* 621 F.2d 471 (2d Cir. 1980), *cert. denied,* 450 U.S. 913, 101 S.Ct. 1352, 67 L.Ed.2d 337 (1981), the Second Circuit upheld a "bull pen" imposed by New York City police, which allowed only twelve persons to protest within a designated area visible from the consulate across the street. All other protestors were required to stay off the block on which the consulate was located, and hence, in areas where they could not be seen from the consulate. Despite evidence that these restrictions made protests ineffective, and thereby chilled speech, the Second Circuit had little difficulty upholding the restrictions:

> The government interest in providing security, safety and silence may, at times, be superior to asserted First Amendment rights. A statute, ordinance or regulation which embodies these interests will be valid even though it infringes on purported constitutional guarantees....
>
> The United States and the New York City Police have a substantial interest in protecting foreign officials and their property. The New York City Police, pursuant to their mandate in § 435 of the New York City

Charter, must "preserve the public peace, ... [disperse] assemblages which obstruct the free passage of public streets, sidewalks, parks and places; [and] protect the rights of persons and property...." This includes the members and property of a Foreign Mission.

The United States is charged by various international obligations to protect diplomatic personnel and has recognized its obligation statutorily. *See, e. g.,* Article 22(2) of the 1961 Vienna Convention on Diplomatic Relations, 23 U.S.T. 3227, 3237, TIAS No. 7502 (protection of missions); Section 16 of the Headquarters Agreement between the United Nations and the United States (61 Stat. 758, 763) (Headquarters of member states to be protected from disturbance); and 18 U.S.C. § 112 (1976) (providing for severe criminal penalties for harassment or assault of foreign officials).

We do not think that the federal statute (18 U.S.C. § 112) was designed to take all power to control demonstrations at Foreign Missions away from local authorities as CJY argues. The relevant provision was enacted "to protect the peace, dignity and security of foreign officials and guests in their embassies, consulates, missions, residences and offices". Sen. Rep. No. 92–1105, 92d Cong., 2d Sess. *reprinted in* U.S. Code Cong. & Admin. News 4316, 4328 (1972). Any actions local authorities may take to aid in protecting foreign officials furthers this intent of Congress in enacting the legislation. The law did not set maximum standards of protection, but rather set minimum standards, and specifically left open the situation where local authorities might use stricter controls....

When the New York City Police instituted these restrictions on demonstrations in front of the Mission, they were simply protecting the Mission and its personnel. There have been numerous instances of violence at the Russian Mission. In 1971 and 1976 shots were fired at and into the Mission. In 1975, containers of red paint were thrown at the Mission splattering paint on walls and doors. Finally, in 1977 and 1978 there were problems with unruly demonstrators in front of the Mission. (Br. of U.S. at 2–3). More recently, the Russian Mission was bombed for the first time.

The Police implemented the restrictions because of this violence and because they were aware that even a peaceful demonstration could be infiltrated by members of a violent group. ...One Co-chairman of CJY admitted that through deceit or inadequate screening by CJY, violent demonstrators could be among their ranks at a protest. ...Finally, one police officer testified that even peaceful demonstrators walking immediately adjacent to the Mission could become stirred to violence, due to the emotional reaction to seeing the Russian Mission. ...Because of the potential violence which might result when persons demonstrate in front of the Mission, the restrictions were properly imposed.

Testimony at trial established that the only reasonable place for the 12 demonstrators would be in the bull pen. ...There they can be seen from the Mission, but do not interfere with Mission personnel or property, and do not interfere with the synagogue, police station, schoolhouse, and firehouse across the street from the Mission. These restrictions are

> no greater than required to maintain the governmental interest involved in this case. . . .

621 F.2d at 474–75 (footnotes omitted). Do you agree that U.S. interests in protecting foreign embassies and diplomatic personnel are such as to make New York's congregation restriction permissible?

BOOS v. BARRY

485 U.S. 312, 108 S.Ct. 1157, 99 L.Ed.2d 333 (1988).

JUSTICE O'CONNOR delivered the opinion of the Court, except as to Part II–A.

The question presented in this case is whether a provision of the District of Columbia Code, § 22–1115, violates the First Amendment. This section prohibits the display of any sign within 500 feet of a foreign embassy if that sign tends to bring that foreign government into "public odium" or "public disrepute." It also prohibits any congregation of three or more persons within 500 feet of a foreign embassy.

I

Petitioners are three individuals who wish to carry signs critical of the Governments of the Soviet Union and Nicaragua on the public sidewalks within 500 feet of the embassies of those Governments in Washington, D.C. Petitioners Bridget M. Brooker and Michael Boos, for example, wish to display signs stating "RELEASE SAKHAROV" and "SOLIDARITY" in front of the Soviet Embassy. Petitioner J. Michael Waller wishes to display a sign reading "STOP THE KILLING" within 500 feet of the Nicaraguan Embassy. All of the petitioners also wish to congregate with two or more other persons within 500 feet of official foreign buildings.

Asserting that D.C. Code § 22–1115 (1981) prohibited them from engaging in these expressive activities, petitioners, together with respondent Father R. David Finzer, brought a facial First Amendment challenge to that provision in the District Court for the District of Columbia. . . .

Congress enacted § 22–1115 in 1938, S.J. Res. 191, ch. 29, § 1, 52 Stat. 30 (1938), pursuant to its authority under Article I, § 8, cl. 10, of the Constitution to "define and punish . . . Offenses against the Law of Nations." Section 22–1115 reads in pertinent part as follows:

> "It shall be unlawful to display any flag, banner, placard, or device designed or adapted to intimidate, coerce, or bring into public odium any foreign government, party, or organization, or any officer or officers thereof, or to bring into public disrepute political, social, or economic acts, views, or purposes of any foreign government, party or organization . . . within 500 feet of any building or premises within the District of Columbia used or occupied by any foreign government or its representative or representatives as an embassy, legation, consulate, or for other official purposes . . . or to congregate within

500 feet of any such building or premises, and refuse to disperse after having been ordered so to do by the police authorities of said District."

The first portion of this statute, the "display" clause, applies to signs tending to bring a foreign government into public odium or public disrepute, such as signs critical of a foreign government or its policies. The display clause applies only to the display of signs, not to the spoken word. ... The second portion of the statute, the "congregation" clause, addresses a different concern. It prohibits congregation, which District of Columbia common law defines as an assemblage of three or more people. ... Both of these prohibitions generally operate within a 500–foot zone surrounding embassies or consulates owned by foreign governments, but the statute also can extend to other buildings if foreign officials are inside for some official purpose.

....

The Court of Appeals considered the two aspects of § 22–1115 separately. First, the court concluded that the display clause was a content-based restriction on speech. Relying, however, upon our decisions in *Perry Education Assn. v. Perry Local Educators' Assn.*, 460 U.S. 37, 45 (1983), and *Carey v. Brown*, 447 U.S. 455, 461–462, 100 S.Ct. 2286, 2290–2291 (1980), the court nonetheless found it constitutional because it was justified by a compelling governmental interest and was narrowly drawn to serve that interest. Second, the Court of Appeals concluded that the congregation clause should be construed to authorize an order to disperse "only when the police reasonably believe that a threat to the security or peace of the embassy is present," and that as construed, the congregation clause survived First Amendment scrutiny. 255 U.S. App. D.C., at 40, 798 F.2d, at 1471.

We granted certiorari, 479 U.S. 1083 (1987). We now reverse the Court of Appeals' conclusion as to the display clause, but affirm as to the congregation clause.

II

A

Analysis of the display clause must begin with several important features of that provision. First, the display clause operates at the core of the First Amendment by prohibiting petitioners from engaging in classically political speech....

Second, the display clause bars such speech on public streets and sidewalks, traditional public fora that "time out of mind, have been used for purposes of assembly, communicating thoughts between citizens, and discussing public questions." *Hague v. CIO*, 307 U.S. 496, 515 (1939) (Roberts, J.). In such places, which occupy a "special position in terms of First Amendment protection," *United States v. Grace*, 461 U.S., at 180, the government's ability to restrict expressive activity "is very limited." Id., at 177.

Third, § 22–1115 is content based. Whether individuals may picket in front of a foreign embassy depends entirely upon whether their picket signs are critical of the foreign government or not. One category of speech has been completely prohibited within 500 feet of embassies. Other categories of speech, however, such as favorable speech about a foreign government or speech concerning a labor dispute with a foreign government, are permitted. See D.C. Code § 22–1116 (1981).

... Both respondents and the United States ... contend that the statute is not content based because the government is not itself selecting between viewpoints; the permissible message on a picket sign is determined solely by the policies of a foreign government.

We reject this contention, although we agree the provision is not viewpoint based. The display clause determines which viewpoint is acceptable in a neutral fashion by looking to the policies of foreign governments. While this prevents the display clause from being directly viewpoint based, a label with potential First Amendment ramifications of its own, ... it does not render the statute content neutral. Rather, we have held that a regulation that "does not favor either side of a political controversy" is nonetheless impermissible because the "First Amendment's hostility to content-based regulation extends ... to prohibition of public discussion of an entire topic." *Consolidated Edison Co. v. Public Service Comm'n,* 447 U.S. 530, 537 (1980). Here the government has determined that an entire category of speech—signs or displays critical of foreign governments—is not to be permitted.

....

B

Our cases indicate that as a *content-based* restriction on *political speech* in a *public forum,* § 22–1115 must be subjected to the most exacting scrutiny. Thus, we have required the State to show that the "regulation is necessary to serve a compelling state interest and that it is narrowly drawn to achieve that end." *Perry Education Assn. v. Perry Local Educators' Assn.,* 460 U.S., at 45....

We first consider whether the display clause serves a compelling governmental interest in protecting the dignity of foreign diplomatic personnel. Since the dignity of foreign officials will be affronted by signs critical of their governments or governmental policies, we are told, these foreign diplomats must be shielded from such insults in order to fulfill our country's obligations under international law.

As a general matter, we have indicated that in public debate our own citizens must tolerate insulting, and even outrageous, speech in order to provide "adequate 'breathing space' to the freedoms protected by the First Amendment." *Hustler Magazine, Inc. v. Falwell,* 485 U.S. 46, 56 (1988). *See also, e.g., New York Times Co. v. Sullivan,* 376 U.S., at 270....

We are not persuaded that the differences between foreign officials and American citizens require us to deviate from these principles here.

The dignity interest is said to be compelling in this context primarily because its recognition and protection is part of the United States' obligations under international law. The Vienna Convention on Diplomatic Relations, April 18, 1961, [1972] 23 U.S.T. 3227, T.I.A.S. No. 7502, which all parties agree represents the current state of international law, imposes on host states

> "[the] special duty to take all appropriate steps to protect the premises of the mission against any intrusion or damage and to prevent any disturbance of the peace of the mission or impairment of its dignity." *Id.*, at 3237–3238, Art. 22.

As a general proposition, it is of course correct that the United States has a vital national interest in complying with international law. The Constitution itself attempts to further this interest by expressly authorizing Congress "[t]o define and punish Piracies and Felonies committed on the high Seas, and Offenses against the Law of Nations." U.S. Const., Art. I, § 8, cl. 10. Cf. The Federalist No. 3, p. 43 (C. Rossiter ed. 1961) (J. Jay). Moreover, protecting foreign emissaries has a long history and noble purpose. In this country national concern for the protection of ambassadors and foreign ministers even predates the Constitution. In 1781 the Continental Congress adopted a resolution calling on the States to enact laws punishing "infractions of the immunities of ambassadors and other public ministers, authorised and received as such by the United States in Congress assembled," targeting in particular "violence offered to their persons, houses, carriages and property." 21 J. Continental Cong. 1136–1137 (G. Hunt ed. 1912).

The need to protect diplomats is grounded in our Nation's important interest in international relations. As a leading commentator observed in 1758, "[i]t is necessary that nations should treat and hold intercourse together, in order to promote their interests,—to avoid injuring each other,—and to adjust and terminate their disputes." E. Vattel, The Law of Nations 452 (J. Chitty ed. 1844) (translation). This observation is even more true today given the global nature of the economy and the extent to which actions in other parts of the world affect our own national security. Diplomatic personnel are essential to conduct the international affairs so crucial to the well-being of this Nation. In addition, in light of the concept of reciprocity that governs much of international law in this area, *see* C. Wilson, Diplomatic Privileges and Immunities 32 (1967), we have a more parochial reason to protect foreign diplomats in this country. Doing so ensures that similar protections will be accorded those that we send abroad to represent the United States, and thus serves our national interest in protecting our own citizens. Recent history is replete with attempts, some unfortunately successful, to harass and harm our ambassadors and other diplomatic officials. These underlying purposes combine to make our national interest in protecting diplomatic personnel powerful indeed.

At the same time, it is well established that "no agreement with a foreign nation can confer power on the Congress, or on any other branch of Government, which is free from the restraints of the Constitution." *Reid v. Covert*, 354 U.S. 1, 16 (1957). See 1 Restatement of Foreign Relations Law of the United States § 131, Comment a, p. 53 (Tent. Draft No. 6, Apr. 12, 1985) ("[R]ules of international law and provisions of international agreements of the United States are subject to the Bill of Rights and other prohibitions, restrictions or requirements of the Constitution and cannot be given effect in violation of them").

Thus, the fact that an interest is recognized in international law does not automatically render that interest "compelling" for purposes of First Amendment analysis. We need not decide today whether, or to what extent, the dictates of international law could ever require that First Amendment analysis be adjusted to accommodate the interests of foreign officials. Even if we assume that international law recognizes a dignity interest and that it should be considered sufficiently "compelling" to support a content-based restriction on speech, we conclude that § 22–1115 is not narrowly tailored to serve that interest. *See, e.g., Perry Education Assn.*, 460 U.S., at 45; *Board of Airport Comm'rs of Los Angeles*, 482 U.S., at 573.

The most useful starting point for assessing § 22–1115 is to compare it with an analogous statute adopted by Congress, which is the body primarily responsible for implementing our obligations under the Vienna Convention. Title 18 U.S.C. § 112(b)(2) subjects to criminal punishment willful acts or attempts to "intimidate, coerce, threaten, or harass a foreign official or an official guest or obstruct a foreign official in the performance of his duties."

Its legislative history reveals that § 112 was developed as a deliberate effort to implement our international obligations. *See, e.g.,* 118 Cong. Rec. 27112–27113 (1972). At the same time, the history reflects a substantial concern with the effect of any such legislation on First Amendment freedoms. For example, the original provision contained a prohibition on willful acts or attempts to "intimidate, coerce, threaten, or harass . . . or obstruct a foreign official," as does the current version of § 112. In a portion with similarities to the display clause, however, it also punished anyone who

> "parades, pickets, displays any flag, banner, sign, placard, or device, or utters any word, phrase, sound, or noise, for the purpose of intimidating, coercing, threatening, or harassing any foreign official or obstructing him in the performance of his duties." Act for Protection of Foreign Official Guests of the United States, Pub.L. 92–539, Title III, § 301(c)(1), 86 Stat. 1070, 1073 (1972).

Concerned with the effects that such a provision might have on First Amendment freedoms, the Senate added a new subsection, which directed:

> "[N]othing contained in this section shall be construed or applied so as to abridge the exercise of rights guaranteed under the first

> amendment to the Constitution of the United States." § 301(e), 86 Stat. 1073.

See S. Rep. No. 92–1105, p. 19 (1972).

After the 1972 passage of § 112 in this form, congressional concerns about its impact on First Amendment freedoms apparently escalated rather than abated. In 1976, Congress revisited the area and repealed the antipicketing provision, leaving in place only the current prohibition on willful acts or attempts to "intimidate, coerce, threaten, or harass a foreign official." § 112(b)(2). In modifying § 112, Congress was motivated by First Amendment concerns:

> "This language [of the original antipicketing provision] raises serious Constitutional questions because it appears to include within its purview conduct and speech protected by the First Amendment." S. Rep. No. 94–1273, p. 8, n. 9 (1976); H.R. Rep. No. 94–1614, p. 6, n. 9 (1976).

Thus, after a careful balancing of our country's international obligations with our Constitution's protection of free expression, Congress has determined that § 112 adequately satisfies the Government's interest in protecting diplomatic personnel outside the District of Columbia. It is the necessary, "appropriate" step that Congress has enacted to fulfill our international obligations. Cf. Vienna Convention on Diplomatic Relations, Art. 22, § 2, 23 U.S.T., at 3237 ("special duty to take all appropriate steps").

Section 112 applies to all conduct "within the United States but outside the District of Columbia." § 112(b)(3). In the legislative history, the exclusion of the District from the statute's reach is explained with reference to § 22–1115; Congress was informed that a "similar" statute already applied inside the District. S. Rep. No. 92–1105, *supra,* at 19; H.R. Rep. No. 92–1268, p. 5 (1972). The two statutes, however, are not identical, and the differences between them are constitutionally significant. In two obvious ways, § 112 is considerably less restrictive than the display clause of § 22–1115. First and foremost, § 112 is not narrowly directed at the content of speech but at any activity, including speech, that has the prohibited effects. Moreover, § 112, unlike § 22–1115, does not prohibit picketing; it only prohibits activity undertaken to "intimidate, coerce, threaten, or harass." Indeed, unlike the display clause, even the repealed antipicketing portion of § 112 permitted peaceful picketing.

Given this congressional development of a significantly less restrictive statute to implement the Vienna Convention, there is little force to the argument that we should give deference to a supposed congressional judgment that the Convention demands the more problematic approach reflected in the display clause. If § 112 is all that is necessary in the rest of the country, petitioners contend it should be all that is necessary in the District of Columbia. The only counter-argument offered by respondents is that the District has a higher concentration of foreign embassies than other locales and that a more restrictive statute is therefore necessary.

But this is arguably factually incorrect (New York City is reported to have a greater number of foreign embassies, missions, or consulates than does the District of Columbia, *see* Note, Regulating Embassy Picketing in the Public Forum, 55 Geo. Wash. L. Rev. 908, 928, n. 140 (1987)), and logically beside the point since the need to protect "dignity" is equally present whether there is one embassy or mission or one hundred. The United States points to Congress' exclusive legislative authority over the District of Columbia, U.S. Const., Art. I, § 8, cl. 17, and argues that this justifies more extensive measures. We fail to see, however, why the potential legislative power to enact more extensive measures makes such measures necessary.

[The Court noted that, indeed, Congress had considered repealing § 22–1115 directly and amending § 112 to include the District, but had refrained in light of potential objections based on "home rule" principles. Instead, Congress settled for a sense-of-the-Congress provision that urged the District to review its laws concerning demonstrations near foreign missions. Such an outcome seemed to reinforce that idea that a less restrictive alternative was available. The Court then proceeded to determine that the congregation clause of § 22–1115 withstood First Amendment overbreadth scrutiny because it did not reach a substantial amount of constitutionally protected conduct, but merely regulated the place and manner of certain demonstrations.]

V

We conclude that the display clause of § 22–1115 is unconstitutional on its face. It is a content-based restriction on political speech in a public forum, and it is not narrowly tailored to serve a compelling state interest. We also conclude that the congregation clause, as narrowed by the Court of Appeals, is not facially unconstitutional. Accordingly, the judgment of the Court of Appeals is reversed in part and affirmed in part.

It is so ordered.

INTRODUCTORY NOTE ON INTERNATIONAL IMMUNITIES FOR GOVERNMENTS

The acknowledgement by U.S. courts of the immunity due to foreign officials (whether diplomats, consular officials, international civil servants, heads of state, or otherwise) shares its roots with the immunity conferred on foreign sovereigns as a whole. For much of U.S. history, U.S. courts adhered to an "absolute" theory of immunity, meaning that foreign sovereigns were completely immune from the jurisdiction of U.S. courts, except in very limited circumstances that rarely arose. By the first half of the twentieth century, the adherence to the absolute theory of immunity became increasingly problematic, especially as foreign governments began to engage in activities that were more commercial in nature, and as the U.S. government began waiving aspects of its own sovereign immunity in U.S. courts. Beginning in 1952, and continuing for nearly twenty-five years, the U.S. Department of State and the U.S. Department of Justice attempted to administer a scheme for determining whether a foreign government's request for immunity should be accepted and for reporting that conclusion to the relevant court.

This background is described in *Verlinden B.V. v. Central Bank of Nigeria, infra*. The immediate predicate for that case, however, was the Foreign Sovereign Immunities Act of 1976 (FSIA) (excerpted below), which both defined the kinds of activity by governments and state enterprises that were entitled to immunity in civil actions and transferred to the federal courts full responsibility for making the relevant determinations. As you read the excerpts from the FSIA, note that there is a general accordance of immunity (§ 1604) and then a series of exceptions when immunity will not be accorded (§ 1605). Why do you think these exceptions were adopted? What are some of the important limitations on the way the exceptions operate? Does the statute distinguish between the ability to bring an action to obtain a judgment and the ability to attach assets and enforce the judgment? If so, why make such a distinction? Are some assets of a foreign government completely off-limits from actions in U.S. courts? If so, why?

FOREIGN SOVEREIGN IMMUNITIES ACT OF 1976, AS AMENDED

28 U.S.C. §§ 1330, 1602–1605A, 1609–1611 (2006).

§ 1330. Actions against Foreign States

(a) The district courts shall have original jurisdiction without regard to amount in controversy of any nonjury civil action against a foreign state as defined in section 1603(a) of this title as to any claim for relief in personam with respect to which the foreign state is not entitled to immunity either under sections 1605–1607 of this title or under any applicable international agreement.

(b) Personal jurisdiction over a foreign state shall exist as to every claim for relief over which the district courts have jurisdiction under subsection (a) where service has been made under section 1608 of this title.

(c) For purposes of subsection (b), an appearance by a foreign state does not confer personal jurisdiction with respect to any claim for relief not arising out of any transaction or occurrence enumerated in sections 1605–1607 of this title.

§ 1602. Findings and Declaration of Purpose

The Congress finds that the determination by United States courts of the claims of foreign states to immunity from the jurisdiction of such courts would serve the interests of justice and would protect the rights of both foreign states and litigants in United States courts. Under international law, states are not immune from the jurisdiction of foreign courts insofar as their commercial activities are concerned, and their commercial property may be levied upon for the satisfaction of judgments rendered against them in connection with their commercial activities. Claims of foreign states to immunity should henceforth be decided by courts of the United States and of the States in conformity with the principles set forth in this chapter.

§ 1603. Definitions

For purposes of this chapter—

(a) A "foreign state", except as used in section 1608 of this title, includes a political subdivision of a foreign state or an agency or instrumentality of a foreign state as defined in subsection (b).

(b) An "agency or instrumentality of a foreign state" means any entity—

(1) which is a separate legal person, corporate or otherwise, and

(2) which is an organ of a foreign state or political subdivision thereof, or a majority of whose shares or other ownership interest is owned by a foreign state or political subdivision thereof, and

(3) which is neither a citizen of a State of the United States as defined in section 1332(c) and (e) of this title, nor created under the laws of any third country.

(c) The "United States" includes all territory and waters, continental or insular, subject to the jurisdiction of the United States.

(d) A "commercial activity" means either a regular course of commercial conduct or a particular commercial transaction or act. The commercial character of an activity shall be determined by reference to the nature of the course of conduct or particular transaction or act, rather than by reference to its purpose.

(e) A "commercial activity carried on in the United States by a foreign state" means commercial activity carried on by such state and having substantial contact with the United States.

§ 1604. Immunity of a Foreign State From Jurisdiction

Subject to existing international agreements to which the United States is a party at the time of enactment of this Act a foreign state shall be immune from the jurisdiction of the courts of the United States and of the States except as provided in sections 1605 to 1607 of this chapter.

§ 1605. General Exceptions to the Jurisdictional Immunity of a Foreign State

(a) A foreign state shall not be immune from the jurisdiction of courts of the United States or of the States in any case—

(1) in which the foreign state has waived its immunity either explicitly or by implication, notwithstanding any withdrawal of the waiver which the foreign state may purport to effect except in accordance with the terms of the waiver;

(2) in which the action is based upon a commercial activity carried on in the United States by the foreign state; or upon an act performed in the United States in connection with a commercial activity of the foreign state elsewhere; or upon an act outside the territory of the United States in connection with a commercial activi-

ty of the foreign state elsewhere and that act causes a direct effect in the United States;

(3) in which rights in property taken in violation of international law are in issue and that property or any property exchanged for such property is present in the United States in connection with a commercial activity carried on in the United States by the foreign state; or that property or any property exchanged for such property is owned or operated by an agency or instrumentality of the foreign state and that agency or instrumentality is engaged in a commercial activity in the United States;

(4) in which rights in property in the United States acquired by succession or gift or rights in immovable property situated in the United States are in issue;

(5) not otherwise encompassed in paragraph (2) above, in which money damages are sought against a foreign state for personal injury or death, or damage to or loss of property, occurring in the United States and caused by the tortious act or omission of that foreign state or of any official or employee of that foreign state while acting within the scope of his office or employment; except this paragraph shall not apply to—

(A) any claim based upon the exercise or performance or the failure to exercise or perform a discretionary function regardless of whether the discretion be abused, or

(B) any claim arising out of malicious prosecution, abuse of process, libel, slander, misrepresentation, deceit, or interference with contract rights;

(6) in which the action is brought, either to enforce an agreement made by the foreign state with or for the benefit of a private party to submit to arbitration all or any differences which have arisen or which may arise between the parties with respect to a defined legal relationship, whether contractual or not, concerning a subject matter capable of settlement by arbitration under the laws of the United States, or to confirm an award made pursuant to such an agreement to arbitrate, if (A) the arbitration takes place or is intended to take place in the United States, (B) the agreement or award is or may be governed by a treaty or other international agreement in force for the United States calling for the recognition and enforcement of arbitral awards, (C) the underlying claim, save for the agreement to arbitrate, could have been brought in a United States court under this section or section 1607, or (D) paragraph (1) of this subsection is otherwise applicable.

§ 1605A. Terrorism Exception to the Jurisdictional Immunity of a Foreign State

(a) In general.—

(1) No immunity.—A foreign state shall not be immune from the jurisdiction of courts of the United States or of the States in any case not otherwise covered by this chapter in which money damages are sought against a foreign state for personal injury or death that was caused by an act of torture, extrajudicial killing, aircraft sabotage, hostage taking, or the provision of material support or resources for such an act if such act or provision of material support or resources is engaged in by an official, employee, or agent of such foreign state while acting within the scope of his or her office, employment, or agency.

(2) Claim heard.—The court shall hear a claim under this section if—

(A)(i)(I) the foreign state was designated as a state sponsor of terrorism at the time the act described in paragraph (1) occurred, or was so designated as a result of such act, and, subject to subclause (II), either remains so designated when the claim is filed under this section or was so designated within the 6-month period before the claim is filed under this section; or

(II) in the case of an action that is refiled under this section by reason of section 1083(c)(2)(A) of the National Defense Authorization Act for Fiscal Year 2008 or is filed under this section by reason of section 1083(c)(3) of that Act, the foreign state was designated as a state sponsor of terrorism when the original action or the related action under section 1605(a)(7) (as in effect before the enactment of this section) or section 589 of the Foreign Operations, Export Financing, and Related Programs Appropriations Act, 1997 (as contained in section 101(c) of division A of Public Law 104–208) was filed;

(ii) the claimant or the victim was, at the time the act described in paragraph (1) occurred—

(I) a national of the United States;

(II) a member of the armed forces; or

(III) otherwise an employee of the Government of the United States, or of an individual performing a contract awarded by the United States Government, acting within the scope of the employee's employment; and

(iii) in a case in which the act occurred in the foreign state against which the claim has been brought, the claimant has afforded the foreign state a reasonable opportunity to arbitrate the claim in accordance with the accepted international rules of arbitration; or

(B) the act described in paragraph (1) is related to Case Number 1:00CV03110 (EGS) in the United States District Court for the District of Columbia.

(b) Limitations.—An action may be brought or maintained under this section if the action is commenced, or a related action was commenced under section 1605(a)(7) (before the date of the enactment of this section) or section 589 of the Foreign Operations, Export Financing, and Related Programs Appropriations Act, 1997 (as contained in section 101(c) of division A of Public Law 104–208) not later than the latter of—

(1) 10 years after April 24, 1996; or

(2) 10 years after the date on which the cause of action arose.

(c) Private right of action.—A foreign state that is or was a state sponsor of terrorism as described in subsection (a)(2)(A)(i), and any official, employee, or agent of that foreign state while acting within the scope of his or her office, employment, or agency, shall be liable to—

(1) a national of the United States,

(2) a member of the armed forces,

(3) an employee of the Government of the United States, or of an individual performing a contract awarded by the United States Government, acting within the scope of the employee's employment, or

(4) the legal representative of a person described in paragraph (1), (2), or (3),

for personal injury or death caused by acts described in subsection (a)(1) of that foreign state, or of an official, employee, or agent of that foreign state, for which the courts of the United States may maintain jurisdiction under this section for money damages. In any such action, damages may include economic damages, solatium, pain and suffering, and punitive damages. In any such action, a foreign state shall be vicariously liable for the acts of its officials, employees, or agents.

. . . .

(h) Definitions.—For purposes of this section—

(1) the term "aircraft sabotage" has the meaning given that term in Article 1 of the Convention for the Suppression of Unlawful Acts Against the Safety of Civil Aviation;

(2) the term "hostage taking" has the meaning given that term in Article 1 of the International Convention Against the Taking of Hostages;

(3) the term "material support or resources" has the meaning given that term in section 2339A of title 18;

(4) the term "armed forces" has the meaning given that term in section 101 of title 10;

(5) the term "national of the United States" has the meaning given that term in section 101(a)(22) of the Immigration and Nationality Act (8 U.S.C. 1101(a)(22));

(6) the term "state sponsor of terrorism" means a country the government of which the Secretary of State has determined, for

purposes of section 6(j) of the Export Administration Act of 1979 (50 U.S.C. App. 2405(j)), section 620A of the Foreign Assistance Act of 1961 (22 U.S.C. 2371), section 40 of the Arms Export Control Act (22 U.S.C. 2780), or any other provision of law, is a government that has repeatedly provided support for acts of international terrorism; and

(7) the terms "torture" and "extrajudicial killing" have the meaning given those terms in section 3 of the Torture Victim Protection Act of 1991 (28 U.S.C. 1350 note).

§ 1609. Immunity From Attachment and Execution of Property of a Foreign State

Subject to existing international agreements to which the United States is a party at the time of enactment of this Act the property in the United States of a foreign state shall be immune from attachment, arrest and execution except as provided in sections 1610 and 1611 of this chapter.

§ 1610. Exceptions to the Immunity From Attachment or Execution

(a) The property in the United States of a foreign state, as defined in section 1603(a) of this chapter, used for a commercial activity in the United States, shall not be immune from attachment in aid of execution, or from execution, upon a judgment entered by a court of the United States or of a State after the effective date of this Act, if—

(1) the foreign state has waived its immunity from attachment in aid of execution or from execution either explicitly or by implication, notwithstanding any withdrawal of the waiver the foreign state may purport to effect except in accordance with the terms of the waiver, or

(2) the property is or was used for the commercial activity upon which the claim is based, or

(3) the execution relates to a judgment establishing rights in property which has been taken in violation of international law or which has been exchanged for property taken in violation of international law, or

(4) the execution relates to a judgment establishing rights in property—

(A) which is acquired by succession or gift, or

(B) which is immovable and situated in the United States: *Provided*, That such property is not used for purposes of maintaining a diplomatic or consular mission or the residence of the Chief of such mission, or

(5) the property consists of any contractual obligation or any proceeds from such a contractual obligation to indemnify or hold harmless the foreign state or its employees under a policy of automo-

bile or other liability or casualty insurance covering the claim which merged into the judgment, or

(6) the judgment is based on an order confirming an arbitral award rendered against the foreign state, provided that attachment in aid of execution, or execution, would not be inconsistent with any provision in the arbitral agreement, or

(7) the judgment relates to a claim for which the foreign state is not immune under section 1605A, regardless of whether the property is or was involved with the act upon which the claim is based.

(b) In addition to subsection (a), any property in the United States of an agency or instrumentality of a foreign state engaged in commercial activity in the United States shall not be immune from attachment in aid of execution, or from execution, upon a judgment entered by a court of the United States or of a State after the effective date of this Act, if—

(1) the agency or instrumentality has waived its immunity from attachment in aid of execution or from execution either explicitly or implicitly, notwithstanding any withdrawal of the waiver the agency or instrumentality may purport to effect except in accordance with the terms of the waiver, or

(2) the judgment relates to a claim for which the agency or instrumentality is not immune by virtue of section 1605(a)(2), (3), or (5), 1605(b), or 1605A of this chapter, regardless of whether the property is or was involved in the act upon which the claim is based.

(c) No attachment or execution referred to in subsections (a) and (b) of this section shall be permitted until the court has ordered such attachment and execution after having determined that a reasonable period of time has elapsed following the entry of judgment and the giving of any notice required under section 1608(e) of this chapter.

(d) The property of a foreign state, as defined in section 1603(a) of this chapter, used for a commercial activity in the United States, shall not be immune from attachment prior to the entry of judgment in any action brought in a court of the United States or of a State, or prior to the elapse of the period of time provided in subsection (c) of this section, if—

(1) the foreign state has explicitly waived its immunity from attachment prior to judgment, notwithstanding any withdrawal of the waiver the foreign state may purport to effect except in accordance with the terms of the waiver, and

(2) the purpose of the attachment is to secure satisfaction of a judgment that has been or may ultimately be entered against the foreign state, and not to obtain jurisdiction.

(e) The vessels of a foreign state shall not be immune from arrest in rem, interlocutory sale, and execution in actions brought to foreclose a preferred mortgage as provided in section 1605(d).

(f)(1)(A) Notwithstanding any other provision of law, including but not limited to section 208(f) of the Foreign Missions Act (22 U.S.C. 4308(f)), and except as provided in subparagraph (B), any property with respect to which financial transactions are prohibited or regulated pursuant to section 5(b) of the Trading with the Enemy Act (50 U.S.C. App. 5(b)), section 620(a) of the Foreign Assistance Act of 1961 (22 U.S.C. 2370(a)), sections 202 and 203 of the International Emergency Economic Powers Act (50 U.S.C. 1701–1702), or any other proclamation, order, regulation, or license issued pursuant thereto, shall be subject to execution or attachment in aid of execution of any judgment relating to a claim for which a foreign state (including any agency or instrumentality or such state) claiming such property is not immune under section 1605(a)(7) (as in effect before the enactment of Section 1605A) or section 1605A.

(B) Subparagraph (A) shall not apply if, at the time the property is expropriated or seized by the foreign state, the property has been held in title by a natural person or, if held in trust, has been held for the benefit of a natural person or persons.

(2)(A) At the request of any party in whose favor a judgment has been issued with respect to a claim for which the foreign state is not immune under section 1605(a)(7) (as in effect before the enactment of Section 1605A) or section 1605A, the Secretary of the Treasury and the Secretary of State should make every effort to fully, promptly, and effectively assist any judgment creditor or any court that has issued any such judgment in identifying, locating, and executing against the property of that foreign state or any agency or instrumentality of such state.

(B) In providing such assistance, the Secretaries—

(i) may provide such information to the court under seal; and

(ii) should make every effort to provide the information in a manner sufficient to allow the court to direct the United States Marshall's office to promptly and effectively execute against that property.

(3) Waiver.—The President may waive any provision of paragraph (1) in the interest of national security.

(g) Property in certain actions.—

(1) In general.—Subject to paragraph (3), the property of a foreign state against which a judgment is entered under section 1605A, and the property of an agency or instrumentality of such a state, including property that is a separate juridical entity or is an interest held directly or indirectly in a separate juridical entity, is subject to attachment in aid of execution, and execution, upon that judgment as provided in this section, regardless of—

(A) the level of economic control over the property by the government of the foreign state;

(B) whether the profits of the property go to that government;

(C) the degree to which officials of that government manage the property or otherwise control its daily affairs;

(D) whether that government is the sole beneficiary in interest of the property; or

(E) whether establishing the property as a separate entity would entitle the foreign state to benefits in United States courts while avoiding its obligations.

(2) United States sovereign immunity inapplicable.—Any property of a foreign state, or agency or instrumentality of a foreign state, to which paragraph (1) applies shall not be immune from attachment in aid of execution, or execution, upon a judgment entered under section 1605A because the property is regulated by the United States Government by reason of action taken against that foreign state under the Trading With the Enemy Act or the International Emergency Economic Powers Act.

(3) Third-party joint property holders.—Nothing in this subsection shall be construed to supersede the authority of a court to prevent appropriately the impairment of an interest held by a person who is not liable in the action giving rise to a judgment in property subject to attachment in aid of execution, or execution, upon such judgment.

§ 1611. Certain Types of Property Immune From Execution

(a) Notwithstanding the provisions of section 1610 of this chapter, the property of those organizations designated by the President as being entitled to enjoy the privileges, exemptions, and immunities provided by the International Organizations Immunities Act shall not be subject to attachment or any other judicial process impeding the disbursement of funds to, or on the order of, a foreign state as the result of an action brought in the courts of the United States or of the States.

(b) Notwithstanding the provisions of section 1610 of this chapter, the property of a foreign state shall be immune from attachment and from execution, if—

(1) the property is that of a foreign central bank or monetary authority held for its own account, unless such bank or authority, or its parent foreign government, has explicitly waived its immunity from attachment in aid of execution, or from execution, notwithstanding any withdrawal of the waiver which the bank, authority or government may purport to effect except in accordance with the terms of the waiver; or

(2) the property is, or is intended to be, used in connection with a military activity and

(A) is of a military character, or

(B) is under the control of a military authority or defense agency.

(c) Notwithstanding the provisions of section 1610 of this chapter, the property of a foreign state shall be immune from attachment and from execution in an action brought under section 302 of the Cuban Liberty and Democratic Solidarity (LIBERTAD) Act of 1996 to the extent that the property is a facility or installation used by an accredited diplomatic mission for official purposes.

VERLINDEN B.V. v. CENTRAL BANK OF NIGERIA

461 U.S. 480, 103 S.Ct. 1962, 76 L.Ed.2d 81 (1983) (some footnotes omitted).

CHIEF JUSTICE BURGER delivered the opinion of the Court.

. . . .

I

On April 21, 1975, the Federal Republic of Nigeria and petitioner Verlinden B.V., a Dutch corporation with its principal offices in Amsterdam, the Netherlands, entered into a contract providing for the purchase of 240,000 metric tons of cement by Nigeria. The parties agreed that the contract would be governed by the laws of the Netherlands and that disputes would be resolved by arbitration before the International Chamber of Commerce, Paris, France.

The contract provided that the Nigerian government was to establish an irrevocable, confirmed letter of credit for the total purchase price through Slavenburg's Bank in Amsterdam. According to petitioner's amended complaint, however, respondent Central Bank of Nigeria, an instrumentality of Nigeria, improperly established an unconfirmed letter of credit payable through Morgan Guaranty Trust Co. in New York.

In August 1975, Verlinden subcontracted with a Liechtenstein corporation, Interbuco, to purchase the cement needed to fulfill the contract. Meanwhile, the ports of Nigeria had become clogged with hundreds of ships carrying cement, sent by numerous other cement suppliers with whom Nigeria also had entered contracts. In mid-September, Central Bank unilaterally directed its correspondent banks, including Morgan Guaranty, to adopt a series of amendments to all letters of credit issued in connection with the cement contracts. Central Bank also directly notified the suppliers that payment would be made only for those shipments approved by Central Bank two months before their arrival in Nigerian waters.

Verlinden then sued Central Bank in United States District Court for the Southern District of New York, alleging that Central Bank's actions constituted an anticipatory breach of the letter of credit. Verlinden alleged jurisdiction under the Foreign Sovereign Immunities Act, 28 U.S.C. § 1330. Respondent moved to dismiss for, among other reasons, lack of subject-matter and personal jurisdiction.

. . . .

[The district court held that the Foreign Sovereign Immunities Act (FSIA) intended to encompass actions brought by foreign plaintiffs and that Article III permitted the exercise of subject matter jurisdiction over suits by foreign corporations against foreign sovereigns. The court, however, dismissed the case on the ground that the none of the exceptions to sovereign immunity applied. The court of appeals affirmed dismissal on different grounds, concluding that the FSIA exceeded Article III, with neither the diversity clause (Art. III, § 2, cl. 1) nor the "arising under" clause (Art. III, § 2, cl. 1) supporting jurisdiction over actions by foreign plaintiffs against a foreign sovereign—thus depriving Congress of the authority to grant federal courts jurisdiction.]

II

For more than a century and a half, the United States generally granted foreign sovereigns complete immunity from suit in the courts of this country. In *The Schooner Exchange v. M'Faddon,* 7 Cranch 116 (1812), Chief Justice Marshall concluded that, while the jurisdiction of a nation within its own territory "is susceptible of no limitation not imposed by itself," *id.,* at 136, the United States had impliedly waived jurisdiction over certain activities of foreign sovereigns. Although the narrow holding of *The Schooner Exchange* was only that the courts of the United States lack jurisdiction over an armed ship of a foreign state found in our port, that opinion came to be regarded as extending virtually absolute immunity to foreign sovereigns. *See, e.g., Berizzi Brothers Co. v. S.S. Pesaro,* 271 U.S. 562 (1926); Von Mehren, The Foreign Sovereign Immunities Act of 1976, 17 Colum. J. Transnat'l L. 33, 39–40 (1978).

As *The Schooner Exchange* made clear, however, foreign sovereign immunity is a matter of grace and comity on the part of the United States, and not a restriction imposed by the Constitution. Accordingly, this Court consistently has deferred to the decisions of the political branches—in particular, those of the Executive Branch—on whether to take jurisdiction over actions against foreign sovereigns and their instrumentalities. *See, e.g., Ex parte Peru,* 318 U.S. 578, 586–590 (1943); *Mexico v. Hoffman,* 324 U.S. 30, 33–36 (1945).

Until 1952, the State Department ordinarily requested immunity in all actions against friendly foreign sovereigns. But in the so-called Tate Letter, the State Department announced its adoption of the "restrictive" theory of foreign sovereign immunity. Under this theory, immunity is confined to suits involving the foreign sovereign's public acts, and does not extend to cases arising out of a foreign state's strictly commercial acts.

The restrictive theory was not initially enacted into law, however, and its application proved troublesome. As in the past, initial responsibility for deciding questions of sovereign immunity fell primarily upon the Executive acting through the State Department, and the courts abided by "suggestions of immunity" from the State Department. As a consequence, foreign nations often placed diplomatic pressure on the State Department in seeking immunity. On occasion, political considerations led to suggestions of immunity in cases where immunity would not have been available under the restrictive theory.

An additional complication was posed by the fact that foreign nations did not always make requests to the State Department. In such cases, the responsibility fell to the courts to determine whether sovereign immunity existed, generally by reference to prior State Department decisions. *See generally* Lowenfeld, Claims against Foreign States—A Proposal for Reform of United States Law, 44 N.Y.U. L. Rev. 901, 909–912 (1969). Thus, sovereign immunity determinations were made in two different branches, subject to a variety of factors, sometimes including diplomatic considerations. Not surprisingly, the governing standards were neither clear nor uniformly applied. *See, e.g., id.*, at 906–909; Weber, The Foreign Sovereign Immunities Act of 1976: Its Origin, Meaning and Effect, 3 Yale Studies in World Public Order 1, 11–13, 15–17 (1976).

In 1976, Congress passed the Foreign Sovereign Immunities Act in order to free the Government from the case-by-case diplomatic pressures, to clarify the governing standards, and to "assur[e] litigants that ... decisions are made on purely legal grounds and under procedures that insure due process," H.R. Rep. No. 94–1487, p. 7 (1976). To accomplish these objectives, the Act contains a comprehensive set of legal standards governing claims of immunity in every civil action against a foreign state or its political subdivisions, agencies, or instrumentalities.

For the most part, the Act codifies, as a matter of federal law, the restrictive theory of sovereign immunity. A foreign state is normally immune from the jurisdiction of federal and state courts, 28 U.S.C. § 1604, subject to a set of exceptions specified in §§ 1605 and 1607. Those exceptions include actions in which the foreign state has explicitly or impliedly waived its immunity, § 1605(a)(1), and actions based upon commercial activities of the foreign sovereign carried on in the United States or causing a direct effect in the United States, § 1605(a)(2). When one of these or the other specified exceptions applies, "the foreign state shall be liable in the same manner and to the same extent as a private individual under like circumstances," § 1606.

The Act expressly provides that its standards control in "the courts of the United States and of the States," § 1604, and thus clearly contemplates that such suits may be brought in either federal or state courts. However, "[i]n view of the potential sensitivity of actions against foreign states and the importance of developing a uniform body of law in this area," H.R. Rep. No. 94–1487, *supra* at 32, the Act guarantees foreign states the right to remove any civil action from a state court to a federal court, § 1441(d). The Act also provides that any claim permitted under the Act may be brought from the outset in federal court, § 1330(a). If one of the specified exceptions to sovereign immunity applies, a federal district court may exercise subject-matter jurisdiction under § 1330(a); but if the claim does not fall within one of the exceptions, federal courts lack subject matter jurisdiction. In such a case, the foreign state is also ensured immunity from the jurisdiction of state courts by § 1604.

. . . .

IV

. . . .

By reason of its authority over foreign commerce and foreign relations, Congress has the undisputed power to decide, as a matter of federal law, whether and under what circumstances foreign nations should be amenable to suit in the United States. Actions against foreign sovereigns in our courts raise sensitive issues concerning the foreign relations of the United States, and the primacy of federal concerns is evident. *See, e.g., Banco Nacional de Cuba v. Sabbatino,* 376 U.S. 398, 423–425 (1964); *Zschernig v. Miller,* 389 U.S. 429, 440–441 (1968).

To promote these federal interests, Congress exercised its Article I powers by enacting a statute comprehensively regulating the amenability of foreign nations to suit in the United States. The statute must be applied by the district courts in every action against a foreign sovereign, since subject matter jurisdiction in any such action depends on the existence of one of the specified exceptions to foreign sovereign immunity, 28 U.S.C. § 1330(a). At the threshold of every action in a district court against a foreign state, therefore, the court must satisfy itself that one of the exceptions applies—and in doing so it must apply the detailed federal law standards set forth in the Act. Accordingly, an action against a foreign sovereign arises under federal law, for purposes of Art. III jurisdiction.

. . . .

[I]n enacting the Foreign Sovereign Immunities Act, Congress expressly exercised its power to regulate foreign commerce, along with other specified Art. I powers. *See* n. 19, *supra.* As the House Report clearly indicates, the primary purpose of the Act was to "se[t] forth comprehensive rules governing sovereign immunity," H.R. Rep. No. 94–1487, p. 12 (1976); the jurisdictional provisions of the Act are simply one part of this comprehensive scheme. The Act thus does not merely concern access to the federal courts. Rather, it governs the types of actions for which foreign sovereigns may be held liable in a court in the United States, federal or state. The Act codifies the standards governing foreign sovereign immunity as an aspect of substantive federal law, *see Ex parte Peru,* 318 U.S., at 588; *Mexico v. Hoffman,* 324 U.S., at 36; and applying those standards will generally require interpretation of numerous points of federal law. Finally, if a court determines that none of the exceptions to sovereign immunity applies, the plaintiff will be barred from raising his claim in any court in the United States—manifestly, "the title or right set up by the party, may be defeated by one construction of the . . . laws of the United States, and sustained by the opposite construction." *Osborn v. Bank of the United States,* 9 Wheat., at 822. That the inquiry into foreign sovereign immunity is labeled under the Act as a matter of jurisdiction does not affect the constitutionality of Congress' action in granting federal courts jurisdiction over cases calling for application of this comprehensive regulatory statute.

Congress, pursuant to its unquestioned Art. I powers, has enacted a broad statutory framework governing assertions of foreign sovereign immunity. In so doing, Congress deliberately sought to channel cases against foreign sovereigns away from the state courts and into federal courts, thereby reducing the potential for a multiplicity of conflicting results among the courts of the 50 States. The resulting jurisdictional grant is within the bounds of Art. III, since every action against a foreign sovereign necessarily involves application of a body of substantive federal law, and accordingly "arises under" federal law, within the meaning of Art. III.

V

A conclusion that the grant of jurisdiction in the Foreign Sovereign Immunities Act is consistent with the Constitution does not end the case. An action must not only satisfy Article III but must also be supported by a statutory grant of subject matter jurisdiction. As we have made clear, deciding whether statutory subject matter jurisdiction exists under the Foreign Sovereign Immunities Act entails an application of the substantive terms of the Act to determine whether one of the specified exceptions to immunity applies.

In the present case, the District Court, after satisfying itself as to the constitutionality of the Act, held that the present action does not fall within any specified exception. The Court of Appeals, reaching a contrary conclusion as to jurisdiction under the Constitution, did not find it necessary to address this statutory question.[23] Accordingly, on remand the Court of Appeals must consider whether jurisdiction exists under the Act itself. If the Court of Appeals agrees with the District Court on that issue, the case will be at an end. If, on the other hand, the Court of Appeals concludes that jurisdiction does exist under the statute, the action may then be remanded to the District Court for further proceedings.

It is so ordered.

REPUBLIC OF ARGENTINA v. WELTOVER

504 U.S. 607, 614–17, 112 S.Ct. 2160, 119 L.Ed.2d 394 (1992).

[In this case, the Supreme Court heard claims arising from Argentina's default on certain bonds issued to foreign creditors, which it claimed were

23. In several related cases involving contracts between Nigeria and other cement suppliers, the Court of Appeals held that statutory subject matter jurisdiction existed under the Act. In those cases, the court held that Nigeria's acts were commercial in nature and "cause[d] a direct effect in the United States," within the meaning of 28 U.S.C. § 1605(a)(2). *Texas Trading & Milling Corp. v. Federal Republic of Nigeria,* 647 F.2d, at 310–313. Each of those actions involved a contract with an *American* supplier operating *within the United States*, however. In the present case, the District Court found that exception inapplicable, concluding that the repudiation of the letter of credit "caused no direct, substantial, injurious effect in the United States." 488 F. Supp., at 1299–1300.

issued in order to alleviate "a domestic credit crisis, and as a component of a program designed to control that nation's critical shortage of foreign exchange." 504 U.S. at 616. Argentina argued that its actions were distinctly political and not commercial and thus it should be entitled to sovereign immunity.]

JUSTICE SCALIA delivered the opinion of the court.

. . . .

[W]e conclude that when a foreign government acts, not as regulator of a market, but in the manner of a private player within it, the foreign sovereign's actions are "commercial" within the meaning of the FSIA. Moreover, because the Act provides that the commercial character of an act is to be determined by reference to its "nature" rather than its "purpose," 28 U.S.C. § 1603(d), the question is not whether the foreign government is acting with a profit motive or instead with the aim of fulfilling uniquely sovereign objectives. Rather, the issue is whether the particular actions that the foreign state performs (whatever the motive behind them) are the *type* of actions by which a private party engages in "trade and traffic or commerce," Black's Law Dictionary 270 (6th ed. 1990). . . .

The commercial character of the Bonods [bonds] is confirmed by the fact that they are in almost all respects garden-variety debt instruments: They may be held by private parties; they are negotiable and may be traded on the international market (except in Argentina); and they promise a future stream of cash income. We recognize that, prior to the enactment of the FSIA, there was authority suggesting that the issuance of public debt instruments did not constitute a commercial activity. *Victory Transport*, 336 F.2d, at 360 (dicta). There is, however, nothing distinctive about the state's assumption of debt (other than perhaps its purpose) that would cause it always to be classified as *jure imperii*, and in this regard it is significant that *Victory Transport* expressed confusion as to whether the "nature" or the "purpose" of a transaction was controlling in determining commerciality, *id.*, at 359–360. Because the FSIA has now clearly established that the "nature" governs, we perceive no basis for concluding that the issuance of debt should be treated as categorically different from other activities of foreign states.

Argentina contends that, although the FSIA bars consideration of "purpose," a court must nonetheless fully consider the *context* of a transaction in order to determine whether it is "commercial." Accordingly, Argentina claims that the Court of Appeals erred by defining the relevant conduct in what Argentina considers an overly generalized, acontextual manner and by essentially adopting a *per se* rule that all "issuance of debt instruments" is "commercial." *See* 941 F.2d, at 151 (" '[I]t is self-evident that issuing public debt is a commercial activity within the meaning of [the FSIA]' "), quoting *Shapiro v. Republic of Bolivia,* 930 F.2d 1013, 1018 (CA2 1991). We have no occasion to consider such a *per se* rule, because it seems to us that even in full context, there is nothing about the issuance of these Bonods (except perhaps its purpose) that is not analogous to a private commercial transaction.

. . . .

Argentina argues that the Bonods differ from ordinary debt instruments in that they "were created by the Argentine Government to fulfill its obligations under a foreign exchange program designed to address a domestic credit crisis, and as a component of a program designed to control that nation's critical shortage of foreign exchange." [Brief for Petitioners] 23–24. In this regard, Argentina relies heavily on *De Sanchez v. Banco Central de Nicaragua,* 770 F.2d 1385 (1985), in which the Fifth Circuit took the view that "[o]ften, the essence of an act is defined by its purpose"; that unless "we can inquire into the purposes of such acts, we cannot determine their nature"; and that, in light of its purpose to control its reserves of foreign currency, Nicaragua's refusal to honor a check it had issued to cover a private bank debt was a sovereign act entitled to immunity. *Id.,* at 1393. Indeed, Argentina asserts that the line between "nature" and "purpose" rests upon a "formalistic distinction [that] simply is neither useful nor warranted." Reply Brief for Petitioners 8. We think this line of argument is squarely foreclosed by the language of the FSIA. However difficult it may be in some cases to separate "purpose" (*i.e.,* the *reason* why the foreign state engages in the activity) from "nature" (*i.e.,* the outward form of the conduct that the foreign state performs or agrees to perform), *see De Sanchez, supra,* at 1393, the statute unmistakably commands that to be done, 28 U.S.C. § 1603(d). We agree with the Court of Appeals, *see* 941 F.2d, at 151, that it is irrelevant *why* Argentina participated in the bond market in the manner of a private actor; it matters only that it did so. We conclude that Argentina's issuance of the Bonods was a "commercial activity" under the FSIA.

CONCLUDING NOTES ON FOREIGN SOVEREIGN IMMUNITY

1. *Sovereign Immunity and Law of Nations.* As with diplomatic immunity, state (or "sovereign") immunity reflects the proposition that in situations where one sovereign could exercise jurisdiction over the acts of another, the interests of international harmony dictate restraint by national courts and other authorities. The doctrine of sovereign immunity emerged as one of the earliest concepts of international law, but until very recently there was no multilateral treaty addressing this area of the law. As such, foreign sovereign immunities remain largely regulated by customary international law. For centuries, customary international law followed the theory of absolute immunity, but uniform state practice began to break down by the early twentieth century. Arguably customary international law then evolved so as to accept certain exceptions to immunity, such as when the state's conduct is commercial in nature.

In 2004, the U.N. General Assembly adopted the U.N. Convention on Jurisdictional Immunities of States and Their Property. G.A. Res. 59/38, annex (Dec. 2, 2004). The convention recognizes a general immunity for states, including their various organs, constituent units or political subdivisions, and their agencies or instrumentalities. At the same time, the convention recognizes certain exceptions, such as when a state engages in commercial transactions (art. 10) or when a state is involved in proceedings related to the determination of intellectual property rights (art. 14). Unlike the FSIA, the convention provides no exception to immunity for a state's expropriation of property, nor for acts of state-sponsored terrorism. In addition, the convention identifies types of state-owned property immune from suit, such as military property, property (including bank accounts) used for diplomatic missions or missions to international organizations, property of the central bank or other monetary authority of the state, and property forming part of the cultural heritage or scientific interest of the state.

The convention was open for signature from January 2005 to January 2007. As of mid-2011, 28 states had signed and 11 states had ratified the convention. The United States has neither signed nor ratified the convention and is not expected to do so. Were the United States to join the convention, it would have to amend the FSIA to bring it into conformity with the convention. To the extent that the convention reflects not just multilateral treaty obligations, but also customary international law on sovereign immunities, then do you think the FSIA may be viewed as non-compliant with customary international law? Or do you think the United States may maintain that it is a "persistent objector" to emergent customary rules and thus is not bound by them? Under any theory is the FSIA "terrorist state" exception (see note 5 below) compatible with customary international law? Since no other state has adopted such an exception to sovereign immunity, is it possible to argue that the exception is permissible under customary international law, new or old?

2. *Waiver Exception.* Under the waiver exception, 28 U.S.C. § 1605(a)(1), a foreign state is subject to U.S. jurisdiction if it has either impliedly or expressly waived its immunity. Once a waiver is made, it cannot be withdrawn except in a manner consistent with the terms of the waiver. An explicit waiver of immunity occurs when a foreign state waives immunity by treaty, by contract with a private party, or by a statement from an authorized official after a dispute arises. *See, e.g.*, Aquamar S.A. v. Del Monte Fresh Produce N.A., Inc., 179 F.3d 1279 (11th Cir. 1999) (giving effect to an express waiver by Ecuador's ambassador to the United States). An implicit waiver may occur when a foreign state agrees to arbitration in another state knowing that U.S. courts can compel or enforce the arbitration, or when the state agrees that the law of another state will govern a contract. Immunity may also be waived by a failure to raise it as a defense in the first responsive pleading.

3. *Commercial Activity Exception.* Recall the definition of "commercial activity" contained in 28 U.S.C. § 1603(d): "The commercial character of an activity shall be determined by reference to the *nature* of the course of conduct or particular transaction or act, rather than by reference to its *purpose*" (emphasis added). How does a determination of commercial "purpose" differ, in practice, from a determination of commercial "nature"? Do you agree with the Supreme Court's assessment in *Republic of Argentina v. Weltover* that the actions taken by Argentina were commercial in nature,

caused a direct effect in the United States, and thus fell under the exception to immunity in 28 U.S.C. § 1605(a)(2)?

The following year, in a case brought by a United States citizen who had been severely beaten and tortured after whistle-blowing about the practices of a Saudi hospital in which he worked, the Supreme Court declined to characterize the Saudi Arabian government's activity as "commercial" and upheld the state's sovereign immunity. Saudi Arabia v. Nelson, 507 U.S. 349, 113 S.Ct. 1471, 123 L.Ed.2d 47 (1993). Nelson was an American recruited to work in Saudi hospitals by an independent corporation, under an agreement signed by the Saudi government. When he discovered safety hazards in some of the hospital's medical equipment and reported the defects, he was arrested by Saudi police and taken to a cell where he alleged that he was tortured and beaten for a prolonged period of time. In bringing suit, Nelson claimed jurisdiction under the FSIA's commercial-activity exception to sovereign immunity, arguing that a nexus existed between the commercial activities of the hospital recruitment and employment and the Saudi government's tortious actions against him. The Court, invoking the "nature" vs. "purpose" reasoning in *Weltover,* rejected this reasoning:

> The conduct boils down to abuse of the power of its police by the Saudi Government, and however monstrous such abuse undoubtedly may be, a foreign state's exercise of the power of its police has long been understood for purposes of the restrictive theory as peculiarly sovereign in nature. ... Exercise of the powers of police and penal officers is not the sort of action by which private parties can engage in commerce.

507 U.S. at 361–62. Do you agree?

4. *Immovable Property Exception.* The limited exception for cases involving rights in immovable property situated in the United States, see 28 U.S.C. § 1605(a)(4), has recently been the subject of pitched litigation involving not only the interests of foreign governments and the United States, as is usually the case, but also states and localities. In *Permanent Mission of India to the United Nations v. City of New York*, 551 U.S. 193, 127 S.Ct. 2352, 168 L.Ed.2d 85 (2007), New York City sought to apply the immovable property exception to pursue millions of dollars in unpaid real estate taxes it had levied on the portion of properties owned by the India's Permanent Mission to the United Nations and the Ministry of Foreign Affairs for the People's Republic of Mongolia that were used for residence of lower-level employees and their families, in accord with municipal law providing that unpaid real estate taxes create a lien that constitutes an interest in such property. The Supreme Court agreed that the literal application of the exception permitted the suits to proceed. Justice Stevens, dissenting, did not disagree as to the literal application of the text, but cautioned that "[a] whole host of routine civil controversies, from sidewalk slip-and-falls to landlord-tenant disputes, could be converted into property liens under local law, and then used—as the tax lien was in this case—to pierce a foreign sovereign's traditional and statutory immunity"; he concluded by stating that "At bottom, this case is not about the validity of the city's title to immovable property, or even the validity of its automatic prejudgment lien. Rather, it is a dispute over a foreign sovereign's tax liability. If Congress had intended the statute to waive sovereign immunity in

tax litigation, I think it would have said so." 551 U.S. at 202, 203–204, 127 S. Ct. at 2358, 2359 (Stevens, J., dissenting).

5. *Tort Exception.* Under the tort exception, 28 U.S.C. § 1605(a)(5), a state is not immune from tort actions involving money damages where the damage occurred in the United States, including actions for personal injury, death, and loss or damage to property caused by a tortious act or omission of the foreign state or its agents. Thus, if a foreign country's embassy driver negligently hits another car in Washington, D.C., the victim can sue the foreign government in federal court, using District of Columbia tort law for the cause of action. One important limitation on this "tort exception" is that the damage or loss must occur in the United States. *See* Argentine Republic v. Amerada Hess Shipping Corp., 488 U.S. 428, 439, 109 S.Ct. 683, 102 L.Ed.2d 818 (1989). Per 28 U.S.C. § 1603(c), the "United States" includes "all territories and waters, continental or insular, subject to the jurisdiction of the United States." U.S. embassies abroad do not fall within this exception because the ground on which an embassy stands remains the territory of the host state. *See* McKeel v. Islamic Republic of Iran, 722 F.2d 582, 588 (9th Cir. 1983).

6. *Terrorist State Exception.* In 1996, Congress amended the Foreign Sovereign Immunities Act to strip states designated as "terrorist states" of their sovereign immunity against suits for extrajudicial killings and torture. Under this "terrorist state" exception, the claimant or victim must have been a U.S. national when the terrorist act occurred and the foreign state must have been designated by the U.S. Secretary of State as a state sponsor of terrorism. As of mid-2011, Cuba, Iran, Sudan, and Syria were designated as terrorist states. Further, claimants must afford foreign states "a reasonable opportunity to arbitrate the claim in accordance with accepted rules of arbitration" if "the act occurred in the foreign state against which the claim has been brought." *See, e.g.,* Simpson v. Socialist People's Libyan Arab Jamahiriya, 326 F.3d 230, 233–34 (D.C. Cir. 2003). Even in situations where the foreign state fails to appear, plaintiffs must establish to the satisfaction of the court that the foreign state was liable for the conduct in question. *See, e.g.,* Ungar v. Islamic Republic of Iran, 211 F.Supp.2d 91, 98 (D.D.C. 2002).

Although Congress quite deliberately established subject-matter jurisdiction over such cases—to the point of identifying one particular case against Iran by docket number in 2001, and correcting a mistake in that reference in 2002—U.S. courts have evidenced considerable caution in inferring causes of action that would enable plaintiffs to take advantage of that jurisdiction so as to sue terrorist states. When creating the exception, Congress also passed a civil liability statute (sometimes referred to as the "Flatow Amendment") that established a cause of action against an agent of a foreign state who acts under the conditions specified in the exception and provided that the agent shall be liable for "money damages which may include economic damages, solatium, pain and suffering, and punitive damages." The Flatow Amendment was, by its terms, more narrow than the terrorist-state exception itself, since it conferred a right of action only against an "official, employee, or agent of a foreign state," not against the foreign state itself. In *Cicippio-Puleo v. Iran*, the D.C. Circuit Court of Appeals affirmed that the Flatow Amendment did not create a private right of action against a foreign government and found that the cause of action was limited to claims against officials in their individual, as opposed to official, capacities. *See* Cicippio–Puleo v. Islamic Republic of Iran, 353 F.3d 1024, 1033–36 (D.C. Cir. 2004). As such, the portion of the claim against the government of Iran was dismissed.

Congress revisited the terrorist state exception again in the National Defense Authorization Act of 2008 ("NDAA"), Pub.L. 110–181, 122 Stat. 3 (2008), resulting in what is now codified at 28 U.S.C. § 1605A, together with a few related provisions. Section 1605A(c) created a private right of action, this time including as against foreign states. But it was again less than a complete solution. In a subsequent case, the U.S. District Court for the District of Columbia held that although the action against Iran specifically referenced in the provisions relating to subject-matter jurisdiction (see § 1605A(a)(2)(B)) was not unambiguously incorporated in the section 1605A(c), leaving the plaintiffs still without recourse against Iran. That court, in keeping with prior decisions, explained its narrow reading of the terrorist state exception as grounded in its reluctance to abrogate the Algiers Accords, Declaration of the Government of the Democratic and Popular Republic of Algeria (Jan. 20, 1981), 20 I.L.M. 224, which prohibit lawsuits arising out of the 1979 hostage-taking in Iran. Roeder v. Islamic Republic of Iran, 742 F.Supp.2d 1 (D.D.C. 2010). Consider, in this connection, the depth of the judicial commitment to the principle that "an act of congress ought never to be construed to violate the law of nations if any other possible construction exists . . ." The Murray v. The Charming Betsy, 6 U.S. (2 Cranch) 64, 118, 2 L.Ed. 208 (1804) (Chapter 2, section 2, *supra*).

As these cases illustrate, the immunity accorded state sponsors of terrorism under U.S. law remains exceptionally complicated, and section 1605A is but part of the statutory apparatus addressing these matters. The Terrorism Risk Insurance Act of 2002 (TRIA), § 201, 116 Stat. 2337, 28 U.S.C. § 1610 note, permits certain holders of terrorism-related judgments against Iran to attach a statutorily-delimited class of "blocked" assets, save when that right has been waived by accepting partial compensation in return for an agreement not to attach property at issue in claims against the United States before an international tribunal—namely, the Iran–U.S. Claims Tribunal arising from the Algiers Accords. *See, e.g.*, Ministry of Def. & Support for the Armed Forces of Iran v. Elahi, 556 U.S. 366, 129 S.Ct. 1732, 173 L.Ed.2d 511 (2009) (holding that arbitral award was not a "blocked asset" under the Terrorism Risk Insurance Act at all relevant times, but that in any event, the plaintiff had waived its right of attachment).

7. *Attachment Provisions.* As *Ministry of Def. & Support for the Armed Forces of Iran v. Elahi* illustrates, the immunity from attachment and execution of the property of foreign states is administered under separate provisions from those for actions for obtaining a judgment and for money damages. *See* 28 U.S.C. §§ 1609–11. While comparable in some regards, these reward careful study. For example, a commercial activity exception to immunity from attachment and execution requires that the property actually be used for the commercial activity upon which the claim is based. *Id.* § 1610(a)(2). Another provision protects certain kinds of property used for diplomatic and other official purposes from the application of this and other exceptions. *Id.* § 1611.

8. *Retroactivity of FSIA.* In *Republic of Austria v. Altmann*, 541 U.S. 677, 124 S.Ct. 2240, 159 L.Ed.2d 1 (2004), a U.S. national, Maria Altmann, sued the government of Austria for the return of five paintings by Altmann's uncle, Gustave Klimt, which were allegedly seized by the Nazis or expropriated by the Austrian government during the World War II. Austria responded that the allegedly wrongful conduct occurred prior to enactment of the FSIA (and even prior to the Tate letter), and thus Austria was entitled to the then-prevailing theory in U.S. courts of absolute immunity. The Supreme Court sided with Altmann, holding that the FSIA, including the expropriation exception contained in 28 U.S.C. § 1605(a)(3), applied to events occurring even before the FSIA's enactment in 1976.

After the Court's decision, Altmann and Austria agreed to submit the claim to binding arbitration. In January 2006, a three-member Austrian arbitration panel found unanimously that the five Klimt paintings must be returned by the Austrian government to Altmann. *See* Richard Bernstein, *Austrian Panel Backs Return of Klimt Works*, N.Y. TIMES, Jan. 17, 2006. At an auction held by Christie's, the recovered paintings set record prices. Art collector and Estee Lauder cosmetics heir Ronald Lauder paid $135 million for "Adele Bloch–Bauer I," a portrait of Altmann's aunt—and one of Klimt's most famous works. *See* Carol Vogel, *$491 Million Sale at Christie's Shatters Art Auction Record*, N.Y. TIMES, Nov. 9, 2006.

9. *Role of the Executive Branch.* In its decision in *Austria v. Altmann,* the Court seemed to re-open the door to judicial reliance on Executive Branch opinions in FSIA cases. The Court framed the issue by distinguishing, on the one hand, between the questions of sovereign immunity that involve statutory interpretation (in which the Executive had no special influence) and, on the other hand, other questions that may bear upon the exercise of jurisdiction over a foreign sovereign (in which case executive opinion might deserve deference). The Court in *Altmann* stated:

> [W]hile we reject the United States' recommendation to bar application of the FSIA to claims based on pre-enactment conduct, . . . nothing in our holding prevents the State Department from filing statements of interest suggesting that courts decline to exercise jurisdiction in particular cases implicating foreign sovereign immunity.[21] The issue now before us, to which the Brief for United States as *Amicus Curiae* is addressed, concerns interpretation of the FSIA's reach—a "pure question of statutory construction . . . well within the province of the Judiciary." INS v. Cardoza–Fonseca, 480 U.S. 421, 446, 448, 107 S.Ct. 1207, 94 L.Ed.2d 434 (1987). While the United States' views on such an issue are of considerable interest to the Court, they merit no special deference. . . . In contrast, should the State Department choose to express its opinion on the implications of exercising jurisdiction over *particular* petitioners in connection with *their* alleged conduct, that opinion might well be entitled to defer-

21. *See, e.g.*, Flatow v. Islamic Republic of Iran, 305 F.3d 1249, 1251–1252, and n. 4 (C.A.D.C. 2002) (statement of interest concerning attachment of property that is owned by a foreign state but located in the United States); Sea Hunt, Inc. v. Unidentified Shipwrecked Vessel or Vessels, 221 F.3d 634, 642 (C.A.4 2000) (statement of interest concerning sovereign immunity of a foreign state's vessels); 767 Third Ave. Assoc. v. Consulate General of Socialist Federal Republic of Yugoslavia, 218 F.3d 152, 157 (C.A.2 2000) (statement of interest concerning successor states to the Socialist Federal Republic of Yugoslavia).

> ence as the considered judgment of the Executive on a particular question of foreign policy.[23] *See, e.g.,* Verlinden, 461 U.S., at 486; American Ins. Assn. v. Garamendi, 539 U.S. 396, 414, 123 S.Ct. 2374, 156 L.Ed.2d 376 (2003) (discussing the President's " 'vast share of responsibility for the conduct of our foreign relations' "). We express no opinion on the question whether such deference should be granted in cases covered by the FSIA.

541 U.S. at 701–702 (some footnotes omitted).

Beyond the circumstances addressed in *Altmann*, the FSIA preserves a decisive role for the executive branch in several circumstances. One involves the operation of the terrorist state exception. Beyond the State Department's role in designating state sponsors of terrorism pursuant to the statutes referenced in 28 U.S.C. § 1605A(h)(6), other provisions of law entitle the President to waive the application of the terrorist state exception to Iraq, so as to permit the successor government to avoid liability for suits stemming from actions of its predecessor—even though the claims against Iraq arose, by the same token, from Iraq's conduct prior to the President's waiver, when it had been duly designated as a state sponsor. *See* Republic of Iraq v. Beaty, ___ U.S. ___, 129 S.Ct. 2183, 173 L.Ed.2d 1193 (2009) (describing and applying statutory scheme, and upholding waiver).

A second, more routine occasion involves determination of immunity for officials. A number of courts of appeals have held that the FSIA applies to suits against foreign officials; such an official could, it was reasoned, be deemed a "foreign state" either because the statutory definition in 28 U.S.C. § 1603(a)–(b) included "an agency or instrumentality of a foreign state" or was nonexclusive in character, and immunizing acts committed by those officials in their official capacity prevented plaintiffs from maintaining suits that were, in reality, against the state itself. *See, e.g.*, El-Fadl v. Central Bank of Jordan, 75 F.3d 668, 671 (D.C. Cir. 1996); In re Terrorist Attacks on September 11, 2001, 538 F.3d 71, 83 (2d Cir. 2008); Byrd v. Corporacion Forestal y Industrial de Olancho S. A., 182 F.3d 380, 388 (5th Cir. 1999); Keller v. Central Bank of Nigeria, 277 F.3d 811, 815 (6th Cir. 2002); Chuidian v. Philippine Nat. Bank, 912 F.2d 1095, 1103 (9th Cir. 1990).

In *Samantar v. Yousuf*, 130 S.Ct. 2278, 176 L.Ed.2d 1047 (2010), the Supreme Court sided with the minority view, established in the Fourth Circuit and the Seventh Circuit, that a foreign official is neither an "agency or instrumentality" of a foreign state nor, like the other types of defendants contemplated, an entity. According to the Court, this did not mean that

---

23. Mislabeling this observation a "constitutional conclusion," the dissent suggests that permitting the Executive to comment on a party's assertion of sovereign immunity will result in "[u]ncertain prospective application of our foreign sovereign immunity law." . . . We do not hold, however, that executive intervention could or would trump considered application of the FSIA's more neutral principles; we merely note that the Executive's views on questions within its area of expertise merit greater deference than its opinions regarding the scope of a congressional enactment. Furthermore, we fail to understand how our holding, which requires that courts apply the FSIA's sovereign immunity rules in *all* cases, somehow injects greater uncertainty into sovereign immunity law than the dissent's approach, which would require, for cases concerning pre–1976 conduct, case-by-case analysis of the status of that law at the time of the offending conduct—including analysis of the existence or nonexistence of any State Department statements on the subject.

plaintiffs might circumvent the FSIA through artful pleading. A state itself or another covered entity might, it noted, be a required party and require dismissal by virtue of its immunity; some actions against an official in his official capacity might be deemed actions against the state as the real party in interest; and some actions may be barred under the common law of immunity. 130 S.Ct. at 2292. Determining whether common law immunity is appropriate is, as we have discovered, a matter on which courts appear to accord complete deference to the executive branch.

8. *Commentary*. For commentary, see Joseph W. Dellapenna, *Suing Foreign Governments and Their Corporations* (2d ed. 2003); Andrew Dickinson et al., *State Immunity: Selected Materials and Commentary* (2004); Hazel Fox, *The Law of State Immunity* (2002); Michael Wallace Gordon, *Foreign State Immunity in Commercial Transactions* (1991) (looseleaf); Charles J. Lewis, *State and Diplomatic Immunity* (3d ed. 1990); William H. Manz, ed., *Foreign Sovereign Immunities Act of 1976, with Amendments: A Legislative History of Pub. L. No. 94–583* (2000) (2 vols.).

SECTION 8. ACT OF STATE DOCTRINE

INTRODUCTORY NOTE

The "act-of-state doctrine" is essentially a rule of judicial self-restraint that has developed in the United States. Under this rule, U.S. courts decline to "sit in judgment" on the acts of a foreign government when those acts are taken within the foreign government's territory. The principal motivation for this self-restraint appears to be a desire that disputes involving the acts of foreign governments in their own territories be resolved through diplomatic means, not through litigation in national courts. *See* Restatement (Third) of the Foreign Relations Law of the United States § 443 rptrs. n. 12 (1987). While the doctrine may not be compelled by customary international law, it is certainly used by many other states in one form or another. Robert Jennings & Arthur Watts eds., *Oppenheim's International Law* 365–71 (9th ed. 1992).

An early application of this doctrine in the United States is illustrated in *Underhill v. Hernandez*, 168 U.S. 250, 18 S.Ct. 83, 42 L.Ed. 456 (1897). In 1892, revolution broke out in Venezuela, led by General Hernandez, who assumed control of the city of Bolivar. Underhill, a U.S. national, wished to leave the city, but was prevented by Hernandez because Underhill had constructed the city's waterworks and was needed to help operate the system. Eventually the revolutionaries succeeded in seizing control of the entire country, and Underhill was able to leave Venezuela. Upon his return to the United States, he sued Hernandez for violations of Venezuelan tort law. The U.S. Supreme Court viewed Hernandez's action as that of a sovereign and so affirmed the dismissal of the case based on the act of state doctrine.

> Every sovereign State is bound to respect the independence of every other sovereign State, and the courts of one country will not sit in judgment on the acts of the government of another done within its own territory. Redress of grievances by reason of such acts must be obtained through the means open to be availed of by sovereign powers as between themselves.

Id. at 252. Later cases have suggested that the doctrine either was required by principles of comity (*see, e.g.*, Oetjen v. Central Leather Co., 246 U.S. 297, 38 S.Ct. 309, 62 L.Ed. 726 (1918); Ricaud v. American Metal Co., 246 U.S. 304, 38 S.Ct. 312, 62 L.Ed. 733 (1918)) or was a special choice of law rule (*see, e.g.*, American Banana Co. v. United Fruit Co., 213 U.S. 347, 29 S.Ct. 511, 53 L.Ed. 826 (1909)).

Since the act-of-state doctrine is frequently invoked in cases in U.S. courts involving foreign governments, discussion of the doctrine is often coupled with discussion of sovereign immunity. It must be emphasized, however, that the act-of-state doctrine is potentially relevant in *any case* where the validity of a foreign government's act, taken in its own territory, is at issue. Hence, such cases may arise even when the foreign government itself is not a party.

BANCO NACIONAL de CUBA v. SABBATINO

376 U.S. 398, 84 S.Ct. 923, 11 L.Ed.2d 804 (1964).

MR. JUSTICE HARLAN delivered the opinion of the Court.

The question which brought this case here, and is now found to be the dispositive issue, is whether the so-called act of state doctrine serves to sustain petitioner's claims in this litigation. Such claims are ultimately founded on a decree of the Government of Cuba expropriating certain property, the right to the proceeds of which is here in controversy. The act of state doctrine in its traditional formulation precludes the courts of this country from inquiring into the validity of the public acts a recognized foreign sovereign power committed within its own territory.

I.

[In 1960 President Eisenhower, acting pursuant to permission from Congress, reduced the sugar quota for Cuba. Cuba retaliated by adopting "Law No. 851," which called the U.S. reduction an "act of aggression" and granted discretionary power to the Cuban President and Prime Minister to nationalize property or enterprises in which American nationals had an interest. The U.S. State Department called this law "manifestly in violation" of international law and "in its essence discriminatory, arbitrary and confiscatory." In August 1960 Cuba seized a sugar shipment belonging to C.A.V., a company in which U.S. nationals had an interest. The sugar had been contracted for by an American commodity broker, Farr, Whitlock & Co, which was then forced to make a new agreement to buy the sugar from an instrumentality of the Cuban government. Upon receiving the shipment in New York, Farr, Whitlock accepted the shipping documents and negotiated the bills of lading to its customers, but refused to deliver the proceeds to Cuba. Instead, it handed the proceeds to Sabbatino, the temporary receiving agent for C.A.V., in exchange for C.A.V.'s promise of indemnity. Cuba's national bank then instituted this proceeding in Federal District Court for the Southern District of New York, alleging conversion of the bills of lading and seeking an injunction against Sabbatino to prevent him from taking the proceeds from the sugar sale.]

. . . .

. . . Upon motions to dismiss and for summary judgment, the District Court, 193 F.Supp. 375, sustained federal *in personam* jurisdiction despite state control of the funds. It found that the sugar was located within Cuban territory at the time of expropriation and determined that under merchant law common to civilized countries Farr, Whitlock could not have asserted ownership of the sugar against C.A.V. before making payment. It concluded that C.A.V. had a property interest in the sugar subject to the territorial jurisdiction of Cuba. The court then dealt with the question of Cuba's title to the sugar, on which rested petitioner's claim of conversion. While acknowledging the continuing vitality of the act of state doctrine, the court believed it inapplicable when the questioned foreign act is in violation of international law. Proceeding on the basis that a taking invalid under international law does not convey good title, the District Court found the Cuban expropriation decree to violate such law in three separate respects: it was motivated by a retaliatory and not a public purpose; it discriminated against American nationals; and it failed to provide adequate compensation. Summary judgment against petitioner was accordingly granted.

The Court of Appeals, 307 F.2d 845, affirming the decision on similar grounds, relied on two letters (not before the District Court) written by State Department officers which it took as evidence that the Executive Branch had no objection to a judicial testing of the Cuban decree's validity. The court was unwilling to declare that any one of the infirmities found by the District Court rendered the taking invalid under international law, but was satisfied that in combination they had that effect. We granted certiorari because the issues involved bear importantly on the conduct of the country's foreign relations and more particularly on the proper role of the Judicial Branch in this sensitive area. 372 U.S. 905. For reasons to follow we decide that the judgment below must be reversed.

[For the Court's discussion of whether there is standing in U.S. court for the instrumentality of a government with whom the United States has no diplomatic relations, see *supra* Section 6.]

. . . .

IV.

The classic American statement of the act of state doctrine, which appears to have taken root in England as early as 1674, *Blad v. Bamfield,* 3 Swans. 604, 36 Eng. Rep. 992, and began to emerge in the jurisprudence of this country in the late eighteenth and early nineteenth centuries, *see e.g., Ware v. Hylton*, 3 Dall. 199, 230; *Hudson v. Guestier*, 4 Cranch 293, 294; *The Schooner Exchange v. M'Faddon,* 7 Cranch 116, 135, 136; *L'Invincible,* 1 Wheat. 238, 253; *The Santissima Trinidad*, 7 Wheat. 283,

336, is found in *Underhill v. Hernandez*, 168 U.S. 250, where Chief Justice Fuller said for a unanimous Court (p. 252):

> "Every sovereign State is bound to respect the independence of every other sovereign State, and the courts of one country will not sit in judgment on the acts of the government of another done within its own territory. Redress of grievances by reason of such acts must be obtained through the means open to be availed of by sovereign powers as between themselves."

. . . .

None of this Court's subsequent cases in which the act of state doctrine was directly or peripherally involved manifest any retreat from *Underhill*. *See American Banana Co. v. United Fruit Co.*, 213 U.S. 347; *Oetjen v. Central Leather Co.,* 246 U.S. 297; *Ricaud v.American Metal Co.,* 246 U.S. 304; *Shapleigh v. Mier*, 299 U.S. 468; *United States v. Belmont,* 301 U.S. 324; *United States v. Pink*, 315 U.S. 203. On the contrary in two of these cases, *Oetjen* and *Ricaud,* the doctrine as announced in *Underhill* was reaffirmed in unequivocal terms.

. . . .

The outcome of this case, therefore, turns upon whether any of the contentions urged by respondents against the application of the act of state doctrine in the premises is acceptable: (1) that the doctrine does not apply to acts of state which violate international law, as is claimed to be the case here; (2) that the doctrine is inapplicable unless the Executive specifically interposes it in a particular case; and (3) that, in any event, the doctrine may not be invoked by a foreign government plaintiff in our courts.

V.

Preliminarily, we discuss the foundations on which we deem the act of state doctrine to rest, and more particularly the question of whether state or federal law governs its application in a federal diversity case.

We do not believe that this doctrine is compelled either by the inherent nature of sovereign authority, as some of the earlier decisions seem to imply, *see Underhill, supra; American Banana, supra; Oetjen, supra,* at 303, or by some principle of international law. If a transaction takes place in one jurisdiction and the forum is in another, the forum does not by dismissing an action or by applying its own law purport to divest the first jurisdiction of its territorial sovereignty; it merely declines to adjudicate or makes applicable its own law to parties or property before it. The refusal of one country to enforce the penal laws of another . . . is a typical example of an instance when a court will not entertain a cause of action arising in another jurisdiction. While historic notions of sovereign authority do bear upon the wisdom of employing the act of state doctrine, they do not dictate its existence.

That international law does not require application of the doctrine is evidenced by the practice of nations. Most of the countries rendering decisions on the subject fail to follow the rule rigidly.[21] No international arbitral or judicial decision discovered suggests that international law prescribes recognition of sovereign acts of foreign governments, see 1 Oppenheim's International Law, § 115aa (Lauterpacht, 8th ed. 1955), and apparently no claim has ever been raised before an international tribunal that failure to apply the act of state doctrine constitutes a breach of international obligation. If international law does not prescribe use of the doctrine, neither does it forbid application of the rule even if it is claimed that the act of state in question violated international law. The traditional view of international law is that it establishes substantive principles for determining whether one country has wronged another. Because of its peculiar nation-to-nation character the usual method for an individual to seek relief is to exhaust local remedies and then repair to the executive authorities of his own state to persuade them to champion his claim in diplomacy or before an international tribunal. *See United States v. Diekelman,* 92 U.S. 520, 524. Although it is, of course, true that United States courts apply international law as a part of our own in appropriate circumstances, *Ware v. Hylton*, 3 Dall. 199, 28; *The Nereide*, 9 Cranch 388, 423; *The Paquete Habana*, 175 U.S. 677, 700, the public law of nations can hardly dictate to a country which is in theory wronged how to treat that wrong within its domestic borders.

Despite the broad statement in *Oetjen* that "The conduct of the foreign relations of our Government is committed by the Constitution to the Executive and Legislative ... Departments," 246 U.S. at 302, it cannot of course be thought that "every case or controversy which touches foreign relations lies beyond judicial cognizance." *Baker v. Carr,* 369 U.S. 186, 211. The text of the Constitution does not require the act of state doctrine; it does not irrevocably remove from the judiciary the capacity to review the validity of foreign acts of state.

The act of state doctrine does, however, have "constitutional" underpinnings. It arises out of the basic relationships between branches of

21. In English jurisprudence, in the classic case of *Luther v. James Sagor & Co.,* (1921) 3 K.B. 532, the act of state doctrine is articulated in terms not unlike those of the United States cases. *See Princess Paley Olga v. Weisz,* [1929] 1 K.B. 718. But see *Anglo-Iranian Oil Co. v. Jaffrate,* [1953] 1 Weekly L.R. 246, [1953] Int'l L. Rep. 316 (Aden Sup. Ct.) (exception to doctrine if foreign act violates international law). Civil law countries, however, which apply the rule make exceptions for acts contrary to their sense of public order. *See, e.g., Ropit* case, Cour de Cassation (France), [1929] Recueil General Des Lois et Des Arrets (Sirey) Part I, 217; 55 Journal Du Droit International (Clunet) 674 (1928), [1927–1928] Ann. Dig., No. 43; Graue, Germany: Recognition of Foreign Expropriations, 3 Am. J. Comp.L. 93 (1954); Domke, Indonesian Nationalization Measures Before Foreign Court, 54 Am. J. Int'l L. 305 (1960) (discussion of and excerpts from opinions of the District Court in Bremen and the Hanseatic Court of Appeals in *N.V. Verenigde Deli–Maatschapijen v. Deutsch–Indonesische Tabak–Handelsgesellschaft m.b.H.,* and of the Amsterdam District Court and Appellate Court in *Senembah Maatschappij N.V. v. Republiek Indonesie Bank Indonesia*); Massouridis, The Effects of Confiscation, Expropriation, and Requisition by a Foreign Authority, 3 Revue Hellenique De Droit International 62, 68 (1950) (recounting a decision of the court of the first instance of Piraeus); *Anglo-Iranian Oil Co. v. S.U.P.O.R. Co.,* [1955] Int'l L. Rep. 19, (Ct. of Venice), 78 Il Foro Italiano Part I, 719; 40 Blatter fur Zurcherische Rechtsprechung No. 65, 172–173 (Switzerland). *See also Anglo–Iranian Oil Co. v. Idemitsu Kosan Kabushiki Kaisha,* [1953] Int'l L. Rep. 312 (High Ct. of Tokyo).

government in a system of separation of powers. It concerns the competency of dissimilar institutions to make and implement particular kinds of decisions in the area of international relations. The doctrine as formulated in past decisions expresses the strong sense of the Judicial Branch that its engagement in the task of passing on the validity of foreign acts of state may hinder rather than further this country's pursuit of goals both for itself and for the community of nations as a whole in the international sphere. . . .

We could perhaps in this diversity action avoid the question of deciding whether federal or state law is applicable to this aspect of the litigation. New York has enunciated the act of state doctrine in terms that echo those of federal decisions decided during the reign of *Swift v. Tyson*, 16 Pet. 1 . . . Thus our conclusions might well be the same whether we dealt with this problem as one of state law, *see Erie R. Co. v. Tompkins*, 304 U.S. 64; *Klaxon Co. v. Stentor Elec. Mfg. Co.*, 313 U.S. 487; *Griffin v. McCoach,* 313 U.S. 498, or federal law.

However, we are constrained to make it clear that an issue concerned with a basic choice regarding the competence and function of the Judiciary and the National Executive in ordering our relationships with other members of the international community must be treated exclusively as an aspect of federal law. It seems fair to assume that the Court did not have rules like the act of state doctrine in mind when it decided *Erie R. Co. v. Tompkins*. Soon thereafter, Professor Philip C. Jessup, now a judge of the International Court of Justice, recognized the potential dangers were *Erie* extended to legal problems affecting international relations.[24] He cautioned that rules of international law should not be left to divergent and perhaps parochial state interpretations. His basic rationale is equally applicable to the act of state doctrine.

The Court in the pre-*Erie* act of state cases, although not burdened by the problem of the source of applicable law, used language sufficiently strong and broad-sweeping to suggest that state courts were not left free to develop their own doctrines (as they would have been had this Court merely been interpreting common law under *Swift v. Tyson, supra*). The Court of Appeals in the first *Bernstein* case, *supra*, a diversity suit, plainly considered the decisions of this Court, despite the intervention of *Erie*, to be controlling in regard to the act of state question, at the same time indicating that New York law governed other aspects of the case. We are not without other precedent for a determination that federal law governs; there are enclaves of federal judge-made law which bind the States. A national body of federal-court-built law has been held to have been contemplated by § 301 of the Labor Management Relations Act, *Textile Workers Union of America v. Lincoln Mills*, 353 U.S. 448. Principles formulated by federal judicial law have been thought by this Court to be necessary to protect uniquely federal interests, *D'Oench, Duhme & Co. v.*

---

24. The Doctrine of Erie Railroad v. Tompkins Applied to International Law, 33 Am. J. Int'l L. 740 (1939).

Federal Deposit Ins. Corp., 315 U.S. 447; *Clearfield Trust Co. v. United States*, 318 U.S. 363. Of course the federal interest guarded in all these cases is one the ultimate statement of which is derived from a federal statute. Perhaps more directly in point are the bodies of law applied between States over boundaries and in regard to the apportionment of interstate waters.

In *Hinderlider v. La Plata River Co.*, 304 U.S. 92, 110, in an opinion handed down the same day as *Erie* and by the same author, Mr. Justice Brandeis, the Court declared, "For whether the water of an interstate stream must be apportioned between the two States is a question of 'federal common law' upon which neither the statutes nor the decisions of either State can be conclusive." Although the suit was between two private litigants and the relevant States could not be made parties, the Court considered itself free to determine the effect of an interstate compact regulating water apportionment. The decision implies that no State can undermine the federal interest in equitably apportioned interstate waters even if it deals with private parties. This would not mean that, absent a compact, the apportionment scheme could not be changed judicially or by Congress, but only that apportionment is a matter of federal law. *Cf. State of Arizona v. State of California*, 373 U.S. 546, 597–598. The problems surrounding the act of state doctrine are, albeit for different reasons, as intrinsically federal as are those involved in water apportionment or boundary disputes. The considerations supporting exclusion of state authority here are much like those which led the Court in *United States v. California*, 332 U.S. 19, to hold that the Federal Government possessed paramount rights in submerged lands though within the three-mile limit of coastal States. We conclude that the scope of the act of state doctrine must be determined according to federal law.[25]

VI.

If the act of state doctrine is a principle of decision binding on federal and state courts alike but compelled by neither international law nor the Constitution, its continuing vitality depends on its capacity to reflect the proper distribution of functions between the judicial and political branches of the Government on matters bearing upon foreign affairs. It should be apparent that the greater the degree of codification or consensus concerning a particular area of international law, the more appropriate it is for the judiciary to render decisions regarding it, since the courts can then focus on the application of an agreed principle to circumstances of fact rather than on the sensitive task of establishing a principle not inconsistent with the national interest or with international justice. It is also

---

25. Various constitutional and statutory provisions indirectly support this determination, *see* U.S. Const., Art I, § 8, cls. 3, 10; Art. II, §§ 2, 3; Art. III, § 2; 28 U.S.C. §§ 1251(a)(2), (b)(1), (b)(3), 1332(a)(2), 1333, 1350–1351, by reflecting a concern for uniformity in this country's dealings with foreign nations and indicating a desire to give matters of international significance to the jurisdiction of federal institutions. *See* Comment, The Act of State Doctrine—Its Relation to Private and Public International Law, 62 Col. L. Rev., 1278, 1297, n. 123; *cf. United States v. Belmont, supra; United States v. Pink, supra.*

evident that some aspects of international law touch much more sharply on national nerves than do others; the less important the implications of an issue are for our foreign relations, the weaker the justification for exclusivity in the political branches. The balance of relevant considerations may also be shifted if the government which perpetrated the challenged act of state is no longer in existence ... for the political interest of this country may, as a result, be measurably altered. Therefore, rather than laying down or reaffirming an inflexible and all-encompassing rule in this case, we decide only that the Judicial Branch will not examine the validity of a taking of property within its own territory by a foreign sovereign government, extant and recognized by this country at the time of suit, in the absence of a treaty or other unambiguous agreement regarding controlling legal principles, even if the complaint alleges that the taking violates customary international law.

There are few if any issues in international law today on which opinion seems to be so divided as the limitations on a state's power to expropriate the property of aliens.[26]

. . . .

... It is difficult to imagine the courts of this country embarking on adjudication in an area which touches more sensitively the practical and ideological goals of the various members of the community of nations.[34]

When we consider the prospect of the courts characterizing foreign expropriations, however justifiably, as invalid under international law and ineffective to pass title, the wisdom of the precedents is confirmed. While each of the leading cases in this Court may be argued to be distinguishable on its facts from this one—*Underhill* because sovereign immunity provided an independent ground and *Oetjen, Ricaud*, and *Shapleigh* because there was actually no violation of international law—the plain implication of all these opinions ... is that the act of state doctrine is applicable even if international law has been violated....

The possible adverse consequences of a conclusion to the contrary of that implicit in these cases is highlighted by contrasting the practices of the political branch with the limitations of the judicial process in matters of this kind. Following an expropriation of any significance, the Executive engages in diplomacy aimed to assure that United States citizens who are harmed are compensated fairly. Representing all claimants of this country, it will often be able, either by bilateral or multilateral talks, by submission

26. *Compare, e.g.*, Friedman, Expropriation in International Law 206–211 (1953); Dawson and Weston, "Prompt, Adequate and Effective": A Universal Standard of Compensation? 30 Fordham L. Rev. 727 (1962), with Note from Secretary of State Hull to Mexican Ambassador, August 22, 1938, V Foreign Relations of the United States 685 (1938); Doman, Postwar Nationalization of Foreign Property in Europe, 48 Col. L. Rev. 1125, 1127 (1948). We do not, of course, mean to say that there is no international standard in this area; we conclude only that the matter is not [meant] for adjudication by domestic tribunals.

34. There are, of course, areas of international law in which consensus as to standards is greater and which do not represent a battleground for conflicting ideologies. This decision in no way intimates that the courts of this country are broadly foreclosed from considering questions of international law.

to the United Nations, or by the employment of economic and political sanctions, to achieve some degree of general redress. Judicial determinations of invalidity of title can, on the other hand, have only an occasional impact, since they depend on the fortuitous circumstance of the property in question being brought into this country. Such decisions would, if the acts involved were declared invalid, often be likely to give offense to the expropriating country; since the concept of territorial sovereignty is so deep seated, any state may resent the refusal of the courts of another sovereign to accord validity to acts within its territorial borders. Piecemeal dispositions of this sort involving the probability of affront to another state could seriously interfere with negotiations being carried on by the Executive Branch and might prevent or render less favorable the terms of an agreement that could otherwise be reached. Relations with third countries which have engaged in similar expropriations would not be immune from effect.

The dangers of such adjudication are present regardless of whether the State Department has, as it did in this case, asserted that the relevant act violated international law. If the Executive Branch has undertaken negotiations with an expropriating country, but has refrained from claims of violation of the law of nations, a determination to that effect by a court might be regarded as a serious insult, while a finding of compliance with international law would greatly strengthen the bargaining hand of the other state with consequent detriment to American interests.

Even if the State Department has proclaimed the impropriety of the expropriation, the stamp of approval of its view by a judicial tribunal, however impartial, might increase any affront and the judicial decision might occur at a time, almost always well after the taking, when such an impact would be contrary to our national interest. Considerably more serious and far-reaching consequences would flow from a judicial finding that international law standards had been met if that determination flew in the face of a State Department proclamation to the contrary. When articulating principles of international law in its relations with other states, the Executive Branch speaks not only as an interpreter of generally accepted and traditional rules, as would the courts, but also as an advocate of standards it believes desirable for the community of nations and protective of national concerns. In short, whatever way the matter is cut, the possibility of conflict between the Judicial and Executive Branches could hardly be avoided.

. . . .

Against the force of such considerations, we find respondents' countervailing arguments quite unpersuasive. Their basic contention is that United States courts could make a significant contribution to the growth of international law, a contribution whose importance, it is said, would be magnified by the relative paucity of decisional law by international bodies. But given the fluidity of present world conditions, the effectiveness of such a patchwork approach toward the formulation of an acceptable body of law concerning state responsibility for expropriations is, to say the least, highly conjectural. Moreover, it rests upon the sanguine presupposition that the decisions of the courts of the world's major capital exporting country and principal exponent of the free enterprise system would be accepted as disinterested expressions of sound legal principle by those adhering to widely different ideologies.

. . . .

However offensive to the public policy of this country and its constituent States an expropriation of this kind may be, we conclude that both the national interest and progress toward the goal of establishing the rule of law among nations are best served by maintaining intact the act of state doctrine in this realm of its application.

W.S. KIRKPATRICK & CO. v. ENVIRONMENTAL TECTONICS CORP.

493 U.S. 400, 110 S.Ct. 701, 107 L.Ed.2d 816 (1990).

[According to respondent's complaint, petitioners obtained a construction contract from the Nigerian Government by bribing Nigerian officials. Nigerian law prohibits both the payment and the receipt of such bribes. Respondent, an unsuccessful bidder for the contract, filed an action for damages against petitioners and others under various federal and state statutes. The District Court ruled that the suit was barred by the act of state doctrine, which in its view precluded judicial inquiry into the motivation of a sovereign act that would result in embarrassment to the sovereign, or constitute interference with the conduct of United States foreign policy. The court granted summary judgment for petitioners because resolution of the case in favor of respondent would require imputing to foreign officials an unlawful motivation (the obtaining of bribes), and accordingly might embarrass the Executive Branch in its conduct of foreign relations. The Court of Appeals reversed and remanded the case for trial, holding that on the facts of this case the doctrine of sovereign immunity did not apply because no embarrassment of the Executive in its conduct of foreign affairs was evident.]

JUSTICE SCALIA delivered the opinion of the Court.

In this case we must decide whether the act of state doctrine bars a court in the United States from entertaining a cause of action that does not rest upon the asserted invalidity of an official act of a foreign sovereign, but that does require imputing to foreign officials an unlawful motivation (the obtaining of bribes) in the performance of such an official act.

. . . .

II

This Court's description of the jurisprudential foundation for the act of state doctrine has undergone some evolution over the years. We once viewed the doctrine as an expression of international law, resting upon "the highest considerations of international comity and expediency," *Oetjen v. Central Leather Co.*, 246 U.S. 297, 303–304 (1918). We have more recently described it, however, as a consequence of domestic separation of powers, reflecting "the strong sense of the Judicial Branch that its engagement in the task of passing on the validity of foreign acts of state may hinder" the conduct of foreign affairs, *Banco Nacional de Cuba v. Sabbatino*, 376 U.S. 398, 423 (1964). Some Justices have suggested possible exceptions to application of the doctrine, where one or both of the foregoing policies would seemingly not be served: an exception, for example, for acts of state that consist of commercial transactions, since neither modern international comity nor the current position of our Executive Branch accorded sovereign immunity to such acts, see *Alfred Dunhill of London, Inc. v. Republic of Cuba*, 425 U.S. 682, 695–706 (1976) (opinion of WHITE, J.); or an exception for cases in which the Executive Branch has represented that it has no objection to denying validity to the foreign sovereign act, since then the courts would be impeding no foreign policy goals, see *First National City Bank v. Banco Nacional de Cuba*, 406 U.S. 759, 768–770 (1972) (opinion of REHNQUIST, J.).

The parties have argued at length about the applicability of these possible exceptions, and, more generally, about whether the purpose of the act of state doctrine would be furthered by its application in this case. We find it unnecessary, however, to pursue those inquiries, since the factual predicate for application of the act of state doctrine does not exist. Nothing in the present suit requires the court to declare invalid, and thus ineffective as "a rule of decision for the courts of this country," *Ricaud v. American Metal Co.*, 246 U.S. 304, 310 (1918), the official act of a foreign sovereign.

In every case in which we have held the act of state doctrine applicable, the relief sought or the defense interposed would have required a court in the United States to declare invalid the official act of a foreign sovereign performed within its own territory. In *Underhill v. Hernandez*, 168 U.S. 250, 254 (1897), holding the defendant's detention of the plaintiff to be tortious would have required denying legal effect to "acts of a military commander representing the authority of the revolutionary party as government, which afterwards succeeded and was recognized by the United States." In *Oetjen v. Central Leather Co., supra*, and in *Ricaud v. American Metal Co., supra*, denying title to the party who claimed through purchase from Mexico would have required declaring that government's prior seizure of the property, within its own territory, legally ineffective. *See Oetjen, supra*, 246 U.S., at 304; *Ricaud, supra*, 246 U.S., at 310. In *Sabbatino*, upholding the defendant's claim to the funds would have required a holding that Cuba's expropriation of goods located in Havana was null and void. In the present case, by contrast, neither the claim nor any asserted defense requires a determination that Nigeria's contract with Kirkpatrick International was, or was not, effective.

Petitioners point out, however, that the facts necessary to establish respondent's claim will also establish that the contract was unlawful. Specifically, they note that in order to prevail respondent must prove that petitioner Kirkpatrick made, and Nigerian officials received, payments that violate Nigerian law, which would, they assert, support a finding that the contract is invalid under Nigerian law. Assuming that to be true, it still does not suffice. The act of state doctrine is not some vague doctrine of abstention but a "principle of decision binding on federal and state courts alike." *Sabbatino, supra,* 376 U.S., at 427 (emphasis added). As we said in *Ricaud,* "the act within its own boundaries of one sovereign State ... becomes ... a rule of decision for the courts of this country." 246 U.S., at 310. Act of state issues only arise when a court must decide—that is, when the outcome of the case turns upon—the effect of official action by a foreign sovereign. When that question is not in the case, neither is the act of state doctrine. That is the situation here. Regardless of what the court's factual findings may suggest as to the legality of the Nigerian contract, its legality is simply not a question to be decided in the present suit, and there is thus no occasion to apply the rule of decision that the act of state doctrine requires. *Cf. Sharon v. Time, Inc.,* 599 F.Supp. 538, 546 (SDNY 1984) ("The issue in this litigation is not whether [the alleged] acts are valid, but whether they occurred").

In support of their position that the act of state doctrine bars any factual findings that may cast doubt upon the validity of foreign sovereign acts, petitioners cite Justice Holmes' opinion for the Court in *American Banana Co. v. United Fruit Co.,* 213 U.S. 347 (1909). That was a suit under the United States antitrust laws, alleging that Costa Rica's seizure of the plaintiff's property had been induced by an unlawful conspiracy. In the course of a lengthy opinion Justice Holmes observed, citing *Underhill,* that "a seizure by a state is not a thing that can be complained of elsewhere in the courts." *Id.,* at 357–358. The statement is concededly puzzling. *Underhill* does indeed stand for the proposition that a seizure by a state cannot be complained of elsewhere—in the sense of being sought to be declared ineffective elsewhere. The plaintiff in *American Banana,* however, like the plaintiff here, was not trying to undo or disregard the governmental action, but only to obtain damages from private parties who had procured it. Arguably, then, the statement did imply that suit would not lie if a foreign state's actions would be, though not invalidated, impugned.

Whatever Justice Holmes may have had in mind, his statement lends inadequate support to petitioners' position here, for two reasons. First, it was a brief aside, entirely unnecessary to the decision. *American Banana* was squarely decided on the ground (later substantially overruled, see *Continental Ore Co. v. Union Carbide & Carbon Corp.,* 370 U.S. 690, 704–705 (1962)) that the antitrust laws had no extraterritorial application, so that "what the defendant did in Panama or Costa Rica is not within the scope of the statute." 213 U.S., at 357. Second, whatever support the dictum might provide for petitioners' position is more than overcome by our later holding in *United States v. Sisal Sales Corp.*, 274 U.S. 268 (1927). There we held that, *American Banana* notwithstanding, the defendant's actions in obtaining Mexico's enactment of "discriminating legislation" could form part of the basis for suit under the United States antitrust laws. 274 U.S., at 276. Simply put, *American Banana* was not an act of state case; and whatever it said by way of dictum that might be relevant to the present case has not survived *Sisal Sales*.

Petitioners insist, however, that the policies underlying our act of state cases—international comity, respect for the sovereignty of foreign nations on their own territory, and the avoidance of embarrassment to the Executive Branch in its conduct of foreign relations—are implicated in the present case because, as the District Court found, a determination that Nigerian officials demanded and accepted a bribe "would impugn or question the nobility of a foreign nation's motivations," and would "result in embarrassment to the sovereign or constitute interference in the conduct of foreign policy of the United States." 659 F.Supp., at 1392–1393. The United States, as amicus curiae, favors the same approach to the act of state doctrine, though disagreeing with petitioners as to the outcome it produces in the present case. We should not, the United States urges, "attach dispositive significance to the fact that this suit involves only the 'motivation' for, rather than the 'validity' of, a foreign sovereign act," Brief for United States as Amicus Curiae 37, and should eschew "any rigid formula for the resolution of act of state cases generally," id., at 9. In some future case, perhaps, "litigation ... based on alleged corruption in the award of contracts or other commercially oriented activities of foreign governments could sufficiently touch on 'national nerves' that the act of state doctrine or related principles of abstention would appropriately be found to bar the suit," id., at 40 (quoting *Sabbatino*, 376 U.S., at 428), and we should therefore resolve this case on the narrowest possible ground, viz., that the letter from the legal advisor to the District Court gives sufficient indication that, "in the setting of this case," the act of state doctrine poses no bar to adjudication....

These urgings are deceptively similar to what we said in *Sabbatino*, where we observed that sometimes, even though the validity of the act of a foreign sovereign within its own territory is called into question, the policies underlying the act of state doctrine may not justify its application. We suggested that a sort of balancing approach could be applied—the balance shifting against application of the doctrine, for example, if the government that committed the "challenged act of state" is no longer in existence. 376 U.S., at 428. But what is appropriate in order to avoid unquestioning judicial acceptance of the acts of foreign sovereigns is not similarly appropriate for the quite opposite purpose of expanding judicial incapacities where such acts are not directly (or even indirectly) involved. It is one thing to suggest, as we have, that the policies underlying the act of state doctrine should be considered in deciding whether, despite the doctrine's technical availability, it should nonetheless not be invoked; it is something quite different to suggest that those underlying policies are a doctrine unto themselves, justifying expansion of the act of state doctrine (or, as the United States puts it, unspecified "related principles of abstention") into new and uncharted fields.

The short of the matter is this: Courts in the United States have the power, and ordinarily the obligation, to decide cases and controversies properly presented to them. The act of state doctrine does not establish an exception for cases and controversies that may embarrass foreign governments, but merely requires that, in the process of deciding, the acts of foreign sovereigns taken within their own jurisdictions shall be deemed valid. That doctrine has no application to the present case because the validity of no foreign sovereign act is at issue.

The judgment of the Court of Appeals for the Third Circuit is *affirmed.*

CONCLUDING NOTES

1. *Rationale for the Doctrine.* According to *Restatement (Third) of the Foreign Relations Law of the United States* § 443, cmt. a:

> The rationale for the doctrine has been variously described. The doctrine was developed by the Court on its own authority, as a principle of judicial restraint, essentially to avoid disrespect for foreign states. "To permit the validity of the acts of one sovereign State to be reexamined and perhaps condemned by the courts of another would very certainly 'imperil the amicable relations between governments and vex the peace of nations.' " *Oetjen v. Central Leather Co.*, 246 U.S. 297, 304 (1918). Thus, the doctrine is related in spirit to the rules of international law that accord to foreign sovereigns large immunity from adjudication in domestic courts. *See* Reporters' Note 11; *see also* §§ 451–460. In *Sabbatino*, the Court said that the act of state doctrine is compelled neither by international law nor by the Constitution, but that it has "constitutional underpinnings," 376 U.S. at 423. The Court referred to the doctrine as "concerned with a basic choice regarding the competence and function of the Judiciary and the National Executive in ordering our relationships with other members of the international community." 376 U.S. at 425. The Court's statement in *Underhill* implies that disputes arising out of foreign acts of state should be resolved between governments. The act of state doctrine therefore also reflects deference to the Executive Branch, akin to the political question doctrine. ... Where the act of a foreign state is challenged under international law, as in *Sabbatino*, the lack of consensus on the relevant content of that law has contributed to the Court's reluctance to entertain such a challenge. ... Courts and commentators have stressed one or another of these bases for the doctrine, and the weight given to the different bases may determine possible limitations or exceptions....

2. *The Role of Congress (the Second Hickenlooper Amendment).* After the *Sabbatino* case was decided by the Supreme Court, Congress enacted the "Second Hickenlooper Amendment," Pub. L. No. 88–633, § 302(d)(2) (1964), amended and codified at 22 U.S.C. § 2370(e)(2) (2006), which states:

Notwithstanding any other provision of law, no court in the United States shall decline on the ground of the federal act of state doctrine to make a determination on the merits giving effect to the principles of international law in a case in which a claim of title or other rights to property is asserted by any party including a foreign state (or a party claiming through such state) based upon (or traced through) a confiscation or other taking after January 1, 1959, by an act of that state in violation of the principles of international law, including the principles of compensation and the other standards set out in this subsection: *Provided*, That this subparagraph shall not be applicable (1) in any case in which an act of a foreign state is not contrary to international law or with respect to a claim of title or other right to property acquired pursuant to an irrevocable letter of credit of not more than 180 days duration issued in good faith prior to the time of the confiscation or other taking, or (2) in any case with respect to which the President determines that application of the act of state doctrine is required in that particular case by the foreign policy interests of the United States and a suggestion to this effect is filed on his behalf in that case with the court.

Courts have upheld the constitutionality of the Hickenlooper Amendment. The matter was considered in *Banco Nacional de Cuba v. Farr,* 243 F.Supp. 957 and 272 F.Supp. 836 (S.D.N.Y. 1965), *aff'd*, 383 F.2d 166 (2d Cir. 1967), *cert. denied,* 390 U.S. 956, 88 S.Ct. 1038, 19 L.Ed.2d 1151 (1968), *reh'g denied,* 390 U.S. 1037, 88 S.Ct. 1406, 20 L.Ed.2d 298 (1968). The district court found that eliminating the act-of-state doctrine in the areas of foreign investment and international trade and commerce, except by contrary Presidential determination, was wholly within the powers of Congress under its commerce-clause authority as well as under the necessary-and-proper clause, Art. I, § 8, cl. 18. The court hinted that such powers were also granted under the define-and-punish clause, Art. I, § 8, cl. 10, or "within the ambit of implied congressional power over foreign relations." Looking to these additional sources was unnecessary, however: "congressional power under the commerce clause is so clear that to discuss these less obvious questions would be merely gilding the lily." The court further rejected the contention that the amendment impinged on the President's foreign relations powers and thus violated separation of powers. 243 F.Supp. at 972–73. If the act-of-state doctrine is a constitutionally based rule of judicial restraint, can Congress alter such a rule? If it is not constitutionally based, what is it?

Note, however, that the effect of congressional (and judicial) paring of *Sabbatino* through the Hickenlooper Amendment has been to project the courts quite extensively into the determination of international legal standards applicable to the seizure of property owned by U.S. interests abroad. *See* Banco Nacional de Cuba v. First National City Bank of New York, 431 F.2d 394 (2d Cir. 1970), *vacated and remanded,* 400 U.S. 1019, 91 S.Ct. 581, 27 L.Ed.2d 630 (1971), on remand, 442 F.2d 530 (2d Cir. 1971), *rev'd*, 406 U.S. 759, 92 S.Ct. 1808, 32 L.Ed.2d 466 (1972); Alfred Dunhill of London, Inc. v. Republic of Cuba, 425 U.S. 682, 96 S.Ct. 1854, 48 L.Ed.2d 301 (1976).

For commentary, see Monroe Leigh and & Michael David Sandler, *Dunhill: Toward a Reconsideration of Sabbatino,* 16 VA. J. INT'L L. 685 (1976); Andreas F. Lowenfeld, *Act of State and Department of State: First National*

City Bank v. Banco Nacional de Cuba, 66 AM. J. INT'L L. 795 (1972); Victor Rabinowitz, *Viva Sabbatino,* 17 VA. J. INT'L L. 697 (1977); Alan C. Swan, *Act of State at Bay: A Plea on Behalf of the Exclusive Doctrine,* 1976 DUKE L.J. 807 (1976). *See also* 6 Marjorie Whiteman, *Digest of International Law* 1–88 (1968). For commentary critical of the *Restatement*'s treatment of the act-of-state doctrine, see Monroe Leigh, *Sabbatino's Silver Anniversary and the Restatement: No Cause for Celebration,* 24 INT'L LAW. 1 (1990).

In other situations, Congress has indicated as part of a congressional record that it does not expect the act-of-state doctrine to be applied. Thus, when enacting the Torture Victim Protection Act, 28 U.S.C. § 1350 note (2006)—which, as discussed in Chapter 3, Section 4, provides a civil remedy to persons who suffer torture or extrajudicial killing by, or under the authority of, a foreign government—a congressional committee indicated that it did not intend the act-of-state doctrine to apply to such claims. *See* S. REP. NO. 102–249, at 8 (1991).

A final example concerns the Cuban Liberty and Democratic Solidarity (Libertad) Act, Pub. L. No. 104–114, 110 Stat. 785, 104th Cong. 2d Sess. (1996), better known as the "Helms–Burton Act." Title III of the Act provides a civil remedy against those "trafficking" in property formerly owned by U.S. citizens and confiscated by the Cuban government on or after January 1, 1959. "Trafficking" was described quite broadly in the Act. In § 302(a)(6), 22 U.S.C. § 6082(a)(6) (2006), the Act precludes courts in the United States from using the act-of-state doctrine as justification for declining to adjudicate the merits of such cases. The Helms–Burton Act provoked intense opposition from foreign states, which viewed it as an impermissible extension of U.S. jurisdiction. Since the law was passed in 1996, both Presidents Bush and President Clinton have applied consistent waivers of Title III's controversial provisions, as permitted under 22 U.S.C. § 6085(b) (2006). Would the law be constitutional had it not included such a waiver provision? For further reading on the act-of-state doctrine and the Helms–Burton Act, see, e.g., Helen Kim, *The Errand Boy's Revenge: Helms–Burton and the Supreme Court's Response to Congress's Abrogation of the Act of State Doctrine*, 48 EMORY L.J. 305 (1999); S. Kern Alexander, *Trafficking in Confiscated Cuban Property: Lender Liability Under the Helms–Burton Act and Customary International Law*, 16 DICK. J. INT'L L. 523 (1998).

3. *The Role of the Executive (The "Bernstein" Exception).* In the interplay between courts and the Executive over recognition policy, courts follow executive policy, often receiving specific instructions from the Department of State. *See supra* Section 6. These instructions as to recognition can also determine the application of act-of-state doctrine since the doctrine can only be applied only to recognized governments. *Sabbatino, supra*, 376 U.S. at 428. A broader question is whether the Executive can generally command the non-application of the act-of-state doctrine.

The Second Circuit followed executive instructions during the course of the *Bernstein* litigation. Bernstein, a German Jew, brought suits after the Second World War to recover damages for property that Nazi officials had compelled him to transfer to third parties. At first, he was unsuccessful because the courts invoked the act-of-state doctrine. Bernstein v. Van Heyghen Freres S.A., 163 F.2d 246 (2d Cir. 1947), *cert. denied,* 332 U.S. 772, 68 S.Ct. 88, 92 L.Ed. 357 (1947); Bernstein v. N.V. Nederlandsche–Amerikaansche Stoomvaart–Maatschappij, 173 F.2d 71 (2d Cir. 1949). Bernstein then procured a letter from the State Department advising that: "The policy of the Executive, with respect to claims asserted in the United States for the restitution of identifiable property (or compensation in lieu thereof) lost through force, coercion, or duress as a result of Nazi persecution in Germany, is to relieve American courts from any restraint upon the exercise of their jurisdiction to pass upon the acts of Nazi officials." 20 DEP'T STATE BULL. 592, 593 (1949).

The Second Circuit, "in view of this supervening expression of Executive policy," remanded the case to the district court, expressly accepting that the act-of-state doctrine was no longer a hindrance. Bernstein v. N.V. Nederlandsche–Amerikaansche Stoomvaart–Maatschappij, 210 F.2d 375 (2d Cir. 1954). However, the *Bernstein* holding can be, and later was, limited to its facts: the Nazi government was both defunct (and therefore could not be offended by American judicial action) and, uniquely, had been condemned universally. *See e.g., Sabbatino, supra*, 376 U.S. at 428.

The issue arose again during the *Sabbatino* litigation. The Second Circuit interpreted two State Department letters as "express[ing] a belief on the part of those responsible for the conduct of our foreign affairs that the courts here should decide the status here of Cuban decrees," and, applying the *Bernstein* exception, the court lifted the act of state bar. Banco Nacional de Cuba v. Sabbatino, 307 F.2d 845, 858 (2d Cir. 1962). When the case reached the Supreme Court, the United States as *amicus curiae* urged reversal, averring that the lower court had misinterpreted the letters. Sabbatino, *supra,* 376 U.S. at 419; 6 M. Whiteman, *Digest of International Law* 24 (1968). In response, the Court expressly declined to apply the *Bernstein* exception. 376 U.S. at 419. Note, however, that Harlan's strong policy stance in favor of the act-of-state doctrine seems to reject executive interventions of the *Bernstein* kind. *Id.* at 432–33.

In *First National City Bank v. Banco Nacional de Cuba,* the Supreme Court reached the *Bernstein* exception issue. 406 U.S. 759, 92 S.Ct. 1808, 32 L.Ed.2d 466 (1972). The litigation involved a loan, secured by collateral, by First National to the pre-revolutionary Cuban government. In 1960, the Castro regime confiscated First National property in Cuba. In retaliation, First National cashed in the collateral, receiving more than was due on the outstanding loan (but less than the Bank's total loss due to confiscation). Banco Nacional brought suit to recover this excess. First National, on the basis of the other confiscations, counterclaimed to the extent of the Cuban claim. The Second Circuit, reversing the district court, asserted that *Sabbatino* prevented judicial consideration of the U.S. bank's counterclaim. Banco Nacional de Cuba v. First National City Bank of New York, 431 F.2d 394 (2d Cir. 1970). The Hickenlooper law did not reverse this result since it only applied to confiscated property brought into the United States. *Id.* at 399–402.

While appeal to the Supreme Court was pending, the State Department intervened. The Department wrote to the Court that "the act of state doctrine should not be applied to bar consideration of a defendant's counterclaim or set-off against the Government of Cuba in this or like cases." *Reprinted in* 442 F.2d at 538. In response, the Supreme Court vacated the circuit court decision and remanded the case. First National City Bank v. Banco Nacional de Cuba, 400 U.S. 1019, 91 S.Ct. 581, 27 L.Ed.2d 630 (1971). Despite the letter, the Second Circuit, re-asserting its previous position in the case, refused to follow the State Department's suggestion. It limited the *Bernstein* exception to its specific circumstances. Banco Nacional de Cuba v. First National City Bank of New York, 442 F.2d 530, 534 (2d Cir. 1971).

On appeal, the Supreme Court reversed in a 5–4 decision. First National City Bank v. Banco Nacional de Cuba, 406 U.S. 759, 92 S.Ct. 1808, 32 L.Ed.2d 466 (1972). The five justices voting for reversal offered divergent rationales. Justice Rehnquist, joined by Chief Justice Burger and Justice White, approved the *Bernstein* exception: "We conclude that where the Executive Branch, charged as it is with primary responsibility for the conduct of foreign affairs, expressly represents to the Court that application of act of state doctrine would not advance the interests of American foreign policy, that doctrine should not be applied by the courts." 406 U.S. at 759, 768. Justice Douglas, concurring, based his opinion on *National City Bank v. Republic of China,* 348 U.S. 356, 75 S.Ct. 423, 99 L.Ed. 389 (1955), elaborating that to allow Cuba to enter U.S. courts and make its claim without that claim being subject to setoff "would permit Cuba to have its cake and eat it too." 406 U.S. at 772. He continued, "It is that principle, not the *Bernstein* exception, which should govern here." *Id.* at 772–73 (footnote omitted). Justice Powell, concurring, also disavowed the *Bernstein* exception, reporting that he "would be uncomfortable with a doctrine which would require the judiciary to receive the Executive's permission before invoking its jurisdiction." *Id.* at 773. The problem for Powell was that he believed *Sabbatino* itself to have been wrongly decided. *Id.* at 774–75. He concluded that "federal courts have an obligation to hear cases such as this ... [u]nless it appears that an exercise of jurisdiction would interfere with delicate foreign relations conducted by the political branches." *Id.* at 775–76.

The dissent, authored by Justice Brennan, calculated that a majority of the Court had rejected the *Bernstein* exception. *Id.* at 776–77. It also argued that *Sabbatino* had implicitly rejected the *Bernstein* exception and, applying Harlan's reasoning in *Sabbatino,* argued that, although the Executive had urged that the act-of-state doctrine not be applied, it had done so only because it "anticipate[d] a favorable ruling," and if the Court upset that expectation, its ruling would "frustrate the conduct of this country's foreign relations." *Id.* at 783–84. Second, the rationale for applying the act-of-state doctrine included other concerns: for example, the lack of international consensus with respect to the law applicable to expropriation, the respect due to an existing and recognized foreign government, and the ability of the Executive to negotiate an overall settlement. *Id.* at 788. Brennan's analysis continued:

> In short, *Sabbatino* held that the validity of a foreign act of state in certain circumstances is a " 'political question' " not cognizable in our courts. ... The Executive Branch, however extensive its powers in the area of foreign affairs, cannot by simple stipulation change a political question into a cognizable claim.

Id. at 787–89. Brennan was also troubled by other ramifications of the decision: making the courts fill the Executive's role in the advocacy of new international norms, giving the Executive wide discretion to pick and choose favored litigants, and ultimately debasing international law, since that law could not be effectively pronounced by courts of the world's "principal exponent of the free-enterprise system" whose "determination of international law is made to depend upon a prior political authorization." *Id. at 790–93. See also* Alfred Dunhill of London, Inc. v. Republic of Cuba, 425 U.S. 682, 96 S.Ct. 1854, 48 L.Ed.2d 301 (1976).

4. *Other Limitations to the Doctrine.* In addition to situations where non-application of the act-of-state doctrine is directed by the Congress (note 2 above) or by the Executive (note 3 above), there are circumstances where courts have declined to apply the doctrine or declared its inherent limitations. Core limitations were articulated in *W.S. Kirkpatrick & Co. v. Environmental Tectonics Corp.*, excerpted above, in which the Supreme Court explained that the cases applying the act-of-state doctrine all "would have required a court in the United States to declare invalid the official act of a foreign sovereign performed within its own territory."

One limitation this suggests, clearly, is the need to declare an official act of a foreign sovereign to be invalid—or, as the Court also put it, the imperative that courts respecting the act-of-state doctrine must deem valid those sovereign acts. In *W.W. Kirkpatrick* itself, the issue before the court was whether an unlawful motivation could be imputed to a foreign official in the performance of his duties so as to satisfy U.S. requirements for a civil recovery by the plaintiff.

Second, the official act concerned must be within the sovereign's territory. Prior case law established that the act-of-state doctrine does not apply where the foreign government seeks to affect property located outside its territory. *See* Republic of Iraq v. First Nat'l City Bank, 353 F.2d 47 (2d Cir. 1965). Situs questions become particularly important in cases involving actions against intangibles, such as credits, debts, or securities.

Third, a clear and countervailing international law principle may contraindicate application of the act-of-state doctrine. *Sabbatino, supra*, explained that "the greater the degree of codification or consensus concerning a particular area of international law, the more appropriate it is for the judiciary to render decisions regarding it." 376 U.S. at 428, 84 S. Ct. at 940. Even the expropriation issue in *Sabbatino* was susceptible to reconsideration under the appropriate circumstances.

In *Kalamazoo Spice Extraction Co. v. Ethiopia*, 729 F.2d 422 (6th Cir. 1984), the district court was asked to decide a counterclaim by a U.S. defendant for the expropriation of his property by the revolutionary government of Ethiopia. Although the U.S.–Ethiopia Treaty of Amity and Economic Relations, U.S.–Eth., Sept. 7, 1951, 4 U.S.T. 2134, 206 U.N.T.S. 41, included a standard of "prompt payment of just and effective compensation" in the event that one party expropriated property belonging to nationals of the other, the district court applied the act-of-state doctrine and dismissed the case. 543 F.Supp. 1224 (W.D.Mich. 1982). Before the appeal was heard, the Department of State transmitted a letter to the Sixth Circuit stating: "When, as in this case, there is a controlling legal standard for compensation, we believe that adjudication would not be inconsistent with foreign policy interests under the Act of State Doctrine." On appeal, the Sixth Circuit accepted the position expressed in the letter.

Increasingly, but not universally, the presence of a "controlling legal standard" is cited as a basis for resisting application of the act-of-state doctrine to cases alleging human rights violations by a foreign government in its territory. *See, e.g.*, Doe I v. Unocal Corp., 395 F.3d 932, 959 (9th Cir. 2002) ("[b]ecause jus cogens violations are, by definition, internationally denounced, there is a high degree of international consensus against them"); Kadic v. Karadzic, 70 F.3d 232, 250 (2d Cir. 1995) (claiming that "it would be a rare case in which the act of state doctrine precluded suit under [the Alien Tort Statute, 28 U.S.C. § 1350]"). Some courts have explained similar results by claiming that at least some acts—for example, torture, extrajudicial killing, and crimes against humanity—"committed in violation of the norms of customary international law, are not deemed official acts for purposes of the act of state doctrine." Lizarbe v. Rondon, 642 F.Supp.2d 473, 488 (D. Md. 2009); *see* Sarei v. Rio Tinto, 487 F.3d 1193, 1208–10 (9th Cir. 2007) (suggesting that jus cogens norms, including claims of racial discrimination, are not public acts subjected to the act-of-state doctrine, but other customary international law violations may be), *vacated*, 499 F.3d 923 (9th Cir. 2007), *vacated*, 499 F.3d 923 (9th Cir. 2007).

Fourth, Sabbatino advised that "the balance of relevant considerations may also be shifted if the government which perpetrated the challenged act of state is no longer in existence." 376 U.S. at 428, 84 S. Ct. at 940. *See, e.g., Bigio v. Coca–Cola Co.*, 239 F.3d 440, 453 (2d Cir. 2001) (declining to dismiss on act-of-state grounds an Alien Tort Statute action alleging nationalization by the Egyptian government during the 1960s, over thirty years prior to suit). What sort of incentives does this create?

Fifth, and finally, *Sabbatino* observed that "the less important the implications of an issue are for our foreign relations, the weaker the justification for exclusivity in the political branches." 376 U.S. at 428, 84 S. Ct. at 940. How adept are courts likely to be at this inquiry?

Other limitations have been suggested more tentatively and appear to have less purchase. For example, it has been suggested that the act-of-state doctrine may not be invoked by counterclaim. In *First National City Bank v. Banco Nacional de Cuba, supra*, a foreign government filed a claim, and a U.S. national responded with a counterclaim. The foreign government raised the act-of-state doctrine as a defense to the counterclaim. The Supreme Court declined to apply the doctrine. Justice Douglas took the position that the act-of-state doctrine should not be applied to counterclaims. 406 U.S. at 770–73 (citing to National City Bank v. China, 348 U.S. 356, 75 S.Ct. 423, 99 L.Ed. 389 (1955)). None of the other justices, however, found that issue dispositive.

In *Alfred Dunhill of London, Inc. v. Cuba, supra*, three justices argued that the act-of-state doctrine did not apply to a foreign sovereign's *commercial* acts, even though those acts were done within its own territory. According to those justices, such acts are incapable of examination in U.S. courts only if U.S. jurisdiction over the conduct is limited under international jurisdictional principles. This possible exception has occasionally been suggested since, but without evident success. *See, e.g.*, *In re Refined Petroleum Products Antitrust Litigation*, 649 F.Supp.2d 572, 595 (S.D. Tex. 2009) (rejecting such a "commercial activities" exception, and noting that "[a]part from *Dunhill*, plaintiffs cite no judicial authority in support of their argument that the act of state doctrine is inapplicable under the facts of this case because the acts of which they complain are purely commercial acts as opposed to sovereign—i.e., governmental—acts.").

5. *Complaints and Criticisms*. Despite the several decades-long history of the act-of-state doctrine and its perhaps diminishing importance in U.S. foreign relations law, some basic questions remain unsettled. Critics have often pointed to the shifting and not-altogether-clear rationales for the act-of-state doctrine; in general, courts seem to have moved from an international comity rationale to a separation-of-powers rationale. *See, e.g. Sabbatino, supra* this section; *Restatement (Third) on the Foreign Relations Law of the United States*, § 443, rptr.'s note 2 (1987). Which is a more convincing rationale for the act-of-state doctrine? One way of thinking about the issue that combines both rationales is to realize that in terms of comity, states "sit in judgment" of the actions of other states under international law all the time—but this judgment is usually exercised by the Executive Branch in its diplomatic dealings with other nations, rather than by the judiciary. Is this as it should be? Why?

Critics also bemoan the lack of a bright-line rule for courts as to when and whether to apply the act-of-state doctrine. Would a such a clear rule be preferable, thereby increasing consistency and predictability (especially for those wishing to engage in commercial transactions involving foreign states), or is judicial discretion appropriate in determining when the court should make forays into the realm of sensitive foreign policy issues, even at some cost to predictability?

For commentary, see Louis Henkin, *Act of State Today: Recollections in Tranquility*, 6 COLUM. J. TRANSNAT'L L. 175 (1967); Malvina Halberstam, *Sabbatino Resurrected: The Act of State Doctrine in the Revised Restatement of U.S. Foreign Relations Law*, 79 AM. J. INT'L L. 68 (1985); Michael J. Bazyler, *Abolishing the Act of State Doctrine*, 134 U. PA. L. REV. 325 (1986). Others suggest alternative ways of looking at the doctrine. Daniel C.K. Chow, *Rethinking the Act of State Doctrine: An Analysis in Terms of Jurisdiction to Prescribe*, 62 WASH. L. REV. 397 (1987); Michael Ramsey, *Acts of State and Foreign Sovereign Obligations*, 39 HARV. INT'L L.J. 1 (1998); Jack L. Goldsmith, *The New Formalism in United States Foreign Relations Law*, 70 U. COLO. L. REV. 1395 (1999); Jake S. Tyshow, *Informal Foreign Affairs Formalism: The Act of State Doctrine and the Reinterpretation of International Comity*, 43 VA. J. INT'L L. 275 (2002); Patrick W. Pearsall, *Means/Ends Reciprocity in the Act of State Doctrine*, 43 COLUM. J. TRANSNAT'L L. 999 (2005).

APPENDIX I

U.S. CONSTITUTION

■ ■ ■

[On September 17, 1787, the U.S. Constitution was adopted by the framers meeting in convention in Philadelphia. The Convention transmitted the Constitution to the Congress then operating under the Articles of Confederation, which approved it. The Congress, in turn, submitted the Constitution to the thirteen states for ratification. After the ninth state (New Hampshire) ratified the Constitution on June 21, 1788, the requirements were met for its entry into force (eventually all thirteen states ratified). On March 4, 1789, the new federal government began operating under the Constitution. Today, the U.S. Constitution is the oldest written constitution that is still in use.

The text that is reproduced below does not include text that has been repealed, but does include amendments adopted since its entry into force. For ease of reference, individual clauses are numbered using square brackets.]

We the People of the United States, in Order to form a more perfect Union, establish Justice, insure domestic Tranquility, provide for the common defence, promote the general Welfare, and secure the Blessings of Liberty to ourselves and our Posterity, do ordain and establish this Constitution for the United States of America.

Article I

Section 1

All legislative Powers herein granted shall be vested in a Congress of the United States, which shall consist of a Senate and House of Representatives.

Section 2

[1] The House of Representatives shall be composed of Members chosen every second Year by the People of the several States, and the Electors in each State shall have the Qualifications requisite for Electors of the most numerous Branch of the State Legislature.

[2] No Person shall be a Representative who shall not have attained to the Age of twenty five Years, and been seven Years a Citizen of the United States, and who shall not, when elected, be an Inhabitant of that State in which he shall be chosen.

[3] Representatives and direct Taxes shall be apportioned among the several States which may be included within this Union, according to their respective Numbers, which shall be determined by adding to the whole Number of free Persons, including those bound to Service for a Term of Years, and excluding Indians not taxed, three fifths of all other Persons. The actual Enumeration shall be made within three Years after the first Meeting of the Congress of the United States, and within every subsequent Term of ten Years, in such Manner as they shall by Law direct. The Number of Representatives shall not exceed one for every thirty Thousand, but each State shall have at Least one Representative; and until such enumeration shall be made, the State of New Hampshire shall be entitled to choose three, Massachusetts eight, Rhode Island and Providence Plantations one, Connecticut five, New York six, New Jersey four, Pennsylvania eight, Delaware one, Maryland six, Virginia ten, North Carolina five, South Carolina five, and Georgia three.

[4] When vacancies happen in the Representation from any State, the Executive Authority thereof shall issue Writs of Election to fill such Vacancies.

[5] The House of Representatives shall choose their Speaker and other Officers; and shall have the sole Power of Impeachment.

Section 3

[1] The Senate of the United States shall be composed of two Senators from each State, chosen by the Legislature thereof, for six Years; and each Senator shall have one Vote.

[2] Immediately after they shall be assembled in Consequence of the first Election, they shall be divided as equally as may be into three Classes. The Seats of the Senators of the first Class shall be vacated at the Expiration of the second Year, of the second Class at the Expiration of the fourth Year, and of the third Class at the Expiration of the sixth Year, so that one third may be chosen every second Year; and if Vacancies happen by Resignation, or otherwise, during the Recess of the Legislature of any State, the Executive thereof may make temporary Appointments until the next Meeting of the Legislature, which shall then fill such Vacancies.

[3] No person shall be a Senator who shall not have attained to the Age of thirty Years, and been nine Years a Citizen of the United States, and who shall not, when elected, be an Inhabitant of that State for which he shall be chosen.

[4] The Vice President of the United States shall be President of the Senate, but shall have no Vote, unless they be equally divided.

[5] The Senate shall choose their other Officers, and also a President pro tempore, in the Absence of the Vice President, or when he shall exercise the Office of President of the United States.

[6] The Senate shall have the sole Power to try all Impeachments. When sitting for that Purpose, they shall be on Oath or Affirmation. When the President of the United States is tried, the Chief Justice shall preside: And no Person shall be convicted without the Concurrence of two thirds of the Members present.

[7] Judgment in Cases of Impeachment shall not extend further than to removal from Office, and disqualification to hold and enjoy any Office of honor, Trust or Profit under the United States: but the Party convicted shall nevertheless be liable and subject to Indictment, Trial, Judgment and Punishment, according to Law.

Section 4

[1] The Times, Places and Manner of holding Elections for Senators and Representatives, shall be prescribed in each State by the Legislature thereof; but the Congress may at any time by Law make or alter such Regulations, except as to the Place of choosing Senators.

[2] The Congress shall assemble at least once in every Year, and such Meeting shall be on the first Monday in December, unless they shall by Law appoint a different Day.

Section 5

[1] Each House shall be the Judge of the Elections, Returns and Qualifications of its own Members, and a Majority of each shall constitute a Quorum to do Business; but a smaller Number may adjourn from day to day, and may be authorized to compel the Attendance of absent Members, in such Manner, and under such Penalties as each House may provide.

[2] Each House may determine the Rules of its Proceedings, punish its Members for disorderly Behavior, and, with the Concurrence of two thirds, expel a Member.

[3] Each House shall keep a Journal of its Proceedings, and from time to time publish the same, excepting such Parts as may in their Judgment require Secrecy; and the Yeas and Nays of the Members of either House on any question shall, at the Desire of one fifth of those Present, be entered on the Journal.

[4] Neither House, during the Session of Congress, shall, without the Consent of the other, adjourn for more than three days, nor to any other Place than that in which the two Houses shall be sitting.

Section 6

[1] The Senators and Representatives shall receive a Compensation for their Services, to be ascertained by Law, and paid out of the Treasury of the United States. They shall in all Cases, except Treason, Felony and

Breach of the Peace, be privileged from Arrest during their Attendance at the Session of their respective Houses, and in going to and returning from the same; and for any Speech or Debate in either House, they shall not be questioned in any other Place.

[2] No Senator or Representative shall, during the Time for which he was elected, be appointed to any civil Office under the Authority of the United States which shall have been created, or the Emoluments whereof shall have been increased during such time; and no Person holding any Office under the United States, shall be a Member of either House during his Continuance in Office.

Section 7

[1] All bills for raising Revenue shall originate in the House of Representatives; but the Senate may propose or concur with amendments as on other Bills.

[2] Every Bill which shall have passed the House of Representatives and the Senate, shall, before it become a Law, be presented to the President of the United States; If he approve he shall sign it, but if not he shall return it, with his Objections to that House in which it shall have originated, who shall enter the Objections at large on their Journal, and proceed to reconsider it. If after such Reconsideration two thirds of that House shall agree to pass the Bill, it shall be sent, together with the Objections, to the other House, by which it shall likewise be reconsidered, and if approved by two thirds of that House, it shall become a Law. But in all such Cases the Votes of both Houses shall be determined by Yeas and Nays, and the Names of the Persons voting for and against the Bill shall be entered on the Journal of each House respectively. If any Bill shall not be returned by the President within ten Days (Sundays excepted) after it shall have been presented to him, the Same shall be a Law, in like Manner as if he had signed it, unless the Congress by their Adjournment prevent its Return, in which Case it shall not be a Law.

[3] Every Order, Resolution, or Vote to which the Concurrence of the Senate and House of Representatives may be necessary (except on a question of Adjournment) shall be presented to the President of the United States; and before the Same shall take Effect, shall be approved by him, or being disapproved by him, shall be repassed by two thirds of the Senate and House of Representatives, according to the Rules and Limitations prescribed in the Case of a Bill.

Section 8

[1] The Congress shall have Power To lay and collect Taxes, Duties, Imposts and Excises, to pay the Debts and provide for the common Defence and general Welfare of the United States; but all Duties, Imposts and Excises shall be uniform throughout the United States;

[2] To borrow Money on the credit of the United States;

[3] To regulate Commerce with foreign Nations, and among the several States, and with the Indian Tribes;

[4] To establish an uniform Rule of Naturalization, and uniform Laws on the subject of Bankruptcies throughout the United States;

[5] To coin Money, regulate the Value thereof, and of foreign Coin, and fix the Standard of Weights and Measures;

[6] To provide for the Punishment of counterfeiting the Securities and current Coin of the United States;

[7] To establish Post Offices and Post Roads;

[8] To promote the Progress of Science and useful Arts, by securing for limited Times to Authors and Inventors the exclusive Right to their respective Writings and Discoveries;

[9] To constitute Tribunals inferior to the supreme Court;

[10] To define and punish Piracies and Felonies committed on the high Seas, and Offences against the Law of Nations;

[11] To declare War, grant Letters of Marque and Reprisal, and make Rules concerning Captures on Land and Water;

[12] To raise and support Armies, but no Appropriation of Money to that Use shall be for a longer Term than two Years;

[13] To provide and maintain a Navy;

[14] To make Rules for the Government and Regulation of the land and naval Forces;

[15] To provide for calling forth the Militia to execute the Laws of the Union, suppress Insurrections and repel Invasions;

[16] To provide for organizing, arming, and disciplining the Militia, and for governing such Part of them as may be employed in the Service of the United States, reserving to the States respectively, the Appointment of the Officers, and the Authority of training the Militia according to the discipline prescribed by Congress;

[17] To exercise exclusive Legislation in all Cases whatsoever, over such District (not exceeding ten Miles square) as may, by Cession of particular States, and the Acceptance of Congress, become the Seat of the Government of the United States, and to exercise like Authority over all Places purchased by the Consent of the Legislature of the State in which the Same shall be, for the Erection of Forts, Magazines, Arsenals, dock-Yards, and other needful Buildings; and

[18] To make all Laws which shall be necessary and proper for carrying into Execution the foregoing Powers, and all other Powers vested by this Constitution in the Government of the United States, or in any Department or Officer thereof.

Section 9

[1] The Migration or Importation of such Persons as any of the States now existing shall think proper to admit, shall not be prohibited by the Congress prior to the Year one thousand eight hundred and eight, but a Tax or Duty may be imposed on such Importation, not exceeding ten dollars for each Person.

[2] The Privilege of the Writ of Habeas Corpus shall not be suspended, unless when in Cases of Rebellion or Invasion the public Safety may require it.

[3] No Bill of Attainder or ex post facto Law shall be passed.

[4] No Capitation, or other direct Tax shall be laid, unless in Proportion to the Census or Enumeration herein before directed to be taken.

[5] No Tax or Duty shall be laid on Articles exported from any State.

[6] No Preference shall be given by any Regulation of Commerce or Revenue to the Ports of one State over those of another: nor shall Vessels bound to, or from, one State, be obliged to enter, clear, or pay Duties in another.

[7] No Money shall be drawn from the Treasury, but in Consequence of Appropriations made by Law; and a regular Statement and Account of the Receipts and Expenditures of all public Money shall be published from time to time.

[8] No Title of Nobility shall be granted by the United States: And no Person holding any Office of Profit or Trust under them, shall, without the Consent of the Congress, accept of any present, Emolument, Office, or Title, of any kind whatever, from any King, Prince or foreign State.

Section 10

[1] No State shall enter into any Treaty, Alliance, or Confederation; grant Letters of Marque and Reprisal; coin Money; emit Bills of Credit; make any Thing but gold and silver Coin a Tender in Payment of Debts; pass any Bill of Attainder, ex post facto Law, or Law impairing the Obligation of Contracts, or grant any Title of Nobility.

[2] No State shall, without the Consent of the Congress, lay any Imposts or Duties on Imports or Exports, except what may be absolutely necessary for executing its inspection Laws: and the net Produce of all Duties and Imposts, laid by any State on Imports or Exports, shall be for the Use of the Treasury of the United States; and all such Laws shall be subject to the Revision and Control of the Congress.

[3] No State shall, without the Consent of Congress, lay any Duty of Tonnage, keep Troops, or Ships of War in time of Peace, enter into any Agreement or Compact with another State, or with a foreign Power, or engage in War, unless actually invaded, or in such imminent Danger as will not admit of delay.

Article II

Section 1

[1] The executive Power shall be vested in a President of the United States of America. He shall hold his Office during the Term of four Years, and, together with the Vice President chosen for the same Term, be elected, as follows:

[2] Each State shall appoint, in such Manner as the Legislature thereof may direct, a Number of Electors, equal to the whole Number of Senators and Representatives to which the State may be entitled in the Congress: but no Senator or Representative, or Person holding an Office of Trust or Profit under the United States, shall be appointed an Elector.

[3] The Electors shall meet in their respective States, and vote by Ballot for two Persons, of whom one at least shall not be an Inhabitant of the same State with themselves. And they shall make a List of all the Persons voted for, and of the Number of Votes for each; which List they shall sign and certify, and transmit sealed to the Seat of the Government of the United States, directed to the President of the Senate. The President of the Senate shall, in the Presence of the Senate and House of Representatives, open all the Certificates, and the Votes shall then be counted. The Person having the greatest Number of Votes shall be the President, if such Number be a Majority of the whole Number of Electors appointed; and if there be more than one who have such Majority, and have an equal Number of Votes, then the House of Representatives shall immediately choose by Ballot one of them for President; and if no Person have a Majority, then from the five highest on the List the said House shall in like Manner choose the President. But in choosing the President, the Votes shall be taken by States, the Representation from each State having one Vote; a quorum for this Purpose shall consist of a Member or Members from two thirds of the States, and a Majority of all the States shall be necessary to a Choice. In every Case, after the Choice of the President, the Person having the greatest Number of Votes of the Electors shall be the Vice President. But if there should remain two or more who have equal Votes, the Senate shall choose from them by Ballot the Vice President.

[4] The Congress may determine the Time of choosing the Electors, and the Day on which they shall give their Votes; which Day shall be the same throughout the United States.

[5] No Person except a natural born Citizen, or a Citizen of the United States, at the time of the Adoption of this Constitution, shall be eligible to the Office of President; neither shall any Person be eligible to that Office who shall not have attained to the Age of thirty-five Years, and been fourteen Years a Resident within the United States.

[6] In Case of the Removal of the President from Office, or of his Death, Resignation, or Inability to discharge the Powers and Duties of the said Office, the Same shall devolve on the Vice President, and the

Congress may by Law provide for the Case of Removal, Death, Resignation or Inability, both of the President and Vice President, declaring what Officer shall then act as President, and such Officer shall act accordingly, until the Disability be removed, or a President shall be elected.

[7] The President shall, at stated Times, receive for his Services, a Compensation, which shall neither be increased nor diminished during the Period for which he shall have been elected, and he shall not receive within that Period any other Emolument from the United States, or any of them.

[8] Before he enter on the Execution of his Office, he shall take the following Oath or Affirmation: "I do solemnly swear (or affirm) that I will faithfully execute the Office of President of the United States, and will to the best of my Ability, preserve, protect and defend the Constitution of the United States."

Section 2

[1] The President shall be Commander in Chief of the Army and Navy of the United States, and of the Militia of the several States, when called into the actual Service of the United States; he may require the Opinion, in writing, of the principal Officer in each of the executive Departments, upon any Subject relating to the Duties of their respective Offices, and he shall have Power to Grant Reprieves and Pardons for Offenses against the United States, except in Cases of Impeachment.

[2] He shall have Power, by and with the Advice and Consent of the Senate, to make Treaties, provided two thirds of the Senators present concur; and he shall nominate, and by and with the Advice and Consent of the Senate, shall appoint Ambassadors, other public Ministers and Consuls, Judges of the supreme Court, and all other Officers of the United States, whose Appointments are not herein otherwise provided for, and which shall be established by Law: but the Congress may by Law vest the Appointment of such inferior Officers, as they think proper, in the President alone, in the Courts of Law, or in the Heads of Departments.

[3] The President shall have Power to fill up all Vacancies that may happen during the Recess of the Senate, by granting Commissions which shall expire at the End of their next Session.

Section 3

He shall from time to time give to the Congress Information of the State of the Union, and recommend to their Consideration such Measures as he shall judge necessary and expedient; he may, on extraordinary Occasions, convene both Houses, or either of them, and in Case of Disagreement between them, with Respect to the Time of Adjournment, he may adjourn them to such Time as he shall think proper; he shall receive Ambassadors and other public Ministers; he shall take Care that the Laws be faithfully executed, and shall Commission all the Officers of the United States.

Section 4

The President, Vice President and all Civil Officers of the United States, shall be removed from Office on Impeachment for, and Conviction of, Treason, Bribery, or other high Crimes and Misdemeanors.

Article III

Section 1

The judicial Power of the United States, shall be vested in one supreme Court, and in such inferior Courts as the Congress may from time to time ordain and establish. The Judges, both of the supreme and inferior Courts, shall hold their Offices during good Behavior, and shall, at stated Times, receive for their Services a Compensation which shall not be diminished during their Continuance in Office.

Section 2

[1] The judicial Power shall extend to all Cases, in Law and Equity, arising under this Constitution, the Laws of the United States, and Treaties made, or which shall be made, under their Authority; to all Cases affecting Ambassadors, other public Ministers and Consuls; to all Cases of admiralty and maritime Jurisdiction; to Controversies to which the United States shall be a Party; to Controversies between two or more States; between a State and Citizens of another State; between Citizens of different States; between Citizens of the same State claiming Lands under Grants of different States, and between a State, or the Citizens thereof, and foreign States, Citizens or Subjects.

[2] In all Cases affecting Ambassadors, other public Ministers and Consuls, and those in which a State shall be Party, the supreme Court shall have original Jurisdiction. In all the other Cases before mentioned, the supreme Court shall have appellate Jurisdiction, both as to Law and Fact, with such Exceptions, and under such Regulations as the Congress shall make.

[3] The Trial of all Crimes, except in Cases of Impeachment, shall be by Jury; and such Trial shall be held in the State where the said Crimes shall have been committed; but when not committed within any State, the Trial shall be at such Place or Places as the Congress may by Law have directed.

Section 3

[1] Treason against the United States, shall consist only in levying War against them, or in adhering to their Enemies, giving them Aid and Comfort. No Person shall be convicted of Treason unless on the Testimony of two Witnesses to the same overt Act, or on Confession in open Court.

[2] The Congress shall have Power to declare the Punishment of Treason, but no Attainder of Treason shall work Corruption of Blood, or Forfeiture except during the Life of the Person attainted.

Article IV

Section 1

Full Faith and Credit shall be given in each State to the public Acts, Records, and judicial Proceedings of every other State. And the Congress may by general Laws prescribe the Manner in which such Acts, Records and Proceedings shall be proved, and the Effect thereof.

Section 2

[1] The Citizens of each State shall be entitled to all Privileges and Immunities of Citizens in the several States.

[2] A Person charged in any State with Treason, Felony, or other Crime, who shall flee from Justice, and be found in another State, shall on Demand of the executive Authority of the State from which he fled, be delivered up, to be removed to the State having Jurisdiction of the Crime.

[3] No Person held to Service or Labour in one State, under the Laws thereof, escaping into another, shall, in Consequence of any Law or Regulation therein, be discharged from such Service or Labour, but shall be delivered up on Claim of the Party to whom such Service or Labour may be due.

Section 3

[1] New States may be admitted by the Congress into this Union; but no new States shall be formed or erected within the Jurisdiction of any other State; nor any State be formed by the Junction of two or more States, or parts of States, without the Consent of the Legislatures of the States concerned as well as of the Congress.

[2] The Congress shall have Power to dispose of and make all needful Rules and Regulations respecting the Territory or other Property belonging to the United States; and nothing in this Constitution shall be so construed as to Prejudice any Claims of the United States, or of any particular State.

Section 4

The United States shall guarantee to every State in this Union a Republican Form of Government, and shall protect each of them against Invasion; and on Application of the Legislature, or of the Executive (when the Legislature cannot be convened) against domestic Violence.

Article V

The Congress, whenever two thirds of both Houses shall deem it necessary, shall propose Amendments to this Constitution, or, on the Application of the Legislatures of two thirds of the several States, shall call a Convention for proposing Amendments, which, in either Case, shall be valid to all Intents and Purposes, as Part of this Constitution, when ratified by the Legislatures of three fourths of the several States, or by

Conventions in three fourths thereof, as the one or the other Mode of Ratification may be proposed by the Congress; Provided that no Amendment which may be made prior to the Year One thousand eight hundred and eight shall in any Manner affect the first and fourth Clauses in the Ninth Section of the first Article; and that no State, without its Consent, shall be deprived of its equal Suffrage in the Senate.

Article VI

[1] All Debts contracted and Engagements entered into, before the Adoption of this Constitution, shall be as valid against the United States under this Constitution, as under the Confederation.

[2] This Constitution, and the Laws of the United States which shall be made in Pursuance thereof; and all Treaties made, or which shall be made, under the Authority of the United States, shall be the supreme Law of the Land; and the Judges in every State shall be bound thereby, any Thing in the Constitution or Laws of any State to the Contrary notwithstanding.

[3] The Senators and Representatives before mentioned, and the Members of the several State Legislatures, and all executive and judicial Officers, both of the United States and of the several States, shall be bound by Oath or Affirmation, to support this Constitution; but no religious Test shall ever be required as a Qualification to any Office or public Trust under the United States.

Article VII

The Ratification of the Conventions of nine States, shall be sufficient for the Establishment of this Constitution between the States so ratifying the Same.

Done in Convention by the Unanimous Consent of the States present the Seventeenth Day of September in the Year of our Lord one thousand seven hundred and Eighty seven and of the Independence of the United States of America the Twelfth.

In Witness whereof We have hereunto subscribed our Names.

George Washington—President and deputy from Virginia

New Hampshire—John Langdon, Nicholas Gilman

Massachusetts—Nathaniel Gorham, Rufus King

Connecticut—William Samuel Johnson, Roger Sherman

New York—Alexander Hamilton

New Jersey—William Livingston, David Brearley, William Paterson, Jonathan Dayton

Pennsylvania—Benjamin Franklin, Thomas Mifflin, Robert Morris, George Clymer, Thomas FitzSimons, Jared Ingersoll, James Wilson, Gouvernour Morris

Delaware—George Read, Gunning Bedford Jr., John Dickinson, Richard Bassett, Jacob Broom

Maryland—James McHenry, Daniel of St Thomas Jenifer, Daniel Carroll

Virginia—John Blair, James Madison Jr.

North Carolina—William Blount, Richard Dobbs Spaight, Hugh Williamson

South Carolina—John Rutledge, Charles Cotesworth Pinckney, Charles Pinckney, Pierce Butler

Georgia—William Few, Abraham Baldwin

Attest: William Jackson, Secretary

Amendment 1 [1791]

Congress shall make no law respecting an establishment of religion, or prohibiting the free exercise thereof; or abridging the freedom of speech, or of the press; or the right of the people peaceably to assemble, and to petition the Government for a redress of grievances.

Amendment 2 [1791]

A well regulated Militia, being necessary to the security of a free State, the right of the people to keep and bear Arms, shall not be infringed.

Amendment 3 [1791]

No Soldier shall, in time of peace be quartered in any house, without the consent of the Owner, nor in time of war, but in a manner to be prescribed by law.

Amendment 4 [1791]

The right of the people to be secure in their persons, houses, papers, and effects, against unreasonable searches and seizures, shall not be violated, and no Warrants shall issue, but upon probable cause, supported by Oath or affirmation, and particularly describing the place to be searched, and the persons or things to be seized.

Amendment 5 [1791]

No person shall be held to answer for a capital, or otherwise infamous crime, unless on a presentment or indictment of a Grand Jury, except in cases arising in the land or naval forces, or in the Militia, when in actual service in time of War or public danger; nor shall any person be subject for the same offence to be twice put in jeopardy of life or limb; nor shall be compelled in any criminal case to be a witness against himself, nor be deprived of life, liberty, or property, without due process of law; nor shall private property be taken for public use, without just compensation.

Amendment 6 [1791]

In all criminal prosecutions, the accused shall enjoy the right to a speedy and public trial, by an impartial jury of the State and district wherein the crime shall have been committed, which district shall have been previously ascertained by law, and to be informed of the nature and cause of the accusation; to be confronted with the witnesses against him; to have compulsory process for obtaining witnesses in his favor, and to have the Assistance of Counsel for his defence.

Amendment 7 [1791]

In Suits at common law, where the value in controversy shall exceed twenty dollars, the right of trial by jury shall be preserved, and no fact tried by a jury, shall be otherwise re-examined in any Court of the United States, than according to the rules of the common law.

Amendment 8 [1791]

Excessive bail shall not be required, nor excessive fines imposed, nor cruel and unusual punishments inflicted.

Amendment 9 [1791]

The enumeration in the Constitution, of certain rights, shall not be construed to deny or disparage others retained by the people.

Amendment 10 [1791]

The powers not delegated to the United States by the Constitution, nor prohibited by it to the States, are reserved to the States respectively, or to the people.

Amendment 11 [1798]

The Judicial power of the United States shall not be construed to extend to any suit in law or equity, commenced or prosecuted against one of the United States by Citizens of another State, or by Citizens or Subjects of any Foreign State.

Amendment 12 [1804]

The Electors shall meet in their respective states, and vote by ballot for President and Vice President, one of whom, at least, shall not be an inhabitant of the same state with themselves; they shall name in their ballots the person voted for as President, and in distinct ballots the person voted for as Vice President, and they shall make distinct lists of all persons voted for as President, and of all persons voted for as Vice President, and of the number of votes for each, which lists they shall sign and certify, and transmit sealed to the seat of the government of the United States, directed to the President of the Senate;

The President of the Senate shall, in the presence of the Senate and House of Representatives, open all the certificates and the votes shall then be counted;

The person having the greatest Number of votes for President, shall be the President, if such number be a majority of the whole number of Electors appointed; and if no person have such majority, then from the persons having the highest numbers not exceeding three on the list of those voted for as President, the House of Representatives shall choose immediately, by ballot, the President. But in choosing the President, the votes shall be taken by states, the representation from each state having one vote; a quorum for this purpose shall consist of a member or members from two-thirds of the states, and a majority of all the states shall be necessary to a choice. And if the House of Representatives shall not choose a President whenever the right of choice shall devolve upon them, before the fourth day of March next following, then the Vice President shall act as President, as in the case of the death or other constitutional disability of the President.

The person having the greatest number of votes as Vice President, shall be the Vice President, if such number be a majority of the whole number of Electors appointed, and if no person have a majority, then from the two highest numbers on the list, the Senate shall choose the Vice President; a quorum for the purpose shall consist of two-thirds of the whole number of Senators, and a majority of the whole number shall be necessary to a choice. But no person constitutionally ineligible to the office of President shall be eligible to that of Vice President of the United States.

Amendment 13 [1865]

Section 1. Neither slavery nor involuntary servitude, except as a punishment for crime whereof the party shall have been duly convicted, shall exist within the United States, or any place subject to their jurisdiction.

Section 2. Congress shall have power to enforce this article by appropriate legislation.

Amendment 14 [1868]

Section 1. All persons born or naturalized in the United States, and subject to the jurisdiction thereof, are citizens of the United States and of the State wherein they reside. No State shall make or enforce any law which shall abridge the privileges or immunities of citizens of the United States; nor shall any State deprive any person of life, liberty, or property, without due process of law; nor deny to any person within its jurisdiction the equal protection of the laws.

Section 2. Representatives shall be apportioned among the several States according to their respective numbers, counting the whole number of persons in each State, excluding Indians not taxed. But when the right to vote at any election for the choice of electors for President and Vice

President of the United States, Representatives in Congress, the Executive and Judicial officers of a State, or the members of the Legislature thereof, is denied to any of the male inhabitants of such State, being twenty-one years of age, and citizens of the United States, or in any way abridged, except for participation in rebellion, or other crime, the basis of representation therein shall be reduced in the proportion which the number of such male citizens shall bear to the whole number of male citizens twenty-one years of age in such State.

Section 3. No person shall be a Senator or Representative in Congress, or elector of President and Vice President, or hold any office, civil or military, under the United States, or under any State, who, having previously taken an oath, as a member of Congress, or as an officer of the United States, or as a member of any State legislature, or as an executive or judicial officer of any State, to support the Constitution of the United States, shall have engaged in insurrection or rebellion against the same, or given aid or comfort to the enemies thereof. But Congress may by a vote of two-thirds of each House, remove such disability.

Section 4. The validity of the public debt of the United States, authorized by law, including debts incurred for payment of pensions and bounties for services in suppressing insurrection or rebellion, shall not be questioned. But neither the United States nor any State shall assume or pay any debt or obligation incurred in aid of insurrection or rebellion against the United States, or any claim for the loss or emancipation of any slave; but all such debts, obligations and claims shall be held illegal and void.

Section 5. The Congress shall have power to enforce, by appropriate legislation, the provisions of this article.

Amendment 15 [1870]

Section 1. The right of citizens of the United States to vote shall not be denied or abridged by the United States or by any State on account of race, color, or previous condition of servitude.

Section 2. The Congress shall have power to enforce this article by appropriate legislation.

Amendment 16 [1913]

The Congress shall have power to lay and collect taxes on incomes, from whatever source derived, without apportionment among the several States, and without regard to any census or enumeration.

Amendment 17 [1913]

The Senate of the United States shall be composed of two Senators from each State, elected by the people thereof, for six years; and each Senator shall have one vote. The electors in each State shall have the qualifications requisite for electors of the most numerous branch of the State legislatures.

When vacancies happen in the representation of any State in the Senate, the executive authority of such State shall issue writs of election to fill such vacancies: *Provided,* That the legislature of any State may empower the executive thereof to make temporary appointments until the people fill the vacancies by election as the legislature may direct.

This amendment shall not be so construed as to affect the election or term of any Senator chosen before it becomes valid as part of the Constitution.

Amendment 18 [1919]

[Prohibition on manufacture, sale, or transportation of intoxicating liquors, which was repealed by Amendment 21]

Amendment 19 [1920]

The right of citizens of the United States to vote shall not be denied or abridged by the United States or by any State on account of sex.

Congress shall have power to enforce this article by appropriate legislation.

Amendment 20 [1933]

Section 1. The terms of the President and Vice President shall end at noon on the 20th day of January, and the terms of Senators and Representatives at noon on the 3d day of January, of the years in which such terms would have ended if this article had not been ratified; and the terms of their successors shall then begin.

Section 2. The Congress shall assemble at least once in every year, and such meeting shall begin at noon on the 3d day of January, unless they shall by law appoint a different day.

Section 3. If, at the time fixed for the beginning of the term of the President, the President elect shall have died, the Vice President elect shall become President. If a President shall not have been chosen before the time fixed for the beginning of his term, or if the President elect shall have failed to qualify, then the Vice President elect shall act as President until a President shall have qualified; and the Congress may by law provide for the case wherein neither a President elect nor a Vice President elect shall have qualified, declaring who shall then act as President, or the manner in which one who is to act shall be selected, and such person shall act accordingly until a President or Vice President shall have qualified.

Section 4. The Congress may by law provide for the case of the death of any of the persons from whom the House of Representatives may choose a President whenever the right of choice shall have devolved upon them, and for the case of the death of any of the persons from whom the Senate may choose a Vice President whenever the right of choice shall have devolved upon them.

Section 5. Sections 1 and 2 shall take effect on the 15th day of October following the ratification of this article.

Section 6. This article shall be inoperative unless it shall have been ratified as an amendment to the Constitution by the legislatures of three-fourths of the several States within seven years from the date of its submission.

Amendment 21 [1933]

Section 1. The eighteenth article of amendment to the Constitution of the United States is hereby repealed.

Section 2. The transportation or importation into any State, Territory, or possession of the United States for delivery or use therein of intoxicating liquors, in violation of the laws thereof, is hereby prohibited.

Section 3. The article shall be inoperative unless it shall have been ratified as an amendment to the Constitution by conventions in the several States, as provided in the Constitution, within seven years from the date of the submission hereof to the States by the Congress.

Amendment 22 [1951]

Section 1. No person shall be elected to the office of the President more than twice, and no person who has held the office of President, or acted as President, for more than two years of a term to which some other person was elected President shall be elected to the office of the President more than once. But this Article shall not apply to any person holding the office of President, when this Article was proposed by the Congress, and shall not prevent any person who may be holding the office of President, or acting as President, during the term within which this Article becomes operative from holding the office of President or acting as President during the remainder of such term.

Section 2. This article shall be inoperative unless it shall have been ratified as an amendment to the Constitution by the legislatures of three-fourths of the several States within seven years from the date of its submission to the States by the Congress.

Amendment 23 [1961]

Section 1. The District constituting the seat of Government of the United States shall appoint in such manner as the Congress may direct:

A number of electors of President and Vice President equal to the whole number of Senators and Representatives in Congress to which the District would be entitled if it were a State, but in no event more than the least populous State; they shall be in addition to those appointed by the States, but they shall be considered, for the purposes of the election of President and Vice President, to be electors appointed by a State; and they shall meet in the District and perform such duties as provided by the twelfth article of amendment.

Section 2. The Congress shall have power to enforce this article by appropriate legislation.

Amendment 24 [1964]

Section 1. The right of citizens of the United States to vote in any primary or other election for President or Vice President, for electors for President or Vice President, or for Senator or Representative in Congress, shall not be denied or abridged by the United States or any State by reason of failure to pay any poll tax or other tax.

Section 2. The Congress shall have power to enforce this article by appropriate legislation.

Amendment 25 [1967]

Section 1. In case of the removal of the President from office or of his death or resignation, the Vice President shall become President.

Section 2. Whenever there is a vacancy in the office of the Vice President, the President shall nominate a Vice President who shall take office upon confirmation by a majority vote of both Houses of Congress.

Section 3. Whenever the President transmits to the President pro tempore of the Senate and the Speaker of the House of Representatives his written declaration that he is unable to discharge the powers and duties of his office, and until he transmits to them a written declaration to the contrary, such powers and duties shall be discharged by the Vice President as Acting President.

Section 4. Whenever the Vice President and a majority of either the principal officers of the executive departments or of such other body as Congress may by law provide, transmit to the President pro tempore of the Senate and the Speaker of the House of Representatives their written declaration that the President is unable to discharge the powers and duties of his office, the Vice President shall immediately assume the powers and duties of the office as Acting President.

Thereafter, when the President transmits to the President pro tempore of the Senate and the Speaker of the House of Representatives his written declaration that no inability exists, he shall resume the powers and duties of his office unless the Vice President and a majority of either the principal officers of the executive department or of such other body as Congress may by law provide, transmit within four days to the President pro tempore of the Senate and the Speaker of the House of Representatives their written declaration that the President is unable to discharge the powers and duties of his office. Thereupon Congress shall decide the issue, assembling within forty-eight hours for that purpose if not in session. If the Congress, within twenty-one days after receipt of the latter written declaration, or, if Congress is not in session, within twenty-one days after Congress is required to assemble, determines by two-thirds vote of both Houses that the President is unable to discharge the powers and duties of his office, the Vice President shall continue to discharge the same as Acting President; otherwise, the President shall resume the powers and duties of his office.

Amendment 26 [1971]

Section 1. The right of citizens of the United States, who are eighteen years of age or older, to vote shall not be denied or abridged by the United States or by any State on account of age.

Section 2. The Congress shall have power to enforce this article by appropriate legislation.

Amendment 27 [1992]

No law varying the compensation for the services of the Senators and Representatives shall take effect until an election of Representatives shall have intervened.

Appendix II

Simulations

■ ■ ■

Simulation for Chapter 2
(Customary International Law)

#1

U.S. relations with the State of Being, a nation in the Western Hemisphere, are in peril. Being's popularly elected government has maintained generally positive relations with the present U.S. administration. But Being suffers a military coup against its government, led by General Specific. The U.S. President has strongly denounced the coup—not least because he feared it would cascade into a series of bloody conflicts across the region—while conservative U.S. critics of the former government's socialist policies rejoiced.

What happened next surprised most observers. Senator Leghorn (South Carolina) summarized developments in the following remarks, delivered on the Senate floor:

> Ladies and Gentleman, the United States stands today in a position of unusual embarrassment. I speak, of course, of the Being situation, and with apologies to those of a tender disposition, let me catalog our offenses.
>
> As you are aware, General Specific was seized from the smoking lounge at Being's principal airport by a Trans American Airways crew, at the direction of Trans American's CEO—who was acting, let us be clear, at the prompting of the U.S. Secretary of Transportation and, I strongly suspect, our own President—and forced onto one of its planes. He was transported against his will to the United States and he is being held incommunicado at Andrews Air Force Base. This kidnaping and arbitrary detention clearly violated customary international law. The Constitution says, and the courts have made this perfectly clear, that customary international law is federal law that constrains every American. Our Secretary of Transportation and our President offended this law, and I have been advised that General Specific has filed suit against both to force his release. I am also informed that he has sued Trans American Airways and its CEO

under something called the Alien Tort Statute. It pains me to say that I wish him success in both endeavors.

Assuming the facts as stated by Senator Leghorn, what are the merits of the objections he has raised, and the strengths and weaknesses of the lawsuits he mentions? Students should assume the roles of: (a) Senator Leghorn; (b) White House Counsel; (c) counsel for General Specific; and (d) counsel for Trans American Airways.

#2

In 2016, Montana voters overwhelmingly approve the "Montana International Law Amendment" to the Montana Constitution. The Amendment reads:

> A. The judicial power of this State shall be vested in the Senate, sitting as a Court of Impeachment, a Supreme Court, the Court of Criminal Appeals, the Court on the Judiciary, and such intermediate appellate and lower courts as may be provided.
>
> B. The Courts provided for in subsection A of this section, when exercising their judicial authority, shall uphold and adhere to the law as provided in the United States Constitution, the Montana Constitution, the United States Code, federal regulations promulgated pursuant thereto, federal common law, Montana Statutes and rules promulgated pursuant thereto, and if necessary the law of another state of the United States provided the law of the other state does not include Sharia Law, in making judicial decisions. Under no circumstance shall such courts shall look to the legal precepts of other nations or cultures, including international or Sharia law.

Abdul Awad, the Executive Director of the Council on American–Islamic Relations in Montana, files a lawsuit against the State of Montana in the federal district court, requesting a preliminary injunction against implementation of the new Amendment and a ruling that the Amendment is unconstitutional. Awad attacks the constitutionality of the Amendment through two arguments. First, he maintains that the Amendment is unconstitutional because it denies the effect of international law as a part of U.S. law. Second, he contends the Amendment is problematic with respect to the freedom of religion clause of the U.S. Constitution. The district court indicates that it intends to proceed initially by only dealing with the first issue; the second issue will be addressed, if necessary, at a later stage in the proceedings.

Students should assume the roles of: (1) counsel for the Council on American–Islamic Relations in Montana (opposing the amendment); (2) counsel representing the Montana Attorney–General's office (defending amendment); and (3) the federal district court judge.

#3

In March 2017, five men set off from Somalia in a heavily-armed seagoing vessel in search of a merchant ship to attack and plunder. Somewhere on the high seas between Somalia and the Seychelles, the men spot what they think is a merchant vessel. They approach the vessel and open fire upon it, but to their surprise, it turns out to be the USS *Intrepid*, a U.S. Navy frigate.

The *Intrepid* returns fire, gives chase, and eventually captures the five men. The men are brought to the United States and indicted under 18 U.S.C. § 1651. The defendants move to dismiss the charge, asserting that their attack on the USS *Nicholas* did not constitute "piracy" under the law of nations, since "piracy" requires a robbery or taking of property on the high seas, and no such robbery occurred. The district court issues an opinion agreeing with the defendants and dismissing the charge. The matter is then appealed to the Ninth Circuit Court of Appeals.

The U.S. President is troubled by the decision and sets up a Commission to propose a new statute (or series of statutes) to address piracy and privateering.

Students should assume the roles of: (1) counsel to the defendants (arguing that the district court decision was correct); (2) counsel for the government (arguing that the decision was incorrect); (3) counsel to the Commission (arguing in favor of and making concrete proposals for expansion and clarification of existing law); (4) counsel representing a group of foreign countries before the Commission (opposing greater extra-territorial application of U.S. law).

SIMULATION FOR CHAPTER 3 (TREATIES AND OTHER INTERNATIONAL AGREEMENTS)

On December 18, 1979, the General Assembly of the United Nations adopted a resolution accepting and commending for signature and ratification by U.N. members the Convention on the Elimination of All Forms of Discrimination Against Women (CEDAW).[1] Article 2 of CEDAW provides:

States Parties condemn discrimination against women in all its forms, agree to pursue by all appropriate means and without delay a policy of eliminating discrimination against women and, to this end, undertake:

(a) To embody the principle of the equality of men and women in their national constitutions or other appropriate legislation if not yet incorporated therein and to ensure, through law and other appropriate means, the practical realization of this principle;

(b) To adopt appropriate legislative and other measures, including sanctions where appropriate, prohibiting all discrimination against women;

(c) To establish legal protection of the rights of women on an equal basis with men and to ensure through competent national tribunals and other public institutions the effective protection of women against any act of discrimination;

1. 1249 U.N.T.S. 13.

(d) To refrain from engaging in any act or practice of discrimination against women and to ensure that public authorities and institutions shall act in conformity with this obligation;

(e) To take all appropriate measures to eliminate discrimination against women by any person, organization or enterprise;

(f) To take all appropriate measures, including legislation, to modify or abolish existing laws, regulations, customs and practices which constitute discrimination against women;

(g) To repeal all national penal provisions which constitute discrimination against women.

As of mid-2011, 186 countries (more than ninety-five percent of the members of the United Nations) are party to the Convention. Although the United States signed CEDAW in July 1980 and President Carter submitted it to the Senate for advice and consent, such consent has not been forthcoming.

The majority leader of the Senate has now decided to bring CEDAW before the full Senate for a vote. The majority leader is concerned, however, about the consequences of U.S. ratification on: (1) the constitutional rights of Congress; (2) the constitutional rights of the states; and (3) the constitutional rights of U.S. citizens. In particular, the majority leader is wondering whether the provisions of CEDAW Article 2, upon ratification, will become part of the supreme law of the United States, whether they are directly enforceable, and, if so, by whom; or whether, if they require implementing legislation, the implementing laws can be enacted by Congress in a form that would be constitutional.

A reservation to the resolution of acceptance has been offered by Senator Abigail Blaghard which states, in part, "None of the provisions of this Convention shall become part of the law of the United States or of the several States unless and until such provisions shall have been enacted into law by the United States or the several states in accordance with the constitutional powers allocated to each that would apply had the Convention not been ratified."

Members of the class are to assume the following roles in simulating a meeting of members of the majority leader's staff:

(1) A member of the staff who will examine the effect the Convention could have, if no reservations were added, on the constitutional rights and privileges of the states, the Congress and U.S. citizens.

(2) Another staffer who will examine whether any of the quoted provisions are self-executing and supreme law of the land, and what the consequences would be if (1) they, or any of them are self-executing; or (2) they are not self-executing. The same staffer shall consider what legislation Congress would have to enact to give effect domestically to the international legal obligations of the Convention and the constitutionality of such laws.

(3) A staffer who will examine the constitutionality and effect on the international legal obligation of the United States of the Blaghard Amendment. The same staffer shall consider what must be required of other states parties to the Convention by way of agreeing to such a reservation and what the legal position would be *vis-a-vis* parties to the Convention which do not agree to this reservation. The same staffer will also address the issue of whether there are alternative methods to achieve some or all of Senator Blaghard's purposes, should the reservation be unconstitutional in its present form.

The simulation consists of meetings between the three staffers and a caucus of interested Senators (i.e., the other members of the class). The Senators may question the staff on their findings, discuss their implications, propose and debate reservations, understandings, or declarations (RUDs), and, finally, indicate whether they intend to vote in favor of consent to CEDAW with such RUDs as command majority support.

SIMULATIONS FOR CHAPTER 4 (THE WAR POWER)

#1

Moraine is a nation in the Middle East governed by Islamic radicals. Its record of human rights abuses is one of the worst in the world. It has verbally threatened other nations in the region, and intelligence reports indicate that it has acquired centrifuges with which it has begun to enrich uranium, although estimates are that Moraine will not have deliverable nuclear devices for at least eight years. Months of direct negotiations have not persuaded Moraine to give up its nuclear enrichment program. Assume that the use of force has not been authorized or prohibited by either statute or treaty. The President argues that he has constitutional power to use force against Moraine without congressional approval. The Senate Foreign Relations Committee has requested the opinion of its staff and the Department of State on whether the use of force under these circumstances would be constitutionally permissible.

Students should assume the roles of: (1) Committee counsel (arguing the negative); (2) the State Department Legal Adviser (arguing the affirmative); and (3) Committee members.

#2

Following the facts set out in simulation #1 above, the United States launches a preemptive strike against Moraine nuclear facilities. In response, Moraine artillery bombards neighboring Imman, a U.S. ally, and invading Moraine troops engage American ground forces stationed in Imman. Full-scale hostilities continue for 78 days following the date of the preemptive strike. Assume that the Senate Foreign Relations Committee is holding a hearing on the issue.

1. Constitutionally, must the President comply with the requirement of the War Powers Resolution to withdraw the armed forces prior to the ninetieth day?
2. If Congress were to adopt a concurrent resolution under section 5(c) of the War Powers Resolution, would the President constitutionally be required to comply with it and to withdraw U.S. forces from Imman?
3. Can the President infer congressional approval from the enactment of previous legislation appropriating funds for the stationing of U.S. troops in Imman, notwithstanding section 8(a)(1) of the War Powers Resolution?

Students should assume the roles of: (1) Committee counsel (arguing in favor of congressional power); (2) the State Department Legal Adviser (arguing in favor of presidential power); and (3) Committee members (from both parties, attempting to find the middle ground).

#3

Moraine is a nation in the Middle East governed by Islamic radicals. Its armed forces have attacked North Arabia. North Arabia is a party to the North Atlantic Treaty. The President argues that he has constitutional power to use force against Moraine without congressional approval because it is authorized by the NATO treaty. Moreover, the U.N. Security Council has adopted a resolution authorizing member states to use armed force against Moraine in defense of North Arabia. The Senate Foreign Relations Committee has requested the opinion of its staff and the Department of State on whether the use of force under these circumstances would be constitutionally permissible.

Students should assume the roles of: (1) Committee counsel (arguing the negative); (2) the State Department Legal Adviser (arguing the affirmative); and (3) Committee members.

SIMULATION FOR CHAPTER 5 (THE POWER OF THE PURSE)

#1

In 2017, a newly-elected Congress is eager to demonstrate its willingness to reduce the federal deficit. At the same time, Congress is very disturbed about various classified documents released by WikiLeaks, including a series of cables from the U.S. Embassy in Caracas demonstrating an Executive Branch willingness to cooperate with Venezuelan strongman Hugo Chavez, rather than pressuring him to improve his human rights records, to allow for a more pluralist democracy, and to depart from his "socialist ways".

The Chair of the House Appropriations Subcommittee on State Department, Foreign Operations, and Related Programs is considering legislation that would:

1. reduce personnel at all U.S. embassies and consulates abroad by 50%, although in no instance would any embassy or consulate have less than 5 persons;
2. reduce personnel at the U.S. Embassy in Caracas by a further 30% (subject to the 5–person minimum), unless the President certifies in writing that U.S. policy to Venezuela seeks improve Venezuela's human rights record, to promote greater democratic participation in Venezuela, and to establish in Venezuela a free market economy; and
3. cut off all foreign aid to Venezuela until such time as the President certifies in writing that Venezuela engages in no significant human rights abuses.

The Chair of the Subcommittee has scheduled a hearing on whether any of these provisions, if enacted into law (perhaps over a Presidential veto), would constitute an unconstitutional encroachment upon Presidential power.

Students should assume the role of: (1) Committee counsel (arguing in favor of congressional power); (2) a representative from the Justice Department's Office of Legal Counsel (arguing in favor of presidential power); (3) an esteemed law professor (no predisposition).

#2

Narco-terrorism has become an enormous problem in Mexico, with transnational implications. For example, after Ricardo Valles de la Rosa, a native of Juárez, Mexico, committed a crime just across the river from Juárez in El Paso, Texas, he was caught and imprisoned in El Paso, where he came into contact with members of the Barrio Azteca, a Mexican narcotics gang. After serving his time, Valles de la Rosa was deported in 2007 from the United States back to Mexico, where he reportedly joined the ranks of Barrio Azteca. In 2010, he allegedly participated in an attempted attack in Juárez on an El Paso prison officer, who lives in Juárez with his wife. Although the prison officer survived the attack unscathed, his wife—an employee of the U.S. Consulate in Juárez—and two other employees of the U.S. Consulate were killed.

Reacting to this and other incidents, Congress adopts a statute in 2017, over the President's veto, entitled the Narcotics Trafficking in Mexico Act (NTMA). Among other things, the statute:

(1) authorizes and appropriates no more than $80 million for Department of Justice programs that train and equip Mexican police involved in anti-narcotics operations;

(2) prohibits the use of any funds in the relevant statute dealing with foreign embassies and consulates (the Foreign Operations, Export Financing, and Related Appropriations Act) for the operation of a consulate in Juárez, given the dangers to consular personnel posted there; and

(3) prohibits the use of any funds to support the sharing of U.S. intelligence information with the Mexican Government on narcotics trafficking in Mexico, due to a concern that such information is being leaked by unknown persons in the Mexican Government to the narcotics traffickers, thereby making it more difficult to thwart their activities.

Once the NTMA is adopted, the President indicates that he views the restrictions contained in the above provisions as "merely advisory in nature, given the inability of Congress to supercede the President's constitutional role as the 'sole voice' in matter of foreign relations." Your law school convenes a conference to hear views on the constitutionality of the statute.

Students should assume the roles of: (1) counsel to the Senate Majority leader; (2) White House counsel; (3) counsel for the Mexican Embassy in Washington, D.C.; and (4) counsel for the Governor of Texas.

SIMULATION FOR CHAPTER 6 (FEDERALISM)

#1

A new Administration and Congress have taken office in Washington, D.C., and both are keenly interested in taking steps to protect the sanctity of life in all aspects. Among other things, the new federal officials note that aliens travel to and reside in the United States, where they are exposed to the death penalty, and where their unborn children have been aborted, and that such matters, as well as the practice of abortion and the death penalty as it affects Americans, have resulted in protests from various foreign governments. Conversely, U.S. nationals have traveled abroad, where they have been convicted and sentenced to death in unjust situations, as well as obtained abortions. The following steps are contemplated:

1. Enacting a federal statute that asserts the sense of the Congress that the practice of abortion and of the death penalty have caused extensive "friction" between the United States and the other nations of the world, and therefore the statute criminalizes such practice in the United States as a matter of federal law; or
2. Ratifying (a) the Second Optional Protocol to the International Covenant on Civil and Political Rights (ICCPR), Dec. 15, 1989, 29 I.L.M. 1464, which prohibits the death penalty; and (b) the American Convention on Human Rights, Nov. 22, 1969, 1144 U.N.T.S. 123, 9 I.L.M. 673, as amended, which provides that "[e]very person has the right to have his life protected . . . , in general, from the moment of conception," followed by enacting a federal statute that, in implementation of the American Convention, criminalizes all abortion; or
3. Having the President issue an executive order stating that it is the foreign policy of the United States to end abortion and the

death penalty worldwide as a means of protecting Americans abroad, avoiding frictions with foreign governments regarding the treatment of aliens in the United States, and promoting a more stable and just world; or

4. Having the U.S. Department of State Legal Adviser issue a declaration that contemporary customary international law forbids the practice of abortion and of the death penalty, and then seeking leave for the Department of Justice to appear as amicus curiae in all cases in U.S. courts where such practice is at issue so as to urge the court to prevent the practice as prohibited under U.S. federal law.

Students should assume the roles of: (1) a U.S. Department of Justice Assistant Attorney–General: (2) the Attorney–General of the State of Texas; (3) a lawyer for a non-governmental organization (People for Choice) which favors a woman's right to choose whether to abort, but opposes the death penalty as a racially-biased and unjust form of punishment; and (4) a lawyer for a non-governmental organization (Stop Crime) which favors allowing the several states to choose whether to use the death penalty, but opposes abortion on moral grounds.

#2

Review the facts of the Simulation for Chapter 5 (#2). Add to those facts that the Governor of Texas and the Governor of Chihuahua (the Mexican State where Juárez is located) sign an instrument that provides the following:

WHEREAS the State of Texas and the State of Chihuahua are experiencing significant levels of violence by persons engaged in narcotics trafficking; and

WHEREAS such persons often operate and cooperate across the border between the State of Texas and the State of Chihuahua in a manner that poses difficulties for police investigation and apprehension of such persons; and

WHEREAS cooperation between police authorities of Texas and Chihuahua is necessary to ensure timely, accurate, and effective investigation of narcotics trafficking, as well as apprehension of those who violate narcotics laws;

THEREFORE, the State of Texas and the State of Chihuahua agree to work cooperatively to the fullest extent possible consistent with their respective laws to ensure that:

1. Each State fully informs the other State regarding its respective investigation and apprehension of persons involved in narcotics trafficking that has a transborder dimension;
2. Each State cooperates on educating the other State about the organization, policies, and tactics of its respective police authori-

ties in addressing narcotics trafficking that has a transborder dimension; and

3. Each State communicates to its national government both its concerns and any concerns of the other State relating to narcotics trafficking that has a transborder dimension.

The Speaker of the House of Representatives believes that the Texas–Chihuahua instrument—which was not authorized by Congress—is constitutionally impermissible. He convenes a hearing on the matter, at which various legal experts testify.

Students should assume the roles of: (1) counsel for the State of Texas; (2) counsel for the House Committee on Foreign Affairs; (2) counsel for the State of Chihuahua; and (4) counsel for the U.S. Department of State Office of the Legal Adviser.

SIMULATION FOR CHAPTER 7 (JUSTICIABILITY AND STANDING)

#1

Congress has passed a law, over a presidential veto, which prohibits the President, or any official of the U.S. government, from assassinating, or planning or otherwise seeking to assassinate, any foreign head of state or of government or any other foreign government official.

The Washington *Tattler* last month carried a report that quotes a telephone call from the President to the Director of the Central Intelligence Agency in which the President reads him a secret directive ordering him to secure the death of Azam Mogul, the dictator of the north-central Asian Republic of Ishtar. Mogul has been responsible for the torture-death of thousands of Ishtar citizens and, most recently, has kidnapped and killed five American Episcopal nuns who had operated a medical facility in the capital, Ishtar City.

The Senate Foreign Relations Committee has held hearings to determine whether the President has acted in violation of the law. At a session with the CIA director, its chair demanded that the director produce any memoranda of this telephone conversation and a copy of the secret directive, if such exists. The director has refused to comply, giving the Committee a copy of a letter from the President claiming executive privilege.

The Senate Committee, last week, voted to bring an action against the President and the director of the CIA asking the U.S. District Court for the District of Columbia to issue an order to the defendants to comply with the Committee's request for production and ordering them also to desist from any actions vis à vis Ishtar in contravention of the law prohibiting assassinations.

Students should assume the roles of: (1) White House Counsel to the President; (2) General Counsel of the CIA; and (3) the Counsel to the Senate Foreign Relations Committee.

#2

In 2017, the Democratic Party controls a bare majority of both the Senate and the House of Representatives. The President is a Republican, and announces on April 1 that the United States will attack Iran with both U.S. air and ground forces on May 1 to eliminate what appears to be a nascent Iranian nuclear weapons program that in the future might be used against the United States and its key allies, such as Israel.

On April 15, both Houses of Congress, by party-line vote, adopt resolutions stating that Congress opposes the President's use of such military force. Further, all Democratic Senate and House members join together to file a suit on April 25 in the District Court for the District of Columbia seeking an injunction that the President shall not proceed in the absence of a Congressional declaration of war or other authorization to use military force.

The District Court finds that the case is justiciable and that the plaintiffs have standing. That decision is taken up on expedited appeal directly to the Supreme Court, given the importance of the issue.

Drawing upon relevant Constitutional, statutory, judicial, or other precedent, students should assume the roles of: (1) counsel for Congress (arguing in favor of justiciability and standing); (2) counsel for the Justice Department (in opposition); (3) counsel for an independent legal think tank (submitting amicus views to the court).

#3

Baltasar Ramdan, a national of Syria, wins a University of Damascus prize to study at Columbia University in New York for one year. He travels to New York with his wife, Lilith, who is a dual U.S.-Syrian national. During that year, he learns about serious human rights abuses by the Syrian Government from reading reports in the Western media and attending academic conferences on the Middle East. Ramdan starts a blog entitled "Syrian Ghosts" in which he reveals extensive details about Syrian Government abuses and calls upon the people of Syria to rise up and depose the Syrian President.

One morning while riding his bicycle to class, Ramdan is gunned down near Columbus Circle by two masked assailants. Though the two men attempt to escape from the scene, they are stopped and apprehended by New York police officers who were having coffee in a nearby shop. The two assailants ultimately confess in great detail that they are agents of the Government of Syria, who were instructed to kill Ramdan by senior Syrian officials at a secret meeting in Damascus.

The next day, Lilith shows up in the law office of Smith & Wesson. She notes that the two men who confessed will be criminally prosecuted for their action, but bringing a civil action against them makes no sense because they are relatively poor and are simply "foot soldiers" of the government. Instead, she wants to sue in a U.S. court both the Government of Syria and the Syrian President. Smith & Wesson agrees to take the case and files suit under the Alien Tort Claims Act, the Torture Victim Protection Act, and New York tort law. When the Syrian President arrives in New York one week later to attend a major fund-raising event for Middle East refugee camps, an employee of Smith & Wesson manages to serve him directly with the relevant court papers. At the same time, the relevant court papers are sent to the Syrian Embassy in Washington, D.C.

A meeting is convened among the relevant counsel to clarify their basic positions. Students should assume the role of: (1) counsel for Smith & Wesson (arguing why the U.S. court has jurisdiction and why plaintiff will prevail on the merits); (2) counsel for the Syrian President (opposing jurisdiction and the merits); (3) counsel for the Government of Syria (also opposing); (4) esteemed law professor (providing an objective view).

SIMULATION FOR CHAPTER 8 (INVESTIGATING AND PROSECUTING THREATS TO NATIONAL SECURITY)

#1

In July 2015, a man named Chris Bethlehem contacts a criminal lawyer in Washington, D.C., with the following story. Bethlehem, a U.S. national, was living in London with his British wife, Lucy Bethlehem. In June 2015, Chris and Lucy leave their London flat and hale a taxi cab on the street. After they enter the cab, the driver turns around and shoots two darts into them. They fall unconscious. When they awake, they are on an airplane en route to what they are told is "another country," where they are held in a dark cell for four weeks and interrogated by masked persons about their links to the terrorist network Al Qaeda. In early July 2015, they are again loaded on an airplane and flown to Washington, D.C., where they are placed in a federal prison.

The U.S. Attorney for Washington, D.C. visits them in their cells and tells them: "The NSA has been tapping your phone in London for over a year; from that, we know all about your connections to Al Qaeda. So, you have been indicted in federal court under various federal statutes concerning aiding and abetting Al Qaeda. Get a lawyer, and tell him or her to call me. I'll tell them whatever they want to know." He then lets Chris make a call and Chris calls a lawyer.

The criminal lawyer takes the case. As a first step, the lawyer must interview: (1) Chris and Lucy Bethlehem; and (2) the U.S. Attorney. The lawyer decides that, for the time being, he (or she) is not going to inquire about whether Chris and Lucy are actually connected with Al Qaeda (i.e, the merits of the government's case); instead, the lawyer is going to focus on information that might help to get the criminal case dismissed by the court before trial. Additionally, the lawyer is interested in obtaining information that might help Chris and Lucy file a civil claim against the U.S. Government for mistreatment.

Students should assume the roles of: (1) the lawyer for Chris/Lucy; (2) the U.S. Attorney; and (3) the federal district court judge. The simulation should focus on the principal lines of inquiry the lawyer should pursue with Chris/Lucy and with the U.S. Attorney, along with discussion of why those lines of inquiry are important in light of any relevant constitutional, statutory, treaty, and case law. The judge should hear and respond to arguments by the lawyer and the U.S. attorney as to whether the case should be dismissed.

#2

Kemal Abdul–Azim was born in 1970 in the United States and is a U.S. citizen. Among other things, he received a B.S. in Civil Engineering from Michigan State University in 1994, where he was President of the Muslim Student Association. After years of studying Islam, Abdul–Azim moved to the New York area, where he became an Islamic lecturer and spiritual leader. After 2014, however, Abdul–Azim leaves New York and travels abroad.

In early 2015, the U.S. Administration concludes that Abdul–Azim—through a blog, a Facebook page, and multiple You Tube videos—is inspiring Islamic terrorism against the West, including against the United States. Among other things, the U.S. Under Secretary of the Treasury for Terrorism and Financial Intelligence advises the President that Abdul–Azim "is extraordinarily dangerous, committed to carrying out deadly attacks on Americans and others worldwide." Though his exact whereabouts are unknown, Abdul–Azim is believed to be residing in a remote area of southeast Somalia.

In April 2015, the U.S. President issues a secret order instructing U.S. intelligence agencies to kill Abdul–Azim, whenever and wherever his location is identified, either by drone (unmanned) aircraft missile attack or other means. The President's order leaks and is widely reported in the press.

Abdul–Azim's father, Nasser Abdul–Azim, is outraged at the President's decision, believing his son to be entirely innocent. A highly educated man (having received a doctorate at the University of Kentucky and worked several years at the University of Maryland), the father files a lawsuit in the U.S. District Court for the Southern District of New York, with the assistance of the Center for Constitutional Rights and the American Civil Liberties Union. The law suit seeks an injunction against the President's proposed action, on grounds that such conduct violates Kemal Abdul–Azim's Fourth Amendment right to be free from unreasonable seizure and his Fifth Amendment right not to be deprived of life without due process of law. The U.S. government does not challenge the standing of Nasser Abdul–Azim nor seeks dismissal for reasons of justiciability, but instead defends on the basis that the states secret doctrine precludes the case going forward.

Students should assume the roles of: (1) counsel for the Center for Constitutional Rights; (2) counsel for the U.S. Department of Justice; (3) a clerk for the U.S. district court.

SIMULATION FOR CHAPTER 9 (NATIONAL SECURITY AND THE CONTROL OF INFORMATION)

Assume that the United States engages in a military intervention in the country of Gondor in 2010, which initially goes well but then turns into an ugly effort to manage an uncontrollable civil war. One day in 2016, the U.S. Attorney–General bursts into a federal judge's chambers in Washington, D.C., and says that the *Washington Post* has obtained a copy of a top secret report prepared by the U.S. Department of State that details various "mistakes" that the U.S. government committed during its military intervention in Gondor from 2010 to 2015, describes current U.S. troop strengths and dispositions in Gondor, and advances several options for getting the United States out of Gondor within the next 12 months. The Attorney–General asserts that publication of the report by the *Washington Post* will cause immediate, grave and serious harm to U.S. national security.

A few minutes later, the publisher of the *Washington Post* appears in the judge's chambers. The publisher says that the information in the report is of extraordinary importance for the public debate on a major foreign policy issue—the U.S. intervention in Gondor—and the U.S. public has a constitutional right to such information. Further, he states that the report in its entirety will be published in the next day's edition of the *Washington Post*. The Attorney–General calmly states: "If you publish that report, I'll see you placed behind bars!"

The judge looks concerned. She says: "We don't have much time. I want to hear argument from both of you right now as to whether the publisher is correct that the *Post*'s readers have a constitutional right to read the report, whether I should issue a preliminary injunction preventing the *Post* from publishing it, and the likelihood that the publisher could be successfully prosecuted if the *Post* publishes it. If you think there is any further information I need before deciding, tell me that."

Students should assume the roles of: (1) the Attorney–General; (2) the publisher, and (3) the federal district court judge.

INDEX

References are to Pages

Page numbers 232–272, 558–748, and 1054–1363, set out below, are found in Franck's Foreign Relations and National Security Law.

References are to Pages

References are to Pages

†